FEDERAL INCOME TAXATION

PRINCIPLES AND POLICIES

REVISED FOURTH EDITION

by

MICHAEL J. GRAETZ
Justus S. Hotchkiss Professor of Law
Yale Law School

DEBORAH H. SCHENK
Marilynn and Ronald Grossman Professor of Law
New York University School of Law

NEW YORK, NEW YORK
FOUNDATION PRESS
2002

COPYRIGHT © 1940, 1946, 1950, 1954, 1955, 1960, 1966, 1976, 1985, 1988, 1995, 2001 FOUNDATION PRESS
COPYRIGHT © 2002 By FOUNDATION PRESS

        395 Hudson Street
        New York, NY 10014
        Phone Toll Free 1–877–888–1330
        Fax (212) 367–6799
        fdpress.com

ISBN 1–58778–423–8

 TEXT IS PRINTED ON 10% POST CONSUMER RECYCLED PAPER

To our students
M.J.G.
D.H.S.

*

PREFACE TO THE REVISED FOURTH EDITION

> *This whole book is but a draught—nay, but the draught of*
> *a draught. Oh, Time, Strength, Cash and Patience!*
> —Herman Melville,
> Moby Dick, ch. 32.

Even with more time, strength, cash, and patience, the Congress, the courts, and the Internal Revenue Service all collaborate to ensure that any book designed for teaching a basic course in Federal Income Taxation will never be more than a draft of a draft. Today, no area of law seems more susceptible to change than federal taxation. Consider the following facts reported by the Staff of the Joint Committee on Taxation: In the period from the enactment of the Tax Reform Act of 1986 until the end of the year 2000, Congress enacted nearly 100 different laws amending the Internal Revenue Code, not counting legislation affecting Social Security, railroad retirement, unemployment compensation, tariffs or customs duties, or the public debt limit. The Code currently contains about 700 provisions affecting individuals and more than 1,500 provisions affecting businesses.

As of May 2000, the Code contained 1.4 million words, making it more than six times longer than *Crime and Punishment* and considerably harder to parse. The regulations contained another 8.6 million words, spanning almost 20,000 pages. During calendar year 2000, the Treasury and IRS published 60 Treasury Decisions (containing final and temporary regulations), 45 sets of proposed regulations, 58 Revenue Rulings, 49 Revenue Procedures, 64 Notices, 100 Announcements, 2,400 Private Letter Rulings and Technical Advice Memoranda, 10 Actions on Decisions, 240 Field Service Advice documents, and a partridge in a pear tree.

For 1999 an individual filing the income tax Form 1040 could file a return with 79 lines, with 11 schedules totaling 443 lines. The schedules refer you to 19 additional worksheets. The instructions to the Form 1040 filled 144 pages of rather small type. In addition to Form 1040, 18 additional forms are commonly used by individuals.

Meanwhile, the courts have decided tens of thousands of tax cases. In 1999 alone, nearly a thousand tax bills were introduced in the Congress. And hardly a day passes without a new proposal for replacing the income tax either with some form of consumption tax or a broader-based, flatter-rate income tax.

Obviously it is impossible—and we think unwise—for a course introducing the income tax to try to instruct students about each of these developments. This book is about the fundamental concepts and forces shaping the income tax, not current events. That is why this edition reflects a remarkable continuity with its ancestor edition, Griswold's *Cases on Federal Taxation*. That book, initially published more than sixty years ago in 1940, was the first law school coursebook devoted exclusively to federal taxation. It appeared at a time when most of the operative statutory provisions were phrased in general terms and many of the basic concepts of federal taxation had not yet matured. Most law schools taught federal taxation only as part of a course that also covered state and local taxation. Nevertheless, this text retains the same overarching organization that Erwin Griswold first brought to the subject. The subsequent adoption of this structure by most income tax coursebooks is a great tribute to Griswold's insights into how the subject of federal taxation should be taught.

The mass of detail that has been added to the statute and the regulations and the burgeoning case law in the intervening six decades has required a substantial rethinking of the purposes of an introductory course in federal taxation and, hence, of this coursebook. For one thing, these details have become so voluminous and the changes so frequent that the student must necessarily strive to understand basic concepts rather than to memorize particular rules. The practice of tax law has become more specialized, and most law schools offer a number of advanced courses in taxation. The student in an introductory course therefore must attain some familiarity not only with the statute, the regulations, and the cases but also with the trends in the tax law, the prospects for change, and the fundamental policy issues that inform such changes. Successful tax lawyering inevitably will involve responding to new and unforeseeable rules and therefore will demand a basic conceptual understanding of income tax principles and policies. Likewise, the nonspecialist needs to be introduced to these fundamental concepts of income taxation, if only to be able intelligently to recognize and monitor his or her clients' tax problems.

The composition of this book has also been influenced by the increasing use of the tax law as an instrument of social and economic policy. The income tax is not merely a revenue-raising device to finance the goods and services provided by the government. The decisions of what to tax, and when, increasingly affect the direction, growth, and overall condition of our economy and the allocation and distribution of resources within our society.

For these reasons, this volume devotes substantial attention to the general principles and policies of federal taxation. Thus, cases have been supplemented with excerpts from congressional reports, administrative pronouncements, and commentaries and analyses of tax issues. In addition, there are explanatory notes introducing fundamental concepts of tax law and shorter notes following the principal cases.

This edition nevertheless continues to reflect the central pedagogical perspective developed in Erwin Griswold's original volume, the preface of which stated:

> Here is an opportunity, almost unique * * *, to study a complete and self-contained system. Here is an opportunity to come into contact with perhaps our most experienced administrative agency. Here is an oppor-

tunity to deal with a statute, not as some excrescence on the common law, but as the law, to trace its growth, to learn how it is given meaning and how that meaning changes. Here is an opportunity to deal with authoritative judicial decisions—or at least, and perhaps more important, to consider how far they are authoritative * * * Here as elsewhere it is understanding and knowledge of the process that is sought.

These opportunities are no less present in this volume than they were in its ancient predecessor.

This edition retains the basic chapter organization of its predecessors. The first chapter contains the basic policy and procedural aspects of income taxation. This chapter includes a brief history of taxation in the United States, an introduction to income tax terminology, and a discussion of the roles of Congress, the executive, and the courts. Subsequent chapters explore the topics "What Is Income?," "Deductions and Credits," "Whose Income Is It?," "Capital Gains and Losses," and "When Is It Income?". Of course, tax problems rarely can be placed into such discrete categories. Hence, there is some overlap of subjects within the chapters. Chapter 7 provides a brief description of the individual minimum tax. Chapter 8, new with this edition, contains an introduction to corporate tax shelters. We have also moved the materials on the ethical responsibilities of tax lawyers to this chapter, thereby providing an appropriate context for their analysis and discussion. The Appendix contains tables of present values.

As every teacher of taxation knows, it has become increasingly difficult to teach an introduction to federal taxation in a single semester, even in a 60-hour course. Compromises between breadth of coverage and treating at least some materials in depth are ever more necessary. Most instructors have learned to maintain limited expectations as to what can reasonably be accomplished in the first course and to assume that students with a genuine interest in taxation will take additional courses in the subject.

This volume continues the layered approach of the prior editions. By selecting from the materials available here, teachers can decide which aspects of income tax law and policy to emphasize and which to skim or even omit in an introductory course. This volume contains enough material to teach not only a four-hour basic course in federal income taxation, but also an additional three-hour course designed to pursue certain issues in greater detail than is possible in the basic course. This means that the instructor must exercise considerable selectivity in teaching any single course from this book. For example, one of us tends to emphasize Chapters 2 and 3, the first two sections of Chapter 4, the first three sections of Chapter 5, and a brief selection from Chapter 6. Another professor, who taught these materials in a two-semester course, skipped certain aspects of Chapters 2 and 3 and used only the introductory sections of Chapters 4 and 5 in the basic course, with the balance of materials used in the second course. Instructors who wish to cover more ground might consider relying on students to read some of the more straightforward materials without classroom discussion.

Designing courses inherently involves personal priorities and choices. The precise materials assigned will depend upon the teacher's individual choices of where to delve deeply into substantive law and policy issues as well as how to trade off in-depth discussions and general coverage. We have attempted here to provide sufficiently comprehensive, interesting, and flexible materials to allow teachers to make a wide variety of satisfactory selections.

Federal income taxation is, of course, primarily a statutory course. In addition to this text, the student will need a current edition of the Internal Revenue Code and probably will also wish to refer to the Income Tax Regulations from time to time. A number of publishers now produce one volume editions of selected statutory and regulatory provisions that may be used along with this text.

Citations and footnotes have been freely omitted and footnotes renumbered from court decisions. Dissenting and concurring opinions frequently have been omitted; however, the existence of these opinions generally has been noted to enable students to find them by consulting the original sources. When brief excerpts from opinions have been used, the page reference has often been omitted.

Preparation of a book of this sort produces many debts. Of course, we are tremendously indebted to Erwin Griswold, whose first six editions of the predecessor book were used by a substantial number of American law students. We also wish to thank both the students and faculty who have used prior editions; their comments and criticisms greatly influenced this edition. In addition to all of those who labored on prior editions to whom we remain indebted, special thanks are due to Edward Vargas, a student at New York University Law School, and to Barbara Ortiz at NYU, who worked with unfailing good humor through the preparation of this manuscript.

MICHAEL J. GRAETZ
DEBORAH H. SCHENK

July 2002

SUMMARY OF CONTENTS

TABLE OF CONTENTS

Sec.

APPENDICES

*

TABLE OF INTERNAL REVENUE CODE SECTIONS

*

TABLE OF TREASURY REGULATIONS

TABLE OF INTERNAL REVENUE RULINGS

Rulings with accompanying text are indicated by bold type.

TABLE OF MISCELLANEOUS RULINGS

*

TABLE OF CASES

Principal cases are in bold type. Non-principal cases are in roman type. References are to Pages.

xli

FEDERAL INCOME TAXATION

PRINCIPLES AND POLICIES

*

CHAPTER 1

INTRODUCTION TO FEDERAL TAXATION

Taxation is the process by which a government transfers resources (almost always money) from the private to the public sector. Individual citizens often resist sacrificing their private wealth to the public fisc, but the citizenry at large demands that government provide goods and services, such as roads and bridges, disability and retirement insurance, education and national defense, all of which ultimately must be financed through taxation. This fundamental conflict—between the public's demand for government provision of goods and services and each person's desire to minimize his own tax burden—works its way through the political process to affect dramatically both the nation's tax laws and government expenditures.

In deciding whom to tax, what to tax, and when, Congress routinely makes fundamental social and economic judgments. Tax policy decisions often affect the general condition of the economy, its direction, and growth. Tax provisions also have a major impact on the use of specific resources: who works and who doesn't, how much the nation spends on this or that and for whom. Today's income tax, for example, favors new development of natural resources over recycling, tells people it is better to own their own homes than to rent, gives a break to families that have one spouse who stays at home rather than those that have both husband and wife in the job market, and makes it cheaper for some people to marry, but cheaper for others to divorce or remain unmarried. Federal alcohol taxes favor wine drinkers over beer drinkers, and both over people who prefer whiskey. President Clinton proposed an energy tax that would have given economic force to fathers' eternal admonitions to their children to turn off the lights, but Congress refused to enact it.

The most fundamental issues of public policy sometimes are raised when Congress enacts tax laws, and the Internal Revenue Code is laden with legislative judgments about social policy. Even the nation's founders recognized that taxation was a "means for shaping the national economy, bringing foreign nations to fair commercial terms, regulating morals, and realizing ... social reforms"—thereby taking a thoroughly modern view of taxation.[1] Issues of equity in taxation raise issues of justice generally. Asking how much revenue to coerce from various classes of individuals in

---

1. Sidney Ratner, Taxation and Democracy in America 18 (1942), citing Wesley C. Mitchell, A History of the Greenbacks (1903).

our society may be a way of asking how much economic inequality society will tolerate.

But even this view of the political role of taxation is too narrow. John Hampden's refusal to pay "ship money" to Charles I of England raised a tax issue, but it also raised a fundamental question of the proper balance of power between the monarch and Parliament that profoundly affected the structure of English government. A tax issue also sparked the Revolutionary War. And the gesture chosen by Henry David Thoreau, and later by Vietnam War protesters, to question the validity of government action was a refusal to pay taxes. In June 1978, when the people of California voted to add to that state's constitution a property tax limitation called Proposition 13, they also transferred substantial power from the local to the state level of government—in the process dramatically changing California's longstanding governmental structure.

Taxation long has been the primary link between the people and their government. In the United States today, far more people file tax returns than vote in presidential elections, and the politics of taxation influences electoral debate at every level of office seeking. A French finance minister once called taxation the art of plucking the goose with the least amount of squawking. Lately we have heard lots of squawking.

In the summer of 1988 George H. Bush sought the presidency with the slogan: "Read my lips, no new taxes!" Many political pundits said that breaking this pledge in the deficit reduction agreement of 1990 was Bush I's political undoing in the 1992 election. His son George W. Bush went one better, promising a tax cut in his (ultimately) successful run for President in the year 2000, a tax cut he convinced Congress to deliver in May 2001. Today no politician seems completely free from fear of political reprisals for suggesting tax increases.

Resistance to taxes is as American as apple pie and can be traced back to the nation's birth. We have always been a tax-hating people. And whenever we have recognized that new taxes or increases in old ones are unavoidable, we always have strived to impose them on someone else. In 1928, when the income tax was just a teenager, a Treasury tax official characterized tax lawmaking as a "group contest in which powerful interests vigorously endeavor to rid themselves of present or proposed tax burdens."[2] Decades later, Russell Long, the Democrat from Louisiana who served as Chairman of the Senate Finance Committee, captured this sentiment nicely when he offered this ditty as the first principle of tax reform: "Don't tax you. Don't tax me. Tax the fellow behind the tree." In 1992, Dan Rostenkowski, then Chairman of the House Ways and Means Committee, added a second stanza, in light of the globalization of the world economy: "Don't tax you. Don't tax me. Tax the companies across the sea."

In the nation's infancy, when adequate revenues could be produced by tariffs, battles were principally among regions in an effort both to shift tax burdens to others and to protect local industries from competition. These kinds of battles still ring familiar two centuries later; for example, in 1993, northeastern legislators fought to avoid energy taxes on home heating oil,

---

2. T.S. Adams, "Ideals and Idealism in Taxation," 18 Amer.Econ.Rev. 1 (1928).

while western senators struggled against large increases in gas taxes, and West Virginians sought preferential treatment for coal. Today, regions battle, industries battle, labor and business interests battle; conflicts to shift tax burdens to others abound.

In tax legislation, personal interests and ideologies conspire to produce arguments for action, justifications for inaction and rationalizations for things done or left undone. Ideology and self-interest generally have little respect for facts, and the abuse and misuse of facts is a standard weapon of the advocates' arsenal. Unfortunately, when Congress is making tax policy, information and misinformation often serve simply as tools for argument. There is a glut of factual controversy, what economists label "empirical uncertainty," about the effects of taxation. Even the most fundamental factual questions about the effects of tax legislation often lack definitive answers. For example, despite almost a century of experience, we still do not know for sure who actually pays the corporate income tax: shareholders, consumers, employees, all owners of capital, or some combination thereof. Firm belief about the consequences of tax policy, however, is omnipresent. Tax facts enjoy an almost religious, mythological character. Whenever adequate facts do not exist or are controversial, the task of ideologues in the political process is made easier. The role of objective policy analysts, if there are such beasts, diminishes.

At a minimum, the anti-tax attitude of the public that has dominated federal policy since the late 1970's has postponed serious consideration of tax policy issues that are fundamental to our nation's future economic well-being: Is the current mix of taxes appropriate to the economic conditions that we face both domestically and internationally as we begin the 21st century? How can we raise the necessary revenues in a manner that is fair to the U.S. people and at the same time facilitates the international competitiveness of our businesses, encourages savings and investment, and nurtures economic growth?

Politicians' fear of increasing taxes—coupled with their unwillingness to limit government spending—made deficits of unprecedented size the dominant fiscal event of the 1980's and early 1990's, in the process shattering the promise of the tax limitation movement: that stemming the supply of tax revenues would constrain government spending and reduce government size. Instead, federal public spending continued to grow, and deficits swelled. With a robust economy, federal deficits gave way to surpluses in the 1990's, and public policy shifted to the question whether to cut taxes, pay down the public debt, or do a bit of both. In the future, deficits seem likely to loom again when the large baby boom generation retires and becomes eligible for Society Security and Medicare.

Whatever the long- or short-term fiscal outlook, the goals of the nation's tax and fiscal policies will be what they always have been: to facilitate growth of the nation's economy and to do justice in the distribution of the burdens and benefits of government, while raising revenues adequate to finance government's expenditures.

And tax policy inevitably will be constrained by the difficulties of achieving political majorities. The tax provisions in force today reflect no more than yesterday's political compromises, but the underlying structural and policy conflicts have changed little over time. A student of taxation must first understand the current tax law and the process for making it; this requires insights into timeless policy and political conflicts and the institutional mechanisms for resolving them. The output itself—the nation's tax law—lives in perpetual motion.

This chapter provides an introduction to the income tax by (1) summarizing the history of taxation in the United States, (2) describing the magnitude and sources of current tax collections, (3) introducing some basic income tax terminology, (4) examining the dominant criteria for evaluating tax systems and tax provisions, (5) exploring "tax expenditure" analysis, and (6) describing the roles of the three branches of government in the formulation and operation of the tax laws.

SECTION 1. BRIEF HISTORY OF TAXATION IN THE UNITED STATES

Early Taxes

In 1791, the first Secretary of the Treasury Alexander Hamilton convinced Congress to impose taxes on distilled spirits and carriages "more as a measure of social discipline than as a source of revenue."[1] Hamilton had the financial purpose of raising money to pay the small national debt, but, more importantly, he wanted the tax imposed to advance and secure the power of the new federal government. This distilled spirits tax produced the "Whiskey Rebellion" of 1794, a tax resistance movement led by farmers of western Pennsylvania and including others from Maryland, Virginia, and North Carolina, who—being consumers as well as producers of substantial quantities of whiskey—regarded themselves as the targets of the tax. In July 1794, about 500 tax protesters burned a tax collector's home and soon thereafter, with the approval of Congress, George Washington sent 13,000 troops into the troubled area. This ended the rebellion. Suppressing these tax protesters demonstrated the ability of the recently formed federal government to enforce its revenue laws within the states. In so doing, it served to secure the power of the national government and to fulfill, at least temporarily, Hamilton's policies.

The carriage tax produced the first Supreme Court case to consider the constitutional validity of an exercise of the taxing power, and the tax was upheld in Hylton v. United States, 3 U.S. (3 Dall.) 171 (1796) on the ground that it was not a "direct tax" required to be apportioned among the states by population under Article 1, Section 2, clause 3 of the Constitution. The first year's receipts from internal taxes netted the federal government a grand total of $208,942.81.

The first "commissioner of the revenue" was appointed on May 8, 1792. Soon thereafter, taxes were imposed on snuff, sugar, auction sales, legal instruments, and bonds. In addition, a direct tax was enacted in 1798

---

1. Samuel E. Morrison, Oxford History of the United States 1783–1917, at 182 (1927).

on real property—houses and land—as well as a tax of fifty cents on all slaves between the ages of twelve and fifty. Like the taxes on distilled spirits, these two taxes proved both unpopular and difficult to collect, and, along with opposition to the Alien and Sedition Acts, contributed to Thomas Jefferson's presidential victory over John Adams in 1800.

In 1802, at the initiative of President Jefferson and his Treasury Secretary Albert Gallatin, all internal taxes (except a tax on salt) were repealed, reflecting Jefferson's determination to reduce federal taxes and expenditures and the national debt. The connection between death and taxes—made famous in an oft-quoted remark, describing them as the only two certain events, first attributed to Benjamin Franklin in 1789—became all too real shortly thereafter, as the nation's major changes in tax policies began their long pattern of accompanying wars.

The War of 1812 demonstrated the risks of Jefferson's policy of relying entirely on tariffs as the sole source of federal government finance. This war also offered the nation's first proof that higher rates need not necessarily produce higher revenues: a doubling of tariff rates in 1812 raised half the pre-enactment revenues in 1814 due to the wartime decline in imports. During this war, virtually all of the previous federal taxes were revived, inaugurating the country's acceptance of the adage "an old tax is a good tax." Not good enough, however. Because of an expected shortage of revenues, Secretary of the Treasury Alexander Dallas in January 1815 proposed an income tax and an inheritance tax, but the Congress, in an early demonstration of politicians' reluctance to enact new taxes, did not act by the war's end in December of that year.

A Century of Tariffs

A peacetime deluge of imports the following year led domestic manufacturers to embrace additional protectionism, and the Tariff Act of 1816 raised duties on imports to a new high. By 1817, the fiscal situation of the federal government had so improved that the wartime taxes were all repealed, and the federal government did not again require revenues from internal taxes until the Civil War. During the interim, the government financed all of its activities from customs duties and sales of public lands. Indeed, trade tariffs remained the most significant single source of federal revenues until 1894. Thus, although Congress had raised some revenues from taxes on internal sources since the first days of the Union, tariffs produced the bulk of the money required to finance federal expenditures for most of this nation's first century.

The federal government's reliance on tariffs as its principal funding source initially suited both the young nation's manufacturers and farmers. High duties on imports served to protect the country's manufacturers from foreign competition and imposed little or no burden on the farmers, who were largely self sufficient from items they produced themselves. Do not think, however, that tariffs avoid imposing burdens similar to those that accompany taxation. Tariffs produce higher prices, for both imported and domestically produced goods that are subject to these duties, and therefore impose significant burdens on consumers, similar to those associated with sales or excise taxes, but varying depending on the linkage between the tariff schedule and each family's mix of purchases of goods and services.

The Civil War Income Tax

The need to finance the Civil War gave rise in 1861 to a direct tax on real property apportioned among the states by population and on July 1, 1862, President Lincoln signed the first income tax imposed by the federal government. It applied to all income in excess of $600, and taxed amounts up to $10,000 at a 3 percent rate with income exceeding that amount taxed at 5 percent. The constitutionality of the income tax was sustained in Springer v. United States, 102 U.S. 586 (1880), against the contention that it was a direct tax that should be apportioned among the states. The 1862 Act also imposed taxes on inheritances in excess of $1,000 with rates graduated from .75 percent to 5 percent depending on how close a relative the beneficiary was to the decedent.

Interestingly, during the Civil War the federal government withheld income taxes from its employees' wages but no withholding was required from the wages of employees of other governments or private employers. Some commentators have suggested that this produced something of an exodus from government jobs to private employers.[2]

The income tax was increased in 1864—with the top rate doubled to 10 percent—reduced in 1867 and again in 1870, when the inheritance tax was repealed, and was repealed in 1872 during the Grant Administration when the federal government was enjoying large budget surpluses. During this time, James A. Garfield proved himself a thoroughly modern politician by railing in 1867 against the income tax he had avidly supported in 1865 and subsequently riding a conservative tide to become President in 1880.

Tariff issues dominated the Presidential campaigns of both 1888 and 1892. Tariffs were increased to an average rate of nearly 50 percent in the McKinley Tariff Act of 1890, but a combination of substantially increased government spending, coupled with lower revenues than had been expected, led to a decline in the federal budget surplus of $85 million in 1890 to less than $10 million in 1892, followed by deficits totalling $61 million by June of 1894. By then it had become apparent that further tariff increases would be counterproductive and that only a decrease in tariff rates would increase revenues.

The next war—with Spain over Cuba and the Philippines—which established the United States as a major world power, demanded additional revenues, and the War Revenue Act of 1898 doubled alcohol and tobacco taxes, enacted a wide range of new excise taxes, and reenacted an inheritance tax. But the usual pattern prevailed, and these taxes were all repealed in 1902 after the crisis had passed.

After intense controversy, the income tax was reinstated at the insistence of the Democrats in 1894 to compensate for the reduction in tariffs anticipated to result from the 1894 Tariff Act. The tax was modelled after the Civil War income tax and imposed a rate of 2 percent on all income over $4,000. In an innovation that since has been lost, gifts and inheritances

---

2. Sidney Ratner, Taxation and Democracy in America 75 (1942).

were taxed as income to the recipient. Contrary to its prior determination in 1880 that the Civil War income tax was constitutionally permissible, in 1895 the Supreme Court struck down the entire income tax as a direct tax not apportioned among the states in conformity with the Constitution. Pollock v. Farmers' Loan & Trust Co., 158 U.S. 601 (1895). That decision was highly controversial, with the Court's majority suffering accusations that they had forgotten they were a court and not a legislature—something courts often are accused of forgetting. The case ultimately led to the adoption of the Sixteenth Amendment in 1913, which permits Congress to tax income "from whatever source derived."

The Twentieth Century: Expansion and Entrenchment of Income and Wage Taxes

Two years before the ratification of the Sixteenth Amendment, the Supreme Court had sustained the constitutional validity of the corporation excise tax of 1909, the forerunner of the general income tax. The Tariff Act of 1909 had imposed a tax of 1 percent of corporate net incomes in excess of $5,000. The Supreme Court upheld this tax on the ground that it was an "excise tax" on the privilege of doing business as a corporation rather than a direct tax on property. Flint v. Stone Tracy Co., 220 U.S. 107 (1911).[3]

The Sixteenth Amendment took effect on February 25, 1913, and it took Congress only until October 3 of that year to enact a tax on the net income of individuals and corporations that was to commence in 1916. The Supreme Court sustained the income tax enacted in 1913 under the explicit power the Sixteenth Amendment granted to Congress to impose income taxes. Brushaber v. Union Pacific Railroad, 240 U.S. 1 (1916).

Congress also enacted taxes on estates in 1916 and enacted a tax on gifts in 1924 (which was repealed in 1926 and reinstated in 1932) and both of these taxes were upheld by the Supreme Court. These are the predecessors of current estate and gift taxes.

During the period 1925–1932, Secretary of the Treasury Andrew Mellon became a role model for President Ronald Reagan by lowering the top income tax rate from its previous high of 73 percent, when he took office in 1921, to 25 percent in 1925. (Six decades later in 1981, President Reagan started three points lower, at 70 percent, and ended three points higher, at 28 percent in 1986.) As we know, the period of a 25 percent top rate, which lasted from 1925 to 1932, was something of a mixed economic bag: times were very good for a while; then times became very bad. During the subsequent five decades from 1932 to 1982—also a period of some very good years and some bad ones—the top rate never dropped below 63 percent. Nevertheless, the notion that low maximum tax rates are critical to the American economy has become an article of unshakeable faith in many quarters.

3. This case is notable now chiefly because of its quaint constitutional distinction between the "subject" (doing business in the corporate form) and the "measure" (income) of a tax—a distinction that also served to uphold the estate tax as an excise on the transfer of property rather than a direct tax on wealth.

By 1932, the Depression had so depleted its revenues that the federal government was experiencing large and growing deficits. In these pre-Keynesian days, agreement was universal that taxes had to be raised. As a result, the Revenue Act of 1932 enacted a major tax increase that served only to prolong the Depression.

From his first days as President, Franklin Delano Roosevelt preached from a populist's hymnal, railing against the rich and big business, but in tax legislation at least, his bark was generally far worse than his bite. In 1936, President Roosevelt proposed a major change in corporate income taxes, but Congress refused to go along, and instead enacted a new tax on undistributed corporate profits. Two years later this tax was reduced to less than one-tenth its original size—from a maximum 27 percent rate to 2½ percent—and soon was completely phased out by the Revenue Act of 1938. From then until taxes were raised to finance the Second World War—with the notable exception of the Social Security revisions of 1939—annual tax legislation had little or no general consequences. In 1944, when peacetime was at hand, Roosevelt proposed reducing taxes on corporations and other businesses by accelerating deductions for depreciation, an idea that was subsequently embraced in the 1950's by President Eisenhower, the 1960's by President Kennedy, the 1970's by President Nixon, the 1980's by President Reagan, and the 1990's by House Speaker Newt Gingrich.

The Enactment of Social Security

Clearly the most significant tax legislation of the years between the First and Second World Wars was the Social Security Act of 1935 and its amendments in 1939. This legislation created the federal retirement, disability, and unemployment insurance system, financed by a flat-rate payroll tax on a specified amount of wages. The system of benefits paid for by this tax is quite progressive.

Whenever there is a surplus in the amount of revenues over expenditures in this mandatory "insurance" system—as there was in its early history and again following major revisions in 1983 through the 1990's—there is an outcry over the burden of this payroll tax on low and moderate wage earners. Originally, the Social Security tax rate was set at 1 percent of wages to grow to 5 percent, split evenly between employees and their employers. Today the combined tax rate on employers and employees exceeds 12 percent and an additional tax of nearly 3 percent of wages is imposed to pay for hospital insurance under Medicare. The share of federal revenues supplied by these payroll taxes has grown substantially over time, and they now account for nearly one-third of federal revenues.

Extension of the Income Tax to Most Americans

The First World War secured for the income tax an important place in this nation's fiscal system, and the Second World War converted this levy of limited scope into a tax on the masses. Although it has long served as the nation's principal source of revenues and greatest cause of springtime headaches, the income tax originally was imposed at low rates and applied to fewer than 400,000 individuals. It was not until World War II that the income tax came to be paid by most Americans. Income tax rates reached their peak of 94 percent during that era. Following the Second World War, taxes—as usual following a war—began to decline, but that trend came to an end with legislation in 1950 and 1951 to finance the Korean War.

Beginning with the election of President Kennedy in 1960, the use of tax policy as a short-term economic stimulus became commonplace, and since the early 1960's, the government has frequently used tax policy to stimulate economic growth. Income taxes were reduced to stimulate a lagging economy in the Revenue Act of 1964, the Revenue Act of 1971, the Tax Reduction Act of 1975, and the Economic Recovery Tax Act of 1981. The 1981 Act provided the largest tax reductions in the nation's history in an attempt to stimulate investment by business and savings by individuals. Ironically, this legislation was followed one year later in 1982 by what was the largest peacetime tax increase in the nation's history until 1993. Tax increases were again enacted in 1984, 1990, and 1993 in an effort to combat large federal deficits. In 2001, President George W. Bush used a faltering economy as a reason to push Congress to enact tax cuts he had promised in his presidential campaign.

The Tax Reform of 1986

With considerable hyperbole, the Tax Reform Act of 1986 was widely heralded as the most significant tax change since the income tax was extended to the masses during the Second World War. This far reaching legislation, however, ultimately proved to be only a slight improvement in tax policy. The 1986 Act was the result of an uneasy political marriage of conservatives' desire for low tax rates and liberals' desire for a broad tax base.[4] Both sides of this compromise immediately came under attack. Its stability, therefore, was precarious from the outset, and although it put an end to a debilitating and escalating tax shelter industry, it ultimately failed to produce a markedly better tax system. By removing or reducing certain tax provisions that had produced very unequal rates of tax on different investments, however, the 1986 legislation probably did improve the economic efficiency of investment decisions and make the economy somewhat more productive. The rate reducing and base broadening contours of the 1986 Act were mimicked throughout the industrialized world.

The ink was barely dry on the 1986 legislation before the compromise began to unravel. An important provision of the act was the repeal of preferential rates on capital gains. Within several years, lower rates on capital gains were reinstated. The key feature of the 1986 Act was base broadening coupled with lower rates. Once again, Congress could not leave well enough alone; it raised rates and enacted new incentive provisions. The 1986 legislation did achieve some simplification for low and some moderate income taxpayers, but even these gains soon were eroded by subsequent legislation.

During the 1900's, President Clinton and Congress used the income tax the way a mother might employ chicken soup: as a magic elixir to solve all the nation's economic and social difficulties. If the nation has a problem

---

4. See generally, Michael J. Graetz, The U.S. Income Tax: What It Is, How It Got   That Way and Where We Go From Here (1999).

in access to education, child care affordability, health insurance coverage, or financing of long-term care, to name just a few, an income tax deduction or credit is the answer.

As its coverage has broadened and its missions have grown more numerous, the income tax has grown more cumbersome. Extraordinary complexity continues to be an income tax hallmark, in no small measure due to the efforts by policymakers to accommodate a variety of competing purposes, although the taxation of business and investment income is inherently complicated. More than 100 different federal tax forms are used each year by individuals. Congress passed legislation in 1997 and 1998 making more than 1,200 substantive changes to the Internal Revenue Code, which now contains more than 1.5 million words. IRS instructions for the Form 1040 grew from 74 pages for 1997 returns to well over 100 pages for 1998 and 1999 returns. This nation's tax law is now more than six times longer than Tolstoy's *War and Peace* and considerably harder to parse. Senator William Roth, the former Chairman of the Senate Finance Committee, added a new wrinkle to the tax law in 1997 by naming the "Roth IRA" after himself. In 2000, outgoing Ways and Means Chairman Bill Archer named a medical savings account provision after himself. If members of Congress all believe they can attach their names to a new tax break, they may add 535 new items each year. There appears to be only a slight political constituency for any major income tax simplification.

The most important aspect of the 1986 Act—the decision to strengthen the income tax rather than to replace it with a consumption tax also was challenged in the 1990's. Several Republican candidates for president in 1996 and Republican members of the House leadership throughout the 1990's urged that the income tax be replaced by some form of consumption tax: a sales tax, a value-added tax, or a so-called flat tax. Republican Congressman Bill Archer of Texas, the Chairman of the House Ways and Means Committee from 1994 until he left Congress after the 2000 election was fond of promising to rip the income tax out by its roots—a guaranteed applause line. But there was no such talk by either of the major presidential candidates in the 2000 election, and, for now at least, the central role of the income tax seems assured.

During the 1990's, the finances of the federal government shifted from large deficits to substantial surpluses. In 1990, after months of tortuous negotiations and machinations, Congress passed a budget act, which, through a combination of tax increases, provisions to slow the growth of federal expenditures, and new budget enforcement procedures, was estimated to reduce deficits by about 500 billion dollars in the subsequent five-year period. The 1990 Act, with tax increases that no doubt contributed to President Bush's failure to win reelection, served as the blueprint for President Clinton's 1993 tax proposals. The 1993 legislation, which ultimately passed by only one vote and with no Republican support, strengthened and extended the budget process adopted in 1990 and raised income taxes, particularly on high-income people. The unprecedented economic growth the country enjoyed from 1992–2000, combined with the budget legislation of the 1990's, converted federal deficits into surpluses, and, as the new millennium began with the inauguration of President George W. Bush, the federal budget outlook was rosy, at least for the near term.

In May 2001, Congress enacted tax cut legislation to be phased in during the years 2001–2010. This legislation reduces income tax rates, increases income tax allowances for children and education, and in 2010 repeals the estate tax. In a cynical move made to comply with budget resolutions, this law rescinds all of its tax reductions in the year 2011 unless extended in subsequent legislation.

SECTION 2.   CURRENT TAXES IN THE UNITED STATES

The Internal Revenue Code of 1986 imposes all federal internal revenue taxes. The 1986 Code superseded the Internal Revenue Code of 1954, which, in turn, had superseded the Internal Revenue Code of 1939. These codes have imposed more than 50 kinds of taxes. The major taxes are the corporate and individual income taxes and the payroll tax. In addition, there are estate and gift taxes and a large number of excise taxes. Over time excise taxes have been imposed on a wide variety of goods, from liquor and cigarettes to oleomargarine and playing cards, and on the manufacture of many articles, including tires, toilet preparations, automobiles, and gasoline, and on telegraph, telephone, radio, and cable messages.

Figure 1.1

Total Federal Revenues vs. Total Federal Outlays, as a Percentage of Gross Domestic Product, 1954 to 1999

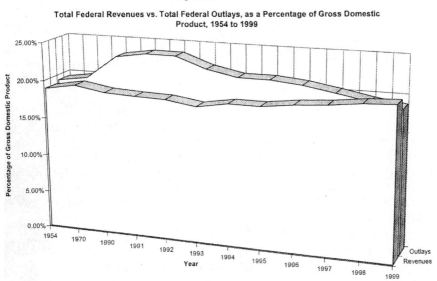

Even though the overall federal tax level has remained relatively constant as a percentage of total national output over a long period of time, the share of Social Security and Medicare employment taxes has increased dramatically relative to GDP, changing substantially the composition of U.S. taxes. Indeed, the most important development in the federal tax structure in the past 60 years has been the growth of the payroll tax to finance social welfare programs, particularly Social Security. These taxes have risen from 10 percent of total budget receipts in 1953 to nearly one-third in 1999. The impact of this increase has been especially dramatic for low and middle income workers, and the promise of future benefits—particularly upon retirement—has not served to offset the public and political perception that the wages of the middle class are being overtaxed. In addition, the current method of funding Social Security may be having an adverse effect on the nation's level of private savings, although whether this is actually occurring is quite controversial.

Figure 1.2

Total Federal/State/local Receipts vs. Total Federal/State/Local Expenditures, as a Percentage of Gross Domestic Product, 1954 to 1999

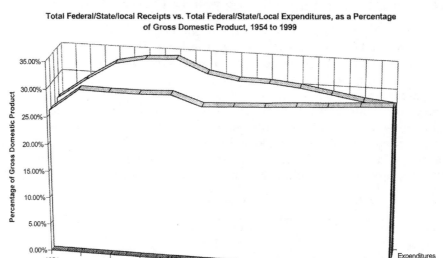

In contrast to the growth in taxes on wages, the past 50 years have witnessed a sharp decline in the percentage of total revenues generated by the corporate income tax. The corporate tax produced 30.3 percent of federal revenues in 1954, but only 8.2 percent in 1986. The 1986 Tax Reform Act reversed this trend, but even after that legislation, the corporate income tax has produced only about 12 percent of federal revenues and is expected to remain at about that level as a share of total income tax receipts.

By contrast, the individual income tax, for a long time, has remained a relatively steady source of federal revenues, producing 42.4 percent of the total in 1954, 45.4 percent in 1986, and 47.6 percent in 1999.

The excise taxes have generated relatively little controversy (and therefore are rarely studied in law school tax courses). Many of these taxes, such as those on tobacco and liquor, are collected routinely on a clearly defined product from a small number of taxpayers (often manufacturers). Although most excise taxes were repealed or reduced in the 1960's, during the 1980's and 1990's, they experienced something of a revival with Congress turning to excise taxes to narrow federal deficits. Whatever their economic merit, many excise taxes meet the test of raising large sums at low administrative costs.

Some comparative figures of federal receipts are given in the following table:

SOURCES OF FEDERAL REVENUES

Table 1–1: 1800–1980 *
(Amounts are in Millions of Dollars)

Year	Customs	Income Taxes	Other	Total Receipts
1800	$ 9.1	...	$ .8	$ 10.8
1870	194.5	$ 37.8	147.1	411.3
1900	233.2	...	295.3	567.2
1920	322.9	3,945.0	1,460.0	6,695.0
1930	587.0	2,411.0	628.0	4,178.0
1940	349.0	2,125.0	3,178.0	5,265.0
1950	423.0	28,263.0	11,186.0	37,045.0
1960	1,123.0	67,125.0	24,650.0	77,763.0
1965	1,478.0	79,792.0	34,643.0	93,072.0
1970	3,430.0	122,241.0	67,136.0	192,807.0
1975	3,676.0	163,007.0	112,407.0	279,090.0
1980	7,200.0	244,100.0	206,243.0	517,112.0

* Because of changes in accounting procedures, the figures for recent years are not wholly comparable with those for earlier years. The chief difference is in the figure for "total receipts," which now includes the figures for federal trust funds, such as the Social Security and highway trust funds.

Table 1–2: 1987–1999
(Amounts in Millions of Dollars)

Year	Excise	Income Taxes	Estate & Gift Taxes	Payroll Taxes	Total Receipts
1987	33,311	568,311	7,668	277,000	886,290
1990	37,374	650,245	11,762	367,219	1,066,600
1995	59,298	850,201	15,144	465,405	1,390,048
1996	56,027	934,368	17,592	492,365	1,500,351
1997	58,689	1,029,513	20,356	528,597	1,637,157
1998	59,231	1,141,336	24,631	557,800	1,782,998
1999	72,076	1,218,511	28,386	598,669	1,917,642

Source: Statistics of Income, Internal Revenue Service

The graph that follows depicts the levels of the individual income tax, the corporate income tax, and payroll taxes as a percentage of total federal revenues for the 45–year period 1954–1999:

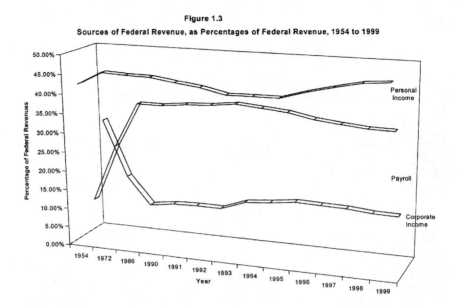

Figure 1.3

Sources of Federal Revenue, as Percentages of Federal Revenue, 1954 to 1999

In addition to federal taxes, taxes in the United States also are levied by state and local governments, with each state or locality administering and enforcing its own tax laws. The fiscal arrangements among the three levels of government are complex. Each raises revenue on its own, but there is also a substantial intergovernmental flow of revenue. The following graph compares total government receipts and total federal receipts for the period 1954–1999:

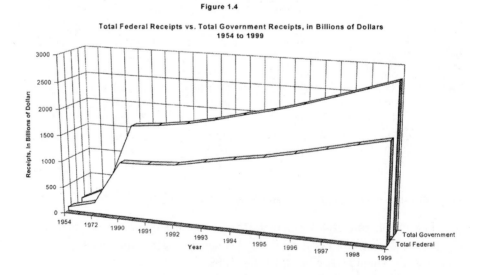

Figure 1.4

**Total Federal Receipts vs. Total Government Receipts, in Billions of Dollars
1954 to 1999**

At the state level, the sales tax and the income tax are the main sources of tax revenue. This represents a dramatic shift from the earlier part of this century when almost half of state tax revenues came from property taxes. The structure of state taxation varies. Most state income tax schemes resemble the federal system. State rates are lower than federal rates, and personal exemptions often are higher. Some states use the amounts reported on federal returns as starting points for completing state returns. Many individual and business taxpayers are required to file more than one state tax return.

Sales taxes are collected by vendors at the point of sale. A variety of exemptions and rate differentials across the states add to the complexity of sales tax systems. For example, many states attempt to soften the regressivity of sales taxes by exempting certain essentials like food or medicine. Sales tax rates now range from 3 percent to 10 percent; by comparison, in 1938 they ranged from 2.5 percent to 3 percent. Sales taxes have come to play an increasing fiscal role for state governments, one that varies more from state to state than it did in the past.

At the local level, the major source of tax revenue is still the property tax, imposed primarily on real property and on business inventory and equipment. There is apparently great variability in the assessments of property of equal value even within the same state, and underassessment seems to be "the rule rather than the exception." As a result, the property tax is the subject of widespread criticism, and there has been some tendency by local governments to diversify their revenue sources by imposing local sales or income taxes if state law allows it.

Although the populace often complains about high taxes, taxes in the United States are lower as a percentage of gross domestic product than in many other countries. When one adds state and local taxes to the federal take, total U.S. taxes are about 30 percent of GDP. This is low by international standards—the average for Organization for Economic Cooperation and Development ("OECD") countries is about 38 percent, with a range from 29–56 percent. Only Turkey enjoys total taxes lower as a percentage of GDP than the United States. But other countries' spending patterns are also different, especially with regard to health and education, where the government's share of spending is much higher than in the United States. The table and graphs below, which were derived from statistics collected by the OECD, show the relative percentage over time:

Table 1–3

Tax Revenues as a Percentage of GDP

United States and Selected Trading Partners

Country	1970	1980	1990	1993	1994	1995	1996	1997	1998
U.S.	27.77	27.00	26.70	26.90	27.30	27.60	27.90	28.30	28.90
Canada	31.20	32.00	36.10	35.50	35.40	35.70	36.10	36.90	37.40
France	35.10	40.60	43.00	43.30	44.70	44.00	45.00	45.20	45.20
Germany	32.90	33.10	32.60	37.90	38.10	38.20	37.40	37.00	37.00
Italy	26.10	30.30	38.90	44.20	41.40	41.20	42.70	44.20	42.70
Japan	19.70	25.40	30.90	28.70	27.80	28.40	28.20	28.70	28.40
U.K.	37.00	35.30	36.00	33.30	34.00	35.20	35.10	35.30	37.20

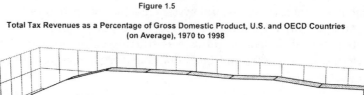

Figure 1.5

Total Tax Revenues as a Percentage of Gross Domestic Product, U.S. and OECD Countries
(on Average), 1970 to 1998

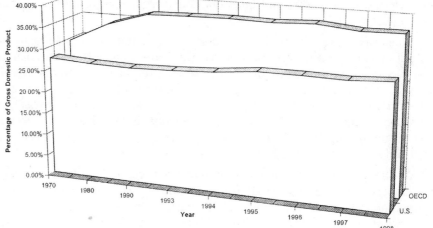

Figure 1.6

Tax Revenues as a Percentage of Gross Domestic Product, U.S. and Selected Trading
Partners, 1970 to 1998

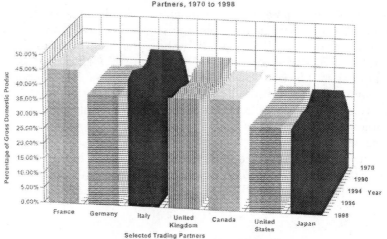

The United States relies more heavily on income and payroll taxes than do our trading partners, many of whom use consumption taxes, such as a value added tax, more extensively.

Table 1–4

Composition of Tax Revenues 1994

Percentage of Total Tax Revenues

Type of tax	Canada	France	Germany	Italy
Indiv. Income	37.8	17.4	25.0	25.0
Corp. Income	10.0	5.9	4.4	7.0
Consumption	23.2	26.0	26.3	24.4
Excise	9.1	8.4	8.4	10.2
Property	10.4	7.3	2.3	4.8
Social Security	13.7	36.2	40.4	29.4
Other	.5	4.0	0.0	5.3

Type of tax	Japan	United Kingdom	United States
Indiv. Income	18.8	27.5	40.5
Corp. Income	13.3	11.0	9.0
Consumption	16.7	30.8	14.1
Excise	7.7	12.8	6.5
Property	10.5	10.7	10.6
Social Security	38.4	17.6	23.7
Other	0.2	0.0	0.0

Figure 1.7

Personal Income Taxes as a Percentage of Gross Domestic Product, U.S. and OECD
Countries (on Average), 1970 to 1998

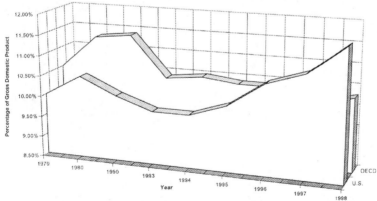

The composition of the tax base reflects important policy decisions. In general, excise and payroll taxes are usually earmarked to fund specific expenditures. For example, our payroll taxes fund retirement, disability, and survivors insurance under the Social Security system and hospital insurance for the elderly under Medicare. General revenue needs are more likely to be funded by income or consumption taxes. Over the last 20 years, the United States has changed the composition of its tax base. Total federal

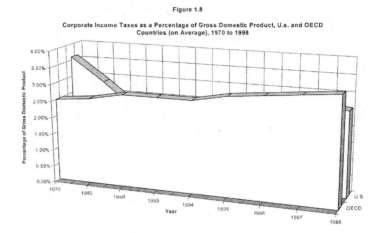

Figure 1.8

Corporate Income Taxes as a Percentage of Gross Domestic Product, U.s. and OECD Countries (on Average), 1970 to 1998

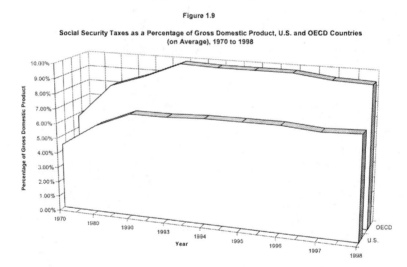

Figure 1.9

Social Security Taxes as a Percentage of Gross Domestic Product, U.S. and OECD Countries (on Average), 1970 to 1998

revenues have increased over time in both real and nominal terms because national output—GDP—has grown consistently over a long period of time. See Figure 1.1, supra at page 11. The important point here is that economic growth has long been the engine of federal revenues—not changes in the kinds or rates of tax, nor a dramatically more burdensome federal tax structure.

NOTE ON THE DISTRIBUTION OF INCOME AND INCOME TAXES

Income is distributed quite unequally in the United States, and during the period from the 1970's to 1992, it grew considerably more unequal. (See Figure 1.11) Researchers attribute this increase in income inequality principally to two factors: first, a greater share of total wages has been going to highly-skilled, trained, and educated workers at the top of the income distribution. This is due both to a shift away from goods-producing industries, which had provided relatively high wage opportunities for relatively low-skilled workers, to technical services industries, which disproportionately employ college graduates, and within-industry shifts in labor demand away from less-educated workers. Other factors are the decline in the proportion of workers who belong to unions, intensifying global competition, and the increasing use of temporary or part-time workers. Second, changes in family composition and living arrangements have increased the differences in families' incomes. Here, the key factor is the shift away from higher income married-couple households toward single-parent households. See Arthur F. Jones & Daniel H. Weinberg, "The Changing Shape of the Nation's Income Distribution, 1947–1998," U.S. Census Bureau, Current Population Report, June, 2000.

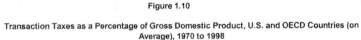

Figure 1.10

Transaction Taxes as a Percentage of Gross Domestic Product, U.S. and OECD Countries (on Average), 1970 to 1998

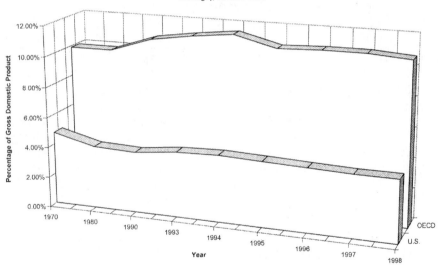

Figure 1.11
Household Shares of Aggregate Income by Quintile, 1975 and 1998

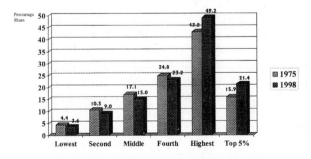

Source: Arthur F. Jones and Daniel H. Weinberg, "The Changing Shape of the Nation's Income Distribution, 1947-1998," U.S. Census Bureau Current Population Reports, June 2000

Students are often surprised at the levels of income at various percentiles of the income distribution. In 1999, for example, according to the Census Bureau, median household income in the United States was $40,816. Twenty percent of households had income of $17,196 or less; 80 percent had income of $79,375 or less. Income of $142,021 or more put a household in the top 5 percent. This is less than the income of a young associate at a large New York or Silicon Valley law firm.

Income for tax purposes is calculated differently from the Census Bureau's measure of household income, but tax data shows a similar dispersion of income. The dispersion of after-tax income is a bit more equal than pretax income because the U.S. tax system is somewhat progressive. The individual income tax is quite progressive as the following data from tax returns filed in 1999, published in the IRS Statistics of Income Bulletin, Fall 2001, demonstrates.

Size of adjusted gross income	Total	$1 under $10,000	$10,000 under $20,000	$20,000 under $30,000	$30,000 under $50,000	$50,000 under $100,000	$100,000 under $200,000	$200,000 under $500,000	$500,000 under $1 million	$1 Million or more
Numer of returns (millions)	127,075	26.328	11.782	18.359	22.958	24.567	7.105	1.876	.348	.205
Adjusted gross income (thousands of dollars)	$5,855,467,909	132,790,126	358,631,220	453,534,866	903,347,940	1,694,924,750	934,766,661	542,447,737	235,700,884	653,184,370
Total income tax (thousands of dollars)	$877,401,489	2,329,470	14,740,651	30,391,767	83,159,567	205,023,349	162,224,990	130,273,941	66,964,769	182,292,689
Tax as a percentage of AGI	15.7	1.7	4.03	6.7	9.2	12.1	17.4	24.0	28.4	27.9

Note that returns with income above $100,000 accounted for 7.5 percent of the returns filed, 40 percent of the total income, and paid 61.7 percent of the income tax. For more detail on the distribution of income and taxes, see Julie–Anne Cronin, "Distributional Analysis Methodology," U.S. Treasury, Office of Tax Analysis, Sept. 1, 1999 (available at 1999 TNT 182–66). For some of the pitfalls in distributional analyses, see Michael J. Graetz, "Paint-by-Numbers Tax Lawmaking," 95 Colum. Law Review 609 (1995).

SECTION 3. INTRODUCTION TO INCOME TAX TERMINOLOGY

This section offers an overview of some of the tax terminology to be used throughout this book. It is important for students to acquire a general familiarity with these terms and concepts early in their study of taxation; the details are provided subsequently.

Income tax is computed by multiplying *taxable income*—that is, *gross income* minus certain *deductions*—by the appropriate *tax rates*. This tax is then reduced by any allowable tax *credits* to determine the amount due.

Gross Income has been broadly defined by the Code and the Supreme Court to encompass "all income from whatever source derived." Thus, an individual's income may include not only wages, commissions, and other compensation for services, but also dividends, alimony payments, sweepstakes winnings, discharges of indebtedness, and so forth. Some receipts, however, that otherwise might be characterized as income—for example certain fringe benefits provided by an employer to its employees, such as health insurance—have been expressly excluded from income by Congress.

Income includes not only cash receipts, but also receipts in the form of services, property, or payments to third parties on the taxpayer's behalf.

Gross income also includes *gains* derived from the sale of securities, real estate, works of art, and other tangible and intangible property. The amount of gain generally is the excess of the price at which the taxpayer sold the property over the price at which she purchased the property. For example, a taxpayer who bought a share of stock for $50 and later sold it for $70 would realize a $20 taxable gain and a $50 nontaxable return of capital. The portion of the sales proceeds that the taxpayer may recover without incurring tax liability is called her *basis* in the property. The owner's *adjusted basis* in a purchased asset typically is her purchase price adjusted upward or downward to reflect subsequent expenditures or tax benefits attributable to the asset. If the adjusted basis exceeds the sales price, there is a *loss,* which sometimes may be taken into account for tax purposes. Gains and losses are not taken into account as they accrue over time, but only when they are *realized* by a sale or other disposition of the property. Gross income issues are examined in Chapter 2.

Various provisions of the Code allow or disallow the *deduction* of certain expenses in the computation of taxable income. For individuals, a distinction is made between expenses incurred in the production of business income, and expenses to earn investment income, which are generally deductible, and personal expenses, which generally are not deductible. Only a few of the latter are deductible without regard to profit-seeking motive—including, for example, home mortgage interest, certain state taxes, medical expenses, and charitable deductions—the so-called *itemized deductions.* First, certain expenses (generally business expenses) are subtracted by individuals from gross income to obtain *adjusted gross income.* Then the deductions for *personal and dependency exemptions* plus either the *standard deduction* or *itemized deductions* are subtracted from adjusted gross income to obtain taxable income. The standard deduction is a flat amount specified by the Code that varies with marital status, which the taxpayer may deduct regardless of actual expenses. If taxpayers are entitled to itemized deductions in excess of the standard deduction, they will claim the itemized deductions rather than the standard deduction. Itemized deductions are defined as all allowable deductions other than the deductions allowable in arriving at adjusted gross income and the personal exemptions. Taxpayers generally prefer deductions from gross income to deductions from adjusted gross income, since they benefit from the latter only when they total more than the applicable standard deduction. In addition, certain itemized deductions can be claimed only when they exceed a percentage of adjusted gross income; by reducing adjusted gross income, a larger itemized deduction sometimes may be claimed. Adjusted gross income, the standard deduction, and itemized deductions are concepts applicable to individual taxpayers; corporations simply subtract all allowable deductions from gross income to obtain taxable income.

Some expenditures incurred in the production of income (for example, the cost of a machine or a building) cannot be deducted immediately in the year paid or accrued. Instead, the expenditure must be *capitalized*—that is, added to the taxpayer's adjusted basis in the property with respect to which the expense was incurred. The taxpayer may recover some of these capital expenditures over a period of years by means of annual deductions for *depreciation* or *amortization;* he may recover other expenditures only upon the sale of the asset, when they will serve to reduce the gain (or increase the loss) he realizes. The following simple example illustrates this principle: A taxpayer pays $30,000 to obtain a piece of land and another $100,000 to construct a fast-food restaurant on the land. Neither expenditure is immediately deductible from income. The structure is a depreciable asset whose cost may be recovered over the first 39 years of its productive life in accordance with a prescribed schedule of annual depreciation deductions. The land, on the other hand, is a nondepreciable asset whose cost may be recovered only upon its sale by the taxpayer. Although the dollar amount of deductions may be the same regardless of when they are allowed to be taken, taxpayers usually prefer earlier deductions because of the resulting opportunity to defer tax liability on an offsetting amount of income and to earn interest on the taxes saved. Deductions are considered in Chapter 3.

The Code accords special tax treatment to *capital gains* and *capital losses* arising from the sale of certain (usually investment) property that the taxpayer has held for a specified period. For most taxpayers, long-term capital gains are taxed at more favorable rates than ordinary income. Capital losses are deductible to a more limited extent than ordinary losses, and generally are allowed to offset only $3,000 a year of an individual's ordinary income, such as wages or dividends. Taxpayers seek to characterize an asset as "capital" or "ordinary" depending upon whether its disposition produces a profit or a loss. This distinction between capital and ordinary gains and losses involves numerous Code sections and has generated a large body of complicated case law. The treatment of capital gains and losses is considered in detail in Chapter 5 of this book, but an awareness that capital gains are treated favorably and that deductions of capital losses are limited is assumed throughout.

Once taxable income is determined, the *tax rates* are applied. Individuals calculate their tax according to one of four tax-rate tables that depend on their filing status (married filing jointly, married filing separately, head of household, or single). The income tax is *progressive* in that the rate of tax applied to an individual's income increases as income increases. Although the income tax has always been somewhat progressive, the degree of progressivity has varied considerably. Prior to 1964, the rates applicable to individuals ranged from 11 percent to 90 percent. After the 2001 Act, these rates range from 10 to 38.6 percent with the top rate falling to 35 percent in 2006. The standard deduction, the personal exemption, and the rate tables are all adjusted for inflation.

It is important to distinguish between the *average rate* of tax applicable to taxable income as a whole and the *marginal rate* applicable to the last dollar of taxable income. Imagine a tax system in which taxpayers paid tax at a rate of 25 percent of their taxable income up to $20,000 and a rate of 50 percent on all taxable income above $20,000. We can now compute the tax of a taxpayer with $50,000 of taxable income:

Tax: .25 × 20,000   = $5,000
         .50 × 30,000   =   <u>15,000</u>
                              $20,000

Average rate = 40 percent (20,000/50,000).
Marginal rate = 50 percent (rate of tax on last dollar).

Suppose this taxpayer is entitled to a $5,000 deduction for business expenses. He will save tax at his marginal rate of 50 percent even though his average rate is 40 percent. His tax bill will go down by $2,500 and, consequently, his average tax rate will go down.

Gross Income			$50,000
Deduction		−	<u>5,000</u>
Taxable Income			$45,000
Tax	.25 × 20,000	=	5,000
	.50 × 25,000	=	<u>12,500</u>
			$17,500

Average rate = 38.89 percent (17,500/45,000).
Marginal rate = 50 percent.

Differences in marginal tax rates become important when income or deductions move the taxpayer into a different marginal bracket. Then the tax effect must be calculated at two different tax rates. The tax savings of additional dollars of deduction and the tax cost of additional income always should be evaluated at the relevant marginal tax rate.

Tax sometimes can be saved by shifting income to a taxpayer in a lower marginal tax bracket or shifting deductions to a taxpayer in a higher bracket. Chapter 4 discusses this shifting. A similar strategy also applies to changes in one taxpayer's marginal rate from year to year. It is to the taxpayer's advantage to report a gain in a year when her marginal tax bracket is low. Moreover, if tax rates do not change, it is better to pay a dollar of tax in the future than now. The longer the tax payment can be deferred, the greater the advantage to the taxpayer who can invest the money and earn interest during the interval. This idea is captured in the concept of present discounted value, which is the value now of money to be received or paid at some future time. Timing issues recur throughout this book and are discussed especially in Chapter 6. A table of present values is set forth in the Appendix.

Taxpayers may reduce their tax liability by the amount of any *credits* for which they are eligible. A credit represents a direct reduction in tax in the amount of the allowable credit, while a deduction represents a reduction in taxable income that, in turn, reduces tax liability by the amount of the allowable deduction multiplied by the taxpayer's marginal rate. Thus, a deduction is of greater dollar value to taxpayers with greater taxable income, while a credit provides similar reductions in tax to all taxpayers. Most credits are nonrefundable, which means they only offset tax liability. A few, like the earned income credit, are refundable, and for those, the taxpayer receives a refund to the extent the credit exceeds the tax liability. Consider, for example, the different effects of a credit and a deduction on the tax liabilities of A, who has taxable income of $200,000, and B, who has taxable income of $15,000. A $1,000 deduction would decrease A's tax liability by $400 ($1,000 multiplied by A's marginal tax rate of 40 percent), but would decrease B's tax liability by only $150 ($1,000 multiplied by B's marginal tax rate of 15 percent). A $200 credit would reduce the tax liability of both A and B by $200. Of course, the difference between the effects of credits and deductions becomes more pronounced as the difference between the bottom and top tax rates widens.

Summary. The description above illustrates the computation of income tax liability. The following five steps summarize that computation. The references to the relevant Internal Revenue Code sections provided parenthetically here are—as you will soon learn—merely a starting point in the determination of the tax. Other Code sections often alter the general rules provided in these section.

STEP ONE: Calculate *gross income* (§ 61).

STEP TWO: Subtract *"above-the-line"* deductions (enumerated in § 62). The resulting figure is known as *adjusted gross income* (§ 62).

STEP THREE: Subtract *"below-the-line"* deductions = the sum of personal exemptions (§§ 151 and 152) and *either* the *standard deduction* or *itemized deductions* (start with §§ 63 and 67). The resulting figure is known as *taxable income* (§ 63).

STEP FOUR: Apply the *tax rate schedules* (found in § 1) to *taxable income* to determine tentative tax liability.

STEP FIVE: Subtract from tentative *tax liability* any available *tax credits*. Bear in mind the important distinction between deductions and credits; deductions reduce income, while credits directly reduce tax liability. The remaining amount is final tax liability.

A second tax computation is required of certain high-income individuals who otherwise might pay little or no tax as a result of so-called items of tax preference that reduce their tax liability. This *alternative minimum tax* imposes tax at a rate of 26 percent on AMT income up to $175,000 and 28 percent on the excess. AMT income is a broader income tax base that is reduced by fewer deductions, exclusions and credits than the regular base. An AMT exemption amount of $49,000 is reduced by 25 percent of the amount by which "alternative minimum taxable income" exceeds $150,000. The exemption is totally phased out when AMT income exceeds $330,000 on a joint return. The AMT includes many items in the broadened tax base that are not included under the regular tax. The minimum tax provisions were intended to improve the fairness of the income tax by ensuring that taxpayers cannot reduce their tax liabilities to zero by combining tax preferences, exclusions, deductions, or credits, but this is achieved only at the cost of considerable complexity. Since the minimum tax must be paid whenever it is greater than the regular tax for which the individual otherwise would be liable, many taxpayers engage in tax planning and tax computations under both the AMT and regular provisions. The minimum tax is discussed in Chapter 7.

The income tax is assessed on an annual basis. The *taxable year* for most individuals and many businesses is simply the calendar year. Income or loss typically is allocated to one taxable year or another according to one of the two basic methods of accounting. The *cash method* generally includes items in income in the year in which they are received and allows items as deductions in the year in which they are paid. The *accrual method* includes items in income when earned, regardless of when they are actually received, and generally allows items as deductions in the year in which they are incurred, regardless of when they actually are paid. Most individuals and many service businesses use the cash method, while manufacturing, wholesale and retail and other corporations use the accrual method. Tax accounting is the subject of Chapter 6.

While the taxation of entities is not the subject of this coursebook, it is helpful to know the basic federal income tax treatment of various entities. Corporations and trusts and estates generally are treated under the Internal Revenue Code as distinct taxpaying entities (although trusts and estates do not pay tax on income currently distributed to beneficiaries). Partnerships and certain small corporations (known as S corporations), in contrast, are treated as mere conduits through which the income or losses of the business flow to the partners (or shareholders) to be included in their individual returns.

Corporations are taxed according to a graduated rate structure. No deduction is allowed a corporation for income distributed as dividends to its shareholders; hence, these distributions often are said to incur "double taxation"—once at the corporate level, and again at the shareholder level— to the extent that both parties are subject to tax.

The undistributed income of trusts and estates is taxed under a separate rate schedule. Trust income, however, may remain taxable to a grantor who retains a reversionary interest in the trust or who has certain powers under the trust instrument. The taxation of trusts and other entities is considered briefly in Chapter 4.

Filling in the details of this introduction to tax terminology is the task of the remainder of this book. As will quickly become clear, this chore frequently becomes quite complex.

SECTION 4. WHY TAX INCOME?

NOTE INTRODUCING CRITERIA FOR EVALUATING TAXES

How do we decide whether a particular tax is "good" or "bad"? There is widespread agreement that the criteria to be used in evaluating taxes are equity, efficiency, and simplicity. There is considerably less agreement, however, as to the precise meaning of these criteria and the relative priorities that they should be accorded, as well as to such underlying "facts" as the party who bears the ultimate burden of a particular tax or the effect of a tax on people's behavior.

The Equity Criterion. Tax equity requires that those with greater ability to pay taxes should pay more tax. It follows that those with equal ability to pay taxes should pay equal amounts of tax. In other words, for a tax to be "fair," it should not impose significantly different burdens on persons in similar economic circumstances.

This requires a determination of what are "similar economic circumstances" so that we can determine the identity of equals. The tax base is used to implement that criterion. Our current tax base is "income." Alternative bases are discussed in a Note, *infra,* at page 33. Thus, in an income tax, people with the same income ordinarily would pay the same amount of tax regardless of the sources and uses of their income, while people with greater income would pay greater amounts of that income in tax. (The first prong of this test often is termed "horizontal equity" while the second is termed "vertical equity.")

Simply because two equals are treated equally does not mean that the system is fair. The equals must be treated in an appropriate way as compared to the unequals. Some standard of distributive justice should determine how unequals should be taxed. For example, imagine four individuals, A and B, both of whom have economic income of $10,000, C, who has economic income of $50,000 and D, who has economic income of $200,000. Suppose our standard of distributive justice is such that D should pay four times as much tax as C and C should pay five times as much tax as A and B. Assume the current tax rules permit C to exclude all of his income from tax and A and B are each subject to $1,000 in taxes. Although A and B would be taxed the same, there would still be an equity violation because the treatment of C is inappropriate. The succeeding note discusses justifications for a progressive rate structure.

Even assuming Congress has agreed on the appropriate distribution of the tax burden and that income best measures ability to pay, there remains the difficult chore of defining income. Fulfilling this task is largely statutory; Chapter 2 explores the parameters of "income." But this definition is not etched in stone. As you think about what is meant by income, you should consider whether two individuals have equal ability to pay. That is, in principle, the definition of income should be such that those with equal ability to pay should be taxed the same and those with unequal ability to pay should be taxed differently.

It is also important that a tax system be perceived to be fair by the populace. If it is not, many observers expect that noncompliance will be widespread.

Finally, the distributional criterion suggested here—that people with greater ability to pay (as measured by income) should bear greater tax burdens is itself controversial. For example, some people claim that ability to pay is better measured by consumption or wealth and that is what should be taxed. Others contend that equity should be based on one's capacity to pay taxes, so that, for example, people with equal capacities to earn income should be taxed the same. And for some, distributional concerns should focus on equality of opportunity rather than the distribution of income.

The Efficiency Criterion. The efficiency criterion requires that a tax interfere as little as possible with people's economic behavior. The benchmark for this analysis typically is the allocation of goods and services that would occur in a market economy in the absence of taxes. In some fundamental sense, however, describing economic efficiency this way is nonsensical because a market economy simply cannot function in the absence of government institutions, which in turn must be financed through taxation. But, under certain idealized circumstances, a market allocation yields maximum total consumer satisfaction, given a distribution of wealth. Even in a world that does not meet these conditions, people are rightly concerned with potential reductions in the economy's ability to satisfy consumer demands because taxes change people's incentives to engage in important economic activities, such as work, savings, domestic or foreign investment, risk taking, or consumption.

Almost all taxes have efficiency costs, that is, they are non-neutral, because they will change the incentives to engage in various activities and this is likely to affect people's behavior and thus the allocation of resources. Sometimes this is desirable and Congress may consciously use a tax to affect behavior or to reallocate resources. But often the distortions are undesirable. There are two essential questions: How does a tax or a tax rule lead people to change their behavior? Why is the change desirable—or objectionable? The first of these questions is empirical, the second normative. Generally, a "good" tax is thought to be one that has as few efficiency costs as possible (given the need to satisfy other criteria, such as equity).

The efficiency criterion sometimes has other meanings. A tax is often said to be efficient when it promotes economic growth and inefficient when it inhibits such growth. Finally, efficiency sometimes refers to the extent to which incentive provisions provide benefits to taxpayers other than the intended beneficiaries. Where, for example, an unintended third party receives a benefit, or where the intended beneficiary receives less than the government loses in tax revenue, the tax provision is said to be inefficient.

On some important issues of tax policy, the norms of equity and efficiency are in harmony. For example, both economic efficiency and equity generally support uniform treatment of all sources and uses of income under an income tax. In other circumstances, however, equity and efficiency conflict. For example, equity might support taxing income when economic efficiency would imply taxing consumption or wages. Likewise, the disincentive for earning income may be increased under a progressive rate structure that applies higher rates to greater amounts of income, but a society's sense of tax justice may demand such progressivity.

The Simplicity Criterion. Simplicity often is viewed not as a separate norm, but as a feature of any tax system that is both equitable and efficient. Complex tax rules are inefficient because taxpayers must divert time from other activities in order to calculate their taxes (or to earn the money to pay for professional tax assistance) and because the government must maintain a large agency to interpret these complex rules and to ensure that taxes are calculated correctly.

Moreover, complexity is inequitable because taxpayers with equal abilities to pay may have different tax burdens because of their unequal abilities to understand or manipulate the tax rules. Generally, wealthier citizens are better able to turn tax ambiguities and complicated rules to their advantage in minimizing tax. Ambiguity and uncertainty also have a tendency to reward the most aggressive adversaries in a self-assessment system of reporting income tax liability such as ours where only a small percentage of returns filed each year are audited by the Internal Revenue Service. Of course, one would never intentionally design a tax system to benefit its strongest adversaries and penalize those most diligent in trying to comply with its requirements.

Adam Smith stated well the simplicity criterion: "The tax which each individual is bound to pay ought to be certain, and not arbitrary. The time of payment, the manner of payment, and the quantity to be paid ought to be clear and plain to the contributor, and to every other person. * * * Every tax ought to be levied at the time or in the manner in which it is most likely to be convenient for the contributor to pay it."

Unfortunately, the Internal Revenue Code—our nation's tax law—is extraordinarily complex. In a far simpler time, Albert Einstein regarded the federal income tax as the hardest thing in the world to understand: completing his own return, Einstein reputedly remarked, "This is too difficult for a mathematician, it takes a philosopher." More than thirty years ago, Judge Learned Hand expressed his frustration with the complexity of our tax laws:

> In my own case the words of such an act as the Income Tax, for example, merely dance before my eyes in a meaningless procession: cross-reference to cross-reference, exception upon exception—couched in abstract terms that offer no handle to seize hold of—leave in my mind only a confused sense of some vitally important, but successfully concealed, purport, which it is my duty to extract, but which is within my power, if at all, only after the most inordinate expenditure of time. I know that these monsters are the result of fabulous industry and ingenuity, plugging up this hole and casting out that net, against all possible evasion; yet at times I cannot help recalling a saying of William James about certain passages of Hegel: that they were no doubt written with a passion of rationality; but that one cannot help wondering whether to the reader they have any significance save that the words are strung together with syntactical correctness.

Learned Hand, The Spirit of Liberty 213 (1952).

As you study the current Internal Revenue Code, you too will quickly become convinced that it is not simple. You should try to understand why it is so complex. Professor David Bradford describes three kinds of complexity: compliance, transactional, and rule complexity. David F. Bradford, Untangling the Income Tax 266–67 (1986). The most easily understood is "rule complexity," which refers to the problems of understanding and interpreting the law. Rule complexity emanates from not only statutes, but also administrative rules (regulations and rulings) and case law. One of the questions we will often return to is whether simple rules (which usually must be interpreted by regulations or the courts) are better than more detailed rules. You should not automatically assume that long complex statutes are necessarily or always problematic. On the other hand, if one cannot understand her obligations (or cannot afford to pay someone to explain them), a rule that covers all the contingencies may be unenforceable.

"Compliance complexity" is the complexity that one encounters in complying with the law, that is, keeping the required records and filling out the appropriate forms. Any tax that requires extensive recordkeeping and perhaps professional tax assistance for ordinary citizens cannot be described as simple. Compliance complexity also refers to the government's ability to administer the law.

"Transactional complexity" is the complexity that arises when taxpayers organize their affairs to minimize taxes. It is created any time the tax law treats similar economic transactions differently. For example, in a particular transaction, the difference between debt and equity, or between a sale and a lease may be economically insignificant, but may have dramatically different tax consequences. Since the stakes are often quite high, a premium is placed on the form of the transaction. Furthermore, the taxation of business and investment income is inherently complicated because the transactions themselves are complex.

The complexity of the tax law is fair game for the jabs of politicians and pundits alike who delight at ridiculing 200–word sentences in the Internal Revenue Code. Simplifying the tax law, however, has proven to be a daunting political task. Despite universal complaints about complexity, there is no effective political constituency for tax simplification, and when Congress must choose between a simplification of the tax law and a complex alternative that either produces additional revenue or is claimed to increase economic efficiency or tax equity, the quest for simplification far too often is abandoned. Thus, complexity will continue to be a hallmark of our tax system.

The Special Problems of Economic Globalization. A nation's ability to impose taxes through a carefully structured compromise among the norms of equity, economic efficiency, and simplicity is severely limited by both flexibility in legal arrangements and the internationalization of economic activity. Because capital, in particular, is extremely mobile across international boundaries, national sovereignty over tax policy is threatened. For example, a nation's view of tax fairness may demand high and steeply progressive rates on capital income, but its ability to implement such a policy can be thwarted by citizens shifting wealth into foreign corporations and other entities employing that capital abroad. If a nation competing for capital investments reduces its taxes on capital or capital income to make such investments more attractive, an international race to the bottom—a "beggar thy neighbor" policy—can result and in the process undermine each nation's independent tax equity goals.

Issues of international taxation are not taken up in this introduction to income taxation, but international conflicts in applying tax policy norms to transactions that cross national borders inevitably must be faced. And these conflicts not only determine the economic burdens that may apply to the individuals that supply the capital for such transactions, but also produce debates about the appropriate sharing of tax revenues among the countries involved. The system of international taxation that governs transactions in today's modern global economy, which is characterized by instantaneous communication and capital transfers, is a relic from the early part of the 20th century, a time that predates both transoceanic flights and telephone calls. Improving this archaic system may well prove the greatest tax policy challenge of our time. Meanwhile, our national ability to collect revenues with fairness and economic efficiency is becoming more difficult.

NOTE: WHY PROGRESSIVE INCOME TAX RATES?

Although the federal income tax has always had a progressive rate structure, the degree of support for progressivity has varied over time. Some academics and policymakers have suggested replacing the progressive income tax rates with a flat-rate tax. Some of these proposals would dramatically redistribute the tax burden from upper income individuals to middle and lower income individuals. It therefore seems appropriate to reassess the arguments for progressivity that have recurred over time.

First, progressive rates are defended as essential to taxation based on ability to pay. This requires one to accept that those with larger incomes are better able to pay taxes than those with smaller incomes. The standard assumption is that equal amounts of income are not of equal value to all recipients. Instead, the incremental value of additional income is assumed to decline as income rises; for example, an additional $100 means less to a person earning $100,000 than to a person earning $10,000 and less to either of them than to a person earning $1,000.

This argument is criticized on the ground that the importance of particular preferences to individual taxpayers cannot be measured objectively. Indeed, there is little reason to assume that the progressive rate schedule is systematically related to the declining marginal utility of income.

Second, progressive rates are defended as a deliberate mechanism for reducing economic inequalities. The progressive income tax, however, has in fact done relatively little to reduce economic disparities in American society.

Third, progressive rates are said to be necessary to produce proportionality of the overall tax burden by offsetting the effects of other, more regressive taxes (such as federal payroll and excise taxes, state and local sales taxes, and perhaps property taxes).

Finally, some analysts defend progressive rates on the ground that the benefits of government expenditures increase progressively with income and wealth. This assertion seems to require acceptance of the view that governmental expenditures on international affairs, national defense, and public order are of special importance to those who are well off. Moreover, today many large government expenditures, particularly transfers through Social Security, Medicare, and Medicaid, benefit the less well-off. For example, taken as a whole, the Social Security system is progressive even though it is financed by a flat-rate payroll tax applicable to wages up to a specified ceiling.

The appropriate distributions of income and wealth, and the appropriate redistributive role of taxation, are controversial issues ultimately grounded in individual value judgments. In 1953, law professors Walter

Blum and Harry Kalven attempted to demonstrate that the case for progressive taxation was "stubborn but uneasy," concluding:

> It is hard to gain much comfort from the special arguments * * * constructed on notions of benefit, sacrifice, ability to pay, or economic stability. The case has stronger appeal when progressive taxation is viewed as a means of reducing economic inequalities. But the case for more economic equality, when examined directly, is itself perplexing. And the perplexity is greatly magnified for those who in the quest for greater equality are unwilling to argue for radical changes in the fundamental institutions of the society.[1]

Compare the response of Professor Boris Bittker:

> I cannot accept the argument that advocacy of socially-prescribed constraints on economic inequality is so inconsistent with a free market that it constitutes, or should if logically pursued lead to, "radical changes in the fundamental institutions of the society." * * * The case for progressive taxation is "uneasy" but it seems no more uneasy than the case for proportionality or for preferring one tax base over another.[2]

Bittker thus questioned the assumption that progressivity "must meet the burden of proof." He found support for his position in an anecdote offered by Dan T. Smith, former assistant secretary of the Treasury and professor of finance at Harvard. Smith had visited a one-room Montana schoolhouse and asked three children what would be a fair tax on a family with an income of $5,000 if a family with an income of $2,000 paid a tax of $200:

> The first child said, "500 dollars," thereby showing a predisposition for proportional burdens and perhaps a desire to make use of a newly acquired familiarity with percentages. A second child immediately disagreed, with the comment that the payment should be more than 500 dollars because "each dollar isn't so important" to the family with the larger income. A third child agreed but with the reservation that the additional tax over 500 dollars shouldn't be "too much more or they won't work so hard."

> In 1998, one of the authors of this book repeated Mr. Smith's experiment in his daughter's fifth grade classroom, and, remarkably, the first three students to speak gave answers identical to the Montana children, in exactly the same order. The intuitions about progressive taxation of the children of the 1990's in a New Haven, Connecticut, school mirrored precisely those of Montana school children in the 1960's. After learning that their answers were identical to those of Montana children three decades earlier, many students commented on how "cool," "neat," "amazing," and weird that was. One student

1. Walter Blum & Harry Kalven, The Uneasy Case for Progressive Taxation 103–04 (1953). Professor Blum, in a 1982 retrospective, concluded: "In the 1950's the case for progressive taxation was not easy. Subsequent developments in our society have made it no less, and perhaps even more uneasy."

Walter Blum, "Revisiting the Uneasy Case for Progressive Taxation," 60 Taxes 16, 21 (1982).

2. Charles Galvin & Boris I. Bittker, The Income Tax: How Progressive Should It Be? 56, 58 (1969).

concluded, "I guess that must be fair if both of the schools got the same answers," echoing Mr. Smith's earlier comment that "elaborate theoretical structures concerning diminishing utility and incentives and disincentives are all really refinements of the quasi-intuitive opinions of these children and may not lead to any greater certainty."[3]

These two experiments might serve as a caution to those who believe that the American public will regard as fair replacing a progressive tax on income with a flat-rate tax on consumption. That sentiment seems likely to last only until the second child speaks.

Indeed, the analytical starting point of most critics of progressive taxation is highly questionable.[4] They begin with the presumption that the market rewards the strong and fails to reward only the lazy, weak, or undeserving. Since income and wealth are regarded as manifestations of merit, they see little reason for taxing such income or wealth in order to fund government programs or redistribution to others.

The assumption that the market distribution is "just" creates the necessity for "making a case" for progressive taxation, indeed for any taxation at all. But there are several reasons not to regard market distributions as inherently fair or as presumptively just.

First, even when the market is functioning perfectly, returns to both capital and labor inputs depend upon the demand for the product or service being produced. People who supply capital or labor to endeavors where demand proves strong will do very well; people who work or risk their capital in endeavors where demand proves weak will do badly. These rewards depend on factors outside an individual's control. For example, the enormous demand for Britney Spears to sing has made her a very wealthy woman. If public tastes were to improve and demand for her services were to decrease, her income would decline dramatically without regard to any change in her ability or work effort.

Second, most production is based upon the joint use of different resources provided by different people. It is usually impossible, as an ethical matter, to determine which person produces what share of the total output.

Third, market returns to capital and labor are attributable in part to social conditions. The existence of public institutions—for example, laws and law-enforcement mechanisms—affects returns to private actors. It therefore might be appropriate to ask what portion of returns to labor and capital should be attributed to the society rather than to the individual.

Fourth, returns to capital and labor are dramatically affected by luck—for example, being born into a family of wealth and education rather than a family of poverty and ignorance. The empirical evidence shows that most of the wealth advantages of the truly rich are attributable to inherited wealth

---

3. Id. at 30–31 (citing Dan T. Smith, "High Progressive Tax Rates: Inequity and Immorality?" 20 U.Fla.L.Rev. 451–52 (1968)).

4. The material that follows is adapted from Michael Graetz, "To Praise the Estate Tax, Not to Bury It," 93 Yale L.J. 259 (1983).

and enormous one-shot gains. Both of these sources of great wealth are typically "morally arbitrary."

This litany is intended to call into question the typical starting point of people who attack the moral validity of progressive taxation by simply assuming that the market distributes rewards to people who deserve them and denies rewards to people who do not. Little of what we own is attributable to individual merit alone. All receipts are joint products, both individual and societal. Because individual and social characteristics are both essential to their joint outcome, there is simply no means by which a percentage of individual and social "desert" can be calculated.

The justification for a market distribution of income and wealth therefore must rely not on ethics, but on economic efficiency and consumer and producer sovereignty. This reflects the belief that a market economy avoids waste and improves the standard of living even for those with a lesser distributional share as well as the view that minimal governmental interference in the market increases freedom of choice and liberty generally.

Four separate liberties seem to be affected by any change in the market's distribution of income and wealth through taxation. The first is the liberty of consumer sovereignty: people's right to buy Britney Spears' records if they wish. The second is the liberty of producer sovereignty: Britney Spears' right to refuse to perform her songs in light of the amount she would be able to retain after taxes. These two important liberties are not constrained by progressivity in taxation.

The third liberty is Ms. Spears' right to keep all that is paid by the consumer for her songs, and the fourth is the right of her heirs to keep whatever of those payments she does not expend before her death. These liberties are not nearly so absolute. Moreover, there are also important conflicting liberties at stake—most significantly, the liberty interests of descendants of other people to start off with a rough equality of opportunity and of initial wealth.

The case for progressive taxation thus becomes far easier when one rejects the strong presumption that the market distribution of income and wealth is necessarily linked to fairness or freedom. Accepting the need for progression does not, however, necessarily require accepting a progressive income tax. For example, some commentators regard the combination of consumption and wealth taxes as superior to a progressive income tax alone.

NOTE ON ALTERNATIVE TAX BASES

The tax levied is the tax rate multiplied by the tax base. Income is only one of several possible bases for the imposition of tax. For example, state and local and foreign governments often impose tax on consumption (for example, by means of a sales or value-added tax) or on wealth (for example, by means of property taxes and taxes on wealth transferred by gift or at death). This Note considers various bases that might provide a significant long-term source of federal revenues.

Perhaps the most economically efficient tax would be a so-called head tax. A flat tax on each adult American above the poverty level in the amount of $5,000 would raise a trillion dollars to fund federal expenditures—assuming 200 million people were taxed. Unlike payroll, consumption, wealth, or income taxes, the amount of a head tax would not vary with work effort or earnings, consumption, savings, risk taking, or investment. A person could lawfully avoid the tax only by dying, emigrating, or becoming poor, so a head tax would have minimal impact in changing people's behavior. Despite the appeal of tax avoidance, very few would commit suicide and only a few more might emigrate; the principal behavioral effect would be other efforts to evade the tax. A head tax is manifestly unfair, however, because it ignores people's different abilities to pay and has never seriously been proposed in the United States.

In 1987, however, after winning a third term, the government of British Prime Minister Margaret Thatcher proposed a head tax on all adults—labelled a "poll tax" and euphemistically referred to as a "community charge"—to replace local residential property taxes. Despite considerable opposition on the grounds that a tax should not be imposed with such disregard for variations in people's ability to pay, the tax was enacted in 1988 and put into effect in Scotland in 1989 and in England and Wales in 1990. The British poll tax was justified by the argument that equal taxation of all persons within the taxing jurisdiction would promote greater political oversight by the citizenry of the spending decisions of local government units. This elevation of concerns for economic efficiency over equity proved a political disaster for Mrs. Thatcher and led to her being replaced as the head of Britain's Conservative party in November, 1990. The tax produced protests, civil unrest, and widespread refusals to pay. As many as one-fifth of all taxpayers required a summons to be issued before making payment. See Peter Smith, "Lessons from the British Poll Tax Disaster," 44 Nat'l Tax J. 421 (1991). The poll tax experience—which apparently married inept implementation to poor policy—made the extremely unpopular local property taxes seem positively benign. This political lesson from across the Atlantic proves both the necessity of public acceptance for tax reform to be successful and the folly of taking the recommendations of the economists too literally.

A tax theoretically could be based on the extent to which people benefit from government goods and services. This concept is currently embodied in the user fees assessed on campers at national parks and, more loosely, in the gasoline tax used to build and maintain federal highways. (The Social Security payroll tax often is portrayed as a sort of user charge through which workers purchase their future retirement benefits; in fact, the current generation of workers generally finances the benefits of the past generation and will have its own benefits financed by the next generation.)

There are major obstacles, both theoretical and practical, to extending this "benefit theory" to the financing of general government services. One is the difficulty of ascertaining the extent and intensity of taxpayers' demands for and use of each public program. How could defense expenditures, for example, be allocated among taxpayers based on the benefit that each receives? The benefit principle clearly would be inappropriate to transfer programs (such as Social Security, Food Stamps, and Medicaid and other welfare programs) that are, by definition, redistributive.

Many people feel that everything but the air they breathe (and sometimes even that) is subjected to tax by some level of government. As we have all come to know through experience, virtually any product or transaction can be taxed, and politicians therefore enjoy limitless potential to do mischief in deciding whom and what to tax. In addition, within any tax, there are myriad possible variations on the amount of tax that can be imposed as specific circumstances change. Moreover, in taxation—unlike other practices, such as discrimination in employment—the Constitution offers people no real protection against the whims of the politicians. The legislative playground frequently produces complexities, unfairness, and economic waste, all of which serve to reinforce the public's anti-tax sentiments.

In sharp contrast to the freedom politicians enjoy in determining how, when and where to impose taxes, financial reality severely limits the kinds of taxes that can serve effectively to finance the expenditures of government. All the governments of the world—including the United States—generally are financed by only three or four kinds of taxes: taxes on income, wages, consumption, or wealth. This is no accident. Income, wages, consumption, and wealth are the four general tax bases sufficiently robust to produce the revenues required that also generally can be said to satisfy the dominant criterion of a good tax, namely that it be fair—that the tax be connected in some way to a person's ability to pay. This basic principle of tax fairness was stated well more than two centuries ago by Adam Smith: "The subjects of every state ought to contribute towards the support of government, as nearly as possible in proportion to their respective abilities." Ability to pay has been measured historically in a variety of ways, although the task has always been essentially the same: to find some way to measure people's relative capacity to finance their government. In medieval England, for example, the tax collector counted the number of windows to determine the homeowner's taxpaying capacity. Perhaps tax avoidance explains the label: "The Dark Ages."

In modern times, each of these four broad tax bases—wages, consumption, income, and wealth—has been considered potentially capable of satisfying the ability-to-pay criterion. In the United States today, income and wage taxes are together the major sources of federal revenues—accounting for nearly 90 percent of all federal revenues—while consumption and wealth taxes have largely been left to state and local governments as a source of finance.

These four tax bases are linked to one another in a variety of ways. Wages, for example, are a form of income as well as a source of consumption and wealth. Wealth is one use of income and a source of both income and consumption. Both wages and wealth are sources of income and income is used for both consumption and wealth creation.

In terms of sources, an income tax base includes both income from labor and income from capital; in terms of uses, an income tax base includes savings as well as consumption. On the contrary, a consumption tax base exempts income that people save from taxation and imposes a burden more like a wage tax than an income tax.

Sometimes arguments for one of these tax bases over another are advanced by asserting "first principles" of fairness in taxation. Probably the most famous among these is John Stuart Mill's proposition that consumption taxes are the most fair because they tax only what individuals have removed from the common societal pool for their own personal consumption. Others claim income to be a superior tax base because it allows the government to claim a share of the returns from both the labor and capital of its citizens and residents—a share of the nation's total output—output that was made possible because of the existence of a variety of government institutions, including such diverse activities, for example, as the protection of property rights through the courts, public education, police and fire protection, and national defense.

Although not at all obvious, the principal distinction among these tax bases is one of timing. An extreme example illustrates the essential point. Imagine, if you will, a society that exists for only one time period. At the beginning of that period, there is no wealth and at the end of the period all remaining wealth has been consumed or is destroyed or, more benignly, is transferred to another society by either gift or bequest. A flat rate tax on wages, income, or consumption will raise the same revenue regardless of which of the tax bases is chosen.

More realistically, over a person's lifetime, she will spend (or consume) all of the income that she does not accumulate as wealth or transfer to others as gifts or bequests. Obviously, if one were willing to adopt a lifetime perspective to measure people's abilities to pay, a combination of a consumption tax and a wealth tax—or a consumption tax that treats gifts and bequests as income—would be quite good substitutes for a tax on income.

Indeed, many who would replace the current income taxes with consumption taxes argue that a lifetime perspective demonstrates that a consumption tax is fairer than an income tax because it treats equally people who consume identical amounts over their lifetimes in contrast to an income tax, which (by taxing income that is both spent and saved) taxes people who consume early in their lifetimes less heavily than those who postpone consumption by saving until later in life.

To the contrary, if fairness in taxation—taxing in accord with people's relative abilities to pay—should be measured over a shorter time horizon, an income tax base is a more comprehensive measure of a person's ability to pay than either wages or consumption. Although most observers agree that some averaging of progressive rates over a time horizon longer than one year is warranted, some analysts contend for an annual measuring rod of peoples' relative ability to pay since governments must collect taxes at least as frequently as annually.

This debate about the proper time horizon for assessing ability to pay will never be resolved to the satisfaction of the opposing camps; an annual period is no doubt too short for assessing people's relative capacity or ability to pay taxes, and a lifetime is probably too long given the contingencies and uncertainties of personal, political, and economic affairs. Some intermediate period over which the ups and downs of income or consumption can be averaged is probably best, but selecting such a time horizon is inevitably arbitrary, thereby shifting this dispute from the moral high ground of arguing about a "true" measure of fairness onto the quagmire of political compromise and debate. Nevertheless, it is revealing that in the income versus consumption tax debate, proponents of consumption taxes tend to emphasize claims grounded in economic efficiency, while income tax adherents stress fairness arguments.

Consumption taxes in the United States consist of selective excise taxes at the federal level and of retail sales taxes at the state and local levels. In Europe, consumption taxes usually take the form of value-added taxes. A value-added tax typically is collected at each stage of the production process as goods and services move from suppliers, to manufacturers, to wholesalers, to retailers. Sales taxes, in contrast, generally are collected only at the retail level.

These consumption taxes usually are imposed at a single rate. Thus, they are proportional with respect to consumption but regressive with respect to income. That is because high income people tend to devote a smaller percentage of their income to consumption than do lower income people. Value-added or sales taxes can be made proportional with respect to income, however, if certain consumption items (such as food, housing and medicine) are excluded from tax.

There have been occasional proposals for an "expenditure tax" that would apply a progressive rate structure to a consumption tax base. Individuals would compute their taxable consumption for the year by subtracting their net savings from their total receipts (including borrowing). Such a plan was proposed by the Treasury Department in 1977 and in 1994 by Senators Nunn and Domenici as an alternative to the income tax.

In 1995 and during the presidential campaign of 1996, polls showed a surprising degree of public support for an uncommon form of consumption tax known as the "flat tax." This tax, which was invented in 1981 by two Stanford professors, Robert Hall and Alvin Rabushka, is a variation on a form of value-added tax that looks a lot like an income tax. Collection of the tax would be split between a business-level tax and an individual-level tax on wages. In combination, the bases of the individual and business taxes equals sales, putting aside any exemptions. The principal advantages of this kind of tax are its relative simplicity for individuals and the fact that dividing the collection of a value-added type tax between businesses and individuals permits the exemption of a certain amount of wages from tax, eliminating for wage earners the regressivity of a standard flat-rate tax on consumption. The political advantage is that this tax looks more like an income tax than standard sales or value-added taxes. (For more, see Robert Hall & Alvin Rabushka, THE FLAT TAX (2d ed. 1995)) and Michael J. Graetz, THE U.S. INCOME TAX: WHAT IT IS, HOW IT GOT THAT WAY, AND WHERE WE GO FROM HERE, ch. 14 (1999).

The federal employment taxes are the most significant wage taxes levied in the United States. Wage taxes exempt from taxation capital and the income from capital, and consumption taxes are sometimes viewed as similar in this regard. See Alvin C. Warren, Jr., "How Much Capital

Income Taxed Under An Income Tax Is Exempt Under a Cash-flow Tax,"
52 Tax L. Rev. 1 (1996). Consequently, many economists have concluded
that wage and consumption taxes are less inhibitive of savings and capital
formation, and therefore are more conducive to economic growth, than are
wealth and income taxes. This perception has contributed to the growing
use of wage and consumption taxes at all levels of government. For
example, Social Security payroll taxes generated only 10 percent of federal
revenues in 1954 but nearly 32 percent of federal revenues in 1999.
Proposals for a national sales tax—typically in the form of a value-added
tax—resurface every several years.

The same factor that has caused some to embrace wage and consumption taxes on grounds of efficiency has caused others to reject these taxes
on grounds of equity: These taxes fail to take into account ability to pay
based on the accumulation of capital or on income derived from capital. A
person who consumes more may have a greater ability to pay than a person
who consumes less, and a person who earns higher wages may have a
greater ability to pay than a person who earns lower wages. But neither of
these measures in isolation may provide an accurate index of overall
economic well-being; consider, for example, the very wealthy person who
lives frugally and earns no wages.

Wealth taxes, which are imposed on capital accumulation, offer one
means of assuring that taxation is based on ability to pay. One lingering
legacy of the constitutional requirement that revenues from direct taxes
must be apportioned to the states in accordance with their population,
however, is that the federal government does not impose a periodic tax on
wealth. Instead, transfers of wealth by gift or bequest are subject to so-
called transfer taxes, better known as estate and gift taxes, which generally
account for only 1.5 percent of federal revenues. The threshold amounts for
imposition of these taxes are set high enough that these taxes are not a
concern for nine out of ten Americans; indeed, the estate tax in recent
years has applied only to the wealthiest one or two percent of Americans
who die each year. Nevertheless, the federal estate and gift taxes historically have made a significant contribution to the overall progressivity of the
tax system. In May 2001, Congress passed legislation to repeal the estate
tax (but not the gift tax), effective in 2010. The other major example of
wealth taxation in this country is the local property tax, which typically is
imposed only on real estate, automobiles, and certain tangible business
property.

Income taxes are imposed, typically at progressive rates, on individuals
and entities (including corporations) at both the federal and state levels.
High income tax rates, however, have been faulted on efficiency grounds for
discouraging savings and investment and perhaps stimulating noncompliance.

Our current federal "income" tax, in fact, has become a "hybrid" that
is part wage or consumption tax and part income tax. Many provisions of
the Internal Revenue Code have the effect of taxing income from capital
more favorably than income from services or of excluding capital income
from the tax base entirely. The hybrid nature of the tax reflects Congress'

compromise of its desire to base taxation on ability to pay, while not unduly inhibiting savings, capital formation, and economic growth.

The case for income as the tax base—rather than other bases discussed in this Note—ultimately is grounded in notions of equity. Notwithstanding its shortcomings, the federal income tax has come to symbolize the nation's commitment to just taxation based on ability to pay. One should not lose sight of this symbolic function of the income tax even while recognizing that there may be considerable dispute about what constitutes greater ability to pay, about the appropriate relationship between greater ability and greater tax burden, and about the appropriate tradeoffs between equity, efficiency, and simplicity.

SECTION 5.   THE TAX EXPENDITURE BUDGET

Excerpt From Estimates Of Federal Tax Expenditures For Fiscal Years 2000–2006

Staff of the Joint Committee on Taxation. January 17, 2002.

I.   THE CONCEPT OF TAX EXPENDITURES

Overview

"Tax expenditures" are defined under the Congressional Budget and Impoundment Control Act of 1974 ("Budget Act") as "revenue losses attributable to provisions of the Federal tax laws which allow a special exclusion, exemption, or deduction from gross income or which provide a special credit, a preferential rate of tax, or a deferral of tax liability." Thus, tax expenditures include any reductions in income tax liabilities that result from special tax provisions or regulations that provide tax benefits to particular taxpayers.

Special income tax provisions are referred to as tax expenditures because they may be considered to be analogous to direct outlay programs, and the two can be considered as alternative means of accomplishing similar budget policy objectives. Tax expenditures are most similar to those direct spending programs that have no spending limits, and that are available as entitlements to those who meet the statutory criteria established for the programs.

Estimates of tax expenditures are prepared for use in budget analysis. They are a measure of the economic benefits that are provided through the tax laws to various groups of taxpayers and sectors of the economy. The estimates also may be useful in determining the relative merits of achieving specified public goals through tax benefits or direct outlays.

The legislative history of the Budget Act indicates that tax expenditures are to be defined with reference to a normal income tax structure (referred to here as "normal income tax law"). The determination of whether a provision is a tax expenditure is made on the basis of a broad concept of income that is larger in scope than "income" as defined under general U.S. income tax principles. The Joint Committee staff has used its judgment in distinguishing between those income tax provisions (and regulations) that can be viewed as a part of normal income tax law and those special provisions that result in tax expenditures. A provision traditionally has been listed as a tax expenditure by the Joint Committee staff if there is a reasonable basis for such classification and the provision results in more than a de minimis revenue loss—which solely for this purpose means a total revenue loss of at least $50 million over the five fiscal years 2000–2006. The Joint Committee staff emphasizes, however, that in the process of listing tax expenditures, no judgment is made, nor any implication intended, about the desirability of any special tax provision as a matter of public policy.

If a tax expenditure provision were eliminated, Congress might choose to continue financial assistance through other means rather than terminate all Federal assistance for the activity. If a replacement spending program were enacted, the higher revenues received as a result of the elimination of a tax expenditure might not represent a net budget gain. A replacement program could involve direct expenditures, direct loans or loan guarantees, regulatory activity, a different form of tax expenditure, or a general reduction in tax rates. Joint Committee staff estimates of tax expenditures do not anticipate such policy responses.

The Budget Act uses the term tax expenditure to refer to the special tax provisions that are contained in the Federal income taxes on individuals and corporations. Other Federal taxes such as excise taxes, employment taxes, and estate and gift taxes may also have exceptions, exclusions, and credits, but those special tax provisions are not included in this report because they are not part of the income tax. Thus, for example, the income tax exclusion for employer-paid health insurance is included, but the Federal Insurance Contributions Act ("FICA") tax exclusion for employer-paid health insurance is not treated as a tax expenditure.

* * *

Comparisons with Treasury Department

The Joint Committee staff and Treasury lists of tax expenditures differ in [one] respect[]. * * * [T]he Treasury uses a different classification of those provisions that can be considered a part of normal income tax law under both the individual and business income taxes. In general, the Joint Committee staff methodology involves a narrower concept of normal income tax law.

* * *

II.   MEASUREMENT OF TAX EXPENDITURES

Tax Expenditure Estimates Generally

A tax expenditure is measured by the difference between tax liability under present law and the tax liability that would result from a recomputation of tax without benefit of the tax expenditure provision. Taxpayer behavior is assumed to remain unchanged for tax expenditure estimate purposes.

* * *

Each tax expenditure is estimated separately, under the assumption that all other tax expenditures remain in the tax code. If two or more tax expenditures were estimated simultaneously, the total change in tax liability could be smaller or larger than the sum of the amounts shown for each item separately, as a result of interactions among the tax expenditure provisions.

Year-to-year differences in the estimates for each tax expenditure reflect changes in tax law, including phaseouts of tax expenditure provisions and changes that alter the definition of the normal income tax structure, such as the tax rate schedule, the personal exemption amount, and the standard deduction. Some of the estimates for this tax expenditure report may differ from estimates made in previous years because of changes in law and economic conditions, the availability of better data, and improved estimating techniques.

Tax Expenditures versus Revenue Estimates

A tax expenditure estimate is not the same as a revenue estimate for the repeal of the tax expenditure provision for [one] reason[]. [T]ax expenditure estimates do not incorporate any changes in taxpayer behavior, whereas revenue estimates incorporate the effects of the behavioral changes that are anticipated to occur in response to the repeal of a tax provision. Second, tax expenditure estimates are concerned with changes in the tax liabilities of taxpayers. Because the tax expenditure focus is on tax liabilities as opposed to Federal government tax receipts, there is no concern for the timing of tax payments. Revenue estimates are concerned with changes in Federal tax receipts which are affected by the timing of tax payments. * * *

TAX EXPENDITURE ESTIMATES

(in billions)

The following chart is an abbreviated version of the Joint Committee's estimates for revenue losses from various tax expenditures for 2003:

National Defense	2.3
International Affairs	18.4
General Science	10.1
Energy	3.0
Natural Resources and Environment	1.2
Agriculture	0.4
Commerce and Housing	
Financial Institutions	0.9
Insurance Companies	30.1
Mortgage Interest	69.8
Property Taxes (homes)	22.1
Deferral of Gain and Exclusion on Homes	13.8
Other Housing	8.7

Capital Gains Rate	57.4
Accelerated Depreciation	
Real Estate	1.7
Equipment	39.4
Expensing	1.6
Carryover of Basis at Death	40.1
Deferral of Gains on Gifts	4.4
Installment Sales	1.0
Like Kind Exchanges	1.9
Transportation	3.8
Community Development	1.7
Education	
Bonds	.9
Tax Credits	4.3
Scholarships	1.4
Exemption for Students	1.0
Charitable Deduction	7.2
Student Loans	0.6
Employer-provided Assistance	0.7
Deduction for higher education expenses	2.1
Deduction for interest on student loans	0.6
Exclusion of earnings on education trusts	0.6
Employment	
Fringe Benefits	7.4
Cafeteria Plans	12.7
ESOPs	1.1
Pension Contributions	87.7
IRAs/Keoughs	21.8
Employee Life Insurance	2.4
Employee Accident and Disability Insurance	2.4
Social Services	
Child Credit	26.9
Charitable Contributions	32.9
Child Care	4.0
Adoption Credit and Foster Care	0.7
Health	
Bonds	0.5
Employer-provided Health Insurance Premiums	75.1
Self-employed Insurance Premiums	2.4
Medical Deduction	6.0
Workers' Comp Medical Care	3.7
Bond Interest	1.4
Charitable Contributions	5.2
Medicare	29.0
Income Security	
Workers Comp	5.6
Damages for personal injury	1.4
Cash Public Assistance	0.7
Standard Deduction for Blind and Elderly	2.1
Earned Income Credit	35.0
Casualty Losses	0.2
Social Security	23.5
Veteran's Benefits	2.6
State and Local Bonds	22.0
State and Local Tax Deduction	46.3

Source: Joint Committee on Taxation, Estimates of Federal Tax Expenditures for Fiscal Years 2000–2006

Excerpt From "Tax Subsidies as a Device For Implementing Government Policy: A Comparison With Direct Government Expenditures"

Hearings before the Subcommittee on Priorities and Economy in Government of the Joint Economic Committee, 92d Cong., 1st Sess., at 48–59 (1972) (Statement of Stanley S. Surrey).

The present federal income tax is replete with tax subsidy provisions. Some were adopted to assist particular industries, business activities, or financial transactions. Others were adopted to encourage nonbusiness activities considered socially useful, such as contributions to charity. Moreover, suggestions are constantly being made that many of our pressing national problems can be solved, or partially met, through the use of income tax subsidies.

It can generally be said that less critical analysis is paid to these tax subsidies than to almost any direct expenditure program one can mention. The tax subsidies tumble into the law without supporting studies, being propelled instead by cliches, debating points, and scraps of data and tables that are passed off as serious evidence. A tax system that is so vulnerable to this injection of extraneous, costly, and ill-considered expenditure programs is in a precarious state from the standpoint of the basic tax goals of providing adequate revenues and maintaining tax equity. It is therefore imperative that the process and substance of these tax subsidies be reexamined.

* * *

The Tax Expenditure Budget enables us to look at the income tax provisions reflected in that Budget in a new light. Once these tax provisions are seen not as inherent parts of an income tax structure but as carrying out programs of financial assistance for particular groups and activities, a number of questions immediately come into focus. Once we see that we are not evaluating technical tax provisions but rather expenditure programs, we are able to ask the traditional questions and use the analytical tools that make up the intellectual apparatus of expenditure experts.

We thus can put the basic question of whether we desire to provide that financial assistance at all, and if so in what amount—a stock question any budget expert would normally ask of any item in the regular Budget. We can inquire whether the program is working well, how its benefits compare with its costs, is it accomplishing its objectives—indeed, what are its objectives? Who is actually being assisted by the program and is that assistance too much or too little? Again, these are stock questions directed by any budget expert at existing programs. They all equally must be asked of the items and programs in the Tax Expenditure Budget.

The fact that the Tax Expenditure Budget summarizes an "expenditure system described in tax language" adds, however, a new dimension to these traditional questions. Each program in that Budget is carried out through a special tax provision. The financial assistance which the program grants is thus determined through the effect of that special provision on the tax liabilities of the persons benefitted. And also, since the persons benefitted are only those within the ambit of the income tax system, the program's assistance is confined to taxpayers and does not extend to non-taxpayers. Individuals whose income amounts are below personal exemption levels, businesses that are losing money rather than making profits, organizations that are tax exempt, being non-taxpayers they do not receive the assistance. As a consequence, before we analyze the tax expenditure program, we must first translate the tax language into expenditure results.

Thus, consider the tax expenditure program for housing represented by the deductibility of mortgage interest and property taxes paid on owner-occupied homes, listed as an item under [Commerce] and Housing. This is a program of assistance estimated at about [$74.1 billion, fiscal 2000]. The translation of the tax language in which the program is framed and the assistance provided—a *deduction* in computing taxable income—tells us first that the wealthier the individual the greater is his assistance under the program. This is because the higher the individual's income and thus the higher the individual's income tax rate, the larger is the tax benefit—the tax reduction—brought about by the deduction. * * * * [A]n individual or family whose income is so low that they are not required to pay an income tax—their income being below their personal exemptions and standard deduction—does not receive any financial assistance, for deductions benefit only taxpayers and not non-taxpayers. * * * *

The process of translation thus gives us the contours of the tax expenditure program for housing—contours that are quite different from the housing assistance programs formulated in direct expenditure terms. But the contrast—and hence the nature of the task of analysis in expenditure terms—can only be appreciated after the translation is made. It is only then that we can really ask the crucial question of how does this tax expenditure program measure up as an "expenditure" program. For then we can restate the tax program as a direct expenditure program and ask whether such a program represents a desirable policy.

The translation and consequent restatement of a tax expenditure program in direct expenditure terms generally shows an upside-down result utterly at variance with usual expenditure policies. Thus, if cast in direct expenditure language, the present assistance for owner-occupied homes under the tax deductions for mortgage interest and property taxes would look as follows [using 1971 tax rates], envisioned as a HUD program:

For a married couple with more than $200,000 in income, HUD would, for each $100 of mortgage interest on the couple's home, pay $70 to the bank holding the mortgage [because of the 70 percent marginal rate then applicable], leaving the couple to pay $30. It would also pay a similar portion of the couple's property tax to the State or city levying the tax.

For a married couple with income of $10,000, HUD would pay the bank on the couple's mortgage $19 [because of the 19 percent rate then applicable] per each $100 interest unit, with the couple paying $81. It would also pay a similar portion of the couple's property tax to the State or city levying the tax.

For a married couple too poor to pay an income tax, HUD would pay nothing to the bank, leaving the couple to pay the entire interest cost. The couple would also have to pay the entire property tax.

One can assume that no HUD Secretary would ever have presented to Congress a direct housing program with this upside-down effect.

Other illustrations exist—in fact almost any of these tax subsidies is seen as woefully unfair or inefficient when cast as a direct expenditure program.

* * *

The fact that a tax expenditure program can be recast as a direct expenditure program really takes us to the heart of tax reform, for it opens up a new way to consider the entire subject. We can regard a major aspect of income tax reform as involving the reexamination of all of the tax expenditure provisions now contained in the income tax. We should start by examining the list of tax expenditures and seeking to decide which should go and which should remain.

* * *

The questions then become:

Which tax programs—which tax expenditures—which tax incentives—which special tax provisions—can simply be dropped without substituting another form of government assistance, because on review it is seen that government policies and priorities do not require the expenditure of federal funds for the purposes involved in these items?

Which tax programs cannot be simply dropped—because government policies and priorities do require the expenditure of federal funds for the purposes involved—but can be readily changed from tax expenditures to direct expenditures, in a way to achieve an improvement in equity and efficiency?

Which tax programs, in the group which cannot simply be dropped, would have to meet special criteria regarding the structure of the substituted direct expenditure program, so that a change must await the development of the latter program?

Finally, which tax programs function much more efficiently and effectively as tax expenditure programs than as direct expenditures so that any consequent loss in tax equity or strain on the tax structure must yield to the need for the use of the tax system in this special case to carry out a particular government policy?

Excerpt From "Accounting For Federal 'Tax Subsidies' In The National Budget"

Boris I. Bittker, 22 National Tax Journal 244, 1969.

For some years, commentators have been asserting that federal income tax exemptions, credits, deductions, and rate reductions are the functional equivalents of federal expenditures, and that the failure to acknowledge this parallelism enables these "tax subsidies" to escape the public and congressional scrutiny that accompanies the appropriation of governmental funds. * * *

[T]hese "tax benefit provisions" will have to be separated from provisions that serve to define income accurately. * * * In the same vein, the Treasury study seeks to identify the provisions of existing law that deviate "from widely accepted definitions of income and standards of business accounting and from the generally accepted structure of an income tax."

To effect a "full accounting," then, we must first construct an ideal or correct income tax structure, departures from which will be reflected as "tax expenditures" in the National Budget.

* * *

The Treasury's "full accounting" will have to select one "correct model" [resolving structural issues that must be decided in any income tax law] against which to measure existing law. Because I see no way to select such an "official" model for these structural provisions, I am not sanguine about the prospects for a "full accounting."

One such area is the rate structure. In 1964, income tax rates were substantially reduced, for the stated purpose of encouraging economic growth. Since an alternative method of accomplishing this objective was a federal subsidy, should the reduction have been reflected in the Treasury's "Tax Expenditure Budget"? The logic of the "full accounting" approach suggests an affirmative response, so that the cost of this effort to increase economic growth by a rate reduction would be constantly brought to public attention, thus encouraging an annual review of both the merits of its objective and its efficiency as compared with other devices and programs to accomplish the same end.

Once it is decided that a rate reduction may be a form of "back door spending," however, we encounter a troublesome—perhaps an insoluble— problem of measurement. The cost of the 1964 experiment in encouraging economic growth by a rate reduction might, I suppose, be ascertained by computing the difference between (a) the revenue actually collected, and (b) the amount that would have been produced if the old rates had been perpetuated. (Ideally, of course, account should be taken of the effect of the reduced rate on the volume of taxable income; but if this is not done for other "tax expenditures," presumably it would not be done in this instance either.) The aggregate cost of the tax reduction would then be allocated among income classes, to reflect the cost of the tax cut for each such group. This process could be repeated for each tax cut in our history, so that the "tax expenditure" section of the National Budget would report, separately, the "cost" of every such change, classified as an aid to investment, a device to encourage consumer spending, and so on, depending on its purpose. The aggregate to be reported for the current year would thus be the difference between the revenue produced by the rates actually in effect, and the amount that would have been produced if the highest rates in history had been preserved. The benchmark year would vary from one taxable income class to another, of course, since the peak rate applicable to each class would be the standard for determining the "cost" of encouraging that group of taxpayers to engage in investment, consumption, or other tax-favored activity.

The computation of "tax expenditures" resulting from tax reductions would be even more forbidding if an attempt were made to distinguish between reductions granted to encourage such economic behavior as investment and consumption, and those reflecting a reduced need for federal revenue or a changed concept of equity. To separate rate reductions designed to serve allocative functions from those concerned with distributive fairness, one would either have to accept the formal statements by the President or the Congressional committees as conclusive, or engage a staff of political scientists and psychoanalysts to ascertain the "real" purpose of the statutory change. If we seek escape from this morass by disregarding the cost of rate reductions, however, we are concomitantly giving up the hope of achieving a "full accounting," and accepting instead a partial one. This slant or bias would be substantial, and it would be especially objectionable in light of the ease with which many deductions, credits and other allowances can be converted into rate reductions (and vice versa).

In an effort to mitigate this defect, we might distinguish between "general" rate reductions (i.e., those that apply to all taxpayers within a given taxable income class), and "special" reductions (i.e., those for which the taxpayer qualifies only by virtue of the type, location, or other characteristics of his activities); and, having made this distinction, we could include the revenue "cost" of the latter category of rate reductions in the "tax expenditure" roster, while disregarding the former category. For myself, however, the adjectives "general" and "special" have no meaning in this context: a rate reduction granted to encourage investment by a group of taxpayers (e.g., those with taxable income above $50,000) because of their propensity to invest their after-tax income seems just as "special" (or "general") to me as a rate reduction granted to taxpayers because of the nature of their investments (e.g., capital assets), the location of their business activities (e.g., Western Hemisphere Trade Corporations), or their political allegiance (e.g., citizens of "treaty countries"). Even if the terms "general" and "special" were meaningful, moreover, they would not describe categories that are relevant to the purpose at hand: the "full accounting" is supposed to report the cost of influencing economic behavior by manipulating the federal income tax structure, a function that can be served interchangeably by rate reductions (whether "general" or "special"), deductions, credits, exclusions, or other allowances.

Another problem * * * equally troublesome to the "full accounting" approach—is the taxable unit to be used in computing the "tax expenditures" that are to be reflected in the National Budget. The problem can be illustrated by a question: should the difference between the tax liability of a married man (or a head of a household) and that of a single individual with the same taxable income be reflected on the expenditure side of the National Budget, as a subsidy to family life, in the interest of a "full accounting"? Does the answer depend upon whether the tax differential exceeds the additional cost of living incurred by a married man? Upon whether the "proper" taxpaying unit is the individual, the married couple, the family, or the clan? Or whether we can properly describe our federal tax system as consisting of three separate taxes (one levied on individuals, the second levied on married couples, and the third levied on heads-of-households), none of which contains any "departures" or "subsidies" because each is imposed solely on its own appropriate constituency?

* * *

The proper classification of tax-exempt organizations presents another problem for the "full accounting" approach. Should the tax exemptions accorded to educational institutions, churches, charitable organizations, social clubs, and other non-profit institutions be reflected as "tax expenditures" to benefit education, religion, charity, and social intercourse? Or is it more appropriate to view the federal income tax as a device by which the government shares in the profits of activities that are carried on for the personal benefit of individual taxpayers, so that the activities of non-profit institutions are not a proper subject for income taxation? So regarded, the tax exemption accorded to these institutions is an acknowledgment of, rather than a departure from, the "true nature" of the federal income tax; and hence it is not a "tax expenditure" required for a "full accounting" in the National Budget. It may be that the Treasury's Tax Expenditure Budget accepts this theory, since it contains no estimate of the revenue cost of exempting non-profit organizations; but perhaps the omission is attributable to an insufficiency of data for a reliable computation.

* * *

To pick and choose among these tax provisions, recording some but not others as "tax expenditures," is a way of compromising on a middle ground, but it falls short of a "full accounting."

* * *

I cannot discern behind the tangle of rules * * * an "ideal," "model," or "correct approach"—modifications of which constitute "tax expenditures." It is obvious, of course, that these provisions favor some taxpayers over others; but if we are to use as a baseline the tax treatment of the least-favored taxpayer, and classify as an expenditure every allowance enjoyed by any other taxpayer, the entire amount of revenue lost under these provisions is an expenditure. Although I doubt that this draconic result is what Mr. Surrey had in mind in calling for a "full accounting," I see no other way to calculate the amount that is "expended". * * *

Yet if we disregard these (and comparable) structural provisions, on the ground that there are no models in this area and hence no departures from normality, the promised "full accounting" becomes seriously lopsided.

* * *

If the lack of an agreed conceptual model makes it impossible to say whether a large number of structural features of the existing federal income tax laws are, or are not, "tax expenditures," the proposed "full accounting" may turn out, in the end, to be only a partial accounting. In this event, it will succeed in bringing some issues to the fore only to conceal others; the same objections now offered to the "burial" of federal expenditures in the Internal Revenue Code will apply, but to a different set of tax concessions. Indeed, the claim that tax subsidies have been exposed to the pitiless glare of publicity will itself help to hide the undisclosed subsidies. Halftruths are often more deceptive than silence. The danger can be illustrated by the Treasury's Tax Expenditure Budget, which [for 1968] reports about $21 billion of tax expenditures on health, labor, welfare, housing, education, and veterans' benefits, as compared with about $16–19 billion for commerce, transportation, agriculture, and natural resources. The inference that is likely to be drawn from this comparison is that "tax expenditures" are of greater benefit to social welfare activities than to business and industry. If the estimate for the business sector had embraced the cost of excluding unrealized appreciation from income, however, an observer would draw a very different conclusion about the allocation of federal resources.

* * *

The proposal is feasible only to the extent that we can agree on a conceptual model, for a "tax expenditure" is nothing more than an estimate of the amount of revenue that would be raised if the tax law conformed to such an agreed model. * * *

The trouble is that * * * any system of income taxation is an aggregation of decisions about a host of structural issues. * * * As to these, one could lock forty tax experts in a room for forty days, and get no agreement—except as a surrender to hunger or boredom * * *. For such issues, every man can create his own set of "tax expenditures," but it will be no more than his collection of disparities between the income tax law as it is, and as he thinks it ought to be. Such compilations would be interesting, but I do not know how we can select one of them for inclusion in the National Budget.

NOTES

(A) *A Continuing Debate.* Both of the foregoing excerpts from Stanley Surrey's testimony and Boris Bittker's article are now more than 30 years old. The figures used are, of course, out of date and today's rate structure is flatter so that taxpayers are no longer arrayed along a series of brackets ranging from 14 percent to 70 percent. Nevertheless, the issues raised in these excerpts continue to have a tremendous impact—both in the literature and in Congress—in debates over revision of the income tax laws.* In some sense, Professor Surrey won the debate since the federal budget now contains as an Appendix each year a tax expenditure list and accounting. In his first budget as President in April 2001, George W. Bush announced that he believed the tax expenditure concept to be of "questionable analytic value" and that his administration would "reconsider this presentation in the future." In any event, Professor Surrey's optimism that such an

---

* For a reply to Professor Bittker's article, see Stanley Surrey & William Hellmuth, "The Tax Expenditure Budget—Response to Professor Bittker," 22 Nat'l Tax J. 528 (1969). For a more comprehensive statement of Professor Surrey's position, see Stanley S. Surrey & Paul R. McDaniel, Tax Expenditures (1985).

accounting would be a first step toward the elimination or rationalization of "tax expenditures" has not proven warranted.

As you go through subsequent materials in this book, it is sometimes helpful to ask whether the provision under study is more appropriately classified as a tax expenditure or as a proper provision in developing a definition of income. Professor Bittker objects to the tax expenditure concept because of the inherent difficulty of defining the "correct model." But it is not necessary to agree on an "official model" to make use of tax expenditure analysis. In order to classify a provision as a tax expenditure, one needs a referent; a tax expenditure is a provision that deviates from the referent. The referent may be, but does not necessarily have to be, an ideal income tax. For example, the Joint Committee's referent excludes certain items on administrative grounds that probably would be included in an "ideal tax."

(B) *Growth of Tax Expenditures.* There has been a rapid increase in the number of tax expenditures and in their revenue cost in the past two decades. The largest tax expenditures, however, are of long standing. The increase in tax expenditures is due both to enactment of new tax credits and deductions and greater use of old provisions.

Little tax expenditures often grow into big ones. For example, the exclusion from employees' income of premiums for medical insurance and medical benefits provided by employers was estimated to cost $1.4 billion in 1970 and $75.1 billion in 2000. Even the smallest and most innocuous proposal for new tax preferences should be scrutinized closely.

(C) *Some Additional Features of Tax Expenditures.* Unlike direct expenditures that can be eliminated only by outright repeal, tax expenditures can be eliminated in two ways—by either repealing the tax expenditure or repealing the tax. Thus, the Tax Expenditure Budget would go to zero if income taxes were repealed.

In some cases, taxpayers make imaginative use of tax expenditure and structural tax provisions to enjoy "negative tax rates" that not only reduce tax on the favored transaction to zero but also achieve an additional reduction. In such cases, the tax laws encourage transactions that would not be made in a world of no taxes. The distinction should be noted between tax preferences that encourage these economically inefficient transactions and tax preferences that reduce barriers to otherwise efficient transactions. This important distinction is often lost in discussions of tax expenditures. This matter is considered in a variety of contexts in subsequent chapters of this book.

(D) *Alternative Government Mechanisms for Reallocating Resources.* The power of the government is often used to alter the allocation of resources within society. Tax expenditure analysis should alert the student to consider the efficacy and equity of achieving these reallocations through income tax provisions rather than direct government subsidies or other government actions. Tax and direct subsidies are not the only potential public- and private-law mechanisms for affecting the allocation of resources. An example will illustrate the variety of policy options available:

Example: The government has determined that it is in the national interest to reduce the consumption of home heating fuels by encouraging the installation of thermal efficiency improvements such as insulation and storm windows in existing homes. As a result, Congress enacted an individual income tax credit equal to 15 percent of the first $2,000 of "energy conservation expenditures," at a substantial cost of revenue lost. How else might this policy have been implemented? What are the advantages and disadvantages of the following alternatives?

(1) Provide an individual income tax deduction that would result in an equivalent revenue loss.

(2) Provide a new income tax credit (or deduction) resulting in an equivalent revenue loss to companies that manufacture and produce storm windows and home insulation materials.

(3) Provide individuals a direct subsidy equal to 15 percent of the first $2,000 of their expenditures on thermal efficiency improvements.

(4) Provide manufacturers of storm windows and home insulation direct subsidies equalling the revenue loss of the tax credit.

(5) Prohibit the distribution of federal funds to any municipality that does not adopt housing code regulations requiring a specified thermal efficiency in homes.

(6) Require a "thermal efficiency certificate" to be provided to all purchasers of housing. The certificate would indicate the type of insulation and estimate the thermal efficiency of the home.

(7) Establish production quotas and maximum prices for storm windows and insulation in order to reduce prices and increase output. (Is this a condemnation? If payments were made to compensate for a taking, would this be different from a subsidy?)

(8) Create a new crime for failure to insulate residences.

(9) Revise the law of trespass and unjust enrichment so that a person who insulates the home of another can collect the value of such insulation.

(E) *A Tax Credit for Laptops.* In his first appearance before the House Ways and Means Committee after becoming Speaker of the House in January 1995, Newt Gingrich recommended a tax credit to fund laptop computers for poor children to help them become more effective in the new "third wave" information age. Later in that week, he called this a "dumb idea." Is it dumb for the government to try to help poor children own computers or dumb to try to enact a tax credit for this purpose? Or is it dumb to simultaneously be opposed to any new government programs to transfer laptops or dollars to people and support a tax credit for that purpose?

For a moment, take the tax credit for laptops idea seriously. How would you design such a credit? Consider the following: How would you limit the credit to people at a specific income level? How would you define income for this purpose? What rules would apply to people with incomes above the specified amounts? Is income sufficient to distinguish those who "deserve" such a credit from those who don't? Should all members of a family qualify for the credit? What qualifies as an eligible "laptop"? For example, are Palms eligible? Does bundled software qualify? Internet connections? Training and technical support? Are you going to include rules to block pornography or violence? How many pages of tax form instructions are you going to add for this tax credit?

Compare the Israeli government's plan to give personal computers to 100,000 poor children. Which is the better policy? Israeli economic commentator Sever Plotzker was skeptical, remarking, "Maybe the most important thing would be to assure them a quiet home for study * * * to give them books, and then more books."

(F) *Tax Penalty Budget.* A "tax penalty budget" would include the revenue Congress is collecting by adopting provisions that increase the tax base above the normative tax base or the referent. For example, although an income tax usually encompasses a deduction for the costs of producing taxable income, the Code prohibits deducting the costs incurred in the sale of illegal drugs. In some cases, the Code also prohibits companies from deducting a salary it pays an executive in excess of $1 million. Such provisions would be included in a tax penalty budget. Neither the Joint Committee nor the Treasury Department prepares a tax penalty budget.

(G) *Oh (sigh!) Those "Liberals."* What is your reaction to the following objection to the "tax expenditure" concept from the editorial page of the Wall Street Journal, March 20, 1975?

As we all should know by now * * * nothing any of us earn really belongs to us. Everything belongs to the federal government. Only because we have a lot of charitable politicians in Washington does it happen that we are permitted to keep a portion of that which we produce. The politicians, after all, are kind enough to write tax laws from time to time that enable all Americans to benefit from their generosity.

If you are in the highest productive category, the government allows you to keep at least 28% of your earnings [now 60 percent]. If you are in the least productive category, the government rewards you with all of your earnings. In between, the government not only showers us with benefits in the form of budget outlays, it also has figured out special ways to let us keep the money we've earned—even though that money belongs to the government. These are called "tax expenditures," or "tax loopholes."

In case we might forget that the government not only gives us good things through budget outlays, but also through tax expenditures, congressional liberals a while back ordered the Office of Management and Budget to tote up the revenues the government was foregoing in this fashion. * * * The liberals are now complaining that nobody in government is studying the "cost effectiveness" of spending money this way. The idea, we suppose, is that maybe the government would do a better job of keeping this money and spending it directly. To look at it this way, maybe we'd be better off if the government kept all of what really belongs to it, $1.3 trillion of personal income, and made all our purchases for us. Now there's a loophole.

(H) *Oh (sigh!) Those "Conservatives."* Contrast the following excerpt from Calvin Trillin, "Taxing Problems," in Uncivil Liberties (35–38):

> For some reason, everybody wants to argue only about how high property taxes are, completely overlooking their potential as an instrument of public policy. For years, the property tax has remained philosophically dormant while the income tax laws expressed the values of the society. Allowing an income-tax deduction for mortgage interest, for instance, is obviously another way of saying that every man should have a castle—or two or three castles if he is able to pick up a deal on a beach house and scrapes up the down payment on a ski chalet. The ceiling on taxation of capital gains reflects the national belief that speculation is a more worthwhile way to make a living than work. The deduction for charitable contributions is simply the government's way of indicating that rich people are in a better position than poor people to decide which eleemosynary institutions are deserving of the taxpayers' support. Why else would coal miners be required to share the cost of a stockbroker's gift to the St. Paul's School's boathouse fund? The laws providing tax shelters reflect the strong philosophical commitment of the Founding Fathers, particularly Alexander Hamilton, to the principle that the public good would be served if dentists owned cattle ranches.

* * *

> For years, I have had a fantasy that helps me fall asleep peacefully. On some cold winter night, a paramilitary strike force of Townies in some place like Nantucket or Edgartown, Martha's Vineyard, ties up all watchmen thought to be loyal to the summer people and then paints every weathered shingle house in town, alternating house by house between turquoise and salmon pink. If property taxes were properly used, there would be no need for such turmoil. The Townies, safely in control of government all winter, would simply assess property owners $14 for each unpainted shingle, and then sit back while every house in town was painted by what one of my predecessors in this line of work referred to as the Invisible Hand. For the sake of such a peaceful transition, I'd even be willing to give up my fantasy about * * * the populists taking over in Beverly Hills.

SECTION 6.   AN OVERVIEW OF THE TAXING PROCESS

The relative impact of the three branches of government—the legislature, the executive, and the judiciary—on the formulation of tax policy has varied over time. Resolution of constitutional issues was critical in the early days of the income tax. The judiciary, performing its traditional function in interpreting the Constitution, was of foremost importance. But since the constitutional validity of the income tax was settled by the ratification of the Sixteenth Amendment in 1913, the general authority of the Congress in the field of taxation has not been significantly challenged. Congress, in turn, has delegated substantial powers to Treasury. Today, the courts function principally to review legal determinations by Treasury.

A pessimist might describe the process as follows: (1) Congress amends the Internal Revenue Code; (2) Treasury interprets the amendment; (3) taxpayers with a financial interest in the outcome disagree with Treasury's interpretation and litigate the issue; (4) after considerable time has passed, one circuit court of appeals agrees with the taxpayers; (5) another circuit court of appeals agrees with the IRS; (6) the Supreme Court denies certiorari and Congress ignores the issue—confusion reigns or (6) the Supreme Court grants certiorari and resolves the conflict; (7) Congress disagrees with the Supreme Court's interpretation and amends the statute; (8) go back six places to (2) above.

The process for formulating tax law is considered in the materials that follow. The section focuses in turn on the legislative, administrative, and judicial processes.

A. Constitutional Provisions

In the early days of the income tax, there were some important constitutional hurdles, and perhaps there will be others in times to come. Currently, however, constitutional issues do not seem nearly as important as they did at an earlier time. The relevant constitutional provisions follow:

Article I, Section 2, clause 3:

"Representatives and direct Taxes shall be apportioned among the several States which may be included within this Union, according to their respective Numbers, which shall be determined by adding to the whole Number of free Persons, including those bound to Service for a Term of Years, and excluding Indians not taxed, three-fifths of all other Persons."*

Article I, Section 7, clause 1:

"All Bills for raising Revenue shall originate in the House of Representatives; but the Senate may propose or concur with amendments as on other Bills."

Article I, Section 8, clause 1:

"The Congress shall have Power To lay and collect Taxes, Duties, Imposts and Excises, to pay the Debts and provide for the common Defence and general Welfare of the United States; but all Duties, Imposts and Excises shall be uniform throughout the United States; * * *."

Article I, Section 9, clauses 4 and 5:

"No Capitation, or other direct, Tax shall be laid, unless in Proportion to the Census or Enumeration herein before directed to be taken.

"No Tax or Duty shall be laid on Articles exported from any State."

---

* The part of this clause relating to the method of apportionment was amended by the Fourteenth Amendment, clause 2, and as to taxes on income by the Sixteenth Amendment, which is quoted below.

Article I, Section 10, clauses 2 and 3:

"No State shall, without the Consent of the Congress, lay any Imposts or Duties on Imports or Exports, except what may be absolutely necessary for executing its inspection Laws: and the net Produce of all Duties and Imposts, laid by any State on Imports, or Exports, shall be for the Use of the Treasury of the United States; and all such Laws shall be subject to the Revision and Controul of the Congress.

"No State shall, without the Consent of Congress, lay any Duty of Tonnage, * * * "

Fifth Amendment:

"No person shall be held to answer for a capital, or otherwise infamous crime, unless on a presentment or indictment of a Grand Jury, except in cases arising in the land or naval forces, or in the Militia, when in actual service in time of War or public danger; nor shall any person be subject for the same offence to be twice put in jeopardy of life or limb; nor shall be compelled in any criminal case to be a witness against himself, nor be deprived of life, liberty, or property, without due process of law; nor shall private property be taken for public use, without just compensation."

Tenth Amendment

"The powers not delegated to the United States by the Constitution, nor prohibited by it to the States, are reserved to the States respectively, or to the people."

Sixteenth Amendment

"The Congress shall have power to lay and collect taxes on incomes, from whatever source derived, without apportionment among the several States, and without regard to any census or enumeration."

The provision of Article I, Section 2, which insists that "direct taxes shall be apportioned among the several states" was rather clearly intended to prevent the more heavily populated manufacturing states from financing the federal government's spending by imposing land taxes that would disproportionately burden the farming states, although even today much mystery still attends the question what—if anything, in addition to a land tax or a head tax—is a direct tax. As the history section of this Chapter described, in 1895, the Supreme Court construed this direct tax clause to hold unconstitutional—without apportionment to the states based on their population—the federal income tax of 1894. That decision was reversed by the adoption of the Sixteenth Amendment in 1913, which permits Congress to tax income "from whatever source derived."

Notwithstanding the striking down of the 1894 income tax, the broad discretion of Congress in the tax field has generally been accepted by the Supreme Court. The Court has on occasion, however, and particularly during the early 20th century, overturned tax statutes designed to accomplish purposes other than raising revenues. One such tax was imposed in 1918 on the profits of employers of child labor. The tax was enacted immediately after the Court had held unconstitutional a statute prohibiting the interstate transportation of goods manufactured at factories where child labor was employed. The Court then struck down the tax statute in the Child Labor Tax Case, 259 U.S. 20 (1922), observing:

> Grant the validity of this law, and all that Congress would need to do, hereafter, in seeking to take over to its control any one of the great number of subjects of public interest, jurisdiction of which the States have never parted with, and which are reserved to them by the Tenth Amendment, would be to enact a detailed measure of complete regulation of the subject and enforce it by a so-called tax upon departures from it. To give such magic to the word "tax" would be to break down all constitutional limitation of the powers of Congress and completely wipe out the sovereignty of the states.

The Court similarly overturned in United States v. Butler, 297 U.S. 1 (1936), a tax on "the first domestic processing" of certain farm commodities. The proceeds from the tax were to be used for agricultural purposes, including payments to farmers who agreed to reduce production of the commodities. The Court observed that, since Congress had no power directly to force farmers to reduce their production, "it may not indirectly accomplish those ends by taxing and spending to purchase compliance."

The Supreme Court, however, began to acknowledge Congress' power to enact such tax statutes beginning in the late 1930's when it became more accommodating of economic regulations generally. This new attitude was made evident, for example, in Mulford v. Smith, 307 U.S. 38 (1939), which sustained the imposition of penalties under the Agricultural Adjustment Act of 1938, and in Sunshine Anthracite Coal Co. v. Adkins, 310 U.S. 381 (1940), which upheld a tax on coal producers who refused to join a code established by the Bituminous Coal Commission. The Court declared in the latter case:

> Clearly this tax is not designed merely for revenue purposes. In purpose and effect it is primarily a sanction to enforce the regulatory provisions of the Act. But that does not mean that the statute is invalid and the tax unenforceable. Congress may impose penalties in aid of the exercise of any of its enumerated powers. The power of taxation, granted to Congress by the Constitution, may be utilized as a sanction for the exercise of another power which is granted it. * * * It is so utilized here.

Following these constitutional hurdles, resolution of constitutional issues remained critical in the early days of the income tax, and the judiciary remained foremost in importance. But, with an important but now archaic exception dealing with the taxation of stock dividends (which we shall examine in Chapter 2), constitutional challenges to the income tax statute have generally failed, and after the constitutional validity of the income tax was settled by the ratification of the Sixteenth Amendment in 1913, the authority of the Congress in the field of taxation has not been significantly challenged. Indeed, today the Constitution seems to stop where the Internal Revenue Code begins.

Consider the "origination" clause, Article I, Section 7, clause 1, which states: "All Bills for raising Revenue shall originate in the House of

Representatives; but the Senate may propose or concur with amendments as on other Bills." In 1982, the House of Representatives passed a minor piece of tax legislation that, in three pages of statutory language, would have lowered revenues by less than $1 billion over the subsequent five-year period. When this legislation got to the Senate, its entire substance was deleted and replaced with more than 500 pages of statutory amendments to the Internal Revenue Code that were estimated to raise about $100 billion during the next three years. The Senate Amendment was accepted virtually intact by a House–Senate conference, was passed by both chambers of Congress, and signed by President Reagan.

Disgruntled taxpayers challenged the constitutional validity of this legislation on the ground that, since the House bill would have reduced revenues, this measure to raise revenues originated in the Senate, in violation of the origination clause. The several courts of appeals that heard these cases all found them without merit and upheld the legislation. Since these cases had not produced a conflict in the lower courts, the Supreme Court saw no need to hear this issue and refused to grant certiorari.

In effect, this episode renders the origination clause a nullity, with no practical significance whatsoever. As one commentator has put it:

> To be sure, the House can prevent the Senate from taking any action on taxation by refraining from originating *any* tax legislation; but even if the Senate were allowed to originate a tax bill, it could not become law without House concurrence, so it hardly matters which chamber acts first. Since it takes two to tango, what difference does it make whose foot first touches the ballroom floor?

Boris I. Bittker, "Constitutional Limits on the Taxing Power of the Federal Government," 41 Tax Law. 3 (1987).

In 1983, the Supreme Court performed an almost equivalent evisceration of the uniformity clause of Article 1, Section 8, which mandates that "all Duties, Imposts and Excises shall be uniform throughout the United States," by upholding, in a unanimous opinion, an exemption for Alaskan oil from the Crude Oil Windfall Profits Tax Act of 1980. United States v. Ptasynski, 462 U.S. 74 (1983). The Court concluded that the exemption was not designed to grant Alaska any "undue preference," but rather was supported by geographic differences that could legitimately—and constitutionally—be taken into account by the Congress in fashioning tax legislation.

Taken together, these decisions—along with other constitutional events that are beyond the scope of this text—suggest that, at least at this moment in our constitutional history, there are few serious procedural or substantive constitutional impediments on congressional power in enacting tax legislation. Exceptions occur only when the tax law interferes with such fundamental rights as the freedoms of speech or religion granted by the First Amendment. Amish adherents, for example, were granted an exception from mandatory Social Security taxes on religious grounds, but victories against a tax statute even on religious grounds are rare indeed. To be sure, the Supreme Court would prohibit Congress from accomplishing a clearly unconstitutional purpose, such as racial discrimination, simply by locating the offending legislative act in a tax statute, but today constitutional questions play a relatively minor role in federal taxation. Constitutional challenges to tax legislation are frequently heard but almost never upheld.

B. THE LEGISLATIVE PROCESS

NOTE ON THE PROCESS FOR ENACTING TAX LEGISLATION

The Constitution grants Congress the power "To lay and collect Taxes, Duties, Imposts and Excises." This congressional power over tax legislation constitutionally is limited only by the President's veto, which, of course, can be overridden by a two-thirds vote of each house.

Despite the emphasis in the Constitution on congressional responsibility, much tax legislation is initiated by the President. Responsibility for tax policy and tax administration generally is vested in the Department of the Treasury. The Secretary of the Treasury delegates to the Internal Revenue Service responsibility for the administration of tax laws, but not for the formulation of tax policy. That job is assigned to the Assistant Secretary for Tax Policy, who oversees a relatively small staff of lawyers, economists, statisticians, and econometricians, who are engaged in the development of tax policy and legislation for the administration. The staff regularly consults with others in the Treasury Department, including the IRS, and with other government departments and agencies. The President retains final authority over tax policy within the administration.

The Constitution provides that all revenue bills shall originate in the House of Representatives and thus, tax legislation is often first considered by the Committee on Ways and Means. Established in 1789, the Ways and Means Committee is one of the oldest House committees. It exercises jurisdiction over legislation concerning taxes, tariffs, foreign trade policy, welfare and health insurance, the level of the public debt, and the Social Security system. Congressional consideration of a major or controversial tax proposal thus usually begins with a public hearing held by the Ways and Means Committee or one of its subcommittees. If the administration has initiated the measure, the Secretary of the Treasury is often the first witness to appear, followed by other administration representatives and then by witnesses from the public. After public hearings, the Ways and Means Committee generally holds "mark-up" sessions on the proposal to determine the general outlines of the bill. The bill, accompanied by a report describing the bill and outlining reasons for the Ways and Means Committee's action, goes to the House for debate. Tax bills are often sent to the floor under a rule permitting very few, if any, amendments, although that determination is made by the House Rules Committee.

After the bill is approved, the process is repeated in the Senate. The counterpart of the House Ways and Means Committee is the Senate Finance Committee. The Finance Committee sometimes does not wait to act on a House bill, but rather holds its own hearings and often works on a bill while the House bill is working its way through the process. The Senate rules provide for unlimited debate when a tax bill is considered on the floor, and generally permit any senator to move to delete or modify any part of the bill or to add new provisions. Under the rules of the Senate, a 60–vote majority is sometimes necessary to pass tax legislation.

When the Senate version of the bill differs from the House version—as it almost always does—the revised bill is returned for House consideration. Though the House may accept the changes made by the Senate, it ordinarily will ask for a conference of senior members of the House Ways and Means and Senate Finance Committees to reconcile the differences. In the conference committee, the House and Senate members each vote on the issues as a unit, the vote of each chamber being controlled by a majority vote of that side.

Once agreement has been reached, a conference report is issued containing the statutory changes and briefly explaining the conference result. The report is presented separately to the Senate and House. Each must either accept or reject the conference version; no amendments are allowed. If approved by both bodies, the bill is sent to the President for signature or veto.

In 1996 President Clinton signed legislation permitting a partial line item veto, which permitted him, after signing a spending or tax bill, to send to Congress a separate message that lists the items he wishes to veto. Those items were deemed automatically rescinded by Congress unless it passed a bill to overturn some or all of them. President Clinton used this authority to cancel two provisions in the Taxpayer Relief Act of 1997. The beneficiaries of the tax breaks challenged the constitutionality of the line item veto and the Supreme Court agreed. It held that the Constitution did not give the President the authority to create a law whose text was not voted on by either the House or the Senate and presented to the President for his signature. Clinton v. City of New York, 524 U.S. 417 (1998).

NOTES

(A) *Joint Committee on Taxation.* The Joint Committee on Taxation (JCT), established in 1926 and made up of members of both houses, meets only about three times a year. The primary importance of the JCT is to provide status for its professional staff of lawyers, economists, accountants and statistical analysts. See §§ 8001–8023 for the organization and functions of the Joint Committee. The Committee provides assistance to both the House Ways and Means Committee and the Senate Finance Committee, and is responsible for estimating the revenue effects of legislative proposals and enacted legislation for the Congress. The JCT produces pamphlets analyzing proposed legislation, and after a bill is enacted, the staff often produces a "General Explanation" of the new law, an important document of legislative history.

(B) *The Code Itself.* The *first* matter to consider in *any* tax case is: What are the exact words of the statute? There is no use in a lawyer's thinking great thoughts about a tax problem unless the thoughts are firmly based on the controlling statute. A certain amount of "common law" of federal taxation has developed and judicial decisions are often very important, but federal taxation is not a common law subject.

The basic statute is the Internal Revenue Code of 1986, which has been amended a number of times. Earlier statutes may be important, however, in showing the history and development of the provisions now contained in the Code—the story of "the Government's [often futile] endeavor to keep pace with the fertility of invention" of taxpayers' lawyers.*

The provisions of the Internal Revenue Code vary greatly in terms of substantive scope, specificity, and drafting style. The student must acquire an ability to deal with the Code in its many vagaries and to master the ability to parse its complexities.

(C) *Legislative History.* Since the chief problems in federal taxation relate to the application and construction of statutes, it is important to be familiar with the materials that may shed light on these questions. They include:

Committee Reports. The reports of the House Ways and Means Committee, the Senate Finance Committee, and the conference committees provide useful explanations of the provision of a revenue bill and the reasons for the changes in the law. The full texts of the reports through 1938 were reprinted in Part 2 of the 1939–1 Cumulative Bulletin. Later reports may be found in subsequent issues of the Cumulative Bulletin and the U.S. Code Congressional and Administrative News. Recent committee reports are in computer databases, and there are a variety of secondary sources.

In addition to the committee reports on legislation, there are other reports on tax issues; the most significant of these are pamphlets and reports issued by the staff of the Joint Committee on Taxation. One of the most useful is the "General Explanation" of various revenue acts.

Hearings. A record is published of the public hearings before the congressional committees. The hearings occasionally yield material that is useful in considering tax questions. On-line databases, such as those maintained by Tax Analysts, often contain statements submitted at congressional hearings and sometimes unofficial hearing transcripts.

Statements on the Floor of Congress. The debates in Congress, recorded in the Congressional Record, are sometimes of moment in the construction of tax statutes.

(D) *Revenue Neutrality.* The soaring deficits of the 1980's and early 1990's and Congress' response to them had a major effect on the course of tax legislation. As part of the deficit reduction process, Congress legislatively imposed on itself the practice that each revenue bill must be "revenue neutral" over each year of a specified "budget period," generally five or ten years. This process, while perhaps a necessary first step towards curbing deficits, sometimes made it difficult to pass legislation that reflects desirable tax policy. "Revenue neutrality" of course depends on the revenue estimates of various provisions. The "science" of scoring a particular provision is quite controversial. There is no agreed upon "best" methodolo-

---

* The phrase comes from Mr. Justice   (1933).
Cardozo in Burnet v. Wells, 289 U.S. 670, 676

gy and many of the issues surrounding revenue estimating have become quite politicized. The mystery surrounding the process and the importance of the estimates in ensuring a bill's passage have led to acrimonious debate. The effect of the budget process and revenue neutrality on tax legislation is outlined in Charles E. McLure Jr., "The Budget Process and Tax Simplification/Complication," 45 Tax L.Rev. 25 (1989) and both revenue estimating and the use of tables purporting to show the distribution across income classes of tax changes are discussed in Michael J. Graetz, "Paint–By–Numbers Tax Lawmaking," 95 Colum.L.Rev. 609 (1995).

(E) *Gucci Gulch.* There has long been concern about the disproportionate influence of so-called "special interests" on the tax legislative process. See, e.g., the 1957 article by Stanley Surrey, "The Congress and the Tax Lobbyist—How Special Tax Provisions Get Enacted," 70 Harv.L.Rev. 1145 (1957). More recently, the advent of political action committees ("PACs") with enormous influence over campaign funding has intensified concerns that special interests now dominate the tax legislative process. Vast sums of money are contributed to members of the tax writing committees of Congress.

When Congress has tax legislation on its agenda, the halls of Capitol Hill are lined with "Gucci-clad" lobbyists, each urging defeat or passage of special provisions that would benefit their clients. Their victories and defeats in the Tax Reform Act of 1986 are described in Jeffrey H. Birnbaum and Alan S. Murray, Showdown at Gucci Gulch: Lawmakers, Lobbyists, and the Unlikely Triumph of Tax Reform (1987).

If lobbyists speak for "special interests," who speaks for the general interest? Sometimes the Treasury Department or the staff of the Joint Committee on Taxation provides nonpartisan tax policy assessment. Occasionally, bar associations and other public interest groups urge Congress to pay close attention to tax policy issues. But their voices—without the accompanying campaign contributions—are usually dwarfed by lobbyists.

As a counterpoint to the vast sums of money contributed to members of the taxwriting committees of Congress, consider the following comments concerning the retirement of George Lefcoe from the Los Angeles County Regional Planning Commission, excerpted from Kaplan, "When He Missed the Ham, He Quit," Los Angeles Times, January 25, 1987 at Part VIII, Page 2:

> [Lefcoe] did say that a mistake might have been that he retired before, and not after, Christmas. "I really missed the cards from engineers I never met, the wine and cheese from development companies I never heard of and, especially, the Honeybaked ham from, of all places, Forest Lawn [a well-known Los Angeles mortuary and cemetery], even though the company was never an applicant before the commission when I was there," Lefcoe said.

> "But because I miss them is why I think it was a good idea I resigned," he added. "I do not think it is wise to stay in public office for too long a time." Lefcoe used the ham from Forest Lawn as an illustration:

"My first Christmas as a commissioner—when I received the ham—I tried to return it at once, though for the record, I did not because no one at Forest Lawn seemed authorized to accept hams, apparently not even for burial. My guess is that no one of the many public servants who received the hams ever had tried to return it," said Lefcoe.

"When I received another ham the next Christmas, I gave it to a worthy charity," Lefcoe recalled. "The next year, some worthy friends were having a party, so I gave it to them. The next year I had a party and we enjoyed the ham."

"In the fifth year, about the 10th of December," said Lefcoe, "I began wondering, where is my ham? Why is it late?"

Lefcoe sighed and laughed. "So much for the seduction of public officials. It was then I thought it was time to retire, though it took me two more hams and three years to finally do it."

C.   THE ADMINISTRATION OF THE TAX LAWS

NOTE ON TAX ADMINISTRATION

Organization of the Internal Revenue Service. From the time of the Civil War, the agency charged with collecting internal taxes was known as the Bureau of Internal Revenue. In 1953, the name was changed to the Internal Revenue Service. Its principal officer is the Commissioner of Internal Revenue, who is nominated by the President and confirmed by the Senate.

The IRS is an extremely large agency, having a budget of approximately $8 billion and employing more than 115,000 people. In 2000, the IRS processed 213 million returns and collected $2 trillion in tax revenues. The cost of collecting each $100 of revenue was 42 cents. Slightly over half a million returns were audited, about .49%.

The central supervisory office where the top officers work, called the National Office, is located in Washington, D.C. The IRS has over 700 field offices located around the United States and in foreign countries. The chief legal advisor to the Commissioner is the Chief Counsel, whose office is responsible for preparing regulations, overseeing tax litigation, and writing rulings. There are regional counsel as well, who are primarily responsible for litigation in the Tax Court. The large field offices are headed by a District Director, and a Regional Commissioner supervises the district offices within each region. Regional Service Centers generally are responsible for collecting taxes and processing tax returns.

Congress has expressly given authority, in many places in the Code, "to the Secretary or his delegate." Much of the power of the Secretary of the Treasury with respect to taxes has been delegated to the Commissioner, and the Commissioner has, in turn, delegated her authority to various officers in the Service. See §§ 7802–7809.

Congress creates the complexities in the tax law, but then blames the IRS for being unable to cope. Concerned that the organizational structure of the IRS made it ill-equipped to efficiently collect revenue, Congress passed the Internal Revenue Service Restructuring and Reform Act of 1998.

The Act provided for a complete reorganization of the IRS and gave the Commissioner powers to assist in the restructuring. It also established within the Treasury Department an IRS Oversight Board. In addition to the Treasury Secretary, the Commissioner, and a full-time Federal employee, the board has six private members. The Board is to oversee the IRS in administration, management, conduct, and execution of the tax laws. The reorganization of the IRS has and will produce significant improvements in the administration of the tax law, but to believe that the IRS can become an effective modern financial services institution without a major overhaul of the tax law it administers is to believe that you can turn a winnebago around without taking it out of its garage.

The Act also creates the post of Treasury Inspector General for Tax Administration, whose job is to evaluate IRS programs and operations and to ferret out fraud, abuse, or misconduct within the IRS.

Treasury Regulations. Congress has delegated substantial rulemaking power to the Treasury. Section 7805(a) provides that "the Secretary shall prescribe all needful rules and regulations for the enforcement" of the internal revenue laws. Regulations issued under the general authority of § 7805(a) are given presumptive validity by the courts. Additional rulemaking authority is specifically delegated to Treasury by specific Code sections. See, e.g., § 385 (delegating to Treasury authority to "prescribe such regulations as may be necessary or appropriate" to determine whether an interest in a corporation is debt or equity). Regulations issued under such broad delegations of legislative authority are virtually always binding on taxpayers.

The regulations are quite extensive in scope and detail. They usually are designated by a number that includes the relevant Code section (for example, § 1.61–2 is a regulation under § 61 of the Code). There are many references to regulations in this book, but no effort has been made to include comprehensive citations.

It is important, but difficult, to get the feel of the regulations—to know what force and effect they have, when they will be followed, and to anticipate the rare instances when they will be disregarded. Although the courts generally follow regulations, their willingness to do so may depend in part on whether it is a legislative regulation, the length of time the provision has been in force, the reenactment of the statute on which it is based, and the consistency with which the regulation has been maintained.

The Secretary of the Treasury has delegated the authority to issue regulations to the Commissioner of Internal Revenue, subject to the approval of the Assistant Secretary of the Treasury for Tax Policy. Typically, a regulation is published in the Federal Register as a notice of proposed rulemaking. Comments from the public are received, and often a public hearing is held, before final regulations are published as a Treasury Decision ("T.D."). When time is limited and the need for guidance is immediate, regulations are issued as temporary regulations without following the notice of rulemaking procedures. In the last 30 years, due to a constant stream of legislation, temporary regulations became more common. In response to the increased use of temporary regulations, Congress enacted a provision that "sunsets" or terminates them after three years if no final regulations are issued; previously, temporary regulations remained in force until permanent regulations were issued.

Revenue Rulings and Revenue Procedures. In addition to the Regulations, the Service publishes a large volume of revenue rulings and revenue procedures. Revenue rulings, which address issues of substantive tax law, arise from various sources, including rulings to taxpayers, technical advice to district offices, studies undertaken by the IRS, court decisions, suggestions from practitioner groups, and so on.

A revenue ruling is the Commissioner's "official interpretation of the law" and generally is binding on revenue agents and other IRS officials. The IRS states that taxpayers generally may rely on published revenue rulings in determining the tax treatment of their own transactions that arise out of similar facts and circumstances. Courts typically give revenue rulings less weight than regulations, but many courts accord them considerable respect. See, e.g., Davis v. United States, 495 U.S. 472 (1990) ("Although the Service's interpretive rulings do not have the force and effect of regulations * * * we give an agency's interpretations and practices considerable weight where they involve a contemporaneous construction of a statute and where they have been in long use.").

Revenue procedures typically reflect the contents of internal management documents, but also may announce practice and procedures for the guidance of the public. From time to time, however, the IRS has issued revenue procedures stating IRS policy on substantive issues. See, e.g., Rev.Proc. 72–18, 1972–1 C.B. 740 (setting forth guidelines for disallowing interest deductions when taxpayers hold tax-exempt state and local bonds). When the IRS chooses to issue a substantive revenue procedure rather than a revenue ruling, the substantive rules set forth in the revenue procedure may be of doubtful validity; there may not have been sufficient support within the IRS to issue a revenue ruling—an "official interpretation of the law."

Private Rulings and Determination Letters to Taxpayers. Taxpayers sometimes can obtain rulings (generally referred to as "private" or "letter" rulings) and determination letters from the Internal Revenue Service. A "ruling" is a written statement issued to a taxpayer by the IRS National Office that interprets and applies the tax laws to a specific set of facts. In some cases (for example, those involving questions of fact), the Service may issue no ruling.

A "determination letter" is a written statement, issued by a District Director in response to a taxpayer's written inquiry, that applies the principles and precedents previously announced by the National Office to a particular set of facts. When the question involves a novel issue, a determination letter will not be issued. Taxpayers are required to pay user fees to the IRS for the issuance of private rulings and determination letters.

Technical advice memoranda are issued in response to a request by the District Director to the National Office for "technical advice" in a case. The taxpayer may file a brief and have a hearing. Technical advice memoranda largely have been replaced by field service advice, which serve a similar function.

Private rulings, technical advice memoranda, and field service advice are available to the public although certain identifying information is deleted. Section 6110(k)(3) provides that these written determinations are to have no precedential value, but taxpayers routinely cite private rulings when it is advantageous to do so and courts occasionally cite them as reflecting the IRS position. The basic tension here is between fairness to similarly situated taxpayers and the administrative necessity to give only a relatively low level of review to private rulings within the IRS.

NOTES

(A) *Administrative Announcements.* Revenue rulings and revenue procedures are published in the weekly Internal Revenue Bulletin. The material in the weekly issues is gathered together semi-annually into a publication titled the Cumulative Bulletin (cited as "C.B."). The IRS also publishes technical information releases (known as TIRs), press releases, pamphlets, tax forms and instructions, and other documents and pronouncements. The Cumulative Bulletin also contains IRS acquiescences or non-acquiescences in Tax Court decisions, Treasury decisions, executive orders, legislative histories, and other related items. The rulings and procedures and many other Service announcements also are found in a variety of privately-published tax services and in computer databases.

(B) *Retroactivity.* Section 7805(b) gives Treasury the power to decide whether regulations, rulings, or changes in regulations or rulings are to be retroactive in effect. This section is stated in the reverse form from normal administrative practice, viz, in such a way as to make "retroactive" rulemaking the norm with provision for discretionary prospective relief.

This is an important power and determinations whether to make pronouncements or changes retroactive are quite frequent. The courts generally have upheld the power unless the Commissioner has abused her discretion. Automobile Club of Michigan v. Commissioner, 353 U.S. 180 (1957). The Courts seldom have considered abuses of discretion to occur, usually only when they perceive unfairness to affected taxpayers. The classic example is International Business Machines Corp. v. United States, 170 Ct.Cl. 357, 343 F.2d 914 (1965), cert. denied 382 U.S. 1028 (1966), in which the court ruled that the IRS could not apply an unfavorable ruling retroactively when it had previously given a favorable ruling to the taxpayer's competitor. Compare Gehl Co. v. Commissioner, 795 F.2d 1324 (7th Cir.1986) (finding the Commissioner to have abused his discretion in making retroactive regulations defining qualifications for certain export tax incentives when a prior IRS announcement had stated that any such regulations would have prospective effect), with CWT Farms, Inc. v. Commissioner, 755 F.2d 790 (11th Cir.1985) (upholding the validity of the retroactive application of the identical regulations in the identical circumstances).

In addition to the technical questions raised by § 7805(b), there is a difficult policy issue as to when taxpayers should be entitled to rely on a tax law remaining unchanged. Can Congress, for example, enact tax laws that will explicitly apply retroactively? In 1993 and 2001, for example, Congress changed the rate structure and applied it retroactively to the beginning of the year. For a general discussion of the policy considerations relating to retroactive changes in the tax laws, see Michael J. Graetz, "Legal Transitions: The Case of Retroactivity in Income Tax Revision," 126 U.Pa.L.Rev. 47 (1977); Michael J. Graetz, "Retroactivity Revisited," 98 Harv.L.Rev. 1820 (1985).

(C) *Freedom of Information Act.* Until the mid–1970's, the IRS made little information available to the public. In response to several lawsuits brought by Tax Analysts under the Freedom of Information Act, the IRS subsequently agreed to release all private letter rulings, technical advise memoranda, General Counsel Memoranda (legal advice on proposed revenue rulings, private letter rulings and technical advice memoranda), and Actions on Decisions (attorneys' recommendations whether to appeal adverse Tax Court or District Court decisions). Other lawsuits resulted in the release of audit guidelines, the Closing Agreement Handbook (which sets forth rules, procedures and guidelines for IRS personnel in entering into certain agreements with taxpayers), and Treasury bill reports (which state Treasury's position on proposed legislation).

The IRS also reversed prior practice whereby people could submit comments on proposed regulations with a request that they be kept confidential. All comments on proposed regulations are now subject to public inspection and copying. Substantial portions of the Internal Revenue Manual are now available and can be very helpful to practitioners.

Before making public certain written determinations, information is to be deleted, including: (1) the taxpayer's name and other identifying characteristics, (2) commercial or financial information that is privileged or confidential, (3) trade secrets, (4) classified matter, (5) information specifically exempted by statutes, (6) information relating to bank regulations, (7) matters relating to personal privacy, and (8) certain geological and geophysical information. Sometimes a taxpayer litigating a normal tax case before the Tax Court may not be able to obtain through discovery information that any other citizen could get through the Freedom of Information Act. In 2000, Congress enacted legislation prohibiting the IRS from releasing information pertaining to certain agreements between taxpayers and the IRS, including closing agreements, certain "refiling agreements," and information arising under treaty obligations.

What limitations, if any, should be imposed upon the publication requirement? Would you extend the publication requirement to audit tolerances, investigative techniques, and other law enforcement materials?

(D) *Disclosure of Tax Return Information.* Section 6103 of the Code generally provides that tax returns and related information cannot be disclosed except under the following specific conditions: (1) to congressional committees, (2) to the President, (3) to the Justice Department, (4) to certain officials of state and local governments, (5) with respect to judicial and administrative tax proceedings, (6) to federal officers or employees involved in the administration of federal laws other than the tax law, (7) to the General Accounting Office, (8) to people designated by the taxpayer, and (9) to other persons having a material interest in the amount of tax due. In most cases, Treasury has the right to refuse to disclose tax return information if it determines that disclosure would impair the administration of the tax laws. Disclosure of return information is permitted in situations where other laws require such disclosure, for example, in connection with child support enforcement. Disclosure of returns or return information to cities is only permitted to the extent it is necessary in the administration of a local jurisdiction tax; disclosure is not permitted to any elected official of the jurisdiction. Public disclosure of all agencies receiving tax return information, the purposes of their requests for information, and the number of cases in which information was disclosed during each year is also required. There are sanctions for unauthorized disclosures of a federal tax return or return information.

Are there any situations where you would require disclosure of tax returns? Of large corporations? Of elected officials? Of your own tax return?

(E) *Stopping Pandora*

In 1997 President Clinton signed the Taxpayer Browsing Protection Act, which makes the unauthorized browsing of taxpayer's returns by federal or state employees a crime. Congress was apparently moved to act after the press extensively reported on activities of two curious IRS employees. The First Circuit overturned the conviction of Richard Czubinski, a contact representative for the IRS Boston office (and a member of the Ku Klux Klan) who made it a habit of browsing the returns of people he knew, although he failed to do anything with the information. The court found browsing "reprehensible," but ruled that it did not rise to the level of a crime. United States v. Czubinski, 106 F.3d 1069 (1st Cir.1997). According to the April 4, 1997 edition of the Chicago Sun–Times, Czubinski's motive was curiosity. "It's human nature to be curious" he said. "That's why we're so far advanced technologically.... It was just like, if you go into somebody's home, have you ever looked in the medicine cabinet?"

Robert M. Patterson, a computer "inputter" on the graveyard shift in the Memphis IRS office, was simply trying to get ahead in his job. Claiming he was not adequately trained, he regularly looked up the returns of famous people (and other people with the same names) in order to get computer experience. Although charged with falsely obtaining Social Security numbers, he was acquitted. The July 1, 1997 issue of Harper's Magazine included the following exchange between Patterson and his attorney Beth Brooks:

BETH BROOKS: Beginning in April of 1992, shortly after you moved to the night shift, did you begin to try to train yourself on the computer?

ROBERT M. PATTERSON: Yes, ma'am. I would punch in celebrity names or names I saw in the newspaper, names I saw on TV, names that just came into my head. I really wasn't going in there with any malicious intent, I was just trying to teach myself. And you know, when something came up on the screen, I would look at it, see what happened, and then I would go on to the next name. Once I had Elvis Presley—it was for an estate or a trust or something. It surprised me, because he has been dead—how many, almost eighteen, nineteen years. I thought, it must be somebody with that same name. Then I got it in my mind: Wouldn't it be funny if there were people with those names, and I just punched in Karen Carpenter to see if there were really people named Karen Carpenter, and I got a whole page of them. You know, I just thought that was odd.

BROOKS: All right. Do you recall whether you had a legitimate purpose that you can remember for accessing other files? For example, Wynonna Judd. Do you remember?

PATTERSON: No.

BROOKS: Naomi Judd?

PATTERSON: No. I had country singers often.

BROOKS: Okay. But you can't say whether you did or did not have a legitimate purpose?

PATTERSON: (Shaking head negatively)

* * *

BROOKS: Bryan Adams? Does that ring a bell?

PATTERSON: I can't say about that. I don't remember.

* * *

BROOKS: Do you remember anything about Elizabeth Taylor?

* * *

PATTERSON: Now, Elizabeth Taylor, that would be like another Karen Carpenter situation.

BROOKS: What about Michael Jordan?

PATTERSON: (Shaking head negatively)

* * *

BROOKS: Lucille Ball?

PATTERSON: No.

BROOKS: Desi Arnaz?

PATTERSON: Well, see, Lucy—these movie stars like Lucille Ball, Desi Arnaz, they're not going to show up, because they're not even in our district. I was just looking to see if anybody else had those names.

BROOKS: Clark Gable?

PATTERSON: He has been dead, you know.

BROOKS: Okay. Lisa Presley?

PATTERSON: You see, those two go together—Lisa and Elvis Presley. If you get into estates, I knew that she has control of his estate now, so I would have to check her out too.

NOTE ON ADMINISTRATIVE RESOLUTION OF TAX DISPUTES

The Filing of a Tax Return. Under our self-assessment system, taxpayers make the initial determination of their tax liability. Section 6012 of the

Code requires that every individual who has gross income in excess of a certain level must file a tax return. See § 6012(a)(1), which sets the level as the sum of the taxpayer's exemptions plus the standard deduction. Section 6012 also requires all corporations subject to income taxation and all estates and trusts with gross income of $600 or more to file returns. Most individuals report their income on a calendar-year basis and must file their returns by April 15 of the following year, but extensions of time until August 15 are routinely permitted.

Final payment of tax for the year is required with the return, but, in most cases, the bulk of the tax liability has already been collected by the IRS through withholding or estimated tax payments. Employers are required to withhold income and payroll taxes from the wages and salaries of employees, to deposit the withheld taxes regularly, and, by January 31 of the following year, to give the employee a statement of the wages paid and the taxes withheld (the Form W–2). Certain gambling winnings and dividend and interest income, where required information has not been submitted, are also subject to withholding. See §§ 3401–3406. Quarterly payment of estimated tax is required from individuals who receive income, such as business income, interest, or dividends, that is not subject to withholding. There are significant penalties for failing to pay estimated tax. See § 6654.

About 75 percent of all individual tax liability is paid through withholding. Much of the balance is secured through estimated tax payments. The filing of a return is, therefore, principally a reconciliation of the amount withheld or paid as an estimate with the taxpayer's final determination of tax liability for the year. An additional payment to the government or a refund to the taxpayer is then made. Because many taxpayers do not base their withholding on the full exemptions to which they are entitled, there is a large amount of overwithholding and as a result, most taxpayers who have only wage income receive refunds.

IRS Review of Returns. Review of the taxpayer's self-assessment of tax liability begins with a computerized check of the tax return for mathematical mistakes. If such mistakes are found, the taxpayer is billed or additional tax is refunded. The IRS also performs computerized matching of information returns, such as Form 1099 reports of interest and dividend payments, and employers' reports of wages, with the taxpayers' returns. In addition, some returns are selected for audit. The specific criteria for selecting returns for audit are not made public, but the IRS focuses the bulk of its audit efforts on returns that are likely to produce significant amounts of revenue. Thus, the IRS audits a higher percentage of returns of individuals with high incomes and about 70 percent of returns from large corporations. Returns also are selected for audit if they contain certain questionable deductions, such as unusually large itemized deductions or a disproportionate ratio of expenses to income. Certain occupations and professions are subjected to greater scrutiny. Section 6103(b)(2) permits the IRS to refuse to disclose to taxpayers the standards used for the selection of tax returns for audit or the data used in developing audit standards.

There is a good deal of public suspicion that sometimes returns are audited for political reasons. Despite protestations from the White House that it had no role in determining who was audited, in 1998 Congress made it unlawful for the President, Vice President, cabinet members, or their employees to request the IRS to conduct or terminate an audit.

In 2000 the percentage of individual tax returns audited was less than one-half of one percent. The limited ability of the IRS to audit tax returns, coupled with the ever-increasing complexity of the income tax law, has given rise to a significant compliance problem known as the "audit lottery." People and companies file tax returns on the assumption that the return will not be selected for audit or that, if selected, the auditing revenue agent will overlook understatements of tax liability. Congress has enacted severe penalties to try to deal with this "compliance gap."

The Audit and Administrative Appeals Process. An audit can be a "correspondence audit" where the taxpayer is asked to mail material to the local district office; an "office audit," where the taxpayer must personally appear at the district office with any material requested; or a "field audit," where the IRS official examines the taxpayer's books and other relevant material at the taxpayer's home or place of business. In the case of a field audit, the taxpayer should determine whether the examining officer is a "revenue agent" or a "special agent." Special agents investigate potential criminal charges, and taxpayers have different rights in dealing with special agents.

The Code requires the IRS to provide taxpayers with a simple nontechnical explanation of their rights and obligations during an audit, their appeal and litigation rights, and procedures for filing taxpayer complaints. The IRS also must explain the procedures it can use to enforce tax collections. Taxpayers are given the right to be represented at all interviews and to record or obtain IRS recordings of interviews. Different provisions apply to criminal investigations by the IRS.

If the taxpayer does not agree with the IRS determination of tax liability on audit, he will receive a "30–day letter" from the IRS that explains his options for further administrative review of the dispute. A written protest is generally required. The IRS permits conferences with its "Appeals Office," a part of the Office of Chief Counsel, at hundreds of locations throughout the country. Most disputes are settled administratively. If there is no settlement or if the taxpayer decides to forgo any administrative review, she may request a "statutory deficiency" notice (known as a 90–day letter because the taxpayer then has only 90 days to file a petition in the Tax Court). If the taxpayer fails to respond to the 30–day letter, she will receive a 90–day letter.

Section 7121 of the Code authorizes the Secretary or his delegate to make binding "closing agreements" with respect to past or future tax liability. Closing agreements are final except where fraud, malfeasance, or misrepresentation of a material fact can be shown. In some cases, the IRS may require a taxpayer to enter into a closing agreement as a condition to obtaining a ruling.

NOTES

(A) *Statute of Limitations.* The IRS generally has three years from the filing of a tax return to send a 90–day letter. § 6501(a). The period is six years if the taxpayer omits an amount from gross income that exceeds 25 percent of the gross income on the return unless there is disclosure. § 6501(e). If no return is filed or the return is false or fraudulent with an intent to evade tax, the time to send a notice is unlimited. § 6501(c). The statute of limitations may be extended by the taxpayer in writing; taxpayers usually agree to do so when requested by the IRS because a failure to agree will result in the immediate issuance of a deficiency letter that is probably erroneous.

The taxpayer has three years from the date a return was filed (or two years from the time the tax was paid, whichever is later) to file for a refund. § 6511. If the taxpayer has filed a waiver to assessment, he also may file a refund claim within the extension plus six months.

(B) *Taxpayer Bill of Rights.* The so-called Taxpayer Bill of Rights, which probably should be given an award for the most exaggerated legislative title of 1988, was a response to taxpayer concerns with tax penalties and perceived IRS abuses. At the most basic level, the Taxpayer Bill of Rights requires the IRS to prepare and disseminate a comprehensive and comprehensible statement explaining taxpayer rights and IRS duties at virtually every stage of the tax administrative process. The Taxpayer Bill of Rights was not as effective as Congress had hoped. As part of the Internal Revenue Service Restructuring and Reform Act of 1998, Congress added additional taxpayer protections.

One of the more nervewracking experiences for any taxpayer is an "interview" with the IRS. The Taxpayer Bill of Rights now requires that the IRS conduct examinations at reasonable times and places. § 7605. The Conference Committee Report indicates that it is generally not reasonable, for example, to force a small business owner to close shop in order to attend an interview. Taxpayers may record interviews, and the Service may record an interview if the IRS official informs the taxpayer prior to the interview and upon request provides the taxpayer with the transcript or recording. § 7521(a). Taxpayers are now empowered to stop an interview in order to consult with an "authorized representative." § 7521(b)(2). For this purpose, an authorized representative includes an attorney, CPA, or any other person allowed to represent a taxpayer before the IRS.

The IRS frequently provides taxpayers with advice that turns out to be incorrect. The Taxpayer Bill of Rights requires the IRS to abate any portion of a penalty that is attributable to a mistake in written advice from the Service. § 6404(f). The taxpayer, however, must make a specific request in writing, provide accurate and complete information, and must reasonably rely on the advice given. Since § 6404(f) applies only to written advice, a taxpayer who relies on inaccurate advice given by the IRS over the phone may be out of luck.

The Taxpayer Bill of Rights also made substantial changes in the rules governing collection procedures, in particular, levies and liens. Section 6331 provides generally that the IRS may levy on a taxpayer's property if taxes remain unpaid ten days after notice and demand for payment. Unless the collection of tax is in jeopardy, however, the IRS must give the taxpayer notice of the proposed levy and wait thirty days after the notice before it levies on the property. § 6331(d)(2). The notice that precedes the levy must be in simple, nontechnical language and must give the taxpayer information on how to avoid or challenge the levy. § 6331(d)(4). The Service now also is required to release a levy if it is causing economic hardship because of the taxpayer's financial status or if certain other conditions are met, for example, the taxpayer has made arrangements to pay the tax on the installment method.

The exemptions from levy for certain personal property are currently $6,250 and $3,125 for books and tools, § 6334(a)(2), and $1,050 for business property, § 6334(a)(3). Under certain conditions, property essential to the taxpayer's trade or business must be released if levy would prevent the taxpayer from conducting that trade or business. § 6334(a)(2). Weekly wages equal to the taxpayer's standard deductions and personal exemptions are exempt from levy. § 6334(d). Some public assistance payments are exempt altogether, such as unemployment benefits, supplemental security income, and worker's compensation. § 6334(a)(4), (7) and (11). A taxpayer's principal residence cannot be seized without prior judicial approval.

Lien procedures also have been modified by the Taxpayer Bill of Rights. Section 6326 allows a taxpayer to seek administrative review of a recorded lien on the ground that it was mistakenly recorded, for example, because the tax was already paid. If the lien is found to be erroneous, it must be released and the IRS must provide a statement saying the lien was erroneous. The Taxpayer Bill of Rights also added a new provision allowing taxpayers to recover damages for failure to release a lien. See §§ 7432 and 7433. The Internal Revenue Service Restructuring and Reform Act of 1998 extended the right to protest a lien to a third party owner of property against which the tax lien has been filed.

A taxpayer who prevails in a tax case in federal court can be awarded reasonable litigation costs if the position of the government is not "substantially justified." Under certain conditions, the taxpayer may recover reasonable administrative costs incurred after the date on which the first letter of proposed deficiency that allows the taxpayer an opportunity for administrative review is sent. § 7430(a)(1). The Internal Revenue Service Restructuring and Reform Act of 1998 increased the amount of allowable fees and generally made it somewhat easier for courts to award fees.

The 1998 legislation created a new National Taxpayer Advocate who is to help taxpayers who suffer hardships because of action taken by the IRS. And it requires the IRS to rewrite several of its publications to make it clearer to taxpayers what their rights are.

(C) *Anyone Can Be Hassled By the Tax Collector.* While the IRS and other tax collection agencies try to be thoughtful and evenhanded in their administration of the tax law, overreaching is inevitable. Consider the following three stories:

On August 2, 1987, David Brinkley closed his show, "This Week with David Brinkley," with the following comments:

> I received from the District of Columbia tax collector a brisk and officious notice that I owed back taxes from the year 1985, which I did not. The amount, they said: 10 cents, one dime. It cost them 22 cents to send me the notice. It gets worse. The notice said that unless the 10

cents was paid immediately by a certified check, the fines and penalties would be $2,137.32. I have paid the 10 cents because it's too much trouble to argue with them. The certified check cost $2.50. With the postage, return receipt and so on, the 10 cents I did not owe has cost me $4. A $2,000 fine for a claimed back tax of 10 cents? That's the law, they said, and that concludes today's lesson in democracy in action.

In 1987 newspapers throughout the land reported the saga of one Gary D. Keefer, a 12–year old whose life savings of $10.35 was seized by the IRS to settle a tax debt owed by his parents. Keefer's parents apparently were delinquent on a $200 monthly overdue tax bill and Gary's account was seized because his mother's Social Security number was on it. Keefer's first salvo was a letter to President Reagan, stating: "Greetings from Virginia. I regret to inform you that there is once again trouble in the colonies." Reagan did not answer, but after many phone calls, the IRS returned Gary's $10.35. On August 4, 1987, the IRS announced that it will no longer ask banks to seize accounts with balances under $100 and will freeze temporarily—rather than seize—any accounts that bear a name in addition to the delinquent taxpayer. Bless the children.

A footnote to this story. Sympathizers of Gary, including patrons of the New Paradise Lounge in Madison, Wisconsin, sent him checks for $10.35 and his account grew. Proving further his perspicacity, Gary said, "The IRS is going to want to tax all of that as income. A piggy bank is awfully inviting, considering they can just go into your account and take it again."

Finally, a tax professor (who for obvious reasons prefers to remain anonymous) reports the following encounter with an IRS revenue agent. The agent, on a question of deductions for medical expenses, was presented canceled checks and evidence that no reimbursement by insurance had occurred. "Not enough," he said, "I need a letter from your doctor indicating dates of treatment, etc."

"What!!" replied Professor X, "Why do you need more?"

The agent turned smugly to the table behind his desk and patted the Internal Revenue Code benignly. "It's in this book; we just have to go by this book," he said.

Professor X, who had not yet identified his line of work, felt a surge of adrenalin. The agent had patted a book he knew something about. Cloaking his voice now with sugar and innocence, the professor asked, "Could I just see what it says?"

The agent promptly flipped the Code open to the contemporaneous recordkeeping requirements of § 274(d). Almost leaping from his seat, the professor noted that § 274(d) was directed at entertainment expenses and a few other specific items, but not medical expenses.

Undaunted, the revenue agent replied, "It may say 'travel and entertainment,' but it means everything."

The professor reports that he then hired an accountant who cost him several thousand dollars to obtain a "no change" letter regarding his tax return from the IRS.

(D) *Tax Penalties.* Unlike some systems, in which the government determines the amount of tax due and sends the taxpayer a bill, the first formal determination of tax liability occurs when taxpayers themselves file their tax returns. The "voluntary" compliance demanded by "self-assessment" depends upon a variety of motivations ranging from the fear of being caught to pleasure of participating in the democratic process. Justice Holmes wrote, "I like to pay taxes. With them I buy civilization." But his is distinctly a minority view. Compare Justice Stone, writing for the Court in Carmichael v. Southern Coal & Coke Co., 301 U.S. 495, 522 (1937): "A tax is not an assessment of benefits. It is * * * a means of distributing the burden of the cost of government."

Should taxpayers, when "self-assessing" the tax due, attempt to sit as a judge, resolving doubtful questions of law and fact according to "legislative intent," or as an adversary, resolving each doubtful issue in their own favor? Many corporations and individuals have adopted an "opening bid" philosophy, resolving every issue in favor of paying less, on the assumption that they will not be audited or that, if they are audited, the revenue agent will overlook or compromise certain issues. At worst, they will pay the taxes due plus interest. On occasion, however, this philosophy is carried too far and a fraudulent return is filed.

Alarmed by the extent of noncompliance, the proliferation of tax shelters and the audit lottery, Congress substantially revised the penalty structure of the Code to try to increase the economic cost of cheating. The tax return accuracy penalty is found in § 6662, which imposes a 20 percent penalty on any portion of an underpayment of tax that is attributable to (1) negligence or disregard of rules or regulations, (2) substantial understatement of income tax liability, or (3) valuation misstatement. § 6662(b). No penalty is imposed with respect to any portion of an underpayment if the taxpayer establishes that there was reasonable cause for that portion of the underpayment and that the taxpayer acted in good faith. § 6664(c).

The Code defines "negligence" to include any failure to make a reasonable attempt to comply with the tax laws. The regulations also indicate that negligence includes a failure to exercise ordinary and reasonable care in the preparation of a return. A taxpayer can avoid the penalty for disregarding rules if he discloses his position on the return *and* the position has a reasonable basis. Reg. § 1.6662–3(b).

The penalty for a substantial understatement of income tax is imposed where the underpayment of tax exceeds the greater of 10 percent of the correct tax liability or $5,000 ($10,000 in the case of a corporation). § 6662(d)(1)(A). No penalty is imposed on an understatement to the extent that it is attributable to a position with respect to which (1) "substantial authority" exists, or (2) the relevant facts concerning tax treatment are "adequately disclosed" on the return or an attached statement and there is a reasonable basis for the opinion.

The substantial authority standard is less stringent than a "more likely than not" standard (where there is a greater than 50 percent chance that the position will be upheld), but more stringent than a reasonable basis standard. Reg. § 1.6662–4(d)(2). The regulations define substantial authority. Authority includes the Internal Revenue Code and other statutes; proposed, temporary, and final regulations; tax treaties and their official explanations; court cases; committee reports and certain other legislative history, including "Blue Book" explanations; private letter rulings; technical advice memoranda; IRS information and press releases; and IRS notices and other announcements published in the Internal Revenue Bulletin. Treatises, legal periodicals, legal opinions, or opinions rendered by tax professionals are not authority. Reg. § 1.6662–4(d)(3)(iii). Authority for a position is substantial if the weight of authorities supporting it is substantial in relation to the weight of authorities supporting a contrary position. Reg. § 1.6662–4(d)(3)(i). A taxpayer may have substantial authority for a position that is supported only by a well-reasoned construction of the applicable statutory provision. Reg. § 1.6662–4(d)(3)(ii). The penalty also may be avoided if the taxpayer acts in good faith and has reasonable cause. § 6664(c). For a discussion of penalties on tax preparers, see page 837 infra.

The accuracy penalty also is triggered by substantial income tax valuation misstatements, substantial overstatements of pension liabilities and substantial estate or gift tax valuation understatements. § 6662(e), (f), and (g). Understatements attributable to these causes are not reduced by the existence of substantial authority or by adequate disclosure.

Taxpayers who evade their tax obligations with criminal intent are subject to prosecution under various criminal provisions of the Code. §§ 7201 *et seq.* In addition, if any portion of an underpayment of tax is attributable to "fraud," the Code provides a civil penalty equal to 75 percent of the portion of the underpayment that is due to fraud. § 6663.

(E) *Interest.* Interest rates on tax underpayments are established twice a year. It is generally the recent short-term Federal rate plus 3% and interest accrues on a compounded daily basis. §§ 6621, 6662. Interest accrues from the date the tax was owed, usually the return filing date. Interest is not suspended while litigation is pending in the Tax Court.

D. THE ROLE OF THE JUDICIARY IN TAX MATTERS

When the administrative process fails to produce agreement between the IRS and the taxpayer, the taxpayer may litigate through any of three procedural avenues. This array of alternatives, and the particular consequences of choosing one or another, cannot be explained in terms of a rational tax judicial system but only as a matter of history.

NOTE ON THE JUDICIAL PROCESS IN TAX CASES

District Courts. First, the taxpayer may, on receipt of a notice of deficiency from the IRS, pay the deficiency assessed, file a claim for a refund, and bring suit to enforce that claim in the appropriate district court under 28 U.S.C.A. § 1346. If the taxpayer loses, he may appeal to the proper court of appeals and ultimately petition the Supreme Court for a writ of certiorari.

The Claims Court. Second, the taxpayer may pay the deficiency, file a claim for a refund, and bring suit to enforce that claim in the Claims Court under 28 U.S.C.A. § 1491. If she loses in the Claims Court, she may take an appeal to the Court of Appeals for the Federal Circuit.* The suit must be filed within two years after the Service has denied the claim for refund. § 6532(a).

The Tax Court. Third, the taxpayer may refuse to pay the deficiency and, within 90 days of receipt of the notice of deficiency, petition the Tax Court for review under §§ 7441–7478 of the Code. Either she or the Service may obtain review of a Tax Court decision in the appropriate court of appeals, §§ 7481–7487, and ultimately petition the Supreme Court for review. Section 7463 provides for a simplified and relatively informal optional procedure for "small" tax cases, involving $50,000 or less. Small cases are typically heard by special trial judges appointed by the chief judge of the Tax Court. See § 7443A. Small claims cases may not be used as precedents for other cases and are not reviewable.

The Tax Court's role and operations are unique to the tax law and often as unfamiliar to experienced tax practitioners as to beginning law students. The following comments of Tax Court Judge Mary Ann Cohen to the University of Southern California Tax Institute provide helpful insights into the court's operations.

> * * * Tax Lawyers sometimes forget that the Tax Court is a trial court, bound by the evidence in the case before it and the applicable statutes as written by Congress. * * *
>
> Tax Court opinions are often difficult to read from beginning to end because of compliance with the statutory admonition that "it shall be the duty of the Tax Court ... to include in its report upon any proceeding its findings of fact or opinion or memorandum opinion." Judges sometimes write opinions and include voluminous facts because of the possibility of appeal. Most would say that they much prefer an outright reversal to a remand for the purpose of finding additional facts.
>
> For these reasons, opinions sometimes seem replete with minutiae and invite the reader to skip over the portion labeled "findings of fact" and to read only the discussion under the heading "opinion." But the detailed facts or the procedural history of the case may well explain a surprising result and [this material] is probably there so that prior or subsequent cases may be distinguished if the same result is not appropriate in other cases.
>
> In that regard it is important to understand and keep in mind the distinction between opinions published in the official Tax Court reports and memorandum opinions published privately by commercial publishers. Only the former are officially recognized as precedents where the full impact of stare decisis is felt binding on the court, although most lawyers and some judges will regularly cite memorandum opinions, especially in analogous fact situations. The so-called division opinions published by the court are those that the chief judge designates as deciding a significant issue of law not previously decided, whereas

---

* The Federal Circuit was created in 1982. Prior to that, its jurisdiction resided in   the United States Court of Claims.

memorandum opinions generally are entirely factual or merely apply settled law to the facts of the case before the court. Thus classification of an opinion as a memorandum opinion may itself be a signal that the case should not be relied on in other circumstances as establishing a rule of law. Of course, if the facts of a case are similar to those in a reported memorandum opinion, the advocate who likes the result should argue that the situations are indistinguishable and the advocate who does not like the result should urge that it be limited to the facts of the case in which it was reached. You, of course, should not say that it is "merely a memorandum opinion of Judge X."

I should acknowledge that memorandum opinions or even bench opinions may sometimes become significant because of appellate action. The famous *Duberstein* case was a memorandum opinion in the Tax Court. * * *

Another aspect of the court that sometimes is not well understood is the relationship between the trial judge hearing the case and the court conference of all 19 judges entitled to vote on a case. The Tax Court is unique in this melding process by which the report of the judge becomes the opinion of the court. The chief judge is central to the process. * * * When a judge tries a case on a trial session, usually in one of approximately sixty places of trial away from Washington, D.C., and unless a bench opinion is rendered at the close of trial, a written report must be prepared. The judge usually will but may not order briefs from the parties as an aid to preparation of the report. When the trial judge has completed the report, it is sent to the chief judge. By statute, section 7460(b), "the report of the division shall become the report of the Tax Court within 30 days after such report by the division, unless within such period the chief judge has directed that such report shall be reviewed by the Tax Court." The parties have no right to affect this action or inaction by the chief judge. The parties do not know whether a case is being reviewed by the court and learn that it has been reviewed only after release of a court reviewed opinion. By that time, the 30–day period invariably has passed.

* * * Past chief judges have adopted rules of thumb by which certain categories of cases will be referred to the court conference for review. * * * The categories include cases invalidating a treasury regulation, overruling a prior case, or re-examining an issue where we have been reversed by a court of appeals in a circuit other than the one in which the case before the court arises.

[Y]ou cannot discount a case because it has not been court reviewed. Any published opinion is the opinion of the Tax Court unless and until it has been overruled. The result reached may have seemed so clearly right and noncontroversial to the chief judge that the consumption of judicial time in the court review process was unwarranted. On the other hand, a case designated as a memorandum opinion by the chief judge may have been regarded as either clearly right and noncontroversial under established law or may involve a unique set of facts not likely to be seen again and therefore not regarded as establishing any precedent.

Each day before a case is served on the parties, copies of the proposed opinion are circulated to the other judges, who thus have an opportunity to raise and negotiate objections with the author or to request that the chief judge reconsider his categorization of the case. Although judges are frequently in travel status and cannot read all proposed opinions before release, the system is designed to maximize reliability of the opinions that reach the public.

Returning then to my point that the Tax Court is first and foremost a trial court, I want to focus on the deference accorded to the trial judge as the finder of fact by the chief judge and the other judges entitled to vote. Cases often depend on credibility of witnesses or weighing conflicting evidence. Although different judges may sometimes see the same facts differently, well established principles of due process as well as collegiality preclude invasion of the fact-finding provinces of the trial judge. Even appellate courts are, at least officially, proscribed from reversing factual determinations unless they are "clearly erroneous." Most of the judges of the Tax Court differentiate their role as reviewers of the legal reasoning of a report from the appellate role of "correcting error." Frequently in court reviewed cases you will see concurring opinions based solely on the trial judge's right to determine factual matters. Sometimes a statement that a judge concurs or dissents, without an opinion, may signify a judge's desire to avoid association with the factual conclusions of the author of the opinion but a reluctance to express publicly such disagreement. Usually if a trial judge ends up writing a dissent to the majority opinion, you will see a statement in the majority opinion or in the dissent that the trial judge's findings of fact have been accepted but the legal analysis is the subject of disagreement.

Prior to 1924, there was no method to obtain judicial review of an IRS determination of tax liability without first paying the tax. Congress then established the Tax Court's predecessor, the Board of Tax Appeals, as "an independent agency in the executive branch." In 1942, the Board's name was changed to the Tax Court of the United States; in 1969, Congress established the Tax Court as an Article I court, exercising the legislative power of Congress, as distinguished from an Article III court, exercising powers under the judicial article of the Constitution. (Article I courts are more limited in jurisdiction than Article III courts, and Article I judges do not enjoy life tenure as do Article III judges.)

The Courts of Appeals. Tax Court and district court decisions are reviewable by the court of appeals for the circuit in which these lower courts sit, and Claims Court decisions are reviewable by the Federal Circuit. Section 7482(a) provides for appellate review of Tax Court decisions "in the same manner and to the same extent as decisions of the district Courts in civil actions tried without a jury." The 13 different circuits are not bound by one another's decisions, and the Tax Court and district courts are bound only by the decisions of the circuit to which the case may be appealed. Consequently, the outcome of a tax case often depends on the circuit in which the trial court is situated; inconsistent holdings among the circuits are not uncommon. The strategy for tax litigators often includes choosing the tribunal with the most favorable precedents.

Supreme Court Review. Review by the Supreme Court in federal cases is ordinarily only by writ of certiorari. 28 U.S.C.A. § 1245(1). Certiorari is granted in only a small proportion of the tax cases in which it is sought— recently far less than 10 percent. Most of these writs are granted on the government's petition. The Court's own formulation of the situations in which certiorari will be granted is found in Rule 19 of the revised Rules of the Supreme Court, 28 U.S.C.A. Rule 19. Certiorari is sometimes granted in situations that do not seem to come within the rules, however, so the tax practitioner often finds it difficult not to submit a petition.

NOTES

(A) *Proposals for Tax Appeals Court.* Variations in tax decisions due to the appellate system often have prompted proposals for a separate Tax Appeals Court. A more uniform appeals process would be a more efficient and logical way to reconcile district court and Tax Court decisions. Since the Supreme Court rarely hears a tax case, a Tax Appeals Court would eliminate the unresolved inconsistencies between the circuits and bring more certainty and consistency to the tax law. On the other hand, the independence of each circuit offers an opportunity for tax issues to be litigated fully throughout the circuits, creating a much more dynamic system for developing tax law. An alternative is reform at the trial court level, either with exclusive jurisdiction in the Tax Court or concurrent jurisdiction in the Tax Court and the district courts.

(B) *The Golsen Rule.* One problem of the current system of review of tax decisions arises when a Tax Court decision has been reversed by a court of appeals. Of course, the decision of the court of appeals is controlling in the particular case. Should the Tax Court also defer to that decision in cases reviewable by other courts of appeals? What should it do in the case of another taxpayer who can take his appeal to the same court of appeals?

In Golsen v. Commissioner, 54 T.C. 742 (1970), affirmed on the merits 445 F.2d 985 (10th Cir.1971), the full Tax Court announced that it would follow the decision of a court of appeals whenever the taxpayer's appeal would lie to that circuit. The Tax Court was faced with the problem of a case involving two or more taxpayers, appealable to more than one circuit, in Kast v. Commissioner, 78 T.C. 1154 (1982). The court followed Ninth Circuit precedent to grant summary judgment in favor of the seven taxpayers whose cases were appealable to that circuit. But the court, citing its disagreement with the Ninth Circuit, refused to grant summary judgment to the one taxpayer whose case was appealable elsewhere.

(C) *"Acquiescence" and "Non–Acquiescence."* After the Commissioner has lost a case in the Tax Court, she may decide, for one reason or another, not to seek further review. She may, for example, conclude that the decision against the IRS is correct. In that event, she may decide to publish her "acquiescence" in the decision. This is done by including the case in a list of "acquiescences" in the Internal Revenue Bulletins, which later are gathered together in the Cumulative Bulletin. The Commissioner's formal "acquiescence" amounts to instructions to all Treasury employees that the decision is to be followed. Thus, it has much the same effect as a revenue ruling.

However, the Commissioner, even though she does not appeal, may announce her "non-acquiescence" in the decision. This, too, is published in the Internal Revenue Bulletin. The procedure of "non-acquiescence" causes some misunderstanding. If the Commissioner does not agree with the decision, why does she not appeal? In the first place, the decision whether to appeal is made by the Solicitor General, who may have refused to follow the Commissioner's recommendation. Or, the Commissioner herself may have recommended against an appeal on the grounds that the case is unimportant or factually weak so that review of the issue by an appellate court should await some other case where the facts are better for the government.

A "non-acquiescence" has something of the status of a revenue ruling against the taxpayer and means that Treasury personnel will not apply the Tax Court's decision. The taxpayer, however, can probably win if he takes his case to the Tax Court unless this case has factual differences, or is appealed, or is affected by an intervening appeal of a similar case.

The Tax Court was a part of the executive branch until it was made an Article I court in 1969. Given the current status of the Tax Court, is there any reason for the Commissioner to publish acquiescences and non-acquiescences only with respect to Tax Court decisions? Would not the procedure make as much sense for district court, claims court, and court of appeals decisions?

(D) *Score one for Pyrrhus.* The decades-old judicially created rule that the taxpayer has the burden of proof in tax cases was curtailed by Congress in the Internal Revenue Service Restructuring and Reform Act of 1998. Now the government has the burden of proof in a judicial proceeding as to a factual issue if the taxpayer introduces credible evidence relevant to determining her tax liability. In order to shift the burden of proof to the government, the taxpayer must (1) comply with any substantiation requirements imposed by the Code, (2) maintain records required by the Code and regulations, and (3) cooperate with IRS requests for meetings, information, documents and the like, including exhausting her administrative remedies. Large corporations, partnerships, and trusts continue to have the burden of proof. Despite the enormous amount of "pro-taxpayer" publicity that accompanied this change, it actually affects only a tiny fraction of the millions of taxpayers filing returns and seems likely to affect the outcome of very few cases, if any. It does create, however, the prospect of some additional litigation over whether the taxpayer really "cooperated," and may make IRS agents somewhat more aggressive in obtaining information during audits.

As this idea was winding its way through Congress, nearly 100 tax law professors—including neither of the editors of this coursebook—sent the taxwriting committees a letter indicating that this was a very bad idea that would "make tax controversies more expensive, more intrusive, and more inconvenient for taxpayers" and also "would erode federal revenues, require higher appropriations for tax enforcement and make tax disputes more acrimonious." We regard the legislation to be neither as bad as our colleagues think nor the victory for the American people that its proponents claim. On the other hand, it doesn't seem "just right" either.

NOTE ON THE ANTI–INJUNCTION ACT AND STANDING REQUIREMENTS

Anti–Injunction Act. The courts often have been asked to resolve tax-related controversies that raise the sorts of constitutional or, at least, political issues with respect to which the judiciary may be less inclined to defer to the expertise of the executive branch. The impetus for increased judicial scrutiny of tax policy frequently has been provided by the IRS treatment of tax-exempt organizations. The Supreme Court has tempered this judicial activism, however, by its strict construction of standing requirements and the Anti–Injunction Act (§ 7421 of the Code).

In Bob Jones University v. Simon, 416 U.S. 725 (1974), the Court held that the Anti–Injunction Act barred an action to enjoin the IRS from revoking a ruling letter that previously had declared the plaintiff university tax-exempt and eligible for deductible charitable contributions despite its refusal to admit blacks as students. The Supreme Court declared that the Act, which provides that "no suit for the purpose of restraining the assessment or collection of any tax shall be maintained in any court," was applicable to the action because the university was seeking to restrain the collection of its own income, FICA and FUTA (employment) taxes as well as the income taxes of its donors, who would be denied charitable contribution deductions under the IRS action. Thus, the university could avoid the inhibitions of the Anti–Injunction Act only by establishing both irreparable injury and certainty of success on the merits; here, the Court found that Bob Jones University had failed to prove that "under no circumstances could the government ultimately prevail."

The Court emphasized that "this is not a case where an aggrieved party has no access at all to judicial review" since an assessment of tax eventually could be contested by the university or a donor in the Tax Court or the federal district courts. The Court observed:

> We do not say that these avenues of review are the best that can be devised. They present serious problems of delay, during which the flow of donations to an organization will be impaired and in some cases perhaps even terminated. But, as the Service notes, some delay may be an inevitable consequence of the fact that disputes between the Service and a party challenging the Service's actions are not susceptible of instant resolution through litigation. And although the congressional restriction to postenforcement review may place an organization claiming tax-exempt status in a precarious financial position, the problems presented do not rise to the level of constitutional infirmities, in light of the powerful government interests in protecting the administration of the tax system from premature judicial interference.

The university did subsequently litigate the issue in a suit for the refund of $21 in unemployment taxes. In Bob Jones University v. United States, 461 U.S. 574 (1983), the Supreme Court denied tax exemptions to religious schools that engage in racially discriminatory practices. For further discussion, see page 456, infra.

The Supreme Court recognized in the first *Bob Jones University* case that "serious problems" may be suffered by organizations whose tax exemption is revoked by the IRS. Similar concerns motivated legislation that now provides for declaratory judgment proceedings in the Tax Court, the Claims Court, or the Federal District Court for the District of Columbia to resolve controversies over an IRS determination or failure to make a determination with respect to an organization's tax-exempt status. See § 7428. A limited number of additional declaratory judgment procedures also have been authorized by Congress. See, e.g., § 7478, providing the Tax Court exclusive jurisdiction to hear cases of actual controversy involving an IRS determination (or failure to make a determination) whether interest on a prospective obligation of a state or local government is exempt from the federal income tax.

Standing. In Simon v. Eastern Kentucky Welfare Rights Organization, 426 U.S. 26 (1976), the Supreme Court held that the Eastern Kentucky Welfare Rights Organization did not have standing to challenge an IRS ruling that exempted hospitals from tax as charitable institutions even though they provided no indigent care facilities or services. The Court held that neither the organization nor its indigent members could show the "actual injury" necessary to establish standing. In reaching its decision, the Court emphasized defects in the complaint, including the fact that, although the hospitals might have caused actual injury to the plaintiffs, the hospitals themselves were not defendants in the case. The Court repeatedly characterized as "speculative" the connection between the plaintiffs' injuries and the challenged actions of the IRS; for example, the court characterized as "speculative" the inference that the hospitals were so dependent on their tax exemption that they would change their treatment policies rather than forgo tax-exempt status.

In a subsequent district court case virtually identical to *Eastern Kentucky* on the facts, plaintiffs attempted to meet all of the pleading requirements suggested by the *Eastern Kentucky* opinion. Lugo v. Simon, 453 F.Supp. 677 (N.D.Ohio 1978). The district judge found that the evidence presented met the *Eastern Kentucky* guidelines and heard the case on its merits, but this grant of standing was reversed on appeal, 640 F.2d 823 (6th Cir.1981). There now appears to be little hope that procedural precision and thoroughness in pleadings will meet the *Eastern Kentucky* guidelines for standing by third-party plaintiffs.

It is almost impossible to obtain standing to challenge an IRS decision not to collect additional taxes. This difficulty was made clear by the Supreme Court in Allen v. Wright, 468 U.S. 737 (1984). The majority, in an opinion by Justice O'Connor, denied standing to a group of parents of black public school children who sought to bring a class action suit against the IRS attempting to challenge IRS grants of tax exemption to racially discriminatory schools. The Court held that the parents' claim of injury was not "fairly traceable" to the government conduct challenged as unlawful, and that the parents therefore lacked standing. The Court found that "[t]he diminished ability of respondents' children to receive a desegregated education would be fairly traceable to unlawful IRS grants of tax exemptions only if there were enough racially discriminatory private schools receiving tax exemptions in respondents' communities for withdrawal of those exemptions to make an appreciable difference in public school integration." The Court further stated that the links in the "chain of causation" between the challenged IRS conduct and the asserted injury were too weak to sustain the parents' standing since it was speculative whether withdrawal of tax exemption would lead the schools to change their segregationist policies.

The Court also resorted to a separation of powers justification for its decision. Saying that most suits challenging public programs established by agencies to carry out their legal obligations are not appropriate for federal court adjudication, Justice O'Connor expressed fear that granting standing would force courts into monitoring "the wisdom and soundness of Executive action." Justice O'Connor felt that the parents sought an inappropriate "restructuring of the apparatus established by the Executive Branch to fulfill its legal duties."

In dissenting in *Allen,* Justice Stevens (joined by Justice Blackmun) referred to statements in *Bob Jones University* as well as to language in Regan v. Taxation With Representation of Washington, 461 U.S. 540, 544 (1983), that a tax exemption is a form of subsidy administered through the tax system. Through what he described as a "restatement of elementary economics," Stevens explained why the grant of such a subsidy by the government could arguably be deemed causative of an injury to the black parents for purposes of standing analysis. Justice Stevens also dismissed the majority's invocation of separation of powers, believing the question of IRS' administrative policy to be well within the competence of the judiciary. (Justice Brennan filed a separate dissent.)

Congressmen fare no better in obtaining standing to challenge tax legislation. The Supreme Court held that six Congressmen who voted against the Line Item Veto Act had no standing to challenge its constitutionality because they had no particularized and personal injury. Raines v. Byrd, 521 U.S. 811 (1997).

NOTES

(A) *Why Wait?* What is to be gained by waiting until suits are filed by those more directly injured by IRS actions? Can it fairly be said that any person who is willing to bear the expenses of litigation will pursue the case "with the kind of vigor that the Article III 'case or controversy' standard requires"?*

(B) *Causation. Allen* seems to suggest that the plaintiffs could not show that the IRS rules *caused* them harm. Does this suggest that IRS constraints on allegedly charitable exemptions have no behavioral consequences, a proposition on which *Allen's* standing analysis seems to rest? If so, one wonders why the Court went to so much trouble a year earlier in *Bob Jones University* to deny the exemption to discriminatory schools. The

---

* Tax Analysts and Advocates v. Shultz,
376 F.Supp. 889 (D.D.C.1974).

majority in *Allen* made a rather feeble effort to distinguish Coit v. Green, 404 U.S. 997 (1971), its summary affirmance of the case that originally developed the no-exemption-for-discriminating-schools principles. The *Allen* Court observed that *Coit* had involved only private schools in Mississippi, where overwhelming evidence documented the use of private schools to frustrate public school desegregation and the importance of tax exemption to these institutions.

After many court proceedings, standing was denied to various individuals and organizations who sued to challenge the tax-exempt status of the Roman Catholic Church asserting that the church's anti-abortion activities violated the Code's prohibition against lobbying by tax-exempt organizations. In re United States Catholic Conference, 885 F.2d 1020 (2d Cir.1989), cert. denied 495 U.S. 918 (1990). See also Apache Bend Apartments, Ltd. v. United States, 987 F.2d 1174 (5th Cir.1993), in which the court held that taxpayers who did not benefit from extensive transition rules enacted as part of the 1986 Act lacked standing to challenge their constitutionality.

(C) *The South Carolina Case. Allen* should be compared with South Carolina v. Regan, 465 U.S. 367 (1984), where the Court permitted a state to invoke its original jurisdiction to decide a question concerning the tax liability of those who would buy bonds from the state. In *South Carolina*, the state wanted the Court to decide the constitutionality of § 103(j) (now § 149) of the Code, which denied owners of state and municipal bonds issued after June 30, 1983, an exclusion for interest unless the issuer has put the obligation in registered form. Although the nominal tax liability under this provision falls on bondholders, issuers would likely bear a portion of the economic consequences of taxation by having to pay higher interest rates. South Carolina in effect claimed *jus tertii* standing to assert its bondholders' rights to avoid tax liability, largely because its own material stakes were closely tied to the bondholders.

In upholding South Carolina's right to sue, the Supreme Court distinguished the *Bob Jones University* case, on the grounds that the loss of tax-exempt status produced some direct liability under the federal unemployment tax that would enable Bob Jones University to obtain post-assessment judicial review of their constitutional claims. In contrast, South Carolina would not owe any taxes to the federal government, no matter what the tax status of its bonds, and had only its bondholders' liability to contest.

Seizing on the non-direct-access opening, the *South Carolina* Court created a new exception to the Anti–Injunction Act. A majority believed that the exception extended to all cases where a person asserted only the tax claims of third parties and therefore had no power to bring a refund suit. It discounted the possibility that bondholders could vindicate the state's interests.

Having swept aside the Anti–Injunction Act, the Court did not look for positive congressional authorization for the suit to proceed. Perhaps it believed no inquiry was necessary, as the case met the requirements of the Court's original jurisdiction, the state had a clear economic interest in the litigation, and the cause of action could be implied directly from the Constitution.

Is it the Court's view that the state's showing of direct economic harm is simply a more important claim than the *Allen* plaintiffs' allegations concerning the nature of their harms? Constitutional history suggests the opposite, but distinguishing the cases on "causation" grounds seems tenuous indeed.

(D) *An Ombudsman?* If the IRS chooses not to enforce a provision of the Code, or interprets it in a clearly erroneous way favorable to the taxpayer, who could challenge the decision? The standing cases seem to suggest that it is virtually impossible to obtain judicial review of IRS determinations that are favorable to the taxpayers whose financial interests are at stake.

One solution might be the creation of an inspector general or ombudsman entity responsible for reviewing Treasury enforcement practice. Should such an entity be granted standing to sue (perhaps only in the Tax Court)? Or should moral authority and publicity be its only tools? How would such an approach compare to a general grant of standing to public interest law firms, other public interest organizations, and groups of plaintiffs such as those in *Allen?*

CHAPTER 2

WHAT IS INCOME?

There is no universally accepted definition of income for the purpose of levying an income tax.

Laymen find it hard to believe that there are major problems in defining income. They are used to thinking in terms of cash wages and salaries, which are easily identified and clearly income. In fact, wages and salaries account for the great bulk of income—however defined—in the U.S. economy; other items like interest and dividends are also easily identified. So it may be fairly said that most of the dollars identified as income in the total economy will be the same under any definition of income.

But as one approaches the edges of the concept of income, there is a substantial grey area. It is small compared with the bulk of income, but this grey area * * * is the focus of much controversy. There is an extensive literature on the subject, beginning before the turn of the century and continuing to the present, with no consensus except that particular definitions may be more practical in certain circumstances than in others.

U.S. Treasury Dep't, Blueprints for Tax Reform 21 (1977).

The term "income" is not defined in the Code or the Regulations. Although a number of courts have attempted to define income, almost 90 years of experience with a Federal income tax have not produced an acceptable definition. Nevertheless, scholars have devoted a great deal of thought to the question, "What is income?" It is valuable to compare some of the definitions proposed by economists with the concept of income for tax purposes by Congress, the Internal Revenue Service, and the courts. A sampling from the economic literature is set out below:

Robert Haig, "The Concept of Income," in The Federal Income Tax 1, 7 (1921): "Income is the money value of the net accretion to one's economic power between two points of time."

Carl Plehn, "Income as Recurrent, Consumable Receipts," 14 Amer. Econ.Rev. 1, 5 (1924): "Income is essentially wealth available for recurrent consumption, recurrently (or periodically) received. Its three essential characteristics are: receipt, recurrence and expendability."

William Hewett, The Definition of Income and its Application in Federal Taxation 22–23 (1925): "Net individual income is the flow of commodities and services accruing to an individual through a period of time and available for disposition after deducting the necessary costs of acquisition."

Henry C. Simons, Personal Income Taxation 50 (1938): "Personal income may be defined as the algebraic sum of (1) the market value of rights exercised in consumption and (2) the change in the value of the store of property rights between the beginning and end of the period in question."

Richard Posner, Economic Analysis of Law 535 (1998): "The broadest definition of income would be all pecuniary and non-pecuniary receipts, including not only leisure and other non-pecuniary income from household production but also gift, bequests and prizes."

The Simons definition, which is considered a refinement of the Haig definition, is the most widely accepted and is usually referred to as the Haig–Simons definition of income. It is used by many economists and lawyers as a basis for testing the equity of the income tax. Simons himself, however, noted that the definition would not serve for all purposes and, without modification, would not describe a workable tax base.

It is not clear that a generally accepted economic definition of income should be accepted by Congress, the Service, and the courts for tax purposes. The selection of income as the base implies that income should provide a measure of an individual's ability to pay tax and any definition should serve to further that purpose. Furthermore, the concept of income must be sufficiently practical to be administered by the IRS.

Gross income is defined in § 61 of the Code as "all income from whatever source derived." That section also includes a non-inclusive list of specific items included in gross income. Sections 71–90 of the Code are concerned with additional items specifically included in gross income, and §§ 101–137 specifically exclude certain items from gross income. But the items cataloged are not an exhaustive list of the receipts included in gross income, and the Service and the courts have attempted to further determine what is within the contours of "income." In Eisner v. Macomber, 252 U.S. 189, 207 (1920), the Supreme Court attempted to define income:

Income may be defined as the gain derived from capital, from labor, or from both combined, provided it be understood to include profit gained through a sale or conversion of capital assets. * * *

This definition of income, while often quoted, was abandoned long ago as being too narrow. For example, it would not include windfalls. The Supreme Court tried again in Commissioner v. Glenshaw Glass Co., 348 U.S. 426 (1955), when it found that punitive damages were included in gross income.

This Court has frequently stated that [the statutory language of the predecessor to § 61] was used by Congress to exert in this field "the full measure of its taxing power." * * * Congress applied no limitations as to the source of taxable receipts, nor restrictive labels as to their nature. * * * Here we have instances of *undeniable accessions to wealth, clearly realized, and over which the taxpayers have complete dominion.* * * * We would do violence to the plain meaning of the statute and restrict a clear legislative attempt to bring the taxing power to bear upon all receipts constitutionally taxable were we to say that the payments in question here are not gross income.

This definition stands for the proposition that "income" should be broadly construed in the absence of a specific congressional directive to the contrary.

In determining *what* is income, we do not focus just on receipts. It is also appropriate to determine *what deductions* are allowed in measuring taxable income. We also must determine *whose* income it is and *when* it is taxable. As you will see, these are not always clearly separated issues; they shade into one another. Nevertheless, the classification is useful and it has been followed as an organizing principle of this book.

This Chapter presents materials primarily on the first question: What is income? Usually there is no question as to *who* has received the benefit or *when* it was received. The fundamental question is which receipts or benefits are income.

SECTION 1. COMPENSATION FOR SERVICES

Section 61 requires that compensation for services be included in gross income. Thus, wages, salaries, fees, commissions, fringe benefits, and similar items are income. Compensation received in the form of royalties, or as a percentage of profits, is also income. It is not necessary that there be an employer-employee relationship; tips, legal and medical fees, and jury fees are all compensation for services includable in gross income. Generally, the form of payment does not affect the inclusion of compensation in gross income. Thus, for example, compensation would include stock, notes, or other property transferred for services; the amount of the income is the fair market value of the transferred property. § 1.61–2(d) and § 83. There are, however, many important exceptions that are considered in this Section.

Not all payments to employees are compensation; the question is whether the payment was compensatory in nature. Sometimes specific Code provisions exclude from gross income certain payments by employers to or for the benefit of employees even if compensatory. This Section of the Chapter provides illustrations of the general rule and its exceptions and limitations.

A. FORM OF RECEIPT

Old Colony Trust Co. v. Commissioner

Supreme Court of the United States, 1929. 279 U.S. 716.

MR. CHIEF JUSTICE TAFT delivered the opinion of the Court.

* * *

The facts certified to us are substantially as follows:

William M. Wood was president of the American Woolen Company during the years 1918, 1919, and 1920. In 1918 he received as salary and commissions from the company $978,725, which he included in his federal income tax return for 1918. In 1919 he received as salary and commissions from the company $548,132.87, which he included in his return for 1919.

August 3, 1916, the American Woolen Company had adopted the following resolution, which was in effect in 1919 and 1920:

"Voted: That this company pay any and all income taxes, State and Federal, that may thereafter become due and payable upon the salaries of all the officers of the company * * * to the end that said persons and officers shall receive their salaries or other compensation in full without deduction on account of income taxes, State or Federal, which taxes are to be paid out of the treasury of this corporation."

This resolution was amended on March 25, 1918, as follows:

"Voted: That, referring to the vote passed by this board on August 3, 1916, in reference to income taxes, State and Federal, payable upon the salaries or compensation of the officers and certain employees of this company, the method of computing said taxes shall be as follows, viz.:

" 'The difference between what the total amount of his tax would be, including his income from all sources, and the amount of his tax when computed upon his income excluding such compensation or salaries paid by this company.' "

Pursuant to these resolutions, the American Woolen Company paid to the collector of internal revenue Mr. Wood's federal income and surtaxes due to salary and commissions paid him by the company, as follows:

Taxes for 1918 paid in 1919 .... $681,169.88
Taxes for 1919 paid in 1920 .... 351,179.27

The decision of the Board of Tax Appeals here sought to be reviewed was that the income taxes of $681,169.88 and $351,179.27 paid by the American Woolen Company for Mr. Wood were additional income to him for the years 1919 and 1920.

* * *

[The first portion of the opinion, in which the jurisdiction of the federal courts to review decisions of the Board of Tax Appeals was sustained, is omitted.]

Coming now to the merits of this case, we think the question presented is whether a taxpayer, having induced a third person to pay his income tax or having acquiesced in such payment as made in discharge of an obligation [of his], may avoid the making of a return thereof and the payment of a corresponding tax. We think he may not do so. The payment of the tax by the employers was in consideration of the services rendered by the employee, and was a gain derived by the employee from his labor. The form of the payment is expressly declared to make no difference. Section 213, Revenue Act of 1918, * * *. It is therefore immaterial that the taxes were directly paid over to the government. The discharge by a third person of an obligation [of his] is equivalent to receipt by the person taxed. The * * * taxes were imposed upon the employee, * * * the taxes were actually paid by the employer and * * * the employee entered upon his duties in the years in question under the express agreement that his income taxes would be paid by his employer. This is evidenced by the terms of the resolution passed August 3, 1916, more than one year prior to the year in which the taxes were imposed. The taxes were paid upon a valuable consideration, namely, the services rendered by the employee and as part of the compensation therefor. We think, therefore, that the payment constituted income to the employee. * * *

Nor can it be argued that the payment of the tax * * * was a gift. The payment for services, even though entirely voluntary, was nevertheless compensation within the statute. This is shown by the case of Noel v. Parrott (C.C.A.) 15 F.2d 669. There it was resolved that a gratuitous appropriation equal in amount to $3 per share on the outstanding stock of the company be set aside out of the assets for distribution to certain officers and employees of the company, and that the executive committee be authorized to make such distribution as they deemed wise and proper. The executive committee gave $35,000 to be paid to the plaintiff taxpayer. The court said * * *:

"In no view of the evidence, therefore, can the $35,000 be regarded as a gift. It was either compensation for services rendered, or a gain or profit derived from the sale of the stock of the corporation, or both; and, in any view, it was taxable as income."

It is next argued against the payment of this tax that, if these payments by the employer constitute income to the employee, the employer will be called upon to pay the tax imposed upon this additional income, and that the payment of the additional tax will create further income which will in turn be subject to tax, with the result that there would be a tax upon a tax. This, it is urged, is the result of the government's theory, when carried to this logical conclusion, and results in an absurdity which Congress could not have contemplated.

In the first place, no attempt has been made by the Treasury to collect further taxes, upon the theory that the payment of the additional taxes creates further income, and the question of a tax upon a tax was not before the Circuit Court of Appeals, and has not been certified to this Court. We can settle questions of that sort when an attempt to impose a tax upon a tax is undertaken, but not now. * * * It is not, therefore, necessary to answer the argument based upon an algebraic formula to reach the amount of taxes due. The question in this case is, "Did the payment by the employer of the income taxes assessable against the employee constitute additional taxable income to such employee?" The answer must be "Yes."

[The dissent by Justice McReynolds is omitted.]

NOTES

(A) *A "Tax on a Tax"?* In *Old Colony*, the government conceded that no further tax (other than the tax sought in the case) was owed and thus the tax on a tax did not arise. Was the government's concession necessary or desirable? If the employer agreed to pay all taxes owed, could it have computed the exact amount of the total tax? See Rev.Proc. 81–48, 1981–2

C.B. 623 and Rev.Rul. 86–14, 1986–1 C.B. 304, both of which require pyramiding of federal income and employment taxes under current law.

(B) *Tax-Inclusive Base.* Section 275 denies any deduction for federal income taxes. Therefore, the federal income tax is imposed on a "tax-inclusive" basis: The amount of tax is included in the amount of taxable income to which rates are applied. This clearly can be seen with our current withholding system. The tax is levied on the gross amount of compensation even though the employee receives a net amount after the appropriate amount of tax has been withheld and sent to the government. If federal taxes were deductible, the income tax would be imposed on a "tax-exclusive" basis. Whether the federal income tax is deductible or not is simply a matter of the rate of tax. Tax-inclusive rates can be converted into tax-exclusive rates (and vice versa) by the following formulas:

$$r_e = \frac{r_i}{1 - r_i} \quad \text{and} \quad r_i = \frac{r_e}{1 + r_e}$$

where r_i is the tax-inclusive rate and r_e is the tax-exclusive rate.

The following table illustrates some tax-inclusive and tax-exclusive rates:

Tax–Inclusive Rates	*Equivalent Tax–Exclusive Rates*
28%	39%
35%	54%
40%	66⅔%
50%	100%
75%	300%
83%	488%

For example, assume an employer wants to pay a salary yielding $30,000 in after-tax income to an employee who is taxable at a 28 percent tax-inclusive rate. Applying the 28 percent rate to the $30,000 of income, produces $8,400 of tax, which in turn (at a 28 percent rate) would produce $2,352 of tax, $659 of tax, $184 of tax, $52 of tax, $15 of tax, $4 of tax, $1 of tax and some additional pennies for a total of $11,667. (These numbers are rounded to the nearest dollar. Those who insist on mathematical precision and are concerned with Zeno's paradox should look at § 7504). Alternatively, the corresponding tax-exclusive rate of 39 percent would also produce a tax of $11,667. The same result would be obtained by applying the 28 percent tax-inclusive rate to a before-tax income of $41,667. The $11,667 tax liability would represent the entire pyramid discussed in *Old Colony.* Algebraically, if an employer wants to pay a specific amount after taxes, the net salary (N) equals the gross salary (G) minus the tax due, which is the gross salary times the tax rate (t). So: $N = G - Gt$ or $N = G(1-t)$, so $G = N/1-t$. Thus at a 28 percent rate, to pay a $30,000 net salary, the employer must pay $30,000/1 - .28$ or $41,667.

In contrast to income taxes, sales taxes generally are applied on a tax-exclusive basis. Why might Congress choose tax-inclusive or tax-exclusive rates?

(C) *Progressivity.* Note that the 1918 amendment in *Old Colony* whereby the company agreed to pay the difference between the employee's total tax and the tax on his non-company income had the effect of "stacking" the employee's salary (on which the company paid tax) on top of his other income. Given a progressive rate schedule, the company thus paid the highest marginal rate of tax. Compare this result to an agreement that computed the tax by stacking non-company income on top of the company salary; in this agreement, the company would calculate Wood's tax liability at the lowest marginal rate. An alternative plan might have required the company to pay a proportion of the employee's total tax equal to the ratio of the company salary to his total income; here the company would pay tax based on Wood's average tax rate. The 1918 agreement was to the employee's benefit when it was adopted, and stacking wages on which the company would pay tax on top of other income would always be to the employee's benefit under a progressive rate schedule.

The distinction between marginal and average rates of tax is important. The marginal rate is the rate that applies to additional dollars of taxable income, and therefore is the rate that affects tax decisions at the margin. The marginal rate tells you how much an additional dollar of income or deduction will change your tax liability. In a progressive rate schedule, marginal tax rates increase as income increases. Often marginal rates are referred to as tax "brackets." The average tax rate is the total tax liability divided by income. Typically, taxable income is used as the denominator for calculating average tax rates, but sometimes other concepts of income—adjusted gross income or some estimate of "economic income"—are used. Average rates measure taxpayers' overall tax burdens and are frequently used to compare tax rates across taxpayers.

(D) *Who Wants to be a Millionaire?* For four episodes beginning on Sunday, February 18, 2001, ABC ran a tax-free version of "Who Wants to be a Millionaire?" The rules state: For the four (4) episodes of the Tax–Free Edition only, which are scheduled to tape on February 13, 14, and 15 (2 episodes), 2001, the Game Sponsor will pay Contestants both their prize money including the Bonus Prize, if any, and, with the support of sponsor H & R Block, an amount equal to the estimated applicable Federal, state and local income taxes in connection with their participation on the Program. How do you think ABC will calculate the taxes it will pay? Is it going to pay a tax on a tax?

(E) *Other Benefits. Old Colony* is not limited to taxes paid by the employer. In theory, any in-kind benefit transferred as compensation for services rendered is income, although Congress has chosen to exempt certain benefits. The employer, for example, could pay the employee's rent or pay school tuition for an employee's child. Generally, the employer's payment of the employee's obligation is equivalent to the receipt of the amount of the obligation. See, e.g., O'Malley v. Commissioner, 91 T.C. 352 (1988) (payment of legal fees); Tennessee Securities Inc. v. Commissioner, 674 F.2d 570 (6th Cir.1982) (payment on guarantee of taxpayer's loan).

B. FRINGE BENEFITS

INTRODUCTORY NOTE ON FRINGE BENEFITS

The term "fringe benefits" is loosely used to describe in-kind benefits transferred to an employee. They may clearly be additional compensation or they may be essential to the performance of the employee's job. An example of the latter is chalk used by a school teacher and an example of the former is an all-expenses-paid vacation. Most fringe benefits fall somewhere in between. They are transferred because the employee has performed services for the employer and thus have a compensatory element, but they also are often for the benefit of the employer.

Which of the following would be "income"? Suppose the employer installs a drinking fountain or supplies free sodas? Suppose air conditioning is provided? What if very expensive art is hung in an executive's office? What about free uniforms furnished to janitors? Or free suits furnished to law firm associates? What about a free limousine that brings an executive to work and back? Or a van that takes workers home who finish work at 2 a.m.? Suppose free parking is provided? Suppose employees are allowed to use a gym on the business premises? Suppose country club dues are paid by the employer? What about health or life insurance? What if only highly-paid employees were eligible for perks? Would it make a difference if the employer reimbursed the employee for any of these items? Would the result be the same if the employer simply paid additional compensation and expected employees to pay for the items?

Many fringe benefits are not subject to the income tax under current law—not because they are not income, but because Congress has chosen to treat them specially. Fringe benefits excluded from the income tax generally also are excluded from the definition of "wages" under the federal payroll taxes, including Social Security tax. In recent years, fringe benefits, including health and pension benefits, have accounted for an increasing percentage of employee compensation. They also are the largest tax expenditures. The most important of these are described in the following section.

1.   TAX EXPENDITURE FRINGE BENEFITS

Several fringe benefits are eligible for specific statutory exclusion from gross income. All of them constitute "income" in an economic sense and thus none can be justified on tax policy grounds. Rather, they must be defended as accomplishing some nontax policy objective.

NOTE ON THE EXCLUSION OF EMPLOYER–PROVIDED HEALTH INSURANCE

Section 106 excludes employer contributions to accident and health plans from the gross income of employees. Under this provision, the cost of employer-provided disability or medical "insurance" is not taxable to employees whether the employer provides the protection through an insurance company or on a self-financed basis. If an employee purchases accident or health insurance himself, no deduction is provided (except to the limited extent an itemized medical expense deduction might be available, see page 458, infra), but the proceeds in the event of sickness or disability would not be taxed. § 104(a)(3).

Section 104 also excludes from gross income compensation for injuries or sickness in the form of workers' compensation, disability pensions and annuities received as a result of active service in the military, foreign service, Coast Guard, or Public Health Service and disability payments received by civilian government employees for injuries attributable to terrorist attacks.

Section 105 excludes benefits paid under an employer's accident and health plan for the medical expenses of employees and their families as well as for permanent disfigurement or "loss of use of a member or function of the body." Sick pay, however, is taxable. Self-insured medical reimbursement plans established by employers must not discriminate in terms of eligibility or benefits in favor of highly-paid employees, officers, or shareholders. § 105(h)(2).

Lump sum payments to employees on the termination of a health and accident plan are taxable as compensation. See Adkins v. United States, 882 F.2d 1078 (6th Cir.1989), where the employees argued that the payments were not taxable as they arose from a health plan. The court found that "accepting [the employees'] theory would provide a very dangerous precedent, an easy way for employees to retain the benefits of a salary while avoiding tax liabilities."

Employer-provided health care benefits are one of the largest tax expenditures. They are estimated to be $75 billion in 2003.

Although enormously popular, the tax exclusion for employer-provided health insurance has been the Titanic of U.S. domestic policy.* It is hard to find a domestic program that rivals the incompetence of U.S. health insurance. While spending nearly twice the OECD average (14 percent versus 7½ percent of GDP), we manage to leave about 45 million Americans without insurance. All of the systems of other OECD countries provide (near) universal access at aggregate costs—both as a percentage of GDP and per capita—below U.S. expenditures. To be sure, certain high tech wonders are available to some Americans that are not available elsewhere. But quality measured in more meaningful terms—real resources (physician and hospital time) devoted to patient care, breadth of covered services, continuity of care, and gross indicators of health (like infant morality and longevity)—points in the direction of at least equal, and sometimes higher, quality care abroad. Basic health indicators like life expectancy at birth and the percentage of babies with low birth weights bear virtually no relationship to a country's health care expenditure level. This suggests that the United States is not getting a significant health quality bang for its huge health care bucks. In a candid assessment, the U.S. system may rank ahead of others only on the proximity of high-tech medical equipment and consumer choice of insurance carrier.

Most of the uninsured are both working age and working at least part-time or part-year. Americans' chances of being uninsured are much higher if their incomes are average or low. Nowhere in America's social insurance world does the combination of unaffordability and inadequacy loom larger than in health insurance.

---

* Much of the following material in this note and the figures are taken from Michael J. Graetz & Jerry L. Mashaw, *True Security:* *Rethinking American Social Insurances* (1999).

This poor record has hardly gone unnoticed by reformers who have peppered the populace, state legislators, and Congress with proposals. During the First World War, a group called the American Association for Labor Legislation tried to persuade a number of state legislatures to adopt health insurance, but to no avail. Franklin Roosevelt's 1944 call for an "economic bill of rights," including a right to adequate medical care, went nowhere. FDR's successor, Harry Truman, consistently supported national health insurance. He proposed action in 1945, made health insurance the centerpiece of his legislative program in 1949, and repeated the effort annually until 1953. Truman was never able even to muster a vote on the floor of the House or Senate. To make this story short, Presidents Nixon, Carter, and Clinton, all advanced plans for universal health insurance. None fared any better than Truman or Roosevelt, although their plans and their political opponents were different.

Since any effort to remake the U.S. health insurance system potentially affects the overlapping and often antagonistic interests of doctors, hospitals, medical equipment manufacturers, pharmaceutical manufacturers, and distributors, other health services providers, private insurers, organized labor, employers, large and small, and their employees, the difficulty of change should not be underestimated. Commenting on the Clinton plan, Charles Schultze, Jimmy Carter's Chairman of the Council of Economic Advisors, remarked that President Clinton was attempting to remake an economic entity as large as the economy of France in one legislative stroke. Moreover, while fears of losing or being denied health insurance coverage are widespread in the United States, virtually all Americans over age 65 enjoy health insurance coverage under Medicare, and nearly 85 percent of other Americans have some coverage, mostly through employer-sponsored health insurance plans and Medicaid. A political system, crafted by the founders to resist large-scale reforms, coupled with public and politicians' fears of a "government takeover" of health care has entrenched our health insurance patchwork in the face of obvious inequities and absurd levels of expenditure.

Following the defeat of President Clinton's health insurance proposals and the Republican takeover of Congress in 1994, which it may have precipitated, the political process has returned to its traditional path of incremental change. In 1996 Congress passed federal legislation adding regulatory protections so that people don't necessarily lose their health insurance when they change jobs or because they have preexisting medical conditions and addressed some of the short-term financials problems of Medicare. In 1997 Congress provided new federal funding to reduce the number of uninsured children from 10 million to 5 million over the next several years through state-based health insurance programs. And in 2001 a prescription drug benefit was added to Medicare.

For the non-elderly population, the source of health insurance coverage varies significantly by the individual's level of income. For example, in 1993, 70 percent of individuals whose family income was below the poverty level were covered by health insurance, and three-quarters of those were covered through a public plan. Employer-sponsored health insurance coverage declines steadily with income. See Figure 2.1. Less than 11 percent of

Figure 2.1

Nonelderly population covered by employer-based health insurance

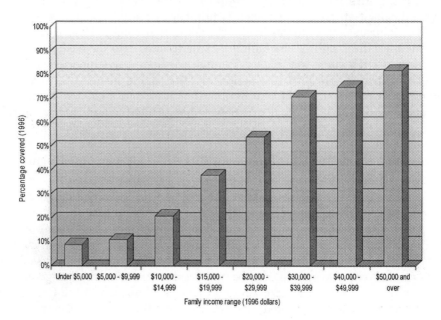

Source: Michael J. Graetz and Jerry L. Mashaw, *True Security* (Yale University Press, 2000)

Figure 2.2
Per capita value of federal tax subsidies
for employer-based health insurance

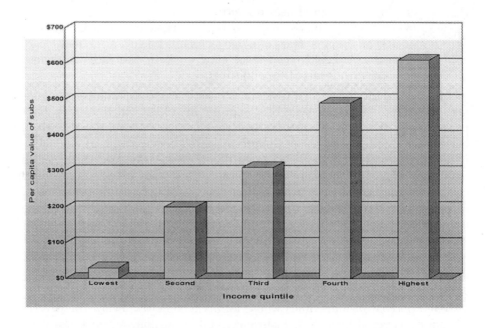

Source: Michael J. Graetz and Jerry L. Mashaw, *True Security* (2000)

poor families are covered through employer plans compared to 64 percent of the overall non-elderly population. Moreover, the value of employer-provided health insurance also increases with income. See Figure 2.2. Voluntary tax-subsidized group insurance is not a good vehicle for increasing the economic security of lower-income families.

Employer-sponsored health insurance also shows considerable regional variation, principally because coverage is concentrated among larger employers. More than 70 percent of Connecticut, Wisconsin, and Utah residents, for example, had employer-sponsored health insurance coverage in 1993, while less than half of Louisiana residents had coverage. Most working Americans who get their insurance through their employer are offered a single plan or a menu in which cost differentials make only one or two plans a realistic option.

Prior to World War II, there was remarkably little private health insurance coverage in the United States; only 9 percent of the population enjoyed such coverage in 1940. By 1950, half of the U.S. population was covered by private health insurance, largely because employment-based health insurance had become a desirable form of paying wages—it was exempt from wartime wage control limitations. Federal income and payroll tax exemptions further stimulated employment-based health insurance coverage as a way of compensating workers. Employer-based coverage, however, has experienced a steady decline beginning in the 1980's. In 1979, for example, 82 percent of full-time civilian employees had employer-sponsored health insurance coverage. That number had declined to 73 percent in little more than a decade. Only about 30 percent of workers in firms with less than 25 employees enjoy employer-sponsored health insurance coverage, compared to 65–70 percent of workers with 1,000 or more employees. Part-time workers are far more likely to be uninsured than full-time workers.

Employer-provided health insurance has been declining for both workers and retirees. And, as Medicare and Medicaid's fiscal challenges increase, public programs are having increasing difficulty taking up the slack.

The Notes that follow describe other tax-expenditure fringe benefits excluded from income.

NOTES

(A) *Retirement Income.* Sections 401–404 and 410–416 provide favorable tax treatment for "qualified" pension, profit-sharing, and stock bonus plans. Employees are not taxed on these plans until they receive payments, usually in retirement, although employers receive immediate deductions for contributions to fund the retirement benefits. In addition, the pension trust or fund that accumulates contributions and income to fund the retirement benefits is tax-exempt. The Code also contain provisions that allow employees to make contributions to retirement savings plans in lieu of receiving cash salary and, by doing so, to receive tax savings comparable to those available to employer-sponsored qualified pension plans. See, e.g., §§ 401(k) and 403(b). Tax-preferred retirement income plans suffer some of the same problems as beset employer-provided health insurance; they tend to provide greater benefits to higher earners and to employees of larger firms. In the case of retirement income, however, the universal coverage of Social Security, whose benefits are skewed in favor of lower-wage workers, provides a universal baseline of retirement security for all. The income taxation of deferred compensation is taken up in Chapter 6 at page 756.

In addition, employers who maintain a qualified pension plan can provide tax-free retirement planning services to their employees. § 132(a)(7).

(B) *Life Insurance.* Generally, if the employer pays life insurance premiums on the life of an employee and the employee's estate or family is the beneficiary, the employer's premium payments are income to the employee. See, e.g., Frost v. Commissioner, 52 T.C. 89 (1969). Where the employer or a charity is the beneficiary, the premium payments are not taxable to the employee. Rev.Rul. 68–99, 1968–1 C.B. 193.

An employee may exclude, however, the value of premiums on a limited amount of group term life insurance provided by an employer. Under § 79, an exclusion from income for group term life insurance premiums paid by an employer is provided for the premiums on an aggregate of $50,000 of insurance. The cost of the excess over $50,000 is subject to tax. Employer payments to group term life insurance plans are eligible for exclusion from employees' income only if the plans do not discriminate in favor of key employees with respect to eligibility or benefits. § 79(d).

While one might think that Congress has included this exclusion in order to encourage employers to provide group insurance, it is not clearly so. The Regulations long contained a provision under which premiums paid on group term life insurance policies for employees were not taxable. Although this exclusion presumably was designed to apply to modest premium payments on relatively small insurance policies covering all or most of a company's employees, the regulatory exclusion was stated in general terms, without any limit in amount, and without any requirement against discriminatory application. It is likely that this provision was based on a de minimis principle, plus the fact that the individual premium would be small and perhaps also difficult to compute.

(C) *Moving Expenses.* Reimbursement by an employer of the expenses incurred by an employee in moving from one location to another are excluded to the extent the employee could have deducted the expenses if paid directly. § 132(a)(6), (g). Generally, an employee can deduct moving costs only if incurred in connection with a new job in a location at least 50 miles from his old job. § 217. An employer's reimbursement of other moving expenses is included in income. § 82.

(D) *Dependent Care.* Payments made by an employer for the care of dependents of its employees are excluded from the employee's income by § 129. The exclusion is limited to $5,000 a year ($2,500 for married individuals filing separately). The definitional limitations closely parallel those for the dependent care credit discussed infra at page 255.

(E) *Educational Benefits.* An employee can exclude up to $5,250 a year for amounts paid by her employer under a "qualified educational assistance program." Educational assistance includes tuition, fees and books but does not include living expenses. §127.

(F) *Adoption Assistance.* Amounts paid under a qualified adoption assistance program provided by an employer are excludible to the extent they are used in connection with the employee's adoption of a child. § 137. The maximum amount excludible is $10,000 and is phased out ratably for employees whose adjusted gross income exceeds $150,000. The exclusion is not available to an employee whose AGI exceeds $190,000. Qualified expenses include adoption fees, attorney fees and court fees.

(G) *Cafeteria Plans.* Plans that allow employees to select from a group of employer-provided taxable and nontaxable fringe benefits have become known as "cafeteria plans." These are considered a valuable compensation device, since the platter of benefits can be selected to reflect the tastes of the particular employee. Section 125 excludes from employee income employer contributions to certain nondiscriminatory cafeteria plans. An employee may choose only among excludable fringe benefits and cash. § 125(d)(1)(B). If the benefits are concentrated on key employees, they will be taxed as if they had received cash.

NOTE ON FRINGE BENEFITS

There is a large incentive to provide a tax-free fringe benefit. An employee subject to a 40 percent marginal tax rate is indifferent as to receiving $60 of desirable tax-free fringe benefits or $100 of taxable wages, but definitely would prefer $61 of benefits to $100 of cash. Employers, needless to say, would prefer paying $61 of benefits to $100 of wages. (As Chapter 3 will detail, the costs of either the benefits or the cash generally are deductible by the employer, regardless of whether they are included in the employees' income). As marginal income tax rates rise, the incentive to substitute tax-free benefits for cash salary increases. (Remember that in addition to the income tax, payroll taxes exceeding 15 percent also apply to most salaries below about $80,000. The examples in this book generally ignore the payroll taxes.)

Equity. Tax-free fringe benefits raise a number of tax policy concerns, including equity issues. If A receives $15,000 cash and B receives $10,000 cash and $5,000 of tax-free airfare, they are not taxed the same even though they may be in the same economic position. This is said to violate horizontal equity because two taxpayers in the same economic situation are taxed differently. In reality, because the airfare is not taxed, B's employer may provide less. Thus, B may receive only $3,000 of benefits, and although he receives $2,000 less than A, he will have the same after-tax benefit as A. In that case A and B are in the same economic position after tax as well. Another equity concern is that untaxed benefits are more valuable and often have been more available to employees in higher tax brackets. Moreover, untaxed fringes may be disproportionately available depending upon the employee's industry or occupation.

Efficiency. Issues of economic efficiency also are involved because the failure to tax benefits induces employers to offer, and employees to select, wage and benefit packages very different from those that they would obtain without the tax benefits. Suppose in the above example, that the employer is willing to offer $5,000 cash compensation or $5,000 in free airfare and, because the cost is the same, is indifferent between the two. If B is not particularly fond of flying, he would choose the $5,000 cash. But assume that the cash is taxable and the airfare is not. If B takes the cash, he will have $3,000 left after paying tax at a 40 percent rate. So long as the air travel is worth more to him than $3,000 (even if it is not worth $5,000), he will choose the airfare. Suppose the airfare is worth only $4,000 to him, although it costs the employer $5,000 to provide it. Economists call the wasted $1,000 a "deadweight loss." But keep in mind that Congress might knowingly prefer this distortion, if, for example, it wanted to provide an incentive to a failing airline industry. There is, however, a cost. If the income tax is to raise a certain amount of revenue, exclusion of fringe benefits requires higher tax rates. Even if the exclusion from income of fringe benefits were defended as a type of rate reduction on labor income, corresponding to exclusion of certain types of capital income, it would be fairer and more efficient to exclude a portion of labor income from tax for all taxpayers regardless of the form in which it is received.

Complexity. The taxation of fringe benefits has been troublesome since the beginning of the income tax in 1913 and has proven to be surprisingly complex. There are two principal reasons for this complexity. First is the inherent difficulty—as a matter both of theory and of administration of the tax laws—in distinguishing in-kind compensation from goods or services related to an employee's work that also provide the employee incidental economic benefits. For example, a free book would constitute noncash compensation to most employees, but might constitute a noncompensatory incident of employment to a book critic.

As noted previously, the concept of income is not self-defining. It is clear that excluding all noncash compensation from income, while simple, would very quickly produce a barter economy for labor income. On the other hand, taxing any economic benefit, no matter how closely related to an employee's work, would violate public perceptions of fairness and would dramatically increase the costs of tax compliance for both the government and taxpayers. Drawing the line between these two unacceptable extremes, however, is necessarily controversial and often arbitrary. Fringe benefit taxation therefore is subject to inevitable change.

Change itself is an additional source of complexity. Many exclusions of "work-related" fringe benefits originated in administrative practice and judicial decisions in the early days of the income tax, when tax rates were low and the income tax was largely confined to upper-income people. By the time a fringe benefit, perhaps long ignored by tax administrators as de minimis, had become an important component of employees' compensation, workers had come to regard the income exclusion as an entitlement.

The second source of complexity is Congress' unwillingness to accept the principle that all noncash compensation designed to reward the employee for services rendered should be subject to income tax. The exclusion from gross income of a number of fringe benefits reflects a variety of policies unrelated to the measurement of income. As we have seen, these exclusions include employer-provided life and health insurance, health, accident and death benefits, dependent care assistance, and some benefits provided to members of the Armed Forces.

Statutory Provisions. The complexity of fringe benefit taxation is reflected in the relevant statutory provisions. Section 61 includes compensation in income, including fringe benefits, and the regulations provide that if services are paid for other than in money, the fair market value of the property or services taken in payment must be included in income. Reg. § 1.61–2(d). Statutory authority for taxing fringe benefits also is found in § 83. Although the purpose of the section was to tax income received as compensation through restricted stock plans, the language is much broader.

Numerous fringe benefits are specifically excluded from income. In addition to those discussed above, Section 132 excludes seven categories of work-related fringe benefits. It is not clear if work-related benefits not meeting the tests of § 132 otherwise might be excludable because they are not "income." In addition to § 132, there are a variety of other specific statutory exclusions for fringe benefits. Section 119 excludes certain work-related meals and lodging. Section 117(d) deals with tuition reduction plans for employees of educational institutions.

2. WORK–RELATED FRINGE BENEFITS

Excerpt From Joint Committee Staff Pamphlet Describing 1984 Amendments Regarding Miscellaneous Fringe Benefits

Staff of the Joint Committee on Taxation, Pamphlet Describing Tax Treatment of Fringe Benefits for Hearings of House Ways and Means Subcommittees, September 17 and 18, 1984.

GENERAL RULE

The Tax Reform Act of 1984 provides a statutory exclusion from income and FICA and other employment taxes for (1) no-additional-cost services; (2) qualified employee discounts; (3) working condition fringes; (4) de minimis fringes; and (5) qualified tuition reductions. No fringe benefit (other than a de minimis fringe) is excluded under the Act if another section of the Code provides rules for the tax treatment of that general type of benefit.

Under the Act, any fringe benefit that does not qualify for a statutory exclusion is expressly includible in gross income, and subject to employment taxes, at the excess of its fair market value over any amount paid by the employee for the benefit.

The rules of the Act do not make any change in existing statutory or regulatory exclusions for benefits for military personnel.

EXCLUSION PROVISIONS

No-additional-cost service.—A service provided to an employee is excluded if—

(1) the employer incurs no substantial cost (including foregone revenue) in providing the service;

(2) the service is provided by the employer or another business with whom the employer has a written reciprocal agreement, and is of the same type ordinarily sold to the public in the line of business in which the employee works;

(3) the service is provided to a current or retired employee, or a spouse or dependent child of either, or a [surviving spouse] or dependent children of a deceased employee; and

(4) for certain highly compensated employees, nondiscrimination requirements are met (see below).

Qualified employee discount.—A discount on merchandise provided to an employee is excluded to the extent it does not exceed the employer's gross profit percentage (in the relevant line of business). The exclusion does not apply to discounts on real property or to discounts on personal property of a kind commonly held for investment.

A discount on services provided to an employee is excluded to the extent it does not exceed 20 percent of the selling price of the services to nonemployee customers (with no gross profit percentage restriction).

The following conditions generally must be satisfied for the exclusion to apply:

(1) the property or service is provided by the employee and is of the same type ordinarily sold to the public in the line of business in which the employee works;

(2) the property or service is provided to a current or retired employee, a spouse or dependent child of either, or to a [surviving spouse] or dependent children of a deceased employee; and

(3) for certain highly compensated employees, nondiscrimination requirements are met. * * *

Working condition fringe.—Property or services provided to an employee are excluded to the extent that they would be deductible as ordinary and necessary business expenses (under Code secs. 162 or 167) if the employee had paid for them.

* * *

De minimis fringe.—Property or services not otherwise tax-free are excluded if their fair market value is so small, taking into account the frequency with which similar fringe benefits (otherwise excludable as de minimis fringes) are provided and other relevant factors, as to make accounting for the benefits unreasonable or administratively impracticable. For example, benefits that generally are excluded as de minimis fringes include the typing of a personal letter by a company secretary, occasional personal use of the company copying machine, monthly transit passes provided at a discount not exceeding $15 [now $60], occasional company cocktail parties or picnics for employees, occasional supper money or taxi fare for employees because of overtime work, and certain holiday gifts of property with a low fair market value.

Subsidized eating facilities operated by the employer also are excluded as a de minimis fringe if located on or near the employer's business premises, if revenue equals or exceeds direct operating costs, and if (for certain highly compensated employees) nondiscrimination requirements are met. * * *

Athletic facilities.—An exclusion is allowed for the value of on-premises athletic facilities provided and operated by an employer for use of its employees. Under Code section 274, the employer is not allowed a deduction for the costs of an athletic facility if the facility is not primarily for the benefit of employees (other than employees who are officers, shareholders or other owners, or highly compensated employees).

Qualified tuition reduction.—The Act provides that a reduction in tuition provided to an employee of an educational institution is excluded for income and employment tax purposes if (1) the tuition is for education below the graduate level provided by the employer or by another educational institution; (2) the education is provided to a current or retired employee, a spouse or dependent child of either, or to [surviving spouse] or dependent children of a deceased employee; and (3) certain nondiscrimination requirements are met. * * * [§ 117(d) of the Code.]

Nondiscrimination requirements.—The exclusions for no-additional-cost services, qualified employee discounts, subsidized eating facilities, and qualified tuition reductions are available to officers, owners, or highly compensated employees only if the property or service is provided on substantially the same terms to each member of a group of employees defined under a reasonable classification, set up by the employer, which does not discriminate in favor of employees who are officers, owners, or highly compensated employees.

Effective dates.—[T]he provisions generally are effective beginning January 1, 1985. * * *

The reasons for adopting this legislation are described in the following excerpt from the Report of the House Ways and Means Committee, which in 1983 developed the rules ultimately enacted as § 132.

Excerpt From Report of the Committee on Ways and Means on the Tax Reform Act of 1983

H.R.Rep. No. 98–432, at 286, 1983.

In providing statutory rules for exclusion of certain fringe benefits for income and payroll tax purposes, the committee has attempted to strike a balance between two competing objectives.

First, the committee is aware that in many industries, employees may receive, either free or at a discount, goods and services which the employer sells to the general public. In many cases, these practices are long established, and have been treated by employers, employees, and the IRS as not giving rise to taxable income. Although employees may receive an economic benefit from the availability of these free or discounted goods or services, employers often have valid business reasons, other than simply providing compensation, for encouraging employees to avail themselves of the products which they sell to the public. For example, a retail clothing business will want its salespersons to wear, when they deal with customers, the clothing which it seeks to sell to the public. In addition, the fact that the selection of goods and services available from a particular employer usually is restricted makes it appropriate to provide a limited exclusion, when such discounts are generally made available to employees, for the income employees realize from obtaining free or reduced-cost goods or services. The committee believes, therefore, that many present practices under which employers may provide to a broad group of employees, either free or at a discount, the products and services which the employer sells or provides to the public do not serve merely to replace cash compensation. These reasons support the committee's decision to codify the ability of employers to continue these practices without imposition of income or payroll taxes.

The second objective of the committee's bill is to set forth clear boundaries for the provision of tax-free benefits. * * * [T]he administrators of the tax law have not had clear guidelines in this area, and hence taxpayers in identical situations have been treated differently. The inequities, confusion, and administrative difficulties for businesses, employees, and the IRS resulting from this situation have increased substantially in recent years. * * *

In addition, the committee is concerned that without any well-defined limits on the ability of employers to compensate their employees tax-free by using a medium other than cash, new practices will emerge that could shrink the income tax base significantly, and further shift a disproportionate tax burden to those individuals whose compensation is in the form of cash. A shrinkage of the base of the social security payroll tax could also pose a threat to the viability of the social security system. * * * Finally, an unrestrained expansion of noncash compensation would increase inequities among employees in different types of businesses, and among employers as well.

The nondiscrimination rule is an important common thread among the types of fringe benefits which are excluded under the bill from income and employment taxes. Under the bill, most fringe benefits may be made available tax-free to officers, owners, or highly compensated employees only if the benefits are also provided on substantially equal terms to other employees. The committee believes that it would be fundamentally unfair to provide tax-free treatment for economic benefits that are furnished only to highly paid executives. Further, where benefits are limited to the highly paid, it is more likely that the benefit is being provided so that those who control the business can receive compensation in a nontaxable form; in that situation, the reasons stated above for allowing tax-free treatment would not be applicable. Also * * * some commentators argue that the current situation—in which the lack of clear rules for the tax treatment of nonstatutory fringe benefits encourages the nonreporting of many types of compensatory benefits—has led to nonreporting of types of cash income which are clearly taxable under present-law rules, such as interest and dividends.

In summary, the committee believes that * * * the bill substantially improves the equity and administration of the tax system.

NOTES

(A) *Distinguishing Working Condition Fringes from Compensation.* Section 132 represents an effort to develop fringe benefit rules that distinguish "working condition benefits" from "in-kind compensation." The former usually are regarded as primarily for the benefit of the employer and therefore not includable in the income of the employee. Thus, an essential prerequisite for exclusion should be the existence of a substantial noncompensatory business purpose on the part of the employer for providing the good or service in question to its employees. A good or service should not be excluded unless it is related to the employee's work and is something ordinarily useful to someone in the employee's position. A benefit provided at the employer's place of business would be more likely to be characterized as a working condition fringe than a benefit provided outside the business premises.

How well does § 132 conform to these principles? Pay particular attention to § 132(b) and (c). How are the following items treated under § 132?

1. a)   An airline baggage handler, allowed to fly free on a space-available basis, flies to Hawaii.
   b)   A salesman is given a free airline ticket to Hawaii.
2. a)   A salesclerk at Macy's is given a 10 percent discount (Macy's profit margin) and purchases a $1,000 television set for $900.
   b)   The owner of a manufacturing company arranges for an employee to buy from the owner's brother a car for $27,000 that he normally sells for $30,000.
3. a)   State University provides a free parking space on campus for all faculty members.
   b)   City University gives each faculty member a one-year subway pass.
4. a)   ABC Bank operates a gym in its basement and permits employees to use it free.
   b)   XYZ Bank pays the YMCA dues and gym fees for each of its employees.

Given your answers to these questions (in each case, (a) is not taxable and (b) is taxable, except for 3 where taxation depends on values), what do you think of the equity and efficiency of § 132? Some cases are easy. The American Bankruptcy Institute Law Review (of all places) reports that the law firm Shearman and Sterling in Menlo Park, California gives its associates an $800 car allowance, whether or not they have a car. See 8 Am. Bkruptcy. Inst. L. Rev. 205, 211 (2000). That amount is included in income, whether or not they have a car.

(B) *Valuation.* What is the amount of income when a fringe benefit is includable in the employee's gross income? The cost to the employer, the fair market value or the subjective value to the employee? The basic rule is that the amount is the fair market value. Reg. § 1.61–2(d). The regulations define fair market value as "the amount that an individual would have to pay for the particular fringe benefit in an arm's length transaction." Reg. § 1.61–21(b)(2).

This may lead to results that might be considered unfair. Suppose the employee receives something that is of little value to him, for example, the vegetarian who receives a holiday turkey or the non-skier who is given a trip to Aspen. The value might be discounted to reflect the possibility that employees might have purchased something else had they received cash or because the item received had less value to them. See Turner v. Commissioner, 13 T.C.M. 462 (1954), where the court refused to require the taxpayer to include the market value of a free trip to South America. The court stated:

> The winning of the tickets did not provide them with something which they needed in the ordinary course of their lives and for which they would have made an expenditure in any event, but merely gave them an opportunity to enjoy a luxury otherwise beyond their means. Their value to the petitioners was not equal to their retail cost.

Generally, however, it would not be feasible to permit taxpayers to prove that a receipt is worth less to them than market value. Rather than taking seriously employee allegations that they would have said to their employers, "Please, don't give me that Mercedes," an income tax generally must include such goods or services in employees' income at their objective fair market value and rely on employees to negotiate for cash when they really prefer it. Of course, an employee generally can reject a benefit and forgo tax.

Suppose the item is more valuable to the recipient than it is to other taxpayers. For example, assume a law professor would rather read the Internal Revenue Code than any other book and receives a free copy. Would it be appropriate to include the excess value in income? Economists describe this excess of satisfaction from property over its market price as consumer surplus. Is it practical to tax consumer surplus?

Are there situations where using fair market value as the touchstone creates inequities? Suppose an executive is allowed to travel free on a space-available basis on the company jet. The value of a seat on a private jet (or the employer's cost of providing the seat) might be ten times higher than the cost of a first class ticket to the same destination. The regulations provide special rules for certain situations. See, e.g., Reg. § 1.61–21(g) (rules for valuing flights on commercial aircraft).

(C) *Nondiscrimination.* In some cases, Section 132 places great weight on a nondiscrimination requirement to insure equity. See § 132(e)(2) and (j). Nondiscrimination rules are also found in § 117(d) and § 274(e)(4). Would vertical equity be achieved by providing each employee the same dollar amount of nontaxable fringe benefits? By providing each employee nontaxable fringes as the same proportion of total compensation?

(D) *Frequent Fliers.* Suppose an employee takes a business trip and his airfare is paid by the employer. The airline awards the employee frequent flier miles, which the employee uses for a personal trip. Do these transactions have any federal income tax consequences? Is there a Code section that clearly dictates the tax treatment of frequent flier miles awarded to customers? If not, what is the economic substance of their frequent flier miles?

After almost a decade of saying nothing about frequent flier miles, the IRS issued a technical advice memorandum in 1995 in which it took the position that employees who were permitted to keep the miles under a written plan of the employer had taxable income. After the business community went apoplectic, the Service announced that it had no "special enforcement plan for frequent flier miles." The following year, the Ninth Circuit held that an employee had taxable income arising from the following complicated scheme: The employee booked a coach seat for a business trip on behalf of a client with a travel agent, who then obtained a first class upgrade with the employee's frequent flier miles (obtained from trips paid for by the employer). When the client reimbursed the first class fare, the travel agent credited the employee's "travel account" with an amount equal to the difference between the coach and first class fares. The court held him taxable on the credited amount, finding the transaction akin to a sale of the frequent flier miles. Although the court said there was no need for it to decide if the miles themselves were taxable, it said that the employee had a zero basis in the miles, an assumption consistent with no taxation on receipt. Charley v. Commissioner, 91 F.3d 72 (9th Cir.1996).

Suppose the amount in the employee's travel account was $2,000, which he used to purchase a round trip ticket to Paris. Is there any economic difference between that transaction and simply using the frequent flier miles to obtain a ticket to Paris?

In 2002 the IRS announced that it will not assert that a taxpayer has gross income because he has received or used frequent flier miles attributable to business travel. Announcement 2002–18, 2002–10 I.R.B. 10. The Service noted that there are many unanswered questions with respect to the miles and until it can figure out the answers, they will go untaxed.

(E) *Computer Research Junkies Beware.* Congress often amends Code sections by deleting or inserting a subsection in the middle, rather than at the end of the section. This then requires relettering all subsequent sections. Section 132 is a good example of this. You should be aware that if you were to do an electronic database search, say on Westlaw or LEXIS for § 132(h), which contains a rule relating to fringe benefits for dependents, you would pick up references to what is now § 132(i) (reciprocal agreements) and also to what is now § 132(j) (special rules). If you wanted all the rulings or cases on the dependents rule, you would also have to search for its former Code sections § 132(g) and § 132(f). But the difficulties accumulate: If you searched for § 132(g), for example, you would pick up not only references to the dependents rule, but also references to the current § 132(g) (moving expenses) and to another former version of § 132(g) (reciprocal agreements). Sometimes doing research the old-fashioned way—with books—may be the only way to get the right answer. Many versions of the complete Internal Revenue Code, for example, include historical footnotes that alert readers to changes such as these.

(F) *Alternatives.* Contrast § 132 with a 1977 Treasury proposal to exclude only items required as a condition of a particular job. Why not just assume that all fringe benefits—other than working condition fringes—are part of the bargain between employers and employees and include their fair market value in employee's income?

Another alternative is to disallow the employer's deduction, particularly where it would be onerous to allocate compensation to particular employees. It often is asserted that the viability of a system of fringe benefit taxation requires that employers be able to calculate the amount of income and withhold tax on that amount, or, at a minimum, inform employees of includable amounts on Form W–2. Even though a fringe benefit is rather clearly compensatory, it may be difficult to allocate the benefit to specific employees. For example, it may be impossible to keep track of the value of subsidized meals in the employee cafeteria. Why not simply disallow the deduction to the employer for the expense? What would be the differences between an employer-deduction disallowance and an employee inclusion in income? Whose marginal rate would apply? This approach often is referred to as "surrogate taxation" because the taxation of the employer is a surrogate for taxing the employee on the fringe benefit. For which employers does this approach not work?

Another possibility is an excise tax on the value of such benefits. The disallowance of a deduction can be the equivalent of an excise tax. How might such an excise tax rate be chosen? See § 4977, which allows employers to elect a 30 percent excise tax on certain "excess fringe benefits" in lieu of taxation to employees under § 132.

(G) *Benefits Provided to Other than an Employee.* Although the general language of § 132 applies only to benefits provided by an employer to an employee, there are many instances where "employee" is very broadly defined. For example, no-additional cost service and qualified employee discount fringes can be excluded by family members of employees. § 132(h). Parents of airline employees get their own exclusion. § 132(h)(3). The regulations treat independent contractors as employees for purposes of working condition fringes, and family members as employees for purposes of on-site athletic facilities. Reg. § 1.132–1(b). And anyone can exclude a de minimis fringe. Reg. § 1.132–1(b)(4). Where does the IRS get the authority to exclude de minimis fringes provided to non-employees? See § 132(m). Why should the parents of airline employees get tax-free air travel while a Greyhound bus driver would have to pay tax on a free ticket provided to his parents? Folklore has it that Ways and Means Chairman Dan Rostenkowski added § 132(h)(3) to the Code because two of his daughters were flight attendants.

(H) *Interest-Free Loans.* Generally, an interest-free (or low-interest) loan from an employer to an employee will be recharacterized to reflect economic reality. The lender is treated as charging a market rate of interest (established by the statute) and making a payment of some or all of that amount to the borrower. This payment is treated as a gift, dividend, contribution to capital or compensation, depending on the circumstances. The borrower is then deemed to transfer the amount of the payment to the lender as interest. § 7872. Loans between individuals of less than $10,000 are generally excluded if the forgone interest is a gift and if the loan proceeds are not used for business or investment purposes. This exception does not apply if one of the principal purposes of the transaction is tax avoidance.

(I) *Benefits Not from Employers*. What is the appropriate tax treatment of benefits provided by a nonemployer that are not covered by § 132? Consider the book critic who receives books unsolicited from publishers. (See *Haverly v. United States*, at page 148 infra). Suppose a law firm associate visits a firm client and the client pays her parking fee and buys her lunch? What if a prospective employer pays a law student's airfare to interview with a firm? See Rev.Rul. 63–77, 1963–1 C.B. 177. The next case deals in part with a transfer by a nonemployer.

United States v. Gotcher

United States Court of Appeals, Fifth Circuit, 1968. 401 F.2d 118.

THORNBERRY, CIRCUIT JUDGE. In 1960, Mr. and Mrs. Gotcher took a twelve-day expense-paid trip to Germany to tour the Volkswagen facilities there. The trip cost $1372.30. His employer, Economy Motors, paid $348.73, and Volkswagen of Germany and Volkswagen of America shared the remaining $1023.53. Upon returning, Mr. Gotcher bought a twenty-five percent interest in Economy Motors, the Sherman, Texas Volkswagen dealership, that had been offered to him before he left. Today he is President of Economy Motors in Sherman and owns fifty percent of the dealership. Mr. and Mrs. Gotcher did not include any part of the $1372.30 in their 1960 income. The Commissioner determined that the taxpayers had realized income to the extent of the $1372.30 for the expense-paid trip and asserted a tax deficiency of $356.79, plus interest. * * * The district court, sitting without a jury, held that the cost of the trip was not income or, in the alternative, was income and deductible as an ordinary and necessary business expense. 259 F.Supp. 340. We affirm the district court's determination that the cost of the trip was not income to Mr. Gotcher ($686.15); however, Mrs. Gotcher's expenses ($686.15) constituted income and were not deductible.

Section 61 of the Internal Revenue Code of 1954 * * * defines gross income as income from whatever source derived and specifically includes fifteen items within this definition. The court below reasoned that the cost of the trip to the Gotchers was not income because an economic or financial benefit does not constitute income under section 61 unless it is conferred as compensation for services rendered. This conception of gross income is too restrictive since it is well-settled that section 61 should be broadly interpreted and that many items, including noncompensatory gains, constitute gross income.

Sections 101–123 specifically exclude certain items from gross income. Appellant argues that the cost of the trip should be included in income since it is not specifically excluded by sections 101–123, reasoning that section 61 was drafted broadly to subject all economic gains to tax and any exclusions should be narrowly limited to the specific exclusions. This analysis is too restrictive since it has been generally held that exclusions from gross income are not limited to the enumerated exclusions. Moreover, the Supreme Court in Rudolph v. United States, 1962, 370 U.S. 269, has indicated, in concurring and dissenting opinions to dismissing the writ of certiorari as improvidently granted, that sections 101–123 are not exhaustive. * * *

In determining whether the expense-paid trip was income within section 61, we must look to the tests that have been developed under this section. The concept of economic gain to the taxpayer is the key to section 61. * * * This concept contains two distinct requirements: There must be an economic gain, and this gain must primarily benefit the taxpayer personally. In some cases, as in the case of an expense-paid trip, there is no direct economic gain, but there is an indirect economic gain inasmuch as a benefit has been received without a corresponding diminution in wealth. Yet even if expense-paid items, as meals and lodging, are received by the taxpayer, the value of these items will not be gross income, even though the employee receives some incidental benefit, if the meals and lodging are primarily for the convenience of the employer. See * * * § 119.

* * *

The trip was made in 1959 when VW was attempting to expand its local dealerships in the United States. The "Buy American" campaign and the fact that the VW people felt they had a "very ugly product" prompted them to offer these tours of Germany to prospective dealers. * * * In 1959, when VW began to push for its share of the American market, its officials determined that the best way to remove the apprehension about this foreign product was to take the dealer to Germany and have him see his investment first-hand. It was believed that once the dealer saw the manufacturing facilities and the stability of the "new Germany" he would be convinced that VW was for him. Furthermore, VW considered the expenditure justified because the dealer was being asked to make a substantial investment of his time and money in a comparatively new product. Indeed, after taking the trip, VW required him to acquire first-class facilities. * * * Apparently these trips have paid off since VW's sales have skyrocketed and the dealers have made their facilities top-rate operations under the VW requirements for a standard dealership.

The activities in Germany support the conclusion that the trip was oriented to business. * * * There is ample support for the trial judge's finding that a substantial amount of time was spent touring VW facilities and visiting local dealerships. VW had set up these tours with local dealers so that the travelers could discuss how the facilities were operated in Germany. Mr. Gotcher took full advantage of this opportunity and even used some of his "free time" to visit various local dealerships. Moreover, at almost all of the evening meals VW officials gave talks about the organization and passed out literature and brochures on the VW story.

Some of the days were not related to touring VW facilities, but that fact alone cannot be decisive. The dominant purpose of the trip is the critical inquiry and some pleasurable features will not negate the finding of an overall business purpose. * * * Since we are convinced that the agenda related primarily to business and that Mr. Gotcher's attendance was prompted by business considerations, the so-called sightseeing complained of by the Government is inconsequential. * * * Indeed, the district court found that even this touring of the countryside had an indirect relation to business since the tours were not typical sightseeing excursions but were connected to the desire of VW that the dealers be persuaded that the German economy was stable enough to justify investment in a German product. We cannot say that this conclusion is clearly erroneous. Nor can we say that the enthusiastic literary style of the brochures negates a dominant business purpose. It is the business reality of the total situation, not the colorful expressions in the literature, that controls. Considering the record, the circumstances prompting the trip, and the objective achieved, we conclude that the primary purpose of the trip was to induce Mr. Gotcher to take out a VW dealership interest.

The question, therefore, is what tax consequences should follow from an expense-paid trip that primarily benefits the party paying for the trip. In several analogous situations the value of items received by employees has been excluded from gross income when these items were primarily for the benefit of the employer. Section 119 excludes from gross income of an employee the value of meals and lodging furnished to him for the convenience of the employer. Even before these items were excluded by the 1954 Code, the Treasury and the courts recognized that they should be excluded from gross income. Thus it appears that the value of any trip that is paid by the employer or by a businessman primarily for his own benefit should be excluded from gross income of the payee on similar reasoning. * * *

In the recent case of Allen J. McDonnell, 26 T.C.M. 115, Tax Ct.Mem. 1967–18, a sales supervisor and his wife were chosen by lot to accompany a group of contest winners on an expense-paid trip to Hawaii. In holding that the taxpayer had received no income, the Tax Court noted that he was required by his employer to go and that he was serving a legitimate business purpose though he enjoyed the trip. The decision suggests that in analyzing the tax consequences of an expense-paid trip one important factor is whether the traveler had any choice but to go. Here, although taxpayer was not forced to go, there is no doubt that in the reality of the business world he had no real choice. The trial judge reached the same conclusion. He found that the invitation did not specifically order the dealers to go, but that as a practical matter it was an order or directive that if a person was going to be a VW dealer, sound business judgment necessitated his accepting the offer of corporate hospitality. So far as Economy Motors was concerned, Mr. Gotcher knew that if he was going to be a part-owner of the dealership, he had better do all that was required to foster good business relations with VW. Besides having no choice but to go, he had no control over the schedule or the money spent. VW did all the planning. In cases involving noncompensatory economic gains, courts have emphasized that the taxpayer still had complete dominion and control over the money to use it as he wished to satisfy personal desires or needs. Indeed, the Supreme Court has defined income as accessions of wealth over which the taxpayer has complete control. Commissioner of Internal Revenue v. Glenshaw Glass Co. Clearly, the lack of control works in taxpayer's favor here.

McDonnell also suggests that one does not realize taxable income when he is serving a legitimate business purpose of the party paying the expenses. * * * Thus, the rule is that the economic benefit will be taxable to the recipient only when the payment of expenses serves no legitimate corporate purpose. * * * The decisions also indicate that the tax consequences are to be determined by looking to the primary purpose of the expenses and that the first consideration is the intention of the payor. The Government in argument before the district court agreed that whether the expenses were income to taxpayers is mainly a question of the motives of the people giving the trip. Since this is a matter of proof, the resolution of the tax question really depends on whether Gotcher showed that his presence served a legitimate corporate purpose and that no appreciable amount of time was spent for his personal benefit and enjoyment.

* * *

The corporate-executive decisions indicate that some economic gains, though not specifically excluded from section 61, may nevertheless escape taxation. They may be excluded even though the entertainment and travel unquestionably give enjoyment to the taxpayer and produce indirect economic gains. When this indirect economic gain is subordinate to an overall business purpose, the recipient is not taxed. We are convinced that the personal benefit to Mr. Gotcher from the trip was merely incidental to VW's sales campaign.

As for Mrs. Gotcher, the trip was primarily a vacation. She did not make the tours with her husband to see the local dealers or attend discussions about the VW organization. This being so the primary benefit of the expense-paid trip for the wife went to Mr. Gotcher in that he was relieved of her expenses. He should therefore be taxed on the expenses attributable to his wife. * * * Nor are the expenses deductible since the wife's presence served no bona fide business purpose for her husband. Only when the wife's presence is necessary to the conduct of the husband's business are her expenses deductible under section 162. * * * Also, it must be shown that the wife made the trip only to assist her husband in his business. A single trip by a wife with her husband to Europe has been specifically rejected as not being the exceptional type of case justifying a deduction. * * *

Affirmed in part; reversed in part.

JOHN R. BROWN, CHIEF JUDGE (concurring):

* * *

Attributing income to the little wife who was neither an employee, a prospective employee, nor a dealer, for the value of a trip she neither planned nor chose still bothers me. If her uncle had paid for the trip, would it not have been a pure gift, not income? Or had her husband out of pure separate property given her the trip would the amount over and above the cost of Texas bed and board have been income? I acquiesce now, confident that for others in future cases on a full record the wife, as now does the husband, also will overcome.

NOTES

(A) *Gotcher and § 132.* If *Gotcher* were decided today, would the result be the same? Presumably the portion of Gotcher's trip paid for by Economy

Motors, his employer, would be covered by § 132, but not that paid for by Volkswagen, which was never his employer. Should both portions be treated the same? See § 132(*l*).

The *Gotcher* court emphasized that the taxpayer "had no real choice" but to take the trip and to follow the planned itinerary. What is the relevance of the taxpayer's lack of control over funds expended by the employer for the employee's personal consumption? Suppose a travel agency requires an employee to take an all-expenses-paid two-week trip to Paris with the itinerary selected by the employer? What if an employer orders an employee to take a prepaid vacation in order to improve his efficiency at work?

(B) *Spouse's Expenses.* Regardless of the test adopted, should the same test also apply to a spouse? In United States v. Disney, 413 F.2d 783 (9th Cir.1969), Roy Disney and his wife were reimbursed by his employer, Walt Disney Productions, for expenses incurred on certain of his business trips. The court found it was necessary for Mrs. Disney to accompany her husband and that she assisted his performance of business duties. The court held that reimbursement of Mrs. Disney's expenses was includable in gross income, but allowed the Disneys to deduct these expenses as business expenses under § 162. Compare Meridian Wood Products Co., Inc. v. United States, 725 F.2d 1183 (9th Cir.1984), where the court distinguished *Disney* and denied business expense deductions because the taxpayer's wife's primary purpose was to "socialize," not to serve the interests of the business. Where a member of the employee's family receives a taxable fringe benefit, it is included in the gross income of the employee, not the family member.

It is now significantly more difficult to deduct the cost of a spouse's travel expenses. Section 274(m)(3) provides that travel expenses are deductible for a spouse or dependent only if the spouse is an employee of the taxpayer, there is a bona fide business purpose, and the expenses otherwise would have been deductible. While it might have been relatively easy to add Mrs. Disney to the payroll, it will not be possible for most businesses to do so. Suppose a corporation or a law firm, for example, picks up the expenses for a non-employee spouse who travels to a meeting and attends dinners with other spouses. Does either spouse have taxable income? Reg. § 1.132–5(t) provides that even if the employer cannot deduct the spouse's expenses, the employee can exclude the reimbursement so long as the spouse's presence had a bona fide business purpose. This is an example of "surrogate taxation," discussed supra at page 108.

3.   MEALS AND LODGING

NOTE ON THE EXCLUSION OF MEALS AND LODGING

In the early versions of the income tax regulations and in a number of early rulings, the Bureau of Internal Revenue exempted from gross income meals and lodging furnished to employees in a variety of circumstances "for the convenience of the employer." These included board and lodging furnished seamen aboard ship, O.D. 265, 1 C.B. 71 (1919); living quarters furnished to employees for the convenience of the employer, Reg. § 45, Art.

33, T.D. 2992, 2 C.B. 76 (1920); and certain cash payments for "supper money," O.D. 514, 2 C.B. 90 (1920).

In Benaglia v. Commissioner, 36 B.T.A. 838 (1937), a manager of two deluxe Hawaiian resorts and a golf club and his wife occupied a suite of rooms and took meals free of charge at the hotel, "entirely for the convenience" of the employer. The Commissioner argued that the fair market value of the meals, $7,845, was income. The Board of Tax Appeals disagreed, stating:

> [P]etitioner's residence at the hotel was not by way of compensation for services, not for his personal convenience, comfort or pleasure, but solely because he could not otherwise perform the services required of him. * * * His duty was continuous and required his presence at a moment's call. * * * Under such circumstances, the value of meals and lodging is not income to the employee, even though it may relieve him of an expense which he would otherwise bear.

The majority accepted the employer's statement that the manager could not perform his job without living in the hotel suite since his job required his presence at a moment's call. The dissenting judge was far more skeptical that acceptance of a suite of rooms in one of the world's most luxurious hotels was really for the convenience of the employer. He noted that the taxpayer managed the other hotel and the golf club without living there and was away from Honolulu for over five months for the year in question.

The Commissioner subsequently followed the *Benaglia* case and permitted certain meals and lodging furnished to an employee to be excluded from income. They had to be furnished "for the convenience of the employer" and could not represent compensation for services rendered.

Section 119, added by the 1954 Code, was the first legislative treatment of the problem. This provision provides that an employee may exclude from income "the value of any meals * * * furnished to him * * * by his employer for the convenience of the employer, but only if * * * the meals are furnished on the business premises of the employer * * *." Taxpayers may also be able to exclude from income the value of meals and lodging furnished to their immediate families under a 1978 amendment to § 119.

Commissioner v. Kowalski

Supreme Court of the United States, 1977. 434 U.S. 77.

MR. JUSTICE BRENNAN delivered the opinion of the Court.

* * *

The starting point in the determination of the scope of "gross income" is the cardinal principle that Congress in creating the income tax intended "to use the full measure of its taxing power." * * * In applying this principle to the construction of § 22(a) of the Internal Revenue Code of 1939 this Court stated that "Congress applied no limitations as to the source of taxable receipts, nor restrictive labels as to their nature [, but intended] to tax all gains except those specifically exempted." Commissioner v. Glenshaw Glass Co., 348 U.S. 426, 429–430 (1955). * * * Although Congress simplified the definition of gross income in § 61 of the 1954 Code, it did not intend thereby to narrow the scope of that concept. * * * In the absence of a specific exemption, therefore, respondent's meal-allowance payments are income within the meaning of § 61 since, like the payments involved in *Glenshaw Glass Co.*, the payments are "undeniabl[y] accessions to wealth, clearly realized, and over which the [respondent has] complete dominion." * * *

Respondent contends, however, that § 119 can be construed to be a specific exemption covering the meal-allowance payments to New Jersey troopers. Alternatively, respondent argues that notwithstanding § 119 a specific exemption may be found in a line of lower-court cases and administrative rulings which recognize that benefits conferred by an employer on an employee "for the convenience of the employer"—at least when such benefits are not "compensatory"—are not income within the meaning of the Internal Revenue Code.

* * *

Section 119 provides that an employee may exclude from income "the value of any meals ... furnished to him by his employer for the convenience of the employer, but only if ... the meals are furnished on the business premises of the employer...." By its terms, § 119 covers meals furnished by the employer and not cash reimbursements for meals. This is not a mere oversight. * * * Accordingly, respondent's meal allowance payments are not subject to exclusion under § 119.

[The Court's detailed examination of the history of the "convenience of the employer" doctrine prior to the 1954 amendments and the legislative history of § 119 are omitted.]

Because § 119 replaces prior law, respondent's further argument—that [a] technical appendix in the Senate Report recognized the existence under § 61 of an exclusion for a class of noncompensatory cash payments—is without merit. If cash meal allowances could be excluded on the mere showing that such payments served the convenience of the employer, as respondent suggests, then cash would be more widely excluded from income than meals in kind, an extraordinary result given the presumptively compensatory nature of cash payments and the obvious intent of § 119 to narrow the circumstances in which meals could be excluded. * * *

Moreover, even if we were to assume with respondent that cash meal payments made for the convenience of the employer could qualify for an exclusion notwithstanding the express limitations upon the doctrine embodied in § 119, there would still be no reason to allow the meal allowance here to be excluded. Under the pre–1954 convenience-of-the-employer doctrine respondent's allowance is * * * income. * * * In any case, to avoid the completely unwarranted result of creating a larger exclusion for cash than kind, the meal allowances here would have to be demonstrated to be necessary to allow respondent "properly to perform his duties." There is not even a suggestion on this record of any such necessity.

Finally, respondent argues that it is unfair that members of the military may exclude their subsistence allowances from income while respondent cannot. While this may be so, arguments of equity have little force in construing the boundaries of exclusions and deductions from income many of which, to be administrable, must be arbitrary. In any case, Congress has already considered respondent's equity argument and has rejected it in the repeal of § 120 of the 1954 Code. That provision as enacted allowed state troopers like respondent to exclude from income up to $5 of subsistence allowance per day. Section 120 was repealed after only four years, however, because it was "inequitable since there are many other individual taxpayers whose duties also require them to incur subsistence expenditures regardless of the tax effect. Thus, it appears that certain police officials by reasons of this exclusion are placed in a more favorable position tax-wise than other individual income taxpayers who incur the same types of expense...." H.R.Rep. No. 775, 85th Cong., 1st Sess., 7 (1957).

Reversed.

[JUSTICE BLACKMUN AND THE CHIEF JUSTICE dissented on the ground that § 119 does not explicitly distinguish cash and in-kind provision of meals and because the business premises of the State of New Jersey, the trooper's employer, are wherever the trooper is on duty in that State. The dissenters were also concerned with the "ironical difference" in tax treatment accorded to the paramilitary New Jersey state troopers and the federal military, whose subsistence allowance is excluded under Reg. § 1.61–2(b).]

NOTES

(A) *More Than One Way to Skin This Cat.* In Christey v. United States, 841 F.2d 809 (8th Cir.1988), the Eighth Circuit permitted state troopers to deduct as ordinary and necessary business expenses under § 162(a) the costs of meals that they were required to eat at public restaurants adjacent to the highway while they were on duty.

The treatment of deductions is taken up subsequently in Chapter 3. As will become clear, the deduction of employee business expenses under § 162 does not afford tax benefits that are necessarily identical to those that would result from an exclusion from income under § 119. For some taxpayers, however, the tax consequences may be the same.

(B) *The In–Kind Requirement.* As *Kowalski* makes clear, a cash payment or cash reimbursement to an employee is not excludable under § 119. Thus, an employee on call who is reimbursed for the sandwich he brings to his desk is taxed, but the employee whose employer brings the sandwich to the desk is not taxed. Any fear that the employee could spend the cash for something other than the meal could be alleviated by requiring the employee to account to the employer.

But *Kowalski* did not lay the issue to rest. Note that § 119(b)(3) excludes certain fixed charges for meals that an employee is required to pay. The meals, however, must still be provided by the employer (rather than the employee). This distinction was muddied by the Ninth Circuit in Sibla v. Commissioner, 611 F.2d 1260 (9th Cir.1980). Firemen were required to eat meals at the firehouse during their 24–hour shifts. The fire department provided the kitchen facilities, but the firemen purchased and prepared the food and assessed members for the costs of the meals. The only question under § 119 was whether the employer "furnished" the meals in kind. The court thought that the *Kowalski* court was only concerned with cash allowances over which the taxpayer has complete dominion. "We do not believe that the Court intended to rule that an allowance otherwise excludable should be denied excludability simply because it was paid in cash." Consider this hypothetical discussed by both the majority and dissenting opinion in *Sibla:* Suppose the fire department issued scrip in the precise amount of the meal assessment and the scrip was redeemable only at the mess. The majority took the position that "such an allowance * * * whether paid in scrip or cash would be [excludable]." The dissent believed the scrip should be taxed because the firemen would be free to "suit their own tastes in the groceries purchased and the food prepared."

A further issue is the definition of "meal." In Tougher v. Commissioner, 51 T.C. 737 (1969), affirmed per curiam 441 F.2d 1148 (9th Cir.1971), the taxpayer, a Federal Aviation Administration employee, was required to include in income groceries that he purchased at a commissary where he was employed. In Jacob v. United States, 493 F.2d 1294 (3d Cir.1974), the taxpayer was able to exclude as "meals" groceries supplied by his employer.

What are the tax consequences (after *Kowalski*) of supper money provided to law firm associates who work at night? Occasional recipients should check Reg. § 1.132–6. In American Airlines, Inc. v. United States, 204 F.3d 1103 (Fed.Cir.2000), the court held $50 American Express vouchers given to employees to use for meals while traveling were not excluded as a de minimis fringe under § 132(e). As a practical matter, the employees could use the vouchers at any time.

(C) *The Business Premises Test.* The requirement that the meals and lodging be on the business premises was designed to eliminate controversy, but it has not been completely successful. Consider the following cases:

The president of a Japanese subsidiary of a U.S. corporation was provided a large company-owned house in a prestigious Tokyo location. The Court of Claims in Adams v. United States, 585 F.2d 1060 (Ct.Cl.1978), rejected a literal reading of § 119 and imposed a "functional rather than a spatial test." In holding that the lodging was excluded from the president's gross income, the court emphasized that the company had built the house specifically for its presidents, with facilities for a home office and substantial business entertaining, that the company president had lived there for 15 years and that the house had become associated with the company, and that the taxpayer was required to live in the house and to perform various business activities there after working hours. The court concluded that the house served important business functions of the company and therefore was part of its business premises.

Similarly, the Tax Court held that a taxpayer who was a manager for a large hotel and was required to live in a house leased by the hotel could exclude the value of the lodging. The house was on the perimeter of property adjacent to the hotel, but across the street. The taxpayer performed significant duties for his employer in the house and was subject to call 24 hours a day. The court held that the house was on the hotel's business premises. Lindeman v. Commissioner, 60 T.C. 609 (1973), acq. 1973–2 C.B. 2. The Service took a similar approach in ruling that state governors are not required to include in gross income the fair market value of their official residences. Rev.Rul. 75–540, 1975–2 C.B. 53.

These results should be contrasted with that in Dole v. Commissioner, 43 T.C. 697 (1965), affirmed 351 F.2d 308 (1st Cir.1965). The superintendent, assistant superintendent, and office manager of a wool manufacturer were told by their employer to live in houses owned by the company and located about one mile from the mill. The officials were required by their jobs to live close to the mill, which operated on a three-shift schedule five days a week and a two-shift schedule on Saturday. The Tax Court held that the fair rental value of the houses, including utilities, was taxable to the officials. The First Circuit affirmed on the basis that the houses, although owned by the employer, were not "on the business premises" of the employer as required by § 119.

This requirement can lead to inefficiencies. Suppose the employer needs to have luncheon meetings so employees can eat together and discuss business, but there are no facilities on the premises. The employer rents a hotel suite and the employees regularly meet there for lunch and business meetings. The Tax Court held that the suite became a part of the business premises of the employer, and that the lunches were tax-free to the employees. Mabley v. Commissioner, 24 T.C.M. 1794 (1965). (Compare Moss v. Commissioner, 80 T.C. 1073 (1983), set forth at page 272, infra, where similar lunches were held to be personal). Suppose, however, the meetings were held in a restaurant on the ground floor of the office building where the employer is located. The value of the meals would be includable in the employees' income.

(D) *Convenience of Employer Test.* The regulations for § 119 provide that meals are provided for the convenience of the employer only if there is a "substantial noncompensatory purpose." The statute requires that lodging must be a condition of employment as well. Will a requirement that the employee live in a particular residence suffice? Suppose a couple requires a nanny to occupy a room in their home, but she is only expected to work fixed hours? Suppose a university president is required to live in the president's house located in a suburb several miles from an urban campus? Does "convenience of the employer" mean that the lodging or meals are essential to the functioning of the business or simply helpful?

Generally, a requirement that an employee be "on call" after business hours establishes that the lodging or meals are for the convenience of the employer. Another way to establish that meals are for the convenience of the employer is to adopt a policy that precludes employees from eating away from the employer's business premise during reasonable meal hours. Ann. 99–77, 1999–32 I.R.B. 243 indicated that the IRS would accept the employer's judgement about restricting the ability of the employees to leave for meals, regardless of the reason, so long as the policy is actually enforced.

In 1998, Congress amended Section 119 to provide that *all* meals furnished to employees at a place of business are treated as furnished for the convenience of the employer if more than one-half of the employees to whom meals are provided are furnished the meals for the convenience of the employer. This provision was the work of a Nevada Congressman who is a former Casino official and the son of the CEO of Circus Circus. Want to guess whom this obscure provision benefits? Apparently large casinos in Las Vegas permit most of their employees to eat in subsidized or free cafeterias. Although it was clear that the meals served to food service employees were for the convenience of the employer, that was not true for exotic dancers and lion tamers. This created an employee relations imbroglio in that the hash slingers got to exclude their free hamburgers while the performers did not. Enter the lobbyists. Through a complex interaction of Sections 119, 132, and 274 (that you do not want to wade through), Congress agreed to the amendment, which essentially provides companies that serve meals to its employees a 100 percent deduction for a fringe benefit that is not taxable to the employees. But that still left employees having to argue that the meals were furnished for the convenience of the employer simply because they had to remain on the premises during their entire shift. The Ninth Circuit dealt them a winning hand. Holding that *Kowalski* does not require that the employee must accept the meals in order to properly perform his duties, the court found the stay-on-the premises policy was sufficient. The court noted that the IRS argument that accepting the meals had to be necessary to perform the specific duties of the employee would "render the test virtually impossible to satisfy; only restaurant critics and dieticians could meet such a test." Boyd Gaming Corp. v. Commissioner, 177 F.3d 1096 (9th Cir.1999).

(E) *Sections 107 and 134.* Note § 107, which exempts from gross income the rental value of a parsonage or a rental allowance paid to a minister. See also § 134 which excludes from gross income benefits to military personnel that were excludable from gross income as of September 9, 1986. The Regulations have long granted an exemption for quarters furnished to military personnel and to commutation in lieu of quarters. Is there any conceivable tax policy justification for these exclusions?

(F) *Is the Exclusion Justified?* Is it good tax policy to exclude from an employee's income the value of items furnished by the employer, such as meals and lodging, which the employee necessarily would otherwise purchase out of after-tax income? If the meals and lodging are for "the convenience of the employer," is this forced consumption? Should it matter if the consumption is different from that which a taxpayer would normally prefer, for example, meals at a fancy hotel or on a merchant marine ship? Note that § 119 also excludes meals and lodging provided to the employee's spouse or dependents, presumably because it is difficult to allocate the cost of meals and lodging provided to family members.

4. SECTION 83

NOTE ON SECTION 83

Section 83 provides additional authority for taxing benefits received by a taxpayer in connection with the performance of services. In addition, that section indicates when such benefits should be taxed and in what amount.

In some instances a taxpayer acquires goods or services at a price below the general market price. For example, a purchaser acquires a valuable antique from junk shop dealer unaware of its value. This so-called bargain purchase is not subject to tax. Where, however, a taxpayer is permitted to purchase property or services at a price below fair market value because the seller is compensating the purchaser for services, the purchaser has gross income in the amount of the discount. § 83(a). The general rule of § 83 also provides that if a person receives property in return for the performance of services, and if the property is nontransferable and subject to a substantial risk of forfeiture at the time of transfer, then the property is treated as still owned by the transferor and no income is realized by the transferee. When the forfeiture risk is removed or the property becomes transferable, the fair market value of the property at that time, less any amount originally paid for it, is includable in income by the person who performed the services. Section 83(c)(1) provides that property is subject to a substantial risk of forfeiture if full enjoyment of the property is conditioned upon the future performance of substantial services by an individual. For example, XYZ Co. permits A, an employee, to purchase shares of XYZ stock for $1,000 at a time when they are valued at $3,000. If, however, A terminates his employment with XYZ at any time in the succeeding five years, A must resell the stock to XYZ for $1,000. The restriction is stamped onto the face of the shares, making them nontransferable. At the end of five years, when the stock is worth $5,000, A's ownership vests. A has no income when he purchases the stock, but has $4,000 income when his interest in the stock vests.

Section 83(b) permits a taxpayer to elect to include the property in gross income when received even though it is subject to a substantial risk of forfeiture or is nontransferable. A taxpayer presumably would make this election if he expected the property to increase in value. Although he must report income on the receipt of the property, he has no further income when the property vests. In the above example, if A made a § 83(b) election, A would have $2,000 of income on the purchase of the stock but no income when the property vested. The additional $2,000 gain on the stock would not be taxed until the stock is sold. Section 83(b) carries with it some risk. If A forfeits the stock and receives his $1,000 back, he does not have a deductible loss even though he previously included $2,000 in income. § 83(b)(1). In order to make such an election, § 83 must apply. It does not apply to stock options unless they have a "readily ascertainable fair market value." § 83(e)(4). The courts have split on whether a zero value election can be made. Compare Pagel, Inc. v. Commissioner, 905 F.2d 1190 (8th Cir.1990) (stock with zero value does not have readily ascertainable fair market value) with Alves v. Commissioner, 734 F.2d 478 (9th Cir.1984) (zero value election permitted).

The employer is entitled to take a deduction under § 162 for the compensation in the year in which the employee includes the property in income. § 83(h). A divided Tax Court held that in order for the employer to take a deduction, the employees must actually have reported the receipt of the property on their tax returns. A failure to do so deprives the employer of the deduction. Venture Funding Ltd. v. Commissioner, 110 T.C. 236 (1998).

SECTION 2.   IMPUTED INCOME

NOTE ON IMPUTED INCOME

Suppose in exchange for legal services performed by a lawyer, a housepainter paints the lawyer's house. Or an individual who owns an apartment building receives a work of art from an artist in exchange for the rent-free use of an apartment by the artist. Both the lawyer and the house painter have gross income equal to the fair market value of the services received. The apartment owner includes the value of the painting in income and the artist has income equal to the fair rental value of the apartment. Rev.Rul. 79–24, 1979–1 C.B. 60.

Suppose, however, that the lawyer paints his own house. The benefits derived from labor on one's own behalf or the benefits from the ownership of property are commonly referred to as "imputed income." Economists generally regard imputed income as income that should be taxed, but these benefits usually are not treated as income for tax purposes. Although the failure to tax imputed income creates inequities and inefficiencies, the practical difficulties in subjecting imputed income to tax make taxation unlikely.

The exclusion of imputed income results in similarly situated taxpayers paying different tax. Assume that Bill and Jill each own a dog. Bill works overtime and earns $10, which he uses to pay someone to walk his dog. Jill leaves work on time and walks her own dog. Bill and Jill are in the same economic situation, but Bill will pay tax on $10 more income than Jill.

The exclusion of imputed income also produces inefficiencies by causing taxpayers to make economic choices different from those that they would have made in a no-tax world. Returning to the lawyer and the house painter, assume the lawyer earns $500 an hour and it will cost him $400 to have his windows painted, a one hour job. If he works for an hour, he will have only $350 left after taxes, assuming a 30 percent tax rate. Thus, the lawyer may paint his windows himself even though he may prefer to work as a lawyer and his work as a lawyer results in greater productivity.

There are a number of reasons for the failure to tax imputed income. The conceptual difficulty with taxing imputed income is determining where to stop. Does the person who shaves himself have imputed income equal to the value of a shave by a barber? What about a person who reads a book rather than have someone read it to him? Can leisure be thought of as a type of imputed income? Presumably someone who chooses leisure values it by the income that she loses by not working. Should income be measured by the amount that a person could earn, rather than what is actually earned? Should a law professor be taxed on the salary she could have earned by practicing on Wall Street? How could we justify taxing services performed by the taxpayer for himself, but not taxing leisure?

There are also practical difficulties in taxing imputed income. Putting aside the political wisdom of a rule that no one would understand or accept, there are still valuation and recordkeeping problems. If I comb my hair and do a lousy job, would my income be the value of a comb-out by a stylist or of my own weak attempt? Would sloppy housekeepers have less income than fastidious ones? Do fastidious housekeepers really have more ability to pay taxes than sloppy ones? Imagine the privacy concerns if the Service had to enforce compliance with a rule that required the taxpayer to account for services performed for one's self.

Although we may think the failure to tax the value of walking one's dog or combing one's hair is of academic interest only, the failure to tax the services provided by homemakers has undoubtedly influenced the decisions of some women to stay at home rather than to enter the work force. Many homemakers cannot earn sufficient income after taxes to pay for an equivalent amount of domestic services. Thus, there is an incentive for one spouse to perform untaxed domestic services. There is a problem of fairness as well. Both spouses of couple AB work outside the home and earn a total of $50,000. They pay $10,000 for domestic help. Only one spouse of couple CD works outside the home and earns $40,000 and the other spouse is a homemaker. Couple AB's taxable income exceeds couple CD's by $10,000 even though they have no economic advantage. Domestic services rendered by homemakers to their families is the largest source of imputed income from services. Since taxing the imputed income from domestic services is impractical and unlikely, are there alternatives? One clearly unacceptable alternative is to provide a deduction to the person who pays someone else to perform any services he could have performed for himself. Such a deduction for personal consumption would allow many taxpayers to eliminate their taxable income and would seriously erode the income tax base. An alternative approach is to allow a tax credit or deduction for families in which both spouses work. Congress did provide for such a deduction for a time. But this may create disparity with the single person who must pay for household services.

It is sometimes very difficult to distinguish imputed income from services that should be taxed. Consider the following definition of imputed income:

> a flow of satisfactions from durable goods owned and used by the taxpayer, or from goods and services arising out of the personal exertions of the taxpayer on his own behalf. Imputed income is non-cash income or income in kind. But all non-cash income, or income in kind, is not * * * imputed income. For example, where income in kind is received in return for services rendered, we have an ordinary market transaction without a transfer of cash but with a direct monetary valuation implied. * * * [The] distinguishing characteristic [of imputed income] is that it arises outside of the ordinary processes of the market.

Donald B. Marsh, "The Taxation of Imputed Income," 58 Pol.Sci.Q. 514 (1943).

The courts have been somewhat inconsistent in their treatment of imputed income. In Morris v. Commissioner, 9 B.T.A. 1273 (1928), acq. VII–2 C.B. 75, the Board of Tax Appeals held that the value of farm products consumed by the owners of the farm is not income, stating:

To include the value of such products, even if [the value] could be determined, * * * to a farmer as compensation would * * * include in income something which Congress did not intend should be so regarded. If products of a farm consumed thereon are income to the producer, it would seem to follow that the rental value of the farmer's home, the gratuitous services of his wife and children, and the value of the power derived from draft animals owned by the farmer and used without cost should also be so considered. It is obvious that such items are comparable to the rental value of a private residence, which has never been regarded as income or as a factor in the determination of tax liability.

Compare Dicenso v. Commissioner, 11 B.T.A. 620 (1928), holding that the owner of a grocery store must include in income groceries used for home consumption. In Commissioner v. Minzer, 279 F.2d 338 (5th Cir.1960), the Fifth Circuit held that an insurance agent was taxable on the usual commission payable on a policy on his own life even if he simply remitted the premiums to the insurance company after subtracting the commission. The court found that he performed the same services for himself that he performed for other insureds. Compare Benjamin v. Hoey, 139 F.2d 945 (2d Cir.1944), where a partner in a brokerage firm received, as part of his share of partnership profits, commissions on transactions for his own account. The Court held that there was no income from these transactions. In Worden v. Commissioner, 2 F.3d 359 (10th Cir.1993), an insurance agent was not taxable where he sold first year coverage on life insurance policies at cost, and remitted only the net premium to the company because he waived his commission in contracts with the clients.

The most significant form of imputed income from property is the imputed rental value of owner-occupied homes. For a while, Britain taxed such income, although it has never been taxed in the United States. The Treasury Department does include such income in measuring "family economic income," which it uses as an income measure to classify families by income levels in evaluating the distribution of taxes and proposed tax changes among people at different levels of income. But even this limited use of imputed income is not well understood by the media, politicians, or the public.

SECTION 3. GIFTS AND BEQUESTS

A. GIFTS

Commissioner v. Duberstein

Supreme Court of the United States, 1960. 363 U.S. 278.

[Two cases were decided in this opinion. No. 376, Commissioner v. Duberstein, involved a Cadillac car given to Duberstein by Berman because Duberstein had been helpful in suggesting customers to Berman. There was no prior arrangement for compensation, and Duberstein did not expect to be paid. The Court of Appeals held that this was not income, reversing the Tax Court.

In No. 546, Stanton v. United States, the taxpayer had been comptroller of Trinity Church and manager of its real estate. He resigned in 1942. The directors then voted him "a gratuity" of $20,000. There was no enforceable right or claim for any such payment. The Court of Appeals held that this was income, reversing the District Court.]

MR. JUSTICE BRENNAN delivered the opinion of the Court.

* * *

First. The Government suggests that we promulgate a new "test" in this area to serve as a standard to be applied by the lower courts and by the Tax Court in dealing with the numerous cases that arise.[1] We reject this invitation. We are of opinion that the governing principles are necessarily general and have already been spelled out in the opinions of this Court, and that the problem is one which, under the present statutory framework, does not lend itself to any more definitive statement that would produce a talisman for the solution of concrete cases. The cases at bar are fair examples of the settings in which the problem usually arises. They present situations in which payments have been made in a context with business overtones—an employer making a payment to a retiring employee; a businessman giving something of value to another businessman who has been of advantage to him in his business. In this context, we review the law as established by the prior cases here.

The course of decision here makes it plain that the statute does not use the term "gift" in the common-law sense, but in a more colloquial sense. This Court has indicated that a voluntary executed transfer of his property by one to another, without any consideration or compensation therefor, though a common-law gift, is not necessarily a "gift" within the meaning of the statute. For the Court has shown that the mere absence of a legal or moral obligation to make such a payment does not establish that it is a gift. Old Colony Trust Co. v. Commissioner, 279 U.S. 716, 730. And, importantly, if the payment proceeds primarily from "the constraining force of any moral or legal duty," or from "the incentive of anticipated benefit" of an economic nature, Bogardus v. Commissioner, 302 U.S. 34, 41, it is not a gift. And, conversely, "[w]here the payment is in return for services rendered, it is irrelevant that the donor derives no economic benefit from it." Robertson v. United States, 343 U.S. 711, 714.[2] A gift in the statutory sense, on the other hand, proceeds from a "detached and disinterested generosity," Commissioner of Internal Revenue v. LoBue, 351 U.S. 243, 246 (1956); "out of affection, respect admiration, charity or like impulses." Robertson v. United States [343 U.S. at 714]. And in this regard, the most critical consideration, as the Court has agreed in the leading case here, is the transferor's "intention." Bogardus v. Commissioner, 302 U.S. 34, 43.
* * *

---

1. The Government's proposed test is stated: "Gifts should be defined as transfers of property made for personal as distinguished from business reasons."

2. The cases including "tips" in gross income are classic examples of this. See, e.g., Roberts v. Commissioner, 176 F.2d 221.

The Government says that this "intention" of the transferor cannot mean what the cases on the common-law concept of gift call "donative intent." With that we are in agreement, for our decisions fully support this. Moreover, the *Bogardus* case itself makes it plain that the donor's characterization of his action is not determinative—that there must be an objective inquiry as to whether what is called a gift amounts to it in reality. 302 U.S., at 40. * * *

Second. The Government's proposed "test," while apparently simple and precise in its formulation, depends frankly on a set of "principles" or "presumptions" derived from the decided cases, and concededly subject to various exceptions; and it involves various corollaries, which add to its detail. Were we to promulgate this test as a matter of law, and accept with it its various presuppositions and stated consequences, we would be passing far beyond the requirements of the cases before us, and would be painting on a large canvas with indeed a broad brush. The Government derives its test from such propositions as the following: That payments by an employer to an employee, even though voluntary, ought, by and large, to be taxable; That the concept of a gift is inconsistent with a payment's being a deductible business expense; That a gift involves "personal" elements; That a business corporation cannot properly make a gift of its assets. The Government admits that there are exceptions and qualifications to these propositions. We think, to the extent they are correct, that these propositions are not principles of law but rather maxims of experience that the tribunals which have tried the facts of cases in this area have enunciated in explaining their factual determinations. * * * The taxing statute does not make nondeductibility by the transferor a condition on the "gift" exclusion; nor does it draw any distinction, in terms, between transfers by corporations and individuals, as to the availability of the "gift" exclusion to the transferee. The conclusion whether a transfer amounts to a "gift" is one that must be reached on consideration of all the factors. * * *

Third. Decision of the issue presented in these cases must be based ultimately on the application of the fact-finding tribunal's experience with the mainsprings of human conduct to the totality of the facts of each case. The nontechnical nature of the statutory standard, the close relationship of it to the data of practical human experience, and the multiplicity of relevant factual elements, with their various combinations, creating the necessity of ascribing the proper force to each, confirm us in our conclusion that primary weight in this area must be given to the conclusions of the trier of fact. * * *

This conclusion may not satisfy an academic desire for tidiness, symmetry and precision in this area, any more than a system based on the determinations of various fact-finders ordinarily does. But we see it as implicit in the present statutory treatment of the exclusion for gifts, and in the variety of forums in which federal income tax cases can be tried. If there is fear of undue uncertainty or over-much litigation, Congress may make more precise its treatment of the matter by singling out certain factors and making them determinative of the matter, as it has done in one field of the "gift" exclusion's former application, that of prizes and awards.

* * * But the question here remains basically one of fact, for determination on a case-by-case basis. * * *

One consequence of this is that appellate review of determinations in this field must be quite restricted. Where a jury has tried the matter upon correct instructions, the only inquiry is whether it cannot be said that reasonable men could reach differing conclusions on the issue. * * * Where the trial has been by a judge without a jury, the judge's findings must stand unless "clearly erroneous." * * * And Congress has in the most explicit terms attached the identical weight to the findings of the Tax Court. I.R.C. § 7482(a).

Fourth. A majority of the Court is in accord with the principles just outlined. And, applying them to the *Duberstein* case, we are in agreement, on the evidence we have set forth, that it cannot be said that the conclusion of the Tax Court was "clearly erroneous." It seems to us plain that as trier of the facts it was warranted in concluding that despite the characterization of the transfer of the Cadillac by the parties and the absence of any obligation, even of a moral nature, to make it, it was at bottom a recompense for Duberstein's past services, or an inducement for him to be of further service in the future. We cannot say with the Court of Appeals that such a conclusion was "mere suspicion" on the Tax Court's part. To us it appears based in the sort of informed experience with human affairs that fact-finding tribunals should bring to this task.

As to *Stanton,* we are in disagreement. To four of us, it is critical here that the District Court as trier of fact made only the simple and unelaborated finding that the transfer in question was a "gift." To be sure, conciseness is to be strived for, and prolixity avoided, in findings; but, to the four of us, there comes a point where findings become so sparse and conclusory as to give no revelation of what the District Court's concept of the determining facts and legal standard may be. * * * For all that appears, the District Court may have viewed the form of the resolution or the simple absence of legal consideration as conclusive. While the judgment of the Court of Appeals cannot stand, the four of us think there must be further proceedings in the District Court looking toward new and adequate findings of fact. In this, we are joined by MR. JUSTICE WHITTAKER, who agrees that the findings were inadequate, although he does not concur generally in this opinion.

Accordingly, in No. 376, the judgment of this Court is that the judgment of the Court of Appeals is reversed, and in No. 546, that the judgment of the Court of Appeals is vacated, and the case is remanded to the District Court for further proceedings not inconsistent with this opinion.

It is so ordered.

MR. JUSTICE HARLAN concurs in the result in No. 376. In No. 546, he would affirm the judgment of the Court of Appeals for the reasons stated by MR. JUSTICE FRANKFURTER.

MR. JUSTICE WHITTAKER, agreeing with *Bogardus* that whether a particular transfer is or is not a "gift" may involve "a mixed question of law and fact," 302 U.S., at 39, concurs only in the result of this opinion.

MR. JUSTICE DOUGLAS dissents, since he is of the view that in each of these two cases there was a gift under the test which the Court fashioned nearly a quarter of a century ago in Bogardus v. Commissioner, 302 U.S. 34.

[The opinion of Justice Black concurring in No. 376 (Duberstein) and dissenting in No. 546 (Stanton) is omitted.]

MR. JUSTICE FRANKFURTER, concurring in the judgment in No. 376 and dissenting in No. 546.

As the Court's opinion indicates, we brought these two cases here * * * primarily on the Government's urging that, in the interest of the better administration of the income tax laws, clarification was desirable for determining when a transfer of property constitutes a "gift" and is not to be included in income for purposes of ascertaining the "gross income" under the Internal Revenue Code. * * *

Despite acute arguments at the bar and a most thorough reexamination of the problem on a full canvass of our prior decisions and an attempted fresh analysis of the nature of the problem, the Court has rejected the invitation of the Government to fashion anything like a litmus paper test for determining what is excludable as a "gift" from gross income. Nor has the Court attempted a clarification of the particular aspects of the problem presented by these two cases, namely, payment by an employer to an employee upon the termination of the employment relation and non-obligatory payment for services rendered in the course of a business relationship. While I agree that experience has shown the futility of attempting to define, by language so circumscribing as to make it easily applicable, what constitutes a gift for every situation where the problem may arise, I do think that greater explicitness is possible in isolating and emphasizing factors which militate against a gift in particular situations.

Thus, regarding the two frequently recurring situations involved in these cases—things of value given to employees by their employers upon the termination of employment and payments entangled in a business relation and occasioned by the performance of some service—the strong implication is that the payment is of a business nature. The problem in these two cases is entirely different from the problem in a case where a payment is made from one member of a family to another, where the implications are directly otherwise. No single general formulation appropriately deals with both types of cases, although both involve the question whether the payment was a "gift." While we should normally suppose that a payment from father to son was a gift, unless the contrary is shown, in the two situations now before us the business implications are so forceful that I would apply a presumptive rule placing the burden upon the beneficiary to prove the payment wholly unrelated to his services to the enterprise. The Court, however, has declined so to analyze the problem. * * *

The Court has made only one authoritative addition to the previous course of our decisions * * * that it is "for the triers of the facts to seek among competing aims or motives the ones that dominated conduct." All this being so in view of the Court, it seems to me desirable not to try to improve what has "already been spelled out" in the opinions of this Court but to leave to the lower courts the application of old phrases rather than to float new ones and thereby inevitably produce a new volume of exegesis on the new phrases.

Especially do I believe this when fact-finding tribunals are directed by the Court to rely upon their "experience with the mainsprings of human conduct" and on their "informed experience with human affairs" in appraising the totality of the facts of each case. Varying conceptions regarding the "mainsprings of human conduct" are derived from a variety of experiences or assumptions about the nature of man, and "experience with human affairs," is not only diverse but also often drastically conflicting. What the Court now does sets fact-finding bodies to sail on an illimitable ocean of individual beliefs and experiences. This can hardly fail to invite, if indeed not encourage, too individualized diversities in the administration of the income tax law. I am afraid that by these new phrasings the practicalities of tax administration, which should be as uniform as is possible in so vast a country as ours, will be embarrassed. By applying what has already been spelled out in the opinions of this Court, I agree with the Court in reversing the judgment in Commissioner v. Duberstein.

But I would affirm the decision of the Court of Appeals for the Second Circuit in Stanton v. United States. * * *

NOTES

(A) *Subsequent History.* On remand of *Stanton,* the District Court, sitting without a jury, held that the payment made to Stanton was a gift. The Second Circuit affirmed, finding that the decision was not clearly erroneous. Stanton v. United States, 186 F.Supp. 393 (E.D.N.Y.1960), affirmed 287 F.2d 876 (2d Cir.1961).

Section 102(c) (added to the Code subsequently) makes it clear that § 102 no longer applies to employer gifts to employees; any exclusion must be as a de minimis fringe benefit under § 132. Furthermore, § 274(b) provides a general maximum deduction of $25 for business gifts that are excludable under § 102. The payor generally would prefer to take a business deduction, defeating a claim of nonbusiness or donative intent.

(B) *The Duberstein Approach.* How much guidance does the *Duberstein* approach provide to lower courts? Are there any limitations on the trier of fact?

Is a diversity of outcomes (or more pointedly, inconsistency of outcomes) troublesome? Is there an explanation for Duberstein's loss and Stanton's victory or is this simply the outcome of tax cases being litigated in many forums? In a dissenting opinion in Estate of Carter v. Commissioner, 453 F.2d 61 (2d Cir.1971), Judge Davis argued that *"Duberstein* contemplated lack of 'symmetry' between 'the variety of forums in which federal income tax cases can be tried.' " The majority opinion in that case reversed a Tax Court opinion holding that a payment to the widow of an employee was income. The Second Circuit noted that the Tax Court generally had considered all payments to survivors of deceased employees to be compensation whereas the district courts have consistently held such payments to be gifts. Finding that the courts of appeals generally had upheld the district court approach rather than the Tax Court approach, the court found the payment to be a gift.

How much assistance does *Duberstein* provide to a lawyer advising a client? How does a donee determine whether the donor has the requisite intent? Why is the donor's intent relevant? Can a donee have a "gift" from an unknown donor? Does a panhandler who collects coins from subway passengers have income? Would it matter if the person who puts the coin in the cup does so out of pity or to encourage the panhandler to move on or with gratitude for the panhandler's saxophone playing?

Would the government's proposed test in *Duberstein* be more workable?

For an example of how the discretion conferred by *Duberstein* still haunts the tax law, see United States v. Harris and Conley, 942 F.2d 1125 (7th Cir.1991). Harris and Conley were two young women who each received $500,000 over a period of years from an elderly man who died before the litigation began. They were convicted of criminal tax evasion for willfully evading their duty to pay taxes on these amounts. The government argued that the payments were for services and the twins argued they were nontaxable gifts. The Seventh Circuit overturned the convictions, holding that the twins could not have intentionally failed to pay taxes unless they knew that the donor's intent was not disinterested generosity. The court pointed out the inherent difficulty of trying to prove a willful tax violation that hinges on the intent of a dead person.

(C) *Some Tips.* Tips are taxable income. See Reg. § 1.61–2(a). Collection of income tax on tip income has proven difficult, however. Tip reporting requirements for employers have increased the likelihood of collection. See §§ 6053(c) and 6722.

In Olk v. United States, 536 F.2d 876 (9th Cir.1976), cert. denied 429 U.S. 920 (1976), the court found that "tokes" received by a craps dealer from casino patrons were income, noting that the payments were motivated by superstition rather than by detached or disinterested generosity. Although the court noted that the amount, regularity, and equal division of the tokes among dealers all indicated that dealers regarded them as compensation for services, that factor does not appear to be relevant under *Duberstein*. The court also noted: "Tribute to the gods of fortune which it is hoped will be returned bounteously soon can only be described as an 'involved and intensely interested' act." If Dad purchases a car for Son when he makes the honor roll, does Son have income?

(D) *Presidential Dresses.* Former First Lady Nancy Reagan may well ultimately be remembered best for her expensive taste in clothes. Apparently unable to just say no, Mrs. Reagan ignored the repeated advice of White House lawyers and accepted the "loan" of virtually an entire wardrobe of designer dresses, the total value of which was estimated at between $1 and $1.4 million, not including similar "loans" of jewelry worth that much again. Aside from the ethical questions raised by her failure to disclose these "loans," there also is the question whether the First Lady should have reported this sartorial splendor as gross income.

Unfortunately for the Reagans, statements made by her benefactors made it unlikely that she would be able to claim the wardrobe was a gift under the *Duberstein* test. One tax lawyer compared the First Lady to a walking billboard. The designers themselves were less metaphorical, but nonetheless were publicly and explicitly delighted with what Mrs. Reagan did for their sales figures. As subjective as the *Duberstein* standard may be, it would be difficult to call these "loans" gifts; the designers' largess was hardly motivated by the detached and disinterested generosity *Duberstein* demands. Arguing that the value of the "loan" or gift was de minimis won't work, as fashion experts agree that, like new cars, high fashion attire depreciates substantially in value as soon as it is donned or removed from the showroom floor.

At the end of the Clinton administration, the Clintons received more than $200,000 in furniture, china, and other goods from political supporters to furnish their new homes in New York and Washington, D.C. Are these amounts includable in their income?

(E) *Political Contributions.* In Revenue Ruling 68–512, 1968–2 C.B. 41, the Service held that political contributions are not taxable to a political candidate to the extent used for expenses of a political campaign. However, any amount diverted for personal use is taxable.

What is the underlying theory of the ruling? What Code section enables the Service to reach this result? Congress subsequently affirmed this ruling, noting that if a payment satisfies a legal obligation of the candidate, including an obligation for federal income taxes, it is a diversion for personal use. See S.Rep. No. 93–1357, 93d Cong., 2d Sess. 31 (1974).

In Stratton v. Commissioner, 54 T.C. 255 (1970), modified on another issue 54 T.C. 1351 (1970), the IRS alleged that Stratton, a former governor of Illinois, had failed to report more than $100,000 in cash contributions used by him for personal purposes. Several major contributors testified that they had made contributions to Stratton without any restrictions whatsoever. The Tax Court concluded that about $40,000 of the contributions were excludable under § 102 as gifts, but that the remainder was taxable income to Stratton. If the exclusion of political contributions is based on § 102, what difference does it make how the funds are used?

(F) *Support and Government Transfer Payments.* Support provided by family members, like intra-family gifts, is not included in gross income. There is no specific statutory authority for this rule, but the Service has never sought to tax family support.

It also has been the longstanding policy of the Service to exclude from income most government benefits and other welfare payments. For example, the IRS has ruled that Social Security payments, unemployment compensation, benefit payments to the blind, and other assistance payments are not includable in the gross income of the recipient. See, e.g., Rev.Rul. 70–280, 1970–1 C.B. 13 (unemployment benefits); Rev.Rul. 70–217, 1970–1 C.B. 12 (Social Security payments); Rev.Rul. 57–102, 1957–1 C.B. 26 (state aid to the blind). The Service's position has been that "disbursements from a general welfare fund in the interest of the general welfare are not includible in gross income." Rev.Rul. 75–271, 1975–2 C.B. 23. The IRS has never cited any statutory authority for this proposition, although it once asserted that this type of payment was not "within the concept of gross income." Rev.Rul. 53–131, 1953–2 C.B. 112. It is clear, however, that Congress can choose to tax such benefits. See § 85 (taxing unemployment payments) and § 86 (taxing a portion of Social Security payments); see also Bannon v. Commissioner, 99 T.C. 59 (1992) (taxing a mother on state assistance received on behalf of her disabled adult daughter). Other payments that are not need-based have been subject to tax. See, e.g., Rev.Rul. 85–39, 1985–1 C.B. 21 (taxing "dividend" payments to Alaska residents out of state's oil income).

What is the justification for excluding these payments from income? If welfare payments were taxed, would the government simply have to increase welfare? Proposals have been made to tax the subsidy under Medicare for physicians' services for people over age 65, at least for those above a specified income threshold. (The subsidy originally was 25 percent of cost and now is 75 percent). Is there any merit to the contention that if the government taxed such benefits, it would merely be paying with one hand and taking back with another? Does the exclusion result in different treatment for similarly situated taxpayers? The case for taxing transfer payments that are wage replacements or deferred compensation can easily be supported on equity grounds. What about other in-kind benefits like free medical care or legal services, police protection, maintained highways, etc.?

(G) *Policy Reasons for Exclusion.* An individual who works is taxed, but one who lives off the munificence of others is not taxed. What is the rationale for not taxing gifts as income? If it is difficult to distinguish between support and gifts, does this justify not taxing gifts?

Consider the three possible ways to treat gifts under an income tax: (1) the gift might be deducted from the income of the donor and included in the income of the donee, (2) the gift might be included in the income of the donor and also in the income of the donee, or (3) the gift might be included in the income of the donor but excluded from the income of the donee.

The first of these treatments taxes the person who uses the gift for personal consumption. The second treatment taxes the person with the wherewithal to make the gift and the person who uses the gift for consumption. The third treatment is that of the income tax, at least with respect to property with no unrealized appreciation at the time the gift is made.

Under the first and third options, there is no separate tax on the transfer of wealth from one taxpayer to another. The tax burdens under those two alternatives, however, will tend to differ with a progressive rate structure, depending on whether or not the marginal tax rate of the donee is higher or lower than the marginal tax rate of the donor. Typically, marginal rates of donors are higher than those of donees, at least at the time of the transfer. (Donees under age 14 are taxed at their parents' tax rates.) Under the second option, the consumption financed by the gift, in effect, is taxed twice, to both the donor and the donee.

(H) *Prizes and Awards.* The recipient of a prize or award generally includes the prize in income even if the transfer was gratuitous. Regulation § 1.102–1(a) has long provided that the gift exclusion under § 102 does not apply to prizes and awards. Under § 74, certain prizes are excludable if they are not retained by the recipient. The award must be in recognition of religious, charitable, scientific, educational, artistic, literary or civic achievement; the recipient must have taken no action to enter the contest; the recipient must not be required to render substantial future services, and the prize or award must be transferred to charity. Under a previous incarnation of § 74, the prize did not need to be donated to charity so long as the other requirements were met. This resulted in frequent and sometimes amusing litigation to determine if a prize was excludable. See, e.g. Wills v. Commissioner, 411 F.2d 537 (9th Cir.1969). The baseball player Maury Wills failed to convince the court that the Hickok belt, given to him for his baseball prowess, was for "civic or artistic achievement." Now that a recipient must donate the prize to charity, why is there any need for limitation on the types of excludable prizes? In many cases, if the recipient were forced to include the prize in income, there would be an offsetting charitable deduction. The current rule, however, permits the recipient of certain prizes to transfer them to a charity without the adverse tax consequence that would occur if the recipient were subject to one of the limitations on the amount of deductible charitable contributions.

Five American Nobel Laureates in science sent the following letter to President Clinton (the letter was reprinted in Tax Notes Today, a daily tax news service, on July 27, 1995):

Dear Mr. President:

The undersigned American Nobel Laureates of 1994 greatly appreciate your and Mrs. Clinton's kindness to invite us to the White House for a reception in our honor. As much as a Nobel Prize is a most rewarding personal recognition, we strongly feel that it also reflects acknowledgment of the continuing strength of American Science and its achievements.

* * *

We perhaps may be allowed to raise a point concerning the Nobel Prizes. According to the Nobel Foundation the US is the only Western country that taxes the prizes. We understand that even the gold medals we are to receive in Stockholm are being taxed by their weight. This is a relatively new policy, introduced in only 1986 during a previous administration. The tax on income from a few Nobel Prizes cannot make much difference for the Treasury but restoring their former tax-free status would show the world that the United States government and the American people do appreciate scientific achievement and do agree that it should receive proper recognition.

We hope that you will agree, Mr. President, that the present policy should be rescinded and that the tax-free status of Nobel Prizes should be restored. We hope that this can be done in a retrospective manner as from October 1, 1994, preferably by an Executive Order or by initiation of Legislative Action if needed. We would very much appreciate your favorable consideration of this matter.

How should the President—or the Treasury's Assistant Secretary for Tax Policy—respond?

(I) *Employee Achievement Awards.* Certain "employee achievement awards" are excludable from income. These are awards of tangible personal property for length-of-service or safety achievements—"gold watch awards." See § 274(j)(3). If the employer's cost does not exceed limits defined in § 274(j) (generally $400), the employee may exclude the full fair market value. Otherwise, the employee must include in income the greater of (1) the excess of the employer's cost over the limitation (but not in excess of fair market value), or (2) the excess of the award's fair market value over the maximum allowable employer deduction.

B. BEQUESTS

NOTE ON THE TAXATION OF BEQUESTS

Like gifts, bequests are excluded from income under § 102, and, as with gifts, questions sometimes arise whether a particular transfer (or class of transfers) qualifies as an excludable bequest. For example, is an attorney required to include in income the amount of a legacy received under the will of a client in lieu of payment of legal fees during the client's lifetime?

In Wolder v. Commissioner, 493 F.2d 608 (2d Cir.1974), the attorney had contracted to perform all legal services that his client would require during her lifetime in exchange for her promise to bequeath to him certain shares of stock or their equivalent. The Commissioner asserted that the fair market value of the property was taxable compensation for services, while the attorney countered that the legacy was excludable under § 102, even though some consideration had flowed from beneficiary to decedent. The Tax Court held for the Commissioner and the Second Circuit affirmed on the ground that the parties had merely agreed to postpone payment for legal services, stating: "[A] transfer in the form of a bequest was the method that the parties chose to compensate Mr. Wolder for his legal services * * * and that transfer is therefore subject to taxation, whatever its label whether by federal or local law may be."

The *Wolder* court distinguished the Supreme Court's decision in United States v. Merriam, 263 U.S. 179 (1923), which held that a bequest made to an executor in lieu of compensation was excludable from income under a predecessor of § 102. The Supreme Court stated that the test was not whether the testator gave the legacies for services but whether the legatees had to perform the services in order to earn the bequests.

Compare Rev.Rul. 67–375, 1967–2 C.B. 60, where A and B agreed to take care of C for the rest of his life. C agreed to leave all of his personal property to A and B, stating that this was in payment for their services. The Service ruled that the amount was taxable as income to A and B. The Tax Court reached the same result in Miller v. Commissioner, 53 T.C.M. 962 (1987).

In Getty v. Commissioner, 913 F.2d 1486 (9th Cir.1990), a son of J. Paul Getty successfully settled with his father's residuary beneficiary to enforce his father's promise to remedy the inequality of financial treatment of the son and his children. The court held that proceeds were received in lieu of a bequest and thus were excludable.

C. SCHOLARSHIPS AND FELLOWSHIPS

NOTE ON THE EXCLUSION OF SCHOLARSHIPS

The exclusion for scholarships and fellowships under § 117 is limited to amounts used by degree candidates for "qualified tuition and related expenses." Qualified expenses are (1) tuition and fees for enrollment or attendance by a student enrolled in a school and (2) fees, books, supplies, and equipment required for the course of study. The recipient is not required to trace dollars of scholarship aid to these particular uses; an exclusion is allowed to the extent that the scholarship or grant received does not exceed these amounts. There is no exclusion for grant or scholarship money used for room and board. The exclusion applies only if the terms of the grant or scholarship do not earmark or designate its use for nonqualified expenses and do not specify that the funds cannot be used for tuition or course-related expenses.

Any portion of a "scholarship" received for teaching, research or other services required as a condition for receiving the scholarship is not excludable. § 117(c). Thus, amounts received for teaching are taxable whether the compensation takes the form of a paycheck, tuition reduction or a scholarship. Note that the Service has emphasized the necessity of a *quid pro quo*. In Revenue Ruling 77–263, 1977–2 C.B. 47, the Service held that an athletic scholarship is excludable if the scholarship "does not require the student to participate in a particular sport, requires no particular activity in lieu of participation, and does not cancel if the student cannot participate."

Why should scholarships be excluded from gross income? If a student works part-time, she will pay her tuition with after-tax dollars. If an individual obtains a student loan rather than a scholarship, the loan is not income at the time of receipt, but it will be repaid out of after-tax income.

If scholarships were taxed, should the value of higher education at state schools provided free or at reduced cost to state residents also be taxed as income? What about a gift from a parent used to pay tuition?

A limited amount of educational assistance provided through a employer-funded plan is exempt from tax. § 127, discussed supra at page 99.

SECTION 4.   CAPITAL APPRECIATION AND RECOVERY OF BASIS

NOTE INTRODUCING THE CONCEPTS OF CAPITAL RECOVERY AND BASIS

Section 61 provides that gross income means income from "whatever source derived," and inherent in the concept of "income" is the notion of net gain. Thus, if A purchases property for $1,000, and it yields no income while he holds it, he must sell it for more than $1,000 to have income or profit. If he sells it for less than $1,000, he has a loss. If he sells it for $1,000, he has merely experienced a "recovery of capital" and does not have any net gain or loss.

In determining income in a business context, the regulations distinguish gross income from gross receipts. Thus, § 1.61–3(a) of the Regulations states that " 'gross income' means the total sales less the costs of goods sold." The Supreme Court recognized this distinction in 1918, when it ruled that, absent any statutory provision authorizing an offset against gross receipts, the income concept implied a deduction for the cost of goods sold. In Doyle v. Mitchell Brothers Co., 247 U.S. 179 (1918), Justice Pitney stated, at 185:

> Whatever difficulty there may be about a precise and scientific definition of "income", it imports * * * something entirely distinct from principal or capital either as a subject of taxation or as a measure of the tax; conveying rather the idea of gain or increase * * * * Understanding the term in this natural and obvious sense, it cannot be said that a conversion of capital assets invariably produces income. If sold at less than cost, it produces rather loss or outgo. * * * In order to determine whether there has been gain or loss, and the amount of the gain, if any, we must withdraw from the gross proceeds an amount sufficient to restore the capital value that existed at the commencement of the period under consideration.

The Code currently reaches this result as follows: Section 61(a)(3) includes in income "gains derived from dealings in property." Section 1001 describes a *gain* as the excess of the *amount realized* from the sale over the taxpayer's *basis* for the property. In the preceding example, the amount realized is the sales price, and the taxpayer's basis is $1,000. *Basis* is a term of art in the tax law,. Section 1012 provides that the basis of property is usually its cost to the taxpayer, except as otherwise provided. Determination of basis is discussed in the next Note. It is important to understand that basis is the technical mechanism by which taxpayers are allowed to recover their capital investment when they sell property. The determination of the "amount realized," the "adjusted basis" and thus, the amount of gain or loss, is in many cases far more difficult than the above discussion would suggest. A more detailed discussion of gain or loss on the disposition of property is found in Chapter 5.

These problems would be hard enough if our system measured gain or loss at the end of each year. But the reckoning of gross income from the ownership of property can take many years, because accounting for gain or loss generally is postponed until property is sold. Thus, there is a significant distinction between the tax concept of "income" and "economic income," which may increase or diminish as the market value of property changes. Rather than requiring a taxpayer to estimate the change in value of his assets each year and to include that amount in income (or to deduct any losses), the Code generally taxes only "realized" gains. The realization requirement, which calls for a realization event before gain is taken into income, is discussed infra at page 144.

The tax-free recovery of capital is a fundamental aspect of income measurement, and the timing and mechanism for recovering capital is one of the most important issues in designing an income tax. Although taxpayers are taxed only on income, and thus will be able to recover capital tax free, the timing of the capital recovery is extremely important.

There are basically three ways in which the taxpayer accounts for costs. First, some expenditures for the production of income are treated as *immediately deductible expenses;* the costs are said to be "expensed." If there is enough income to offset the deductions, the tax-free recovery of such income-producing expenses is immediate. Other expenses must be *capitalized* and the purchase price or cost taken into account only when the asset is sold or exchanged. In the case of stock, for example, the cost or basis is taken into account only when the stock is sold or exchanged. Dividend income received while the stock is held is taxed in full without any offset for the capital invested. Finally, other assets may be *depreciated;* that is periodic deductions are allowed for the asset's cost. Suppose a cab driver purchases a $10,000 cab for her business. The $10,000 cost of the cab must be capitalized, but periodic deductions will be allowed for depreciation. For example, if the cab was useful in her business for five years, she might be permitted to take one-fifth of her cost or $2,000 a year as a depreciation deduction. Which costs are immediately deductible and which must be capitalized is discussed in Chapter 3, infra at page 284. The rules for determining the tax allowance for depreciation also are considered in detail in Chapter 3.

It is critical to understand that so long as a tax-free recovery of capital is allowed, the same total net income will be taxed over the entire period the asset is held, but there may be great variations in annual income depending upon the timing of the offset for capital recovery.

Thus, it should not be surprising that tax deferral is one of the principal tax planning functions. We shall return to the issue of deferral throughout the course. We next explore in more detail the concepts of basis and realization.

NOTE ON THE DETERMINATION OF THE BASIS OF PROPERTY

Basis of Purchased Property. The basis of property is its cost, except as otherwise provided. § 1012. This rule is simple where a taxpayer purchases a piece of property for cash—her basis is the amount of cash paid. Where the taxpayer receives property in exchange for services, his basis is the fair market value of the property received. Reg. § 1.61–2(d)(2)(i). In effect, it is as if the employee had received compensation in cash and had used the cash to purchase the property. The term "tax cost" is sometimes used to describe the basis of property that was not purchased, but whose fair market value the taxpayer included in income.

Basis generally is cost even if the taxpayer has "underpaid" or "overpaid" for the property. If the property is purchased at less than its fair market value, the purchaser takes a cost basis and is not taxed on the gain until she disposes of the property at its fair market value. Similarly, if the taxpayer overpays for property, the basis is the amount paid, and the loss will be realized only when she sells the property for its fair market value.

Sometimes, however, a bargain purchase occurs as a result of a relationship between the parties. For example, an employer might allow an employee to purchase an asset at less than the market value as a form of compensation. A bargain purchase might also occur between companies and their shareholders as a substitute for dividends or between landlords and tenants as a substitute for rent or between family members as a way of making a gift. In general, courts will examine the facts and circumstances in an effort to recharacterize the transaction to reflect its substance. Often, the substance of the transaction is the sale of property in exchange for cash and services. Where a bargain purchase is in substance a substitute for salary, the amount of price reduction is included in income and the purchaser is treated as acquiring the asset for fair market value. The cost basis of the asset would then be its recharacterized purchase price: the amount actually paid plus the amount included in income as salary. For example, if Employee is permitted to purchase stock worth $100 for $80, Employee would be taxed on $20 and his basis in the stock would be $100.

Basis also must be determined where the taxpayer acquires property in exchange for other property. Generally, an arm's length transaction will involve an exchange of properties of equal value and any difference in the values of the properties exchanged will be accounted for by the transfer of cash. The exchange usually will be a "realization" event and any gain or loss on either side of the transaction will be "recognized." As to the basis of the property purchased, courts have construed cost to mean the value of the property received. See, e.g. Philadelphia Park Amusement Co. v. United States, 126 F.Supp. 184 (Ct.Cl.1954) (holding that where the value of the property given up differs from the value of the property received, the taxpayer's basis in the property received is its value). By contrast, where the taxpayer transfers property in exchange for a release of marital rights, the gain or loss is not recognized and the recipient takes a fair market value basis in the property. See *Farid-Es–Sultaneh* infra at p. 486.

There are a number of instances where the taxpayer acquires property in a transaction where gain or loss is not "recognized." Where such "nonrecognition" provisions apply, recognition of gain or loss generally is postponed until the taxpayer's investment is significantly altered. Almost always, there are special basis rules that apply when the taxpayer has entered into a nonrecognition transaction. These rules are considered in some detail in Chapter 5.

Finally, the basis of property acquired with borrowed funds in considered infra at page 187.

Basis of Property Acquired by Gift. Section 1015 provides that, for all gifts and transfers in trust since 1921, the basis of property for computing gain in the hands of a donee shall be the same as the basis in the hands of the donor. This treatment is commonly known as "carryover basis" or technically as "transferred basis." § 7701(a)(42) and (43). This carryover basis provision reflects a congressional determination not to tax accrued income at the time of a gift, but to preserve the basis so that the tax is triggered upon subsequent disposition. The basis for determining loss, however, is either the donor's basis or the fair market value at the time of the gift, whichever is lower. For example, suppose Mom buys property for

$100, she gives it to her son when it is worth $150, and he subsequently sells it for $175. The son's basis is $100; thus, when the asset is sold, he will report a $75 gain: the $50 gain that had accrued at the time of the gift as well as the $25 appreciation that accrued while he held the asset. If, however, the value of the property were $80 at the time of the gift and the son subsequently sold it for $75, he would recognize only a $5 loss. The loss of $20 that had accrued at the date of the gift would disappear. Suppose the value of the property at the date of the gift was $50 and the son sold it for $75?

The Supreme Court upheld the constitutionality of requiring the donee to pay tax on the gain accrued by the donor. Taft v. Bowers, 278 U.S. 470 (1929). Of course, the donee did not question the appropriateness of receiving a basis in the gifted property when she had no cost.

In combination, the basis rules for gifts permit the transfer of tax on accrued gains to the donee, but not the transfer of the tax benefit of losses. Which should be of more concern? Does it matter if the donor and donee are in different income tax brackets?

What if a taxpayer cannot establish the donor's basis? See § 1015(a), which provides that the donee must attempt to attain such facts from the donor and if impossible, the basis will be the fair market value at the date the property was acquired by the donor.

Basis of Property Acquired From a Decedent. The basis rules are quite different when a taxpayer acquires property from a decedent. Section 1014 provides that the basis of property acquired from a decedent is "the fair market value of the property at the date of the decedent's death." This section reflects a policy decision that death is an inappropriate time to tax accrued gain on property passing to others from the decedent. The result of this decision is a "stepped-up" (or stepped-down) basis for the transferee and the accrued gain (or loss) on the property will never be subjected to income tax (or available to reduce tax).

Because so much appreciation on property transferred at death escapes income tax, proposals to eliminate the stepped-up basis rule have been advanced for many years. Proponents of reform argue that § 1014 is inequitable because it produces a different tax burden depending on whether a decedent's estate is composed of unrealized appreciation or of previously taxed income. In addition, proponents argue that a carryover basis provision or an income tax on appreciation at death would mitigate the so-called "lock-in" effect that occurs when owners of appreciated property, aware of the stepped-up basis that will be given to their heirs under § 1014, refuse to sell appreciated property prior to death. Many analysts contend that the repeal of the step-up in basis would eliminate the advantage of holding assets until death. A carryover basis rule, however, might amplify the "lock-in" effect, because once an asset passes to a beneficiary, he might become particularly reluctant to sell it, since he would have to pay tax on gain that accrued during the decedent's lifetime as well as any gain that accrued subsequently. In the 1970's, Congress enacted a carryover basis provision, but compromises embodied in the provision resulted in an enormously complex set of rules. Ultimately, Congress repealed this provision before it became effective. In the tax reduction legislation enacted in May 2001, Congress once again repealed the step-up in basis of § 1014, § 1014(f), and enacted a "modified carryover basis" to take effect in the year 2010, when the repeal of the estate tax also occurs under this legislation. § 1022. A minimum basis equal to fair market value of assets transferred at death or $1.3 million, whichever is smaller, is provided so that for most decedents the step-up in basis rules will still apply. It also remains to be seen whether this change will take effect as enacted.

NOTE ON ADJUSTED BASIS

Events subsequent to the acquisition of property may require "adjustments to basis" before gain or loss is determined. See §§ 1001(a), 1011, 1016. These adjustments reflect the history of the asset in the hands of the taxpayer or, in the case of a "transferred basis," of a person or asset whose basis has been "carried over." Capitalized expenditures, untaxed receipts, and certain losses are reflected as adjustments to basis. Depreciation also requires adjustments to basis. In general, such adjustments increase basis to reflect capital expenditures and reduce basis to reflect the tax benefits allowed to taxpayers while they hold the property. Further detail is provided by the regulations under § 1016.

NOTE ON ALLOCATION OF BASIS

Where a taxpayer sells less than her whole interest in an asset, it may be difficult to allocate basis to the portion sold and the portion retained. Early recovery of basis defers the realization of income, while late basis recovery can accelerate gross income for tax purposes.

When a person acquires property and then sells part of it, there are two possible ways to handle the transaction: (1) She could apply the amount realized against the basis for the entire property, and not report any gain until the aggregate amount realized exceeds her entire basis, or (2) she could allocate the basis of the whole between the part sold and the part retained in some reasonable manner, and compare the amount realized with the portion of the total basis allocated to the part sold. Reg. § 1.61–6(a) provides that when a portion of property is sold, the basis must be divided among the parts. Furthermore, the gain or loss on each component part must be determined at the time of the sale of each part and cannot be deferred until the entire property has been sold. See, e.g., Gladden v. Commissioner, 262 F.3d 851 (9th Cir.2001) (allocation of basis to water rights associated with land); see infra at page 608. For example, if a person buys Blackacre and later sells a portion of it, the portion sold and the portion retained must be appraised and the original basis allocated to the two portions in proportion to their values. Allocation of basis is routinely required when a single price is paid for a building and land held for investment or used in a trade or business. As we shall see, the basis allocated to the building can be depreciated, but the land cannot.

It is occasionally impossible to allocate basis in a reasonable way. In that case, the consideration received on the sale may be credited against the basis for the entire property. For example, if the taxpayer receives an amount for an easement that affects the entire property, the basis of the entire property is offset against the payment and the basis is reduced. Foster v. Commissioner, 80 T.C. 34, 218–19 (1983), vacated in part 756 F.2d 1430 (9th Cir.1985). Consider the following example based on the case of Inaja Land Co. v. Commissioner, 9 T.C. 727, 735 (1947):

In 1940, a taxpayer paid $100 to buy land and the fishing rights on a river in order to establish a fishing club. In 2000, the taxpayer received $20 in settlement of a lawsuit against a city up river that had polluted the river. In 2001, the taxpayer sold the fishing club for $120.

The taxpayer's overall gain (amounts received minus amounts paid) is $40 (i.e., $20 + $120 – $100). If that total gain ultimately is to be taxed, the decision to include or not include the $20 of damages in income in 2000 must affect the measurement of subsequent gain. The income tax uses the concept of basis for this purpose.

Suppose the taxpayer can prove that $5 of the $100 originally paid to establish the fishing club was for the right to have a river free of pollution by the city. In that case, the amount of gain (amount realized minus basis) taxable in 2000 would presumably be $15 (i.e., $20 – $5). As the taxpayer used $5 of basis in 2000, there would remain $95 of basis to be subtracted from the amount realized in 2001, when the taxable gain would be $25 (i.e., $120 – $95), so the total amount of gain taxed over the years would be $40.

Suppose that the full $20 of damages is taxed that year. In that case, the $100 basis would remain unchanged and amount taxed in 2001 would be $20 (i.e., $120 – $100), so the total amount of gain taxed would again be $40.

Suppose finally that the $20 receipt is not taxed in 2000. In order to tax the total gain of $40 when the taxpayer sells the fishing club in 2001, the taxpayer's basis would be reduced in 2000 by the $20 amount received but excluded in 2000 (i.e., $100 – $20 = $80). With this adjustment to basis the full $40 would be taxed in 2001 (i.e., $120 amount realized minus the $80 basis).

The key point here is the relationship between taxation (or not) of a receipt and the way basis is adjusted and taken into account in future transactions. The assumption of the example was that we wanted ultimately to tax the full $40 of gain. Consider the basis consequences of the decision not to tax the $20 receipt in 1990 if we assume that this portion of the taxpayer's gain should never be taxed. In such a case, the $20 would be excluded from income without any reduction in basis.

It is occasionally impossible to allocate basis in a reasonable way. In that case, the consideration received on the sale may be credited against the basis for the entire property. For example, if the taxpayer receives an amount for an easement that affects the entire property, the basis of the entire property is offset against the payment and the basis is reduced. Foster v. Commissioner, 80 T.C. 34, 218–19 (1983), vacated in part 756 F.2d 1430 (9th Cir.1985); Inaja Land Co. v. Commissioner, 9 T.C. 727, 735 (1947).

Determination of basis also can be difficult where the taxpayer has acquired similar assets at different times. Problems often occur with the sale of securities. If a taxpayer cannot adequately identify the lot from which the stock sold or transferred was taken, the stock sold will be charged against the earliest lots of such stock acquired by the taxpayer to determine basis and gain or loss. Reg. § 1.1012–1(c)(1). A taxpayer who can adequately identify the assets to be sold will be able to escape the unfavorable consequences of this "first-in, first-out" rule. Reg. § 1.1012–1(c).

In a part-gift, part-sale transfer, the transferor generally can allocate basis to the portion of the transfer that constitutes a sale. For example, suppose Mom sells property with an adjusted basis of $80 and a value of $100 to Son for $75. Regulation § 1.1015–4 provides that the initial basis of the transferee is the greater of the amount paid by the transferee for the property or the transferor's basis under § 1015(d). Thus, the son's basis is $80. For determining a subsequent loss, however, the basis is never greater than the fair market value of the property at the time of the transfer. When, however, a taxpayer makes a part-gift, part-sale to a charity, § 170(e) and Reg. § 1.1011–2 require an allocation of basis between the gift and sale portions in proportion to their respective values. In the above example, $60 of mom's basis (three-quarters) would be allocated to the sale, producing a $15 gain. Mom would have made a charitable contribution of $25, the difference between the value of the property and the purchase price. Is there any reason for having different rules, depending only on the identity of the donee?

Hort v. Commissioner

Supreme Court of the United States, 1941. 313 U.S. 28.

Mr. Justice Murphy delivered the opinion of the Court.

We must determine whether the amount petitioner received as consideration for cancellation of a lease of realty in New York City was ordinary gross income as defined in § 22(a) of the Revenue Act of 1932 (47 Stat. 169, 178), and whether, in any event, petitioner sustained a loss through cancellation of the lease which is recognized in § 23(e) of the same Act (47 Stat. 169, 180).

Petitioner acquired the property, a lot and ten-story office building, by devise from his father in 1928. At the time he became owner, the premises were leased to a firm which had sublet the main floor to the Irving Trust Co. In 1927, five years before the head lease expired, the Irving Trust Co. and petitioner's father executed a contract in which the latter agreed to lease the main floor and basement to the former for a term of fifteen years at an annual rental of $25,000, the term to commence at the expiration of the head lease.

In 1933, the Irving Trust Co. found it unprofitable to maintain a branch in petitioner's building. After some negotiations, petitioner and the Trust Co. agreed to cancel the lease in consideration of a payment to petitioner of $140,000. Petitioner did not include this amount in gross income in his income tax return for 1933. On the contrary, he reported a loss of $21,494.75 on the theory that the amount he received as consideration for the cancellation was $21,494.75 less than the difference between the present value of the unmatured rental payments and the fair rental value of the main floor and basement for the unexpired term of the lease. He did not deduct this figure, however, because he reported other losses in excess of gross income.

The Commissioner included the entire $140,000 in gross income, disallowed the asserted loss, made certain other adjustments not material here, and assessed a deficiency. The Board of Tax Appeals affirmed. 39 B.T.A. 922. The Circuit Court of Appeals affirmed per curiam on the authority of Warren Service Corp. v. Helvering, 110 F.2d 723. 112 F.2d 167. Because of conflict with Commissioner v. Langwell Real Estate Corp., 7 Cir., 47 F.2d 841, we granted certiorari limited to the question whether, "in computing net gain or loss for income tax purposes, a taxpayer [can] offset the value of the lease canceled against the consideration received by him for the cancellation". 311 U.S. 641.

Petitioner apparently contends that the amount received for cancellation of the lease was capital rather than ordinary income and that it was therefore subject to [the sections] which govern capital gains and losses. Further, he argues that even if that amount must be reported as ordinary gross income he sustained a loss which § 23(e) authorizes him to deduct. We cannot agree.

The amount received by petitioner for cancellation of the lease must be included in his gross income in its entirety. Section 22(a), * * * expressly defines gross income to include "gains, profits, and income from * * * rent, * * * or gains or profits and income derived from any source whatever". Plainly this definition reached the rent paid prior to cancellation just as it would have embraced subsequent payments if the lease had never been canceled. *It would have included a prepayment of the discounted value of unmatured rental payments whether received at the inception of the lease or at any time thereafter.* Similarly, it would have extended to the proceeds of a suit to recover damages had the Irving Trust Co. breached the lease instead of concluding a settlement. * * * That the amount petitioner received resulted from negotiations ending in cancellation of the lease rather than from a suit to enforce it cannot alter the fact that basically the payment was merely a substitute for the rent reserved in the lease. So far as the application of § 22(a) is concerned, it is immaterial that petitioner chose to accept an amount less than the strict present value of the unmatured rental payments, rather than to engage in litigation, possibly uncertain and expensive.

The consideration received for cancellation of the lease was not a return of capital. We assume that the lease was "property" whatever that signifies abstractly. Presumably the bond in Helvering v. Horst, 311 U.S. 112, and the lease in Helvering v. Bruun, 309 U.S. 461, were also "property" but the interest coupon in *Horst* and the building in *Bruun* nevertheless were held to constitute items of gross income. Simply because the lease was "property" the amount received for its cancellation was not a return of capital, quite apart from the fact that "property" and "capital" are not necessarily synonymous in the Revenue Act of 1932 or in common usage. Where, as in this case, the disputed amount was essentially a substitute for rental payments which § 22(a) expressly characterizes as gross income, it must be regarded as ordinary income, and it is immaterial that for some purposes the contract creating the right to such payments may be treated as "property" or "capital".

For the same reasons, that amount was not a return of capital because petitioner acquired the lease as an incident of the realty devised to him by his father. Theoretically, it might have been possible in such a case to value realty and lease separately and to label each a capital asset. * * * But that would not have converted into capital the amount petitioner received from the Trust Co. since [the statute] would have required him to include in gross income the rent derived from the property, and [the statute] does not distinguish rental payments and a payment which is clearly a substitute for rental payments.

We conclude that petitioner must report as gross income the entire amount received for cancellation of the lease without regard to the claimed disparity between that amount and the difference between the present value of the unmatured rental payments and the fair rental value of the property for the unexpired period of the lease. The cancellation of the lease involved nothing more than relinquishment of the right to future rental payments in return for a present substitute payment and possession of the leased premises. Undoubtedly it diminished the amount of gross income petitioner expected to realize, but to that extent he was relieved of the duty to pay income tax. Nothing in [the statute] indicates that Congress intended to allow petitioner to reduce ordinary income actually received and reported by the amount of income he failed to realize. * * * We may assume that petitioner was injured insofar as the cancellation of the lease affected the value of the realty. But that would become a deductible loss only when its extent had been fixed by a closed transaction. Regulations No. 77, Art. 171, p. 46; United States v. White Dental Mfg. Co., 274 U.S. 398.

The judgment of the Circuit Court of Appeals is affirmed.

NOTES

(A) *Basis.* In the Court's view, what is Hort's basis in the lease? Is it implicit in the Court's decision (although certainly not explicit) that his entire basis in the property was allocated to the land and building? Does this seem appropriate in light of the factual circumstances of the case? Might a different result be called for if, for example, the taxpayer purchased a building with an outstanding lease with a rent far in excess of the rental value of the property? Remember, in *Hort* the building was inherited in 1928 subject to the lease, and the lease was canceled in 1933. Something happened to the U.S. economy during that interval. Under current law, no portion of the basis of property acquired subject to a favorable lease may be allocated to the lease. § 167(c)(2). Purchase of a lease only, without acquiring any ownership in the building, however, does give the purchaser a basis in the lease equal to the amount paid.

(B) *Other Issues.* In addition to issues of basis, the *Hort* case raises questions of characterizing gain as capital gain or ordinary income, and this aspect of the case is considered infra at page 588.

SECTION 5.   THE REALIZATION REQUIREMENT

NOTE INTRODUCING THE REALIZATION REQUIREMENT

As prior sections of this Chapter have made clear, amounts do not need to be received in cash to be included in gross income under § 61. The fair market value of property received is often included in income at the time of receipt. On the other hand, the Code normally has not been interpreted as including unrealized appreciation in income. Thus, gains and losses in the value of property generally are reflected in taxable income only when "realized." For example, if the taxpayer buys a painting for $100 and it increases in value to $1,000, she has no income until the painting is sold. Similarly, if she bought the painting at an auction and it turns out to be worth $5,000 more than she paid for it, the $5,000 gain will not be income until the painting is sold. As the succeeding cases indicate, however, the time of realization is not always crystal clear.

The nontaxation of unrealized appreciation is one of the most fundamental aspects of the federal income tax. The realization requirement provides taxpayers with considerable flexibility in the timing of taxation of gains and losses. This ability to accelerate or postpone gains and losses is one of the major tools of tax planning. In periods of high interest rates and high tax rates, the tax stakes of deferring income or accelerating deductions are magnified. As will be seen throughout this book, the realization requirement often produces tremendous complexity, primarily because taxpayers try to arrange their affairs to take advantage of deferral. Important consequences often turn on arbitrary and insignificant distinctions and this is one of the major problems with our income tax. In fact, William Andrews has concluded that the realization requirement is the "Achilles heel" of the income tax and is a fundamental reason to abandon the income tax in favor of a consumption tax (under which such timing questions are largely eliminated). See William Andrews, "The Achilles Heel of Income Taxation," in Taxation for the 1980's (Charls Walker, ed. 1983).

Despite the problems created by the realization requirement, including the potential for abuse, it is widely believed to be a necessary evil. The realization requirement is justified on the grounds that periodic taxation of accrued gains (and losses) would cause three problems that, in the view of the Treasury, "taken together, appear insurmountable": "(1) The administrative burden of annual reporting; (2) the difficulty and cost of determining asset values annually; and (3) the potential hardship of obtaining the funds to pay taxes on accrued but unrealized gains." U.S. Treasury Dep't, Blueprints for Tax Reform 82–83 (1977).

Although these concerns are sufficiently serious that we are not likely to abandon the realization requirement, some scholars (and occasionally Congress) have come to realize that they do not apply to all assets and all situations. For example, it is relatively easy to determine the value of some assets annually. Some commentators have suggested taxing unrealized gains and losses of securities traded on major stock exchanges. Furthermore, administrative, valuation, and cash flow problems are present on the receipt of any in-kind benefit, and yet we generally do not exempt in-kind transfers from tax. In addition, liquidity cannot be the only concern. Taxpayers could too easily avoid tax if the rule was that income is never realized until cash is received. The failure to include in-kind amounts in income at the time of receipt would give taxpayers too much control over the timing of tax liabilities and too many incentives to exchange property or services in lieu of cash. Taxpayers who use the accrual method of accounting, for example, are routinely required to include amounts in income before cash is received.

Over the last several decades, Congress has made some inroads on the realization requirement. For example, bondholders are required to include in income annually an interest amount, known as "original issue discount" that is not payable until the bond matures and is redeemed. (Original issue discount is discussed, infra at page 748). Another more complicated case is a tax straddle, where taxpayers own property with offsetting positions (for example both an option to purchase and an option to sell a commodity). Certain stock and stock option transactions are also subject to a "mark-to-market" rule requiring most taxpayers to include in gross income all unrealized gains and losses from straddle contracts. (Section 1256, dealing with certain straddle transactions, is discussed infra at page 585). Further deviations from the realization requirement may be likely, particularly with respect to financial instruments.

Despite these efforts, the realization requirement continues to play an important role in the income tax and to present serious questions of equity and efficiency. In many instances, the requirement violates horizontal equity. Consider A who earns $1,000 in salary and B who owns a building that increases in value from $50,000 to $51,000 during the taxable year. Each has $1,000 of economic income, but only A will be taxed currently. Although B ultimately will pay tax on the income when he disposes of the property, he has enjoyed the tax benefit of deferral. The incentive to acquire assets that produce unrealized, and therefore untaxed, appreciation distorts investment decisions. If a taxpayer in a 30 percent tax bracket has the choice to invest $10,000 in a bond producing 10 percent annual interest or a share of stock that increases in value 10 percent a year, he is likely to choose the latter. At the end of two years, the taxpayer with the bond will have $11,450 (the bond will grow in value to $11,450 at an after-tax rate of return of 7 percent). If the taxpayer with the stock sells it, he will have $11,470 (the stock will have increased in value to $11,000 in the first year and to $12,100 in the second year, producing a $2,100 gain, which, if taxed at 30 percent, will result in $630 in taxes). Ignoring risk, in order to attract a buyer, the interest rate on the bond will have to increase. Actually, throughout most of our history, the tax rate on the stock has been less than the rate on bond interest (due to lower rates on capital gains), creating a wider disparity.

The following cases illustrate the difficulty in determining when there has been a realization event. We will return to this subject throughout the book.

Cesarini v. United States

United States District Court, N.D.Ohio, 1969.
296 F.Supp. 3, affirmed 428 F.2d 812 (6th Cir.1970).

YOUNG, DISTRICT JUDGE. [Plaintiffs purchased a used piano for $15 in 1957. In 1964 they found $4,467 in cash in the piano. They paid the tax on that sum in their original return and sued for a refund, claiming that the windfall was not includible in gross income under § 61.]

After a consideration of the pertinent provisions of the Internal Revenue Code, Treasury Regulations, Revenue Rulings, and decisional law in the area, this Court has concluded that the taxpayers are not entitled to a refund of the amount requested * * *.

The starting point in determining whether an item is to be included in gross income is, of course, Section 61(a) of Title 26 U.S.C.A., and that section provides in part:

> "Except as otherwise provided in this subtitle, *gross income means all income from whatever source derived,* including (but not limited to) the following items: * * * " (Emphasis added.)

Subsections (1) through (15) of Section 61(a) then go on to list fifteen items specifically included in the computation of the taxpayer's gross income, and Part II of Subchapter B of the 1954 Code (Sections 71 et seq.) deals with other items expressly included in gross income. While neither of these listings expressly includes the type of income which is at issue in the case at bar, Part III of Subchapter B (Sections 101 et seq.) deals with items specifically *excluded* from gross income, and found money is not listed in those sections either. This absence of express mention in any of the code sections necessitates a return to the "all income from whatever source" language of Section 61(a) of the code, and the express statement there that gross income is "not limited to" the following fifteen examples. Section 1.61–1(a) of the Treasury Regulations, the corresponding section to Section 61(a) in the 1954 Code, reiterates this broad construction of gross income, providing in part:

> "Gross income means all income from whatever source derived, unless excluded by law. *Gross income includes income realized in any form,* whether in money, property, or services. * * * " (Emphasis added.)

The decisions of the United States Supreme Court have frequently stated that this broad all-inclusive language was used by Congress to exert the full measure of its taxing power under the Sixteenth Amendment to the United States Constitution. Commissioner of Internal Revenue v. Glenshaw Glass Co., 348 U.S. 426, 429 (1955) * * *.

In addition, the Government in the instant case cites and relies upon an I.R.S. Revenue Ruling which is undeniably on point:

> "The finder of treasure-trove is in receipt of taxable income, for Federal income tax purposes, to the extent of its value in United States currency, for the taxable year in which it is reduced to undisputed possession." Rev.Rul. 61, 1953–1, Cum.Bull. 17.

The plaintiffs argue that the above ruling does not control this case for two reasons. The first is that subsequent to the Ruling's pronouncement in 1953, Congress enacted Sections 74 and 102 of the 1954 Code, § 74 expressly *including* the value of prizes and awards in gross income in most cases, and § 102 specifically *exempting* the value of gifts received from gross income. From this, it is argued that Section 74 was added because prizes might otherwise be construed as non-taxable gifts, and since no such section was passed expressly taxing treasure-trove, it is therefore a gift which is non-taxable under Section 102. This line of reasoning overlooks the statutory scheme previously alluded to, whereby income from all sources is taxed unless the taxpayer can point to an express exemption. Not only have the taxpayers failed to list a specific exclusion in the instant case, but also the Government *has* pointed to express language covering the found money, even though it would not be required to do so under the broad language of Section 61(a) and the foregoing Supreme Court decisions interpreting it.

* * *

Although not cited by either party, and noticeably absent from the Government's brief, the following Treasury Regulation appears in the 1964 Regulations, the year of the return in dispute:

"§ 1.61–14 Miscellaneous items of gross income.

"(a) In general. In addition to the items enumerated in section 61(a), there are many other kinds of gross income * * *. *Treasure trove, to the extent of its value in United States currency, constitutes gross income for the taxable year in which it is reduced to undisputed possession.*"

Identical language appears in the 1968 Treasury Regulations, and is found in all previous years back to 1958. This language is the same in all material respects as that found in Rev.Rul. 61–53–1, 1961–1, Cum.Bull. 17, and is undoubtedly an attempt to codify that ruling into the Regulations which apply to the 1954 Code. This Court is of the opinion that Treas.Reg. § 1.61–14(a) is dispositive of the major issue in this case if the $4,467.00 found in the piano was "reduced to undisputed possession" in the year petitioners reported it, for this Regulation was applicable to returns filed in the calendar year of 1964. * * *

[The portions of the opinion holding that the cash was income in the year found and not the year the piano was purchased and that the amount was taxable as ordinary income and not as capital gain have been omitted.]

NOTES

Would Mrs. Cesarini have had gross income if, instead of finding cash in the piano, she had discovered a diamond ring worth $5,000? If she had discovered that the piano was a Steinway Concert Grand worth $5,000 more than she paid for it? Suppose she discovered that one of the keys was solid gold and worth $5,000?

Suppose a taxpayer purchases a house and subsequently, while digging in the backyard, uncovers thousands of tulip bulbs. What if he uncovered a chest of gold coins? Suppose he discovered an underground stream with gold nuggets?

Suppose the taxpayer is unable to reduce the item to "undisputed possession" because it does not belong to him? Where the taxpayer converts or uses the money for his own benefit, it is clearly taxable even if he later must return it. Consider the case of William H. Irvin. A short time after being discharged from the Army, Irvin went to a lonely road and prayed that he would become self-sufficient. His prayers were answered shortly thereafter, when the Army, which owed him $183.69, mistakenly issued a Treasury check in the amount of $836,939.19. Irvin testified that he thought the check was a nontaxable miracle and proceeded to spend $340,000 before the government detected the error. Miracle or not, the check was taxable. United States v. Irvin, 67 F.3d 670 (8th Cir.1995). Suppose Irvin returns the money? It is deductible when paid. This issue is discussed infra at page 174.

Haverly v. United States

United States Court of Appeals, Seventh Circuit, 1975. 513 F.2d 224, cert. denied 423 U.S. 912 (1975).

HASTINGS, SENIOR CIRCUIT JUDGE. This case presents for resolution a single question of law which is of first impression: whether the value of unsolicited sample textbooks sent by publishers to a principal of a public elementary school, which he subsequently donated to the school's library and for which he claimed a charitable deduction, constitutes gross income to the principal within the meaning of Section 61 of the Internal Revenue Code of 1954, 26 U.S.C. § 61. * * *

During the years 1967 and 1968 Charles N. Haverly was the principal of the Alice L. Barnard Elementary School in Chicago, Illinois. In each of these years publishers sent to the taxpayer unsolicited sample copies of textbooks which had a total fair market value at the time of receipt of $400. The samples were given to taxpayer for his personal retention or for whatever disposition he wished to make. The samples were provided, in the hope of receiving favorable consideration, to give taxpayer an opportunity to examine the books and determine whether they were suitable for the instructional unit for which he was responsible. The publishers did not intend that the books serve as compensation.

In 1968 taxpayer donated the books to the Alice L. Barnard Elementary School Library. The parties agreed that the donation entitled the taxpayer to a charitable deduction under 26 U.S.C. § 170, in the amount of $400, the value of the books at the time of the contribution.

The parties further stipulated that the textbooks received from the publishers did not constitute gifts within the meaning of 26 U.S.C. § 102 since their transfer to the taxpayer did not proceed from a detached and disinterested generosity nor out of affection, respect, admiration, charity or like impulses.

Taxpayer's report of his 1968 income did not include the value of the textbooks received, but it did include a charitable deduction for the value of the books donated to the school library. The Internal Revenue Service assessed a deficiency against the taxpayer representing income taxes on the value of the textbooks received. Taxpayer paid the amount of the deficiency, filed a claim for refund and subsequently instituted this action to recover that amount.

The amount of income, if any, and the time of its receipt are not issues here since the parties stipulated that if the contested issue of law was decided in the taxpayer's favor, his taxable income for 1968 as determined by the Internal Revenue Service would be reduced by $400.00.

* * * The district court issued a memorandum opinion which held that receipt of the samples did not constitute income. Haverly v. United States, N.D.Ill., 374 F.Supp. 1041 (1974). The court subsequently ordered, in accordance with its decision, that plaintiffs recover from the United States the sum of $120.40 plus interest. The United States appeals from that judgment. We reverse.

Section 61(a) of Title 26 of the United States Code provides: "Except as otherwise provided in this subtitle, gross income means all income from whatever source derived, including (but not limited to) the following items:" The section thereafter enumerates fifteen items none of which, the government concedes, encompass the receipt of sample textbooks. The taxpayer concedes that receipt of the books does not fall within any of the specific exclusions from gross income set out in Sections 101 through 124 of Title 26. The only question remaining is whether the value of the textbooks received is included within "all income from whatever source derived."

The Supreme Court has frequently reiterated that it was the intention of Congress "to use the full measure of its taxing power" and "to tax all gains except those specifically exempted." James v. United States, 366 U.S. 213, 218–219 (1961). The Supreme Court has also held that the language of Section 61(a) encompasses all "accessions to wealth, clearly realized, and over which the taxpayers have complete dominion." Id. at 219; Commissioner v. Glenshaw Glass Co., 348 U.S. 426, 431 (1955).

There are no reported cases which have applied these definitions of income to the question of the receipt of unsolicited samples. The parties have cited to the court a number of cases applying income definitions to other fact situations. We have considered these cases, but we find them of no particular assistance in resolving the question before us. In view of the comprehensive conception of income embodied in the statutory language and the Supreme Court's interpretation of that language, we conclude that when the intent to exercise complete dominion over unsolicited samples is demonstrated by donating those samples to a charitable institution and taking a tax deduction therefor, the value of the samples received constitutes gross income.

The receipt of textbooks is unquestionably an "accession to wealth." Taxpayer recognized the value of the books when he donated them and took a $400 deduction therefor. Possession of the books increased the taxpayer's wealth. Taxpayer's receipt and possession of the books indicate that the income was "clearly realized." Taxpayer admitted that the books were given to him for his personal retention or whatever disposition he saw fit to make of them. Although the receipt of unsolicited samples may sometimes raise the question of whether the taxpayer manifested an intent to accept the property or exercised "complete dominion" over it, there is no question that this element is satisfied by the unequivocal act of taking a charitable deduction for donation of the property.

The district court recognized that the act of claiming a charitable deduction does manifest an intent to accept the property as one's own. It nevertheless declined to label receipt of the property as income because it considered such an act indistinguishable from other acts unrelated to the tax laws which also evidence an intent to accept property as one's own, such as a school principal donating his sample texts to the library *without* claiming a deduction. We need not resolve the question of the tax consequences of this and other hypothetical cases discussed by the district court and suggested by the taxpayer. To decide the case before us we need only hold, as we do, that when a tax deduction is taken for the donation of unsolicited samples the value of the samples received must be included in the taxpayer's gross income.

This conclusion is consistent with Revenue Ruling 70–498, 1970–2 Cum.Bull. 6, in which the Internal Revenue Service held that a newspaper's book reviewer must include in his gross income the value of unsolicited books received from publishers which are donated to a charitable organization and for which a charitable deduction is taken. This ruling was issued to supersede an earlier ruling, Rev.Rul. 70–330, 1970–1 Cum.Bull. 14, that mere retention of unsolicited books was sufficient to cause them to be gross income.

The Internal Revenue Service has apparently made an administrative decision to be concerned with the taxation of unsolicited samples only when failure to tax those samples would provide taxpayers with double tax benefits. It is not for the courts to quarrel with an agency's rational allocation of its administrative resources.

In light of the foregoing, the judgment appealed from is reversed and the case is remanded to the district court with directions to enter judgment for the United States. Reversed.

NOTES

(A) *Double Dipping*. The Service's objection to excluding the books from income and allowing a tax deduction for the contribution of the books to charity can be seen from the following example: Assume the taxpayer's salary is $20,000, he sells the books for $1,000, and donates the $1,000 to the charity. T would have $21,000 of gross income ($20,000 salary plus the $1,000 from the sale of the books) and a charitable contribution deduction that would reduce taxable income to $20,000. But if the books were donated directly to charity, T would have taxable income of $19,000 ($20,000 salary minus the charitable deduction). T would be allowed a deduction for something whose value was never included in income.

What would have been the tax consequences if Haverly had sold the books rather than giving them to charity? What is the basis in the books? What if he had simply put them on his bookshelf? Suppose he had used them to prepare for class? What is the theory of *Haverly*? Is giving the books to charity a realization event, but receiving them is not?

(B) *Other Windfalls.* What if, instead of books, Haverly had received and consumed unsolicited samples of toothpaste or soap? Would it matter whether the sample was an item that he ordinarily would purchase with after-tax income? What difference would it make if, instead of a sample of toothpaste, the taxpayer received a coupon entitling him to a 50-cent discount on toothpaste?

Eisner v. Macomber

Supreme Court of the United States, 1920. 252 U.S. 189.

MR. JUSTICE PITNEY delivered the opinion of the court.

This case presents the question whether, by virtue of the Sixteenth Amendment, Congress has the power to tax, as income of the stockholder and without apportionment, a stock dividend. * * *

It arises under the Revenue Act of September 8, 1916, * * * which, in our opinion * * * plainly evinces the purpose of Congress to tax stock dividends as income.

* * *

In Pollock v. Farmers' Loan & Trust Co., 158 U.S. 601, * * * it was held that taxes upon rents and profits of real estate and upon returns from investments of personal property were in effect direct taxes upon the property from which such income arose, imposed by reason of ownership; and that Congress could not impose such taxes without apportioning them among the States according to population, as required by Art. I, § 2, cl. 3, and § 9, cl. 4, of the original Constitution.

Afterwards, and evidently in recognition of the limitation upon the taxing power of Congress thus determined, the Sixteenth Amendment was adopted, in words lucidly expressing the object to be accomplished: "The Congress shall have power to lay and collect taxes on incomes, from whatever source derived, without apportionment among the several States, and without regard to any census or enumeration."

* * *

In order, therefore, that the clauses cited from Article I of the Constitution may have proper force and effect, save only as modified by the Amendment, and that the latter also may have proper effect, it becomes essential to distinguish between what is and what is not "income," as the term is there used; and to apply the distinction, as cases arise, according to truth and substance, without regard to form. * * *

The fundamental relation of "capital" to "income" has been much discussed by economists, the former being likened to the tree or the land, the latter to the fruit or the crop; the former depicted as a reservoir supplied from springs, the latter as the outlet stream, to be measured by its flow during a period of time. For the present purpose we require only a clear definition of the term "income," as used in common speech, in order to determine its meaning in the Amendment; and, having formed also a correct judgment as to the nature of a stock dividend, we shall find it easy to decide the matter at issue.

After examining dictionaries in common use * * * we find little to add to the succinct definition adopted in two cases arising under the Corporation Tax Act of 1909 (Stratton's Independence v. Howbert, 231 U.S. 399, 415; Doyle v. Mitchell Bros. Co., 247 U.S. 179, 185)—"Income may be defined as the gain derived from capital, from labor, or from both combined," provided it be understood to include profit gained through a sale or conversion of capital assets, to which it was applied in the Doyle Case. * * *

Brief as it is, it indicates the characteristic and distinguishing attribute of income essential for a correct solution of the present controversy. The Government, although basing its argument upon the definition as quoted, placed chief emphasis upon the word "gain," which was extended to include a variety of meanings; while the significance of the next three words was either overlooked or misconceived. *"Derived—from—capital ";* * * * Here we have the essential matter: *not* a gain *accruing to* capital; not a *growth* or *increment* of value *in* the investment; but a gain, a profit, something of exchangeable value *proceeding from* the property, *severed from* the capital, however invested or employed, and *coming in,* being *"derived,"*—that is, *received* or *drawn by* the recipient (the taxpayer) for his *separate* use, benefit and disposal—*that* is income derived from property. Nothing else answers the description.

The same fundamental conception is clearly set forth in the Sixteenth Amendment—"incomes from whatever source derived"—the essential thought being expressed with a conciseness and lucidity entirely in harmony with the form and style of the Constitution.

Can a stock dividend, considering its essential character, be brought within the definition? * * * [A stock dividend] does not alter the pre-existing proportionate interest of any stockholder or increase the intrinsic value of his holding or of the aggregate holdings of the other stockholders as they stood before. The new certificates simply increase the number of the shares, with consequent dilution of the value of each share.

* * *

Far from being a realization of profits of the stockholder, [a stock dividend] tends rather to postpone such realization, in that the fund represented by the new stock has been transferred from surplus to capital, and no longer is available for actual distribution.

The essential and controlling fact is that the stockholder has received nothing out of the company's assets for his separate use and benefit; on the contrary, every dollar of his original investment, together with whatever accretions and accumulations have resulted from employment of his money and that of the other stockholders in the business of the company, still remains the property of the company, and subject to business risks which may result in wiping out the entire investment. Having regard to the very truth of the matter, to substance and not to form, he has received nothing that answers the definition of income within the meaning of the Sixteenth Amendment.

* * *

It is said that a stockholder may sell the new shares acquired in the stock dividend; and so he may, if he can find a buyer. It is equally true that if he does sell, and in doing so realizes a profit, such profit, like any other, is income, and so far as it may have arisen since the Sixteenth Amendment is taxable by Congress without apportionment. The same would be true were he to sell some of his original shares at a profit. But if a shareholder sells dividend stock he necessarily disposes of a part of his capital interest, just as if he should sell a part of his old stock, either before or after the dividend. What he retains no longer entitles him to the same proportion of future dividends as before the sale. His part in the control of the company likewise is diminished. Thus, if one holding $60,000 out of a total of $100,000 of the capital stock of a corporation should receive in common with other stockholders a 50 per cent stock dividend, and should sell his part, he thereby would be reduced from a majority to a minority stockholder, having six-fifteenths instead of six-tenths of the total stock outstanding. * * * Yet, without selling, the shareholder, unless possessed of other resources, has not the wherewithal to pay an income tax upon the dividend stock. Nothing could more clearly show that to tax a stock dividend is to tax a capital increase, and not income, than this demonstration that in the nature of things it requires conversion of capital in order to pay the tax.

* * *

Conceding that the mere issue of a stock dividend makes the recipient no richer than before, the Government nevertheless contends that the new certificates measure the extent to which the gains accumulated by the corporation have made him the richer. There are two insuperable difficulties with this: In the first place, it would depend upon how long he had held the stock whether the stock dividend indicated the extent to which he had been enriched by the operations of the company; unless he had held it throughout such operations the measure would not hold true. Secondly, and more important for present purposes, enrichment through increase in value of capital investment is not income in any proper meaning of the term.

* * *

It is said there is no difference in principle between a simple stock dividend and a case where stockholders use money received as cash dividends to purchase additional stock contemporaneously issued by the corporation. But an actual cash dividend, with a real option to the stockholder either to keep the money for his own or to reinvest it in new shares, would be as far removed as possible from a true stock dividend, such as the one we have under consideration, where nothing of value is taken from the company's assets and transferred to the individual ownership of the several stockholders and thereby subjected to their disposal.

* * *

[The Sixteenth] Amendment applies to income only, and what is called the stockholder's share in the accumulated profits of the company is capital, not income. As we have pointed out, a stockholder has no individual share in accumulated profits, nor in any particular part of the assets of the corporation, prior to dividend declared.

Thus, from every point of view, we are brought irresistibly to the conclusion that neither under the Sixteenth Amendment nor otherwise has Congress power to tax without apportionment a true stock dividend * * * as income of the stockholder. The Revenue Act of 1916, in so far as it imposes a tax upon the stockholder because of such dividend, contravenes the provisions of Article I, § 2, cl. 3, and Article I, § 9, cl. 4, of the Constitution, and to this extent is invalid notwithstanding the Sixteenth Amendment.

Judgment affirmed.

MR. JUSTICE HOLMES, dissenting. * * * I think that the word "incomes" in the Sixteenth Amendment should be read in "a sense most obvious to the common understanding at the time of its adoption." * * * The known purpose of this Amendment was to get rid of nice questions as to what might be direct taxes, and I cannot doubt that most people not lawyers would suppose when they voted for it that they put a question like the present to rest. * * *

MR. JUSTICE DAY concurs in this opinion.

MR. JUSTICE BRANDEIS, dissenting. Financiers, with the aid of lawyers, devised long ago two different methods by which a corporation can, without increasing its indebtedness, keep for corporate purposes accumulated profits, and yet, in effect, distribute these profits, among its stockholders. One method is a simple one. The capital stock is increased; the new stock is paid up with the accumulated profits; and the new shares of paid-up stock are then distributed among the stockholders pro rata as a dividend. * * * The other method is slightly more complicated. Arrangements are made for an increase of stock to be offered to stockholders pro rata at par, and, at the same time, for the payment of a cash dividend equal to the amount which the stockholder will be required to pay to the company, if he avails himself of the right to subscribe for his pro rata of the new stock. If the stockholder takes the new stock, as is expected, he may endorse the dividend check received to the corporation and thus pay for the new stock. In order to ensure that all the new stock so offered will be taken, the price at which it is offered is fixed far below what it is believed will be its market value. If the stockholder prefers ready money to an increase of his holdings of stock, he may sell his right to take new stock pro rata, which is evidenced by an assignable instrument. In that event the purchaser of the rights repays to the corporation, as the subscription price of the new stock, an amount equal to that which it had paid as a cash dividend to the stockholder.

* * *

It is conceded that if the stock dividend paid to Mrs. Macomber had been made by the more complicated method * * * [it] would have been taxable. * * * But it is contended that, because the simple method was adopted * * *, the new stock is not to be deemed income. * * * If such a different result can flow merely from the difference in the method pursued, it must be because Congress is without power to tax as income * * * the stock received * * *; for Congress has, by the provisions in the Revenue Act of 1916, expressly declared its purpose to make stock dividends, by whichever method paid, taxable as income. * * *

Hitherto powers conferred upon Congress by the Constitution have been liberally construed, and have been held to extend to every means appropriate to attain the end sought. In determining the scope of the power the substance of the transaction, not its form has been regarded. * * * Is there anything in the phraseology of the Sixteenth Amendment or in the nature of corporate dividends which should lead to a departure from these rules of construction and compel this court to hold, that Congress is powerless to prevent a result so extraordinary as that here contended for by the stockholder? * * *

NOTES

(A) *Terminology.* Some students are confused by the terminology of the *Macomber* case. A "dividend" generally can be thought of as a distribution of cash or property based on the ownership of stock. (If you insist on technical perfection, take a glance at §§ 301 and 316 for the conditions under which a "distribution" will be taxed as a "dividend.") Usually a distribution is in cash, but corporations sometimes distribute other assets. A "stock dividend" is a distribution of additional shares of stock in the distributing corporation based on shareholders' outstanding ownership. Thus, if a corporation declares a stock dividend of 10 percent, it will distribute 10 new shares of stock for every 100 shares owned. After a stock dividend, there are more shares outstanding (110 percent in the example), but each shareholder's proportionate ownership interest remains the same until some shareholders begin buying or selling shares. It has long been clear that a cash dividend is gross income under § 61; the question in the case was whether a stock dividend—Mrs. Macomber received additional shares of stock and no cash at all—triggers tax.

Mrs. Macomber would have been taxed had she received a cash dividend that she then used to purchase more shares of Standard Oil. Why? Because she received cash rather than a distribution in kind? Is her economic position any different from that where she receives a stock dividend? When will Mrs. Macomber's unrealized appreciation be taxed?

Although the general principles announced in *Macomber* have been subjected to qualification, the result of the case remains the law today. A simple pro rata "common on common" stock dividend, in which the stockholder receives shares identical to those producing the dividend and has no option to choose cash, produces no taxable income. § 305. The rules governing other stock dividends are quite complex, reflecting the variety of potential transactions between a corporation and its shareholders.

(B) *Constitutional Nature of the Realization Requirement.* In no case since *Macomber* has the Supreme Court ruled that a federal revenue statute violated the Sixteenth Amendment, although in the two decades following the decision, the Court reaffirmed the constitutional basis of the holding. See, e.g., Edwards v. Cuba Railroad Co., 268 U.S. 628 (1925); Helvering v. Independent Life Ins. Co., 292 U.S. 371, 378–79 (1934). Although the Court has not overruled *Macomber,* it has confined the decision to its facts. See Commissioner v. Glenshaw Glass Co., 348 U.S. 426 (1955). The Ninth Circuit has held that the mark-to-market rules found in Section 1256 (relating to certain financial instruments) are constitutional. Murphy v. United States, 992 F.2d 929 (9th Cir.1993). The continuing vitality of *Macomber* as a constitutional precedent is doubtful.

Cottage Savings Ass'n v. Commissioner

Supreme Court of the United States, 1991. 499 U.S. 554.

JUSTICE MARSHALL delivered the opinion of the Court.

The issue in this case is whether a financial institution realizes tax-deductible losses when it exchanges its interests in one group of residential mortgage loans for another lender's interests in a different group of residential mortgage loans. We hold that such a transaction does give rise to realized losses.

Petitioner Cottage Savings Association (Cottage Savings) is a savings and loan association (S & L) formerly regulated by the Federal Home Loan Bank Board (FHLBB). Like many S & L's, Cottage Savings held numerous long-term, low-interest mortgages that declined in value when interest rates surged in the late 1970's. These institutions would have benefitted from selling their devalued mortgages in order to realize tax-deductible losses. However, they were deterred from doing so by FHLBB accounting regulations, which required them to record the losses on their books. Reporting these losses consistent with the then-effective FHLBB accounting regulations would have placed many S & L's at risk of closure by the FHLBB.

The FHLBB responded to this situation by relaxing its requirements for the reporting of losses. In a regulatory directive known as "Memorandum R–49," dated June 27, 1980, the FHLBB determined that S & L's need not report losses associated with mortgages that are exchanged for "substantially identical" mortgages held by other lenders. The FHLBB's acknowledged purpose for Memorandum R–49 was to facilitate transactions that would generate tax losses but that would not substantially affect the economic position of the transacting S & L's.

This case involves a typical Memorandum R–49 transaction. On December 31, 1980, Cottage Savings sold "90% participation interests" in 252 mortgages to four S & L's. It simultaneously purchased "90% participation interests" in 305 mortgages held by these S & L's.[1] All of the loans involved

---

1. By exchanging merely participation interests rather than the loans themselves, each party retained its relationship with the individual obligors. Consequently, each S & L

in the transaction were secured by single-family homes, most in the Cincinnati area. The fair market value of the package of participation interests exchanged by each side was approximately $4.5 million. The face value of the participation interests Cottage Savings relinquished in the transaction was approximately $6.9 million.

On its 1980 federal income tax return, Cottage Savings claimed a deduction for $2,447,091, which represented the adjusted difference between the face value of the participation interests that it traded and the fair market value of the participation interests that it received. As permitted by Memorandum R–49, Cottage Savings did not report these losses to the FHLBB * * * *

Rather than assessing tax liability on the basis of annual fluctuations in the value of a taxpayer's property, the Internal Revenue Code defers the tax consequences of a gain or loss in property value until the taxpayer "realizes" the gain or loss. The realization requirement is implicit in § 1001(a) of the Code * * * As this Court has recognized, the concept of realization is "founded on administrative convenience." Helvering v. Horst, 311 U.S. 112, 116 (1940). Under an appreciation-based system of taxation, taxpayers and the Commissioner would have to undertake the "cumbersome, abrasive, and unpredictable administrative task" of valuing assets on an annual basis to determine whether the assets had appreciated or depreciated in value. * * *

Section 1001(a)'s language provides a straightforward test for realization: to realize a gain or loss in the value of property, the taxpayer must engage in a "sale or other disposition of [the] property." The parties agree that the exchange of participation interests in this case cannot be characterized as a "sale" under § 1001(a); the issue before us is whether the transaction constitutes a "disposition of property." The Commissioner argues that an exchange of property can be treated as a "disposition" under § 1001(a) only if the properties exchanged are materially different. The Commissioner further submits that, because the underlying mortgages were essentially economic substitutes, the participation interests exchanged by Cottage Savings were not materially different from those received from the other S & L's. Cottage Savings, on the other hand, maintains that any exchange of property is a "disposition of property" under § 1001(a), regardless of whether the property exchanged is materially different. Alternatively, Cottage Savings contends that the participation interests exchanged were materially different because the underlying loans were secured by different properties.

We must therefore determine whether the realization principle in § 1001(a) incorporates a "material difference" requirement. If it does, we must further decide what that requirement amounts to and how it applies in this case. We consider these questions in turn.

Neither the language nor the history of the Code indicates whether and to what extent property exchanged must differ to count as a "disposition of property" under § 1001(a). Nonetheless, we readily agree with the Com-

---

continued to service the loans on which it had transferred the participation interests and made monthly payments to the participation-interest holders.

missioner that an exchange of property gives rise to a realization event under § 1001(a) only if the properties exchanged are "materially different." The Commissioner himself has by regulation construed § 1001(a) to embody a material difference requirement:

"Except as otherwise provided * * * the gain or loss realized from the conversion of property into cash, or from the exchange of property for other property differing materially either in kind or in extent, is treated as income or as loss sustained." Treas.Reg. § 1.1001–1. * * *

Precisely what constitutes a "material difference" for purposes of § 1001(a) of the Code is a more complicated question. The Commissioner argues that properties are "materially different" only if they differ in economic substance. To determine whether the participation interests exchanged in this case were "materially different" in this sense, the Commissioner argues, we should look to the attitudes of the parties, the evaluation of the interests by the secondary mortgage market, and the views of the FHLBB. We conclude that § 1001(a) embodies a much less demanding and less complex test.

* * * We must look to the case law from which the test derives and which we believe Congress intended to codify in enacting and reenacting the language that now comprises § 1001(a). * * *

We start with the classic treatment of realization in Eisner v. Macomber. * * *

In three subsequent decisions—United States v. Phellis, 257 U.S. 156 (1921); Weiss v. Stearn, 265 U.S. 242 (1924); and Marr v. United States, 268 U.S. 536 (1925)—we refined Macomber's conception of realization in the context of property exchanges. In each case, the taxpayer owned stock that had appreciated in value since its acquisition. And in each case, the corporation in which the taxpayer held stock had reorganized into a new corporation, with the new corporation assuming the business of the old corporation. While the corporations in Phellis and Marr both changed from New Jersey to Delaware corporations, the original and successor corporations in Weiss both were incorporated in Ohio. In each case, following the reorganization, the stockholders of the old corporation received shares in the new corporation equal to their proportional interest in the old corporation.

The question in these cases was whether the taxpayers realized the accumulated gain in their shares in the old corporation when they received in return for those shares stock representing an equivalent proportional interest in the new corporations. In Phellis and Marr, we held that the transactions were realization events. We reasoned that because a company incorporated in one State has "different rights and powers" from one incorporated in a different State, the taxpayers in Phellis and Marr acquired through the transactions property that was "materially different" from what they previously had. United States v. Phellis, 257 U.S., at 169–173; see Marr v. United States, supra, at 540–542 (using phrase "essentially different"). In contrast, we held that no realization occurred in Weiss. By exchanging stock in the predecessor corporation for stock in the newly reorganized corporation, the taxpayer did not receive "a thing really different from what he theretofore had." Weiss v. Stearn, supra, at 254. As we explained in Marr, our determination that the reorganized company in Weiss was not "really different" from its predecessor turned on the fact that both companies were incorporated in the same State. See Marr v. United States, supra, at 540–542 (outlining distinction between these cases).

Obviously, the distinction in Phellis and Marr that made the stock in the successor corporations materially different from the stock in the predecessors was minimal. Taken together, Phellis, Marr, and Weiss stand for the principle that properties are "different" in the sense that is "material" to the Internal Revenue Code so long as their respective possessors enjoy legal entitlements that are different in kind or extent. * * * No more demanding a standard than this is necessary in order to satisfy the administrative purposes underlying the realization requirement in § 1001(a). See Helvering v. Horst, 311 U.S. at 116. For, as long as the property entitlements are not identical, their exchange will allow both the Commissioner and the transacting taxpayer easily to fix the appreciated or depreciated values of the property relative to their tax bases.

In contrast, we find no support for the Commissioner's "economic substitute" conception of material difference. According to the Commissioner, differences between properties are material for purposes of the Code only when it can be said that the parties, the relevant market (in this case the secondary mortgage market), and the relevant regulatory body (in this case the FHLBB) would consider them material. Nothing in Phellis, Weiss, and Marr suggests that exchanges of properties must satisfy such a subjective test to trigger realization of a gain or loss.

Moreover, the complexity of the Commissioner's approach ill serves the goal of administrative convenience that underlies the realization requirement. In order to apply the Commissioner's test in a principled fashion, the Commissioner and the taxpayer must identify the relevant market, establish whether there is a regulatory agency whose views should be taken into account, and then assess how the relevant market participants and the agency would view the transaction. The Commissioner's failure to explain how these inquiries should be conducted further calls into question the workability of his test. * * *

Under our interpretation of § 1001(a), an exchange of property gives rise to a realization event so long as the exchanged properties are "materially different"—that is, so long as they embody legally distinct entitlements. Cottage Savings' transactions at issue here easily satisfy this test. Because the participation interests exchanged by Cottage Savings and the other S & L's derived from loans that were made to different obligors and secured by different homes, the exchanged interests did embody legally distinct entitlements. Consequently, we conclude that Cottage Savings realized its losses at the point of the exchange.

The Commissioner contends that it is anomalous to treat mortgages deemed to be "substantially identical" by the FHLBB as "materially different." The anomaly, however, is merely semantic; mortgages can be substantially identical for Memorandum R–49 purposes and still exhibit "differences" that are "material" for purposes of the Internal Revenue

Code. Because Cottage Savings received entitlements different from those it gave up, the exchange put both Cottage Savings and the Commissioner in a position to determine the change in the value of Cottage Savings' mortgages relative to their tax bases. Thus, there is no reason not to treat the exchange of these interests as a realization event, regardless of the status of the mortgages under the criteria of Memorandum R–49. * * *

NOTES

(A) *Aftermath of* Cottage Savings. The scope of *Cottage Savings* is not certain. Both of the tests for realization considered by the Court—changes in economic vs. legal aspects—have difficulties. Any such general rule for triggering realization on an exchange of assets or liabilities has the potential both to create tax planning opportunities to accelerate losses or defer gains and at the same time to create traps for the unwary.

The lack of clarity of the meaning of *Cottage Savings* has been felt most acutely in the area of debt modifications. Some observers believed that *Cottage Savings* implies that a change in any legal rights or powers of either the creditor or the debtor would create a realization event, triggering tax consequences. The creditor would recognize gain or loss because the creditor's basis in the note would be different from the fair market value. The debtor may have discharge of indebtedness income because the principal amount of the new debt instrument is less than the principal amount of the original obligation. See discussion at page 176 infra. This is a distinct change from the law in effect before *Cottage Savings,* under which a realization was not deemed to occur unless there has been a "material modification" of the debt. See Reg. § 1.1001–1(a). In order to quell fears that *Cottage Savings* might have created a "hair trigger" test for realization on the modification of debt instruments, the IRS issued regulations defining what constitutes a "significant modification" of a debt instrument such that the parties are deemed to have exchanged a modified instrument for the original debt. For example, if the parties agree to change the yield by more than a quarter of 1 percent, an exchange would be deemed to have occurred. Reg. § 1.1001–3(e)(2)(ii)(a). Obviously, the IRS does not read *Cottage Savings* as prohibiting an examination of changes in economic factors. But other debt modifications would not be treated as "significant" and there would be no tax consequences to either debtor or creditor. Because *Cottage Savings* did not deal with debt modification, it is not clear whether these regulations, which would not treat all modifications that involve changes in legal obligations as exchanges, are consistent with the Court's holding.

(B) *Leasehold Improvements.* Suppose a taxpayer leases land to a tenant who constructs a a building that will pass to the lessor at the termination of the lease. When should the landlord realize gain attributable to tenant improvements of leased property? When the tenant constructs the improvements? Ratably over the remaining lease term as periodic rent? At the end of the lease when the landlord gains possession of the building? Or only when the landlord sells the property and improvements? In Helvering v. Bruun, 309 U.S. 461 (1940), the Supreme Court held that the landlord had income when he gained possession of the building. Section 109 now provides, however, that the lessor does not include in income the value of the leasehold improvements constructed by the lessee on the termination of the lease. By virtue of § 1019, the landlord's basis is unaffected, so that the value of the improvements is recaptured on disposition because a lower basis yields increased gain (or decreased loss).

SECTION 6.   ANNUITIES AND LIFE INSURANCE

The concepts of realization, basis, and cost recovery are further illustrated by the tax treatment of annuities and life insurance. Annuities are governed by § 72 of the Code. Regulations issued under that provision cover both annuities and life insurance proceeds paid while the insured is still living. Section 101 and the regulations thereunder govern life insurance proceeds paid on account of the death of the insured.

A.   ANNUITIES

NOTE ON THE TAXATION OF ANNUITIES

When a person transfers money or other property and receives from the transferee a promise to pay certain sums at intervals, the amount so paid is likely to be an annuity. It is clearly an annuity if the period of payment is measured by a life or lives. It may be an annuity if it is for a fixed period of years. Annuities often relate to a person's life expectancy. For example, you can buy an annuity that will pay you $100 each year for the rest of your life. The seller will use a table of average life expectancies to decide what you should pay for such an annuity. An individual may wish to provide for a constant flow of income after retirement. He might then purchase an annuity for a fixed premium that would pay him a constant sum each month from age 65 until his death. The amount of the premium will be determined by (1) the individual's life expectancy and (2) the return the insurance company expects to receive from investing the premium. The amount actually received by the individual under such an arrangement will depend on how long he lives.

Allocating the Cost. For tax purposes, the annuitant has income to the extent he receives more than he paid for the annuity. The investment in the annuity is, in effect, his "basis," which is recovered as annuity payments are received. It is therefore necessary to determine what portion of each payment is treated as tax-free recovery of basis and what portion is the taxable return on the investment.

Suppose the taxpayer purchases an annuity for $267.30 that will pay $100 a year for three years (an interest rate of 6 percent). It is clear that the total income from this transaction is $32.70, the excess of the $300 received over the $267.30 paid. The question is how this income is allocated to each of the three years of the annuity. There are several methods that might be used to determine the income tax consequences of annuity payments:

(1) There might be no tax on the receipts until the aggregate of receipts equalled the amount paid, after which everything would be taxable. Thus, basis is recovered first. This was the method used before there was any special provision for taxing annuities. See Burnet v. Logan, 283 U.S. 404, 414 (1931). In the above example, the taxpayer would report nothing for the first two years and $32.70 in the third year.

(2) A portion of each annuity payment could be treated as a recovery of investment and a portion could be treated as a taxable return. This is the approach of § 72, under which the entire amount that is expected to be received under the annuity is compared to the amount paid for the annuity. A ratable portion of each payment received is excluded from income in an amount expected to restore the capital in full when the final payment is received. The amount of payment excluded from income is determined by the "exclusion ratio," where the numerator is the investment in the contract and the denominator is the expected return. § 72(b). In the example above, the exclusion ratio is 89.1 percent and 89.1 percent of each payment is a recovery of capital. Thus, the taxpayer would report $10.90 each year.

(3) The third method is best seen by comparing the annuity to a bank account. Suppose a bank paid 6 percent interest on savings accounts, and the taxpayer put $267.30 into the bank and withdrew $100 at the end of each of the following three years. In a year, she would earn $16.04 of taxable interest, resulting in $283.34 in the account. If she then withdrew $100, she would still have $183.34 in the bank. After another year, she would earn $11 of taxable interest on the $183.34, for a total of $194.34. After withdrawing $100, she would have $94.34 in the bank. In a year, that sum would earn $5.66 of taxable interest, for a total of $100, which she would withdraw.:

Deposit Beginning of Year	Interest	Total	Withdrawal	Deposit Year–End
$267.30	$16.04	$283.34	$100	$183.34
183.34	11.00	194.34	100	94.34
94.34	5.66	100.00	100	0

If the taxpayer makes a loan of $267.30 at a 6 percent rate of interest to be paid back $100 a year for three years, the annual loan payments would be taxed just as the bank account above. A simple annuity works the same way, i.e., if 6 percent were an appropriate market rate of interest, the taxpayer could buy an annuity for $267.30. The annuity could be taxed just as the interest on a bank account or a loan would be: $16.04 of income in Year 1, $11 of income in Year 2 and $5.66 of income in Year 3.

It is the timing of the income inclusions that is important. Although the aggregate income reported is the same, the present value of the tax liabilities under the first and second methods are of course less than they are under the third method. This timing difference between the income inclusions of annuities and other economically similar transactions has produced efforts to disguise bank deposits, mutual funds, and other arrangements as annuities and countermoves by Congress and the Service. It is possible, for example, to buy an annuity with investment returns similar to a mutual fund, where the amounts distributed under the contract depend on the investment results. The result is extraordinary complexity. See, e.g. §§ 817(h), 72(q) and (u). Why doesn't Congress just tax an annuity as the interest accrues and avoid this complexity?

Deferred Annuities. Suppose the taxpayer purchases an annuity with payments to begin at some point in the future, for example, at retirement. During the period between the purchase date and the date when annuity payments begin, interest accrues on the annuity and typically the insurance company treats it as a return on the purchaser's investment. The interest, however, is not taxable as it accrues, but rather is taxed to the annuitant as he receives payment. § 72(b).

Under prior law, a withdrawal of an amount prior to the annuity starting date was treated as a return of capital and thus tax-free until the taxpayer's entire investment had been received. Insurance companies marketed these annuities, primarily because of the benefits of the tax deferral of the interest and the favorable treatment of early withdrawals. Apparently interested in protecting this tax advantage only when it fulfills long-term retirement goals, but not short-term investments, Congress added § 72(e), which treats cash withdrawals before the annuity starting date as income to the extent the cash value of the contract exceeds the owner's investment. Thus, when cash is withdrawn, interest is taxed first. In addition, § 72(q) imposes a penalty on amounts withdrawn before retirement. The penalty is 10 percent of the amount includible in income. The penalty does not apply if the payments are made after the annuitant has reached age 59½ or if by reason of the annuitant's death. Note that neither of these rules changes the deferral of interest if there is no cash withdrawal.

Why should annuities be treated more favorably than other investments producing interest? From time to time, Treasury has proposed taxing the annuitant currently on the interest on the grounds that the investment income is similar to that earned on other savings vehicles, that the rules favor insurance companies over other financial institutions and that generally only high income people with disposable income are able to take advantage of the rules.

There are other tax-favored vehicles for specific investment purposes. Individual retirement accounts, for example, are treated even more favorably than annuities; IRAs are taken up at page 773 infra. Section 529, for another example, provides for qualified state tuition programs, under which earnings are not taxed either as when they are earned or when distributed. Interest on U.S. government savings bonds can be included in income either as it accrues or when the bond is surrendered. § 454(c).

Mortality Gains and Losses. When the annuity is payable each year of a person's life, it is not certain from the outset how much will be received. The statute provides that, in such a case, the aggregate amount to be received, for determining the annual inclusion in income, is based on the life expectancy of the person or persons whose lives measure the period of the annuity. § 72(c)(3). Of course, the actual payments may be more or less than the amount determined based on the life expectancies. When the annuitant outlives the life expectancy, he is said to have a mortality gain on which he is taxed. § 72(b)(2). Where the annuitant dies prior to the expectancy, he has mortality losses and is able to deduct his unrecovered investment on his last income tax return. § 72(b)(3). Compare the treatment (or lack thereof) of mortality gains and losses on life insurance, discussed in the next Section. Is there a policy reason why they should be treated differently? With an annuity, mortality gains occur when the annuitant outlives her life expectancy; with life insurance the gains occur if the insured dies young. Perhaps Congress thought it would be easier to explain the tax in the annuity case.

B.   LIFE INSURANCE PROCEEDS

NOTE ON THE PREFERENTIAL TREATMENT OF LIFE INSURANCE SAVINGS

Life insurance generally consists of two elements.* The first is "pure insurance"—protection against the event of death during the period of coverage. The insured (or someone else) pays a premium in return for which a specified sum will be paid to his survivors in the event of his death. This generally is referred to as "term insurance." Term insurance involves essentially a gamble of the insurance premium on the odds that the insured will live through the term or period covered by the insurance. If the insured survives the period, his beneficiaries do not collect on the policy, and they "lose" their insurance gamble. But if the insured dies during the period covered by the term insurance, his beneficiaries receive the value for which his life was insured. Term insurance thus represents a bet against the mortality averages through which the insured endeavors to provide for his heirs.

All actual insurance, however, combines such pure term insurance with a savings element. The size of the savings component relative to the pure (or term) insurance component varies. In some life insurance contracts (for example, one- or five-year term policies), the savings element is small; in others (for example, whole life policies), it may be quite large.

The savings element easily can be seen in "ordinary life insurance"— the most popular form of cash-value life insurance—which involves the payment of a uniform annual premium throughout the life of the insured and matures at death. The annual premium (per dollar of coverage) of annual term insurance would rise over time because of the increasing likelihood of death. Eventually the cost of the term coverage would become quite burdensome. A uniform premium payable throughout the life of the insured (or over some specified shorter period) exceeds the actuarial cost of term insurance in the early years of the policy. A reserve is built up against the time when the actuarial cost of insurance would exceed the flat annual premium. The reserve is invested by the insurance company and increases over time because of interest earnings and because the premiums exceed the actuarial cost of insurance in the early years of the policy. The savings element, represented by the reserve accumulation, becomes apparent if one compares purchasing whole life insurance to purchasing pure term insur-

---

* This description of life insurance is drawn largely from Charles E. McLure, Jr. "The Income Tax Treatment of Interest Earned on Savings in Life Insurance" in Joint Economic Committee, the Economics of Federal Subsidy Programs: A Compilation of Papers, 92d Cong., 2d Sess. 370–92, July 15, 1972.

ance and investing the difference in cost in a bank account or other investment vehicle.

In recent years, a product that explicitly combines term insurance and savings has been marketed widely. This is so-called universal life insurance, whereby a person simultaneously purchases a contract for life insurance and deposits a sum with the insurance company. On a monthly basis, the life insurance company deducts from the amount deposited that month's premium for insurance (plus "loading and administrative fees") and then credits the insured's account with investment income on the balance. The insured is permitted to withdraw the balance in his account at any time, but if he fails to do so, it is paid to his beneficiaries at his death. (A penalty may be charged if the insured withdraws the balance in his account soon after it is opened.) There are also "variable life insurance" policies, where the premiums paid are invested in the stock market by the life insurance company and the proceeds payable on the death of the insured vary depending upon the success of the investments.

Earnings on savings invested in most kinds of interest-bearing assets are subject to income tax, either as they accrue or as they are realized. (An important exception is interest earned on investments in state and local bonds, discussed infra at page 212). Thus, interest on corporate bonds and on savings accounts with banks and savings and loan associations is taxable in the year earned. On the other hand, interest earned on the savings element of life insurance is largely or totally excluded from federal income taxation.

The basic rule about life insurance proceeds is that amounts paid "by reason of the death of the insured" are not subject to income tax—regardless of the amount of gain that actually may be involved. § 101(a). Thus, the interest earned on savings through life insurance, or any other return on the taxpayer's investment, and the portion of proceeds representing the amount covering the life insurance risk, are free of income tax if received by reason of the death of the insured.

Proceeds received upon the termination of a cash value policy through surrender, rather than because of the death of the insured, are taxable to the extent that they exceed the total cost of the policy. The proceeds received upon surrender of a policy consist of the return of the taxpayer's savings portion of policy premiums and the compound interest earned on those savings. Total policy costs consist of the cost of pure insurance protection enjoyed up to the time of surrender, the "loading fee" (the cost of writing the policy) and the savings portion of the premiums paid up to the surrender date. Thus, allowance of tax-free recovery of total policy costs implies that, for income tax purposes, the owner of the life insurance policy can offset the personal cost of insurance against the interest earned on the savings. Stated alternatively, he can reduce his interest income for tax purposes by the amount of his personal expenditure for insurance protection (up to the limit of the interest income earned). If, at the time of surrender, the total policy cost exceeds proceeds, interest earned on savings accumulated in cash value insurance is totally excluded from income for tax purposes. And even if proceeds from surrender of a cash value policy exceed the total cost of the policy, only the excess of proceeds over cost is taxed.

As a practical matter, therefore, taxpayers are not taxed annually on the investment income earned under a life insurance contract, even when amounts are withdrawn prior to death. Thus, whether realized through death or through surrender of the policy during the lifetime of the insured, interest earned on savings in life insurance receives favorable treatment under the income tax relative to the earnings on many other forms of saving. This preferential treatment is not offset by more burdensome than average corporate taxation of life insurance companies. The marketing of life insurance products often emphasizes its tax-advantaged quality.

Life insurance contracts are defined in § 7702 of the Code. This definition was added to the Code in an effort to limit the preferential treatment of life insurance proceeds to cases where an insurance element is genuinely present and significant. Such a provision was necessary to curb the proliferation of investment-oriented programs marketed with a minor life insurance element to take advantage of the tax preference for life insurance. The definition does not limit, however, the application of the § 101 exclusion to traditional whole life policies that accumulate based on reasonable interest rates. The intention is to disqualify contracts that build up excessive amounts of cash value relative to insurance risk. If a policy fails at any time to satisfy this life insurance definition, the policy is treated as a combination of term life insurance and an investment fund, with the income generated by the investment fund taxed to the policyholder.

Because of the exclusion of investment earnings, the attractiveness of life insurance rises with a taxpayer's marginal tax rate, and hence with income level and wealth. In order to get this exemption, however, it is necessary to purchase some insurance as well as the investment component of life insurance. Except to provide liquid assets in the event of death, the very wealthy may be less in need of life insurance than those in the lower and middle income groups; therefore, so long as the insurance component is relatively significant, the wealthy might find the pure insurance and investment package relatively unattractive because of the expenditure required for the pure risk component. For example, for taxpayers in the highest tax brackets, state and local bonds may be more attractive than cash value life insurance, because municipal bonds do not require a (possibly unwanted) expenditure on pure insurance protection and tend to allow more financial flexibility. This advantage diminishes, however, to the extent that life insurance can be designed as a tax-free investment vehicle—and even with the current statutory definition, it is sometimes possible (with interest rates in the 10 percent range) to have investment earnings as much as eight times as large as the cumulative insurance costs.

NOTES

(A) *Policy of the Exclusion.* Unlike annuities, mortality gains and losses on life insurance are ignored for tax purposes. This might be justified for both life insurance and annuities because, in the aggregate, the mortality gains and losses even out. Suppose for example, three individuals A, B, and C purchase $3,000 of term insurance for one year, paying a premium of $1,000. Assume further that the life insurance company expects that one will die within the year. If A dies, he has a mortality gain of $2,000 because $1,000 is a recovery of capital. B and C each have a mortality loss of $1,000. The mortality gains and losses wash out and thus, ignoring them for tax purposes could be defended as "rough justice." Taxing these gains when someone dies young seems harsh.

Interest earned on the savings in cash value life insurance, however, clearly receives preferential income tax treatment. Earnings on other types of savings are often fully taxed. What arguments would you advance for the preferential treatment of savings through life insurance? Is life insurance an especially important form of savings since it provides death benefits in the event of the untimely death of the insured and savings for retirement if the insured does not die early?

As part of its 1984 proposals for broadening the income tax base and lowering rates, the Treasury recommended that policyholders be required to include in current income increases in the cash surrender value of life insurance policies. The amount of income so computed would have been offset by the amount of the taxpayer's investment excluding the costs of term insurance. U.S. Treasury Dep't, Report to the President, Tax Reform for Fairness, Simplicity and Economic Growth, Vol. 2, at 258–62 (1984).

(B) *Case Law Requirement of Insurance Risk.* A person bought a life insurance policy and a life annuity contract at the same time, paying a single premium for the two contracts. The single premium was equal to the face value of the insurance contract. The taxpayer could not have bought the life insurance contract separately. He made his daughter beneficiary of the life policy and assigned the policy to her after it was issued. The Treasury ruled that since the required purchase of the annuity contract eliminated any risk to the insurer of premature death of the insured, the life policy was not insurance, and the proceeds were not excludable from gross income under § 101(a). Rev.Rul. 65–57, 1965–1 C.B. 56. See also Helvering v. Le Gierse, 312 U.S. 531, 539 (1941) ("risk shifting and risk distributing" are the heart of insurance).

(C) *Abusive Transactions.* In 1988, Congress took a step toward eliminating some of the tax benefits for certain policies, which it regarded as "abusive," now called "modified endowment contracts." See §§ 72(e) and 7702A. Essentially, these are policies more like investments than true insurance because they are funded more rapidly than would be needed to pay for the death benefits they provide. The basic test for determining whether a policy is a modified endowment contract looks to the amount of premiums paid during the first seven years and asks whether that amount paid is greater than what would have been paid had the contract provided for paid-up future life insurance benefits after seven level premiums. See § 7702A(b).

In general, amounts received under modified endowment contracts are treated first as income to the extent of the difference between the policy's cash surrender value and the taxpayer's investment. See § 72(e). Amounts received in excess of that difference are considered to be a recovery of capital. This reverses the usual rule that provides that amounts received under life insurance policies are treated first as a recovery of basis. In effect, this means that modified endowment contracts are treated like annuities with respect to amounts received prior to death; all such withdrawals are now taxable to the extent of accumulated income. Moreover, there is a 10 percent penalty on early withdrawals, and loans under these policies are considered income. § 72(e)(4) and (v).

By overstating certain charges to policyholders that were used to determine whether a policy qualified as life insurance, companies offered policies that passed the § 7702 test, but still afforded considerable tax deferred build-up. The statute now requires that these charges be tested under a reasonableness standard pursuant to regulations issued by Treasury. § 7702(c)(3).

(D) *Payments Before Death.* Congress amended Section 101 in 1996 to permit the exclusion of death benefits paid out to terminally ill insureds. Similarly, amounts received by a terminally ill taxpayer from the sale or assignment of any portion of a death benefit under a life insurance contract to a qualified person are also excluded from gross income. The purpose of this exclusion is to permit terminally ill patients—such as those with AIDS—to obtain the benefits of their insurance policy tax-free when they need it most, before death when expenses are high.

SECTION 7.   TRANSACTIONS INVOLVING BORROWED FUNDS

The income tax treatment of borrowing and lending is one of the most complex and conceptually difficult aspects of income taxation. The taxation of loans raises problems of universal application. Tax planners have contributed greatly to the confusion and complexity by taking advantage of the difficulty of distinguishing loans from other transactions that have similar economic consequences but dramatically different tax consequences. Thus, they have structured legal relationships as loans when favorable tax consequences flow from that characterization and as something else—for example, leases or ownership interests—when a loan would produce less favorable tax consequences.

This Section is an introduction to some of the issues that arise in answering the question "what is income?" when loans are involved. More detail about the deductibility of interest payments is found in Chapter 3, which deals with deductions and credits. Lending and borrowing transactions also raise questions about when income should be recognized and deductions should be allowed and those issues are largely deferred until Chapter 6. In addition, loans raise issues of assignment and allocation of income and deductions and some of these issues are taken up in Chapters 3 and 4. Finally, the tension between interest income, which is considered ordinary income, and capital gain is considered in Chapter 5.

A borrower does not realize income upon receipt of a loan, regardless of how the loan proceeds are used. Similarly, he has no deduction when he makes principal payments on the loan. Likewise, the lender does not have a deductible loss upon making the loan and does not realize income on the repayment of the loan principal; the repayment is a recovery of capital. These results are appropriate because there is no change in the net worth of either party. It may be useful to refer to the lender and borrower's balance sheets. The increase in the borrower's assets is offset by an equivalent liability to repay. When the borrower pays off the loan, his assets decrease, but so do his liabilities. The decrease in the lender's assets is offset by the borrower's promise to pay. In entering into an arm's length transaction, the parties have merely exchanged one form of property for another—that is, a sum of money for a promise to repay that sum at a future date. As time passes, the lender will earn income on the transaction in the form of interest, a payment for the use or forbearance of money.

Suppose the borrower does not pay back the loan. If his debt is paid by another, he would have income under *Old Colony Trust Co.*, or it might be a nontaxable gift. If, however, the debt is subsequently cancelled for less than its face value, he is considered to have income. § 61(a)(12). For example, a taxpayer whose $10,000 debt is cancelled upon payment of $7,000 generally is deemed to have $3,000 cancellation of indebtedness income. As the following case demonstrates, people who have embezzled or extorted funds from another have sometimes attempted to exclude the proceeds as "borrowing."

A. ILLEGAL INCOME

Collins v. Commissioner

United States Court of Appeals, Second Circuit, 1993. 3 F.3d 625.

CARDAMONE, CIRCUIT JUDGE:

Collins was employed as a ticket vendor and computer operator at an Off–Track Betting (OTB) parlor in Auburn, New York. OTB runs a network of 298 betting parlors in New York State that permit patrons to place legal wagers on horse races without actually going to the track. Operating as a cash business, OTB does not extend credit to those making bets at its parlors. It also has a strict policy against employee betting on horse races. Collins, an apparently compulsive gambler, ignored these regulations and occasionally placed bets on his own behalf in his computer without paying for them. Until July 17, 1988 he had always managed to cover those bets without detection. On that date, appellant decided he "would like some money" and on credit punched up for himself a total of $80,280 in betting tickets.

* * *

[After betting on 10 races] Collins was behind $38,105 for the day. At the close of the races Collins put his $42,175 in winning tickets in his OTB drawer and reported his bets and his losing ticket shortfall to his supervisor, who until then had not been aware of Collins' gambling activities. She called the police, and in police custody Collins signed an affidavit admitting what he had done. On October 27, 1988 he pled guilty to one count of grand larceny. * * *

A. General Principles

In addressing the argument Collins raises regarding the tax treatment of his illegal actions, we believe it useful to set out initially the basic principles underlying the definition of gross income. Internal Revenue Code § 61 defines gross income broadly as "all income from whatever source derived." It then categorizes 15 common items that constitute gross income, a list that includes interest, rents, royalties, salaries, annuities, and dividends, among others. Gross income, as § 61 specifically states, is "not limited to" the enumerated items.

Defining gross income as "all income" is admittedly somewhat tautological. In the early days of the tax code, the Supreme Court recognized this problem and attempted to provide a more workable and perhaps somewhat more limited definition for the term. It defined income in Eisner v. Macomber, 252 U.S. 189 (1920), " 'as gain derived from capital, from labor, or from both combined,' provided it be understood to include profit gained through a sale or conversion of capital assets * * *." Id. at 207 (quoting Doyle v. Mitchell Bros. Co., 247 U.S. 179, 185 (1918)).

It soon became evident that this definition created more problems than it solved. Under the Eisner formulation questions arose as to whether gains from cancellation of indebtedness or embezzlement—which do not fall neatly into either the labor or capital categories—constituted gross income * * * Acknowledging the defects in the Eisner definition, the Supreme Court began to steer away from it. For example, in United States v. Kirby Lumber Co., 284 U.S. 1, 3 (1931), it held that gains from the retirement of corporate bonds by their issuer at less than their issuing price were includable in gross income. Justice Holmes, writing for the Court, reached this conclusion despite the fact that the gains were not clearly derived from either capital or labor. In so doing he adverted to the futility of attempting to capture the concept of income and encapsulate it within a phrase.

The Court finally abandoned the stilted capital-labor formulation of gross income and jettisoned its earlier attempts to define the term in Commissioner v. Glenshaw Glass Co., 348 U.S. 426, 430–31 (1954). There the taxpayers had received treble damage awards from successfully prosecuting antitrust suits. They argued that two-thirds of these awards constituted punishment imposed on the wrongdoer and, under the gross income definition of Eisner, this punitive portion of the damages could not be treated as income derived from either labor or capital. In rebuffing this proposition, the Court ruled the damage awards taxable in their entirety. It cast aside Eisner's definition of income stating that it was "not meant to provide a touchstone to all future gross income questions." Instead the Court stated, "Congress applied no limitations as to the source of taxable receipts, nor restrictive labels as to their nature." Id. at 429–30. The legislature intended to simply tax "all gains," which the Court effectively described as all "accessions to wealth, clearly realized, and over which the taxpayers have complete dominion."

Since Glenshaw Glass the term gross income has been read expansively to include all realized gains and forms of enrichment, that is, "all gains except those specifically exempted." Id. at 430. Under this broad definition, gross income does not include all moneys a taxpayer receives. It is quite plain, for instance, that gross income does not include money acquired from borrowings. Loans do not result in realized gains or enrichment because any increase in net worth from proceeds of a loan is offset by a corresponding obligation to repay it.

This well-established principle on borrowing initially gave rise to another nettlesome question on how embezzled funds were to be treated. The Supreme Court once believed that money illegally procured from another was not gross income for tax purposes when the acquiror was legally obligated, like a legitimate borrower, to return the funds. See Commissioner v. Wilcox, 327 U.S. 404, 408–09 (1946). In Rutkin v. United States, 343 U.S. 130, 136–38 (1952), the Court partially and somewhat unsatisfactorily abandoned that view, holding that an extortionist, unlike an embezzler, was obligated to pay tax on his ill-gotten gains because he was unlikely to be asked to repay the money.

Rutkin left the law on embezzlement in a murky state. This condition cleared in James v. United States, 366 U.S. 213, 218 (1961). There the Court stated unequivocally that all unlawful gains are taxable. It reasoned that embezzlers, along with others who procure money illegally, should not be able to escape taxes while honest citizens pay taxes on "every conceivable type of income." Id. at 221. Thus, under James, a taxpayer has received income when she "acquires earnings, lawfully or unlawfully, without the consensual recognition, express or implied, of an obligation to repay and without restriction as to their disposition * * *." Id. at 219. This income test includes all forms of enrichment, legal or otherwise, but explicitly excludes loans.

Distinguishing loans from unlawful taxable gains has not usually proved difficult. Loans are identified by the mutual understanding between the borrower and lender of the obligation to repay and a bona fide intent on the borrower's part to repay the acquired funds. Accordingly, in Buff v. Commissioner, 496 F.2d 847, 849 (2d Cir.1974), we found an embezzler who confessed to his crime and within the same year signed a judgment agreeing to make repayment had received a taxable gain as opposed to a loan because he never had any intention of repaying the money. The embezzler's expressed consent to repay the loan, we determined, "was not worth the paper it was written on." Id. The mere act of signing such a consent could not be used to escape tax liability.

It is important to note, in addition, that though an embezzler must under the James test include as taxable income all amounts illegally acquired, the taxpayer may ordinarily claim a tax deduction for payments she makes in restitution. Such a deduction is available for the tax year in which the repayments are made. See § 165(c); James, 366 U.S. at 220 * * *

B. Principles Applied

With this outline of the relevant legal principles in mind, we have little difficulty in holding that Collins' illegal activities gave rise to gross income. Under the expansive definitions of income advanced in Glenshaw Glass and James, larceny of any kind resulting in an unrestricted gain of moneys to a wrongdoer is a taxable event. Taxes may be assessed in the year in which the taxpayer realizes an economic benefit from his actions. In this case, Collins admitted to stealing racing tickets from OTB on July 17, 1988. This larceny resulted in the taxpayer's enrichment: he had the pleasure of betting on horses running at the Finger Lakes Race Track. Individuals purchase racing tickets from OTB because these tickets give them the pleasure of attempting to make money simply by correctly predicting the outcomes of horse races. By punching up tickets on his computer without paying for them, Collins appropriated for himself the same benefit that patrons of OTB pay money to receive. This illegally-appropriated benefit, as the tax court correctly concluded, constituted gross income to Collins in 1988.

The taxpayer raises a series of objections to this conclusion. He first insists that such a holding cannot be correct because at the end of the day he was in debt by $38,105. He asserts that a tax is being assessed on his losses rather than on any possible gain. What may seem at first glance a rather anomalous result is explained by distinguishing between Collins' theft and his gambling activities. Collins took illegally acquired assets and spent them unwisely by betting on losing horses at a racetrack.

Although the bets gave rise to gambling losses, the taxpayer gained from the misappropriation of his employer's property without its knowledge or permission. The gambling loss is not relevant to and does not offset Collins' gain in the form of opportunities to gamble that he obtained by virtue of his embezzlement. Collins' situation is quite the same as that of any other individual who embezzles money from his employer and subsequently loses it at the racetrack. Such person would properly have his illegally-acquired assets included in his gross income. Further, taxpayer would not be able to deduct gambling losses from theft income because the Internal Revenue Code only allows gambling losses to offset gambling winnings. See § 165(d). Collins is being treated the same way.

The taxpayer next contends his larceny resulted in no taxable gain because he recognized that he had an obligation to repay his employer for the stolen tickets. He posits that recognition of a repayment obligation transformed a wrongful appropriation into a nontaxable transaction. In effect, Collins tries to revive pre-James law under which an embezzler's gain could be found nontaxable due to the embezzler's duty to repay stolen funds. Yet, the Supreme Court has clearly abandoned the pre-James view and ruled instead that only a loan, with its attendant "consensual recognition" of the obligation to repay, is not taxable. See James, 366 U.S. at 219 (emphasis added). There was no loan of funds, nor was there any "consensual recognition" here: OTB never gave Collins permission to use betting tickets. * * * His unilateral intention to pay for the stolen property did not transform a theft into a loan within the meaning of James. * * *

The taxpayer then avers this case is analogous to Gilbert v. Commissioner, 552 F.2d 478 (2d Cir.1977), in which we found a consensual recognition of the obligation to repay despite the absence of a loan agreement. Taxpayer Edward Gilbert, as president and a director of E.L. Bruce Company, acquired on margin a substantial personal stake in the stock of a rival company, Celotex Corporation, intending to bring about a merger between Celotex and E.L. Bruce. The stock market declined after Gilbert bought these shares, and he was required to meet several margin calls. Lacking personal funds to meet these obligations, Gilbert instructed the corporate secretary of E.L. Bruce to make $1.9 million in margin payments on his behalf. A few days later, Gilbert signed secured promissory notes to repay the funds; but, the corporation's board of directors refused to ratify Gilbert's unauthorized withdrawal, demanded his resignation, and called in his notes. The board also declined to merge with Celotex, and soon thereafter the Celotex stock that Gilbert owned became essentially worthless. Gilbert could not repay his obligations to E.L. Bruce, and he eventually pled guilty to federal and state charges of unlawfully withdrawing funds from the corporation.

The IRS claimed that Gilbert's unauthorized withdrawal of funds constituted income to the taxpayer. It asserted that there was no consensual recognition of a repayment obligation because E.L. Bruce Company's board of directors was unaware of and subsequently disapproved Gilbert's actions. Citing the highly atypical nature of the case, we held that Gilbert did not realize income under the James test because (1) he not only "fully" intended but also expected "with reasonable certainty" to repay the sums taken, (2) he believed his withdrawals would be approved by the corporate board, and (3) he made prompt assignment of assets sufficient to secure the amount he owed. These facts evidenced consensual recognition and distinguished Gilbert from the more typical embezzlement case where the embezzler plans right from the beginning to abscond with the embezzled funds.

Plainly, none of the significant facts of Gilbert are present in the case at hand. Collins, unlike Gilbert, never expected to be able to repay the stolen funds. He was in no position to do so. The amount he owed OTB was three times his annual salary—a far cry from Gilbert, where the taxpayer assigned to the corporation enough assets to cover his unauthorized withdrawals. Also in contrast to Gilbert, Collins could not have believed that his employer would subsequently ratify his transactions. He knew that OTB had strict rules against employee betting. Moreover, while Gilbert was motivated by a desire to assist his corporation, Collins embezzled betting tickets because he wanted to make some money. Collins' purpose makes this a garden variety type of embezzlement case, not to be confused with a loan. Gilbert is therefore an inapposite precedent.

Finally, appellant complains of the root unfairness and harshness of the result, declaring that the imposition of a tax on his July 17 transaction is an attempt to use the income tax law to punish misconduct that has already been appropriately punished under the criminal law. Although we are not without some sympathy to the taxpayer's plight, we are unable to adopt his claim of unfairness and use it as a basis to negate the imposition of a tax on his income. The Supreme Court has repeatedly emphasized that taxing an embezzler on his illicit gains accords with the fair administration of the tax law because it removes the anomaly of having the income of an honest individual taxed while the similar gains of a criminal are not. See James, 366 U.S. at 218; Rutkin, 343 U.S. at 137–38. Thus, there is no double penalty in having a taxpayer prosecuted for the crime that resulted in his obtaining ill-gotten gains and subsequently being required to pay taxes on those illegal gains. Such is not an unduly harsh result because Internal Revenue Code § 165 provides that once the taxpayer makes restitution payments to OTB or its insurer, he will be able in that year to deduct the amount of those payments from his gross income. See § 165(c).

* * *

Having determined that the July 17 transaction resulted in a taxable gain to Collins, we next consider how that gain should be measured. It is well-settled that income received in a form other than cash is taxed at its fair market value at the time of its receipt. * * *

Based on this measure the value of Collins' tickets was the price at which they would have changed hands between legitimate bettors and OTB. This price was the retail price or face value of the tickets. Accordingly, the Tax Court properly found that the stolen tickets were worth $80,280, their retail price, and this amount was correctly included in the taxpayer's gross income, as a gain from theft. From that figure Collins was entitled to a deduction for restitution he made to OTB in 1988. Collins returned to his till on July 17 winning tickets with a face value of $42,175.

* * *

NOTES

(A) *Getting Caught Quickly Does Not Solve the Tax Problems.* What if the embezzler is caught while he still has some or all of the money? The taxpayer/embezzler is entitled to a deduction in the year in which he actually repays or forfeits the illegally obtained gains. Rev. Rul. 65–254, 1965–2 C.B. 50, held that a deduction is available under § 165(c)(2).; Stephens v. Commissioner, 905 F.2d 667 (2d Cir.1990) allowed a deduction under § 162(c). In Ianniello v. Commissioner, 98 T.C. 165 (1992), the taxpayer, known as "Matty the Horse," was convicted of a RICO violation for skimming restaurant receipts. The court held that the receipts were taxable income even though title to the receipts vested in the United States immediately. Thus, the taxpayer has income in the year of embezzlement, followed by a deduction in the year of forfeiture. Does that ordinarily make the taxpayer whole?

(B) *Embezzlement vs. Loans.* In Hobson v. Commissioner, 63 T.C.M. 3085 (1992), the taxpayer, a branch manager of a bank, surreptitiously deposited funds in the account of a long-time, but uncreditworthy customer. These amounts were not repaid although the court, suspending disbelief, took at face value the customer's statement that he knew the illegitimate deposits were advances required to be repaid. Thus, the court found that this case was like *Gilbert,* discussed in *Collins,* because there was a consensual obligation to repay. In an extraordinary—and not likely to be followed—narrowing of *James,* the court interpreted that case to apply only when the embezzler personally benefits from the funds.

(C) *Consensual Agreement.* In *James,* the Court requires a consensual recognition of an obligation to repay. Why? Doesn't an embezzler (or for that matter an armed robber) have a legal obligation to repay regardless of whether the victim knows of the "theft"? *James* implies that the usual loan rule has no application because the embezzler has no intention to repay.

The taxes collected from the thief usually come from the stolen funds that would otherwise be returned to the victim. In the usual case, the claim for taxes has priority over the victim's claim for the stolen funds. See § 6321.

(D) *Illegal Income*. The fact that gain arises out of illegal activity does not result in its exclusion from income. For example, in United States v. Sullivan, 274 U.S. 259 (1927), the Supreme Court held that the income of a bootlegger was subject to tax notwithstanding its illegal origin. The Court stated: "We see no reason * * * why the fact that a business is unlawful should exempt it from paying the taxes that if lawful it would have to pay."

(E) *Constitutional Implications*. The taxation of illegal income raises several questions of constitutional dimensions. The Supreme Court has held that the requirement that an individual disclose illegal income on a tax return does not constitute compulsory self-incrimination under the Fifth Amendment. In United States v. Sullivan, supra, the Court said:

> If the form of the return provided called for answers that the defendant was privileged from making he could have raised the objection in the return, but could not on that account refuse to make any return at all.

If the taxpayer has income from drug dealing, for example, he is required to file a return and required to disclose the amount of taxable income, but is not required to reveal its source.

In Couch v. United States, 409 U.S. 322 (1973), the Supreme Court rejected the taxpayer's attempt to invoke her Fifth Amendment claim of self-incrimination against an IRS summons directing her to produce business and tax records in the possession of her accountant. The Court emphasized the "personal" nature of the Fifth Amendment privilege, noting that the privilege "adheres basically to the person, not to information that may incriminate him." Notwithstanding these decisions, however, the precise scope of the self-incrimination privilege in connection with tax return information remains uncertain.

(F) *Enforcement of Criminal Laws to Get Tax Information*. The taxpayer in United States v. Baggot, 463 U.S. 476 (1983), was the target of a grand jury investigation into a scheme to use sham commodities transactions to create paper losses that were deducted on his tax returns. He was never indicted, but he pled guilty to two misdemeanor violations of the Commodities Exchange Act. The Supreme Court rejected the government's attempts to obtain grand jury transcripts and documents for use in an audit to determine Baggot's tax liability. In dissent, Chief Justice Burger argued that the decision would require agencies to duplicate investigations and prevent potentially meritorious administrative actions.

(G) *Enforcement of Nontax Criminal Laws*. From time to time, criminal tax violations have been used principally to enforce nontax criminal statutes. The two most famous instances involve Al Capone's criminal tax conviction, his only criminal conviction, and the resignation of Spiro Agnew as Vice President of the United States following a plea of nolo contendere to a criminal tax charge for failure to report income from bribes and kickbacks.

The use of federal tax laws to enforce state criminal laws was criticized by Justice Black in his dissenting opinion in Rutkin v. United States, 343 U.S. 130, 139–41 (1952):

> To all intents and purposes, bootleggers and gamblers are engaged in going businesses and make regular business profits which should be taxed * * *. However, in my judgement it stretches previous tax interpretations too far to classify the sporadic loot of an embezzler, an extortioner or a robber as taxable earnings gained from a business, trade or profession. I just do not think Congress intended to treat the plunder of such criminals as theirs.

> It seems illusory to believe, as the majority apparently does, that the burden on honest American taxpayers will be lightened by a governmental policy of pursuing extortioners in futile efforts to collect income taxes. I venture the guess that this one trial has cost United States taxpayers more money than the Government will collect in taxes from extortioners in the next twenty-five years. If this statute is to be interpreted on the basis of what is financially best for honest taxpayers, it probably should be construed so as to save money by eliminating federal prosecutions of state crimes under the guise of punishing tax evaders.

> * * *

> [Today's decision gives] Washington more and more power to punish purely local crimes such as embezzlement and extortion. [It] illustrates an expansion of federal criminal jurisdiction into fields of law enforcement heretofore wholly left to states and local communities. I doubt if this expansion is wise from the standpoint of the United States or the states.

Is it wrong for the federal government to use enforcement of the tax law to convict individuals who have engaged in nontax crimes? Should it matter whether a state or federal crime is involved?

B.   DISCHARGES OF INDEBTEDNESS

In an early case, the Supreme Court found that a corporation had taxable income when it repurchased in the market at less than par bonds that had been issued earlier in the year at par. United States v. Kirby Lumber, 284 U.S. 1 (1931). The *Kirby Lumber* principle is codified in § 61(a)(12), which provides that gross income includes "income from discharge of indebtedness." This result could be reached by either of two approaches. Using a balance sheet analogy, taxation becomes appropriate when the net worth of the taxpayer is increased by the cancellation of indebtedness—that is, the liability is erased without decreasing assets. This approach suggests that taxation may not be warranted if there is no increase in net worth; for example, if the taxpayer is insolvent before and after the transaction. Under a second view, immediate inclusion in income of the loan proceeds was not required on the grounds that the loan will be repaid. If it is not, the failure to repay is a taxable event. Under this theory, characterization of the original transaction as a loan may be critical. Section 108 contains a number of statutory exceptions to the *Kirby Lumber* rule and to § 61(a)(12), some of which are discussed in the following case and the notes following. Where the original consideration for the borrower's debt is not cash equal to the face amount of the debt, the courts have had more difficulty determining if there is cancellation of indebtedness income, as the following case illustrates.

Zarin v. Commissioner Of Internal Revenue

United States Tax Court, 1989. 92 T.C. 1084.

COHEN, JUDGE: * * * * David Zarin (petitioner) occasionally stayed at Resorts International Hotel, Inc. (Resorts), in Atlantic City. * * * In June 1978, petitioner applied to Resorts for a $10,000 line of credit to be used for gambling. After a credit check, which included inquiries with petitioner's banks and "Credit Central," an organization that maintains records of individuals who gamble in casinos, the requested line of credit was granted, despite derogatory information received from Credit Central.

The game most often played by petitioner, craps, creates the potential of losses or gains from wagering on rolls of dice. When he played craps at Resorts, petitioner usually bet the table limit per roll of the dice. Resorts quickly became familiar with petitioner. At petitioner's request, Resorts would raise the limit at the table to the house maximum. * * *

By November 1979, petitioner's permanent line of credit had been increased to $200,000. Despite this increase, at no time after the initial credit check did Resorts perform any further analysis of petitioner's credit-worthiness. Many casinos extend complimentary services and privileges ("comps") to retain the patronage of their best customers. Beginning in the late summer of 1978, petitioner was extended the complimentary use of a luxury three-room suite at Resorts. Resorts progressively increased the complimentary services to include free meals, entertainment, and 24–hour access to a limousine. * * *

Once the line of credit was established, petitioner was able to receive chips at the gambling table. Patrons of New Jersey casinos may not gamble with currency, but must use chips provided by the casino. Chips may not be used outside the casino where they were issued for any purpose.

Petitioner received chips in exchange for signing counter checks, commonly known as "markers." The markers were negotiable drafts payable to Resorts drawn on petitioner's bank. The markers made no reference to chips, but stated that cash had been received.

Petitioner had an understanding with Gary Grant, the credit manager at Resorts, whereby the markers would be held for the maximum period allowable under New Jersey law, which at that time was 90 days, whereupon petitioner would redeem them with a personal check. At all times pertinent hereto, petitioner intended to repay any credit amount properly extended to him by Resorts and to pay Resorts in full the amount of any personal check given by him to pay for chips or to reduce his gambling debt. Between June 1978 and December 1979, petitioner incurred gambling debts of approximately $2.5 million. Petitioner paid these debts in full. * * *

After [problems with the state casino control commission arose], Resorts began a policy of treating petitioner's personal checks as "considered cleared." Thus, when petitioner wrote a personal check it was treated as a cash transaction, and the amount of the check was not included in determining whether he had reached his permanent credit limit. * * *

By January 1980, petitioner was gambling compulsively at Resorts. Petitioner was gambling 12–16 hours per day, 7 days per week in the casino, and he was betting up to $15,000 on each roll of the dice. Petitioner was not aware of the amount of his gambling debts.

On April 12, 1980, Resorts increased petitioner's permanent credit line to $215,000, without any additional credit investigation. During April 1980, petitioner delivered personal checks and markers in the total amount of $3,435,000 that were returned to Resorts as having been drawn against insufficient funds. On April 29, 1980, Resorts cut off petitioner's credit. Shortly thereafter, petitioner indicated to the Chief Executive Officer of Resorts that he intended to repay the obligations.

On November 18, 1980, Resorts filed a complaint in New Jersey state court seeking collection of $3,435,000 from petitioner based on the unpaid personal checks and markers. On March 4, 1981, petitioner filed an answer, denying the allegations and asserting a variety of affirmative defenses.

On September 28, 1981, petitioner settled the Resorts suit by agreeing to make a series of payments totaling $500,000. Petitioner paid the $500,000 settlement amount to Resorts in accordance with the terms of the agreement. The difference between petitioner's gambling obligations of $3,435,000 and the settlement payments of $500,000 is the amount that respondent alleges to be income from forgiveness of indebtedness.

* * *

Income From the Discharge of Indebtedness

In general, gross income includes all income from whatever source derived, including income from the discharge of indebtedness. Sec. 61(a)(12). Not all discharges of indebtedness, however, result in income. See sec. 1.61–12(a), Income Tax Regs., "The discharge of indebtedness, in whole or in part, *may* result in the realization of income." (Emphasis supplied.) The gain to the debtor from such discharge is the resultant freeing up of his assets that he would otherwise have been required to use to pay the debt. See United States v. Kirby Lumber Co., 284 U.S. 1 (1931).

Respondent contends that the difference between the $3,435,000 in personal checks and markers that were returned by the banks as drawn against insufficient funds and the $500,000 paid by petitioner in settlement of the Resorts suit constitutes income from the discharge of indebtedness. Petitioner argues that the settlement agreement between Resorts and himself did not give rise to such income because, among other reasons, the debt instruments were not enforceable under New Jersey law and, in any event, the settlement should be treated as a purchase price adjustment that does not give rise to income from the discharge of indebtedness.

Enforceability

* * *

Petitioner received credit of $3,435,000 from Resorts. He treated these amounts as a loan, not reporting any income on his 1980 tax return. * * * The parties have stipulated that he intended to repay the amounts received. Although Resorts extended the credit to petitioner with the expectation that he would continue to gamble, theoretically petitioner could have redeemed the chips for cash. Certainly if he had won, rather than lost, at gambling, the amounts borrowed would have been repaid.

Petitioner argues that he did not get anything of value when he received the chips other than the "opportunity to gamble," and that, by reason of his addiction to gambling, he was destined to lose everything that he temporarily received. Thus, he is in effect arguing, * * * that the settlement merely reduced the amount of his loss and did not result in income.

We have no doubt that an increase in wealth from the cancellation of indebtedness is taxable where the taxpayer received something of value in exchange for the indebtedness.

We conclude here that the taxpayer did receive value at the time he incurred the debt and that only his promise to repay the value received prevented taxation of the value received at the time of the credit transaction. When, in the subsequent year, a portion of the obligation to repay was forgiven, the general rule that income results from forgiveness of indebtedness, section 61(a)(12), should apply.

Legal enforceability of an obligation to repay is not generally determinative of whether the receipt of money or property is taxable. James v. United States, 366 U.S. 213, 219 (1961).

Here the timing of recognition was set when the debt was compromised. The amount to be recognized as income is the part of the debt that was discharged without payment. The enforceability of petitioner's debts under New Jersey law did not affect either the timing or the amount and thus is not determinative for Federal income tax purposes. We are not persuaded that gambling debts should be accorded any special treatment for the benefit of the gambler—compulsive or not.

* * *

Disputed Debt

Petitioner also relies on the principle that settlement of disputed debts does not give rise to income. * * * Prior to the settlement, the amount of petitioner's gambling debt to Resorts was a liquidated amount. * * * There is no dispute about the amount petitioner received. The parties dispute only its legal enforceability, i.e., whether petitioner could be legally compelled to pay Resorts the fixed amount he had borrowed. A genuine dispute does not exist merely because petitioner required Resorts to sue him before making payment of any amount on the debt. In our view, petitioner's arguments concerning his defenses to Resorts' claim, which apparently led to Resorts' agreement to discount the debt, are overcome by (1) the stipulation of the parties that, at the time the debt was created, petitioner agreed to and intended to repay the full amount, and (2) our conclusion that he received full value for what he agreed to pay, i.e., over $3 million worth of chips and the benefits received by petitioner as a "valued gambling patron" of Resorts.

Deductibility of Gambling Losses

In several different ways, petitioner argues that any income from discharge of his gambling debt was income from gambling against which he may offset his losses; thus, he argues, he had no net income from gambling.

Section 165(d) provides that "Losses from wagering transactions shall be allowed only to the extent of the gains from such transactions." Neither section 165(d) nor section 1.165–10, Income Tax Regs., defines what items are included as gains from wagering transactions. The regulation, however, provides that wagering losses "shall be allowed as a deduction but only to the extent of the gains *during the taxable years* from such transactions." (Emphasis supplied.) Petitioner incurred gambling losses in 1980, but his gain from the discharge of his gambling debts occurred in 1981. That gain is separate and apart from the losses he incurred from his actual wagering transactions. We have no evidence of his actual wagering gains and losses for either year. If we were to effectively allow petitioner to deduct the value of the lost chips from the value of the discharged debt, we would ignore annual accounting and undermine section 165(d) by in effect allowing gambling losses in excess of gambling winnings.

Purchase Money Debt Reduction

Petitioner argues that the settlement with Resorts should be treated as a purchase price adjustment that does not give rise to income from the discharge of indebtedness. * * * All gambling must be done with chips provided by the casino. Such chips are property which are not negotiable and may not be used to gamble or for any other purpose outside the casino where they were issued. Respondent argues that petitioner actually received "cash" in return for his debts. * * *

For a reduction in the amount of a debt to be treated as a purchase price adjustment under section 108(e)(5), the following conditions must be met: (1) The debt must be that of a purchaser of property to the seller which arose out of the purchase of such property; (2) the taxpayer must be solvent and not in bankruptcy when the debt reduction occurs; and (3) except for section 108(e)(5), the debt reduction would otherwise have resulted in discharge of indebtedness income. * * *

In addition to the literal statutory requirements, the legislative history indicates that section 108(e)(5) was intended to apply only if the following requirements are also met: (a) The price reduction must result from an agreement between the purchaser and the seller and not, for example, from a discharge as a result of the bar of the statute of limitations on enforcement of the obligation; (b) there has been no transfer of the debt by the seller to a third party; and (c) there has been no transfer of the purchased property from the purchaser to a third party. * * *

It seems to us that the value received by petitioner in exchange for the credit extended by Resorts does not constitute the type of property to which section 108(e)(5) was intended to or reasonably can be applied. Petitioner argued throughout his briefs that he purchased only "the opportunity to gamble" and that the chips had little or no value. We agree with his description of what he bargained for but not with his conclusion about the legal effect.

Petitioner [asserts he] purchased the opportunity to gamble as he received chips in exchange for his markers. * * * Petitioner [also asserts that] in entering into the gaming transactions with Resorts, [he] did not receive any item of tangible value. In support of an argument that "A debt incurred by a casino patron to acquire gambling opportunity is not a typical commercial debt and as such should not be treated as a typical commercial debt," petitioner argues:

> In addition to the character of the gambling debt being different than a typical commercial debt, the Petitioner–Resorts gambling transactions did not occur in the normal commercial debtor-creditor relationship in which a debtor borrows funds from a creditor and uses the loan proceeds elsewhere or uses the funds as purchase money for which he acquires something of value. Petitioner received gambling chips from Resorts. He then promptly gambled and lost the entire amount of chips at Resorts. Petitioner received no consideration from Resorts and was, in fact, $500,000 poorer from his transactions, while Resorts parted with nothing. * * * Accordingly, the only value represented by the chips is their potential income earning power. * * *

The "opportunity to gamble" would not in the usual sense of the words be "property" transferred from a seller to a purchaser. The terminology used in section 108(e)(5) is readily understood with respect to tangible property and may apply to some types of intangibles. Abstract concepts of property are not useful, however, in deciding whether what petitioner received is within the contemplation of the section. * * *

We conclude that petitioner's settlement with Resorts cannot be construed as a "purchase-money debt reduction" arising from the purchase of property within the meaning of section 108(e)(5).

TANNENWALD, J., dissenting: The foundation of the majority's reasoning is that Mr. Zarin realized income in an amount equal to the amount of the credit extended to him because he was afforded the "opportunity to gamble." Based upon that theory, the majority concludes that Mr. Zarin is seeking to reduce the amount of his loss. * * *

I think it highly significant that in all the decided cases involving the cancellation of indebtedness, the taxpayer had, in a prior year when the indebtedness was created, received a nontaxable benefit clearly measurable in monetary terms which would remain untaxed if the subsequent cancellation of the indebtedness were held to be tax free. Such is simply not the case herein. The concept that petitioner received his money's worth from the enjoyment of using the chips (thus equating the pleasure of gambling with increase in wealth) produces the incongruous result that the more a gambler loses, the greater his pleasure and the larger the increase in his wealth. Under the circumstances, I think the issue of enforceability becomes critical. In this connection, the repeated emphasis by the majority on the stipulation that Mr. Zarin intended to repay the full amount at the time the debt was created is beside the point. If the debt was unenforceable under New Jersey law, that intent is irrelevant.

In resolving that issue, I think it significant that because the debts involved herein were unenforceable *from the moment that they were created,* there was no freeing up of petitioners' assets when they were discharged, see United States v. Kirby Lumber Co., supra, and therefore there was no increase in petitioners' wealth that could constitute income. Cf. Commissioner v. Glenshaw Glass Co., supra. This is particularly true in light of the fact that the chips were given to Mr. Zarin with the expectation that he would continue to gamble and, therefore, did not constitute an increase in his wealth when he received them in the same sense that the proceeds of a non-gambling loan would. Cf. Rail Joint Co. v. Commissioner, 22 B.T.A. 1277 (1931), affd, 61 F.2d 751 (2d Cir.1932) (cited in Commissioner v. Tufts, 461 U.S. at 209 n. 6), where we held that there was no income from the discharge on indebtedness when the amount paid for the discharge was in excess of the value of what had been received by the debtor at the time the indebtedness was created even though the face amount of the indebtedness and hence the taxpayer's liability was reduced; Fashion Park, Inc. v. Commissioner, 21 T.C. 600 (1954) (same holding). * * *

JACOBS, J., dissenting: In my opinion, petitioner's obligation to Resorts was void ab initio, and therefore, I would first hold that petitioner realized income (herein referred to as chip income) in 1980 (a year at issue) to the extent of the value of the chips received.

It is apparent that petitioner left the chips he obtained through the extension of credit by Resorts on Resorts' gambling tables. For had he won, his markers undoubtedly would have been paid, and this case would not be before us. Accordingly, I would next hold that the amount of petitioner's losses from wagering activities in 1980 equalled or exceeded the amount of chip income.

I recognize that section 165(d) limits losses from wagering transactions to the extent of gains from such transactions. In my opinion, for purposes of section 165(d), the chip income constitutes gain from a wagering transaction, because no such income would have been realized but for the wagering transactions in which petitioner's losses occurred. Thus, I would hold that petitioner is entitled to deduct in 1980 his gambling losses to the extent of the chip income.

While I believe the preceding analysis resolves the tax consequences of petitioner's transaction with Resorts, I feel compelled to address the majority's holding that petitioner had income from discharge of gambling indebtedness in 1981.

Section 61(a)(12) provides that gross income includes income from the discharge of indebtedness. However, as the majority recognizes, not all discharges of indebtedness result in income.

In my opinion, for tax purposes, an unenforceable debt is a contradiction in terms, an oxymoron. It is like shooting craps without dice. For interest on indebtedness to be deductible under section 163, it is well recognized that the indebtedness must be enforceable. I am unable to discern why the majority imposes a different rule for the inclusion of discharge of indebtedness income. Accordingly, for 1981, I would hold petitioner did not realize discharge of indebtedness income.

The result reached by the majority is tantamount to taxing petitioner on his losses.

Ruwe, J., dissenting: Although I agree with much of the majority's reasoning in this case, I dissent from that portion of the opinion which holds that section 108(e)(5) is inapplicable to the transaction at issue. I find no support in the language of the statute or the accompanying legislative history for the majority's determination that the gambling chips purchased by petitioner do not constitute "property" for purposes of section 108(e)(5). Because I believe that petitioner acquired "property" from the casino on credit and subsequently negotiated a reduction of his debt to the casino, I would apply section 108(e)(5) in this case.

NOTES

(A) *More Theories.* The Third Circuit overruled the Tax Court. 916 F.2d 110 (3d Cir.1990). The Appeals Court noted that one cannot have cancellation of indebtedness income without a loan. It found that since Zarin's loan was unenforceable under New Jersey law, Zarin, therefore, did not have income from the discharge of a debt. Furthermore, the court held that the chips were not property to which a debt related. Alternatively, the court applied the so-called contested liability doctrine, under which, if a taxpayer disputes the amount of a debt, a subsequent settlement is treated as the actual amount of indebtedness. The dissent found that the casino was selling for cash "the exhilaration and the potential for profit inherent in games of chance." Zarin made this purchase on credit in exchange for which Resorts provided chips that entitled him to participate in Resorts' gambling activity on the same basis as others who had paid cash. To not tax Zarin, it argued, was incompatible with the fundamental principle that "anything of commercial value received by a taxpayer is taxable unless expressly excluded from gross income."

The Tax Court stuck to its original position in *Zarin* in Rood v. Commissioner, 71 T.C.M. 3125 (1996), and held that a patron who gambled on credit had income when the casino discharged his debt. Unlike *Zarin*, the court found that the debt was not in dispute and thus Rood had discharge of indebtedness income when he settled with the casino for less than the amount he owed. The Eleventh Circuit affirmed in a per curiam opinion. 122 F.3d 1078 (1997). Suppose in order to attract high-rollers, the casino agrees in advance to discount any losses, but to pay the full amount of the winnings?

The numerous opinions in *Zarin* do not exhaust the possibilities as to how to approach this case. For example, one could argue that Zarin should not be taxed on the full value of his income because of the offsetting negative utility of his gambling addiction. See Daniel N. Shaviro, The Man Who Lost Too Much: *Zarin v. Commissioner* and the Measurement of Taxable Consumption, 45 Tax L.Rev. 215 (1990). Alternatively, Zarin might have no income because this is simply a bargain purchase of consumption that should not be taxable. See Joseph M. Dodge, *Zarin v. Commissioner: Musings about Debt Cancellations and "Consumption" in an Income Tax Base*, 45 Tax L.Rev. 677 (1990). Or perhaps Zarin has no income because his failure to pay for his chips was a recovery of his prior nondeductible gambling losses and under the tax benefit rule, the recovery is exempt. See Calvin Johnson, *Zarin* and the Tax Benefit Rule: *Tax Models for Gambling Losses and the Forgiveness of Gambling Debts*, 45 Tax L.Rev. 697 (1990).

Suppose Zarin had received the ultimate bargain purchase—Resorts gave him $2.5 million in chips with which to gamble and he could keep his winnings and did not need to pay anything back if he lost. Would he have had gross income? Suppose instead Zarin had run up a $2.5 million tab at the hotel in lodging and meal costs, never paid it and ultimately Resorts wrote it off. What result?

(B) *Comparing* Collins *and* Zarin. Students and commentators are often sympathetic to Zarin, although they have little trouble concluding that Collins, supra at 169, had income when he gambled and lost with OTB money. In both cases the inability to offset the income (whether from embezzlement or cancellation of indebtedness) with gambling losses, due to the limitation of § 165(d), means that both of these losers may have to pay income tax. Is the difference in results—income to Collins, no income to Zarin—justifiable?

Collins relied on the Third Circuit's decision in *Zarin* to argue that the stolen tickets were essentially valueless for tax purposes. He insisted that like Zarin he stole opportunities to gamble and that his stolen racing tickets—like Zarin's gambling chips—had no intrinsic economic value. The court was not sympathetic to Collins' claim, and distinguished *Zarin:*

> [W]e observe that the statement in Zarin regarding the value of the casino's gambling chips was offered as part of the appellate court's interpretation of the narrow income exclusion provision of § 108(d) of the Code. * * * We are not convinced that the Third Circuit's reasoning is applicable outside the context of § 108 and the specific facts of that case where nothing was stolen and there was no embezzlement. * * * Zarin may have been written differently had the Third Circuit been confronted with the separate question of whether to include as gross income under § 61 the face value of stolen gambling opportunities.

(C) *Exceptions to COD Rule.* Although cancellation of indebtedness often results in income to the debtor, there are a number of important exceptions. They have emerged largely as a response to the perceived harshness of imposing a tax on debtors at a time when they have not received cash income and under circumstances where the very fact giving rise to taxable income—a cancellation of indebtedness for less than its face value—may well suggest that the debtor is in a precarious financial condition.

Insolvency of the Debtor. If a taxpayer who is insolvent or who is the subject of bankruptcy proceedings settles with his creditors at a discount, § 108(a) permits him to exclude the debt cancellation from income to the extent of his insolvency. The amount excluded is limited to the extent to which his liabilities exceed his assets. For example, a taxpayer who has liabilities of $20,000 and assets with a fair market value of $13,000, and whose debts are discharged for $10,000, recognizes income of only $3,000. The quid pro quo for nonrecognition is that the taxpayer must reduce certain tax benefits (for example, net operating loss carryovers) or the basis in his property by the amount of the debt cancellation. § 108(b).

Note that other forms of income received by insolvent taxpayers are taxable to them. See, e.g., Parkford v. Commissioner, 133 F.2d 249 (9th Cir.1943), which held that salary paid to an insolvent individual is income. Should there be a general exclusion for all income of insolvent taxpayers? If not, why is cancellation of indebtedness income different?

Lost Deductions. Section 108(e)(2) excludes from income the discharge of a debt if its payment would have given rise to a deduction. This puts the taxpayer in the same position he would have been in had the discharge of the debt been included in income and a deduction allowed for it.

Purchase Price Reduction. If the seller of specific property reduces the debt of the buyer arising out of the purchase, the reduction is treated by both parties as an adjustment of the purchase price. § 108(e)(5). Suppose for example, A owes B $10,000 for property he acquired from B that later turns out to be a lemon. A and B settle by agreeing that A owes B only $7,000. A has no income on the settlement, but his purchase price (and basis) for the property is now $7,000. This provision does not apply if the purchaser is insolvent or the subject of bankruptcy proceedings, if the seller has transferred the debt to a third party or if the purchaser has transferred the property to a third party. The § 108(e)(5) provision is very similar to the contested liability doctrine used by the Third Circuit in *Zarin.* Either approach eliminates COD income when the buyer and seller of goods or services reduce the debt as a purchase price adjustment.

The reduction of the principal amount of an undersecured nonrecourse debt that arose in connection with the sale of property by the holder of the debt (who was not the seller) results in COD income because the debt reduction is not treated as a purchase price adjustment. Rev.Rul. 92–99, 1992–2 C.B. 35. For example, suppose a taxpayer borrowed $200,000 to purchase a building. At a time when the building is worth only $150,000, the lender agrees to reduce the principal amount to $150,000. The taxpayer has $50,000 of COD income.

Corporate Debt to Shareholder. If a shareholder forgives a debt owed him by a corporation, § 108(e)(6) treats this as if the corporation had satisfied the debt with an amount of money equal to the shareholder's basis in the debt. Thus, in the usual case, where the shareholder's basis is equal to the face amount of the debt, the corporation would have no discharge of indebtedness income.

Corporate Stock Issued in Exchange for Debt. Section 108(e)(8) provides that a corporation that is not insolvent or in bankruptcy proceedings realizes discharge of indebtedness income when it issues stock in cancellation of its debt to the extent that the value of the stock is less than the principal amount of the debt.

Discharge of Indebtedness Treated as Gift. Despite the Supreme Court's ruling in Helvering v. American Dental Co., 318 U.S. 322 (1943), that a gratuitous cancellation of indebtedness in a business context was a gift excluded from income, it now seems clear that in a commercial setting, a discharge of indebtedness is not a gift. The Senate Finance Committee in its report on the Bankruptcy Tax Act of 1980 expressed its intention that "there will not be any gift exception in a commercial context (such as a shareholder-corporation relationship) to the general rule that income is realized on the discharge of indebtedness."

In a noncommercial setting, such as a loan between family members, a discharge may be treated as a gift excludable under § 102. If a party who is related to the debtor acquires the debt from an unrelated party, the debt is treated as acquired by the debtor, which may result in COD income to the debtor and the debtor is treated as issuing a new debt to the related party. § 108(e)(4). (For a definition of related party, see § 267(b)).

Qualified Farm Indebtedness. Under certain circumstances, gross income does not include the discharge of "qualified farm indebtedness." The incurably curious should consult §§ 108(a)(1) and 108(g).

Real Estate Business Debt. Those interested in the power of lobbyists should take a look at § 108(a)(1)(D). This provision permits individual taxpayers to elect to exclude from gross income the discharge of real property business indebtedness in exchange for reducing the basis of property. The mortgage must be either acquisition indebtedness or have been incurred or assumed before 1993. This exception presumably will benefit those who suffered when the real estate market crashed and the value of unoccupied office buildings and shopping malls plummeted in the late 1980's and early 1990's.

Student Loan Forgiveness. Section 108(f) provides that gross income does not include any amount from the forgiveness of certain student loans (generally made by a government agency), provided the forgiveness is contingent on the student's working for a certain period of time in certain professions for any of a broad class of employers (e.g., providing health care services to a nonprofit organization). Gross income also does not include forgiveness of student loans made by tax-exempt charities (such as universities) where a condition of the loan is that the student (or former student) must fulfill a public service requirement. The statute defines this as an occupation or working in an area with unmet needs so long as the work is performed for or under the direction of a tax-exempt charitable organization or a government entity. The proceeds of the loan can be used to pay tuition and expenses or to refinance outstanding student loans. This latter rule would cover lawyers who participate in public service student loan programs that required them to work for public service organizations or the government for a period of time. Generally, a portion of the student loan is forgiven each year the student works in a public interest job. Under § 108(f), there is no taxable income when the law school forgives the loan.

(D) *Nature of the Consideration.* In 1932, the Second Circuit held that no income was produced where a corporation issued bonds as a dividend to its shareholders and later bought some of the bonds at less than par. Commissioner v. Rail Joint Co., 61 F.2d 751 (2d Cir.1932). The court reasoned that the corporation received nothing in return. Accord, Fashion Park, Inc. v. Commissioner, 21 T.C. 600 (1954).

SECTION 8. THE EFFECT OF DEBT ON BASIS AND AMOUNT REALIZED

NOTE ON ACQUISITION AND DISPOSITION OF PROPERTY ENCUMBERED BY DEBT

This Section deals with the treatment of debt used to purchase or carry assets. Where a taxpayer purchases an asset for cash, the basis, as described earlier, is equal to the cash paid. Many taxpayers finance acquisitions with debt, however, and the basis of such assets must be determined to assess the tax consequences—such as depreciation deductions and the amount realized upon a disposition of the assets.

There are two general types of borrowing: (1) recourse debt, where the borrower is personally liable for repayment of the debt, and (2) nonrecourse debt, where the borrower is not personally liable and the lender can look only to the assets that secure the debt for repayment. Upon default of a recourse debt, the lender can look not only to any asset securing the debt, but also to the borrower's other assets for repayment. Upon default of a nonrecourse debt, the lender can obtain satisfaction of the obligation only from the property securing the debt. If, when a nonrecourse loan comes due, the value of the property is adequate to satisfy the amount owed, the lender will be paid in full. If, on the other hand, the value of the property is inadequate to satisfy the debt—either because the property declined in value after the loan was made or because the property was overvalued at the time of the loan—the lender, not the borrower, will suffer the economic loss. Where the borrower has other financial resources, the economic consequences will be quite different than if the borrower had been personally liable. The borrower's lack of personal liability might arise in a variety of ways. For example, the lender might agree that the loan will be nonrecourse; a straw or dummy might be used in the conveyance; the purchaser might take property subject to a mortgage without assuming personal liability; or guarantees or other similar arrangements might protect the borrower from personal liability.

The appropriate tax treatment of borrowed amounts in determining basis and amount realized is a serious issue for the income tax. The classic case of Crane v. Commissioner, 331 U.S. 1 (1947), established as a general principle that recourse and nonrecourse debt will be treated alike. A loan, whether recourse or nonrecourse, is included in the basis of the asset it finances. This creates parity between a purchaser who borrows from a bank and pays the seller cash and a purchaser who uses seller financing. Thus, if A acquires a building for $1 million by paying $100,000 in cash and assuming a $900,000 mortgage, his basis is $1 million whether he borrows the $900,000 from a bank or the seller or assumes an outstanding $900,000 mortgage on the property. When property is sold (or otherwise disposed of), any balance of the recourse or nonrecourse debt is included in the amount realized. Thus, if B purchases A's building for $1.1 million by transferring

$300,000 cash and assuming the mortgage with an outstanding principal amount of $800,000, A's amount realized is $1.1 million. The combination of these rules creates a significant benefit for the taxpayer. First, if the property is eligible for depreciation deductions, including the borrowed amount in basis enables a taxpayer to recover costs that she has not yet paid or assumed directly. Second, if the money for buying the property is borrowed through a nonrecourse mortgage for which the taxpayer has no personal liability, it may be possible for her to recover through depreciation putative acquisition costs for which she may never have to put up any of her own money. Third, although the amount of the outstanding debt will be included in the taxpayer's amount realized upon an eventual sale (offsetting the earlier depreciation deductions), the taxpayer enjoys the time value of the depreciation deductions. For example, suppose A purchases property for $100,000, giving the seller a nonrecourse note calling for no principal payments for 20 years. A has a $100,000 basis and takes $100,000 in depreciation deductions over the 20–year life of the property. Her basis will be reduced by the deductions so that at the end of 20 years, her adjusted basis will be zero. Suppose the seller forecloses at that time because A makes no principal payment. The amount realized will be the outstanding principal of the debt or $100,000 and A will have a gain of like amount. Although the total deductions equal the gain on the foreclosure, A has enjoyed the tax benefits of the depreciation well in advance of the time when she must pay tax on the gain. The typical loan, of course, will not defer all payments of principal for as long as 20 years, so the foregoing is a somewhat extreme example of the deferral potentially available, but the principle it illustrates holds and the amounts borrowed may be far greater.

In the *Crane* case, which is described further in the *Tufts* case which follows, the taxpayer had inherited an apartment building subject to a nonrecourse mortgage equal to the value of the property. Applying the predecessor of § 1014, she originally calculated her basis as equal to the value of the building without reduction for the mortgage. Over the course of six years, she deducted about a tenth of this figure as depreciation. She made no payments on the mortgage and, in the face of a foreclosure threat, she sold the building, subject to the mortgage for a small cash sum. The Court rejected her claim that the nonrecourse debt should not have counted in calculating her basis and that the amount she realized on the sale should not include her relief from the mortgage obligation. Instead the Court ruled that, in calculating basis, a taxpayer must treat a nonrecourse mortgage as equivalent to a cash investment, and that, in determining the amount realized upon disposition of property, the taxpayer must include relief from the obligation to repay a mortgaged nonrecourse debt.

The principal effect of the government's "victory" in *Crane* was to increase and accelerate the amount of depreciation deductions allowed to owners of property financed from debt. If, as Crane had argued, property was defined as "equity," she would have been entitled to zero depreciation while she held the property.

In a famous footnote (famous in some quarters at least), number 37, the *Crane* court left open the question whether the transfer of property subject to a nonrecourse mortgage in excess of the value of the property securing it should produce the same results. That issue is resolved in the following case.

Commissioner v. Tufts

Supreme Court of the United States, 1983. 461 U.S. 300.

JUSTICE BLACKMUN delivered the opinion of the Court.

Over 35 years ago, in Crane v. Commissioner, 331 U.S. 1 (1947), this Court ruled that a taxpayer, who sold property encumbered by a nonrecourse mortgage (the amount of the mortgage being less than the property's value), must include the unpaid balance of the mortgage in the computation of the amount the taxpayer realized on the sale. The case now before us presents the question whether the same rule applies when the unpaid amount of the nonrecourse mortgage exceeds the fair market value of the property sold.

I

On August 1, 1970, respondent Clark Pelt, a builder, and his wholly owned corporation, respondent Clark, Inc., formed a general partnership. The purpose of the partnership was to construct a 120–unit apartment complex in Duncanville, Tex., a Dallas suburb. Neither Pelt nor Clark, Inc., made any capital contribution to the partnership. Six days later, the partnership entered into a mortgage loan agreement with the Farm & Home Savings Association (F & H). Under the agreement, F & H was committed for a $1,851,500 loan for the complex. In return, the partnership executed a note and a deed of trust in favor of F & H. The partnership obtained the loan on a nonrecourse basis: neither the partnership nor its partners assumed any personal liability for repayment of the loan. Pelt later admitted four friends and relatives, respondents Tufts, Steger, Stephens, and Austin, as general partners. None of them contributed capital upon entering the partnership.

The construction of the complex was completed in August 1971. During 1971, each partner made small capital contributions to the partnership; in 1972, however, only Pelt made a contribution. The total of the partners' capital contributions was $44,212. In each tax year, all partners claimed as income tax deductions their allocable shares of ordinary losses and depreciation. The deductions taken by the partners in 1971 and 1972 totalled $439,972. Due to these contributions and deductions, the partnership's adjusted basis in the property in August 1972 was $1,455,740.

In 1971 and 1972, major employers in the Duncanville area laid off significant numbers of workers. As a result, the partnership's rental income was less than expected, and it was unable to make the payments due on the mortgage. Each partner, on August 28, 1972, sold his partnership interest to an unrelated third party, Fred Bayles. As consideration, Bayles agreed to reimburse each partner's sale expenses up to $250; he also assumed the nonrecourse mortgage.

On the date of transfer, the fair market value of the property did not exceed $1,400,000. Each partner reported the sale on his federal income tax return and indicated that a partnership loss of $55,740 had been sustained.[1] The Commissioner of Internal Revenue, on audit, determined that the sale resulted in a partnership capital gain of approximately $400,000. His theory was that the partnership had realized the full amount of the nonrecourse obligation.[2]

Relying on Millar v. Commissioner, 577 F.2d 212, 215 (CA3), cert. denied 439 U.S. 1046 (1978), the United States Tax Court, in an unreviewed decision, upheld the asserted deficiencies. 70 T.C. 756 (1978). The United States Court of Appeals for the Fifth Circuit reversed, 651 F.2d 1058 (1981). That court expressly disagreed with the Millar analysis, and, in limiting Crane v. Commissioner, supra, to its facts, questioned the theoretical underpinnings of the Crane decision. We granted certiorari to resolve the conflict. 456 U.S. 960 (1982).

II

Section 752(d) of the Internal Revenue Code of 1954, 26 U.S.C. § 752(d), specifically provides that liabilities incurred in the sale or exchange of a partnership interest are to "be treated in the same manner as liabilities in connection with the sale or exchange of property not associated with partnerships." Section 1001 governs the determination of gains and losses on the disposition of property. Under § 1001(a), the gain or loss from a sale or other disposition of property is defined as the difference between "the amount realized" on the disposition and the property's adjusted basis. Subsection (b) of § 1001 defines "amount realized": "The amount realized from the sale or other disposition of property shall be the sum of any money received plus the fair market value of the property (other than money) received." At issue is the application of the latter provision to the disposition of property encumbered by a nonrecourse mortgage of an amount in excess of the property's fair market value.

A

In Crane v. Commissioner, supra, this Court took the first and controlling step toward the resolution of this issue. Beulah B. Crane was the sole beneficiary under the will of her deceased husband. At his death in January 1932, he owned an apartment building that was then mortgaged for an amount which proved to be equal to its fair market value, as determined for federal estate tax purposes. The widow, of course, was not personally liable on the mortgage. She operated the building for nearly seven years, hoping to turn it into a profitable venture; during that period, she claimed income tax deductions for depreciation, property taxes, interest, and operating expenses, but did not make payments upon the mortgage principal. In computing her basis for the depreciation deductions, she included the full

---

1. The loss was the difference between the adjusted basis, $1,455,740, and the fair market value of the property, $1,400,000. On their individual tax returns, the partners did not claim deductions for their respective shares of this loss. In their petitions to the Tax Court, however, the partners did claim the loss.

2. The Commissioner determined the partnership's gain on the sale by subtracting the adjusted basis, $1,455,740, from the liability assumed by Bayles, $1,851,500. [leaving as a] resulting figure, $395,760 * * *.

amount of the mortgage debt. In November 1938, with her hopes unfulfilled and the mortgagee threatening foreclosure, Mrs. Crane sold the building. The purchaser took the property subject to the mortgage and paid Crane $3,000; of that amount, $500 went for the expenses of the sale.

Crane reported a gain of $2,500 on the transaction. She reasoned that her basis in the property was zero (despite her earlier depreciation deductions based on including the amount of the mortgage) and that the amount she realized from the sale was simply the cash she received. The Commissioner disputed this claim. He asserted that Crane's basis in the property, under [the predecessor of] § 1014 of the 1954 Code * * * was the property's fair market value at the time of her husband's death, adjusted for depreciation in the interim, and that the amount realized was the net cash received plus the amount of the outstanding mortgage assumed by the purchaser.

In upholding the Commissioner's interpretation * * * the Court observed that to regard merely the taxpayer's equity in the property as her basis would lead to depreciation deductions less than the actual physical deterioration of the property, and would require the basis to be recomputed with each payment on the mortgage. 331 U.S., at 9–10. The Court rejected Crane's claim that any loss due to depreciation belonged to the mortgagee. The effect of the Court's ruling was that the taxpayer's basis was the value of the property undiminished by the mortgage. Id., at 11.

The Court next proceeded to determine the amount realized under [the predecessor of] § 1001(b) of the 1954 Code. * * * In order to avoid the "absurdity," see 331 U.S., at 13, of Crane's realizing only $2,500 on the sale of property worth over a quarter of a million dollars, the Court treated the amount realized as it had treated basis, that is, by including the outstanding value of the mortgage. To do otherwise would have permitted Crane to recognize a tax loss unconnected with any actual economic loss. The Court refused to construe one section of the Revenue Act so as "to frustrate the Act as a whole." Ibid.

Crane, however, insisted that the nonrecourse nature of the mortgage required different treatment. The Court, for two reasons, disagreed. First, excluding the nonrecourse debt from the amount realized would result in the same absurdity and frustration of the Code. Id., at 13–14. Second, the Court concluded that Crane obtained an economic benefit from the purchaser's assumption of the mortgage identical to the benefit conferred by the cancellation of personal debt. Because the value of the property in that case exceeded the amount of the mortgage, it was in Crane's economic interest to treat the mortgage as a personal obligation; only by so doing could she realize upon sale the appreciation in her equity represented by the $2,500 boot. The purchaser's assumption of the liability thus resulted in a taxable economic benefit to her, just as if she had been given, in addition to the boot, a sum of cash sufficient to satisfy the mortgage.

In [footnote 37], pertinent to the present case, the Court observed:

> "Obviously, if the value of the property is less than the amount of the mortgage, a mortgagor who is not personally liable cannot realize a benefit equal to the mortgage. Consequently, a different problem might

be encountered where a mortgagor abandoned the property or transferred it subject to the mortgage without receiving boot. That is not this case."

Id., at 14, n. 37.

B

This case presents that unresolved issue. We are disinclined to overrule Crane, and we conclude that the same rule applies when the unpaid amount of the nonrecourse mortgage exceeds the value of the property transferred. Crane ultimately does not rest on its limited theory of economic benefit; instead, we read Crane to have approved the Commissioner's decision to treat a nonrecourse mortgage in this context as a true loan. This approval underlies Crane's holdings that the amount of the nonrecourse liability is to be included in calculating both the basis and the amount realized on disposition. That the amount of the loan exceeds the fair market value of the property thus becomes irrelevant.

When a taxpayer receives a loan, he incurs an obligation to repay that loan at some future date. Because of this obligation, the loan proceeds do not qualify as income to the taxpayer. When he fulfills the obligation, the repayment of the loan likewise has no effect on his tax liability.

Another consequence to the taxpayer from this obligation occurs when the taxpayer applies the loan proceeds to the purchase price of property used to secure the loan. Because of the obligation to repay, the taxpayer is entitled to include the amount of the loan in computing his basis in the property; the loan, under § 1012, is part of the taxpayer's cost of the property. Although a different approach might have been taken with respect to a nonrecourse mortgage loan,[5] the Commissioner has chosen to accord it the same treatment he gives to a recourse mortgage loan. The Court approved that choice in Crane, and the respondents do not challenge it here. The choice and its resultant benefits to the taxpayer are predicated on the assumption that the mortgage will be repaid in full.

When encumbered property is sold or otherwise disposed of and the purchaser assumes the mortgage, the associated extinguishment of the mortgagor's obligation to repay is accounted for in the computation of the

---

5. The Commissioner might have adopted the theory, implicit in Crane's contentions, that a nonrecourse mortgage is not true debt, but, instead, is a form of joint investment by the mortgagor and the mortgagee. On this approach, nonrecourse debt would be considered a contingent liability, under which the mortgagor's payments on the debt gradually increase his interest in the property while decreasing that of the mortgagee. * * * Because the taxpayer's investment in the property would not include the nonrecourse debt, the taxpayer would not be permitted to include that debt in basis. * * *

We express no view as to whether such an approach would be consistent with the statutory structure and, if so, and Crane were not on the books, whether that approach would be preferred over Crane's analysis. We note only that the Crane Court's resolution of the basis issue presumed that when property is purchased with proceeds from a nonrecourse mortgage, the purchaser becomes the sole owner of the property. 331 U.S., at 6. Under the Crane approach, the mortgagee is entitled to no portion of the basis. Id., at 10, n. 28. The nonrecourse mortgage is part of the mortgagor's investment in the property, and does not constitute a coinvestment by the mortgagee. * * *

amount realized. * * * Because no difference between recourse and nonrecourse obligations is recognized in calculating basis,[7] Crane teaches that the Commissioner may ignore the nonrecourse nature of the obligation in determining the amount realized upon disposition of the encumbered property. He thus may include in the amount realized the amount of the nonrecourse mortgage assumed by the purchaser. The rationale for this treatment is that the original inclusion of the amount of the mortgage in basis rested on the assumption that the mortgagor incurred an obligation to repay. Moreover, this treatment balances the fact that the mortgagor originally received the proceeds of the nonrecourse loan tax-free on the same assumption. Unless the outstanding amount of the mortgage is deemed to be realized, the mortgagor effectively will have received untaxed income at the time the loan was extended and will have received an unwarranted increase in the basis of his property.[8] The Commissioner's interpretation of § 1001(b) in this fashion cannot be said to be unreasonable.

C

The Commissioner in fact has applied this rule even when the fair market value of the property falls below the amount of the nonrecourse obligation. Treas.Reg. § 1.1001–2(b), 26 CFR § 1.1001–2(b) (1982); Rev. Rul. 76–111, 1976–1 Cum.Bull. 214. Because the theory on which the rule is based applies equally in this situation, * * * [W]e have no reason, after Crane, to question this treatment.[11]

7. The Commissioner's choice in Crane "laid the foundation stone of most tax shelters," Bittker, Tax Shelters, Nonrecourse Debt, and the Crane Case, 33 Tax.L.Rev. 277, 283 (1978), by permitting taxpayers who bear no risk to take deductions on depreciable property. Congress recently has acted to curb this avoidance device by forbidding a taxpayer to take depreciation deductions in excess of amounts he has at risk in the investment. * * * Real estate investments, however, are exempt from this prohibition. § 465(c)(3)(D) * * *. Although this congressional action may foreshadow a day when nonrecourse and recourse debts will be treated differently, neither Congress nor the Commissioner has sought to alter Crane's rule of including nonrecourse liability in both basis and the amount realized.

8. * * * Our analysis applies even in the situation in which no deductions are taken. It focuses on the obligation to repay and its subsequent extinguishment, not on the taking and recovery of deductions. * * *

11. Professor Wayne G. Barnett, as amicus in the present case, argues that the liability and property portions of the transaction should be accounted for separately. Under his view, there was a transfer of the property for $1.4 million, and there was a cancellation of the $1.85 million obligation for a payment of $1.4 million. The former resulted in a capital loss of $50,000, and the latter in the realization of $450,000 of ordinary income. Taxation of the ordinary income might be deferred under § 108 by a reduction of respondents' bases in their partnership interests.

Although this indeed could be a justifiable mode of analysis, it has not been adopted by the Commissioner. Nor is there anything to indicate that the Code requires the Commissioner to adopt it. We note that Professor Barnett's approach does assume that recourse and nonrecourse debt may be treated identically.

The Commissioner also has chosen not to characterize the transaction as cancellation of indebtedness. We are not presented with and do not decide the contours of the cancellation-of-indebtedness doctrine. We note only that our approach does not fall within certain prior interpretations of that doctrine. In one view, the doctrine rests on the same initial premise as our analysis here—an obligation to repay—but the doctrine relies on a freeing-of-assets theory to attribute ordinary income to the debtor upon cancellation. See Commissioner v. Jacobson, 336 U.S. 28, 38–40 (1949);

Respondents received a mortgage loan with the concomitant obligation to repay by the year 2012. The only difference between that mortgage and one on which the borrower is personally liable is that the mortgagee's remedy is limited to foreclosing on the securing property. This difference does not alter the nature of the obligation; its only effect is to shift from the borrower to the lender any potential loss caused by devaluation of the property.[12] If the fair market value of the property falls below the amount of the outstanding obligation, the mortgagee's ability to protect its interests is impaired, for the mortgagor is free to abandon the property to the mortgagee and be relieved of his obligation.

This, however, does not erase the fact that the mortgagor received the loan proceeds tax-free and included them in his basis on the understanding that he had an obligation to repay the full amount. See Woodsam Associates, Inc. v. Commissioner, 198 F.2d 357, 359 (C.A.2 1952); Bittker, 33 Tax.L.Rev. at 284. When the obligation is canceled, the mortgagor is relieved of his responsibility to repay the sum he originally received and thus realizes value to that extent within the meaning of § 1001(b). From the mortgagor's point of view, when his obligation is assumed by a third party who purchases the encumbered property, it is as if the mortgagor first had been paid with cash borrowed by the third party from the mortgagee on a nonrecourse basis, and then had used the cash to satisfy his obligation to the mortgagee.

1.   Moreover, this approach avoids the absurdity the Court recognized in Crane. Because of the remedy accompanying the mortgage in the nonrecourse situation, the depreciation in the fair market value of the property is relevant economically only to the mortgagee, who by lending on a nonrecourse basis remains at risk. To permit the

United States v. Kirby Lumber Co., 284 U.S. 1, 3 (1931). According to that view, when nonrecourse debt is forgiven, the debtor's basis in the securing property is reduced by the amount of debt canceled, and realization of income is deferred until the sale of the property. * * * Because that interpretation attributes income only when assets are freed, however, an insolvent debtor realizes income just to the extent his assets exceed his liabilities after the cancellation. Lakeland Grocery Co. v. Commissioner, 36 B.T.A. 289, 292 (1937). Similarly, if the nonrecourse indebtedness exceeds the value of the securing property, the taxpayer never realizes the full amount of the obligation canceled because the tax law has not recognized negative basis.

Although the economic benefit prong of Crane also relies on a freeing-of-assets theory, that theory is irrelevant to our broader approach. In the context of a sale or disposition of property under § 1001, the extinguishment of the obligation to repay is not ordinary income; instead, the amount of the canceled debt is included in the amount realized, and enters into the computation of gain or loss on the disposition of property. Accord-

ing to Crane, this treatment is no different when the obligation is nonrecourse: the basis is not reduced as in the cancellation-of-indebtedness context, and the full value of the outstanding liability is included in the amount realized. Thus the problem of negative basis is avoided.

12.   In his opinion for the Court of Appeals in Crane, Judge Learned Hand observed:

"[The mortgagor] has all the income from the property; he manages it; he may sell it; any increase in its value goes to him; any decrease falls on him, until the value goes below the amount of the lien.... When therefore upon a sale the mortgagor makes an allowance to the vendee of the amount of the lien, he secures a release from a charge upon his property quite as though the vendee had paid him the full price on condition that before he took title the lien should be cleared...." 153 F.2d 504, 506 (C.A.2 1945).

taxpayer to limit his realization to the fair market value of the property would be to recognize a tax loss for which he has suffered no corresponding economic loss.[13] Such a result would be to construe "one section of the Act * * * so as * * * to defeat the intention of another or to frustrate the Act as a whole." 331 U.S., at 13.

In the specific circumstances of Crane, the economic benefit theory did support the Commissioner's treatment of the nonrecourse mortgage as a personal obligation. The footnote in Crane acknowledged the limitations of that theory when applied to a different set of facts. Crane also stands for the broader proposition, however, that a nonrecourse loan should be treated as a true loan. We therefore hold that a taxpayer must account for the proceeds of obligations he has received tax-free and included in basis. Nothing in either § 1001(b) or in the Court's prior decisions requires the Commissioner to permit a taxpayer to treat a sale of encumbered property asymmetrically, by including the proceeds of the nonrecourse obligation in basis but not accounting for the proceeds upon transfer of the encumbered property. * * *

[The Court's discussion rejecting the taxpayer's argument that § 752 expressly requires a different result for partnership dispositions is omitted.]

IV

When a taxpayer sells or disposes of property encumbered by a nonrecourse obligation, the Commissioner properly requires him to include among the assets realized the outstanding amount of the obligation. The fair market value of the property is irrelevant to this calculation. We find this interpretation to be consistent with Crane v. Commissioner, 331 U.S. 1 (1947), and to implement the statutory mandate in a reasonable manner. * * *

The judgment of the Court of Appeals is therefore reversed.

It is so ordered.

JUSTICE O'CONNOR, concurring.

I concur in the opinion of the Court, accepting the view of the Commissioner. I do not, however, endorse the Commissioner's view. Indeed, were we writing on a slate clean except for the *Crane* decision, I would take quite a different approach—that urged upon us by Professor Barnett as *amicus*.

---

13. In the present case, the Government bore the ultimate loss. The nonrecourse mortgage was extended to respondents only after the planned complex was endorsed for mortgage insurance under §§ 221(b) and (d)(4) of the National Housing Act, 12 U.S.C. § 17151(b) and (d)(4) * * *. After acquiring the complex from respondents, Bayles operated it for a few years, but was unable to make it profitable. In 1974, F & H foreclosed, and the Department of Housing and Urban Development paid off the lender to obtain title. In 1976, the Department sold the complex to another developer for $1,502,000. The sale was financed by the Department's taking back a note for $1,314,800 and a nonrecourse mortgage. To fail to recognize the value of the nonrecourse loan in the amount realized, therefore, would permit respondents to compound the Government's loss by claiming the tax benefits of that loss for themselves.

Crane established that a taxpayer could treat property as entirely his own, in spite of the "coinvestment" provided by his mortgagee in the form of a nonrecourse loan. That is, the full basis of the property, with all its tax consequences, belongs to the mortgagor. That rule alone, though, does not in any way tie nonrecourse debt to the cost of property or to the proceeds upon disposition. I see no reason to treat the purchase, ownership, and eventual disposition of property differently because the taxpayer also takes out a mortgage, an independent transaction. In this case, the taxpayer purchased property, using nonrecourse financing, and sold it after it declined in value to a buyer who assumed the mortgage. There is no economic difference between the events in this case and a case in which the taxpayer buys property with cash; later obtains a nonrecourse loan by pledging the property as security; still later, using cash on hand, buys off the mortgage for the market value of the devalued property; and finally sells the property to a third party for its market value.

The logical way to treat both this case and the hypothesized case is to separate the two aspects of these events and to consider, first, the ownership and sale of the property, and, second, the arrangement and retirement of the loan. Under Crane, the fair market value of the property on the date of acquisition—the purchase price—represents the taxpayer's basis in the property, and the fair market value on the date of disposition represents the proceeds on sale. The benefit received by the taxpayer in return for the property is the cancellation of a mortgage that is worth no more than the fair market value of the property, for that is all the mortgagee can expect to collect on the mortgage. His gain or loss on the disposition of the property equals the difference between the proceeds and the cost of acquisition. Thus, the taxation of the transaction *in property* reflects the economic fate of the *property*. If the property has declined in value, as was the case here, the taxpayer recognizes a loss on the disposition of the property. The new purchaser then takes as his basis the fair market value as of the date of the sale. * * *

In the separate borrowing transaction, the taxpayer acquires cash from the mortgagee. He need not recognize income at that time, of course, because he also incurs an obligation to repay the money. Later, though, when he is able to satisfy the debt by surrendering property that is worth less than the face amount of the debt, we have a classic situation of cancellation of indebtedness, requiring the taxpayer to recognize income in the amount of the difference between the proceeds of the loan and the amount for which he is able to satisfy his creditor. 26 U.S.C. § 61(a)(12). The taxation of the financing transaction then reflects the economic fate of the loan.

The reason that separation of the two aspects of the events in this case is important is, of course, that the Code treats different sorts of income differently. A gain on the sale of the property may qualify for capital gains treatment, §§ 1202, 1221 * * * while the cancellation of indebtedness is ordinary income, but income that the taxpayer may be able to defer. §§ 108, 1017 * * *. Not only does Professor Barnett's theory permit us to accord appropriate treatment to each of the two types of income or loss present in these sorts of transactions, it also restores continuity to the system by making the taxpayer-seller's proceeds on the disposition of property equal to the purchaser's basis in the property. Further, and most important, it allows us to tax the events in this case in the same way that we tax the economically identical hypothesized transaction.

Persuaded though I am by the logical coherence and internal consistency of this approach, I agree with the Court's decision not to adopt it judicially. We do not write on a slate marked only by Crane. The Commissioner's longstanding position, Rev.Rul. 76–111, 1976–1 C.B. 214, is now reflected in the regulations. Treas.Reg. § 1.1001–2, 26 CFR § 1.1001–2 (1982). In the light of the numerous cases in the lower courts including the amount of the unrepaid proceeds of the mortgage in the proceeds on sale or disposition, * * * it is difficult to conclude that the Commissioner's interpretation of the statute exceeds the bounds of his discretion. As the Court's opinion demonstrates, his interpretation is defensible. One can reasonably read § 1001(b)'s reference to "the amount realized *from* the sale or other disposition of property" (emphasis added) to permit the Commissioner to collapse the two aspects of the transaction. As long as his view is a reasonable reading of § 1001(b), we should defer to the regulations promulgated by the agency charged with interpretation of the statute. * * * Accordingly, I concur.

NOTES

(A) *The Taxpayer is Still Ahead.* By resolving the ambiguity of *Crane*'s footnote 37 and making clear the symmetrical treatment of mortgage indebtedness in basis and amount realized, *Tufts* demonstrates that the *total amount* of income from such property transactions will be the same whether the mortgage debt is included in both basis and amount realized or excluded from both. The difference between the two rules is a question of timing of tax liabilities. The ability to obtain accelerated and larger depreciation deductions offsets the inclusion of the deductions in income upon disposition. Even if the taxpayer's marginal tax rate has not changed, the subsequent increase in tax liability by the amount of the earlier reduction is not adequate to make either the government or taxpayers indifferent. The deferral of tax is of major advantage to taxpayers because the present value of the future tax liability is less than its nominal value. *Crane* served as the foundation of tax shelter investments based on increasing the amount of tax deferred through borrowing or "leverage." The value of deferral is discussed infra at page 285.

(B) *The "Joint Venture" Analysis.* In Footnote 5 of *Tufts* the Court raises but does not adopt a joint venture analysis of an acquisition of property with debt. The Court felt constrained by its earlier decision in *Crane,* which treated the borrower as the sole owner of the property. The *Crane* court was clearly influenced by its view that depreciation deductions reflect wear and tear of the asset rather than a recovery of the taxpayer's capital investment. If, however, the Court had regarded depreciation as a device for the recovery of the taxpayer's actual investment in the property, depreciation might be allowed only to a taxpayer who suffers an economic loss due to the decline in the value of the property over time. That, of course, does not describe an owner of property subject to a nonrecourse mortgage. The lender who provides the nonrecourse mortgage bears this economic risk and thus might be entitled to basis in the property and depreciation deductions.

The lender, however, is not exactly like a participant in a joint venture because, unless he has an "equity kicker," he will not enjoy the benefits if the property appreciates in value. The borrower/"owner" has something akin to an option—he can walk away without further loss if the property declines in value, but will retain the property and enjoy the benefits if it increases in value. But this analogy is not perfectly apt either because the borrower usually can manage and control the use of the property whereas the optionholder typically will have no management powers. The question of who should be treated as the "owner" of the property and thus who should have basis is quite difficult. The *Crane* rule, therefore, influences not only timing, but also the allocation of income and deductions among taxpayers by treating loans differently from other economically similar transactions.

The *Crane* rule also may affect the amount of gain treated as ordinary income or capital gain. This is taken up in Chapter 5.

Estate of Franklin v. Commissioner

United States Court of Appeals, Ninth Circuit, 1976. 544 F.2d 1045.

SNEED, CIRCUIT JUDGE:

This case involves another effort on the part of the Commissioner to curb the use of real estate tax shelters. In this instance he seeks to disallow deductions for the taxpayers' distributive share of losses reported by a limited partnership with respect to its acquisition of a motel and related property. These "losses" have their origin in deductions for depreciation and interest claimed with respect to the motel and related property. These deductions were disallowed by the Commissioner on the ground either that the acquisition was a sham or that the entire acquisition transaction was in substance the purchase by the partnership of an option to acquire the motel and related property on January 15, 1979. The Tax Court held that the transaction constituted an option exercisable in 1979 and disallowed the taxpayers' deductions. Estate of Charles T. Franklin, 64 T.C. 752 (1975). We affirm this disallowance although our approach differs somewhat from that of the Tax Court.

The interest and depreciation deductions were taken by Twenty–Fourth Property Associates (hereinafter referred to as Associates), a California limited partnership of which Charles T. Franklin and seven other doctors were the limited partners. The deductions flowed from the purported "purchase" by Associates of the Thunderbird Inn, an Arizona motel, from Wayne L. Romney and Joan E. Romney (hereinafter referred to as the Romneys) on November 15, 1968.

Under a document entitled "Sales Agreement," the Romneys agreed to "sell" the Thunderbird Inn to Associates for $1,224,000. The property would be paid for over a period of ten years, with interest on any unpaid balance of seven and one-half percent per annum. "Prepaid interest" in the amount of $75,000 was payable immediately; monthly principal and interest installments of $9,045.36 would be paid for approximately the first ten years, with Associates required to make a balloon payment at the end of the ten years of the difference between the remaining purchase price, forecast as $975,000, and any mortgages then outstanding against the property.

The purchase obligation of Associates to the Romneys was nonrecourse; the Romneys' only remedy in the event of default would be forfeiture of the partnership's interest. The sales agreement was recorded in the local county. A warranty deed was placed in an escrow account, along with a quitclaim deed from Associates to the Romneys, both documents to be delivered either to Associates upon full payment of the purchase price, or to the Romneys upon default.

The sale was combined with a leaseback of the property by Associates to the Romneys; Associates therefore never took physical possession. The lease payments were designed to approximate closely the principal and interest payments with the consequence that with the exception of the $75,000 prepaid interest payment no cash would cross between Associates and Romneys until the balloon payment. The lease was on a net basis; thus, the Romneys were responsible for all of the typical expenses of owning the motel property including all utility costs, taxes, assessments, rents, charges, and levies of "every name, nature and kind whatsoever." The Romneys also were to continue to be responsible for the first and second mortgages until the final purchase installment was made; the Romneys could, and indeed did, place additional mortgages on the property without the permission of Associates. Finally, the Romneys were allowed to propose new capital improvements which Associates would be required to either build themselves or allow the Romneys to construct with compensating modifications in rent or purchase price.

In holding that the transaction between Associates and the Romneys more nearly resembled an option than a sale, the Tax Court emphasized that Associates had the power at the end of ten years to walk away from the transaction and merely lose its $75,000 "prepaid interest payment." It also pointed out that a *deed* was never recorded and that the "benefits and burdens of ownership" appeared to remain with the Romneys. Thus, the sale was combined with a leaseback in which no cash would pass; the Romneys remained responsible under the mortgages, which they could increase; and the Romneys could make capital improvements. The Tax Court further justified its "option" characterization by reference to the nonrecourse nature of the purchase money debt and the nice balance between the rental and purchase money payments.

Our emphasis is different from that of the Tax Court. We believe the characteristics set out above can exist in a situation in which the sale imposes upon the purchaser a genuine indebtedness within the meaning of section 167(a), Internal Revenue Code of 1954, which will support both interest and depreciation deductions. * * *

In none of [the cases sustaining such transactions], however, did the taxpayer fail to demonstrate that the purchase price was at least approximately equivalent to the fair market value of the property. Just such a failure occurred here. The Tax Court explicitly found that on the basis of the facts before it the value of the property could not be estimated. 64 T.C. at 767–768.[4] In our view this defect in the taxpayers' proof is fatal.

Reason supports our perception. An acquisition such as that of Associates if at a price approximately equal to the fair market value of the property under ordinary circumstances would rather quickly yield an equity in the property which the purchaser could not prudently abandon. This is the stuff of substance. It meshes with the form of the transaction and constitutes a sale.

No such meshing occurs when the purchase price exceeds a demonstrably reasonable estimate of the fair market value. Payments on the principal of the purchase price yield no equity so long as the unpaid balance of the purchase price exceeds the then existing fair market value. Under these circumstances the purchaser by abandoning the transaction can lose no more than a mere chance to acquire an equity in the future should the value of the acquired property increase. While this chance undoubtedly influenced the Tax Court's determination that the transaction before us constitutes an option, we need only point out that its existence fails to supply the substance necessary to justify treating the transaction as a sale *ab initio*. It is not necessary to the disposition of this case to decide the tax consequences of a transaction such as that before us if in a subsequent year

---

4. The Tax Court found that appellants had "not shown that the purported sales price of $1,224,000 (or any other price) had any relationship to the actual market value of the motel property...." 64 T.C. at 767.

Petitioners spent a substantial amount of time at trial attempting to establish that, whatever the actual market value of the property, Associates acted in the good faith *belief* that the market value of the property approximated the selling price. However, this evidence only goes to the issue of sham and does not supply substance to this transaction. "Save in those instances where the statute itself turns on intent, a matter so real as taxation must depend on objective realities, not on the varying subjective beliefs of individual taxpayers." * * *

In oral argument it was suggested by the appellants that neither the Tax Court nor they recognized the importance of fair market value during the presentation of evidence and that this hampered the full and open development of this issue. However, upon an examination of the record, we are satisfied that the taxpayers recognized the importance of presenting objective evidence of the fair market value and were awarded ample opportunity to present their proof; appellants merely failed to present clear and admissible evidence that fair market value did indeed approximate the purchase price. Such evidence of fair market value as was relied upon by the appellants, viz. two appraisals, one completed in 1968 and a second in 1971, even if fully admissible as evidence of the truth of the estimates of value appearing therein, does not require us to set aside the Tax Court's finding. As the Tax Court found, the 1968 appraisal was "error-filled, sketchy" and "obviously suspect." 64 T.C. at 767 n. 13. The 1971 appraisal had little relevancy as to 1968 values. On the other side, there existed cogent evidence indicating that the fair market value was substantially less than the purchase price. This evidence included (i) the Romneys' purchase of the stock of two corporations, one of which wholly-owned the motel, for approximately $800,000 in the year preceding the "sale" to Associates ($660,000 of which was allocable to the sale property, according to Mr. Romney's estimate), and (ii) insurance policies on the property from 1967 through 1974 of only $583,200, $700,000, and $614,000. 64 T.C. at 767–768.

Given that it was the appellants' burden to present evidence showing that the purchase price did not exceed the fair market value and that he had a fair opportunity to do so, we see no reason to remand this case for further proceedings.

the fair market value of the property increases to an extent that permits the purchaser to acquire an equity.

Authority also supports our perception. It is fundamental that "depreciation is not predicated upon ownership of property *but rather upon an investment in property.* * * * " No such investment exists when payments of the purchase price in accordance with the design of the parties yield no equity to the purchaser. * * * In the transaction before us and during the taxable years in question the purchase price payments by Associates have not been shown to constitute an *investment in the property.* Depreciation was properly disallowed. Only the Romneys had an investment in the property.

Authority also supports disallowance of the interest deductions. This is said even though it has long been recognized that the absence of personal liability for the purchase money debt secured by a mortgage on the acquired property does not deprive the debt of its character as a bona fide debt obligation able to support an interest deduction. * * * However, this is no longer true when it appears that the debt has economic significance only if the property substantially appreciates in value prior to the date at which a very large portion of the purchase price is to be discharged. Under these circumstances the purchaser has not secured "the use or forbearance of money." * * * Nor has the seller advanced money or forborne its use. * * * Prior to the date at which the balloon payment on the purchase price is required, and assuming no substantial increase in the fair market value of the property, the absence of personal liability on the debt reduces the transaction in economic terms to a mere chance that a genuine debt obligation may arise. This is not enough to justify an interest deduction. To justify the deduction the debt must exist; potential existence will not do. For debt to exist, the purchaser, in the absence of personal liability, must confront a situation in which it is presently reasonable from an economic point of view for him to make a capital investment in the amount of the unpaid purchase price. * * * Associates, during the taxable years in question, confronted no such situation. Compare Crane v. Commissioner, 331 U.S. 1, 11–12 (1947).

Our focus on the relationship of the fair market value of the property to the unpaid purchase price should not be read as premised upon the belief that a sale is not a sale if the purchaser pays too much. Bad bargains from the buyer's point of view—as well as sensible bargains from buyer's, but exceptionally good from the seller's point of view—do not thereby cease to be sales. * * * We intend our holding and explanation thereof to be understood as limited to transactions substantially similar to that now before us.

Affirmed.

NOTES

(A) *Effect of* Franklin *on Basis.* Where at the time of purchase the amount of a nonrecourse loan exceeds the value of the property securing it, should the indebtedness be excluded completely from basis, or rather be limited to the value of the property?

The Service, following *Estate of Franklin*, takes the position that an inadequately secured nonrecourse loan generally is too contingent to merit characterization as indebtedness and hence will not allow any portion of the loan to be considered an acquisition cost includable in basis. Rev.Rul. 77–110, 1977–1 C.B. 58. See also Rev.Rul. 84–5, 1984–1 C.B. 32 (denying interest deductions on a 30–year nonrecourse obligation with a large final "balloon" payment on the grounds that the obligation "does not constitute a valid indebtedness") A number of courts have explicitly agreed with the entire exclusion of loans from basis. See, e.g., Brannen v. Commissioner, 722 F.2d 695 (11th Cir.1984); Brountas v. Commissioner, 692 F.2d 152 (1st Cir.1982).

In Pleasant Summit Land Corp. v. Commissioner, 863 F.2d 263 (3d Cir.1988), cert. denied sub nom. Commissioner v. Prussin, 493 U.S. 901 (1989), the Third Circuit disagreed with the conclusion of *Estate of Franklin* that all depreciation and interest deductions should be disallowed whenever nonrecourse debt significantly exceeds the fair market value of property. Instead the court allowed the taxpayer to deduct depreciation and interest attributable to the portion of the nonrecourse debt that did not exceed the fair market value of the property. The court reasoned that the creditor has no incentive to foreclose if the debtor offers to settle the debt for the fair market value and thus, it was appropriate to regard that amount of the debt as genuine. See Lebowitz v. Commissioner, 917 F.2d 1314 (2d Cir.1990) (rejecting *Pleasant Summit*).

(B) *Tufts and Franklin Reconciled. Tufts* should be understood as holding only that a taxpayer must treat a nonrecourse mortgage consistently when he accounts for basis and amount realized. Thus, in an *Estate of Franklin* situation, where the amount of the mortgage exceeds the fair market value of the property securing it when the debt was first incurred, the mortgage is not included in the basis and thus will not be included in the amount realized upon disposition, generally foreclosure. In the *Tufts* situation, where the value of the security exceeded the debt initially, the debt is included in the basis and likewise is included in the amount realized upon foreclosure, even if the amount of debt then exceeds the fair market value of the property.

Generally, where there is an unrelated third party lender, the *Estate of Franklin* issue will not arise. A commercial lender, for example, will not extend nonrecourse debt where the value of the underlying security is insufficient. The seller of the property, however, is not so constrained because he does not actually transfer cash to the borrower. (Furthermore, as we shall see later, because of the installment sale rules, the seller reports no gain unless he actually receives payment on the debt).

What if a purchaser assumes a nonrecourse mortgage that exceeds the security? Reconsider the facts in *Tufts*. What is the basis of the purchaser from Tufts who assumed the $1.8 million nonrecourse mortgage and agreed to reimburse Tufts and his partners for the sale expenses when the "fair market value" of the property was only $1.4 million? Since the purchaser was an unrelated third party, is what he paid (the assumption of the debt and the reimbursement of the expenses) really the fair market value? Or is the debt excluded from his basis under *Franklin* because the value of the security is less than the debt?

(C) *Comparison of Discharge of Indebtedness Income and Gain.* A taxpayer who settles a debt at a discount generally has discharge of indebtedness income. United States v. Kirby Lumber Co., 284 U.S. 1 (1931). Where a taxpayer disposes of property secured by the debt, the debt is included in the amount realized. As *Tufts* indicates, this is true regardless of the value of the underlying security so long as the debt is nonrecourse. Where the debt is recourse, however, the transaction is bifurcated if the amount of the indebtedness exceeds the value of the property. Where a taxpayer transfers property with a fair market value that exceeds the basis, but is less than the outstanding debt, the value of the property is the amount realized and the extent to which it exceeds the basis is gain. Any excess debt that is discharged is income from the discharge of indebtedness. Reg. § 1.1001–2(c) (Ex. 8); Rev.Rul. 90–16, 1990–1 C.B. 12. This may be important if the discharge of indebtedness income is excluded from income by virtue of § 108, where, for example, the debtor is insolvent. The extent to which the fair market value of the property exceeds the basis is taxable income even if the debtor is insolvent. See Gehl v. Commissioner, 102 T.C. 784 (1994), aff'd in unpublished opinion, 50 F.3d 12 (8th Cir.1995).

For example, suppose A has property with an adjusted basis of $10, that is subject to a recourse mortgage of $45. At a time when the fair market value of the property is $30, the lender forecloses. The disposition of the property will satisfy $30 of the debt and the borrower will have a $20 gain. If the lender is unable to obtain assets to satisfy the remainder of the debt, A will have $15 of discharge of indebtedness income. If the debt were nonrecourse, the amount realized would include the entire debt and A would have $35 of gain. Generally, the amount received on a foreclosure sale is treated as the amount realized. Aizawa v. Commissioner, 99 T.C. 197 (1992).

Where a taxpayer is discharged from all or a portion of a nonrecourse liability, but does not dispose of the collateral, there is discharge of indebtedness income. There is no effect on the basis of the property used as security. Gershkowitz v. Commissioner, 88 T.C. 984 (1987); Rev.Rul. 91–31, 1991–1 C.B. 19. Note, however, that if the debt reduction is considered a reduction of the purchase price of the asset, there is no cancellation of indebtedness income. § 108(e)(5).

The interplay of these provisions is nicely illustrated by Preslar v. Commissioner, 167 F.3d 1323 (10th Cir.1999). The Preslars bought a ranch financed by a local bank. They subdivided and sold lots and turned the proceeds over to the bank to pay down the debt. The bank was declared insolvent and the FDIC took over the loan. When it refused to accept lot sale contracts, the Preslars made no more payments. Ultimately, they settled and their total payments on a $1 million debt were $550,000. The Preslars argued that they had no discharge of indebtedness income because the debt was disputed. (Recall the discussion of the disputed liability doctrine in *Zarin*, supra, at p. 177). The Tenth Circuit ruled that the mere fact that the taxpayers challenged the enforceability of the debt does automatically shield them from income on the resolution of the debt. The underlying amount of the debt was not in dispute, only the method of payment. The court also held that § 108(e)(5) did not apply because neither the bank nor the FDIC was the seller of the property. The result was that the Preslars had $450,000 of discharge of indebtedness income and retained their original cost basis.

(D) *Borrowing in Excess of Basis.* Suppose A purchases real estate for $50,000. At a time when the market value of this asset is $100,000, A takes out a nonrecourse loan for $80,000 secured only by the real estate. Does A have income? In Woodsam Associates, Inc. v. Commissioner, 198 F.2d 357 (2d Cir.1952), the court held that a loan, even when secured only by untaxed appreciation in property, does not constitute realized income to the borrower. The borrowing is not a realization event. The taxpayer (in a role reversal, having to do with a corporate tax provision) had argued that the loan, which allowed the borrower to receive cash without assuming any personal obligation to repay, constituted a partial disposition of the property that resulted in a realization of gain. This is another example of a timing advantage. The borrower does not include the amount of the loan in her basis because it is not an acquisition cost. She will either pay off the loan or, if it is assumed or discharged, it will be included in her amount realized. In the meantime, however, the taxpayer has the use of the money without a tax liability.

(E) *Post-Acquisition Indebtedness.* Suppose the taxpayer builds up additional equity in property and obtains post-acquisition indebtedness, either a second mortgage or an equity loan. The debt is not included in basis because it is not part of the "cost" of acquisition. § 1012. If, however, the taxpayer uses the proceeds to add to or improve the property, the amount expended would increase basis. § 1016. On disposition, regardless of whether the debt was included in basis, the outstanding amount of the indebtedness would be included in the amount realized. This reflects the fact that the taxpayer withdrew an amount of cash equal to the principal of the loan, which was not taxed on receipt under *Woodsam.*

(F) *Contingent Liabilities.* As the opinion in *Estate of Franklin* intimates, a loan should not increase basis where it is unclear whether the borrower will ever actually make principal payments. Thus, contingent liabilities are not included in basis until payments is made. In Rev.Rul. 78–29, 1978–1 C.B. 62, the IRS ruled that "an obligation, the payment of which is so speculative as to create a contingent liability, cannot be included in the basis of the property." For example, where the purchaser of a business agrees to pay the seller a percentage of profits, his basis does not include this liability until payments are made. Albany Car Wheel Co. v. Commissioner, 40 T.C. 831 (1963), aff'd per curiam, 333 F.2d 653 (2d Cir.1964). See also Gibson Products Co. v. United States, 637 F.2d 1041 (5th Cir.1981) (holding that nonrecourse debt secured by oil and gas leases, drilling equipment, and future production too contingent to be included in basis).

(G) *A Taxable Gift.* Recall that generally a transfer of property by gift is not a realization event. If, however, the donee transfers consideration, in exchange there is a part-sale, part-gift. The consideration may be the assumption of a liability of the donor. In Diedrich v. Commissioner, 457

U.S. 191 (1982), infra at page 634, the Court held that the transfer of stock on condition that the donees pay the federal gift tax owed on the transaction by the donor resulted in gross income to the donors to the extent that the gift tax exceeded basis. The Court determined that the taxpayers should treat the discharge of the gift tax liability as equivalent to the amount realized on a sale of the stock, and that they could offset this amount with their adjusted basis.

SECTION 9.   DAMAGES

It is the nature of the injury for which compensation is made that determines the tax consequences of the damages received by the taxpayer. It is difficult, but essential, to distinguish between business and personal damages because the Code provides preferential treatment for certain personal damages.

A.   DAMAGES TO BUSINESS INTERESTS

NOTE ON BUSINESS DAMAGES

The tax consequences of a compensatory damages award or reimbursement depend on the tax treatment of the item for which the reimbursement is intended to substitute. In Hort v. Commissioner, supra at page 141, the payment resulting from a negotiated settlement of a canceled lease was taxable because "basically the payment was merely a substitute for the rent reserved in the lease." In rejecting the taxpayer's contention that the income was capital gain, the Court noted that because the settlement payment "was essentially a substitute for rental payments which [§ 61] expressly characterizes as gross income, it must be regarded as ordinary income."

In Raytheon Production Corp. v. Commissioner, 144 F.2d 110, 113–14 (1st Cir.1944), cert. denied 323 U.S. 779 (1944), the court of appeals further detailed the principles governing the taxation of business damages:

Damages recovered in an antitrust action are not necessarily nontaxable as a return of capital. As in other types of tort damage suits, recoveries which represent a reimbursement for lost profits are income. * * * The reasoning is that since the profits would be taxable income, the proceeds of litigation which are their substitute are taxable in like manner.

Damages for violation of the anti-trust acts are treated as ordinary income where they represent compensation for loss of profits. * * *

The test is not whether the action was one in tort or contract but rather the question to be asked is "In lieu of what were the damages awarded?" * * * Where the suit is not to recover lost profits but is for injury to good will, the recovery represents a return of capital and, with certain limitations * * * is not taxable.

* * *

Since the suit was to recover damages for the destruction of the business and good will, the recovery represents a return of capital. Nor does the fact that the suit ended in a compromise settlement change the nature of the recovery; "the determining factor is the nature of the basic claim from which the compromised amount was realized."

* * *

But, to say that the recovery represents a return of capital in that it takes the place of the business good will is not to conclude that it may not contain a taxable benefit. Although the injured party may not be deriving a profit as a result of the damage suit itself, the conversion thereby of his property into cash is a realization of any gain made over the cost or other basis of the good will prior to the illegal interference.

Raytheon presented no evidence to establish the basis in its lost goodwill. Since a zero basis was determined for the goodwill, the entire amount recovered for its destruction was realized income.

Where the taxpayer receives an amount to compensate him for the loss of property that has an adjusted basis, the amount of income equals the amount by which the amount received exceeds his adjusted basis. For example, if the taxpayer's truck that he uses in his business has a basis of $10,000 and is destroyed and the tortfeasor gives the taxpayer $15,000, he has income to the extent that amount exceeds his adjusted basis of $10,000 or $5,000.

Where the taxpayer receives an amount to compensate for lost profits, he has no basis (usually because his costs have been deducted) and thus the entire amount is taxable. Similarly, punitive damages are entirely taxable. In Commissioner v. Glenshaw Glass, 348 U.S. 426 (1955), the Court held that money received as exemplary damages for fraud or as the punitive two-thirds portion of a treble damage recovery must be included in gross income under § 61. In that opinion, which is widely quoted for its definition of income, quoted supra at page 87, the Court also said:

> The mere fact that the payments were extracted from the wrongdoers as punishment for unlawful conduct cannot detract from their character as taxable income to the recipients. Respondents concede, as they must, that the recoveries are taxable to the extent that they compensate for damages actually incurred. It would be an anomaly that could not be justified in the absence of clear congressional intent to say that a recovery for actual damages is taxable but not the additional amount extracted as punishment for the same conduct which caused the injury. And we find no such evidence of intent to exempt these payments.

Where the taxpayer settles a claim for damages, what she is being compensated for must be determined. In Revenue Procedure 67–33, 1967–2 C.B. 659, the Service established procedures for determining tax liability for settlement of claims for damages. The tax treatment of settlements, like the tax treatment of damages, depends on the treatment of the amounts for which the settlement is a substitute. To the extent the settlement is attributable to a taxpayer's claim for the trebling of actual damages, therefore, it will be included in the taxpayer's gross income. But no amount will be attributed to punitive damages if the taxpayer can reasonably establish that actual damages exceeded the amount of the settlement (less legal expenses). In allocating the settlement amount between compensation for lost profits (taxable as ordinary income) and restoration of capital (treated as recovery of basis or, if in excess of basis, perhaps capital gain), however, the taxpayer may not attribute to capital an amount that exceeds the adjusted basis of the assets involved in the suit. The basis of the assets must be decreased to reflect the restoration of capital resulting from the settlement.

Section 186 permits taxpayers to reduce their taxable damages to reflect earlier losses that they have not been able to deduct fully (for example, because they had insufficient income at the time the injury occurred and net operating loss carryovers expired before they could use the deductions). This provision was intended to prevent injured parties who could not realize the benefit of loss deductions from being exposed to full tax liability for the compensation they received. It allows a deduction in the amount of the lesser of the compensation received (minus legal expenses) or the unrecovered losses sustained from the injury. Recoveries may be deducted only in the amount of actual economic injury; no deduction is permitted for punitive damages or for the noncompensatory two-thirds of treble damage antitrust awards. Reg. § 1.186–1.

B. Damages for Personal Injury

NOTE ON DAMAGES FOR PERSONAL INJURIES

The need to distinguish between personal and business damages is occasioned by § 104(a)(2), which excludes from income "the amount of any damages received (whether by suit or agreement and whether as lump sums or as periodic payments) on account of personal physical injuries or illness." This task is complicated by the fact that tort law, which generates compensation eligible for the § 104 exclusion, usually is indifferent to the personal-business distinction. The modern trend, to the extent one exists, involves the consolidation of contract and tort liability into a single compensation system. Even when the underlying substantive law permits assignment of an injury to a business or personal category, a principal measurement for compensation will be lost income, which rests on the impairment of income-producing capacity. As a result, rules implementing this personal-business distinction often appear artificial.

Prior to 1996, § 104(a)(2) excluded "the amount of any damages received * * * on account of personal injuries or sickness." This simple language led to a tremendous amount of litigation, primarily revolving around nonphysical personal injuries and punitive damages.

After decades of struggle by the lower courts to determine whether a particular injury—such a defamation or age discrimination—was a personal injury, the Supreme Court twice entered the fray to try to craft a definition. See United States v. Burke, 504 U.S. 229 (1992) (holding that back pay received on account of sex discrimination was taxable because personal injury involves only tort-like rights); Commissioner v. Schleier, 515 U.S. 323 (1995) (holding that back pay received on account of age discrimination was not on account of a personal injury). The decision to interpret personal injury to mean tort-like injuries did little to quell the controversy given the increasing coalescence of tort and contract claims. In 1996, Congress substantially narrowed the scope of § 104 by limiting the exclusion to personal *physical injury*. Thus, amounts received for defamation, sexual harassment, age discrimination, racial discrimination and the like—some of which previously had been excludible—are now taxable.

Section 104(a) also provides that emotional distress is not to be treated as "physical injury" or "sickness." Damages not in excess of the amount paid for medical care attributable to emotional distress are, however, excludible. Legislative history indicates that damages for physical injury or sickness resulting from emotional distress (headaches, insomnia) may not be excluded but damages for emotional distress resulting from physical injury may be. Legislative history indicates that damages from loss of consortium or emotional distress arising from a physical injury to one's spouse are excluded.

Although the IRS had always taken the position that punitive damages were taxable, some recipients had convinced the courts that the broad language "amounts received on account of personal injury" excluded punitive damages. Shortly after Congress amended Section 104 to make it clear that all punitive damages are taxable, the Supreme Court ruled that the prior language did not exclude punitive damages. O'Gilvie v. United States, 519 U.S. 79 (1996).

Unlike awards for business damages, an award for lost wages arising out of physical injury is excludible under § 104(a)(2). Rev.Rul. 85–97, 1985–2 C.B. 50. The Service has been thwarted in its attempt to divide an award between personal injury and back pay. See, e.g., Metzger v. Commissioner, 845 F.2d 1013 (3d Cir.1988); Downey v. Commissioner, 97 T.C. 150 (1991) (holding that all amounts received for personal injury, including back pay, are excludible). If, however, there are multiple claims, and one of them is not a personal injury claim, the award can be allocated between the taxable and nontaxable portions. See Stocks v. Commissioner, 98 T.C. 1 (1992).

NOTES

(A) *Damages*. "Personal injury" is not the only ambiguous term in § 104(a). In response to novel arguments, courts have begun to explore the meaning of "damages." Is a severance payment "damages" if a legal release of claims must be signed in order to receive it? In Taggi v. United States, 35 F.3d 93 (2d Cir.1994), the court required a laid-off AT&T employee to include in income a termination payment that was conditioned on "a full legal release" of claims against the employer. It found that the payment did not constitute a settlement agreement in lieu of such prosecution. A down-sized IBM employee met a similar fate in Abrahamsen v. United States, 228 F.3d 1360 (Fed.Cir.2000). The court pointed out that there were no claims outstanding when the release was signed and that the payment was based on two factors only: wages and tenure of service. Note that the taxpayers would have no claim under current law because their injuries were not physical.

(B) *Interest.* With the exception of certain tax-exempt interest (which is discussed in the next Section), interest generally is taxable to the recipient. Because the injury may occur long before payment is made by the tortfeasor, the parties may agree that the settlement amount should include interest on the amount of damages from the time of injury. Some state statutes mandate that interest accrue on the award before it is paid. Relying on *Schleier*, the Tenth Circuit determined that prejudgement interest was not excludible because it was not "damages received on account of personal injury." Rather it was to compensate the victim for the lost time value of money. Brabson v. United States, 73 F.3d 1040 (10th Cir.1996). This interpretation puts the taxpayer in the same position he would have been in had he received the excludible damages on the date of the injury and invested the proceeds.

Suppose the injured party and the tortfeasor simply agree on a lump sum amount of "damages," which is to be paid several years after the injury. If they do not explicitly state that the amount reflects a time value element, is anything taxable? In Delaney v. Commissioner, 99 F.3d 20 (1st Cir.1996), the court determined that a portion of the damages was nonexcludible prejudgement interest even though a settlement reached during the appeals process stated "No interest. No costs." The court clerk had added prejudgement interest to the jury award. If, however, no interest is stated, periodic payments are excluded under § 104(a) even though a portion of each payment is the economic equivalent of interest. E.g., Rev.Rul. 79–220, 1979–2 C.B. 74 (recipient of annuity in satisfaction of a personal injury claim can exclude entire amount).

(C) *Jury Instructions as to Exclusion of Damage Awards.* In Norfolk and Western Ry. Co. v. Liepelt, 444 U.S. 490 (1980), a wrongful death case arising out of the Federal Employers' Liability Act, the Supreme Court held that the jury should be instructed that "your award will not be subject to any income taxes and you should not consider such taxes in fixing the amount of your award." The plaintiff's expert witness had computed the amount of pecuniary loss at about $302,000, and the jury awarded damages of $775,000. The majority assumed that most jurors would be sufficiently "tax conscious" to assume the award would be taxable and therefore would increase the amount of the award by the "imaginary tax" they expected would be due. The Court concluded that the requested instruction was brief and easily understood by the jury, would not be prejudicial to either party, and would "merely eliminate an area of doubt or speculation that might have an improper impact on the computation of damages." Such an instruction "can certainly help by preventing the jury from inflating the award and thus overcompensating the plaintiff on the basis of an erroneous assumption that the judgment will be taxable."

In a vigorous dissent (joined by Justice Marshall), Justice Blackmun argued that "by mandating adjustment of the award by way of reduction for [taxes] on his earnings, the Court appropriates for the tortfeasor a benefit intended to be conferred on the victim or his survivors."

Justice Blackmun suggested that Congress had two likely purposes in not taxing wrongful death awards:

First, [that it] is simply not worthwhile to enact a complex and administratively burdensome system in order to approximate the tax treatment of the income if, in fact, it had been earned over a period of time by the decedent. Second, Congress may have intended to confer a humanitarian benefit on victim or the victims of the tort.

* * *

Whichever of these concerns it was that motivated Congress, transfer of the tax benefit to the * * * tortfeasor-defendant is inconsistent with that purpose.

Assume, in Norfolk and Western Ry. Co. v. Liepelt that the jury would have awarded $300,000 of damages with an instruction and $775,000 without such an instruction. If Congress, in fact, intended the first purpose suggested by Justice Blackmun, to approximate the tax treatment if the income had been earned over a period of time, then the appropriate award is the after-tax income stream. Is Justice Blackmun correct that this appropriates the tax savings to the tortfeasor? If the jury were blissfully ignorant of § 104, presumably they would award the before-tax income stream. In that case, can it be said that the failure to give an instruction about the excludability of damage awards would impose an additional and unwarranted "penalty" on tortfeasors by requiring damages greater than necessary to make the victim whole?

On the other hand, suppose Congress had the second purpose mentioned by Justice Blackmun, "to confer a humanitarian benefit on the victim." The implication is that Congress intended to put the victim in a better position than he would have been in had he not suffered the injury and received the compensation as salary, for example. In that case, would the failure to give the instruction penalize or benefit the victim? Does evaluating and choosing whether such an instruction should be given depend on whether § 104(a)(2) should be characterized as a tax expenditure provision, or, alternatively, as a provision appropriate in measuring net income?

(D) *Policy Justifications for Exclusion.* A number of justifications have been offered for the § 104 exclusion, none of which is entirely satisfactory.

Taxing an award for pain and suffering is offensive. Some have asserted that taxing a recovery due to pain and suffering is offensive and the victim should be assisted rather than taxed. This might be a justification for a tax expenditure, but § 104 then is a peculiar way to accomplish it. There clearly are items exempted by § 104 that do not involve pain and suffering.

A recovery for expenses should not be taxed. If a taxpayer incurred expenses and is reimbursed for them, there should be no income (unless he took a deduction in a prior year). In theory, this justifies excluding expenses that otherwise would be deductible, such as medical expenses, but, as we shall see, many taxpayers are unable to deduct their medical expenses because of various limitations. It certainly does not justify excluding wages, which otherwise would be taxed.

A recovery of human capital should not be taxed. If an award is a replacement of human capital, it should not be taxed because the taxpayer has no gain; he has an offsetting economic loss. Thus, payments received for a lost limb, for example, should be exempt. This is akin to a property recovery, although the taxpayer would have no income only if his basis were deemed to be equal to the amount received. It is possible—although mysterious and without statutory authority—that a taxpayer is born with a basis in his body, reputation, etc. The Supreme Court has held, for example, that a spouse has a basis in marital rights equal to their value. United States v. Davis, 370 U.S. 65, 73 n. 7 (1962). If this is Congress' reason for exempting recoveries, § 104 creates an inequity for a victim without insurance or one who is unable to recover from the tortfeasor: the taxpayer who loses an arm, but receives no recovery has no deduction for a loss of human capital. Furthermore, a taxpayer has no loss for a decline in value of his human capital.

Recoveries for nontaxable items should be tax-free. In many circumstances, the recovery is to compensate the taxpayer for a loss of an item which is itself nontaxable. For example, possessing good health, the use of one's body, enjoying one's reputation, privacy, civil rights and the freedom from harassment and discrimination are all "psychic benefits" that are untaxed. Recall the discussion on the failure to tax imputed income from services. The payment made by the tortfeasor can be likened to a transfer equal to the imputed income stream from these items that would be untaxed. There is an essential difference, however; imputed income generally is untaxed due to the absence of a market transaction. The services are not taxed because we would have trouble identifying or valuing them. When the taxpayer converts the services into cash, however, she is taxed. Perhaps, then, when the taxpayer converts body parts or reputation, for example, into cash, she should be taxed. In United States v. Garber, 589 F.2d 843 (5th Cir.1979), reversed in part on rehearing 607 F.2d 92 (5th Cir.1979), the Fifth Circuit held that income derived from the sale of blood plasma is taxable, whether giving blood is classified as a personal service or as the sale of a product. The court held that the substantial amount the taxpayer received for her blood, which contained a rare antibody, was taxable because it produced an economic gain not excluded by statute. Section 104(a)(2) was held not to be applicable.

Wages should be untaxed so the victim will be in the position he would have been in had there been no injury. If the damages are calculated on an after-tax basis using an after-tax discount rate and tax rates are assumed to be constant over time, exemption of the proceeds puts the taxpayer in the identical position he would have been had he earned the wages. As the above discussion of jury instructions makes clear, however, a jury may be told about the tax consequences, but apparently is permitted to calculate damages on either a before-or after-tax basis. If the jury were to calculate damages on a before-tax basis, the taxpayer economically would be in a better position than he would have been without the injury. Note the unequal treatment of a taxpayer who receives "sick pay" or a continuation of wages from an insurance plan or from the employer. Under § 105, the wages are taxable. If, however, a tortfeasor makes a payment that includes lost wages, they are exempt under § 104(a)(2).

(E) *September 11 Tax Provisions.* Congress occasionally chooses to provide special tax benefits to those who have been injured in combat or disasters or to those who lost property in a federally-declared disaster area. In 2002 Congress enacted generous benefits to those affected by the September 11 terrorist attack. It forgave the federal income tax liabilities for 2000 and 2001 for all those who died in the September 11 attack, as well as the anthrax attacks in the fall of 2001 and the Oklahoma City bombing in 1995. If the victim's tax liability was less than $10,000, the difference was refunded. Also excluded from income are disaster relief payments, disability payments, employer death benefits paid to survivors' families, and payments made by the federal September 11 Victims' Compensation Fund.

SECTION 10.   TAX-EXEMPT INTEREST

Section 103 generally excludes from income interest on state and local obligations. Such a tax exemption has been provided ever since the federal income tax was adopted in 1913.

The exemption allows state and local governments to pay lower rates of interest on their debt than that paid on taxable corporate bonds of comparable risk. For example, if the market rate of interest is 10 percent on a comparable corporate bond, a municipality could pay only 6 percent on its debt and a purchaser in a 40 percent marginal tax bracket would be indifferent between the municipal and the corporate bond, since the after-tax interest rate on the corporate bond is 6 percent. The municipal bond is sometimes said to be subject to an implicit tax. In the above example, the bond is subject to an implicit tax of 40 percent. Although the federal government forfeits the 4 percent differential, the state or local government saves the same amount. Taking into account the implicit tax, there is no violation of horizontal equity since the two taxpayers with the same economic income receive the same after-tax return.

Historically, the ratio of yields on tax-exempt issues to taxable issues has generally been about 75 percent, but in some years it has been as high as 92 percent. The ratio of yields has varied in response to the general availability of credit, the demand for credit, and the relative demand of state and local governments for credit in the total market. If high-income taxpayers do not purchase the entire tax-exempt bond market, the ratio of the yields on tax-exempt bonds to taxable bonds must rise. In the above example, a taxpayer in the 20 percent bracket would not purchase the municipal bond with a 6 percent interest rate because his after-tax yield on the corporate bond would be 8 percent. Thus, in order to attract purchases by 20 percent–bracket taxpayers, the municipality would need to pay at least 8 percent. Notice that a 40 percent–bracket taxpayer who purchased an 8 percent municipal bond would receive a 2 percent windfall—an amount not needed to get him to purchase the bond. As a result of high ratios of tax-exempt to taxable bond yields, high-income taxpayers otherwise subject to high income tax rates (who constitute a major portion of the market for tax-exempt state and local securities) often receive significantly greater tax benefits than necessary for them to prefer tax-exempt to taxable bonds. On the 8 percent bond purchased by that taxpayer, the federal government will lose the 4 percent that it would have received had the taxpayer purchased a 10 percent taxable bond, but the state or local government would receive only a 2 percent interest-savings benefit. Estimates are that the annual saving in interest charges to state and local governments is generally roughly two-thirds of the annual revenue loss to the federal government. Thus, the subsidy can be said to be inefficient because it provides benefits to third parties (i.e., the high-income investors) in addition to the benefits to the local government; the revenue cost to the federal government is substantially greater than the savings in interests costs to state and local governments.

Distributional Aspects of the Tax Exemption. It is clear that if the present tax exemption were eliminated, the entire burden would not be borne by the purchasers of taxable state and local bonds, who would, as a statutory matter, pay the tax on the interest from the bonds. Elimination of the tax exemption would undoubtedly require higher interest rates for state and local bonds. The benefits of the tax exemption are, in effect, shared by the bondholders and the taxpayers of state and local governments and thus, both would also share the burden of the elimination of the tax exemption.

But descriptions of the distributional effects that would result from repeal of the tax exemption often ignore the effects on interest rates.* The sharing of benefits of the tax exemption between bond owners and state and local governments is not taken into account in determining the burdens of such repeal. Official estimates that ignore the interest savings to state and local governments show that more than 50 percent of the benefits from the tax exemption accrue to individuals with adjusted gross income over $100,000 and only about 19 percent of the benefits go to individuals with adjusted gross income of $20,000 or less.** But when the interest saving is taken into account, the benefits from the tax exemption appear to be spread far more evenly through the income classes. About half of the benefits flow to individuals with adjusted gross incomes of $20,000 or less, and less than one-third of the revenue loss benefits individuals with adjusted gross incomes over $100,000.***

---

* This discussion is based on Michael J. Graetz, "Assessing the Distributional Effects of Income Tax Revision: Some Lessons from Incidence Analysis," 4 J. of Legal Studies 351 (1975).

** See, e.g., Congressional Research Service, Tax Expenditures: Compendium of Background Material on Individual Provisions, 102d Cong., 2d Sess., November 1992; Staff of Treasury Dep't and Joint Comm. on Taxation, Estimates of Federal Tax Expenditures, 92d Cong., 2d Sess. 9 tbl. 2 (Comm. Print 1972), reprinted in Panel Discussions on General Tax Reform before the House Ways and Means Committee, 93d Cong., 1st Sess., pt. 1 at 31–34.

*** These figures are based on the assumption that state and local governments will finance the increased interest costs which would result from repeal of the tax exemption through general revenues. They are a rough approximation of a distribution of benefits from the tax exemption. They are based on the assumption that 70 percent of the revenue loss from the tax exemption would be reflected in lower interest costs to state and local governments and that this 70 percent benefits income classes of individuals in proportion to their burdens of general state and local tax revenues. In other words, it assumes that repeal of the exemption would increase interest costs to state and local governments and that these govern-

Would you expect to see a similar shifting of other income tax benefits from one party to another? Can you think of examples?

Constitutional Implications. Although there is a body of opinion that regards it as unconstitutional for the federal government to tax interest on state and local governments, recent decisions of the Supreme Court have made it clear that the Constitution grants Congress power to repeal the tax exemption for interest in state and local bonds. In State of South Carolina v. Baker, 485 U.S. 505 (1988), the Court upheld a provision that taxes interest on state and local bonds unless the bonds are issued in registered (as opposed to bearer) form. The Court rejected the argument that the statute interfered with the state's right to borrow, made borrowing more expensive and therefore impaired its exercise of sovereign powers.

Private Activity Bonds. Primarily as a response to the increasing issuance of bonds by state and local governments to finance activities other than general government operations or governmentally owned and operated facilities, Congress has substantially limited the issuance of such bonds. Sections 141–150 contain restrictions on the general exclusion for certain types of private activity or industrial development bonds, arbitrage bonds and other special types of bonds.

An arbitrage bond is one used by a state or local government to acquire other securities with a higher rate of return. This return would not be taxed to the government because it is tax-exempt. Section 148 imposes severe restrictions on these bonds, so that in most cases the interest on the bond would not be tax-exempt. § 103(b)(2).

An industrial development bond (IDB) is often used as a way to attract a business to a state or locality. The local government is simply a conduit. It borrows the funds, in order to obtain the tax exemption, but the payment of the debt service on the bond is the responsibility of the user of the facility acquired with the bond proceeds. Alarmed at the increasing use of these private activity bonds, Congress limited their use when (1) more than 10 percent of the proceeds is for direct or indirect use in a trade or business of anyone other than a governmental unit (with certain further restrictions); or (2) more than 5 percent of the proceeds of the issue is used to make or finance loans to entities other than state or local governments. § 141(b). Bonds which are used for traditional public activities—such as schools, roads and bridges, and sewers—continue to be exempt without limitation. There are also a number of exceptions to the private activity bond limitations. One important example is for exempt-facility bonds, those where the proceeds are used to provide airports, docks and wharves, mass commuting facilities, facilities for the furnishing of water, sewage facilities, solid waste disposal facilities, qualified residential rental projects, facilities for the furnishing of electric energy or gas, local district heating or cooling facilities, qualified hazardous waste facilities or high-speed intercity rail

ments would finance the increased interest costs out of general revenues. Of course, the impact of repeal of the exemption would vary from state to state but no attempt has been made to take interstate differences into account. The lowering of the top rate from 70 percent in the 1970's to about 38 percent today has increased the share of the tax benefits going to state and local governments, so the 70 percent number may now be a bit low, but the principle of the illustration holds.

facilities. § 142(a). In addition, certain mortgage bonds, small issue bonds, student loan bonds, redevelopment bonds and bonds where the proceeds are to be used by a charity are also exempt. § 143–147. These exemptions are subject to many definitional and other limitations. These arcane rules are of mind-boggling complexity and best left to tax-exempt bond specialists.

Tax Expenditure Considerations. The justification for the exemption is that it provides a subsidy to state and local governments in the form of lower interest rates on their borrowings. This could also be accomplished by a direct subsidy. What differences would there be between a direct subsidy and the tax exemption?

Note that the tax exemption for general purpose bonds provides an unlimited subsidy. In general, there is no limitation on the number of bonds issued or the amount a government may borrow. It is highly unlikely that Congress would pass an unlimited direct subsidy. Furthermore, the federal government does not exercise control over what projects are funded or what states or municipalities are subsidized. Are these advantages or disadvantages of a subsidy in the form of tax exemption?

CHAPTER 3

DEDUCTIONS AND CREDITS

This Chapter discusses questions that arise in reducing gross income to taxable income by subtracting allowable deductions. Many deductions are necessary to measure income accurately. The deduction for ordinary and necessary business expenses, § 162, is essential if we are to tax net income. Other deductions are not necessary to obtain an accurate measurement of net income, but rather are tax subsidies for certain activities or investments. An example is the immediate writeoff for expenses to remove architectural and transportation barriers to the handicapped and elderly found in § 190. Certain deductions, however, are very difficult to categorize. For example, tax experts have hotly debated whether the charitable deduction and medical deduction are subsidies or whether they are needed to properly determine net income.

A deduction is closely related to an exclusion from income; both remove amounts from taxable income. A deduction of an item related to personal consumption may have the same effect as an exclusion from income. If, for example, a taxpayer receives $10,000 of salary and a $1,000 excludable fringe benefit, he will have the same net economic and taxable income if he receives $11,000 of salary and spends $1,000 on a benefit that produces a deduction. As we shall see, in many cases a taxpayer may prefer an exclusion to a deduction because of limits imposed on deductions.

For corporations, allowable deductions serve to reduce gross income to taxable income; for individuals, the computation of taxable income is more cumbersome. The first computational step for individuals is to subtract those deductions allowable in reducing gross income to "adjusted gross income" (AGI) as defined in § 62. Then AGI is reduced to "taxable income" by subtracting "itemized deductions." Itemized deductions are allowable only to the extent they exceed the standard deduction, specified in § 63(c). The standard deduction is taken in lieu of itemized deductions. Itemized deductions are, in some cases, fully allowable. In others, they are allowable only to the extent of certain related types of income or only to the extent they exceed certain floors—typically, specified percentages of AGI. Furthermore, certain itemized deductions, called "miscellaneous itemized deductions," are subject to further limitation. Only the amount of miscellaneous itemized deductions that exceeds 2 percent of the taxpayer's AGI may be deducted. § 67(a). This limitation applies in addition to any specific statutory limitation on a particular deduction. High income taxpayers have some itemized deductions disallowed (as a backhand way of increasing their tax rate). § 68. Deductions exceeding a certain amount are not allowable at all. § 68(a), although this provision is effective only through 2009. Finally, certain itemized deductions are disallowed in computing the alternative minimum tax. The alternative minimum tax is discussed in Chapter 7.

In addition to deductions that reduce taxable income, this Chapter also considers several income tax credits that offset tax liability. A dollar of tax credit saves a dollar of taxes, while a dollar of deduction saves a fraction of that amount, depending on the taxpayer's tax bracket. For example, a $100 deduction for a taxpayer in the 30 percent bracket saves $30 in taxes whereas a $100 credit saves $100 in taxes regardless of the taxpayer's rate bracket. Typically, a tax credit is allowed only for a specified percentage of the expenditure that qualifies for the credit.

Generally, a taxpayer can use deductions only to the extent of her income for the taxable year. In some cases, the deductions are preserved and carried over to be used in a succeeding taxable year. In other situations, the deductions are lost. Similarly, a credit that is usable only to the extent of the tax liability for the taxable year is nonrefundable. A few credits are refundable, meaning that the taxpayer will receive a check from the government even if he has no tax liability. Some credits can be carried over to a succeeding year.

One of the major issues in connection with deductions is timing, especially those deductions relating to capitalization of costs and their recovery, such as through depreciation allowances. Timing issues are extremely important both to tax policy and tax planning. Indeed, as will be detailed subsequently, acceleration of a deduction may be equivalent to a full or partial exclusion of the income generated by the deductible expense.

Is there is a constitutional right to deductions? Could Congress deny all deductions and impose a tax on gross income? Would a tax on gross income constitute a direct tax on wealth that must be apportioned among the states? Or does the Sixteenth Amendment doom such an argument? See Helvering v. Independent Life Insurance Co., 292 U.S. 371, 381 (1934) ("Unquestionably Congress has power to condition, limit or deny deductions from gross income in order to arrive at the net that it chooses to tax."). See also Pedone v. United States, 151 F.Supp. 288, 291 (Ct.Cl.1957) (Congress may "provide that certain costs, the incurring of which is in violation of law or public policy, shall be disregarded in computing gains.").

Courts often state that deductions should be narrowly construed. The usual phrase is "an income tax deduction is a matter of legislative grace and the burden of clearly showing the right to the claimed deduction is on the taxpayer." It is true that the taxpayer bears the burden of proving his right to a deduction, but the question should not be approached in terms of a "narrow" construction or "legislative grace." The clear intent of Congress to impose the tax on "taxable income" requires recognition of deductions as well as gross income. When Congress wants to limit deductions, it can do so explicitly.

SECTION 1. BUSINESS EXPENSES

NOTE ON ORDINARY AND NECESSARY BUSINESS EXPENSES

There are a number of Code sections that provide for a deduction for expenses or losses incurred by a business. The primary provision is § 162, which allows a deduction for "all the ordinary and necessary expenses paid or incurred during the taxable year in carrying on any trade or business." This section permits a wide-ranging number of deductions, most of which are commonplace and noncontroversial. The regulations give as examples of deductible business expenses employee wages, annual insurance premiums on business assets, office rent, utilities, and the like.

Section 162 permits deductions only in connection with a trade or business. Section § 212 permits individuals to deduct "ordinary and necessary" expenses stemming from income producing activities that do not qualify as a trade or business. Section 212 was Congress' response to Higgins v. Commissioner, 312 U.S. 212 (1941), in which the Supreme Court held that an investor could not treat the management of his own investments as a trade or business and therefore could not deduct the salaries of his assistants, office rent, and similar outlays.

Although § 212 is very similar to § 162, it differs in two important respects. Section 212 applies only to individuals and generally is only a deduction from AGI to obtain taxable income; consequently, the taxpayer must have itemized deductions that exceed the standard deduction in order to take advantage of § 212 expenses. (Deductions attributable to rents and royalties, however, are deductible from gross income in determining adjusted gross income. § 62(a)(4)). Second, § 212 expenses are miscellaneous itemized deductions and thus are subject to the 2 percent limitation, discussed above and at page 243 infra.

These distinctions (as well as others, see, e.g., §§ 163(d), 166(d), 172(d)(4), 469, 1221, and 1231) make it important to know whether an activity is a "trade or business" or an income producing activity. In Commissioner v. Groetzinger, 480 U.S. 23 (1987), the Supreme Court held that a professional gambler engages in a trade or business if "involved in the activity with continuity and regularity" and with the primary purpose of earning income or profit, even if there is no sale of goods or services. The Seventh Circuit has noted that a taxpayer cannot simply call itself a "business" and make it so:

> The concept of "trade or business" is plastic, CIR v. Groetzinger * * *, but it hardly follows that anything goes. The taxpayers take a "magic words" approach to the subject: if the * * * documents contain the right language, then all is well. The [question is] whether the [taxpayers] reasonably anticipated availing themselves of the privileges they possessed on paper. That is the right question; pen and ink divorced from reasonable business expectations do not a "trade or business" make.

Levin v. Commissioner, 832 F.2d 403, 406 (7th Cir.1987) (holding that passive investors in a partnership to develop "bacon board dispensers" were not entitled to research deduction because they had no intention of going into business).

Sections 165(a) and (c) permit deductions for losses incurred in a trade or business or in a profit seeking activity. In practice the distinction between § 162 and § 165 can become blurred.

The cases and materials presented here do not exhaust the issues arising under § 162, but they do illustrate the more important issues. Section 162 permits a deduction for "all the ordinary and necessary expenses paid or incurred during the taxable year in carrying on any trade or business." Three types of general questions have arisen: (1) To what extent does the phrase "ordinary and necessary" imply that there is a class of nondeductible business expenses? (2) What distinguishes a "trade or business" expense from a personal expense? (3) What separates a deductible expense from a capital outlay?

The latter two questions are essential in defining net income. In contrast, deciding that some expenses are "extraordinary" or "unnecessary," even though they are not capital expenditures and are expended to advance the taxpayer's business, is a departure from the concept of net income in pursuit of some other policy.

The *Welch* case, which follows, is widely cited as putting flesh on the meaning of the phrase "ordinary and necessary;" *Gilliam*, which follows *Welch* is less typical.

Welch v. Helvering

Supreme Court of the United States, 1933. 290 U.S. 111.

MR. JUSTICE CARDOZO delivered the opinion of the Court.

The question to be determined is whether payments by a taxpayer, who is in business as a commission agent, are allowable deductions in the computation of his income if made to the creditors of a bankrupt corporation in an endeavor to strengthen his own standing and credit.

In 1922 petitioner was the secretary of the E.L. Welch Company, a Minnesota corporation, engaged in the grain business. The company was adjudged an involuntary bankrupt, and had a discharge from its debts. Thereafter the petitioner made a contract with the Kellogg Company to purchase grain for it on a commission. In order to reestablish his relations with customers whom he had known when acting for the Welch Company and to solidify his credit and standing, he decided to pay the debts of the Welch business so far as he was able. In fulfilment of that resolve, he made payments of substantial amounts during five successive years. * * * The Commissioner ruled that these payments were not deductible from income as ordinary and necessary expenses, but were rather in the nature of capital expenditures, an outlay for the development of reputation and good will. The Board of Tax Appeals sustained the action of the Commissioner (25 B.T.A. 117), and the Court of Appeals for the Eighth Circuit affirmed. 63 F.2d 976. The case is here on certiorari.

"In computing net income there shall be allowed as deductions * * * all the ordinary and necessary expenses paid or incurred during the taxable year in carrying on any trade or business." [citing predecessors of § 162.]

We may assume that the payments to creditors of the Welch Company were necessary for the development of the petitioner's business, at least in the sense that they were appropriate and helpful. McCulloch v. Maryland, 4 Wheat. 316. He certainly thought they were, and we should be slow to override his judgment. But the problem is not solved when the payments are characterized as necessary. Many necessary payments are charges upon capital. There is need to determine whether they are both necessary and ordinary. Now, what is ordinary, though there must always be a strain of constancy within it, is nonetheless a variable affected by time and place and circumstance. Ordinary in this context does not mean that the payments must be habitual or normal in the sense that the same taxpayer will have to make them often. A lawsuit affecting the safety of a business may happen once in a lifetime. The counsel fees may be so heavy that repetition is unlikely. Nonetheless, the expense is an ordinary one because we know from experience that payments for such a purpose, whether the amount is large or small, are the common and accepted means of defense against attack. * * * The situation is unique in the life of the individual affected, but not in the life of the group, the community, of which he is a part. At such times there are norms of conduct that help to stabilize our judgment, and make it certain and objective. The instance is not erratic, but is brought within a known type.

The line of demarcation is now visible between the case that is here and the one supposed for illustration. We try to classify this act as ordinary or the opposite, and the norms of conduct fail us. No longer can we have recourse to any fund of business experience, to any known business practice. Men do at times pay the debts of others without legal obligation or the lighter obligation imposed by the usages of trade or by neighborly amenities, but they do not do so ordinarily, not even though the result might be to heighten their reputation for generosity and opulence. Indeed, if language is to be read in its natural and common meaning * * *, we should have to say that payment in such circumstances instead of being ordinary is in a high degree extraordinary. There is nothing ordinary in the stimulus evoking it, and none in the response. Here, indeed, as so often in other branches of the law, the decisive distinctions are those of degree and not of kind. One struggles in vain for any verbal formula that will supply a ready touchstone. The standard set up by the statute is not a rule of law; it is rather a way of life. Life in all its fullness must supply the answer to the riddle.

The Commissioner of Internal Revenue resorted to that standard in assessing the petitioner's income, and found that the payments in controversy came closer to capital outlays than to ordinary and necessary expenses in the operation of a business. His ruling has the support of a presumption of correctness, and the petitioner has the burden of proving it to be wrong. * * * Unless we can say from facts within our knowledge that these are ordinary and necessary expenses according to the ways of conduct and the forms of speech prevailing in the business world, the tax must be confirmed. But nothing told us by this record or within the sphere of our judicial notice permits us to give that extension to what is ordinary and necessary. Indeed, to do so would open the door to many bizarre analogies. One man has a family name that is clouded by thefts committed by an ancestor. To add to his own standing he repays the stolen money, wiping off, it may be, his income for the year. The payments figure in his tax return as ordinary expenses. Another man conceives the notion that he will be able to practice his vocation with greater ease and profit if he has an opportunity to enrich his culture. Forthwith the price of his education becomes an expense of the business, reducing the income subject to taxation. There is little difference between these expenses and those in controversy here. Reputation and learning are akin to capital assets, like the good will of an old partnership. * * * For many, they are the only tools with which to hew a pathway to success. The money spent in acquiring them is well and wisely spent. It is not an ordinary expense of the operation of a business.

Many cases in the federal courts deal with phases of the problem presented in the case at bar. To attempt to harmonize them would be a futile task. They involve the appreciation of particular situations, at times with borderline conclusions. * * *

The decree should be

Affirmed.

NOTES

(A) *The Ordinary and Necessary Standard.* Does "life in all its fullness" supply an answer to the riddle of the meaning of "ordinary and necessary"? "Ordinary" and "necessary" are terms of art; it is quite clear that an expense that is neither "ordinary" nor "necessary" in the dictionary sense may still be deductible.

Although the Court in Deputy v. du Pont, 308 U.S. 488, 494 (1940), says that "ordinary" has the "connotation of normal, usual, or customary," it also notes that an expense can be ordinary even though it happens only once in a person's life. It must be, however, common or a frequent occurrence in the type of business involved. Does this mean that the first taxpayer to incur a particular business expense may not deduct it? "Necessary" does not mean essential; it appears to mean appropriate and helpful for the development of the taxpayer's business.

Others have interpreted *Welch* to mean that a capital expenditure is not an ordinary and necessary business deduction. This principle is codified in § 263, which explicitly prohibits a deduction under § 162 for capital expenditures. The Service had argued in *Welch* that the expenses "came closer to capital outlays than to ordinary and necessary expenses in the operation of a business." See also Raymond Bertolini Trucking Co. v. Commissioner, 736 F.2d 1120 (6th Cir.1984), where the court allowed deduction of legal kickback payments, stating that "[t]he central issue in *Welch* was * * * whether the expenditure should have been deducted currently or capitalized; the question of whether the expenditure was 'normal' is a tool for getting at this prime question." Perhaps the Court could have decided *Welch* without reference to the "ordinary and necessary" language simply by applying the predecessor of § 263 to this expenditure and denying a deduction on the ground that it was capital. Capital expenditures are treated infra at page 284.

(B) *Deduction for Payment of Another's Expenses. Welch* has not led to a general rule that forbids taxpayers from deducting all reimbursements of another's losses. Where such payments are made to protect the payor's own business, they are frequently deductible. If, however, the payor incurs the expense due to a moral obligation, there is no deduction. For example, in Friedman v. Delaney, 171 F.2d 269 (1st Cir.1948), a lawyer made a payment on behalf of a client when the client would not pay the amount for which the lawyer had settled a case. The lawyer felt that the payment was a moral obligation, although it was not legally enforceable. The court held that the payment was not deductible. Compare Jenkins v. Commissioner, 47 T.C.M. 238 (1983), where Conway Twitty, the late country music star, made payments to investors in a defunct restaurant business called Twitty Burger, Inc. The court determined that Twitty made the payments (on behalf of the corporation) to protect his personal business reputation as a country music performer. Although the court did not believe that Twitty's personal sense of morality was paramount, it apparently did accept Twitty's testimony that country music fans insist on integrity and allowed the deduction based on the "unique facts of this case."

Gilliam v. Commissioner

United States Tax Court, 1986. 51 T.C.M. 515.

CHABOT, JUDGE: * * * Gilliam is, and was at all material periods, a noted artist. His works have been exhibited in numerous art galleries throughout the United States and Europe * * * In addition, Gilliam is, and was at all material periods, a teacher of art. On occasion, Gilliam lectured and taught art at various institutions.

Gilliam accepted an invitation to lecture and teach for a week at the Memphis Academy of Arts in Memphis, Tennessee. On Sunday, February 23, 1975, he flew to Memphis to fulfill this business obligation.

Gilliam had a history of hospitalizations for mental and emotional disturbances and continued to be under psychiatric care until the time of his trip to Memphis.

Before his Memphis trip, Gilliam created a 225–foot painting for the Thirty-fourth Biennial Exhibition of American Painting at the Corcoran Gallery of Art (hereinafter sometimes referred to as "the Exhibition"). The Exhibition opened on Friday evening, February 21, 1975. In addition, Gilliam was in the process of preparing a giant mural for an outside wall of the Philadelphia Museum of Art for the 1975 Spring Festival in Philadelphia. The budget plans for this mural were due on Monday, February 24, 1975.

On the night before his Memphis trip, Gilliam felt anxious and unable to rest. * * * On Sunday, February 23, 1975 * * * he boarded American Airlines flight 395 at Washington National Airport, Washington, D.C., bound for Memphis. About one and one-half hours after the airplane departed Washington National Airport, Gilliam began to act in an irrational manner. He talked of bizarre events and had difficulty in speaking. According to some witnesses, he appeared to be airsick and held his head. Gilliam began to feel trapped, anxious, disoriented, and very agitated. Gilliam said that the plane was going to crash and that he wanted a life raft. Gilliam entered the aisle and, while going from one end of the airplane to the other, he tried to exit from three different doors. Then Gilliam struck * * * another passenger, several times with a telephone receiver. Gilliam also threatened the navigator and a stewardess, called for help, and cried * * *.

On arriving in Memphis, Gilliam was arrested by Federal officials. On March 10, 1975, Gilliam was indicted. * * * Gilliam entered a plea of not guilty to the criminal charges. * * * [T]he district court granted Gilliam's motion for a judgment of acquittal by reason of temporary insanity. Petitioners paid $8,250 and $8,600 for legal fees in 1975 and 1976.

Petitioners contend that they are entitled to deduct the amounts paid in defense of the criminal prosecution and in settlement of the related civil claim under section 162. Petitioners maintain that the instant case is directly controlled by our decision in Dancer v. Commissioner, 73 T.C. 1103 (1980). According to petitioners, "[t]he clear holding of Dancer is * * * that expenses for litigation arising out of an accident which occurs during a business trip are deductible as ordinary and necessary business expenses." Respondent contends that the legal fees paid are not deductible under either section 162 or section 212 because the criminal charges against Gilliam were neither directly connected with nor proximately resulted from his trade or business and the legal fees were not paid for the production of income. Respondent maintains that "the criminal charges which arose as a result of * * * [the incident on the airplane], could hardly be deemed 'ordinary,' given the nature of [Gilliam's] profession." Respondent contends "that the provisions of section 262 control this situation." We agree with respondent that the expenses are not ordinary expenses of Gilliam's trade or business. * * * In Deputy v. du Pont, the Supreme Court set forth a guide for application of the statutory requirement that the expense be "ordinary", as follows (308 U.S. at 494–497):

> * * * Ordinary has the connotation of normal, usual, or customary. To be sure, an expense may be ordinary though it happen but once in the taxpayer's lifetime * * * Yet the transaction which gives rise to it must be of common or frequent occurrence in the type of business involved. Hence, the fact that a particular expense would be an ordinary or common one in the course of one business * * * does not necessarily make it such in connection with another business. One of the extremely relevant circumstances is the nature and scope of the particular business out of which the expense in question accrued.

Gilliam is a noted artist and teacher of art. It undoubtedly is ordinary for people in Gilliam's trades or businesses to travel (and to travel by air) in the course of such trades or businesses; however, we do not believe it is ordinary for people in such trades or businesses to be involved in altercations of the sort here involved in the course of any such travel. The travel was not itself the conduct of Gilliam's trades or businesses. Also, the expenses here involved are not strictly a cost of Gilliam's transportation. Finally, it is obvious that neither the altercation nor the expenses were undertaken to further Gilliam's trades or businesses.

We conclude that Gilliam's expenses are not ordinary expenses of his trades or businesses.

It is instructive to compare the instant case with Dancer v. Commissioner, supra, upon which petitioners rely. * * * Dancer, the taxpayer was driving an automobile; he caused an accident which resulted in injuries to a child. The relevant expenses were the taxpayer's payments to settle the civil claims arising from the accident.

In Dancer, we stated as follows:

> It is true that the expenditure in the instant case did not further petitioner's business in any economic sense; nor is it, we hope, the type of expenditure that many businesses are called upon to pay. Nevertheless, neither factor lessens the direct relationship between the expenditure and the business. Automobile travel by petitioner was an integral part of this business. * * * As unfortunate as it may be, lapses by drivers seem to be an inseparable incident of driving a car. Costs incurred as a result of such an incident are just as much a part of overall business expenses as the cost of fuel.

Dancer is distinguishable.

NOTES

(A) *Carrying on a Trade or Business.* As *Gilliam* states, an expense must be incurred in carrying on a trade or business in order to be deductible under § 162. Note that the court says that the travel itself was not the conduct of Gilliam's business. Suppose at the lecture in Memphis Gilliam had slugged someone who had disparaged his art? Could he have deducted expenses in connection with that altercation? This issue is closely related to distinguishing between personal and business expenses, which is discussed infra at page 246.

(C) *Legal Expenses.* Although one might argue that litigation costs are inherently profit motivated, at least whenever money will change hands as a result of the litigation, the courts have not provided such generous tax treatment for legal fees. In United States v. Gilmore, 372 U.S. 39 (1963), the taxpayer sought to deduct legal expenses incurred in contesting a divorce property settlement. The Court developed an "origin of the claim" test to distinguish deductible from nondeductible litigation expenses; the spouse's claim originated in the marital relationship, so the costs of opposing it were personal and nondeductible.

Where the litigation is criminal rather than civil, the courts have made deductibility turn on the origin of the government's charges. Taxpayers may deduct only the cost of defending against prosecutions that stem from profit seeking activities. Compare Commissioner v. Tellier (deduction allowed for unsuccessful defense against securities act violations by underwriter), with Hylton v. Commissioner, 32 T.C.M. 1238 (1973) (no deduction for successful defense against murder charges resulting from domestic dispute). Expenses to defend against criminal charges that would result in a loss of employment are not deductible if the conduct that gave rise to the charges did not arise in the course of business. For example, in Nadiak v. Commissioner, 356 F.2d 911 (2d Cir.1966), an airline pilot could not deduct the legal expenses in defending assault and battery charges even though conviction would result in the loss of his license because the charges arose out of disputes with his former wife.

A.   REASONABLE ALLOWANCE FOR SALARIES

Exacto Spring Corporation v. Commissioner
196 F.3d 833 (7th Cir.1999).

POSNER, CHIEF JUDGE. This appeal from a judgment by the Tax Court requires us to interpret and apply § 162(a)(1), which allows a business to deduct from its income its "ordinary and necessary" business expenses, including a "reasonable allowance for salaries or other compensation for personal services actually rendered." In 1993 and 1994, Exacto Spring Corporation, a closely held corporation engaged in the manufacture of precision springs, paid its cofounder, chief executive, and principal owner, William Heitz, $1.3 and $1.0 million, respectively, in salary. The Internal Revenue Service thought this amount excessive, that Heitz should not have been paid more than $381,000 in 1993 or $400,000 in 1994, * * * The Tax Court * * * found that the maximum reasonable compensation for Heitz would have been $900,000 in the earlier year and $700,000 in the later one. * * *

In reaching its conclusion, the tax court applied a test that requires the consideration of seven factors: "(1) the type and extent of the services rendered, (2) the scarcity of qualified employees, (3) the qualifications and prior earning capacity of the employee, (4) the contributions of the employee to the business venture, (5) the net earnings of the employer, (6) the prevailing compensation paid to employees with comparable jobs, and (7) the peculiar characteristics." it is apparent that this test, though it or variants of it (one of which has the astonishing total of 21 factors), * * * are encountered in many cases, * * * leaves much to be desired—being, like many other multi-factor tests, "redundant, incomplete, and unclear." * * *

To begin with, it is nondirective. No indication is given of how the factors are to be weighed in the event they don't all line up on one side. And many of the factors, such as the type and extent of services rendered, the scarcity of qualified employees, and the peculiar characteristics of the employer's business, are vague.

Second, the factors do not bear a clear relation either to each other or to the primary purpose of section 162(a)(1), which is to prevent dividends (or in some cases gifts), which are not deductible from corporate income, from being disguised as salary, which is. Suppose that an employee who let us say was, like Heitz, a founder and the chief executive officer and principal owner of the taxpayer rendered no services at all but received a huge salary. It would be absurd to allow the whole or for that matter any part of his salary to be deducted as an ordinary and necessary business expense even if he were well qualified to be CEO of the company, the company had substantial net earnings, CEOS of similar companies were paid a lot, and it was a business in which high salaries are common. The multifactor test would not prevent the Tax Court from allowing a deduction in such a case even though the corporation obviously was seeking to reduce its taxable income by disguising earnings as salary. The court would not allow the deduction, but not because of anything in the multi-factor test; rather because it would be apparent that the payment to the employee was not in fact for his services to the company. Treas. Reg. § 1.162–7(a).

Third, the seven-factor test invites the Tax Court to set itself up as a superpersonnel department for closely held corporations, a role unsuitable for courts. * * * The test * * * invites the court to decide what the taxpayer's employees *should* be paid on the basis of the judges' own ideas of what jobs are comparable, what relation an employee's salary should bear to the corporation's net earnings, what types of business should pay abnormally high (or low) salaries, and so forth. The judges of the Tax Court are not equipped by training or experience to determine the salaries of corporate officers; no judges are.

Fourth, since the test cannot itself determine the outcome of a dispute because of its nondirective character, it invites the making of arbitrary decisions based on uncanalized discretion or unprincipled rules of thumb. The Tax Court in this case essentially added the IRS's determination of the maximum that Mr. Heitz should have been paid in 1993 and 1994 to what he was in fact paid, and divided the sum by two. It cut the baby in half. One would have to be awfully naive to believe that the seven-factor test generated this pleasing symmetry.

Fifth, because the reaction of the Tax Court to a challenge to the deduction of executive compensation is unpredictable, corporations run unavoidable legal risks in determining a level of compensation that may be indispensable to the success of their business.

The drawbacks of the multi-factor test are well illustrated by its purported application by the Tax Court in this case. With regard to factor (1), the court found that Heitz was "indispensable to Exacto's business" and "essential to Exacto's success." Heitz is not only Exacto's CEO; he is also the company's chief salesman and marketing man plus the head of its research and development efforts and its principal inventor. The company's entire success appears to be due on the one hand to the research and development conducted by him and on the other hand to his marketing of these innovations (though he receives some additional compensation for his marketing efforts from a subsidiary of Exacto). The court decided that factor (1) favored Exacto.

Likewise factor (2), for, as the court pointed out, the design of precision springs, which is Heitz's specialty, is "an extremely specialized branch of mechanical engineering, and there are very few engineers who have made careers specializing in this area," let alone engineers like Heitz who have "the ability to identify and attract clients and to develop springs to perform a specific function for that client. * * * It would have been very difficult to replace Mr. Heitz." Notice how factors (1) and (2) turn out to be nearly identical.

Factors (3) and (4) also supported Exacto, the court found. "Mr Heitz is highly qualified to run Exacto as a result of his education, training, experience, and motivation. Mr. Heitz has over 40 years of highly successful experience in the field of spring design." And his "efforts were of great value to the corporation." So factor (4) duplicated (2), and so the first four factors turn out to be really only two.

With regard to the fifth factor—the employer's (Exacto's) net earnings—the tax court was noncommittal. Exacto had reported a loss in 1993 and very little taxable income in 1994. But it conceded having taken some improper deductions in those years unrelated to Heitz's salary. After adjusting Exacto's income to remove these deductions, the court found that Exacto had earned more than $1 million in each of the years at issue net of Heitz's supposedly inflated salary.

The court was noncommittal with regard to the sixth factor—earnings of comparable employees—as well. The evidence bearing on this factor had been presented by expert witnesses, one on each side, and the court was critical of both. The taxpayer's witness had arrived at his estimate of Heitz's maximum reasonable compensation in part by aggregating the salaries that Exacto would have had to pay to hire four people each to wear one of Heitz's "hats," as chief executive officer, chief manufacturing executive, chief research and development officer, and chief sales and marketing executive. * * * [S]alaries are determined not by the method of comparable worth but, like other prices, by the market, which is to say by conditions of demand and supply. * * *

The Internal Revenue Service's expert witness sensibly considered whether Heitz's compensation was consistent with Exacto's investors' earning a reasonable return (adjusted for the risk of Exacto's business), which he calculated to be 13 percent. * * *

What is puzzling is how disallowing deductions and thus increasing the taxpayer's tax bill could increase the investors' return. What investors care about is the corporate income available to pay dividends or be reinvested; obviously money paid in taxes to the Internal Revenue Service is not available for either purpose. The reasonableness of Heitz's compensation thus depends not on Exacto's taxable income but on the corporation's profitability to the investors. * * * Both parties, plus the Tax Court, based their estimates of investors' returns on the after-tax income shown on Exacto's tax returns * * * rather than on Exacto's real profits. * * * The approach is inconsistent with a realistic assessment of the investors' rate of return, but as no one in the case questions it we shall not make an issue of it.

Finally, under factor (7) ("peculiar characteristics"), the court first and rightly brushed aside the IRS's argument that the low level of dividends paid by Exacto (zero in the two years at issue, but never very high) was evidence that the corporation was paying Heitz dividends in the form of salary. The court pointed out that shareholders may not want dividends. They may prefer the corporation to retain its earnings, causing the value of the corporation to rise and thus enabling the shareholders to obtain corporate earnings in the form of capital gains taxed at a lower rate than ordinary income. The court also noted that while Heitz, as the owner of 55 percent of Exacto's common stock, obviously was in a position to influence his salary, the corporation's two other major shareholders, each with 20 percent of the stock, had approved it. They had not themselves been paid a salary or other compensation, and are not relatives of Heitz; they had no financial or other incentive to allow Heitz to siphon off dividends in the form of salary.

Having run through the seven factors, all of which either favored the taxpayer or were neutral, the court reached a stunning conclusion: "We have considered the factors relevant in deciding reasonable compensation for Mr. Heitz. On the basis of all the evidence, we hold that reasonable compensation for Mr. Heitz" was much less than Exacto paid him. The court's only effort at explaining this result when Heitz had passed the seven-factor test with flying colors was that "we have balanced Mr. Heitz' unique selling and technical ability, his years of experience, and the difficulty of replacing Mr. Heitz with the fact that the corporate entity would have shown a reasonable return for the equity holders, after considering petitioners' concessions." But "the fact that the corporate entity would have shown a reasonable return for the equity holders" after the concessions is on the same side of the balance as the other factors; it does not favor the Internal Revenue Service's position. The government's lawyer was forced to concede at the argument of the appeal that she could not deny the possibility that the Tax Court had pulled its figures for Heitz's allowable compensation out of a hat.

The failure of the Tax Court's reasoning to support its result would alone require a remand. But the problem with the court's opinion goes deeper. The test it applied does not provide adequate guidance to a rational decision. We owe no deference to the tax court's statutory interpretations, its relation to us being that of a district court to a court of appeals, not that of an administrative agency to a court of appeals. The federal courts of appeals, whose decisions do of course have weight as authority with us even when they are not our own decisions, have been moving toward a much simpler and more purposive test, the "independent investor" test. * * * We applaud the trend and join it.

Because judges tend to downplay the element of judicial creativity in adapting law to fresh insights and changed circumstances, the cases * * * prefer to say * * * that the "independent investor" test is the "lens" through which they view the seven (or however many) factors of the orthodox test. But that is a formality. The new test dissolves the old and returns the inquiry to basics. The Internal Revenue Code limits the amount of salary that a corporation can deduct from its income primarily in order to prevent the corporation from eluding the corporate income tax by paying dividends but calling them salary because salary is deductible and dividends are not. (Perhaps they should be, to avoid double taxation of corporate earnings, but that is not the law.) In the case of a publicly held company, where the salaries of the highest executives are fixed by a board of directors that those executives do not control, the danger of siphoning corporate earnings to executives in the form of salary is not acute. The danger is much greater in the case of a closely held corporation, in which ownership and management tend to coincide; unfortunately, as the opinion of the Tax Court in this case illustrates, judges are not competent to decide what business executives are worth.

There is, fortunately, an indirect market test, as recognized by the Internal Revenue Service's expert witness. A corporation can be conceptualized as a contract in which the owner of assets hires a person to manage them. The owner pays the manager a salary and in exchange the manager works to increase the value of the assets that have been entrusted to his management; that increase can be expressed as a rate of return to the owner's investment. The higher the rate of return (adjusted for risk) that a manager can generate, the greater the salary he can command. If the rate of return is extremely high, it will be difficult to prove that the manager is being overpaid, for it will be implausible that if he quit if his salary was cut, and he was replaced by a lower-paid manager, the owner would be better off; it would be killing the goose that lays the golden egg. The service's expert believed that investors in a firm like Exacto would expect a 13 percent return on their investment. Presumably they would be delighted with more. They would be *overjoyed* to receive a return more than 50 percent greater than they expected—and 20 percent, the return that the tax court found that investors in Exacto had obtained, is more than 50 percent greater than the benchmark return of 13 percent.

When, notwithstanding the CEO's "exorbitant" salary (as it might appear to a judge or other modestly paid official), the investors in his company are obtaining a far higher return than they had any reason to expect, his salary is presumptively reasonable. We say "presumptively" because we can imagine cases in which the return, though very high, is not due to the CEO's exertions. Suppose Exacto had been an unprofitable company that suddenly learned that its factory was sitting on an oil field, and when oil revenues started to pour in its owner raised his salary from $50,000 a year to $1.3 million. The presumption of reasonableness would be rebutted. There is no suggestion of anything of that sort here and likewise no suggestion that Mr. Heitz was merely the titular chief executive and the company was actually run by someone else, which would be another basis for rebuttal.

The government could still have prevailed by showing that while Heitz's salary may have been no greater than would be reasonable in the circumstances, the company did not in fact intend to pay him that amount as salary, that his salary really did include a concealed dividend though it need not have. This is material (and the "independent investor" test, like the multifactor test that it replaces, thus [is] incomplete, though invaluable) because any business expense to be deductible must be, as we noted earlier, a bona fide expense as well as reasonable in amount. The fact that Heitz's salary was approved by the other owners of the corporation, who had no incentive to disguise a dividend as salary, goes far to rebut any inference of bad faith here, which in any event the Tax Court did not draw and the government does not ask us to draw.

Reversed.

NOTES

(A) *Reasonable Allowance.* If the language "a reasonable allowance for salaries or other compensation" were not in the Code, would the result in

Exacto Spring have been any different? Since the general language of § 162 would surely permit a deduction for salaries, the more specific language generally is thought to limit the deduction for salaries that exceed a reasonable amount. Why is such a limitation necessary? Legislative history indicates that the language originally was added to permit taxpayers to take deductions for salaries greater than the amounts actually paid to employees in order to reduce the World War I excess profits tax. See Erwin Griswold, "New Light on 'A Reasonable Allowance for Salaries'," 59 Harv.L.Rev. 286 (1943).

Despite its original purpose, the language has come to serve as a check on salary deductions where the taxpayer is attempting to substitute compensation for a nondeductible expenditure. There are two situations where it might be appropriate to recharacterize the "unreasonable salary" as something else. Corporate earnings distributed to shareholders as dividends are taxed twice, once at the corporate level and again at the shareholder level. This "double taxation" is unusual; profits of trusts, partnerships, and proprietorships generally are taxed only once, whether distributed or retained. Amounts paid by corporations to employees as salary, however, are deductible to the corporation and are taxed only to the employee. A payment is taxed twice if the payor is denied a deduction (because the amount is "unreasonable") while the recipient nevertheless must include the amount in income. Since a single tax at the individual level is always less than two levels of tax, regardless of rates, there is an incentive for a corporation to give a shareholder/employee salary rather than a dividend distribution. An amount paid to a shareholder that does not actually represent compensation for services rendered is, under our system, subject to double, rather than single taxation.

Today, however, the double taxation of corporate income is essentially limited to large publicly held companies. Closely held enterprises can be formed as limited liability companies, which escape corporate tax since the tax law treats them as partnerships, or can elect Subchapter S status, which also avoids any corporate-level tax. The only closely held businesses now subject to the corporate tax are pre-existing companies, which do not want to pay the tax on unrealized appreciation of its assets, which is required, or for other reasons fail to convert to Subchapter S status. Even though the statute itself draws no distinction between publicly and closely held corporations, the IRS never challenges as unreasonable—no matter how large—salaries paid to executives of large publicly held companies, where the double corporate tax has its principal force. Corporate governance mechanisms, independent directors, and shareholder rights, along with the stock market itself, presumably are thought to guard against the payment of unreasonable amounts to executives. But at today's levels, it seems likely that a portion of many executives' salaries is a diversion of amounts that otherwise would be paid to shareholders as dividends. And the amounts at stake are far greater than those at issue in cases like *Exacto Spring*. See generally Edward A. Zelinsky, Reasonable Compensation: A Study in Doctrinal Obsolescence, available at http://papers.ssrn.com/pa-per.taf?abstract_did=254928.

Income transferred by gift is also taxed once to the donor, who is not allowed a deduction, but not again to the donee who enjoys the § 102 exclusion. Thus, there is no question of double taxation. But where two employees are related, there is an incentive to overcompensate the taxpayer in the lower bracket to minimize the total taxes on the two family members. Similarly, putting a family member on the corporate payroll may permit the taxpayer to make support payments out of pretax income.

If the disguised salary is unreasonable, how does that affect the taxation of the recipient? A shareholder is taxed on the receipt of a dividend. § 61(a)(7). A gift, however, is excluded. But see § 102(c). Would the donor have the requisite disinterested generosity? See Smith v. Manning, 189 F.2d 345 (3d Cir.1951) (payments made by owner to daughters who worked in the business that were held to be unreasonable could not be treated as excludible gifts because there was no donative intent).

Except where a gift or dividend is masquerading as salary, why should the IRS or the courts question the reasonableness of the amount of compensation? What policy is served by a general limitation on salary deductions? Why should the Service second guess a business judgment as to salary? As the court points out in *Exacto Spring*, one result of the factors approach is to set the court up as a "superpersonnel department," substituting the court's judgement as to what is a reasonable salary for that of the business. The court may have a entirely different view about an individual's worth than does the market. It may also bring to the decision some questionable judgments. Consider Thomas A. Curtis, M.D., Inc. v. Commissioner, 67 T.C.M. 1958 (1994). The Service questioned the payment of roughly $500,000 in salary to Ellen Curtis, a registered nurse with extensive training, who organized and ran the business, which provided psychiatric treatment and reports to the court with respect to worker's compensation cases. The court detailed Ms. Curtis' training, background, and work hours (60–70 per week). It also noted that she had set up the six-office operation, hired all the psychologists, and supervised the 60–80 employees. Among other laudatory statements, the court said, "Ms. Curtis' efforts have been a primary reason for the corporation's success" and "[i]n the case at hand, the importance of Ms. Curtis' role cannot be questioned," and her "vision * * * and ability * * * have been of paramount importance." Nevertheless, without really explaining its decision, the court found that only $239,000 of Ms. Curtis' salary was reasonable. Her husband, *Dr.* Curtis (the corporation's other shareholder), was paid an identical salary but the IRS failed to question its reasonableness. The taxpayer argued that the IRS had "taken an inconsistent position by questioning Ms. Curtis' amount of compensation but not the compensation paid to Dr. Curtis," contending that the IRS position "is 'antediluvian' and constitutes sexual discrimination." The Tax Court said it would not look behind IRS's decision to challenge the salary of only the female nurse and not the male doctor.

(B) *Absence of Dividends.* A failure to pay dividends is an important, although not conclusive factor. The IRS has rejected an approach that would require a reasonable return on capital, Rev.Rul. 79–8, 1979–1 C.B. 92, but a number of courts have noted that an absence of dividends is troubling. See, e.g., Charles McCandless Tile Service v. United States, 422 F.2d 1336 (Ct.Cl.1970). In *McCandless,* the Court of Claims held that even though compensation paid to two shareholder-employees was reasonable in amount, the payments "necessarily" contained disguised dividends because the closely held corporation had been profitable but had never paid dividends since its formation. This holding has been referred to as the "automatic dividend" rule. It has been criticized by commentators and rejected by other courts. As Judge Posner notes in *Exacto Spring,* investors may prefer (perhaps for tax reasons) that the corporation retain and reinvest its earnings and therefore would neither demand nor want that earnings be distributed as dividends. Other courts have continued to look at the factors criticized in the principal case, but have viewed them from the perspective of an investor.

In Dexsil Corp. v. Commissioner, 147 F.3d 96 (2d Cir.1998), the Court of Appeals vacated and remanded a Tax Court decision holding a part of compensation paid to Ted Lynn, the company's founder, key officer, and its majority shareholder, to be unreasonable because the Tax Court had failed to assess "the entire tableau from the perspective of an independent investor." The Second Circuit stated:

> The independent investor test is not a separate autonomous factor; rather, it provides a lens through which the entire analysis should be viewed. * * * Thus, if the company's earnings on equity, when viewed in relation to such factors as the company's overall performance and levels of compensation, "remain at a level that would satisfy an independent investor, there is a strong indication that management is providing compensable services and that profits are not being siphoned out of the company disguised as salary."

Unlike the Second and Sixth Circuits, however, the Tax Court and the ~~Seventh~~ Circuit [10th] refused to follow the independent investor test and instead rely on the traditional multi-part factor test rejected in *Exacto Spring.* Eberl's Claim Service, Inc. v. Commissioner, 249 F.3d 994 (10th Cir.2001), aff'g 77 T.C.M. 2336 (1999).

The *McCandless* rule, thus, may not be dead. What if the salary is reasonable in amount but the employer does not have the requisite compensatory intent? Suppose one of the employer's motives is to avoid paying nondeductible dividends? In O.S.C. & Associates, Inc. v. Commissioner, 187 F.3d 1116 (9th Cir.1999), the court held that to be deductible, the employer's purpose for making the payments must be compensatory. In *O.S.C. & Associates,* the corporation adopted an incentive compensation plan and payments were made to two shareholder-employees according to their stock ownership. The court determined that most of the payments were disguised dividends, intended to be a distribution of excess profits, even though the total amount did not exceed an amount determined by the IRS to be reasonable compensation. Thus, even if the compensation is reasonable, it will not be deductible unless the employer possesses the necessary compensatory intent.

(C) *Repayment of Unreasonable Salary.* Suppose the employee is required to repay any salary that is held to be unreasonable. At least one court has implied that a repayment agreement is evidence of "unreasonableness." Charles Schneider & Co. v. Commissioner, 500 F.2d 148, 155 (8th Cir.1974). But see Rev.Rul. 69–115, 1969–1 C.B. 50 (allowing a deduction where the repayment is made pursuant to an agreement entered into prior to the payment).

(D) *Executive Compensation.* Section 162(m) denies a deduction for compensation in excess of $1 million paid to the chief executive officer or the four most highly compensated employees of a publicly held corporation unless the compensation is performance-based. Payments to a qualified retirement plan and fringe benefits are not subject to the deduction limitation.

The Code contains an elaborate definition of performance-based compensation, which is not subject to limitation. In general, it includes any remuneration payable on a commission basis attributable to income generated by the applicable employee. It also includes compensation paid for reaching performance goals so long as the goals are established by a compensation committee comprised solely of two or more outside directors, the terms are approved by the shareholders, and the compensation committee certifies that the goals have been met before the compensation has been paid. Although the rules are cumbersome, well-advised corporations have little difficulty meeting them and deducting the entire compensation.

Is a provision such as § 162(m) appropriate in an income tax? If a business determines that $2 million is the proper salary for an executive, why should the government require the business to jump through these hoops in order to take a deduction? If compensation is a necessary business expense and very few deductions are likely to be denied, why would Congress adopt such a provision? Note that § 162(m) does not apply to compensation paid to anyone other than executives of publicly held corporations. Thus, there is no limitation on salaries paid to doctors, lawyers, professional athletes, or rock stars. Does this distinction make sense?

(E) *Undercompensation.* Section 162(a)(1) has never been interpreted to prevent undercompensation. Suppose, for example, a shareholder/employee is not adequately compensated. This might be done where the corporate tax rate was less than the individual rate and the shareholder had no need to withdraw funds for the foreseeable future. In that case, the income would be shifted to the lower-taxed corporation. In the case of a pass-through entity, the incentive is to undercompensate a high bracket shareholder or partner in order to shift income to a related shareholder or partner. The Service has the authority to prevent the shift. See §§ 706, 1366(e).

(F) *Payments Other than Salaries.* The issue whether a payment that is denominated as an item deductible under § 162 is actually a nondeductible expense arises in other contexts as well. See, e.g., Tulia Feedlot, Inc. v. United States, 513 F.2d 800 (5th Cir.1975), where a corporation was not allowed to deduct under § 162 a payment to a shareholder for personally guaranteeing a corporate loan. The court found the payment was a dividend even though the corporation needed the loan and the fee was reasonable in relation to existing interest rates. Cf. Tulia Feedlot, Inc. v. United States, 3 Cl.Ct. 364 (1983) (holding such fees deductible where company was unable to obtain financing without the shareholders' guarantees); Fong v. Commissioner, 48 T.C.M. 689 (1984) (denying deduction for similar fees).

Payments that are denominated as rent, but that are, in fact, dividends or gifts are not deductible. See Capital Refrigeration, Inc. v. Commissioner, 31 T.C.M. 428 (1972). It also is well established that excessive rent paid to a related lessor will be disallowed. See, e.g., Mackinac Island Carriage Tours, Inc. v. Commissioner, 455 F.2d 98 (6th Cir.1972). Is the problem whether the payment is excessive or whether the payment is for something other than rent?

B. EXPENSES CONTRARY TO PUBLIC POLICY

Commissioner v. Tellier

Supreme Court of the United States, 1966. 383 U.S. 687.

MR. JUSTICE STEWART delivered the opinion of the Court.

The question presented in this case is whether expenses incurred by a taxpayer in the unsuccessful defense of a criminal prosecution may qualify for deduction from taxable income under § 162(a) of the Internal Revenue Code of 1954, which allows a deduction of "all the ordinary and necessary expenses paid or incurred during the taxable year in carrying on any trade or business * * * " The respondent, Walter F. Tellier, was engaged in the business of underwriting the public sale of stock offerings and purchasing securities for resale to customers. In 1956 he was brought to trial upon a 36–count indictment that charged him with violating the fraud section of the Securities Act of 1933 and the mail fraud statute, and with conspiring to violate those statutes. He was found guilty on all counts and was sentenced to pay an $18,000 fine and to serve four and a half years in prison. The judgment of conviction was affirmed on appeal. In his unsuccessful defense of this criminal prosecution, the respondent incurred and paid $22,964.20 in legal expenses in 1956. He claimed a deduction for that amount on his federal income tax return for that year. The Commissioner disallowed the deduction and was sustained by the Tax Court. T.C.Memo. 1963–212, 22 CCH Tax Ct.Memo. 1062. The Court of Appeals for the Second Circuit reversed in a unanimous *en banc* decision, 342 F.2d 690, and we granted certiorari. 382 U.S. 808. We affirm the judgment of the Court of Appeals.

There can be no serious question that the payments deducted by the respondent were expenses of his securities business under the decisions of this Court, and the Commissioner does not contend otherwise. * * *

The Commissioner also concedes that the respondent's legal expenses were "ordinary" and "necessary" expenses within the meaning of § 162(a). Our decisions have consistently construed the term "necessary" as imposing only the minimal requirement that the expense be "appropriate and helpful" for "the development of the [taxpayer's] business." Welch v. Helvering, 290 U.S. 111, 113. The principal function of the term "ordinary" in § 162(a) is to clarify the distinction, often difficult, between those expenses that are currently deductible and those that are in the nature of capital expenditures, which, if deductible at all, must be amortized over the useful life of the asset. Welch v. Helvering, supra, at 113–16. The legal expenses deducted by the respondent were not capital expenditures. They were incurred in his defense against charges of past criminal conduct, not in the acquisition of a capital asset. Our decisions establish that counsel fees comparable to those here involved are ordinary business expenses, even though a "lawsuit affecting the safety of a business may happen once in a lifetime." Welch v. Helvering, supra, at 114.

It is therefore clear that the respondent's legal fees were deductible under § 162(a) if the provisions of that section are to be given their normal effect in this case. The Commissioner and the Tax Court determined, however, that even though the expenditures meet the literal requirements of § 162(a), their deduction must nevertheless be disallowed on the ground of public policy. That view finds * * * no support * * * in any regulation or statute or in any decision of this Court, and we believe no such "public policy" exception to the plain provisions of § 162(a) is warranted in the circumstances presented by this case.

We start with the proposition that the federal income tax is a tax on net income, not a sanction against wrongdoing. That principle has been firmly imbedded in the tax statute from the beginning. One familiar facet of the principle is the truism that the statute does not concern itself with the lawfulness of the income that it taxes. Income from a criminal enterprise is taxed at a rate no higher and no lower than income from more conventional sources. "[T]he fact that a business is unlawful [does not] exempt it from paying the taxes that if lawful it would have to pay." United States v. Sullivan, 274 U.S. 259, 263. * * *

With respect to deductions, the basic rule, with only a few limited and well-defined exceptions, is the same. During the Senate debate in 1913 on the bill that became the first modern income tax law, amendments were rejected that would have limited deductions for losses to those incurred in a "legitimate" or "lawful" trade or business. Senator Williams, who was in charge of the bill, stated on the floor of the Senate that

> "[T]he object of this bill is to tax a man's net income; that is to say, what he has at the end of the year after deducting from his receipts his expenditures or losses. It is not to reform men's moral characters; that is not the object of the bill at all. The tax is not levied for the purpose of restraining people from betting on horse races or upon 'futures,' but the tax is framed for the purpose of making a man pay upon his net income, his actual profit during the year. The law does not care where he got it from, so far as the tax is concerned, although the law may very properly care in another way." 50 Cong.Rec. 3849.

The application of this principle is reflected in several decisions of this Court. As recently as Commissioner v. Sullivan, 356 U.S. 27, we sustained the allowance of a deduction for rent and wages paid by the operators of a gambling enterprise, even though both the business itself and the specific rent and wage payments there in question were illegal under state law. In rejecting the Commissioner's contention that the illegality of the enterprise required disallowance of the deduction, we held that, were we to "enforce as federal policy the rule espoused by the Commissioner in this case, we

would come close to making this type of business taxable on the basis of its gross receipts, while all other business would be taxable on the basis of net income. If that choice is to be made, Congress should do it." Id., at 29.
* * *

Deduction of expenses falling within the general definition of § 162(a) may, to be sure, be disallowed by specific legislation, since deductions "are a matter of grace and Congress can, of course, disallow them as it chooses." * * * But * * * only where the allowance of a deduction would "frustrate sharply defined national or state policies proscribing particular forms of conduct" have we upheld its disallowance. * * * Further, the "policies frustrated must be national or state policies evidenced by some *governmental* declaration of them." * * * Finally, the "test of nondeductibility always is the severity and immediacy of the frustration resulting from allowance of the deduction." Tank Truck Rentals v. Commissioner, 356 U.S. 30, 35. In that case, as in Hoover Express Co. v. United States, 356 U.S. 38, we upheld the disallowance of deductions claimed by taxpayers for fines and penalties imposed upon them for violating state penal statutes; to allow a deduction in those circumstances would have directly and substantially diluted the actual punishment imposed.

The present case falls far outside that sharply limited and carefully defined category. No public policy is offended when a man faced with serious criminal charges employs a lawyer to help in his defense. That is not "proscribed conduct." It is his constitutional right. In an adversary system of criminal justice, it is a basic [tenet] of our public policy that a defendant in a criminal case have counsel to represent him.

Congress has authorized the imposition of severe punishment upon those found guilty of the serious criminal offenses with which the respondent was charged and of which he was convicted. But we can find no warrant for attaching to that punishment an additional financial burden that Congress has neither expressly nor implicitly directed. To deny a deduction for expenses incurred in the unsuccessful defense of a criminal prosecution would impose such a burden in a measure dependent not on the seriousness of the offense or the actual sentence imposed by the court, but on the cost of the defense and the defendant's particular tax bracket. We decline to distort the income tax laws to serve a purpose for which they were neither intended nor designed by Congress.

The judgment is affirmed.

NOTES

(A) *Other Cases.* In *Tank Truck Rentals v. Commissioner,* discussed in the principal case, the Supreme Court refused to permit a trucking company to deduct fines levied by Pennsylvania for violation of its weight limits. Surrounding states had much higher limits, which meant that the truckers faced three choices: (1) drive around Pennsylvania at great expense; (2) carry light loads at greater proportional costs; or (3) violate the weight limit. The last of these choices was the universal industry practice. The state did not require overweight trucks to unload or impose any nonmonetary penalties, and its own regulatory agency required the companies to record the fines on their books as business expenses. Nevertheless, the Court found that allowance of a deduction for these expenses would undermine Pennsylvania's weight limit policy; the fines therefore did not qualify as ordinary and necessary business expenses.

In *Commissioner v. Sullivan,* also discussed in *Tellier* and decided the same day as *Tank Truck,* the Court allowed a deduction for salaries and rents paid by a bookmaker, even though the applicable state law made these payments a separate criminal offense. The Court explained that salaries and rent were part of the "normal" costs of doing business. Could a state be said to have a policy forbidding bookmakers to pay salary and rents? If so, why are these expenses any more ordinary and necessary than those at stake in *Tank Truck?*

(B) *Statutory Provisions.* Perhaps in response to the confusion created by these cases, Congress amended § 162 to specifically deny five types of expenditures: (1) fines or similar penalties paid to a government for the violation of any law, § 162(f); (2) a portion of treble damage payments under the antitrust laws following a related criminal conviction (or plea of guilty or nolo contendere), § 162(g); (3) bribes or kickbacks paid to public officials, § 162(c)(1); (4) bribes or referral fees for Medicaid and Medicare patients, § 162(c)(3); and (5) any other illegal bribe, kickback or payment under any law if such law is generally enforced and it subjects the payor to a criminal penalty or the loss of license or privilege to engage in a trade or business. § 162(c)(2).

(C) *Tax Penalties.* The denial of a deduction for a business expense that is contrary to public policy can be seen as a "tax penalty" (or excise tax). These provisions are the reverse of tax expenditure provisions, discussed supra at page 39. They are departures from the net income concept; business expenses ought to be deductible in defining income in an income tax. The practical effect of the denial varies with the taxpayer's marginal tax rate, rather than with the importance of the underlying policy goal. Is a tax penalty less objectionable if Congress carved out the exception to the net income concept or if the courts take the initiative?

(D) *Questions on the Margins of Statutory Language.* Notwithstanding the legislative efforts to make more precise the contours of the disallowance of business deductions on public policy grounds, the courts continue to struggle at the margins. For example, in Mason and Dixon Lines, Inc. v. United States, 708 F.2d 1043 (6th Cir.1983), a trucking company was allowed to deduct "liquidated damages" levied by a state following conviction for weight violations. The court stressed that these fines supplemented criminal penalties and were calculated with the aim of measuring highway damage. See generally Reg. § 1.162–21(b)(1), which provides that civil as well as criminal penalties are subject to § 162(f) and Reg. § 1.162–21(b)(2), which states that "compensatory" damages paid to the government are not "fines or penalties." Were the fines in *Tank Truck* compensatory or retributive penalties? At least one court has refused to make such distinctions. In Colt Industries, Inc. v. United States, 880 F.2d 1311 (Fed.Cir. 1989), the court held that no distinction could be drawn between compensatory and retributive civil penalties. It refused to permit the taxpayer to deduct payments made to settle a suit with the Environmental Protection

Agency, saying that ascertaining whether payments were compensatory would require the courts to determine the underlying purpose of every civil penalty. Taking a different approach, the Tenth Circuit found that if there are "deterrent and retributive function[s]" to a penalty, it cannot be deducted even if it also has "compensatory and remedial aspects." True v. United States, 894 F.2d 1197 (10th Cir.1990).

In Huff v. Commissioner, 80 T.C. 804 (1983), the Tax Court distinguished nondeductible civil penalties "imposed for purposes of enforcing the law and as punishment for the violation thereof" from deductible civil penalties "imposed to encourage prompt compliance with a requirement of the law or as a remedial measure to compensate another party for expenses incurred as a result of the violation." The former were considered "similar" to criminal penalties while the latter were not. The civil penalties imposed in this case were not deductible because the Supreme Court of California had characterized them as designed to penalize past illegal conduct.

(E) *Payments to Third Parties.* Because § 162(f) prohibits deductions only for fines or penalties paid to a government, damages or payments made to a private party for a violation of law or for violating private rules are deductible. Where, however, the payments to private parties are akin to a fine, deduction has been disallowed. See, e.g., Rev.Rul. 81–151, 1981–1 C.B. 74 (corporate officer who caused the corporation to make illegal campaign contributions resulting in a fine could not deduct restitution he was required to make to corporation). Similarly, restitution made to the victims of fraud or theft is not deductible where the repayment serves a punitive purpose. Kraft v. United States, 991 F.2d 292 (6th Cir.1993). In Allied–Signal Inc. v. Commissioner, 54 F.3d 767 (3d Cir.1995), the court refused to permit a corporation to deduct the contribution it made to an environmental endowment fund in lieu of paying a fine for releasing toxic chemicals. A company that makes a court-ordered charitable contribution in lieu of a criminal fine may not take a business deduction under § 162 or a charitable deduction under § 170. The IRS regards the contribution as a nondeductible fine under § 162(f) and not gratuitous as required for deductibility under § 170. Rev.Rul. 79–148, 1979–1 C.B. 93.

(F) *Vitality of Common Law Public Policy Exception.* Congress apparently intended that the provisions of § 162 denying deductions for payments that were deemed to violate public policy be exclusive. "Public policy, in other circumstances, generally is not sufficiently clearly defined to justify the disallowance of deductions." See Staff of the Joint Committee on Taxation, General Explanation of the Tax Reform Act of 1969, 91st Cong., 1st Sess. 233–35 (1969). See also Reg. § 1.162–1(a): "A deduction for an expense * * * which would otherwise be allowable under section 162 shall not be denied on the grounds that allowance of such deduction would frustrate a sharply defined public policy. See section 162(c), (f), and (g) * * *." Most courts have so found, but not all. The Sixth Circuit, which seems genuinely confused about the public policy limitation, disallowed a deduction for a kickback that did not violate either state or federal law or subject the payor to loss of its business license. Car–Ron Asphalt Paving Co., Inc. v. Commissioner, 758 F.2d 1132 (6th Cir.1985). The taxpayer paid

$90,000 in kickbacks to the supervisor of construction of a shopping mall that secured about $1 million in contracts for the company. In the previous year, however, the same court permitted another taxpayer to deduct similar payments to the same individual. Raymond Bertolini Trucking Co. v. Commissioner, 736 F.2d 1120 (6th Cir.1984). The panel in *Car-Ron* neither overruled *Bertolini* nor did it forthrightly explain the difference between the cases. The majority distinguished the earlier case by saying that the Tax Court had found the payments in *Car-Ron* were not necessary, even though the Tax Court's definition of "necessary" in this case seemed to include only "essential" expenses—a definition that is clearly wrong as a matter of law and that, in any event, seemed to have been met in the case. The good news is that the recipient of the kickbacks was convicted for federal tax fraud for failing to report the kickbacks as income, a conviction that probably never would have occurred if the payments had not been revealed by Bertolini and Car–Ron's deducting them.

(G) *Other Public Policy Limitations.* The general public policy limitation lives on, however, in other Code sections. The Tax Court imported into § 165 the limitation on the deductibility of losses that would "frustrate sharply defined national or state policies proscribing particular types of conduct" (the language of *Tellier*). See, e.g., Blackman v. Commissioner, 88 T.C. 677, 682 (1987), affirmed in an unpublished order 867 F.2d 605 (1st Cir.1988) (no loss deduction where individual intentionally set fire to his residence); see also Rev.Rul. 77–126, 1977–1 C.B. 47, 48 (public policy limitation in § 165 not affected by amendments to § 162).

Stretching the public policy limitation to its limits, the Tax Court denied a loss to a taxpayer who had given $20,000 to someone who claimed to have a machine that reproduced money. The man was about to demonstrate the machine to the gullible victim Mazzei when the man's confederates burst into the room impersonating law enforcement officers. They took the Mazzei cash on the pretext of seizing evidence of counterfeiting. A majority of the Tax Court held that allowing a deduction to Mazzei under these circumstances would frustrate public policy because the loss bore a "direct relationship" to what the taxpayer had believed to be an illegal act. Mazzei v. Commissioner, 61 T.C. 497 (1974). A dissenting opinion argued that Congress had intended to reserve for itself the power to limit deductions on public policy grounds.

Treasury also has issued regulations stating that taxpayers may not deduct under § 212 (investment expenses) or § 471 (inventory costs) items that would be nondeductible under § 162. Regs. §§ 1.212–1(p), 1.471–3(d). But in Max Sobel Wholesale Liquors v. Commissioner, 630 F.2d 670 (9th Cir.1980), the court permitted the taxpayer to deduct illegal kickbacks paid to its supplier.

Consider also § 280E, which denies any deduction for business expenses related to illegal drug trafficking. The legislative history emphasizes that Congress did not intend to bar drug traffickers from offsetting the cost of obtaining drugs against the gross receipts of their illegal business. Is there a justification for the distinction between the cost of goods to be sold and the other expenses of running an illegal business? Why should only drug dealers lose their business deductions? Should operators of illegal businesses be taxed on gross receipts rather than net income?

The expenses of other illegal profit-seeking ventures are deductible. For example, John DiFronzo was the "crew chief" in a crime syndicate that attempted to control gaming operations of the Rincon Band of Mission Indians. He paid a lawyer $50,000 to defend him but he was convicted anyway of participating in a criminal venture. The Tax Court permitted him to deduct his legal fees, finding that he had a "genuine intention of making a profit." DiFronzo v. Commissioner, 75 T.C.M. 1693 (1998). What is the logic behind the public policy limitation?

C. LOBBYING EXPENSES

NOTES ON LOBBYING EXPENSES

History. One of the earliest uses of the "ordinary and necessary" requirement as a basis for denying business deductions involved expenses for lobbying, propaganda, and campaign contributions. The Supreme Court upheld regulations disallowing such deductions in Textile Mills Securities Corp. v. Commissioner, 314 U.S. 326 (1941), which rejected a deduction for the costs of persuading Congress to compensate foreign businesses that had lost property during World War I under the Trading with the Enemy Act. In Cammarano v. United States, 358 U.S. 498 (1959), the Court reaffirmed the regulations and refused to permit a beer distributor to deduct the costs of opposing a referendum that would have abolished private alcohol distribution in the state.

In response, Congress in 1962 added § 162(e), which permits deductions for certain types of lobbying expenses and disallows others. Congress permitted a deduction for certain ordinary and necessary expenses in carrying on a trade or business incurred for appearances before and communications with legislative, administrative, and judicial bodies. In 1993, Congress amended § 162(e) to eliminate the deduction for expenses incurred in lobbying federal or state legislators or certain executive branch officials. Expenses in connection with lobbying local governing bodies (e.g., a city council or a county legislature) remain deductible. There is also a de minimis exception: If a taxpayer's total in-house lobbying expenditures do not exceed $2,000, they are deductible. Expenses incurred to attempt to influence the general public with respect to legislative matters, elections or referendums are not deductible.

Legislative history does not explain why Congress retained a deduction for the cost of lobbying local officials. In recent years, lobbyists have become ubiquitous on Capitol Hill, particularly while tax legislation is being considered, and their ability to influence the course of legislation has been legendary. Perhaps Congress thought that eliminating the deduction for lobbying expenses was a relatively painless way of turning a deaf ear to their pleas. They also apparently thought that local officials were able to exercise more self-control. Denying income tax deductions for lobbying seems to have had little or no effect on the amount of lobbying of Congress that occurs.

Requirements. In order for the lobbying expense to be deductible, the taxpayer must have a trade or business and the legislation must be of direct interest to that business. Thus, no matter how deeply a taxpayer may feel about a particular piece of legislation, if it does not affect his business, he may not deduct the expenses of lobbying either for or against its passage.

Although lawmaking in some states can occur through public initiatives and referenda, § 162(e)(1)(C) does not permit a business to deduct the costs of influencing these elections on issues related to its business. The Tax Court has rejected the argument that the general electorate acts as a legislative body. Southern Pacific Transportation Co. v. Commissioner, 90 T.C. 771 (1988).

Constitutional Limitations. The limitations on deductibility contained in § 162(e)(2) mean that taxpayers may not deduct some indisputably business-related expenses solely because they involve politics. Justice Douglas, concurring in *Cammarano,* appeared troubled by the possibility that singling out political expenses for nondeductibility might constitute a violation of the First Amendment. He concluded that no constitutional problems existed, however, because "[d]eductions are a matter of grace, not of right;" moreover, he found that nondeductibility reflects "a complete hands-off policy on the part of government [that] is at times the only course consistent with First Amendment rights." Cammarano v. United States, 358 U.S. 498, 515 (1959). Does departure from the rule that nonpersonal, noncapital business expenses normally are deductible reflect a "hands-off" policy? Is nondeductibility justified on the ground that an opposite rule would favor political activity by pro-business interests? Is it appropriate for government to restrict the political power of the wealthy to enhance the power of the less wealthy? Cf. Buckley v. Valeo, 424 U.S. 1, 49 (1976) ("The First Amendment's protection against governmental abridgment of free expression cannot properly be made to depend on a person's financial ability to engage in public discussion."); First National Bank of Boston v. Bellotti, 435 U.S. 765, 784 (1978) (rejecting "the proposition that speech that otherwise would be within the protection of the First Amendment loses that protection simply because its source is a corporation").

Charities eligible for deductible contributions face substantial limits on the extent of legislative lobbying that they may undertake. These rules are discussed below. In Regan v. Taxation With Representation, 461 U.S. 540 (1983), the Court upheld these restrictions against First Amendment and equal protection attacks. By characterizing the charitable exemption as a kind of subsidy, the Court fit the limitations within the principle that the government may not penalize, but need not subsidize, the exercise of free speech. This characterization also permitted the Court to apply a less demanding form of equal protection scrutiny; the Court therefore could uphold as rational the different treatment of lobbying by business, charitable and veterans' groups.

Advertising vs. Other Efforts to Influence the Public. The Treasury regulations interpreting § 162(e) distinguish between deductible institutional or goodwill advertising and nondeductible efforts to influence the public on particular issues of legislative significance. Reg. § 1.162–20. How easy is it to separate the presentation of "views on economic, financial, social, or other subject of a general nature" from propaganda on matters of particular legislative significance? May an oil company deduct the costs of newspaper ads contending that gasoline price controls are economically unsound? May an electric utility deduct advertisements detailing the benefits of nuclear power?

In Geary v. Commissioner, 235 F.3d 1207 (9th Cir.2000), in order to improve his relationship with the community, Geary, a police officer, took a puppet, Officer O'Smarty, to work. (This did not take place in NYC). Forbidden from patrolling with the puppet, Geary formed a committee to put the issue on the local ballot and advertised in voting materials. The measure was approved and O'Smarty went back on the beat, but Geary lost his deduction. The advertising was intended to influence the general public and thus was nondeductible.

Lobbying by Charitable Organizations. In general, a charity may not engage in a substantial amount of lobbying or it will lose its tax exemption or forfeit the right of contributors to a deduction, although a public charity may engage in a limited amount of lobbying without losing its tax exemption. See §§ 501(h) and 4911. The limitation is based on a percentage of a charity's total annual expenditures, starting at 20 percent of the first $500,000 and decreasing until a ceiling of $1 million in political expenses is reached. An excise tax of 25 percent is imposed on political expenses in excess of the ceiling, and frequent violation of the ceiling will result in loss of the tax exemption. In addition, there is an excise tax on organizations that lose their exemptions. §§ 4912 and 4955. Attempting to influence the executive or judicial branch about the enforcement and interpretation of legislation does not constitute "influencing legislation" in violation of the rule against political activity.

A charitable organization can lobby the general public, although no more than a quarter of the permitted lobbying expenses can be devoted to this activity. Note that this permits contributors to some charities to deduct the cost of grassroots lobbying for which § 162(e)(1)(C) forbids a business deduction. In order to prevent an end-run around this rule, § 162(e)(3) disallows deductions for the portion of dues paid to a tax-exempt organization allocable to the organization's lobbying expenses. Is the disparity in the treatment of businesses and charities proper? On the other hand, both businesses and charities can deduct the cost of their efforts to influence public policy through administrative agencies or the courts. Why is lawmaking through the administrative or adjudicative process different from lawmaking through the legislative process?

"Neutrality." Even with restrictions, does § 162(e) give businesses an advantage over individuals? Assume that a corporation saves $10,000 a year by polluting the Mississippi River rather than avoiding such pollution. What is the maximum amount that the corporation would spend to lobby against anti-pollution legislation if such expenses were deductible? If they were nondeductible? Assume that a citizens' group supporting the legislation values the cleaner water at $10,000 per year. How much would the group spend if such expenses were deductible? Nondeductible? Would your answers to the preceding question change if the lobbying related to a

business's effort to obtain a substantial loan from the government at favorable interest rates? A direct government subsidy? An especially favorable federal income tax provision?

D. EMPLOYEE BUSINESS EXPENSES

NOTE ON EMPLOYEE BUSINESS EXPENSES

An employee who incurs deductible business expenses must follow a tortuous route through the statute to determine the amount of the allowable deduction. First, the employee must determine whether the expenses are ordinary and necessary in carrying on a trade or business. Second, expenses that are allowable under § 162 must be further characterized as "above the line" expenses (deductible from gross income in determining adjusted gross income) or alternatively as itemized deductions. Third, certain itemized deductions are subject to limitation and may not be deductible in full.

Deductible Employee Expenses. Expenses incurred by an employee in connection with a trade or business are deductible under § 162, provided they are ordinary and necessary. Performing your job is considered the trade or business of an employee. Quite often the issue is whether the expenses are actually personal in nature. This issue is discussed in detail infra at page 246. The regulations indicate that professional expenses may be deducted. Examples include supplies, dues to professional societies and unions, subscriptions to professional journals, and the expenses incurred in using an automobile to make business calls. Reg. § 1.162–6. Travel expenses incurred by employees are subject to special limitations and are taken up infra at page 262.

Itemized Deductions. Generally, whether employee business expenses are deducted "above the line" or are taken as itemized deductions depends on whether the employer reimburses the deduction. Reimbursed expenses are deductible above the line, which means the employee may deduct them even if she takes the standard deduction. § 62(a)(2)(A). The employee must, however, provide substantiation to the person providing reimbursement and cannot be reimbursed for more than the deductible expense. § 62(c). All unreimbursed expenses are deductible only if the employee itemizes deductions. Displaying an inexplicable favoritism, however, Congress made this rule inapplicable to performing artists, whose employee business expenses are deductible in computing adjusted gross income. § 62(a)(2)(B). Note that a self-employed "independent contractor" (as contrasted to an employee) can deduct all business expenses above the line. § 62(a)(1). While the line between independent contractor and employee status is frequently difficult to apply, this independent contractor status does not apply to employees of the ordinary sort, including associates in a law firm.

The 2 Percent Floor. Under § 67, a taxpayer can deduct "miscellaneous itemized deductions" only to the extent that, in the aggregate, they exceed 2 percent of the taxpayer's adjusted gross income for the year. The Code defines "miscellaneous itemized deductions" by exclusion, detailing what is not a miscellaneous itemized deduction. Excluded are the itemized deductions for interest, taxes, casualty and wagering losses, charitable donations, medical expenses, and several other deductions. Section 67 applies primarily to unreimbursed employee business expenses and investment expenses under § 212. For example, a taxpayer with $100,000 of salary and $2,500 of unreimbursed employee business expenses could treat only $500 as an itemized deduction; the remaining $2,000 is not deductible.

The 3 Percent Haircut. Section 68 caps the total amount of certain itemized deductions for high bracket taxpayers. In 2001 once adjusted gross income exceeds $132,950, itemized deductions (other than medical expenses, investment interest, gambling, and casualty losses) are reduced by 3 percent of the excess AGI. The reduction cannot exceed 80 percent of the deductions. For example, a taxpayer with an AGI of $200,000 and $40,000 of the relevant deductions could deduct only $37,988 [$2,012 or ($200,-000 − $132,950) x 3% would be disallowed.] If the relevant deductions were only $2,000, the haircut would have been limited to $1,600, but because of state income taxes alone, most taxpayers have enough itemized deductions that this rule does not come into play. Note that the effect is the same as raising the top marginal tax rate on the affected taxpayers without changing the nominal tax rates. Why do you suppose Congress chose to change the top rates in this manner?

In 2001, as part of an act reducing tax rates, Congress repealed § 68. The repeal is phased in, however, beginning in 2006 and does not become fully effective until 2010. Thus, both the simplicity gains and the revenue loss from the repeal are postponed for almost a decade (and they are lost again as these changes are scheduled to be terminated in 2011).

Congress justified these byzantine rules on simplicity grounds, thereby confirming Will Rogers' famous adage that when Congress makes a joke, it's a law. Essentially, the 2 percent floor and the 3 percent haircut were added to raise revenue. In fact, the 2 percent rule may promote simplification in some cases because few taxpayers will have sufficient expenses to exceed the floor. That may eliminate a recordkeeping burden for taxpayers whose expenses are consistently below the floor and an auditing burden for the IRS. Disallowing a percentage of income producing expenses, however, often means that more than net income is taxed. Do the simplification benefits warrant such a departure from basic income tax principles?

Recall the discussion of fringe benefits in Chapter 2. Where business expenses are paid by the employer, the reimbursement can be excluded from income. Section 132(d) defines as a working condition fringe benefit any "property or services provided to an employee of the employer to the extent that, if the employee paid for such property or services, such payment would be allowable as a deduction under § 162 or § 167." Must the employee include in income any working condition fringe that would not be deductible because of the 2 percent floor? The regulations indicate that the 2 percent limitation can be ignored for purposes of § 132. Reg. § 1.132–5(a)(vi).

This rule, combined with the fact that reimbursed expenses are above the line, has resulted in pressure on employers to reimburse expenses. Consider the following cases (which assume a 30 percent tax rate):

Case A: The taxpayer has $100,000 of salary and receives $2,000 of working condition fringes.

Case B: The taxpayer has $100,000 of salary and has $2,000 of employee business expenses that are reimbursed by the employer.

Case C: The taxpayer has $102,000 of salary and the employee is not reimbursed for $2,000 of business expenses.

	Case A	Case B*	Case C
AGI	$100,000	$100,000	$102,000
Deductible Bus. Ex.	0	0	0
Taxable Income	100,000	100,000	102,000
Tax Paid	30,000	30,000	30,600
After-tax income	70,000	70,000	69,400

As the above example shows, the tax law now provides different consequences depending on whether employee business expenses are reimbursed by the employer, provided as working condition fringes by the employer or paid directly by the employee. There is no way to justify such disparate treatment.

Congress seems to understand this and sometimes treats certain professions preferentially by permitting taxpayers to deduct unreimbursed expenses "above the line" so that they are subject to neither the 2% or 3% rule. See, e.g., § 62(A)(2)(B) (special rule for performing artists). In 2002, Congress adopted a provision permitting full-time teachers to deduct up to $250 in unreimbursed expenses for classroom supplies. Teachers could have deducted the cost of such supplies as a miscellaneous itemized deduction but the effect of the 2% rule was that almost no one received any benefit. The new deduction is above the line so that teachers can deduct the expenses even if they do not itemize.

The 2 percent limitation of § 67 also applies to deductions taken under § 212. As a result, most taxpayers are unable to deduct employee business expenses and expenses for the production of income under § 212. This can lead to the taxpayer's tax bill being larger than her net income. This bizarre result is illustrated nicely by the situation where a plaintiff pays his attorney on a contingency basis. Suppose the litigation arises in connection with the plaintiff's employment, such as employment discrimination under Title VII or is not job-related, such as a personal automobile accident. The amount of the judgement or settlement paid to the attorney as a fee would be an itemized deduction subject to the 2 percent floor. (The deduction is also disallowed for alternative minimum tax purposes. See Chapter 7, infra.) The interaction of these statutory rules almost always strips the plaintiff of a deduction. Not surprisingly, taxpayer-plaintiffs have looked for a back door solution, arguing that the amount paid to the attorney is not gross income to the plaintiff. Three circuit courts of appeal have agreed.

---

* Technically, the taxpayer, who is reimbursed by his employer for $2,000 of employee business expenses, has $2,000 of gross income and $2,000 of business expenses, deductible in determining adjusted gross income. The regulations, however, permit the employee to exclude the income and omit the deduction, provided there is adequate accounting to the employer. Reg. § 1.162–2.

The Fifth Circuit in Cotnam v. Commissioner, 263 F.2d 119 (1959), held that since the attorney had a lien on his portion of the contingency fee, the plaintiff never had a right to the entire recovery. The Sixth Circuit followed suit, noting that the value of the plaintiff's suit was speculative and was dependent on the services of the attorney. The claim was an "intangible, contingent expectancy." Estate of Clarks v. United States, 202 F.3d 854 (6th Cir.2000); see also Foster v. United States, 249 F.3d 1275 (11th Cir.2001). The Third, Fourth, Seventh, Ninth, Tenth and Federal circuit courts and the Tax Court disagreed. The Tax Court followed a long line of cases holding attorneys' fees were not excludable but were only deductible. The court expressed a good deal of sympathy with the taxpayer's plight, but noted that the unfairness was created by Congress and only Congress could rewrite the statute. Kenseth v. Commissioner, 114 T.C. 399 (2000). The Seventh Circuit affirmed. 259 F.3d 881 (2001). All courts determined that the plaintiff had a right to the entire amount of the recovery, a portion of which was used to satisfy the plaintiff's personal obligation to pay the attorney's fee. O'Brien v. Commissioner, 319 F.2d 532 (3d Cir.1963); Baylin v. United States, 43 F.3d 1451 (Fed.Cir.1995); Coady v. Commissioner, 213 F.3d 1187 (9th Cir.2000); Young v. Commissioner, 240 F.3d 369 (4th Cir.2001); Hukkanen–Campbell v. Commissioner, 274 F.3d 1312 (10th Cir.2001). The Fifth Circuit in Srivastava v. Commissioner, 220 F.3d 353 (2000), felt constrained to follow *Cotnam*, but noted that if it were writing on a clean slate, it would find the portion attributable to the contingent fee was taxable to create parity with a claimant who pays the attorney on a noncontingent basis.

The basic problem is that the 2 percent floor disallows deductions appropriate to measure net income. Short of repeal, one way to solve this particular dilemma is to exempt litigation expenses from the definition of miscellaneous itemized expenses. To be a complete solution, Congress also would have to eliminate the reduction of the deduction by § 68 and eliminate the effect of the alternative minimum tax.

SECTION 2. DISTINCTION BETWEEN DEDUCTIBLE BUSINESS OR INVESTMENT EXPENSES AND NONDEDUCTIBLE PERSONAL, LIVING OR FAMILY EXPENSES

NOTE INTRODUCING THE BUSINESS OR INVESTMENT–PERSONAL CONSUMPTION DISTINCTION[1]

Since an individual can at once obtain income and satisfy personal needs, the line between deductible and nondeductible expenses is often hard to draw. Some business expenses have little or no personal connection, but most personal expenses can be linked, at least tenuously, to business. Taxpayers often find ways to mix personal pleasure with potentially de-

---

1. Much of the material in this note is taken from Michael J. Graetz, "Expenditure Tax Design" in What Should Be Taxed: In- come or Expenditure? 222–27 (Joseph Pechman ed., 1979).

ductible business. The annual congregation of corporate jets at the Kentucky Derby and the Super Bowl is not accidental.

We would have difficulty performing our jobs or other income producing tasks if we did not eat, obtain housing or take an occasional vacation. Thus, much basic consumption performs some "income producing" function. Money often is spent not only to provide personal satisfaction but also to make more money. Marvin Chirelstein accurately assesses the difficulty of the tax collector's task when he observes that "the notion of a sharp division between pleasure-seeking and profit-seeking is alien to human psychology and essentially unrealistic."[2]

Boris Bittker has remarked on the dilemma in greater detail:

There is, unfortunately, no theoretically satisfactory boundary between business expenses that provide incidental personal benefits and personal expenditures that incidentally serve business purposes. No matter how generously the Code defines business expenses in an effort to insure that all business-related expenses can be deducted, there will always be some non-deductible items beyond the line that contribute in some way to the production of income, whether it is the basic cost of living—one cannot work, after all, unless one is fed and housed—or the cost of luxuries that contribute to the taxpayer's willingness to work and to his initiative and reliability while on the job. On the other hand, no matter how severely the term "business expense" is defined, many items will continue to qualify for deduction although they confer "personal" benefits on the taxpayer. Taxpayers may be forbidden to deduct entertainment expenses because they are suspected of enjoying dinners and theater parties with their business customers, for example, but even the most puritanical definition of business expense is not likely to prevent self-employed taxpayers from deducting the cost of air conditioning their offices, upholstering their swivel chairs, or adding gadgets to their telephones, even if they derive personal pleasure from these amenities.[3]

Chirelstein's and Bittker's emphasis on indeterminacy is in sharp contrast to Daniel Halperin's conclusion:

The position that a deduction ought to be allowed for all income-generating expenses, while quite correct, is really beside the point. If such expenditures actually provide personal satisfaction, the amount of such satisfaction ought to be included in income. The fairest income tax would take account of income from "whatever source derived." On-the-job entertainment, traveling expenses and other expenditures which but for their connection with income-generating activities would be considered to provide personal satisfaction should not be distinguished from other forms of enjoyment.

An indirect way of taxing these benefits is to deny a deduction to the extent personal satisfaction has been obtained from the expendi-

---

2. Marvin A. Chirelstein, Federal Income Taxation: A Law Student's Guide to the Leading Cases and Concepts 97 (rev. 8th ed., 1997).

3. Boris Bittker, "Income Tax Deductions, Credits and Subsidies for Personal Expenditures," 16 J. Law and Econ. 203–04 (1973).

ture. If satisfaction were equal to cost, this approach would suggest complete disallowance. This reasoning is the foundation of [my] conclusion * * * that, assuming perfect information and absence of administrative problems, a deduction should be permitted only to the extent that the costs incurred exceed the personal benefit obtained. The proposal does not, therefore, represent a challenge to the right to a deduction for expenditures intended to produce income.

Despite [measurement difficulties] * * * it is not necessary to have complete assurance that personal satisfaction equals cost in order to make this assumption for purposes of taxation. While undoubtedly this will lead to overtaxation in some circumstances, such a result is far more acceptable than the understatement of income which results from ignoring the personal benefit. Of course, there will be many circumstances in which the matter is completely in doubt, and some sort of arbitrary allocation or partial taxation may be the best solution available.[4]

Notwithstanding the conceptual difficulties, the income tax law must distinguish business from personal expenses. If personal expenses could be deducted, personal consumption would be omitted from the tax base; in contrast, if business deductions were not allowed, gross income, not net income, would be taxed. The problems of equity and efficiency that emerge from the necessity of drawing the business-personal line are quite similar to those that emerge in connection with fringe benefits. (In fact, an employee's fringe benefit may be a self-employed person's business deduction.)

Unwarranted business deductions would permit taxpayers to finance personal consumption from pretax rather than after-tax dollars. To a taxpayer subject to a 40 percent marginal tax rate, a $50 fully deductible meal has the same after-tax cost as a $30 nondeductible meal. Allowing business deductions for personal consumption produces both horizontal and vertical inequities; taxpayers with similar incomes have different abilities to obtain these deductions depending on their occupations, while taxpayers with higher income often have more opportunities to obtain these deductions than do people with lower incomes. Such deductions also induce a misallocation of resources as spending flows toward deductible forms of consumption.

For many years, the struggle to distinguish deductible business or investment expenses from nondeductible personal, family or living expenses was left to the IRS and the courts. More recently, however, Congress has responded to what it perceives as "abuses" by imposing restrictions on or disallowing certain deductions. Congress has also limited certain mixed motive expenses in order to raise revenue. See, e.g., § 280A (disallowing deduction of certain expenses in connection with home office and vacation homes, discussed infra at page 280), § 280F (limiting depreciation deductions and investment tax credits for "luxury" automobiles and personal property not used primarily for business purposes), § 183 (limiting deduc-

---

4. Daniel Halperin, "Business Deductions for Personal Living Expenses: A Uni-   form Approach to an Unsolved Problem," 122 U.Pa.L.Rev. 859 (1974).

tions with respect to "activities not engaged in for profit"). (Section 183 is discussed infra at page 416.)

Travel and entertainment expenses, in particular, have a large consumption element. Congress has imposed numerous restrictions on their deductibility. See, e.g., § 274(n) (limiting the deduction for business meals and entertainment to 50 percent of cost); § 274(m)(1)(A) (limiting the deduction for "luxury" water travel); § 274(k)(1)(A) (limiting the deduction for "lavish or extravagant" business meals); § 274(*l*) (limiting deductions for entertainment and sports event tickets to face value and restricting deductions for skyboxes).

In the absence of statutory rules, the IRS and the courts have applied various tests for deductibility. These tests are not uniform; they depend on the type of expenses involved. For some expenses, the courts allow the deduction whenever the expense is appropriate and helpful to the taxpayer's business or income producing activity. For other expenses, courts disallow the deduction unless the taxpayer's "primary purpose" in incurring the expense was profit seeking (or, in some cases, unless the expense would not have been made "but for" a business or investment motive). The courts occasionally require that the taxpayer's expenditures be "reasonable" even if they were clearly incurred for profit-oriented rather than personal reasons. Courts sometimes have allowed a deduction only for the "additional expenses" due to the needs of the taxpayer's business or income producing activities. Expenses sometimes are allocated between business and personal use, with deduction permitted only for the amount allocated to business use. Some types of expense have been regarded by the courts as "inherently personal" and nondeductible even if shown to enhance profit-making activity. It is difficult to know when the courts will apply any of these tests. The cost of haircuts, for example, is nondeductible under the "inherently personal" test, but the cost of books is deductible if "appropriate and helpful" to the taxpayer's business. In some cases, the IRS, in regulations, has provided specific, and somewhat arbitrary rules for the deduction of certain mixed-motive expenses. Neither the IRS nor the courts, however, has developed an overarching theory.

Because logical reasoning often will not provide the answer, there is no substitute for examining the precedents or regulations relating to the particular type of expense at issue. Many of the rules are illustrated in the materials that follow. Sometimes the question is made more difficult by issues of timing, for example, whether an expenditure is a currently deductible "expense" or a nondeductible capital expenditure. In reading the materials that follow, reflect upon the following questions: Should a single test govern the line between profit seeking and personal expenses, or are multiple tests desirable or at least inevitable? Are some tests clearly superior to others?

Pevsner v. Commissioner

United States Court of Appeals, Fifth Circuit, 1980. 628 F.2d 467.

SAM D. JOHNSON, CIRCUIT JUDGE:

This is an appeal by the Commissioner of Internal Revenue from a decision of the United States Tax Court. The tax court upheld taxpayer's business expense deduction for clothing expenditures in the amount of $1,621.91 for the taxable year 1975. We reverse.

Since June 1973 Sandra J. Pevsner, taxpayer, has been employed as the manager of the Sakowitz Yves St. Laurent Rive Gauche Boutique located in Dallas, Texas. The boutique sells only women's clothes and accessories designed by Yves St. Laurent (YSL), one of the leading designers of women's apparel. * * *

As manager of the boutique, the taxpayer is expected by her employer to wear YSL clothes while at work. In her appearance, she is expected to project the image of an exclusive lifestyle and to demonstrate to her customers that she is aware of the YSL current fashion trends as well as trends generally. Because the boutique sells YSL clothes exclusively, taxpayer must be able, when a customer compliments her on her clothes, to say that they are designed by YSL. In addition to wearing YSL apparel while at the boutique, she wears them while commuting to and from work, to fashion shows sponsored by the boutique, and to business luncheons where she represents the boutique. * * *

Although the clothing and accessories purchased by the taxpayer were the type used for general purposes by the regular customers of the boutique, the taxpayer is not a normal purchaser of these clothes. * * *

Although taxpayer's employer has no objection to her wearing the apparel away from work, taxpayer stated that she did not wear the clothes during off-work hours because she felt that they were too expensive for her simple everyday lifestyle. * * * Taxpayer did admit at trial, however, that a number of the articles were things she could have worn off the job and in which she would have looked "nice."

* * *

The principal issue on appeal is whether the taxpayer is entitled to deduct as an ordinary and necessary business expense the cost of purchasing and maintaining the YSL clothes and accessories worn by the taxpayer in her employment as the manager of the boutique. This determination requires an examination of the relationship between Section 162(a) of the Internal Revenue Code of 1954, which allows a deduction for ordinary and necessary expenses incurred in the conduct of a trade or business, and Section 262 of the Code, which bars a deduction for all "personal, living, or family expenses." Although many expenses are helpful or essential to one's business activities—such as commuting expenses and the cost of meals while at work—these expenditures are considered inherently personal and are disallowed under Section 262. * * *

The generally accepted rule governing the deductibility of clothing expenses is that the cost of clothing is deductible as a business expense only if: (1) the clothing is of a type specifically required as a condition of employment, (2) it is not adaptable to general usage as ordinary clothing, and (3) it is not so worn. Donnelly v. Commissioner, 262 F.2d 411, 412 (2d Cir.1959).[1]

In the present case, the Commissioner stipulated that the taxpayer was required by her employer to wear YSL clothing and that she did not wear such apparel apart from work. The Commissioner maintained, however, that a deduction should be denied because the YSL clothes and accessories purchased by the taxpayer were adaptable for general usage as ordinary clothing and she was not prohibited from using them as such. The tax court, in rejecting the Commissioner's argument for the application of an objective test, recognized that the test for deductibility was whether the clothing was "suitable for general or personal wear" but determined that the matter of suitability was to be judged subjectively, in light of the taxpayer's lifestyle. Although the court recognized that the YSL apparel "might be used by some members of society for general purposes," it felt that because the "wearing of YSL apparel outside work would be inconsistent with * * * [taxpayer's] lifestyle," sufficient reason was shown for allowing a deduction for the clothing expenditures.

[The court's discussion of the Tax Court's reliance on a similar case, Yeomans v. Commissioner, 30 T.C. 757 (1958) (where the taxpayer was allowed to deduct expensive work clothing not suitable to her lifestyle) is omitted.]

Notwithstanding the tax court's decision in *Yeomans,* the Circuits that have addressed the issue have taken an objective, rather than subjective, approach. * * * Under an objective test, no reference is made to the individual taxpayer's lifestyle or personal taste. Instead, adaptability for personal or general use depends upon what is generally accepted for ordinary street wear.

The principal argument in support of an objective test is, of course, administrative necessity. The Commissioner argues that, as a practical matter, it is virtually impossible to determine at what point either price or style makes clothing inconsistent with or inappropriate to a taxpayer's lifestyle. Moreover, the Commissioner argues that the price one pays and the styles one selects are inherently personal choices governed by taste, fashion, and other unmeasurable values. Indeed, the tax court has rejected the argument that a taxpayer's personal taste can dictate whether clothing is appropriate for general use. * * * An objective test, although not perfect, provides a practical administrative approach that allows a taxpayer or revenue agent to look only to objective facts in determining whether clothing required as a condition of employment is adaptable to general use as ordinary street wear. Conversely, the tax court's reliance on subjective factors provides no concrete guidelines in determining the deductibility of clothing purchased as a condition of employment.

In addition to achieving a practical administrative result, an objective test also tends to promote substantial fairness among the greatest number

---

1. When the taxpayer is prohibited from wearing the clothing away from work a deduction is normally allowed. See Harsaghy v. Commissioner, 2 T.C. 484 (1943). However, in the present case no such restriction was placed upon the taxpayer's use of the clothing.

of taxpayers. As the Commissioner suggests, it apparently would be the tax court's position that two similarly situated YSL boutique managers with identical wardrobes would be subject to disparate tax consequences depending upon the particular manager's lifestyle and "socio-economic level." This result, however, is not consonant with a reasonable interpretation of Sections 162 and 262.

For the reasons stated above, the decision of the tax court * * * is

Reversed.

NOTES

(A) *Clothing.* The Tax Court had permitted Ms. Pevsner to deduct the cost of her clothes, apparently being much more sympathetic to her claim that she would not wear the clothes outside of work. The court found that the question of suitability was a subjective one to be answered by the taxpayer. If the taxpayer had prevailed, what kinds of clothing would be deductible? Suits worn by laid-back attorneys? The Fifth Circuit accepted the Commissioner's objective test: If the clothing was adaptable for general usage, it was not deductible. This test is derived from several rulings that permit a deduction for "uniforms" if (1) they are specifically required as a condition of employment and (2) they are not adaptable to general wear. Rev.Rul. 70–474, 1970–2 C.B. 34; Rev.Rul. 67–115, 1967–1 C.B. 30.

The extent to which the fisc might be raided if taxpayers were permitted to treat clothing, grooming, and the like as a deductible business expense is nicely illustrated by Irwin v. Commissioner, 72 T.C.M. 1148 (1996). Pennel Phlander Irwin, author of the unpublished novels "Great Woods Poppy" and "Positively People," attempted to deduct many of life's costs including a television, a hot tub, the expenses of traveling to his mother's funeral, his daughter's dorm expenses at college, and the costs of his home. He explained to the court: "For fiction writing all personal experiences and observations are all business experiences and observations. * * * (Example: Upon awaking in the morning the toiletry and dressing process carried out by myself, and observed in others, is research whose end observations are included in the fictional writing for similar actions carried on by the various characters; and therefore, different grooming products would be justifiable research expenses as well as different clothing that conveys fit and feel.)" The following exchange from the trial transcript gives the flavor of Irwin's approach to research and its relationship to his tax return:

The Court: Mr. Irwin, please explain your research expenses.

Irwin: * * * Interview research expenses are incurred when I am trying to gain information on different types of subject matter. For instance, Scott Keithley is listed under interview research materials. Scott Keithley happens to be a dentist, and I was getting information on dental hygiene and dental practice, which I learned about firsthand.

The Court: Was he your dentist?

Irwin: Scott Keithley? Yes. So part of the service I'm paying for—

The Court: * * * What did Scott Keithley do for you? Did he clean your teeth?

* * *

Irwin: Okay, well, when I'm paying for a service, I prefer—I pay for the physical service as well as for the information that person provides. * * *

Irwin chose not to deduct all food and toiletries however, in part so that he would not have to reveal the contents of works in progress. Despite his largess, the court found all the expenses inherently personal and not deductible. The Ninth Circuit affirmed. 80 AFTR2d 8006 (9th Cir.1997).

Consider also Ralph Vitale, who in preparation for his upcoming retirement, decided to write a book about legal brothels in Nevada. He researched his subject by visiting brothels, paying prostitutes in cash, and keeping a detailed journal. Because he behaved in a business-like manner and actually received royalties, the Tax Court concluded that he had a profit motive. Despite that victory, most of his expenses were not deductible. He apparently forgot to ask for receipts and therefore his expenses were unsubstantiated. And the cash payments to the prostitutes? They were "so personal in nature as to preclude their deductibility." Vitale v. Commissioner, 47 T.C.M. 1869 (1999), aff'd per curiam 217 F.3d 843 (4th Cir.)

Would a better alternative be to assume that all costs of clothing and grooming are inherently personal and thus nondeductible? To whom would that be unfair? Perhaps someone who derived no pleasure from the activity and for whom the expenses played a substantial role in her trade or business. A piano soloist required to wear formal attire? See W.J. Fisher v. Commissioner, 23 T.C. 218 (1954) (permitting a deduction for tuxedos). A professional tennis player who wears out court shoes every three weeks? See Mella v. Commissioner, 52 T.C.M. 1216 (1986) (denying a deduction and rejecting taxpayer's statement that tennis pros do not wear tennis shoes off the court). A model whose hair is styled? See Wilson v. Commissioner, 32 T.C.M. 407 (1973) (denying a deduction because styling provided personal benefits). A soldier whose fatigues cannot be worn off duty? See Rev.Rul. 67–115, 1967–1 C.B. 30 (allowing deduction for fatigues that do "not merely take the place of articles required in civilian life"). TV actors who had to purchase clothing worn by "an average American family" although some of it was too hot to wear in southern California? See Nelson v. Commissioner, 25 T.C.M. 1142 (1966) (permitting deduction for some of Ozzie's sweaters and Harriet's dresses). Is it important that (almost) everyone purchases clothes for work and incurs grooming expenses? Is it fair that a lawyer can deduct a legal pad but a tennis pro cannot deduct shoes?

Could Ms. Pevsner avoid paying for her YSL attire out of after-tax dollars if her employer provided such clothing to her as a fringe benefit? Which, if any, of the exclusions of § 132 would apply?

(B) *The Inherently Personal Standard.* In Trebilcock v. Commissioner, 64 T.C. 852, aff'd 557 F.2d 1226 (6th Cir.1977), the court disallowed deductions for payments by a businessman to a minister for business and personal advice based on prayer. A similar result was reached in Fred W.

Amend Co. v. Commissioner, 55 T.C. 320 (1970), aff'd 454 F.2d 399 (7th Cir.1971), where a businessman hired a Christian Science practitioner who provided spiritual guidance on both business and personal matters. In both cases, the courts disallowed deduction on the ground that the expenditures were "inherently personal in nature." Would it have made any difference if other similar businesses "ordinarily" consulted ministers or Christian Science practitioners? Would it have made any difference if the advice given via prayer and spiritual counseling always resulted in significantly increased profits? If they had received identical advice from a "business consultant," would the payment of the consultant's fee have been deductible? The court in *Trebilcock* noted that "all benefits provided by ministers are inherently personal by nature." Are benefits provided by sports psychologists inherently personal? By aerobics teachers? Stress managers? Does the inherently personal standard provide much guidance? See Kelly v. Commissioner, 62 T.C.M. 1406 (1991). The taxpayer, a CPA who did tax work, sought to deduct the cost of athletic equipment he acquired to build up the stamina needed for a tax practice. The court, rejecting the taxpayer's inherently believable position, found the exercise equipment inherently personal.

(C) *Comparison to Fringe Benefits.* Reconsider § 132. Does the exclusion of § 132(a)(3) for "working condition fringes" defined in § 132(d) as property or services, which, if paid for by the employee, would be deductible under § 162, simply shift the inquiry to the employee level? In Henderson v. Commissioner, 46 T.C.M. 566 (1983), the Tax Court denied a deduction for a $35 framed print and a $35 plant purchased by a South Carolina assistant attorney general for her office, finding they were personal expenses. If Ms. Henderson had been assigned an office with a print and a plant, would she have had income?

(D) *Public Employees.* Although, in general, a trade or business expense must be profit-seeking, a limited exception has been carved out for public employees. In Frank v. United States, 577 F.2d 93 (9th Cir.1978), a businessman who also worked as a virtually uncompensated aide to a United States Senator was allowed to deduct food, lodging, and transportation expenses for trips taken on the Senator's behalf. In some years, the taxpayer's expenses were more than thirty times his salary as an aide. The court recognized that not every public office could be considered a trade or business, but concluded that a position that entailed "a definite work assignment" and was not undertaken "as a tax dodge" would qualify as a trade or business and its expenses could be deducted. See also Rev.Rul. 84–110, 1984–2 C.B. 35, which interprets § 7701(a)(26) to provide an exception for public officeholders to the requirement of a profit motive for a trade or business.

(E) *Unreimbursed Expenses.* The courts tend to be suspicious of any expense paid by an employee not reimbursed by the employer, presumably on the ground that if it were sufficiently appropriate and helpful, the employer would have covered the cost. For example, in Tesar v. Commissioner, 73 T.C.M. 2709 (1997), the taxpayer—a high school math teacher and an apparent comic book fanatic—attempted to deduct almost $30,000 he spent on 16,000 comic books he bought for the school comic book club.

Although the Service argued that the expense was not ordinary because other teachers/sponsors commonly bought only snacks and not necessary because he did not have to sponsor a club, the taxpayer appears to have lost his deduction because he took all the comics with him when he left his job.

An employee who fails to seek reimbursement to which she is entitled also may lose a deduction. The Tax Court takes the position that a deduction is not allowable to an employee to the extent she is entitled to reimbursement from her employer. Cavitt v. Commissioner, 60 T.C.M. 160 (1990).

(F) *Domestic Services and Child Care.* Prior to the adoption of § 21, taxpayers argued that the cost of child care during work hours was an ordinary and necessary expense in carrying on a trade or business. In Smith v. Commissioner, 40 B.T.A. 1038 (1939), affirmed per curiam 113 F.2d 114 (2d Cir.1940), the court held that such amounts paid by a two-earner married couple were "inherently personal" and were not deductible. In effect, the court treated the decision to have a child as an "inherently personal" one, without which no child care expenses would have been incurred. Although there had previously been a deduction for child care expenses, § 21 currently provides a tax credit for qualifying child care expenses. Taxpayers with adjusted gross income of $15,000 or less may offset tax liability by 35 percent of their employment-related dependent care expenses. That percentage is reduced one percentage point for each additional $2,000 of adjusted gross income of the taxpayer, until it reaches 20 percent for taxpayers with incomes above $28,000. The amount of creditable expenses is limited to the income of the lower-earning spouse or, in the case of a single person, to earned income. Students are deemed to earn a limited amount of income. There is a ceiling on creditable expenses of $2,400 ($3,000 after 2002) for one dependent and $4,800 ($6,000 after 2002) for more than one. Thus, the credit cannot exceed $720 ($900 after 2002) for one dependent or $1,440 ($1,800 after 2002) for two or more dependents. The credit is not refundable if the taxpayer has insufficient tax liability to take full advantage of it.

Is the child care credit appropriately classified as a tax expenditure or is it necessary to a proper measurement of income? Do the phase-down and phase-out of the credit and the overall dollar limitation inform your answer? Do the following distinctions lend support to either view? (1) The credit is limited to expenses incurred for dependents under age 13. (2) Expenses of sending a child to preschool are deductible, but elementary school tuition is not. But see Zoltan v. Commissioner, 79 T.C. 490 (1982) (partial cost of "educational" trip to Washington, D.C. during spring vacation was qualifying expense). (3) The cost of overnight camp is ineligible for the credit, but the expense of day camp is creditable. (4) The employee's motive in incurring the child care expenses is apparently irrelevant. See Brown v. Commissioner, 73 T.C. 156 (1979) (employment motive need not be exclusive or even dominant). Thus, it does not appear to matter whether the taxpayer worked in order to hire a babysitter or hired a babysitter in order to work. (5) So long as there is a qualifying individual in the home, expenses for "household services" are creditable.

Consider also § 129 which permits an employee to exclude up to $5,000 any taxable year in dependent care costs. The maximum amount of the dependent care credit under § 21 is reduced by the amounts excluded under § 129. Is § 129 consistent with the policy reflected in § 21?

In 2001 Congress added a provision that permits a credit for employer-provided child care facilities. Employers receive a credit equal to 25 percent of qualified expenses for child care for employees and 10 percent of expenses for child care resource and referral services. The maximum credit is $150,000 each taxable year. § 45F.

Section 23 permits an adopting parent to take a credit of up to $10,000 for the expenses of adopting a minor child who is not the child of a spouse. Taxpayers with AGI above $150,000 are not eligible for the credit. Taxpayers can also exclude up to $10,000 of employer-provided adoption assistance. § 137. This exclusion is phased out for taxpayers with more than $150,000 of AGI.

(G) *The Costs of Being an Employee.* As the above notes indicate, the general costs of being an employee usually are not deductible, on the grounds that these expenses are inherently personal. For example, the cost of purchasing work clothes, eating lunch in a restaurant, and commuting to work (discussed in the next Section) are not offset against an employee's wages. Is this fair? A, who earns $20,000 in wages, is obviously going to be left with fewer after-tax dollars than B, who collects $20,000 in interest from bonds. Why has Congress chosen not to permit a deduction for these normal expenses of being employed?

A.   TRAVEL EXPENSES

1.   TRANSPORTATION EXPENSES

Transportation expenses, such as airfare, taxicab fare or the cost of operating a car, generally are deductible when the taxpayer is traveling on business. This may be the cost of traveling from one city to another, but it also may be the cost of traveling from one business engagement to another within one metropolitan area. For example, cab fare from the taxpayer's law firm to the courthouse would be deductible.

These deductions should be contrasted with the rule that the cost of commuting from home to work and back are nondeductible personal expenses. Reg. § 1.162–2(e). This rule has been defended on the grounds that the work location is fixed and the decision to live beyond walking distance is a personal one. See, e.g., Commissioner v. Flowers, 326 U.S. 465 (1946), discussed in the following case. A strict denial of commuting deductions avoids difficult factual inquiries, but may seem unfair where the taxpayer cannot avoid commuting (for example, if she works at a weapons testing facility in the desert) or incurs significant additional expenses. Even though the disallowance of commuting deductions is well settled, questions have remained about special commuting costs that some taxpayers must incur because of the nature of their work. The following case illustrates how the courts and the IRS have wrestled with these issues.

McCabe v. Commissioner

United States Court of Appeals, Second Circuit, 1982. 688 F.2d 102.

CARDAMONE, CIRCUIT JUDGE:

The appellant, Dennis McCabe, a police officer employed by the City of New York, was required to carry his service revolver at all times while in the City. To reach his place of employment the most direct route from his home in Suffern, New York is through the State of New Jersey. New Jersey will allow an officer such as petitioner to carry a weapon only by permit. Stating that he could not expect to obtain a New Jersey permit, appellant carried his service revolver on his person and used his own automobile as his mode of transportation to and from work. * * *

* * *

[T]he cost of operating the vehicle by carrying a revolver was the same as it would have been had he commuted to his job by automobile without the revolver. But the record clearly establishes that appellant's commuting costs could have been reduced had he been able to travel through New Jersey. The record further shows that ample public transportation existed from Suffern to New York City. Since much of the convenient public transportation went through New Jersey, appellant would have again been faced with the need for a New Jersey gun permit.

On his 1976 income tax return appellant claimed $2,950 in automobile expenses [for] the commuting costs of driving 17,600 miles between Suffern and New York City * * *. The Commissioner of Internal Revenue disallowed the entire deduction and the Tax Court affirmed.

* * *

[T]he question becomes whether petitioner's additional expenses were appropriate, helpful, normal and expected under the circumstances or so personal in nature as to be non-deductible under I.R.C. § 262 (1976).

One well-established rule in tax law is that expenses incurred as a result of commuting from home to work are personal and not deductible under section 162. * * * The controlling precedent on this issue is Commissioner v. Flowers, 326 U.S. 465 (1946).

In *Flowers* the Court was faced with a case involving a taxpayer who lived in Jackson, Mississippi and worked in Mobile, Alabama. The taxpayer tried to deduct the travel expenses incurred in his excursions between the two cities and also claimed his expenditures for meals and hotel accommodations while in Mobile. The Supreme Court ruled that the additional expenses, including the commuting expenses, were not deductible. Although *Flowers* was concerned mostly with what is now I.R.C. § 162(a)(2), the Court's general analysis of section 162 sheds illumination on the question before us. In setting forth the final prong of a three-part test of travel expense deductibility,[1] the Court stated that the "expense must be

---

1. The first two prongs which must be satisfied before a traveling expense deduction may be taken under section 162(a)(2) are:

(1) The expense must be a reasonable and necessary traveling expense, as that term is generally understood. This in-

incurred in pursuit of business." This means that there must be a direct connection between the expenditure and the carrying on of the trade or business of the taxpayer or of his employer. Moreover, such an expenditure must be necessary or appropriate to the development and pursuit of the business or trade. 326 U.S. at 470. The Court concluded that the traveling expenses were "not incurred in pursuit of the business of the taxpayer's employer." Id. at 473. Further, the added costs were said to be "unnecessary and inappropriate" to the development of the employer's business. Id. The Court was of the view that the sole cause of the expense was the taxpayer's personal desire to reside in Jackson, "a factor irrelevant to the maintenance and prosecution of the [employer's] legal business." Id. Thus, personal convenience cannot be the motivating factor behind a section 162(a) deduction. Where one chooses to live is generally a matter of personal convenience. * * *

An exception to the commuting rule appears in Fausner v. Commissioner, 413 U.S. 838 (1973). *Fausner* acknowledged that commuting expenses are not deductible. * * * The brief *per curiam* states, however, that "[a]dditional expenses may at times be incurred for transporting job-required tools and material to and from work. Then an allocation of costs between 'personal' and 'business' expenses may be feasible." [413 U.S. at 839.] While the Court provided little or no guidance as what kind of circumstances should trigger such an allocation, its specific reference to the commuter rule would indicate that the requirements of section 162(a)—ordinary and necessary—must first be established before reaching the additional step of allocating.

The Internal Revenue Service in Revenue Ruling 75–380, 1975–2 C.B. 59 sought to explain *Fausner*. It stated that for additional expenses to be deductible the taxpayer must first establish "the necessity of transporting work implements to and from work." 1975–2 C.B. at 60. Giving the word "necessity" its usual meaning in tax law, it again appears that the taxpayer must establish that the additional expenses were appropriate and helpful to the employer's legal business and not personal in nature.

With this background in mind we may resolve the case presently before us. Appellant has argued that he may deduct the additional traveling expense incurred by reason of the use of his automobile in transporting his police revolver. However, a majority of the Tax Court ruled, sitting *en banc:*

> that petitioner's additional commuting expenses were not directly connected with the pursuit of his employer's business, but were principally the result of his decision to reside in a comparatively remote suburb adjacent to New Jersey. Accordingly, petitioner is entitled to no deduction for his commuting expenses under section 162(a), I.R.C. 1954, since such expenses were not necessary for the conduct of his employer's business.

McCabe v. Commissioner, 76 T.C. 876, 881 (1981).

---

cludes such items as transportation fares and food and lodging expenses incurred while traveling.

(2) The expense must be incurred "while away from home."

Commissioner v. Flowers, 326 U.S. 465, 470 (1946).

We are persuaded that the critical finding of the Tax Court, as set out above, is adequately based on permissible inferences derived from the stipulated facts. The New York City requirement that police officers be armed within city limits presented a problem for appellant simply because of the location of his home. * * * The Police Department required that officers be armed within New York City limits; it did not require them to be armed otherwise. Thus, the added expense incurred by appellant did not further the New York City Police Department's business of preventing crime within the City itself.

Finally, appellant's argument that he falls within the ambit of *Fausner* is fatally defective. Although concededly he incurred additional expense, in order to deduct it he must first show that it was ordinary and necessary. As noted, the location of one's home is personal and did not serve to further the business of the taxpayer's employer in this case.

The judgment is affirmed.

MESKILL, CIRCUIT JUDGE (dissenting):

I respectfully dissent.

I cannot agree with the majority's conclusion that McCabe's additional commuting costs were entirely a result of his personal choice of residence. In Fausner v. Commissioner, 413 U.S. 838 (1973) (per curiam), the Supreme Court disallowed a deduction for commuting costs where the taxpayer, a commercial airlines pilot, claimed that his "automobile expenses were incurred to transport his flight bag and overnight bag and thus constituted ordinary and necessary business expenses." Id. at 838. Because the taxpayer would have driven to work via the same route in any event, the Court found that no "allocation of costs between 'personal' and 'business' expenses" was feasible. Id. at 839 * * *.

This case is factually distinguishable from *Fausner*. Had McCabe driven to work without his firearm, he could have travelled through New Jersey. As a result of his alleged inability to secure a New Jersey gun permit, however, McCabe was forced to take a circuitous route, adding fifty cents in tolls and fifteen miles to his commute. * * * Certainly, these additional costs were caused by his employer's requirement that he carry his firearm at all times while within New York City and can be allocated as "business" expenses under *Fausner*.

The majority's reasoning, that "the location of one's home is personal and did not serve to further the business of the taxpayer's employer," * * *, drawn to its logical extreme, would disallow or render meaningless almost all *Fausner*-type deductions. A taxpayer can almost always reduce or eliminate his excess commuting costs by living closer to his work location. The real issue is whether, given the location of McCabe's residence and his selection of a reasonable mode of travel, he incurred additional "ordinary and necessary" commuting costs "in the pursuit of the business of the taxpayer's employer." Commissioner v. Flowers, 326 U.S. 465 (1946). To the extent that McCabe's change in route of travel was necessary to satisfy his employer's requirement that he carry his firearm while in New York

City, I believe that he is entitled to a deduction under section 162(a) of the Internal Revenue Code.

* * *

NOTES

(A) *Tools of the Trade.* In Revenue Ruling 75–380, cited in the principal case, the IRS asserted that it would permit a deduction "for only the portion of the cost of transporting the work implements by the mode of transportation used which is in excess of the cost of commuting by the same mode of transportation without the work implements." It illustrated this position with the following example:

> A taxpayer commuted to and from work by public transportation before the taxpayer had to carry necessary work implements. It cost $2 per day to commute to and from work. When it became necessary to carry the implements to and from work, it cost $3 per day to drive a car and an additional $5 per day to rent a trailer in which the implements were carried. The allowable deduction would be the $5 per day additional expense that the taxpayer incurred in renting the trailer to carry the work implements.

Under this formulation, what expense would the IRS approve other than the cost of renting a trailer? Suppose an employer ordered an employee to take 50 pounds of documents home to read over the weekend. If the employee took a cab rather than his usual mode of travel, the cab fare would not be deductible. But if the employee took the subway and put the documents in the cab, the cab fare would be deductible. Is this efficient?

(B) *Working and Driving.* In Pollei v. Commissioner, 877 F.2d 838 (10th Cir.1989), the court ruled that police officers, who began active patrol when they left home, were engaged in their jobs while driving to and from the stationhouse. Therefore, the commuting expenses allocable to that time were deductible. The government argued that allowing this deduction would lead to a flood of claims from people who during their commute work on dictaphones or telephones. The court, however, found that the nature of police work allowed it to be distinguished.

Can a meaningful line be drawn between the police officer in this case and a lawyer, who while driving to work, telephones a client or listens to educational tapes?

(C) *Commuting to Temporary Employment.* The IRS has promulgated the following rules: (1) A taxpayer may deduct daily transportation expenses incurred in going between the taxpayer's residence and a temporary work location outside the metropolitan area where the taxpayer lives and normally works. Generally, however, daily transportation expenses incurred in going between the taxpayer's residence and a temporary work location within the metropolitan area are nondeductible commuting expenses. (2) If a taxpayer has one or more regular work locations away from the taxpayer's residence, the taxpayer may deduct daily transportation expenses incurred in going between the taxpayer's residence and a temporary work location in the same trade or business, regardless of the distance.

(3) If a taxpayer's residence is the taxpayer's principal place of business within the meaning of § 280A(c)(1)(A), the taxpayer may deduct daily transportation expenses incurred in going between the residence and another work location in the same trade or business, regardless of whether the other work location is regular or temporary and regardless of the distance. Rev. Rul. 99–7, 1999–1 C.B. 361. A temporary place of business is a location at which the taxpayer performs services on an irregular or short-term basis (usually days or weeks). Rev.Rul. 90–23, 1990–1 C.B. 28.

Thus, if an accountant drives from her house to her office, and subsequently travels to see a client, the cost of traveling to the office is a nondeductible commuting expense while the cost of traveling from the office to the client is deductible. If she drives from her house to see a client before going to the office, the cost is deductible. Is this rational? Should all commuting expenses be allowed as a deduction, or should trips from the taxpayer's residence always be disallowed?

Interpreting the Service's position literally, the Tax Court permitted a logger to deduct his commuting costs in going to various job sites in a national forest, even though his home was clearly not his "principal" place of business, although it was his "regular" place of business. The Supreme Court, in *Soliman,* discussed at page 282 infra, held a home office deduction could be taken only for a principal place of business. In a ruling that city slickers will never understand, the Tax Court also found that the Black Hills National Forest constituted a metropolitan area. Walker v. Commissioner, 101 T.C. 537 (1993).

Suppose an employee is required to use a car for business purposes during working hours. Can the cost of getting the car (and not coincidentally the driver/employee) to work be deducted? In an aptly named case, Fillerup v. Commissioner, 55 T.C.M. 362 (1988), the court permitted a doctor to deduct the cost of driving his Mercedes from one hospital to another, but not the cost of driving to the first hospital. See also Croughan v. Commissioner, 55 T.C.M. 1273 (1988) (taxpayer denied deduction because she was required to use a car at work, but was not required to take it home at night). If the taxpayer had paid to garage the car overnight near the office, would the parking have been deductible?

(F) *Commuting at the Midnight Hour.* If an employer pays for an employee's commuting expenses, the payments generally constitute gross income. Section 132(d) does not apply because the amount would not be deductible if paid by the employee. The regulations permit the cost of transportation provided by the employer to employees paid on an hourly basis to be valued at $1.50 (regardless of actual value) if the transportation is furnished solely due to unsafe conditions. Unsafe conditions exist if a reasonable person would not consider it safe to walk or take public transportation at the applicable time of day. Reg. § 1.61–21(k). The IRS probably did not intend this rule to apply to commuting expenses in New York City at all hours.

(G) *Luxury Expenses.* Even when a taxpayer travels on business, the style of transportation may be so luxurious as to produce clear personal benefits. Nevertheless, Congress has acted to limit deductions in only a few cases. Deductions for "luxury" water travel (i.e., cruise ships) are limited to twice the highest per diem allowable to employees of the executive branch of the U.S. government while away from home but serving in the United States. § 274(m). Section 280F limits deductions for "luxury" car expenses.

2.   FOOD AND LODGING

Section 162(a)(2) allows a deduction for travel expenses incurred "while away from home in the pursuit of a trade or business." Deductible expenses include not only transportation but also meals and lodging "while away from home." An employee's unreimbursed travel expenses are deductible as a miscellaneous itemized deduction and are subject to the 2 percent adjusted gross income floor of § 67. Travel expenses reimbursed by the employer (as well as those incurred by self-employed individuals) are deductible from gross income under § 62(a)(2)(A) and are not subject to the 2 percent floor. In United States v. Correll, 389 U.S. 299 (1967), the Supreme Court upheld the Commissioner's rule that the phrase "away from home" does not include any trip not requiring "sleep or rest" no matter how far the taxpayer travels. The Court concluded that the Commissioner's "overnight" rule for deductions of meals has "achieved not only ease and certainty of application, but also substantial fairness" by placing "all one-day travelers on a similar tax footing, rather than discriminating against intra-city travelers and commuters."

Does an "overnight" requirement aid in the basic determination whether meals should be deductible? In Barry v. Commissioner, 435 F.2d 1290 (1st Cir.1970), the taxpayer was not away from home overnight, but stopped at the side of the road for naps. The First Circuit disallowed the taxpayer's deductions for the cost of his meals, holding that the naps were not sleep or rest under *Correll*. In Rev.Rul. 75–168, 1975–1 C.B. 58, the Service permitted deduction of a truck driver's unreimbursed expenses for meals and lodging during eight-hour layovers provided so that he could sleep or rest, but disallowed deduction of the cost of meals purchased during layovers of approximately one-half hour.

Thus, if a taxpayer takes the first shuttle from Washington to New York and the last shuttle back the same day, eating breakfast, lunch, and dinner in New York, meals are not deductible. if, however, the taxpayer spends the night in New York, returning to Washington early the following day, all three meals are deductible. Note that the taxpayer bears any extra cost of eating in restaurants whether or not she stays overnight.

The following case further explores what is meant by "away from home in the pursuit of a trade or business."

Hantzis v. Commissioner

United States Court of Appeals, First Circuit, 1981. 638 F.2d 248, cert. denied 452 U.S. 962 (1981).

LEVIN H. CAMPBELL, CIRCUIT JUDGE.

The Commissioner of Internal Revenue (Commissioner) appeals a decision of the United States Tax Court that allowed a deduction under 26

U.S.C. § 162(a)(2) (1976) for expenses incurred by a law student in the course of her summer employment. * * *

In the fall of 1973 Catharine Hantzis (taxpayer) * * * entered Harvard Law School in Cambridge, Massachusetts, as a full-time student. During her second year of law school she sought unsuccessfully to obtain employment for the summer of 1975 with a Boston law firm. She did, however, find a job as a legal assistant with a law firm in New York City, where she worked for ten weeks beginning in June 1975. Her husband, then a member of the faculty of Northeastern University with a teaching schedule for that summer, remained in Boston and lived at the couple's home there. At the time of the Tax Court's decision in this case, Mr. and Mrs. Hantzis still resided in Boston.

On their joint income tax return for 1975, Mr. and Mrs. Hantzis reported the earnings from taxpayer's summer employment ($3,750) and deducted [under § 162] the cost of transportation between Boston and New York, the cost of a small apartment rented by Mrs. Hantzis in New York and the cost of her meals in New York ($3,204). * * *

The Commissioner disallowed the deduction on the ground that taxpayer's home for purposes of section 162(a)(2) was her place of employment and the cost of traveling to and living in New York was therefore not "incurred * * * while away from home." The Commissioner also argued that the expenses were not incurred "in the pursuit of a trade or business." Both positions were rejected by the Tax Court, which found that Boston was Mrs. Hantzis' home because her employment in New York was only temporary and that her expenses in New York were "necessitated" by her employment there. The court thus held the expenses to be deductible under section 162(a)(2).

In asking this court to reverse the Tax Court's allowance of the deduction, the Commissioner has contended that the expenses were not incurred "in the pursuit of a trade or business." We do not accept this argument; nonetheless, we sustain the Commissioner and deny the deduction, on the basis that the expenses were not incurred "while away from home."

I.

Section 262 of the Code * * * declares that "except as otherwise provided in this chapter, no deductions shall be allowed for personal, living, or family expenses." Section 162 provides less of an exception to this rule than it creates a separate category of deductible business expenses. This category manifests a fundamental principle of taxation: that a person's taxable income should not include the cost of producing that income. * * *

The test by which "personal" travel expenses subject to tax under section 262 are distinguished from those costs of travel necessarily incurred to generate income is embodied in the requirement that, to be deductible under section 162(a)(2), an expense must be "incurred ... in the pursuit of a trade or business." In *Flowers* the Supreme Court read this phrase to mean that "[t]he exigencies of business rather than the personal conveniences and necessities of the traveler must be the motivating factors." 326

U.S. at 474. Of course, not every travel expense resulting from business exigencies rather than personal choice is deductible; an expense must also be "ordinary and necessary" and incurred "while away from home." 26 U.S.C. § 162(a)(2) (1976); *Flowers,* 326 U.S. at 470. But the latter limitations draw also upon the basic concept that only expenses necessitated by business, as opposed to personal, demands may be excluded from the calculation of taxable income.

With these fundamentals in mind, we proceed to ask whether the cost of taxpayer's transportation to and from New York, and of her meals and lodging while in New York, was incurred "while away from home in the pursuit of a trade or business."

II.

The Commissioner has directed his argument at the meaning of "in pursuit of a trade or business." He interprets this phrase as requiring that a deductible traveling expense be incurred under the demands of a trade or business which predates the expense, i.e., an "already existing" trade or business. Under this theory, section 162(a)(2) would invalidate the deduction taken by the taxpayer because she was a full-time student before commencing her summer work at a New York law firm in 1975 and so was not continuing in a trade or business when she incurred the expenses of traveling to New York and living there while her job lasted.[1] The Commissioner's proposed interpretation erects at the threshold of deductibility under section 162(a)(2) the requirement that a taxpayer be engaged in a trade or business *before* incurring a travel expense. Only if that requirement is satisfied would an inquiry into the deductibility of an expense proceed to ask whether the expense was a result of business exigencies, incurred while away from home, and reasonable and necessary.

Such a reading of the statute is semantically possible and would perhaps expedite the disposition of certain cases. Nevertheless, we reject it as unsupported by case law and inappropriate to the policies behind section 162(a)(2).

* * *

Nor would the Commissioner's theory mesh with the policy behind section 162(a)(2). As discussed, the travel expense deduction is intended to exclude from taxable income a necessary cost of producing that income. Yet the recency of entry into a trade or business does not indicate that travel expenses are not a cost of producing income. To be sure, the costs incurred by a taxpayer who leaves his usual residence to begin a trade or business at another location may not be truly *travel* expenses, i.e., expenses incurred while "away from home," see infra, but practically, they are as much incurred "in the pursuit of a trade or business" when the occupation is new as when it is old.

* * *

1. The taxpayer has not argued that being a law student constitutes a trade or business and so we do not address the issue. See generally Reisinger v. Commissioner, 71 T.C. 568 (1979); Rev.Rul. 68–591, 1968–2 C.B. 73.

Accordingly, we turn to the question whether, in the absence of the Commissioner's proposed threshold limit on deductibility, the expenses at issue here satisfy the requirements of section 162(a)(2) as interpreted in Flowers v. Commissioner.

III.

As already noted, *Flowers* construed section 162(a)(2) to mean that a traveling expense is deductible only if it is (1) reasonable and necessary, (2) incurred while away from home, and (3) necessitated by the exigencies of business. Because the Commissioner does not suggest that Mrs. Hantzis' expenses were unreasonable or unnecessary, we may pass directly to the remaining requirements. Of these, we find dispositive the requirement that an expense be incurred while away from home. As we think Mrs. Hantzis' expenses were not so incurred, we hold the deduction to be improper.

The meaning of the term "home" in the travel expense provision is far from clear. When Congress enacted the travel expense deduction now codified as section 162(a)(2), it apparently was unsure whether, to be deductible, an expense must be incurred away from a person's residence or away from his principal place of business. * * * This ambiguity persists and courts, sometimes within a single circuit, have divided over the issue. * * * It has been suggested that these conflicting definitions are due to the enormous factual variety in the cases. * * * We find this observation instructive, for if the cases that discuss the meaning of the term "home" in section 162(a)(2) are interpreted on the basis of their unique facts as well as the fundamental purposes of the travel expense provision, and not simply pinioned to one of two competing definitions of home, much of the seeming confusion and contradiction on this issue disappears and a functional definition of the term emerges.

We begin by recognizing that the location of a person's home for purposes of section 162(a)(2) becomes problematic only when the person lives one place and works another. Where a taxpayer resides and works at a single location, he is always home, however defined; and where a taxpayer is constantly on the move due to his work, he is never "away" from home. * * * However, in the present case, the need to determine "home" is plainly before us, since the taxpayer resided in Boston and worked, albeit briefly, in New York.

We think the critical step in defining "home" in these situations is to recognize that the "while away from home" requirement has to be construed in light of the further requirement that the expense be the result of business exigencies. The traveling expense deduction obviously is not intended to exclude from taxation every expense incurred by a taxpayer who, in the course of business, maintains two homes. Section 162(a)(2) seeks rather "to mitigate the burden of the taxpayer who, *because of the exigencies of his trade or business, must* maintain two places of abode and thereby incur additional and duplicate living expenses." * * *

Consciously or unconsciously, courts have effectuated this policy in part through their interpretation of the term "home" in section 162(a)(2). Whether it is held in a particular decision that a taxpayer's home is his residence or his principal place of business, the ultimate allowance or disallowance of a deduction is a function of the court's assessment of the reason for a taxpayer's maintenance of two homes. If the reason is perceived to be personal, the taxpayer's home will generally be held to be his place of employment rather than his residence and the deduction will be denied. * * *

If the reason is felt to be business exigencies, the person's home will usually be held to be his residence and the deduction will be allowed. * * * We understand the concern of the concurrence that such an operational interpretation of the term "home" is somewhat technical and perhaps untidy, in that it will not always afford bright line answers, but we doubt the ability of either the Commissioner or the courts to invent an unyielding formula that will make sense in all cases. The line between personal and business expenses winds through infinite factual permutations; effectuation of the travel expense provision requires that any principle of decision be flexible and sensitive to statutory policy.

Construing in the manner just described the requirement that an expense be incurred "while away from home," we do not believe this requirement was satisfied in this case. Mrs. Hantzis' *trade or business* did not require that she maintain a home in Boston as well as one in New York. Though she returned to Boston at various times during the period of her employment in New York, her visits were all for personal reasons. It is not contended that she had a business connection in Boston that necessitated her keeping a home there; no professional interest was served by maintenance of the Boston home—as would have been the case, for example, if Mrs. Hantzis had been a lawyer based in Boston with a New York client whom she was temporarily serving. The home in Boston was kept up for reasons involving Mr. Hantzis, but those reasons cannot substitute for a showing by *Mrs.* Hantzis that the exigencies of *her* trade or business required *her* to maintain two homes. Mrs. Hantzis' decision to keep two homes must be seen as a choice dictated by personal, albeit wholly reasonable, considerations and not a business or occupational necessity. We therefore hold that her home for purposes of section 162(a)(2) was New York and that the expenses at issue in this case were not incurred "while away from home."

We are not dissuaded from this conclusion by the temporary nature of Mrs. Hantzis' employment in New York. Mrs. Hantzis argues that the brevity of her stay in New York excepts her from the business exigencies requirement of section 162(a)(2) under a doctrine supposedly enunciated by the Supreme Court in Peurifoy v. Commissioner, 358 U.S. 59 (1958) (per curiam).[2] The Tax Court here held that Boston was the taxpayer's home

---

2. In *Peurifoy,* the Court stated that the Tax Court had "engrafted an exception" onto the requirement that travel expenses be dictated by business exigencies, allowing "a deduction for expenditures * * * when the taxpayer's employment is 'temporary' as contrasted with 'indefinite' or 'indeterminate.'" 358 U.S. at 59. Because the Commissioner did not challenge this exception, the Court did not rule on its validity. It instead upheld the circuit court's reversal of the Tax Court and disallowance of the deduction on the basis of the adequacy of the appellate court's review. The Supreme Court agreed that the Tax Court's finding as to the temporary nature of taxpayer's employment was clearly erroneous. Id. at 60, 61.

Despite its inauspicious beginning, the exception has come to be generally accepted.

because it would have been unreasonable for her to move her residence to New York for only ten weeks. At first glance these contentions may seem to find support in the court decisions holding that, when a taxpayer works for a limited time away from his usual home, section 162(a)(2) allows a deduction for the expense of maintaining a second home so long as the employment is "temporary" and not "indefinite" or "permanent." * * *

The temporary employment doctrine does not, however, purport to eliminate any requirement that continued maintenance of a first home have a business justification. We think the rule has no application where the taxpayer has no business connection with his usual place of residence. If no business exigency dictates the location of the taxpayer's usual residence, then the mere fact of his taking temporary employment elsewhere cannot supply a compelling business reason for continuing to maintain that residence. Only a taxpayer who lives one place, works another and has business ties to *both* is in the ambiguous situation that the temporary employment doctrine is designed to resolve. In such circumstances, unless his employment away from his usual home is temporary, a court can reasonably assume that the taxpayer has abandoned his business ties to that location and is left with only personal reasons for maintaining a residence there. Where only personal needs require that a travel expense be incurred, however, a taxpayer's home is defined so as to leave the expense subject to taxation. * * * Thus, a taxpayer who pursues temporary employment away from the location of his usual residence, but has no business connection with that location, is not "away from home" for purposes of section 162(a)(2). * * *

On this reasoning, the temporary nature of Mrs. Hantzis' employment in New York does not affect the outcome of her case. She had no business ties to Boston that would bring her within the temporary employment doctrine. By this holding, we do not adopt a rule that "home" in section 162(a)(2) is the equivalent of a taxpayer's place of business. Nor do we mean to imply that a taxpayer has a "home" for tax purposes only if he is already engaged in a trade or business at a particular location. Though both rules are alluringly determinate, we have already discussed why they offer inadequate expressions of the purposes behind the travel expense deduction. We hold merely that for a taxpayer in Mrs. Hantzis' circumstances to be "away from home in the pursuit of a trade or business," she must establish the existence of some sort of business relation both to the location she claims as "home" and to the location of her temporary employment sufficient to support a finding that her duplicative expenses are necessitated by business exigencies. This, we believe, is the meaning of the statement in *Flowers* that "[b]usiness trips are to be identified *in relation to* business demands and the traveler's business headquarters." 326 U.S. at 474 (emphasis added). On the uncontested facts before us, Mrs.

Some uncertainty lingers, however, over whether the exception properly applies to the "business exigencies" or the "away from home" requirement. * * * In fact, it is probably relevant to both.

    * * *

Because we treat these requirements as inextricably intertwined, * * * we find it unnecessary to address this question; applied to either requirement, the temporary employment doctrine affects the meaning of both.

Hantzis had no business relation to Boston; we therefore leave to cases in which the issue is squarely presented the task of elaborating what relation to a place is required under section 162(a)(2) for duplicative living expenses to be deductible.

Reversed.

KEETON, DISTRICT JUDGE, concurring in the result.

Although I agree with the result reached in the court's opinion, and with much of its underlying analysis, I write separately because I cannot join in the court's determination that New York was the taxpayer's home for purposes of 26 U.S.C. § 162(a)(2). In so holding, the court adopts a definition of "home" that differs from the ordinary meaning of the term and therefore unduly risks causing confusion and misinterpretation of the important principle articulated in this case.

In adopting section 162(a)(2), Congress sought "to mitigate the burden of the taxpayer who, because of the exigencies of his trade or business, must maintain two places of abode and thereby incur additional and duplicate living expenses."

* * *

In the present case, the taxpayer does not contend that she maintained her residence in Boston for business reasons. Before working in New York, she had attended school near her home in Boston, and she continued to do so after she finished her summer job. In addition, her husband lived and worked in Boston. Thus, on the facts in this case, I am in agreement with the court that the taxpayer's deductions must be disallowed because she was not required by her trade or business to maintain both places of residence. However rather than resting its conclusion on an interpretation of the language of section 162(a)(2) taken as a whole, which allows a deduction for ordinary and necessary expenses incurred "while away from home in the pursuit of trade or business," the court reaches the same result by incorporating the concept of business-related residence into the definition of "home," thereby producing sometimes, but not always, a meaning of "home" quite different from ordinary usage.

* * *

The court enters [the] conflict among circuits with a "functional" definition of home not yet adopted by any other circuit. I read the opinion as indicating that in a dual residence case, the Commissioner must determine whether the exigencies of the taxpayer's trade or business require her to maintain both residences. * * * If so, the Commissioner must decide that the taxpayer's *principal residence* is her "home" and must conclude that expenses associated with the secondary residence were incurred "while away from home," and are deductible. If not, as in the instant case, the Commissioner must find that the taxpayer's *principal place of business* is her "home" and must conclude that the expenses in question were not incurred "while away from home." The conclusory nature of these determinations as to which residence is her "home" reveals the potentially confusing effect of adopting an extraordinary definition of "home."

* * *

The result reached by the court can easily be expressed while also giving "home" its ordinary meaning, and neither Congress nor the Supreme Court has directed that "home" be given an extraordinary meaning in the present context. * * *

In analyzing dual residence cases, the court's opinion advances compelling reasons that the first step must be to determine whether the taxpayer has business as opposed to purely personal reasons for maintaining both residences. This must be done in order to determine whether the expenses of maintaining a second residence were, "necessitated by business, as opposed to personal, demands," * * * and were in this sense incurred by the taxpayer "while away from home in pursuit of trade or business." Necessarily implicit in this proposition is a more limited corollary that is sufficient to decide the present case: When the taxpayer has a business relationship to only one location, no traveling expenses the taxpayer incurs are "necessitated by business, as opposed to personal demands," regardless of how many residences the taxpayer has, where they are located, or which one is "home."

* * *

NOTES

(A) *The "Away–From–Home" Test.* The obvious task of § 162(a)(2) is to distinguish everyday living expenses from those occasioned by business travel. Does the phrase "away from home" adequately differentiate business from personal expenses? The current rule essentially ignores the personal consumption element of business travel, unless the food and lodging are lavish and extravagant, a limitation seldom, if ever, applied.

(B) *A House Is Not Necessarily a Home.* The Service's position is that a taxpayer's "home" for purposes of § 162(a)(2) is the taxpayer's regular or principal place of business. If the taxpayer has no principal place of business, then his "tax home" is his regular place of abode. Rev.Rul. 75–432, 1975–2 C.B. 60. Several Courts of Appeals have adopted this position. See, e.g., Markey v. Commissioner, 490 F.2d 1249 (6th Cir.1974). The Second Circuit, however, has concluded that your house is indeed your home. Using the approach that a taxpayer's residence is his home, the court shifted the focus to whether the expenses were inquired in pursuit of business. Rosenspan v. United States, 438 F.2d 905 (2d Cir.1971). As the dissent suggests, the court in *Hantzis* seems to create a "third way."

If the taxpayer has no regular abode, there is no deduction. In James v. United States, 308 F.2d 204 (9th Cir.1962) the court disallowed any deduction for an itinerant salesman without a regular home on the ground that the statute is applicable only "when the taxpayer has a 'home' the maintenance of which involves substantial continuing expenses which will be duplicated by expenditures he must make when required to travel elsewhere for business purposes."

In Henderson v. Commissioner, 143 F.3d 497 (1998), a divided Ninth Circuit rejected an attempt by a lighting technician for a traveling ice skating show to claim Boise Idaho as his tax home. Boise was where his parents lived and they let him stay there rent-free between tours. The majority found that he had no tax home because he did not incur duplicative living expenses in Boise. The court said he was a "tax turtle." Dissenting in "the name of family values," Judge Kozinski noted that if the parents had actually charged him rent, Henderson undoubtedly would have been permitted a deduction. He argued that the fact that Henderson compensated his parents with filial affection was none of the IRS' business and he was being hit with extra taxes because his lifestyle did not conform to the IRS' idea of normalcy. "Leave it to the IRS to turn a family reunion into a taxable event."

(C) *Multiple Businesses.* Suppose Hantzis had worked part-time during the school year at the Boston office of the New York City firm where she spent the summer? Would it make any difference if she had returned to the job during her third year? Would it matter how much she earned or how many hours she worked in Boston? Note that Hantzis netted, after expenses, $546, for her 10 weeks in New York, far less than the minimum wage. Even if she had retained a "tax home" in Boston, would her expenses be "necessitated by business exigencies"?

Where a taxpayer has two businesses, it is clear that she can deduct the costs of travelling between them and meals and lodging when she is away from home. Is she always "away from home"? Or is she in that status in only one location? The Service's position is that "home" is the principal place of business and thus meals and lodging can be deducted only when the taxpayer is at her minor place of business. Rev.Rul. 63–82, 1963–1 C.B. 33. In Rev.Rul. 75–432, 1975–2 C.B. 60, the IRS applied this rule to seasonal workers, such as baseball players, who alternate between two bases every year.

Note the special exception in § 162(a) for legislators. Most members of Congress must maintain residences in their home districts. Section 162 provides that the home district will be treated as a member's tax home, but that no more than $3,000 in "living expenses" can be deducted each year. Is this exception justified on policy grounds? Compare the even more generous treatment of state legislators under § 162(h).

(D) *Temporary vs. Indefinite Employment.* Where a taxpayer leaves his regular place of employment to take a temporary job at another location, the taxpayer may treat his regular residence or place of employment as "home" and deduct the costs of food and lodging at his temporary job. If the duration of the new job is "indefinite," however, the taxpayer may not deduct his expenses. Section 162(a) provides that the taxpayer is not treated as being temporarily away from home if the period of employment exceeds one year. The IRS has interpreted this to mean that expenses attributable to employment which is realistically expected to last for more than a year are not deductible regardless of how long the employment actually lasts. Expenses relating to employment expected to last for less than a year that in fact do last for less than a year are deductible, but if the expectation changes, only the expenses until that date are deductible. Rev.Rul. 99–7, 1999–1 C.B. 361. A taxpayer who is temporarily away from home on business for 370 days, for example, would be able to deduct none of her travel expenses. If you were out-of-town "temporarily" assigned to a case, what should you consider doing on the 364th day?

(E) *Two-Earner Families.* As *Hantzis* illustrates, two-earner families can face particular problems as a result of the "tax home" concept. See, e.g., Daly v. Commissioner, 662 F.2d 253 (4th Cir.1981), in which a salesman maintained a home in Virginia near his wife's place of employment, but spent most of his time in and around Philadelphia where many of his customers were located. Reversing a panel decision, the en banc court held that Philadelphia was the taxpayer's "home" for purposes of § 162(a)(2) and disallowed deductions for travel between Philadelphia and Virginia and for meals and lodging consumed in Philadelphia. The decision not to live separately from his wife was considered personal. A concurring opinion argued for legislative reform to accommodate the particular problems of working couples.

(F) *Mixed Personal–Business Trips.* Once the taxpayer establishes a "tax home," he must be away from that home "in pursuit of a trade or business." If a trip is for mixed business and personal reasons, travel costs are deductible only if the trip is primarily for business purposes. The relative amount of time spent on business as opposed to pleasure is important, but not determinative, as to the primary purpose. Suppose a doctor attends a continuing education program for physicians at a ski resort, attends classes from 8–10 a.m. and skis for the rest of the day? (See § 274(c) for special rules relating to foreign travel.)

(G) *Foreign Conventions.* Concerned that nominally business-motivated foreign travel, particularly conventions held at resorts, had substantial potential for abuse, Congress imposed limitations on foreign conventions. No deduction is allowed for expenses allocable to a convention, seminar or similar meeting held outside the North American area unless, taking into account certain factors, it is "as reasonable" for the meeting to be held outside the North American area as within it. (The North American area includes the United States, its possessions, Canada, Mexico, and the Trust Territory of the Pacific Islands and, in certain circumstances, the countries of the Caribbean.) § 274(h)(3) and (6). The factors that will be taken into account are: (1) the purpose of the meeting and its activities; (2) the purposes and activities of the sponsoring groups; and (3) the residence of the active members of the sponsoring groups and the places at which other meetings have been held. Expenses for conventions reasonably held outside North America are treated like any other business expense and not disallowed unless they are extravagant.

In general, the expenses of attending a convention in the United States (even if at a ski resort or oceanside paradise) are deductible. Deduction is not permitted, however, for the cost of attending investment seminars and conventions under § 212. § 274(h)(7).

What is the logic of rules that would permit a deduction for attendance at a convention of U.S. swimming pool dealers in Alaska but not for high school art teachers in France?

(H) *Duplication.* Why should meals and lodging ever be deductible? Although the IRS has steadfastly tried to apply a mechanical rule to determine when the taxpayer is away from home, the courts increasingly look to the purpose behind the deduction. In the view of the First Circuit, a taxpayer may deduct expenses when business reasons require him to duplicate expenses. See Andrews v. Commissioner, 931 F.2d 132 (1st Cir.1991), where a taxpayer spent several months of the year operating a pool construction business in Massachusetts and the rest of the year maintaining a stable of race horses in Florida. The court rejected the Service's argument that he was never away from home because he had two tax homes, finding that he had one tax home and could deduct his duplicate expenses while away on business. It is difficult, however, to see how food expenses could be duplicative. An individual must have food and lodging whether she engages in business or not, although the price of these items might rise as business constraints limit her choices. To the extent the expense substitutes for, rather than duplicates, personal consumption, it might be classified as inherently personal. Alternatively, why not limit deductions for meals to verifiable "additional expenses?" Consider also the excludability of meals under § 119, see supra at page 113, and their deductibility as business entertainment, infra in the next section.

B.   ENTERTAINMENT AND BUSINESS MEALS

Moss v. Commissioner

Tax Court of the United States, 1983. 80 T.C. 1073.

WILBUR, JUDGE: * * *

Petitioner is a partner in a Chicago law firm that met every business day in 1976 and 1977 at the Café Angelo for lunch. Current litigation problems, scheduling, assignments, and settlement of cases were discussed at that time. The firm paid for the meals of those lawyers who ate during the firm meetings. The issue for decision is whether petitioner may deduct his share of those expenses in calculating his taxable income.

Petitioner contends that the luncheon meeting expenses are deductible under section 162 as ordinary and necessary business expenses. * * * Respondent, conversely, claims that the lunches are a personal and therefore nondeductible expense. We agree with respondent.

The broad purpose of the Internal Revenue Code is to tax all accessions to wealth, "from whatever source derived." Sec. 61(a). The goal being to tax income, business expenses reduce taxable income. Sec. 162. Funds spent on personal consumption, on the other hand, are not deductible. Sec. 262. The boundary line dividing personal expenses from business expenses, often obscurely marked, has been a fertile field of battle. * * * In close contests, it is essential to bear in mind that the provisions of section 262 take priority over section 162.

The expense in question is close to that evanescent line dividing personal and business expenses. From the perspective of the partnership, the lunches were a cost incurred in earning their income. The lawyers needed to coordinate assignments and scheduling of their case load, and the noon hour was a logical, convenient time at which to do so. They considered the meeting to be part of their working day, not as an hour of reprieve from business affairs. The individuals did not feel free to make alternate plans, or to eat elsewhere. For this firm, petitioner argues, the meeting was both ordinary and necessary.

The Commissioner focuses not on the circumstances bringing the partnership together each day, but rather on the fact that the individuals were eating lunch while they were together. Rather than to section 162, he looks to section 262, and the regulations which specifically categorize meals as personal expenses. Sec. 1.262–5, Income Tax Regs. The respondent, in essence, argues that while the meeting may have been ordinary and necessary to the business, the outlay was for meals, a personal item.

The dual nature of the business lunch has long been a difficult problem for legislators and courts alike. The traditional view of the courts has been that if a personal living expense is to qualify under section 162, the taxpayer must demonstrate that it was "different from or in excess of that which would have been made for the taxpayer's personal purposes." Sutter v. Commissioner, 21 T.C. 170, 173 (1953).[1]

Following the *Sutter* formula, numerous taxpayers have attempted to deduct the cost of meals eaten under unusual or constraining circumstances. The claims have been denied almost invariably. See, e.g., Fife v. Commissioner, 73 T.C. 621 (1980) (attorney may not deduct cost of meals eaten in restaurants due to late client meetings); Ma–Tran Corp. v. Commissioner, 70 T.C. 158 (1978) (corporation may not deduct cost of officer's locally consumed meals absent travel or compliance with section 274); Drill v. Commissioner, 8 T.C. 902 (1947) (construction worker cannot deduct cost of dinners on nights he worked overtime). Daily meals are an inherently personal expense, and a taxpayer bears a heavy burden in proving they are routinely deductible.

Petitioner relies on Wells v. Commissioner, 626 F.2d 868 (9th Cir. 1980), affg. without published opinion T.C.Memo. 1977–419, in support of his position. In *Wells*, we denied a deduction claimed by a public defender for the cost of occasional lunch meetings with his staff. The Court noted, however, that in a law firm, "an occasional luncheon meeting with the staff to discuss the operation of the firm would be regarded as an 'ordinary and necessary expense.'" We note, first, that this statement is dictum in a memorandum opinion, and thus not controlling. Second, that case referred to occasional lunches, a far cry from the daily sustenance involved in the case at bar. Even assuming that *Wells* is of any assistance to petitioner, we need not decide where the line between these two cases should be drawn,

---

1. * * * The present circumstances do not require an exploration of the dimensions of our opinion in Sutter v. Commissioner, 21 T.C. 170 (1953). We note, however, that in the case of business meals, *Sutter* permits a deduction where the expense is "different from *or* in excess of" the personal expenditure the taxpayer would otherwise have made. This language is in the disjunctive. Business meals have received extensive con-gressional consideration through the years. Accordingly, Congress is presumed to be aware of the administrative practice permitting the entire expense of a business meal to be deducted without fragmentation. In essence, where a proper business purpose and relationship are established, the expenses are presumed to be different from one the taxpayer would normally have made.

for we are convinced that outlays for meals consumed 5 days per week, 52 weeks per year would in any event fall on the nondeductible side of it.

The only recent cases where deductions were allowed for meals taken on a regular basis were Sibla v. Commissioner, 611 F.2d 1260 (9th Cir. 1980), affg. 68 T.C. 422 (1977), and Cooper v. Commissioner, 67 T.C. 870 (1977). Those cases involved Los Angeles firemen who were required to contribute to a meal fund for each day they were on duty, regardless of whether they ate or even were present at the fire station. This Court allowed them to deduct the expense under section 162; a concurring opinion would have allowed the expense by analogy to section 119. Cooper v. Commissioner, supra at 874–876. On appeal, the Ninth Circuit approved of both theories, stating that because the taxpayer's situation was both unusual and unique, the expense was business rather than personal.

The decision by the Ninth Circuit implies that similar considerations are involved in determining whether a meal is a business expense under section 162 and whether the value of a meal supplied by an employer should be included in gross income under section 61. Section 119 provides a limited exception to section 61 by allowing an employee to exclude such amounts if the meal is furnished on the business premises for the convenience of the employer. The cases decided under section 119 have focused on the degree to which the employee's actions are restricted by his employer's demands. * * * Language referring to compliance with the demands of one's employer can also be found in section 162 cases decided by this Court. * * *

Petitioner relies on this notion of restriction in contending that the cost of the lunches, like the cost of the firehouse mess in *Sibla* and *Cooper,* should be deductible. He argues that the attorneys "considered the luncheon meetings as a part of their regular work day," and that the firm incurred the expense "solely for the benefit of its practice and not for the personal convenience of its attorneys."

Petitioner has not explained, however, how this "restriction" is any different than that imposed on an attorney who must spend his lunch hour boning up on the Rules of Civil Procedure in preparation for trial or reading an evidence book to clarify a point that may arise during an afternoon session. In all these cases, the lawyer spends an extra hour at work. The mere fact that this time is given over the noon hour does not convert the cost of daily meals into a business expense to be shared by the Government.

* * *

In agreeing with the Commissioner on this point, we are well aware that business needs dictated the choice of the noon hour for the daily meeting. In a very real sense, these meetings contributed to the success of the partnership. But other costs contributing to the success of one's employment are treated as personal expenses. Commuting is obviously essential to one's continued employment, yet those expenses are not deductible as business expenses. * * *

In the instant case, we are convinced that petitioner and his partners and associates discussed business at lunch, that the meeting was a part of their working day, and that this time was the most convenient time at which to meet. We are also convinced that the partnership benefited from the exchange of information and ideas that occurred.

But this does not make his lunch deductible any more than riding to work together each morning to discuss partnership affairs would make his share of the commuting costs deductible. If only the four partners attended the luncheons, petitioner's share of the expenses (assuming they were coequal partners) would have corresponded to his share of the luncheons. This is not an occasion for the general taxpayer to share in the cost of his daily sustenance. Indeed, if petitioner is correct, only the unimaginative would dine at their own expense.

* * *

STERRETT, J., concurring: I concur in the result in this particular case, but I want to make it clear that I do not view this opinion as disallowing the cost of meals in all instances where only partners, co-workers, etc., are involved. We have here findings that the partners met at lunch because it was "convenient" and "convenient" 5 days a week, 52 weeks a year.

TANNENWALD, FAY, GOFFE, WHITAKER, KÖRNER, SHIELDS, HAMBLEN, and COHEN, JJ., agree with this concurring opinion.

NOTES

(A) *Employer-Subsidized Meals.* The *Sutter* case, cited in *Moss,* is the leading case disallowing deductions for regular business meals. In Christey v. United States, 841 F.2d 809 (8th Cir.1988), however, the Eighth Circuit Court of Appeals permitted state troopers to deduct as ordinary and necessary business expenses under § 162(a) the cost of meals that they were required to eat at public restaurants adjacent to the highway while they were on duty. By treating such expenses as deductible employee business expenses, the court achieved results somewhat similar, but not precisely identical, to the exclusion under § 119 that the Supreme Court rejected in *Kowalski,* which is reprinted at page 114 of the coursebook.

Are the lunches of the associates at Moss's law firm taxable to them? Omitted Footnote 13 of *Moss* indicates that the meals may be compensation. Might they be excludable under § 119? Would the answer be different if the meals were provided on the business premises? According to the October 28, 1986 edition of the Chicago Tribune, the Moss law firm subsequently hired its favorite waiter at Café Angelo to cook meals in a new dining room at the firm. Is there any reason why the results under § 119 and § 162 should be different?

Consider also § 132(e)(2) for what appears to be an alternative means of providing employer-subsidized meals.

(B) *Meals with Clients.* How do you think the Tax Court would view a case where a law partner eats lunch with a client and pays for both meals? The cost of the client's meal would be deductible under § 274(a) if it is "directly related" or "associated with the active conduct of a trade or business." Legislative history indicates that a business meal is directly related to the active conduct of the taxpayer's trade or business if (1) the taxpayer has more than a general expectation of deriving income or a specific business benefit; (2) the taxpayer engaged in business discussions during or directly before or after the meal or entertainment; and (3) the principal reason for the expense was the active conduct of the taxpayer's trade or business. Would you expect these requirements to significantly limit the number of client meals that are deductible?

(C) *The Taxpayer's Meal.* May the taxpayer who accompanies the client to dinner deduct his own meal? If the cost is reimbursed by the employer, must he report his own meal as income? See Rev.Rul. 63–144, 1963–2 C.B. 129, which provides in part as follows:

31. Question: Several of these questions and answers refer to the cost of a taxpayer entertaining a business customer at lunch or dinner. To what extent is the cost of the taxpayer's own meal deductible?

Answer: Judicial decisions under established law, applying the statutory rules that deductions are not allowed for personal expenses, hold that a taxpayer cannot obtain a deduction for the portion of his meal cost which does not exceed an amount he would normally spend on himself. The Service practice has been to apply this rule largely to abuse cases where taxpayers claim deductions for substantial amounts of personal living expenses. The Service does not intend to depart from this practice.

Why should the taxpayer's own meal be deductible if he eats with a client? *Moss* was affirmed by the Seventh Circuit. 758 F.2d 211 (7th Cir.1985). Writing for the court, Judge Posner noted:

Suppose a theatrical agent takes his clients out to lunch at the expensive restaurants that the clients demand. Of course he can deduct the expense of their meals, from which he derives no pleasure or sustenance, but can he also deduct the expense of his own? He can, because he cannot eat more cheaply; he cannot munch surreptitiously on a peanut butter and jelly sandwich brought from home while his client is wolfing down tournedos Rossini followed by soufflé au grand marnier. No doubt our theatrical agent, unless concerned for his longevity, derives personal utility from his fancy meal, but probably less than the price of the meal. He would not pay for it if it were not for the business benefit; he would get more value from using the same money to buy something else; hence the meal confers on him less utility than the cash equivalent would.

Why should the taxpayer's meal be deductible if he eats with a client, but not if he eats with a co-worker? Judge Posner explained that dichotomy:

[I]t is undeniable that eating together fosters camaraderie and makes business dealings friendlier and easier. It thus reduces the costs of transacting business, for these costs include the frictions and the failures of communication that are produced by suspicion and mutual misunderstanding, by differences in tastes and manners, and by lack of rapport. A meeting with a client or customer in an office is therefore not a perfect substitute for a lunch with him in a restaurant. But it is different when all the participants in the meal are coworkers, as essentially was the case here (clients occasionally were invited to the firm's daily luncheon, but Moss has made no attempt to identify the occasions). They know each other well already; they don't need the social lubrication that a meal with an outsider provides—at least don't need it daily. If a large firm had a monthly lunch to allow partners to get to know associates, the expenses of the meal might well be necessary, and would be allowed by the Internal Revenue Service * * *. But Moss's firm never had more than eight lawyers (partners and associates), and did not need a daily lunch to cement relationships among them.

(D) *"Three–Martini Lunches."* What President Carter labeled the businessman's "three-martini lunch" and other entertainment expenses have long been visible targets for tax reform. Congress has tried a number of methods to limit deductions for business expenses with a strong personal element.

Section 274(d) imposes substantiation rules, requiring the taxpayer to retain adequate documentation. This rule effectively repealed the so-called *Cohan* rule, which had allowed approximations of the amount of expenditures when there was evidence of a deductible expenditure in some amount. See Cohan v. Commissioner, 39 F.2d 540 (2d Cir.1930); Reg. § 1.274–5(c)(3). See also Rev.Proc. 83–71, 1983–2 C.B. 590, which provides that taxpayers may claim a specified amount per day for meals instead of substantiating the actual cost of each meal.

Congress also has flatly prohibited the deduction of certain kinds of entertainment. For example, no deduction may be taken with respect to hunting lodges, yachts, and other entertainment facilities. § 274(a)(1)(B). Section 274(*l*)(2) limits the deduction for luxury leased skyboxes in sports stadiums rented for more than one event to the sum of the face value of regular box seat tickets for the number of seats in the skybox. There is no deduction for club dues even if the primary purpose for using the club is the furtherance of the taxpayer's trade or business. § 274(a)(3). Legislative history indicates that this rule was meant to cover airline and hotel clubs as well as clubs organized for business, pleasure, recreation or social purposes. An employee whose club dues are reimbursed, however, may continue to exclude the portion of the dues attributable to business use. Reg. § 1.132–5(s).

Even if the entertainment expense meets the "directly related" test of § 274, it still must be an ordinary and necessary expense. The limits under § 274 have not eliminated taxpayer attempts to deduct lavish entertainment or to mix pleasure with business. Consider the efforts of the Danville Plywood Corporation, which tried to take a business expense deduction for taking 58 customers, a group of employees, and everyone's spouse and children on a weekend Mississippi River cruise to the Super Bowl. The Federal Circuit concluded that the central purpose of the trip was entertainment, not business. Danville Plywood Corp. v. United States, 899 F.2d 3 (Fed.Cir.1990). Of what relevance is this determination? Suppose Danville had given rebates to its best customers or increased the salary of its employees in an amount equal to the cost of the trip to the Super Bowl. Would the rebates and salary have been deductible?

A more direct attack on the personal element of meals and entertainment is found in § 274(n), which now limits the deduction to 50 percent of cost. This provision is intended, in a rough way, to reflect Congress' judgment that an element of personal consumption is inherent in such meals and is a reaction to the public sentiment that government is subsidizing expense account living. In effect, Congress arbitrarily treats the consumption as one-half the cost of the meal. The report of the Senate Finance Committee, S.Rep. No. 313, 99th Cong., 1st Sess. 68 (1986) (discussing an amendment that had limited the deduction to 80 percent) noted:

> The committee believes that present law, by not focusing sufficiently on the personal-consumption element of deductible meal and entertainment expenses, unfairly permits taxpayers who can arrange business settings for personal consumption to receive, in effect a Federal tax subsidy for such consumption that is not available to other taxpayers. * * * For example, when executives have dinner at an expensive restaurant following business discussions and then deduct the cost of the meal, the fact that there may be some bona fide business connection does not alter the imbalance between the treatment of those persons, who have effectively transferred a portion of the cost of their meal to the Federal Government, and other individuals, who cannot deduct the cost of their meals.
>
> The significance of this imbalance is heightened by the fact that business travel and entertainment often may be more lavish than comparable activities in a nonbusiness setting. * * * This disparity is highly visible, and contributes to public perceptions that the tax system is unfair.

The 50 percent limitation also applies to meals while away from home overnight on business. It does not apply to, among other things: food or beverage expenses excludable from the gross income of an employee under § 132, traditional recreational expenses for employees, such as a holiday party or summer outing, meals fully taxed to the recipient as compensation, and meals sold to customers (e.g., a restaurant can fully deduct the cost of meals sold to patrons). § 274(e).

If a taxpayer is reimbursed for the cost of business meals or entertainment (and makes an adequate accounting), the 50 percent limitation applies to the one who makes the reimbursement, not the taxpayer. Thus, for example, if a law firm separately bills and is reimbursed by a client for meal and entertainment expenses, the client, and not the law firm, is subject to the 50 percent limitation on these expenses. Likewise, an employee who spends amounts on business-related meals and is reimbursed by his employer is not taxed on this amount, but the employer is allowed to deduct only 50 percent of the cost of the meals. Reg. § 1.62–2(h).

If the employee is not reimbursed by the employer, the expenses for meals and entertainment are subject to not only the 50 percent limitation, but also the 2 percent floor of § 67. Suppose, for example, an employee with an adjusted gross income of $50,000 spends $3,000 on unreimbursed business meals and has no other miscellaneous itemized deductions. He can deduct only $500 if he itemizes deductions [$3,000 − $1,500 (.50 × $3,000)− $1,000 (.02 × $50,000 AGI)]. If, however, the employer reimbursed himfor the full amount, the results would be quite different. Because the 50 percent reduction applies at the employer level and the 2 percent limitation does not apply to reimbursed expenses, the employee could deduct the entire $3,000, or exclude the reimbursements from income. Reg. § 1.162–2(c).

From time to time, more restrictive limitations on the deduction for meals and entertainment have been proposed. Treasury proposals in 1984 recommended elimination of deductions for entertainment expenses other than business meals. The Treasury would have permitted deductions only for "ordinary and necessary business meals furnished in a clear business setting," and the deduction would have been limited to fixed amounts for each meal. 2 Treasury Dep't, Report to the President, Tax Reform for Fairness, Simplicity and Economic Growth 81–85 (1984).

(E) *Reform Strategy.* Considerations of equity seem to dominate efforts to restrict entertainment and business meal deductions. The most equitable result would be to prohibit a deduction for the personal consumption portion of a meal or entertainment expense. Congress seems to recognize the folly of actually inquiring about the personal consumption component of business meal and entertainment expenses and instead has adopted a number of arbitrary rules. What do you think is the best strategy for dealing with business meals and entertainment—the strict substantiation rules embodied in § 274, flat prohibitions of certain kinds of expenses, specific dollar limits on allowable deductions as recommended by Treasury, or limits on the proportion of costs that can be deducted? Are percentage limitations arbitrary, even if simple to comply with? Does the burden of substantiation requirements fall disproportionately on those who take fewer deductions and therefore have less incentive to maintain careful records? Does a flat prohibition substitute Congress' judgment as to what are helpful costs in trying to maximize profits?

Despite the limitations, the liberal allowance of the deduction for meals and entertainment is in sharp contrast to the restrictions on deduction of many other business-related costs, such as work clothing and commuting. Is the case for characterizing expenditures as "inherently personal" stronger or weaker for entertainment than for work clothing or grooming?

Is it important that high income individuals generally are thought to capture most of the benefits of the meal and entertainment deductions? Note that if a corporate executive takes a client/friend to dinner and the theater, the costs are deductible, but if a blue-collar laborer has a hot dog at the ball game with a co-worker, the cost is not deductible even if they talk about their jobs during the seventh-inning stretch.

Restrictions on deductions for meals and entertainment are usually opposed by unions representing restaurant employees. Charles Clotfelder has offered the following estimate of the economic effects of disallowing business deductions for travel and entertainment:

> Proposals to limit deductibility * * * would undoubtedly cause sharp declines in employment in hotels, restaurants, and some entertainment sectors. The * * * estimates * * * imply that halving the deduction for

entertainment could cause spending on entertainment by proprietorships to drop by 50 percent.

Charles Clotfelder, "Tax–Induced Distortions and the Business–Pleasure Borderline: The Case of Travel and Entertainment," 73 Am.Econ.Rev. 1053 (1983). Whether or not Clotfelder's estimates are accurate, some shifting of the sort he describes no doubt occurs. It is no accident that the strongest opponent in 1993 of proposed reductions of deductions for business meals and entertainment was a Nevada Senator.

C.   HOME OFFICE EXPENSES

Commissioner v. Soliman

Supreme Court of the United States, 1992. 506 U.S. 168.

JUSTICE KENNEDY delivered the opinion of the Court.

Nader E. Soliman, an anesthesiologist, spent 30 to 35 hours per week with patients, dividing that time among three hospitals. About 80 percent of the hospital time was spent at one hospital. At the hospitals, Soliman administered the anesthesia, cared for patients after surgery, and treated patients for pain. None of the three hospitals provided him with an office. Soliman's residence had a spare bedroom which he used exclusively as an office. Although he did not meet patients in the home office, he spent two to three hours per day there on a variety of tasks such as contacting patients, surgeons, and hospitals by telephone; maintaining billing records and patient logs; preparing for treatments and presentations; satisfying continuing medical education requirements; and reading medical journals and books.

Section 162(a) of the Internal Revenue Code allows a taxpayer to deduct "all the ordinary and necessary expenses paid or incurred * * * in carrying on any trade or business." 26 U.S.C. § 162(a). That provision is qualified, however, by various limitations, including one that prohibits otherwise allowable deductions "with respect to the use of a dwelling unit which is used by the taxpayer * * * as a residence." § 280A(a). Taxpayers may nonetheless deduct expenses attributable to the business use of their homes if they qualify for one or more of the statute's exceptions to this disallowance. * * * In deciding whether a location is "the principal place of business," the common sense meaning of "principal" suggests that a comparison of locations must be undertaken. * * * Courts cannot assess whether any one business location is the "most important, consequential, or influential" one without comparing it to all the other places where business is transacted. * * * The statute refers * * * to the "principal place" of business. It follows that the most important or significant place for the business must be determined.

In determining the proper test for deciding whether a home office is the principal place of business, we cannot develop an objective formula that yields a clear answer in every case. The inquiry is more subtle, with the ultimate determination of the principal place of business being dependent upon the particular facts of each case. There are, however, two primary considerations in deciding whether a home office is a taxpayer's principal place of business: the relative importance of the activities performed at each business location and the time spent at each place.

* * * Although variations are inevitable in case-by-case determinations, any particular business is likely to have a pattern in which certain activities are of most significance. If the nature of the trade or profession requires the taxpayer to meet or confer with a client or patient or to deliver goods or services to a customer, the place where that contact occurs is often an important indicator of the principal place of business. [T]he point where goods and services are delivered must be given great weight in determining the place where the most important functions are performed. * * *

Unlike the Court of Appeals, we do not regard the necessity of the functions performed at home as having much weight in determining entitlement to the deduction. In many instances, planning and initial preparation for performing a service or delivering goods are essential to the ultimate performance of the service or delivery of the goods, just as accounting and billing are often essential at the final stages of the process. But that is simply because, in integrated transactions, all steps are essential. Whether the functions performed in the home office are necessary to the business is relevant to the determination of whether a home office is the principal place of business in a particular case, but it is not controlling. Essentiality, then, is but part of the assessment of the relative importance of the functions performed at each of the competing locations.

We reject the Court of Appeals' reliance on the availability of alternative office space as an additional consideration in determining a taxpayer's principal place of business. * * *

In addition to measuring the relative importance of the activities undertaken at each business location, the decisionmaker should also compare the amount of time spent at home with the time spent at other places where business activities occur. This factor assumes particular significance when comparison of the importance of the functions performed at various places yields no definitive answer to the principal place of business inquiry. This may be the case when a taxpayer performs income-generating tasks at both his home office and some other location.

The comparative analysis of business locations required by the statute may not result in every case in the specification of which location is the principal place of business; the only question that must be answered is whether the home office so qualifies. There may be cases when there is no principal place of business, and the courts and the Commissioner should not strain to conclude that a home office qualifies for the deduction simply because no other location seems to be the principal place. The taxpayer's house does not become a principal place of business by default. * * *

Under the principles we have discussed, the taxpayer was not entitled to a deduction for home office expenses. The practice of anesthesiology requires the medical doctor to treat patients under conditions demanding immediate, personal observation. So exacting were these requirements that all of respondent's patients were treated at hospitals, facilities with special characteristics designed to accommodate the demands of the profession.

The actual treatment was the essence of the professional service. We can assume that careful planning and study were required in advance of performing the treatment, and all acknowledge that this was done in the home office. But the actual treatment was the most significant event in the professional transaction. The home office activities, from an objective standpoint, must be regarded as less important to the business of the taxpayer than the tasks he performed at the hospital.

A comparison of the time spent by the taxpayer further supports a determination that the home office was not the principal place of business. The 10 to 15 hours per week spent in the home office measured against the 30 to 35 hours per week at the three hospitals are insufficient to render the home office the principal place of business in light of all of the circumstances of this case. That the office may have been essential is not controlling.

JUSTICE STEVENS, dissenting.

The test applied by the Tax Court, and adopted by the Court of Appeals, is both true to the statute and practically incapable of abuse. In addition to the requirements of exclusive and regular use, those courts would require that the taxpayer's home office be essential to his business and be the only office space available to him. Respondent's home office is the only place where he can perform the administrative functions essential to his business. Because he is not employed by the hospitals where he works, and because none of those hospitals offers him an office, respondent must pay all the costs necessary for him to have any office at all. In my judgment, a principal place of business is a place maintained by or (in the rare case) for the business. As I would construe the statute in this context, respondent's office is not just the "principal" place of his trade or business; it is the only place of his trade or business.

* * * A self-employed person's efficient use of his or her resources should be encouraged by sound tax policy. When it is clear that no risk of the kind of abuse that led to the enactment of § 280A is present, and when the taxpayer has satisfied a reasonable, even a strict, construction of each of the conditions set forth in § 280A, a deduction should be allowed for the ordinary cost of maintaining his home office.

NOTES

(A) *Principal Place of Business Exception.* Justice Thomas, in his concurring opinion in *Soliman,* noted that although certiorari had been granted to clarify a recurring issue in the tax law, "this issue is no clearer today than it was before."

The *Soliman* decision was controversial, particularly with small business, who persuaded Congress that the decision had created havoc. § 280A now provides that a home office can qualify as a principal place of business if the taxpayer uses the office to conduct administrative or management activities and there is no other fixed location of the business where the taxpayer conducts substantial administrative or management activities.

Although this provision provides short-term relief, it may provide a long-term trap for the unwary. Taxpayers generally may exclude $500,000 of gain on the sale of a principal residence. (This provision is described at page 652.) Gain attributable to the portion of the house used for rental or business purposes is taxable, however.

In Sengpiehl v. Commissioner, 75 T.C.M. 1604 (1998), the Tax Court denied a deduction for the dining room even though it was used exclusively for legal practice during working hours because family occasionally used it for meals after working hours. See also Drucker v. Commissioner, 715 F.2d 67 (2d Cir.1983) (home practice studio of a musician for the Metropolitan Opera who performed approximately 12 hours per week at Lincoln Center and practiced approximately 32 hours per week in a musical study in his home was principal place of business.)

(B) *Other Requirements.* As *Soliman* discusses, § 280A permits a taxpayer to deduct expenses of a home office where it is used by patients, clients or customers in meeting with the taxpayer. In Green v. Commissioner, 707 F.2d 404 (9th Cir.1983), the court refused to allow a deduction for a home office used exclusively to receive telephone calls from clients.

If the taxpayer is an employee, the home office must be provided for the convenience of the employer. Can that test ever be met if the employer provides the employee with another office? Compare Weissman v. Commissioner, 751 F.2d 512 (2d Cir.1984) (university professor permitted to deduct home office when he was required to share employer-provided office with several others) with Strasser v. Commissioner, 42 T.C.M. 1125 (1981) (denying deduction upon finding that professor's university office and not her home office was her principal place of business). Section 280A(c)(6) denies a home office deduction for expenses attributable to the rental by an employee of all or part of his home to his employer if the employee uses the rented portion to perform the services of an employee.

The deductible home office expenses are limited to the gross income from the use of the home office less deductions associated with the residence that are allowable regardless of use (such as mortgage interest, real property taxes, and casualty losses) and other deductible expenses attributable to the business (such as the cost of supplies and wages paid to others). In effect, then, home office deductions may not exceed the net income from the activity. Disallowed deductions may be carried forward to succeeding years, subject to continuing application of the gross income limit.

(C) *Rationale.* Legislative history suggests two reasons for the enactment of § 280A. First, prior law often allowed a business deduction for expenses attributable to the home even though no additional costs resulted from the business use. The typical case was a taxpayer/employee who occasionally read work-related material in an armchair in the family den and deducted the costs of maintaining the den. Second, the various standards applied by the courts and the IRS were considered confusing to taxpayers. Congress perceived a "great need for definitive rules." Section 280A and the cases interpreting that provision seem to demonstrate that this latter purpose has not been achieved. Is this failure the result of faulty statutory draftsmanship or the incredible variety of facts and circumstances? Might the results have been clearer if Congress had sacrificed some equity for greater simplicity? For example, what if no deduction at all was available for a home office? Or might the results have been clearer if Congress had enacted rules even more detailed than § 280A? Would explicitly requiring taxpayers to prove "additional or incremental" expenses be more definitive or simpler? Would it be fair? Or would such a rule merely shift the nature of the controversies rather than eliminating or reducing them? If so, does this make you terminally pessimistic about a "simple" income tax? Wildly optimistic about the prospects of making a good living practicing tax law?

(D) *Vacation Homes.* Section 280A also applies to vacation homes. A "vacation home" essentially is a dwelling unit used by the taxpayer for more than the greater of 14 days or 10 percent of the number of days the unit is rented. § 280A(d)(1). If so classified, the taxpayer prorates expenses other than interest and taxes and can deduct these expenses up to the amount of rent reduced by the appropriate share of interest and taxes. § 280A(c)(5). If the unit is used for personal purposes for less than the specified number of days, pro rata deductions are allowed. § 280A(e). There is a de minimis exception for those who use the property for personal purposes for a sufficient amount of time, but rent the property for less than 15 days. The owner forfeits any deductions other than interest and taxes, but need not include the rental income. Consider the owner of a home in Louisville who each year rents it only for the first weekend in May to Derby enthusiasts for $10,000. Is there a rationale for not taxing this income?

(E) *Listed Property.* Dual use property is not limited to home offices and vacation homes. Cars, computers, and cell phones often serve both functions. Congress has tackled the problem with respect to these items quite differently than it did with respect to homes. Section 280F limits depreciation deductions and lease payments with respected to "listed property," which includes vehicles, boats, airplanes, computers, and cell phones. Generally, any listed property, other than automobiles, which is used more than 50 percent for business is exempt from the limitations.

SECTION 3.   THE DISTINCTION BETWEEN DEDUCTIBLE BUSINESS AND INVESTMENT EXPENSES AND NONDEDUCTIBLE CAPITAL EXPENDITURES

Section 263 specifically disallows deduction of a "capital expenditure." When an amount must be capitalized, it is added to the taxpayer's basis in the asset with respect to which the expenditure is incurred. This amount either will be recovered when the asset is sold or over some period of time during which the asset is held, through a series of deductions for depreciation or amortization. Distinguishing deductible business or investment expenses from nondeductible capital expenditures can be as difficult as distinguishing business expenses from personal expenses. The distinction is nevertheless essential to an income tax. If all expenditures made for business or investment purposes were immediately deductible, the tax would be imposed on consumption, rather than income. In a tax where consumption is the base, all savings and investment would be subtracted from receipts to measure an individual's consumption during the taxable period. Under a consumption tax, therefore, a deduction would be allowed immediately for all business and investment expenditures, including such classic capital expenditures as purchased shares of stock, equipment, and real estate. The need for an income tax to distinguish capital expenditures from business or investment expenses also can be demonstrated by the equivalence, under certain conditions, of immediate deduction of a capital investment to exemption from tax of the income from the investment. The relationship between immediate deduction of capital expenditures and the exemption of yield is examined in the Note on Tax Deferral, which follows.

Tax planners are well aware of the distinction between nondeductible capital expenditures and deductible business or investment expenses. If an expenditure that should be capitalized is permitted to be deducted immediately, the taxpayer will postpone tax liability on the income offset by the deduction. Especially in times of high interest rates, such tax deferrals are very valuable to taxpayers.

In addition, if long-term capital gains are treated preferentially while long-term capital losses are not as readily deductible as ordinary losses, the total tax may be very different depending on whether an expense is treated as deductible or a capital expenditure. These two advantages—deferral of tax and conversion of ordinary income into capital gains—are the chief functions of tax planning; for example, they were central features of "tax shelters" used in the 1980's to enable high income taxpayers to reduce their tax liability substantially. Both Congress and the courts have struggled to define the line between deductible expenses and capital expenditures to prevent taxpayers from inappropriately using deferral and conversion to reduce income. This Section concerns the kinds of expenditures that must be capitalized. It is important to remember that when capitalization is required, the taxpayer will be permitted to account for his cost; the issue is when. Because the advantage of an immediate deduction is much greater than offsetting sales proceeds with the taxpayer's cost when an asset is sold, or even allowing deductions for costs during the time the asset is held through depreciation, the stakes are quite high.

A.   TAX DEFERRAL—THE TAX IMPACT OF THE CAPITALIZATION REQUIREMENT

Before turning to the specific rules for distinguishing deductible expenses and capital expenditures and for recovering capital expenditures over time, it is worthwhile to examine in greater detail the impact of income tax timing decisions on both taxpayers and the government. In Chapter 2, we explored the concept that a taxpayer is entitled to a tax-free recovery of capital. The timing and mechanism for recovering capital is one of the most important issues in designing an income tax. Although the same total net income will be taxed over the period the asset is held, income will vary depending on the timing of the offset for capital recovery.

To make this point clear, consider the following example:

Example: Assume T purchases an asset for $10,000 that will produce $3,000 of income each year for five years and then at the end of Year 5 will be worthless and disposed of. Consider three possible tax treatments for the recovery of the cost of the asset: (1) immediate expensing, (2) depreciation of equal amounts over the five-year period, and (3) cost recovery only when the asset is disposed of.

Case 1 (Immediate Expensing)

	Year 1	Year 2	Year 3	Year 4	Year 5
Gross Income	3,000	3,000	3,000	3,000	3,000
Deductions	10,000	0	0	0	0
Net Income	(7,000)	3,000	3,000	3,000	3,000

Case 2 (Ratable Depreciation)

	Year 1	Year 2	Year 3	Year 4	Year 5
Gross Income	3,000	3,000	3,000	3,000	3,000
Deductions	2,000	2,000	2,000	2,000	2,000
Net Income	1,000	1,000	1,000	1,000	1,000

Case 3 (Recovery on Disposition)

	Year 1	Year 2	Year 3	Year 4	Year 5
Gross Income	3,000	3,000	3,000	3,000	3,000
Deductions	0	0	0	0	10,000
Net Income	3,000	3,000	3,000	3,000	(7,000)

The total net income for the five-year period is $5,000 in each of the three cases, but the allocation of taxable gain or loss to each year, and therefore, the timing of tax payments is very different. The precise stream of tax payments depends on the rules for deducting losses. If the total deduction for any year exceeds the income, there is a loss. Such losses generally may be used to offset other unrelated income. For example, in Case 1, the taxpayer might use the $7,000 loss in Year 1 to offset dividend income. In some cases, losses from one type of activity cannot be used against other income. If the taxpayer has no income in a particular year against which to offset the loss, the taxpayer may be able to carry forward or carry back the loss to offset income from other years. If there is no income during the entire statutory period when losses are eligible for carryover, the recovery of capital deductions may be useless to the taxpayer. A detailed discussion of the deductibility of losses begins infra at page 374.

Assuming that the losses in the above example reduce taxes in the year that they occur (Year 1 in Case 1 and Year 5 in Case 3), at a 30 percent marginal tax rate, the tax results for each case would be as follows:

Tax Liability

	Year 1	Year 2	Year 3	Year 4	Year 5	Present Value (8 percent)
Case 1	(2,100)	900	900	900	900	815
Case 2	300	300	300	300	300	1,198
Case 3	900	900	900	900	(2,100)	1,551

Given the flat rate of tax assumed in the example, the total tax for the five-year period is the same in each case, $1,500 (30 percent x $5,000). But the stream of payments is quite different. If the stream of tax payments is discounted to present value, assuming an 8 percent interest rate (and that tax payments are made at the end of each year), Case 1 is best for the taxpayer and Case 3 is the worst. This example should make clear that timing differences will produce significant variations in the real tax burdens in the three cases.

The Note that follows explores in greater detail the value of tax deferral. Here, we treat the value of tax deferral alone, putting aside for the moment the prospects for "conversion" from combining ordinary deductions with capital gains and for "tax arbitrage" or "leverage" from combining borrowing with exclusions from income or accelerated or immediate deductions (an issue that was briefly described in connection with the *Tufts* case, supra at page 189, and that will be examined further in subsequent materials).

NOTE ON TAX DEFERRAL[1]

The ability to accelerate deductions, and thereby defer tax, is of major advantage to taxpayers. In some instances, deferral may exempt income from tax permanently; for example, most property held until death is given a stepped-up basis equal to its fair market value. In other cases, deferral may cause income to be taxed at lower rates, for example, when the taxpayer is subsequently in a lower tax bracket or when the income is eligible for favorable capital gains treatment. Tax deferral is valuable even if the tax on the income in a later year is identical in amount to the tax saved from a deduction in an earlier year. In some ways, the deferral advantage is well understood. It is clear that you would be wealthier if the IRS allowed you to wait until 2005 to pay $100,000 of taxes owned for 2002. You could put the $100,000 in the bank and earn interest, or invest it in other productive assets, or pay off a loan and avoid interest expenses. The value of postponing tax by deferring income or accelerating deductions depends upon tax rates, interest rates, and the length of deferral. The following paragraphs attempt to describe and quantify the benefits of tax deferral by analogies to (1) an interest-free loan, (2) tax forgiveness, and (3)

1. This note is largely adapted from materials found in Stanley S. Surrey, "The Tax Reform Act of 1969—Tax Deferral and Tax Shelters," 12 Bost.Coll.Ind. & Comm. L.Rev. 307 (1971); William Andrews, "A Consumption–Type or Cash–Flow Personal Income Tax," 87 Harv.L.Rev. 1113, 1123–28 (1974); Michael Graetz, "Implementing a Progressive Consumption Tax," 92 Harv. L.Rev. 1575, 1597–23 (1979); and conversations with Daniel I. Halperin and Alvin C. Warren, Jr.

a tax-free return on the amount invested. The third is the most difficult to understand.

1. *Equivalence to an Interest–Free Loan.*

One way to think of the value of deferral is by analogy to an interest-free loan. Assume a taxpayer T in a 50 percent tax bracket invests $100 in an asset that will be sold in ten years and that will produce ordinary income at the time of sale. If the cost could be deducted in the year of acquisition, the immediate deduction would save T $50 in taxes. When sold, the asset will produce $100 more ordinary income than if the cost of the asset had been capitalized because the basis is zero; thus, T will repay, at the time of sale, the $50 of tax saved in the year of acquisition. It is as if the government made a ten-year interest-free loan of $50 to T. (The amount of the loan depends upon the taxpayer's tax bracket, and its duration depends upon the length of deferral.)

2. *Equivalence to a Reduction of Tax Rates or Tax Forgiveness.*

In the above example, T arranges to defer $50 of tax for ten years. Assume that the market rate of interest on T's borrowing, saving or lending is 12 percent (or 6 percent after tax). If T puts $27.92 in the bank at a 12 percent interest rate, he will have accumulated $50 at the end of ten years after withdrawing enough money each year to pay taxes (at a 50 percent rate) on each year's interest income. The ten-year deferral is thus the equivalent of paying only $27.92 in taxes in the initial year. The difference of $22.08 in taxes is, in effect, forgiven, and T's tax rate effectively has been reduced from 50 percent to 27.9 percent.

This is just another way of saying that the interest-free loan is worth $22.08 to T—the present value of after-tax earnings of 6 percent in interest each year for ten years. This equivalence can be seen by assuming that borrowing the $50 would have cost T 12 percent interest, or $6 a year. Assuming a tax deduction is allowed for interest, the $6 interest before tax would cost $3 a year after tax. T thus saves a total of $30 in interest costs by virtue of the immediate deduction (the "interest-free loan"). Expressed in terms of the present value of money, the acceleration of the deduction from year ten to year one is worth $22.08 to T. (This amount was computed by applying a discount rate of 6 percent to the total $30 interest costs, assuming T can borrow at that after-tax rate.)

3. *The Immediate Deduction–Yield Exemption Equivalence.*

The tax savings that occur when the cost of an investment is deductible immediately, under certain conditions, can be described as equivalent to disallowing the deduction initially but exempting from tax the income from the investment.

The concept originated in an article by Professor E. Cary Brown more than 50 years ago, and appears in the standard public finance texts.[2]

---

2. E. Cary Brown, "Business–Income Taxation and Investment Incentives," in Income, Employment and Public Policy: Essays in Honor of Alvin E. Hansen 330–416 (1948). See also Stanley S. Surrey, Pathways to Tax Reform 123 (1973); Carl S. Shoup, Public Finance 302 (1969).

Although difficult to grasp—and only true under limited conditions—this equivalence often provides a useful analytical tool. The equivalence also helps to explain the relationship between income taxes and consumption taxes.

Here we approach this equivalence first by setting out some examples to demonstrate the relationship of immediate deduction and exemption of yield, then by outlining the conditions (or assumptions) necessary for the equivalence to hold, and finally by demonstrating its implications for the distinction between income taxes and consumption taxes.

Example 1: Consider a taxpayer who pays $100 for Greenacre, which is sold five years later for $200. The tax rate is 30 percent.

Capitalized Expenditure

If the purchase price is capitalized, the 30 percent tax reduces the investor's rate of profit from 100 to 70 percent as expected.

	Year 1 Investment	Year 5 Disinvestment	Profit	Rate of Profit
Pre-tax	100	200	100	100%
Tax (reduction)	——·	30*		
After-tax	100	170	70	70%

* This amount is computed as follows: Amount realized of $200 less basis of $100 equals gain of $100, which is taxed at 30 percent for a tax of $30.

Immediately Deductible Capital Cost—Same Pre-tax Investment

If the $100 purchase price can be deducted in the year of purchase, there is an immediate tax savings of $30, so the taxpayer's net investment is only $70. The investment doubles, even after taxes, by year 5. There is no difference between the pre-tax and after-tax rate of profit.

	Year 1 Investment	Year 5 Disinvestment	Profit	Rate of Profit
Pre-tax	100	200	100	100%
Tax (reduction)	(30)	60*		
After-tax	70	140	70	100%

* This amount is computed as follows: Amount Realized of $200 less zero basis equals gain of $200, which is taxed at 30 percent for a tax of $60.

Immediately Deductible Capital Cost—Same After-tax Investment

Assume now that the taxpayer wanted to increase his investment in Greenacre using not only his $100, but also the tax savings from deducting the purchase price. He would be able to invest $143 in Greenacre and would have $200 after paying taxes in year 5.

	Year 1 Investment	Year 5 Disinvestment	Profit	Rate of Profit
Pre-tax	143*	286	143	100%
Tax (reduction)	(43)	86**		
After-tax	100	200	100	100%

* The pre-tax investment is calculated as follows: The post-tax investment of $100 is divided by one minus the tax rate [$100/(1–t) = $100/(1–.3) = $143].

** This amount is calculated as follows: The amount realized of $286 less a basis of zero equals a gain of $286, which is taxed at 30 percent rate for a tax of $86.

The after-tax rate of profit of 100%, when the purchase price of Greenacre is deducted immediately is equal to the pre-tax profit of 100%, the same result as if there is no tax. In other words, with expensing, the pre-tax and after-tax rates of return are the same.

Example 2: The Treasury Department has described the value of deferral in a slightly different fashion, stating that "permitting the capital cost of an asset to be expensed has the effect of exempting the income from ownership of the asset from taxation." The Treasury used the following example to illustrate the point:[3]

> An intuitive explanation of this somewhat surprising result takes the following form: A $1,000 asset will generate some stream of revenue over its life; if the cost is expensed and the tax rate is 48 percent, the net cost of the asset to the owner * * * is only $520, after tax. However, in the future, each $1 of revenue will be taxed fully, with no allowance for depreciation, leaving $0.52 of net return on the $520 investment, the same ratio as $1 to $1,000 as if there were no tax. Incidentally, in those cases, as in minerals taxation, where the total present value of expensing and depletion deductions may actually exceed the cost of the investment, the effective tax rate is negative. That is, in some instances the tax rate equivalent of an investment tax incentive is a tax rate less than zero.

Example 3:[4] Assume a taxpayer with $1000, who faces a tax rate of 50 percent, could invest the $1,000 in a tax-exempt savings account that yielded 10 percent annually and have $100 to consume each year after taxes. If that taxpayer could instead invest $2,000 in a deductible asset or account (by virtue of $1,000 in tax savings from the deduction) that yielded a fully taxable return of 10 percent, this also would leave the investor $100 to consume each year after taxes. Withdrawal of the balances from the accounts would leave the taxpayer with $1,000 after taxes in both cases, because the $2,000 amount would be fully taxable as a result of the previous deduction of that amount.

(b) *Conditions for the Equivalence to Hold.*

A number of conditions are necessary for the immediate deduction-yield exemption equivalence to hold.[5] For example:

3. The quotation and example are from a 1970 Treasury Department Study on Tax Depreciation Policy, set forth at 116 Cong. Rec. 6963–75 (daily ed. July 23, 1970). Both are reproduced and discussed in Surrey, supra note 1, at 313.

4. This example is from American Bar Association, Section of Taxation, Simplifica-

tion Committee, "Report on the Bradley–Gephardt and Kemp–Kasten Bills," 38 Tax Law. 381 (1985).

5. For a slightly different statement of the formal conditions in the economics literature, see Graetz, supra note 1, at 1602.

(i) The applicable tax rates must remain constant—rates can be neither progressive nor change over time. Tax, therefore, is saved from the deduction and collected at an identical rate on the earnings from an asset immediately deducted and on amounts received at the close of the transaction (whether by the disposition of the asset or by some other event.)

(ii) The deduction must produce an immediate tax savings equal to the taxpayer's marginal rate multiplied by the deduction. This means that the deduction must offset income from other sources and cannot be either lost or delayed by carryover requirements.

(iii) The tax savings is assumed to be invested so as to yield a return identical to that of the original investment. It is assumed that the opportunities for investment at the assumed rate of return are unlimited.

The government may be regarded as automatically becoming a joint venturer in the taxpayer's investment by permitting its immediate deduction. In effect, the government invests a percentage equal to the taxpayer's marginal tax rate in the deductible venture. For example, if the taxpayer's marginal rate is 40 percent, the taxpayer receives an initial tax savings of 40 percent of the investment, and the government receives 40 percent of the gain or contributes 40 percent of the loss.

(c) *An Implication of the Equivalence: The Difference Between an Income Tax and an Expenditure (or Progressive Consumption) Tax Is Only Timing.*

Under a consumption tax, all investments would be immediately deductible; consumption would be determined by subtracting all savings and investments from all receipts. The equivalence of an immediate deduction of investments to an exemption of their yield has led a number of commentators to note that a consumption tax does not reduce the before-tax return from investments. The Meade Commission, for example, has stated:

> It is indeed the characteristic feature of [a consumption] tax as contrasted with an income tax that, at any given constant rate of tax, the former will make the rate of return to the saver on his reduced consumption equal to the rate of return which can be earned on the investment which his savings finances, whereas the income tax will reduce the rate of return to the saver below the rate of return which the investment will yield.[6]

Professor Alvin Warren has used the equivalence to demonstrate that a consumption tax can be viewed as exemption of all capital income from tax and therefore as equivalent to a wage tax.[7]

In any event, this analysis of tax deferral confirms the need under an income tax to distinguish immediately deductible expenses from capital expenditures, notwithstanding the difficulties of doing so. The analysis also

---

6. Institute for Fiscal Studies, the Structure and Reform of Direct Taxation 37 (United Kingdom, 1978) (also known as the "Meade Report" after the Chairman of the Commission that prepared the Report.)

7. Alvin C. Warren, Jr., "Fairness and a Consumption–Type or Cash–Flow Personal Income Tax," 88 Harv.L.Rev. 931 (1975). This equivalence between a consumption tax and a wage tax ignores the potential effect of the former on returns from pre-existing capital investments that had not been deductible.

suggests that too rapid deduction of capital expenditures may seriously undermine the income tax. Finally, as each of the three approaches illustrates, tax deferral can be of great value to taxpayers. For a large part of the history of the income tax, those responsible for tax policy overlooked the immense revenue losses that can result from tax deferral alone. Some efforts to redress this problem have occurred in recent times. These basic issues will be explored further in the next Section in connection with the rules for distinguishing capital expenditures from deductible expenses and the provisions for the recovery of capital, and also in connection with accounting provisions discussed in Chapter 6. Many opportunities for the deferral of tax still exist; the deduction of expenses that should be capitalized is but one important example.

NOTE INTRODUCING THE DISTINCTION BETWEEN DEDUCTIBLE EXPENSES AND CAPITAL EXPENDITURES

Certain categories of expenditures are routinely required to be capitalized. These include expenditures to purchase an asset, including financial assets, such as stock or bonds, real estate, tangible personal property, such as machinery and equipment, and intangible assets, such as player contracts purchased and sold by sports franchises. Similarly, the costs incurred by a company in raising capital by issuing debt or stock or of reorganizing a company's capital structure are capital expenditures. Likewise, the costs of entering into a new trade or business or of acquiring the stock or assets of a new trade or business are capital expenditures. In these cases, the issues that arise tend to be factual. For example, is an expenditure made in order to enter a new trade or business or to expand an existing trade or business? Sometimes disputes also arise over what costs must be capitalized. The most difficult legal issues, however, tend to occur in connection with expenditures for operating or expanding an existing business.

The materials that follow provide an introduction to and overview of the kinds of questions that arise. In general the materials move from circumstances where the case for capitalization is relatively clear to more controversial circumstances. Sometimes the courts will ask whether the immediate or long-term benefits dominate. Courts are also more willing to allow deduction of recurring than nonrecurring expenditures. The question whether particular expenditures must be capitalized became more contentious following the Supreme Court's decision in *INDOPCO v. Commissioner*, set forth at page 299 infra. The IRS national office and Treasury personnel often asserted that the *INDOPCO* case did not change the longstanding principles for determining whether an expenditure is capital or deductible. Many IRS agents and litigators, however, regarded the *INDOPCO* decision as an invitation to capitalize any expenditure that is likely to produce a "significant future benefit" and urged capitalization of expenditures that businesses had previously deducted without challenge. The Tax Court largely agreed with this reading of *INDOPCO*, but the courts of appeals reversed some of the Tax Court's decisions. In response to the confusion and controversy, the Treasury announced that it would propose regulations with an eye towards providing consistent and administrable standards.

B. ACQUISITION AND DISPOSITION OF ASSETS

Nondeductible capital expenditures typically include the acquisition of business or investment assets that will last longer than the taxable year. The regulations provide that the costs incurred in the acquisition of an asset must be capitalized. Reg. § 1.263(a)–2(a). Thus, a taxpayer can immediately deduct the purchase of a legal pad, but must capitalize the cost of machinery and equipment, land and buildings, and intangibles such as stocks and bonds. As the following materials demonstrate, however, the question whether expenses are incurred to acquire assets is not always an easy one.

Woodward v. Commissioner

Supreme Court of the United States, 1970. 397 U.S. 572.

MR. JUSTICE MARSHALL delivered the opinion of the Court.

This case and United States v. Hilton Hotels Corp., 397 U.S. 580, involve the tax treatment of expenses incurred in certain appraisal litigation.

Taxpayers owned or controlled a majority of the common stock of the Telegraph–Herald, an Iowa publishing corporation. * * * On June 9, 1960, taxpayers voted their controlling shares of the stock of the corporation in favor of a perpetual extension of the charter. A minority stockholder voted against the extension. Iowa law requires "those [stockholders] voting for such renewal * * * [to] purchase at its real value the stock voted against such renewal." Iowa Code, § 491.25 (1966).

Taxpayers attempted to negotiate purchase of the dissenting stockholder's shares, but no agreement could be reached on the "real value" of those shares. Consequently, in 1962 taxpayers brought an action in state court to appraise the value of the minority stock interest. The trial court fixed a value * * * In July 1965, taxpayers purchased the minority stock interest at the price fixed by the court.

During 1963, taxpayers paid attorneys', accountants', and appraisers' fees of over $25,000, for services rendered in connection with the appraisal litigation. On their 1963 federal income tax returns, taxpayers claimed deductions for these expenses, asserting that they were "ordinary and necessary expenses paid * * * for the management, conservation, or maintenance of property held for the production of income" deductible under § 212 of the Internal Revenue Code of 1954. The Commissioner of Internal Revenue disallowed the deduction "because the fees represent capital expenditures incurred in connection with the acquisition of capital stock of a corporation." The tax court sustained the Commissioner's determination, with two dissenting opinions, 49 T.C. 377 (1968), and the Court of Appeals affirmed, 410 F.2d 313 (C.A. 8th Cir.1969). We granted certiorari, 396 U.S. 875 (1969), to resolve the conflict over the deductibility of the costs of appraisal proceedings between this decision and the decision of the Court of Appeals for the Seventh Circuit in United States v. Hilton Hotel Corp., supra. We affirm.

Since the inception of the present federal income tax in 1913, capital expenditures have not been deductible. See Internal Revenue Code * * *, § 263. Such expenditures are added to the basis of the capital asset with respect to which they are incurred, and are taken into account for tax purposes either through depreciation or by reducing the capital gain (or increasing the loss) when the asset is sold. If an expense is capital, it cannot be deducted as "ordinary and necessary," either as a business expense under § 162 of the Code or as an expense of "management, conservation, or maintenance" under § 212.

It has long been recognized, as a general matter, that costs incurred in the acquisition or disposition of a capital asset are to be treated as capital expenditures. The most familiar example of such treatment is the capitalization of brokerage fees for the sale or purchase of securities, as explicitly provided by a longstanding Treasury regulation, Treas.Reg. on Income Tax 1.263(a)–2(e), and as approved by this Court in Helvering v. Winmill, 305 U.S. 79 (1938), and Spreckels v. Commissioner, 315 U.S. 626 (1942). * * *

The regulations do not specify other sorts of acquisition costs, but rather provide generally that "[t]he cost of acquisition * * * of * * * property having a useful life substantially beyond the taxable year" is a capital expenditure. Treas.Reg. on Income Tax 1.263(a)–2(a). Under this general provision, the courts have held that legal, brokerage, accounting and similar costs incurred in the acquisition or disposition of such property are capital expenditures. * * * The law could hardly be otherwise, for such ancillary expenses incurred in acquiring or disposing of an asset are as much part of the cost of that asset as is the price paid for it.

* * *

Taxpayers * * * argue [that] the costs here in question were properly deducted, since the legal proceedings in which they were incurred did not directly involve the question of title to the minority stock, which all agreed was to pass to taxpayers, but rather was concerned solely with the value of that stock.

* * *

* * * In our view application of the [regulation which makes the "cost of acquisition" of a capital asset a capital expense] to litigation expenses involves the simpler inquiry whether the origin of the claim litigated is in the process of acquisition itself.

A test based upon the taxpayer's "purpose" in undertaking or defending a particular piece of litigation would encourage resort to formalisms and artificial distinctions. For instance, in this case there can be no doubt that legal, accounting and appraisal costs incurred by taxpayers in *negotiating* a purchase of the minority stock would have been capital expenditures. * * * Under whatever test might be applied, such expenses would have clearly been "part of the acquisition cost" of the stock. * * * Yet the appraisal proceeding was no more than the substitute which state law provided for the process of negotiation as a means of fixing the price at which the stock was to be purchased. Allowing deduction of expenses incurred in such a proceeding, merely on the ground that title was not directly put in question in the particular litigation, would be anomalous.

Further, a standard based on the origin of the claim litigated comports with this Court's most recent ruling on the characterizing of litigation expenses for tax purposes. In United States v. Gilmore, 372 U.S. 39 (1963), this Court held that the expense of defending a divorce suit was a nondeductible personal expense, even though the outcome of the divorce case would affect the taxpayer's property holdings, and might affect his business reputation. The Court rejected a test that looked to the consequences of the litigation, and did not even consider the taxpayer's motives or purposes in undertaking defense of the litigation, but rather examined the origin and character of the claim against the taxpayer, and found that the claim arose out of the personal relationship of marriage.

The standard here pronounced may, like any standard, present borderline cases, in which it is difficult to determine whether the origin of particular litigation lies in the process of acquisition. This is not such a borderline case. Here state law required taxpayers to "purchase" the stock owned by the dissenter. In the absence of agreement on the price at which the purchase was to be made, litigation was required to fix the price. Where property is acquired by purchase, nothing is more clearly part of the process of acquisition than the establishment of a purchase price. Thus the expenses incurred in that litigation were properly treated as part of the cost of the stock which the taxpayers acquired.

Affirmed.

NOTES

(A) *Costs of Constructing Property.* Suppose instead of purchasing property, the taxpayer constructs it. What is the proper treatment of the taxpayer's construction costs? In order to provide parity with the purchaser of property, the costs of constructing a capital asset must be capitalized. Thus, costs that otherwise would be deductible, such as wages paid to construction workers, must be capitalized and included in the asset's basis when they are paid in connection with the construction of a capital asset. The recovery of such costs then depends on the applicable rules governing depreciation or amortization of the constructed asset.

For some expenses, this result follows from the explicit language of § 263(a)(1), which disallows a deduction for "[a]ny amount paid out for new buildings or for permanent improvements or betterments made to increase the value of any property or estate." The treatment of other costs is not so clear. For example, in Commissioner v. Idaho Power Co., 418 U.S. 1 (1974), a public utility used equipment for the construction of its own facilities. It depreciated the equipment over a ten-year useful life, the appropriate period for equipment. The Commissioner argued that under § 263, insofar as the equipment was used in constructing capital facilities, depreciation deductions should be disallowed and the disallowed amounts added to the taxpayer's adjusted basis in the new facilities. The adjusted basis of the facility (which would include the cost of using the equipment) would be depreciated over its useful life, then 30 years or more. The

Supreme Court upheld the Commissioner's position, stating (at 418 U.S. 13–14):

> There can be little question that other construction-related expense items, such as tools, materials, and wages paid construction workers, are to be treated as part of the cost of acquisition of a capital asset. The taxpayer does not dispute this. Of course, reasonable wages paid in the carrying on of a trade or business qualify as a deduction from gross income. Section 162(a)(1) of the 1954 Code, 26 U.S.C. § 162(a)(1). But when wages are paid in connection with the construction or acquisition of a capital asset, they must be capitalized and are then entitled to be amortized over the life of the capital asset so acquired. * * *

> Construction-related depreciation is not unlike expenditures for wages for construction workers. The significant fact is that the exhaustion of construction equipment does not represent the final disposition of the taxpayer's investment in that equipment; rather, the investment in the equipment is assimilated into the cost of the capital asset constructed. * * * The taxpayer's own accounting procedure reflects this treatment, * * * on its books the construction-related depreciation was capitalized * * *. By the same token, this capitalization prevents the distortion of income that would otherwise occur if depreciation properly allocable to asset acquisition were deducted from gross income currently realized. * * *

> An additional pertinent factor is that capitalization of construction-related depreciation by the taxpayer who does its own construction work maintains tax parity with the taxpayer who has its construction work done by an independent contractor. The depreciation on the contractor's equipment incurred during the performance of the job will be an element of cost charged by the contractor for his construction services, and the entire cost, of course, must be capitalized by the taxpayer having the construction work performed.

The rule of *Idaho Power* was codified in § 263A, which generally requires capitalization of virtually all indirect costs, in addition to all direct costs, allocable to the construction or production of real property or tangible personal property. Section 263A imposes specific rules with respect to certain items, but it also gives the IRS the authority to allocate other direct and indirect costs. See Noël B. Cunningham & Deborah H. Schenk, How to Tax the House That Jack Built, 43 Tax L.Rev. 447 (1988).

(B) *Capitalization to Avoid "Conversion."* The decision whether an expense is required to be capitalized or is deductible immediately may affect the total amount of income that will be characterized as capital gain (or loss) as opposed to ordinary gain (or loss). Since capital gains are taxed less heavily than ordinary income, a deduction of expenses against ordinary income, combined with the taxation of the gain at favorable capital gains rates, can result in extraordinary tax savings. For example, in Schultz v. Commissioner, 50 T.C. 688, aff'd per curiam 420 F.2d 490 (3d Cir.1970), the taxpayers claimed deductions under § 212 for a four-year prepayment of storage charges, insurance premiums, and state ad valorem taxes in conjunction with their nonbusiness purchase of substantial quantities of bulk whiskey, which they intended to sell. If these deductions were allowed, the taxpayer would have offset income otherwise taxable as ordinary income while the difference between the purchase and sale price of the whiskey would be taxed favorably as capital gain. The Tax Court stated:

Initially, we note that petitioner sought to have the benefit of deductions against ordinary income and long-term capital gain treatment for his ultimate profit. But this blessing, which respondent finds so abhorrent, is sanctioned in many areas of the tax law and certainly does not make petitioner's position malum in se. The presence of such a pattern of tax benefits may erect a yellow caution signal on our road to decision. * * * But it should not become a red stoplight against the petitioner if the statute permits him the benefits he seeks. * * *

[T]he situation herein fits neither the classic pattern of capital expenditure nor deductible expense. Petitioner's expenditures in and of themselves did not add to the value of the whisky. But they certainly provided the opportunity for a "permanent improvement" in the whisky. * * *

The question is a close one, but, under the circumstances herein, we hold that petitioner sought to acquire 4–year-old bourbon whisky and that the expenditures for insurance, storage charges, and estimated Kentucky ad valorem taxes are required to be capitalized and are not deductible as expenses under 212.

In a similar case, a taxpayer was prohibited from amortizing and deducting the cost of building access roads to timber, which produced capital gain when sold. United States v. Regan, 410 F.2d 744, cert. denied, 396 U.S. 834 (1969). The following example demonstrates the potential for "negative" tax rates from "conversion," that would have occurred if the taxpayer had been permitted to deduct the cost of building the roads:

Assume that the timber cost $10,000, that the only additional expense was a road costing $5,000, and that the timber would be sold for $19,000. Assume that a marginal tax rate of 40 percent applies to the taxpayer's ordinary income and that capital gains are taxed at 20 percent. The total pre-tax profit on the transaction would be $4,000 ($19,000 sales price minus $10,000 cost of timber and minus $5,000 cost of road). Applying the favorable 20 percent rate to this profit would produce a tax liability of $800. But if the cost of the road were deducted, the result would be as follows:

(1) Allowing a deduction of $5,000 for the road at the taxpayer's 40 percent marginal rate would produce a tax savings of $2,000.

(2) The profit on the sale of timber would be $9,000 ($19,000 sales price minus $10,000 basis—since the cost of the road was deducted, it would not be added to basis). This gain would be taxed at a 20 percent rate, producing a tax liability of $1,800.

(3) The total tax effect would be a tax savings of $2,000 from the deduction of the cost of the road and a tax liability of $1,800 from the capital gain on the timber sale. Thus, there would be a net tax of negative $200 on a $4,000 economic profit when there should have been an $800 tax at the favorable capital gains rate.

Contrast the result in *Schultz* with that in Heaven Hill Distilleries, Inc. v. United States, 476 F.2d 1327 (Ct.Cl.1973), and Van Pickerill & Sons, Inc. v. United States, 445 F.2d 918 (7th Cir.1971). The taxpayer in *Heaven Hill* was a manufacturer of whiskey and the taxpayer in *Van Pickerill* was a distributor of whiskey. As in *Schultz,* each wanted to deduct storage costs and insurance charges while the whiskey aged. Although the IRS argued that these expenses should be capitalized into the cost of the whiskey, each court permitted the taxpayer to deduct the costs. Both the manufacturer and the distributor would have ordinary income, rather than capital gains, on the sale of the whiskey. Should that difference be important in determining whether an expense is properly capitalized?

There are many instances where taxpayers take ordinary deductions while holding an asset that will qualify for capital gain on sale. Generally, the IRS questions the deductions or attempts to deny capital gains treatment only where the expenditures are at least arguably capital in nature.

(C) *Costs of Disposition.* As the opinion in *Woodward* suggests, the typical costs of disposing of property—for example, a broker's selling commission—are not deductible under §§ 162 or 212 as ordinary and necessary business or investment expenses. Rather they are capitalized and added to the asset's basis, thereby reducing the amount of gain or increasing the loss from the asset's disposition. Thus, if the asset qualifies for capital gain treatment, the broker's commission will reduce that gain rather than offset ordinary income.

(D) *Costs of Demolition.* The costs of demolition are analogous to the costs of asset dispositions, but unlike a sale, no income ordinarily is immediately received. For example, land may be acquired and a building demolished to make way for another. Section 280B disallows deduction of any expenses for the demolition of structures and requires that such expenses be added to the basis of the land on which the demolished structures were located.

(E) *Costs of Defense of Title to Property and of Recovering Property.* Expenses incurred in the defense or perfection of title or property cannot be deducted as current expenses, but must be capitalized and added to the property's basis. This rule follows from the general rule requiring the costs of asset acquisition or disposition to be capitalized. See Regs. §§ 1.263(a)–2, 1.212–1(k). Any lawsuit, however, might affect a taxpayer's title to property and this has produced what the *Woodward* opinion (in a portion omitted here) described as a "melange of decisions" that it would be "idle to suggest * * * can be reconciled." See, e.g., Georator Corp. v. United States, 485 F.2d 283 (4th Cir.1973), cert. denied 417 U.S. 945 (1974) (requiring capitalization of legal fees incurred while resisting a petition to cancel registration of a trademark); Medco Products Co., Inc. v. Commissioner, 523 F.2d 137 (10th Cir.1975) (requiring capitalization of legal expenses incurred by plaintiff in a trademark infringement suit even though the company was a going concern); Cruttenden v. Commissioner, 644 F.2d 1368 (9th Cir.1981) (permitting deduction of legal expenses to recover securities loaned under a subordination agreement to a securities brokerage firm and rejecting the Commissioner's argument that the legal expenses served to remove "clouds" on title, which should be capitalized under the same reasoning that requires capitalization of the expenses of perfecting title); Nickell v. Commissioner, 831 F.2d 1265 (6th Cir.1987) (requiring capitalization of legal fees in connection with the recovery of investment property despite a possible suggestion to the contrary in Reg. § 1.212–1(k)).

In *Gilmore*, discussed in *Woodward*, the court required the taxpayer to look to the origin of the claim in determining whether to deduct legal expenses. If the claim does not arise in connection with business or profit-seeking activities, it is not deductible. If, however, the legal expenditure is capital in nature, it may be capitalized and added to the basis of property, thus reducing the future gain or increasing the loss.

C.   ACQUISITION OF INTANGIBLE ASSETS OR BENEFITS

INDOPCO, Inc. v. Commissioner
Supreme Court of the United States, 1992. 503 U.S. 79.

JUSTICE BLACKMUN delivered the opinion of the Court. [The petitioner, formerly National Starch, was the target of a friendly takeover by Unilever and incurred significant investment banking and legal fees as well as other acquisition expenses which it sought to deduct as ordinary and necessary business expenses.]

In this case we must decide whether certain professional expenses incurred by a target corporation in the course of a friendly takeover are deductible by that corporation as "ordinary and necessary" business expenses under § 162(a) of the federal Internal Revenue Code.

* * *

Section 162(a) of the Internal Revenue Code allows the deduction of all the "ordinary and necessary expenses paid or incurred during the taxable year in carrying on any trade or business." In contrast, § 263 of the Code allows no deduction for a capital expenditure—an amount paid out for new buildings or for permanent improvements or betterments made to increase the value of any property or estate. The primary effect of characterizing a payment as either a business expense or a capital expenditure concerns the timing of the taxpayer's cost recovery: While business expenses are currently deductible, a capital expenditure usually is amortized and depreciated over the life of the relevant asset, or, where no specific asset or useful life can be ascertained, is deducted upon dissolution of the enterprise. * * * Through provisions such as these, the Code endeavors to match expenses with the revenues of the taxable period to which they are properly attributable, thereby resulting in a more accurate calculation of net income for tax purposes.

* * *

In exploring the relationship between deductions and capital expenditures, this Court has noted the familiar rule "that an income tax deduction is a matter of legislative grace and that the burden of clearly showing the right to the claimed deduction is on the taxpayer." * * * The notion that deductions are exceptions to the norm of capitalization finds support in various aspects of the Code. Deductions are specifically enumerated and thus are subject to disallowance in favor of capitalization. See §§ 161 and 261. Nondeductible capital expenditures, by contrast, are not exhaustively enumerated in the Code; "rather than providing a complete list of nondeductible expenditures," * * * § 263 serves as a general means of distinguishing capital expenditures from current expenses.

* * *

National Starch contends that the decision in [Commissioner v.] Lincoln Savings [403 U.S. 345 (1971)] * * * announced an exclusive test for identifying capital expenditures, a test in which "creation or enhancement of an asset" is a prerequisite to capitalization, and deductibility under § 162(a) is the rule rather than the exception. * * * We do not agree, for we conclude that National Starch has overread Lincoln Savings. * * *

Lincoln Savings stands for the simple proposition that a taxpayer's expenditure that "serves to create or enhance * * * a separate and distinct" asset should be capitalized under § 263. It by no means follows, however, that only expenditures that create or enhance separate and distinct assets are to be capitalized under § 263. We had no occasion in Lincoln Savings to consider the tax treatment of expenditures that * * * did not create or enhance a specific asset, and thus the case cannot be read to preclude capitalization in other circumstances. In short, Lincoln Savings holds that the creation of a separate and distinct asset well may be a sufficient but not a necessary condition to classification as a capital expenditure. * * *

Although the mere presence of an incidental future benefit—*some future aspect*—may not warrant capitalization, a taxpayer's realization of benefits beyond the year in which the expenditure is incurred is undeniably important in determining whether the appropriate tax treatment is immediate deduction or capitalization. * * * Indeed, the text of the Code's capitalization provision, § 263(a)(1), which refers to "permanent improvements or betterments," itself envisions an inquiry into the duration and extent of the benefits realized by the taxpayer.

In applying the foregoing principles to the specific expenditures at issue in this case, we conclude that National Starch has not demonstrated that the investment banking, legal, and other costs it incurred in connection with Unilever's acquisition of its shares are deductible as ordinary and necessary business expenses under § 162(a).

Although petitioner attempts to dismiss the benefits that accrued to National Starch from the Unilever acquisition as "entirely speculative" or "merely incidental," * * * the Tax Court's and the Court of Appeals' findings that the transaction produced significant benefits to National Starch that extended beyond the tax year in question are amply supported by the record.

* * *

Courts long have recognized that expenses such as these, incurred for the purpose of changing the corporate structure for the benefit of future operations are not ordinary and necessary business expenses. * * *

NOTES

(A) *Hostile Takeovers.* National Starch incurred its expenses in completing a friendly takeover. The Court does not mention a hostile takeover. In A.E. Staley Manufacturing Co. v. Commissioner, 119 F.3d 482 (7th Cir.1997), the Seventh Circuit permitted the taxpayer to deduct the fees in unsuccessfully fighting a hostile takeover. The court rejected the Tax Court's position that the hostile nature of the takeover did not distinguish the case from *INDOPCO*. Rather, it found that Staley, unlike National Starch, did not create a new asset or add future value. Because the fees were not to facilitate a change in ownership but to protect the existing structure, the court applied what it described as a longstanding rule that costs incurred to defend a business were deductible, adding that the court in *INDOPCO* "did not purport to be creating a talismanic test that an expenditure must be capitalized if it creates some future benefit."

The court in *Staley* cited cases holding that expenses to protect a current business were deductible (see the discussion in Note (D) at page 303 infra), but did not cite cases holding that expenses in defending title to property were not deductible (see Note (E) on page 298 supra). Can these cases be reconciled?

(B) *Other Acquisition Costs.* In Dana Corp. v. United States, 174 F.3d 1344 (Fed.Cir.1999), the taxpayer paid the law firm Wachtell, Lipton $100,000 each year to ensure that Wachtell would not represent a hostile company in a takeover attempt. For the first eight years, Wachtell performed minimal or no legal services, but kept the retainer. In two subsequent years, Dana Corp. completed a takeover of another company. In each case, Wachtell provided legal representation and Dana credited the $100,000 retainer against the fees owed. The court rejected Dana's argument that $100,000 of the legal fees was an ordinary and necessary expense of preventing a takeover. The court reasoned that it was more appropriate to look at the transaction to which the legal fees actually related rather than the original motive for incurring the fee and therefore the retainer must be capitalized as the cost of acquiring a capital asset.

Suppose a corporation pays a large retainer each year to have a major law firm on call for the purpose of fighting any hostile takeover. Each year the retainer is applied against routine legal fees, including the acquisition of capital assets. Is the retainer deductible?

(C) *Officers' Salaries.* In Wells Fargo & Co. v. Commissioner, 224 F.3d 874 (8th Cir.2000), rev'g 112 T.C. 89 (1999), the court of appeals reversed a Tax Court decision (when the case was entitled Norwest v. Commissioner) requiring capitalization of $150,000 of officers' salaries on the ground that they were only incidentally related to a merger, stating:

> Lest one should doubt that paying salaries to corporate officers is a transaction "of common or frequent occurrence" in the business world, we note that courts have traditionally permitted current deductions for expenses attributable to salaries similar to those at issue here. * * * However, *INDOPCO*, which signaled that the Supreme Court's previously announced tests for capitalization were not exhaustive, may well have been viewed by the IRS as a green light to seek capitalization of

costs that had previously been considered deductible in a number of businesses and industries.

The Tax Court erred when it so easily dismissed a major distinction between the instant case and *INDOPCO*. The *INDOPCO* case addressed costs which were *directly* related to the acquisition, while the instant case involves costs which were only *indirectly* related to the acquisition. * * * According to cases which explain and apply the "origin of the claim doctrine", such a distinction effects the outcome of the case. *See Woodward v. Commissioner*, 397 U.S. 572 * * *.

Payments made by an employer are deductible when they are made to employees, are compensatory in nature, and are directly related to the employment relationship (and only indirectly related to the capital transaction, which provides the long term benefit). Likewise, it is true that, a deductible expense is not converted into a capital expenditure solely because the expense is incurred as part of the terms of a corporate reorganization. Rather, the important consideration in determining the nature of an expenditure for tax purposes is the origin and character of the claim for which the expenditure is incurred. In the present case, * * * the origin of the payments was not the acquisition, but rather the employment relationship between the taxpayer and [its employees].

Thus the distinction between the case at hand, and the *INDOPCO* case lies in the relationship between the expense at issue and the long term benefit. In *INDOPCO*, the expenses in question were directly related to the transaction which produced the long term benefit. Accordingly, the expenses had to be capitalized. * * * We conclude that if the expense is *directly* related to the capital transaction (and therefor, the long term benefit), then it should be capitalized. In this case, there is only an *indirect* relation between the salaries (which originate from the employment relationship) and the acquisition (which provides the long term benefit).

* * *

Upon consideration of the facts and circumstances of this case, we determine that [the] salary expenses are directly related to (and arise out of) the employment relationship, and are only indirectly related to the acquisition itself.

But *see Vornado Realty Trust v. Commissioner*, Order, August 11, 2000, denying taxpayer's notion for summary judgment on deductibility of compensation in form of stock options on the ground that it was an issue of fact whether the options were intended to compensate the employee for services in connection with various capital transactions over a thirteen-year period.

With regard to the legal fees also at issue in *Wells Fargo*, the Eighth Circuit held that the expenses incurred before the "final decision" to merge were deductible "investigatory" expenses of an ongoing business but that the fees incurred after that date were incurred to "facilitate consummation" of the merger transaction and therefore must be capitalized. Nearly $28,000 of the $111,000 paid to attorneys was required to be capitalized.

(D) *Expenses With Respect to a New Business*. The usual issue raised with respect to expenses incurred in entering a new business is whether an expense was incurred to maintain an existing business or to change or expand to a new business. If the former, the expense generally is deductible; if the latter, it usually must be capitalized.

Income tax law has had considerable difficulty with the treatment of expenses that would be deductible by an ongoing business but that are incurred prior to the time the business becomes a "going concern." In general, start-up costs or expenditures incurred prior to entering a new business have been required to be capitalized. For example, in Richmond Television Corp. v. United States, 345 F.2d 901 (4th Cir.), vacated and remanded on another issue, 382 U.S. 68 (1965), the court required capitalization of job training and related expenses incurred before the company obtained its operating license from the Federal Communications Commission and began broadcasting. The court held that Richmond Television was not "carrying on a trade or business" until the license was obtained. Likewise, in a widely-followed decision, Frank v. Commissioner, 20 T.C. 511 (1953), the taxpayer sought to deduct travel and legal expenses incurred in the search for and investigation of newspaper and radio properties. The deduction under the predecessor of § 162(a) was disallowed on the grounds that the statute presupposed an existing business with which the taxpayer was connected. The taxpayer's expenses were characterized as investigatory and preparatory to entering a business and therefore not deductible.

Although § 212 does not require that the taxpayer be "carrying on a trade or business" as § 162 does, the courts have held that the pre-opening expenses doctrine applies as well to § 212. See, e.g., Sorrell v. Commissioner, 882 F.2d 484 (11th Cir.1989) (investor services fee paid by a limited partnership prior to commencing business must be capitalized); Fishman v. Commissioner, 837 F.2d 309 (7th Cir.1988) (pre-opening expenses including rentals must be capitalized). The court in *Sorrell* noted that the "carrying on" language was only one justification for the doctrine. Pre-opening expenses were part of the cost of acquiring a capital asset and thus must be capitalized, and that requirement applies to someone who was never going to operate a business.

Section 195 allows taxpayers to elect to amortize certain start-up expenses over a five-year period. This includes expenditures in connection with the investigation or creation of an active trade or business that would be deductible if incurred in connection with the operation of an existing trade or business, as well as expenditures incurred in connection with a § 212 activity in "anticipation of such activity becoming an active trade or business." § 195(c)(1). The requirement that start-up expenses be deductible if incurred by an existing business has caused controversy and limited the simplification benefits of the five-year amortization provided by § 195. The question when an active trade or business begins is left to the regulations. § 195(c)(2). The IRS has interpreted this to mean that expenditures incurred as part of a general search for, or an investigation of, an active trade or business, for example, expenditures paid to determine whether to enter a new business and which new business to enter are investigatory costs that are start-up expenditures eligible for amortization under § 195. Costs incurred in the attempt to acquire a specific business are capital in nature and thus must be capitalized without eligibility for amortization under § 195. Rev. Rul. 99–23, 1999–10 C.B. 998. Interest, taxes, and research and development expenses continue to be immediately deductible under §§ 163, 164, and 174, respectively.

Ironically, although expenses to start-up a new business can generally be amortized over a 5–year period under § 195 and expenses to purchase intangible assets of an existing business can be amortized over a 15–year period (under § 197, discussed infra at page 347), capital expenditures of an ongoing business in some cases may not be recoverable through amortization unless the taxpayer can convince the IRS or the court of its useful life. If it cannot, expenses may not be recovered until the business is sold.

(E) *Expenses of an Ongoing Business.* Courts have struggled with the distinction between expanding an existing business and entering a new business. As indicated above, courts and the IRS have been more willing to allow deduction of expenses attributable to the former, but those attributable to the latter must be capitalized. For example, the courts of appeal split on whether expenses in connection with new bank branches must be capitalized. In Central Texas Savings & Loan Association v. United States, 731 F.2d 1181 (5th Cir.1984), the Fifth Circuit held that the expenditures made to investigate and establish new branches had to be capitalized. The Fourth Circuit, on the other hand, held that such expenses could be deducted immediately because they were incurred in expanding the bank's existing business. NCNB v. United States, 684 F.2d 285 (4th Cir.1982). The court in NCNB relied on a number of cases that allowed banks an immediate deduction for the costs of initiating bank card services. See, e.g., Colorado Springs National Bank v. United States, 505 F.2d 1185 (10th Cir.1974) (permitting deduction because bank was not entering into a new business but merely carrying on its old business of lending in a new way). The Eleventh Circuit, in requiring capitalization of the expenses of acquiring the stock of a new subsidiary, noted the anomaly that would result if the cost of a subsidiary must be capitalized, but the cost of a branch could be deducted. Ellis Banking Corp. v. Commissioner, 688 F.2d 1376 (11th Cir.1982).

To some extent, the diversity of results in these cases turned on differing interpretations of the Supreme Court's holding in Commissioner v. Lincoln Savings and Loan Association, 403 U.S. 345 (1971), which seemed to require the existence of a new asset for capitalization. The separate asset requirement of *Lincoln Savings* was overruled by *INDOPCO v. Commissioner,* supra at page 299, thereby clouding somewhat the value of these cases as precedents, although the IRS has cited them, along with *Briarcliff Candy*, discussed below, favorably in a number of post-*INDOPCO* revenue rulings. In addition to the *Lincoln Savings* precedent, the courts in *NCNB* and *Central Texas Savings* looked to the nonrecurring nature of the expenses and the life of the new branches to determine if the expenditures should be capitalized. Which approach do you think will better serve the purposes of the capitalization requirement? Should expenses of such expansions normally be immediately deductible?

In Briarcliff Candy Corp. v. Commissioner, 475 F.2d 775 (2d Cir.1973), the taxpayer, a manufacturer, wholesaler, and retailer of candy, expended more than $300,000 reorganizing its sales force, entering into franchise contracts with retailers and advertising its products. The Second Circuit, while describing the capital-deductible boundary as "imprecise," permitted a deduction of these expenses, emphasizing that they were related to an advertising and promotional campaign, where deduction is the norm. As *PNC*, infra, and the Notes following indicate, it is not clear what effect, if any, *INDOPCO* might have on similar future cases.

As the Note on page 310 infra suggests, after the *INDOPCO* decision the IRS repeatedly issued rulings stating that *INDOPCO* did not change the basic law of capitalization but the IRS's litigating position became much more aggressive in contending for capitalization of expenses that businesses historically had deducted. The language in *INDOPCO* suggesting that a taxpayer must capitalize costs that produce significant benefits beyond the taxable year is quite broad. As the next case illustrates, both the IRS and the courts struggled to determine what business expenses continue to be deductible after *INDOPCO*.

PNC Bancorp, Inc. v. Commissioner

212 F.3d 822 (3d Cir.2000).

RENDELL, CIRCUIT JUDGE.

In this appeal from a decision of the Tax Court, we are asked to determine whether certain costs incurred by banks for marketing, researching and originating loans are deductible as "ordinary and necessary expenses" as provided by section 162 of the Internal Revenue Code, or whether these expenses must be capitalized under section 263 of the Code. Two banks that were predecessors in interest of appellant PNC Bancorp, Inc. deducted these costs as ordinary business expenses. The Internal Revenue Service disallowed the deductions. * * * The Tax Court determined that the expenses in question were not deductible, but, instead, must be capitalized and amortized over the life of the subject loans. PNC now appeals from this determination.

We hold that the costs at issue were deductible as "ordinary and necessary" expenses of the banking business within the meaning of *Internal Revenue Code section 162*, and that these costs do not fall within the purview of section 263. Accordingly, we will reverse the judgment of the Tax Court. * * *

The costs that the banks seek to deduct are the internal and external costs that they incur in connection with the issuance of loans to their customers. These costs * * * are a routine part of the banks' daily business, and the services procured with these outlays have been integral to the basic execution of the banking business for decades.

The general contours of banks' involvement in making loans have not changed dramatically in recent years, and the relevant sections of the Tax Code have remained largely unchanged. Historically, the costs at issue have been deductible in the year that they are incurred; however, the Commissioner rejected this tax treatment by PNC. Why is the Commissioner now insisting upon capitalization of these costs?

There are two relatively recent developments that appear to have emboldened the Internal Revenue Service to pursue capitalization of such costs. One of these developments is the Supreme Court's opinion in *INDOPCO, Inc. v. Commissioner,* 503 U.S. 79, 117 L. Ed. 2d 226, 112 S. Ct. 1039 (1992), in which the Court held that expenses incurred by a target corporation in the course of its friendly acquisition by another entity were not currently deductible. *INDOPCO,* which signaled that the Supreme Court's previously announced tests for capitalization were not exhaustive, may well have been viewed by the IRS as a green light to seek capitalization of costs that had previously been considered deductible in a number of businesses and industries. * * * Thus, *INDOPCO* ushered in an era of generally more aggressive IRS pursuit of capitalization.

An additional development may have prompted the IRS's assertive posture in the more specific case of the loan origination costs at issue here. This second development was the Financial Accounting Standards Board's promulgation of a new standard for financial accounting treatment of loan origination costs, Statement of Financial Accounting Standards No. 91 ("SFAS 91"). Beginning in the late 1980s, SFAS 91 required for the first time that, for financial accounting purposes, loan fee income and the costs incurred in connection with loan origination should be deferred and recognized over the life of the loan, rather than being recognized in full in the year the loan closed. The FASB's authority extends only to financial accounting standards and not to tax accounting standards. For the first few years of SFAS 91's existence, the IRS did not require capitalization of the loan origination costs described in this financial accounting standard. However, the IRS apparently viewed *INDOPCO* as a reason to pursue capitalization of the costs that SFAS 91 requires to be deferred. Thus, the stage for this litigation was set.

* * *

The costs challenged in this appeal were incurred by both banks in connection with the origination of loans. There are two categories of such "loan origination costs," as they have been called. The first category includes payments made to third parties for activities that help the bank determine whether to approve a loan (credit screening, property reports, and appraisals) and for the recording of security interests when the bank decides to issue a secured loan. The second category consists of internal costs, namely that portion of employee salaries and benefits that can be attributed to time spent completing and reviewing loan applications, and to other efforts connected with loan marketing and origination.

* * *

Two sections of the Internal Revenue Code address the deductibility vel non of expenditures such as those incurred by FNPC and UFB. [Sections 162 and 263]. * * * It is true that these two sections are neither all-inclusive nor mutually exclusive. For example, it is possible that an expense that might appear to be deductible under section 162(a) might instead be required to be capitalized because it also properly falls under the description provided by section 263(a). If an expense were to fall under the language of section 263(a), that section would "trump" the deductibility provision of section 162(a) and the expense would have to be capitalized. Thus, in order to be deductible, the expense must both be "ordinary and necessary" within the meaning of section 162(a) and fall outside the group of capital expenditures envisioned by section 263(a). Nonetheless, the two sections represent the archetypes of the two opposing alternatives for tax treatment of expenditures—deduction and capitalization—and, ordinarily, an expenditure will fall under one or the other section, not both.

* * * In order to demonstrate deductibility under section 162(a) of the Code, the taxpayer must meet a five-part test. "To qualify as an allowable deduction under § 162(a) * * *, an item must (1) be 'paid or incurred during the taxable year,' (2) be for 'carrying on any trade or business,' (3) be an 'expense,' (4) be a 'necessary' expense, and (5) be an 'ordinary' expense." *Commissioner v. Lincoln Sav. & Loan Ass'n*, 403 U.S. 345, 352, 29 L. Ed. 2d 519, 91 S. Ct. 1893 (1971). It is clear that PNC's loan origination expenses can satisfy the first four parts of this test. The question before us under § 162, then, is whether these expenses qualify as "ordinary" business expenses within the meaning of that section.

In determining what expenditures qualify as "ordinary," we must look to the particular facts of the case before us, including the particular puzzle posed by the circumstances of the banking industry. As Justice Cardozo stated nearly seventy years ago in interpreting an earlier version of this long-standing Code provision, ordinariness is "a variable affected by time and place and circumstance." *Welch v. Helvering*, 290 U.S. 111, 113–14 (1933). In interpreting the Code, we should not stray from the moorings of the "natural and common meaning" of the term "ordinary," and in doing so must examine the nature of the day-to-day operations of the particular business being considered. * * * Accordingly, we pursue a real-life inquiry into whether the expenditures associated with loan marketing and origination are "ordinary" expenses incurred in the day-to-day maintenance of a bank's business.

The Commissioner has conceded that loan interest was the banks' largest revenue source during the period in question, and that interest payments on deposits and other borrowing were their largest expense. There is no reason to suppose that this time period was any different from any other in this regard. Further, maximizing the "net interest margin"— the difference between interest received and interest paid out—is the principal manner in which banks earn their keep. As the Tax Court stated, "the principal businesses of [the banks] consisted of accepting demand and time deposits and using the amounts deposited, together with other funds, to make loans." Given this context, the ordinary nature of the costs at issue, routinely incurred in the banks' businesses, would seem clear. In order to ensure deductibility, however, we must also ascertain whether these costs were expended for betterments to increase the value of property in a way that would require these costs' capitalization under § 263. We cannot conclude that in performing credit checks, appraisals, and other tasks intended to assess the profitability of a loan, the banks "stepped out of [their] normal method of doing business" so as to render the expenditures at issue capital in nature. * * * The facts before us demonstrate that loan operations are the primary method of income production for the subject banks. We have no doubt that the expenses incurred in loan origination were normal and routine "in the particular business" of banking.

* * *

In the case at bar, the Tax Court concluded without any elaboration that the consumer and commercial loans "clearly" were separate and distinct assets of the banks, and that the costs incurred in originating and processing the loans "created" these separate and distinct assets. We believe that the Tax Court took * * * an overbroad reading of what can be said to "create" such assets.

* * * The Tax Court * * * essentially treats the term "separate and distinct asset" as if it extends to cover any identifiable asset. We do not subscribe to this reading of Lincoln Savings.

Furthermore, we do not agree that the marketing and origination activities actually "created" the banks' loans * * *. In the instant case, the Tax Court proceeded from the clearly accurate premise that the expenses in question were associated with the loans, incurred in connection with the acquisition of the loans, or "directly related to the creation of the loans," * * * to the faulty conclusion that these expenses themselves created the loans. * * * We conclude that the term "create" does not stretch this far. * * * In PNC's case, * * * the expenses are merely costs associated with the origination of the loans; the expenses themselves do not become part of the balance of the loan. PNC argues persuasively that the Tax Court's interpretation * * * is inappropriately expansive: * * *

* * * [B]oth the Tax Court and the government effectively have transformed * * * a test based on whether a cost "creates" a separate and distinct asset, into a much more sweeping test that would mandate capitalization of costs incurred "in connection with" or "with respect to" the acquisition of an asset.

* * * We decline to follow the Tax Court's broad interpretation, for to do so would be to expand the type of costs that must be capitalized so as to drastically limit what might be considered as "ordinary and necessary" expenses. We conclude, therefore, that the loan origination expenses were ordinary expenses and that they did not "create or enhance a separate and distinct asset" * * *

Nor do we view the Supreme Court's decision in *INDOPCO* as requiring a different result regarding the deductibility of the banks' costs. In *INDOPCO*, the Supreme Court required capitalization of the expenditures incurred by the target corporation during a planned friendly takeover by another company.

The Supreme Court was careful to emphasize in *INDOPCO*, as it had in Lincoln Savings, that the capitalization versus deductibility inquiry was heavily fact-based. The Supreme Court in *INDOPCO* downplayed the importance of the "creation of a separate and distinct asset" described in Lincoln Savings.

* * *

We also conclude that the Tax Court erred in its interpretation of the "future benefit" analysis by relying on the fact that the loan itself was usually of several years' duration and by reasoning that the loan origination costs were, thus, essentially directed at future benefit. The Tax Court stated: "While the useful life of a credit report and other financial data may be of short duration, the useful life of the asset they serve to create is not." However, that analysis depends on the Tax Court's earlier assumption that the loan origination expenses actually created a "separate and distinct asset." Stripped of this assumption, the Tax Court's analysis is not supportable.

In addition, we must remember that the "future benefit" analysis adopted in *INDOPCO* is not meant as a talismanic, bright-line test. Rather, the *INDOPCO* analysis demonstrates the contextual, case-by-case approach to determining whether an expenditure better fits under the "ordinary and necessary" language of section 162(a) or the "permanent improvements or betterments" language of 263(a). We conclude that the loan origination expenses incurred by UFB and FNPC have the characteristics of the former, rather than the latter, statutory language. As described above, the loan marketing activities at issue here lie at the very core of the banks' recurring, routine day-to-day business. The Commissioner has not been able to articulate a principled reason why these normal costs of doing business must be capitalized, while other ordinary banking costs need not be. * * *

The remaining question, then, is whether either the Financial Accounting Standards Board's adoption of SFAS 91 or the Supreme Court's pronouncement on deductibility in *INDOPCO*, * * * would alter the calculus of deductibility versus capitalization in PNC's case. We conclude that the existence of SFAS 91 has little, if any, bearing on the appropriate tax analysis, and that the Supreme Court's decision in INDOPCO, while clearly relevant, does not change the result in the case at bar.

The Supreme Court has held that financial accounting standards such as SFAS 91 do not dictate tax treatment of income and expenditures. See *Thor Power Tool Co. v. Commissioner,* 439 U.S. 522 (1979) (discussing the "vastly different objectives that financial and tax accounting have" and stating that "given this diversity, even contrariety, of objectives, any presumptive equivalency between tax and financial accounting would be unacceptable" and would "create insurmountable difficulties of tax administration"). * * * [A]s with the financial accounting standards at issue in *Thor Power*, it is clear that the reasons for SFAS 91's requirement that loan origination costs be deferred are reasons wholly specific to the realm of financial accounting,[1] and thus those financial accounting standards do not affect our tax analysis.

---

1. SFAS 91 was motivated by a concern that the structure of certain banks' loan agreements could lead to the illusion that these banks and their customers were in better financial condition than they actually were.

The Supreme Court has noted that "capitalization prevents the distortion of income that would otherwise occur if depreciation properly allocable to asset acquisition were deducted from gross income currently realized." *Commissioner v. Idaho Power Co.*, 418 U.S. 1, 14 (1974). In the case of the costs at issue here, there need be no concern about a distortion of income because of the regularity of these expenses.

Finally, we emphasize that the key to the deductibility inquiry remains the statutory language of sections 162(a) and 263(a). The analyses set forth in *INDOPCO* and Lincoln Savings provide us with two applications of that statutory language. Like the Supreme Court in *INDOPCO* and Lincoln Savings, we do not here attempt to define once and for all a bright line between deduction and capitalization that will hold true for all factual situations. * * * Resorting to that language, we find the case before us today to be much farther from the heartland of the traditional capital expenditure (a "permanent improvement or betterment") than are the scenarios at issue in *INDOPCO* and Lincoln Savings. We will not mechanistically apply phrases from those precedents in ignorance of the realities of the facts before us. We see no principled distinction between the costs at issue here and other costs incurred as "ordinary expenses" by banks. * * *

NOTES

(A) *Left Hand Ignorant of Right Hand.* Post-*INDOPCO,* the IRS continued to interpret the capitalization requirement quite broadly and took very aggressive positions in litigation. In FMR Corp. v. Commissioner, 110 T.C. 402 (1998), the court required a corporation (the parent of Fidelity Mutual Funds) that provided investment management services to regulated investment companies to capitalize its expenditures in setting up new mutual funds. These costs included such things as research, legal, and regulatory fees, and the preparation of offering documents that for existing mutual funds would have been ordinary and necessary expenses. The Court allowed no amortization of these amounts because it rejected the company's attempt to show a short useful life.

In Lychuk v. Commissioner, 116 T.C. 374 (2001), the Tax Court required a company in the business of acquiring automobile installment loans from automobile dealers to capitalize the costs of acquisition of the loans, including employees' salaries, which mostly paid for checks of the creditworthiness of the borrowers. The court allowed deduction of overhead costs—such as rent, telephone and utilities—distinguishing the salaries from the overhead costs on the ground that the former were "directly related" to the acquisition of separate and distinct assets, while the latter were not. The court held that the salaries were part of the "process of acquisition" under *Woodward* (supra at p. 293). The Tax Court distinguished *Wells Fargo*, supra, on the ground that the employees whose salaries were at issue in *Lychuk* all spent "a significant portion of [their] time (in fact, in 8 of the 15 cases, all of [their] time) working on capital asset acquisitions which occurred in the ordinary course of [the company's] business." The court rejected the Third Circuit's holding in *PNC* that "normal and routine" expenses—the everyday and recurring costs of running the business—could be deducted. The court explicitly refused to follow *PNC*, which it regarded as essentially indistinguishable, holding that the loans were separate assets with substantial benefits extending beyond a year, citing *INDOPCO*. Although a majority of the court joined in this decision, two judges would have allowed deduction of all the costs at issue, while six judges would have required the corporation to capitalize both the salaries and the overhead costs.

The people who determined the IRS litigating position during this period seemed to be blissfully unaware of the IRS stance in revenue rulings interpreting *INDOPCO*. These rulings narrowly interpreted the case, identifying numerous categories of expenses that remain deductible. See, e.g. Rev. Rul. 94–77, 1994–2 C.B. 19 (permitting severance payments made to employees to be deducted); Rev. Rul. 96–62, 1996–2 C.B. 9 (training costs generally are deductible); Rev. Rul. 2000–4, 2000–1 C.B. 331 (permitting the costs of obtaining and maintaining a certification for a quality management system to be deducted); Rev. Rul. 2000–7, 2000–1 C.B. 712 (cost of removing an asset to replace it does not have to be capitalized). In each case, the IRS noted that the fact that the expenditure may produce a future benefit did not require capitalization, a statement that appears to conflict with the position it was taking in litigation.

(B) *Amortization*. In cases in which the expenditure does not create a separate and distinct asset, but nevertheless must capitalized, the taxpayer supposedly accounts for the cost by amortizing it over its useful life. But, as the FMR case demonstrates, the taxpayer has the burden of proving the appropriate useful life for amortization. This means that "permanent capitalization," with no recovery of costs until the business is sold, may result if capitalization is required. This makes the stakes very high for taxpayers in cases where the IRS asserts that capitalization is required. What if the expenditure involves the expansion of a business (as for example in *Briarcliff Candy*, supra at page 305)? If the costs were capitalized, over what period should they be amortized?

(C) *Advertising and Promotional Expenses*. Historically, advertising and promotional expenses have been deducted despite the fact that a particular ad campaign might last several years. Reg. § 1.162–20. For example, in Rev. Rul. 68–561, 1968–2 C.B. 117, a natural gas company, as part of a program to increase gas consumption, gave cash allowances to builders and apartment owners who used only gas, and also conducted an advertising campaign. The Service ruled that the cash allowances were capital in nature since they secured benefits that were likely to have a value extending beyond the year incurred. The advertising expenses, however, were currently deductible since they were less directly and less significantly productive of benefits having a value beyond the taxable year. Does this distinction hold up analytically? Compare E.H. Sheldon & Co. v. Commissioner, 214 F.2d 655 (6th Cir.1954) (permitting taxpayer to deduct the cost of an advertising catalogue published every five years), with Cleveland Electric Illuminating Co. v. United States, 7 Cl.Ct. 220 (1985) (advertising costs incurred to ally public opposition to license to construct a nuclear power plant must be capitalized).

To quell fears that *INDOPCO* would require capitalization of expenses commonly deducted, the Service announced that the decision did not affect the longstanding treatment of advertising costs. Rev. Rul. 92–80, 1992–2 C.B. 7, stating: "Only in the unusual circumstance where advertising is directed towards obtaining future benefits significantly beyond those traditionally associated with ordinary product advertising or with institutional or goodwill advertising, must the costs of that advertising be capitalized." If a corporation ran a television ad for a two-year period, should the costs of producing the ad be deductible in the first year?

The fact that advertising is generally deductible has not stopped the IRS from trying to limit the impact of the advertising "exception." In RJR Nabisco Inc. v. Commissioner, 76 T.C.M. 71 (1998), the IRS urged the Tax Court to require the R.J. Reynolds Tobacco Co. to capitalize its costs for graphic and package design for cigarette packages. The Service had issued a revenue ruling providing a five-year amortization of package design costs. Rev. Rul. 89–23, 1989–1C.B. 85. The IRS conceded that under its regulations, advertising was deductible, but argued that graphic and package design must be capitalized because they provided benefits that extended for more than a year. The court found that the design costs were not severable from the advertising campaign and thus were deductible. Could the IRS change the result in *RJR* by amending the regulations?

Department of the Treasury
Guidance Regarding Deduction and Capitalization of Expenditures

January 23, 2002.

* * *

The IRS and Treasury Department are reviewing the application of section 263(a) of the Internal Revenue Code to expenditures that result in taxpayers acquiring, creating, or enhancing intangible assets or benefits. This document describes and explains rules and standards that the IRS and Treasury Department expect to propose in 2002 in a notice of proposed rulemaking.

A fundamental purpose of section 263(a) is to prevent the distortion of taxable income through current deduction of expenditures relating to the production of income in future taxable years. See Commissioner v. Idaho Power Co., 418 U.S. 1, 16 (1974). Thus, the Supreme Court has held that expenditures that create or enhance separate and distinct assets or produce certain other future benefits of a significant nature must be capitalized under section 263(a). See INDOPCO, Inc. v. Commissioner, 503 U.S. 79 (1992); Commissioner v. Lincoln Savings & Loan Ass'n, 403 U.S. 345 (1971).

The difficulty of translating general capitalization principles into clear, consistent, and administrable standards has been recognized for decades. See Welch v. Helvering, 290 U.S. 111, 114–15 (1933). Because courts focus on particular facts before them, the results reached by the courts are often difficult to reconcile and, particularly in recent years, have contributed to substantial uncertainty and controversy. The IRS and Treasury Department are concerned that the current level of uncertainty and controversy is neither fair to taxpayers nor consistent with sound and efficient tax administration.

Recently, much of the uncertainty and controversy in the capitalization area has related to expenditures that create or enhance intangible assets or benefits. To clarify the application of section 263(a), the forthcoming notice of proposed rulemaking will describe the specific categories of expenditures incurred in acquiring, creating, or enhancing intangible assets or benefits that taxpayers are required to capitalize. In addition, the forthcoming notice of proposed rulemaking will recognize that many expenditures that create or enhance intangible assets or benefits do not create the type of future benefits for which capitalization under section 263(a) is appropriate, particularly when the administrative and record keeping costs associated with capitalization are weighed against the potential distortion of income.

To reduce the administrative and compliance costs associated with section 263(a), the forthcoming notice of proposed rulemaking is expected to provide safe harbors and simplifying assumptions including a "one-year rule," under which expenditures relating to intangible assets or benefits whose lives are of a relatively short duration are not required to be capitalized, and "de minimis rules," under which certain types of expenditures less than a specified dollar amount are not required to be capitalized. The IRS and Treasury Department are also considering additional administrative relief, for example, by providing a "regular and recurring rule," under which transaction costs incurred in transactions that occur on a regular and recurring basis in the routine operation of a taxpayer's trade or business are not required to be capitalized.

The proposed standards and rules described in this document will not alter the manner in which provisions of the law other than section 263(a) (e.g., sections 195, 263(g), 263(h), or 263A) apply to determine the correct tax treatment of an item. Moreover, these standards and rules will not address the treatment of costs other than those to acquire, create, or enhance intangible assets or benefits, such as costs to repair or improve tangible property. The IRS and Treasury Department are considering separate guidance to address these other costs.

The following discussion describes the specific expenditures to acquire, create, or enhance intangible assets or benefits for which the IRS and Treasury Department expect to require capitalization in the forthcoming notice of proposed rulemaking. The IRS and Treasury Department anticipate that other expenditures to acquire, create, or enhance intangible assets or benefits generally will not be subject to capitalization under section 263(a).

A.   Amounts Paid to Acquire Intangible Property

1.   Amounts paid to acquire financial interests.

Under the expected regulations, capitalization will be required for an amount paid to purchase, originate, or otherwise acquire a security, option, any other financial interest described in section 197(e)(1), or any evidence of indebtedness. For a discussion of related transaction costs see section C of this document.

For example, a financial institution that acquires portfolios of loans from another person or originates loans to borrowers would be required to capitalize the amounts paid for the portfolios or the amounts loaned to borrowers.

2.   Amounts paid to acquire intangible property from another person.

Under the expected regulations, capitalization will be required for an amount paid to another person to purchase or otherwise acquire intangible property from that person. For a discussion of related transaction costs see section C of this document.

For example, an amount paid to another person to acquire an amortizable section 197 intangible from that person would be capitalized. Thus, a taxpayer that acquires a customer base from another person would be required to capitalize the amount paid to that person in exchange for the customer base. On the other hand, a taxpayer that incurs costs to create its own customer base through advertising or other expenditures that create customer goodwill would not be required to capitalize such costs under this rule.

B.   Amounts Paid to Create or Enhance Certain Intangible Rights or Benefits

1.   12–month rule.

The IRS and Treasury Department expect to propose a 12–month rule applicable to expenditures paid to create or enhance certain intangible rights or benefits. Under the rule, capitalization under section 263(a) would not be required for an expenditure described in the following paragraphs 2 through 8 unless that expenditure created or enhanced intangible rights or benefits for the taxpayer that extend beyond the earlier of (i) 12 months after the first date on which the taxpayer realizes the rights or benefits attributable to the expenditure, or (ii) the end of the taxable year following the taxable year in which the expenditure is incurred.

The IRS and Treasury Department request comments on how the 12–month rule might apply to expenditures paid to create or enhance rights of indefinite duration and contracts subject to termination provisions. For example, comments are requested on whether costs to create contract rights that are terminable at will without substantial penalties would not be subject to capitalization as a result of the 12–month rule.

2.   Prepaid items.

Subject to the 12–month rule, the IRS and Treasury Department expect to propose a rule that requires capitalization of an amount prepaid for goods, services, or other benefits (such as insurance) to be received in the future.

For example, a taxpayer that prepays the premium for a 3–year insurance policy would be required to capitalize such amount under the rule. Similarly, a calendar year taxpayer that pays its insurance premium on December 1, 2002, for a 12–month policy beginning the following February would be required to capitalize the amount of the expenditure. The 12–month rule would not apply because the benefit attributable to the expenditure would extend beyond the end of the taxable year following the taxable year in which the expenditure was incurred. On the other hand, if the insurance contract had a term beginning on December 15, 2002, the taxpayer could deduct the premium expenditure under the 12–month rule because the benefit neither extends more than 12 months beyond December 15, 2002 (the first date the benefit is realized by the taxpayer) nor beyond the taxable year following the year the expenditure was incurred.

3. Certain market entry payments.

Subject to the 12–month rule, the IRS and Treasury Department expect to propose a rule that requires capitalization of an amount paid to an organization to obtain or renew a membership or privilege from that organization.

For example, subject to the 12–month rule, the rule would require capitalization of costs to obtain a stock trading privilege, admission to practice medicine at a hospital, and access to the multiple listing service. The rule does not contemplate requiring capitalization for costs to obtain ISO 9000 certification or similar costs.

4. Amounts paid to obtain certain rights from a governmental agency.

Subject to the 12–month rule, the IRS and Treasury Department expect to propose a rule that requires capitalization of an amount paid to a governmental agency for a trade name, trademark, copyright, license, permit, or other right granted by that governmental agency.

For example, under the rule, a restaurant would be required to capitalize the amount paid to a state to obtain a license to serve alcoholic beverages that is valid indefinitely.

5. Amounts paid to obtain or modify contract rights.

Subject to the 12–month rule, the IRS and Treasury Department expect to propose a rule that requires capitalization of amounts in excess of a specified dollar amount (e.g., $5,000) paid to another person to induce that person to enter into, renew, or renegotiate an agreement that produces contract rights enforceable by the taxpayer, including payments for leases, covenants not to compete, licenses to use intangible property, customer contracts and supplier contracts. The IRS and Treasury Department request comments on whether there are standards other than the standard described above that would be more appropriate for determining whether expenditures related to the creation or enhancement of contractual rights should be capitalized.

Subject to the 12–month rule, this rule would require a lessee to capitalize an amount paid to a lessor in exchange for the lessor's agreement to enter into a lease. This rule also would require a lessee to capitalize an amount paid to a lessor in exchange for the lessor's agreement to terminate a lease and enter into a new lease. See, e.g., U.S. Bancorp v. Commissioner, 111 T.C. 231 (1998). However, this rule would not require a lessee to capitalize an amount paid to a lessor to terminate a lease where the parties do not enter into a new or renegotiated agreement. This rule also would not require a taxpayer to capitalize a payment that does not create enforceable contract rights but, for example, merely creates an expectation that a customer or supplier will maintain its business relationship with the taxpayer. See, e.g., Van Iderstine Co. v. Commissioner, 261 F.2d 211 (2d Cir.1958).

6. Amounts paid to terminate certain contracts.

Subject to the 12–month rule, the IRS and Treasury Department expect to propose a rule that requires capitalization of an amount paid by a lessor to a lessee to induce the lessee to terminate a lease of real or tangible personal property or by a taxpayer to terminate a contract that grants another person the exclusive right to conduct business in a defined geographic area.

For example, under the rule, a lessor that pays a lessee to terminate a lease of real property with a remaining term of 24 months would be required to capitalize such payment. See, e.g., Peerless Weighing and Vending Machine Corp. v. Commissioner, 52 T.C. 850 (1969). On the other hand, if the lease had a remaining term of 6 months, the 12–month rule would apply, and the taxpayer would not be required to capitalize the termination payment under the rule.

As a further example, where a taxpayer grants another person the exclusive right to develop the taxpayer's motel chain in four states, and the taxpayer later pays that other person to terminate such right at a time when the remaining useful life of the right is 5 years, the taxpayer would be required to capitalize the termination payment under the rule. See Rodeway Inns of America v. Commissioner, 63 T.C. 414 (1974).

7. Amounts paid in connection with tangible property owned by another.

Subject to the 12–month rule, the IRS and Treasury Department expect to propose a rule that requires capitalization of amounts in excess of a specified dollar amount paid to facilitate the acquisition, production, or installation of tangible property that is owned by a person other than the taxpayer where the acquisition, production, or installation of the tangible property results in the type of intangible future benefit to the taxpayer for which capitalization is appropriate. This rule would apply even though there is no contractual relationship between the taxpayer and the other person. This rule is intended to require capitalization of expenditures that produce intangible future benefits similar to those that were in issue in Kauai Terminal Ltd. v. Commissioner, 36 B.T.A. 893 (1937) (expenditure incurred to construct a publicly owned breakwater for the purpose of increasing taxpayer's freight lighterage operation). The IRS and Treasury Department request comments on standards that can be established to ensure that the expenditures described in this rule result in the type of future benefits that are similar to those in Kauai Terminal and therefore should be capitalized. The IRS and Treasury Department also request comments on whether safe harbors or dollar thresholds should be used to determine whether capitalization of such expenditures is appropriate under section 263(a).

8. Defense or perfection of title to intangible property.

Subject to the 12–month rule, the IRS and Treasury Department expect to propose a rule that requires capitalization of amounts paid to defend or perfect title to intangible property.

For example, under the rule, if a taxpayer and another person both claim title to a particular trademark, the taxpayer must capitalize any amount paid to the other person for relinquishment of such claim. See, e.g., J.J. Case Company v. United States, 32 F.Supp. 754 (Ct.Cl.1940).

C. Transaction Costs

The IRS and Treasury Department expect to propose a rule that requires a taxpayer to capitalize certain transaction costs that facilitate the taxpayer's acquisition, creation, or enhancement of intangible assets or benefits described above (regardless of whether a payment described in sections A or B of this document is made). In addition, this rule would require a taxpayer to capitalize transaction costs that facilitate the taxpayer's acquisition, creation, restructuring, or reorganization of a business entity, an applicable asset acquisition within the meaning of section 1060(c), or a transaction involving the acquisition of capital, including a stock issuance, borrowing, or recapitalization. However, this rule would not require capitalization of employee compensation (except for bonuses and commissions that are paid with respect to the transaction), fixed overhead (e.g., rent, utilities and depreciation), or costs that do not exceed a specified dollar amount, such as $5,000. The IRS and Treasury Department request comments on how expenditures should be aggregated for purposes of applying the de minimis exception, whether the de minimis exception should allow a deduction for the threshold amount where the aggregate transaction costs exceed the threshold amount, and whether there are certain expenditures for which the de minimis exception should not apply (e.g., commissions).

The IRS and Treasury Department are considering alternative approaches to minimize uncertainty and to ease the administrative burden of accounting for transaction costs. For example, the rules could allow a deduction for all employee compensation (including bonuses and commissions that are paid with respect to the transaction), be based on whether the transaction is regular or recurring, or follow the financial or regulatory accounting treatment of the transaction. The IRS and Treasury Department request comments on whether the recurring or nonrecurring nature of a transaction is an appropriate consideration in determining whether an expenditure to facilitate the transaction must be capitalized under section 263(a) and, if so, what criteria should be applied in distinguishing between recurring and nonrecurring transactions. In addition, the IRS and Treasury Department request comments on whether a taxpayer's treatment of transaction costs for financial or regulatory accounting purposes should be taken into account when developing simplifying assumptions.

For example, under the rule described above, a taxpayer would be required to capitalize legal fees in excess of the threshold dollar amount paid to its outside attorneys for services rendered in drafting a 3–year covenant not to compete because such costs facilitated the creation of the covenant not to compete. Similarly, the rule would require a taxpayer to capitalize legal fees in excess of the threshold dollar amount paid to its outside attorneys for services rendered in defending a trademark owned by the taxpayer.

Conversely, a taxpayer that originates a loan to a borrower in the course of its lending business would not be required to capitalize amounts paid to secure a credit history and property appraisal to facilitate the loan where the total amount paid with respect to that loan does not exceed the threshold dollar amount. The taxpayer also would not be required to capitalize the amount of salaries paid to employees or overhead costs of the taxpayer's loan origination department.

In addition, the rule would require a corporate taxpayer to capitalize legal fees in excess of the threshold dollar amount paid to its outside counsel to facilitate an acquisition of all of the taxpayer's outstanding stock by an acquirer. See, e.g., INDOPCO, Inc. v. Commissioner, 503 U.S. 79 (1992). However, the rule would not require capitalization of the portion of officers' salaries that is allocable to time spent by the officers negotiating the acquisition. Cf. Wells Fargo & Co. v. Commissioner, 224 F.3d 874 (8th Cir.2000).

The rule also would not require capitalization of post-acquisition integration costs or severance payments made to employees as a result of an acquisition transaction because such costs do not facilitate the acquisition.

D.   Other Items on Which Public Comment Is Requested

1.   Other costs of creating, acquiring or enhancing intangible assets or benefits that require capitalization.

The IRS and Treasury Department are considering what general principles of capitalization should be used to identify the costs of acquiring, creating, or enhancing intangible assets or benefits that should be capitalized under section 263(a) but are not described above. The IRS and Treasury Department anticipate that these general principles will apply in rare and unusual circumstances to require capitalization of costs that are similar to those described above. Comments are requested on capitalization principles (for example, a separate and distinct asset test or a significant future benefit test) that can be used to identify other costs that should be capitalized under section 263(a) and the administrability of such principles. The IRS and Treasury Department also request comments on other categories of costs associated with intangible assets or benefits that should be capitalized under section 263(a), but are not described above.

2.   Book–Tax conformity.

The IRS and Treasury Department request comments on whether there are types of expenditures other than those discussed above for which the taxpayer's treatment for financial or regulatory accounting purposes should be taken into account in determining the treatment for federal income tax purposes or to simplify tax reporting.

3.   Amortization periods.

Certain intangibles have readily ascertainable useful lives that can be determined with reasonable accuracy, while others do not. The IRS and Treasury Department expect to provide safe harbor recovery periods and methods for certain capitalized expenditures that do not have readily ascertainable useful lives. Comments are requested regarding whether guidance should provide one uniform period or multiple recovery periods and what the recovery periods and methods should be.

4.   De minimis rules.

The IRS and Treasury Department request comments on whether there are types of expenditures other than those discussed above for which it would be appropriate to prescribe de minimis rules that would not require capitalization under section 263(a). If there are such categories or thresholds, comments are requested on how expenditures would be aggregated in applying these de minimis rules.

5.   Costs of software.

The IRS and Treasury Department request comments on what rules and principles should be used to distinguish acquired software from developed software and the administrability of those rules and principles. See Rev. Proc. 2000–50, 2000–2 C.B. 601.

NOTES

(A) *Theory and Administrability*. As Treasury notes, the post-*INDOPCO* litigation is hard to reconcile and has produced a good deal of uncertainty and controversy. The government was under a good deal of pressure by the business community to put an end to the chaos. In doing so, it eschewed the test suggested by the Supreme Court in *INDOPCO* that would require capitalization of all expenditures providing a future benefit. Instead, it accepted some of the case law (e.g. *Wells Fargo*), deferred to custom (e.g. expensing advertising and the one-year rule), and adopted some rules purely for administrative ease (e.g. expensing all employee compensation and the first $5,000 of many expenses). Theory does not imply expensing the first $5,000 of legal fees in connection with a corporate acquisition and capitalizing the excess. This is a concession to administrability and perhaps the hope that the rules will be accepted by those who must live by them.

(B) *In the Meantime*. The "advance notice of proposed rulemaking" is exactly that—at some point in the future the IRS will issue proposed regulations providing guidance for the capitalization of intangibles. The ANPRM is something like a trial balloon in which Treasury reveals its current thinking on the subject and solicits comments about the future rules. In order to provide more certainty before the regulations are finalized, the IRS subsequently issued a notice announcing a change in its litigating position with respect to *INDOPCO* cases. The Service will no longer assert that certain employee compensation, fixed overhead, or de minimis transaction costs related to the acquisition, creation, or enhancement of intangible assets must be capitalized. The notice also adopts the $5,000 de minimis threshold. This has the result of putting many of the proposed rules into effect immediately.

(C) *The "One–Year" Guidepost.* As the Court notes in *INDOPCO,* the capitalization requirement is in part concerned with accurately matching a taxpayer's income and expenses to measure net income for the relevant period of time. Thus, where an expenditure is expected to produce income over a period of time rather than only in the current year, capitalization, accompanied by a recovery of capital as the income is earned, is thought to reflect each year's income more accurately than immediate deduction of the expenditure.

This is the notion behind a line of cases, of which *INDOPCO* is an example, that deal with expenditures that do not involve the acquisition, construction, or manufacture of a separate asset. Capitalization, nevertheless, is sometimes required if the expenditure is expected to produce benefits beyond the year in which the expenditure occurred. On the other hand, if the economic benefit will be exhausted by the expiration of the current period, immediate deduction results in the proper measure of current net income. This "one-year rule" therefore often is used as a "guidepost" for the ultimate resolution of the essentially factual issue of the relative weight of an expenditure's current benefit as compared to its future value in producing income. For example, in Fall River Gas Appliance Co. v. Commissioner, 349 F.2d 515 (1st Cir.1965), the court required the taxpayer to capitalize the costs of installing gas appliances that it leased to customers. Despite the fact that the leases initially lasted only a year and the appliances could be removed at will, the court found that the expenditure was made "in anticipation of a continuing economic benefit over a period of years." Without any proof on the issue, the court allowed the costs to be recovered through amortization over a twelve-year period.

The one-year cutoff has been a guidepost rather than a rigid rule. As the Ninth Circuit noted in Zaninovich v. Commissioner, 616 F.2d 429 (9th Cir.1980), there is an automatic deduction arm of the rule, but not an automatic capitalization arm. If the expenditure provides a benefit that has a useful life of less than one year, it can be deducted. But if it provides a benefit beyond the taxable year, capitalization may be required, but capitalization is not inevitable. In *Zaninovich* the court allowed deduction in the year paid of an expenditure lasting eleven months beyond the end of the taxable year. In the ANPRM, the IRS proposes to include a version of the one-year rule in regulations, which would make it mandatory rather than a guidepost.

The one-year rule is often blurred with tax accounting requirements, including the rule of § 446(b) that the taxpayer's method of accounting must "clearly reflect income." This rule is considered in the chapter on accounting provisions, Chapter 6.

(D) *The Nonrecurring Expenditure Standard.* In Encyclopaedia Britannica v. Commissioner, 685 F.2d 212 (7th Cir.1982), the taxpayer decided to publish a book, titled The Dictionary of Natural Sciences, which it ordinarily would have prepared in-house. Being temporarily short-handed, however, it hired David–Stewart Publishing Company to do all necessary research work and to prepare, edit, and arrange the manuscript. The contract contemplated that David–Stewart would turn over a complete manuscript that would be copyrighted, published, and sold by Encyclopaedia Britannica and, in exchange, David–Stewart would receive advances against the royalties that Encyclopaedia Britannica expected to earn from the book.

Encyclopaedia Britannica treated these advances as ordinary and necessary business expenses deductible in the years when they were paid, though it had not yet obtained any royalties. The IRS disallowed the deductions, but the Tax Court held that the expenditures were for "services" rather than for the acquisition of an asset and could be deducted immediately. The opinion by Judge Posner, reversing the Tax Court, emphasized the nonrecurring quality of the expenditure although he also referred to the one-year rule as a reason for requiring capitalization:

> The work was intended to yield Encyclopaedia Britannica income over a period of years. The object of sections 162 and 263 of the Code, read together, is to match up expenditures with the income they generate. Where the income is generated over a period of years the expenditures should be classified as capital, contrary to what the Tax Court did here. * * * It would make no difference under this view whether Encyclopaedia Britannica hired David–Stewart as a mere consultant to its editorial board, which is the Tax Court's conception of what happened, or bought outright from David–Stewart the right to a book that David–Stewart had already published. If you hire a carpenter to build a tree house that you plan to rent out, his wage is a capital expenditure to you.

> * * *

> It is also relevant that the commissioning of the manuscript from David–Stewart was somewhat out of the ordinary for Encyclopaedia Britannica. * ** Most of the "ordinary," in the sense of recurring, expenses of a business are noncapital in nature and most of its capital expenditures are extraordinary in the sense of nonrecurring.

> * * *

> If one really takes seriously the concept of a capital expenditure as anything that yields income, actual or imputed, beyond the period (conventionally one year * * *) in which the expenditure is made, the result will be to force the capitalization of virtually every business expense. It is a result courts naturally shy away from. * * * It would require capitalizing every salesman's salary, since his selling activities create goodwill for the company and goodwill is an asset yielding income beyond the year in which the salary expense is incurred. The administrative costs of conceptual rigor are too great. The distinction between recurring and nonrecurring business expenses provides a very

crude but perhaps serviceable demarcation between those capital expenditures that can feasibly be capitalized and those that cannot be.

* * *

[What Encyclopaedia Britannica] was buying was indeed a product, a complete manuscript. This was a turnkey project, remote from what is ordinarily understood by editorial consultation. While maybe some creators or buyers of capital goods * * * may deduct as current expenses what realistically are capital expenditures, they may not do so * * * when the expense is tied to producing or acquiring a specific capital asset.

As the preceding excerpt suggests, nonrecurring expenses are likely to be required to be capitalized. But as the ANPRM suggests, it is sometimes very difficult to determine whether an expense is recurring. The notice suggests that some expenses, such as employee compensation are clearly recurring and would be deductible. Suppose Encyclopaedia Britannica contracted out its books regularly so that the expenses were recurring? Should they be deductible?

(E) *Authors' Expenses.* The *Encyclopaedia Britannica* decision is in sharp contrast to the decision in Hadley v. Commissioner and Garrison v. Commissioner, 819 F.2d 359 (2d Cir.1987), where the court held that writers can deduct in the year paid or incurred expenses of creating literary property. § 263A codified this decision by exempting writers, photographers, and artists from its capitalization requirements. § 263A(h).

The rule provides—for reasons that are difficult to understand, but nevertheless are welcomed, at least by authors—that only expenses incurred by an individual in the trade or business of being a writer, photographer or artist qualify for the exemption. And this individual must either be self-employed or own substantially all the stock of a personal service corporation. See § 263A(h)(2). Congress apparently was concerned that this exception would be construed too broadly, so the statute defines a writer as any individual whose personal efforts create or may reasonably be expected to create a literary manuscript, a musical composition or a dance score. Photographers and artists are similarly defined by reference to the fruits of their personal efforts. Section 263A(h) further indicates that whether an individual is in the trade or business of being an artist is to be determined in part by whether the item created is original and unique, and whether aesthetic or utilitarian values are predominant. Does this limitation serve to disqualify authors of tax coursebooks? Of all coursebooks? Of all tax books? Never mind.

The House Committee Report, by way of example, says that expenses for the production of jewelry, silverware, pottery, furniture, and other household items are not to be considered paid or incurred in the trade or business of being an artist. Expenses related to printing, photographic plates, motion pictures, video tapes, and similar items also are specifically excluded from the benefits of this exemption. Are writers typically poorer than potters? Or simply more worthy?

D.   DEDUCTIBLE REPAIRS VS. NONDEDUCTIBLE REHABILITATION OR IMPROVEMENTS

A frequently disputed issue is whether the expenses of repairing or improving an existing asset must be capitalized or are immediately deductible. In general, expenses associated with preserving assets and keeping them in efficient operating condition are deductible as repairs under §§ 162 or 212, and expenditures for replacement of property or "permanent" improvements made to increase the value or prolong the life of property are capital expenditures, similar to the purchase of a new asset. See Reg. § 1.162–4. Of course any repair increases the value of an unrepaired building and prolongs its life. What the regulations must mean is that the "repair" does not prolong the original expected life of the assets. For example, if the taxpayer purchases a building with a useful life of 30 years, he expects that there will be maintenance costs that will be necessary to actually produce 30 years of productive use.

The IRS has attempted to clarify the distinction between deductible repairs and capital improvements in the following Revenue Ruling.

Revenue Ruling 2001–4

2001–1 C.B. 295.

ISSUE

Are costs incurred by a taxpayer to perform work on its aircraft airframe, including the costs of a "heavy maintenance visit," deductible as ordinary and necessary business expenses under section 162 of the Internal Revenue Code, or must they be capitalized under sections 263 and 263A?

FACTS

X is a commercial airline engaged in the business of transporting passengers and freight throughout the United States and abroad. To conduct its business, X owns or leases various types of aircraft. As a condition of maintaining its operating license and airworthiness certification for these aircraft, X is required by the Federal Aviation Administration ("FAA") to establish and adhere to a continuous maintenance program for each aircraft within its fleet. * * * The maintenance manuals require a variety of periodic maintenance visits at various intervals during the operating lives of each aircraft. The most extensive of these for X is termed a "heavy maintenance visit" * * * which is required to be performed by X approximately every eight years of aircraft operation. The purpose of a heavy maintenance visit, according to X's maintenance manual, is to prevent deterioration of the inherent safety and reliability levels of the aircraft equipment and, if such deterioration occurs, to restore the equipment to their inherent levels. In each of the following three situations, X reasonably anticipated at the time the aircraft was placed in service that the aircraft would be useful in its trade or business for up to 25 years, taking into account the repairs and maintenance necessary to keep the aircraft in an ordinarily efficient operating condition. * * *

Situation 1

In 2000, X incurred $2 million for the labor and materials necessary to perform a heavy maintenance visit on the airframe of Aircraft 1, which X acquired in 1984 for $15 million (excluding the cost of engines). To perform the heavy maintenance visit, X extensively disassembled the airframe, removing items such as its engines, landing gear, cabin and passenger compartment seats, side and ceiling panels, baggage stowage bins, galleys, lavatories, floor boards, cargo loading systems, and flight control surfaces. * * * X then performed certain tasks on the disassembled airframe for the purpose of preventing deterioration of the inherent safety and reliability levels of the airframe. * * *

Whenever the execution of a task revealed cracks, corrosion, excessive wear, or dysfunctional operation, X was required by the maintenance manual to restore the airframe to an acceptable condition. * * *

X also performed additional work as part of the heavy maintenance visit for Aircraft 1. This work included applying corrosion prevention and control compounds; stripping and repainting the aircraft exterior; and cleaning, repairing, and painting airframe interior items such as seats, carpets, baggage stowage bins, ceiling and sidewall panels, lavatories, galleys, and passenger service units. * * *

None of the work performed by X as part of the heavy maintenance visit * * * for Aircraft 1 resulted in a material upgrade or addition to its airframe or involved the replacement of any (or a significant portion of any) major component or substantial structural part of the airframe. This work maintained the relative value of the aircraft. The value of the aircraft declines as it ages even if the heavy maintenance work is performed.

After 45 days, the heavy maintenance visit was completed, and Aircraft 1 was reassembled, tested, and returned to X's fleet. X then continued to use Aircraft 1 for the same purposes and in the same manner that it did prior to the performance of the heavy maintenance visit. The performance of the heavy maintenance visit did not extend the useful life of the airframe beyond the 25–year useful life that X anticipated when it acquired the airframe.

Situation 2

Also in 2000, X incurred costs to perform work in conjunction with a heavy maintenance visit on the airframe of Aircraft 2. The heavy maintenance visit on Aircraft 2 involved all of the same work described in Situation 1. In addition, X found significant wear and corrosion of fuselage skins of Aircraft 2 that necessitated more extensive work than was performed on Aircraft 1. Namely, X decided to remove all of the skin panels on the belly of Aircraft 2's fuselage and replace them with new skin panels. The replaced skin panels represented a significant portion of all of the skin panels of Aircraft 2, and the work performed materially added to the value of the airframe. Because Aircraft 2 was already out of service and its airframe disassembled for the heavy maintenance visit, X also performed certain modifications to the airframe. These modifications involved installing a cabin smoke and fire detection and suppression system, a ground proximity warning system, and an air phone system to enable passengers to send and receive voice calls, faxes, and other electronic data while in flight.

Situation 3

Also in 2000, X decided to make substantial improvements to Aircraft 3, which was 22 years old and nearing the end of its anticipated useful life, for the purpose of increasing its reliability and extending its useful life. X's improvement of Aircraft 3 involved many modifications to the structure, exterior, and interior of the airframe. The modifications included removing all the belly skin panels on the aircraft's fuselage and replacing them with new skin panels; replacing the metal supports under the lavatories and galleys; removing the wiring in the leading edges of both wings and replacing it with new wiring; removing the fuel tank bladders, harnesses, wiring systems, and connectors and replacing them with new components; opening every lap joint on the airframe and replacing the epoxy and rivets used to seal the lap joints with a non-corrosive sealant and larger rivets; reconfiguring and upgrading the avionics and the equipment in the cockpit; replacing all the seats, overhead bins, sidewall panels, partitions, carpeting, windows, galleys, lavatories, and ceiling panels with new items; installing a cabin smoke and fire detection system, and a ground proximity warning system; and painting the exterior of the aircraft. * * *

In order to upgrade the airframe to the desired level, X performed much of the same work that would be performed during a heavy maintenance visit (as described in Situation 1). The result of the work performed on Aircraft 3 was to materially increase the value of the airframe and substantially prolong its useful life.

LAW

Section 162 and section 1.162–1(a) of the Income Tax Regulations allow a deduction for all the ordinary and necessary expenses paid or incurred during the taxable year in carrying on any trade or business, including "incidental repairs."

Section 1.162–4 allows a deduction for the cost of incidental repairs that neither materially add to the value of the property nor appreciably prolong its useful life, but keep it in an ordinarily efficient operating condition. However, section 1.162–4 also provides that the cost of repairs in the nature of replacements that arrest deterioration and appreciably prolong the life of the property must be capitalized and depreciated in accordance with section 167.

Section 263(a) provides that no deduction is allowed for (1) any amount paid out for new buildings or permanent improvements or betterments made to increase the value of any property or estate or (2) any amount expended in restoring property or in making good the exhaustion thereof for which an allowance has been made. See also section 1.263(a)–1(a).

Section 1.263(a)–1(b) provides that capital expenditures include amounts paid or incurred to (1) add to the value, or substantially prolong the useful life, of property owned by the taxpayer, or (2) adapt property to a new or different use. However, that regulation also provides that amounts paid or incurred for incidental repairs and maintenance of property within the meaning of section 162 and section 1.162–4 are not capital expenditures under section 1.263(a)–1.

Section 263A provides that the direct and indirect costs properly allocable to real or tangible personal property produced by the taxpayer must be capitalized. Section 263A(g)(1) provides that, for purposes of section 263A, the term "produce" includes construct, build, install, manufacture, develop, or improve.

The United States Supreme Court has specifically recognized that the "decisive distinctions [between capital and ordinary expenditures] are those of degree and not of kind," and a careful examination of the particular facts of each case is required. *Deputy v. du Pont*, 308 U.S. 488, 496 (1940), quoting *Welch v. Helvering*, 290 U.S. 111, 114 (1933). To determine whether certain costs should be classified as capital expenditures or as repair and maintenance expenses, "it is appropriate to consider the purpose, the physical nature, and the effect of the work for which the expenditures were made." *American Bemberg Corp. v. Commissioner*, 10 T.C. 361, 376 (1948), aff'd, 177 F.2d 200 (6th Cir.1949).

Any properly performed repair, no matter how routine, could be considered to prolong the useful life and increase the value of the property if it is compared with the situation existing immediately prior to that repair. Consequently, courts have articulated a number of ways to distinguish between deductible repairs and non-deductible capital improvements. For example, in *Illinois Merchants Trust Co. v. Commissioner*, 4 B.T.A. 103, 106 (1926), acq., V–2 C.B. 2, the court explained that repair and maintenance expenses are incurred for the purpose of keeping the property in an ordinarily efficient operating condition over its probable useful life for the uses for which the property was acquired. Capital expenditures, in contrast, are for replacements, alterations, improvements, or additions that appreciably prolong the life of the property, materially increase its value, or make it adaptable to a different use. In *Estate of Walling v. Commissioner*, 373 F.2d 190, 192–193 (3d Cir.1967), the court explained that the relevant distinction between capital improvements and repairs is whether the expenditures were made to "put" or "keep" property in ordinary efficient operating condition. In *Plainfield-Union Water Co. v. Commissioner*, 39 T.C. 333, 338 (1962), nonacq. on other grounds, *1964–2 C.B. 8.*, the court stated that if the expenditure merely restores the property to the state it was in before the situation prompting the expenditure arose and does not make the property more valuable, more useful, or longer-lived, then such an expenditure is usually considered a deductible repair. In contrast, a capital expenditure is generally considered to be a more permanent increment in the longevity, utility, or worth of the property. The Supreme Court's decision in *INDOPCO, Inc. v. Commissioner*, 503 U.S. 79 (1992) does not affect these general principles. * * *

Even if the expenditures include the replacement of numerous parts of an asset, if the replacements are a relatively minor portion of the physical structure of the asset, or of any of its major parts, such that the asset as whole has not gained materially in value or useful life, then the costs incurred may be deducted as incidental repairs or maintenance expenses. The same conclusion is true even if such minor portion of the asset is replaced with new and improved materials. * * *

If, however, a major component or a substantial structural part of the asset is replaced and, as a result, the asset as a whole has increased in value, life expectancy, or use then the costs of the replacement must be capitalized. * * *

In addition, although the high cost of the work performed may be considered in determining whether an expenditure is capital in nature, cost alone is not dispositive. * * *

Similarly, the fact that a taxpayer is required by a regulatory authority to make certain repairs or to perform certain maintenance on an asset in order to continue operating the asset in its business does not mean that the work performed materially increases the value of such asset, substantially prolongs its useful life, or adapts it to a new use. * * *

The characterization of any cost as a deductible repair or capital improvement depends on the context in which the cost is incurred. Specifically, where an expenditure is made as part of a general plan of rehabilitation, modernization, and improvement of the property, the expenditure must be capitalized, even though, standing alone, the item may be classified as one of repair or maintenance. *United States v. Wehrli*, 400 F.2d 686, 689 (10th Cir.1968). Whether a general plan of rehabilitation exists, and whether a particular repair or maintenance item is part of it, are questions of fact to be determined based upon all the surrounding facts and circumstances, including, but not limited to, the purpose, nature, extent, and value of the work done. *Id.* at 690. The existence of a written plan, by itself, is not sufficient to trigger the plan of rehabilitation doctrine. See *Moss v. Commissioner*, 831 F.2d 833, 842 (9th Cir.1987). * * *

In general, the courts have applied the plan of rehabilitation doctrine to require a taxpayer to capitalize otherwise deductible repair and maintenance costs where the taxpayer has a plan to make substantial capital improvements to property and the repairs are incidental to that plan. * * *

On the other hand, the courts and the Service have not applied the plan of rehabilitation doctrine to situations where the plan did not include substantial capital improvements and repairs to the same asset, the plan primarily involved repair and maintenance items, or the work was performed merely to keep the property in an ordinarily efficient operating condition. * * *

ANALYSIS

In Situation 1, the heavy maintenance visit on Aircraft 1 primarily involved inspecting, testing, servicing, repairing, reconditioning, cleaning, stripping, and repainting numerous airframe parts and components. The heavy maintenance visit did not involve replacements, alterations, improvements, or additions to the airframe that appreciably prolonged its useful life, materially increased its value, or adapted it to a new or different use. Rather, the heavy maintenance visit merely kept the airframe in an ordinarily efficient operating condition over its anticipated useful life for the uses for which the property was acquired. * * * The fact that the taxpayer was required to perform the heavy maintenance visit to maintain its airworthiness certificate does not affect this determination. * * *

Although the heavy maintenance visit did involve the replacement of numerous airframe parts with new parts, none of these replacements required the substitution of any (or a significant portion of any) major components or substantial structural parts of the airframe so that the airframe as a whole increased in value, life expectancy, or use. * * * Thus, the costs of the heavy maintenance visit constitute expenses for incidental repairs and maintenance under section 1.162–4.

Finally, the costs of the heavy maintenance visit are not required to be capitalized under sections 263 or 263A as part of a plan of rehabilitation, modernization, or improvement to the airframe. Because the heavy maintenance visit involved only repairs for the purpose of keeping the airframe in an ordinarily efficient operating condition, it did not include the type of substantial capital improvements necessary to trigger the plan of rehabilitation doctrine. * * * Accordingly, the costs incurred by X for the heavy maintenance visit in Situation 1 may be deducted as ordinary and necessary business expenses under section 162.

In Situation 2, in addition to performing all of the work described in Situation 1 on Aircraft 2, X replaced all of the skin panels on the belly of the fuselage and installed a cabin smoke and fire detection and suppression system, a ground proximity warning system and an air phone system. Because the replacement of the skin panels involved replacing a significant portion of the airframe's skin panels (which in the aggregate represented a substantial structural part of the airframe) thereby materially adding to the value of and improving the airframe, the cost of replacing the skin panels must be capitalized. * * * In addition, the additions and upgrades to Aircraft 2 in the form of the fire protection, air phone, and ground proximity warning systems must be capitalized because they materially improved the airframe. * * * Accordingly, the costs incurred by X for labor and materials allocable to these capital improvements must be treated as capital expenditures under section 263. * * *

Further, the mere fact that these capital improvements were made at the same time that the work described in Situation 1 was performed on Aircraft 2 does not require capitalization of the cost of the heavy maintenance visit under the plan of rehabilitation doctrine. Whether a general plan of rehabilitation exists is a question of fact to be determined based on all the facts and circumstances. * * * X's plan in Situation 2 was not to rehabilitate Aircraft 2, but merely to perform discrete capital improvements to the airframe. * * * Accordingly, the costs of the work described in Situation 1 are not part of a general plan of rehabilitation, modernization, or improvement to the airframe. The costs incurred by X for the work performed on Aircraft 2 must be allocated between capital improvements, which must be capitalized under sections 263 and 263A, and repairs and maintenance, which may be deducted under section 162.

In Situation 3, X is required to capitalize under section 263 the costs of all the work performed on Aircraft 3. The work in Situation 3 involved replacements of major components and significant portions of substantial structural parts that materially increased the value and substantially prolonged the useful life of the airframe. * * * In addition, the value of Aircraft 3 was materially increased as a result of material additions, alterations and upgrades that enabled X to operate Aircraft 3 in an improved way. * * * In contrast to Situation 1, the extensiveness of the work performed on Aircraft 3 constitutes a restoration within the meaning of section 263(a)(2). * * *

X performed much of the same work on Aircraft 3 that would be performed during a heavy maintenance visit (as described in Situation 1) ("Situation 1—type work"). Although these costs, standing alone, generally are deductible expenses under section 162, in this context, they are incurred as part of a general plan of rehabilitation, modernization, and improvement to the airframe of Aircraft 3 and X is required to capitalize under sections 263 and 263A the costs of that work. * * * In this situation, X planned to perform substantial capital improvements to upgrade the airframe of Aircraft 3 for the purpose of increasing its reliability and extending its useful life. * * * The Situation 1—type work was incidental to X's plan to upgrade Aircraft 3. * * * The effect of all the work performed on Aircraft 3, including the inspection, repair, and maintenance items, is to materially increase the value of the airframe and substantially prolong its useful life. Thus, all the work performed by X on Aircraft 3 is part of a general plan of rehabilitation, modernization, and improvement to the airframe and the costs associated with this work must be capitalized under section 263. * * *

The conclusions in this ruling would be the same whether X transported only freight or only passengers.

NOTES

(A) *Other Cases.* In United States v. Wehrli, 400 F.2d 686 (10th Cir.1968), which is cited in Rev. Rul. 2001–4, the court of appeals required a jury instruction that expenditures that are part of a "general plan of rehabilitation, modernization and improvement of property must be capitalized," even though certain items standing alone would be deductible repair expenses. The court regarded the "one-year rule" as:

> intended to serve as a mere guidepost for the resolution of the ultimate issue, not as an absolute rule requiring the automatic capitalization of every expenditure providing the taxpayer with a benefit enduring for a period in excess of one year. Certainly the expense incurred in the replacement of a broken windowpane, a damaged lock, or a door, or even a periodic repainting of the entire structure, may well be treated as a deductible repair expenditure even though the benefits endure quite beyond the current year.

Contrast Moss v. Commissioner, 831 F.2d 833 (9th Cir.1987), also cited with approval in Rev. Rul. 2001–4. The court permitted the owners of a hotel to deduct a substantial portion of $2 million spent on carpeting, drapes, hotel furnishings, and dining and kitchen furnishings on the grounds that the expenditures were necessary repairs "of the type a hotel must make to remain competitive and in first class condition." The Service relied on *Wehrli* to argue that the expenditures (which were expected to last for three to five years) had to be recovered over the hotel's 30–year useful life because they were part of a plan to remodel the hotel. The court, however, noted that there was neither a plan of total rehabilitation or a structural improvement to the hotel.

In Plainfield–Union Water Co. v. Commissioner, 39 T.C. 333 (1962), the cleaning and cement lining of a water main did not increase the useful life, strength, value or capacity of the main, and therefore were deductible. The Court said the proper time to ask the key question whether the expenditure increased the property's useful life or materially increased its value was immediately prior to the condition that necessitated the repair. The Court stated: "An expenditure which returns property to the state it was in before the situation prompting the expenditure arose, and which does not make the relevant property more valuable, more useful, or longer lived is usually deemed a deductible repair. A capital expenditure is generally considered to be a more permanent increment in the longevity, utility or worth of the property."

In Ingram Industries, Inc. v. Commissioner, 80 T.C.M. 532 (2000), the Tax Court allowed deduction of expenditures of $100,000 each to repair a number of towboat engines. The Court held that capitalization would be required only if the expenditures "(1) adapted the property for a new or materially different use, (2) appreciably prolonged the useful life of the property, or (3) materially added to the value of the property." The Court found that the expenditures did none of these, even though the failure to do the work could have hurt the engines. The engines were not expected to last longer than their originally estimated life of 40 years.

(B) *Environmental Cleanup.* In Rev. Rul. 94–38, 1994–1 C.B. 35, the IRS permitted a taxpayer to deduct costs incurred to clean up hazardous waste attributable to its manufacturing operations. The ruling held that soil remediation expenses need not be capitalized because they merely brought the land back to its state before the contamination. The IRS said the appropriate test was to compare the status of the asset after the expenditure to the status before the condition arose that created the need for the expenditure. In another ruling, the IRS noted that *INDOPCO* does not affect the deduction for incidental repairs "even though they have some future benefit." Rev. Rul. 94–12, 1994–1 C.B. 36. In Rev. Rul. 98–25, 1998–1C.B. 998, costs of removing, cleaning, and disposing of old underground storage tanks and filling and monitoring new underground storage tanks were held to be deductible business expenses under § 162.

The courts have refused to extend the rule in Rev. Rul. 94–38 to cases where the taxpayer purchases contaminated property rather than contaminates the property itself. Dominion Resources Inc. v. United States, 219 F.3d 359 (4th Cir.2000); United Dairy Farmers Inc. v. United States, 267 F.3d 510 (6th Cir.2001). The courts reasoned that deduction was inappropriate in the latter case because the expenses put the property in usable condition as opposed to keeping the property in such condition.

E. EXPENSES THAT INVOLVE BOTH THE PERSONAL–BUSINESS AND CAPITAL–NONCAPITAL BOUNDARIES: JOB–SEEKING AND EDUCATION EXPENSES

1. JOB–SEEKING EXPENSES

Revenue Ruling 75–120
1975–1 C.B. 55.

* * *

[I]t is now the position of the Service that expenses incurred in seeking new employment in the same trade or business are deductible under § 162 of the Code if directly connected with such trade or business as determined by all the objective facts and circumstances.

However, such expenses are not deductible if an individual is seeking employment in a new trade or business even if employment is secured. If the individual is presently unemployed, his trade or business would consist of the services previously performed for his past employer if no substantial lack of continuity occurred between the time of the past employment and the seeking of the new employment. Such expenses are not deductible by an individual where there is a substantial lack of continuity between the time of his past employment and the seeking of new employment, or by an individual seeking employment for the first time. Such expenses are not deductible under section 212(1) of the Code which applies only to expenses incurred with respect to an existing profit-seeking endeavor not qualifying as a trade or business.

NOTES

(A) *New Trade or Business.* What is the rationale for not permitting a deduction when an employee seeks employment in a new trade or business? Is it merely a statutory interpretation question as to the meaning of "carrying on a trade or business" or is there a policy distinction? Drawing this line puts pressure on the definition of a "new" trade or business and results in rather arbitrary distinctions. For example, a corporate executive in the oil industry who incurs costs in looking for a job as an executive in the retailing industry can deduct the costs, but a lawyer who incurs similar costs in looking for a teaching position cannot. In Davis v. Commissioner, 65 T.C. 1014, 1019 (1976), in deciding whether an education expenditure qualified the taxpayer for a "new trade or business," the Tax Court described itself as applying a "commonsense approach":

> If substantial differences exist in the tasks and activities of various occupations or employments, then each such occupation or employment constitutes a separate trade or business.

Why should fees paid to an employment agency by a graduate of Harvard Business School seeking her first job not be deductible? Does § 195 allow the amortization of job-seeking or education expenses for a new trade or business? Should it? In Snell v. Commissioner, 38 T.C.M. 635 (1979), the taxpayer incurred expenses of a nonrefundable entrance fee, deed preparation, and a trip to London for a personal interview to become a member of Lloyd's of London. The Tax Court disallowed the taxpayer's deduction of expenses, but allowed him to amortize them over his life expectancy. The taxpayer's assertion that he intended to resign in seven years was not enough to establish a shorter useful life for the membership. Compare Harman v. Commissioner, 72 T.C. 362 (1979) (initiation fee paid to become a member of the New York Stock Exchange added to the cost basis of the membership, but not amortized).

Job-seeking and education expenses often are linked because both raise the new vs. old business issue. The notes following the next case explore this issue further.

(B) *Expenses of Seeking Public Office.* In McDonald v. Commissioner, 323 U.S. 57 (1944), the court held that a state judge could not deduct assessments that had to be paid to a political party fund if the taxpayer was to obtain the support of the party organization for his election campaign. The court held that if campaign expenditures were to be deductible, the policy should be more clearly stated by Congress. See also Nichols v. Commissioner, 511 F.2d 618 (5th Cir.1975), where the Fifth Circuit, sitting en banc, held that a candidate for judicial office could not deduct a fee enabling him to be placed on a ballot for a primary election. Five judges dissented.

The Tax Court reaffirmed its *McDonald* position in Estate of Rockefeller v. Commissioner, 83 T.C. 368 (1984), where it denied a deduction under § 162 for $550,160 of legal fees and other expenses paid by Nelson Rockefeller in connection with investigations and hearings for his confirmation as Vice President of the United States. The Tax Court rejected the argument that "holding public offices" constitutes a single trade or business and instead viewed the office of Vice President as a "unique position * * * with vastly different tasks, activities, and responsibilities from the offices previously held by Mr. Rockefeller." After denying any deduction for the expenses on the ground that they were incurred in seeking a job in a new business, the court concluded:

> The extent to which tax-deductible dollars are to be spent in attaining nominations and congressional confirmations is a policy issue which should be decided by Congress, not the courts. As the law now stands, the courts have no guidance on where to draw the line. Not until Congress provides that guidance should the courts sanction the allowance of deductions for expenses incurred in attaining public office.

2. EDUCATION EXPENSES

Ruehmann v. Commissioner

United States Tax Court, 1971. 30 T.C.M. 675.

SCOTT, JUDGE. Respondent determined a deficiency in petitioners' income tax for the calendar year 1967 in the amount of $307.17.

The [issue for decision is]:

Whether petitioner is entitled to deduct as ordinary and necessary business expenses [amounts] paid in connection with attending the University of Georgia Law School from January to June 1967 and $1,257 paid in attending Harvard Law School from September through December 1967.

* * *

Albert C. Ruehmann III (hereinafter referred to as petitioner) * * * entered the University of Georgia Law School as a full-time student in September 1964. In 1966, after having completed 2 years of the study of law at the University of Georgia, petitioner took the Georgia Bar examination.[1] On or about December 10, 1966, petitioner was notified that he had passed the Georgia State bar examination and on December 16, 1966, he became a member of the State Bar of Georgia, authorized to practice law in the State of Georgia. In September of 1966 petitioner returned as a third-year student to the University of Georgia Law School. * * *

During the summer of 1966 petitioner was employed in Atlanta, Georgia as a law clerk by the law firm of Kilpatrick, Cody, Rogers, McClatchey and Regenstein (hereinafter referred to as the Kilpatrick Firm). He received a bimonthly salary of $225. Petitioner was again employed by the Kilpatrick Firm during his Christmas vacation from law school in 1966. Petitioner informed the Kilpatrick Firm that he had passed the Georgia Bar Examination and had been admitted to the State of Georgia Bar. Petitioner received a salary for his work during his Christmas vacation on the basis of $270 bimonthly.

In the fall of 1966 petitioner applied for admission to Harvard Law School as a graduate law student working toward his LL.M. degree [and was] accepted as a graduate student at Harvard Law School.

* * *

While attending the University of Georgia Law School as a full-time student during the winter and spring quarters of 1967 petitioner taught a course in business law in a vocational and technical school in Clarke County. He did research work for one of the professors at the University of Georgia and worked as a student assistant librarian at the University of Georgia.

Commencing immediately after receiving his LL.B. degree from the University of Georgia in June 1967 and continuing until the first of September 1967, petitioner was employed by the Kilpatrick Firm. He was employed as a lawyer, paid the same salary as other beginning lawyers who were members of the Bar, and assigned the same type of work that other lawyers of comparable experience in the Kilpatrick Firm were assigned.

* * *

In the fall of 1966 the members of the Kilpatrick Firm agreed that they wished to employ petitioner in 1967 on a full-time basis. * * * It was the custom of the Kilpatrick Firm to offer permanent employment to graduating law students even though the student planned to spend one year in a clerkship or in attending law school as a graduate student as a candidate for an LL.M. degree. * * * However, where an individual had a military obligation which would extend over a period of 2 to 4 years, no definite commitment with respect to employment after completion of that obligation would be made to that individual. However, the Kilpatrick Firm had

---

1. Ga.Code Ann. Sec. 9–103, prior to its amendment in 1966, required only 2 years of law school study for an applicant to be permitted to take the Georgia Bar examination. As amended in 1966 the statute required receipt of an LL.B. degree or its equivalent for a person to be permitted to take the bar examination except that any person who was enrolled in law school when the statute was amended was exempt from the provisions of the amendment.

an understanding with petitioner that if he were required to discharge his military obligation, he could return as an associate with the Kilpatrick Firm when he completed his military service if circumstances had not changed. * * *

Petitioner attended Harvard Law School from September 1967 through June 1968, receiving his LL.M. degree from that school in June 1968. Shortly prior to the time he graduated from Harvard Law School petitioner was notified that he would be called to active duty in the Army within a few months and assigned to the office of the Judge Advocate General of the Department of the Army.

The Kilpatrick Firm has over 40 lawyers and has various individuals assigned in specialized fields of legal work. Petitioner's work with that firm included corporate and commercial law problems, securities problems, insurance problems, and labor law problems. The courses which petitioner took in his graduate work at Harvard Law School were Business Planning, Collective Bargaining, Financial Planning, Creditor's Rights, Insurance, and Securities Regulations.

It was customary for persons who took and passed the Bar examination in the State of Georgia after completing 2 years of law school to complete their third year of school and this was generally expected of students who were to be employed by firms such as the Kilpatrick Firm in Atlanta.

During the calendar year 1967 petitioner was paid a total of $2,100 for his work in the Kilpatrick Firm, $86.40 for teaching the course in Clarke County, $180 for the research work he did for a professor at the University of Georgia and $315.75 for working as an assistant librarian at the University of Georgia. Petitioner did not work during the fall of 1967 other than his work as a student attending graduate classes at Harvard Law School.

In the spring of 1968 petitioner did research for four different law firms in Boston, receiving $410, $122, $350, and $125, respectively, from those firms.

When petitioner received notice at approximately the time he received his LL.M. degree from Harvard Law School that he would have to report in September to discharge his military obligation, he obtained a position for the period between his graduation and September with the law firm of Epstein & Salloway in Boston. He was not admitted to the Bar of the State of Massachusetts when he was employed by this law firm. He was paid $2,705 for his summer's work and in September 1968 he entered the military service as a captain in the office of the Judge Advocate General of the Department of the Army. In this capacity in the Army, he did legal work.

Petitioners on their joint Federal income tax return for the year 1967 claimed a deduction for educational expenses of $2,065, composed of $808 which petitioner expended in attending the University of Georgia Law School from January 1 through June 3, 1967 and $1,257 which petitioner expended in attending Harvard Law School during the period September 15, 1967 to December 31, 1967.

Respondent in his notice of deficiency disallowed this claimed deduction with the explanation that during the year 1967 petitioner was a full-time undergraduate and graduate law student and was not then currently employed or otherwise gainfully engaged in a trade or business within the meaning of section 162(a), I.R.C.1954, and the related regulations and additionally because the expenses were incurred primarily for personal rather than business purposes in that they were incurred in preparing petitioner to enter the legal profession. Respondent further determined that the $808 which petitioner expended at the University of Georgia Law School was not deductible because it was incurred for the purpose of meeting the minimum standards of education generally required by the legal profession.

* * *

Section 162(a) provides for the deduction of ordinary and necessary business expenses. Section 1.162–5, Income Tax Regs., as amended by T.D. 6918, 1967–1 C.B. 36, provides for deductions under the circumstances therein stated of expenses for education. This regulation allows expenditures made by an individual for education to be deducted if the education "maintains or improves skills required by the individual in his employment or other trade or business" unless the expenditures are made for education which is required of the individual in order to meet the minimum educational requirements "for qualification in his employment or other trade or business" or are expenditures made by an individual for education which is "part of a program of study being pursued by him which will lead to qualifying him in a new trade or business."

* * * [F]or the deduction of educational expenses to be allowable, the expense must be an ordinary and necessary business expense. Therefore, this deduction is allowable only to a person who is engaged in a trade or business. In our view petitioner's work while he was a law student at the University of Georgia was secondary to his attendance at law school and did not place him in the trade or business of being a lawyer. * * *

From the facts in this case we have concluded that petitioner's attendance at the University of Georgia Law School from January 1 through June 3, 1967, when he received his LL.B. degree was education generally required of a lawyer to meet the minimum educational requirements for qualification for employment in a law firm of the type by which petitioner was employed in 1967. It is obvious that since petitioner was admitted to the Bar in December 1966, he could have practiced law in the State of Georgia, had he not continued with his law school work until receipt of his LL.B. degree. However, from the testimony in this record, we conclude that the last two quarters of petitioner's work toward his LL.B. degree were a part of a program of study which was being pursued by him which would lead to qualifying him as a lawyer. He had entered the University of Georgia Law School on the 3–year legal program. The final two quarters of that program were required in the program of study he was pursuing leading to receipt of his LL.B. degree. Even though because of the law in Georgia at the time he was able to be admitted to the Bar before actually receiving his LL.B. degree, it was customary for lawyers in Georgia to obtain an LL.B. degree before beginning the practice of law.

We therefore hold that petitioner is not entitled to deduct the $808 spent by him in connection with completing the work for his LL.B. degree in the winter and spring quarters of 1967.

Whether the $1,257 spent by petitioner in attending the graduate law program at Harvard Law School is deductible by petitioner as an educational expense has been narrowed by respondent's concession in his reply brief to the question of whether petitioner "was engaged in the trade or business of practicing law prior to entering Harvard." In his reply brief, respondent makes the following statement in this respect:

> With respect to Albert's LL.M. degree, *respondent concedes that under the 1967 regulations petitioners may deduct these expenses if the Court finds that Albert was engaged in the trade or business of practicing law prior to entering Harvard.* * * * In the instant case, petitioners should be denied the deduction for Albert's LL.M. expenses, not because he is pursuing a specialty, but because he has never engaged in a trade or business. (Underscoring supplied.)

We view respondent's concession to be of more than ordinary significance since it is with respect to his interpretation of his own regulations. We interpret respondent's statement, which we have quoted, to be a concession by respondent that the work taken by petitioner at Harvard Law School did improve the skills required in the practice of law, that this graduate work in law was not necessary to meet the minimum educational requirements of a legal position or the legal profession and was not a program of study in law which qualified petitioner in a new trade or business within the meaning of the new regulations.

We also interpret respondent's reply brief as conceding that if petitioner was engaged in the practice of law prior to entering Harvard Law School as a graduate student, he continued to be engaged in that trade or business while attending graduate school at Harvard. On all the facts in this record and with particular reference to the fact that petitioner was a member of the Bar of Georgia prior to June 1967 and did the same work as other inexperienced lawyers in the firm by which he was employed in the summer of 1967, we conclude that petitioner was engaged in the trade or business of practicing law from June to September 1967. Therefore, in light of respondent's concessions, we hold that petitioner is entitled to deduct the $1,257 he spent in attending Harvard Law School in the fall of 1967.

* * *

NOTES

(A) *The Business–Personal Distinction.* All education involves an element that is personal: knowledge is imparted that may not be directly related to the production of income. The regulations distinguish between education that maintains or improves skills in a trade or business and education that leads to qualification for a new trade or business. How well does that test serve to distinguish between personal and business expenses? Were Ruehmann's Harvard Law School expenses more business-related than his Georgia Law School expenses? Are the former expenses more clearly profit-motivated than the latter? If Ruehmann had not practiced before attending Harvard, his expenses would not have been deductible. Does that make them less business-related? Suppose Ruehmann had practiced only long enough to earn money to go to graduate school? Would it matter if Ruehmann admitted that his principal purpose in attending graduate school at Harvard was to extend his student deferment, which protected him against being drafted to fight in the war in Vietnam? Would the law be better if it tried to take into account motivation or is the Service's new vs. old business test acceptable?

(B) *Capital Expenditure Analysis.* Why should any education expense be immediately deductible even if it is directly related to a trade or business? Education provides a "permanent" benefit lasting beyond the taxable year. The distinction between qualification for a new business and maintenance of skills for an old business corresponds to the requirement that start-up expenses be capitalized. If so, why not capitalize education expenses and amortize them? Over what period of time? When should the recovery of costs begin? What result would be appropriate if the education expense was personal in nature?

(C) *When Does a Trade or Business Begin?* As a technical matter, education expenses are not deductible unless they are "incurred in carrying on" a trade or business. Expenses that are incurred prior to beginning a business or career are not deductible. The level of activity necessary to establish a trade or business is an oft-litigated question. Compare *Ruehmann* with Wassenaar v. Commissioner, 72 T.C. 1195 (1979), where an individual was denied a deduction for the costs of a master's degree program in taxation begun within months of his graduation from law school. Since the taxpayer had held only a summer job during his second summer of law school, the court held he had not begun the practice of law and thus had no trade or business. In Link v. Commissioner, 90 T.C. 460 (1988), aff'd 869 F.2d 1491 (6th Cir.1989), the taxpayer was denied a deduction for the expenses of obtaining an MBA because he had worked for only one summer after graduating from college. Taking a long view and examining the taxpayer's activities since high school, the court found that his employment was a "temporary hiatus between academic endeavors" that was "more in the nature of a sporadic and isolated deviation from his 'career' as a student."

In Ford v. Commissioner, 56 T.C. 1300 (1971), aff'd 487 F.2d 1025 (9th Cir.1973), the taxpayer worked as a substitute teacher before and while pursuing a graduate degree in anthropology. He also taught English, Spanish, and history full-time for one semester. Then he spent a year in Norway during which he studied Norwegian, linguistic analysis, and cultural anthropology. He returned to the United States to become a full-time teacher of high school English and social studies. The court allowed him to deduct the expense of his Norwegian education. The six dissenters argued that the taxpayer had not been carrying on the trade or business of teaching prior to the trip but instead in Norway was pursuing studies for a new trade as an anthropologist. Even granting the taxpayer's teaching status, however, the dissenters maintained that the purpose of the trip was primarily personal rather than to maintain or improve his skills as a teacher.

If the taxpayer were to change from teaching English and social studies in high school to teaching physics, would he remain within the same trade or business? See Reg. § 1.162–5(b)(3)(i) (stating that an employee's change of duties is not a new trade or business).

(D) *Minimum Educational Requirements.* The regulations do not permit a taxpayer to deduct minimum education requirements for "qualification in his employment or other trade or business." Thus, education that qualifies the taxpayer for a new trade or business is not deductible even if the taxpayer never intended or never did enter the new business. Reg. § 1.162–5(b)(2).

In Toner v. Commissioner, 71 T.C. 772 (1979), the taxpayer worked as a teacher in a parochial elementary school. The minimum education required by her employer was a high school diploma, but teachers without a bachelor's degree also were required to earn six hours of college credit each year. Teachers in the public elementary schools generally were required to have a bachelor's degree in order to begin teaching. While teaching, the taxpayer took fifteen college hours, received her degree, and claimed a deduction for the educational expenses. The Tax Court denied the deductions, finding that the degree met the minimum educational requirement "for qualification in his employment" as expressed in the regulations. The seven dissenters argued that the language of the regulation should be controlled by the "requirements of the employer," not the standards of the profession (the public school system). In addition, the dissent argued that teaching in the public schools would not be a new trade or business within the meaning of Reg. § 1.162–5(b)(3). The Third Circuit reversed under reasoning similar to the Tax Court dissents. Toner v. Commissioner, 623 F.2d 315 (3d Cir.1980).

The courts and the Service have had a great deal of difficulty determining what is a new trade or business. Lawyers have not fared well. See, e.g., Sharon v. Commissioner, 66 T.C. 515 (1976), aff'd 591 F.2d 1273 (9th Cir.1978), cert. denied 442 U.S. 941 (1979) (New York attorney could not deduct the expenses incurred in studying for and taking the California bar exam because the practice of law in California was a new business, but the expenses could be amortized over his life expectancy); Rev.Rul. 75–412, 1975–2 C.B. 62 (the holder of a foreign law degree cannot deduct a law school course necessary to take a state bar exam because it would enable him to become a U.S. lawyer); Johnson v. United States, 332 F.Supp. 906 (E.D.La.1971) (lawyer could not deduct the expense of attending graduate school to obtain an LL.M. in taxation because it prepared him for a new business, i.e. being a tax lawyer); O'Donnell v. Commissioner, 62 T.C. 781 (1974), aff'd 519 F.2d 1406 (7th Cir.1975) (CPA could not deduct costs of attending law school even though he was already in the business of being a "tax accounting professional").

On the other hand, the cost of an MBA is often deductible because the degree is not the minimum requirement for any particular profession and thus a recipient is not qualified for a new trade or business. See, e.g., Beatty v. Commissioner, 40 T.C.M. 438 (1980) (engineer whose duties involved management, interpersonal, and administrative skills could deduct expense of obtaining an MBA). This line drawing is often quite arbitrary. Compare *Sharon* and Robinson v. Commissioner, 78 T.C. 550 (1982) (licensed practical nurse cannot deduct the cost of nursing school that will qualify her to be a registered nurse), with Rev.Rul. 71–58, 1971–1 C.B. 55 (a teacher in one state may deduct the cost of courses necessary to qualify to teach in another state) and Reg. § 1.162–5(b)(3) (Ex. 4) (psychiatrist may deduct the cost of study at a psychoanalytic institute that will qualify him to practice psychoanalysis).

(D) *General Self–Improvement.* Although all education has aspects of general self-improvement, in some cases that aspect is so predominant that a deduction is denied. Generally, the costs of obtaining an undergraduate degree or taking "college" courses is not deductible, in part because it is the minimum education requirement for so many businesses, but also because there is a large personal consumption element that would be helpful to any trade or business. But see Glasgow v. Commissioner, 31 T.C.M. 310 (1972), aff'd 486 F.2d 1045 (10th Cir.1973), in which a Baptist minister was allowed to deduct the cost of obtaining a college degree. The court found that the study for this degree maintained skills—such as public speaking, English, drama, accounting, psychology, history, and education—that are required for a pastor to carry out his varied duties effectively.

In Love Box Co. v. Commissioner, 842 F.2d 1213 (10th Cir.1988), cert. denied 488 U.S. 820 (1988), a divided panel of the Tenth Circuit affirmed the Tax Court's disallowance of deductions for a company's expenses in connection with a series of seminars the company held to educate its employees with respect to the virtues of the free-enterprise system. The court regarded the five-day seminars as likely to contribute to the employees being more "trustworthy" and "reliable," but, nevertheless, held that the seminar expenses were not deductible as ordinary and necessary education expenses of employees because they did not maintain or improve the job skills of the employees in a way that directly contributed to the company's wood and fiberboard business. The court regarded these expenses as analogous to nondeductible expenses for general education. The court also held that the seminar expenses were not deductible as ordinary and necessary advertising expenses because the company failed to meet its burden of showing a direct relationship between the seminar's focus upon individual character development and the solicitation of new customers.

(E) *Travel Expenses.* Although travel expenses in connection with otherwise deductible education are themselves deductible, there is no deduction for travel as education. § 274(m)(2). Thus, although traveling in Europe visiting art museums may improve the skills of an art history teacher, the travel is not deductible.

(F) *Employer Subsidies.* An employee whose education costs are subsidized through an educational assistance program has no gross income even if he would not have been able to deduct the costs if he has paid it himself. Section 127 permits an employee to exclude reimbursement of undergraduate or graduate school expenses paid by his employer. Only $5,250 may be excluded each taxable year. Reg. § 1.162–5 is designed to distinguish between the costs of producing income and personal consumption. Section 127 is a tax expenditure designed to subsidize the cost of education.

(G) *General Education Deduction.* A taxpayer may deduct up to $3,000 for college tuition and related expenses for himself, a spouse or a dependent. § 222. Taxpayers whose adjusted gross income exceeds $65,000 (or $130,000 if married filing jointly) are not eligible to take a deduction and neither are students who are claimed as dependents on their parents' return. In 2004 and 2005 up to $4,000 of education expenses may be deducted up to those income levels and $2,000 may be deducted by people with AGI between $65,000 and $80,000 ($130,000 and $160,000 respectively in the case of taxpayers who are married filing jointly). No deduction is allowed for married couples filing separately. This provision terminates in 2006.

Unlike the deduction for education expenses under § 162, discussed above, this education does not need to be business-related. In order to prevent a double benefit, this deduction must be coordinated with other education benefits, discussed infra at page 434. For example, if a taxpayer elects to take a Hope Credit, she cannot deduct education expenses. Because the amount of the benefit and the phase-out ranges are not identical, taxpayers must calculate the benefits under the various educational provisions before determining which to use.

Section 222 is a particularly egregious example of a "cliff effect." A taxpayer who has $64,999 of AGI can deduct $3,000 of education expenses whereas a taxpayer with an AGI of $65,000 can deduct zero. Better watch out for that last dollar of income.

F.   OPTION TO DEDUCT OR CAPITALIZE

In a number of situations, Congress has given the taxpayer the option of deducting items otherwise required to be capitalized or capitalizing items otherwise deductible. Current examples where deduction is permitted include:

Circulation Expenses. Under § 173, expenses to establish, maintain or increase the circulation of a newspaper, magazine or other periodical are deductible. The expenses may, however, be capitalized and amortized over a three-year period at the election of the taxpayer.

Research and Experimental Expenditures. Section 174 allows research and experimental expenditures (except those for land or depreciable property) to be deducted immediately, to be capitalized, or to be deducted over a period of five years. See also § 59(e) permitting 10–year amortization and § 41 which provides a 20 percent tax credit for increases in research and experimental expenditures.

Soil and Water Conservation Expenditures. Section 175 allows farmers to deduct certain expenditures of a limited amount of depreciable tangible personal property for soil and water conservation.

Qualified Clean Fuel Vehicles. Section 179A permits taxpayers to elect to deduct a portion of the costs of a qualified clean fuel motor vehicle (such as an electric car) even if the vehicle is not used in a trade or business.

Expenditures by Farmers for Fertilizer. Under § 180 farmers may deduct expenditures for fertilizer or other materials to enrich, neutralize or condition land.

Option to Deduct Costs of Removing Architectural and Transportation Barriers for the Handicapped and Elderly. Section 190 allows taxpayers to elect to deduct currently up to $15,000 per year of expenditures for making any facility or public transportation vehicle used in a trade or business more usable by handicapped and elderly people.

A taxpayer who is likely to have no income against which to take a deduction would prefer to capitalize rather than deduct expenses that otherwise would be deductible. Section 266, for example, permits a taxpayer to capitalize otherwise deductible interest, taxes, and carrying charges with respect to property.

Why might Congress permit a taxpayer to deduct an item that otherwise would be capitalized? Should the decision whether expenses will be capitalized or immediately deducted be left to the taxpayer? What results would you expect from allowing taxpayers to determine whether various expenditures should be capitalized or deducted? The decision to deduct rather than capitalize produces, at a minimum, a deferral of tax that otherwise would be paid currently. How would the availability of a capital gains preference on the sale of the asset affect your decision whether to provide an option to deduct currently expenses that ordinarily would be capitalized?

SECTION 4.   RECOVERY OF CAPITAL EXPENDITURES

The prior Section of this Chapter focused primarily on the distinction between immediate deduction and capitalization. We now consider in detail the principal mechanisms for recovery of capitalized expenditures over a number of years: depreciation, amortization, and depletion. The following materials illustrate that the precise timing of such deductions has varied dramatically from time to time and with the kind of asset at issue. This Section also considers the role of several special tax credits available to businesses. Historically, the most important of these has been the investment tax credit, in effect from time to time in various forms from 1962 to 1986.

A.   DEPRECIATION

NOTE ON DEPRECIATION

An allowance for depreciation has been a part of the tax law since 1909. With the exception of salaries, depreciation has long been the largest single amount of deduction on corporate tax returns. The history of the annual depreciation allowance has been marked by frequent change and considerable controversy.

Section 167 of the Code permits as a depreciation deduction a "reasonable allowance for the exhaustion, wear and tear (including a reasonable allowance for obsolescence)'' of assets used in a trade or business or held for the production of income.

Section 168 provides a mandatory system of depreciation (the Modified Accelerated Cost Recovery System or "MACRS") for tangible personal property and real property placed in service in 1981 and subsequent years. Taxpayers who have assets dating from before 1981 will use a different depreciation system for those assets. Section 167 provides that, for assets placed in service in 1981 or later, the depreciation allowance of § 168 shall be the only "reasonable allowance" for property described in that section. The rules of section 168 were substantially modified in 1986. In addition, the calculation of depreciation on various assets for purposes of the alternative minimum tax (discussed in Chapter 7) is performed in yet a different manner. Many taxpayers therefore have to contend with at least three depreciation systems.

The depreciation deduction allows taxpayers to deduct in determining taxable income an allocable part of the cost of business or investment assets that have a limited life. No depreciation allowance is provided for assets acquired for personal use, since to do so would undermine the prohibition against the deduction of personal expenses. A taxpayer is allowed to deduct from income each year ("expense") regularly recurring business or income-producing expenditures such as repairs, consumable supplies, heat, electricity, and salaries and wages. The cost of a machine is also an expense of doing business that must be deducted from gross income if the taxpayer is to recover its capital investment. Since the machine has a life that extends over a period of years, however, its cost must be capitalized and recovered over a number of years.

An allocation of costs to the related income is essential to the clear reflection of income. The cost of the machine cannot be deducted entirely in the year of acquisition because that would understate income for that year. Neither can the deduction of the cost be spread over too long a period because income then would be overstated during the actual productive life of the machine. The depreciation deduction is intended to allocate the cost of the machine over the proper period of time.

Economic Depreciation. It has been demonstrated that "economic depreciation"—which would allow deduction for the actual decline in an asset's value during the taxable period—would provide "appropriate" results under an income tax. Such a depreciation system would more properly measure net economic income for the period and would impose an effective rate of tax equal to the statutory rate for all assets. Economic depreciation would not distort taxpayers' choices among assets to be used in the production of income; taxpayers would acquire the same assets under an income tax as they would in the absence of an income tax.* Thus, economic depreciation can serve as a useful analytical benchmark to assess actual income tax rules.

The income tax, however, has never attempted to measure economic depreciation directly. Such measurement would be impossible as a practical

---

* This result was demonstrated in Paul Samuelson, "Tax Deductibility of Economic Depreciation to Insure Invariant Valuations," 72 J. Pol. Econ. 604 (1964).

matter because of the need to measure annually the change in value of a massive number of business and investment assets. Such an annual valuation also would conflict with the realization requirement, which generally ignores annual changes in asset values. For administrative reasons, Congress and the IRS have long endeavored to establish a single depreciation schedule to be used when an asset is first placed in service and followed throughout its useful life. Finally, depreciation allowances often have been used not to just measure income, but also as a subsidy to affect the overall level of investment in plant and equipment for fiscal and economic policy reasons.

Income Tax Rules. The annual depreciation allowance is applied to the *depreciable base.* This is usually the property's basis, which is determined under § 1011. Basis is often cost, but as discussed supra at page 136, other rules sometimes apply. The depreciable base includes any capital expenditures, which have been added to basis under § 1016. The basis is reduced periodically by the amount of allowable depreciation. The result, referred to as adjusted basis, thus reflects the recovery of the taxpayer's capital investment over time. Depreciation deductions increase the gain or decrease the loss realized by the taxpayer on disposition.

The depreciation allowance depends on the depreciation *rate.* This rate is a function of both the *method* of depreciation and of the depreciation period, which generally is referred to as the *recovery period.* The recovery method may be a function of the asset's "useful life" or it may not be.

The simplest method of allocating the cost of an asset over the recovery period is the *straight line method.* Under this method, the cost of an asset is allocated in equal amounts over its useful life. The straight line rate is the reciprocal of the useful life; for example, a 10-year life produces a straight line rate of 10 percent (⅒). Thus, a $100 asset with an estimated five-year life would be depreciated under the straight line method at the rate of 20 percent or $20 in each of the five years.

The *declining balance method* allocates a larger portion of the cost to the earlier years and a lesser portion to the later years. Under this method, a constant percentage is used, but it is applied each year to the amount remaining after the depreciation of previous years has been charged off. The double declining balance method (so named, because it uses double the straight line rate) would depreciate a $100 five-year asset in amounts of $40 in the first year (twice 20 percent, or 40 percent × $100), $24 in the second year (40 percent × the balance of $60), $14.40 in the third year (40 percent × the balance of $36), and so on. Methods, like the declining balance method that result in larger depreciation charges in the earlier years, are often referred to as accelerated depreciation.

Determining the recovery period or useful life of an asset is necessarily an estimate or a prognostication of the period of time during which the asset will be economically productive. For administrative reasons, this estimate of useful life must be made when the asset is placed in service and, therefore, must take into account future events that are often unpredictable. These include engineering and economic factors, technological developments in the industry, future market conditions, and other variables. Over the years, a number of methods have been used to make such estimates. One method looks to a variety of facts and circumstances, but relies heavily on evidence of the length of time that similar assets have been used by the taxpayer. Another method looks to the average length of time that similar assets have been used throughout the economy. Yet another method estimates useful life based upon industry-wide experiences.

The *salvage value* of an asset is the amount the taxpayer would expect to recover when he stops using the asset for the production of income. Theoretically, the portion of the taxpayer's cost allocable to salvage value should not be depreciated. This, however, requires an estimate of salvage value when an asset is first placed in service, even if the asset is expected to be used in the business for many years. Frequent controversies about the amount of salvage value have led Congress to ignore salvage value limitations and permit the entire cost of an asset to be depreciated or to assume an arbitrary amount of salvage value.

Brief History of Depreciation. Until the early 1960's, most assets were depreciated using the straight line method. For more than 20 years after the introduction of the corporate tax in 1909, taxpayers generally were free to determine the useful lives of their assets. This changed, however, as a result of the wrongheaded desire to raise revenue during the Depression. In 1934, the Treasury Department shifted the burden of proof as to depreciable lives to the taxpayer. Thereafter, useful life was determined largely by reference to standardized lives prescribed by the IRS. The taxpayer had a heavy burden of proof to sustain any shorter life on individual assets and there was frequent controversy as to proper depreciation allowances.

In 1954, Congress authorized the use of the double declining balance method of depreciation as well as certain other forms of accelerated depreciation. In 1962, the Service produced a fundamental change in the means of determining useful lives by promulgating a list of guideline lives for 75 broad classes of assets, mostly based on the industries in which the assets were used. Under this procedure, taxpayers were advised that they would not be challenged as long as their total depreciation deductions for all assets within a particular class did not exceed the total that would be obtained by aggregating the guideline lives of each asset in that class. These lives, which were shorter than those previously used, were meant to simplify depreciation accounting and to provide a stimulus for investment. The new procedure abandoned the asset-by-asset approach that had required a particularized determination of the useful life of each item of depreciable property. Broad industrial categories were given a single guideline life. In 1971, Congress approved an Asset Depreciation Range (ADR) system that allowed taxpayers to select useful lives from a range, generally 20 percent above or below the guideline lives.

In 1981, Congress substantially altered the depreciation rules. Finding that the real value of depreciation allowances had been eroded by inflation and wanting to stimulate capital formation through the tax system (especially investment in equipment and real estate), Congress adopted the Accelerated Cost Recovery System ("ACRS"). This system provided for the recovery of capital costs over specified periods that generally were far shorter than the useful lives of prior law. For example, the cost of eligible personal property was recovered over a 15–year, ten-year, five-year or three-year period, depending on the type of property. Most eligible personal property was in the five-year class. Eligible real property was originally in a separate 15–year real property class but, in 1984, the depreciation period for most real property was extended to 18 years. Longer recovery periods were provided as an option to allow taxpayers a certain amount of flexibility. The ACRS system eliminated the salvage value limitations of prior law and allowed recovery of the entire cost or other basis of eligible property. In general, the annual ACRS depreciation deduction was determined by applying a percentage set forth in the statute to the unadjusted basis of the property. The applicable percentage to be applied each year to the property's unadjusted basis depended on the property's class and the number of years since the year in which the taxpayer placed the property in service. The schedule that was generally in effect was constructed to approximate the benefits of a 150 percent declining balance method for the early years and the straight line method for the later years. For real property, the statute provided for a table in accordance with the use of a 175 percent declining balance schedule.

Current Rules. Under the current system, which came into effect in 1986, the Modified Accelerated Cost Recovery System, "MACRS," depreciable assets are assigned to recovery classes. There are eight classes with class lives from three years to 39 years. For example, most personal property with a guideline class life of more than four years but less than 10 years is depreciated over a five-year recovery period. Residential rental property is in the 27.5 year class, and commercial real property is in the 39 year class.

MACRS prescribes one of three depreciation methods for each class of property. Property in the three-, five-, seven-, and ten-year classes is depreciated using the 200 percent declining balance method. The taxpayer switches to a straight line method that allocates the cost ratably over the remaining recovery period in the year in which that method produces a larger deduction. § 168(b)(1). Property in the 15– and 20–year classes is depreciated using the 150 percent declining balance method, with a switch to the straight line method in the year that straight line recovery produces a larger deduction. § 168(b)(2). This permits a full recovery of basis. Straight line depreciation must be used for real estate. § 168(b)(3). The taxpayer may elect to use the straight line method for any class of property. § 168(b)(3)(C) and (b)(5). In all cases, salvage value is not taken into account. § 168(b)(4).

Because property is seldom purchased on the first day of the year or disposed of on the last day of the year, some rule must be adopted to determine the depreciation allowance when the property is not used for the entire year. For personal property, a half-year convention is used, meaning that one-half year's depreciation is allowed in both the year of acquisition and the year of disposition, regardless of how long the taxpayer actually held the property. Thus, if the taxpayer, for example, purchased a machine on September 20, he would take one-half of the total depreciation allowance for the year of purchase. § 168(d)(1). Obviously, there is an advantage to purchasing property late in the year. Where the taxpayer purchases a significant amount of depreciable property in the last quarter, a mid-quarter convention applies, meaning the property is deemed to have been purchased at the midpoint of the quarter. § 168(d)(3). For real property, a mid-month convention is used, meaning the taxpayer takes one-half a month's depreciation for the month of acquisition and disposition. If real property was placed in service on October 20, the taxpayer would take a depreciation allowance for 2½ months of the first year. § 168(d)(2).

Section 179 permits a taxpayer to elect to deduct immediately $24,000 of the cost of certain tangible business property where the taxpayer's annual total investment in qualified property is $200,000 or less. The amount that can be expensed increases to $25,000 in 2003. Any additional amount is subject to the usual depreciation rules. This deduction is phased out dollar for dollar for taxpayers who place in service more than $200,000 of such property in any one taxable year. The effect is to permit many small businesses to deduct the cost of business assets rather than to capitalize them. Congress justified this as a subsidy for small business. Recall the earlier note on the benefits of tax deferral that explains why this is a subsidy.

To assist in the economic recovery following the September 11 terrorist attacks, in 2002 Congress adopted an additional depreciation incentive. In addition to the deduction provided by § 179, a taxpayer can take a first-year depreciation deduction equal to 30 percent of the basis of certain property. Eligible property includes property eligible for MACRS with a recovery period of 20 years or less and certain computer software. To spur investment, the original use of the property must commence with the taxpayer after September 11, 2001. Thus, used property is not eligible. This provision expires on September 11, 2004. Suppose, for example, that a business owner purchases property with a five-year recovery period in 2003 for $100,000. In 2003, he would be entitled to a § 179 deduction of $25,000 and an additional first-year depreciation deduction of $22,500 (30% x $75,000). He would also be entitled to MACRS depreciation, using a depreciation basis of $52,500 ($100,000–$25,000–$22,500). Since his first-year MACRS deduction will be $11,000, he will have written off more than one-half of his cost in the first year alone.

Amortization of Intangibles. Historically, when a taxpayer purchased a business, the portion of the purchase price allocated to goodwill was not depreciable. Taxpayers often argued that, in fact, they had purchased other intangible assets with a determinable useful life that could be depreciated. Examples included customer or subscriber lists, a trained workforce in place, and "core deposits" of financial institutions. The cases often turned on costly expert evidence that a particular intangible had a value independent of goodwill and a limited useful life. The cases were often battles of experts on either side. In Newark Morning Ledger v. United States, 507 U.S. 546 (1993), the Supreme Court allowed amortization of a newspaper's list of subscribers, holding that if a taxpayer could prove that an asset could be valued and that the asset had a limited useful life that could be ascertained with reasonable accuracy, the taxpayer may depreciate the value over the useful life even if the asset seems to reflect the expectancy of continued patronage usually associated with goodwill. Because the Court also noted, however, that the taxpayer's burden of proof "often will prove too great to bear," controversy over the treatment of intangible assets was expected to continue.

Congress struck a blow for certainty by adopting rules to account for the cost of intangibles. In general, under § 197, most intangibles, including goodwill, are amortized on a straight line basis over a 15–year period. This is something of a "rough justice" approach, sacrificing any attempt at accuracy for simplicity. Many intangibles will be amortized over a period that is either longer or shorter than their actual useful lives. But the former controversy ended. There is no longer any incentive to try to distinguish goodwill from other assets since both are now amortizable. Furthermore, there is no longer a need to determine (and ultimately litigate) the useful life of an asset since § 197 arbitrarily assigns a uniform useful life to intangibles.

Section 197 is very broad. In addition to goodwill, it applies to acquired intangibles such as going concern value, workforce in place, information base, know how, customer lists, government licenses, covenants not to compete, franchises, and trademarks. Section 197, however, does not apply to any intangible created by the taxpayer unless it was created in connection with the acquisition of a trade or business.

Although this provision has resulted in much simplification in practice, § 197 itself is not simple. In addition to very complex rules defining a "section 197 intangible," there are complicated provisions dealing with the disposition of such an intangible before the recovery period expires, the acquisition of intangibles in nonrecognition transactions, the holding of intangibles in a pass-through entity, such as a partnership, and an election to apply the provision retroactively. Like the passive loss rules of § 469, § 197 is a good example of rule complexity coupled with transactional simplicity. That is, although § 197 appears on its face to be quite complex (an idea easily confirmed by quickly perusing it), it contributes to overall simplification by eliminating much transactional planning and litigation.

Start-Up Expenses. As previously discussed, a taxpayer may elect under § 195 to amortize start-up expenses in connection with a trade or business over a five-year period.

Organizational Expenses. Section 248 permits a corporation to elect to amortize organizational expenses over a five-year period.

NOTES

(A) *Recapture.* Current depreciation rules often provide a write-off of cost that exceeds economic depreciation (the actual decline in value). For example, suppose the taxpayer purchases an asset for $1,000, deducts $300 of depreciation and sells the asset for $800. The taxpayer's adjusted basis is $700 and he will report $100 of gain, which represents the $100 in depreciation that exceeded the asset's actual $200 decline in value. Although, after taking the gain into account, the total amount of deductions equals the asset's economic depreciation, the taxpayer has enjoyed the time value of money, via taking depreciation in an earlier year and "paying it back" in a later year. Sections 1245 and 1250 provide that certain amounts previously deducted as depreciation will be "recaptured" as ordinary income rather than characterized as capital gain when depreciable property is sold. These provisions are treated in connection with the material on capital gains, infra in Chapter 5.

(B) *Property for Personal Use.* Section 167 permits depreciation only for assets used in a trade or business or an income producing activity. Thus, there is no depreciation for property used for personal purposes. If an item is used for both personal and income producing purposes (for example, renting out a floor of a personal residence or using   car for both business and personal purposes), the property's basis must be allocated between the business and personal uses. If personal use property is converted to business use, the basis for depreciation is the lesser of the fair market value of the property at the date of conversion or the property's adjusted basis. Reg. § 1.167(g)–1.

(C) *Land.* Land is not depreciable. Reg. § 1.167(a)–2. Buildings, however, are subject to depreciation. When land and buildings are bought together, as they often are, the purchase price (or other basis) must be allocated between land and buildings in proportion to their respective fair market values. Two justifications typically are offered for disallowing depreciation for the cost of land. The first is that land does not wear out or become obsolete. The second—which seems simply a different way of saying that land does not wear out—is that land has "no ascertainable useful life."

(D) *Antiques.* The IRS has taken the position that antiques are not depreciable because they do not have a determinable useful life defined by the physical condition of the art work. Rev.Rul. 68–232, 1968–1 C.B. 79. Thus, a professional musician who acquired a Stradivarius violin for performances would be unable to offset depreciation against his income. See Browning v. Commissioner, 890 F.2d 1084 (9th Cir.1989) where the court found it impossible to believe that a 200–year old violin had a remaining useful life of 12 years.

In striking contrast is Simon v. Commissioner, 103 T.C. 247 (1994). The court permitted the taxpayers—professional musicians—to depreciate two 19th century Tourte violin bows that they had purchased for $30,000 and $21,500. The court accepted evidence that the bows can suffer wear and tear and that they would become "unplayable" with use. The IRS argued that the bows, which were 175 years old at the time of purchase, had no ascertainable useful life. The court rejected the argument, explaining that useful life was irrelevant under current law. Under § 168, to be depreciable, property must be "recovery property," which means that the "property must be of a character subject to an allowance for depreciation." The court defined that to mean that it must "suffer exhaustion, wear and tear or obsolescence." Furthermore, the court pointed out that the useful life of the bows as playable instruments was limited.

In response to evidence the bows had appreciated in value substantially since purchased, the court stated that:

> depreciation accounting reflects the daily diminution in value of the underlying asset through other than market conditions. Accounting for changes in the values of depreciable property because of market

conditions, on the other hand, is reportable as gain or loss upon the sale of the depreciable asset.

One dissent took the position that the taxpayer had no "cost" in holding the bows because they were not wasting assets and retained their value. Another dissent thought both positions were wrong in that the bows had an intrinsic value and the issue was the effect of the wear and tear on that value. In explaining why a portion of the taxpayer's cost should be deductible, Judge Gerber gave the following example:

> [A]ssume that Elvis Presley had purchased a guitar for $1,000. Due to his fame, however, the value of the guitar immediately increases to $11,000. If Elvis Presley had used the guitar in his business, he would have been entitled to depreciate the $1,000 amount. * * * If, however, another musician purchases Elvis' guitar for $11,000, the portion of the guitar which would be subject to wear and tear * * * would be about $1,000, more or less, depending upon how much Elvis had used it and/or the cost of a similar quality guitar at the time of purchase. The fact that it had been Elvis' guitar will sustain a premium value which is attributable to the guitar's intrinsic collector's value. Even if Elvis's guitar became unusable for commercial purposes, collectors would be willing to pay for the intrinsic value because it had belonged to Elvis. * * * That intrinsic value could be affected by wear and tear, but the wear and tear will not necessarily eliminate the intrinsic value. Accordingly, under section 167 the remaining value would be the equivalent of "salvage value."

Is Judge Gerber correct? Suppose another rock musician purchased Elvis' guitar and played it daily for one year, slamming it on the floor at the end of each concert. At the end of the year, the damaged guitar could no longer be used to produce music and the rock musician was forced to buy another guitar. The instrument retained value, however, because it was still "Elvis' guitar." Should the rock star have a deduction? Does the logic of *Simon* apply only to assets that can be "used up" or subject to "wear and tear" through physical use? Suppose, for example, a business buys a collectible painting to hang on a wall. Should the business be allowed any deduction for depreciation?

Simon was affirmed by the Second Circuit. 68 F.3d 41 (2d Cir.1995). The Third Circuit, in a related case, permitted the owner of a valuable bass violin to take depreciation deductions because the violin suffered wear and tear making it no longer usable, although it had increased in value. Liddle v. Commissioner, 65 F.3d 329 (3d Cir.1995).

The Second Circuit answered the question concerning the painting as follows:

> For example, paintings that hang on the wall of a law firm merely to be looked at—to please connoisseur clients or to give the appearance of dignity to combative professionals—do not generally suffer wear or tear. More to the point, the Simons' Tourte bows were playable for a time precisely because they had been kept in a private collection and were relatively unused since their manufacture. Indeed, it appears that one had never been played at all. Had that collection been displayed at

a for-profit museum, the museum could not have depreciated the bows * * * because, although the bows were being used in a trade or business, they were not subject to wear and tear.

(E) *Investment Tax Credit.* At various times, Congress has adopted a credit against tax of a fixed percentage (typically seven to ten percent) of the cost of depreciable personal property purchased or constructed by the taxpayer. The credit was first adopted in 1962 to stimulate purchases of new machinery and equipment and has been utilized from time to time as an instrument of fiscal policy. Although Congress most recently repealed the credit in 1986, proposals to resurrect it keep resurfacing.

The investment tax credit has been both complex and controversial. Proponents regard the credit as an effective stimulus to business investment, which they believe provides more economic bang for the buck than alternative forms of business tax reduction. In contrast to a general reduction in corporate tax rates, for example, the investment tax credit can be limited to property newly placed in service or even to particular types of investments. Detractors focus primarily on the fact that the credit is available only for limited categories of investment—principally business equipment—and therefore induces a shift away from other sectors of the economy where the cost of investing is not subsidized. Empirical evidence suggests that the principal effect of the credit has been on the timing, not the level, of investment in equipment, but this may well be due to its frequent on-and-off history. A more general complaint is that the credit favors capital-intensive over labor-intensive industries.

(F) *Need for an Ownership Interest.* Only an owner of property who has a capital investment is entitled to depreciation deductions; the owner is thought to be the one who enjoys the economic benefits of ownership and bears the economic burden of the decline in value. Recall *Estate of Franklin*, supra at page 198 in which the court determined that the putative owners had no real economic investment in the property. The practical effect of the decision was to deny depreciation deductions to the taxpayers.

(G) *Depreciation as a Subsidy.* As noted previously, if the goal of the tax system is to accurately measure net income, then only economic depreciation, based on the annual change in an asset's value, is accurate. An allowance greater than economic depreciation understates income and one less overstates income. But economic depreciation is not practical and Congress may also have other goals in mind, intentionally choosing to overstate depreciation (and thus understate income) in order to provide an incentive for certain activities.

There are a number of ways to overstate depreciation, all of which have been used at some point in the history of the income tax. First, allowing a taxpayer to expense an asset that otherwise would be capitalized clearly understates income. Section 179 is one such example. Second, Congress may permit the taxpayer to write off more than actual cost. Under prior law, when an investment tax credit was available for a percentage of the purchase price of an asset, the combination of the credit and depreciation resulted in cost recovery deductions that actually exceeded the taxpayer's cost for the asset. Third, Congress can allow a taxpayer to recover the cost of an asset over a period shorter than the economic life of the asset. The use of abbreviated useful lives or arbitrary recovery periods means that taxable income will be less than economic income during the early years of the asset's life and greater in the later years. Fourth, Congress can use accelerated methods of depreciation so that more than the actual cost of using the asset is allocated to the earlier years of its economic life. For example, declining balance depreciation generally is assumed to provide a writeoff that is faster than economic depreciation. Fifth, salvage value can be ignored, as it is under current law. This has the effect of permitting a deduction larger than the economic cost of using the asset. Finally, an arbitrary convention allowing a specified amount of depreciation for years of acquisition and disposition may produce an understatement of income if the allocation results in a deduction reflecting a period greater than the taxpayer's holding period in the year of acquisition or disposition.

Congress may also choose to forsake accuracy for simplicity. For example, the current convention and salvage value rules are quite simple and eliminate potential litigation.

Section 5.   Depletion

In the case of mineral or oil and gas exploration and development, the capitalized costs of the income producing property are recovered through allowances for depletion, a concept closely related to depreciation. Section 611 provides for a "reasonable allowance for depletion * * * according to the peculiar conditions in each case." Depletion allowances are used in situations where it is difficult to determine what portion of property has been removed from the ground and sold and what has been retained. Suppose, for example, a taxpayer purchases an oil well for $2 million and extracts and sells the oil. Although it is difficult or even impossible to estimate the total amount of oil that will be removed, at some point the well will run dry and become worthless.

There are two types of depletion allowance. The amount deductible is either "cost depletion" or "percentage depletion." Cost depletion estimates the total amount of natural resource in the property and allows deduction of its cost in proportion to each year's extractions. The taxpayer estimates the total number of units to be recovered (for example, barrels of oil) and each year deducts the basis per unit times the number of units sold. Thus, for example, if 100,000 barrels of oil were estimated as the total for a property, and 10,000 barrels were recovered, 10 percent of the basis would be deductible as cost depletion. Adjustments are made in succeeding years if the estimate proves to be wrong.

"Percentage depletion", which has been in the tax law since 1924, allows the deduction of a specified percentage of the gross income from the property year after year without regard to the recovery of cost. It remains deductible even after the basis (the capital actually invested) has been recovered. Percentage depletion allowances range from 5 percent for gravel and sand, for example, to 22 percent for sulphur, uranium, and a host of other minerals. See § 613(b). Percentage depletion is limited to 50 percent of the taxable income from the property for minerals other than oil and gas. In 1975, following an energy crisis, which involved an embargo of shipments to the United States of foreign-produced oil and produced a substantial increase in the price of gasoline and other petroleum products and a boom in oil company profits, Congress repealed percentage depletion for oil and gas wells of major oil companies. Independent domestic oil and gas producers may use percentage depletion for 1,000 barrels of average daily production at a 15 percent rate. §§ 613(a); 613A(b)(1). Percentage depletion was also retained for regulated and certain other natural gas, for certain geothermal deposits and for many varieties of minerals. Although cost depletion is similar to depreciation, percentage depletion serves an additional purpose. Because it permits a taxpayer to deduct more than actual cost, it provides a subsidy for the activities to which it applies, and a stimulus to natural resource exploration and development.

Percentage depletion is calculated with respect to the "gross income from the property." Depletion is permitted only with respect to the amount received for the extraction of the minerals, not the amount attributable to processing or manufacturing the minerals. The regulations provide complicated rules for determining the receipts attributable to extraction. See Reg. §§ 1.613–3, 1.613–4. In 1986, Congress modified percentage depletion slightly by forbidding inclusion in gross income for computing percentage depletion lease bonuses, royalty payments, and other amounts payable without regard to actual production.

Only a taxpayer with an "economic interest" in the minerals is entitled to a depletion deduction. An economic interest is not limited to "ownership" of the minerals; other arrangements qualify. For example, in United States v. Swank, 451 U.S. 571 (1981), the Court held that a lessee under a mineral lease that could be terminated without cause by the lessor on 30 days notice had an economic interest. But a licensee who simply has the right to extract the minerals does not have an economic interest. See, e.g., Missouri River Sand Co. v. Commissioner, 774 F.2d 334 (8th Cir.1985).

NOTES

(A) *Water.* Cost depletion, but not percentage depletion, has been allowed for water. In United States v. Shurbet, 347 F.2d 103 (5th Cir.1965), the record showed that the geological structure of the Southern High Plains is such that underground water that is drawn out will not be replaced. Thus, the water supply eventually will disappear, irrigation will no longer be possible, and the land will be of little value. The court held that a taxpayer owning land in this area could take cost depletion for the water used. The IRS acquiesced in this decision. Rev.Rul. 65–296, 1965–2 C.B. 181.

(B) *"Ordinary Treatment Processes."* For minerals, the percentage deduction is not limited to the value of the mineral itself as it is taken from the ground; the deduction also includes the value of "the ordinary treatment processes normally applied by mine owners or operators in order to obtain the commercially marketable mineral product or products." § 613(c). See United States v. Cannelton Sewer Pipe Co., 364 U.S. 76

(1960) (holding that mining stops when the mineral is "in such a state that [it is] ready for industrial use or consumption").

(C) *Intangible Drilling Costs.* A deduction is allowed for so-called intangible drilling costs. When an oil well is drilled, there are a variety of expenses. Some relate to tangible property—a derrick, a shed, and so on. The costs of this property are recovered through depreciation deductions. But a large part of drilling expenses goes into the intangible costs of putting a hole in the ground. These include expenditures for items such as labor, fuel, repairs, hauling, and supplies. The taxpayer is given an option either to immediately deduct these costs—which typically amount to 65 to 85 percent of total drilling costs—or to capitalize and recover the costs through depletion. Intangible drilling costs normally are deducted since percentage depletion is a fixed deduction—relating to income—and is not limited to basis, so that deduction ordinarily is not any greater if intangible drilling costs are capitalized. The taxpayer thus is allowed to deduct production costs as well as percentage depletion. § 263(c); Reg. § 1.612–4. A corporation that is an integrated oil company may deduct immediately "only" 70 percent of intangible drilling costs. Those costs that are not immediately deductible must be deducted ratably over the 60 months following the expenditure. § 291(b).

(D) *Recapture.* Section 1254 provides that amounts deducted as intangible drilling expenses will be "recaptured" as ordinary income rather than capital gain when certain oil, gas, and geothermal properties are sold. Cost depletion deductions under § 611 are also subject to § 1254 recapture. Recapture is discussed generally, in Chapter 5, infra at page 570.

(E) *Other Incentives.* The incentives provided to the oil and gas industry by percentage depletion and the deduction for intangible drilling costs are not the only tax benefits provided to the natural resources industry. Others include:

Exploration and Development Expenditures. Section 617 permits taxpayers to deduct currently certain expenditures incurred in the exploration or development of ores or minerals in the United States that otherwise would be capitalized into the depletable basis. A taxpayer who makes this election must recapture the deductions when the mine begins to produce, by including the deductions in income or reducing the income used to calculate the percentage depletion deduction.

Mine Development Expenditures. Section 616(a) allows the taxpayer to deduct all the expenses of developing a mine (other than an oil or gas well) after minerals have been discovered. Corporate taxpayers may deduct only 70 percent of mine development costs and the remaining 30 percent may be deducted ratably over a 60–month period. § 291(b)(1).

Tertiary Injectants. Certain qualified expenditures for tertiary injectants (which are used in oil and natural gas recovery processes) may be deducted immediately under § 193.

Reforestation Expenditures. Under § 194, a taxpayer can elect to amortize reforestation expenditures relating to qualified timber property over a seven-year period. The election is limited to $10,000 per taxable year.

(F) *Recycling.* Some commentators have suggested that the tax subsidies for exploration of natural resources—such as those discussed above—have created an incentive to "waste" natural resources and a disincentive for recycling them. Similar subsidies for recycling have been proposed to cure this alleged imbalance. Would you support such subsidies? Should the Code be amended to accomplish this result? If so, how?

SECTION 6.   INTEREST

1.   THE GENERAL STRUCTURE OF THE INTEREST DEDUCTION

NOTE PROVIDING AN OVERVIEW OF THE INTEREST DEDUCTION

Interest on borrowing by individuals historically has been deductible as an itemized deduction regardless of the use to which the borrowed funds were put. This principle has eroded over time until it seems to have become the exception rather than the rule. In the process, the income tax treatment of interest expenses has evolved from one of the simplest issues in the Code—when virtually all interest was deductible when paid or incurred—into one of the most complex. Currently, deductibility of interest turns generally on the purpose of the indebtedness—a question that is often unanswerable since taxpayers generally borrow both to acquire new assets and to keep everything they have.

Interest expense should be regarded as a cost to the taxpayer of holding assets that are used in a business, for investment or for personal consumption. The proper treatment of interest is controversial because the taxation of assets financed with borrowed funds is uneven: The realization requirement precludes taxation of annual increases in asset values; imputed returns from housing and other assets used for consumption are not taxed; and a wide variety of both business and investment assets enjoy tax-favored treatment.

Business Interest. Interest on indebtedness used to operate a trade or business is a cost to the taxpayer of doing business and thus is deductible like any other business expense, § 163(a), except in circumstances where interest is required to be capitalized, for example, when allocable to an asset the taxpayer is constructing, § 263A(f). Trade or business interest generally is deducted without limit, § 163(a), except to the extent the taxpayer is subject to the passive loss rules, discussed infra at page 418.

Investment Interest. The deduction of interest on debt incurred by individuals to purchase or carry investment property is limited to net investment income (with an indefinite carryforward of interest disallowed under this provision). § 163(d). Net investment income is total investment income less investment expenses. § 163(d)(4). Interest incurred in connection with a "passive activity" is not treated as investment interest but instead is subject to the rules of § 469, which limit the deduction of passive losses (discussed at page 418). This investment interest limitation is somewhat analogous to requiring that investment interest be capitalized and deducted only as ordinary income is produced.

Section 163(d) was added to prevent both a mismatch of income and expense and conversion of ordinary income into capital gain. Suppose, for example, a taxpayer bought a growth stock paying no dividends for $30,000 and funded the purchase with debt. He paid $3,000 in interest for two years and then sold the stock for $40,000 at the beginning of the third year. His net profit is $4,000. Absent § 163(d), the interest would be deductible each year against ordinary income, but because of the realization requirement, the gain would not be reported until the third year and then taxed at preferential capital gains rates.

Investment income does not include net capital gains unless the taxpayer elects to forgo the 20 percent preferential rate on capital gains (discussed infra at page 543). § 1(h)(3). This rule prevents a taxpayer from deducting investment interest at the top ordinary rate against the lower capital gains rate.

The amount of disallowed investment interest that can be carried forward to a succeeding year is not limited by the taxpayer's taxable income in the current year. Sharp v. United States, 14 F.3d 583 (Fed.Cir. 1993); Rev.Rul. 95–16, 1995–1 C.B. 9. Since there is no general carryover of an individual's interest expenses, this has the curious result of permitting the taxpayer to deduct more than would have been deductible had the limitations of § 163(d) never been enacted.

The matching of investment interest deductions with investment income creates a "basket" of income and expenses, analogous to the "basket" created by the matching of passive activity losses and income, discussed infra at page 418. As a result, some legitimate investment interest expenses may not be deductible in the year paid or incurred. This basket approach marks a shift away from a strict net income concept, under which noncapital expenses incurred in a profit-seeking activity would be fully deductible when paid or incurred.

The distinction between a business or an investment is important, for example, in connection with interest on debt used to purchase securities. Business interest is fully deductible, but if the taxpayer's activities in connection with the securities do not rise to the level of a business, the interest deduction is limited to the amount of investment income under § 163(d). The management of one's own securities investments typically is not a business. See, e.g., Estate of Yaeger v. Commissioner, 889 F.2d 29 (2d Cir.1989). Even though the taxpayer made over 2,000 trades for his own account over a two-year period, and spent evenings and many days researching investments and placing orders, his activity was not a business. The critical factor, however, appeared to be that Yaeger did not churn his portfolio. The court noted that the two fundamental criteria distinguishing traders from investors are the length of the holding period and the source of the profit.

> Investors are engaged in the production of income. * * * Traders are those "whose profits are derived from the 'direct management of purchasing and selling.' " * * * Investors derive profit from the interest, dividends, and capital appreciation of securities. * * * They are "primarily interested in the long-term growth potential of their stocks." * * * Traders, however, buy and sell securities "with reason-

able frequency in an endeavor to catch the swings in the daily market movements and profit thereby on a short term basis." * * * The activity of holding securities for a length of time to produce interest, dividends, and capital gains fits the abuse targeted by Section 163(d): investing for postponed income and current interest deduction.

Interest to Earn Tax–Exempt Income. The deduction of interest expended to earn tax-exempt or tax-preferred investment income has long been controversial. Congress has limited interest deductions in several of these contexts. For example, § 264 forbids deduction of interest on borrowing with respect to certain life insurance or annuity contracts; § 265(a)(2) prohibits deduction of interest on indebtedness to purchase or hold bonds that yield tax-exempt interest; §§ 1277 and 1282 defer the deduction of interest on indebtedness to purchase or hold certain bonds purchased at a discount until the "interest" income from the bond is taxed at maturity or upon disposition (see page 748, infra); and, as discussed above, § 163(d) limits the deduction of investment interest to investment income. Deductions of prepayments of interest are restricted, § 461(g) (discussed infra at page 700); and interest incurred in connection with the construction of certain types of real property and tangible personal property must be capitalized and amortized, § 263A(f). In the computation of the alternative minimum tax under § 55, limitations on deductions for personal interest are more restrictive than under the regular tax computations, although much home mortgage interest is deductible. § 56(b)(1). Current tax jargon uses the term "tax arbitrage" to describe deductions of interest in circumstances where related income is tax-exempt or tax-preferred. This issue is considered in some detail, infra at page 360.

Personal Interest. The propriety of interest deductions on borrowing for personal consumption has long been disputed. Some analysts regard interest charged on credit purchases of consumer goods and services simply as an additional element of the cost of consumption; as such, interest is no more entitled to deduction than is the rest of the item's price. A second view defends interest deductibility as necessary for equity between those who finance consumption purchases with debt and those who use their own assets. Taxpayers with investment assets producing taxable income could sell those assets and, for example, invest that equity in a residence, automobile or other consumer good, the returns from which are not taxed. This suggests that the negative income—interest—of those who finance consumption with debt should be deductible to offset the advantage that otherwise would accrue to those who finance consumption with forgone earnings. The former can be said to be poorer, to have less ability to pay, than the latter.

Compare A who liquidates his $100,000 investment account and purchases a house and B who retains an identical account that earns $10,000, borrows $100,000, which he invests in a home, and pays $10,000 interest. If A and B were taxed on the imputed income on the use of the home, a deduction for B clearly would be appropriate as it would be a cost of producing taxable income; each then would have $10,000 of net income. Even without taxing imputed income, however, an interest deduction is necessary to create parity between A and B. Without an interest deduction, there would be a difference between the borrower-buyer B, who would have $10,000 of taxable income, and the cash buyer A, who would have no taxable income. Thus,

> the role of interest expense in income computation is analytically independent of the use to which the borrowed funds are put. The deductibility of interest expense follows simply from the fact that debt, a negative asset, is a source of negative income. In the logic of income computation, interest expense, however it arises in household or business finance, is properly deductible.*

Nevertheless, under § 163(h), personal nonbusiness interest generally is not deductible. Personal interest is defined by omission to include any interest that is *not*: (a) interest paid or incurred in connection with a trade or business (not including for this purpose the trade or business of performing services as an employee), (b) investment interest, (c) interest that would be deductible in connection with a § 469 passive activity, (d) "qualified residence interest" (as defined in § 163(h)(3) and discussed below), or (e) interest on certain deferred estate tax payments. Interest on an income tax deficiency is personal interest. See § 163(h)(1). Every circuit court so far has held that this rule applies even where the income subject to the deficiency arose in a trade or business. E.g., Miller v. United States, 65 F.3d 687 (8th Cir.1995); Redlark v. Commissioner, 141 F.3d 936 (9th Cir.1998); Allen v. United States, 173 F.3d 533 (4th Cir.1999); Kikalos v. Commissioner, 190 F.3d 791 (7th Cir.1999); McDonnell v. United States, 180 F.3d 721 (6th Cir.1999).

The Tax Court found that interest on indebtedness incurred as part of a divorce was not required to be treated per se as nondeductible personal interest. In Seymour v. Commissioner, 109 T.C. 279 (1997), the wife transferred an interest in stock, commercial property, and a home to the husband, who signed a promissory note and conveyed a mortgage secured by the home. The court found that the interest on the note was deductible. The recipient spouse could not use § 1041, which excludes marital transfers from tax, because the interest was not the marital property being transferred. Gibbs v. Commissioner, 73 T.C.M. 2669 (1997). If the interest had been unstated—that is, the amount to be transferred in the future was simply increased—the entire amount would be excluded under § 1041.

Home Mortgage Interest. The major exception to the disallowance of personal interest is the deduction allowed for home mortgage interest. Legislative history indicates that Congress believed that "encouraging home ownership is an important policy goal." Why would Congress want to provide an incentive for owning rather than renting a home? Recall B above who has a $100,000 bank account but borrows $100,000 to purchase a home. His interest deduction washes out his investment income. Compare him to C who uses the interest income from the account to pay $10,000 rent or D who uses the investment income to pay interest on a loan to purchase a car. C and D are taxed on $10,000 income. What is the justification for the difference?

---

* Melvin I. White, "Proper Income Tax Treatment of Deductions for Personal Expense" in Tax Revision Compendium, Committee on Ways and Means 365–66 (1959).

Two categories of home mortgage interest are provided under § 163(h) rules: (1) "acquisition indebtedness" and (2) "home equity indebtedness." Interest is deductible on up to $1 million of debt used to acquire, construct or substantially improve either a principal residence or second home. This acquisition indebtedness limit is reduced as principal is repaid on the loan and refinancing does not increase this amount unless used for acquisition or improvement of a home. § 163(h)(3)(B). In addition to interest on acquisition indebtedness, interest may be deducted on home equity indebtedness of up to $100,000, regardless of the purpose or use of the loan, so long as the debt does not exceed the fair market value of the home. § 163(h)(3)(C). In both cases, the debt must be secured by the residence to be qualified residence interest.

These rules governing interest deductibility affect tax planning. Many taxpayers convert personal indebtedness into qualified residence indebtedness through home equity loans. The fungibility of money makes it virtually impossible to enforce limits on the deduction of interest incurred for certain purposes. Taxpayers may borrow against their residences to purchase consumer goods and circumvent the elimination of the deduction for consumer interest. Hence, this provision grants a further advantage to homeowners as against renters. An economic downturn, however, may cause some overextended taxpayers who have shifted indebtedness to their residence to lose not only their credit ratings but also their homes.

Note that taxpayers may borrow amounts on appreciated residences in excess of the amount paid for the residence and obtain deductible interest even though the appreciation in the value of the residence may never be recognized for tax purposes.*

Interest on Education Loans. Certain taxpayers may take an above-the-line deduction for up to $2,500 of interest paid on education loans. The indebtedness must be incurred to pay for college tuition for the taxpayer, the taxpayer's spouse or a dependent. The amount of the indebtedness is reduced by any other education benefit (such as the Hope Credit, the Lifetime Learning Credit, or distributions from an education savings account, discussed at page 434 *infra*). The deduction is phased out for single taxpayers with income of $50,000 to $65,000 and married taxpayers with income of $100,000 to $130,000. See § 221.

Tracing Interest. Full deduction for interest has often been defended as necessary due to the administrative difficulties of tracing borrowed money to its use. For example, an individual might borrow money secured by investments to finance personal consumption, or might borrow against a personal residence to purchase investment assets. Borrowing to purchase an asset is really for two purposes: to acquire the new asset and to avoid disposing of assets already on hand. But, as indicated above, the Code currently disallows or limits interest deductions when indebtedness is used for certain purposes, and consequently requires tracing such indebtedness

---

* Appreciation in the value of a taxpayer's appreciated residence is rarely taxed due to two other tax preferences: First, § 121 allows taxpayers to exclude from income up to $250,000 of gain ($500,000 if married filing jointly) from the sale of a principal residence. Second, § 1014 provides a basis step-up to fair market value of any property held until death.

to its use. Alternatively, the law might require borrowing (and interest expense) to be allocated against all assets although this, too, would be difficult administratively, or provide an ordering rule to treat certain expenditures as made with borrowed funds. No one has yet offered a convincing rationale for preferring any of the three approaches.

Nevertheless, taxpayers frequently are required by the Code to "know" the purpose for which interest expense (and the related borrowing) was paid or incurred. As the foregoing discussion makes clear, a variety of provisions limit interest deductions based on the purpose of the loan. The Code requires the impossible; since money is fungible, there is no "correct" way to determine, with any degree of certainty, the purpose for which funds were borrowed. Obviously, the taxpayer borrows for the purpose of keeping everything she has and at the same time making whatever new expenditure is desired or required.

The impossibility of the task, however, has not deterred Congress or the regulation writers at the Treasury Department. See Temp.Reg. § 1.163–8T (tracing principles for allocation of loan proceeds to specific purposes) and § 1.163–10T(n) (definition of qualified residence interest). In general, the purpose of these rules is to tell taxpayers how to determine whether interest deductions will be disallowed or limited under § 163(d) (investment interest), § 163(h) (personal interest) or § 469 (passive activity interest), or fully deductible. "Qualified residence interest" is not subject to the tracing rules of Temp.Reg. § 1.163–8T at all, and other rules may trump these regulations by allocating interest to some other specific purpose, for example, to a trade or business purpose.

Generally, the rules determine the purpose of an interest expense by tracing loan proceeds to their use. It is the expenditure of the loan proceeds and (with the exception of qualified residence interest) not the security of the debt that governs. Thus, for example, if the taxpayer pledges an automobile as security for funds borrowed and used to buy corporate stock for investment, the interest paid on the loan is investment interest, and, contrariwise, if the taxpayer pledges corporate stock as security for loan proceeds that are used to buy an automobile for personal use, the interest expense on the loan is personal interest. Since investment and business interest may be deductible and personal interest is not, a well-informed taxpayer generally would arrange her affairs so as to use loan proceeds for investment or business purposes.

Compound interest and interest on funds borrowed to pay interest on other loans did not trouble the regulation writers; these are simply traced to the use of the original borrowing. Temp.Regs. §§ 1.163–8T(c)(2)(ii)(B) and 1.163–8T(c)(6)(ii). This approach, of course, works best when the lending institution forwards the loan proceeds directly to the seller of a particular asset. Fun can be had when the loan proceeds are paid to the taxpayer and commingled with other funds, for example, by being deposited in a bank account that contains other funds of the taxpayer. The regulations here provide that expenditures from bank accounts containing commingled funds are deemed to have been made first from borrowed funds and then from unborrowed funds, and proceeds from different loans (which, of course, may have differing interest rates) are used in the order that the loan proceeds are deposited. The order that checks are written generally determines the tracing of the use of proceeds, but for checks written on the same day, the taxpayer may designate the order, and a special rule allows taxpayers to designate any expenditure made within 15 days of the borrowing as the specific use of the funds. Temp.Reg. § 1.163–8T(c)(4).

For more fun than this, you will have to delve into the regulations yourself. Needless to say, the tracing approach of the regulations contains tax savings opportunities for those who plan their transactions carefully and tax increases or, more likely, random tax consequences for the unknowing or unwary and people with better ways to spend their time. Those who pay no attention at all seem likely to enjoy tax savings or tax increases depending upon their luck.

2.   INTEREST PAID TO EARN TAX–PREFERRED INCOME: THE PROBLEM OF "TAX ARBITRAGE"

NOTE ON TAX ARBITRAGE

The treatment of assets and debt under the current income tax has resulted in a problem often labelled "tax arbitrage." This arises when assets eligible for favored tax treatment are acquired with debt.

Many income tax rules can be characterized as imposing a zero rate of tax on the income from important categories of assets. These have included investments in equipment, which, during the period of 1981–1986, essentially could be immediately expensed by a combination of accelerated cost recovery deductions and the investment tax credit, natural resource exploration and development, where immediate expensing is generally permitted, real estate, which prior to 1986 often produced negative income tax rates, owner-occupied houses, retirement savings, tax-exempt state and local bonds, and all assets held by tax-exempt organizations, such as pension funds or by taxable corporations with large operating losses. It has been estimated that in 1983 as much as 80 percent of the $10.5 trillion of assets held by individuals qualified for such favored treatment. Harvey Galper & Eugene Steuerle, "Tax Incentives for Savings," 2 Brookings Rev. 19–20 (Winter 1983).

A negative rate of tax can be achieved when a taxpayer can obtain both an interest deduction and the equivalent of a zero rate of tax on the income from the asset purchased with debt. Borrowing to purchase tax-exempt municipal bonds presents the classic case. Assume, for example, that a taxpayer subject to a 40 percent marginal tax rate simultaneously borrows at an interest rate of 7 percent to purchase municipal bonds yielding tax-exempt interest of 6 percent. Before tax, the transaction loses 1 percent. After tax, the net interest cost is 4.2 percent, which is 1.8 percentage points less than the after-tax yield of 6 percent. The 1 percent before-tax loss has become a 1.8 percent after-tax gain, a result that may be characterized as a negative tax.

Section 265(a)(2) bars tax arbitrage in such a case by disallowing interest deductions on borrowing to purchase or carry tax-exempt bonds. Section 163(d) likewise operates to disallow interest deductions on borrowing to purchase growth stocks that yield little or no current investment income. In computing the alternative minimum tax base under § 55, nonbusiness interest is deductible only if it is related to owner-occupied housing or if it is no greater than net investment income.

Tax arbitrage also may occur where the Code allows immediate expensing of the cost of assets. This may be equivalent to exempting the yield from such an asset. See discussion supra at page 288. As with § 265(a)(2), disallowing interest deductions would eliminate the tax-system profit—or negative tax—in such a case. The Code, however, generally does not do so. For example, taxpayers are permitted to deduct the interest on a loan the proceeds of which are used to purchase business property that is expensed under § 179.

More subtle examples of tax arbitrage occur when the return from the asset takes the form of the use of the asset. For example, when a person owns a residence subject to a mortgage, the interest is deductible but the imputed rental value of the house is not included in taxable income.

In any circumstance where interest expense is entirely deductible and the income from the preferred asset is entirely excluded from income, taxpayers often will find that their total tax liability is negative—less than zero—on a fully leveraged investment. This may be true even when the transaction produces a gain before tax. As long as the after-tax rate of return on the preferred asset is greater than the after-tax rate of interest on the borrowing, the taxpayer will find such tax arbitrage profitable. See Eugene Steuerle, "Tax Arbitrage, Inflation, and the Taxation of Interest Payments and Receipts," 30 Wayne L.Rev. 991 (1984).

The problem of tax arbitrage, of course, would disappear if the income from the asset side of the above transaction were not subject to differential tax treatment—for example, if capital gains were not taxed more favorably than ordinary income and if gains were taxed when they accrue rather than when they are realized; if municipal bond interest were not exempt from tax; if depreciation were limited to economic depreciation; and if the imputed rental value of housing and home-equity financed consumer durables were not excluded from taxable income. It is unlikely, however, that these tax preferences will be repealed. If not, the only feasible means of preventing tax arbitrage (and negative tax rates) will be the disallowance of interest deductions in a wide variety of circumstances.* This is probably the best explanation of many of the limitations on interest deductibility. The desirability of such an approach is not treated in detail here, but a closer look at § 265(a)(2) is worthwhile.

Return to our earlier example of the taxpayer in the 40 percent bracket who borrows at 7 percent to purchase municipal bonds yielding tax-exempt interest income of 6 percent. As illustrated above, full deduction of interest produces an after-tax gain of 1.8 percent from a before-tax loss of 1 percent. Section 265(a)(2) maintains the before-tax loss by denying any deduction

---

* Subjecting taxpayers to a minimum tax that both includes many forms of tax-preferred income and limits interest deductibility may be something of an alternative, although the current minimum tax is not comprehensive—it excludes most state and local bond interest, for example—and is imposed at a lower tax rate. See generally Chapter 7.

for interest; this ensures that taxpayers will not incur interest expense greater than the tax-exempt yield to purchase municipal bonds.

Recall, however, from our earlier discussion of the tax-exempt bonds, supra at page 212, that such bonds generally bear an "implicit tax" in that their interest rate is lower than taxable corporate bonds of equal risk, reflecting the tax advantage. Where that is the case, arguably the taxpayer should be permitted to deduct interest offset by this implicit income, which would have been taxed if received. Suppose in the above example, that a corporate bond of similar risk bears interest at 10 percent. A taxpayer who borrowed at 7 percent would have a 1.8 percent after-tax return. The taxpayer who borrows at 7 percent to purchase the tax-exempt bond with a 6 percent return would also have a 1.8 percent return if interest were deductible. If not, he loses 1 percent.

Inhibiting borrowing to purchase tax-exempt bonds may reduce the volume of bonds purchased by high-bracket taxpayers. State and local governments then might pay greater interest on their bonds to attract lower-bracket investors and as a consequence increase the return to high-bracket investors who purchase the bonds with their own funds. Such windfall gains to high-bracket taxpayers are discussed at page 213, supra. If § 265(a)(2) were repealed, high-bracket taxpayers would enjoy after-tax profits as long as the yield on the tax-exempt bonds exceeded the after-tax cost of the borrowed funds (4.2 percent in the above example). This would increase demand for tax-exempt bonds so that state and local government could pay lower rates of return on the bonds and thereby receive more of the benefits from the tax exemption.

The general point is that interest-disallowance provisions permit wealthy taxpayers to obtain relatively greater benefits from tax-favored assets because they can acquire tax-favored assets by liquidating their existing assets. This choice is not available to less wealthy taxpayers who would have to borrow the funds necessary to acquire the tax-favored assets. As indicated earlier in this Section, this is an important element of the general defense of the interest deduction.

The variety of limitations on interest deductions are controversial and often produce inconsistent results. The continuing ability to deduct home mortgage interest on indebtedness equal to the cost of two homes so far seems to be politically secure and not likely to be restricted through future "tax reform." On the other hand, the Code disallows deductions for interest on indebtedness for certain purposes and for much investment interest and requires capitalization of trade or business interest in a number of important circumstances. Targeted efforts to deal with tax arbitrage by limiting interest deductions seems likely to continue in the future and are guaranteed to produce uneven results and increased complexity.

NOTES

(A) *Tracing.* Denying an interest deduction on indebtedness used for a specific purpose requires tracing the indebtedness to its use. Section 265(a)(2) requires the IRS to establish a direct connection between the taxpayer's borrowing and his purchasing or holding of tax-exempt securities. For example, interest on indebtedness where the proceeds are directly used to purchase tax-exempt debt is disallowed. The use of tax-exempt obligations as collateral for indebtedness is evidence of a purpose to carry the obligations. On the other hand, the IRS does not consider the purchase of tax-exempt bonds at a time when the taxpayer holds a home mortgage as evidence of "carrying" the bonds. Rev.Proc. 72–18, 1972–1 C.B. 740.

(B) *Nonrecourse Liabilities.* Interest on a mortgage secured by real estate paid by the owner of the property is deductible even if there is no personal liability. Reg. § 1.163–1(b). Recall Crane v. Commissioner, supra at page 187, and Commissioner v. Tufts, supra at page 189, which confirmed that nonrecourse debt generally is treated the same as recourse debt for tax purposes.

(C) *Expenses to Produce Tax–Exempt Income.* Interest is not the only type of expense that could be used for arbitrage. Deducting any type of expense attributable to tax-exempt income also can create a negative rate of tax. Section 265(a)(1) generally prohibits the deduction of the expenses of producing tax-exempt income. See, e.g., Rev.Rul. 87–102, 1987–2 C.B. 78 (denying deduction for legal fees to obtain tax-exempt Social Security payments); Rugby Productions Ltd. v. Commissioner, 100 T.C. 531 (1993) (denying deduction for premiums on disability policy, the proceeds of which would have been exempt under § 104(a)(3)); Induni v. Commissioner, 990 F.2d 53 (2d Cir.1993) (denying deduction for home mortgage interest where taxpayer received tax-exempt federal housing allowance). The regulations define exempt income as that exempt under a specific statutory provision and thus does not include items such as imputed income. Reg. § 1.265–1(b).

3. SHAMS AND TRANSACTIONS WITH NO "ECONOMIC PURPOSE"

Knetsch v. United States

Supreme Court of the United States, 1960. 364 U.S. 361.

MR. JUSTICE BRENNAN delivered the opinion of the Court.

This case presents the question of whether deductions from gross income claimed on petitioners' 1953 and 1954 joint federal income tax returns, of $143,465 in 1953 and of $147,105 in 1954, for payments made by petitioner, Karl F. Knetsch, to Sam Houston Life Insurance Company, constituted "interest paid * * * on indebtedness" within the meaning of § 23(b) of the Internal Revenue Code of 1939 * * * and § 163(a) of the Internal Revenue Code of 1954. * * * The Commissioner of Internal Revenue disallowed the deductions and determined a deficiency for each year. The petitioners paid the deficiencies and brought this action for refund in the District Court for the Southern District of California. The District Court rendered judgment for the United States, and the Court of Appeals for the Ninth Circuit affirmed, 272 F.2d 200. Because of a suggested conflict with the decision of the Court of Appeals for the Fifth Circuit in United States v. Bond, 258 F.2d 577, we granted certiorari, 361 U.S. 958.

On December 11, 1953, the insurance company sold Knetsch ten 30–year maturity deferred annuity savings bonds, each in the face amount of $400,000 and bearing interest at 2½% compounded annually. The purchase price was $4,004,000. Knetsch gave the Company his check for $4,000, and signed $4,000,000 of nonrecourse annuity loan notes for the balance. The notes bore 3½% interest and were secured by the annuity bonds. The interest was payable in advance, and Knetsch on the same day prepaid the first year's interest, which was $140,000. Under the Table of Cash and Loan Values made part of the bonds, their cash or loan value at December 11, 1954, the end of the first contract year, was to be $4,100,000. The contract terms, however, permitted Knetsch to borrow any excess of this value above his indebtedness without waiting until December 11, 1954. Knetsch took advantage of this provision only five days after the purchase. On December 16, 1953, he received from the company $99,000 of the $100,000 excess over his $4,000,000 indebtedness, for which he gave his notes bearing 3½% interest. This interest was also payable in advance and on the same day he prepaid the first year's interest of $3,465. In their joint return for 1953, the petitioners deducted the sum of the two interest payments, that is $143,465, as "interest paid * * * within the taxable year on indebtedness," under § 23(b) of the 1939 Code.

The second contract year began on December 11, 1954, when interest in advance of $143,465 was payable by Knetsch on his aggregate indebtedness of $4,099,000. Knetsch paid this amount on December 27, 1954. Three days later, on December 30, he received from the company cash in the amount of $104,000, the difference less $1,000 between his then $4,099,000 indebtedness and the cash or loan value of the bonds of $4,204,000 on December 11, 1955. He gave the company appropriate notes and prepaid the interest thereon of $3,640. In their joint return for the taxable year 1954 the petitioners deducted the sum of the two interest payments, that is $147,105, as "interest paid * * * within the taxable year on indebtedness," under § 163(a) of the 1954 Code.

The tax years 1955 and 1956 are not involved in this proceeding, but a recital of the events of those years is necessary to complete the story of the transaction. On December 11, 1955, the start of the third contract year, Knetsch became obligated to pay $147,105 as prepaid interest on an indebtedness which now totalled $4,203,000. He paid this interest on December 28, 1955. On the same date he received $104,000 from the company. This was $1,000 less than the difference between his indebtedness and the cash or loan value of the bonds of $4,308,000 at December 11, 1956. Again he gave the company notes upon which he prepaid interest of $3,640. Petitioners claimed a deduction on their 1955 joint return for the aggregate of the payments, or $150,745.

Knetsch did not go on with the transaction for the fourth contract year beginning December 11, 1956, but terminated it on December 27, 1956. His indebtedness at that time totalled $4,307,000. The cash or loan value of the bonds was the $4,308,000 value at December 11, 1956, which had been the basis of the "loan" of December 28, 1955. He surrendered the bonds and his indebtedness was canceled. He received the difference of $1,000 in cash.

The contract called for a monthly annuity of $90,171 at maturity (when Knetsch would be 90 years of age) or for such smaller amount as would be produced by the cash or loan value after deduction of the then existing indebtedness. It was stipulated that if Knetsch had held the bonds to maturity and continued annually to borrow the net cash value less $1,000, the sum available for the annuity at maturity would be $1,000 ($8,388,000 cash or loan value less $8,387,000 of indebtedness), enough to provide an annuity of only $43 per month.

The trial judge made findings that "[t]here was no commercial economic substance to the * * * transaction," that the parties did not intend that Knetsch "become indebted to Sam Houston," that "[n]o indebtedness of [Knetsch] was created by any of the * * * transactions," and that "[n]o economic gain could be achieved from the purchase of these bonds without regard to the tax consequences * * *." His conclusion of law, based on this Court's decision in Deputy v. du Pont, 308 U.S. 488, was that "[w]hile in form the payments to Sam Houston were compensation for the use or forbearance of money, they were not in substance. As a payment of interest, the transaction was a sham."

We first examine the transaction between Knetsch and the insurance company to determine whether it created an "indebtedness" within the meaning of § 23(b) of the 1939 Code and § 163(a) of the 1954 Code, or whether, as the trial court found, it was a sham. We put aside a finding by the District Court that Knetsch's "only motive in purchasing these 10 bonds was to attempt to secure an interest deduction."[1] As was said in Gregory v. Helvering, 293 U.S. 465, 469: "The legal right of a taxpayer to decrease the amount of what otherwise would be his taxes, or altogether avoid them, by means which the law permits, cannot be doubted * * *. But the question for determination is whether what was done, apart from the tax motive, was the thing which the statute intended."

When we examine "what was done" here, we see that Knetsch paid the insurance company $294,570 during the two taxable years involved and received $203,000 back in the form of "loans." What did Knetsch get for the out-of-pocket difference of $91,570? In form he had an annuity contract with a so-called guaranteed cash value at maturity of $8,388,000, which would produce monthly annuity payments of $90,171, or substantial life insurance proceeds in the event of his death before maturity. This, as we have seen, was a fiction, because each year Knetsch's annual borrowings kept the net cash value, on which any annuity or insurance payments would depend, at the relative pittance of $1,000.[2] Plainly, therefore, Knetsch's transaction with the insurance company did "not appreciably affect his beneficial interest except to reduce his tax * * *." Gilbert v. Commissioner, 2 Cir.248 F.2d 399, 411 (dissenting opinion). For it is patent

---

1. We likewise put aside Knetsch's argument that, because he received ordinary income when he surrendered the annuities in 1956, he has suffered a net loss even if the contested deductions are allowed, and that therefore his motive in taking out the annuities could not have been tax avoidance.

2. Petitioners argue further that in 10 years the net cash value of the bonds would have exceeded the amounts Knetsch paid as "interest." This contention, however, is predicated on the wholly unlikely assumption that Knetsch would have paid off in cash the original $4,000,000 "loan."

that there was nothing of substance to be realized by Knetsch from this transaction beyond a tax deduction. What he was ostensibly "lent" back was in reality only the rebate of a substantial part of the so-called "interest" payments. The $91,570 difference retained by the company was its fee for providing the facade of "loans" whereby the petitioners sought to reduce their 1953 and 1954 taxes in the total sum of $233,297.68. There may well be single premium annuity arrangements with nontax substance which create an "indebtedness" for the purposes of § 23(b) of the 1939 Code and § 163(a) of the 1954 Code. But this one is a sham.

[The Court then rejected the taxpayer's argument that Congress had implicitly allowed deductions for such payments made prior to the 1954 enactment of § 264(a)(2), which denies a deduction for amounts paid on indebtedness incurred to purchase or carry single premium annuity contracts purchased after March 1, 1954.]

* * *

MR. JUSTICE DOUGLAS, with whom MR. JUSTICE WHITTAKER and MR. JUSTICE STEWART concur, dissenting. I agree with the views expressed by Judge Moore in Diggs v. Commissioner, 281 F.2d 326, 330–332, and by Judge Brown, writing for himself and Judge Hutcheson, in United States v. Bond, 258 F.2d 577.

It is true that in this transaction the taxpayer was bound to lose if the annuity contract is taken by itself. At least the taxpayer showed by his conduct that he never intended to come out ahead on that investment apart from this income tax deduction. Yet the same may be true where a taxpayer borrows money at 5% or 6% interest to purchase securities that pay only nominal interest; or where, with money in the bank earning 3%, he borrows from the self-same bank at a higher rate. His aim there, as here, may only be to get a tax deduction for interest paid. Yet as long as the transaction itself is not hocus-pocus, the interest charges incident to completing it would seem to be deductible under the Internal Revenue Code as respects annuity contracts made prior to March 1, 1954, the date Congress selected for terminating this class of deductions. 26 U.S.C.A. § 264. The insurance company existed; it operated under Texas law; it was authorized to issue these policies and to make these annuity loans. While the taxpayer was obligated to pay interest at the rate of 3½% per annum, the annuity bonds increased in cash value at the rate of only 2½% per annum. The insurance company's profit was in that 1–point spread.

Tax avoidance is a dominating motive behind scores of transactions. It is plainly present here. Will the Service that calls this transaction a "sham" today not press for collection of taxes[3] arising out of the surrender of the annuity contract? I think it should, for I do not believe any part of the transaction was a "sham." To disallow the "interest" deduction because the annuity device was devoid of commercial substance is to draw a line which will affect a host of situations not now before us and which, with

---

3. Petitioners terminated this transaction in 1956 by allowing the bonds to be cancelled and receiving a check for $1,000. The termination was reflected in their tax return for 1956. It might also be noted that the insurance company reported as gross income the interest payments which it received from petitioners in 1953 and 1954.

all deference, I do not think we can maintain when other cases reach here. The remedy is legislative. Evils or abuses can be particularized by Congress. We deal only with "interest" as commonly understood and as used across the board in myriad transactions. Since these transactions were real and legitimate in the insurance world and were consummated within the limits allowed by insurance policies, I would recognize them tax-wise.

NOTES

(A) *"Sham" vs. Tax Avoidance Motive.* Must a court find a "sham" in order to disallow interest deductions? Or will a "tax avoidance" motive or absence of any "business purpose" suffice?

In Goldstein v. Commissioner, 364 F.2d 734 (2d Cir.1966), cert. denied 385 U.S. 1005 (1967), a taxpayer who won $140,000 in the Irish Sweepstakes paid 4 percent interest to borrow money with which she purchased Treasury notes yielding annually about 1.5 percent interest income payable over a number of years. The taxpayer prepaid interest in the year she won the Sweepstakes and tried to deduct that prepayment. Although the taxpayer paid more interest than she would earn, the tax savings from, in effect, spreading the Sweepstakes winnings over a number of years would have made the transaction profitable. The court found no "sham" but nevertheless disallowed the interest deduction on the grounds that there was "no purposive reason, other than the securing of a deduction." The court then stated that allowing the deduction "would encourage transactions that have no economic utility and that would not be engaged in but for the system of taxes imposed by Congress."

What are the limits of the *Goldstein-Knetsch* analysis? Does *Goldstein* imply that the courts might deny interest deductions in any "tax arbitrage" situation?

Some courts have found no need to determine if transactions were fictitious, so long as there was no economic motive. For example, in Lifschultz v. Commissioner, 393 F.2d 232 (2d Cir.1968), the court examined a transaction in which the taxpayers purchased bonds paying 2 percent from a seller who did not own the bonds. The seller borrowed funds, which it used to purchase the bonds, using the bonds as collateral for the loan. The interest on the note was 4 percent. The court found it unnecessary to determine if the transactions were genuine because there was no realistic opportunity for profit. Since the bonds were U.S. treasury bonds near maturity, the only possibility for gain was if the bonds increased in value and such a fluctuation so close to maturity was unlikely. In examining an agreement involving the purchase and repurchase of Treasury bills, the Tax Court noted that "financing transactions will merit respect and give rise to deductible interest only if there is some tax-independent purpose of the transaction." Sheldon v. Commissioner, 94 T.C. 738, 752 (1990).

(B) *Validity of Loan.* An important element of many "tax shelters" is the availability of an interest deduction. One way to attack the transaction is to question whether the indebtedness is valid. Recall *Estate of Franklin,* discussed supra at page 198 in which the Ninth Circuit refused to treat a "loan" that exceeded the value of the property when undertaken as valid indebtedness and therefore held the loan proceeds were not includible in the purchaser's basis. Another consequence of the court's finding that the debt was invalid was that interest deductions were denied. Thus, even if a transaction is not a "sham," interest deductions may be disallowed because the debt is invalid. See, e.g., Rev.Rul. 84–5, 1984–1 C.B. 32 (denying interest deductions on a 30–year nonrecourse obligation with a large final balloon payment on the grounds that the obligation "does not constitute a valid indebtedness"). Another strategy is to invalidate the entire transaction on the grounds that it lacks economic purpose (as the court did in *Knetsch*), which has the effect of eliminating the interest deduction. This approach has been used in corporate tax shelter cases, such as Winn Dixie Stores, Inc. v. Commissioner, 113 T.C. 254 (1999), discussed in Chapter 8, infra. A third option is to recharacterize the transaction for tax purposes to better reflect its "economic reality" as the Tax Court did in *Estate of Franklin* when it recharacterized the "prepaid interest" as a payment to purchase an option.

4.   WHAT IS INTEREST?

NOTE ON DISTINGUISHING INTEREST FROM OTHER PAYMENTS

Often it is difficult to know whether a particular payment is for interest or something else. The distinction will be crucial when interest is deductible but another characterization will produce no deduction.

The Supreme Court has defined interest as "the amount which one has contracted to pay for the use of borrowed money," Old Colony Railroad Co. v. Commissioner, 284 U.S. 552, 560 (1932), and as "compensation for the use or forbearance of money," Deputy v. du Pont, 308 U.S. 488, 498 (1940). The courts frequently have said that whether a payment is compensation for the use or forbearance of money is a factual determination, and that the labels or terminology used by the parties are not controlling. For example, in Rev. Rul. 74–187, 1974–1 C.B. 48, the IRS held that a late payment charge assessed by a public utility was interest where there were no specific services performed in connection with the customer's account. But in a case that the Tax Court judge found not easy to distinguish from that revenue ruling, a 4% fee for home mortgage payments made to a bank more than 15 days after the due date was held not to be deductible interest. The court found that although the late charges were imposed partially to compensate the bank for lost earnings or interest, their primary function was to recoup costs attendant to the bank's attempt to collect the delinquent loans. West v. Commissioner, 61 T.C.M. 1694 (1991). Even assuming that to be true, however, was the payment not an "amount which one has contracted to pay for the use of borrowed money" or as "compensation for the use or forbearance of money"? Would the result have been different if the amount of the delinquency payment increased each month? Points on home mortgages (a fee paid up front for obtaining the loan) are treated as interest. § 461(g) (2).

See also § 163(b), allowing an interest deduction under certain circumstances where carrying charges are imposed, even though the actual amount of interest cannot be determined, and § 216, which allows a tenant-stockholder in a cooperative building to deduct a pro rata share of interest (as well as property taxes).

Consider also § 7872, discussed at page 753 infra, which recharacterizes as interest amounts designated otherwise on a variety of no-interest or below-market interest transactions.

As further evidence of the courts' reluctance to characterize as interest payments that are not labelled as such, consider Consolidated Edison Co. of N.Y., Inc. v. United States, 10 F.3d 68 (2d Cir.1993). Con Ed accepted New York City's offer to prepay its real estate taxes and the prepayment extinguished its entire tax liability. Con Ed claimed that, in effect, the prepayment was a loan to the city, which the latter repaid with interest to Con Ed, that satisfied its tax liability. Since the "borrower" was a municipality, Con Ed attempted to exclude the discount as tax-exempt interest and deduct the entire real estate tax. The Court rejected the characterization. Although the court noted the appeal of this non-formalistic approach, it found that the discounts were compensation for the early payment of taxes and not "interest." It determined that the taxpayer was bound by the form of the transaction, which was not a "loan."

In Albertson's, Inc. v. Commissioner, set forth at page 762 infra, the court held that certain "additional amounts" paid to reflect the time value of money on compensation employees were entitled to currently but agreed to defer were not deductible as interest. The court determined that allowing a deduction for these amounts as interest would contravene the rules and policies with respect to the taxation of nonqualified deferred compensation, an issue taken up in Chapter 6.

Distinguishing Debt from Equity. Allowing a deduction for interest paid on borrowing, but not for other payments to suppliers of capital, notably dividends paid to corporate equity suppliers, creates considerable controversy between taxpayers and the IRS as to whether particular payments are "interest." Lender-borrower relationships must be distinguished from other relationships, most importantly from those involving ownership. Moreover, deductible payments of interest must be distinguished from nondeductible payments of principal—a chore made more difficult in times of inflation.

In United States v. Mississippi Chemical Corp., 405 U.S. 298 (1972), the Supreme Court rejected the taxpayer farmers' arguments that "stock purchases" based directly upon the amount of below-market interest payments due on loans were actually additional interest payments and therefore deductible. The Farm Credit Act required farmers who borrowed from cooperative banks to make quarterly purchases of bank stock, in proportion to the interest owed on the loans. This so-called Class C stock paid no dividends and was rarely transferable. Further, additional shares conferred no additional voting power, and Class C stock was redeemable only after all other classes of stock had been redeemed. All of these characteristics would make normal commercial stock undesirable and made the market for the Class C stock virtually nonexistent.

All in all, the required purchases of Class C stock economically resembled additional interest far more than typical equity purchases. Since the interest rates to farmers' cooperatives were lower than the market interest rates, and the amount of Class "C" stock required to be purchased was a percentage (15 percent) of the interest due, taxpayers' contention that their payments for the stock for the "use or forbearance of money" seems persuasive. What weight would you give to the nonvoting character and nontransferability of the stock? The government conceded, and the Court agreed, that the stock was not worth the full $100 per share; the taxpayer contended that $99 of the $100 was interest. Would a more equitable result have been to permit an interest deduction for part of the $100, say $50? Would such a result be a proper construction of the statute?

Nevertheless, the Court rejected the taxpayers' effort to deduct $99 of every $100 stock purchase required as additional interest and held that the purported stock was indeed stock, noting Congress' goal of ensuring adequate bank capitalization and stability and continuity in the farm credit program. In one of those rather remarkable comments that give counsel something to quote when there is little of economic substance on their side, the Court remarked: "The taxpayers and the Government each allege that the other is looking at form rather than substance. At some point, however, the form in which a transaction is cast must have considerable impact." 405 U.S. at 311.

The *Mississippi Chemical* and *Knetsch* cases seem to reflect two quite different approaches by the Supreme Court to the question whether the form or substance of a transaction should govern for tax purposes. The problem of distinguishing between form and substance most frequently arises when, as in *Knetsch,* taxpayers select the form of economic transactions to minimize tax. This occurs in a variety of contexts, some of which are illustrated throughout this book. The courts routinely pay homage to the tax maxim that, absent explicit statutory provisions, the substance of a transaction, not its form, will determine its tax consequences, but there is considerable force to the Court's observation in *Mississippi Chemical* that "[a]t some point, however, the form in which a transaction is cast must have considerable impact." Tax planning and tax administration routinely involve contests over moving that point.

Distinguishing Corporate Debt from Equity. The difficulties of distinguishing debt and equity transactions have long plagued the corporate income tax, which permits deduction of interest on debt but not of dividends on equity. Many cases have recharacterized "loans" as shareholders' contributions of capital, and thus recharacterized deductible "interest" payments as nondeductible dividends. The debt-equity distinction became increasingly important in the 1980's. Companies then converted large amounts of equity capital into debt through a variety of financial transactions, including so-called leveraged buy-outs and leveraged recapitalizations. Conversely, cases also occasionally are encountered in which "dividends" payable on "stock" are held to be deductible as interest payments.

The Tax Reform Act of 1969 attempted to respond to the difficulty of making such distinctions with § 385, which authorizes Treasury to prescribe by regulation how to ascertain whether an interest in a corporation is stock or debt. A number of relevant factors are listed in this Code section, but Treasury explicitly is not limited to these. The difficult determinations necessary to distinguish debt from equity were made no easier by delegating the task to Treasury. Indeed, notwithstanding several false starts beginning with proposed regulations issued in March, 1980, the Treasury has never issued final regulations under § 385 and has withdrawn all regulations it has proposed. The 1969 enactment of § 385 delegating to the Treasury the responsibility to issue regulations distinguishing debt from equity surely by now has proved a failure.

Limitations enacted in 1969 on the deduction of interest in connection with certain corporate mergers and acquisitions (§ 279) also proved largely ineffective. New approaches to this issue now seem essential. Rather than attempting to draw undrawable distinctions based upon the kinds of rights that accompany various corporate financial instruments, new avenues should be explored. See, e.g., § 163(e)(5) (treating a portion of the "interest" on high yield discount obligations as a nondeductible dividend). Serious attention should be given to new limitations on corporate interest deductions, to limitations on the percentage of corporate capital that will be recognized for tax purposes as debt, and to treating as equity all corporate financial instruments traded or tradeable for equity. Revenues from the corporate income tax are far too important for Congress to allow the ongoing disappearance of the corporate income tax base through leveraging.

Distinguishing Interest from Principal. Because interest is often deductible and principal is not, it is important to be able to distinguish between the two. The designation by the parties of an amount as something other than interest, however, does not necessarily preclude an interest deduction. Conversely, the fact that the parties designate an amount paid as interest may not be decisive, especially if the parties are related or have different tax characteristics.

Suppose the buyer and seller contract on January 1 for the sale of property but the closing date can occur no later than August 1. In the interim, the purchaser will obtain a zoning variance. The purchaser makes a "down payment" on the contract date, which the seller will retain as liquidated damages if the sale does not close. The contract calls for an increase in the sales price to be calculated daily based on a market rate of interest from the contract date to the closing date. May the purchaser deduct this increase as "interest" or must it be treated as part of the cost of the property? In Halle v. Commissioner, 83 F.3d 649 (4th Cir.1996), the court permitted a deduction. It rejected the Service's argument that the interest the purchaser held was akin to an option to purchase and the total payments represented the sales price when the option was exercised. The court disagreed, holding that even though the sale was contingent in the sense that it might not be completed, because the purchase price set on the contract date was equal to value, the payment was more in the nature of interest on a fixed obligation.

Sections §§ 1271–1278 also provide rules for allocating principal and interest on deferred-payment transactions. These provisions are treated in some detail in Chapter 6 at page 748.

NOTES

(A) *Equity-Kicker Loans.* During much of this century, interest rates were reasonably constant; lenders therefore were willing to engage in long-term financing arrangements at fixed rates of interest. Unexpected and fluctuating rates of inflation in recent decades, however, have resulted in wide swings in interest rates. In response, lenders devised new financing techniques involving varying or adjustable rates of interest, or in some instances, sharing between lender and borrower of any appreciation realized when the property securing the loan is sold. These "equity-kicker" loans, which have been quite common in real estate transactions, may permit the "lender" to obtain a variety of "equity-type" economic rights or risks, including:

(1) the right to share in appreciation of the property,

(2) the right to a portion of any cash flow generated by operation of the property,

(3) the risk of a decline in the value of the property because the "loan" is nonrecourse,

(4) the power to manage and control the property,

(5) the right to prohibit or insist upon sale or other disposition of the property, and

(6) the right to purchase the property at some future date.

Where financing arrangements provide the lender with such "equity-type" risks or rights, the IRS may argue for recharacterization of an arrangement labelled a "loan" as some form of equity, such as a joint venture or partnership interest. The cases generally have emphasized the parties' intent to enter into a debtor/creditor relationship (rather than a partnership or joint venture, for example) as the most critical factor in determining whether a "loan" will be recharacterized as "equity." However, the law in this area is unsettled.

(B) *Distinguishing a Lender from an Owner.* The characterization of the transaction as a loan or a joint venture not only determines the availability of the interest deduction, but, since basis includes borrowed amounts, this characterization also determines the amount of depreciation deductions allowable.

The IRS and the courts often have relied on the parties' intent and their labels in determining whether a "loan" will be recharacterized as "equity" in order to assure consistent treatment on both sides of the transaction. Interest deductions to the "borrower" are interest income to the "lender"; allocation of the entire depreciable basis to the "borrower" defeats the "lender's" claim to any depreciation deductions. It was long thought that such "matching" of tax consequences without more would protect the federal fisc; thus, the IRS and the courts routinely accepted not only the taxpayers' characterization of the transaction as a loan but also their allocation of annual payments between interest and principal.

The "matching" approach does not suffice, however, where the tax characteristics of the parties are significantly different, such as when the "lender" is a tax-exempt entity or a corporation that is nontaxable because of excess losses. A tax-exempt organization suffers no adverse tax consequences from receiving ordinary interest income in lieu of capital gain or forgoing depreciation deductions. This cautions against undue reliance on the parties' intent, labels, and characterization of such transactions. There often will be no substitute for attempting to ascertain whether the "economic substance" of the transaction creates a debtor-creditor relationship or something more akin to a joint venture.

5. INFLATION AND THE INTEREST DEDUCTION

NOTE ON INFLATION AND THE INTEREST DEDUCTION

Inflation is not systematically accounted for under the income tax; the fluctuating inflation since the 1960's has created a variety of problems for the income tax. Congress has enacted a number of provisions designed to take inflation into account. See, e.g., § 1(f) (adjusting the rate brackets for inflation). None of them deals directly with assets or liabilities, although a variety of provisions have been enacted partly in response to inflation. For example, one of the justifications for rapid depreciation allowances under MACRS and the preferential capital gain rate preference was to counterbalance inflation.

Meanwhile, problems caused by inflation with respect to debt have been largely ignored, although it is widely recognized that inflation results in overstatement of both interest income and interest deductions, a portion of which should be recharacterized as principal. For example, if a one-year loan of $10,000 has an interest rate of 9 percent, in the absence of inflation, the lender will have real income of $900 and the borrower will pay real interest of $900. If the inflation rate is 5 percent during that period, however, the lender has suffered a real loss of $500 because the borrower will repay $10,000, which is worth only $9,500 in Year 2 dollars. Similarly, the borrower has gained $500. In effect, the $10,000 principal of the loan was reduced by $500 due to the 5 percent inflation. One way to accurately treat this transaction is to give the lender a deductible loss of $500 and to tax the borrower on $500 of discharge of indebtedness income. Another alternative is to treat a portion of each interest payment as a return of principal. For example, the lender would treat $500 of the $900 payment by the borrower as principal and report only $400 of interest income; conversely, the borrower would deduct only $400 of interest expense. Adjusting for inflation would be quite complex.

Ignoring inflation's impact on the tax treatment of debt has largely been justified on the theory that the undertaxation of debtors (which results from overstating the interest deductions) in the aggregate will be compensated for by overtaxation of creditors (which results from overstating the interest income).* But this is unlikely to be true. The creditors are likely to be low-bracket taxpayers or tax-exempt and the borrowers are likely to be high-bracket taxpayers. Because the borrowers save more than the creditors pay in taxes, the fisc loses.

Congress' priorities in responding to the distortion of income caused by inflation no doubt reflect political considerations. Only the Treasury loses

* In 1977, for example, Treasury justified its proposal to index assets but not debt on this ground. U.S. Treasury Dep't, Blueprints for Tax Reform (1977).

when Congress acts to reduce the inflationary overtaxation of owners of capital assets. Any effort to redress the overtaxation of lenders, however, would simultaneously require an effort to redress the undertaxation of the far more numerous borrowers. Moreover, there has been little demand among lenders for Congress to take such actions. Taxable institutional lenders, such as banks and insurance companies, can shelter much of their overstated income, and tax-exempt lenders, such as pension funds and university endowment funds, are indifferent to income overstatement. Influential commentators have contributed to the imbalance by noting the practical difficulties of income tax indexing, particularly of indexing debt, and by focusing on the inhibiting effect of asset overtaxation on capital formation.

Where assets are indexed or treated favorably, but debt is not, the taxpayer can engage in a form of tax arbitrage. By overstating the interest deduction on debt used to purchase an asset, he can create a tax savings where there is no economic return. Suppose, for example, T borrows $1,000 and invests the entire amount in stock that pays an annual dividend of $50. T pays interest at the annual rate of 5 percent plus inflation. During the year, there is 10 percent inflation and the value of the stock goes up to $1,100. T sells the stock and uses the sales proceeds plus the dividend to pay off the loan and accrued interest. Although there are no economic consequences to this transaction, as T will have no profit on the stock, there would be a tax loss. As the basis of the stock would be indexed to $1,100, T would have no gain. He would report the $50 dividend and have a $150 interest deduction, resulting in a net $100 tax loss.

The 1984 Treasury Report to the President recommended rather comprehensive income tax adjustments for inflation. See 2 Treasury Dep't, Report to the President, Tax Reform for Fairness, Simplicity and Economic Growth 193–200 (1984). These included indexation of depreciation allowances, the basis of capital assets, and inventories. Interest would have been indexed for inflation by excluding a fractional amount of interest receipts from income and denying deduction of a corresponding fraction of interest payments. Congress did not adopt Treasury's proposal or any other when it considered comprehensive tax reform in 1986. For a comprehensive discussion of inflation, see Reed Shuldiner, Indexing the Tax Code, 48 Tax L.Rev. 537 (1993).

The failure of Congress to revise the taxation of debt to account for inflation, together with its capriciousness in revising the taxation of assets, has created an income tax that is often incapable of accurately measuring the income of asset owners, debtors, or creditors. Because Polonius' admonition to "neither a borrower nor a lender be" is universally ignored in modern American society, the wrong tax burden has been imposed on virtually every individual and corporation.

SECTION 7. LOSSES

A. IN GENERAL

Section 165 of the Code permits deductions for certain losses not compensated for by insurance. Generally, § 165, consistent with §§ 162 and 212, allows deductions for losses incurred in connection with a trade or business or a transaction entered into for profit. See § 165(a), (c)(1) and (c)(2). There can be important tax differences, however, depending on whether a loss is a business loss or a loss arising from income producing activities that fall short of a trade or business. The latter may be treated as capital losses and subject to limitations that do not apply to ordinary business losses. Losses that are connected with neither a trade or business nor profit seeking activity are personal in nature and generally not deductible. Section 165 allows a deduction, however, for certain personal casualty and theft losses. See § 165(c)(3), (d) and (e). Other sections of the Code deny deductions for losses in specific circumstances.

This Section organizes these specific limitations on deductions for losses into three categories: (1) losses that might be considered personal, (2) losses related to unrealized gains, and (3) tax shelter losses. Three limitations designed to enforce the nondeductibility of personal losses are considered by taking a slightly different look at the now familiar distinction between personal and income producing activities. Limitations on deductions for gambling losses under § 165(d), and for so-called hobby losses under § 183, are treated first, followed by an examination of deductibility of casualty losses, the major exception to the general policy that losses incurred on assets related to personal consumption are not deductible. Next follows a discussion of loss deduction limitations that have been enacted to protect against taxpayers' efforts to take advantage of the realization requirement by realizing losses for tax purposes without fully parting with the asset, for example, by so-called wash sales (§ 1091), and sales to related parties (§ 267). Limitations to restrict a rather elaborate tax planning scheme, "straddles," which take advantage of the realization requirement, also are briefly described here. However, a detailed discussion of capital losses is postponed until Chapter 5.

The limitations on deductions for tax shelter losses—for example, the passive loss rules of § 469—are intended primarily to preclude taxpayers from using losses derived from tax shelter investments to reduce taxes on earned income and on investment income such as dividends and interest. These rules are described at the end of this Section.

Before turning to the various limitations on losses, the following Note considers the general issues of when and whether a loss exists and in what amount.

NOTE DISCUSSING WHEN AND WHETHER A LOSS EXISTS AND IN WHAT AMOUNT

1. WHEN DO LOSSES OCCUR?

As should be clear from prior materials, neither gains nor losses are taken into account for tax purposes as they accrue. Instead, they produce tax consequences only when they are realized. Thus, a mere decline in value is insufficient to create a loss for tax purposes. The time of realization is clear when property is sold, exchanged, or otherwise disposed of. But a taxpayer may dispose of property without actually suffering an economic loss, where he sells to a related party or where he is under an obligation to repurchase the property. For example, in Scully v. United States, 840 F.2d 478 (7th Cir.1988), the court held there was no genuine economic loss arising from a sale of property between two trusts with the same fiduciaries and beneficiaries. This issue is discussed further infra at page 394. Losses sometimes are allowed when property becomes worthless, an issue that troubled the Supreme Court in the early days of the income tax. For example, in United States v. S.S. White Dental Manufacturing Co., 274 U.S. 398 (1927), the Court held that a loss was realized in 1918, when the German government seized the taxpayer's wholly-owned German branch, despite the possibility that some sort of claim might subsequently be presented against the German government. The Court said:

> The quoted regulations, consistently with the statute, contemplate that a loss may become complete enough for deduction without the taxpayer's establishing that there is no possibility of an eventual recoupment. * * * The Taxing Act does not require the taxpayer to be an incorrigible optimist.

Section 165(g) allows deduction for a loss when certain securities become worthless. In Boehm v. Commissioner, 326 U.S. 287 (1945), the Court held that a loss on a security was sustained when the security actually became worthless and not when the taxpayer in good faith believed that it had become worthless. In other words, an "objective" rather than a "subjective" test applies to this question. This test has produced many disputes. Section 6511(d) provides a seven-year statute of limitations for refund claims under § 165(g). The former three-year limit caused much litigation because the Commissioner often claimed the proper year for deducting the loss was a year barred by the statute.

A casualty is treated as a realization event, even if it does not cause a total loss. See, e.g., Alcoma Association v. United States, 239 F.2d 365 (5th Cir.1956) (allowing casualty loss deduction for citrus grove partially destroyed by hurricane).

The courts tend to fix the time of loss by looking to a "definitive" or "identifiable" event or to conduct indicating a "closed transaction" or "no reasonable prospect of recovery." The test is a "flexible practical one," not dependent upon "any single factor," thus requiring the courts to look to "realism and practicality" for the answer. The mere failure to use property is not enough, although it is not necessary to give up legal title. There must be some action evincing an intent to abandon property or the prospects of its recovery. Most cases have held that a loss deduction may not be taken on account of loss of goodwill until the taxpayer has disposed of the entire business. In general, no deduction is allowed for the loss of anticipated income.

2.   AMOUNT OF LOSS DEDUCTION

Although taxpayers think of losses in terms of market value, § 165(b) provides that the amount of the loss deduction is the adjusted basis of the property. The amount of deductible loss may not be obvious when the loss is partially compensated for by insurance. In Kraus v. Commissioner, 10 T.C.M. 1071 (1951), for example, the taxpayer owned a residence that had cost $10,000. The value of the house rose to $18,000 before it was destroyed by fire. The taxpayer received $7,000 in insurance proceeds. The taxpayer argued that he should be entitled to deduct $10,000. His contention was that his overall loss was $18,000 (since the property had no salvage value after the fire). He then applied the $7,000 insurance payment against the $18,000 value to obtain a net loss of $11,000. He argued that he could then deduct the lower of his net loss ($11,000) or his basis ($10,000). The Tax Court held that the deductible loss was $3,000—the difference between the $10,000 basis and the $7,000 insurance payment.

3. THE DISTINCTION BETWEEN BUSINESS AND NONBUSINESS PROFIT–SEEKING LOSSES

Business losses under § 165(c)(1) may receive more favorable tax treatment over time—in the form of net operating loss carryforwards or carrybacks provided by § 172—than investment or transaction-for-profit losses under § 165(c)(2). Trade or business losses are deductible from gross income rather than from adjusted gross income and therefore can be taken even if the taxpayer does not itemize deductions. § 62(a)(2). Section 165(c)(2) losses can be deducted in computing adjusted gross income only if they result from a sale or exchange of property or are attributable to property that produces rent or royalties. § 62(a)(3), (4). Otherwise, these loss deductions must be itemized and are allowed only if the taxpayer's total "allowable itemized deductions" exceed the standard deduction. Moreover, many nonbusiness losses are "capital losses" whose deductibility is limited, while business losses are more likely to be "ordinary losses" deductible in full against ordinary income. The definition and treatment of capital losses are considered in Chapter 5.

Differences such as those described above can make it important to know whether a loss was incurred in business or a nonbusiness profit-seeking activity. For example, in Yerkie v. Commissioner, 67 T.C. 388 (1976), the taxpayer argued that his repayment to his employer of embezzled funds was a business loss, which could be carried back and forward under § 172 as a net operating loss, because he was in the trade or business of being a salaried employee (although not the trade or business of embezzlement). The Tax Court recognized that, while being an employee is treated as a trade or business under the Code, the loss in this case was incurred in an unrelated profit-seeking activity, and allowed deduction for repayment of embezzlement proceeds as an itemized deduction subject to the limitations of § 165(c)(2).

A more typical example is presented by the case of Reese v. Commissioner, 35 T.C.M. 1228 (1976), which involved losses on the general contracting and financing of a manufacturing plant for a company of which the taxpayer was president, treasurer, chairman of the board of directors, and a principal stockholder. In finding that the loss was a nonbusiness loss, the court stated:

> In order for petitioner to qualify for a loss deduction under section 165(c)(1) the loss must be sustained in a trade or business. It is clear that the taxpayer may be engaged in more than one trade or business.

* * * Whether the taxpayer's activities constitute a trade or business is a question of fact. * * *

Petitioner was primarily engaged in the business of a corporate executive. Petitioner contends, however, that he was also engaged in another business—that of general contractor. * * * We must consequently determine whether his activities in regard to that project constituted a trade or business.

Prior to [this] project petitioner admittedly had not been engaged as a general contractor nor was he so engaged on any subsequent project. Moreover, the record does not support a conclusion that petitioner did more than provide the financing for [this] project. In addition, no evidence regarding either the amount of time petitioner devoted to the project or specific tasks preformed by petitioner in pursuit of the alleged trade or business was presented.

Petitioner was clearly motivated by a desire to make a profit. The profit motive is in itself insufficient to transform financing activities into a trade or business. Thus, the loss is not deductible under section 165(c)(1) as a loss incurred in a trade or business. Nevertheless, since petitioner's primary motive was to obtain a profit, the loss is deductible under section 165(c)(2) as a loss incurred in a transaction entered into for profit.

B.   THE DISTINCTION BETWEEN PROFIT-SEEKING (OR BUSINESS) AND PERSONAL LOSSES

NOTE INTRODUCING THE DISTINCTION BETWEEN PROFIT-SEEKING (OR BUSINESS) AND PERSONAL LOSSES

1.   IN GENERAL

Section 165 denies a deduction for personal losses other than theft and casualty losses. To a large extent, this rule corresponds to the rule of § 262 disallowing any deduction for personal expenses.

Under § 165, the problem of distinguishing nondeductible personal losses from deductible income-seeking losses sometimes arises with regard to residential property that has been used or offered for use for both purposes. In Austin v. Commissioner, 298 F.2d 583 (2d Cir.1962), for example, the court asked whether the taxpayer's primary motive in acquiring and holding residential property was to earn a profit; the Second Circuit upheld the Tax Court's finding that a loss was not deductible because it was incurred on the sale of property "purchased by [the taxpayer] primarily for a residence and secondarily to generate a profit." The taxpayer had purchased a $28,000 home in Poughkeepsie, N.Y. in anticipation of his company's announced relocation from New York City. He immediately undertook a $40,000 renovation of the house. The company cancelled its relocation plans after the taxpayer had sold his previous home and moved into the new home. He immediately offered the home for sale and also offered it for rental one year later. When the house and land were finally sold, the taxpayer claimed a large loss deduction. In upholding the Tax Court's disallowance of the loss, the Second Circuit stated:

The logical interrelationship of § 165 and § 262 [disallowing deductions for personal expenses] requires a decision as to which of the two motives was dominant, so that one or the other section can be applied. * * * This court has repeatedly held that, in determining the deductibility of a loss, the primary motive must be ascertained and given effect.

The same result typically is reached where the property first was acquired for rental purposes and so used, but then was used as a personal residence up to the time of the sale. This result also may be reached even though the taxpayer had ceased for some time before the sale to occupy the premises as a residence, had made efforts to rent it, and had expended substantial sums to place it in a more saleable condition. Is a loss deductible if the property was lived in, then rented for a period, and then sold? Reg. § 1.165–9(b)(1) permits a deduction if the property has been "appropriated to income-producing purposes." See also Rechnitzer v. Commissioner, 26 T.C.M. 298 (1967) (residence converted to rental property; loss allowed under § 165(c)(2)).

When part of a property is used for one purpose and part for another, or when the same property is used at different times for different purposes, losses from the sale of the property must be allocated between the different uses. The deduction is allowed in proportion to the business or income-producing use in the same way that a taxpayer's basis in property is allocated between personal and business uses for calculating depreciation. For example, the taxpayer in Sharp v. United States, 199 F.Supp. 743 (D.Del.1961), aff'd per curiam 303 F.2d 783 (3d Cir.1962), owned an airplane that cost $54,000. The airplane was used 75 percent for personal matters and 25 percent for business. The taxpayer took depreciation totaling $13,000 on one-fourth of the cost. The question was the amount of gain or loss realized by the taxpayer on the sale of the airplane for $35,000.

The taxpayer said that, since the cost was $54,000 and the depreciation allowed was $13,000, his adjusted basis was $41,000. Consequently, he claimed a loss of $6,000 when the plane was sold for $35,000. He did not contend that this loss was deductible. The government's contention was that three-fourths of the cost, or $40,500, was personal and remaining one-fourth, or $13,500, was business. The $13,000 depreciation was allocable only against this business portion of the plane, leaving an adjusted basis of $40,500 for the personal portion and $500 for the business portion. This produced a nondeductible loss of $14,250 on the personal portion and a taxable gain of $8,250 on the business portion ($8,750 less the $500 remaining basis on that portion). The court agreed.

2. GAMBLING LOSSES

A gambling loss is a classic example of a loss that is presumed to involve a component of personal consumption. To prevent taxpayers from using such consumption-related losses to reduce the tax otherwise payable on other unrelated income and to permit the deduction of losses only when incurred in business or profit-seeking activities, § 165(d) allows gambling losses to be deducted only to the extent of gambling gains. This technique—limiting deductions to the amount of related income—has become quite common in the Code. Similar rules, for example, apply with respect to vacation homes, § 280A, hobby losses, § 183, and passive losses, § 469. Hobby losses are considered infra at page 416 and passive losses at page 418.

NOTES

(A) *Proving Gambling Losses.* The issue most frequently litigated in gambling loss cases is the adequacy of the taxpayer's proof of his losses. For example, in Green v. Commissioner, 31 T.C.M. 592 (1972), the taxpayer submitted $23,680 in losing tickets, all allegedly purchased by him or on his behalf within a period of less than six weeks. The court noted that "[s]everal of the losing tickets submitted unmistakably bear heel marks," and disallowed a portion of the losses claimed. See also DeMonaco v. Commissioner, 41 T.C.M. 718 (1981) (gambling losses disallowed; uncashed losing race tickets had no heel marks but were purchased at ticket windows to which taxpayer had no access, purchased at multiple windows for the same race, and were nonsequential).

Gamblers often have inadequate records and attempt to rely on the so-called *Cohan* rule that permits a deduction based on estimates where the court believes that an expense actually was undertaken. Cohan v. Commissioner, 39 F.2d 540 (2d Cir.1930), is a classic case in the tax law. In that case, the Board of Tax Appeals noted that George M. Cohan had spent considerable sums of money in entertaining actors, employees, and drama critics, but disallowed any deduction on the grounds that it was impossible to tell how much he had spent because his records were inadequate. The Second Circuit reversed in an opinion by Judge Learned Hand and instructed the Board to "make as close an approximation as it can." The case was expressly overruled for entertainment expenses by § 274 of the Code, which requires adequate records to support all entertainment expenses, but the *Cohan* rule lives on in other contexts.

(B) *Why Limit Gambling Losses?* Section 165(d) allows wagering losses to be deducted only to the extent of wagering gains. What is the rationale for this rule? Is it likely that consistent losers are gambling for personal, rather than profit-seeking reasons? Or, is there at least a subjective expectation of profit? Compare the business-personal borderline, supra at page 246, and the "hobby loss" restrictions of § 183, infra at page 416. Should there at least be some ability to carry forward gambling losses to offset them against winnings in a subsequent year? How do the problems of proof affect this question?

(C) *Gambling Professionally.* Is a professional gambler—a full-time gambler who bets solely for his own account and does not act as a bookmaker or hold himself out in any way as offering goods or services to others—engaged in a trade or business?

The Supreme Court, in Commissioner v. Groetzinger, 480 U.S. 23 (1987), held that a professional gambler engages in a trade or business if "involved in the activity with continuity and regularity" and with the primary purpose of earning income or profit. A sporadic activity, a hobby or an amusement diversion does not qualify. In resolving a conflict on this issue among the circuits, the Court rejected the reasoning of the Second

Circuit in Gajewski v. Commissioner, 723 F.2d 1062 (2d Cir.1983), cert. denied 469 U.S. 818 (1984), that selling goods or services was a necessary element of engaging in a trade or business, a standard the Second Circuit had adopted from a statement in a concurring opinion by Justice Frankfurter in Deputy v. du Pont, 308 U.S. 488 (1940). The Supreme Court viewed full-time, professional gambling to be as much of a profit-making enterprise as any other activity, for example, active trading of securities. In cases following the *Groetzinger* decision, the Tax Court has held that professional gamblers' gambling losses and other expenses are deductible under § 162 as ordinary and necessary business expenses. This would permit any excess of gambling losses over gambling winnings to be carried back and forward to other taxable years under § 172, notwithstanding the limitations of § 165(d). See, e.g., Bathalter v. Commissioner, 54 T.C.M. 902 (1987) (treating full-time gambler as being in a trade or business for purposes of § 172).

(D) What Are Gambling Gains? Section 165(d) provides that "Losses from wagering transactions shall be allowed only to the extent of the gains from such transactions." Note that the statute does not say gambling "winnings." Does that mean that something other than winning bets might be used to offset gambling losses?

In Allen v. Commissioner, 976 F.2d 975 (5th Cir.1992), the court refused to permit a blackjack dealer to offset "tokes" against his gambling losses. The court determined that the tokes were given to the dealer by the gambling patrons for services rendered and they did not constitute a wagering transaction. In Boyd v. United States, 762 F.2d 1369 (9th Cir. 1985), a professional poker player was not permitted to use his losses to offset the fees he was paid by the house to play cards as a shill.

In a somewhat surprising opinion, a taxpayer was permitted to offset gambling losses with the $2.5 million in comps (free cars) that he received from an Atlantic City casino. Libutti v. Commissioner, 71 T.C.M. 2343 (1996). Judge Laro interpreted "gains" to mean any increases to the gambler's wealth that arose out of wagering transactions. Recall that in *Zarin*, set out supra at page 177, one of the dissenting opinions argues that any income Zarin had when the debt was discharged should be offset against his gambling losses in the same year. Is the discharge of indebtedness income properly considered a gain from gambling transactions when the indebtedness occurs due to gambling activities?

3. HOBBY LOSSES: LIMITED DEDUCTIBILITY OF EXPENSES INCURRED IN NOT–FOR–PROFIT ACTIVITIES

Section 183 is another provision designed to restrict the deduction of losses under § 165 to those incurred in the course of a business or profit-seeking activity. Losses incurred in the course of personal consumption are disallowed to the extent they exceed income from the activity. The "hobby loss" provisions of § 183 exemplify this rule.

Plunkett v. Commissioner

United States Tax Court, 1984. 47 T.C.M. 1439.

GOFFE, JUDGE:

Petitioner H. Connely Plunkett is an architectural engineer and a partner of an architectural firm located in Jackson, Mississippi. He also is in the business of building homes. Extensive income generated by these businesses partially paid for petitioner's mud-racing and truck-pulling activities.

Mud racing is a relatively new entrant to the American sporting scene. It generally involves speed competition amongst four-wheel drive vehicles on a circular track which has been intentionally transformed into a mudhole. * * *

Mud-racing drivers compete in four different classes: (1) vehicles with six-cylinder engines, (2) "V–8 stock," i.e., eight-cylinder vehicles whose engines and remaining components are substantially unchanged from the factory, (3) "street-modified," i.e., eight-cylinder vehicles whose engines are modified for racing but the remainder is substantially unchanged, and (4) "super-modified" which encompasses generally unrestricted multi-cylinder vehicles. * * *

Truck pulling is an entirely different sporting event. Although it also includes similar classes of four-wheel drive vehicles which have been modified for pulling, the participants complete by attempting to tow a large weighted sled along a straight dirt runway. * * *

As in mud racing, each truck-pulling participant competes in as many different classes as he has qualifying vehicles. Unlike mud racing, however, participation in a truck-pulling contest is by invitation only and there usually is no registration fee. Most truck-pulling events involve several days of competition. Cash awards are distributed to the winners and other high finishers at the end of each day of competition. Depending upon the size of the total purse, a truck-pulling competitor can win up to $1,000 per day in the "super-modified" class and possibly even $2,000 over a weekend. * * *

Petitioner began to mud race in 1975 without ever having been a spectator at such an event. Petitioner competed in only one mud race during the 1975 season yet won $100 on his debut. During the 1976, 1977 and 1978 mud-racing seasons, petitioner entered 10, 20 and 26 races, respectively. Petitioner generally competed in the "super-modified" class while mud racing.

During 1977, petitioner became increasingly interested in truck pulling. * * * Petitioner's interest in mud racing waned as his truck-pulling activities increased. This was largely the result of his realization that he had increased likelihood of winning more money in truck pulling. Truck-pulling contests generally have larger purses and this sport is increasing in popularity. Many truck pulls draw over 15,000 paying spectators.

Petitioner drove all of the vehicles he entered in mud races and truck pulls. He never had any formal training for these activities; he acquired expertise through participation. Petitioner did not employ any crew or experienced personnel to assist him in either competition format. Petitioner performed most of the maintenance work on his vehicles although he did employ a machinist to assist him in preparing and repairing various engine components. His 11–year-old son occasionally assisted him. Petitioner devoted approximately 500 hours per year to his mud-racing and truck-pulling activities during the years in issue.

Petitioner enjoyed mud racing and truck pulling. When petitioner began to mud race, he anticipated that it would take him three years to recover his initial outlays. * * *

Section 183(a) provides that, except as otherwise permitted in that section, individual taxpayers will not be allowed deductions which are attributable to activities that are "not engaged in for profit." Section 183(b)(1) provides that deductions which would be allowable without regard to whether such activity is engaged in for profit shall be allowed. Section 183(b)(2) further provides that deductions which would be allowable only if such activity is engaged in for profit shall be allowed "but only to the extent that the gross income derived from such activity for the taxable year exceeds the deductions allowable by reason of paragraph (1)." * * *

The standard * * * is: did the individual engage in the activity "with the actual and honest objective of making a profit"? Dreicer v. Commissioner, 78 T.C. 642, 645 (1982), aff'd without published opinion, 702 F.2d 1205 (D.C.Cir.1983). Although a taxpayer's expectation of profit need not be reasonable, the facts and circumstances must indicate that the taxpayer had the requisite profit objective. Dreicer v. Commissioner, supra at 645. * * *

The question of whether petitioner's mud-racing and truck-pulling activities fall within the purview of section 183(a) is one of fact which must be resolved on the basis of all of the facts and circumstances and not just one factor. * * *

Section 1.183–2(b), Income Tax Regs., lists some of the relevant factors, derived principally from case law, which "should normally be taken into account" in determining whether an activity is engaged in for profit. The factors include: (1) the manner in which the taxpayer carries on the activity, (2) the expertise of the taxpayer or his advisors, (3) the time and effort expended by the taxpayer in carrying on the activity, (4) the expectation that the assets used in the activity may appreciate in value, (5) the success of the taxpayer in carrying on other similar or dissimilar activities, (6) the taxpayer's history of income or loss with respect to the activity, (7) the amount of occasional profits, if any, which are earned, (8) the financial status of the taxpayer, and (9) whether elements of personal pleasure or recreation are involved.

Upon examination of petitioner's mud-racing activities in light of the nine objective criteria set forth in the regulations, we hold that such endeavors constitute an activity "not engaged in for profit" within the scope of section 183(a). Although petitioner was experienced in mechanics and racing and had been "playing with automobiles" since he was 12, he had no prior experience in four-wheel drive vehicle competition prior to the start of his mud-racing activities. The racing of four-wheel drive vehicles through specially built mudholes also involves a great deal of recreational characteristics. Further, the profit potential from mud racing is generally low. Each participant must successfully complete numerous heats to even be eligible for the cash awards, thus significantly increasing the likelihood of elimination or damage to the mud racer. Finally, even assuming petitioner had won every mud race he entered (which is totally unsupported by petitioner's actual track record), his total winnings would have been significantly less than his attendant expenses; therefore, petitioner did not have an actual and honest objective of making a profit from his mud-racing activities during the years in issue. Sec. 1.183–2(a), Income Tax Regs.; Dreicer v. Commissioner, supra. Accordingly, all of petitioner's mud-racing expenses during the years in issue shall be governed by the provisions of section 183.

Upon review of petitioner's truck-pulling activities, however, we hold that such endeavors were engaged in for profit during petitioner's taxable year 1978. Petitioner carried on his truck-pulling activities in a workman-like fashion, guided by the additional racing experience he gained during his mud-racing competition. Through his diligence and devotion of large amounts of time and effort, petitioner was ultimately ranked 35th in the nation by Truck–O–Rama, a national truck-pulling promoter. Petitioner also converted some of his mud-racing vehicles into truck-pulling devices, thus limiting his recreational use of such vehicles in future mud races, with no assurance that he would even be able to compete since participation in truck pulls is by invitation only. Finally, petitioner expanded into this new activity only after realizing that it had a greater profit potential than mud racing. Truck pulling differs from mud racing in several significant respects concerning its profitability potential. Truck-pulling contests generally have larger total purses and class prizes and this pasttime is increasing in popularity. The truck-pulling circuit is also national in scope while mud racing is generally confined to the southeastern portions of the country. A truck-pulling participant's chances of elimination or damage to his vehicle is also significantly less than a mud racer's because a truck-pulling competitor's finish and eligibility for cash awards is determined by a single pulling attempt while mud racing involves numerous elimination heats.

While some of the objective criteria listed in the regulations weigh against the petitioner, we do not consider them significant enough to offset the criteria which weigh in his favor. Although petitioner did not maintain a formal set of records concerning his truck-pulling endeavors, he generally conducted this activity in a fashion similar to his construction business which was also engaged in for profit. * * * Further, the fact that petitioner's truck-pulling activities were not immediately profitable does not alter our opinion that petitioner had a bona fide objective of making a profit when he began to compete in truck-pulling contests. The regulations specifically acknowledge that losses can be incurred during the formative years of profit-oriented activities. Sec. 1.183–2(b)(6), Income Tax Regs. * * * Finally, the fact that truck-pulling competition and the related preparatory activities involve some elements of recreation and pleasure for petitioner, who liked to work on cars, is not determinative.

NOTES

(A) *Purpose of Section 183.* Section 183 itself does not permit a deduction for a loss. Section 165(c), however, requires that losses be incurred in a business or in a transaction entered into for profit. Section 183 provides guidelines for determining whether an activity is entered into for profit. There is a rebuttable presumption that an activity was engaged in with the requisite profit motive if the activity produced profits for three out of five consecutive years ending with the year in question. If an activity cannot meet the presumption, a taxpayer may still attempt to prove the activity was engaged in for profit by using the regulation's factors, which are described in *Plunkett*.

If an activity is not engaged in for profit, certain deductions are permitted in any event. First, a taxpayer may deduct those amounts that are deductible without regard to whether there was a profit motive, for example, taxes under § 164. Second, any amount that would have been deductible if there had been the requisite profit motive is deductible to the extent of gross income from the activity minus the first sort of deductions.

(B) *The Legal Standard.* In Dreicer v. Commissioner, 78 T.C. 642 (1982), cited in *Plunkett,* the Tax Court reconsidered a decision that had been reversed and remanded by the Court of Appeals for the District of Columbia Circuit because an erroneous legal standard had been applied in determining whether a taxpayer's activities were engaged in for profit. Dreicer v. Commissioner, 665 F.2d 1292 (D.C.Cir.1981). The Tax Court had found that the taxpayer's activities were not engaged in for profit and had disallowed large loss deductions, principally for travel expenses that the taxpayer claimed had been incurred in the course of his writing and lecturing activities. The Tax Court described the grounds for the Court of Appeals' reversal as follows:

> On appeal, Mr. Dreicer argued that we had applied an incorrect legal standard, in that we predicated our decision on his profit expectation rather than his profit objective. The Court of Appeals examined the legislative history of section 183 and determined that the proper standard was whether the taxpayer engaged in the activity with the objective of making a profit, not whether he had a reasonable expectation of making a profit. The proper standard was expressed by that court as "when profit is actually and honestly his objective though the prospect of achieving it may seem dim." The Court of Appeals found that rather than focusing our analysis on whether Mr. Dreicer had an objective of making a profit, we focused on whether he had "a bona fide expectation of profit." The court apparently feared that we were equating a bona fide expectation of profit with a reasonable expectation of profit. Thus, it held that we had applied an erroneous legal standard in determining whether Mr. Dreicer's activities were engaged in for profit.

78 T.C. at 644.

The Tax Court agreed with the Court of Appeals' statement of the proper standard and indicated that it had intended its use of the term "bona fide expectation of profit" to have the same meaning as "an actual and honest profit objective." In reexamining the *Dreicer* record, the court found that this standard was not satisfied by the taxpayer's contention that he was "like the wildcat driller or the inventor * * * continuing his endeavors in the face of adverse results in the hope of one day reaping a large profit." Instead, the court found that "[f]or many years, [this taxpayer] sustained large losses; there was no realistic possibility that he could ever earn sufficient income from his activity to offset such losses; * * * he was able to continue to bear such losses only because of his large resources," and "[r]ather, there is a strong indication that he enjoyed his life of travel." The court again disallowed the deductions and its decision was upheld on appeal in an unpublished opinion.

(C) *The Cases Turn on Their Facts.* Section 183 cases are highly fact-specific. What may be a profit-seeking activity for one taxpayer may not be for another. Compare Cornfeld v. Commissioner, 797 F.2d 1049 (D.C.Cir. 1986) (taxpayer had honest profit objective in connection with his aircraft leasing activities), with Worley v. Commissioner, 39 T.C.M. 1090 (1980) (no profit motive existed with respect to aircraft leasing). Furthermore, a taxpayer may have the proper motive one year and have abandoned it in a future year. See, e.g., Kartrude v. Commissioner, 925 F.2d 1379 (11th Cir.1991) (stunt flier lacked proper profit motive although he previously had operated the activity as a business).

Dentists seem to have a lot of time on their hands. In Zdun v. Commissioner, 76 T.C.M. 278 (1998), aff'd per curiam 229 F.3d 1161 (9th Cir.2000), the taxpayer attempted to combine a holistic dental practice with an organic apple orchard. When the latter lost money, he claimed it was part of the profitable dental practice because he sold the apples to his patients. The court found it was a separate activity not conducted for profit. The dentist in Morley v. Commissioner, 76 T.C.M. 363 (1998), was more successful. The court permitted him to deduct the losses from his Arabian horse breeding, remarking:

> Mr. Morley's work on the farm was difficult, and it often precluded him from spending time with his family. Mrs. Morley credibly testified that she and her children missed her husband and that she would have preferred it if Mr. Morley had been at home instead of working on the horse-breeding activity. Mr. Morley arrived home after dark, very tired, in a bad mood, and dirty with "a certain aroma" from his work on the farm. It appeared to the Court that Mrs. Morley resented the amount of time Mr. Morley spent on the horse-breeding activity and that she was unhappy that her husband came home every night dirty and smelly. We are not convinced that Mr. Morley would subject himself to such rigors solely for recreation or pleasure.

(D) *Tax Shelters.* Traditionally, the hobby loss problem involved activities that were unrelated to a taxpayer's primary business activities and that arguably provided a means of securing business deductions for what were in reality personal consumption expenditures. See, e.g., Benz v. Commissioner, 63 T.C. 375 (1974) (expenses of a businessman who lost money breeding and training dogs). More recent cases have applied § 183 to tax shelters and represent an evolution of the original hobby loss concept. The use of § 183 as a weapon in the battles against tax shelters is discussed infra at page 416.

4. CASUALTY LOSSES

NOTE ON CASUALTY LOSSES

Section 165(c)(3) allows deductions for personal losses arising from "fire, storm, shipwreck, or other casualty, or from theft." Only uninsured casualty losses exceeding $100 are taken into account. Deductions for casualty and theft losses equal to casualty and theft gains are deductible from gross income. Excess casualty losses are limited to the amount that exceeds 10 percent of adjusted gross income and are deductible only as itemized deductions. § 165(h)(2). No deduction is permitted if the taxpayer does not file a timely insurance claim to the extent the policy would provide reimbursement.

The deduction for casualty and theft losses may seem at odds with the policy of disallowing personal losses, but the allowance may be motivated by ability-to-pay considerations. Suppose the taxpayer's $2,000 paycheck is stolen. Has the taxpayer therefore lost the opportunity to consume $2,000 or should he be taxed because he had the opportunity to consume $2,000 but was unable to do so? Is the answer different if he lost his paycheck?

The 10 percent floor ensures that only large and uninsured losses are deductible. Therefore, taxpayers who have sustained a severe, unexpected and nonvolitional loss will bear less tax than other taxpayers who have not experienced such losses. The reports of the House and Senate on the Revenue Act of 1964 state:

> [I]n the case of nonbusiness casualty and theft losses, it is appropriate in computing taxable income to allow the deduction only of those losses which may be considered extraordinary, nonrecurring losses, and which go beyond the average or usual losses incurred by most taxpayers in day-to-day living. * * * This means that * * * casualty and theft losses will continue to be deductible * * * in those cases where they are sufficient in size to have a significant effect upon an individual's ability to pay Federal income taxes. * * *

The casualty loss rule is comparable to the medical expenses deduction, which is limited to amounts in excess of 7.5 percent of AGI. In each case, the loss or expense is considered to be largely beyond the taxpayer's control and not the result of a personal consumption choice, unlike gambling losses, where even very large net losses are not deductible. Some observers, however, regard the widespread availability of casualty insurance as adequate protection and would repeal the casualty loss deduction.

A great deal of litigation has occurred over the meaning of the word "casualty" in § 165(c)(3), particularly what is meant by "other casualty." For example, Kielts v. Commissioner, 42 T.C.M. 238 (1981), allowed a casualty loss deduction for the adjusted basis of a $20,000 diamond lost from a ring, based on expert testimony that the ring had suffered from a "fairly strong blow" on one side of the ring. Mrs. Kielts had absolutely no recollection of any such event. The court added, "absent willfulness, negligence has no bearing on whether a casualty has occurred." The same result was reached in White v. Commissioner, 48 T.C. 430 (1967), where the taxpayer irretrievably lost a diamond in her gravel driveway while shaking her hand in pain after a car door was slammed on it. The court concluded that the "events giving rise to the loss were 'sudden, unexpected, violent and not due to deliberate or willful actions'" by the taxpayer. A similar "sudden event" occurred in Carpenter v. Commissioner, 25 T.C.M. 1186 (1966), where the taxpayer's husband emptied the contents of a glass, which included her ring in a soaking solution, into a garbage disposal.

Contrast these cases with Keenan v. Bowers, 91 F.Supp. 771 (E.D.S.C. 1950). There a wife wrapped her diamond ring in a tissue and placed it on the nightstand. In the morning, her husband, who had used several tissues to blow his nose during the night, collected all the tissues and flushed them down the toilet. The court held that the event was not sudden and denied any deduction. Similarly, in Stevens v. Commissioner, 6 T.C.M. 805 (1947), a duck-hunting taxpayer was denied a deduction for the loss of a ring that fell in the water while he was retrieving a decoy.

Attempts to develop a definition of "suddenness" have led to bizarre results. The court notes that Anne Kielts' loss "would be considered sudden, whether 'suddenness' is determined with reference to the event itself or measured by the time interval between the cause of a loss and manifestation of an effect." The suddenness requirement often goes hand in hand with a requirement that the event be unforeseen.

Cases and rulings involving animals give the flavor of the sometimes irrational way these two standards have been interpreted. For example, in Revenue Ruling 63–232, 1963–2 C.B. 97, the IRS changed its position on the deductibility of losses resulting from termite damage. The Service previously had followed court rulings that damage caused by termites over periods up to 15 months after infestation constituted a deductible casualty. But then the Service, after "extensive examination of scientific data regarding the habits, destructive power and other factors peculiar to termites," found that "authorities agree that termite infestation and the resulting damage cannot be inflicted with the suddenness comparable to that caused by fire, storm or shipwreck." Contrast that holding with the one in Revenue Ruling 79–174, 1979–1 C.B. 99, where the Service found that an attack of southern pine beetles on pine trees was a casualty, citing evidence that pine beetles killed their quarry within five to 30 days. Slow-moving pests apparently do not cause deductible casualties. See, e.g., Banigan v. Commissioner, 10 T.C.M. 561 (1951) (denying a deduction for rat infestation); Rev.Rul. 55–327, 1955–1 C.B. 25 (denying a deduction for carpet beetles).

The IRS has also suggested that an advance warning that animals might behave in a particular manner precludes a deduction. For example, in Revenue Ruling 73–123, 1973–1 C.B. 76, the Service denied a deduction for the loss caused by a horse who stripped the bark from ornamental trees, causing their death. The damage was said to be "not unexpected or unusual." The Tax Court appears to agree. In Dyer v. Commissioner, 20 T.C.M. 705 (1961), the court refused to treat as a casualty damage to an expensive vase caused by the taxpayer's cat "having a fit." It rejected the taxpayer's argument that the damage was not caused by "the cat's ordinary perambulations on the top of the particular piece of furniture, but by its extraordinary behavior there in the course of having its first fit." Similarly, in Ltr. Rul. 8133097, a taxpayer was not permitted to deduct the damage to a roof caused by squirrels because it was "common knowledge that squirrels are destructive." Is that position consistent with a decision permitting a deduction for damage to trees due to ice storms or hurricanes? See Hollington v. Commissioner, 15 T.C.M. 668 (1956) (permitting deduction for storm damage to roof of house and shrubs).

This distinction may be attributable to the fact that courts permit any loss attributable to "fire, storm or shipwreck," casualties specified by the statute, but are more stringent in defining other casualties. Compare Portman v. United States, 683 F.2d 1280 (9th Cir.1982) (no deduction for damage due to heavy rainfall because it was not beyond the range of foreseeable weather conditions), with Butschky v. United States, 82–1 U.S.T.C. ¶ 9139 (D.Md.) (damage caused to house by heavy rainfall during hurricane deductible).

Suddenness may be necessary, but it is not sufficient. A mere decline in value does not give rise to a deduction unless there is actual physical damage. For example, two of O.J. Simpson's neighbors claimed a casualty loss due to the decline in value of their Brentwood properties because of the murders and the subsequent media attention and influx of onlookers. In each case, the deduction was denied because there was no physical damage to the property and because as the Tax Court put it, the claim was based on a long period of public attention "more akin to a steadily operating cause than to a casualty." Chamales v. Commissioner, 79 T.C.M. 1428 (2000); Caan v. United States, 99–1 USTC ¶ 50,349 (C.D.Cal.1999).

The suddenness and physical damage requirements probably should be viewed as backstops to the realization requirement and depreciation rules. Recall that generally a taxpayer cannot take a deduction for the decline in value of property until the loss is "realized." Similarly, the depreciation deduction for ordinary wear and tear is unavailable for personal use property. A casualty deduction for anything less than a sudden event involving physical damage would circumvent these other limitations.

Amount of Loss. The amount of deduction on personal property is limited to the lesser of the fair market value before the casualty minus the fair market value after the casualty or the property's adjusted basis. § 1.165–7(b). Suppose, for example, the taxpayer's car is totally destroyed. The taxpayer paid $20,000 for the car, but at the time of the accident, it is worth only $8,000. The deductible loss is $8,000. The remaining $12,000 of basis is not a loss at all, but rather is attributable to the taxpayer's consumption, which is not deductible. On the other hand, suppose a painting worth $75,000 and purchased by the taxpayer for $30,000, is stolen. The deductible loss is $30,000. The remaining $45,000 represents untaxed appreciation.

It is necessary to disallow a loss deduction for unrealized gains in order to prevent the double benefit that otherwise would result since the gain was never taken into income. Treating the loss as an occasion for both the realization of gain and the deduction of the entire value of property would have the same effect in such circumstances as limiting the deduction to basis.

The amount of a casualty loss must be reduced by insurance or any other recovery. Reg. § 1.165–1(d)(2). If at the end of the taxable year in which the casualty occurs, there is a reasonable prospect of recovery, the taxpayer is not permitted to take a deduction. The Tenth Circuit set a high barrier for the taxpayer in finding that in order to take the deduction, the taxpayer must prove that it could be ascertained that the loss would never be recovered. Jeppsen v. Commissioner, 128 F.3d 1410 (10th Cir.1997).

Thus, even though the defendant disclaimed liability and no lawyer would even take the victim's claim on a contingency basis, no casualty deduction was permitted because at year end the taxpayer had not abandoned his claim.

NOTES

(A) *Theft Losses.* A theft loss is deductible in the year of discovery. Proving to the IRS that a theft loss occurred is often not straightforward. For example, in Krahmer v. United States, 810 F.2d 1145 (Fed.Cir.1987), the Federal Circuit held that the taxpayer had not shown that he was entitled to a theft loss deduction when a painting he purchased that bore the signature of W.M. Chase turned out not to be an original Chase. The court stated that the existence of the forged signature is not sufficient as a matter of law, and that the taxpayer must "prove that the seller defrauded him by knowingly and intentionally misattributing the painting to the artist." Swell.

(B) *Section 123.* Section 123 of the Code excludes from gross income amounts received under an insurance contract to reimburse the taxpayer for living expenses when his residence is destroyed by fire or other casualty.

(C) *Public Policy Limitation.* A taxpayer is entitled to take a deduction even if the casualty results from her negligence, but not if it is intentional or results from gross negligence. In Blackman v. Commissioner, 88 T.C. 677 (1987), the Tax Court explained that permitting such a deduction would frustrate national or state public policy. The taxpayer returned to his home and found another man living with his wife. After quarreling, the taxpayer gathered some of his wife's clothes and set fire to them on the stove. Although he claimed to have tried to douse the fire, it spread and the house and most of its contents (but not all of the clothes) were destroyed. He was charged with arson and malicious destruction because he "did willfully and maliciously destroy, injure, deface and molest clothing." The court found Mr. Blackman's actions amounted to gross negligence and that to permit a deduction would frustrate the state's public policy against arson, burning, and domestic violence.

If a taxpayer's house is destroyed by fire resulting from her smoking in bed, may she deduct the loss? If a taxpayer damages his car while driving under the influence of alcohol, may he deduct the loss? If a taxpayer builds a house near the San Andreas fault, may he deduct any earthquake damage?

(D) *Insurance.* Does the tax deduction for casualty losses have any bearing on the desirability of maintaining insurance? If a taxpayer has no insurance, is the government acting as insurer? Does the answer to the previous question depend upon an individual's tax bracket? Should the premiums for insurance against destruction of one's personal possessions be deductible? Consider the following comments from Boris Bittker, "Income Tax Deductions, Credits, and Subsidies for Personal Expenditures," 16 J. Law & Econ. 193, 197–98 (1973):

In a statistical sense, of course, destruction by fire is one of the hazards of home ownership, "voluntarily" assumed when the taxpayer chooses to buy a personal residence. But if a dog can distinguish between being kicked and being stumbled over, as Holmes asserted, we can properly distinguish between the minor frustrations of life—a cigarette burn in a rug, a dented fender, a quarter lost when fumbling for change to put in a parking meter—and major casualties ("sudden, unexpected, and unusual" events that do not "commonly occur in the ordinary course of day-to-day living)," (to quote a recent Revenue Ruling).

* * *

Casualties undeniably reduce the taxpayer's net worth—and should therefore presumptively reduce his income * * *.

A more cogent criticism of the casualty deduction is that taxpayers should be encouraged to insure against such losses and that the deduction mitigates the cost of neglecting this sensible precaution. Whatever its strength, this line of argument does not prove that a taxpayer whose uninsured home is destroyed by fire has the same "income" as an otherwise identical taxpayer whose house escapes. The first taxpayer's loss is real, no matter how stupid, pigheaded, or foolhardy his failure to insure. One might wish to deny him a deduction as a penalty for improvidence, as a warning to others, or as a mode of raising revenue; but these objectives should be openly acknowledged, not disguised as an effort to "define income" or to achieve horizontal equity.

Is the limitation on casualty loss deductions only to the extent they exceed 10 percent of adjusted gross income consistent with the position that Professor Bittker expresses? Is a floor based on a percentage of income preferable to a dollar amount limitation?

C. Limitations on Losses to Protect Against Abuses of the Realization Requirement

Fender v. United States

United States Court of Appeals, Fifth Circuit, 1978. 577 F.2d 934.

Ainsworth, Circuit Judge:

Harris R. Fender, an experienced investment banker, established two trusts for his two sons and in 1969 the trusts had large capital gains from the sale of certain Continental Telephone stock. To offset those gains, Harris Fender, co-trustee of the trust, attempted to sell an installment of Bender Road Improvement District WW and SS Combination Tax and Revenue Bonds ("Bender Bonds") owned by the trusts. These bonds, along with the bond market as a whole, had substantially declined in value as a result of a rise in interest rates. The bonds were purchased by the trusts for the amount of $435,017 and had a par value of $445,000. Because the bonds were unrated, they could not be sold in the public bond market. On December 26, 1969, Fender completed an over-the-counter sale of the

Bender Bonds to the Longview National Bank & Trust Company, Longview, Texas, for $225,000 (approximately 50% of par value) plus accrued interest. This resulted in a $106,258.35 loss for each of the trusts. At the time of the sale, Fender controlled 40.7% of the Longview National Bank's stock either individually or through the two trusts. Shortly thereafter, on January 15, 1970, the stock interest of Fender and the trusts in the Longview Bank increased to 50.15%. On February 6, 1970, 42 days after their transfer to the bank, the trusts repurchased the bonds from the bank for $224,735 (approximately 50.5% of par value) plus accrued interest. Both transactions were made at the fair market value of the bonds, though the bonds had limited marketability since they were unrated. The Internal Revenue Service disallowed the loss deduction claimed in connection with the transfer of the Bender Bonds and this litigation ensued.

A taxpayer is allowed a deduction for "any loss sustained during the taxable year * * *." I.R.C. § 165(a). However, not every transaction purporting to result in a loss is deductible. "Only a bona fide loss is allowable. Substance and not mere form shall govern in determining a deductible loss." Treas.Reg. § 1.165–1(b). The burden of showing that the loss was bona fide is on the taxpayer. See Rand v. Helvering, 8 Cir., 1935, 77 F.2d 450. Further, the district court's conclusion that the transfer of the Bender Bonds to the Longview Bank was a bona fide sale is a conclusion of law which this Court may fully review. * * *

In deciding to sell the Bender Bonds, the taxpayers were motivated by the possibility of tax avoidance. Standing alone such a motive is an insufficient basis for disallowing a deduction. The legal right of a taxpayer to decrease the amount of what would otherwise be his taxes, or to altogether avoid them, by means which the law permits, cannot be doubted. * * * But the question for determination is whether what was done, apart from the tax motive, was the thing which the statute intended. Gregory v. Helvering, 293 U.S. 465, 469 (1935). The circumstances of this case establish that the taxpayers did not in substance experience the loss that is necessary for a deduction under section 165, and that the sole purpose of the transaction was to create a tax loss in the year 1969.

Apart from the tax motive, there was no apparent reason for the taxpayers to sell the Bender Bonds. While increased interest rates had caused the market value of the bonds to decline, the issuer of the Bender Bonds remained financially sound and capable of continuing to pay current interest and the full par value of the bonds at maturity. Hence, a bondholder would experience no loss if the bonds were held to maturity. Although the trusts appeared to sustain a significant loss by transferring the bonds to the bank during a depressed bond market, the ability to repurchase these bonds meant that the trusts would eventually be paid their original investment in the bonds and would suffer no real loss from the sale.

Hence, in determining whether the taxpayers suffered a genuine loss in the alleged sale to the bank, we examine the circumstances to see whether the taxpayers were exposed to a real risk of not being able to repurchase the bonds in a short period of time and thus of not being able to recover the apparent loss from the December 26 sale to the bank. This, in turn, depends on whether the taxpayers were able effectively to control the

Longview Bank sufficiently to assure a resale of the bonds to the trusts. In support of the loss deduction, Fender claims that there was no agreement for the trusts to repurchase the bonds from the bank.[1] Further, Fender contends that although the plaintiffs owned 50.15% of the bank's stock when the bonds were repurchased, the plaintiffs lacked sufficient control of the Longview Bank to assure the repurchase of the bonds when the bonds were initially sold to the bank since the plaintiffs then owned less than 50% of the bank's stock.[2]

This contention is invalid since a transaction may not be bona fide even if the seller does not completely control the buyer as he does in the situation where he owns a majority of the stock.

> To divest a sale of its fundamental incident of finality plainly requires a controlled or sympathetic vendee. Such dominion might be * * * accomplished boldly through contracts or options to repurchase and the creation of fictitious entities or it might be * * * accomplished through the more subtle tie of affectionate interest found among families and friends, business or otherwise.

DuPont v. Commissioner of Internal Revenue, 3 Cir., 1941, 118 F.2d 544, 545, cert. denied, 314 U.S. 623 (1941). In DuPont v. Commissioner of Internal Revenue, two friends sold each other about the same amount of stock at a loss at the end of the year and repurchased the stock from one another at the start of the next year. Both sales were for the fair market value of the stock. Although the friends had no legal obligation to repurchase the stock, the court concluded that sufficient dominion existed to assure repurchase and thus to prevent bona fide sale. Another court denied a loss deduction to a taxpayer who sold and repurchased stock from one of his employees. See Rand v. Helvering, 8 Cir., 1935, 77 F.2d 450.

The circumstances of this case demonstrate that the taxpayers had sufficient influence over the Longview Bank to remove any substantial risk that the trusts would be unable to repurchase the Bender Bonds and thus eliminate the apparent loss on the sale to the bank. The taxpayers then controlled 40.7% of the bank's stock, the largest single block of stock. In addition, Fender had greatly assisted the bank recently in dealing with a series of financial difficulties. It appears that Longview Bank would not have agreed to the transaction absent a special relationship with Fender. The Bender Bonds were unrated and were of a maturity that the Longview Bank did not normally purchase. Another bank, Peoples National Bank, where Fender lacked similar influence, had refused to accept the offer to purchase the bonds. Further, since the Bender Bonds were unrated bonds and had limited marketability the Longview Bank would have had difficulty

---

1. Fender stated that there was an agreement that the Bender Bonds would not be resold to the trusts within 31 days of the sale. Such an agreement was necessary to prevent a deduction from being disallowed under the provisions of section 1091 of the Internal Revenue Code.

2. If the taxpayer had controlled more than 50% of the bank's stock, a deduction would automatically be disallowed as a sale to a related party. I.R.C. § 267(a)(1), (b)(2). However, section 267 is not an exclusive condition for denying a deduction. A deduction is also disallowed for any transaction which is not bona fide "even though section 267 does not apply to the transaction." Treas.Reg. 1.267(1)–1(c).

in selling the bonds to a buyer other than the taxpayers. Although the transaction was in the form of a sale to Longview Bank, the trusts allowed the money received from the sale to remain deposited in the Longview Bank until the bonds were repurchased. Finally, Norman Taylor, President of the Longview Bank at that time, in his deposition testified that the transaction was an accommodation to Fender and that he understood that the trusts would repurchase the Bender Bonds within ninety days.[3]

Because the taxpayers had sufficient dominion over the Longview Bank to ensure that the apparent loss from the sale of Bender Bonds on December 26 could be recaptured through a repurchase of the bonds, we conclude that the taxpayers did not suffer a real economic loss as is necessary for a deduction under section 165.

NOTES

(A) *Has There Been a Loss?* Several provisions of the Code are designed to prevent the deduction of losses in circumstances where a loss has not actually been realized. In *Fender,* neither § 267 (transfer to a related party) or § 1091 (wash sale) applied. These sections are discussed below. The court, however, finds that even where there are no statutory limitations, no loss is permitted unless there is a "bona fide sale." Is the court correct that the seller's control over the purchaser precludes a bona fide sale? Suppose interest rates had fallen and the value of the Bender bonds had risen. Could the bank, a regulated institution, have sold the bonds back to Fender at less than their market value? If there is an agreement to resell the property to its original owner, § 1091 would disallow the deduction. What if the agreement is informal or otherwise hidden from the Service? What evidence would indicate that there was no bona fide sale? Suppose T "parked" assets with A in exchange for $100,000 and six months later A "resold" the assets to T for $105,000?

(B) *Transactions Between Related Taxpayers.* Section 267 disallows deductions for losses from sales or exchanges of property, whether direct or indirect, between certain related people, such as family members or corporations and their majority (more than 50 percent) shareholders. What is the policy behind this provision? How easy would it be for the Commissioner to show whether there was a bona fide sale between such related persons and what the real price was? Suppose that a wife sells her husband some property at a price lower than her purchase price. In general, loss deductions are not allowed until a loss is realized. Has the wife realized a loss in this situation? Is it appropriate to view the wife and husband as a single economic unit for this purpose?

The seller's loss generally is lost permanently under § 267 because the purchaser's basis for computing loss when he sells the property is his cost. If, however, he ultimately sells the property for a gain, the purchaser's cost basis is increased by the seller's disallowed loss. § 267(d). For example, suppose a mother sells property she purchased for $10,000 to her son for

---

3. The testimony of Norman Taylor, president of the bank and the only disinterested witness, indicates that an agreement to repurchase existed although the time and price for the repurchase was [sic] not fixed. * * * *

$6,000. Her $4,000 loss is disallowed. If, however, the son subsequently sells the property for $13,000, the son reports only $3,000 gain (his $7,000 gain is offset by mom's $4,000 disallowed loss).

Several courts have found that the use of an intermediary results in a prohibited "indirect" sale. See, e.g., McWilliams v. Commissioner, 331 U.S. 694 (1947) (use of intermediary to effectuate sale to related party); Hassen v. Commissioner, 599 F.2d 305 (9th Cir.1979) (foreclosure sale followed by prearranged but not binding repurchase by controlled corporation).

(C) *Wash Sales.* Section 1091 disallows a loss from a sale preceded or followed by a purchase of substantially identical securities (including options) within a 30–day period. The basis of the stock purchased is that of the stock sold, plus any additional amount paid on the repurchase, so that losses are deferred, not lost. For example, if the taxpayer sells for $500 a share of XYZ stock he purchased for $700 and repurchases a share of XYZ stock 15 days later for $550, the $200 loss on the sale is disallowed and the basis in his new share is $750. Similar rules apply to short sales of stock or securities. Note that § 1091 does not apply to gains nor does it apply if the securities are not "substantially identical." At year end, a taxpayer can sell a bond that has declined in value and purchase a similar bond from another issuer. Section 1091 will not prevent deduction of the loss because the issuers are not the same.

Is the approach of § 267, which permanently disallows the loss, or of § 1091, which defers the loss, more appropriate?

(D) *Capital Losses.* Probably the most important limitation on the deduction of losses is the restriction on the deduction of capital losses. Capital losses are deductible by individuals only to the extent of capital gains plus $3,000 of ordinary income. § 1211. Any capital losses not allowed in the current year may be carried forward indefinitely by individuals. § 1212. Capital losses are discussed in greater detail in Chapter 5.

Despite the limitation, taxpayers in many cases are able to deduct their losses while, at the same time, deferring their gains. This strategy, known as cherrypicking, is discussed infra at page 551.

(E) *Straddles.* Where a taxpayer retains related assets with unrealized gains, she can use tax losses to obtain optimum tax treatment, regardless of the effect on her overall economic position or the economic substance of the transactions. Straddles are an example of this ploy.

In a typical tax straddle, the taxpayer acquires offsetting positions in commodity futures contracts. For example, she might enter into contracts to both buy and sell the same quantity of January wheat. Any changes in the prices of the contracts will offset each other; a loss on one contract will offset any gain on the other, so the taxpayer's economic position does not change. Each contract or "leg" of the straddle will show either a loss or gain. By selling one leg while holding the other, the taxpayers have been able to obtain two tax benefits: deferral and conversion.

To achieve deferral, the taxpayer sells the loss leg in the current tax year, while retaining the gain leg until the next year. Hence, the loss is accelerated while the offsetting gain is deferred. In a sophisticated straddle, the gain may be deferred almost perpetually by subsequent purchases of offsetting positions.

Under pre–1986 law, net short-term gain was taxed at ordinary income rates, while long-term gain was taxed at 40 percent of the ordinary income rate. The holding period for long-term gain was six months. To achieve conversion,—i.e., the conversion of short-term capital gain into long-term capital gain—then, the taxpayer would hold the loss leg less than six months. He could use the short-term capital loss to shelter short-term capital gain (that otherwise would be taxed at the same rate as ordinary income) or a limited amount of ordinary income. The gain leg would be held more than six months, so that any gain eventually realized would be taxed at preferential long-term capital gain rates.

Section 1092 was enacted to address the straddle problem. In general, that section limits the deduction of losses from straddles to the amount by which losses exceed unrecognized gains on offsetting positions. Section 1092 applies to certain commodity future contracts, and stock and stock option transactions where offsetting positions are held in similar or related properties. Complementing the straddle rules of § 1092 are the "mark-to-market" rules of § 1256. Section 1256 requires that certain stock and commodities options and other contracts be "marked to market" at the end of the year, whether or not the taxpayer holds offsetting positions. That is, each such contract the taxpayer holds is treated as if it is sold at year's end. Gain or loss is fully recognized. Thus, under the mark-to-market rules, realized losses on investments subject to § 1256 are offset by unrealized gains so that only the net loss, if any, is available to reduce income from unrelated sources. See also §§ 1233, 1234, 1234A, and 1236. The mark-to-market rules of § 1256 provide a very limited accrual tax system.

The Service has applied the principle of § 1092 to transactions that are not explicitly covered by the straddle rules. Assume the taxpayer purchases two debt instruments at the same time. Each of them has a provision that the interest will be reset if a particular event occurs. If the event occurs, the interest on one note will go up and the interest on the other will go down and if the event does not occur, the opposite happens. On the reset date, the taxpayer sells the note whose value falls when the interest falls and holds the note that increases in value. The IRS held that the taxpayer cannot take a loss on the note that was sold. It did not realize an actual economic loss because the purported loss on the sale of one note is substantially offset by the unrealized gain in the other note. Rev. Rul. 2000–12, 2000–1 C.B. 744.

D.   TAX SHELTER LOSSES

Investments in so-called tax shelters typically produce losses that can offset or "shelter" other income, such as wages, interest, or dividends that were neither produced by nor related to the income produced by the investment. A tax shelter combines various provisions of the Code to reduce taxes. In some cases, tax shelters result from tax benefits designed to encourage particular economic or social activities. In others, they result from basic structural provisions in the income tax system.

The materials that follow describe typical tax shelters and the methods used by the courts and Congress to combat their use. In the 1980's, tax shelters became ubiquitous and a significant percentage of the Tax Court's docket was tax shelter controversies. Because shelters threatened to undermine the tax base, Congress and the IRS began to wage war on shelters. The Service initially attacked transactions perceived to be without economic substance. When that failed to stem the tide, Congress responded with a variety of devices designed to limit tax shelter losses. After the 1986 Act, which contained a number of tax shelter limitations, the proliferation of shelters used by individuals abated. It is nevertheless useful to be familiar with the tax shelter phenomenon and the responses to it because the basic conflicts and structural issues remain and a study of tax shelters enables the student to perceive interrelationships within the Code and among seemingly discrete tax provisions. Finally, some of the issues that arose in connection with individual shelters have resurfaced in corporate tax shelters, which are discussed in Chapter 8, infra.

NOTE ON DEFINING A TAX SHELTER

Like pornography, a tax shelter is something that people know when they see it. The term has proved somewhat difficult to define, and whether an "abusive tax shelter" exists often depends upon who is watching.

Although the Code contains a number of technical tax shelter definitions, they all involve essentially the same characteristics. Tax shelters are passive investments; the investor is typically not actively involved in managing the activities. Tax shelter investments are often structured as limited partnerships in order to provide investors both the benefits of limited liability and conduit taxation (whereby the income and losses of the partnership are passed through to the partners). In general, a tax shelter may include any investment or transaction that produces a tax savings greater than that which would be appropriate given its economic income or loss. Tax shelter investments typically involve a mismatching of deductions and income to produce net losses that offset unrelated income. Alternatively, in some cases, the investment produces tax credits that shelter taxes that otherwise would be due on unrelated income.

Tax shelters have been grouped into two broad categories: (1) legitimate tax shelters and (2) abusive tax shelters. Legitimate tax shelters usually involve tax-favored investments clearly sanctioned by the tax laws, typically where tax benefits have been enacted expressly as incentives for particular activities (for example, oil exploration and real estate). In other cases, the result sought by taxpayers may be available under current law, but the tax preference is unintended.

Abusive tax shelters, on the other hand, typically involve transactions that, if the facts were known, would not be upheld in court. These investments enable taxpayers to take a reporting position for claiming deductions or credit that, while not ultimately allowable, may produce significant tax savings either because the return will not be examined by the IRS, or, if it is examined and the claimed deduction is disallowed, the tax will be deferred at a low interest cost. Abusive tax shelter investments are entered into primarily, if not exclusively, to reduce federal income tax liability. Often they yield negligible returns (and sometimes negative returns) before tax, but offer significant after-tax returns.

Tax shelters raise fairness concerns because they create horizontal inequities by permitting individuals with similar economic incomes to pay very different amounts of tax. They also decrease tax progressivity by reducing the tax burden of high income individuals. Tax shelters are inefficient because they often create incentives for taxpayers to engage in economically unproductive transactions. Even those activities that the government has sought to encourage through preferential tax treatment might be encouraged more effectively by alternative means, such as direct loans or subsidies. In addition, tax shelters may shift the ownership of certain assets from low-bracket individuals to high-bracket individuals who may be able to pay a higher price for assets. Because they can make better use of tax deductions, they may bid up the price of assets and force others out of business.

Finally, tax shelters are said to undermine taxpayer confidence in the fairness of the tax system and to encourage other forms of tax evasion and avoidance. When shelters proliferate, there are often calls for a more neutral tax system—one that is fairer and more economically efficient. Abusive tax shelter investments generate great concern among policymakers, enforcement officials, and taxpayers.

NOTE ON COMMON TAX SHELTER TECHNIQUES

Tax shelters rely on five basic techniques to reduce tax liability: income shifting, exemption, deferral, conversion, and leverage. (The last, in combination with exemption, deferral, or conversion, is often labelled arbitrage.) Each method is discussed in more detail elsewhere in this coursebook.

Income shifting involves structuring transactions to ensure that income, deductions, or credits are allocated among taxpayers in the manner that produces the lowest net tax liability. Generally, this means that deductions and credits are allocated to those in the highest brackets or to those who have offsetting income. Conversely, income is allocated to those in the lowest brackets or to those with expiring losses. Income shifting is explored at length in Chapter 4.

Furthermore, the income tax produces great incentives for undertaxed assets to be held by taxpayers subject to the highest marginal rates and for overtaxed assets, such as loans that produce taxable interest, to be held by low-bracket taxpayers and tax-exempt entities. Structural provisions of the Code, designed for a simpler era, allowed transactions to be planned to maximize arbitrage opportunities and thereby to achieve large tax savings.

Excessive or accelerated deductions create opportunities for taxpayers to have tax deductions that exceed current income from an investment. For example, during the 1980's, the tax savings generated by the combination of accelerated depreciation and the investment tax credit were likely to exceed the income produced by the asset in its early years. Profitable companies could use such tax losses to shelter other income, but new companies or companies with business losses were not able to use the increased deductions. Likewise, individuals with substantial amounts of unrelated income could use these deductions to shelter income, for example, when the losses were passed through to the individuals by a partnership.

Since the income tax is not refundable, taxable income is, in effect, a ceiling on the extent to which tax benefits can be obtained. One way to avoid that limitation is to sell the property to a taxpayer who can use all the tax benefits. In order to retain the ability to continue to use the property, the selling taxpayer would lease the property back. Because the rental payments generally were intended to cover all the purchaser's costs, the purchaser in a sale-leaseback was often merely purchasing tax benefits. The *Estate of Franklin* case, at page 198 supra, is an example of such a transaction. At one time, Congress provided for a fictionalized "safe-harbor leasing" of depreciable property that effectively sanctioned sales of the tax savings from depreciation and the investment tax credit by firms that could not benefit from them to firms that could. In response to the public outcry generated by widely publicized safe-harbor leases among major corporations, this provision was repealed. Taxpayers with unused losses, however, continued to use leasing to transfer benefits. The often tenuous distinction between a lender and an owner assumed overwhelming importance for tax purposes at the same time it was blurred for economic and legal purposes by new lending practices, especially equity participation.

Exemption involves receipt of economic income that is not subject to tax. Exemptions under current law include, for example, the exclusion of interest on state and local bonds and interest earned on individual retirement accounts, and qualified employer pensions.

Deferral of tax from the current year to a future year is achieved by accelerating deductions and credits or by postponing recognition of income. Deferral often results from an investment that generates deductions in early years to offset unrelated income and that generates income, if at all, only in later years. For example, the taxpayer may take advantage of special provisions that allow the immediate deduction of capital expenditures that will produce income over a number of years.

Recall that the deferral of tax has been analogized to an interest-free loan from the government to the taxpayer. It also has been analogized to imposing tax currently but exempting from tax the earnings that are subsequently generated by investment of the amount that remains after tax. See the Note on Tax Deferral, supra at page 287.

Although Congress has attempted to curb the use of deferral by a variety of measures, major opportunities for deferral remain, for example, in the depreciation schedules for much equipment as well as in special provisions governing recovery of the costs of oil, gas, and mineral exploration and extraction.

Conversion of ordinary income into tax-preferred income is typically achieved where the investment generates both deductions against ordinary income and income that will be taxed at lower rates for example, as long-term capital gains. This technique is discussed in Chapter 5.

Leverage is the use of borrowed funds to increase the size of deductible expenditures. The *Crane* rule, discussed supra at page 187, may allow the taxpayer to obtain deductions based not only on a cash investment but also on indebtedness incurred incident to the investment. For example, a taxpayer who is subject to income tax at a 40 percent rate makes a tax shelter investment of $100,000—$10,000 of his own funds and $90,000 in borrowed funds. If the investment produces a $30,000 tax loss in the first year, the taxpayer may save $12,000 in taxes on a $10,000 cash investment.

The ability to acquire large depreciation deductions for a comparatively small cash investment has long been an integral aspect of most tax shelters. The taxpayer may be able to use depreciation deductions on a large basis not only to offset any income from the property but also to offset unrelated income. Without borrowing, taxpayers may deduct only the amount of their investment; with borrowing, taxpayers may deduct much greater amounts and thereby recover their investments through tax savings in a short period of time. The tax cost of leverage is the gain to be realized from treating the unamortized mortgage balance as part of the amount realized when the investment is liquidated.

The combination of leveraging and high deductions can even produce negative rates of return. This point can be illustrated by an example that, for simplicity, uses immediate expensing of assets in lieu of other deductions.* Assume a tax rate of 40 percent, an interest rate of 10 percent, and a before-tax yield on investment of 10 percent. Without taxes, of course, there would be zero return from borrowing at 10 percent to finance an asset that yields 10 percent. In the current tax regime, however, assume the taxpayer borrows $60 to finance an investment of $100, which is immediately expensed for tax purposes. The $100 immediate deduction saves $40 in taxes, so the taxpayer has no out-of-pocket cost for the investment. From the $10 annual yield on the investment, he must pay interest of $6 and taxes of $1.60 ($10 income less $6 deductible interest leaves $4 taxable income taxed at 40 percent equals $1.60 taxes). This would leave him an annual after-tax return of $2.40 on a zero investment. Graduated rates further complicate the story but, in general, will tend to induce a concentration of tax-favored investments in the hands of upper-bracket taxpayers. Disallowing interest deductions would eliminate the profit in the above example. If the interest in the example were nondeductible, the tax would be $4 and the after-tax return zero ($4 of tax plus $6 of interest equal the $10 yield on the asset)—a result that we might expect given the taxpayer's out-of-pocket investment of zero.

It is true that the taxpayer eventually may have to repay the loan or to recognize income from the cancellation of indebtedness. The present value of his loan, however, may be significantly less than the present value of his tax savings, especially if he is not obligated to make repayment until a date in the distant future. Moreover, the taxpayer may be able to deduct his interest payments—at least to the extent of his investment income—under § 163. The advantages of leverage are greatest where the taxpayer is not

---

* This example is derived from Alvin Warren & Alan Auerbach, "Transferability of Tax Incentives and the Fiction of Safe Harbor Leasing," 95 Harv.L.Rev. 1752 (1982); see also Calvin Johnson, "Tax Shelter Gain: The Mismatch of Debt and Supply Side Depreciation," 61 Tex. L. Rev. 1013 (1983).

personally liable on the indebtedness. See the Note on Tax Arbitrage, supra at page 360.

Real estate is a good example of a tax shelter that often has combined the major tax shelter components: deferral, leverage, conversion of ordinary income into capital gain, and shifting of tax benefits to those who can best use them. Tax deferral was accomplished principally because the depreciation allowed for tax purposes was much more rapid than actual economic depreciation. Deductions were accelerated to a current year, while the investment was recovered (perhaps with some profit) in a subsequent taxable year. Real estate tax shelters were typically highly leveraged, i.e., a great percentage of the cost was financed with borrowed funds. This increased the taxpayer's basis for depreciation, which permitted deductions in excess of his equity in the property. These deductions often were converted into capital gains on a sale of the property, where the gain (the difference between the amount received and the depreciated basis) was eligible for preferential treatment. Shifting the tax benefit to investors who may best use them generally was accomplished through special partnership allocations or through sale-leaseback transactions.

1. JUDICIAL RESPONSE

Frank Lyon Co. v. United States

Supreme Court of the United States, 1978. 435 U.S. 561.

MR. JUSTICE BLACKMUN delivered the opinion of the Court.

This case concerns the federal income tax consequences of a sale-and-leaseback in which petitioner Frank Lyon Company (Lyon) took title to a building under construction by Worthen Bank & Trust Company (Worthen) of Little Rock, Ark., and simultaneously leased the building back to Worthen for long-term use as its headquarters and principal banking facility.

I

* * *

Lyon is a closely held Arkansas corporation engaged in the distribution of home furnishings, primarily Whirlpool and RCA electrical products. Worthen in 1965 was an Arkansas-chartered bank and a member of the Federal Reserve System. Frank Lyon was Lyon's majority shareholder and board chairman; he also served on Worthen's board. Worthen at that time began to plan the construction of a multistory bank and office building to replace its existing facility in Little Rock. About the same time Worthen's competitor, Union National Bank of Little Rock, also began to plan a new bank and office building. Adjacent sites on Capitol Avenue, separated only by Spring Street, were acquired by the two banks. It became a matter of competition, for both banking business and tenants, and prestige as to which bank would start and complete its building first.

Worthen initially hoped to finance, to build, and to own the proposed facility at a total cost of $9 million for the site, building, and adjoining parking deck. * * * Worthen's plan, however, had to be abandoned for two significant reasons:

1. As a bank chartered under Arkansas law, Worthen legally could not pay more interest on any debentures it might issue than that specified by Arkansas law. But the proposed obligations would not be marketable at that rate.

2. Applicable statutes or regulations of the Arkansas State Bank Department and the Federal Reserve System required Worthen, as a state bank subject to their supervision, to obtain prior permission for the investment in banking premises of any amount (including that placed in a real estate subsidiary) in excess of the bank's capital stock or of 40% of its capital stock and surplus. * * * Worthen, accordingly, was advised by staff employees of the Federal Reserve System that they would not recommend approval of the plan by the System's Board of Governors.

Worthen therefore was forced to seek an alternative solution that would provide it with the use of the building, satisfy the state and federal regulators, and attract the necessary capital. In September 1967 it proposed a sale-and-leaseback arrangement. The State Bank Department and the Federal Reserve System approved this approach, but the Department required that Worthen possess an option to purchase the leased property at the end of the 15th year of the lease at a set price, and the federal regulator required that the building be owned by an independent third party.

Detailed negotiations ensued with investors that had indicated interest, namely, Goldman, Sachs & Company; White, Weld & Co.; Eastman Dillon; Union Securities & Company; and Stephens, Inc. Certain of these firms made specific proposals.

Worthen then obtained a commitment from New York Life Insurance Company to provide $7,140,000 in permanent mortgage financing on the building, conditioned upon its approval of the titleholder. At this point Lyon entered the negotiations and it, too, made a proposal. [Lyon was ultimately selected as the investor by Worthen and approved by the state and federal regulators, by First National City Bank for the construction financing, and by New York Life, as the permanent lender.]

In the meantime, on September 15, before Lyon was selected, Worthen itself began construction.

In May 1968 Worthen, Lyon, City Bank, and New York Life executed complementary and interlocking agreements under which the building was sold by Worthen to Lyon as it was constructed, and Worthen leased the completed building back from Lyon.

1. Agreements between Worthen and Lyon. Worthen and Lyon executed a ground lease, a sales agreement, and a building lease.

Under the ground lease dated May 1, 1968, Worthen leased the site to Lyon for 76 years and 7 months through November 30, 2044. The first 19 months were the estimated construction period. The ground rents payable by Lyon to Worthen were $50 for the first 26 years and 7 months and thereafter in quarterly payments:

12/1/94 through 11/30/99	(5 years)—$100,000 annually
12/1/99 through 11/30/04	(5 years)—$150,000 annually
12/1/04 through 11/30/09	(5 years)—$200,000 annually
12/1/09 through 11/30/34	(25 years)—$250,000 annually
12/1/34 through 11/30/44	(10 years)—$10,000 annually.

Under the sales agreement dated May 19, * * *, Worthen agreed to sell the building to Lyon, and Lyon agreed to buy it, piece by piece as it was constructed, for a total price not to exceed $7,640,000, in reimbursements to Worthen for its expenditures for the construction of the building.

Under the building lease dated May 1, 1968, * * *, Lyon leased the building back to Worthen for a primary term of 25 years from December 1, 1969, with options in Worthen to extend the lease for eight additional 5-year terms, a total of 65 years. During the period between the expiration of the building lease (at the latest, November 30, 2034, if fully extended) and the end of the ground lease on November 30, 2044, full ownership, use, and control of the building were Lyon's, unless, of course, the building had been repurchased by Worthen * * *. Worthen was not obligated to pay rent under the building lease until completion of the building. For the first 11 years of the lease, that is, until November 30, 1980, the stated quarterly rent was $145,581.03 ($582,324.12 for the year). For the next 14 years, the quarterly rent was $153,289.32 ($613,157.28 for the year), and for the option periods the rent was $300,000 a year, payable quarterly * * *. The total rent for the building over the 25-year primary term of the lease thus was $14,989,767.24. That rent equaled the principal and interest payments that would amortize the $7,140,000 New York Life mortgage loan over the same period. When the mortgage was paid off at the end of the primary term, the annual building rent, if Worthen extended the lease, came down to the stated $300,000. Lyon's net rentals from the building would be further reduced by the increase in ground rent Worthen would receive from Lyon during the extension.[1]

The building lease was a "net lease," under which Worthen was responsible for all expenses usually associated with the maintenance of an office building, including repairs, taxes, utility charges, and insurance, and was to keep the premises in good condition, excluding, however, reasonable wear and tear.

Finally, under the lease, Worthen had the option to repurchase the building at the following times and prices:

> 11/30/80 (after 11 years)—$6,325,169.85
> 11/30/84 (after 15 years)—$5,432,607.32
> 11/30/89 (after 20 years)—$4,187,328.04
> 11/30/94 (after 25 years)—$2,145,935.00

---

1. This, of course, is on the assumption that Worthen exercises its option to extend the building lease. If it does not, Lyon remains liable for the substantial rents prescribed by the ground lease. This possibility brings into sharp focus the fact that Lyon, in a very practical sense, is at least the ultimate owner of the building. If Worthen does not extend, the building lease expires and Lyon may do with the building as it chooses.

The Government would point out, however, that the net amounts payable by Worthen to Lyon during the building lease's extended terms, if all are claimed, would approximate the amount required to repay Lyon's $500,000 investment at 6% compound interest. Brief for United States 14.

These repurchase option prices were the sum of the unpaid balance of the New York Life mortgage, Lyon's $500,000 investment, and 6% interest compounded on that investment.

2. Construction financing agreement. By agreement dated May 14, 1968, * * * City Bank agreed to lend Lyon $7,000,000 for the construction of the building. This loan was secured by a mortgage on the building and the parking deck, executed by Worthen as well as by Lyon, and an assignment by Lyon of its interests in the building lease and in the ground lease.

3. Permanent financing agreement. By Note Purchase Agreement dated May 1, 1968, * * * New York Life agreed to purchase Lyon's $7,140,000 6¾% 25–year secured note to be issued upon completion of the building. Under this agreement Lyon warranted that it would lease the building to Worthen for a noncancelable term of at least 25 years under a net lease at a rent at least equal to the mortgage payments on the note. Lyon agreed to make quarterly payments of principal and interest equal to the rentals payable by Worthen during the corresponding primary term of the lease. The security for the note was a first deed of trust and Lyon's assignment of its interests in the building lease and in the ground lease. * * * Worthen joined in the deed of trust as the owner of the fee and the parking deck.

In December 1969 the building was completed and Worthen took possession. At that time Lyon received the permanent loan from New York Life, and it discharged the interim loan from City Bank. The actual cost of constructing the office building and parking complex (excluding the cost of the land) exceeded $10,000,000.

Lyon filed its federal income tax returns on the accrual and calendar year basis. On its 1969 return, Lyon accrued rent from Worthen for December. It asserted as deductions one month's interest to New York Life; one month's depreciation on the building; interest on the construction loan from City Bank; and sums for legal and other expenses incurred in connection with the transaction.

On audit of Lyon's 1969 return, the Commissioner of Internal Revenue determined that Lyon was "not the owner for tax purposes of any portion of the Worthen Building," and ruled that "the income and expenses related to this building are not allowable * * * for Federal income tax purposes." * * * He also added $2,298.15 to Lyon's 1969 income as "accrued interest income." This was the computed 1969 portion of a gain, considered the equivalent of interest income, the realization of which was based on the assumption that Worthen would exercise its option to buy the building after 11 years, on November 30, 1980, at the price stated in the lease, and on the additional determination that Lyon had "loaned" $500,000 to Worthen. In other words, the Commissioner determined that the sale-and-leaseback arrangement was a financing transaction in which Lyon loaned Worthen $500,000 and acted as a conduit for the transmission of principal and interest from Worthen to New York Life.

* * *

After trial without a jury, the District Court, in a memorandum letter-opinion setting forth findings and conclusions, ruled in Lyon's favor and held that its claimed deductions were allowable. * * * It concluded that the legal intent of the parties had been to create a bona fide sale-and-leaseback in accordance with the form and language of the documents evidencing the transactions. It rejected the argument that Worthen was acquiring an equity in the building through its rental payments. It found that the rents were unchallenged and were reasonable throughout the period of the lease, and that the option prices, negotiated at arm's length between the parties, represented fair estimates of market value on the applicable dates. It rejected any negative inference from the fact that the rentals, combined with the options, were sufficient to amortize the New York Life loan and to pay Lyon a 6% return on its equity investment. It found that Worthen would acquire an equity in the building only if it exercised one of its options to purchase, and that it was highly unlikely, as a practical matter, that any purchase option would ever be exercised. It rejected any inference to be drawn from the fact that the lease was a "net lease." It found that Lyon had mixed motivations for entering into the transaction, including the need to diversify as well as the desire to have the benefits of a "tax shelter."

The United States Court of Appeals for the Eighth Circuit reversed. 536 F.2d 746 (1976). It held that the Commissioner correctly determined that Lyon was not the true owner of the building and therefore was not entitled to the claimed deductions. It likened ownership for tax purposes to a "bundle of sticks" and undertook its own evaluation of the facts. It concluded, in agreement with the Government's contention, that Lyon "totes an empty bundle" of ownership sticks. * * * It stressed the following: (a) The lease agreements circumscribed Lyon's right to profit from its investment in the building by giving Worthen the option to purchase for an amount equal to Lyon's $500,000 equity plus 6% compound interest and the assumption of the unpaid balance of the New York Life mortgage.[2] (b) The option prices did not take into account possible appreciation of the value of the building or inflation.[3] (c) Any award realized as a result of destruction or condemnation of the building in excess of the mortgage balance and the $500,000 would be paid to Worthen and not Lyon.[4] (d) The building rental payments during the primary term were exactly equal to

---

2. Lyon here challenges this assertion on the grounds that it had the right and opportunities to sell the building at a greater profit at any time; the return to Lyon was not insubstantial and was attractive to a true investor in real estate; the 6% return was the minimum Lyon would realize if Worthen exercised one of its options, an event the District Court found highly unlikely; and Lyon would own the building and realize a greater return than 6% if Worthen did not exercise an option to purchase.

3. Lyon challenges this observation by pointing out that the District Court found

the option prices to be the negotiated estimate of the parties of the fair market value of the building on the option dates and to be reasonable. * * *

4. Lyon asserts that this statement is true only with respect to the total destruction or taking of the building on or after December 1, 1980. Lyon asserts that it, not Worthen, would receive the excess above the mortgage balance in the event of total destruction or taking before December 1, 1980, or in the event of partial damage or taking at any time. Id., at 408–410, 411.

the mortgage payments.[5] (e) Worthen retained control over the ultimate disposition of the building through its various options to repurchase and to renew the lease plus its ownership of the site.[6] (f) Worthen enjoyed all benefits and bore all burdens incident to the operation and ownership of the building so that, in the Court of Appeals' view, the only economic advantages accruing to Lyon, in the event it were considered to be the true owner of the property, were income tax savings of approximately $1.5 million during the first 11 years of the arrangement.[7] Id. * * *[8] The court concluded, * * *, that the transaction was "closely akin" to that in Helvering v. Lazarus & Co., 308 U.S. 252 (1939). "In sum, the benefits, risks, and burdens which [Lyon] has incurred with respect to the Worthen building are simply too insubstantial to establish a claim to the status of owner for tax purposes. * * * The vice of the present lease is that all of [its] features have been employed in the same transaction with the cumulative effect of depriving [Lyon] of any significant ownership interest." 536 F.2d at 754.

We granted certiorari, 429 U.S. 1089 (1977), because of an indicated conflict with American Realty Trust v. United States, 498 F.2d 1194 (C.A.4 1974).

II

This Court, almost 50 years ago, observed that "taxation is not so much concerned with the refinements of title as it is with actual command over the property taxed—the actual benefit for which the tax is paid." Corliss v. Bowers, 281 U.S. 376, 378 (1930). In a number of cases, the Court has refused to permit the transfer of formal legal title to shift the incidence of taxation attributable to ownership of property where the transferor continues to retain significant control over the property transferred. E.g., Commissioner v. Sunnen, 333 U.S. 591 (1948); Helvering v. Clifford, 309 U.S. 331 (1940). In applying this doctrine of substance over form, the Court

---

5. Lyon concedes the accuracy of this statement, but asserts that it does not justify the conclusion that Lyon served merely as a conduit by which mortgage payments would be transmitted to New York Life. It asserts that Lyon was the sole obligor on the New York Life note and would remain liable in the event of default by Worthen. It also asserts that the fact the rent was sufficient to amortize the loan during the primary term of the lease was a requirement imposed by New York Life, and is a usual requirement in most long-term loans secured by a long-term lease.

6. As to this statement, Lyon asserts that the Court of Appeals ignored Lyon's right to sell the building to another at any time; the District Court's finding that the options to purchase were not likely to be exercised; the uncertainty that Worthen would renew the lease for 40 years; Lyon's right to lease to anyone at any price during the last 10 years of the ground lease; and

Lyon's continuing ownership of the building after the expiration of the ground lease.

7. In response to this, Lyon asserts that the District Court found that the benefits of occupancy Worthen will enjoy are common in most long-term real estate leases, and that the District Court found that Lyon had motives other than tax savings in entering into the transaction. It also asserts that the net cash after-tax benefit would be $312,220, not $1.5 million.

8. Other factors relied on by the Court of Appeals, 536 F.2d, at 752, were the allocation of the investment credit to Worthen, and a claim that Lyon's ability to sell the building to a third party was "carefully circumscribed" by the lease agreements. The investment credit by statute is freely allocable between the parties, § 48(d) of the 1954 Code, 26 U.S.C.A. § 48(d), and the Government has not pressed either of these factors before this Court.

has looked to the objective economic realities of a transaction rather than to the particular form the parties employed. * * * Nor is the parties' desire to achieve a particular tax result necessarily relevant. * * *

In the light of these general and established principles, the Government takes the position that the Worthen–Lyon transaction in its entirety should be regarded as a sham. The agreement as a whole, it is said, was only an elaborate financing scheme designed to provide economic benefits to Worthen and a guaranteed return to Lyon. The latter was but a conduit used to forward the mortgage payments, made under the guise of rent paid by Worthen to Lyon, on to New York Life as mortgagee. This, the Government claims, is the true substance of the transaction as viewed under the microscope of the tax laws. Although the arrangement was cast in sale-and-leaseback form, in substance it was only a financing transaction, and the terms of the repurchase options and lease renewals so indicate. It is said that Worthen could reacquire the building simply by satisfying the mortgage debt and paying Lyon its $500,000 advance plus interest, regardless of the fair market value of the building at the time; similarly, when the mortgage was paid off, Worthen could extend the lease at drastically reduced bargain rentals that likewise bore no relation to fair rental value but were simply calculated to pay Lyon its $500,000 plus interest over the extended term. Lyon's return on the arrangement in no event could exceed 6% compound interest (although the Government conceded it might well be less * * *). Furthermore, the favorable option and lease renewal terms made it highly unlikely that Worthen would abandon the building after it in effect had "paid off" the mortgage. The Government implies that the arrangement was one of convenience which, if accepted on its face, would enable Worthen to deduct its payments to Lyon as rent and would allow Lyon to claim a deduction for depreciation, based on the cost of construction ultimately borne by Worthen, which Lyon could offset against other income, and to deduct mortgage interest that roughly would offset the inclusion of Worthen's rental payments in Lyon's income. If, however, the Government argues, the arrangement was only a financing transaction under which Worthen was the owner of the building, Worthen's payments would be deductible only to the extent that they represented mortgage interest, and Worthen would be entitled to claim depreciation; Lyon would not be entitled to deductions for either mortgage interest or depreciation and it would not have to include Worthen's "rent" payments in its income because its function with respect to those payments was that of a conduit between Worthen and New York Life.

The Government places great reliance on Helvering v. Lazarus & Co., supra, and claims it to be precedent that controls this case. The taxpayer there was a department store. The legal title of its three buildings was in a bank as trustee for land-trust certificate holders. When the transfer to the trustee was made, the trustee at the same time leased the buildings back to the taxpayer for 99 years, with option to renew and purchase. The Commissioner, in stark contrast to his posture in the present case, took the position that the statutory right to depreciation followed legal title. The Board of Tax Appeals, however, concluded that the transaction between the taxpayer and the bank in reality was a mortgage loan and allowed the taxpayer depreciation on the buildings. This Court, as had the Court of

Appeals, agreed with that conclusion and affirmed. It regarded the "rent" stipulated in the leaseback as a promise to pay interest on the loan, and a "depreciation fund" required by the lease as an amortization fund designed to pay off the loan in the stated period. Thus, said the Court, the Board justifiably concluded that the transaction, although in written form a transfer of ownership with a leaseback, was actually a loan secured by the property involved.

The *Lazarus* case, we feel, is to be distinguished from the present one and is not controlling here. Its transaction was one involving only two (and not multiple) parties, the taxpayer-department store and the trustee-bank. The Court looked closely at the substance of the agreement between those two parties and rightly concluded that depreciation was deductible by the taxpayer despite the nomenclature of the instrument of conveyance and the leaseback. See also Sun Oil Co. v. Commissioner, 562 F.2d 258 (C.A.3 1977) (a two-party case with the added feature that the second party was a tax-exempt pension trust).

The present case, in contrast, involves three parties, Worthen, Lyon, and the finance agency. The usual simple two-party arrangement was legally unavailable to Worthen. Independent investors were interested in participating in the alternative available to Worthen, and Lyon itself (also independent from Worthen) won the privilege. Despite Frank Lyon's presence on Worthen's board of directors, the transaction, as it ultimately developed, was not a familial one arranged by Worthen, but one compelled by the realities of the restrictions imposed upon the bank. Had Lyon not appeared, another interested investor would have been selected. The ultimate solution would have been essentially the same. Thus, the presence of the third party, in our view, significantly distinguishes this case from *Lazarus* and removes the latter as controlling authority.

III

It is true, of course, that the transaction took shape according to Worthen's needs. As the Government points out, Worthen throughout the negotiations regarded the respective proposals of the independent investors in terms of its own cost of funds. * * * It is also true that both Worthen and the prospective investors compared the various proposals in terms of the return anticipated on the investor's equity. But all this is natural for parties contemplating entering into a transaction of this kind. Worthen needed a building for its banking operations and other purposes and necessarily had to know what its cost would be. The investors were in business to employ their funds in the most remunerative way possible. And, as the Court has said in the past, a transaction must be given its effect in accord with what actually occurred and not in accord with what might have occurred. * * *

There is no simple device available to peel away the form of this transaction and to reveal its substance. The effects of the transaction on all the parties were obviously different from those that would have resulted had Worthen been able simply to make a mortgage agreement with New York Life and to receive a $500,000 loan from Lyon. Then *Lazarus* would apply. Here, however, and most significantly, it was Lyon alone, and not

Worthen, who was liable on the notes, first to City Bank, and then to New York Life. Despite the facts that Worthen had agreed to pay rent and that this rent equaled the amounts due from Lyon to New York Life, should anything go awry in the later years of the lease, Lyon was primarily liable. No matter how the transaction could have been devised otherwise, it remains a fact that as the agreements were placed in final form, the obligation on the notes fell squarely on Lyon. Lyon, an ongoing enterprise, exposed its very business well-being to this real and substantial risk.

The effect of this liability on Lyon is not just the abstract possibility that something will go wrong and that Worthen will not be able to make its payments. Lyon has disclosed this liability on its balance sheet for all the world to see. Its financial position was affected substantially by the presence of this long-term debt, despite the offsetting presence of the building as an asset. To the extent that Lyon has used its capital in this transaction, it is less able to obtain financing for other business needs.

In concluding that there is this distinct element of economic reality in Lyon's assumption of liability, we are mindful that the characterization of a transaction for financial accounting purposes, on the one hand, and for tax purposes, on the other, need not necessarily be the same. * * * But in this case accepted accounting methods, as understood by the several parties to the respective agreements and as applied to the transaction by others, gave the transaction a meaningful character consonant with the form it was given. Worthen was not allowed to enter into the type of transaction which the Government now urges to be the true substance of the arrangement. Lyon and Worthen cannot be said to have entered into the transaction intending that the interests involved were allocated in a way other than that associated with a sale-and-leaseback.

Other factors also reveal that the transaction cannot be viewed as anything more than a mortgage agreement between Worthen and New York Life and a loan from Lyon to Worthen. There is no legal obligation between Lyon and Worthen representing the $500,000 "loan" extended under the Government's theory. And the assumed 6% return on this putative loan—required by the audit to be recognized in the taxable year in question—will be realized only when and if Worthen exercises its options.

The Court of Appeals acknowledged that the rents alone, due after the primary term of the lease and after the mortgage has been paid, do not provide the simple 6% return which, the Government urges, Lyon is guaranteed. * * * Thus, if Worthen chooses not to exercise its options, Lyon is gambling that the rental value of the building during the last 10 years of the ground lease, during which the ground rent is minimal, will be sufficient to recoup its investment before it must negotiate again with Worthen regarding the ground lease. There are simply too many contingencies, including variations in the value of real estate, in the cost of money, and in the capital structure of Worthen, to permit the conclusion that the parties intended to enter into the transaction as structured in the audit and according to which the Government now urges they be taxed.

It is not inappropriate to note that the Government is likely to lose little revenue, if any, as a result of the shape given the transaction by the parties. No deduction was created that is not either matched by an item of income or that would not have been available to one of the parties if the transaction had been arranged differently. While it is true that Worthen paid Lyon less to induce it to enter into the transaction because Lyon anticipated the benefit of the depreciation deductions it would have as the owner of the building, those deductions would have been equally available to Worthen had it retained title to the building. The Government so concedes. * * * The fact that favorable tax consequences were taken into account by Lyon on entering into the transaction is no reason for disallowing those consequences.[9] We cannot ignore the reality that the tax laws affect the shape of nearly every business transaction. * * * Lyon is not a corporation with no purpose other than to hold title to the bank building. It was not created by Worthen or even financed to any degree by Worthen.

The conclusion that the transaction is not a simple sham to be ignored does not, of course, automatically compel the further conclusion that Lyon is entitled to the items claimed as deductions. Nevertheless, on the facts, this readily follows. As has been noted, the obligations on which Lyon paid interest were its obligations alone, and it is entitled to claim deductions therefor under § 163(a) * * *.

As is clear from the facts, none of the parties to this sale and-leaseback was the owner of the building in any simple sense. But it is equally clear that the facts focus upon Lyon as the one whose capital was committed to the building and as the party, therefore, that was entitled to claim depreciation for the consumption of that capital. The Government has based its contention that Worthen should be treated as the owner on the assumption that throughout the term of the lease Worthen was acquiring an equity in the property. In order to establish the presence of that growing equity, however, the Government is forced to speculate that one of the options will be exercised and that, if it is not, this is only because the rentals for the extended term are a bargain. We cannot indulge in such speculation in view of the District Court's clear finding to the contrary. We therefore conclude that it is Lyon's capital that is invested in the building according to the agreement of the parties, and it is Lyon that is entitled to depreciation deductions, under § 167 * * *.

IV

We recognize that the Government's position, and that taken by the Court of Appeals, is not without superficial appeal. One, indeed, may theorize that Frank Lyon's presence on the Worthen board of directors; Lyon's departure from its principal corporate activity into this unusual venture; the parallel between the payments under the building lease and the amounts due from Lyon on the New York Life mortgage; the provisions relating to condemnation or destruction of the property; the nature and presence of the several options available to Worthen; and the tax benefits,

---

9. Indeed, it is not inevitable that the transaction, as treated by Lyon and Worthen, will not result in more revenues to the Government rather than less. Lyon is gambling that in the first 11 years of the lease it will have income that will be sheltered by the depreciation deductions, and that it will be able to make sufficiently good use of the tax dollars preserved thereby to make up for the income it will recognize and pay taxes on during the last 14 years of the initial term of the lease and against which it will enjoy no sheltering deduction.

such as the use of double declining balance depreciation, that accrue to Lyon during the initial years of the arrangement, form the basis of an argument that Worthen should be regarded as the owner of the building and as the recipient of nothing more from Lyon than a $500,000 loan.

We, however, as did the District Court, find this theorizing incompatible with the substance and economic realities of the transaction: the competitive situation as it existed between Worthen and Union National Bank in 1965 and the years immediately following; Worthen's undercapitalization; Worthen's consequent inability, as a matter of legal restraint, to carry its building plans into effect by a conventional mortgage and other borrowing; the additional barriers imposed by the state and federal regulators; the suggestion, forthcoming from the state regulator, that Worthen possess an option to purchase; the requirement, from the federal regulator, that the building be owned by an independent third party; the presence of several finance organizations seriously interested in participating in the transaction and in the resolution of Worthen's problem; the submission of formal proposals by several of those organizations; the bargaining process and period that ensued; the competitiveness of the bidding; the bona fide character of the negotiations; the three-party aspect of the transaction; Lyon's substantiality and its independence from Worthen; the fact that diversification was Lyon's principal motivation; Lyon's being liable alone on the successive notes to City Bank and New York Life; the reasonableness, as the District Court found, of the rentals and of the option prices; the substantiality of the purchase prices; Lyon's not being engaged generally in the business of financing; the presence of all building depreciation risks on Lyon; the risk, born by Lyon, that Worthen might default or fail, as other banks have failed; the facts that Worthen could "walk away" from the relationship at the end of the 25–year primary term, and probably would do so if the option price were more than the then-current worth of the building to Worthen; the inescapable fact that if the building lease were not extended, Lyon would be the full owner of the building, free to do with it as it chose; Lyon's liability for the substantial ground rent if Worthen decides not to exercise any of its options to extend; the absence of any understanding between Lyon and Worthen that Worthen would exercise any of the purchase options; the nonfamily and nonprivate nature of the entire transaction; and the absence of any differential in tax rates and of special tax circumstances for one of the parties—all convince us that Lyon has far the better of the case.[10]

In so concluding, we emphasize that we are not condoning manipulation by a taxpayer through arbitrary labels and dealings that have no economic significance. Such, however, has not happened in this case.

---

10. Thus, the facts of this case stand in contrast to many others in which the form of the transaction actually created tax advantages that, for one reason or another, could not have been enjoyed had the transaction taken another form. See, e.g., Sun Oil Co. v. Commissioner, 562 F.2d 258 (C.A.3 1977) (sale-and-leaseback of land between taxpayer and tax-exempt trust enabled the taxpayer to amortize, through its rental deductions, the cost of acquiring land not otherwise depreciable). Indeed, the arrangements in this case can hardly be labeled as tax-avoidance techniques in light of the other arrangements being promoted at the time.

In short, we hold that where, as here, there is a genuine multiple-party transaction with economic substance which is compelled or encouraged by business or regulatory realities, is imbued with tax-independent considerations, and is not shaped solely by tax-avoidance features that have meaningless labels attached, the Government should honor the allocation of rights and duties effectuated by the parties. Expressed another way, so long as the lessor retains significant and genuine attributes of the traditional lessor status, the form of the transaction adopted by the parties governs for tax purposes. What those attributes are in any particular case will necessarily depend upon its facts. It suffices to say that, as here, a sale-and-leaseback, in and of itself, does not necessarily operate to deny a taxpayer's claim for deductions.

The judgment of the Court of Appeals, accordingly, is reversed.

It is so ordered.

MR. JUSTICE WHITE dissents and would affirm the judgment substantially for the reasons stated in the opinion in the Court of Appeals for the Eighth Circuit. 536 F.2d 746 (1976).

MR. JUSTICE STEVENS, dissenting.

In my judgment the controlling issue in this case is the economic relationship between Worthen and petitioner, and matters such as the number of parties, their reasons for structuring the transaction in a particular way, and the tax benefits which may result, are largely irrelevant. The question whether a leasehold has been created should be answered by examining the character and value of the purported lessor's reversionary estate.

For a 25–year period Worthen has the power to acquire full ownership of the bank building by simply repaying the amounts, plus interest, advanced by the New York Life Insurance Company and petitioner. During that period, the economic relationship among the parties parallels exactly the normal relationship between an owner and two lenders, one secured by a first mortgage and the other by a second mortgage. If Worthen repays both loans, it will have unencumbered ownership of the property. What the character of this relationship suggests is confirmed by the economic value that the parties themselves have placed on the reversionary interest.

All rental payments made during the original 25–year term are credited against the option repurchase price, which is exactly equal to the unamortized cost of the financing. The value of the repurchase option is thus limited to the cost of the financing, and Worthen's power to exercise the option is cost-free. Conversely, petitioner, the nominal owner of the reversionary estate, is not entitled to receive *any* value for the surrender of its supposed rights of ownership. Nor does it have any power to control Worthen's exercise of the option.

"It is fundamental that 'depreciation is not predicated upon ownership of property *but rather upon an investment in property.* 'No such investment exists when payments of the purchase price in accordance with the design of the parties yield no equity to the purchaser." Estate of Franklin v. Commissioner, 544 F.2d 1045, 1049 (C.A.9 1976) (citations omitted; emphasis in original). Here, the petitioner has, in effect, been guaranteed that it will receive its original $500,000 plus accrued interest. But that is all. It incurs neither the risk of depreciation,[11] nor the benefit of possible appreciation. Under the terms of the sale-leaseback, it will stand in no better or worse position after the 11th year of the lease—when Worthen can first exercise its option to repurchase—whether the property has appreciated or depreciated.[12] And this remains true throughout the rest of the 25-year period.

Petitioner has assumed only two significant risks. First, like any other lender, it assumed the risk of Worthen's insolvency. Second, it assumed the risk that Worthen might *not* exercise its option to purchase at or before the end of the original 25-year term.[13] If Worthen should exercise that right *not* to repay, perhaps it would *then* be appropriate to characterize petitioner as the owner and Worthen as the lessee. But speculation as to what might happen in 25 years cannot justify the *present* characterization of petitioner as the owner of the building. Until Worthen has made a commitment either to exercise or not to exercise its option, I think the Government is correct in its view that petitioner is not the owner of the building for tax purposes. At present, since Worthen has the unrestricted right to control the residual value of the property for a price which does not exceed the cost of its unamortized financing, I would hold, as a matter of law, that it is the owner.

I therefore respectfully dissent.

NOTES

(A) *Determining the Owner.* As *Frank Lyon* illustrates, many tax consequences (for example, who gets depreciation deductions) turn on who is the owner of the property. It is often difficult to determine the owner for tax purposes, particularly of property that is subject to an arrangement that the parties have characterized as a lease. The Service and the courts traditionally have attempted to distinguish between true leases, whereby the lessor owns the property for tax purposes, and conditional sales or financing arrangements, whereby the user of the property is the owner for tax purposes. The rules for making this distinction are not in the Code, but

---

11. Petitioner argues that it bears the risk of depreciation during the primary term of the lease, because the option price decreases over time. This is clearly incorrect. Petitioner will receive $500,000 plus interest, and no more or less, whether the option is exercised as soon as possible or only at the end of 25 years. Worthen, on the other hand, does bear the risk of depreciation, since its opportunity to make a profit from the exercise of its repurchase option hinges on the value of the building at the time.

12. After the 11th year of the lease, there are three ways that the lease might be terminated. The property might be condemned, the building might be destroyed by act of God, or Worthen might exercise its option to purchase. In any such event, if the property had increased in value, the entire benefit would be received by Worthen and petitioner would receive only its $500,000 plus interest.

13. The possibility that Worthen might not exercise its option is a risk for petitioner because in that event petitioner's advance would be amortized during the ensuing renewal lease terms, totaling 40 years. Yet there is a possibility that Worthen would choose not to renew for the full 40 years or that the burdens of owning a building and paying a ground rental of $10,000 during the years 2034 through 2044 would exceed the benefits of ownership.

rather are contained in a series of revenue rulings, revenue procedures, and court decisions.

Consider first the various factors that established—at least to the satisfaction of the Supreme Court—that the transaction in *Frank Lyon* was not a loan but a sale (followed by a leaseback). For example, what is the significance to this inquiry of the existence of competing bids on the acquisition of the building? Might not the parties have been competing only for the tax benefits incident to ownership of the building?

Of what importance is the fact that there were three parties to the transaction rather than only two? It is difficult to understand why the result should have differed if Lyon had possessed sufficient resources to construct the building without the assistance of New York Life. This distinction would appear to be relevant only in cases such as *Estate of Franklin,* supra at page 198, where the valuation of the property is an important issue.

What of the distant possibility that Worthen would go bankrupt or refuse to renew its lease in future years? Do not these risks assumed by Lyon more closely resemble those typically assumed by a lender of money rather than by a buyer of property? Does the Court do an adequate job of distinguishing the economic risks of an owner from those of a lender, such as a holder of a second mortgage? Is there any other way to separate the "substance" from the "form" of the transactions?

Note that the Court found support for its decision in the fact that "the Government is likely to lose little revenue" because the deductions taken by Lyon "would have been equally available to Worthen had it retained title to the building." Does this argue for a different result if Worthen and Lyon were taxed at different marginal rates? Perhaps if Worthen were tax-exempt because of operating losses? Consider also the following comment:

> One might say that Worthen and Lyon were in the same tax circumstances because both corporations were subject to the same schedule of tax rates under § 11 of the Internal Revenue Code. But that would be misleading. Worthen was in a "special tax circumstance" because it was a commercial bank. Commercial banks comprise the only class of taxpayers permitted to deduct the interest expenses incurred in holding state and local bonds that yield tax-exempt interest income. * * * [W]ithin limits commercial banks like Worthen can predict their taxable income, and they can alter it by shifting their mix of taxable and tax-exempt investments, while Lyon and other ordinary business corporations are less free to do so. Commercial banks can keep their taxable income below the level at which the maximum statutory rate (48 percent at the time of the Lyon–Worthen transaction) becomes applicable by carefully managing their investment portfolios. * * * It is not credible that Worthen and Lyon * * * were unaware of their differing tax needs and the way each might be helpful to the other at the expense of only the United States Treasury.

Bernard Wolfman, "The Supreme Court in the *Lyon*'s Den," 66 Cornell L.Rev. 1075, 1095–96, 1098 (1981).

The IRS has relied less on the form, and more on the substance of the transaction to determine who is the owner of property for tax purposes. A purported lease is required to have economic substance aside from the transfer of tax benefits.

In general, the owner of property must possess meaningful burdens and benefits of ownership as determined by the facts and circumstances. This inquiry focuses on which party experiences gains, or losses, when the property fluctuates in value. Thus, lease treatment may be denied, and the lessee will be treated as the owner, if the lessee has the option to acquire the property at the end of the lease for a price that is small in relation to the total lease payments or to the value of the property at the time the option is exercisable. In such cases, the lessor will be viewed as having transferred full ownership of the property in exchange for the rental payments because of the likelihood that the lessee will exercise the option. The IRS has issued two revenue procedures—Rev.Proc. 2001–28, 2001–19 I.R.B. 1156, and Rev. Proc. 2001–29, 2001–19 I.R.B. 1160—to provide objective guidelines for structuring leveraged leases of personal property. The courts, however, as *Frank Lyon* indicates, have not been as rigid as the IRS is in requiring a lessor to bear the economic burdens and benefits of ownership to qualify as an "owner" for tax purposes.

(B) *Some Other Cases.* The *Frank Lyon* case might be compared with Rice's Toyota World v. Commissioner, 81 T.C. 184 (1983), aff'd in part and rev'd in part, 752 F.2d 89 (4th Cir.1985). The taxpayer in that case was an auto dealer that purchased a six-year-old computer from a computer leasing company. The purchase was financed by $250,000 in recourse notes payable over a three-year period and $1,205,227 in nonrecourse notes payable over an eight-year period. The taxpayer then leased the computer back to the seller at an amount calculated to produce a $10,000 net annual cash flow to the taxpayer. There was evidence that the computer would have little residual value at the end of eight years.

The Tax Court, in disallowing the taxpayer's interest and depreciation deductions, first engaged in a subjective inquiry and ascertained that the taxpayer had no business purpose for the transaction other than tax avoidance. The court then engaged in an objective inquiry to find that the transaction also had no "economic substance"—that is, no "realistic hope of profit"—apart from its beneficial tax consequences. The court adopted the rationale of *Estate of Franklin,* supra at page 198, to hold that the nonrecourse liability did not represent a genuine investment because the taxpayer would find it prudent at the end of the eight-year period to abandon property that no longer had substantial value. The court excluded from the taxpayer's basis not only the nonrecourse debt but also the initial installment on the recourse debt, which was held to be "akin to a fee to purchase tax savings." The court also disallowed interest deductions on both the recourse and nonrecourse debt. On appeal, the Fourth Circuit upheld the Tax Court in disallowing depreciation deductions based on the inclusion of the recourse and nonrecourse notes in basis and in disallowing interest deductions on the nonrecourse notes; however, the appellate court did allow the deduction of interest payments on the recourse debt.

See also Hilton v. Commissioner, 74 T.C. 305 (1980), aff'd 671 F.2d 316 (9th Cir.1982), which disallowed interest and depreciation deductions on the sale and leaseback of a store between the Broadway department store chain and a single-purpose finance corporation. The court noted that the finance corporation was not an independent third party. Moreover, the court emphasized that, since Broadway would have continued to lease the building as long as it had substantial residual value, the finance company never would have found it economically imprudent to abandon the building and thus did not have an ownership interest.

2.   SECTION 183

NOTE ON THE USE OF THE "HOBBY LOSS" LIMITATION TO COMBAT TAX SHELTERS

The IRS employed the limitations of § 183 (for deductions of losses on activities "not engaged in for profit") in its efforts to shut down tax shelters. For example, in Brannen v. Commissioner, 722 F.2d 695 (11th Cir.1984), the court applied the multi-factor test of the § 183 regulations (see the *Plunkett* case supra at page 381) to disallow losses claimed by a doctor on an investment in a movie tax shelter partnership. Dr. Brannen had invested $20,000 for a promised $43,000 tax savings with respect to a movie aptly titled "Beyond the Law," a poorly dubbed "spaghetti western" filmed in Italy. The film opened and played briefly at the Red River Drive–In in Lubbock, Texas and showed also at other theaters in Texas, North Carolina, and South Carolina, but did not enjoy the protections of a U.S. copyright. The partnership had claimed depreciation deductions (and resulting losses) of $1,730,000 on the film, which earned a total of $17,180.02 in income.

Although the Service won a number of hobby loss decisions in addition to *Brannen*, § 183 did not prove to be an effective weapon against tax shelters. Inquiries into profit motive tend to turn on the particular facts of the case, and taxpayers were willing to try to prove that they had the requisite profit motive. Ultimately, § 183 did little or nothing to stem the tide of tax shelter litigation.

In many § 183 cases, the Commissioner argued that the transactions were not entered into primarily for profit and that the taxpayer's motive was entirely or primarily for tax reasons. Why is a profit motive (other than the tax benefits) required? Consider the following from Fox v. Commissioner, 82 T.C. 1001 (1984):

> We believe that section 165(c)(2) requires a primary profit motive if a loss from a particular transaction is to be deductible.

> Petitioner, however, points out that a multitude of transactions which are likely to be motivated primarily by tax reasons is nonetheless sanctioned under the tax laws. Examples of such transactions are the purchase of tax-exempt securities; purchases of property motivated by the availability of accelerated depreciation, the investment credit, and the deductibility of interest; safe-harbor leasing; renovation of historical structures; location of subsidiaries in Puerto Rico because of tax credits; acquiring interests in low income housing partnerships;

and many others. Indeed, some of these transactions are arguably *solely* tax motivated.

We acknowledge that many such tax-motivated transactions are congressionally approved and encouraged. We therefore relax our holding that section 165(c)(2) permits loss deductions only from transactions entered into primarily for profit to allow for those essentially tax-motivated transactions which are unmistakably within the contemplation of congressional intent. The determination whether a transaction is one Congress intended to encourage will require a broad view of the relevant statutory framework and some investigation into legislative history. The issue of congressional intent is raised only upon a threshold determination that a particular transaction was entered into primarily for tax reasons.

Professor Alvin Warren has argued that no economic profit requirement should apply where a court determines that a special tax subsidy is intended. See Alvin Warren, "The Requirement of Economic Profit in Tax–Motivated Transactions," 59 Taxes 985 (1981). How could one determine that a subsidy was intended? Should it matter whether Congress intended to provide the equivalent of a direct subsidy or merely to eliminate tax barriers to the investment?

Assuming it is proper to require a profit motive, what should be the standard? Any pre-tax profit? A pre-tax profit in present value terms equivalent to that on U.S. Treasury bills or that generally available on activities of similar risk (an "economically appropriate" rate of return)? A pre-tax profit that is large relative to the anticipated tax benefits? A pre-tax profit large enough to constitute the principal purpose of entering into the transaction?

3. THE "AT–RISK" LIMITATION OF SECTION 465

The advantages of leverage are greatest where the taxpayer is not personally liable on the indebtedness. By using nonrecourse debt, a tax shelter investment may produce tax losses (often from large depreciation deductions) for taxpayers who invest little of their own money in an asset and bear little genuine economic risk of loss.

The size of the tax benefit is exaggerated if the value of the property (and therefore the amount of the loan) is overstated. As previously noted, the IRS had been successful in disallowing deductions on investments financed with nonrecourse debt on the grounds that the purchase price was too inflated to permit the nominal buyer to obtain actual ownership of the property or that the debt was too contingent. See, e.g. *Estate of Franklin v. Commissioner*, supra at page 198. Because of the difficulty of making a careful inquiry as to value on a case-by-case basis and because nonrecourse debt made shelters attractive even where the value was not inflated, Congress decided to try a statutory attack.

Opportunities to obtain tax losses through nonrecourse financing were severely curtailed by the enactment of § 465. This provision allows the taxpayer to deduct losses on an investment only in the amount "at risk" with respect to that investment. § 465(a). A taxpayer is considered "at risk" only to the extent of (1) his investment of cash in the activity, (2) the adjusted basis of property contributed, (3) debt on which he is personally liable for repayment and (4) the net fair market value of his personal assets that secure nonrecourse borrowings (apart from the investment). The taxpayer is not considered at risk with respect to losses for which he is guaranteed reimbursement. § 465(b). Deductions reduce the amount the taxpayer is considered to have at risk. If deductions and/or a decrease in the value of the collateral reduce the at-risk figure below zero, the taxpayer must recapture his deductions by including an offsetting amount in income. § 465(e).

Section 465 initially was limited to farming, oil and gas, motion pictures, and equipment leasing, but later was extended to all investments. The limitation applies to real estate activities as well, except for certain loans from parties actively engaged in the financing business, such as commercial banks. See § 465(b)(6).

Section 465 does not directly change the *Crane* rule and thus does not prohibit the inclusion of nonrecourse debt in basis. Rather, it limits loss deductions (including those due to depreciation) from the property to the amount the owner has at risk. Needless to say, § 465 inspired many creative tax plans to convert nonrecourse liabilities into loans where the taxpayer was considered "at risk" and even led to much substitution of recourse for nonrecourse financing.

4. THE "PASSIVE LOSS" LIMITATION OF SECTION 469

When administrative and judicial efforts and various statutory provisions, including new penalties and compliance measures enacted in 1982 and 1984, failed to stem the tide of tax shelters, Congress responded in the 1986 Act with an extremely broad-based attack that limits the deduction of losses from "passive activities." This section was intended primarily to preclude taxpayers from using losses derived from tax shelter investments to reduce taxes on earned income and on investment income, such as interest and dividends. The passive loss rules are very complex, but they have been largely successful in shutting down tax shelters marketed to individuals. Since, despite its complexity, the statute does not define many of the critical statutory concepts, the regulations are extremely important.

The Mechanics. Section 469 provides that aggregate deductions from "passive activities" may be used only to offset the aggregate income from these activities. Passive activity losses in excess of passive activity income are not deductible, but may be carried forward to offset passive activity income of subsequent years. § 469(b). In effect, passive income and related deductions are placed in a separate "basket," and walled off from other forms of income. Passive activity losses therefore cannot shelter other forms of income.

Passive activities are defined by § 469(c) to include (1) the conduct of a trade or business in which the taxpayer does not materially participate and (2) rental activities.

Section 469 provides that an investment is a passive activity only if the taxpayer does not "materially participate" in the activity. The statute requires that the taxpayer be involved in the activity's operations on a "regular, continuous, and substantial" basis. The regulations provide seven alternative tests for determining whether "material participation" exists. A taxpayer materially participates in the activity if she meets any of the following conditions: (1) she spends more than 500 hours per taxable year on the activity, (2) she performs substantially all of the activities performed by all of the individuals involved in the activity for a taxable year, (3) she spends more than 100 hours per taxable year on the activity where that equals or exceeds the participation of any other individual, (4) she has "significant participation" with respect to this activity (more than 100 hours, but less than that required for material participation) and her combined participation in all such activities exceeds 500 hours, (5) she materially participated in the activity for any five of the last ten prior taxable years, or (6) she materially participated in a "personal service activity" in any one of the three prior taxable years (where a "personal service activity" is a trade or business in which capital is not an income producing factor). To further complicate things, a seventh alternative provides that the taxpayer may show material participation by "facts and circumstances" that demonstrate that she participates in the activity on a regular, continuous, and substantial basis. See § 469(h)(1) and § 1.469–5T.

The Regulations go on to provide that the work done to qualify under the above alternatives must be the type of work typically done by an owner of the activity and that the work may not be performed simply to avoid the passive loss rules. Work typically performed by investors, for example, such as reviewing financial statements, preparing summaries of finances or operations, or monitoring finances does not count. A limited partner is never treated as materially participating unless she spends more than 500 hours in the taxable year, meets the five-year or three-year material participation test, or is also a general partner. Participation in an activity for less than 100 hours a year can never constitute material participation.

As if the material participation requirements of the Internal Revenue Code itself were lacking in complexity, the regulations have introduced the new concept of "significant participation activities" for the purpose of identifying a number of situations where a taxpayer will not be considered to have passive income. For example, if a taxpayer participates for more than 100 hours in an activity, but does not "materially participate," net income from the activity will not be treated as passive, even though losses from the activity are. See § 1.469–1(f)(2)(i)(C). The purpose of this rule is to ensure that it will not be easy for a taxpayer to create passive income (which can be offset against other passive losses). The losses from significant participation activities will continue to be treated as passive. The government has been criticized for this rule as "heads we win, tails you lose."

Another area of regulatory concern involves the definition of rental activities. A rental activity is passive even if the taxpayer participates materially in the management of the rental activity. § 469(c)(2). The regulations list a number of activities that will not constitute rental activities for purposes of the passive loss rules. See Reg. § 1.469–1(e)(3). For example, income from renting property for less than seven days will not be considered rent, nor will income from renting property for less than 30 days if significant personal services are provided.

These rules are substantially different with regard to real estate professionals. A rental real estate activity in which the taxpayer materially participates is not treated as passive if he meets certain eligibility requirements. Generally, the taxpayer must be involved in development, construction, acquisition, conversion, management, leasing or brokering of the real property. Furthermore, the taxpayer must be involved on essentially a full-time basis: More than half of his services and more than 750 hours worth of services must be performed during the year in real estate businesses in which he materially participates. § 469(c)(7).

In the case of rental real estate activities, a special rule contained in § 469(i) provides that up to $25,000 of losses can be used against nonpassive income if the taxpayer is an "active participant." The $25,000 of allowable loss, however, is phased out beginning with taxpayers with adjusted gross income of $100,000 and is not available if AGI exceeds $150,000. This exception is designed to permit deduction of losses by some individuals with small scale rental activities who actively manage them. A favorite example is a New York firefighter who rents out a portion of her brownstone.

The definition of "activity" is important for two reasons. Material participation is defined with respect to each activity. Thus, if "activity" is narrowly defined, it may be difficult for a taxpayer to show material participation with respect to that activity. On the other hand, a narrow definition may make it easy for the taxpayer to completely dispose of an activity and thereby obtain the deduction of suspended losses. § 469(g).

The regulations use a facts and circumstances approach to identify a single activity. The primary factors that the regulations indicate will be used to treat several businesses as an activity are the types of businesses, common control, common ownership, geographical location, and business interdependence. § 1.469–4(c). Generally, a rental activity may not be grouped with another business and a real estate rental activity may not be grouped with an activity that rents personal property. § 1.469–4(d).

Passive activity income typically does not include "portfolio income," such as interest earned on bonds, dividends on stocks or income from other securities, annuities or royalties. § 469(e)(1). Thus, passive losses cannot offset certain types of investment income. The distinctions between "portfolio" income, "passive activity" income, and "active" income are exceedingly complex. For example, the regulations provide that income from licensing intangible property will be treated as income from a trade or business, and hence not as passive income, only if the taxpayer receiving the royalties created the property or performed substantial services in its development or marketing.

The passive loss rules must be coordinated with the at-risk rules of § 465 and the capital loss provisions. In general, whether a loss is subject to the passive loss limitations of § 469 is determined after applying the at-risk limitations of § 465. The interaction of the capital loss limitations and the passive loss rules is not nearly so straightforward. In general, both rules are applied simultaneously. In determining the income or loss from a passive activity, capital gains and losses are treated the same as ordinary gains and losses. If a capital loss is suspended under the passive loss rules, it is not offset against capital gains. Capital gains and losses from passive activities that are not limited by § 469 are mixed with other capital gains and losses in calculating the limitations on the deduction of capital losses. Carryover rules generally operate similarly. See § 1.469–1(d). There are also instances where limitations on basis, for example, under the partnership provisions, interact with the passive loss rules. In general, if a loss is prohibited from being deducted under those basis rules, the loss is ignored under § 469 and a loss permitted by the § 469 rules is still subject to these other basis limitations. Further discussion of those rules here, however, would forever bar this course from being called "baby tax."

Policy Issues. The passive activity rules mark a major extension of a "basket" approach to income taxation. A basket approach also is illustrated by § 165(d)'s limitation of gambling loss deductions to gambling income and § 163(d)'s limitation of deductions for investment interest to investment income.

A "basket" approach generally divides income into certain categories or "baskets" and limits deductions against that income to expenses related in some manner to the production or receipt of that income. Inevitably, the use of baskets of income requires applications of criteria to distinguish between different forms of income and "tracing rules" to match deductions to related income sources. As a practical matter, a "basket" approach introduces substantial complexities into the tax law because taxpayers often have flexibility to change the form of business and investment transactions and business and investment entities. For example, by changing a transaction from a "loan" to a "lease" with similar economic effects, interest income may be transformed into rents.

The use of baskets of income also in some circumstances will create a divergence between taxable and economic income. For example, a taxpayer who earns $10,000 of income in a passive activity but who has real economic expenses of $30,000 under § 469 would be able to deduct only one-third of the expenses in the year incurred. Carrying the losses forward would not fully compensate the taxpayer for the economic loss because of the cost of deferring the tax reduction. On the other hand, many tax shelter losses deducted by taxpayers against unrelated income under prior law were artificial losses generated by favorable tax rules, and did not reflect a genuine diminution in the taxpayer's economic income. Such losses, for example, often were due to accelerated depreciation. The passive loss rules restrict the availability of deductions for such artificial losses, but the trade-off may be restrictions on deductions for real economic losses.

SECTION 8.   BAD DEBTS

United States v. Generes

Supreme Court of the United States, 1972. 405 U.S. 93.

JUSTICE BLACKMUN delivered the opinion of the Court.

[Generes owned 44 percent of the stock of a corporation engaged in the construction business, for which he had originally invested $38,900. He was also president of the corporation for which he received an annual salary of $12,000. To help the company through financial difficulties Generes directly and indirectly loaned it more than $300,000. The company nevertheless went into receivership and Generes was never repaid. He claimed a business bad debt deduction, asserting that he made the loans to protect his job and salary—a legitimate business reason—rather than his investment.]

* * *

We conclude that in determining whether a bad debt has a "proximate" relation to the taxpayer's trade or business, as the Regulations specify, and thus qualifies as a business bad debt, the proper measure is that of dominant motivation, and that only significant motivation is not sufficient. We reach this conclusion for a number of reasons.

The Code itself carefully distinguishes between business and nonbusiness items. It does so, for example, in § 165 with respect to losses, in § 166 with respect to bad debts, and in § 162 with respect to expenses. It gives particular tax benefits to business losses, business bad debts, and business expenses, and gives lesser benefits, or none at all, to nonbusiness losses, nonbusiness bad debts, and nonbusiness expenses. It does this despite the fact that the latter are just as adverse in financial consequence to the taxpayer as are the former. But this distinction has been a policy of the income tax structure ever since the Revenue Act of 1916, § 5(a), 39 Stat. 759, provided differently for trade or business losses than it did for losses sustained in another transaction entered into for profit. And it has been the specific policy with respect to bad debts since the Revenue Act of 1942 incorporated into § 23(k) of the 1939 Code the distinction between business and nonbusiness bad debts. 56 Stat. 820.

The point, however, is that the tax statutes have made the distinction, that the Congress therefore intended it to be a meaningful one, and that the distinction is not to be obliterated or blunted by an interpretation that tends to equate the business bad debt with the nonbusiness bad debt. We think that emphasis upon the significant rather than upon the dominant would have a tendency to do just that.

Application of the significant-motivation standard would also tend to undermine and circumscribe the Court's holding in Whipple [v. Commissioner, 373 U.S. 193 (1963)] and the emphasis there that a shareholder's mere activity in a corporation's affairs is not a trade or business. As Chief Justice Lumbard pointed out in his separate and disagreeing concurrence in Weddle [v. Commissioner, 325 F.2d 849 (2d Cir.1963)], at 852–853, both motives—that of protecting the investment and that of protecting the salary—are inevitably involved, and an inquiry whether employee status [which is a "business" status] provides a significant motivation will always produce an affirmative answer and result in a judgment for the taxpayer.

* * *

The dominant-motivation test strengthens and is consistent with the mandate of § 262 of the Code * * * that "no deduction shall be allowed for personal, living, or family expenses" except as otherwise provided. It prevents personal considerations from circumventing this provision.

The dominant-motivation approach to § 166(d) is consistent with that given the loss provisions in § 165(c)(1), see, for example, Imbesi v. Commissioner of Internal Revenue, 361 F.2d 640, 644 (C.A.3 1966), and in § 165(c)(2), see Austin v. Commissioner of Internal Revenue, 298 F.2d 583, 584 (C.A.2 1962). In these related areas, consistency is desirable. See also, Commissioner of Internal Revenue v. Duberstein, 363 U.S. 278, 286 (1960).

* * *

The conclusion we have reached means that the District Court's instructions, based on a standard of significant rather than dominant motivation, are erroneous and that, at least, a new trial is required. We have examined the record, however, and find nothing that would support a jury verdict in this taxpayer's favor had the dominant-motivation standard been embodied in the instructions. Judgment n.o.v. for the United States, therefore, must be ordered. * * *

As Judge Simpson pointed out in his dissent, 427 F.2d, at 284–285, the only real evidence offered by the taxpayer bearing upon motivation was his own testimony that he signed the indemnity agreement "to protect my job," that "I figured in three years' time I would get my money out," and that "I never once gave it [his investment in the corporation] a thought."

The statements obviously are self-serving. In addition, standing alone, they do not bear the light of analysis. What the taxpayer was purporting to say was that his $12,000 annual salary was his sole motivation, and that his $38,900 original investment, the actual value of which prior to the misfortunes of 1962 we do not know, plus his loans to the corporation, plus his personal interest in the integrity of the corporation as a source of living for his son-in-law and as an investment for his son and his other son-in-law, were of no consequence whatever in his thinking. The comparison is strained all the more by the fact that the salary is pre-tax and the investment is taxpaid. With his total annual income about $40,000, Mr. Generes may well have reached a federal income tax bracket of 40% or more for a joint return in 1958–1962. Sections 1 and 2 of the 1954 Code, 68A Stats. 5 and 8. The $12,000 salary thus would produce for him only about $7,000 net after federal tax and before any state income tax. This is the figure, and not $12,000, that has any possible significance for motivation purposes, and it is less than ⅙ of the original stock investment.

We conclude on these facts that the taxpayer's explanation falls of its own weight, and that reasonable minds could not ascribe, on this record, a dominant motivation directed to the preservation of the taxpayer's salary as president of Kelly–Generes Construction Co., Inc.

* * *

NOTES

(A) *Code Requirements.* A business bad debt is deductible in full as an ordinary loss. A partially worthless business debt can be deducted to the extent charged off by the taxpayer on his books. § 166(a). An individual may deduct a wholly worthless nonbusiness bad debt only as a short-term capital loss, which is not as valuable as an ordinary loss, since, unlike ordinary losses, capital losses can be deducted only to the extent of capital gains plus $3,000. § 166(d)(1). Taxpayers always prefer business bad debts to nonbusiness bad debts, which can be deducted only as capital losses and only when entirely worthless. It is sometimes advantageous for a taxpayer to attempt to achieve deduction as a § 165 loss, instead of a bad debt. A nonbusiness profit-seeking transaction that produces a loss may be deductible against ordinary income under § 165. The Supreme Court has held that §§ 165 and 166 are mutually exclusive. Spring City Foundry Co. v. Commissioner, 292 U.S. 182 (1934). The treatment of capital losses is taken up in Chapter 5.

(B) *Cases Finding Dominant Business Motivation.* As *Generes* suggests, the question whether a bad debt resulted from a loan made for a dominant business motive typically turns on the particular facts and circumstances, when both investment and business reasons are present. Contrast Hough v. Commissioner, 882 F.2d 1271 (7th Cir.1989) (dominant motive in making loan to corporation was taxpayer's investment interest as a shareholder and not to protect business he received from corporation), with Garlove v. Commissioner, 24 T.C.M. 1049 (1965) (attorney made loans to client corporation of which he was a shareholder so that it would remain with him as a fee-paying client; dominant purpose was business-related). In Estate of Mann, 731 F.2d 267 (5th Cir.1984), the appellate court affirmed a jury verdict allowing business bad debt deductions for several million dollars of unpaid loans from a broker to a holding company owned principally by his brother, a businessman. The government argued that the taxpayer had made the loans to protect his significant minority investment in the company and to aid family members—his brother and a nephew—who were financially dependent on the company. In upholding the jury verdict as not "patently incorrect," the court emphasized that the two brothers "conducted their business transactions as businessmen," that at the time the loans were made (as opposed to the time of default), the lending brother had no substantial investment in the company, and that his profit from the business—brokerage commissions from transactions involving the company—was substantial.

(C) *The Trade or Business of Lending.* In Estate of Bounds v. Commissioner, 46 T.C.M. 1209 (1983), the taxpayer made 16 loans to business and social acquaintances as well as to entities in which he had an investment interest. The Tax Court denied his deduction of five bad debts as business bad debts. The court rejected the taxpayer's claim that his lending activities were sufficiently extensive and continuous to place him in the trade or business of lending money, stating:

> The [taxpayer's] lending activities * * * lacked most of the attributes common to the carrying on of a trade or business. First of all, it does not appear that these activities occupied a substantial amount of the decedent's time and effort during this period. On the contrary, most of his time was divided between his duties as an employee and later a consultant * * * and, to a lesser extent, as an officer and

director of several corporations. The [taxpayer] himself stated at trial that he devoted very little time to the making of loans. Such passive conduct is not at all characteristic of the operation of a trade or business. * * * The [taxpayer] did not advertise his lending activities and did not maintain what could fairly be considered a separate office for such activities. Moreover, he did not keep books and records reflecting his lending activities. For this reason, the [taxpayer] was unable to reconstruct his purported "business" activities with any degree of accuracy. These factors all weigh against him. * * * It is also enlightening that the [taxpayer] apparently did not consider himself in the money-lending business * * * as evidenced by the fact that he listed his occupation on his tax returns as that of executive * * *

Although the occasional lending of large amounts of money indicates a hope of generating substantial income from such activity, it does not transform intermittent transactions into the operation of a trade or business any more than does the making of large, isolated investments in the stock market. * * * We do not believe this is the "exceptional situation" where the [taxpayer's] lending activities were sufficiently extensive and continuous to elevate them to the status of a separate business.

(D) *Loans to Family and Friends.* In his concurring opinion in *Generes,* Justice Marshall said that

[t]he major congressional purpose in distinguishing between business and nonbusiness bad debts was to prevent taxpayers from lending money to friends or relatives who they knew would not repay it and then deducting against ordinary income a loss in the amount of the loan. * * * A related congressional purpose in enacting the predecessor of § 166 was "to put nonbusiness investments in the form of loans on a footing with other nonbusiness investments."

Compare Davis v. Commissioner, 60 T.C.M. 1256 (1990) (as there were no formal indicia of a loan such as interest, collateral or documentation, advance was considered a gift), with Hunt v. Commissioner, 57 T.C.M. 919 (1989) (evidence indicated family transfer was a bona fide loan). See also Vaughters v. Commissioner, 55 T.C.M. 1150 (1988) (transfer by mother to son's farming operation did not create a debtor-creditor relationship when repayment was contingent on profits); Reg. § 1.166–1(c) (generally treating losses on debts to friends or family members as gifts).

Should there be a deduction for bad debts arising out of personal loans to friends or relatives? Recall the tax treatment of a donor who simply gives money to a family member or friend. Should it make any difference if a loan to a family member bore adequate interest?

(E) *Was There a Loan? Did It Have Basis?* Section 166 presupposes the existence of a bona fide debt. A debtor-creditor relationship must exist based on a valid and enforceable obligation to pay a fixed or determinable sum of money. Reg. § 1.166–1(c).

No deduction is allowed for a debt that was worthless when acquired. Putnam v. Commissioner, 352 U.S. 82 (1956). No bad debt deduction is allowed for a claim for unpaid wages or rent because such debts are treated as having a zero basis. These amounts would be fully included in income if collected, so the taxpayer's loss when they are unpaid is adequately reflected for tax purposes by excluding them from income. A deduction would add an unwarranted double benefit. See, e.g., Perry v. Commissioner, 92 T.C. 470 (1989), affirmed in an unpublished opinion 912 F.2d 1466 (5th Cir.1990), cert. denied 499 U.S. 938 (1991) (no bad debt deduction for unpaid alimony because wife has no basis in the obligation).

If, however, the taxpayer is an accrual basis taxpayer, then she will have included the item in gross income when the unconditional right to receive it accrues. In that case, the taxpayer has a basis, and if the item is not paid, there is a bad debt deduction. The distinction between the accrual and cash methods of accounting is taken up in Chapter 6.

(F) *Loan Guarantees.* A taxpayer who sustains a loss from guaranteeing a loan is treated in the same manner as a taxpayer who sustains a loss from a loan that she made directly. If the guaranty agreement relates to the guarantor's trade or business, the guarantor may treat the transaction as a business bad debt. If the guaranty agreement is unrelated to the guarantor's trade or business but related to a transaction entered into for profit, any resulting loss will be treated as a nonbusiness bad debt. Payments on loan guarantees based on personal motivation are not deductible. Reg. § 1.166–9. The taxpayer must have received reasonable consideration for making the guarantee and where the debtor is the taxpayer's spouse, dependent or close relative, cash or property consideration must have changed hands.

The taxpayer obtains a deduction only in the year in which she actually makes payment on the guarantee and then only in the amount actually paid. A transfer of the guarantor's note does not give rise to a deduction. Black Gold Energy Corp. v. Commissioner, 99 T.C. 482 (1992).

(G) *Political Contributions.* Section 271 specifically disallows deductions for the worthlessness of debts owed by a political party. This rule was designed to overcome a common practice whereby taxpayers loaned a large sum to a political organization and then deducted it as a bad debt. In this way, taxpayers obtained deductions for what were in substance nondeductible campaign contributions. The single exception to § 271 allows a deduction for worthless debts resulting from a bona fide sale of goods or services to a political party or campaign committee in the ordinary course of the seller's trade or business. This exception is permitted only if the taxpayer made substantial efforts to collect the debt and if more than 30 percent of its total business for the year in which the debt accrued was with political parties. See § 271(c).

(H) *Voluntary Cancellation.* A taxpayer who voluntarily cancels a debt is not entitled to a bad debt deduction. However, if the voluntary cancellation is for a business purpose, a deduction under § 162(a) may be taken.

(I) *Timing.* Section 166(a) allows a deduction for "any debt which becomes worthless within the taxable year." This presents the often difficult question of determining the year in which the debt actually became worthless. The taxpayer must prove that the debt had some value at the beginning and none at the end of the year in which the deduction is claimed. Under the normal three-year statute of limitations, taxpayers would often lose deductions because they could not establish, or established too late, the year in which the worthlessness occurred. Since 1942, however, § 6511(d) has provided a special seven-year statute of limitations with respect to refund claims based on the deduction of bad debts. This usually enables the taxpayer to get a deduction in one of the seven years.

SECTION 9.   PERSONAL DEDUCTIONS

Taxpayers whose income is below a threshold amount are not thought to have the ability to pay income taxes. Some mechanism must be used to exempt them from the universe of taxpayers. Currently, three such devices are employed—the standard deduction, the personal exemption, and the earned income credit. The standard deduction and the personal exemptions, are available to higher-income taxpayers and thus do not serve only to exempt low income taxpayers. For provisions designed principally to benefit presumably the least sophisticated citizens, these allowances are extraordinarily complex.

A.   THE STANDARD DEDUCTION

A taxpayer may deduct either itemized deductions or a standard deduction. The latter is a flat amount that varies with marital status and may be taken regardless of whether the taxpayer actually had expenditures. § 63(c). By contrast, itemized deductions are a specific set of expenses, generally personal in nature. Since the standard deduction is the amount that taxpayers may deduct in lieu of itemized deductions, it effectively provides a floor for itemized deductions. Most high income taxpayers itemize deductions rather than taking the standard deduction. Itemized deductions are discussed in the next Section.

The standard deduction is $5,000 on a joint return, $4,400 for a head of household, $3,000 for unmarried individuals, and $2,500 for married individuals filing separately. The standard deduction is indexed annually for inflation. In 2002 the deduction is $7,850 for married couples filing jointly, $6,900 for heads of household, and $4,700 for singles. Note that current law creates a "marriage penalty" in that the standard deduction decreases when a couple marries, as they will be entitled to the deduction for couples filing jointly (currently $7,850) rather than two standard deductions for singles (currently twice $4,700 or $9,400). Beginning in 2009 the standard deduction for a married couple filing a joint return will be twice the standard deduction for an individual filing a single return. This creates a "marriage bonus," however, when only one of the spouses has income since the standard deduction will double simply because the couple marries. This issue is discussed further infra at page 472.

Additional amounts of standard deduction are allowed for people over age 65 and for the blind. In 2002 married taxpayers can each deduct an additional $900 for each such status and unmarried taxpayers can deduct $1,150 for each such status. § 63(f). Like the regular standard deductions, these additional allowances are not allowed to taxpayers who itemize deductions.

The standard deduction of an individual who can be claimed as a dependent by another taxpayer (see infra at page 430) is limited to the lesser of the usual standard deduction or the greater of $750 or the individual's earned income plus $250. § 63(c)(5).

Some taxpayers are required to itemize deductions even if their deductions are less than the standard deduction. The standard deduction is not available, for example, to married taxpayers filing separate returns where either spouse itemizes deductions, to nonresident aliens, to U.S. citizens with income from U.S. possessions, and to estates, trusts, common trust funds, or partnerships.

Congress has increased the amount of the standard deduction from time to time, in part to promote simplicity. Taxpayers who do not itemize may not need to keep records and this makes compliance easier. In turn, the standard deduction promotes administrative compliance because the IRS does not need to audit it.

There are two rationales typically offered for the standard deduction. First, it may be viewed as a substitute for itemized deductions for those taxpayers whose itemized deductions would be of relatively small amounts. Under this view, the standard deduction is justified on grounds of simplifying both tax administration and taxpayer recordkeeping. Alternatively, the standard deduction may be viewed as an adjustment of the tax rate schedules. The amount of the standard deduction, in conjunction with the personal exemption (and certain other provisions such as the earned income tax credit), reflects Congress' determination of the level of income below which no tax should be imposed. In fact, for awhile, the standard deduction was called the "zero bracket amount."

Policy arguments with respect to other provisions of the Code often turn on which of these two views of the standard deduction is being advanced. One often hears the argument—in the context of the charitable contribution deduction, for example—that providing only an itemized deduction for charitable contributions deprives nonitemizers of the benefit of the deduction. When the charitable deduction for nonitemizers was repealed by the 1986 Act, some said the change unfairly harmed nonitemizers. This is true if one thinks the standard deduction serves principally to determine the level of income below which no tax should be imposed.

If, however, the standard deduction is intended to substitute for itemized deductions for most taxpayers or to serve as a floor that itemized deductions must exceed to be allowed, this "unfairness" disappears. A taxpayer is a nonitemizer only if the total of his itemizable deductions is less than the standard deduction. Suppose a single taxpayer's total deductions, including charitable contributions, is $500. That taxpayer should be happy with a standard deduction of $4,550. She can be viewed as getting $4,050 of "extra" deductions. The taxpayer's true deductions are allowed, plus an extra amount that arises from the need to set the standard deduction at a level sufficiently high that the bulk of taxpayers will not itemize in order to achieve the administrative and taxpayer recordkeeping simplifications accorded by the standard deduction. Under this view of the standard deduction, there should be no unfairness in failing to provide any charitable deduction (or other itemized deduction) for nonitemizers.

Of course, deductions available only as itemized deductions have no marginal incentive effects on nonitemizers. An itemized deduction for charitable contributions does not create similar incentives for itemizers and nonitemizers; if the itemizer and nonitemizer both increase their charitable giving, additional contributions save taxes for the former, but not for the latter. The nonitemizer takes only the standard deduction until her charitable giving is sufficient to make her an itemizer. Thus, whenever itemized deductions are intended to encourage particular behavior, there is a conflict between the incentive intentions of Congress and simplification concerns. Incentive considerations argue for making the deduction available to itemizers and nonitemizers alike, while simplification argues for limiting the deduction to itemizers. In 2001, President Bush proposed once again allowing a limited charitable deduction to nonitemizers. This provision did not make it into the 2001 Act, but Congress did add deductions for education expenses and interest on education loans, which are above-the-line deductions, available to nonitemizers. See page 216 supra.

NOTES

(A) *Filing Status.* A number of Code provisions (such as the standard deduction and the earned income credit) turn on the taxpayer's filing status. There are five possibilities: married filing jointly, married filing separately, surviving spouse, head of household, and single.

Married couples who choose to do so may combine income and deductions on one return. This is generally advantageous. For example, the tax rates and the standard deduction for a married couple filing jointly are more favorable than those that apply if the couple filed separately although some of these differences are phased out beginning in 2005. On the other hand, if the couple is not married and thus each files as a single taxpayer, their tax liability may be less in some circumstances, depending on the relative incomes of the two people. This dichotomy is discussed further infra at page 470.

A taxpayer whose spouse has died in either of the two years preceding the current year continues to be treated as a married taxpayer. § 2(a). In order to qualify as a "surviving spouse," however, the taxpayer must maintain and reside in a household in which a dependent child or grandchild resides for the entire taxable year. Congress apparently wanted to provide a transition from married filing jointly status to single status, but it is not clear why it thought a child was necessary.

Another intermediate status is "head of household;" the applicable rates and the amount of the standard deduction lie between those for a married couple and a single person. Such a taxpayer must be unmarried for federal tax purposes and must maintain a household in which she lives that is also the principal place of residence for more than one-half the taxable year of a child or a dependent. Alternatively, the taxpayer can maintain a separate residence for her mother or father so long as the parent qualifies as a dependent. § 2(b). "Maintaining a household" "child," "dependent," and "unmarried" are all words of art and the Code and regulations contain quite complex definitions.

B. PERSONAL EXEMPTION

Each taxpayer is entitled to a personal exemption of $2,000. § 151. The amount is indexed annually for inflation. In 2002, the exemption equals $3,000.

Taxpayers also are entitled to an exemption for each dependent. The term "dependent" is defined in § 152 to include children, grandchildren, parents, and other relatives, as well as unrelated members of the taxpayer's household, more than half of whose support for the taxable year was provided by the taxpayer. An individual with gross income equal to or more than the exemption amount cannot qualify as a dependent unless he or she is a child of the taxpayer and is either under age 19 or a student under age 24. This exception does not apply if the child is married and files a joint return. An additional exception to this income limit applies to individuals who earn income incidental to their medical treatment at sheltered workshops for the disabled. § 151(c).

A taxpayer who can be claimed as a dependent by another taxpayer (usually a parent) cannot claim a personal exemption. The theory is that the exemption represents an amount spent on support that is unavailable to pay taxes. The person who actually pays the support should claim the deduction, not the person who receives the support. Amounts transferred as support generally are not includible in the income of the recipient. This rule mainly affects minor children with unearned income and college students who work part-time but are supported by their parents.

Exemptions are phased out for taxpayers with income above certain levels. A taxpayer whose income is at a threshold amount reduces the deduction for exemptions by 2 percent of each $2,500 over the threshold. § 151(d). For example on a joint return, the deduction for the exemptions is reduced when income reaches $199,450 and is completely eliminated when income reaches $321,950. These thresholds are indexed annually for inflation. The effect of phasing out the exemptions is to create a so-called "rate bubble." The first $122,500 of taxable income above the threshold is taxed at a marginal rate in excess of the statutory maximum rate. In fact, some taxpayers with a large number of dependents are subjected to higher marginal tax rates than taxpayers with equal income and fewer dependents. This restriction on the use of personal exemptions is phased out beginning in 2006 and is repealed as of 2010. This change was part of the 2001 Act, which reduced rates generally, and has the effect of decreasing the marginal rate of high income taxpayers even further.

Section 24 entitles a taxpayer to a $600 credit for each dependent child (son or daughter, stepson or stepdaughter or eligible foster child) who is under age 17. The amount of the credit increases gradually to $1,000 by 2010. The credit is phased out for single taxpayers whose AGI exceeds $75,000 or married taxpayers whose AGI exceeds $110,000. The credit is refundable to the extent of 10 percent (15 percent in 2005) of the taxpayer's earned income in excess of $10,000 (indexed for inflation). For example, suppose a couple with two children earned $20,000 and owed no taxes against which to offset the $1,200 in child credits due to other deductions and credits . They would still receive a check for $1,000 [10 percent × ($20,000 – $10,000)]. Families with three or more children are forced to make additional calculations. Their refundable credit is equal to the amount by which their Social Security taxes exceed their earned income tax credit (discussed infra at page 432) if that amount is greater than the above calculation.

Like the standard deduction, there are two theories supporting personal exemptions and they have different implications for its structure. Some view the personal exemption as setting the amount of a taxpayer's income that should be taxed at a zero rate. Under that view, every taxpayer should have the same level of personal exemption regardless of income and a phase-out is inappropriate. Others view the personal exemption as a mechanism to exempt a subsistence level of income from taxation. The need for an exemption decreases as income rises and a flat exemption for all taxpayers provides a windfall for those in high brackets. One's view of the dependency exemption depends on how family size should be taken into account. If children or families are viewed as a form of consumption, there is no need to adjust exemptions by family size. On the other hand, if the exemptions are intended to exempt subsistence income from tax or to distinguish families based on ability to pay, family size is obviously relevant.

NOTES

(A) *Support.* The support requirement has generated considerable controversy. For example, a parent cannot claim an exemption for a child if more than half of the child's support was furnished by public assistance payments. Lutter v. Commissioner, 61 T.C. 685 (1974), affirmed per curiam 514 F.2d 1095 (7th Cir.1975), cert. denied 423 U.S. 931 (1975). An adult offspring likewise cannot claim an exemption for a parent more than half of whose support was furnished by state old-age assistance. Carter v. Commissioner, 55 T.C. 109 (1970). The IRS similarly has held that Social Security benefits must be attributed to the recipient rather than the taxpayer to determine whether the taxpayer has provided the requisite 50 percent support. Rev.Rul. 57–344, 1957–2 C.B. 112.

(B) *Unrelated Individuals.* An unrelated individual can be claimed as a dependent only if that individual makes his or her principal residence in the household of the taxpayer. Section 152(b)(5) states that an unrelated individual is not a member of the household for exemption purposes if the relationship between the individual and the taxpayer is "in violation of local law." The Tax Court consequently has held that an individual cannot qualify as a dependent if his or her relationship to the taxpayer constitutes "cohabitation" in violation of a state statute. Peacock v. Commissioner, 37 T.C.M. 177 (1978).

(C) *Divorced Parents and Multiple Support Agreements.* The dependency exemption in the event of divorce or separation is allocated to the parent who has custody of the child. § 152(e). This rule is waived, however, for written agreements that permit the noncustodial parent to take the deduction, for multiple support agreements or for certain pre–1985 agreements allocating the dependency exemption to the noncustodial parent.

Multiple support agreements may be used, for example, when several taxpayers together provide more than half of the support of an elderly parent. The agreement can allocate the dependency exemption to one of the taxpayers, or to the children on a rotating basis, although none of them alone provides more than half of the parent's support. § 152(c).

C.   EARNED INCOME TAX CREDIT

Section 32 provides a credit to low income individuals who have earnings. The credit is refundable, which means that people with no tax liability can receive a credit; they file a tax return to receive a cash payment.

In 2002, for example, taxpayers with one qualifying child obtained a credit of 34 percent of the first $7,370 of earned income. The maximum credit is $2,506 and is reduced by 16 percent of earned income in excess of $14,520. The maximum credit for taxpayers with two or more qualifying children is $4,140. Eligible taxpayers are married individuals who maintain a household for their minor children or grandchildren or single taxpayers between the ages of 25 and 65 who are not another taxpayer's dependent. The credit is substantially less for the latter group than that for a taxpayer with a child. The childless taxpayer receives a credit of 7.65 percent of the first $4,910 of earned income; the maximum credit is $376.

Because the EITC is so much larger for a taxpayer with a child, the definition of "child" becomes quite important. A child is a (1) son, daughter, stepchild (or a descendant of these individuals), (2) a brother, sister, step-sibling (or a descendant of these individuals) for whom the taxpayer cares as her own child or (3) a foster child. Obviously, one child could qualify different taxpayers for the EITC (a child of divorced parents, for example, or a child living with his grandmother) and § 32 contains complex tie-breaking rules.

The phaseouts create the potential for enormous marriage penalties. For example, suppose a man a woman, each earning $13,090 and each with two children got married. Before the wedding, each owed no taxes and received an EITC refund of $4,008. After marriage, they owed taxes of $177 and have one EITC of $1,252 for a net refund of $1,070. Their taxes therefore increased by $6,946 or by more than 600 percent simply by getting married! To alleviate this problem, the 2001 Act increased the beginning and ending of the phase-out amounts for married couples beginning in 2002 and again in 2005 and 2008. Although this will decrease the penalty, it will not eliminate it.

The EITC originally was enacted primarily to reduce the burden of Social Security taxes on the working poor. It was used in 1986, in 1990 and again in 1993, however, to help remove people with poverty-level incomes from the income tax rolls and to provide a subsidy to low-wage workers. Many purposes are claimed for the EITC; in 1990, for example, the expansion of the EITC was claimed to be a means of increasing federal support for child care expenses of the working poor.

Increasingly, the EITC is seen not only as a way to remove low-wage workers from the income tax rolls, but also as a way to help assure a minimum standard of living to the working poor. Thus, some have advocated the EITC as a form of a "negative tax" or a "wage subsidy" as the primary way to transfer government benefits to the working poor. Is it good to use the income tax system in this way?

The EITC has become something of a pawn in the political battle over welfare. Those who favor government transfer payments generally support the EITC as a way to protect those below the poverty line, in part because of its pro-work character. Those who want to scale back transfer payments generally favor tightening eligibility requirements. For example, the 1996 Act adjusted the earned income and phaseout amounts upward to take inflation into account, but also provided that individuals who are not authorized to work in the United States cannot claim the credit.

A taxpayer can receive an advance payment of the EITC through a reduction in withholding on his wages. Only about 10,000 taxpayers have chosen this option, a very small fraction of those eligible. Since taxpayers clearly would benefit from early payment, why do you suppose this option has been utilized so infrequently? Many of those who receive the EITC as a lump sum in the form of a tax refund apparently purchase consumer durable goods or put the money, at least temporarily, into savings. Consider also the complexity of § 32. The various eligibility rules have been thought necessary to prevent undeserving taxpayers from receiving unwarranted largess. But the complexity also prevents some targeted beneficiaries from receiving the credit. For a critique of provisions affecting low income taxpayers and proposals for change, see Deborah H. Schenk, Old Wine in Old Bottles: Simplification of Family Status Tax Issues, 91 Tax Notes 1437 (2001); Anne L. Alstott, "The Earned Income Tax Credit and the Limitations of Tax–Based Welfare Reform," 108 Harv. L. Rev. 533 (1995). For a discussion of the economic effects of the EITC, see the special issue of the National Tax Journal, "The Earned Income Tax Credit," Volume 53, No. 4, Part 2, Dec., 2000.

D. CREDIT FOR THE ELDERLY AND DISABLED

Individuals who are 65 or older or who are permanently and totally disabled may qualify for a credit of 15 percent of their income up to a specified maximum. § 22(a). Such a credit (formerly the "retirement income credit") was added to the Code in 1954 because of concern that those receiving Social Security benefits, which generally are excluded from gross income, were favored over others receiving comparable forms of retirement income, which is includible in gross income.

The maximum amount of income against which the credit can be taken is $5,000 for single individuals and married couples where only one spouse is 65 or older, $7,500 for married couples where both spouses are 65 or older, and $3,750 for married individuals filing separately. The maximum for disabled individuals is the amount received as disability income.

The credit base is reduced dollar for dollar by any Social Security and Railroad Retirement benefits and other tax-exempt retirement income. The base also is reduced by 50 percent of the taxpayer's adjusted gross income in excess of $7,500 for single individuals, $10,000 for married individuals filing jointly and $5,000 for married individuals filing separately. § 22(c). As a result of these offsets and the expansions in Social Security coverage since the credit was first enacted, few elderly now benefit from this credit.

E.   EDUCATION CREDITS

In recent years, Congress added a number of astonishingly complex credits designed to offset the cost of college tuition. Because these credits are nonrefundable and are phased out at moderate levels of income, they are aimed primarily at middle-income taxpayers.

The fancifully-named Hope Credit enables a taxpayer to take a credit of up to 100 percent on the first $1,000 and 50 percent on the next $1,000 of tuition paid for the first two years of college for a taxpayer, a spouse or a dependent. § 25A(b). The maximum credit thus is $1,500. The credit is nonrefundable so that it is not available to anyone who does not owe taxes and it is phased out for single taxpayers with income between $40,000 and $50,000 and married taxpayers with income between $80,000 and $100,000. The Hope Credit is indexed for inflation.

Taxpayers also have the option of taking the equally fancifully named Lifetime Learning Credit. Unlike the Hope Credit, the lifetime credit can be used for undergraduate or graduate education at any point in the taxpayer's (or spouse's or dependent's) life. An eligible student must attend at least half-time or be taking courses to acquire or improve job skills. The credit, which can be taken for an unlimited number of years, is 20 percent of tuition and fees up to $5,000 ($10,000 beginning in 2003). This credit is also phased out. § 25A(c).

A taxpayer is ineligible to take a deduction for education expenses for an individual if the taxpayer or any other person elects to take either the Hope or Lifetime Credits for that individual. See the discussion of § 222 supra at page 340. Because the amount of the benefits and the phase-out ranges for the credits and the deduction differ, taxpayers need to calculate all possibilities before deciding which provision to use.

As if choosing between the Hope and the Lifetime Learning Credits and the education deduction were not complicated enough, taxpayers have a third option of contributing to an Education Savings Account. Up to $2,000 a year can be contributed to an investment account created to pay for education expenses, including fees, books, and room and board for a taxpayer, the taxpayer's spouse or a dependent. The distributions from an education IRA may be used to pay for elementary and secondary school expenses as well as higher education. The use of an ESA is phased out for taxpayers with an AGI between $190,000 and $220,000.

> The distributions from an education IRA may be used to pay for elementary and secondary school expenses as well as higher education. The use of this IRA is phased out for taxpayers with AGI between

$95,000 and $110,000 ($190,000 to $220,000 for married taxpayers). § 530.

Distributions to a beneficiary from an education IRA are excludible from gross income. A taxpayer may claim a Hope or Lifetime Credit and exclude distributions from an education IRA on behalf of the same student so long as the distributions are not used to pay the expenses for which the credit was claimed.

Taxpayers also have the option of contributing to qualified tuition programs maintained by many states and some colleges. Under these plans, a person (usually a parent or grandparent) contributes to an account that will be used to pay college tuition at any university or purchases tuition credits at a designated university. Both the earnings and distributions are exempt from the income of the beneficiary and the contributor. § 529. A taxpayer can claim a Hope or Lifetime Credit and exclude the proceeds of a qualified tuition account so long as the distribution is not used to pay the expenses for which the credit was claimed.

And if these options are not confusing enough, a taxpayer must also consider the effect using these provisions would have on any deduction for interest on education loans. See the discussion at page 358 supra.

Taxpayers who pay for college education not only must decide which of the above three options is preferable but also must consider the effect on any deduction for interest on education loans.

SECTION 10.   PERSONAL ITEMIZED DEDUCTIONS

As noted previously, taxpayers may deduct certain expenses—known as itemized deductions—if they exceed the standard deduction. We have already explored several itemized deductions, such as employee business expenses, casualty losses, mortgage interest, and bad debts. This Section explores other deductions not related to a trade or business or income-producing activity.

Section 68 places a cap on certain itemized deduction for high income taxpayers. Where AGI exceeds $100,000, the affected itemized deductions are reduced by 3 percent of the excess of AGI over $100,000. This threshold is indexed annually for inflation and in 2002 was $137,300. The reduction cannot exceed 80 percent of the deductions. This cap applies to all itemized deductions except medical expenses, investment interest, gambling losses and casualty losses. The 2 percent limitation on miscellaneous itemized deductions applies before the cap. For most taxpayers subject to the cap, this limitation is simply an increase in the marginal tax rate, although it is based on adjusted gross income rather than taxable income. For example, for a taxpayer subject to tax at a marginal rate of 38.6 percent, the cap increases taxable income by 3 percent of AGI and increases tax by 1.2 percent of AGI, in effect raising the marginal tax rate to nearly 40 percent.

In 2001 Congress repealed the 3 percent haircut effective in 2010—although it is uncertain whether the repeal will actually take effect since the 2001 Act contains a provision repealing all changes made by the Act in 2011.

A. TAXES

NOTE ON THE DEDUCTION FOR TAXES AND THE FOREIGN TAX CREDIT

Section 164 permits deductions for the amount of certain tax payments to states and localities, to foreign countries and their political subdivisions, and to the federal government. Some taxes (for example, federal or state gasoline taxes) are deductible only if they are attributable to business or investment activity; other taxes (for example, state or local property taxes on one's residence) are deductible regardless of whether they are incurred in a personal or a profit seeking context. In allowing deduction of state and local income and property taxes without regard to profit seeking, § 164 thus constitutes an exception to the general rule of § 262 that no deductions from income are allowed for "personal, living, or family expenses."

Tax payments that are not related to business or investment activity must be deducted from adjusted gross income. Consequently, the deduction is allowed only to taxpayers who itemize. The deduction for income and property taxes is not subject to the 2 percent AGI floor on "miscellaneous itemized deductions" of § 67. § 67(b)(2).

Some taxes cannot be deducted whether incurred in a personal or a profit-seeking context. These include the federal income tax itself as well as employees' Social Security taxes and estate, inheritance and gift taxes imposed at the federal, state and local levels. § 275. Taxes that are deductible only if incurred in connection with trade, business or investment activity include federal excise taxes and customs duties, as well as state and local sales taxes, stock transfer taxes, gasoline taxes and licensing fees.

The income tax enacted in 1913 allowed the deduction of "all national, state, county, school and municipal taxes paid within the year, not including those assessed against local benefits." The provision was extended to foreign taxes in 1916. The Internal Revenue Code of 1954 and subsequent tax legislation have significantly limited the deductibility of tax payments unrelated to income-seeking activity. Section 164 restricts this deduction to the following categories of taxes:

State, Local and Foreign Taxes on Real Property. The deduction is allowable for "taxes imposed on interests in real property and levied for the general public welfare" but not for "taxes assessed against local benefits." § 164(c)(1).

In Revenue Ruling 79–180, 1979–1 C.B. 95, the IRS held that tenants could not deduct payments of property taxes passed along to them by their landlords as provided by a state statute. It was significant that the taxing authority would look to the owner in the event of the renter's nonpayment and would enforce payment against the owner's interest in the entire property. The so-called "renters' tax" was viewed by the IRS not as a tax on the tenant but as additional nondeductible rent.

State and Local Taxes on Personal Property. A tax must meet three criteria in order to be deductible under § 164 as a tax on personal property. First, the tax must be ad valorem, or based on the value of the property. Second, the tax must be imposed on an annual basis even if collected more or less frequently. Third, the tax must be on personal property. Reg. § 1.164–3(c).

For example, automobile registration fees may constitute deductible personal property taxes if based on the value of the car but not if based on its age, weight or horsepower. If the fee is based on more than one of these factors, the taxpayer may deduct the portion that is attributable to the value of the vehicle.

State, Local and Foreign Income, War Profits and Excess Profits Taxes. No deduction is allowed for federal income taxes, but, as described supra at page 91, the disallowance of a deduction for the tax itself is simply a matter of tax rates being imposed on a tax-inclusive rather than tax-exclusive, base. Section 275 also bars employees from deducting their payroll taxes to fund Social Security. Employers can deduct their matching contributions so long as they represent a cost of producing income; however, a taxpayer cannot deduct Social Security taxes paid on behalf of a person employed for personal rather than business reasons. See, e.g., Opper v. Commissioner, 31 T.C.M. 485 (1972) (taxpayer could not deduct Social Security taxes on wages paid workers who built his personal residence). To achieve parity with employees, self-employed individuals are permitted to deduct one-half of their Social Security taxes.

Employers and employees can deduct their contributions to state disability and unemployment compensation funds. However, employees cannot deduct amounts withheld from wages for contributions to a private plan for payment of nonoccupational disability benefits. See Rev.Ruls. 81–191 to 81–194, 1981–2 C.B. 49. Employees are also barred from deducting social security taxes imposed by foreign governments that have entered into agreements with the United States government pursuant to § 233 of the Social Security Act. See, e.g., Revenue Ruling 79–291, 1979–2 C.B. 273 (employees cannot claim deduction or credit for social security taxes assessed by government of Italy).

Several courts have held the corporate minimum tax (§§ 55–59) to be a nondeductible income tax rather than a deductible excise tax on business. See, e.g., Standard Oil (Indiana) v. Commissioner, 77 T.C. 349 (1981).

The Foreign Tax Credit. Income taxes of a foreign country, subject to certain limitations, may be allowed as a credit against domestic income tax liability instead of as a deduction. See §§ 901–08; § 164(b)(3). This credit is designed to prevent double taxation of foreign source income. Its general effect is that foreign income is taxed at the higher of the foreign or the domestic rate. The credit typically is more beneficial than a deduction because U.S. tax liability is reduced dollar for dollar rather than based on their marginal domestic rate.

Environmental Tax. Corporations may deduct any tax liability imposed under § 59A. This tax, imposed on modified alternative minimum taxable income over $2 million, is dedicated to the Hazardous Substance Superfund.

Capitalization Requirement. Certain state and local taxes incurred in connection with the acquisition or disposition of property must be capitalized. Such taxes are treated as a cost of acquisition and serve to increase the taxpayer's basis in the acquired property. Taxes paid upon disposition decrease the amount realized. See the last sentence of § 164(a). The capitalization requirement does not apply to: (1) state, local and foreign real property taxes, (2) state and local personal property taxes, (3) state, local and foreign income taxes, or (4) the environmental tax of § 59A. § 164(a). See also § 263A which now requires capitalization of costs (including taxes) in connection with the construction or production of certain types of real and personal property and with respect to inventory.

Minimum Tax. A so-called alternative minimum tax imposes a tax on an individual's "alternative minimum taxable income" if that tax is greater than the tax computed under the normal rules. For purposes of computing alternative minimum taxable income, no deduction is permitted for state and local real or personal property taxes or income taxes. § 56(b)(1)(A)(ii). See Chapter 7 infra.

Tax Refunds. Taxpayers may be required to include in income the refund of a tax for which they claimed a deduction or credit in an earlier year. Congress has attempted to increase compliance with this previously ignored obligation by requiring state and local governments to file information returns reporting refunds to individuals of more than $10. See § 6050E. A refund must be included in income, however, only to the extent that the earlier tax payment served to reduce tax liability. See § 111. This is an application of the "tax benefit rule," discussed infra in Chapter 6 at page 663.

NOTE ON POLICIES REGARDING THE DEDUCTIBILITY OF TAXES

Two principal reasons have been advanced for allowing deductions for taxes that are not incurred in an income seeking context. The first is that the deduction produces a more accurate measurement of taxable income. For example, Boris Bittker contends that, because state and local tax payments are compelled rather than voluntary, the deduction "may therefore be defended as a mode of refining the concept of income." Boris Bittker, "Income Tax Deductions, Credits and Subsidies for Personal Expenditures," 16 J.L. & Econ. 193, 200–01 (1973). Others have argued that state and local income taxes are a direct cost of earning income that will be taxed at the federal level. Like other costs, these taxes thus should be deductible since the federal income tax is imposed only on net income. (This would suggest repeal of the deduction for state and local property taxes because they are not a direct cost of earning income.) On the other hand, the Treasury has argued that the deduction for state and local taxes provides a federal subsidy for the public services provided by state and local governments that is not available when taxpayers acquire similar services by nondeductible private purchases. Treasury contended that voting at the polls and voting with one's "feet" provided sufficient voluntariness to justify taxation. See 2 Treasury Dep't, Report to the President, Tax Reform for Fairness, Simplicity and Economic Growth 62–68 (1984).

Evaluating the justification for the deduction should depend—at least in part—on the role of the deduction in the context of the entire system of intergovernmental financial assistance. State-local tax deductibility is but one of the three major methods by which the federal government subsidizes state-local activities. The other sources are grants-in-aid and the subsidy to borrowing through the exclusion of state and local bond interest from federal income taxation. State tax deductibility and the exclusion for bond interest may be less efficient than grants because they provide less than a dollar of revenue to state and local governments for each dollar of federal cost, but grants often require the state or local government to make expenditures specified by the federal government.

B.   CHARITABLE CONTRIBUTIONS

Since 1917, the income tax has allowed a deduction for charitable contributions. Section 170 allows deduction for a transfer by an individual or a corporation of cash or, in some cases, for the fair market value of property transferred, but not for a contribution of services. The amount deductible is subject to a variety of limitations. Individuals generally are allowed a charitable contribution deduction of no more than 50 percent of adjusted gross income. § 170(b). Although Congress provides incentives for individuals to donate significant portions of their income to charities, it does not believe individuals should be permitted to eliminate their tax liability entirely by transferring all of the current year's income to charity. Certain gifts of appreciated property are limited to 30 percent of a taxpayer's adjusted gross income. Limitations are also imposed on gifts to private foundations. The charitable deduction is not subject to the 2 percent floor on miscellaneous itemized deductions of § 67, but is subject to the reduction of itemized deductions under § 68.

A corporation's charitable deduction is limited to 10 percent of its taxable income. § 170(b)(2). Neither individuals nor corporations may deduct as a business expense charitable contributions in excess of the percentage limitations.

NOTES

(A) *Why Allow the Deduction?* Is the charitable deduction a tax expenditure? Some have argued that the choice to give property to a charity is itself a form of consumption and therefore the deduction is inappropriate. Others contend that a contribution deduction is justified by the fact that the amount given to charity will not be consumed by the taxpayer. Income generally is defined as the year's earnings that are available for consumption or savings. Is it appropriate to give a deduction to taxpayers who serve merely as conduits for funds to be consumed by someone else? Should the charity or the ultimate consumer be taxed instead of the donor? Would taxing the recipient of charitable largess be consistent with exempting other gifts from tax? Would it be administratively possible to tax the recipients? Many of those who benefit from charitable gifts are not subject to income tax because their income is below the taxable threshold. In such cases, it seems inappropriate to tax the amount of the gift at the donor's tax rate and a deduction for the donor seems justified. But many beneficiaries (such as patrons of the Metropolitan Opera or law students) would not be taxed at a zero rate. If the value of the benefit they receive from the contributed amounts cannot be taxed, why should the donor be allowed a deduction?

If a charitable deduction is an appropriate adjustment in measuring the donor's net income, is it appropriate to allow it only as an itemized deduction? Those who take a standard deduction are taxed on the dollars given to charity. From time to time, nonitemizers have been allowed to deduct a portion of charitable contributions that would have been deductible if they itemized.

(B) *Efficiency of the Deduction.* Is the deduction an efficient means of encouraging gifts to charity? Economists differ on whether the deduction efficiently encourages gifts. Some believe that the deduction increases charitable giving by significantly more than the amount of lost revenue. Others believe that it may subsidize gifts that would have been made in any event.

To use an analogy, bread costs $1 a loaf. A buys three loaves of bread per week at a cost of $3. Suppose the price of bread falls to 50 cents per loaf. Which of the following describes A's likely behavior. Do you need more information?

(1) A continues to buy three loaves, spending $1.50.

(2) A gets six loaves for his $3.

(3) The price of bread is so cheap that A substitutes bread for potatoes and buys ten loaves at $5 per week.

Similarly, if the charitable deduction reduces the cost of giving $1 to charity to 60 cents for a taxpayer in the 40 percent bracket, what is the likely behavior of a taxpayer who gave $3 to charity before taxes? Will he give $5, keeping his out-of-pocket costs at $3 or reduce his out-of-pocket costs to $1.80, maintaining the total benefit to charity of $3? Conversely, once a charitable deduction is permitted, limiting or repealing the deduction will raise the price of the donation. What would be the effect on charitable contributions of retaining the deduction but lowering tax rates, as was done in the 1986 Act?

In considering the equity and efficiency of the deduction, how would you assess the following alternatives:

(1) Retain the charitable deduction;

(2) Repeal the charitable deduction and replace it with a tax credit;

(3) Repeal the charitable deduction and replace it with a matching grant program under which the federal government would provide the charity a direct grant equal to a specified percentage of the individual's gift;

(4) Repeal the charitable deduction and lower tax rates generally to offset the revenue increase; or

(5) Repeal the charitable deduction and replace it with direct federal subsidies.

1. WHEN IS A TRANSFER TO A CHARITY A CONTRIBUTION?

Hernandez v. Commissioner

Supreme Court of the United States, 1989. 490 U.S. 680.

JUSTICE MARSHALL delivered the opinion of the Court.

Section 170 of the Internal Revenue Code of 1954 * * * permits a taxpayer to deduct from gross income the amount of a "charitable contribution." The Code defines that term as a "contribution or gift" to certain eligible donees, including entities organized and operated exclusively for religious purposes. We granted certiorari to determine whether taxpayers may deduct as charitable contributions payments made to branch churches of the Church of Scientology (Church) in order to receive services known as "auditing" and "training." We hold that such payments are not deductible.

I

Scientology was founded in the 1950's by L. Ron Hubbard. It is propagated today by a "mother church" in California and by numerous branch churches around the world. The mother church instructs laity, trains and ordains ministers, and creates new congregations. Branch churches, known as "franchises" or "missions," provide Scientology services at the local level, under the supervision of the mother church. Church of Scientology of California v. Commissioner, 823 F.2d 1310, 1313 (C.A.9 1987), cert. denied, 486 U.S. 1015 (1988).

Scientologists believe that an immortal spiritual being exists in every person. A person becomes aware of this spiritual dimension through a process known as "auditing." Auditing involves a one-to-one encounter between a participant (known as a "preclear") and a Church official (known as an "auditor"). An electronic device, the E-meter, helps the auditor identify the preclear's areas of spiritual difficulty by measuring skin responses during a question and answer session. Although auditing sessions are conducted one-on-one, the content of each session is not individually tailored. The preclear gains spiritual awareness by progressing through sequential levels of auditing, provided in short blocks of time known as "intensives." 83 T.C. 575, 577 (1984), aff'd, 822 F.2d 844 (C.A.9 1987).

The Church also offers members doctrinal courses known as "training." Participants in these sessions study the tenets of Scientology and seek to attain the qualifications necessary to serve as auditors. Training courses, like auditing sessions, are provided in sequential levels. Scientologists are taught that spiritual gains result from participation in such courses. 83 T.C., at 577.

The Church charges a "fixed donation," also known as a "price" or a "fixed contribution," for participants to gain access to auditing and training sessions. These charges are set forth in schedules and prices vary with a session's length and level of sophistication. In 1972, for example, the general rates for auditing ranged from $625 for a 12½-hour auditing intensive, the shortest available, to $4,250 for a 100-hour intensive, the longest available. Specialized types of auditing required higher fixed donations: a 12½-hour "Integrity Processing" auditing intensive cost $750; a 12½-hour "Expanded Dianetics" auditing intensive cost $950. This system of mandatory fixed charges is based on a central tenet of Scientology known as the "doctrine of exchange," according to which any time a person receives something he must pay something back. Id., at 577–578. In so doing, a Scientologist maintains "inflow" and "outflow" and avoids spiritual decline. 819 F.2d 1212, 1222 (C.A.1 1987).

The proceeds generated from auditing and training sessions are the Church's primary source of income. The Church promotes these sessions not only through newspaper, magazine, and radio advertisements, but also through free lectures, free personality tests, and leaflets. The Church also encourages, and indeed rewards with a 5% discount, advance payment for these sessions. 822 F.2d, at 847. The Church often refunds unused portions of prepaid auditing or training fees, less an administrative charge.

The petitioners in these consolidated cases each made payments to a branch church for auditing or training sessions. They sought to deduct these payments on their federal income tax returns as charitable contributions under § 170. Respondent Commissioner of the Internal Revenue Service (Commissioner or IRS) disallowed these deductions, finding that the payments were not charitable contributions within the meaning of § 170. * * *

For over 70 years, federal taxpayers have been allowed to deduct the amount of contributions or gifts to charitable, religious, and other eleemosynary institutions. Section 170, the present provision, was enacted in 1954; it requires a taxpayer claiming the deduction to satisfy a number of conditions. The Commissioner's stipulation in this case, however, has narrowed the statutory inquiry to one such condition: whether petitioners' payments for auditing and training sessions are "contribution[s] or gift[s]" within the meaning of § 170.

The legislative history of the "contribution or gift" limitation, though sparse, reveals that Congress intended to differentiate between unrequited payments to qualified recipients and payments made to such recipients in return for goods or services. Only the former were deemed deductible. The House and Senate Reports on the 1954 tax bill, for example, both define "gifts" as payments "made with no expectation of a financial return commensurate with the amount of the gift." S.Rep. No. 1622, 83d Cong., 2d Sess., 196 (1954); H.R.Rep. No. 1337, 83d Cong., 2d Sess., A44 (1954). Using payments to hospitals as an example, both Reports state that the gift characterization should not apply to "a payment by an individual to a hospital *in consideration of* a binding obligation to provide medical treatment for the individual's employees. It would apply only if there were no expectation of any *quid pro quo* from the hospital." S.Rep. No. 1622, supra, at 196 (emphasis added); H.Rep. No. 1337, supra, at A44 (emphasis added).

In ascertaining whether a given payment was made with "the expectation of any *quid pro quo*," the Internal Revenue Service (IRS) has customarily examined the external features of the transaction in question. This practice has the advantage of obviating the need for the IRS to conduct imprecise inquiries into the motivations of individual taxpayers. The lower courts have generally embraced this structural analysis.

In light of this understanding of § 170, it is readily apparent that petitioners' payments to the Church do not qualify as "contribution[s] or gift[s]." As the Tax Court found, these payments were part of a quintessential quid pro quo exchange: in return for their money, petitioners received an identifiable benefit, namely, auditing and training sessions. The Church established fixed price schedules for auditing and training sessions in each branch church; it calibrated particular prices to auditing or training sessions of particular lengths and levels of sophistication; it returned a refund if auditing and training services went unperformed; it distributed "account cards" on which persons who had paid money to the Church could monitor what prepaid services they had not yet claimed; and it categorically barred provision of auditing or training sessions for free. Each of these practices reveals the inherently reciprocal nature of the exchange.

Petitioners do not argue that such a structural analysis is inappropriate under § 170, or that the external features of the auditing and training transactions do not strongly suggest a quid pro quo exchange. * * * Petitioners argued instead that they are entitled to deductions because a quid pro quo analysis is inappropriate under § 170 when the benefit a taxpayer receives is purely religious in nature. Along the same lines, petitioners claim that payments made for the right to participate in a religious service should be automatically deductible under § 170.

We cannot accept this statutory argument for several reasons. First, it finds no support in the language of § 170. Whether or not Congress could, consistent with the Establishment Clause, provide for the automatic deductibility of a payment made to a church that either generates religious benefits or guarantees access to a religious service, that is a choice Congress has thus far declined to make. Instead, Congress has specified that a payment to an organization operated exclusively for religious (or other eleemosynary) purposes is deductible only if such a payment is a "contribution or gift." § 170(c). The Code makes no special preference for payments made in the expectation of gaining religious benefits or access to a religious service. * * *

Second, petitioners' deductibility proposal would expand the charitable contribution deduction far beyond what Congress has provided. Numerous forms of payments to eligible donees plausibly could be categorized as providing a religious benefit or as securing access to a religious service. For example, some taxpayers might regard their tuition payments to parochial schools as generating a religious benefit or as securing access to a religious service; such payments, however, have long been held not to be charitable contributions under § 170. * * * Taxpayers might make similar claims about payments for church-sponsored counseling sessions or for medical care at church-affiliated hospitals that otherwise might not be deductible. Given that, under the First Amendment, the IRS can reject otherwise valid claims of religious benefit only on the ground that a taxpayers' alleged beliefs are not sincerely held, but not on the ground that such beliefs are inherently irreligious, see United States v. Ballard, 322 U.S. 78 (1944), the resulting tax deductions would likely expand the charitable contribution provision far beyond its present size. We are loath to effect this result in the absence of supportive congressional intent.

Finally, the deduction petitioners seek might raise problems of entanglement between church and state. If framed as a deduction for those payments made in connection with a religious service, petitioners' proposal would force the IRS and the judiciary into differentiating "religious" services from "secular" ones. We need pass no judgment now on the constitutionality of such hypothetical inquiries, but we do note that "pervasive monitoring" for "the subtle or overt presence of religious matter" is a central danger against which we have held the Establishment Clause guards.

Accordingly, we conclude that petitioners' payments to the Church for auditing and training sessions are not "contribution[s] or gift[s]" within the meaning of that statutory expression.

[The Court rejects petitioners' constitutional claims based on the Establishment Clause and the Free Exercise Clause of the First Amendment. It finds that § 170 does not create an unconstitutional denominational preference by according disproportionately harsh tax status to those religions that raise funds by imposing fixed costs for participation in certain religious practices nor does § 170 threaten excessive governmental entanglement.]

JUSTICE O'CONNOR, with whom JUSTICE SCALIA joins, dissenting.

The Court today acquiesces in the decision of the Internal Revenue Service (IRS) to manufacture a singular exception to its 70–year practice of allowing fixed payments indistinguishable from those made by petitioners to be deducted as charitable contributions. Because the IRS cannot constitutionally be allowed to select which religions will receive the benefit of its past rulings, I respectfully dissent. * * *

It must be emphasized that the IRS' position here is not based upon the contention that a portion of the knowledge received from auditing or training is of secular, commercial, nonreligious value. * * * Here the IRS denies deductibility solely on the basis that the exchange is a *quid pro quo*, even though the quid is exclusively of spiritual or religious worth. The Government cites no instances in which this has been done before, and there are good reasons why.

When a taxpayer claims as a charitable deduction part of a fixed amount given to a charitable organization in exchange for benefits that have a commercial value, the allowable portion of that claim is computed by subtracting from the total amount paid the value of the physical benefit received. If at a charity sale one purchases for $1,000 a painting whose market value is demonstrably no more than $50, there has been a contribution of $950. The same would be true if one purchases a $1,000 seat at a charitable dinner where the food is worth $50. An identical calculation can be made where the quid received is not a painting or a meal, but an intangible such as entertainment, so long as that intangible has some market value established in a noncontributory context. Hence, one who purchases a ticket to a concert, at the going rate for concerts by the particular performers, makes a charitable contribution of zero even if it is announced in advance that all proceeds from the ticket sales will go to charity. The performers may have made a charitable contribution, but the audience has paid the going rate for a show.

It becomes impossible, however, to compute the "contribution" portion of a payment to a charity where what is received in return is not merely an intangible, but an intangible (or, for that matter a tangible) that is not bought and sold except in donative contexts so that the only "market" price against which it can be evaluated is a market price that always includes donations. Suppose, for example, that the charitable organization that traditionally solicits donations on Veterans' Day, in exchange for which it gives the donor an imitation poppy bearing its name, were to establish a flat rule that no one gets a poppy without a donation of at least $10. One would have to say that the "market" rate for such poppies was $10, but it would assuredly not be true that everyone who "bought" a poppy for $10 made no contribution. Similarly, if one buys a $100 seat at a prayer breakfast—receiving as the quid pro quo food for both body and soul—it would make no sense to say that no charitable contribution whatever has occurred simply because the "going rate" for all prayer breakfasts (with equivalent bodily food) is $100. The latter may well be true, but that "going rate" includes a contribution.

Confronted with this difficulty, and with the constitutional necessity of not making irrational distinctions among taxpayers, and with the even higher standard of equality of treatment among religions that the First Amendment imposes, the Government has only two practicable options with regard to distinctively religious quids pro quo: to disregard them all, or to tax them all. Over the years it has chosen the former course. * * *

The IRS reaffirmed its position in 1970, ruling that "[p]ew rents, building fund assessments and periodic dues paid to a church * * * are all methods of making contributions to the church and such payments are deductible as charitable contributions." Rev.Rul. 70–47, 1970–1 Cum.Bull. 49. Similarly, notwithstanding the "form" of Mass stipends as fixed payments for specific religious services, * * * the IRS has allowed charitable deductions of such payments. See Rev.Rul. 78–366, 19782–2 Cum.Bull. 241.

These rulings, which are "official interpretation[s] of [the tax laws] by the [IRS]," * * * flatly contradict the Solicitor General's claim that there "is no administrative practice recognizing that payments made in exchange for religious benefits are tax deductible."

There can be no doubt that at least some of the fixed payments which the IRS has treated as charitable deductions, or which the Court assumes the IRS would allow taxpayers to deduct, are as "inherently reciprocal," as the payments for auditing at issue here. In exchange for their payment of pew rents, Christians receive particular seats during worship services. * * * Similarly, in some synagogues attendance at the worship services for

Jewish High Holy Days is often predicated upon the purchase of a general admission ticket or a reserved seat ticket. * * * Religious honors such as publicly reading from Scripture are purchased or auctioned periodically in some synagogues of Jews from Morocco and Syria. * * * Mormons must tithe ten percent of their income as a necessary but not sufficient condition to obtaining a "temple recommend," i.e., the right to be admitted into the temple. * * * A Mass stipend—a fixed payment given to a Catholic priest, in consideration of which he is obliged to apply the fruits of the Mass for the intention of the donor—has similar overtones of exchange. * * *

This is not a situation where the IRS has explicitly and affirmatively reevaluated its longstanding interpretation of § 170 and decided to analyze all fixed religious contributions under a quid pro quo standard. There is no indication whatever that the IRS has abandoned its 70–year practice with respect to payments made by those other than Scientologists. In 1978, when it ruled that payments for auditing and training were not charitable contributions under § 170, the IRS did not cite—much less try to reconcile—its previous rulings concerning the deductibility of other forms of fixed payments for religious services or practices. See Rev.Rul. 78–189, 1978–1 Cum.Bull. 68 (equating payments for auditing with tuition paid to religious schools).

Nevertheless, the Government now attempts to reconcile its previous rulings with its decision in these cases by relying on a distinction between direct and incidental benefits in exchange for payments made to a charitable organization. This distinction * * * recognizes that even a deductible charitable contribution may generate certain benefits for the donor. As long as the benefits remain "incidental" and do not indicate that the payment was actually made for the "personal accommodation" of the donor, the payment will be deductible. It is the Government's view that the payments made by petitioners should not be deductible under § 170 because the "unusual facts in these cases * * * demonstrate that the payments were made primarily for 'personal accommodation.'" Specifically, the Solicitor General asserts that "the rigid connection between the provision of auditing and training services and payment of the fixed price" indicates a quid pro quo relationship and "reflect[s] the value that petitioners expected to receive for their money."

There is no discernable reason why there is a more rigid connection between payment and services in the religious practices of Scientology than in the religious practices of the faiths described above. * * *

In my view, the IRS has misapplied its longstanding practice of allowing charitable contributions under § 170 in a way that violates the Establishment Clause. It has unconstitutionally refused to allow payments for the religious service of auditing to be deducted as charitable contributions in the same way it has allowed fixed payments to other religions to be deducted. Just as the Minnesota statute at issue in Larson v. Valente, 456 U.S. 228 (1982), discriminated against the Unification Church, the IRS' application of the *quid pro quo* standard here—and only here—discriminates against the Church of Scientology. I would reverse the decisions below.

NOTES

(A) *Hernandez Fallout.* In an unusual ruling the Service obsoleted an earlier ruling and held that the Church of Scientology and its related entities are tax-exempt churches and that contributions to them are deductible. The ruling did not mention *Hernandez,* which denied the deduction. Rev. Rul. 93–73, 1993–2 C.B. 75. The closing agreement with the church was not made public.

Congress added its two cents when it added substantiation requirements to the Code in 1993. Section 170(f)(8) states that in providing a receipt a donor should note if only "intangible religious benefits" were received, which are defined as a benefit "provided by an organization organized exclusively for religious purposes and which generally is not sold in a commercial transaction outside the donative context."

What if the benefit is religious education? In Sklar v. Commissioner, 282 F.3d 610 (9th Cir.2002), the taxpayers attempted to deduct a portion of the private school tuition for their children equal to the value of religious education received. The Appeals Court rejected any reliance on § 170(f) and instead followed *Hernandez.* The Sklars also argued that the IRS violated the Establishment Clause of the Constitution by permitting members of the Church of Scientology to deduct amounts paid for auditing but denying the deduction for the costs of religious education for other sects. Although the court remarked that it was impermissible for the IRS to withhold the closing agreement with the Church of Scientology and that such an agreement violates the Establishment Clause by favoring one religion, they nevertheless denied the Sklars their deduction. First, they were unwilling to order a deduction for all religious training absent Congressional approval and because the court believed doing so was unconstitutional. Second, they found that the Sklars had not made a "dual payment" whose cost exceeded the benefits of the secular education received. Thus, the court's findings with respect to the constitutionality of the *Hernandez* closing agreement became dicta.

(B) *Detached and Disinterested Generosity. Hernandez* is a difficult application of the longstanding rule that a charitable contribution is limited to the excess of the amount transferred to the charity over the value of any benefit received by the donor. For example, if one sends a contribution to the local public television station and receives umbrella in return, the taxpayer must subtract the value of the umbrella from the amount contributed.

Courts have increasingly supported the notion that a deductible charitable contribution must meet the *Duberstein* test ("detached and disinterested generosity", see page 123 supra) for what constitutes a gift. See, e.g., Babilonia v. Commissioner, 681 F.2d 678 (9th Cir.1982), where the parents of figure skater Tai Babilonia attempted to deduct the costs of accompanying her to various international competitions as expenses incurred in performing services for a charitable organization. The deduction was denied on the ground that the taxpayers' primary purpose was to advance their daughter's career rather than to advance the Olympic team in general.

Suppose a taxpayer makes a purchase from an online retailer listed on the site of a Web-based "charity mall" and the mall makes a charitable contribution of 5 percent of purchase price to a tax-exempt organization. Can the purchaser take a charitable deduction? Would it make any difference if the purchaser could choose the charity? Would it make a difference if the amount of the purchase was characterized as a rebate transferred to the purchaser who transfers it to the charity?

The *Duberstein* standard is somewhat more difficult to apply where the donor is a business. For example, the Supreme Court applied the *Duberstein* test in United States v. American Bar Endowment, 477 U.S. 105 (1986), to disallow charitable deductions for payments to purchase insurance policies from a tax-exempt organization because the taxpayers were unable to show that they could have purchased comparable insurance policies elsewhere for less than the amount they paid.

In United States v. Transamerica Corp., 392 F.2d 522, 524 (9th Cir.1968), the court held that a deduction could be taken where there was an indirect business benefit "such as one incidental to the public use or to public recognition of its act of generosity," but not where there was a direct economic benefit.

(C) *Seats at College Sporting Events.* The *Duberstein* gift analysis has been used to combat fundraising tactics that encourage giving for motives that could hardly be classified as "disinterested generosity." For example, colleges and universities often provide choice football or basketball seats to those who contribute in excess of a specific amount. The Code allows an 80 percent deduction whenever a contribution makes the donor eligible to obtain athletic tickets. § 170(*l*). This provision was adopted after the Service issued an unpopular ruling that no deduction could be taken where the donor was eligible to purchase tickets that otherwise would not be available. If the opportunity to purchase tickets is made available only to those who contribute $200, why should $160 be deductible? Why is § 170(*l*) limited only to athletic events? If a donor contributes a sufficient amount that the football stadium is named after him, should the entire amount be deductible?

If you have ever underestimated the power of sports and college alumni, consider the following: Section 274(*l*) limits a deduction for a skybox at a stadium to the face value of non-luxury box seat tickets. This provision was aimed at business entertainment deductions for skyboxes at professional sports stadiums. But it wasn't long before football powerhouses like Nebraska and Penn State also saw money in skyboxes. At some colleges, large contributions entitle donors to purchase the seats in a skybox. Believing that a tax deduction was essential to fundraising, the NCAA joined with one Rod French, an Iowa State booster who gave the university $200,000 to guarantee his seats, to convince the IRS that 170(*l*) and not 274(*l*) applied to university skyboxes. They scored a touchdown. Mr. French and others can deduct 80 percent of the contribution despite the fact that skybox leases are rumored to have a value of $50,000–$80,000. See 1999 Tax Notes Today 141–4.

(D) *Gifts to Schools and Nursing Homes.* In Winters v. Commissioner, 468 F.2d 778 (2d Cir.1972), the Second Circuit considered the deductibility of a couple's "contribution" of more than $2,000 to a church education fund that was used to support schools attended by their children. Although the taxpayers were active members of the church and were not required to pay tuition or otherwise to contribute to the schools, the court denied the deduction on the grounds that the gift was made with the "anticipation of economic benefit" rather than from "detached and disinterested generosity."

Revenue Ruling 83–104, 1983–2 C.B. 46, provides six examples of donations to private schools operated by charitable organizations. In each of the six situations, a taxpayer, who is a parent of a child who attends the school, makes a payment to the charitable organization operating the school. The cost of educating the child in the school is not less than the payments made by the parent to the organization. The ruling states:

> Whether a transfer of money by a parent to an organization that operates a school is a voluntary transfer that is made with no expectation of obtaining a commensurate benefit depends upon whether a reasonable person, taking all the facts and circumstances of the case into account, would conclude that enrollment in the school was in no manner contingent upon making the payment, that the payment was not made pursuant to a plan (whether express or implied) to convert nondeductible tuition into charitable contributions, and that receipt of the benefit was not otherwise dependent upon the making of the payment.

> In determining this issue, the presence of one or more of the following factors creates a presumption that the payment is not a charitable contribution: the existence of a contract under which a taxpayer agrees to make a "contribution" and which contains provisions ensuring the admission of the taxpayer's child; a plan allowing taxpayers either to pay tuition or to make "contributions" in exchange for schooling; the earmarking of a contribution for the direct benefit of a particular individual; or the otherwise unexplained denial of admission or readmission to a school of children of taxpayers who are financially able, but who do not contribute.

> In other cases, although no single factor may be determinative, a combination of several factors may indicate that a payment is not a charitable contribution: * * * (1) the absence of a significant tuition charge; (2) substantial or unusual pressure to contribute applied to parents of children attending a school; (3) contribution appeals made as part of the admissions or enrollment process; (4) the absence of significant potential sources of revenue for operating the school other than contributions by parents of children attending the school; (5) and other factors suggesting that a contribution policy has been created as a means of avoiding the characterization of payments as tuition.

Compare Dowell v. United States, 553 F.2d 1233 (10th Cir.1977) and Estate of Wardwell v. United States, 301 F.2d 632 (8th Cir.1962). In both cases, elderly taxpayers made donations to nursing homes. The taxpayers received no enforceable property rights and no legal obligations were imposed on the donee nursing homes. Ms. Wardwell, shortly after giving her gift, moved into the nursing home at a rental charge that was reduced because of her donation. Nevertheless, the court held the entire donation deductible. Ms. Dowell had already been accepted as a resident in the home at the time her donation was made although she did not receive any lower rate than did nondonors. The court allowed her deduction in full, stressing that the taxpayer's motive was of primary importance and that the appellate court would not overturn the trial court's finding on the issue of motive unless it was clearly erroneous.

(E) *Gifts Earmarked for Individuals.* Ending a split among the circuits, the Supreme Court in Davis v. United States, 495 U.S. 472 (1990), denied the parents of missionaries of the Mormon Church a deduction for payments used to support the missionary activities of their children. The Court noted that § 170 permits a deduction only if the contribution is made "to or for the use of" the charity. In *Davis,* the payments were made directly to the children and although the church required them to account for the funds, it had neither possession nor control of the funds. The Court concluded that: "a gift or contribution is 'for the use of' a qualified organization when it is held in a legally enforceable trust for the qualified organization or a similar legal arrangement."

The Court also rejected the parents' argument that the payments were deductible under Reg. § 1.170A–1(g), which permits the deduction of unreimbursed expenditures incident to the rendition of charitable services. The Court ruled that taxpayers may claim deductions only for expenditures undertaken in connection with their own contributions of services.

(F) *Gifts of Services.* Since 1920, the IRS has consistently maintained, and the courts have agreed, that a taxpayer cannot deduct the value of services rendered to charitable institutions. A person may, however, deduct unreimbursed out-of-pocket expenses incurred in connection with donating services to a charitable organization. See, e.g., McCollum v. Commissioner, 37 T.C.M. 1817 (1978), where the Tax Court allowed deductions for meals, motor home operation, ski uniforms, ski equipment repairs, and lift tickets purchased by the taxpayer and his family, members of the National Ski Patrol, a voluntary organization engaged in policing ski slopes. The court was "unimpressed" with the IRS's argument that the deductions should be disallowed because the taxpayer "enjoyed skiing, enjoyed the work * * * and enjoyed the camaraderie of the other members of the ski patrol." But see, e.g., Churukian v. Commissioner, 40 T.C.M. 475 (1980) (church choir singer denied deduction for costs of traveling to choir practice). A taxpayer can claim a deduction for paying third parties to assist them in providing charitable services. See Rockefeller v. Commissioner, 676 F.2d 35 (2d Cir.1982) (deduction permitted for salaries taxpayers paid to employees who provided services to charities that taxpayers supported).

In Lary v. United States, 787 F.2d 1538 (11th Cir.1986), the court denied deduction for contributions of blood. The IRS had maintained that the contribution of blood was a service, but the Eleventh Circuit did not decide whether the contribution of blood was a service or a gift of property, noting that no charitable deduction would be available even in the latter case since the taxpayers could not prove the holding period or the basis of the blood or the amount or type of gain that would occur if the blood were sold rather than contributed. See the discussion of § 170(e) infra.

How does the failure to allow any deduction for services compare to the treatment the taxpayer would receive if he were compensated for the services and donated the payment to charity?

(G) *Substantiation.* Auctions of donated goods and services by charitable organizations have become commonplace. If a taxpayer bids $1,000 and wins a vacation at a ski resort, there is no charitable contribution at all unless the vacation normally sells for less than $1,000. Nevertheless, many purchasers of such items have deducted their purchases. In response, Congress strengthened substantiation requirements in an effort to curtail bogus charitable contributions. For gifts of $250 or more, the taxpayer must provide a written contemporaneous statement from the charity that includes information as to whether goods or services have been provided to the donor in exchange for the gift, and an estimate of their value. Charities also must indicate whether the taxpayer received "intangible religious benefits," although the charity need not value them. Perhaps in an attempt to define the parameters of *Hernandez,* § 170(f)(8) defines an intangible religious benefit as something "provided by an organization organized exclusively for religious purposes and which generally is not sold in a commercial transaction outside the donative context."

2.   GIFTS OF APPRECIATED PROPERTY

A taxpayer who gives appreciated property to charity generally does not realize gain, as she would have if she had sold the property for its fair market value. Nevertheless, the Code generally allows the taxpayer to deduct the full fair market value of the appreciated property. (A taxpayer also does not realize loss for tax purposes when depreciated property is given to charity; but the loss may be realized if she first sells the depreciated asset, realizing the loss for tax purposes, and then contributes the proceeds.)

The tax law thus confers a generous benefit upon contributors of appreciated property. This benefit is limited by § 170(e), which, in some circumstances, reduces the charitable contribution by the amount of the unrealized gain. Section 170(e) applies generally to all contributions of property that would produce ordinary income or short-term capital gain if sold and to contributions of property that would produce long-term capital gain if the property were sold where the donee is a private foundation or if the contributed property is tangible personal property unrelated to the exempt function of the charity. § 170(e)(1). Charitable contributions to public charities of appreciated securities or real estate therefore are deductible in full if they would produce long-term capital gain if sold.

The generous treatment of gifts of appreciated property to charity has long been a source of controversy. In 1984, for example, the Treasury recommended that the deduction for any charitable donation be limited to the lesser of the fair market value or the basis of the property, stating:

> The current treatment of certain charitable gifts of appreciated property is unduly generous and in conflict with basic principles governing the measurement of income for tax purposes. In other circumstances where appreciated property is used to pay a deductible expense, or where such property is the subject of a deductible loss, the deduction

allowed may not exceed the taxpayer's adjusted basis plus any gain recognized. Thus, a taxpayer generally may not receive a tax deduction with respect to untaxed appreciation in property. The current tax treatment of certain charitable gifts departs from this principle by permitting the donor a deduction for the full value of the property, including the element of appreciation with respect to which the donor does not realize gain.

2 Treasury Dep't, Report to the President, Tax Reform for Fairness, Simplicity, and Economic Growth 72–74 (1984).

The charities respond, however, that the deduction by donors for the fair market value of contributed appreciated property is essential to their continued well-being. Universities point out that while large gifts typically account for less than 5 percent of the number of gifts, large gifts of appreciated property account for nearly half of the total amount of donations received. The universities argue: "Even if granting a deduction for appreciated property favors the high-bracket taxpayer who can afford to make such gifts, this theoretical inequity is dwarfed by the benefits to higher education of the appreciated property rules and the potentially ruinous loss of private support that could result from change in those rules. * * * Making it more costly for a rich man to give money to charity does not make it less costly for a poor man to do so; such tax changes will only reduce the amount flowing to charity from those who can best afford it." Report of the Association of American Universities, Tax Reform and the Crisis of Financing Higher Education 8 (1973).

NOTES

(A) *Section 170(e)*. The amount of the charitable deduction for a donation of appreciated property depends on whether the recipient is a private foundation or a public charity, whether the appreciation would be taxed as capital gain or ordinary income if the property were sold, and whether the gift consists of tangible property or securities.

A contribution of any property other than marketable securities (defined in § 170(e)(5)) to a private foundation (defined in § 509) gives rise to a deduction equal to the fair market value of the property minus any capital gain or ordinary income—in other words, the deduction is generally limited to the basis of the property. The deduction for a contribution of property to a public charity is generally the fair market value minus the amount of gain that would not have been long-term capital gain. If, however, the property is tangible personal property that will not be used by the donee in its charitable function, the deduction is the fair market value reduced by the full amount of the appreciation. The following four examples illustrate the application of § 170(e):

(1) T contributes stock to the Red Cross, a public charity. The stock has an adjusted basis of $100 and has a fair market value of $300 when donated to the charity. If the stock has been held for more than a year, it would have produced long-term capital gain when sold and thus T's charitable deduction is $300. If the stock had been held for only six months, the $300 fair market value is reduced by the appreciation of

$200 which would have been treated as a short-term capital gain had the stock been sold. Thus, T's deduction is limited to his basis of $100.

(2) T contributes a painting to the Red Cross with an adjusted basis of $100 and a fair market value at the time of the donation of $300. The Red Cross does not intend to hang the painting. Since T held the painting for more than a year, the appreciation would have been taxed as long-term capital gain if the painting had been sold. Because, however, the charity does not intend to use this tangible personal property in its charitable function, the deduction is limited to $300 minus the long-term capital gain or $100.

(3) T contributes the same painting to an art museum. If T held the painting for a year or less, the amount of the charitable deduction is only $100 because the fair market value is reduced by the short-term capital gain. If, however, T held the painting for more than a year, the deduction is the full $300 because the appreciation would be treated as long-term capital gain and the donee will use the painting in its charitable function.

(4) T contributes real estate with a basis of $100 and a fair market value of $300 to a private foundation. Because property other than marketable securities has been donated to a private foundation, the deduction is reduced by the full amount of the capital gain. Thus, T's deduction is $100.

Note that if the painting in (2) and (3) had been donated by the artist, the gain would have been ordinary income. See § 1221(a)(3). Regardless of the identity of the charity, the donation would have been the fair market value minus the ordinary income or $100. Note that a donee who receives the painting from the artist as a gift is treated the same as the artist under § 1221(a)(3). The painting in his hands is not a capital asset and the deduction is limited to basis under § 170(e).

(B) *Tax Planning.* Charitable giving can be important in the tax planning of high-income taxpayers. Great care is necessary in counseling such individuals. Well-advised taxpayers will, if they can, make charitable contributions of appreciated stock, real estate or other noncash assets qualifying for full deduction. You should try to understand why they do so, as well as why the advantages of doing so may be lost under § 170(e). The following example should clarify the underlying logic of § 170(e):

Assume that a person in the 40 percent bracket paid $2,000 for stock that now has a market value of $10,000. The stock is not as valuable to the taxpayer as $10,000 in cash, because taxes will have to be paid if it is sold. Assume that the income would be long-term capital gain, subject to tax at a maximum 20 percent rate.

Fair Market Value:	$10,000
Basis	2,000
Taxable Gain	8,000
Tax Payable	1,600
Net Proceeds	8,400

If the taxpayer gives the stock to charity instead of selling it, the $10,000 deduction saves $4,000 of tax on other income. Thus, she receives only $4,400 ($8,400 − $4,000) less than she would from a sale of stock and retention of the proceeds. In contrast, the out-of-pocket cost of a cash gift of $10,000 would be $6,000. (Some commentators, including representatives of charities, contend that a comparison between a charitable gift and sale is not apt because taxpayers instead could hold the property until death and avoid any tax on the appreciation under § 1014.)

The costs of giving cash and appreciated securities would be the same if the gift to charity were a taxable event triggering payment of the tax on the gain. The deduction reduction of § 170(e) (in the limited situations where it applies) accomplishes this goal indirectly. Instead of taxing the gain, § 170(e) reduces the charitable deduction by the amount that taxable income would be increased if the gain were taxable. Under § 170(e), the gain is not recognized, but the charitable deduction may be reduced to $2,000.

(C) *Gift of Property That Has Declined in Value.* In Withers v. Commissioner, 69 T.C. 900 (1978), the taxpayer made a charitable contribution of corporate stock that had depreciated in value. The court limited the deduction to the fair market value of the stock at the date of contribution, rather than allowing a larger deduction equal to basis. Thus, taxpayers should first sell depreciated assets to realize the loss and then give the proceeds to charity.

(E) *Valuation.* The value of a gift to a charity must be measurable with reasonable accuracy. The regulations state that the fair market value of property donated to a charity is the "price at which the property would change hands between a willing buyer and a willing seller, neither being under any compulsion to buy or sell and both having a reasonable knowledge of relevant facts." Reg. § 1.170A–1(c)(2).

Appraisals to establish the fair market value of charitable contributions—especially works of art—have produced many disputes between taxpayers and the IRS. Some tax shelter arrangements—involving buying at wholesale and giving at retail—have tried to inflate charitable deductions through overvaluation. The IRS has attempted to deal with the problem through such efforts as establishing an Advisory Group on the valuation of works of art. Congress further responded to the problem by mandating independent appraisals where the deduction exceeds a specific amount and by imposing new penalties on tax reductions due to overvaluations and on appraisers who deliberately inflate values. See also § 6662(e) for rules dealing with valuation overstatements in the case of charitable contributions. When his tax returns were released on assuming the Presidency, they showed that Bill Clinton had deducted $2 a pair for underwear donated to the Salvation Army. This seems a bit high for a Governor of Arkansas who had not yet told an MTV audience about his preference for boxers over briefs. Wonder what they would be worth now. See also, e.g., Rev. Rul. 80–69, 180–1 C.B. 55 (disallowing deductions of gems donated 13 months after purchase for three times the "wholesale" purchase price.)

3.   TAX–EXEMPT ORGANIZATIONS

NOTE ON TAX–EXEMPT ORGANIZATIONS

Organizations eligible for deductible charitable contributions are described in §§ 170(c) and 501(c)(3) of the Code. These organizations—as well as certain other organizations whose donors are not entitled to charitable deductions under § 170—are also exempt from income tax under § 501. Tax-exempt organizations that are eligible to receive deductible contributions are defined by § 501(c)(3) as follows:

> Corporations, and any community chest, fund, or foundation, organized and operated exclusively for religious, charitable, scientific, testing for public safety, literary, or educational purposes, or to foster national or international amateur sports competition (but only if no part of its activities involve the provision of athletic facilities or equipment), or for the prevention of cruelty to children or animals.

Regulation § 1.501(c)(3)–1(d)(2) provides that the term "charitable" is to be used in its generally accepted legal sense and is not limited by the enumeration in § 501(c)(3) of other tax-exempt purposes that may fall within the broad outlines of "charity" as developed by judicial decisions. Charity includes relief of the poor and distressed; advancement of religion, education or science; erection or maintenance of public buildings, monuments and works; lessening of the burdens of government; and promotion of social welfare by the reduction of neighborhood tensions, the elimination of prejudice or discrimination, the defense of human or civil rights, or the combatting of community deterioration or juvenile delinquency. In Rev. Proc. 71–39, 1971–2 C.B. 575, the IRS allowed a tax exemption under § 501(c)(3) for public-interest law firms.

No part of the net earnings of the organization may inure to the benefit of any private shareholder or individual. No substantial part of its activities may consist of carrying on propaganda, attempting to influence legislation (except as otherwise provided), or participating in, or intervening in (including the publishing or distributing of statements), any political campaign on behalf of any candidate for public office. Such an organization may not participate in any political campaign in opposition to any candidate for public office.

If an organization fails to comply with these requirements, its exemption will be revoked unless the prohibited activities are insubstantial or incidental to the organization's primary function. The existence of a substantial nonexempt purpose will defeat an organization's tax exemption even if it also has many exempt purposes.

Other organizations are exempt from tax under § 501, but contributions to these organizations do not qualify for deduction under § 170. See §§ 501(c)(2) and (c)(4)-(19). These organizations include, for example, certain social welfare organizations, labor unions, business leagues, agricultural organizations, professional football leagues, fraternal lodges and nonprofit cemetery companies. The critical restriction here, as under § 501(c)(3), is the prohibition against inurement to private individuals.

Section 502 denies exemption to any organization operated for the primary purpose of carrying on a trade or business for profit even if the organization pays all of its profits to another organization that is exempt under § 501. These so-called "feeder organizations" are subject to tax unless their eligibility for an exemption is preserved by one of the three special rules in § 502. Sections 511–514 impose a tax—designed to match the corporate income tax—on income received by an exempt organization from an unrelated trade or business, which is defined as a regular activity that is not substantially related to the organization's performance of its exempt function. An organization does not lose its exempt status by engaging in such an unrelated trade or business, but it must pay tax on the proportion of its total income derived from nonexempt activities.

Organizations exempt from tax under § 501(c)(3) are divided into two general categories: private foundations and publicly supported organizations. See § 509 for the definition of private foundation. The law governing the taxation of private foundations is detailed and complex. Private foundations are subject to an excise tax on their net investment income and are required to distribute a specified portion of their income. Limitations are imposed on certain business holdings by private foundations, and self-dealing provisions prohibit specific transactions between foundations and certain "disqualified" persons. Foundations cannot engage in certain political activities, including lobbying and electioneering. The penalties for failure to comply with these restrictions are onerous, generally taking the form of a three-tiered set of taxes. See §§ 4940–4948.

Considerable litigation has occurred over the conditions that organizations must meet in order to receive tax-exempt status and qualify for deductible gifts. A few of the more important developments are summarized below:

(1) *Segregated Schools.* The Supreme Court denied tax-exempt status to a private school that engaged in racial discrimination. Bob Jones University v. United States, 461 U.S. 574 (1983). The university argued that the IRS had improperly determined that racially discriminatory private schools violated public policy, and that, even if the determination was proper, the IRS did not have the authority to alter the scope of §§ 170 and 501(c)(3) to include the additional requirement that an organization not violate established public policy.

To the university's first contention over proper determination of public policy, the Supreme Court held, however, that "there can no longer be any doubt that racial discrimination in education violates deeply and widely accepted views of elementary justice." To the university's second argument, involving the IRS's authority to deny charitable status notwithstanding the organization's fulfillment of all statutory requirements, the Court responded: "In an area as complex as the tax system, the agency Congress vests with administrative responsibility must be able to exercise its authority to meet changing conditions and new problems." The Court also rejected the university's challenge that the IRS determination, even if valid and properly, could not be applied to schools that engage in racial discrimination on the basis of sincerely held religious beliefs. The Court stated that:

However, "[not] all burdens on religion are unconstitutional. * * * The state may justify a limitation on religious liberty by showing that it is essential to accomplish an overriding governmental interest."

* * *

The government interest at stake here is compelling. * * * [T]he Government has a fundamental, overriding interest in eradicating racial discrimination in education—discrimination that prevailed, with official approval, for the first 165 years of this Nation's constitutional history.

(2) *Lobbying.* As discussed at page 242 supra, a tax-exempt organization may elect a limitation on lobbying expenditures equal to a percentage of its total expenditures. An organization's lobbying expenditures cannot exceed the lesser of $1 million or 20 percent of total expenditures relating to its tax-exempt purpose. Within these limitations, no more than 25 percent of the lobbying expenditures may be for "grassroots" lobbying. If an organization that elects these rules exceeds the allowable amount of lobbying expenditures, an excise tax is imposed. An organization that evinces a pattern of excessive lobbying expenditures may lose its tax-exempt status. An excise tax is imposed on lobbying expenditures in any year in which the organization is not exempt because of excessive lobbying expenditures. See §§ 501(h), 504, 4911, 4912, and 4955. The Supreme Court in Regan v. Taxation With Representation of Washington, 461 U.S. 540 (1983), held that the Code's prohibition against substantial lobbying by tax-exempt organizations does not violate the First Amendment or the Equal Protection Clause of the Fifth Amendment.

(3) *Educational Organizations.* There has been great controversy over what is "educational" within § 501(c)(3). Charitable organizations that publish newspapers and magazines often obtain tax-exempt status because they are considered educational. In Big Mama Rag v. United States, 631 F.2d 1030 (D.C.Cir.1980), however, the IRS denied the organization tax-exempt status on the ground that its newspaper was not "educational," because it included articles and editorials promoting lesbianism. The Court of Appeals accepted Big Mama Rag's contention that the "full and fair exposition" test used by the IRS to define "educational" was unconstitutionally vague and thus led to discriminatory application.

After *Big Mama Rag,* the IRS formulated a new "methodology test," which focuses on the method of presentation, rather than the content, to define "educational" within § 501(c)(3). This test was upheld by the same circuit that decided *Big Mama Rag* in National Alliance v. United States, 710 F.2d 868 (D.C.Cir.1983). The court characterized the new test as a carefully-charted middle course that reduces the vagueness found unconstitutional in *Big Mama Rag* and thereby the potential censorship of the content of expression. The court denied tax-exempt status after finding the National Alliance's racist publication to be outside the range of any definition of "educational" promulgated by Congress or the IRS. The newsletter was found to advocate violence to "disadvantage or to injure persons who are members of named racial, religious or ethnic groups."

C.   MEDICAL EXPENSES

Section 213 allows deductions for medical and dental expenses paid during the taxable year for the taxpayer, her spouse, her children and her other dependents. The deduction includes payments for medical care, defined as the diagnosis, cure, mitigation, treatment or prevention of disease. Amounts paid for medical insurance are also deductible, as are the costs of transportation primarily for and essential to medical care. Medical expenses can be deducted only if they are not compensated by insurance or reimbursed by employers. Medical expenses are deductible only to the extent they exceed 7.5 percent of adjusted gross income; this floor is intended to disallow deduction for normal medical expenses such as annual physical and dental check-ups and supplies for the home medicine chest. The deduction is therefore limited to those taxable years when a person's medical expenses uncompensated by insurance are extraordinary. Furthermore, medical expenses are deductible only if together with other itemized deductions they exceed the standard deduction.

Is the medical expense deduction a subsidy to health care? Or is it a proper means of calculating an individual's net income? Contrast the treatment of medical expenses covered by a tortfeasor due to an accident or injury and payment made pursuant to a health insurance plan funded by the taxpayer, § 104, or by the taxpayer's employer, § 105. Recall that these payments are excluded from income without limitation. This is equivalent to including the payments in income and deducting the full amount. Does the Code create an incentive for health insurance?

The Code's definition of medical care is easily applied to most payments to doctors, nurses and hospitals. The difficult cases involve distinguishing medical expenses that are deductible under § 213 from personal expenses that are nondeductible under § 262. Consider whether the tests of deductibility are the same when an expenditure arises out of mixed personal and medical reasons as when it arises out of mixed personal and business reasons. Should the tests be the same?

Revenue Ruling 87–106

1987–2 C.B. 67.

Section 213(a) of the Code allows a deduction in computing taxable income for expenses paid during the taxable year, not compensated for by insurance or otherwise, for medical care of the taxpayer, the taxpayer's spouse, or a dependent (as defined in section 152) to the extent that the expenses exceed 7.5 percent of the taxpayer's adjusted gross income.

Section 213(d)(1) of the Code defines the term "medical care" to include amounts paid for the diagnosis, cure, mitigation, treatment, or prevention of disease, or for the purpose of affecting any structure or function of the body.

Section 1.213–1(e)(1)(ii) of the regulations provides, in part, that deductions for expenditures for medical care allowable under section 213 of the Code will be confined strictly to expenses incurred primarily for the prevention or alleviation of a physical or mental defect or illness. An expenditure that is merely beneficial to the general health of an individual is not an expenditure for medical care.

Section 1.213–1(e)(1)(iii) of the regulations provides, in part: Capital expenditures are generally not deductible for Federal income tax purposes. See section 263 and the regulations thereunder. However, an expenditure which otherwise qualifies as a medical expense under section 213 shall not be disqualified merely because it is a capital expenditure. For purposes of section 213 and this paragraph, a capital expenditure made by the taxpayer may qualify as a medical expense, if it has as its primary purpose the medical care (as defined in subdivisions (i) and (ii) of this subparagraph) of the taxpayer, his spouse, or his dependent. Thus, a capital expenditure which is related only to the sick person and is not related to permanent improvement or betterment of property, if it otherwise qualifies as an expenditure for medical care, shall be deductible; for example, an expenditure for eye glasses, a seeing eye dog, artificial teeth and limbs, a wheel chair, crutches, an inclinator or an air conditioner which is detachable from the property and purchased only for the use of a sick person, etc. Moreover, a capital expenditure for permanent improvement or betterment of property which would not ordinarily be for the purpose of medical care (within the meaning of this paragraph) may, nevertheless, qualify as a medical expense to the extent that the expenditure exceeds the increase in the value of the related property, if the particular expenditure is related directly to medical care. Such a situation could arise, for example, where a taxpayer is advised by a physician to install an elevator in his residence so that the taxpayer's wife who is afflicted with heart disease will not be required to climb stairs. If the cost of installing the elevator is $1,000 and the increase in the value of the residence is determined to be only $700, the difference of $300, which is the amount in excess of the value enhancement, is deductible as a medical expense. If, however, by reason of this expenditure, it is determined that the value of the residence has not been increased, the entire cost of installing the elevator would qualify as a medical expense.

In making a capital expenditure that would otherwise qualify as being for medical care, any additional expenditure that is attributable to personal motivation does not have medical care as its primary purpose and is not related directly to medical care for purposes of section 213 of the Code. Such personal motivations include, for instance, architectural or aesthetic compatibility with the related property. Consequently, such additional expenditures are not deductible under section 213. Ferris v. Commissioner, 582 F.2d 1112 (7th Cir.1978), reversing and remanding T.C.M. 1977–186. In Ferris, the taxpayer had incurred additional costs for architectural and aesthetic reasons in building an enclosed pool that otherwise qualified as an expenditure for medical care. A deduction for the additional costs was denied.

In Jacobs v. Commissioner, 62 T.C. 813 (1974), the Tax Court held that for an expense to be deductible under section 213 of the Code it both must be an essential element of treatment and must not have otherwise been incurred for nonmedical reasons. An expenditure failing either test would be a nondeductible personal, living, or family expense under section 262.

* * * In Jacobs, the taxpayer attempted to deduct lawyer's fees in obtaining a divorce that had been recommended by his psychiatrist. The court denied the deduction because the divorce would have been obtained even without the psychiatrist's recommendation.

* * * Congress expressed a desire to clarify that certain capital expenditures generally do not increase the value of a personal residence and thus generally are deductible in full as medical expenses. These expenditures are those made for removing structural barriers in a personal residence for the purpose of accommodating it to the handicapped condition of the taxpayer or the taxpayer's spouse or dependents who reside there.

The Internal Revenue Service has determined that expenditures for the following purposes generally do not increase the fair market value of a personal residence and thus generally are eligible in full for the medical expense deduction when made for the primary purpose of accommodating a personal residence to the handicapped condition of the taxpayer, the taxpayer's spouse, or dependents who reside there:

1.   constructing entrance or exit ramps to the residence;

2.   widening doorways at entrances or exits to the residence;

3.   widening or otherwise modifying hallways and interior doorways;

4.   installing railing, support bars, or other modifications to bathrooms;

5.   lowering of or making other modifications to kitchen cabinets and equipment;

6.   altering the location of or otherwise modifying electrical outlets and fixtures;

7.   installing porch lifts and other forms of lifts (Generally, this does not include elevators, as they may add to the fair market value of the residence and any deduction would have to be decreased to that extent. See section 1.213–1(e)(1)(iii) of the regulations.);

8.   modifying fire alarms, smoke detectors, and other warning systems;

9.   modifying stairs;

10.   adding handrails or grab bars whether or not in bathrooms;

11.   modifying hardware on doors;

12.   modifying areas in front of entrance and exit doorways; and

13.   grading of ground to provide access to the residence.

NOTES

(A) *Swimming Pools.* Many of the litigated cases involve swimming pools. Following the regulations, the Service has held that a pool is "an expenditure incurred for the primary purpose of, and is directly related to, the taxpayer's medical care and, to the extent the expenditure exceeds the increase in value of [the taxpayer's] property as a result of the installation, is deductible." Rev.Rul. 83–33, 1983–1 C.B. 70. For example, in Cherry v. Commissioner, 46 T.C.M. 1031 (1983), the taxpayers were allowed deductions under § 213 for operating and maintenance costs of their indoor heated pool even though it had a deep end and a diving board and was also used for recreational purposes. The primary purpose of the 80 degree pool was to mitigate Cherry's emphysema and bronchitis. Thus, heating oil, chemicals, electricity and insurance costs related to the pool were all deductible in the year incurred. But see Lerew v. Commissioner, 44 T.C.M. 918 (1982) (buyers of home with medically necessary pool denied deduction for difference between what it would have cost to construct a pool and the allegedly lesser amount by which the pool enhanced the value of their new property).

The costs of building a pool were held not deductible in Evanoff v. Commissioner, 44 T.C.M. 1394 (1982), where taxpayers for $250 a year could have used one of many nearby community swimming pools. The taxpayers in that case built their own pool because their religious beliefs kept their daughter from swimming with children of the opposite sex. The court held that the expenditure was personal rather than medical if motivated by religious convictions and other personal considerations. In Letter Ruling 8326095, the IRS held that the fees and transportation costs related to using a public pool for medically necessary exercise were deductible.

(B) *Other Exercise.* Can a taxpayer who must exercise to treat his emphysema deduct transportation costs to and from a golf course? In Altman v. Commissioner, 53 T.C. 487 (1969), a deduction was denied because the taxpayer had failed to prove why he had to golf instead of engage in another activity that could have been conducted closer to home. See also France v. Commissioner, 40 T.C.M. 508 (1980) (no deduction allowed for dance lessons prescribed by physician where same results were achievable with any physical activity); Taylor v. Commissioner, 54 T.C.M. 129 (1987) (deduction denied for costs of mowing the lawn of a taxpayer whose doctor advised him to avoid lawn care due to severe allergy). Why do you suppose the court is willing to substitute its judgement for a doctor's as to what constitutes medical care?

(C) *Milieu and Other Therapy.* In Rabb v. Commissioner, 31 T.C.M. 476 (1972), the taxpayer attempted to deduct costs of "milieu therapy" prescribed by a psychiatrist for his wife's neurotic disorder. The "milieu therapy" was designed "through the use of increased socialization and participation in appropriate recreational, social, and other activities, to encourage and reinforce [her] existing emotional resources, and to allow her to better cope with her inner stresses." The "milieu therapy" consisted of more than $23,000 of specially tailored clothing, department store charges, remodeling of a lake cottage, apartment improvements, new furniture and appliances, etc. The court stated:

> It is not enough to show that Betty was mentally ill, which indeed she was, nor is it enough in addition thereto to show that the expenses were incurred upon the recommendation of the psychiatrist. It is essential to show the proximate relationship of the expenses to the necessary treatment of the illness. Although Brown stated he "encour-

aged shopping excursions" there is no claim by him that these excursions were an essential element of the treatment, nor is there any evidence in the record of the degree to which such shopping excursions varied either in frequency or dollar amount from that which would have occurred without his specific "encouragement." We may take judicial notice of the generally therapeutic effect that shopping with unlimited charge accounts offers a housewife, even one in Betty's obviously ill state, but without a more explicit statement of the medical purpose from the psychiatrist, and without additional proof from petitioner that of his $86,000 annual income, Betty would not have spent the $2,600 for clothing and $4,300 for other department store charge account items claimed herein, notwithstanding the absence of professional recommendation, we are unconvinced that the amounts claimed for clothing and charge accounts bore the requisite relationship to the treatment.

The court was also "unconvinced" on the other expenditures and upheld the Commissioner's disallowance of all deductions.

The expenses of treatment to combat alcohol and drug abuse have been held deductible. See Rev. Rul. 73–325, 1973–2 C.B. 72 (alcoholism) and Rev. Rul. 72–226, 1972–1 C.B. 96 (drug addiction). The IRS has also held that the costs of smoking-cessation programs are deductible even when the smoker has not been diagnosed with any specific disease. Prescription drugs to combat the effects of nicotine withdrawal are deductible but the cost of non-prescription nicotine gum and patches are not. Rev.Rul. 99–28, 1999–1 C.B. 1269. Similarly, the Service has sanctioned deduction of the costs of weight-loss programs as treatment for a specific disease, including obesity. Rev. Rul. 2002–19, 2202–1 C.B. 778. On the other hand, the costs of diet food are not deductible. Nor are the costs of participating in a weight loss program to improve general health or appearance. Rev. Rul. 79–151. 1979–1 C.B. 116. See Reg. § 1.213–1(e)(1)(ii), which disallows a deduction for an outlay incurred merely to promote general health.

Although the costs of psychiatric treatment generally are deductible, the Service has taken the position that marriage counselling is inherently personal. Rev.Rul. 75–319, 1975–2 C.B. 88. See also Jacobs v. Commissioner, 62 T.C. 813 (1974), where a medical expense deduction was denied a taxpayer for expenses incurred in obtaining a divorce recommended by his psychiatrist.

(D) *Birth Control.* In Revenue Ruling 73–200, 1973–1 C.B. 140, the IRS permitted deduction for birth control pills prescribed by a physician and reversed its prior practice of allowing a deduction for oral contraceptives only if essential to protect a woman's health. The IRS simultaneously issued Revenue Ruling 73–201, 1973–1 C.B. 140, which holds that the cost of a vasectomy or lawful abortion is a deductible medical expense. Subsequently, the IRS issued Revenue Ruling 73–603, 1973–2 C.B. 76, permitting a medical deduction for female sterilization. Are expenses for birth control methods not covered by these rulings also deductible? What is the authority for allowing deductions only for legal abortions? Regs. § 1.213(e)(1)(ii) prohibits deductions for any illegal operation or treatment. Recall the materials on the public policy limitations on business expense deductions, supra at page 238. Is a similar limitation implicit in § 213? In all sections of the Code?

(E) *Cosmetic Improvements*. Cosmetic surgery is generally not deductible and reimbursements for such surgery from an employer-funded medical plan are not excludable from gross income. Cosmetic surgery is defined as any procedure "which is directed at improving the patient's appearance and does not meaningfully promote the proper function of the body or prevent or treat illness or disease." Cosmetic surgery does not include a procedure necessary to ameliorate a deformity attributable to a congenital abnormality, a personal injury due to accident or a disfiguring disease. § 213(d)(9).

If a well-known rock star has his eyes widened or an actor has his nose thinned, could he deduct the cost as a business expense?

(F) *Medical vs. Business Deductions*. Revenue Ruling 75–316, 1975–2 C.B. 54, held that payments by blind employees to readers for services relating to the employees' work are deductible as business expenses, not as medical expenses. Revenue Ruling 75–317, 1975–2 C.B. 57, provides examples of situations where amounts paid by handicapped persons for travel, meals and lodging, and for companions for their business trips, are deductible as business expenses under § 162 or medical expenses under § 213. Why does it matter which section allows the deduction?

(G) *Schools and Retirement Homes*. Where a payment to a school or retirement home covers medical costs, the taxpayer is permitted to deduct a portion of the fee. For example, in Urbauer v. Commissioner, 63 T.C.M. 2492 (1992), the court sanctioned a deduction for a portion of the fee for a prep school where the child attended principally to benefit from the treatment for behavior and drug problems. Compare Rev.Rul. 78–340, 1978–2 C.B. 124 (a portion of tuition deductible for special school designed for children with neurological disorders resulting in learning disabilities) with Martin v. Commissioner, 548 F.2d 633 (6th Cir.1977) (no deduction for tuition for deaf child to attend school that had no special medical facilities or doctors or teachers on staff who specialized in teaching the deaf).

(H) *In-Home Attendants*. In Kohen v. Commissioner, 44 T.C.M. 1518 (1982), the court denied a deduction for the expense of hiring a "baby nurse" to assist a mother in caring for her newborn baby. The fact that the employee was a nurse did not alone transform the performance of the essentially routine functions of bathing and feeding the baby into deductible medical care. In Borgmann v. Commissioner, 438 F.2d 1211 (9th Cir.1971), the court disallowed expenditures for a housekeeper employed on a doctor's advice by an individual who had suffered a heart attack. The court found that the duties "were not primarily those of a nurse and thus did not constitute 'medical care' within the meaning of § 213(e)(1) of the 1954 code." May a taxpayer deduct the costs of maintaining young children in boarding school in order to alleviate the emotional distress of their mother and to help prevent the recurrence of the illness from which she was suffering? No deduction was allowed in Ochs v. Commissioner, 195 F.2d 692 (2d Cir.1952), cert. denied 344 U.S. 827 (1952). Does it make sense that a seriously ill person who needs an attendant can obtain the medical deduction only if he hires a trained nurse? How does this rule comport with nontax health care policies?

(I) *Meals and Lodging.* Section 213(d)(1)(B) defines medical care to include transportation primarily for and essential to medical care. Commissioner v. Bilder, 369 U.S. 499 (1962), involved an unsuccessful attempt by a taxpayer to include his lodging expenses within this subsection. Bilder had suffered four heart attacks in eight years and was advised by a heart specialist to spend the winter season in a warm climate. He proceeded, along with his wife and three-year-old daughter, to Ft. Lauderdale, where he spent a total of five winter months in 1954 and 1955. His transportation costs were considered deductible, but the Supreme Court, overruling the Tax Court and the Court of Appeals, held that the rental payments for the months spent in a Florida apartment were not deductible as medical expenses.

The extent to which costs for care in an institution other than a hospital constitute deductible medical expenses tends to depend upon the services provided. In Kelly v. Commissioner, 440 F.2d 307 (7th Cir.1971), the taxpayer had suffered an appendicitis attack and was hospitalized. Subsequently, he was discharged because the hospital needed his room but was advised by his doctor to stay in a nearby hotel. The court held that the taxpayer's condition caused him to stay in the hotel, where he received continuous daily nursing care and was near his doctor. The court held that the hotel bill was a deductible medical expense for care rendered in a substitute institution.

In Levine v. Commissioner, 695 F.2d 57 (2d Cir.1982), the taxpayer's son suffered from mental illness and had been treated at a hospital clinic. When the son became too old to remain in the clinic, he refused to move to another hospital and insisted on remaining close to his original therapist. He stayed in an apartment rented by his parents and used the clinic as an outpatient. The court held that "only those medically necessary away-from-home living arrangements which involve continuous daily medical care on the premises may give rise to favorable tax treatment for the cost of meals and lodging." The court therefore denied the deduction after finding that, in the two-year period at issue, the taxpayer's son had received medical care only once at the apartment.

Do *Bilder, Kelly,* and *Levine* also apply to meal and lodging expenses incurred while traveling to or staying at a place of medical attention? Section 213(d)(2) treats up to $50 per night for lodging as a deductible medical expense if it is incurred to obtain significant medical care in a licensed hospital or its equivalent and there is no element of "personal pleasure, recreation or vacation in the travel away from home." This provision was enacted to provide deductions for lodging away from home in situations where people travel to receive outpatient medical care. In Montgomery v. Commissioner, 428 F.2d 243 (6th Cir.1970), the court extended the definition of "transportation" deductible under § 213 to include the cost of meals and lodging necessarily incurred in transporting the patient to and from the place of treatment. Holding that *Bilder* and subsequent cases applied only to meals and lodging *at* the place of medical care, the court found no congressional intent to deny deductions for the costs of food and lodging incurred in traveling to the place of treatment.

Distinguishing travel that is itself therapeutic, such as a vacation in a more desirable climate, from travel required to bring a patient to a place of medical care, the Tax Court in Pfersching v. Commissioner, 46 T.C.M. 424 (1983) relied on *Montgomery* and allowed a deduction for meal and lodging expenses incurred by the taxpayer and his son in traveling from Nevada to Kentucky, where the son was to receive a special operation.

(J) *Inconsistent Treatment.* The tax treatment of medical care is not consistent. Recall that the premiums on health insurance plans provided by employers as well as payments for medical care under those plans is tax-exempt. §§ 105, 106. Self-employed individuals can deduct 70 percent of the cost of health insurance (100% in 2003), and medical care provided by the plan is exempt. § 162(*l*). Millions of Americans cannot use these provisions, however, either because their employers do not provide health insurance or because they do not work. If they purchase health insurance, the premiums are deductible each year only to the extent they itemize deductions and the costs exceed 7.5% of adjusted gross income. For many, this means no deduction. As a result, the after-tax cost of health insurance for these taxpayers is much greater than it is for those whose employers provide this benefit.

(K) *Alternative Minimum Tax.* For purposes of computing individuals' alternative minimum taxable income, only medical expenses in excess of 10 percent of adjusted gross income (rather than 7.5 percent of AGI under the regular income tax), are deductible. § 56(b)(1)(B).

CHAPTER 4

WHOSE INCOME IS IT?

In addition to knowing whether income is taxed, one must know to whom it is taxed. This requires a decision as to the appropriate taxable unit. One possibility is the individual taxpayer, without regard to her marital status or dependents. Another option is to tax a family unit on its aggregate income. Alternatively, the income of married couples might be aggregated, or an "economic unit," such as the household, might be used. So long as there is a progressive rate structure, the definition of the taxable unit will be important.

Throughout the history of the income tax, a major tax planning technique has been to shift income from people or entities to whom it would be taxed at a high marginal rate to people or entities subject to low or zero rates of tax. Conversely, tax may be saved by shifting deductions or in some cases, credits from low- or zero-rate taxpayers to high-rate taxpayers.

Shifting of income and deductions is advantageous when there is any progressivity in the rate structure of the income tax. The wider the spread in rates, the greater the incentive to divide income among family members or other entities, such as trusts. It is often advantageous to create new taxpayers—for example, trusts, partnerships or corporations—to employ income and deduction shifting.

The existence of tax-exempt entities—including pension funds, Native American tribes, educational and religious organizations, and governmental units—produces opportunities for saving tax. As we saw in the last Chapter, so does the existence of businesses with tax losses that they cannot use immediately to offset taxable income. Various financing arrangements, such as those examined in the tax shelter material, supra at 396, were designed to shift deductions and credits from individuals or corporations that could not use them to high-bracket individuals or profitable corporations that could. Opportunities for moving income and deductions to the taxpayer who can use them to greatest advantage are increased by variations in the effective tax rates that apply to different types of income.

This Chapter explores various efforts by taxpayers to save tax by shifting deductions and splitting income among family members and other entities. First, the basic provisions governing the taxation of the family are described. The following Section deals with gratuitous assignments of both labor and capital income, and the next Section discusses intrafamily assignments for consideration. A final Section describes the use of entities for income shifting.

SECTION 1.   THE TAXABLE UNIT

Many of the questions about assignments of income historically have arisen out of efforts to keep income in lower brackets by dividing it among several members of a family. The student therefore must understand the basic provisions governing the taxation of the family before proceeding to the other materials on assignments of income. One of the most fundamental issues, which has plagued the income tax since its inception, is the appropriate treatment of single people, married couples, and dependent children.

A.   TAXATION OF THE FAMILY

Druker v. Commissioner

United States Court of Appeals, Second Circuit, 1982.
697 F.2d 46, certiorari denied 461 U.S. 957 (1983).

FRIENDLY, CIRCUIT JUDGE:

* * *

The principal issue on the taxpayers' appeal is the alleged unconstitutionality of the so-called "marriage penalty". The issue relates to the 1975 and 1976 income tax returns of James O. Druker and his wife Joan. During the tax years in question James was employed as a lawyer, first by the United States Attorney for the Eastern District of New York and later by the District Attorney of Nassau County, New York, and Joan was employed as a computer programmer. For each of the two years they filed separate income tax returns, checking the status box entitled "married filing separately". In computing their respective tax liabilities, however, they applied the rates in I.R.C. § 1(c) for "Unmarried individuals" rather than the higher rates prescribed by § 1(d) for "Married individuals filing separate returns". Prior to undertaking this course of action, James consulted with the United States Attorney for the Eastern District and with members of the Intelligence Division of the IRS, explaining that he and his wife wanted to challenge the constitutionality of the "marriage penalty" without incurring liability for fraud or willfulness. Following these conversations they filed their returns as described, attaching to each return a letter explaining that, although married, they were applying the tax tables for single persons because they believed that the "income tax structure unfairly discriminates against working married couples" in violation of the equal protection clause of the fourteenth amendment. The Tax Court rejected this constitutional challenge, sustaining the Commissioner's determination that the Drukers were subject to tax at the rates provided in § 1(d) for married persons filing separately.

Determination of the proper method for federal taxation of the incomes of married and single persons has had a long and stormy history. See generally, Bittker, Federal Income Taxation and the Family, 27 Stan.L.Rev. 1389, 1399–1416 (1975). From the beginning of the income tax in 1913 until 1948 each individual was taxed on his or her own income regardless of marital status. Thus, as a result of the progressive nature of the tax, two married couples with the same aggregate income would often have very different tax liabilities—larger if most of the income belonged to one spouse, smaller as their incomes tended toward equality. The decision in Poe v. Seaborn, 282 U.S. 101 (1930), that a wife was taxable on one half of community income even if this was earned solely by the husband, introduced a further element of geographical inequality, since it gave married couples in community property states a large tax advantage over similarly situated married couples with the same aggregate income in common law states.

After *Poe* the tax status of a married couple in a community property state differed from that of a married couple in a common law state in two significant respects. First, each community property spouse paid the same tax as an unmarried person with one-half the aggregate community income, whereas each common law spouse paid the same tax as an unmarried person with the same individual income. Consequently, marriage usually reduced a couple's tax burden if they resided in a community property state but was a neutral tax event for couples in common law states. Second, in community property states all married couples with the same aggregate income paid the same tax, whereas in common law states a married couple's tax liability depended on the amount of income each spouse earned. * * *

The decision in *Poe* touched off something of a stampede among common law states to introduce community property regimes and thereby qualify their residents for the privilege of income splitting. The Supreme Court's subsequent decision in Commissioner v. Harmon, 323 U.S. 44 (1944), that the income-splitting privileges did not extend to couples in states whose community property systems were elective, slowed but did not halt this movement. The result was considerable confusion and much upsetting of expectations founded on long experience under the common law. Congress responded in 1948 by extending the benefits of "income splitting" to residents of common law as well as community property states. * * * Pursuant to this Act, every married couple was permitted to file a joint return and pay twice the tax that a single individual would pay on one-half of their total income. This in effect taxed a married couple as if they were two single individuals each of whom earned half of the couple's combined income. The Act not only reduced the tax burden on married couples in common law states; it also ensured that all married couples with the same aggregate income paid the same tax regardless of the state in which they lived ("geographical uniformity") and regardless of the relative income contribution of each spouse ("horizontal equity").

While the 1948 Act was good news for married couples, it placed singles at a serious disadvantage. The tax liability of a single person was now sometimes as much as 41% greater than that of a married couple with the same income. * * * Although constitutional challenges to the "singles' penalty" were uniformly rejected, * * * the single taxpayer obtained some relief from Congress. The Tax Reform Act of 1969 * * * increased the number of tax schedules from two to four: § 1(a) for marrieds filing jointly;

§ 1(b) for unmarried heads of households; § 1(c) for unmarried individuals; and § 1(d) for married individuals filing separately.[1] The schedules were set so that a single person's tax liability under § 1(c) would never be more than 120% that of a married couple with the same income filing jointly under § 1(a).

The 1969 reform spawned a new class of aggrieved taxpayers—the two wage-earner married couple whose combined tax burden, whether they chose to file jointly under § 1(a) or separately under § 1(d), was now greater than it would have been if they had remained single and filed under § 1(c). It is this last phenomenon which has been characterized, in somewhat loaded fashion, as the "marriage penalty" or "marriage tax".[2] Here, again, while constitutional attack has been unavailing, * * * Congress has acted to provide relief. The Economic Recovery Tax Act of 1981 * * * allows two-earner married couples a deduction from gross income, within specified limits, equal to 10% of the earnings of the lesser-earning spouse.

* * * [T]he Supreme Court made explicit in Zablocki v. Redhail, 434 U.S. 374 (1978), what had been implicit in earlier decisions, that the right to marry is "fundamental". The Court, however, * * * took care to explain that it did "not mean to suggest that every state regulation which relates in any way to the incidents of or prerequisites for marriage must be subjected to rigorous scrutiny. To the contrary, reasonable regulations that do not significantly interfere with decisions to enter into the marital relationship may be legitimately imposed." 434 U.S. at 386. Whereas differences in race, religion, and political affiliation are almost always irrelevant for legislative purposes, "a distinction between married persons and unmarried persons is of a different character". "Both tradition and common experience support the conclusion that marriage is an event which normally marks an important change in economic status."

We do not doubt that the "marriage penalty" has some adverse effect on marriage; indeed, James Druker stated at argument that, having failed thus far in the courts, he and his wife had solved their tax problem by divorcing but continuing to live together. The adverse effect of the "marriage penalty", however, * * * is merely "indirect"; while it may to some extent weight the choice whether to marry, it leaves the ultimate decision to the individual. * * * The tax rate structure of I.R.C. § 1 places "no direct legal obstacle in the path of persons desiring to get married". * * * Nor is anyone "absolutely prevented" by it from getting married * * *. Moreover, the "marriage penalty" is most certainly not "an attempt to interfere with the individual's freedom [to marry]". * * * It would be altogether absurd to suppose that Congress, in fixing the rate schedules in 1969, had any invidious intent to discourage or penalize marriage—an estate enjoyed by the vast majority of its members. Indeed, as has been

---

1. The rates set under § 1(d) were the pre-1969 rates for single taxpayers. So disadvantageous is this schedule that only about 1% of married couples file separately. * * * As a general rule, married taxpayers file separately only when they are so estranged from one another that they do not wish to sign a joint return or when separate filing enables one spouse to exceed the [now 7.5%] of income floor for medical deductions. * * *

2. Not all married couples are so "penalized". For the couple whose income is earned primarily or solely by one partner, marriage still offers significant tax savings. * * *

shown, the sole and express purpose of the 1969 reform was to provide some relief for the single taxpayer. * * * Given this purpose Congress had either to abandon the principle of horizontal equity between married couples, a principle which had been established by the 1948 Act and the constitutionality of which has not been challenged, or to impose a "penalty" on some two-earner married couples. It was put to this hard choice because, as Professor Bittker has shown, supra, 27 Stan.L.Rev. at 1395–96, 1429–31, it is simply impossible to design a progressive tax regime in which all married couples of equal aggregate income are taxed equally and in which an individual's tax liability is unaffected by changes in marital status.[3]

* * *

Faced with this choice, Congress in 1969 decided to hold fast to horizontal equity, even at the price of imposing a "penalty" on two-earner married couples like the Drukers. There is nothing in the equal protection clause that required a different choice. Since the objectives sought by the 1969 Act—the maintenance of horizontal equity and progressivity, and the reduction of the differential between single and married taxpayers—were clearly compelling, the tax rate schedules in I.R.C. § 1 can survive even the "rigorous scrutiny" reserved by *Zablocki* for measures which "significantly interfere" with the right to marry. * * *

Clearly, the alternative favored by the Drukers, that married persons be permitted to file under § 1(c) if they so wish, would entail the loss of horizontal equity.

In the area of family taxation every legislative disposition is "virtually fated to be both overinclusive and underinclusive when judged from one perspective or another". The result, as Professor Bittker has well said, is that there "can be no peace in this area, only an uneasy truce." * * * Congress must be accorded wide latitude in striking the terms of that truce. The history we have reviewed makes clear that Congress has worked persistently to accommodate the competing interests and accomplish fairness.

[W]hat the Drukers choose to call the "marriage penalty" deprived them of no constitutional right. Whether policy considerations warrant a further narrowing of the gap between the schedules applied to married and unmarried persons is for Congress to determine in light of all the relevant legislative considerations. * * *

NOTES

(A) *Both Ends of a Seesaw Cannot Be Up at the Same Time.* Judge Friendly observes in *Druker* that "it is simply impossible to design a

---

3. Professor Bittker puts it thus, 27 Stan.L.Rev. at 1430–31:

Another way to describe this collision of objectives is that the tax paid by a married couple must be (a) greater than they paid before marriage, in which event they are subject to a marriage penalty, (b) less than they paid before marriage, in which event unmarried persons are subject to a singles penalty, or (c) unchanged by marriage, in which event equal-income married couples are subject to unequal taxes.

progressive tax regime in which all married couples of equal aggregate income are taxed equally and in which an individual's tax liability is unaffected by changes in marital status." This fact was demonstrated mathematically by Edwin S. Cohen, then Assistant Secretary of the Treasury for Tax Policy, in 1972 testimony before the House Ways and Means Committee:

Case 1 is a single person who earns $20,000.

Case 2, two single persons each earn $10,000.

Case 3, a husband earns $20,000 and a wife earns zero.

Case 4, a husband and wife each earn $10,000.

If we want no penalty on remaining single—and a large group insists upon this—Case 1 must pay the same tax as Case 3. A single person earning $20,000 pays the same tax as a married couple earning $20,000.

If we want no penalty on marrying, Case 2 must pay the same tax as Case 4. Two single persons earning $10,000 each pay the same tax as a married couple each earning $10,000.

If we want husband and wife to pay the same tax however they contribute to the family earnings Case 3 pays the same tax as Case 4.

To summarize the tax results:

Case 1 equals Case 3.

Case 2 equals Case 4.

Case 3 equals Case 4.

Based on the fundamental mathematical principle that things equal to the same thing must be equal to each other, the result should then be that Case 1 equals Case 2, or in other words, that the tax on a single person earning $20,000 equals the tax on two single persons each earning $10,000.

But that cannot be so if we are going to have a progressive income tax structure, and progressive taxation is a basic tenet of our income tax system. The tax on a single person earning $20,000—Case 1—must be greater than the total tax on two single persons each earning $10,000 if we are to have a progressive rate structure.

* * *

[I]t becomes apparent from this analysis that you cannot have each of these principles operating simultaneously, and that there is no one principle of equity that covers all of these cases. No algebraic equation, no matter how sophisticated, can solve this dilemma. * * * All that we can hope for is a reasonable compromise.

Hearings on Tax Treatment of Single Persons and Married Persons where Both Spouses are Working, before the House Ways and Means Committee, 93d Cong., 1st Sess. (1972).

(B) *The Marriage Penalty.* Under current law, many couples in which each spouse earns relatively equal amounts of income suffer a "marriage penalty," that is, they pay more tax than they would if they remained single or divorced. This is largely due to the relationship between the tax rate schedules applicable to married couples and those applicable to single people and "heads of households," and to special allowances such as the earned income tax credit. For example, in 2000, if A and B were single and each earned $30,000, they each would pay taxes of $3,420 (each has an exemption of $2,800 and a standard deduction of $4,400 and pays tax at a 15 percent rate) for a total tax of $6,840. If they had been married, their total tax would be: $7,473 (total income of $60,000 minus a standard deduction of $7,350 and two personal exemptions totaling $5,600). Another way to view this is that A and B's effective tax rate if they remain single is 11.4 percent whereas it escalates to 12.5 percent if they marry. This difference arises because the second earner's salary is taxed at a higher marginal rate when a couple is married and because two standard deductions for singles exceed that allowable to a married couple.

The tax penalty is greatly exacerbated for some low income taxpayers who are eligible for the earned income credit. For example, in 2000, two single parents each earning $15,000 are eligible for an earned income credit for two children of $3,396 or a total of $6,792. They would have owned no taxes and received a refund of $6,792. If they married, their taxes would be $878 and they would have a credit of only $237 for a net tax liability of $641. The combination of the two marriage penalties has the effect of dramatically increasing their effective tax rate. The effective tax rate if single is a negative 23 percent; if married it is 2 percent. Marriage increases their effective tax rate by 25 percent. For a proof that solving the marriage problem under the earned income tax credit is fraught with same difficulties as achieving neutrality under a progressive income tax generally, see Anne L. Alstott, "The Earned Income Tax Credit and the Limitations of Tax–Based Welfare Reform," 108 Harv.L.Rev. 533, 562 n1 (1995).

The phase-out of dependency exemptions (see page 430 supra) and the reduction of itemized deductions under § 68 (see p. 435 supra) also contain marriage penalties. In 2000, the phase-out of dependency exemptions begins at $128,950 for single taxpayers and at $161,150 for married taxpayers. Two single taxpayers with $125,000 of income, for example, would be able to deduct dependency exemptions in full; if they married, their exemptions would be phased out. The 3 percent itemized deduction haircut of § 68 is particularly harsh because the phase-out begins in 2000 at $128,950 regardless of filing status. (The 2001 tax legislation repeals both the phase-out of dependency exemptions and the itemized deduction haircut over a five-year period beginning in 2006.)

In contrast to the income tax, a married couple's income is not aggregated for purposes of the Social Security payroll tax. The tax is levied on a flat rate up to a ceiling on an individual's earnings. Although taxes are determined on an individual basis, marital status is taken into account in setting benefits and generally single earner couples receive higher benefits relative to their taxes than two-earner couples.

(C) *The Marriage Bonus.* Some taxpayers enjoy a marriage bonus. Where one taxpayer in a couple earns substantially more than the other, their combined taxes will decline if they marry. If, for example, in 2000, A and B were single and A earned $40,000 and B had no taxable income, A would owe taxes of $5,471 and B would owe nothing. If A and B married, their combined taxes would be $3,806.

(D) *Eliminating the Marriage Penalty.* Testifying before the House Ways and Means Committee in January, 1995, Speaker of the House Newt Gingrich urged a rewrite of the earned income credit to remove its anti-marriage bias. "That's something staff should be able to do in a week." The Speaker had a limited understanding of the necessary political tradeoffs since Congress still has been unable to eliminate marriage penalties, and eliminating marriage penalties in the EITC has not been a priority among the marriage penalty proposals seriously considered by Congress.

The marriage penalty would be eliminated by permitting married couples to file separate returns using the single rate schedules. But this would create differences between married couples based on their relative earnings and whether they live in a community property state. The marriage penalty also would be eliminated if the rate brackets for married filing jointly were twice as wide as those for single taxpayers and the standard deduction and phase-outs were twice as big for married couples as for singles. But that would create a penalty on remaining single because two unmarried persons would pay more than a married couple with the same income. This unmarried person disadvantage could be eliminated by having mandatory joint returns with a one rate schedule for individuals and married couples, but that would recreate a marriage penalty.

As *Druker* notes, in 1981, Congress enacted a deduction for two-earner couples equal to 10 percent of the earnings of the lesser-earning spouse, up to a maximum of $3,000. This deduction was repealed in 1986. Congress justified repeal because of changes in the standard deduction and rate schedules. This deduction for two-earner couples abandoned the principle that married couples with the same joint income will have the same tax burden, regardless of the division of earnings.

An alternative to the two-earner deduction would be to tax all individuals, whether married or single, on their separate earnings. There are several practical problems with this approach. First, to avoid serious geographical disparities, it would be necessary to provide that, in community property states, earnings would be taxed to the person who earned them, regardless of who owns them as a matter of state law. Second, it might be necessary to prevent couples from diverting investment income to the spouse with the smaller earned income in order to get the maximum benefit out of splitting the income on two separate returns. Finally, it also would be necessary to provide rules for the allocation of certain personal deductions—such as the deduction for the medical expenses of the couple's children—between the two spouses.

On the other hand, mandatory individualized filing would achieve marriage neutrality so that important tax consequences would no longer turn on whether a person was single or married. It also would eliminate some of the disincentive of marriage to second earners—a disincentive that now occurs because the marginal tax rate applicable to the second earner in a married couple depends on the marginal rate of the first earner. However, such a regime would make income tax equality among married couples depend upon the similarity of relative incomes of each spouse rather than similarity in aggregate income of couples.

The 2001 tax legislation contained three provisions that Congress described as "Marriage Penalty Relief Provisions." They include changes in the standard deduction, revisions to the rate schedule for married taxpayers filing joint returns, and adjustments to the earned income tax credit phase-out schedule. Like so much of this legislation, these changes were delayed and phased-in in order to meet revenue constraints imposed by budget resolutions of the Senate. (And like the rest of this legislation, any changes that are in effect on September 30, 2011 cease to apply beginning October 1, 2011 unless extended by a subsequent Congress.)

The 2001 Act increased the standard deduction for a married couple filing a joint return to twice the standard deduction for single people, and it also increased the size of the 15 percent tax rate bracket for married couples filing joint returns to twice the size of the 15 percent rate bracket for single people. Neither of these changes begins to take effect until 2005 and both are not fully effective until 2009. See §§ 63(b) and 1(f)(8). These changes will reduce taxes of married couples whether they are subject to marriage penalties because both spouses are earning relatively similar incomes or instead already enjoy marriage bonuses due to income splitting. These provisions were adopted in lieu of President Bush's proposal for a deduction of a specified amount of income when both spouses work. Obviously, Congress was willing to devote only a limited amount of revenue to redress "marriage penalties." Which approach is better targeted to that problem?

Congress also increased the earned income tax credit phase-out for married couples by $1,000 for the years 2002, 2003, and 2004; $2,000 for the years 2005, 2006, and 2007, and $3,000 beginning in 2008. The 2001 Act also simplified somewhat the EITC's definition of earned income and of an eligible child for a parent to qualify for the credit. And, as indicated above, the 2001 legislation repeals both the personal exemption phaseout and the itemized deduction haircut effective in 2010.

(E) *Why are Married Couples Different?* A number of justifications have been offered for treating married couples differently.

Income Pooling. One historical argument for treating married couples differently is that marriage is an equal partnership in which the couples pool their income and jointly share it. Thus income should be aggregated for tax purposes regardless of how it is actually earned. This treats the couple as an economic unit. It is likely that the extent of income pooling within a marriage has declined over time as spouses are likely to keep separate checking or investment accounts. In addition there are cohabitation arrangements other than marriage in which income is pooled although it would be very difficult to develop a workable definition of an economic unit in which income was shared.

Costs of Children. Another argument for treating married couples differently relates to the additional costs of raising children. Thus, for example, a married couple with children should have a larger standard deduction than a single with the same income. As noted in Chapter 3, supra at page 428, however, the dependency exemption and allowances for child care compensate somewhat for differences in family size (except for high income taxpayers whose exemptions are phased out at least until this rule is repealed in 2010). The personal exemptions alone could be used to differentiate between individuals and families with children; for example, economist Joseph Pechman observed that:

> [i]t would be possible to differentiate among taxpayer units by varying the personal exemptions with the size of income as well as the number of persons in the unit with both a minimum and maximum. This procedure could be used to achieve almost any desired degree of differentiation among families while avoiding [most of] the anomalies produced by income splitting. The tax rates for single persons and married couples could be equalized * * *.

Joseph A. Pechman, Federal Tax Policy 105 (5th ed. 1983).

Does an "additional expenses" rationale suggest that the child care allowance should be a deduction rather than a credit? If the child care credit provides only limited tax relief with respect to these costs, is it appropriate to take these costs into account in setting the rates? How does the special rate schedule in § 1(b) for unmarried heads of households (defined in § 2(b) as taxpayers who maintain households for certain eligible dependents) relate to these issues? Can that provision's lowering of rates be regarded as a surrogate for additional deductions or credits for dependents? If so, what is the special concern here for unmarried individuals?

Recall the discussion of the dependent care credit at page 255 supra. One justification for the credit is to offset dependent care costs that permit a taxpayer to be employed. But another justification is to help to create parity with a stay-at-home parent whose imputed income is untaxed. A prior version of § 21 provided a *deduction* for dependent care expenses incurred by a "woman or widower or * * * a husband whose wife is incapacitated." Charles Moritz, a single man who had never married, paid someone to care for his 89–year old invalid mother, who lived with him. He challenged the constitutionality of a provision that permitted women and widowers to take a deduction but not a single man. The Tenth Circuit agreed that this was invidious discrimination and invalidated the statute. Moritz v. Commissioner, 469 F.2d 466 (10th Cir.1972). This is apparently the only time since *Eisner v. Macomber* was decided in 1920 that a court has invalidated a section of the income tax law on constitutional grounds.

Imputed Income. The failure to tax imputed income is also a major factor in the taxation of married couples. The imputed income, typically from domestic services, in the case of a married couple where only one spouse works for compensation, is not counted along with the other spouse's income either for purposes of determining the applicable bracket or for purposes of calculating the earned income credit threshold. Which couple has more income—and thus more ability to pay taxes: a couple in which one spouse earns $20,000 and the other "earns" nothing but provides $10,000 of domestic services or a couple in which each spouse earns $10,000 and the second wage earner's salary is used to purchase domestic services? Note that under current law, they are taxed the same. An alternative to the administratively impossible task of taxing the imputed income would be to reduce the taxable income of the two-earner couple, with a deduction for the second wage-earner.

This failure to tax imputed income has significant efficiency effects. It may be prohibitively expensive for the second spouse (usually the wife) to enter the labor market. Not only would her salary be subject to income tax, but it will be taxed at a rate set by the primary earner's rate, i.e., her wages are placed on top of the husband's wages in determining the rate bracket. This may skew labor market decisions and reinforce gender bias. These issues are discussed in detail in Edward J. McCaffery, Taxation and the Family: A Fresh Look at Behavioral Gender Biases in the Code, 40 UCLA L.Rev. 983 (1993).

Costs of Working. One argument often made in favor of treating married couples differently is that there are greater costs in earning two incomes than in earning one. Are there such differences that should be taken into account in measuring net income? Is this issue limited to a two-worker couple or does it apply equally well to a single laborer? Aren't these the costs of employment, unrelated to marital status? Doesn't a single person who lives off investment income have greater economic income than a single person who must go to work everyday? In the periods 1924–1931 and 1934–1943 the Code allowed a special earned-income deduction to all taxpayers, without regard to marital status.

(F) *Family or Individual?* If an income tax is to be based on "ability to pay," then an initial question is whose ability to pay is relevant—that of the individual or the family. For equity purposes, this translates to whether we want to compare the economic wherewithal of families or individuals. Even if it might be more equitable to compare families, that might be administratively difficult. What should count as a family for this purpose? An unmarried cohabiting couple? A same-sex couple? A couple and an elderly mother-in-law?

Those who favor taxing the consolidated income of a family unit emphasize that the ability of parents to pay taxes differs depending on whether their children have income of their own. The parents' obligation to provide food, clothing, and other items of support for their children may well decrease as the children's own earnings increase. The parents of Aaron Carter, for example, probably have a greater ability to pay than do the parents of a less successful child.

Proposals for a family unit of taxation have been criticized for placing a burden on parents to account for the babysitting and paper route earnings of their children. Who should be penalized if parents unwittingly fail to report the income of their teenager from dealing in marijuana or other drugs? See, e.g., Bassett v. Commissioner, 100 T.C. 650 (1993), where the parents of the actress Skye Bassett were subject to a negligence penalty for failing to file a return reporting her acting fees. Some have argued that family taxation might create a disincentive to productive employment among the children of wealthy families because the earnings of a rich child with a paper route would be taxed more heavily than would the earnings of a poor child with a paper route.

Under current law, a child is considered a separate taxpayer and the child's earned income is not aggregated with the rest of the family even if it pooled to pay household expenses. § 73. The income tax liability of a minor child generally is computed in the same manner as that of an adult. The child is entitled to a personal exemption and standard deduction, except that this latter amount cannot exceed the child's earned income if the child can be claimed as a dependent by another taxpayer. If the parents are entitled to claim the exemption—even if they do not actually do so—the dependent child may not. § 151(d)(2).

If, however, the taxation of the child were wholly divorced from the parent's treatment, any unearned income of the child, such as dividend or interest income, in excess of the amount of the personal exemption would be taxable to the child at his or her marginal rate. This would produce a significant incentive for high income parents (and grandparents) to shift income producing assets to their lower-bracket children.

The so-called "kiddie tax," § 1(g), is a major step in the direction of taxation based on family income, by providing restrictions on the intrafamily shifting of income and tax benefits and a rate structure under which the same rate is likely to apply to the income of all family members. The section provides that "net unearned income" of children under age 14 (as of the end of the taxable year) is taxed at their parents' top marginal rate, regardless of the source of the unearned income. Net unearned income for this purpose is unearned income in excess of $650 reduced by the greater of $650 or the amount of allowable deductions that are directly connected with the production of the unearned income. The two amounts are adjusted for inflation. Note that investment income on a gift from Dad is treated identically to interest income on a savings account funded with the earnings of a paper route.

In combination, these rules mean that a minimum of $1,200 of a child's unearned income is not subject to the kiddie tax and is taxed at the child's rather than the parent's marginal tax rate. Any greater amount of unearned income, however, is taxed at the parent's rate, thus eliminating the income-shifting incentive. Once the child reaches the age of 14, the incentive to shift income is present. (Perhaps this reflects Congress' understanding that parents should be entitled to a tax reduction for having a teenager in the household).

Under limited circumstances, parents may elect to report the gross income of a child in excess of $1,000 on their own return. § 1(g)(7). Under this election, the first $650 of unearned income is still not taxed; the next $650 is taxed at 15 percent, and any excess is taxed at the parents' marginal rate. § 1(g)(7)(B). Such an election generally excuses the child from filing her own return. The election is permitted where the child has income between $500 and $5,000 only from interest and dividends. (A good exercise in reading the Code is to determine where the $5,000 amount comes from.)

(G) *Innocent Spouse.* Where income and deductions are reported correctly, spouses are jointly and severally liable for the tax liability when a joint return is filed. Where, however, there is an understatement of tax due to the omission of income or erroneous deductions by one spouse and the "innocent" spouse did not and had no reason to know of the mistakes, the innocent spouse is not responsible for the liability attributable to the errors. § 6015. Generally, the innocent spouse must show that she or he did not benefit from the omitted items.

Section 66 relieves a so-called "innocent spouse" from taxation on community income received but not shared by the other spouse. The taxpayer is not required to report such income if he establishes that he had no knowledge of his spouse's income and that it would be inequitable to include the item in his income (for example, because he did not benefit from the income). The provision does not apply if the spouses filed a joint return.

B.   DISSOLUTION OF THE FAMILY—SEPARATION AND DIVORCE

Having decided that marital status is relevant in determining tax liability, it is obviously necessary to determine whether a taxpayer is married. Recall the discussion in Chapter 3, supra at 429, in which the various provisions relating to the determination of marital status were outlined. The Code provides that a couple will no longer be considered "married" for federal tax purposes if they are divorced. § 7703(a)(2). As we previously saw, where the earnings of both spouses are approximately equal, there will be a marriage penalty if the spouses file jointly. Thus, there is an incentive to divorce for tax purposes. The following ruling deals with tax-motivated divorces.

Revenue Ruling 76–255

Internal Revenue Service, 1976. 1976–2 C.B. 40.

* * *

Advice has been requested concerning the marital status of certain taxpayers for Federal income tax purposes under the circumstances described below.

SITUATION 1

A and B were married in 1975 and filed a joint 1975 Federal income tax return on April 15, 1976, which included their combined incomes. On April 16, 1976, a state court of competent jurisdiction annulled the marriage and decreed that no valid marriage ever existed.

SITUATION 2

C and D were married in 1964 and filed joint Federal income tax returns for the years 1964 through 1974. In 1975, C and D determined that for Federal income tax purposes it would be advantageous for them to be unmarried so that each of them could file a separate Federal income tax return as an unmarried individual.

On December 30, 1975, C and D secured a divorce under the laws of a foreign jurisdiction. For purposes of this ruling, it is assumed that such divorce was valid. However, at the time of the divorce, they intended to remarry each other and did so in January 1976.

Section 143(a)(1) of the Internal Revenue Code of 1954 provides generally that the determination of whether an individual is married shall be made as of the close of the taxable year.

Section 6013 of the Code permits a husband and wife to file a joint income tax return.

Section 1.143–1(a) and section 1.6013–4(a) of the Income Tax Regulations provide that status as husband and wife under these sections is determined as of the close of the year for two individuals having the same taxable year. These sections also provide that an individual shall be considered as married even though living apart from the individual's spouse unless legally separated under a decree of divorce or separate maintenance.

Rev.Rul. 67–442, 1967–2 C.B. 65, provides that the Internal Revenue Service generally will not question for Federal income tax purposes the validity of any divorce decree until a court of competent jurisdiction declares the divorce to be invalid.

In *Situation 1,* a state court having competent jurisdiction has annulled the marriage and, in accordance with state law, has decreed that no valid marriage ever existed.

Accordingly, since no valid marriage ever existed *A* and *B* were single individuals as of the close of the taxable year 1975. Thus, they must file amended Federal income tax returns for 1975 as unmarried individuals.

In *Situation 2,* although *C* and *D* were divorced under the laws of the foreign jurisdiction, the divorce was not intended by them to have effect except to enable them to qualify as unmarried individuals who would be eligible to file separate returns. In addition, *C* and *D* intended to and did remarry each other early in the succeeding taxable year.

The true nature of a transaction must be considered in light of the plain intent and purpose of the statute. Such transaction should not be given any effect for Federal income tax purposes if it merely serves the purpose of tax avoidance. In determining whether it serves the purpose of tax avoidance all of the surrounding facts and circumstances are to be considered. Neither section 143 nor section 6013 of the Code or the applicable regulations thereunder contemplates a "sham transaction" designed to manipulate for Federal income tax purposes an individual's marital status as of the close of a taxable year. See Gregory v. Helvering, 293 U.S. 465 (1935), XIV–1 C.B. 193 (1935).

Accordingly, *C* and *D* for purposes of sections 143 and 6013 of the Code were married individuals as of the close of the taxable year 1975. Therefore, for 1975 they must file either a joint Federal income tax return or separate returns using rules for married individuals filing separate returns.

NOTES

(A) *Marital Status.* The Code contains special rules for determining marital status and they do not always conform to state law. For example, an individual's marital status is generally determined at year end. Thus, a taxpayer who marries on New Year's Eve is treated as having been married for the entire year. Similarly, a taxpayer whose spouse dies midyear is treated as married at year end. Conversely, a taxpayer who divorces before the end of the year is treated as being unmarried for the entire year. § 7703(a).

In some circumstances, taxpayers who are married for state law purposes are treated as if they were unmarried for federal tax purposes. For example, a taxpayer married to a nonresident alien can qualify for head of household status because he is treated as not being married. § 2(b)(2)(C). In the case of married individuals living apart, the Code often treats one spouse very favorably and the other less so. A married spouse who for the last six months of the taxable year did not live with a spouse, but did maintain for more than one-half the taxable year a home in which s/he lived with a dependent child is not considered married. § 7703(b). Ironically, if the other spouse does not live with a child, he continues to be treated as married. In a scheme Groucho Marx would appreciate, this results in a taxpayer being married to someone who is not considered his spouse.

A number of Code provisions rely on a determination that the taxpayer and his spouse "live apart." See, e.g. § 21(e)(4) and § 2(c). When it is to his benefit, a taxpayer may argue that he and his spouse are not members of the same household even though they live in the same house. This generally involves the introduction of fairly sordid testimony about sleeping habits and the like. The courts generally decline to weigh such evidence, preferring to take at face value the relationship of a married couple under one roof. See, e.g, McAdams v. Commissioner, 118 T.C. No. 24 (2002) (in responding to the taxpayer's argument that separate bedrooms constituted "living apart," the judge "declined to explore the quality of a marriage").

(B) *Sham Divorces.* This ruling abandons the notion that local law will be used to determine marital status and instead appears to create a federal definition of "divorce." See also Boyter v. Commissioner, 74 T.C. 989 (1980), remanded 668 F.2d 1382 (4th Cir.1981). Although the Tax Court adopted much of the reasoning of Rev.Rul. 76–255, the Fourth Circuit remanded for consideration of the applicability of the sham transaction doctrine. In other contexts, the sham transaction doctrine has been used to invalidate a transaction that has no real economic substance other than the tax consequences. Recall *Knetsch,* discussed supra at page 363. Is a "sham" divorce a transaction in which there are no significant nontax effects? In *Boyter,* the couple was divorced for 32 days during the first year in issue and 79 days during the second year. If Mr. Boyter had died during that period, it is unlikely that "Mrs." Boyter could have collected his pension. Nor would Mr. Boyter have been entitled to a marital deduction on his estate tax return for amounts left to "Mrs." Boyter.

(C) *Decree of Divorce.* What is a "decree of divorce" as that term is used in § 7703? Estate of Borax v. Commissioner, 349 F.2d 666 (2d Cir.1965), cert. denied 383 U.S. 935 (1966), involved a couple who had been married in New York. Later they separated and entered into a separation agreement. Thereafter, the husband obtained an ex parte divorce in Mexico. The wife had been notified of the Mexican proceeding, but did not appear there. The husband then married another woman, first in Mexico and later in Connecticut.

The first wife promptly brought an action in New York for a declaratory judgment that she was still married to the husband. This was fully litigated in New York and resulted in a decree in favor of the first wife. The husband nevertheless continued to live with the second wife and to make periodic payments to the first wife as provided in the separation agreement. The IRS disallowed the deduction of alimony payments to the first wife on the ground that they were not made under a separation agreement "incident to * * * a decree of divorce." The Second Circuit ruled that the payments were deductible although the divorce had been held invalid in New York. Cf. Ry Cooder, "It's a Sin to Get a Mexican Divorce," Paradise and Lunch (1971); hear also Steely Dan, "Haitian Divorce," The Royal Scam (1976).

But see Rev.Rul. 67–442, 1967–2 C.B. 65, indicating that, where a state court with jurisdiction declares a prior divorce to be invalid, the IRS will usually follow this declaration, rather than the prior divorce decree, for federal tax purposes. Likewise, the Ninth Circuit has held that the law of the state of the taxpayer's domicile should be used to determine marital status for purposes of the federal income tax. See Lee v. Commissioner, 550 F.2d 1201 (9th Cir.1977); see also Estate of Goldwater v. Commissioner, 539 F.2d 878 (2d Cir.1976) (acknowledging that the Second Circuit opinion in *Borax* had been criticized by legal scholars and might have "cavalierly ignore[d] local law" and emphasizing that *"Borax* explicitly limits its holding to the income tax issue there involved and does not purport to set forth a universal rule of tax code construction").

NOTE ON THE TAX TREATMENT OF ALIMONY AND CHILD SUPPORT PAYMENTS AND PROPERTY SETTLEMENTS UPON DIVORCE

When the family unit dissolves, difficult issues arise in determining who should be taxed on the income. Suppose, for example, that the husband is ordered to pay alimony out of his wages to the former wife and to make child support payments. Should the husband be taxed on the wages because he earned them or should the wife and/or children be taxed because they enjoyed the consumption? Suppose that the husband transfers appreciated property as part of a property settlement in exchange for the wife's marital rights. Should the gain on the property be taxed? The Code now provides answers to these questions, but in many respects, divorced spouses have considerable leeway in allocating the tax burden between themselves. Since both parties always are concerned with their after-tax economic position, tax planning is an important aspect of legal advice relating to divorce. Technical expertise and great care in structuring separation and divorce agreements remain necessary.

1.   ALIMONY AND SUPPORT PAYMENTS

Throughout most of the history of the income tax, payments made from a spouse to a former spouse have been taxable to one, but not both, spouses. Prior to 1942, alimony paid to a divorced spouse was not includible in the recipient's gross income and was treated as a nondeductible personal expense of the payor. See Gould v. Gould, 245 U.S. 151 (1917). In 1942, Congress reversed that rule by requiring that certain alimony payments be included in the recipient spouse's income and permitting the payor-spouse to deduct those payments. Although Congress has tinkered with those rules on a number of occasions since, that pattern—taxation of the recipient of alimony and a deduction for the payor—essentially still holds. On the other hand, payments for child support and property settlements are generally nondeductible to the payor and excludable by the recipient.

Section 71 permits payments—whether in discharge of alimony or support obligations or property rights—to be treated as deductible alimony so long as (1) the payments are in cash rather than property or services; (2) the parties do not earmark payments as nondeductible to the payor and nontaxable to the payee; (3) the parties do not live in the same household if they are already legally divorced or separated; (4) there is no liability for any payment after the death of the payee; and (5) the payments do not constitute child support. Alimony that is taxable to the recipient is deductible to the payor. § 215.

Prior to the adoption of current § 71, there was much controversy over whether payments were alimony or property settlements. The current requirements provide arbitrary, but usually certain results. The requirement that payments be in cash reflects the fact that alimony is generally payable in cash, whereas property settlements are often in kind. All transfers of property are covered by § 1041 (discussed below) and are neither deductible by the transferor nor includible by the transferee. The requirement that alimony payments cease at the recipient spouse's death (although not at the payor's death) replaced an often-controversial requirement of prior law that alimony payments be periodic. An agreement to pay the other spouse's attorney fees generally would not be deductible because the obligation would not be extinguished on the death of the spouse.

Parties may elect to treat alimony payments as nondeductible to the payor and nontaxable to the payee so that the two parties will pay the lowest total tax. § 71(b)(1)(B). This election simplifies tax planning by allowing a lower-bracket payor to make nondeductible excludable payments to a higher-bracket recipient spouse. This is relatively rare, but might occur, for example, where the payor is effectively tax-exempt because of business losses. The couple cannot agree to treat as deductible/includible payments that do not otherwise qualify as alimony.

Payments that are designated for the support of the couple's children are nondeductible to the payor and nontaxable to the payee. Thus, alimony must be distinguished from child support. It is sometimes unclear whether payments are intended for the support of the former spouse, the children or both.

The statute treats as nondeductible child support any amount that will be reduced (1) upon the occurrence of events relating to the child specified in the divorce instrument, such as marriage, graduation from school or attainment of a certain age or income level or (2) at a time "clearly associated" with such an event. § 71(c).

Section 71(f) contains an additional limitation to prevent the parties from structuring a property settlement to qualify as alimony. Property settlements are usually paid in a lump sum shortly after the divorce while alimony generally is paid over a longer period of time. Section 71(f) prevents a payor from frontloading alimony payments, i.e., making "alimony" payments shortly after the divorce that are significantly larger than payments in later years. Any excess alimony payments must be included in the payor's gross income in the third post-separation year and the recipient can deduct a like amount. There may be excess alimony in the first post-separation year as well as the second post-separation year and both are included in income in the third year. The "excess alimony" for the second post-separation year is the excess of the second-year payments over the sum of the third-year payments plus $15,000. The "excess alimony" for the first post-separation year is the excess of the first-year payment over the average of the second and third year payments plus $15,000. The average of the second and third year payments is computed by reducing the second-year payment by any recapture amount. The following example illustrates how the recapture rule works:

> *Example*: The actual payments made by W to H are $40,000 in Year 1, $25,000 in Year 2 and zero in Year 3. The excess alimony in Year 2 is $10,000 (the excess of $25,000 over [0 + $15,000]). The average alimony for Year 2 and Year 3 is $7,500 [($25,000 − $10,000) + 0 /2]. The excess alimony for Year 1 is therefore $27,500 [$50,000 − ($7,500 + $15,000)]. In Year 3, W recaptures $37,500 ($10,000 + $27,500), which she reports as gross income. H would have a deduction of $37,500 in Year 3 as well.

This recapture rule does not apply if annual alimony payments are less than $15,000, apparently to relieve low and moderate income families from the complexities. Even the underlying logic of the rules is somewhat mysterious. Although the provision is intended to preclude deductions of property settlements as alimony, there seems to be no good reason either to require alimony payments not to vary by more than $10,000, or to require the payments not to vary by more than $15,000 for three years, as the provision does.

Payments to a third party on behalf of one's former spouse—as for tuition, rent or taxes—may qualify as alimony if made pursuant to a divorce or separation agreement. Premiums for term or whole life insurance on the life of the payor similarly may be treated as alimony to the extent that the former spouse is the owner of the policy.

Alimony is deducted from gross income in determining adjusted gross income. Thus, the deduction can be claimed even by taxpayers who do not itemize their deductions. § 62(a)(10). As a result, alimony is allowed as a deduction in addition to the standard deduction and is not subject to the 2 percent floor for miscellaneous itemized deductions.

2. PROPERTY SETTLEMENTS

Under prior law, a taxpayer recognized gain (but not loss) on the transfer of property to a spouse (or former spouse) in exchange for the release of marital claims. The recipient received a basis in the property equal to its fair market value. United States v. Davis, 370 U.S. 65 (1962). These rules did not apply to the equal division of community property or to the partition of jointly-held property. This distinction produced considerable litigation and caused some states to amend their property laws in an attempt to avoid the *Davis* result.

Section 1041 now provides that no gain or loss is to be recognized on any transfer of property between spouses or on a transfer incident to divorce between former spouses. This rule applies regardless of whether the transfer was of community or separately-owned property or whether it was for consideration. The recipient takes a carryover basis in the property equal to the adjusted basis of the transferor. This rule is different from the usual rule treating the satisfaction of a debt with appreciated property as a taxable transaction. In effect, the transfer between spouses is treated the same as a gift, regardless of the transferor's motivation or intent. The transferee's basis is a carryover basis regardless of the value of the transferred property. Thus, unlike the gift basis rule of § 1015, one spouse can transfer a loss to another spouse.

The reasons for these changes were explained in the House Ways and Means Committee Report as follows:

> The committee believes that, in general, it is inappropriate to tax transfers between spouses. This policy * * * reflects the fact that a husband and wife are a single economic unit.

> The current rules governing transfers of property between spouses or former spouses incident to divorce have not worked well and have led to much controversy and litigation. Often the rules have proved a trap for the unwary * * *.

> Furthermore, in divorce cases, the government often gets whipsawed. The transferor will not report any gain on the transfer, while the recipient spouse, when he or she sells, is entitled under the *Davis* rule to compute his or her gain or loss by reference to a basis equal to the fair market value of the property at the time received.

H.Rep. 432, 98th Cong., 2d Sess. 1491–92 (1984).

Under § 1041, a transfer is treated as incident to divorce if it occurs within one year after the marriage ceased or if it is related to the cessation of the marriage. Temporary regulations state that a transfer of property generally will be treated as related to the cessation of the marriage if it is made under a divorce or separation instrument and occurs not more than six years after the end of the marriage. Temp. Reg. § 1.1041–1T(b) Q–7.

While these rules reduce a divorcing couple's immediate overall tax liability, they are generally favorable to transferors, who do not have to recognize gain on the transfer of appreciated property, and unfavorable to transferees, who are required to recognize larger capital gains or recapture ordinary income when they ultimately dispose of the property in a taxable transaction. Bargaining between the parties should take this consequence into account.

A spouse may discharge an alimony obligation by creating or transferring a beneficial interest in a trust. Indeed, wealthy taxpayers originated such "alimony trusts" as an income-shifting device in the era before an alimony deduction was permitted by the Code.

The taxation of alimony trusts now is governed by the general trust rules of § 682. The income from the trust is generally taxable to the recipient spouse—unless, for example, no tax is imposed because the income is derived from tax-exempt sources such as municipal bonds. See Ellis v. United States, 416 F.2d 894 (6th Cir.1969) (tax-exempt trust income is not taxable to payee spouse). The grantor receives no deduction for the creation of the trust, but is not taxable on income generated by the trust corpus. The grantor is taxable, however, on the income of a trust established to discharge his or her child support obligations. Section 1041(e) provides that in the case of a transfer in trust where the liabilities assumed by the trust plus the amount of the liabilities to which the property is subject exceed the adjusted basis of the property, the transferor must recognize the excess as gain, and the transferee's basis will be adjusted upward to reflect the gain recognized.

NOTES

(A) *Decree or Written Separation Agreement.* Payments are deductible as alimony only if made pursuant to a court decree or a written separation agreement. For example, the husband in Harlow v. Commissioner, 48 T.C.M. 661 (1984), sent his estranged wife a letter stating that he would pay her $1,500 a month. She did not acknowledge the letter, but did accept the money. The Tax Court held that the letter was merely a unilateral offer to make support payments and did not qualify as a written separation agreement under § 71. See also Rev.Rul. 82–155, 1982–2 C.B. 36 (taxpayer denied alimony deduction once his legal obligation to make payments was terminated by remarriage of his former wife, whether he knew of her remarriage or not).

(B) *Delinquent Payments.* Section 71(c)(3) provides that delinquent payments by a former spouse are to be applied first against past-due child support and then against past-due alimony. If the payor spouse fails to make the alimony or child support payments, does the disappointed spouse have a bad debt deduction? Since the recipient, generally a cash basis taxpayer, has not included the missing payments in income, she has no basis and thus is not entitled to a deduction under § 166. Perry v. Commissioner, 92 T.C. 470 (1989), affirmed 912 F.2d 1466 (5th Cir.1990), cert. denied, 499 U.S. 938 (1991).

(C) *Dependency Exemptions and Medical Deductions.* The tax implications of divorce settlements also involve the entitlement to the dependency exemption for the couple's children. This deduction goes to the custodial parent unless the parties agree that it is to go to the noncustodial parent. § 152(e)(1).

A parent who pays the medical bills of his or her child can qualify for the medical expense deduction if the child is a dependent of either parent. § 213(a)(4). The 7.5 percent floor for medical expense deductions bars deduction for most such expenses; however, it typically will be easier for the parent with lower adjusted gross income to meet this floor and take the deduction.

(D) *Why Allow an Alimony Deduction?* Are the alimony provisions structured appropriately? The fundamental question is which treatment—deduction/inclusion or nondeduction/exclusion—better reflects the abilities of the former spouses to meet their tax liabilities. Is the deduction for the payor an inappropriate departure from the notion that earnings should be taxed to the earner? Or would a failure to tax the recipient be a departure from the usual rule that one who consumes or saves should be taxed? Can the deduction be justified as an incentive to former spouses to satisfy their obligations to make alimony payments?

Now that spouses can elect either treatment, is there likely to be unwarranted shifting of income from those in higher tax brackets to those in lower tax brackets? How much opportunity is there for income shifting?

C.   ANTENUPTIAL AGREEMENTS

Farid–Es–Sultaneh v. Commissioner

United States Court of Appeals for the Second Circuit, 1947. 160 F.2d 812.

CHASE, JUDGE:

* * *

In December 1923 when the petitioner, then unmarried, and S. S. Kresge, then married, were contemplating their future marriage, he delivered to her 700 shares of the common stock of the S. S. Kresge Company which then had a fair market value of $290 per share. The shares were * * * to be held by the petitioner 'for her benefit and protection in the event that the said Kresge should die prior to the contemplated marriage between the petitioner and said Kresge.' The latter was divorced from his wife on January 9, 1924, and on or about January 23, 1924 he delivered to the petitioner 1800 additional common shares of S. S. Kresge Company which * * * were to be held by the petitioner for the same purposes as were the first 700 shares he had delivered to her. On April 24, 1924, and when the petitioner still retained the possession of the stock so delivered to her, she and Mr. Kresge executed a written ante-nuptial agreement wherein she acknowledged the receipt of the shares 'as a gift made by the said Sebastian S. Kresge, pursuant to this indenture, and as an ante-nuptial settlement, and in consideration of said gift and said ante-nuptial settlement, in consideration of the promise of said Sebastian S. Kresge to marry her, and in further consideration of the consummation of said promised marriage' she released all dower and other marital rights, including the right to her support to which she otherwise would have been entitled as a matter of law when she became his wife. They were married in New York immediately after the ante-nuptial agreement was executed and continued to be husband and wife until the petitioner obtained a final decree of absolute divorce from him on, or about, May 18, 1928. No alimony was claimed by, or awarded to, her.

* * * Her adjusted basis for the stock she sold in 1938 was $10.66 2/3 per share computed on the basis of the fair market value of the shares which she obtained from Mr. Kresge. * * * His adjusted basis for the shares she sold in 1938 would have been $0.159091.

When the petitioner and Mr. Kresge were married he was 57 years old with a life expectancy of 16 ½ years. She was then 32 years of age with a life expectancy of 33 3/4 years. He was then worth approximately $375,000,000 and owned real estate of the approximate value of $100,000,000.

The Commissioner determined the deficiency on the ground that the petitioner's stock * * * was acquired by gift within the meaning of that word as used in [§ 102], and * * * used as the basis for determining the gain on her sale * * * the basis it would have had in the hands of the donor. This was correct if [§ 1015] * * * is applicable, and the Tax Court held it was * * *.

[A] transfer * * * solely in consideration of [a prospective wife's] promise of marriage, and to compensate her for loss of trust income which would cease upon her marriage, was not for an adequate and full consideration in money or money's worth within the meaning of the [the gift tax statute] the Tax Court having found that the transfer was not one at arm's length made in the ordinary course of business. But we find nothing in this decision to show that a transfer, taxable as a gift under the gift tax, is ipso facto to be treated as a gift in construing the income tax law.

* * * Although Congress in 1932 also expressly provided that the release of marital rights should not be treated as a consideration in money or money's worth in administering the estate tax law, and failed to include [such] a provision in the gift tax statute [the Supreme Court] held that the gift tax law should be construed to the same effect.

We find in this decision no indication, however, that the term "gift" as used in the income tax statute should be construed to include a transfer which, if made when the gift tax were effective, would be taxable to the transferor as a gift merely because of the special provisions in the gift tax statute defining and restricting consideration for gift tax purposes. * * *

In our opinion the income tax provisions are not to be construed as though they were in pari materia with either the estate tax law or the gift tax statutes. They are aimed at the gathering of revenue by taking for the public use given percentages of what the statute fixes as net taxable income. Capital gains and losses are * * * factors in determining net taxable income. What is known as the basis for computing gain or loss on transfers of property is established by statute in those instances when the resulting gain or loss is recognized for income tax purposes. * * * When Congress provided that gifts should not be treated as taxable income to the donee there was, without any correlative provisions fixing the basis of the gift to the donee, a loophole which enabled the donee to make a subsequent transfer of the property and take as the basis for computing gain or loss its value when the gift was made. Thus it was possible to exclude from taxation any increment in value during the donor's holding and the donee might take advantage of any shrinkage in such increment after the acquisition by gift in computing gain or loss upon a subsequent sale or exchange. It was to close this loophole that Congress provided that the donee should take the donor's basis when property was transferred by gift. * * * Because of this we think that a transfer which should be classed as a gift under the gift tax law is not necessarily to be treated as a gift income-tax-wise. Though such a consideration as this petitioner gave for the shares of stock she acquired from Mr. Kresge might not have relieved him from liability for a gift tax, had the present gift tax then been in effect, it was nevertheless a fair consideration which prevented her taking the shares as a gift under the income tax law since it precluded the existence of a donative intent.

Although the transfers of the stock * * * by Mr. Kresge to this taxpayer are called a gift in the ante-nuptial agreement later executed and were to be for the protection of his prospective bride if he died before the marriage was consummated, the "gift" was contingent upon his death before such marriage, an event that did not occur. Consequently, it would appear that no absolute gift was made before the ante-nuptial contract was executed and that she took title to the stock under its terms, viz: in consideration for her promise to marry him coupled with her promise to relinquish all rights in and to his property which she would otherwise acquire by the marriage. Her inchoate interest in the property of her affianced husband greatly exceeded the value of the stock transferred to her. It was a fair consideration under ordinary legal concepts of that term for the transfers of the stock by him. She performed the contract under the terms of which the stock was transferred to her and held the shares not as a donee but as a purchaser for a fair consideration.

* * *

Decision reversed.

CLARK, CIRCUIT JUDGE (dissenting):

The opinion accepts two assumptions, both necessary to the result. The first is that definitions of gift under the gift and estate tax statutes are not useful, in fact are directly opposed to, definitions of gift under the capital-gains provision of the income tax statute. The second is that the circumstances here of a transfer of the stock some months before the marriage showed, contrary to the conclusions of the Tax Court, a purchase of dower rights, rather than a gift. The first I regard as doubtful; the second, as untenable.

It is true that [the Supreme Court decisions] which would require the transactions here to be considered a gift, dealt with estate and gift taxes. But no strong reason has been advanced why what is a gift under certain sections of the Revenue Code should not be a gift under yet another section.* * * The Congressional purpose would seem substantially identical—to prevent a gap in the law whereby taxes on gifts or on capital gains could be avoided or reduced by judicious transfers within the family or intimate group.

But decision on that point might well be postponed, since, in my mind, the other point should be decisive. Kresge transferred the stock to petitioner more than three months before their marriage. Part was given when Kresge was married to another woman. At these times petitioner had no dower or other rights in his property. If Kresge died before the wedding, she could never secure dower rights in his lands. Yet she would nevertheless keep the stock. Indeed the specifically stated purpose of the transfer was to protect her against his death prior to marriage. It is therefore difficult to perceive how her not yet acquired rights could be consideration for the stock. Apparently the parties themselves shared this difficulty, for in their subsequent instrument releasing dower rights they referred to the stock transfer as a gift and an antenuptial settlement.

If the transfer be thus considered a sale, as the majority hold, it would seem to follow necessarily that this valuable consideration (equivalent to one-third for life in land valued at one hundred million dollars) should have yielded sizable taxable capital gains to Kresge, as well as a capital loss to petitioner when eventually she sold. I suggest these considerations as pointing to the unreality of holding as a sale what seems clearly only intended as a stimulating cause to eventual matrimony.

NOTES

(A) *Tax Consequences to Doris Farid–Es–Sultaneh.* Ms. Farid–Es–Sultaneh apparently did not realize any gain on the transfer of her marital rights in exchange for the stock. Why? Rev.Rul. 67–221, 1967–2 C.B. 63 held that there is no gain when marital rights are relinquished, but provides no analysis of why there is no gain. Is there any statutory authority for this exclusion? It seems that Ms. Farid–Es–Sultaneh did not strike a particularly good bargain, i.e., the value of what she might have inherited or received on divorce from Kresge was much greater than the value of the Kresge stock. Does that matter?

(B) *Tax Consequences to S.S. Kresge.* What were the tax consequences to Mr. Kresge in 1924 when he transferred the stock to Ms. Farid–Es–Sultaneh? Recall the discussion of *United States v. Davis*, supra at page 484. If Mr. Kresge had died after the stock transfer but before marrying Ms. Farid–Es–Sultaneh, what would he have received "in exchange" for the stock? Could Mr. Kresge claim that he had made a gift?

(C) *Section 1041.* Section 1041 only applies to transfers between spouses or transfers incident to a divorce. It generally therefore would not apply to a transfer made prior to marriage pursuant to an antenuptial agreement. If the antenuptial agreement had been signed at the conclusion of the wedding ceremony or had provided that Ms. Farid–Es–Sultaneh would receive the stock only after her marriage to Kresge, would the result be the same under current law?

Is there any justification for the disparate treatment between antenuptial agreements and transfers between spouses (or former spouses)? Is there a reason why transfers in contemplation of marriage should not be treated similarly to gifts under § 1041?

(D) *Unmarried Cohabitants.* There are no special provisions to govern the tax treatment of support payments or property settlements upon separation of unmarried cohabitants. Support payments thus would not be deductible to the payor and would be taxable to the recipient if determined to be something other than a gift.

Professor Michael Asimow suggests that the parties would not have to recognize gain or loss on an equal division of jointly-held property but might have to do so if one party took some pieces of jointly-held property while the other party took the remainder. The principle of *Davis* presumably would require the recognition of gain or loss on the transfer of separately-held property. Section 1041 does not apply. It is possible that the full value of the property might have to be included in the income of the recipient as a contractual payment or a "windfall" or compensation, rather than a gift, especially if the property division was hotly disputed. Professor Asimow points out that "cohabitants might consider getting married solely for the purpose of making a tax-free property division." Michael Asimow, Practice Under the 1984 Domestic Relations Tax Reform Act (1984).

In Reynolds v. Commissioner, 79 T.C.M. 1376 (2000), a woman had no gain when her former companion of 24 years transferred property to her in exchange for her interest in the property. The court agreed with the IRS that § 1041 did not apply and noted that there would be gain if the sales price exceeded her basis. Nevertheless, her basis was deemed to be at least equal to value. Rejecting the IRS argument that her relationship was a business arrangement and that she was paid for services rendered to the companion, the court found that she had acquired her interest as a gift and therefore her basis was equal to his basis.

SECTION 2.   ASSIGNMENTS OF INCOME IN GENERAL

This Section of this Chapter details the basic income tax rules that govern the attribution of income to taxpayers. In general, two basic principles emerge from the materials that follow: (1) earned income is taxable to the person who earns it and (2) income from property is taxable to the owner of the property. The classic cases that produced these basic rules are presented here along with some modern applications.

A.   INCOME FROM SERVICES

Lucas v. Earl

Supreme Court of the United States, 1930. 281 U.S. 111.

MR. JUSTICE HOLMES delivered the opinion of the Court.

This case presents the question whether the respondent, Earl, could be taxed for the whole of the salary and attorney's fees earned by him in the years 1920 and 1921, or should be taxed for only a half of them in view of a contract with his wife which we shall mention. The Commissioner of Internal Revenue and the Board of Tax Appeals imposed a tax upon the whole, but their decision was reversed by the Circuit Court of Appeals, 30 F.(2d) 898. * * *

By the contract, made in 1901, Earl and his wife agreed "that any property either of us now has or may hereafter acquire * * * in any way, either by earnings (including salaries, fees, etc.), or any rights by contract or otherwise, during the existence of our marriage, or which we or either of us may receive by gift, bequest, devise, or inheritance, and all the proceeds, issues, and profits of any and all such property shall be treated and considered, and hereby is declared to be received, held, taken, and owned by us as joint tenants, and not otherwise, with the right of survivorship." The validity of the contract is not questioned, and we assume it to be unquestionable under the law of the State of California, in which the parties lived. Nevertheless we are of opinion that the Commissioner and Board of Tax Appeals were right.

The Revenue Act of 1918 * * * imposes a tax upon the net income of every individual including "income derived from salaries, wages, or compensation for personal service * * * of whatever kind and in whatever form paid," sec. 213(a). The provisions of the Revenue Act of 1921 * * * are similar to those of the above. A very forcible argument is presented to the effect that the statute seeks to tax only income beneficially received, and that taking the question more technically the salary and fees become the joint property of Earl and his wife on the very first instant on which they were received. We well might hesitate upon the latter proposition, because however the matter might stand between husband and wife he was the only party to the contracts by which the salary and fees were earned, and it is somewhat hard to say that the last step in the performance of those contracts could be taken by anyone but himself alone. But this case is not to be decided by attenuated subtleties. It turns on the import and reasonable construction of the taxing act. There is no doubt that the statute could tax salaries to those who earned them and provide that the tax could not be escaped by anticipatory arrangements and contracts however skillfully devised to prevent the salary when paid from vesting even for a second in the man who earned it. That seems to us the import of the statute before us and we think that no distinction can be taken according to the motives leading to the arrangement by which the fruits are attributed to a different tree from that on which they grew.

Judgment reversed.

THE CHIEF JUSTICE took no part in this case.

NOTES

(A) *Relationship to the Joint Return Provisions.* The tax results that Mr. and Mrs. Earl could not achieve by contract today routinely are achieved by married couples through use of the joint return provisions described in the first Section of this Chapter. Consider also the decision of the Supreme Court in Poe v. Seaborn, 282 U.S. 101 (1930), discussed in the *Druker* case, supra at page 467, which held that, in community property states, each spouse was taxable on one-half of community income, even if it was earned solely by one of the spouses.

The principle of *Lucas v. Earl* nonetheless continues to prevent taxpayers from otherwise assigning earned income to those whose services did not produce the income. Was Mrs. Earl also taxed on the receipt of the income? If not, why not?

(B) *Income Splitting and Assignments Between Unmarried Cohabitants.* Unmarried cohabitants are required to file separate tax returns using the single or head of household rate schedule, whichever is appropriate. This rule operates to their advantage if their incomes are relatively equal because they would incur a "marriage penalty" if they formalized their relationship.

What if the cohabitants entered into an income-pooling agreement similar to that in *Lucas v. Earl*? Income shifted as a result of such an arrangement would be taxed to the person who earned it and again to the person who received it unless the payments could be shown to have resulted from "detached and disinterested generosity" and therefore be excluded under § 102 as a gift. See Pascarelli v. Commissioner, 55 T.C. 1082 (1971), affirmed 485 F.2d 681 (3d Cir.1973) (holding that gifts made by taxpayer to a woman with whom he was living were gifts and not compensation for services rendered to his business).

(C) *Other Assignments of Earned Income.* In Armantrout v. Commissioner, 67 T.C. 996, affd 570 F.2d 210 (7th Cir.1978), the taxpayer's employer ("Hamlin") made payments to the "Educo" trust to fund college expenses (up to a maximum of $10,000) of children of key employees. Typically payments were made directly by the trust to the college, although sometimes payments were made to employees to reimburse them for college expenses of their children. The court rejected the taxpayers' argument that the doctrine of *Lucas v. Earl* did not apply because they neither received nor possessed a right to receive the amounts distributed to their children by the Educo trust, stating:

> It is fundamental that anticipatory arrangements designed to deflect income away from the proper taxpayer will not be given effect to avoid tax liability. In substance, by commencing or continuing to be employed by Hamlin, petitioners have allowed a portion of their earnings to be paid to their children. Petitioners have acquiesced in an arrangement designed, at least in part, to shift the incidence of tax liability to third parties unconnected in any meaningful way with their performance of services.

> * * * By accepting employment or continuing to be employed by Hamlin, cognizant of the trust payments, petitioners in effect consented to having a portion of their earnings paid to third parties. There is no evidence to indicate that petitioners were unable to bargain with Hamlin about the terms of their employment and the available avenues of compensation. Hamlin could have made available a direct salary benefit to those employees who so desired * * * We also think significant petitioners' power, whether exercised or not, to designate which of their children would be enrolled in the Educo plan. Under the facts of this case, such power lends substantial compensatory flavor to the Educo arrangement. Petitioners were in a position to influence the manner in which their compensation would be paid; choosing to

acquiesce in the payments to the Educo plan was in our view tantamount to an "anticipatory arrangement" prohibited by Lucas v. Earl.

* * *

* * * Accordingly, we hold that the amounts paid by the Educo trust constituted additional compensation to petitioners and, therefore, are includable in gross income.

If Armantrout's employer had been a university and his children had received tuition reductions, would he have been taxed? See § 117(d). Is this fair? Recall § 132(a), discussed supra at page 101.

The taxpayer in Saunders v. Commissioner, 720 F.2d 871 (5th Cir. 1983) was the majority shareholder and only physician of a professional corporation engaged in the practice of medicine. After *Armantrout,* the corporation amended its own educational benefit plan to provide for loans rather than scholarships to the Saunders children. The loans would be forgiven, however, if the child maintained a "superior scholastic record," engaged in volunteer work or pursued one of several specified careers, such as teaching, after graduation. The Tax Court held that educational payments on behalf of the children constituted income to the father under the rule of *Armantrout* because no valid debtor-creditor relationship had been established. The Fifth Circuit affirmed, citing "the exceedingly generous forgiveness of loan clauses, the restricted scope of actual recipients [the children of other corporate employees could not qualify], the ease with which recipients qualified for cancellation of loan advances, all coupled with the fact that after the *Armantrout* decision the plan was revised, not as to recipients or qualifications or benefits, but merely to change the title of the funds distributed from scholarship to loan."

The taxpayer in *Armantrout* had relied upon Teschner v. Commissioner, 38 T.C. 1003 (1962), where the taxpayer entered a contest in which only people under age 17 were eligible to receive prizes. Pursuant to the contest rules, Teschner designated his daughter to receive the prize if his entry was selected. He won and his daughter received the prize. The Tax Court rejected the Commissioner's argument that the prize was taxable to the father under *Lucas v. Earl* because the contest rules forbid him from receiving any prize. The right to select the recipient was held not sufficient to tax the income to him.

(D) *Who Is the Earner?* In Hundley v. Commissioner, 48 T.C. 339 (1967), the taxpayer had entered into an agreement with his father to share equally any bonus he might receive for signing a professional baseball contract. This amount was to compensate Hundley's father for coaching efforts and for acting as Hundley's agent in contract negotiations. In 1960, Hundley entered into a contract providing for a bonus of $110,000 to be paid over five years. In each of the five years, $11,000 was paid to Hundley and $11,000 to his father. The Commissioner contended that the $11,000 paid to his father was includible in Hundley's gross income. The Tax Court determined that the amount paid by Hundley to his father was reasonable in amount and held that Hundley, while required to include the $11,000 payment in his gross income, was entitled to an $11,000 business expense deduction under § 162. But see Allen v. Commissioner, 50 T.C. 466 (1968), affirmed 410 F.2d 398 (3d Cir.1969), which held that bonus payments to a player's mother were not deductible since, unlike Hundley's father, she "had nothing whatever to do with her son's development as a baseball player and in fact knew nothing about baseball or financial matters."

The taxpayer in United States v. Scott, 660 F.2d 1145 (7th Cir.1981), cert. denied 455 U.S. 907 (1982), was a former attorney general of Illinois. It was established at trial that a Chicago businessman had made payments during 1972 to a woman whom Scott married in 1974; the evidence indicated that the woman had been placed on the businessman's payroll at Scott's request, but that she had done nothing to earn her salary. The government contended that the payments actually had been intended for Scott because, as attorney general, he had regulatory and enforcement powers over many of the businessman's enterprises. The appellate court found sufficient evidence from which the jury could have inferred that the payments were "motivated by Scott's office or in anticipation of services to be rendered." Hence, Scott had "earned" the income and was obligated to report it on his 1972 tax return.

The golfer Bobby Jones contracted with Warner Brothers to make a series of golf films in exchange for $120,000 and a 50 percent royalty on net receipts from the distribution and sale of the films. Before he made the films, Jones contracted to sell his services to his father for six years at $1,000 per year and transferred his rights under the Warner Brothers contract to his father. The father then transferred his rights under that contract to himself as trustee for the golfer's children. The payments from Warner Brothers were taxable to Jones. Jones v. Page, 102 F.2d 144 (5th Cir.1939), cert. denied 308 U.S. 562 (1939). The court observed:

> It would be absurd to say that any reasonable man having a contract from which he was to receive a minimum of $100,000 would in good faith transfer it to another for merely $6,000. Appellant could have set up the trust in favor of his children without the intervention of his father. The conclusion is inescapable that he used his father simply as a conduit in an attempt to reduce or avoid taxes that would be otherwise assessable against compensation derived from his own personal services.

Revenue Ruling 74–581

Internal Revenue Service, 1974. 1974–2 C.B. 25.

Advice has been requested concerning the Federal income tax treatment of payments received for services performed by a faculty member or a student of a university's school of law under the circumstances described below.

The university's school of law has as part of its regular teaching curriculum several clinical programs. The clinics include programs in Constitutional Litigation, Urban Legal Problems, Women's Rights, Prisoner's Rights and Corrections, and from time to time other clinical programs as well. Each program is supervised and conducted by full-time faculty members of the school of law's teaching staff.

At times, various clinics in the law school program handle criminal matters wherein faculty members are assigned as counsel. On occasion, the faculty member is appointed * * * pursuant to the provisions of the Criminal Justice Act of 1964, * * *, which authorizes the payment of compensation of attorneys appointed to represent indigent defendants. In the cases for which an appointment under the Criminal Justice Act is made, the students in the clinical programs assist the attorney-faculty member in investigation of the case, research of the case, and preparation of the litigation papers as the case may require. In other circumstances, the individual student may be able to participate directly in the legal represen- tation of the client * * *.

When an attorney-faculty member is appointed in a criminal case by the Federal Courts pursuant to the Criminal Justice Act, the attorney is entitled to submit a voucher for the expenditure of time and for disburse- ments incident to the representation. With regard to the clinical programs of the law school, each faculty member has agreed, as a condition of participation in the program, that since the time spent in supervising work of students on these cases and in the representation of the client is part of the faculty member's teaching duties for which the faculty member is compensated by a total annual salary, all amounts received under the Criminal Justice Act will be endorsed over to the law school. The attorney- faculty members involved are working solely as agents of the law school, while supervising the law students within the scope of the clinical pro- grams, and realize no personal gain from payments for their services in representing the indigent defendants.

Although the Criminal Justice Act itself does not specify that the monies may not be paid directly to the law school, the Clerk of the District Court has taken the generally acknowledged position that under the Criminal Justice Act payment cannot be arranged through the law school or its clinical programs. Therefore, as a matter of practice, the vouchers would be submitted by the attorney-faculty member to the appropriate Federal court in the name of the faculty member, and upon receipt of the check, he would endorse it over to the university's law school accounts.

Section 61(a) of the Internal Revenue Code of 1954 provides that, unless excluded by law, gross income means all income from whatever source derived including (but not limited to) compensation for services, including fees and similar items.

The Supreme Court of the United States has stated that the dominant purpose of the revenue laws is the taxation of income to those who earn or otherwise create the right to receive it and enjoy the benefit of it when paid. Helvering v. Horst, 311 U.S. 112 (1940), 1940-2 C.B. 296. Consistent with this, it is well established that a taxpayer's anticipatory assignment of a right to income derived from the ownership of property will not be effective to redirect that income to the assignee for tax purposes. See the *Horst* case and Lucas v. Earl, 281 U.S. 111 (1930).

However, the Internal Revenue Service has recognized that amounts that would otherwise be deemed income are not, in certain unique factual situations, subject to the broad rule of inclusion provided by section 61(a) of the Code.

For example, Rev.Rul. 65–282, 1965–2 C.B. 21, holds that statutory legal fees received by attorneys for representing indigent defendants are not includible in gross income where the attorneys, pursuant to their employment contracts, immediately turn the fees over to their employer, a legal aid society.

Rev.Rul. 58–220, 1958–1 C.B. 26, holds that the amount of the checks received by a physician from patients he has treated in the hospital by which he is employed full-time, which checks he is required to endorse over to the hospital, is not includible in his gross income.

Similarly, Rev.Rul. 58–515, 1958–2 C.B. 28, considers a situation where a police officer, in the performance of duties as an employee of the police department, entered into private employment for the purpose of obtaining certain information for the department. Pursuant to the rules and proce-dures of the department, the officer remitted to the police pension fund the compensation he received from the private employer. That Revenue Ruling holds that the officer was acting as an agent of the department while privately employed and that the compensation remitted to the pension fund is not includible in his gross income.

In similar circumstances, Rev.Rul. 69–274, 1969–1 C.B. 36, holds that faculty physicians of a medical school who provide medical services to indigent patients at a hospital are not required to include in their income fees collected and remitted to the university in accordance with the univer-sity policy and agreement.

Accordingly, in the instant case, amounts received for services per-formed by a faculty member or a student of the university's school of law under the clinical programs and turned over to the university are not includible in the recipient's income.

NOTES

(A) *What's a "Unique Factual Situation?"* How can the position of the IRS in Revenue Ruling 74–581 and other "unique factual situations" be reconciled with *Lucas v. Earl* and its progeny? What would be the effect of including amounts received under the Criminal Justice Act in the law professor's income? May the professor take a charitable contribution deduc-tion when she turns the proceeds over to the law school? Or may she take a deduction as an ordinary and necessary business expense? Compare Rev. Rul. 66–377, 1966–2 C.B. 21 (fees received from private professional prac-tice by faculty members of a university's school of medicine are includible in the gross income of those earning the fee even though under the contracts of employment such fees are required to be turned over promptly to the school), with Rev.Rul. 76–479, 1976–2 C.B. 20 (physician's fees paid by patients of limited income on "teaching cases" that had to be turned over to a foundation were not income to the physicians because doctors had no control over fees charged or disbursements). When they are included in income, the fees actually turned over to the school are deductible as an ordinary and necessary business expense. See also Rev.Rul. 70–161, 1970–1 C.B. 15, holding that Medicare fees earned by staff physicians of a hospital, but collected and used by a tax-exempt hospital, are includible in the physicians' gross income, but that such amounts are deductible as charitable contributions. How can these rulings be distinguished from Revenue Ruling 74–581 and the rulings cited therein?

Under current law, allowing an employee to deduct as a business expense the fees turned over to the employer would nevertheless result in tax to the employee. Employee business expenses are deductible only as itemized deductions and are subject to the 2 percent floor on itemized deductions under § 67.

(B) *Assignments to Charities.* Where an employee performs services, is paid directly, and turns the funds over to the employer, the employee is not taxed because she is an agent of the employer. The IRS also has applied this "agency" theory (which was reflected in Revenue Ruling 74–581) to determine whether earnings received by members of a religious order who have taken vows of poverty must be included in their gross income. For example, Rev.Rul. 76–323, 1976–2 C.B. 18, concerned two such individuals who turned over to their tax-exempt religious order all of their earnings from outside employment less an amount necessary for living expenses. The IRS required the members to include all of their earnings in gross income because they were not acting as agents of the order. The Service explained that a member performs services as an agent of a religious order only if the order itself performs the services as a principal. The members were entitled to charitable contribution deductions (to the extent allowable under § 170) for amounts turned over to the order.

See also Rev.Rul. 79–132, 1979–1 C.B. 62, which holds that an agency relationship is established when it appears from all the facts and circumstances that the payor of the income is looking to the religious order, rather than to the member individually, for the performance of services. It is not sufficient merely for the member to have taken a vow of poverty. These principles generally have been accepted by the courts, although application of the IRS's agency theory is frequently controversial. See, e.g., Fogarty v. United States, 780 F.2d 1005 (Fed.Cir.1986) (Catholic priest taxable on income earned as an associate professor at the University of Virginia even though income turned over to religious order); Schuster v. Commissioner, 800 F.2d 672 (7th Cir.1986) (same result for income earned by Catholic nun in performing health care services, but turned over to her religious order).

The Second Circuit has held that to prove an assignment of income on an agency theory, the taxpayer "must show that a contractual relationship existed between their secular employer and the religious order and that the religious order controlled or restricted the taxpayer's use of the money purportedly turned over to the order." Mone v. Commissioner, 774 F.2d 570 (2d Cir.1985). In that case and a number of others, tax protesters set up churches and turned over all their property and earnings to a church that then paid all of the taxpayer's living expenses. In *Mone*, one of the taxpayers was an electrical engineer with Con Ed in New York and assigned all of his wages to the Order of Almighty God of the Life Science Church. The court found that Con Ed had paid his wages to him in his individual capacity, rather than as an agent of the church. Assuming the wages are income to the employee, a further question is whether the taxpayer can take a charitable deduction for the amounts assigned to the church. The deduction is usually denied by courts that express skepticism about the validity of the church. For example, in Page v. Commissioner, 823 F.2d 1263 (8th Cir.1987), the court taxed Mr. Page on wages assigned to the Basic Bible Church of America. The church was located on the first floor of the taxpayer's home and had a workshop, office and chapel; in the chapel were "two pews, some chairs, a bookshelf and a pool table."

(C) *Imputed Income.* Suppose the faculty member in Revenue Ruling 74–581 provides the legal services gratuitously. Is he taxed on the value of his services? Consider the limitation on charitable deductions found in § 170, § 68, and the alternative minimum tax. Suppose a rock singer performs for free at a political fundraising event. See Rev.Rul. 68–503, 1968–2 C.B. 44 (performer at a political fundraising event is not taxable on any of the income raised by admission fee). What result if the singer is paid and makes a political contribution of the fee? Why are the results different where the services are performed gratuitously?

In sharp contrast is Commissioner v. Giannini, 129 F.2d 638 (9th Cir.1942), where the taxpayer was president and a director of a large corporation. On July 22, 1927, the taxpayer notified the board of directors that he would accept no further compensation for 1927 and "suggested that the corporation do something worthwhile with the money." On January 20, 1928, the board adopted a resolution reciting that the taxpayer was entitled to $1.5 million, that he refused to take it, and that the amount would be paid to the University of California to establish a Foundation of Agricultural Economics. It was expressly provided that the foundation should be named after the taxpayer. The court held that the money used to establish the foundation was not beneficially received by the taxpayer and thus not includible in his income. Would it have been more consistent with the other cases in this Section for the amount to be includible in Giannini's income but deductible as a charitable contribution? Is this case distinguishable because the corporation, rather than Giannini, designated the recipient of the forgone income?

B.   INCOME FROM PROPERTY

As noted previously, the general rule is that income from property is taxed to the owner. A gift of property serves to shift the income from the property to the transferee. A gift of the income from property, however, does not shift the tax. In reading the next two cases, see if you can determine why the transfer in *Blair* was respected but the transfer in *Horst* was not.

Blair v. Commissioner

Supreme Court of the United States, 1937. 300 U.S. 5.

MR. CHIEF JUSTICE HUGHES delivered the opinion of the Court.

This case presents the question of the liability of a beneficiary of a testamentary trust for a tax upon the income which he had assigned to his children prior to the tax years and which the trustees had paid to them accordingly.

The trust was created by the will of William Blair, a resident of Illinois who died in 1899, and was of property located in that State. One-half of the net income was to be paid to the donor's widow during her life. His son, the petitioner Edward Tyler Blair, was to receive the other one-half and, after the death of the widow, the whole of the net income during his life. In 1923, after the widow's death, petitioner assigned to his [children], an interest amounting to * * * $9000 in each calendar year thereafter, in the net income which the petitioner was then or might thereafter be entitled to receive during his life. * * * In later years, by similar instruments, he assigned to these children additional interests * * * in the net income. The trustees accepted the assignments and distributed the income directly to the assignees.

The * * * Commissioner of Internal Revenue ruled that the income was taxable to the petitioner. The Board of Tax Appeals held the contrary. 18 B.T.A. 69. The Circuit Court of Appeals reversed the Board, holding that under the law of Illinois the trust was a spendthrift trust and the assignments were invalid. Commissioner v. Blair, 60 F.2d 340. We denied certiorari. 288 U.S. 602.

[Subsequent litigation in the Illinois Courts held that the assignments were valid and the Court acknowledged that it must respect that decision.]

* * * The question remains whether, treating the assignments as valid, the assignor was still taxable upon the income under the federal income tax act. That is a federal question.

Our decisions in *Lucas v. Earl*, 281 U.S. 111, and *Burnet v. Leininger*, 285 U.S. 136, are cited. In the Lucas case the question was whether an attorney was taxable for the whole of his salary and fees earned by him in the tax years or only upon one-half by reason of an agreement with his wife by which his earnings were to be received and owned by them jointly. We were of the opinion that the case turned upon the construction of the taxing act. We said that "the statute could tax salaries to those who earned them and provide that the tax could not be escaped by anticipatory arrangements and contracts however skillfully devised to prevent the same when paid from vesting even for a second in the man who earned it." That was deemed to be the meaning of the statute as to compensation for personal service and the one who earned the income was held to be subject to the tax. In *Burnet v. Leininger*, supra, a husband, a member of a firm, assigned future partnership income to his wife. We found that the revenue act dealt explicitly with the liability of partners as such. The wife did not become a member of the firm; the act specifically taxed the distributive share of each partner in the net income of the firm; and the husband by the fair import of the act remained taxable upon his distributive share. These cases are not in point. The tax here is not upon earnings which are taxed to the one who earns them. Nor is it a case of income attributable to a taxpayer by reason of the application of the income to the discharge of his obligation. * * * There is here no question of evasion or of giving effect to statutory provisions designed to forestall evasion; or of the taxpayer's retention of control. * * *

In the instant case, the tax is upon income as to which, in the general application of the revenue acts, the tax liability attaches to ownership. * * *

The Government points to the provisions of the revenue acts imposing upon the beneficiary of a trust the liability for the tax upon the income distributable to the beneficiary. But the term is merely descriptive of the one entitled to the beneficial interest. These provisions cannot be taken to preclude valid assignments of the beneficial interest, or to affect the duty of the trustee to distribute income to the owner of the beneficial interest, whether he was such initially or becomes such by valid assignment. The one who is to receive the income as the owner of the beneficial interest is to pay the tax. If under the law governing the trust the beneficial interest is assignable, and if it has been assigned without reservation, the assignee thus becomes the beneficiary and is entitled to rights and remedies accordingly. We find nothing in the revenue acts which denies him that status.

The decision of the Circuit Court of Appeals turned upon the effect to be ascribed to the assignments. The court held that the petitioner had no interest in the corpus of the estate and could not dispose of the income until he received it. Hence it was said that "the income was *his*" and his assignment was merely a direction to pay over to others what was due to himself. The question was considered to involve "the date when the income became transferable." * * * The Government refers to the terms of the assignment—that it was of the interest in the income "which the said party of the first part now is, or may hereafter be, entitled to receive during his life from the trustees." From this it is urged that the assignments "dealt only with a right to receive the income" and that "no attempt was made to assign any equitable right, title or interest in the trust itself." This construction seems to us to be a strained one. We think it apparent that the conveyancer was not seeking to limit the assignment so as to make it anything less than a complete transfer of the specified interest of the petitioner as the life beneficiary of the trust, but that with ample caution he was using words to effect such a transfer. That the state court so construed the assignments appears from the final decree which described them as voluntary assignments of interests of the petitioner "in said trust estate," and it was in that aspect that petitioner's right to make the assignments was sustained.

The will creating the trust entitled the petitioner during his life to the net income of the property held in trust. He thus became the owner of an equitable interest in the corpus of the property. * * * By virtue of that interest he was entitled to enforce the trust, to have a breach of trust enjoined and to obtain redress in case of breach. The interest was present property alienable like any other, in the absence of a valid restraint upon alienation * * *. The beneficiary may thus transfer a part of his interest as well as the whole. * * *

We conclude that the assignments were valid, that the assignees thereby became the owners of the specified beneficial interests in the income, and that as to these interests they and not the petitioner were taxable for the tax years in question. * * *

Reversed.

Helvering v. Horst

Supreme Court of the United States, 1940. 311 U.S. 112.

MR. JUSTICE STONE delivered the opinion of the Court.

The sole question for decision is whether the gift, during the donor's taxable year, of interest coupons detached from the bonds, delivered to the donee and later in the year paid at maturity, is the realization of income taxable to the donor.

In 1934 and 1935 respondent, the owner of negotiable bonds, detached from them negotiable interest coupons shortly before their due date and delivered them as a gift to his son who in the same year collected them at maturity. The Commissioner ruled that * * * the interest payments were taxable, in the years when paid, to the respondent donor who reported his income on the cash receipts basis. The circuit court of appeals reversed the order of the Board of Tax Appeals sustaining the tax. We granted certiorari, because of the importance of the question in the administration of the revenue laws and because of an asserted conflict in principle of the decision below with that of Lucas v. Earl, 281 U.S. 111, and with that of decisions by other circuit courts of appeals. * * *

The Court below thought that as the consideration for the coupons had passed to the obligor, the donor had, by the gift, parted with all control over them and their payment, and for that reason the case was distinguishable from *Lucas v. Earl, supra,* and *Burnet v. Leininger,* 285 U.S. 136, where the assignment of compensation for services had preceded the rendition of the services, and where the income was held taxable to the donor.

The holder of a coupon bond is the owner of two independent and separable kinds of right. One is the right to demand and receive at maturity the principal amount of the bond representing capital investment. The other is the right to demand and receive interim payments of interest on the investment in the amounts and on the dates specified by the coupons. Together they are an obligation to pay principal and interest given in exchange for money or property which was presumably the consideration for the obligation of the bond. Here respondent, as owner of the bonds, had acquired the legal right to demand payment at maturity of the interest specified by the coupons and the power to command its payment to others which constituted an economic gain to him.

Admittedly not all economic gain of the taxpayer is taxable income. From the beginning the revenue laws have been interpreted as defining "realization" of income as the taxable event rather than the acquisition of the right to receive it. And "realization" is not deemed to occur until the income is paid. But the decisions and regulations have consistently recognized that receipt in cash or property is not the only characteristic of realization of income to a taxpayer on the cash receipts basis. Where the taxpayer does not receive payment of income in money or property realization may occur when the last step is taken by which he obtains the fruition of the economic gain which has already accrued to him. * * * This may occur when he has made such use or disposition of his power to receive or control the income as to procure in its place other satisfactions which are of economic worth. The question here is, whether because one who in fact receives payment for services or interest payments is taxable only on his receipt of the payments, he can escape all tax by giving away his right to income in advance of payment. If the taxpayer procures payment directly to his creditors of the items of interest or earnings due him, * * * or if he sets up a revocable trust with income payable to the objects of his bounty, * * * he does not escape taxation because he did not actually receive the money. * * *

Underlying [this] reasoning * * * is the thought that income is "realized" by the assignor because he, who owns or controls the source of the income, also controls the disposition of that which he could have received himself and diverts the payment from himself to others as the means of procuring the satisfaction of his wants. The taxpayer has equally enjoyed the fruits of his labor or investment and obtained the satisfaction of his desires whether he collects and uses the income to procure those satisfactions, or whether he disposes of his right to collect it as the means of procuring them. * * *

Although the donor here, by the transfer of the coupons, has precluded any possibility of his collecting them himself he has nevertheless, by his act, procured payment of the interest, as a valuable gift to a member of his family. Such a use of his economic gain, the right to receive income, to procure a satisfaction which can be obtained only by the expenditure of money or property, would seem to be the enjoyment of the income whether the satisfaction is the purchase of goods at the corner grocery, the payment of his debt there, or such non-material satisfactions as may result from the payment of a campaign or community chest contribution, or a gift to his favorite son. Even though he never receives the money he derives money's worth from the disposition of the coupons which he has used as money or money's worth in the procuring of a satisfaction which is procurable only by the expenditure of money or money's worth. The enjoyment of the economic benefit accruing to him by virtue of his acquisition of the coupons is realized as completely as it would have been if he had collected the interest in dollars and expended them for any of the purposes named. * * *

In a real sense he has enjoyed compensation for money loaned or services rendered and not any the less so because it is his only reward for them. To say that one who has made a gift thus derived from interest or earnings paid to his donee has never enjoyed or realized the fruits of his investment or labor because he has assigned them instead of collecting them himself and then paying them over to the donee, is to affront common understanding and to deny the facts of common experience. Common understanding and experience are the touchstones for the interpretation of the revenue laws.

The power to dispose of income is the equivalent of ownership of it. The exercise of that power to procure the payment of income to another is the enjoyment and hence the realization of the income by him who exercises it. We have had no difficulty in applying that proposition where the assignment preceded the rendition of the services, *Lucas v. Earl, supra; Burnet v. Leininger, supra,* for it was recognized in the *Leininger* case that in such a case the rendition of the service by the assignor was the means by which the income was controlled by the donor and of making his assignment effective. But it is the assignment by which the disposition of income is controlled when the service precedes the assignment and in both cases it is the exercise of the power of disposition of the interest or compensation with the resulting payment to the donee which is the enjoyment by the donor of income derived from them.

This was emphasized in *Blair v. Commissioner*, 300 U.S. 5, on which respondent relies, where the distinction was taken between a gift of income derived from an obligation to pay compensation and a gift of income-producing property. In the circumstances of that case the right to income from the trust property was thought to be so identified with the equitable ownership of the property from which alone the beneficiary derived his right to receive the income and his power to command disposition of it that a gift of the income by the beneficiary became effective only as a gift of his ownership of the property producing it. Since the gift was deemed to be a gift of the property, the income from it was held to be the income of the owner of the property, who was the donee, not the donor, a refinement which was unnecessary if respondent's contention here is right, but one clearly inapplicable to gifts of interest or wages. Unlike income thus derived from an obligation to pay interest or compensation, the income of the trust was regarded as no more the income of the donor than would be the rent from a lease or a crop raised on a farm after the leasehold or the farm had been given away. * * * We have held without deviation that where the donor retains control of the trust property the income is taxable to him although paid to the donee. * * *

The dominant purpose of the revenue laws is the taxation of income to those who earn or otherwise create the right to receive it and enjoy the benefit of it when paid. * * * The tax laid by the 1934 Revenue Act upon income "derived from * * * wages or compensation for personal service, of whatever kind and in whatever form paid, * * *; also from interest * * *" therefore cannot fairly be interpreted as not applying to income derived from interest or compensation when he who is entitled to receive it makes use of his power to dispose of it in procuring satisfactions which he would otherwise procure only by the use of the money when received.

* * *

Reversed.

The separate opinion of MR. JUSTICE McREYNOLDS.

* * *

The unmatured coupons given to the son were independent negotiable instruments, complete in themselves. Through the gift they became at once the absolute property of the donee, free from the donor's control and in no way dependent upon ownership of the bonds. No question of actual fraud or purpose to defraud the revenue is presented.

Neither Lucas v. Earl, 281 U.S. 111, nor Burnet v. Leininger, 285 U.S. 136, support petitioner's view. Blair v. Commissioner, 300 U.S. 5, 11, 12, shows that neither involved an unrestricted completed transfer of property.

* * *

The general principles approved in Blair v. Commissioner, 300 U.S. 5, are applicable and controlling. The challenged judgment should be affirmed.

The CHIEF JUSTICE and MR. JUSTICE ROBERTS concur in this opinion.

NOTES

(A) *Taxation of Bonds and Other Income Producing Property.* The specific result in *Horst* has been overruled by statute. Section 1286 now provides that where a taxpayer disposes of unmatured coupons or the naked bond, the basis of the bond is allocated between the retained portion and the portion sold. The transferor and the transferee are then subject to the original issue discount rules, discussed infra at page 748. Each year, the holder of the coupons reports the increase in value of each coupon as it nears payment. The holder of the bond annually reports the increase in value as it nears maturity. The total amount of income reported is the same as in *Horst*, but, instead of being taxed solely to the transferor, it is allocated between the transferor and transferee.

Should *Horst* continue to apply where the property transferred is neither a bond nor its coupons? The Court apparently felt compelled to find that either the transferor or the transferee (but not both) should be taxed on the income. This reflects the Court's assumption that there is only one owner of the bond. As a financial matter, however, both the transferor and the transferee own an interest in the property, each of which produces economic income annually. Requiring the transferor to report all of the income permits the transferee to shift income to the transferor. The realization rule, however, currently prevents taxation of the increase in value in the remainder interest (the bond) and this may explain the need to tax the transferor on the entire income.

Section 1286 is limited to bonds. What would the result be if Dad gives stock to his son? What if he gives the stock to his daughter and the dividend rights to his son? What if the son subsequently transferred the dividend rights to his child? For criticism of *Horst* and a recommendation that the § 1286 approach be extended far more widely, see Noël B. Cunningham & Deborah H. Schenk, "Taxation Without Realization: A 'Revolutionary' Approach to Ownership," 47 Tax L.Rev. 725 (1992).

In Irwin v. Gavit, 268 U.S. 161 (1925), the Court held that the beneficiary of an income interest in a trust could not exclude the gift under § 102. One implication of the decision is that § 102 applies only to the remainderman of a trust. If the Court had permitted the exclusion of *both* the corpus and the income, the § 102 exclusion would be greater for divided interests than it would be for a single gift of the property. As with the holder of the bond in *Horst*, the increase in value of the remainder escapes tax.

(B) *Trees and Fruits.* Justice Holmes' metaphor—the fruits of a taxpayer's labor cannot be attributed "to a different tree from that on which they grew"—has given rise to a whole body of case law that has attempted to jam the facts into the metaphor. *Blair*, for example, is said to stand for the proposition that one cannot avoid taxation by giving away simply the fruit (i.e., the income). If, however, the entire tree (i.e., the property) is transferred, the fruit (income) is taxable to the transferee. *Blair* should be contrasted with Harrison v. Schaffner, 312 U.S. 579 (1941), in which a trust income beneficiary assigned a portion of the income for one year with the donor retaining subsequent trust income. There the Court found that only fruit—and not the tree—had been transferred. In *Schaffner* and *Horst,* the taxpayer carved out an interest, retaining a remainder, whereas in *Blair,* there was no carve-out. Distinguishing the cases where there has been a carve-out and where there has been a complete transfer is not easy. For example, in McGinnis v. Commissioner, 65 T.C.M. 1870 (1993), the taxpayer transferred a 45 percent interest in a leasehold to a trust and argued that he had transferred a share of the entire property, a part of the tree. The court disagreed, finding that the income came not from the leasehold, but from the property itself, which the taxpayer retained.

Even where the taxpayer has transferred the entire tree, any "ripe fruit" usually is taxable to the transferor. For example, the donor of an apartment building is taxed on any accrued but unpaid rents. This concept applies as well to services income. In Helvering v. Eubank, 311 U.S. 122 (1940), decided on the same day as *Horst,* a taxpayer who had been a general agent for a life insurance company, was taxed on renewal commissions that he had assigned after he left employment. As the Supreme Court noted in *Schaffner:*

> one who is entitled to receive, at a future date, interest or compensation for services and who makes a gift of it by an anticipatory assignment, realizes taxable income quite as much as if he had collected the income and paid it over to the object of his bounty.

A taxpayer owned stock in a closely-held corporation. After the declaration of a dividend, but before the record date, he made a gift of the shares. The Tax Court held that the dividend was taxable to the donor. Anton v. Commissioner, 34 T.C. 842 (1960), affirmed sub nom. Smith's Estate v. Commissioner, 292 F.2d 478 (3d Cir.1961). The Fifth Circuit reached the opposite conclusion, rejecting the notion that the taxpayer had earned the income. Disparaging, but nevertheless using, the fruit and tree metaphor, the court noted: "We fail to see why the ripeness of the fruit matters, so long as the entire tree is transplanted before the fruit is harvested." Caruth v. United States, 865 F.2d 644 (5th Cir.1989).

In Rev.Rul. 72–312, 1972–1 C.B. 22, the IRS ruled that interest accrued on bonds prior to their transfer to a trust was taxable to the cash basis donor in the year it was received by the trust. Interest accruing after the transfer was taxable to the trust.

(C) *Transfer of Appreciated Property.* Consider the Court's statement in *Horst* that

> [t]o say that one who has made a gift thus derived from interest or earnings paid to his donee has never enjoyed or realized the fruits of his investment or labor, because he has assigned them instead of collecting them himself and then paying them over to the donee, is to

affront common understanding and to deny the facts of common experience.

Does not the same reasoning apply to any gift of appreciated property? Recall § 1015.

(D) *Some Applications of Horst and Eubank.* The holder of a sweepstakes ticket made an oral assignment of a two-thirds interest to members of his family. He made the assignment after the ticket was selected but before the sweepstakes. The proceeds were paid according to the transfer. The court held that all of the proceeds were taxable to the transferor. Riebe v. Commissioner, 41 B.T.A. 935 (1940), affirmed 124 F.2d 399 (6th Cir. 1941). Compare Braunstein v. Commissioner, 21 T.C.M. 1132 (1962), where the taxpayers transferred their interest in an Irish Sweepstakes ticket to a trust for their children two days before the race; the donors were taxable on the $2,137 guaranteed value of the ticket, but not on the remainder of their $136,000 prize.

A taxpayer transferred his interest in a Court of Claims judgment against the United States to his wife and children after the Supreme Court had denied certiorari in the case. The donor was held taxable on the proceeds of the judgment. The court observed that the family members

> had to wait (and that not for long) for the expected benefits to fall (and they did quickly fall) right into their economic laps. They well knew (as did [the taxpayer]) that a rare piece of good fortune was "right around the corner" without even the necessity of their going to meet it; or, in a picturesque phrase of the Blue Ridge mountaineers, they could well smile in clear anticipation that "It was about to snow in their hats."

Doyle v. Commissioner, 147 F.2d 769 (4th Cir.1945), aff'g 3 T.C. 1092 (1944).

In C.M. Thibodaux Co. v. United States, 915 F.2d 992 (5th Cir.1990), a corporation transferred to its shareholders the right to receive bonuses and rentals from mineral leases on corporate property. The court found that the corporation, by retaining the underlying property, retained significant control over the income flow and thus had anticipatorily assigned income.

C. IS INCOME FROM PROPERTY OR SERVICES?

As the preceding materials suggest, income from property can be more readily transferred to another taxpayer than income from services. By transferring the property itself, the taxpayer ordinarily may shift the tax on income from the property to the transferee. In some cases, however, it is difficult to determine whether income is from property or from services, or whether the property has been transferred or retained. These problems arise frequently in the context of patents and copyrights.

Heim v. Fitzpatrick

United States Court of Appeals, Second Circuit, 1959. 262 F.2d 887.

SWAN, CIRCUIT JUDGE:

This litigation involves income taxes of Lewis R. Heim, for the years 1943 through 1946. On audit of the taxpayer's returns, the Commissioner of Internal Revenue determined that his taxable income in each of said years should be increased by adding thereto patent royalty payments received by his wife, his son and his daughter. * * *

Plaintiff was the inventor of a new type of rod end and spherical bearing. In September 1942 he applied for a patent thereon. On November 5, 1942 he applied for a further patent on improvements of his original invention. Thereafter on November 17, 1942 he executed a formal written assignment of his invention and of the patents which might be issued for it and for improvements thereof to The Heim Company.[1] This was duly recorded in the Patent Office and in January 1945 and May 1946 plaintiff's patent applications were acted on favorably and patents thereon were issued to the Company. The assignment to the Company was made pursuant to an oral agreement, subsequently reduced to a writing dated July 29, 1943, by which it was agreed (1) that the Company need pay no royalties on bearings manufactured by it prior to July 1, 1943; (2) that after that date the Company would pay specified royalties on 12 types of bearings; (3) that on new types of bearings it would pay royalties to be agreed upon prior to their manufacture; (4) that if the royalties for any two consecutive months or for any one year should fall below stated amounts, plaintiff at his option might cancel the agreement and thereupon all rights granted by him under the agreement and under any and all assigned patents should revert to him, his heirs and assigns; and (5) that this agreement is not transferable by the Company. * * *

[Heim then assigned 25 percent interests in the agreement to his wife, son and daughter.] The Company was notified of [these assignments] and thereafter it made all royalty payments accordingly. * * *

The Commissioner of Internal Revenue decided that all of the royalties paid by the Company to plaintiff's wife and children during the taxable years in suit were taxable to him. * * *

The appellant contends that the assignments to his wife and children transferred to them income-producing property and consequently the royalty payments were taxable to his donees, as held in Blair v. Commissioner of Internal Revenue, 300 U.S. 5. Judge Anderson, however, was of [the] opinion that (151 F.Supp. 576):

> "The income-producing property, i.e. the patents, had been assigned by the taxpayer to the corporation. What he had left was a right to a portion of the income which the patents produced. He had the power to dispose of and divert the stream of this income as he saw fit."

Consequently he ruled that the principles applied by the Supreme Court in Helvering v. Horst, 311 U.S. 112, and Helvering v. Eubank, 311 U.S. 122, required all the royalty payments to be treated as income of plaintiff.

---

1. The stock of The Heim Company was owned as follows: plaintiff 1%, his wife 41%, his son and daughter 27% each, and his daughter-in-law and son-in-law 2% each.

The question is not free from doubt, but the court believes that the transfers in this case were gifts of income-producing property and that neither *Horst* nor *Eubank* requires the contrary view. * * *

In the present case more than a bare right to receive future royalties was assigned by plaintiff to his donees. Under the terms of his contract with The Heim Company he retained the power to bargain for the fixing of royalties on new types of bearings, i.e. bearings other than the 12 products on which royalties were specified. This power was assigned and the assignees exercised it as to new products. Plaintiff also retained a reversionary interest in his invention and patents by reason of his option to cancel the agreement if certain conditions were not fulfilled. This interest was also assigned. The fact that the option was not exercised in 1945, when it could have been, is irrelevant so far as concerns the existence of the reversionary interest. We think that the rights retained by plaintiff and assigned to his wife and children were sufficiently substantial to justify the view that they were given income-producing property.

[The court also rejected the argument that, because Heim's wife and daughter owned 68 percent of the stock of the Heim Company, Heim retained sufficient control over the invention and the royalties to make it reasonable to treat him as owner of that income for tax purposes.] * * *

For the foregoing reasons we hold that the judgment should be reversed and the cause remanded with directions to grant plaintiff's motion for summary judgment.

So ordered.

NOTES

(A) *Transfers of Patents and Copyrights.* As the preceding case suggests, difficult questions arise with respect to patents. Similar problems sometimes occur with copyrights. A sale or a gift of the entire interest in the patent or copyright transfers the property, and, in the absence of special circumstances, the income is thereafter taxable to the transferee. On the other hand, a bare license of a patent or copyright produces royalties that are taxable as ordinary income to the transferor. Thus, for example, if a parent transfers a patent or copyright to children, the income typically will be taxed to the children. Rev.Rul. 54–599, 1954–2 C.B. 52. This may occur even if the patent or copyright has been licensed prior to the transfer to the children. But if the patent or copyright has been transferred to a third party, a further transfer of only the right to the receipts from that transfer is not a valid assignment of income.

Due to the many variations of such arrangements, there may be considerable difficulty in telling whether a given transaction is properly treated as a sale or gift or as a license with royalties reserved. For example, there has been a tendency to hold that patents and copyrights are divisible. Thus, the transferor is not taxable on income shifted by means of an exclusive right to use the patent in a particular area, or to use the copyright in a particular medium (such as a book, the radio, or motion pictures) for the life of the patent or copyright. This question is considered further infra at page 571 in connection with capital gains issues.

(B) *Retention of Power and Control.* Compare *Heim* to Commissioner v. Sunnen, 333 U.S. 591 (1948), in which the taxpayer owned 89 percent of the stock of a corporation to which he licensed the patents for certain of his inventions. He then assigned the royalty contracts to his wife as a gift. The taxpayer contended that the licenses relieved him of tax liability on future royalty income. The Supreme Court phrased the crucial question as "whether the assignor retains sufficient power and control over the assigned property or over receipt of the income to make it reasonable to treat him as the recipient of the income for tax purposes." The Court concluded that the taxpayer had been left with "more than a memory" of the license contracts because he retained the power, as controlling shareholder of the corporation, to cancel or regulate the payment of royalties to his wife. It was also relevant that the licenses were nonexclusive. Thus, the transfer did not shift the tax to his wife.

SECTION 3. USING ENTITIES

Taxpayers sometimes have created corporations, partnerships or trusts for the purpose of shifting income to later years or to lower tax brackets.

Corporations generally are treated as separate taxable entities distinct from their shareholders. In contrast, partnerships are treated as conduits through which items of income and deduction flow to the various partners to be reported on their individual tax returns. The income of some trusts is taxed to an individual (or individuals) who is treated as the "owner" of the trust property; the income of other trusts is taxed to the beneficiaries if it is currently distributed but, at least initially, to the trust as a separate taxpayer if it is accumulated at the trust level.

The taxation of corporations, partnerships and trusts is not considered in detail in this book. The following materials are designed to offer only a brief introduction to the taxation of these entities and to some of the income-shifting issues that they raise.

A. CORPORATIONS

NOTE ON THE FUNDAMENTALS OF CORPORATE TAXATION

A corporation, unlike a partnership or a sole proprietorship, is taxed on its earnings as a distinct entity apart from its shareholders. The corporation cannot deduct any dividends distributed to its shareholders, and the shareholders generally must include these dividends in their own gross income. Thus, corporate earnings distributed to shareholders often are said to be subject to a "double tax"—first at the corporate level and again at the shareholder level.

The corporate tax rates are graduated, ranging from 15 percent on the first $50,000 of taxable income, to 35 percent on $10 million of taxable income. § 11(b). The graduated rates are denied to personal service corporations, which are defined as corporations doing business in law, accounting, health, engineering, performing arts, architecture, actuarial science or consulting where virtually all of the shareholders of the corporation work in the business. These corporations are taxed at a flat 35 percent rate. §§ 11(b)(2); 448(d)(2). Corporations, like individuals, must calculate their capital gains and losses separately, but net capital gains are taxed at ordinary income rates. Corporations are also subject to an alternative minimum tax.

Certain tax provisions—especially incentives for particular industries and accelerated depreciation—have permitted many corporations to reduce their tax burden far below the statutory rate. Moreover, corporations in different industries—as well as corporations within the same industry— sometimes pay different effective rates of tax depending on their ability to generate deductions and tax-preferred income.

In general, a corporation determines taxable income in the same manner as does an individual. Of course, a corporation cannot receive certain items of income (for example, scholarships, alimony, and combat pay) or claim certain deductions (for example, the personal exemptions, medical expenses or gambling losses). The Code explicitly distinguishes certain items of corporate income and deduction from those of individuals. See, e.g., § 118 (allowing corporations, but not individuals, to exclude contributions to capital from income), § 1201 (taxing capital gains of corporations), § 243 (the dividends received deduction) and § 1211 (treating capital losses of corporations differently than capital losses of individuals). Moreover, corporations take all of their deductions from gross income to obtain taxable income; in contrast, individuals may take only certain deductions "above the line" from gross income and must take the remainder (if greater than the standard deduction) "below the line" from adjusted gross income.

Some distributions by a corporation are taxable to the shareholders as ordinary income, other distributions are taxable as capital gains, and still other distributions may not be taxable to the shareholders at all. The typical dividend of cash or property is taxable to the shareholder as ordinary income. A distribution is not treated as ordinary income, however, to the extent that it exceeds the corporation's current or accumulated "earnings and profits." The concept of earnings and profits is closely related to economic income and to the accounting concept of earned surplus. It therefore includes some items that are excluded from the corporation's taxable income and excludes some items that are deductible from the corporation's taxable income. A distribution in excess of the corporation's earnings and profits first reduces the shareholder's basis in his stock and then, to the extent that the distribution exceeds basis, is taxed as capital gain. This treatment reflects the theory that earnings from capital are subject to tax whereas recoveries of capital are not.

A distribution likewise generally is treated first as a recovery of capital and then as a capital gain if it represents a significant redemption of a shareholder's stock or is a distribution in full or partial liquidation of the corporation. That is because the taxpayer appears in either case to be cashing in all or part of his investment in the corporation. A redemption is accorded such treatment so long as it is "not equivalent to a dividend." A redemption, however, after which the shareholder retains essentially the same interest as before the distribution is taxed as a dividend.

The general rule—enunciated first in *Eisner v. Macomber,* supra at page 151 and subsequently codified—is that a shareholder is not taxable on a proportional distribution of the stock, or the rights to acquire the stock, of the distributing corporation. The basis of the old stock is allocated between the new and the old stock in proportion to their fair market values. A stock distribution, however, may be taxed under many other circumstances: for example, the distribution is taxable if the shareholder has the option of receiving cash or other property instead of stock.

The distinction between dividend and nondividend distributions from corporations has been important principally because a dividend is taxed as ordinary income, while a nondividend distribution often benefitted from the tax advantage accorded capital gains and also because dividends are taxable in full, while nondividend distributions typically are taxable to the shareholder only if the amount realized exceeds the taxpayer's basis in the corporation's stock. As a result, the corporate provisions of the Code are replete with complex rules designed to prevent corporations from disguising dividends as nontaxable or as returns of capital.

The "double" tax on distributed corporate earnings might become a triple or quadruple tax if corporations were taxed in full on the dividends that they receive from other corporations. Consequently, § 243 allows most corporations to deduct 70 percent of the dividends that they receive from domestic corporations; a corporation is entitled to a 100 percent deduction for dividends received from certain affiliated corporations. On the other hand, the deduction for dividends received by corporations has provided unwarranted opportunities for corporate tax reductions and there are several provisions designed to curb abuse. There are also a significant number of provisions designed to ensure that a corporation recognizes gain when it either sells or distributes appreciated property.

The materials that follow illustrate that, notwithstanding the general prohibition of *Lucas v. Earl* against the shifting of income from one's labor, the Code sometimes affords the taxpayer opportunities to accumulate personal services income in a corporation. Indeed, the opportunity to shift income is greater with corporations than with partnerships. This accumulated income eventually may be distributed—perhaps as capital gain—to the taxpayer's children or other relatives.

The taxpayer's ability to shift personal services income to a corporation nevertheless has been restricted by Congress, the IRS, and the courts. Some of these restrictions are considered in the cases and notes that follow. The desirability of such a shift depends on the relationship of the top corporate rate to the top individual rate. During much of the history of the income tax, the top individual rate has been higher than the corporate rate, although that relationship was reversed during the period 1986–1992 when the corporate rate exceeded the top individual rate. In periods where the corporate rate is less than the individual rate, tax planning efforts are worthwhile. This stratagem, however, is somewhat limited by § 11(b)(2), which taxes a personal service corporation at a flat 35 percent rate, rather than graduated rates. This, however, is still less than the maximum individual rate of 38.6 percent (reduced to 35 percent in 2006 by legislation enacted in 2001). The Tax Equity and Fiscal Responsibility Act of 1982 made a number of important changes concerning pensions and annuities that were designed principally to make the benefits available to self-employed individuals comparable to those available to corporate employees. This eliminated some of the impetus to shift income to corporations.

The following case illustrates the tension between the basic assignment of income doctrine and the corporation as a separate taxpaying entity.

Johnson v. Commissioner

United States Tax Court, 1982. 78 T.C. 882, affirmed 734 F.2d 20 (9th Cir.1984), cert. denied 469 U.S. 857 (1984).

Fay, Judge:

[Charles Johnson was a professional basketball player for the Golden State Warriors. In 1974, he signed an agreement granting the right to his services in professional sports to Presentaciones Musicales (PMSA), a Panamanian corporation. The agreement gave PMSA the right to control Johnson's services with respect to professional sports and obligated PMSA to pay Johnson $1,500 per month. PMSA licensed its rights and obligations under the agreement to EST International, a British Virgin Islands company. Presumably the companies were not subject to U.S. tax on Johnson's earnings or were taxable at a lower rate than would have applied to Johnson himself.

The Warriors refused to sign a contract for Johnson's services with any one other than Johnson himself. The team did, however, agree to remit his compensation to EST after he executed a formal assignment of contract rights. Johnson was later acquired by the Washington Bullets, which likewise refused to enter into a contract with EST but agreed to remit all contract payments to the company rather than to Johnson.]

* * *

At issue is whether amounts paid by the Warriors with respect to petitioner's services as a basketball player are income to petitioner or to the corporation to which the amounts were remitted. Respondent, relying on the rule of Lucas v. Earl, 281 U.S. 111 (1930), that income must be taxed to its earner, contends petitioner was the true earner. Petitioner maintains this is a "loan-out" case like Fox v. Commissioner, 37 B.T.A. 271 (1938), and that Lucas v. Earl is inapplicable. We find Lucas v. Earl indistinguishable in any meaningful sense and hold for respondent.

In Lucas v. Earl, the taxpayer executed an agreement with his wife that any property acquired by either of them, including wages and salary, would be considered joint property. The U.S. Supreme Court accepted the validity of that contract, but held the taxpayer earned the salary in issue therein and must be taxed on it. * * *

However, the realities of the business world prevent an overly simplistic application of the Lucas v. Earl rule whereby the true earner may be identified by merely pointing to the one actually turning the spade or dribbling the ball. Recognition must be given to corporations as taxable entities which, to a great extent, rely upon the personal services of their employees to produce corporate income. When a corporate employee performs labors which give rise to income, it solves little merely to identify the actual laborer. Thus, a tension has evolved between the basic tenets of Lucas v. Earl and recognition of the nature of the corporate business form.[1]

While the generally accepted test for resolving the "who is taxed" tension is who actually earns the income, that test may easily become sheer sophistry when the "who" choices are a corporation or its employee. Whether a one-person professional service corporation or a multi-faceted corporation is presented, there are many cases in which, in a practical sense, the key employee is responsible for the influx of moneys. Nor may a workable test be couched in terms of for whose services the payor of the income intends to pay. In numerous instances, a corporation is hired solely in order to obtain the services of a specific corporate employee.

Given the inherent impossibility of logical application of a per se actual earner test, a more refined inquiry has arisen in the form of who controls the earning of the income. * * * An examination of the case law from Lucas v. Earl hence reveals two necessary elements before the corporation, rather than its service-performer employee, may be considered the controller of the income. First, the service-performer employee must be just that— an employee of the corporation whom the corporation has the right to direct or control in some meaningful sense. * * * Second, there must exist between the corporation and the person or entity using the services a contract or similar indicium recognizing the corporation's controlling position. * * *

In the case before us, we accept arguendo that the PMSA-petitioner agreement was a valid contract which required the payments with respect to petitioner's performance as a basketball player ultimately to be made to PMSA or EST. * * * We also accept arguendo that the PMSA–petitioner agreement gave PMSA a right of control over petitioner's services, although respondent maintains the agreement's control provisions systematically were ignored. * * * Thus, the first element is satisfied. However, the second element is lacking, and that is what brings this case within Lucas v. Earl rather than the cases relied on by petitioner.

In Fox v. Commissioner, 37 B.T.A. 271 (1938), the taxpayer was a cartoonist who formed a corporation. He transferred to the corporation cash and property and assigned to the corporation copyrights and his exclusive services for a number of years. The corporation executed a contract with a syndicate giving the syndicate the right to use the taxpayer's cartoons in return for a percentage of gross sales. The amount the corporation thus received greatly exceeded the amount the corporation paid

---

1. That tension is most acute when a corporation operates a personal service business and has as its sole or principal employee its sole or principal shareholder. In those cases where sec. 482 applies, resort to general sec. 61 principles usually is not necessary since sec. 482 provides a smoother route to the same "who is taxed" result. * * *

the taxpayer for his services. The Court held the excess amounts were not the taxpayer's income. Lucas v. Earl was inapplicable because the employment relationships existed between the corporation and the syndicate and between the corporation and the taxpayer and not between the taxpayer and the syndicate.

In Laughton v. Commissioner, 40 B.T.A. 101 (1939), the taxpayer, an actor, formed a corporation. He contracted with the corporation to receive a weekly payment and certain expense payments in return for his exclusive services. The corporation executed contracts with two film studios whereby the taxpayer's services were loaned to the film studios. The Court held the taxpayer was not taxable on the amounts paid to the corporation by the studios because those amounts were paid "under contracts between it [the corporation] and the studios" and there simply was no assignment of income by the taxpayer. * * *

Petitioner herein stands upon vastly different ground than did the taxpayers in *Fox* and *Laughton*. While petitioner had a contract with PMSA, and by assignment, EST, he also had an employment contract with the Warriors. Crucial is the fact that there was no contract or agreement between the Warriors and PMSA or EST. Nor can any oral contract between those entities be implied. * * * The Warriors adamantly refused to sign any contract or agreement with any person or entity other than petitioner. Thus, the existing employment relationships were between petitioner and PMSA/EST and between petitioner and the Warriors. The relationship between PMSA/EST and the Warriors necessary for PMSA/EST to be considered actually in control of the earnings was not present. * * *

Nor may the assignments of earnings executed by petitioner suffice to make PMSA/EST the taxable party. Such assignments merely demonstrate petitioner's control over the earnings such as would an ordinary assignment of wages to a bank. Nor is it important that petitioner contractually was obligated to pay his earnings to PMSA/EST. The U.S. Supreme Court in Lucas v. Earl accepted the validity of the contract involved therein requiring transmission of one-half to Mrs. Earl, but nevertheless held Mr. Earl taxable as the true earner.

In summary, we find petitioner, rather than PMSA or EST, actually controlled the earning of the amounts paid by the Warriors with respect to petitioner's services. Thus, those amounts were income to petitioner under section 61(a)(1).

To reflect the foregoing,

Decisions will be entered for the respondent.

NOTES

(A) *Formalities vs. Control.* The court in *Johnson* emphasizes that the Warriors had a contract for personal services with Johnson himself, describing as "crucial" the fact that the Warriors had no contract or agreement with PMSA or EST. As the discussion of the *Fox* and *Laughton* cases suggests, a different result might obtain if the third party had contracted with the taxpayer's corporation—and not the taxpayer—for his personal services. Shifting personal service income to a corporation therefore clearly depends on complying with the formalities and, at a minimum, requires the person or entity that obtains services to do business with the corporation rather than with the individual who actually provides the services. Often this requires an actual contract between the "employer" and the corporation. See, e.g., Evatt v. Commissioner, 63 T.C.M. 3194 (1992) (real estate commissions taxable to sole shareholder and not personal services corporation in the absence of a contract between corporation and entity using the services).

Should such formal distinctions govern the tax consequences, or would a better result look to who "actually controls" the individual's performance of services? Notions of "control" have been significant in the context of efforts to shift the taxation of income through the use of so-called grantor trusts. When you have studied those materials, consider whether the differences between formalities and control are as important as they first seemed. When the legal formalities are met—and the corporation cannot simply be said to be the taxpayer's alter ego—it becomes difficult to show that events are in the taxpayer's actual control.

Johnson should be contrasted with Sargent v. Commissioner, 929 F.2d 1252 (8th Cir.1991). The court taxed income to the professional service corporations of two hockey players because the corporation, rather than the players, contracted with the club to provide services. The Tax Court had ignored the formalities, looking instead to who controlled the individual's performances and determined that in team sports, it was the team and the coach, not the player. The Eighth Circuit rejected that view, finding instead that the corporation controlled the players. In a subsequent case appealable to a different circuit, the Tax Court refused to follow the formalities approach adopted by the Eighth Circuit. Leavell v. Commissioner, 104 T.C. 140 (1995). Leavell, a guard with the Houston Rockets, formed a personal service corporation that entered into an arrangement that was very similar to the one used by Sargent. The Tax Court, obviously believing that the language in the standard contract with the PSC did not reflect reality, stuck to a control approach. It quoted the dissenting judge in *Sargent*: "The idea that the coach issued orders to Sargent [and another player] in their capacity as corporate officers, which order they then relayed to themselves as corporate employees, is fanciful."

In Norman E. Duquette, Inc. v. Commissioner, 81 T.C.M. 951 (2001), the taxpayer attempted to use a corporation owned by himself and his wife to obtain deductions for otherwise nondeductible expenses, such as a dinner "Board of Directors" meeting between the two of them. Judge Halpern of the Tax Court not only disallowed the deductions but also assessed negligence penalties, stating:

> We allow no deduction with respect to the $310 claimed for "Board of Directors Meetings" * * *. [T]he Duquettes were petitioner's only directors. On January 1, 1994, the Duquettes met, as directors, to discuss corporate matters * * *. The January 1 meeting took place at a restaurant called "The Mansion at Turtle Creek," and the February 1 meeting took place at a restaurant called "The Riviera." The charge

for dinner at the first restaurant was $162 and the charge for dinner at the second restaurant was $148. Petitioner claimed a deduction for both dinners * * *. Norman exercised poor judgment. He had been a Government auditor, and he had passed his C.P.A. exams. Undoubtedly, he understood that he wore more than one hat with respect to his corporation, as shareholder, director, and employee, and that an expenditure to benefit a shareholder directly is not a deductible corporate expense. There is ample evidence that Norman abused his dual status, exploiting his director and employee roles in order to shortchange the tax collector; for example, by deducting dinners at expensive restaurants to discuss with his wife matters over which he had complete control or deducting as corporate relocation expenses personal costs incident to his divorce and his wife's relocation to Florida. * * * [P]etitioner has failed to convince us that it did not act negligently * * *.

(B) *Sections 482 and 269A.* Section 482 allows the Commissioner to reallocate income between two or more businesses (whether or not incorporated) controlled by the same interests where "necessary in order to prevent evasion of taxes or clearly to reflect * * * income." Although § 482 has its most significant application in monitoring prices among related multinational companies, its application was upheld in Borge v. Commissioner, 405 F.2d 673 (2d Cir.1968), where Victor Borge contracted to perform entertainment and promotional services for his wholly-owned poultry business that had been operating at a loss. The corporation (Danica) was able to offset its poultry losses against its entertainment profits and thus to avoid the $50,000 per year loss limitation then imposed. The court, after accepting the Service's assertion that Borge controlled both an entertainment business and a poultry business, found:

> substantial evidence that the income of Borge's two businesses has been distorted through Borge's having arranged for Danica to receive a large part of his entertainment income although Danica did nothing to earn that income, and the sole purpose of the arrangement was to permit Danica to offset losses from the poultry business with income from the entertainment business.

Id. at 677. The court held that the $75,000 per year reallocated by the IRS from Danica to Borge under § 482 was "entirely reasonable—indeed generous—in view of the fact that Danica's annual net income from Borge's entertainment services averaged $166,465 during the years in question."

In Keller v. Commissioner, 77 T.C. 1014 (1981), aff'd 723 F.2d 58 (10th Cir.1983), a clinical pathologist formed a professional corporation of which he was the sole shareholder and director. He then entered into an employment contract with the corporation at an annual salary of $60,000. The IRS sought to tax Keller on all of the income received by the corporation under both the assignment-of-income doctrine and the reallocation provisions of § 482. The Tax Court rejected as "arbitrary and capricious" the Service's attempt to allocate all of the income of the corporation to Keller as an individual. It noted that the taxpayer's total compensation was essentially equivalent to what it had been before the corporation was established. The court emphasized that "section 482 does not authorize an allocation which would, in effect, disregard the existence of the corporation * * * so long as the corporation actually conducts business." The court regarded § 482 as a particularized application of the assignment-of-income doctrine to corporations that are treated by their taxpayer-shareholders as separate entities. A dissenting judge queried:

> As between the collection of meaningless paper going by the name of Keller, Inc., and Dr. Keller, can there be any doubt on the facts before us who is the true earner of the income at issue? My answer to that is Dr. Keller, and I would apply the assignment of income doctrine to directly tax him on the income earned.

Congress expressly sought to overturn the result of cases such as *Keller* by enacting § 269A in 1982. This provision allows the IRS to allocate income, deductions, credits, and other tax benefits between certain personal-service corporations and their employee-owners if (1) the principal purpose for the formation or use of the corporation is tax avoidance, (2) substantially all of the services of the corporation are performed for one other corporation or business entity, and (3) allocation is necessary to prevent avoidance or evasion of taxes or to clearly reflect the income of the personal service corporation or any of its employee-owners. An employee-owner is defined as any employee who owns more than 10 percent of the stock of the corporation.

(D) *Personal Holding Companies.* "Amounts received under a contract under which the corporation is to furnish personal services" may subject a corporation to the additional income tax on personal holding companies. See § 543(a)(7). For an application of this provision to a one-person personal services corporation, see Morrison v. Commissioner, 44 T.C.M. 1459 (1982) (corporation held to be personal holding company in years in which 60 percent of its total income was received from contracts engaging the services of its sole shareholder).

B. PARTNERSHIPS

NOTE ON THE FUNDAMENTALS OF PARTNERSHIP TAXATION

Partnerships are not subject to taxation. Instead, the income and losses of the partnership pass through to the individual partners. The income of the partnership therefore is taxed directly to the partners, whether or not it is distributed to them.

Each partner separately takes into account specific items—for example, long-term and short-term capital gains and losses—in determining his share of the partnership results for income tax purposes. This allows the specific items of income and deduction derived from the partnership to be combined on the partner's tax return with similar items from his other income-producing activities. The partnership thus generally is treated as a "conduit" whereas the corporation is treated as a separate taxpaying entity.

The Code nevertheless treats the partnership as an entity distinct from its partners for a number of purposes other than the actual collection of tax. This sometimes occurs for reasons of administrative convenience. For example, the partnership must calculate partnership taxable income and file an "informational" partnership tax return. The determination whether a partner realizes gain or loss for the year is therefore made at the partnership level. Moreover, most elections that determine the method of calculating taxable income—for example, the selection of depreciation periods or accounting methods—are made at the partnership level and cannot be modified by the individual partners.

The partnership also is treated as an entity in a variety of more substantive contexts, including the formation and termination of a partnership, the transfer of a partnership interest and the determination of special allocations of income and deductions among partners. In addition, the character of certain items of partnership income, loss, deduction, and credit is determined at the partnership level. Assume, for example, that a partnership sells real estate at a profit, which qualifies as a long-term capital gain at the partnership level. A partner will likewise have capital gain on her distributive share of the sale proceeds even if she is a real estate dealer who would have recognized ordinary income, not capital gain, if she had sold the property individually.

A partner has a basis in her partnership interest that limits the extent to which she can recognize the income and losses of the partnership. This is similar to the basis that a landowner has in a piece of real estate or that a shareholder has in stock of a corporation. The partner's initial basis in her partnership interest is generally equal to the sum of the cash that she contributed to the partnership, the adjusted basis of any property that she contributed and the gain that she recognized in contributing that property.

Her basis is subsequently increased by her share of partnership income and liabilities. Any increase in a partner's share of partnership liabilities is treated as a contribution of money by the partner to the partnership. Her basis is decreased by any cash and the basis of any property that she receives in a distribution from the partnership as well as by her share of partnership losses. A decrease in partnership liabilities decreases the partner's basis in her partnership interest.

The partner cannot deduct partnership losses that exceed the basis of her partnership interest. She is permitted, however, to deduct any excess losses in a later year if her basis has since increased above zero. Partnership losses are subject to the "at risk" restrictions of § 465 and the passive loss limits of § 469, discussed at pages 417 and 418 supra.

A partner's distributive share of income, gain, loss, deduction or credit is determined by the partnership agreement. If the partnership agreement does not provide for the distributive shares of these items, or if the allocations do not have "substantial economic effect," a partner's distributive share is determined with reference to the partner's interest in the partnership, taking into account all facts and circumstances. A partner's distributive share of each item has "substantial economic effect" if the allocation actually affects the dollar amounts received by the partners independent of any tax consequences. The parties cannot allocate taxable income and loss differently from economic income and loss as reflected in the capital accounts that determine their respective shares of partnership assets upon liquidation. In order to avoid shifting income and deductions, a partner's distributive share must reflect his varying interests in the partnership during the taxable year.

The foregoing rules illustrate the fundamental "conduit" vs. "entity" tension in the taxation of partnerships. Partnerships sometimes are treated as mere surrogates for their individual partners and sometimes as entities separate and distinct from their partners. This tension has produced much uncertainty and complexity in the taxation of partnerships. It also has afforded unwarranted opportunities for the shifting of income and deductions among partners to achieve tax advantages and contributed to the proliferation of tax shelter partnerships. Additional tax-planning opportunities have arisen from the possibility that activities that are essentially equivalent economically will produce significantly different tax consequences depending on whether they are conducted by proprietorships, partnerships or corporations.

Family Partnerships. The family partnership has been a popular means by which taxpayers have attempted to shift income generated by their own property or services to their children or to other individuals in lower tax brackets. A particularly egregious case involved a former IRS agent who attempted—ultimately unsuccessfully—to form a law and accounting partnership with his one-day old child. See Tinkoff v. Commissioner, 120 F.2d 564 (7th Cir.1941).

The Supreme Court first took up this issue in a pair of cases involving husband-wife partnerships that predated the joint return provisions described earlier in this Chapter. The Court held that the failure of the wives to contribute either "original capital" or "vital services" could be considered in evaluating the validity of the partnerships for tax purposes. Commissioner v. Tower, 327 U.S. 280 (1946); Lusthaus v. Commissioner, 327 U.S. 293 (1946).

The Court revisited the issue of family partnerships three years later in the famous case of Commissioner v. Culbertson, 337 U.S. 733 (1949). The taxpayer in *Culbertson* transferred a partnership interest in his cattle ranch to his four sons in return for their interest-bearing notes payable out of proceeds from the operation of the ranch. The Tax Court held that the entire income from the partnership could be taxed to the father on the ground that the sons had contributed neither vital services nor capital originating with them.

These tests were deemed by the Supreme Court to be persuasive but not determinative. Instead, the Court held that:

> [i]f, upon a consideration of all the facts, it is found that the partners joined together in good faith to conduct a business, having agreed that the services or capital to be contributed presently by each is of such value to the partnership that the contributor should participate in the distribution of profits, that is sufficient.

The case was remanded to the Tax Court for a determination as to whether there was "a bona fide intent that [the sons] be partners in the conduct of the cattle business, either because of services to be performed during those years, or because of contributions of capital of which they were the true owners."

The *Culbertson* decision, while intended to clarify the tax treatment of family partnerships, produced much confusion among the lower courts. Congress responded to this confusion by enacting a provision that recognizes for tax purposes a partnership in which the partner owns a capital interest, whether or not that interest was acquired by purchase or gift from any other person, including a member of the family.

The Committee Report emphasized that the purpose of the provision was "to harmonize the rules governing interests in the so-called family partnership with those generally applicable to other forms of property or business * * * [and to make clear] that, however the owner of a partnership interest may have acquired such interest, the income is taxable to the owner, if he is the real owner." Thus, in effect, family partnerships are recognized under the Code.

Even a minor child of the donor may be considered a partner if he is "competent to manage his own property and participate in partnership activities" or if his interest is vested in an independent trustee.

The distributive share of a partner may not be "determined without allowance of reasonable compensation for services rendered to the partnership by the donor," and the distributive share of a donee attributable to donated capital may not be "proportionately greater than the share of the donor attributable to the donor's capital." The effect of this rule is to attribute and tax to the donor the income that reflects the value of his personal services and capital contributions.

Moreover, the rule applies only to partnerships in which "capital is a material income-producing factor." The *Culbertson* case continues to govern whenever a donee owns an interest in a partnership in which capital is not a significant factor. The regulations provide that capital is not considered a material income-producing factor if the partnership earns its income primarily from "fees, commissions or other compensation for personal services." It therefore must be demonstrated that the members of such a partnership "in good faith and acting with a business purpose intended to join together in the present conduct of the enterprise" as required by *Culbertson*.

The family partnership rules, therefore, generally incorporate the distinction previously observed in this Chapter between assignments of income from services and assignments of income from property: (1) income from property is taxed to the owner of the property and (2) income from services is taxed to the person who renders the services. Taxpayers have a far greater ability to shift earnings to others if the partnership is one in which capital is a "material income producing factor."

Subchapter S Corporations. Certain corporations may elect to be taxed under a pass-through regime. These corporations, known as S corporations because the rules governing them are found in Subchapter S of the Code, are not subject to tax at the entity level. Instead, the income or loss flows through and is taxed to the shareholders. An S corporation may have no more than 75 shareholders and only individuals, estates, certain trusts, and tax-exempt organizations may hold stock. The corporation may issue only one class of stock. Although an S corporation is taxed somewhat like a partnership, it is not able to use some of the more advantageous, although complicated, provisions available to partnerships. Use of an S corporation generally sacrifices flexibility for simplicity.

Limited Liability Companies. The states have enacted legislation permitting the creation of a form of business organization designed to combine the federal tax advantages of partnerships with the limited liability of a corporation. The IRS has held that a "limited liability company" is to be treated as a partnership for federal tax purposes. Thus, it is not subject to the corporate tax at the entity level and the tax benefits flow through to the owners. An LLC is more advantageous than a Subchapter S corporation because there are no limitations on the number and types of owners and no restrictions on its capital structure.

The tension between the partnership provisions and the assignment of income doctrine is nicely illustrated by the next case.

Schneer v. Commissioner

United States Tax Court, 1991. 97 T.C. 643.

Gerber, Judge:

Until February 25, 1983, petitioner was an associate with the law firm of Ballon, Stoll & Itzler (BSI). BSI was a partnership. Petitioner was not a partner in BSI and he did not share in general partnership profits. Petitioner's financial arrangement with BSI consisted of a fixed or set salary and a percentage of any fees which arose from clients petitioner brought or referred to the firm. * * *

When petitioner left BSI he had an understanding that he would continue to receive his percentage of fees which arose from clients he had referred when he was an associate with BSI. Petitioner was expected to consult regarding clients he referred to BSI and whose fees were to be shared by petitioner. Petitioner would have become entitled to his percentage of the fees even if he had not been called upon to consult.

After petitioner left BSI and while he was a partner of two other law partnerships (other than BSI) he consulted on numerous occasions concerning BSI clients. * * * The services provided by petitioner to BSI consisted of legal advice and consultation on legal matters.

Late in February 1983, petitioner became a partner in the law firm of Bandler & Kass (B & K), and on August 1, 1985, petitioner became a partner in the law firm of Sylvor, Schneer, Gold & Morelli (SSG & M). * * * [P]etitioner agreed to turn over to the [B & K and SSG & M] partnership all legal fees received after joining the partnership, regardless of whether the fees were earned in the partnership's name or from the partnership's contractual relationship with the client. The same agreement existed between the partners of SSG & M, including petitioner.

During 1984 and 1985, BSI remitted $21,329 and $10,585 to petitioner. The amounts represented petitioner's percentage of fees from BSI clients that he had referred to BSI at a time when he was an associate with BSI. * * * Petitioner, pursuant to his agreements with B & K and SSG & M, turned those amounts over to the appropriate partnership. B & K and SSG & M, in turn, treated the amounts as partnership income which was distributed to each partner (including petitioner) according to the partner's percentage share of partnership profits. * * *

We consider here basic principles of income taxation. There is agreement that the amounts paid to petitioner by his former employer-law firm are income in the year of receipt. The question is whether petitioner (individually) or the partners of petitioner's partnerships (including petitioner) should report the income in their respective shares.

The parties have couched the issue in terms of the anticipatory assignment-of-income principles. See Lucas v. Earl, 281 U.S. 111 (1930). Equally important to this case, however, is the viability of the principle that partners may pool their earnings and report partnership income in amounts different from their contribution to the pool. See sec. 704(a) and (b). The parties' arguments bring into focus potential conflict between these two principles and compel us to address both.

First, we examine the parties' arguments with respect to the assignment-of-income doctrine. Respondent argues that petitioner earned the income in question before leaving BSI, despite the fact that petitioner did not receive that income until he was a partner in B & K and, later, SSG & M. According to respondent, by entering into partnership agreements requiring payment of all legal fees to his new partnerships, petitioner anticipatorily assigned to those partnerships the income earned but not yet received from BSI. * * *

Petitioner contends that the income in question was not earned until after he left BSI and joined B & K and SSG & M. He argues that the income received from BSI is reportable by the partners of the B & K and SSG & M partnerships (including petitioner) in their respective shares. * * *

[The court then finds that the majority of the fees were earned after the taxpayer left BSI and while he was a partner of B & K or SSG & M.]

Two additional related questions remain for our consideration. First, respondent argues that irrespective of when petitioner earned the income from BSI, "there was no relationship * * * [between] the past activity of introducing a client to * * * [BSI], and the petitioner's work as a partner with * * * [B & K or SSG & M]." According to respondent, petitioner should not be allowed to characterize as partnership income fees that did not have a requisite or direct relationship to a partnership's business. In making this argument, respondent attempts to limit and modify his long-standing and judicially approved position in Rev.Rul. 64–90, 1964–1 C.B. 226 (Part 1). [In Rev.Rul. 64–90, the IRS ruled that "fees received by a partner for similar services performed in his individual capacity" are partnership income if paid to the partnership]. See also Bufalino v. Commissioner, T.C.Memo. 1976–110; Brandschain v. Commissioner, 80 T.C. 746

(1983), both involving partnership agreements similar to the one described in Rev.Rul. 64–90. * * *

These final two questions bring into focus the true nature of the potential conflict in this case—between respondent's revenue ruling and the assignment-of-income doctrine. Both questions, in their own way, ask whether any partnership agreement—under which partners agree in advance to turn over to the partnership all income from their individual efforts—can survive scrutiny under the assignment-of-income principles.

Respondent's rulings have approved as partnership income fees generated by partners serving in individual capacities only tangentially related to the partner's employment in his or her partnership. See Rev.Rul. 80–338, 1980–2 C.B. 30 (accounting partner serving as executor); Rev.Rul. 54–223, 1954–1 C.B. 174 (partner working for another organization as a school bus driver).

There is no need for us to adopt a broader view of petitioner's partnership in this case. His referral fee income was clearly earned through activities "within the ambit" of the business of his new partnerships. Their business was the practice of law as was petitioner's consulting activity for BSI. His work was incident to the conduct of the business of his partnerships. * * *

Thus, we arrive at the final question in this case. We have already held that petitioner had not yet earned the majority of the income in question when he joined his new partnerships. Additionally, petitioner's fee income from his BSI clients qualifies, under the case law and respondent's rulings, as income generated by services sufficiently related to the business conducted by petitioner's new partnerships. If we decide that petitioner's partnerships should report the income in question, petitioner would be taxable only to the extent of his respective partnership share. This would allow petitioner, through his partnership agreements with B & K and SSG & M, to assign income not yet earned from BSI. Thus, the case law and respondent's rulings permit (without explanation), in a partnership setting, the type of assignment addressed by Lucas v. Earl, 281 U.S. 111 (1930). We must reconcile the principle behind Rev.Rul. 64–90, 1964–1 C.B. 226 (Part 1), with *Lucas v. Earl*, supra. The question is whether income not yet earned and anticipatorily assigned under certain partnership agreements are without the reach of the assignment-of-income principle.

The Internal Revenue Code of 1954 provided the first comprehensive statutory scheme for the tax treatment of partners and partnerships. No section of the 1954 Code, successive amendments or acts, nor the legislative history specifically addresses the treatment of income earned by partners in their individual capacity but which is pooled with other partnership income. It is implicit in subchapter K, however, that the pooling of income and losses of partners was intended by Congress. This question is more easily answered where the partnership contracts with the client for services which are then performed by the partner. The question becomes more complex where the partner contracts and performs the services when he is a partner.

Moreover, no opinion contains a satisfactory rationale as to why partnership pooling agreements do not come within the holding of *Lucas v. Earl.*

The fundamental theme penned by Justice Holmes [in *Lucas v. Earl*] provides that the individual who earns income is liable for the tax. It is obvious that the partnership, as an abstract entity, does not provide the physical and mental activity that facilitates the process of "earning" income. Only a partner can do so. The income earned is turned over to the partnership due solely to a contractual agreement, i.e., an assignment, in advance, of income.

The provisions of subchapter K tacitly imply that the pooling of income is permissible. Said implication may provide sufficient reason to conclude that a partnership should be treated as an entity for the purpose of pooling the income of its partners. Under an entity approach, the income would be considered that of the partnership rather than the partner, even though the partner's individual efforts may have earned the income. If the partnership is treated as an entity earning the income, then assignment-of-income concepts would not come into play.

In this regard, an analysis of personal service corporations (PSC's) may provide, by way of analogy, some assistance in reconciling the principles inherent in Rev.Rul. 64–90 with those underlying *Lucas v. Earl.* Keeping in mind Justice Holmes' desire to tax the "earner" of the income, we consider the assignment-of-income doctrine in the context of personal service corporation cases. In partnerships and personal service corporations an individual performs the services that earn income. In both, a separate entity—the partnership or personal service corporation—is cast as the "earner" for tax purposes. That characterization in both situations is, in essence, an assignment of income. If, in either situation, the transfer to the entity is of income earned before an agreement to turn it over is entered into, the assignment-of-income doctrine will serve to invalidate the transfer. In both the context of a PSC or partnership, transfers prior to the performance of a partner's services may be subject to the partner's or employee's control—in that either may refuse to perform.

[The court discusses *Johnson v. Commissioner*, set forth supra at page 512.]

Thus, an employee of a personal service corporation, or other corporate entity, is outside the holding of Lucas v. Earl, to some degree because of the "entity concept." The business entity is cast as the earner of the income, obviating the need to analyze whether there has been an assignment of income.

The same type of approach may be used with respect to partners of a partnership. In the same manner that a corporation is considered the earner of income gained through the labor of its employees, a partnership, with an appropriate partnership agreement, may be considered the earner of income. Income earned prior to such an agreement, of course, remains within the principles and holding of *Lucas v. Earl*, supra. The link between respondent's Rev.Rul. 64–90 and *Lucas v. Earl* must be the entity concept as it relates to partnerships. * * *

The principle we must analyze in this case involves the role of the partnership with respect to the function of earning income. A general partnership is "an association of two or more persons to carry on as co-owners a business for profit." Either a partnership or a corporation may enter into a contract with clients to perform services. In a partnership, however, either the entity or the individual may enter into contracts. The question we seek to answer is whether this distinction should be treated differently.

For purposes of an entity concept approach to partnerships, we must consider the type and source of income which should be included. Because we have already determined that the type of activity generating the income is relevant to an assignment-of-income analysis in the partnership setting, we focus our analysis of partnerships as entities in situations where the income is of a type normally earned by the partnership. Only in such situations has a partner acted as part of the partnership entity.

The entity concept as it relates to partnerships is based, in part, on the concept that a partner may further the business of the partnership by performing services in the name of the partnership or individually. The name and reputation of a professional partnership plays a role in the financial success of the partnership business. If the partners perform services in the name of the partnership or individually they are, nonetheless, associated with the partnership as a partner. This is the very essence of a professional service partnership, because each partner, although acting individually, is furthering the business of the partnership. * * *

The lack of structure inherent in the partnership form does not lend itself to easy resolution of the assignment-of-income question. A partnership's characteristics do, however, militate in favor of treating a partner's income from services performed in an individual capacity, which are contractually obligated to the partnership for allocation in accord with the pre-established distributive shares, in the same manner as income earned through partnership engagement.

Accordingly, in circumstances where individuals are not joining in a venture merely to avoid the effect of *Lucas v. Earl*, supra, it is appropriate to treat income earned by partners individually, as income earned by the partnership entity, i.e., partnership income, to be allocated to partners in their respective shares. To provide the essential continuity necessary for the use of an entity concept in the partnership setting, the income should be earned from an activity which can reasonably be associated with the partnership's business activity. * * *

There is no apparent attempt to avoid the incidence of tax by the formation or operation of the partnerships in this case. Petitioner, in performing legal work for clients of another firm, was a partner with the law firms of B & K and SSG & M. In view of the foregoing, we hold that, * * * the fee income from BSI was correctly returned by the two partnerships in accord with the respective partnership agreements.

HALPERN, J., dissenting:

[The majority's] analysis wholly ignores the doctrine of agency. When a partner, acting as agent for the partnership, performs services for a client, the partnership is the earner of the income: the instrumentality (in this case the partner) through which the partnership has earned its fee is of no consequence. Therefore, the focus of the anticipatory assignment-of-income analysis ought to be on whether the partner acted for himself individually or as agent of the partnership. This is entirely consistent with the latitude accorded partnerships to disproportionately distribute partnership income: the pertinent requirement is merely that the partnership income so distributed have been earned by the partnership. In this case, it is quite clear that petitioner earned the fees in question pursuant to an agreement he entered into, on his own behalf, with Ballon, Stoll & Itzler—an agreement that was consummated before petitioner's relationship with Bandler & Kass. Consequently, petitioner is the true earner of the income and should not escape taxation by means of an anticipatory assignment. Lucas v. Earl, 281 U.S. 111 (1930).

The majority's "resolution" of the perceived conflict is unsatisfactory. The majority considers the determinative question to be whether the income is "of a type normally earned by the partnership. Only in such situations has the partner acted as part of the partnership entity."

The majority's distinction is unprincipled. The majority observes that "The name and reputation of a professional partnership plays a role in the financial success of a partnership business" suggesting that partners, even acting individually, can further the business of the partnership by adding to its reputation. But, that may be so even if the partner acts individually, doing work entirely dissimilar to that normally performed by the partnership. In any event, the majority fails to explain why such an obviously incidental benefit to the partnership should permit us to frustrate the assignment-of-income doctrine. * * *

NOTES

(A) *More Fruit.* In the usual case, two lawyers may join together to form a partnership and will be taxed on their share of the partnership income according to the agreement, regardless of who performed the services. How well does Justice Holmes' oft-cited statement about not attributing fruit to "a different tree from that on which it grew" apply to those facts?

(B) *Scope of Schneer.* Law firm partnership agreements often require lawyers to turn over lecture fees, teaching compensation or book royalties to the firm. After *Schneer,* is the income taxable to the partner? Does it matter what the lecture or book topic is?

C.   TRUSTS

NOTE ON THE FUNDAMENTALS OF TRUST TAXATION

Tax liability on trust income could be imposed on any of three parties—the settlor (or grantor), the trust itself or the beneficiary. Since income from property normally is taxed to the person who owns the property, the first issue to be considered is whether the grantor has retained sufficient control over the trust property (or has transferred control for such a temporary period) that he should be treated as the owner of the property for income tax purposes.

1.   GRANTOR TRUSTS

Sections 671 and 672 set forth general rules relating to the taxation of grantor trusts. The last sentence of § 671 expressly provides that liability cannot be asserted against the grantor of a trust under § 61 or any other provision of the Code on the grounds of his dominion and control over the trusts. Section 671 is not controlling, however, when the grantor is subject to tax for reasons other than his dominion and control over the trust property. See, e.g., Iber v. United States, 409 F.2d 1273 (7th Cir.1969), where the grantor was held taxable on rental income from a lease transferred to a trust on the ground that the transfer amounted to an anticipatory assignment of income. The *Iber* court did not rely at all on the grantor trust provisions.

Sections 673–677 and 679 define the circumstances under which income of a trust is taxed to a grantor. Section 673, which is the most important of these provisions, taxes the grantor on any part of the trust in which she has a reversionary interest of 5 percent in either the income or corpus. In general, the other grantor trust provisions tax the grantor if she (or a "nonadverse party") has (1) certain powers to affect beneficial enjoyment of income or the trust corpus; (2) specified unusual administrative powers, or (3) if the trust is a foreign trust with U.S. beneficiaries. Any interests and powers of the grantor's spouse are treated as belonging to the grantor, if the spouse was living with the grantor when the spouse's interest or power was created. § 672(e).

Where the grantor has a reversionary interest, he is taxed on the value of the trust in which he has a reversionary interest of at least 5 percent of the total value.* The Senate Finance Committee report on § 673 amplifies this requirement by stating that this provision taxes to the grantor income from a trust "where there is more than a five percent possibility that any of the proscribed powers or interests will become effective in the grantor after the transfer to the trust." The value of the grantor's interest is determined by assuming the maximum exercise of discretion by the fiduciary in favor of the grantor. The possibility that an interest may revert to the grantor or grantor's spouse solely through the intestacy laws may be ignored when determining whether a 5 percent reversionary interest exists.

Section 674 provides that if the grantor or a nonadverse party can control disposition of some or all of the trust income or principal, he or she

---

* Prior to 1986, § 673 provided that the grantor would be treated as the owner of any portion of a trust in which she had a reversionary interest in income or principal that was (or was reasonably expected) to take effect within ten years. The grantor was not treated as owner of a trust where his reversionary interest was not to take effect until after the death of the beneficiary or within ten years. These trusts were often called Clif-ford trusts after a leading Supreme Court case. Because the effective date rules of the revision of § 673, discussed in the text, exempted all pre-existing trusts, the rules of prior law may apply to allocate the income of many trusts long after the change in the rules. The rate changes and kiddie tax rules of the 1986 Act, however, eliminated much of the tax savings potential of these trusts.

is treated as the owner of that portion of the trust. However, § 674 permits substantial flexibility. Subsection (b) lists powers that can be vested in any trustee, including the grantor or the grantor's spouse, without subjecting him to tax; subsection (c) permits broad powers for "independent" trustees; and subsection (d) permits trustees who are relatives or employees of the grantor to exercise certain discretionary powers if limited by "a reasonably definite external standard."

Section 675 provides that the grantor is treated as the owner of the trust or a portion thereof if he or a nonadverse party has certain unusual administrative powers, such as a power to deal with the trust for less than adequate consideration or a power to use the trust assets for voting control of a corporation.

Section 676 provides that the grantor is treated as the owner of the trust or a portion thereof if he or a nonadverse party has the power to revest title to the trust property in the grantor.

Section 677 provides that the grantor is treated as the owner of any portion of a trust whose income may be distributed to the grantor or used to discharge a legal obligation of the grantor. Section 677 also taxes the grantor on income that can be distributed or held for future distribution to the grantor's spouse as well as to the grantor himself. This provision prevents deferral of tax through the use of a trust to accumulate income for the grantor's spouse. Section 677(a)(3) provides that the grantor is taxed on trust income that may be applied to pay premiums for insurance on the life of the grantor or the grantor's spouse.

Where trust income may be used to discharge a legal obligation, the grantor generally is taxed whether or not the income is actually so used. In the case of support obligations, however, the grantor generally is taxed only if income is actually distributed to discharge the obligation. See § 677(b). This allows trust income to be accumulated for the benefit of the grantor's child until a specified age or event (such as marriage) with discretion in the trustee to divert the trust income for the child's current support. The grantor is not taxed unless the income is actually used to discharge the grantor's obligation to support the beneficiaries. Much of the controversy under § 677 concerns whether an obligation of support exists, whether the obligation can be discharged by trust income, and whether a distribution in fact discharged a support obligation. See, e.g., Braun v. Commissioner, 48 T.C.M. 210 (1984) (trust distributions used for the college and private high school expenses of grantor's six children were payments that discharged a support obligation because under state law parents should contribute, if financially able, to the college and even post-graduate education of their children; private high school expenses are "within the scope of parental obligation.")

Controversies under § 677 are not limited to obligations of support. For example, the IRS taxes the grantor on the payment by a trust of interest or principal on a mortgage for which the grantor is personally liable. See Rev.Rul. 54–516, 1954–2 C.B. 54. Similarly, a transfer in trust where the donee is obligated to pay gift tax is taxable, see Diedrich v. Commissioner, 457 U.S. 191 (1982).

Section 679 provides that a U.S. taxpayer who transfers property to a foreign trust is treated as the owner of such property and taxed currently on its income in each taxable year during which the trust has a U.S. beneficiary. In addition, capital gains of a foreign trust are taxed in the same manner as ordinary income. See § 643(a)(6).

In certain cases, § 679 will tax the grantor of a foreign trust on the trust income to which he irrevocably relinquished any rights prior to the enactment of § 679. Does this raise any constitutional problems?

2. TRUSTS WHERE SOMEONE OTHER THAN THE GRANTOR IS TREATED AS OWNER

Someone other than the grantor may possess sufficient control over trust property to be treated as the owner of such property for tax purposes. See § 678. Thus a beneficiary who has an absolute right to immediate enjoyment of the entire trust property will be taxed on the trust income whether or not he chooses to receive it. For example, in Mallinckrodt v. Nunan, 146 F.2d 1 (8th Cir.1945), cert. denied 324 U.S. 871 (1945), A died, leaving property in trust with the income to X for life and remainder to Y. The will provided, however, that the income should be paid to B in whole or in part throughout his life if he asked for it. It was held that the income was taxable to B whether he asked for it or not. See also Spies v. United States, 180 F.2d 336 (8th Cir.1950), where three trustees who had the power to distribute income among several beneficiaries, including themselves, were taxed on the trust income.

Rev.Rul. 81–6, 1981–1 C.B. 385, holds that a minor beneficiary can be the owner of a trust under § 678 even though he is prevented by local law from exercising the power to withdraw principal or income in the absence of an appointed guardian. The IRS considered it immaterial that no guardian had been appointed for the beneficiary.

Section 678(d) allows a person who holds a power that would make the trust income taxable to him to avoid such taxation by renouncing or disclaiming the power within a reasonable time after learning of its existence.

3. INCOME NOT TAXABLE TO THE GRANTOR OR ANOTHER PERSON AS AN OWNER

In most cases neither the settlor nor another person is treated as the owner and taxed on the income. The settlor may be dead, for example, or otherwise may not come within the rules of §§ 671–678. In such situations the tax on trust income could be imposed on either the beneficiary or the trust itself.

A trust may have more than one grantor and often will have more than one beneficiary, for example, where one beneficiary has a life or term interest and another has a remainder interest.

The statutory provisions deal first with what are often called "simple" trusts—that is, trusts where all income must be distributed currently to beneficiaries, where no distributions are made from the trust corpus, and where there are no charitable beneficiaries. These trusts are covered in

§§ 651 and 652. More "complex" trusts are dealt with in §§ 661–668. Complex trusts allow the trustees to accumulate income or distribute principal.

The reason for this approach to taxing trust income is clear. The trust often is simply a conduit. The trustee receives the income and pays it out to the beneficiary. In such a case, the income should be taxable to the beneficiary and not to the trustee. Suppose, however, the trustee is required to accumulate the income and to pay it out to any of the grantor's children who are living 20 years after the grantor's death. No income is paid out currently, and no beneficiary is assured of ever getting any of the income. The income would escape current tax if tax liability is limited to beneficiaries.

The Code therefore treats such a trust as a taxpayer and requires the trustee to pay its tax. The same rule applies to estates before all the assets are distributed to beneficiaries. The taxable income of the estate or trust is computed in the same manner as the income of an individual. But the trust is allowed an additional deduction for the amount of income that it is required to distribute currently. That amount is included in the income of the beneficiary, whether or not actually distributed. Income that is not required to be distributed is taxed to the trust. Such income may be distributed to a beneficiary in a later year without further tax liability to the trust. The tax rates applicable to trusts are set forth in § 1(e).

Under these provisions, the income of trusts and estates is taxed at rates from 15 percent to 39.6 percent. All income over $7,650 is taxed at the highest rate. No standard deduction is allowed to trusts or estates. Thus, opportunities for reducing tax through the use of trusts that had existed under prior law's more generous trust rate schedules now have been eliminated.

The taxation of trusts that accumulate income is complicated by the need to distinguish distributions of income from distributions of trust corpus. This is necessary to allocate income among beneficiaries and to effectuate the rule of § 102, which excludes from a donee's gross income gifts of property but not gifts of income from property.

"Distributable net income," or DNI, is the taxable income of the trust with certain modifications, such as the exclusion of capital gains that are not actually distributed within the taxable year. § 643(a). DNI also reflects deductions allowed to the trust such as trustee's fees for taking care of the principal. The beneficiary of the trust is taxed on his share of DNI. All distributions are considered to be from DNI, rather than from principal, to the extent that DNI is available. The income has the same character—whether capital gain or loss, tax-exempt interest or ordinary income—for the beneficiary as for the trust. §§ 652(b) and 661(b). The concept of DNI thus reflects the principle that trusts are mere conduits through which income flows to the beneficiaries except where the income is accumulated for future distribution.

The allocation of income among beneficiaries is determined under §§ 652 and 662. Section 652 applies only to simple trusts where no principal is distributed and all income may be required to be distributed currently. Income is allocated among beneficiaries in accordance with their respective interests in the trust. The allocation of income is usually more complicated in a complex trust where income is required to be distributed to some beneficiaries but not to others.

The calculation of tax becomes even more complicated when a beneficiary receives income in the current year that was accumulated by the trust during prior years. Unless the income was accumulated when the beneficiary had not yet been born or was a minor, the tax on the beneficiary is determined in such cases under the so-called "throwback rule." This rule is an effort to approximate the taxes on the beneficiary if he had received the accumulated income in the years in which it was earned. See §§ 665, 666 and 667. But, although the beneficiary gets a credit for any taxes previously paid by the trust with respect to this income, the beneficiary cannot receive a credit if the tax paid by the trust was greater than would have been payable had the amounts been distributed. § 666(e).

4. MULTIPLE TRUSTS

Taxpayers long ago recognized that the income-splitting advantages available from the use of one trust might be multiplied through the use of several trusts. The progressive rate structure made it possible to reduce tax substantially by establishing multiple trusts having the same grantor and the same or similar beneficiaries. For example, a taxpayer might secure a significantly lower rate of tax on undistributed trust income by establishing ten identical trusts rather than a single trust.

Section § 643(e) treats two or more trusts as one trust if (1) the trusts have substantially the same grantor or grantors and substantially the same beneficiaries and (2) the trusts have as a principal purpose the avoidance of federal income tax. In determining whether a trust has substantially the same grantors or beneficiaries, a husband and wife are treated as one person.

By taxing income of trusts in excess of $7,650 at the maximum rate generally applicable to individuals, any remaining advantage of multiple trusts essentially is eliminated. The costs of administering multiple trusts, including the cost of filing separate tax returns and making separate quarterly estimated tax returns, will tend to exceed the relatively small tax savings that might be possible.

5. CHARITABLE TRUSTS

Taxpayers have used the trust device to make so-called "split interest gifts" whereby a charitable beneficiary receives the income interest and a noncharitable beneficiary receives the remainder, or vice versa. The *charitable remainder trust* involves a transfer of property to a trust with the income to be paid to a private person for life or a specified period of time and the remainder to be paid to charity. The *charitable lead trust* provides for the income to be paid to a charity for a period of years with the remainder to go to a noncharitable beneficiary, such as a family member. See §§ 170(f), 642 and 664. The statute allows a charitable deduction only where the trust is either a charitable remainder annuity trust or a charitable remainder unitrust, or, in the case of a charitable lead trust where the income interest is either a guaranteed annuity or reflects minimum interest rate based on the fair market value of trust assets paid at least annually. An annuity trust requires that a fixed dollar amount be distributed each year, while a unitrust requires that a fixed percentage of the fair market value of the property be distributed annually. These rules were designed to limit the ability of the trustee to favor the noncharitable beneficiary over the charitable beneficiary by manipulating the trust's investments. An exception to these rules is provided for a gift of a charitable remainder interest in trust that takes the form of a transfer of property to a pooled income fund maintained by the charity.

Deductions are allowed for irrevocable gifts to a donor-advised investment fund where amounts accumulated for subsequent distribution to charity and the donor retains the right to advise the fund regarding the timing of and charitable recipient of distributions from the fund's assets. The Clinton Administration proposed legislation to set standards for the administration of donor-advised funds.

NOTE

Abusive Use of Trusts. Unscrupulous promoters have frequently told taxpayers that they can avoid all individual taxes by setting up "family" or "estate" trusts. The IRS has obtained criminal convictions in some cases. Schulz v. Commissioner, 686 F.2d 490 (7th Cir.1982), is a good example of a case holding such a trust to be an ineffective attempt to shift tax liability. There the taxpayers created a trust to which they conveyed all of their real and personal property, including the farming and office equipment that the husband used to earn a living as a dairyman and real estate agent, as well as the wife's right to receive her salary as a county employee. In return, the couple and their children received shares representing 100 percent of the beneficial interest in the trust. The court rejected the taxpayers' effort to have the trust pay income tax on its net income—that is, the accumulations to the trust minus the expenses of administration (which included everything from the husband's salary as a consultant in running the dairy farm and real-estate business to license fees for a boat and a dog). See also O'Donnell v. Commissioner, 726 F.2d 679 (11th Cir.1984) (family trust "schemes have been universally condemned by the courts.").

SECTION 4.   INTRAFAMILY ASSIGNMENTS INVOLVING CONSIDERATION

The preceding Sections of this Chapter have focused on taxpayers' gratuitous attempts to shift the taxation of income to lower-rate taxpayers, primarily in the family setting. This Section considers assignments of income or losses involving consideration.

A taxpayer may have a variety of motives when she considers transferring money or property to other members of her family. For example, she may wish to confer a gift on her children, to shift income to those in lower tax brackets, to create deductions or to prevent the loss of otherwise unusable deductions, to defer income until later taxable years, and/or to reduce the inheritance taxes that ultimately may be assessed against her estate or her heirs. At the same time, she may wish to retain some benefit from, or some control over, the property transferred. The basic technique is to shift or divide the ownership of assets or capital to achieve favorable tax consequences while retaining management control satisfactory to the transferor, who typically is a member of the senior generation of the family.

Estate Of Stranahan v. Commissioner

United States Court of Appeals, Sixth Circuit, 1973. 472 F.2d 867.

PECK, CIRCUIT JUDGE:

* * * On March 11, 1964, the decedent, Frank D. Stranahan, entered into a closing agreement with the Commissioner of Internal Revenue Service (IRS) under which it was agreed that decedent owed the IRS $754,815.72 for interest due to deficiencies in federal income, estate and gift taxes regarding several trusts created in 1932. Decedent, a cash-basis taxpayer, paid the amount during his 1964 tax year. Because his personal income for the 1964 tax year would not normally have been high enough to fully absorb the large interest deduction, decedent accelerated his future income to avoid losing the tax benefit of the interest deduction. To accelerate the income, decedent executed an agreement dated December 22, 1964, under which he assigned to his son, Duane Stranahan, $122,820 in anticipated stock dividends from decedent's Champion Spark Plug Company common stock (12,500 shares). At the time both decedent and his son were employees and shareholders of Champion. As consideration for this assignment of future stock dividends, decedent's son paid the decedent $115,000 by check dated December 22, 1964. The decedent thereafter directed the transfer agent for Champion to issue all future dividend checks to his son, Duane, until the aggregate amount of $122,820 had been paid to him. Decedent reported this $115,000 payment as ordinary income for the 1964 tax year and thus was able to deduct the full interest payment from the sum of this payment and his other income. During decedent's taxable year in question, dividends in the total amount of $40,050 were paid to and received by decedent's son. No part of the $40,050 was reported as income in the return filed by decedent's estate for this period. Decedent's son reported this dividend income on his own return as ordinary income subject to the offset of his basis of $115,000, resulting in a net amount of $7,282 of taxable income.

Subsequently, the Commissioner sent appellant (decedent's estate) a notice of deficiency claiming that the $40,050 received by the decedent's son was actually income attributable to the decedent. * * * The Tax Court concluded that decedent's assignment of future dividends in exchange for the present discounted cash value of those dividends "though conducted in the form of an assignment of a property right, was in reality a loan to [decedent] masquerading as a sale and so disguised lacked any business purpose; and, therefore, decedent realized taxable income in the year 1965 when the dividend was declared paid."

As pointed out by the Tax Court, several long-standing principles must be recognized. First, under Section 451(a) of the Internal Revenue Code of 1954, a cash basis taxpayer ordinarily realizes income in the year of receipt rather than the year when earned. Second, a taxpayer who assigns future income for consideration in a bona fide commercial transaction will ordinarily realize ordinary income in the year of receipt. Third, a taxpayer is free to arrange his financial affairs to minimize his tax liability; thus, the presence of tax avoidance motives will not nullify an otherwise bona fide transaction. We also note there are no claims that the transaction was a sham, the purchase price was inadequate or that decedent did not actually receive the full payment of $115,000 in tax year 1964. And it is agreed decedent had the right to enter into a binding contract to sell his right to future dividends. * * *

The Commissioner's view regards the transaction as merely a temporary shift of funds, with an appropriate interest factor, within the family unit. He argues that no change in the beneficial ownership of the stock was effected and no real risks of ownership were assumed by the son. Therefore, the Commissioner concludes, taxable income was realized not on the formal assignment but rather on the actual payment of the dividends.

It is conceded by taxpayer that the sole aim of the assignment was the acceleration of income so as to fully utilize the interest deduction. Gregory v. Helvering, 293 U.S. 465 (1935), established the landmark principle that the substance of a transaction, and not the form, determines the taxable consequences of that transaction. * * * In the present transaction, however, it appears that both the form and the substance of the agreement assigned the right to receive future income. What was received by the decedent was the present value of that income the son could expect in the future. On the basis of the stock's past performance, the future income could have been (and was) estimated with reasonable accuracy. Essentially, decedent's son paid consideration to receive future income. Of course, the fact of a family transaction does not vitiate the transaction but merely subjects it to special scrutiny. * * *

We recognize the oft-stated principle that a taxpayer cannot escape taxation by legally assigning or giving away a portion of the income derived from income producing property retained by the taxpayer. * * * Here, however, the acceleration of income was not designed to avoid or escape recognition of the dividends but rather to reduce taxation by fully utilizing a substantial interest deduction which was available.[1] As stated previously, tax avoidance motives alone will not serve to obviate the tax benefits of a transaction. Further, the fact that this was a transaction for good and sufficient consideration, and not merely gratuitous, distinguishes the instant case from the line of authority beginning with *Helvering v. Horst*.

* * *

The Commissioner also argues that the possibility of not receiving the dividends was remote, and that since this was particularly known to the

---

1. By accelerating income into the year 1964, when it would be offset by the interest deduction, decedent could reduce his poten- tial tax liability for the future years in which the dividends would be paid.

parties as shareholders and employees of the corporation, no risks inured to the son. The Commissioner attempts to bolster this argument by pointing out that consideration was computed merely as a discount based on a prevailing interest rate and that the dividends were in fact paid at a rate faster than anticipated. However, it seems clear that risks, however remote, did in fact exist. The fact that the risks did not materialize is irrelevant. Assessment of the risks is a matter of negotiation between the parties and is usually reflected in the terms of the agreement. Since we are not in a position to evaluate those terms, and since we are not aware of any terms which dilute the son's dependence on the dividends alone to return his investment, we cannot say he does not bear the risks of ownership.

Accordingly, we conclude the transaction to be economically realistic, with substance, and therefore should be recognized for tax purposes even though the consequences may be unfavorable to the Commissioner. The facts establish decedent did in fact receive payment. Decedent deposited his son's check for $115,000 to his personal account on December 23, 1964, the day after the agreement was signed. The agreement is unquestionably a complete and valid assignment to decedent's son of all dividends up to $122,820. The son acquired an independent right against the corporation since the latter was notified of the private agreement. Decedent completely divested himself of any interest in the dividends and vested the interest on the day of execution of the agreement with his son.

* * *

The judgment is reversed and * * * remanded for further proceedings consistent with this opinion.

NOTES

(A) *Sale vs. Loan.* The principal case distinguished Martin v. Commissioner, 56 T.C. 1255 (1971), which held that an assignment of future rents for consideration in a nonfamily setting was not effective to create income to the partnership "seller" on receipt of the consideration. In *Martin,* the assignor received the full amount of future rents and agreed to pay the assignee 7 percent annual interest on the unpaid balance. This interest obligation functioned as a substitute for discounting future income to present value. The assignor agreed to continue renting the apartments for two years, but the assignment agreement explicitly negated any guarantee by the assignor of continued collection of the assigned rents. The Tax Court considered the transaction to be in substance a loan with interest. Do the differences between the *Martin* and *Stranahan* transactions justify the different results?

In Mapco Inc. v. United States, 214 Ct.Cl. 389, 556 F.2d 1107 (1977), the taxpayer had a net operating loss carryover of approximately $4.7 million that would expire at the end of that year if not offset by income earned in 1966, and a loss carryover of approximately $550,000 that would expire at the end of 1967 if not offset by income earned in 1966 or 1967. Mapco attempted to obtain enough income to offset the loss carryover that would expire in 1966 by agreeing on December 22, 1966, to "sell" $4 million of future pipeline revenues. It then included this $4 million in its income for 1966, and offset it against the loss carryover. In 1967, 75 percent of Mapco's pipeline revenues were paid over in accordance with the 1966 assignment and were not reported as income for tax purposes. The IRS argued that the transaction was a loan, not a genuine sale. The court agreed, and distinguished *Stranahan* as follows:

> * * * [I]n *Stranahan* the seller of the future income was not under any obligation whatever to produce such income for the benefit of the purchaser, who was compelled to look solely to a third person (the corporation which issued the stock) for the future income that he had purchased. * * *
>
> * * * Here, the plaintiff was obligated to produce the future pipeline revenues that [the "purchaser"] was to receive under the agreement of December 22, 1966. Although the plaintiff did not, in terms, guarantee the repayment of the $4,000,000 principal sum to [the purchaser], plus the interest equivalent of 6⅜ percent, plus reimbursement for [the purchaser's] expenses, the plaintiff, in substance, obligated itself to such a program. The plaintiff specifically obligated itself to continue to operate the pipeline system properly during the life of the agreement, and also obligated itself to use its best efforts not only to maintain the pipeline revenues at their then-current level (which would be sufficient to liquidate the transaction by July 1967) but to increase such revenues, if possible. Thus, when the agreement of December 22, 1966, was entered into, it was certain, as a practical matter, that the plaintiff would itself repay the $4,000,000 principal sum, plus the interest equivalent, plus reimbursement for [the purchaser's] expenses, within a matter of several months. The agreement of December 22, 1966, therefore, was more in the nature of a loan-and-repayment transaction than it resembled a sale-and-purchase transaction.
>
> Moreover, it is at least worthy of some consideration that the transaction of December 22, 1966, was contrived solely for income tax purposes. The plaintiff did not need or use the $4,000,000 * * * for any business purpose, except the attempt to create in 1966 taxable income to offset the net operating loss carryover which otherwise was scheduled to expire at the end of 1966.

(B) *Alternative Treatment.* The taxpayer in *Stranahan* produced taxable income because none of his basis in the stock was allocated to the dividend income. Recall *Hort v. Commissioner,* supra at page ___. Having carved out an income interest, Stranahan retained a remainder interest in the stock, which increased in value as the time approached when the income interest lapsed. As noted previously, this economic income is not taxed under current law because of the realization requirement. A more realistic treatment of Stranahan would be to assign a portion of his basis in the stock to the carved-out interest equal to the fair market value, which would eliminate the income on the sale, and to tax the increase in value of the remainder as it accrues. The net income would be the same as under the loan characterization advocated by the IRS.

(C) *Gift-Leasebacks*. Taxpayers have sometimes used gift-leasebacks as a mechanism for shifting income among family members. Typically, a taxpayer will place business property—for example, an office building or professional equipment—into a trust for the benefit of his children. The taxpayer then will lease back the equipment from the trust and deduct his payments as an ordinary and necessary business expense. He thus may succeed in shifting an amount of income equal to the annual rental expense, which will be deductible to the payor.

The basic purpose of most gift-leaseback arrangements is to shift income to family members in lower brackets, particularly in circumstances where the taxpayer does not have investment property that simply can be transferred outright or in trust to other family members. Most professionals will have equipment or furniture, if not real property, that may be used in a gift-leaseback. (Another purpose of such transactions may be to remove appreciating real property from the taxpayer's estate. Neither the gift nor estate tax consequences of such transactions will be considered here.) In some instances—for example, where fully depreciated business property is transferred—a gift-leaseback also may produce additional business deductions for rent that otherwise would not be available.

The circuits are divided as to whether family gift-leasebacks may give rise to business deductions. The majority of the circuits that have addressed the issue, have allowed the deduction if the leaseback was motivated by a "business purpose." Rosenfeld v. Commissioner, 706 F.2d 1277 (2d Cir.1983); Brown v. Commissioner, 180 F.2d 926 (3d Cir.1950), cert. denied 340 U.S. 814 (1950); Skemp v. Commissioner, 168 F.2d 598 (7th Cir.1948); Quinlivan v. Commissioner, 599 F.2d 269 (8th Cir.1979), cert. denied 444 U.S. 996 (1979); Brooke v. United States, 468 F.2d 1155 (9th Cir.1972).

Other circuits, most notably the Fourth and Fifth, allow the deduction only where the entire transaction was motivated by a business purpose. See, e.g., Perry v. United States, 520 F.2d 235 (4th Cir.1975), cert. denied 423 U.S. 1052 (1976); Van Zandt v. Commissioner, 341 F.2d 440 (5th Cir.1965), cert. denied 382 U.S. 814 (1965).

(D) *Learned Hand Is on My Side*. Both the majority and dissent in the Second Circuit's decision in *Rosenfeld*, supra, invoked quotations from Learned Hand to support their conclusions. The majority remarked (at 1278):

> As Judge Learned Hand eloquently noted, "one may so arrange his affairs that his taxes shall be as low as possible; he is not bound to choose that pattern which will best pay the Treasury; there is not even a patriotic duty to increase one's taxes." Helvering v. Gregory, 69 F.2d 809, 810 (2d Cir.1934) * * *.

The dissent countered (at 1283):

> In the words of Judge Learned Hand: The Income Tax imposes liabilities upon taxpayers based upon their financial transactions and it is of course true that the payment of the tax is itself a financial transaction. If, however, the taxpayer enters into a transaction that does not appreciably affect his beneficial interest except to reduce his tax, the law will disregard it; for we cannot suppose that it was part of

the purpose of the act to provide an escape from the liabilities that it sought to impose. Gilbert v. Commissioner, 248 F.2d 399, 411 (2d Cir.1957) (L. Hand, J., dissenting).

(E) *Sale-Leasebacks.* The validity of a sale-leaseback in a family setting was upheld in Hudspeth v. Commissioner, 509 F.2d 1224 (9th Cir.1975). The taxpayer parents in that case were farmers who were restricted by law to owning no more than 320 acres of federally irrigated land. The government could withdraw irrigation from any excess land and force the farmer to sell the land at a bargain price. The taxpayers sought to avoid this rule by transferring their additional land to their three sons in exchange for notes and mortgages representing the fair market value of the land. The children's indebtedness was to be satisfied by cash gifts and rental payments that they were to receive each year from their parents.

The Tax Court upheld the IRS's disallowance of interest deductions to the children on the ground that the transaction was not a bona fide sale but an installment gift designed to take advantage of the annual gift tax exclusion. The Tax Court also noted that the children would have lacked sufficient funds to meet their repayment obligations had they not received the annual payments from their parents.

The Ninth Circuit reversed on the ground that the children were legally obligated to continue their mortgage payments regardless of whether the parents continued to make their gifts. The children were allowed interest deductions equal to the amount of the rental payments received from their parents. (For example, one son received a $3,000 rental payment and a $9,000 gift: $5,760 of his mortgage obligation for the year represented interest and the balance represented principal. He was allowed an interest deduction of $3,000.)

CHAPTER 5

CAPITAL GAINS AND LOSSES

Probably no subject relating to income taxation has been as much discussed and debated as the taxation of capital gains. During the early years of the federal income tax, leading economists disagreed sharply whether a comprehensive definition of income encompassed capital gains. And for some time there was uncertainty whether the power granted to Congress by the Sixteenth Amendment to tax "income" was broad enough to authorize a tax on gains derived from a sale of property, but the issue was settled in favor of the power to tax in Merchants' Loan and Trust Co. v. Smietanka, 255 U.S. 509 (1921). Thus, the sale or exchange of an asset for more than its cost generally produces taxable income.

Throughout almost the entire history of the income tax, however, Congress has treated certain gains preferentially. These gains have been labelled "capital gains." Congress has never satisfactorily explained why certain gains should be treated better than other types of income. Congressional actions over the years reveal a lack of any comprehensive theoretical framework for taxing capital gains, and there is every reason to suspect that Congress's rather bewildering tinkering will continue in the future.

The distinction between capital gain (and loss) and ordinary income (and loss) has been one of the major sources of income tax complexity. That is in part because the concept of a "capital gain" is a creature of the tax law, without a direct analogue in either economics or accounting. If you are able to discern a bright-line distinction between capital gain and ordinary income after reading this Chapter, you should remove your rose-colored glasses and take another look at the cases.

NOTE: AN HISTORICAL OVERVIEW OF CAPITAL GAINS TAXATION

Capital gains have been accorded some sort of preferential tax treatment since 1921, when the tax was limited to 12½ percent on gains from sales of capital assets held for more than two years. In 1924, the deduction for capital losses was correspondingly limited to a maximum of 12½ percent of the loss. This basic pattern of preferential treatment for capital gains and limited deductibility of capital losses has continued in effect for most of the period the income tax has been in place.

The Revenue Act of 1934 provided for a decreasing percentage of gain to be taxable the longer the asset was held, ranging from 100 percent if the asset were held a year or less to only 30 percent of the gain if the asset had been held for more than 10 years. Losses were deductible only to the extent of recognized gains plus $2,000.

The 1938 Revenue Act combined features of the 1921 and 1934 legislation by allowing taxpayers to choose either to be taxed at a flat maximum rate or to include in income a varying percentage of gain depending upon the length of time they had held the asset. In 1942, the holding period to qualify for capital gains treatment was reduced to six months; gains and losses on property held by individuals for six months or less were fully taxed, while only 50 percent of gains and losses on property held more than six months was included in taxable income. The 1942 amendments also allowed short-term and long-term capital losses to offset both short-term and long-term capital gains, permitted capital losses to offset no more than $1,000 a year of ordinary income, and provided an alternative maximum 25 percent capital gains tax rate for corporations as well as individuals.

The next major change came in the Tax Reform Act of 1969, which limited the alternative 25 percent maximum rate for individual taxpayers to the first $50,000 of gain. Since one-half of capital gains was excluded from taxable income, the maximum rate on capital gains was 35 percent (one-half of 70 percent). This legislation also provided that $2 of net long-term capital loss would be required to offset $1 of ordinary income up to a maximum of $1,000; thus, it took $2,000 of net long-term capital loss to produce $1,000 of deduction. Individuals could carry over any excess loss to offset capital gains and ordinary income in future years. The 1969 Act also imposed an additional tax—the "minimum tax"—on certain "tax preferences" (including the portion of capital gains otherwise excluded from the taxable income of high-income taxpayers). The minimum tax had the effect of increasing the maximum rate applicable to long-term capital gains from 35 percent to 36.5 percent. In addition, under the 1969 Act, capital gains decreased the amount of earned income that otherwise was eligible for a special 50 percent rate of tax, in effect producing a maximum 49.9 percent rate of tax on capital gains for some taxpayers.

The 1976 Act increased the amount of capital losses that could be deducted against ordinary income to $3,000 and increased the long-term holding period to one year.

By 1978, however, Congress was concerned about redressing overtaxation due to inflation and encouraging investment and "capital formation." Congress believed the tax burden on capital gains was unacceptably high and lowered the top capital gains rate to 28 percent. This was done, first, by increasing the capital gains exclusion from 50 to 60 percent of long-term gains (while the maximum rate on ordinary income was 70 percent), and second, by eliminating capital gains as an item of tax preference subject to the additional minimum tax and as an offset to the 50 percent maximum tax. Congress established an alternative minimum tax on capital gains and adjusted itemized deductions, which applied an independent rate schedule to a broader tax base that included capital gains in full, but the top capital gains rate never exceeded 28 percent under either the minimum tax or the regular tax.

When the Economic Recovery Tax Act of 1981 lowered the maximum rate on all ordinary income from 70 percent to 50 percent, the highest marginal rate on capital gains became 20 percent (a top 50 percent rate applied to the included 40 percent of capital gains). The Deficit Reduction Act of 1984 reduced to six months the period for which an asset must be held before qualifying as a long-term capital gain or loss.

As part of a major reform of the Code in 1986 that significantly broadened the tax base in exchange for lower rates, Congress repealed the preferential tax rate for capital gains. The top tax rate on ordinary income as well as capital gains was 28 percent. Capital losses continued to be deductible without limit against capital gains and the limitation on net capital losses of individuals deductible annually against ordinary income remained at $3,000, but capital losses (whether short-term or long-term) offset ordinary income dollar for dollar up to that limit.

The repeal of the capital gains preference was short-lived. In 1990, Congress increased the maximum marginal tax rate for individuals to 31 percent but left the maximum rate on capital gains at 28 percent. Supporters claimed that reduced rates were needed to promote capital investment. Critics complained that additional complexity was renewed with no evidence that the 3 percent differential would in fact spur investment. The relatively small difference in rates was not thought to be of major significance. The capital gains preference was increased, however, in 1993. The 1993 Act increased the top marginal rate to 39.6 percent, but again left the maximum rate on capital gains at 28 percent, resulting in a meaningful differential in the tax treatment of ordinary income and capital gains for people whose ordinary income is taxed at a rate greater than 28 percent. In addition, Congress added a special capital gains preference for the stock of start-up companies.

The 1997 Act reduced the maximum rate on net capital gain to 20 percent, except for assets that otherwise would be taxed at 15 percent, in which case the rate is 10 percent. The 1997 legislation required a taxpayer to have held an asset for eighteen months to obtain these favorable rates. But in 1998, Congress decreased the holding period for assets eligible for the 10 and 20 percent capital gains rates to twelve months. The gain on the sale or exchange of certain collectibles is taxed at a 28 percent rate. Some gains on certain real estate that has been depreciated and that is held for more than twelve months are taxed at a 25 percent rate. This provision is discussed further at page 570 infra.

The rate on assets held for more than five years is only 18 percent, provided the asset's holding period began after December 31, 2000. A taxpayer holding a capital asset or an asset used in her trade or business on January 1, 2001 may elect to treat the asset as sold for its fair market value, recognizing gain (but not loss) and triggering a new holding period. Beginning in 2001 assets that otherwise would be taxed at 15 percent are taxed at 8 percent regardless of when acquired. Finally, assets held less than a year are taxed at the ordinary income rates. See § 1(h).

Under current law, there are now nine different rates on capital gains of individuals, as summarized below:

   7.5% Small business stock (§ 1202), subject to a 50 percent exclusion, if otherwise taxable at 15%

8%   Assets held for more than 5 years if otherwise taxable at 10% or 20%

10%   Assets held for more than one year if otherwise taxable at 15%

14%   Small business stock (§ 1202), subject to 50% exclusion, if otherwise taxable at 28% or higher rate

15%   Assets held for more than one year otherwise subject to a 28% or 25% rate if the taxpayer is otherwise not taxed at a 28% or higher rate

18%   Assets held for more than 5 years, with a holding period beginning after 12/31/00 if taxpayer is otherwise taxable at a 20% rate on capital gain

20%   Assets held for more than one year if the taxpayer otherwise taxable at a 28% or higher rate

25%   Gain to the extent of depreciation on real estate held for more than one year if the taxpayer is otherwise taxable at a 28% or higher rate.

28%   Gain on collectibles held for more than one year if the taxpayer is otherwise taxable at a 28% or higher rate.

Surely there is no coherent policy explanation for this byzantine system. The historical summary suggests that the current treatment of capital gains mirrors nothing more than current thinking on the subject. Congress changed the capital gains tax six times during the two decades culminating with the 1986 Act. Whereas the 1969 and 1976 legislation appeared to move toward elimination of any distinction between capital gains and ordinary income, the 1978 legislation moved in the opposite direction. Then, in 1986, Congress repealed the preferential rate when substantially cutting the top tax rate on ordinary income. Congress flip-flopped again almost immediately, with a differential tax rate on capital gains reintroduced in 1990. The current system taxes most capital gain at a top rate of 20 percent while the top rate on ordinary income is 38.6 percent (to be reduced to 35 percent in 2006 under legislation enacted in 2001). Replacing the multiple rates on capital gains with the old exclusion from income of half the gain would nevertheless be a major simplification.

The tax advantages accorded capital gains coupled with the tax disadvantages of capital losses have generated many contests between the government and taxpayers concerning whether a particular item qualifies as a capital gain or loss. The interpretation of the general statutory definition has been left to the Treasury, the courts, and in the first instance to taxpayers (and their attorneys). The task has been made more difficult by the failure of Congress to adopt any consistent theory of what should qualify as capital gains and losses.

As you will see from the following material, both the mechanics and the attempt to distinguish capital gains from ordinary income are extremely complicated. Furthermore, the rate differentials create a powerful incentive to structure transactions to obtain capital gains. Although it is far from clear on which kinds of gains Congress wishes to bestow preferential treatment, Congress wants to limit the ability of taxpayers to convert ordinary income into capital gain.

SECTION 1. THE MECHANICS OF THE TREATMENT OF CAPITAL GAINS AND LOSSES

The mechanics of the taxation of capital gains and losses are found in §§ 1001–1288 of the Code. Particularly important for present purposes are §§ 1(h), 1001, 1011, 1012, 1016, 1211, 1212, 1221–1231, and 1245 and 1250. These sections should be read carefully.

First, the Code requires a taxable event that causes the taxpayer to "realize" a gain or loss, as taxation is limited to realized gains. The Code contains no definition of "realization," but gain is defined in § 1001(a) as the "excess of the amount realized * * * over the adjusted basis of the property." No realization occurs when property merely appreciates in value; the property must be sold or otherwise disposed of for a taxable event to occur. Recall the discussion of the realization requirement in Chapter 2.

In some cases, there may be a realization event, but the resulting gain or loss nevertheless is not "recognized." Section 1001(c) provides that all gains or losses are recognized in full unless "otherwise provided." Congress has provided a number of nonrecognition provisions and these are discussed later in this Chapter.

After it has been determined that the taxpayer has realized gain or loss and that the gain or loss is recognized, the character of the gain or loss must be determined. All gains and losses are divided into two classes: capital and ordinary. All gains and losses that are not capital in nature fall into the "ordinary" classification. Taxpayers generally prefer capital gains because they are often taxed at lower rates, but they also prefer ordinary losses, which are deductible in full from ordinary income while capital losses generally are deductible only to the extent of capital gains plus (for individuals) a limited amount of ordinary income.

A. NONCORPORATE TAXPAYERS

Capital gains and losses are subdivided into two classes—short-term and long-term. The current dividing line (known as the holding period) is twelve months. The taxpayer must have held property for more than twelve months before any gain from its sale qualifies as a long-term capital gain subject to the lowest rates—currently 20 percent (or 8 percent if the asset otherwise would be taxed at 15 percent). §§ 1222 and 1223.

Because short-term gains and losses historically have been treated differently from long-term gains and losses, determining the tax on an individual's capital gains involves a two-stage netting process. First, the taxpayer must separately net short-term gains against short-term losses. If short-term gains exceed short-term losses, there is a net short-term gain; if short-term losses are greater, there is a net short-term loss. § 1222(5) and

(6). Likewise, the netting of long-term gains and long-term losses produces either a net long-term gain or net long-term loss. § 1222(7) and (8).

The short-term gain or loss then is netted against the long-term gain or loss. If the net short-term capital gains exceed net long-term capital losses, the excess short-term gain is taxable in full as ordinary income. If the net long-term capital gain exceeds the net short-term capital loss, the excess ("net capital gain") is taxed at the preferential capital gains rate. When the taxpayer has both a net short-term gain and a net long-term gain, the former is taxed in full as ordinary income, and the latter is subject to the favorable rate.

Where the losses exceed the gains, the excess capital loss offsets up to $3,000 of ordinary income each taxable year. Any excess not allowed in one taxable year is carried forward indefinitely until it is completely utilized. The losses carried over keep their character; for example, the excess of net short-term capital loss over long-term capital gain is a short-term capital loss in the following year. For this purpose, the "excess capital loss" is the lesser of the amount that exceeds the ordinary income deduction or "adjusted taxable income." Adjusted taxable income for this purpose is taxable income increased by the amount of ordinary income deductions and the deduction for personal exemptions. §§ 1211 and 1212.

Examples of the Mechanics of Capital Gains and Losses

Example 1: The taxpayer has taxable income of $100,000 for the year excluding capital gains and losses. His capital gains and losses are as follows:

Long-term capital gain	$5,000	
Long-term capital loss	($1,000)	
Net long-term capital gain		$4,000
Short-term capital gain	$2,000	
Short-term capital loss	($3,500)	
Net short-term capital loss		($1,500)
Net capital gain		$2,500

The taxable income of $100,000 (excluding the capital gains) is taxed at the ordinary income rates. The net capital gain of $2,500 is taxed at a 20 percent rate (assuming the assets have not been held for five years).

Example 2: The taxpayer has taxable income of $100,000 for the taxable year excluding capital gains and losses. Her capital gains and losses are as follows:

Long-term capital gain	$5,000	
Long-term capital loss	($1,000)	
Net long-term capital gain		$4,000
Short-term capital gain	$2,000	
Short-term capital loss	($500)	
Net short-term capital gain		$1,500

The taxpayer's taxable income of $100,000 plus the net short-term capital gain of $1,500 is taxed at the ordinary income rates. The net long-term capital gain of $4,000 is taxed at a 20 percent rate (assuming the assets have not been held for five years).

Example 3: The taxpayer has taxable income for the taxable year of $100,000 excluding capital gains and losses. His capital gains and losses are as follows:

Long-term capital gain	$1,000	
Long-term capital loss	($5,000)	
Net long-term capital loss		($4,000)
Short-term capital gain	$2,000	
Short-term capital loss	($500)	
Net short-term capital gain		$1,500
Net capital loss		($2,500)

The taxpayer is permitted to net the $2,500 capital loss against up to $3,000 of ordinary income. Thus, the taxpayer has $97,500 taxable income taxed at ordinary income rates.

Example 4: The taxpayer has taxable income for the taxable year of $100,000 excluding capital gains and losses. Her capital gains and losses are as follows:

Long-term capital gain	$1,000	
Long-term capital loss	($5,000)	
Net long-term capital loss		($4,000)
Short-term capital gain	$1,000	
Short-term capital loss	($3,000)	
Net short-term capital loss		($2,000)
Net capital loss		($6,000)

The taxpayer is permitted to use $3,000 of the $6,000 capital loss against up to $3,000 of ordinary income. Thus, the taxpayer has $97,000 of taxable income taxed at ordinary income rates. In addition, she will carry over to the following year $3,000 of long-term capital loss. For purposes of determining the character of the losses carried over to a subsequent year, any short-term losses are deemed to offset ordinary income before long-term losses. § 1212(b)(2).

B.   CORPORATE TAXPAYERS

Net capital gains and losses are calculated in the same way by corporate and noncorporate taxpayers, but they produce different tax consequences.

There is no rate difference between ordinary income and capital gains for corporations. A corporation's taxable income is taxed at the rates listed in § 11.

Capital losses are only deductible to the extent of capital gains. Corporations are permitted a three-year carryback and a five-year carryover of capital losses to be used against past or future capital gains. Each amount carried back or carried forward is treated as a short-term capital loss. It must be carried back to the earliest permitted year, with the unused excess then carried to more recent years and then carried forward until it is fully used. The corporation forfeits losses not used within the permissible period.

C. A WORD OF CAUTION

The preceding discussion of the mechanics of capital gains taxation is intended merely to provide beginning students of federal taxation with a straightforward overview. Many details ignored here may complicate the taxation of a particular transaction. In addition, there may be important interactions with other provisions of the Code. For example, capital gains and losses may be passive gains or losses, subject to the limitation on passive losses of § 469, discussed supra at page 418.

SECTION 2.   THE POLICY OF PREFERENTIAL TREATMENT OF CAPITAL GAINS

Although preferential treatment for capital gains has been a distinctive feature of the U.S. income tax since 1921, the congressional purposes for the favorable treatment always have seemed uncertain and often contradictory. Congress has never clearly articulated a set of policy objectives for this preference. The note that follows sets forth the most commonly raised policy arguments and examines some of their implications for defining "capital" transactions. A more detailed discussion of each of the arguments can be found in Noël B. Cunningham & Deborah H. Schenk, "The Case for a Capital Gains Preference," 48 Tax L.Rev. 319 (1993).

NOTE ON POLICY ARGUMENTS FOR AND AGAINST PREFERENTIAL TREATMENT OF CAPITAL GAINS

Arguments Favoring Preferential Treatment:

(1) *Capital Gains Are Not Income.* This is the most fundamental ground offered for excluding capital gains from the income tax base. The argument concentrates on two common features of capital gains: (a) they are not recurring and (b) they sometimes simply reflect changes in interest rates.

(a) *Capital Gains Are Nonrecurring.* This argument reflects the view that a progressive income tax should be imposed only on recurring items, and generally should exclude extraordinary gains or windfalls.

The Critic's Response. This narrow view of income, which enjoyed considerable favor in the early days of the income tax, was rejected in the Supreme Court's decision in *Glenshaw Glass* (treating punitive damage awards as income, discussed supra at page 87). Including only recurring items in income would conflict with the notion that the income tax base should reflect differences in people's ability to pay tax, even where one person's greater ability is due to a windfall or other extraordinary event. A dollar of capital gain has the same purchasing power as any other dollar of income and this implies no special treatment for capital gains (or for capital losses).

(b) *Asset Value Changes Due to Interest Rate Fluctuations Are Not Income.* The notion that changes in asset values that simply reflect changes in interest rates should not be considered income is more complicated. When interest rates fall, the price of a bond or other fixed-income asset will rise so that its yield will be comparable to that of similar assets paying the new lower rate of interest. The rise in price does not affect the owner's interest income. For example, assume that a bond paying a 12 percent rate of interest rises in value from $1,000 to $1,200 when the market rate of interest falls to 10 percent. The taxpayer who sells such a bond and invests the entire proceeds in a new bond yielding 10 percent will continue to earn interest income of $120 a year (10 percent on a principal amount of $1,200). He will be no better off, notwithstanding the price rise (i.e. the capital gain).

The Critic's Response. That much is true. However, the investor who has enjoyed the price increase is in a better economic position than people whose capital value remained unchanged. He can now purchase $1,200 rather than $1,000 of goods or services and, if he keeps it invested, his capital will produce a greater return than the capital of people who had not invested in such fixed-income assets before the drop in interest rates. Those people, with only $1,000 of capital, will be able to earn only the lower interest rate on new investments, but will not have enjoyed the increase in capital value. The fact that he invested sooner and reaped the benefits in the form of an increase in capital value made him better off.

(2) *Bunching.* Proponents of a capital gains preference often defend it as ameliorating bunching: the realization rule forces a taxpayer to report in the year of the asset's sale capital gains that have accrued over a period of years, and thus the gain on the sale may be subject to a higher marginal rate than would have applied had the gains been reported each year as they accrued.

The Critic's Response. First, bunching is a problem only in a system with graduated tax rates and only if the taxpayer is in a higher bracket on the disposition date than she was when the income accrued. Second, the argument fails to take into account the benefit the taxpayer enjoyed from deferring the tax on the gain until the asset was sold; the deferral attributable to the realization requirement may offset the bunching effect completely. Finally, a lower capital gains rate is an extremely crude mechanism for what is essentially income averaging. A better solution would be to permit the taxpayer to allocate the gain or loss realized to the number of years the asset has been held and compute the tax liability on that fraction at the appropriate marginal rate.

(3) *Inflation.* In an inflationary period, a portion of the capital gain is inflation, rather than "real" gain, and, to the extent it merely reflects the rise in general prices, it does not add to one's economic purchasing power. Thus, it does not represent economic income, and should not be part of the tax base. For example, if A purchases an asset for $100 and prices rise 5 percent during the year, A will report $5 of gain on a sale of the asset even though the $105 sales proceeds reflect no real economic gain.

The Critic's Response. It is true that gain on assets held during a long period of inflation will be mismeasured when current dollars realized upon sale are compared to prior years' dollars of basis. The amount of overtaxation of inflationary gains therefore depends upon the rate of inflation and the period the asset was held. A rate preference for capital gains is a poor solution because it bears no relation to either factor. Furthermore, the inflation may be offset by the benefit of deferring the tax on the gain until realization. The lower tax rate will be of no use to a taxpayer who experiences an economic loss.

Finally, it is somewhat hard to defend an adjustment for inflationary capital gains without comprehensive income tax adjustments for inflation. Congress has taken some steps in this direction by indexing certain items, such as tax brackets, the standard deduction, and the earned income credit. Accelerated depreciation is sometimes defended on the ground that it ameliorates the effects of inflation, but Congress has never adopted inflation indexing of the basis of assets (or debt), i.e., adjusting the basis to reflect general price increases during the holding period. Such indexation is widely viewed as being extraordinarily complex.

(4) *Taxation of Capital Gains on Corporate Stock Is Double Taxation.* This is because gains that typically have been taxed once as income to the corporation are taxed again when a shareholder realizes them on the sale of stock when the increase in the stock value reflects retained earnings of the corporation, which have already been taxed.

The Critic's Response. Taxing gains on the sale of stock constitutes double taxation when the retained earnings already have been subject to corporate income tax. But this is also true of dividends (which are not deductible by the corporation) and is regarded as a problem of corporate taxation rather than capital gains. A more equitable and more efficient solution to this problem would be to integrate corporate and personal income taxes, with the aim of taxing all corporate income alike and taxing corporate source income in the same manner as all other income. In any event, even if this argument were accepted, it would support a preference for gains only on corporate stock attributable to retained earnings, not other capital assets or gains attributable to untaxed appreciation at the corporate level.

(5) *Disincentive to Risk Taking.* Taxing capital gains makes investors less willing to make risky investments because the tax reduces the expected return. This reduces economic welfare because investors may shift their portfolios toward less risky assets from those they would retain in a nontax world. High-risk investments are sometimes thought to perform particularly valuable social functions, such as funding new businesses, which are a source of jobs and innovation, and inherently risky, but essential ventures, such as agriculture.

The Critic's Response. It is not clear that an income tax would significantly discourage risk taking if there is a complete tax offset for losses. If losses are fully deductible, the government shares in the downside risk as well as the upside potential of investments. But generally neither business losses nor capital losses always produce tax refunds. There are significant limitations on the deduction for capital losses in order to limit "cherrypicking," i.e., realizing losses to obtain deductions but deferring gains. A more generous allowance of loss offsets against ordinary income might provide a better incentive for risk taking. Furthermore, the general capital gains preference is not limited to risky assets. The special advantage of § 1202 for small business stock, however, is one attempt to target a capital gains preference toward risky investments.

(7) *Disincentive to Savings.* People's consumption behavior generally is thought to depend more on average lifetime income, or expected long-term income, than on annual income. Thus, a once-in-a-lifetime capital gain is likely to be spent, if at all, over the entire lifetime of a rational spender. Gain that is taxed immediately will be spent by the government whereas it would have been saved (at least temporarily) by the taxpayer. In a growing economy, that means a continuing drain on savings. Taxation of capital gains impinges more heavily on savings than on consumption, since these gains would tend to be saved. Such taxation is therefore more likely to reduce overall savings and investment than other means of raising revenue.

The Critic's Response. The concern that capital gains taxation impinges upon savings generally supports taxation of consumption, rather than income. A consumption tax would exclude all savings from the tax base without regard to the taxpayer's sources of income. Limiting the favorable treatment of savings to capital gain income may be particularly unfair, because assets eligible for capital gains treatment may be more likely than other forms of savings to be held by upper-income taxpayers.

Furthermore, it is not clear that raising the rate of return on savings by not taxing amounts saved would increase the amount of private savings. Some savers are target savers—they save to accumulate a certain amount, say for education or retirement—and will save only until they reach their goal. An increase in the rate of return would enable these savers to achieve their goal more quickly and thus, they might save less. Even assuming an increase in private savings, it is not certain that this would lower the cost of capital and increase domestic investment. In an open economy, foreign investment might be increased instead.

(7) *Lock-in.* To avoid the taxation of the gain on appreciated assets, taxpayers will refrain from selling assets, even when market conditions otherwise would favor sales. This "lock-in" effect reduces liquidity, impairs the mobility of capital, and may lead to broader fluctuations in market prices. A preference for capital gains reduces the tax barriers to economically-motivated shifts in investments.

The Critic's Response. The lock-in effect is real, but a large percentage of capital gains are never subject to tax. The small number of realizations is due primarily to § 1014, which in many cases permits heirs to step up the basis of inherited property to its fair market value, thus permitting the gain to escape tax permanently.

The lock-in problem could be eliminated either by not taxing gains on the sales of assets or by taxing unrealized gains as they accrue. Under a so-called mark-to-market system, a taxpayer would be required to report the value of his property at the end of each year and treat as gain (or loss) the increase (or decrease) in value since the end of the preceding year. Although many proponents of an income tax contend that taxing accrued gains is theoretically correct, they have long considered proposals to do so administratively impractical. But some advocates of cutting back or eliminating the realization requirement do not regard the administrative problems as insurmountable. In fact, some commentators argue that such a system would simplify the income tax; they contend that although accrual taxation would be complicated by valuation and liquidity problems, these disadvantages would be outweighed by the reduction in tax planning complexities, the need for adjustments for inflation, and the possible elimination of the corporate income tax.

Not taxing capital gains at all is inappropriate in an income tax. An alternative to not taxing gains is nonrecognition or rollover of gain on sales. Rollover proposals are designed to encourage capital mobility, but they would be a major step toward taxing consumption rather than income, since gains would be taxed only when they were consumed, not when they are reinvested. A consumption tax, however, would exclude all savings from the tax base, not just capital gains.

Arguments Opposing Preferential Treatment:

(1) *A Dollar of Capital Gain Is the Same as Any Other Dollar of Economic Gain.* Because a dollar of capital gain has the same purchasing power as any other dollar of income, there should be no special treatment for capital gains (or for capital losses).

The Critic's Response. A dollar of capital gain is different for all of the reasons set forth above.

(2) *The Preferential Treatment of Capital Gains Is a Great Source of Income Tax Complexity.* Many provisions in the Code deal with the special treatment of capital gains and losses. Tax planning to achieve capital gain status, including "conversion" of ordinary income into capital gain, has induced bizarre and complex arrangements and transactions.

The Critic's Response. Much of the complexity attributed to the special treatment of capital gains does not disappear by taxing capital gains as ordinary income. The complexity largely is due to the need to measure gain or loss—for example, through basis computations and adjustments—and to determine when income should be taxed (or loss allowed). Moreover, if the realization requirement is retained, some limitations on capital loss deductions remain necessary; otherwise, individuals with accrued gains and losses would realize only the losses, which they could offset without limitation against salaries or other unrelated income. Any remaining restriction on capital losses would require that "capital" transactions be distinguished from "ordinary" transactions, thereby retaining much of the definitional complexity.

(3) *The Capital Gains Preference Creates Too Much Inequity and Too Little "Bang for the Buck."* The preference for capital gains primarily benefits high-bracket taxpayers. In addition, it produces too little additional savings and risk taking for the revenue cost.

The Critic's Response. The revenue cost from capital gains taxation is overstated. When capital gains rates are high, people defer realizations of gains, thereby both decreasing revenues and inhibiting economic growth. Indeed, no matter what the capital gains tax rate, wealthy people, who have a sizable portfolio of stocks and other capital assets, have always enjoyed great discretion about when to pay capital gains taxes or even whether to pay them. This occurs because they control the timing of their sales of assets and thereby the timing of the payment of capital gains tax. If they need cash, they can borrow against assets that have appreciated in value, rather than selling them, and avoid capital gains taxes. People who have assets with both capital gains and capital losses in their portfolios, a common occurrence among the wealthy, can avoid or postpone capital gains taxes by timing their sales of the loss assets.

Given the great flexibility many people have in selling or holding appreciated assets, what rate of capital gains taxation maximizes the government's revenue? Although one cannot be certain about the precise level of the revenue-maximizing tax rate for capital gains, considerable economic evidence suggests that it currently lies somewhere between 19 and 28 percent. Treasury Department economists have believed this rate to be about 20 percent, while key congressional staff economists have regarded it as closer to 28 percent. Perhaps the 25 percent top rate in effect during the 1940's, 1950's, and 1960's was a pretty good approximation. In fact, when the top tax rates on ordinary income were increased above that level in both the 1990 and 1993 Budget Acts, the maximum capital gains rates was retained at 28 percent in order not to lose revenues.

NOTE ON JUSTIFICATION FOR THE LIMITATION ON LOSSES

In a system without a realization requirement, there would be no need for a limitation on losses—all gains and losses would be taxed as they accrue. If, however, gains are deferred until realized, loss limitations are thought to be necessary to prevent selective realization of losses. Otherwise, taxpayers could dispose of assets with losses and hold on to those with gains and use the losses to offset other income. Although the taxpayer's portfolio may reflect a net gain overall, she may realize a loss. If allowed, this practice would be especially egregious when the taxpayer has hedged her investments, i.e., she has purchased assets expected to move in opposite directions. Assume, for example, that A acquires an asset that has a 50 percent chance of increasing in value by 10 and a 50 percent chance of decreasing in value by 10. Assume A also acquires an asset that is a perfect hedge of the first asset, that is, if the first asset increases in value by 10, the second asset will decline in value by 10 and vice versa. A has no chance of an overall loss. Suppose the first asset increases in value and the second asset declines in value. Absent limitations on losses, A would sell the second asset but retain the first, thereby creating a tax loss although she has no economic loss.

In order to limit "cherrypicking" of losses, § 1211 generally limits the deduction for capital losses to the amount of realized gains during a taxable year plus $3,000. Corporations may deduct capital losses only to the extent of capital gains. Thus, taxpayers who want to deduct capital losses will have to also realize gains in order to enjoy the current value of the loss deduction. The capital loss limitation rules apply, however, regardless of whether the taxpayer has appreciated assets in his portfolio or has ever enjoyed the capital gains preference.

The limitation on losses applies to both short-term and long-term capital losses whereas the capital gains preference applies only to long-term capital gains. In addition, capital losses in excess of capital gains are deductible dollar for dollar against $3,000 whereas capital gains generally are taxed at about 50 percent of the regular rate. Finally, the limit on losses creates a bias against risky investments whereas one of the arguments for preferential treatment for gains was to encourage risk-taking. The justification for the capital loss limitation and alternative approaches to the cherrypicking problem are discussed in Robert H. Scarborough, "Risk, Diversification and the Design of Loss Limitations Under a Realization–Based Income Tax," 48 Tax L.Rev. 677 (1993).

NOTE ON DEFINING A "CAPITAL" TRANSACTION

That the words "capital," "gain," and "loss" have a familiar ring often misleads students into feeling unduly comfortable with the phrase "capital gain or loss." The capital gain concept is an artificial creation of the tax law that has no firm theoretical grounding in accounting or economics.

Moreover, the Code provides only a skeletal guide for drawing the necessary distinctions between transactions that produce capital gain (or loss) and those that produce ordinary gain (or loss). Congress has identified those transactions qualifying for favorable capital gains treatment by requiring that a transaction meet three conditions: (1) the transaction must involve "property" that is a "capital asset," (2) the property must be transferred in a "sale or exchange," and (3) the minimum holding period must be met.

A lower tax on capital gains than on ordinary income induces taxpayers to endeavor mightily to qualify profitable transactions for capital gains treatment, and the loss limitations encourage attempting to qualify losing transactions for ordinary treatment. The courts have played an important role in drawing the capital-ordinary distinction, but their results often seem inconsistent, even contradictory.

These inconsistencies are to be expected, given the general nature of the statutory rules and the variety of policy justifications for the preferential income tax treatment of capital gains. The diverse justifications for the capital gains preference, set forth in the preceding Note, have each contributed in some way to the issues that have emerged. Courts often endeavor to match a relevant policy argument to their conclusions characterizing particular transactions as capital or ordinary. For example, the desire to prevent "bunching" has been used to support capital gains treatment for income that accrues over time but is recognized in one period. The concern about "lock-in" has been advanced to limit capital gain treatment to situations involving a "transfer" of the underlying property rather than those involving a sale of a "carved-out" portion of a larger interest. The policy of creating incentives for savings, investment, and risk-taking has been argued to limit preferential treatment to gains from an investment rather than compensation for services, to rewards for risk rather than interest resulting from the mere passage of time, and to market fluctuations rather than normal business profits. For example, the sale of stock typically produces capital gain, while the compensation earned by the corporation's employees, the interest earned by the corporation's creditors, and the profits earned by the corporation on its sales of inventory all give rise to ordinary income. In determining whether the requisite "investment" or "property" is present, the courts often seek guidance not from tax policy concerns but rather from common law concepts of "property" and "ownership."

The distinction between capital gain and ordinary income cannot be so flexible as to allow taxpayers unlimited freedom to structure transactions to their best advantage. Taxpayers must be restricted from converting ordinary income into capital gain and recharacterizing capital losses as ordinary deductions. Many such restrictions are contained in the Code, the regulations, and the case law. The entire process is greatly complicated by the ability of taxpayers to create a variety of ownership-like legal relationships (sale-leasebacks, for example) as well as by the existence of corporations and other legal entities, whose ordinary income transactions (dividends, for example) must be distinguished from capital transactions (certain redemptions, reorganizations, liquidations, and recapitalizations, for example).

SECTION 3.   WHAT IS A CAPITAL ASSET?

We now turn to an examination of the statutory provisions and judicial opinions that have attempted to distinguish capital gain from ordinary income. The statutory scheme is intricate and complex. Capital gains or losses are derived only from the "sale or exchange" of property constituting a "capital asset." § 1222. Section 1221 defines capital asset broadly to include all property held by the taxpayers with certain exceptions. The general statutory exceptions are:

1) the stock in trade or inventory of a business, or property that is held primarily for sale to customers in the ordinary course of a trade or business,

2) depreciable or real property used in a trade or business,

3) literary or artistic property held by its creator,

4) accounts or notes receivable acquired in the ordinary course of the taxpayer's trade or business,

5) U.S. government publications received from the government at a price less than that which the general public is charged,

6) commodities derivative financial instruments held by commodities derivative dealers,

7) identified hedging transactions under rules provided in regulations, and

8) supplies regularly consumed by the taxpayer in the ordinary course of the trade or business.

The exclusion provided by § 1221(a)(2) for real and depreciable property used in the taxpayer's trade or business is affected by § 1231. The principal effect of § 1231 is to characterize net gain on sales of depreciable or real property used in a business as capital gain and net losses on sales of such assets as ordinary losses. Section 1245, however, often "recaptures" as ordinary income amounts that otherwise would be treated as capital gain under § 1231. Sections 1231 and 1245 are considered explicitly, infra at pages 567 and 570.

The exclusions of § 1221, in general, are intended to produce ordinary income treatment for proceeds from everyday business activities and from personal labor and capital gains treatment for investment gains. The scope of the statutory exclusions under § 1221 and their application to varying factual contexts have been the subject of much litigation. Taxpayers have exerted great efforts to structure transactions to avoid the statutory exclusions and thus to obtain capital gain treatment. As a result, the courts have construed the exclusions broadly and, in some cases, expanded them beyond the statutory language. These interpretations then have been used by other taxpayers to obtain ordinary—rather than capital—loss treatment on transactions involving property that otherwise would qualify under the statute as a capital asset. The materials that follow will give the student a feel for some of the problems that the courts have faced. This Section considers first the specific statutory exceptions and then the cases that expand the exceptions beyond a literal construction of the statutory language.

A.   THE STATUTORY FRAMEWORK

1.   PROPERTY HELD FOR SALE TO CUSTOMERS

Section 1221(a)(1) exempts from the definition of capital asset property "held by the taxpayer primarily for sale to customers in the ordinary course of his trade or business." Section 1231(b)(1)(B) likewise excludes such assets from § 1231 treatment. Thus, any gain or loss from the sale or exchange of such property will be ordinary gain or loss. These exclusions apply only if the taxpayer is engaged in a trade or business that ordinarily sells the property in question.

Malat v. Riddell

Supreme Court of the United States, 1966. 383 U.S. 569.

PER CURIAM.

Petitioner was a participant in a joint venture which acquired a 45–acre parcel of land, the intended use for which is somewhat in dispute. Petitioner contends that the venturers' intention was to develop and operate an apartment project on the land; the [Commissioner's] position is that there was a "dual purpose" of developing the property for rental purposes or selling, whichever proved to be the more profitable. In any event, difficulties in obtaining the necessary financing were encountered, and the interior lots of the tract were subdivided and sold. The profit from those sales was reported and taxed as ordinary income.

The joint venturers continued to explore the possibility of commercially developing the remaining exterior parcels. Additional frustrations in the form of zoning restrictions were encountered. These difficulties persuaded petitioner and another of the joint venturers of the desirability of terminating the venture; accordingly, they sold out their interests in the remaining property. Petitioner contends that he is entitled to treat the profits from this last sale as capital gains; the [Commissioner] takes the position that this was "property held by the taxpayer primarily for sale to customers in the ordinary course of his trade or business," and thus subject to taxation as ordinary income.

The District Court made the following finding:

"The members of [the joint venture], as of the date the 44.901 acres were acquired, intended either to sell the property or develop it for rental, depending upon which course appeared to be most profitable. The venturers realized that they had made a good purchase price-wise and, if they were unable to obtain acceptable construction financing or rezoning * * * which would be prerequisite to commercial development, they would sell the property in bulk so they wouldn't get hurt. The purpose of either selling or developing the property continued during the period in which [the joint venture] held the property."

The District Court ruled that petitioner had failed to establish that the property was not held *primarily* for sale to customers in the ordinary course of business, and thus rejected petitioner's claim to capital gain treatment for the profits derived from the property's resale. The Court of Appeals affirmed, 9 Cir. 347 F.2d 23. We granted certiorari (382 U.S. 900) to resolve a conflict among the courts of appeals with regard to the meaning of the term "primarily" as it is used in [§ 1221(a)(1)] of the Internal Revenue Code.

* * *

The statute denies capital gain treatment to profits reaped from the sale of "property held by the taxpayer *primarily* for sale to customers in the ordinary course of his trade or business." (Emphasis added.) The [Commissioner] urges upon us a construction of "primarily" as meaning that a purpose may be "primary" if it is a "substantial" one.

As we have often said, "the words of statutes—including revenue acts—should be interpreted where possible in their ordinary, everyday senses." Crane v. Commissioner, 331 U.S. 1, 6. * * * Departure from a literal reading of statutory language may, on occasion, be indicated by relevant internal evidence of the statute itself and necessary in order to effect the legislative purpose. * * * But this is not such an occasion. The purpose of the statutory provision with which we deal is to differentiate between the "profits and losses arising from the everyday operation of a business" on the one hand (Corn Products Refining Co. v. Commissioner, 350 U.S. 46, 52) and "the realization of appreciation in value accrued over a substantial period of time" on the other. * * * A literal reading of the statute is consistent with this legislative purpose. We hold that, as used in [§ 1221(a)(1)], "primarily" means "of first importance" or "principally."

Since the courts below applied an incorrect legal standard, we do not consider whether the result would be supportable on the facts of this case had the correct one been applied. We believe, moreover, that the appropriate disposition is to remand the case to the District Court for fresh fact-findings, addressed to the statute as we have now construed it.

Vacated and remanded.

MR. JUSTICE BLACK would affirm the judgments of the District Court and the Court of Appeals.

NOTES

(A) *Application of Malat.* As the Supreme Court stated in *Malat*, the purpose of the § 1221(a)(1) exclusion is to distinguish profits and losses "arising from the everyday operation of a business" from those resulting from changes "in value accrued over a substantial period of time." But as *Malat* illustrates, application of the exclusion to particular facts has caused great difficulty for the courts. At what point do investment activities become business activities?

Contrary to the initial expectations of some analysts, *Malat* has had little impact on later lower court determinations. In situations involving a change of purpose from rental to sale, lower courts often have indicated that the time for determining the taxpayer's "purpose" is the time of sale. It is tautological that at the time of sale, sale is "of first importance." See, e.g., Bynum v. Commissioner, 46 T.C. 295 (1966), where the Tax Court, finding ordinary income in a real estate case, noted: "[W]e are not dealing with * * * a dual purpose as concerned the Supreme Court in *Malat*, but with a change in purpose * * *."

Malat was thought to have the most significance in the "dual-purpose" context involving assets held for both rental and sale, but the lower courts have had little difficulty in molding the semantics of *Malat* to avoid characterizing "everyday business profits" as capital gains. Sometimes the courts find two "businesses"—a rental business and a sales business. It naturally follows that the sale is "of first importance" to the sales business. See, e.g., Continental Can Co. v. United States, 190 Ct.Cl. 811, 422 F.2d 405 (1970), cert. denied 400 U.S. 819 (1970), where the taxpayer manufactured and sold cans for food and other products and leased to its customers machines for sealing the cans. An antitrust decree then required Continental to permit its customers to purchase the canning machines. The taxpayer contended that capital gains treatment was proper on sales of machines to customers who previously had leased the machines. The machines purchased by these lessees averaged 16.6 years of age. The court distinguished *Malat:*

> Where there is a change in the purpose of the holding of an asset, as there was here * * * [t]he basic question is the primary purpose of holding as of the date of the sale * * *. And where a company is, at such date, regularly engaged in the dual business of selling and renting its machines, then income resulting from either activity satisfies the "primarily" concept since it is "a part of" the "normal stream * * * of the taxpayer's business" and not "outside" * * * [or] separate from the main-stream of the enterprise. * * * *Malat* itself was an altogether different kind of case. It did not involve a taxpayer in two separate businesses, such as is plaintiff.

See also Rev.Rul. 80–37, 1980–1 C.B. 51, requiring ordinary income treatment for sales of equipment to leasing customers by a taxpayer who is "regularly engaged in the dual business of renting and selling such equipment;" International Shoe Machine Corp. v. United States, 491 F.2d 157 (1st Cir.), cert. denied, 419 U.S. 834 (1974), finding ordinary income where sales to customers were an ongoing and regular part of the business even though the taxpayer's major source of revenue was rental of machines, and sales accounted for only 7 and 2 percent of gross revenues in the years at issue.

Courts often allow capital gain treatment in "rental obsolescence" cases, where equipment is sold only after its rental income producing potential has ended. See, e.g., Mafco Equipment Co. v. Commissioner, 47 T.C.M. 88 (1983), where the Tax Court treated as capital gain the proceeds received by an equipment lessor from sales of equipment that was no longer appropriate for rental because of age, condition or obsolescence.

(B) *The Present Value of a Stream of Ordinary Income.* In *International Shoe Machine,* supra, the court distinguished the sale of machinery that retained the potential of rental income from the liquidation of inventory that generally produced capital gain. The court observed that "the sale of such machinery, for a price which included the present value of [the] future ordinary income [that the machines would generate], cannot be considered the liquidation of an investment outside the scope of the ordinary course of * * * business." Is not the sales price of any asset—whether a patent, a share of stock or a piece of real estate—the present value of an expected stream of future ordinary income? Would this rationale, if carried to an extreme, deny capital gains treatment on any asset sale?

The cases interpreting § 1221(a)(1), many of which involve real estate, tend to turn on their facts, but three issues predominate. Often the issue is whether the nature of the taxpayer's dealings in property classify the taxpayer as a dealer who is holding the property primarily for sale to customers in the ordinary course of business. In other cases, it is clear that the taxpayer acquired the property for investment but changed his purpose and the issue is whether the change resulted in his being treated as a dealer. And third, in some cases, the taxpayer has a dual purpose—perhaps to sell or to rent or to hold for appreciation or sell to customers—or perhaps no set purpose other than to make money. The issue is which purpose controls. The case that follows illustrates the difficulties.

Bramblett v. Commissioner

United States Court of Appeals, Fifth Circuit, 1992. 960 F.2d 526.

E. Grady Jolly, Circuit Judge:

This tax appeal arises out of a series of transactions entered into by a partnership and a related corporation. The partnership, Mesquite East, and the corporation, Town East, are owned by the same four people, and each person has the same ownership interest in the corporation as he does in the partnership. Mesquite East bought several parcels of land for the stated purpose of investment. It then sold almost all of this land to Town East, which developed it and sold it to various third parties. Mesquite East reported the income from the sale of land at issue as capital gain, arguing that it held the land as a capital asset. The commissioner asserted a deficiency * * * arguing that the profit should be taxed as ordinary income, because in the light of the activities of Town East and their relationship to Mesquite East, Mesquite East was really in the business of selling land. The tax court affirmed the deficiency, holding that the totality of circumstances supported the conclusion that Mesquite East was in the business of selling land.

We hold that Mesquite East was not directly in the business of selling land, that Town East was not the agent of Mesquite East, and that the activities of Town East cannot be attributed to Mesquite East. Thus, Mesquite did hold the land as a capital asset and is entitled to capital gains treatment. Therefore, we reverse the decision of the tax court.

I

On May 16, 1979, William Baker, Richard Bramblett, Robert Walker, and John Sexton formed the Mesquite East Joint Venture. Baker, Bramblett, Walker, and Sexton had respective 50%, 22%, 18%, and 10% interests in the joint venture. The stated purpose of the joint venture was to acquire vacant land for investment purposes. On June 4, 1979, the same four individuals formed Town East Development Company, a Texas corporation, for the purpose of developing and selling real estate in the Mesquite, Texas area. The shareholders' interests in Town East mirrored their interests in Mesquite East.

In late 1979 and early 1980, Mesquite East acquired 180.06 acres of land from Bramco, a corporation of which Bramblett was the sole shareholder. Also, in late 1979, Mesquite East acquired 84.5 acres of land from an unrelated third party, bringing its acquisitions to a total of 264.56 acres. Subsequent to its acquisition of the property and prior to the sale at issue here, Mesquite East made four separate sales of its acquired land. In three of the four instances, Mesquite East initially sold the property to Town East, which then developed it and sold it to third parties. In each of these instances, prior to the time Town East purchased the property from Mesquite East, it already had a binding sales agreement with the third party. In the fourth transaction, Mesquite East sold property directly to Langston R & B Financial Joint Venture No. 1. Mesquite East's gross profit on these four transactions was $68,394.80 and it reported this amount as ordinary income on its 1981 partnership tax return.

Following these transactions, Town East still owned 121 acres. In 1982, Baker * * * entered into five contingent contracts of sale for portions of this property. Mesquite East consulted its attorneys and accountants seeking advice on how to structure the transactions to avoid ordinary income tax on the sale. In December 1982, Mesquite East sold the property to Town East in exchange for two promissory notes totaling $9,830,000.00, the amount an appraiser determined to be the fair market value of the land. The notes provided for an interest rate of twelve percent per annum on the unpaid balance and an annual principle payment of $1.5 million. Town East proceeded to develop the property and sold most of it to unrelated third parties in eight different transactions. Town East made no payments on the notes until after the property had been sold to third parties. Town East paid the entire principal amount by the end of 1984, but it did not make the required interest payments.

Mesquite East characterized its profits from this sale as long-term capital gain on its 1983 and 1984 partnership tax returns. On audit, the Commissioner of Internal Revenue determined that the profits constituted ordinary income * * *.

II

* * * The tax court upheld the deficiencies, finding that the sale of land was the business of Mesquite East, and that, therefore, the profits were ordinary income. The tax court stated that this was true whether the business was conducted directly or through Town East. The tax court noted that the businessmen were owners in proportionate shares of the joint venture and the corporation, that the corporation was formed less than a month after the joint venture, that the corporation routinely entered into contracts of sale to third parties before buying the property from the joint venture, that the corporation made no payments to the joint venture until funds were received from third parties, that the corporation did not make the required interest payments and that the corporation only developed land that it bought from the joint venture. * * * The court * * * stated that "the point to be made here, however, is that evidence of the corporation's activities and their correlation with activities of the joint venture is proof of the nature of the business of the joint venture. * * * The totality of the evidence supports the conclusion that the business of the joint venture was the sale of land and that the resulting gains should be taxed as ordinary income." The Brambletts now appeal the decision of the tax court.

III

On appeal, the Brambletts argue that Town East was not the agent of Mesquite East, and that, therefore, its activities cannot be attributed to Mesquite East. They further argue that Mesquite East itself was not in the business of selling property, making the tax court's determination that the profits are ordinary income incorrect. The commissioner argues that under the well-known principle of "substance over form," the business of Town East, selling property, can be attributed to Mesquite East, making its profits ordinary income.

IV

In order to qualify for favorable treatment as long-term capital gain, * * * the gain must arise from the sale or exchange of a "capital asset" held more than one year. "Property held by the taxpayer primarily for sale to customers in the ordinary course of his trade or business" cannot be a capital asset. It is well settled that the definition of a capital asset is to be construed narrowly. Corn Products Refining Co. v. Commissioner, 350 U.S. 46, 52, 76 S. Ct. 20, 24, 100 L. Ed. 29 (1955). The determination of whether Mesquite East was directly involved in the business of selling land is a factual determination, to be reversed only if clearly erroneous. Byram v. United States, 705 F.2d 1418, 1423–24 (5th Cir.1983).

The tax court's opinion is in some respects, not very clear. At one point, the court stated that the facts support the conclusion that Mesquite East was in the business of selling land, directly or through Town East. Later, the court mentioned the agency principle, but did not specifically hold that Town East was the agent of Mesquite East. Finally, the court stated that the totality of evidence supports the conclusion that the business of the joint venture was the sale of land. The commissioner argues that what the tax court meant, was that under the substance over form principle, the activities of Town East can be attributed to Mesquite East.

* * *

V

The tax court held that Mesquite East was in the business of selling land, either directly or through Town East. This court has developed a framework to be used in determining whether sales of land are considered sales of a capital asset or sales of property held primarily for sale to customers in the ordinary course of a taxpayer's business. Three principal questions must be considered:

(1) Was the taxpayer engaged in a trade or business, and if so, what business?

(2) Was the taxpayer holding the property primarily for sale in that business?

(3) Were the sales contemplated by the taxpayer "ordinary" in the course of that business?

Seven factors which should be considered when answering these three questions are: (1) the nature and purpose of the acquisition of the property and the duration of the ownership, (2) the extent and nature of the taxpayer's efforts to sell the property, (3) the number, extent, continuity and substantiality of the sales, (4) the extent of subdividing, developing, and advertising to increase sales, (5) the use of a business office for the sale of the property, (6) the character and degree of supervision or control exercised by the taxpayer over any representative selling the property, and (7) the time and effort the taxpayer habitually devoted to the sales. The frequency and substantiality of sales is the most important factor.

A review of these factors indicates that any finding by the tax court that Mesquite East was directly in the business of selling land is clearly erroneous. Mesquite East did not sell land frequently and the only substantial sale was the sale at issue. It conducted a total of five sales over a three-year period; two in 1979, one in 1980, one in 1981, and the one at issue in 1982. As a result of the first four transactions, Mesquite East made a profit of $68,394.80. On the sale at issue, Mesquite East made a profit of over seven million dollars. This record of frequency does not rise to the level necessary to reach the conclusion that the taxpayer held the property for sale rather than for investment [Suburban Realty Co. v. U.S., 615 F.2d 171, 174 (5th Cir.1980)] (taxpayer made 244 sales over a thirty-two year period);

Biedenharn [Realty Co. v. U.S., 526 F.2d 409, 411–12 (5th Cir.1976)] (during thirty-one year period, taxpayer sold 208 lots and twelve individual parcels from subdivision in question; 477 lots were sold from other properties); [U.S. v.] Winthrop [417 F.2d 905, 907 (5th Cir.1969)] (taxpayer sold 456 lots over a nineteen-year period).

In *Byram*, this court affirmed the district court's finding that even though taxpayer made twenty-two sales over a three-year period, netting $3.4 million, he did not hold the property in question for sale: Though these amounts are substantial by anyone's yardstick, the district court did not clearly err in determining that 22 such sales in three years were not sufficiently frequent or continuous to compel an inference of intent to hold the property for sale rather than investment. This is particularly true in a case where the other factors weigh so heavily in favor of the taxpayer. "Substantial and frequent sales activity, standing alone, has never been held to automatically trigger ordinary income treatment."

In *Byram*, the taxpayer did not initiate the sales, he did not maintain an office, he did not develop the property and he did not devote a great deal of time to the transactions. The taxpayer held the property for six to nine months. In the case at hand, all of the other factors also weigh heavily in favor of the taxpayers. The stated purpose of Mesquite East was to acquire the property for investment purposes. It sought advice as to how to structure the transaction to preserve its investment purpose. Mesquite East held the property in question for over three years. Mesquite East did not advertise or hire brokers, it did not develop the property and it did not maintain an office. The partners did not spend more than a minimal amount of time on the activities of Mesquite East. In the light of the fact that all of these factors weigh so heavily in favor of the taxpayers, and in the light of the fact that Mesquite East made only one substantial sale and four insubstantial sales over a three-year period, any finding by the tax court that Mesquite East was directly in the business of selling land is clearly erroneous. Therefore, we cannot affirm the tax court's decision on this ground.

VI

It is not clear from the tax court's opinion whether the court found that Town East was the agent of Mesquite East, and that therefore, Mesquite East was in the business of selling land through Town East, or whether it attributed the activities of Town East to Mesquite East based on a "substance over form" principle.

* * *

Whether the corporation operates in the name and for the account of the principal, binds the principal by its actions, transmits money received to the principal, and whether the receipt of income is attributable to the services of the employees of the principle and to assets belonging to the principal are some of the relevant considerations in determining whether a true agency exists. If the corporation is a true agent, its relations with its principal must not be dependent upon the fact that it is owned by the principal, if such is the case. Its business purpose must be the carrying on of the normal duties of an agent.

The Supreme Court [has] held that the subsidiaries were not agents of the corporation simply when the business arrangement arose because of ownership and domination by the parent. The Court acknowledged that the arrangement would not have been the same if third parties owned the subsidiaries.

* * * There is no evidence that Town East ever acted in the name of or for the account of Mesquite East. Town East did not have authority to bind Mesquite East. Town East did transfer money to Mesquite East, but it was the amount of the agreed upon fair market value of the property at the time of the sale. Town East realized a profit from its development that was much larger than a typical agency fee. The receipt of income by Town East was not attributable to the services of employees of Mesquite East or assets belonging to the joint venture. * * * [C]ommon ownership of both entities is not enough to prove an agency relationship. * * * It is clear that Town East was not carrying on the normal duties of an agent; it was not selling or developing the property on behalf of Mesquite East because Town East retained all of the profit from development. Thus, * * * Town East was not an agent of Mesquite East. Nor are there any other factors, * * * that indicate that Town East was the agent of Mesquite East. Therefore, we cannot affirm the tax court's decision on the grounds that Town East was the agent of Mesquite East.

VII

The Commissioner argues that the tax court correctly attributed the activities of Town East to Mesquite East. He further argues that the well known principle of substance over form supports this attribution. The Supreme Court recently stated that in applying the principle of substance over form: the Court has looked to the objective economic realities of a transaction, rather than to the particular form the parties employed. The Court has never regarded "the simple expedient drawing up of papers," as controlling for tax purposes when the objective economic realities are to the contrary. "In the field of taxation, administrators of the laws and the courts are concerned with substance and realities, and formal rigid documents are not rigidly binding." Nor is the parties' desire to achieve a particular tax result necessarily relevant. Frank Lyon Co. v. United States, 435 U.S. 561, 573, 98 S. Ct. 1291, 1298, 55 L. Ed. 2d 550 (1978) (internal citations omitted). The Supreme Court further stated, however, that in cases where the form chosen by the taxpayer has a genuine economic substance, "is compelled or encouraged by business or regulatory realities, is imbued with tax-independent considerations, and is not shaped solely by tax-avoidance features," *Frank Lyon*, 435 U.S. at 583–84, the government should honor the tax consequences effectuated by the taxpayer.

The Commissioner argues that when determining what the partnership's purpose was for holding the land, the tax court correctly looked to the economic substance of the transactions as a whole and attributed the activity of Town East to Mesquite East. We disagree. The business of a corporation is not ordinarily attributable to its shareholders. Neither the tax court nor the Commissioner argue that Town East is a sham corporation whose corporate shield can be pierced. Indeed, the tax court recognized and the Commissioner contends that both are separate taxable entities. Moreover, there was clearly at least one major independent business reason to form the corporation and have it develop the land and sell it—that reason being to insulate the partnership and the partners from unlimited liability from a multitude of sources. Furthermore, there is no substantial evidence that the transaction was not an arm's length transaction or that business and legal formalities were not observed. Finally, the partnership bought the real estate as an investment, hoping its value would appreciate. The partnership, however, bore the risk that the land would not appreciate. Therefore, the tax court erred in finding that the activity of Town East can be attributed to Mesquite East and, consequently, that Mesquite East was in the business of selling land. Mesquite East held the land as an investment and is therefore entitled to capital gains treatment on the gain realized by the sale.

VIII

Thus, we conclude. Any finding by the tax court that Mesquite East was directly in the business of selling land is clearly erroneous. Neither the frequency nor the substantiality of the sales made by Mesquite East supports the conclusion that Mesquite East was directly in the business of selling land. The tax court's opinion cannot be affirmed on the grounds that Town East was the agent of Mesquite East. * * * Town East was not acting as the agent of Mesquite East. * * * Finally, the activities of Town East may not be attributed to Mesquite East when determining whether Mesquite East was in the business of selling land. The corporation is not a sham; there was at least one major independent reason to form the corporation. Furthermore, the partners did invest in a capital asset in the sense that they bore the risk that the land would not appreciate. Therefore, the partnership held the land as a capital asset and is entitled to capital gains treatment. The decision of the tax court is

REVERSED.

NOTES

(A) *General Approach.* In the *Byram* case, discussed in *Bramblett*, the appellate court's opinion begins, "If a client asks you in any but an extreme case whether, in your opinion, his sale will result in capital gain, your answer should probably be, 'I don't know, and no one else in town can tell you.'" The *Bramblett* case once again confirms this "hackneyed truism," in the context of sales of real estate. In *Byram* the Fifth Circuit allowed almost a million dollars of tax refunds attributable to taxing the sales over a three-year period of 22 parcels of real property for over $9 million, resulting in a profit of over $2.5 million. As in *Bramblett*, the court in *Byram* applied the seven factors (which it described as "the seven pillars of capital gains") set forth at page 560. In *Byram*, the taxpayer was rewarded because the strength of the market allowed him to make the sales without any significant sales efforts. In *Bramblett* the court rewards clever tax planning.

Determinations whether real estate is "held for sale to customers" tend to turn on their particular facts, and there is diversity among the courts concerning the precise factors to be considered and much diversity over the relative importance of each.

The court in *Byram* held that the purpose for holding property was a question of "pure fact" and implied that the appellate review by the court in *Suburban Realty* and *Biedenharn* was too broad. Thus, the continuing vitality of the largely factual inquiries such as those engaged in by appellate courts may be called into question.

(B) *Frequency and Substantiality of Sales.* The most important factor cited in many cases is the number, frequency, and substantiality of sales. Courts suggest that numerous sales that extend over a long period of time are more likely to have occurred in the ordinary course of business, while sales that are few and isolated are more likely to have resulted from investment activity.

For example, in emphasizing the importance of frequent and substantial sales, the Fifth Circuit in *Suburban Realty Co.* noted,

> A taxpayer who engages in frequent and substantial sales is almost inevitably engaged in the real estate business. The frequency and substantiality of sales are highly probative on the issue of holding purpose because the presence of frequent sales ordinarily belies the contention that property is being held "for investment" rather than "for sale." And the frequency of sales may often be a key factor in determining the "ordinariness" question.

The court was following the Fifth Circuit's en banc decision in *Biedenharn Realty Co.,* which held that a realty company had realized ordinary income rather than capital gain from the sale of subdivided real estate. The court placed primary emphasis on the frequency and substantiality of the taxpayer's sales and secondary emphasis on improvements, including streets, sewage and utilities, that the taxpayer had made to the property. The court, in finding that the taxpayer's purpose for holding the property had changed over time from investment to sales, observed that "once an investment does not mean always an investment."

Although frequency of sales is clearly an important factor, the fact that the taxpayer engaged in only occasional sales does not guarantee that she is not a dealer. Other factors are important as well.

(C) *The Seller's Passivity.* In Adam v. Commissioner, 60 T.C. 996 (1973), the court suggested that a taxpayer would seldom be found to have engaged in a trade or business where he had done little, if anything, to acquire, improve, or market his properties. A rather extreme case emphasizing the taxpayer's passivity, Williams v. United States, 84–1 U.S.T.C. ¶ 9384 (N.D.Tex.1983), refused to impute the activity of the seller's usual broker and partner to the taxpayer. The court found it significant that he (1) did not seek out sellers or buyers of property (brokers brought him sellers and buyers without his asking), (2) rarely negotiated prices but merely accepted or rejected bids, (3) did not have a real estate license, and (4) devoted no more than 56 hours over the several years to his real estate holdings. As *Williams* involved sales of 118 parcels over a seven-year period, the case illustrates the proposition that "the frequency and substantiality of sales activity *standing alone*" does not "*automatically* * * * trigger ordinary income treatment" (emphasis added).

Williams should be contrasted with *Biedenharn Realty,* where the Fifth Circuit, after the taxpayer had attempted to minimize the importance of its own sales and advertising activities, observed that "even one inarguably in the real estate business need not engage in promotional exertions in the face of a favorable market. * * * [W]e do not always require a showing of active solicitation where 'business * * * [is] good, indeed brisk.' "

(D) *Relative Earnings.* The court in *Adam* attached considerable importance to the fact that the taxpayer's real estate activities produced relatively little of his income. In the three years at issue, the net gain from real estate activities constituted 5 percent, 16 percent, and 30 percent of the taxpayer's income. The court noted, "The significant difference in income generated by the two activities tends to show that [the taxpayer's] real estate dealings were investment activities." Why does the difference in relative incomes matter? Adam was an accountant. Should the outcome have differed if Adam was a mechanic earning only $10,000 a year from employment?

Adam should be compared with Goodman v. United States, 390 F.2d 915 (Cl.Ct.1968), which involved the characterization of gain and loss on sales by attorneys of 32 real estate interests over a three-year period. The court noted that individuals may be engaged in more than one trade or business and concluded that buying and selling real estate was one of the businesses of the attorneys. In fact, it was their biggest business in terms of income, although their activities in this connection were relatively slight. The court emphasized the number and frequency of sales in excluding the real estate from the capital asset classification of § 1221(a)(1) and therefore held that the sales produced ordinary income.

(E) *Bulk Sales.* The emphasis in cases such as *Suburban Realty* and *Biedenharn* on the frequency and substantiality of sales suggests that taxpayers are more likely to obtain capital gains treatment if they dispose of their land in a single bulk sale rather than in many smaller sales. This lesson was obviously taken seriously by the taxpayers in *Bramblett.* The *Biedenharn* court observed in a footnote, however, that it was "not prepared to tell taxpayers that in all cases a single bulk sale provides the only road to capital gains." The court suggested that capital gains treatment might remain appropriate when "the change from investment holding to sales activity results from unanticipated, externally induced factors which make impossible the continued pre-existing use of the realty." These factors might include, for example, "acts of God, condemnation of part of one's property, new and unfavorable zoning regulations, or other events forcing alteration of taxpayer's plans * * *."

Would an "externally induced factor" that increased the property's value be compatible with capital gains treatment on sales of parcels of the property? Suppose that creeping suburbanization so increases the value of farmland held as investment property that the owner cannot pay her property taxes without selling pieces of the property. Is it appropriate to require the investor to sell the land in bulk to others who will develop it in order to obtain favorable treatment?

(F) *Liquidation of Investments*. Courts may be more willing to allow capital gains treatment on sales of real estate where the taxpayer can establish that he subdivided his land merely to liquidate his investment more profitably. In liquidating an investment, the seller may engage in the same activities as a dealer but may retain his original investment motive. This is particularly true where the sale has not been preceded by significant development activity. See, e.g., Buono v. Commissioner, 74 T.C. 187, 204 (1980), where the Tax Court allowed capital gain treatment on the sale of subdivided land on the ground that the taxpayer was not a dealer but rather an investor who had "merely subdivided the land in order to make it more marketable and enhance its value."

(G) *Stock and Securities*. The same asset can be either capital or ordinary depending on the holder's relationship to the asset. Since most assets ultimately are held for sale, the courts must distinguish between those held "primarily for sale to customers" and those that are not. Particularly in dealing with stocks or securities, the courts have identified three classes of taxpayers holding stock—dealers, traders, and investors. Consider the following definitions:

> A dealer is a person who purchases the securities or commodities with the expectation of realizing a profit not because of a rise in value during the interval of time between purchase and resale, but merely because they have or hope to find a market of buyers who will purchase from them at a price in excess of their cost. This excess or mark-up represents remuneration for their labors as a middle man bringing together buyer and seller, and performing the usual services of retailer or wholesaler of goods. Dealers have customers for purposes of section 1221.
>
> Traders, on the other hand, are sellers of securities or commodities who "depend upon such circumstances as a rise in value or an advantageous purchase to enable them to sell at a price in excess of cost." A trader performs no merchandising functions nor any other service which warrants compensation by a price mark-up of the securities he or she sells. "[A] trader will be deemed to be engaged in a trade or business if his or her trading is frequent and substantial." Generally, both dealers and traders will be engaged in a trade or business; only a dealer, however, has customers.
>
> An investor is very similar to a trader. Like a trader, an investor "makes purchases for capital appreciation and income." Unlike a trader, however, an investor makes such purchases "usually without regard to short-term developments that would influence prices on the daily market." An investor, on the other hand, will never be considered to be engaged in a trade or business with respect to his or her investment activities, no matter how extensive his or her activities might be.

United States v. Wood, 943 F.2d 1048 (9th Cir.1991) (citations omitted).

Section 1236 permits securities dealers to receive capital gains treatment on securities they earmark as investment assets. Most dealers must identify their investment securities by the end of the day of acquisition, while floor traders have seven business days to designate securities in which they are registered specialists. An ordinary loss cannot be taken on any security that previously has been identified as an investment asset.

In Marrin v. Commissioner, 147 F.3d 147 (2d Cir.1998), the court refused to permit a former securities trader to treat any of his loss on stock sales as ordinary because he was trading for his own account. Although he had a full-time job, he spent nearly 40 hours a week researching trades. Nevertheless, the court found that this did not rise to the level of a trade or business. While the gains on a day trader's profitable sales thus would be capital, they would be short-term and therefore not entitled to preferential treatment.

(H) *Bifurcated Ordinary Income and Capital Gain Treatment.* Where the taxpayer has a dual or changed motive, it might be theoretically preferable to bifurcate the character of the gain. For example, the gain that accrued while the taxpayer held the property as an investment would be capital and the gain that accrued during the period the taxpayer held the property primarily for sale to customers would be ordinary. Such a provision would be extremely difficult to administer. Section 1237, however, under which a taxpayer can preserve capital gains treatment for at least a portion of the profits when she subdivides or develops land, does take a bifurcated approach. Section 1237 establishes conditions under which land will not be deemed to have been "held primarily for sale to customers in the ordinary course of trade or business" solely because it has been subdivided. The taxpayer must have held the land for a period of at least five years. He must not have previously held the land primarily for sale to customers in the ordinary course of business and must not have made any improvement "that substantially enhances the value of the lot or parcel." Gain from the sale of the sixth and subsequent parcels from the same tract of land nevertheless will be taxed as ordinary income to the extent of 5 percent of the selling price. Does the *Bramblett* decision, which allows the taxpayers to bifurcate based on fair market value if they separate the sales into two different entities undermine the bifurcation approach of § 1237?

2.   DEPRECIABLE PERSONAL PROPERTY AND REAL PROPERTY USED IN A TRADE OR BUSINESS

NOTE ON THE MECHANICS OF § 1231

Section 1221(a)(2) excludes from the definition of capital assets depreciable personal property and real property used in a trade or business. Section 1231, however, allows real and depreciable property used in a trade or business to yield capital gain when disposed of at a gain and ordinary loss when disposed of at a loss. This combination of options "constitutes in the tax solar system, the best of all possible worlds."

The predecessor to § 1231 was enacted in 1942 to provide for favorable treatment on dispositions of ships and other property used in the war effort, which due to war needs had greatly appreciated in value. At the same time, Congress retained ordinary treatment for losses on business assets in order to encourage the replacement of obsolete assets.

Section 1231 applies to the disposition of real or depreciable property—such as land, buildings, machinery, and fixtures—excluded from the definition of capital assets by § 1221(a)(2). The property must have been held by the taxpayer for at least one year.

These so-called "quasi-capital assets" do not include, however, other business assets that are denied capital gains treatment by § 1221; thus, § 1231 does not apply to inventory or other property held primarily for sale to customers, copyrights, artistic compositions, or letters produced by or for the taxpayer, government documents obtained below cost, commodity derivatives held by dealers, or hedging transactions. On the other hand, several types of business property—including certain livestock, timber, coal, minerals, and unharvested crops sold with the land—are specifically made eligible for "quasi-capital asset" treatment by § 1231. See § 1231(b)(2), (3), and (4).

Three types of dispositions may give rise to § 1231 treatment: (1) gain or loss from sales and exchanges of property used in a trade or business, (2) gain or loss arising from condemnations and involuntary conversions (such as casualty or theft losses) of property used in a trade or business and (3) gain or loss from condemnations and involuntary conversions of capital assets held in connection with a trade or business or in a profit seeking activity.

Section 1231 requires a two-stage netting process. First, the taxpayer nets her gains from casualty and theft losses (from insurance proceeds, for example) against her losses from such involuntary conversions. If losses exceed gains, § 1231 does not apply to either the losses or the gains. There is deemed to be no "sale or exchange," so the gains are taxable as ordinary income and the losses are deductible from ordinary income. If gains exceed losses, however, both gains and losses are carried over into the second stage of the netting process. See § 1231(a)(4). This first stage of netting is often called the "firepot," since it deals with conversions from fire, storm or other similar casualties.

Second, the taxpayer compares her total gains with her total losses from (1) involuntary conversions carried over from the first stage "firepot," and (2) condemnations, and sales and exchanges of business property. This second stage of netting is often referred to as the "hotchpot." If losses exceed gains, the gains are includible in ordinary income and the losses are deductible from ordinary income. If gains exceed losses, however, the gains are treated as long-term capital gains and the losses are treated as long-term capital losses; these gains and losses then are carried to the tax return to be combined with long-term capital gains and long-term capital losses from other sources. See § 1231(a)(1), (2), and (3).

The following examples illustrate the application of § 1231.

Example 1:

Involuntary Dispositions		*Gains*	*Losses*
Factory building destroyed by fire			
Adjusted basis of building	$100,000		
Insurance proceeds	50,000		
(Loss)	($50,000)		($50,000)
Theft of uninsured equipment			(10,000)
Total in firepot			($60,000)
Other Dispositions			
Sale of real estate used in business		$100,000	
Sale of truck used in business			($5,000)
Condemnation of rental property			
Adjusted basis of building	$30,000		
Compensation	35,000		
Gain	$5,000	5,000	
Total in hotchpot		$105,000	($5,000)

In this example, the application of § 1231 leaves the taxpayer with a long-term capital gain of $105,000 to be added to other long-term capital gains (from the sale of stock, for example) and $5,000 of long-term capital losses to be added to other long-term capital losses. The $60,000 of theft and casualty losses in the firepot is not added to the hotchpot because there is a net loss. Thus, the $60,000 loss is deductible from ordinary income.

Example 2:

Involuntary Dispositions		*Gains*	*Losses*
Factory building destroyed by fire			
Adjusted basis of building	$100,000		
Insurance proceeds	160,000		
Gain	$60,000	$60,000	
Theft of uninsured equipment			($5,000)
Other Dispositions			
Sale of real estate used in business			($75,000)
Sale of truck used in business			(5,000)
Condemnation of rental property			
Adjusted basis of property	$30,000		
Compensation	35,000		
Gain	$5,000	5,000	
Total in hotchpot		$65,000	($85,000)

In Example 2, the application of § 1231 leaves the taxpayer with a gain of $65,000 that is taxed as ordinary income and a loss of $85,000 deductible from ordinary income. Note that the gains and loss from the firepot are included in the hotchpot because there was a net gain.

The application of § 1231 is limited in order to prevent taxpayers from bunching their gains from "quasi-capital assets" into one year and their losses into another. A taxpayer may be required to treat as ordinary income the excess in any year of his gains on § 1231 property over his losses on § 1231 property. This provision applies only to the extent that the taxpayer's § 1231 gains for that year and for the preceding five years do not exceed his losses for the same period. See § 1231(c). Suppose, for example, that T has a net § 1231 loss of $5,000 in Year 1, which is treated as ordinary and in Year 2 has a net § 1231 gain of $8,000. Only $3,000 of that gain is capital and $5,000 is "recaptured" as ordinary. Note that is the identical result if the net loss and net gain had occurred in the same year.

The recapture provisions described below may require amounts that would otherwise be capital gain (or § 1231 gain) on depreciable property nevertheless to be reported as ordinary income.

NOTE ON RECAPTURE PROVISIONS

If depreciation accurately measured the actual decline in value of an asset, a taxpayer's basis would be approximately equal to its fair market value and thus a sale would produce neither gain nor loss. Current depreciation rules, however, make no real attempt to accurately measure decline in value and thus a taxpayer may realize a gain or loss. When the taxpayer realizes a gain on depreciable property, he has been permitted to take depreciation exceeding the economic cost of holding the asset. (Conversely, if a loss is realized, the depreciation allowance has been too limited.)

If the taxpayer were able to enjoy depreciation deductions (which offset ordinary income) and obtain capital gain treatment on sale via § 1231, he would be able to convert ordinary income into capital gain. Section 1245 was enacted to prohibit such conversion on the sale of depreciable property at a gain by requiring the "recapture" of previously deducted depreciation as ordinary income. The ordinary gain "pays back" the excess depreciation, although the taxpayer has enjoyed the time value of the earlier depreciation deductions.

If depreciable property is sold for more than its adjusted basis, any gain not exceeding the total depreciation allowed is taxed as ordinary income. Section 1245 also recaptures as ordinary income amounts deducted under § 179 in lieu of depreciation, amortization deductions (such as under § 197) and other deductions under §§ 190 or 193. Property subject to recapture under § 1245 is generally tangible personal property. § 1245(a)(3).

The following examples illustrate the application of § 1245:

Example 1: In Year 1, A purchased a machine for $100,000 to use in his manufacturing business. After taking depreciation deductions of $61,600, A sells the machine in Year 3 for $90,000. His entire gain of $51,600 on the sale ($90,000 sales proceeds minus his $38,400 adjusted basis) will be taxed as ordinary income because the amount of his depreciation deductions exceeded the amount of the gain. The depreciation deductions that he has taken against ordinary income must be fully "recaptured"—that is, taxed as ordinary income.

Example 2: If the sales price of the machine had been $105,000, A's gain would be $66,600, of which $61,200 would be ordinary income and $5,000 would be capital gain. The additional gain after the recapture of all depreciation represents an increase in market value and is capital gain.

Section 1250, provides a comparable, but less complete, "recapture" mechanism for dispositions of real property. It recaptures the excess of accelerated depreciation over straight line depreciation on certain real estate. Real estate currently is only depreciated using the straight line method, and there is no § 1250 recapture on property that has only been allowed straight line depreciation. Gain up to the amount of depreciation allowed on real property held for more than twelve months is taxed at a special capital gains rate of 25 percent. While this is more advantageous than taxing the gain at ordinary rates, which can be as high as 39.1 percent, it is not as beneficial as the usual capital gains rate of 20 percent or less.

Other recapture provisions aimed at limiting the conversion of ordinary income into long-term capital gains include:

(1) § 1252, requiring recapture of a portion of deductions taken for soil and water conservation on farmland held for less than 10 years;

(2) § 1254, recapturing expensed intangible drilling costs and mining exploration and development costs (under §§ 263, 616, and 617) and depletion (under § 611) for oil and gas properties, certain geothermal wells and mineral properties;

(3) § 1255, which provides for the recapture at the time of sale of amounts received as tax-free grants (under § 126) and used to improve property that is sold less than 20 years after receipt of the grant;

(4) § 1245(a)(4), which requires recapture of depreciation and loss deductions with respect to contracts of players when an entire sports franchise is sold or exchanged; and

(5) § 467, which provides for taxation as ordinary income of a portion of gain on payments made in connection with sales of property that the seller had previously leased. This provision is intended to prevent conversion into long-term capital gain of payments that actually represent rental or interest income relating to a period prior to the sale. Compare § 1258 discussed infra at 592, which explicitly denies capital gain treatment for a specific category of "conversion" transactions.

3.   COPYRIGHTS, LITERARY, MUSICAL AND ARTISTIC COMPOSITIONS, AND PATENTS

NOTE ON THE TREATMENT OF COPYRIGHTS, LITERARY, MUSICAL AND ARTISTIC COMPOSITIONS, AND PATENTS

Sections 1221(a)(3) and 1231(b)(1)(C) exclude from the definition of a capital asset copyrights, literary, musical and artistic compositions, and letters or memoranda prepared by or for the taxpayer. The exclusion from capital gains treatment is limited to dispositions of property held by its creator or by a taxpayer whose basis is determined by reference to the creator's basis (for example, the recipient of a gift of the copyright). This creates parity between one who is paid for his services in creating an artistic composition and one who sells the actual composition. Copyrights and literary, musical, or artistic creations are capital assets, however, in the hands of buyers or most legatees unless they are held for sale to customers in the ordinary course of a trade or business.

Shortly after Congress enacted § 1221(a)(3), it enacted § 1235, which permits capital gain treatment on the sale of a patent by the inventor even when he is a "professional" who makes the sale in the ordinary course of his business. Section 1235 allows capital gain treatment even if the consideration received by the inventor is dependent upon the transferee's sales or use and even if the minimum holding period is not satisfied. The favorable treatment of § 1235 also applies to those who have financed the inventor's work.

Section 1235 requires that the inventor transfer "all substantial rights" in a patent in order to qualify for capital gains treatment. The regulations provide that this requirement will not be satisfied by a transfer of a patent for a period less than its remaining term or by a transfer of rights limited geographically within the country of issuance or limited to less than all the economic fields of use. See Reg. § 1.1235–2(b).

Can the disparity between the ordinary income treatment of copyrights and artistic creations and the capital gains treatment of patents be justified analytically? Apparently, Congress believed that the need for an incentive for inventors outweighed the general policy of taxing as ordinary income profits generated by personal efforts. Research and development expenses are also given favorable income tax treatment.

NOTES

(A) *Scope of § 1221(a)(3)*. The exclusion applies not only to letters and memoranda, but also to "similar property." The regulations define this broadly to include "a draft of a speech, a manuscript, a research paper, an oral recording, * * * a personal or business diary, a log or journal, a corporate archive, * * * office correspondence, a financial record, a drawing, a photograph or a dispatch." Reg. § 1.1221–1(c)(2). In Chronicle Publishing Co. v. Commissioner, 97 T.C. 445 (1991), the Tax Court held that this literally covered the "morgue" or library of newspaper clippings held by a newspaper, but questioned whether Congress intended to include the library within the scope of the exclusion.

The "similar property" exclusion is now important with respect to computer software whether or not it is copyrighted. The software creator has ordinary income on the sale of the program.

(B) *Scope of § 1235*. Section 1235 applies only to transfers of patents by individuals. The general rules of §§ 1221 and 1231 apply in other cases. For example, corporations that are not dealers in patents can receive "quasi-capital gains" treatment on such transfers because patent rights are considered to be depreciable property within the terms of § 1231(b)(1). Because patents used in the trade or business are depreciable, they are subject to recapture under § 1245. Thus, a portion of any gain on the sale of a patent may be recaptured as ordinary income.

Section 1235 applies only to patents, but several courts have analogized to that section to hold that § 1221(a)(3) does not cover trade secrets, know-how, or a trade name and thus those are capital assets as well.

(C) *Inventor-Employees.* Where the inventor is an employee who has contracted to assign any patents to her employer, payments from the employer to the employee typically will be treated as compensation. See, e.g., Beausoleil v. Commissioner, 66 T.C. 244 (1976). But if the employee has not contracted away her rights to the patent, payments she receives for assigning the patent to her employer may qualify for capital gains treatment under § 1235. See, e.g., Ofria v. Commissioner, 77 T.C. 524 (1981).

4.   ACCOUNTS AND NOTES RECEIVABLE

Section 1221(a)(4) excludes from the definition of capital assets "accounts or notes receivable acquired in the ordinary course of trade or business for services rendered or from the sale of property" held for sale to customers in the ordinary course of business. The provision further illustrates the general congressional intent to exclude from capital gain or loss treatment transactions arising out of a taxpayer's everyday business activities.

An accrual basis taxpayer includes an account receivable as ordinary income at the time of its receipt; a cash basis taxpayer would include the payments as ordinary income. (Accounting methods are discussed in detail in Chapter 6, infra). Thus, if the note is subsequently sold for less than the amount included, there will be an ordinary loss. If sold for more than basis, there will be an ordinary gain.

5.   GOVERNMENT PUBLICATIONS RECEIVED FREE OR AT A DISCOUNT

Section 1221(a)(5) excludes from the capital asset definition government publications received by taxpayers without charge or at a reduced price. An example would be copies of the Congressional Record received free by members of Congress. This provision, as well as the exclusion of § 1221(a)(3) for letters and memoranda prepared by or for the holder, was designed to deprive taxpayers of charitable deductions for the fair market value of such materials when they are contributed to a charity such as a university or a library. Before these provisions were enacted, politicians routinely took charitable deductions for the fair market value of gifts of such items to charities. Recall § 170(e), discussed, supra, at pages 451.

6.   DERIVATIVES, HEDGING TRANSACTIONS, AND SUPPLIES USED IN A BUSINESS

Section 1221(a)(1) and (2) excludes from capital gains treatment many, but not all, of the assets used in a trade or business. Suppose a bakery purchases flour to use in making bread and subsequently sells flour that it discovers it does not need. Or suppose the bakery is concerned about the wholesale price of flour and purchases wheat futures to hedge its costs. Neither the flour nor the futures is inventory or depreciable property. They generally, however, would be ordinary assets under §§ 1221(a)(7) and (8), provisions adopted in the wake of the *Arkansas Best* case that follows at page 576.

Corn Products Refining Co. v. Commissioner

Supreme Court of the United States, 1955. 350 U.S. 46.

MR. JUSTICE CLARK delivered the opinion of the Court.

This case concerns the tax treatment to be accorded certain transactions in commodity futures.[1] In the Tax Court, petitioner Corn Products Refining Company contended that its purchases and sales of corn futures in 1940 and 1942 were capital-asset transactions under § 117(a) of the Internal Revenue Code of 1939 [the predecessor of Section 1221]. * * * [F]or the year 1942 both the Tax Court and the Court of Appeals for the Second Circuit held that the futures were not capital assets under § 117. We granted certiorari because of an asserted conflict with holdings in the Courts of Appeal for the Third, Fifth, and Sixth Circuits. * * *

Petitioner is a nationally known manufacturer of products made from grain corn. It manufactures starch, syrup, sugar, and their by-products, feeds and oil. Its average yearly grind of raw corn during the period 1937 through 1942 varied from thirty-five to sixty million bushels. Most of its products were sold under contracts requiring shipment in thirty days at a set price or at market price on the date of delivery, whichever was lower. * * *

In 1934 and again in 1936 droughts in the corn belt caused a sharp increase in the price of spot corn. With a storage capacity of only 2,300,000 bushels of corn, a bare three weeks' supply, Corn Products found itself unable to buy at a price which would permit its refined corn sugar, cerelose, to compete successfully with cane and beet sugar. To avoid a recurrence of this situation, petitioner, in 1937, began to establish a long position in corn futures "as a part of its corn buying program" and "as the most economical method of obtaining an adequate supply of raw corn" without entailing the expenditure of large sums for additional storage facilities. At harvest time each year it would buy futures when the price appeared favorable. It would take delivery on such contracts as it found necessary to its manufacturing operations and sell the remainder in early summer if no shortage was imminent. If shortages appeared, however, it sold futures only as it bought spot corn for grinding. In this manner it reached a balanced position with reference to any increase in spot corn prices. It made no effort to protect itself against a decline in prices.

In 1940 it netted a profit of $680,587.39 in corn futures, but in 1942 it suffered a loss of $109,969.38. In computing its tax liability Corn Products reported these figures as ordinary profit and loss from its manufacturing operations for the respective years. It now contends that its futures were "capital assets" under § 117 and that gains and losses therefrom should have been treated as arising from the sale of a capital asset. In support of this position it claims that its futures trading was separate and apart from its manufacturing operations and that in its futures transactions it was acting as a "legitimate capitalist." * * *

---

1. A commodity future is a contract to purchase some fixed amount of a commodity at a future date for a fixed price. Corn futures, involved in the present case, are in terms of some multiple of five thousand bushels to be delivered eleven months or less after the contract.

Both the Tax Court and the Court of Appeals found petitioner's futures transactions to be an integral part of its business designed to protect its manufacturing operations against a price increase in its principal raw material and to assure a ready supply for future manufacturing requirements. Corn Products does not level a direct attack on these two-court findings but insists that its futures were "property" entitled to capital-asset treatment under § 117 and as such were distinct from its manufacturing business. We cannot agree.

We find nothing in this record to support the contention that Corn Products' futures activity was separate and apart from its manufacturing operation. On the contrary, it appears that the transactions were vitally important to the company's business as a form of insurance against increases in the price of raw corn. Not only were the purchases initiated for just this reason, but the petitioner's sales policy, selling in the future at a fixed price or less, continued to leave it exceedingly vulnerable to rises in the price of corn. Further, the purchase of corn futures assured the company a source of supply which was admittedly cheaper than constructing additional storage facilities for raw corn. Under these facts it is difficult to imagine a program more closely geared to a company's manufacturing enterprise or more important to its successful operation.

Likewise the claim of Corn Products that it was dealing in the market as a "legitimate capitalist" lacks support in the record. * * * [P]etitioner ignores the testimony of its own officers that in entering that market the company was "trying to protect a part of [its] manufacturing costs"; that is entry was not for the purpose of "speculating and buying and selling corn futures" but to fill an actual "need for the quantity of corn [bought] * * * in order to cover * * * what [products] we expected to market over a period of fifteen or eighteen months." It matters not whether the label be that of "legitimate capitalist" or "speculator"; this is not the talk of the capital investor but of the far-sighted manufacturer. For tax purposes petitioner's purchases have been found to "constitute an integral part of its manufacturing business" by both the Tax Court and the Court of Appeals, and on essentially factual questions the findings of two courts should not ordinarily be disturbed. * * *

Petitioner also makes much of the conclusion by both the Tax Court and the Court of Appeals that its transactions did not constitute "true hedging." It is true that Corn Products did not secure complete protection from its market operations. Under its sales policy petitioner could not guard against a fall in prices. It is clear, however, that petitioner feared the possibility of a price rise more than that of a price decline. It therefore purchased partial insurance against its principal risk, and hoped to retain sufficient flexibility to avoid serious losses on a declining market.

Nor can we find support for petitioner's contention that hedging is not within the exclusions of § 117(a). Admittedly, petitioner's corn futures do not come within the literal language of the exclusions set out in that section. They were not stock in trade, actual inventory, property held for sale to customers or depreciable property used in a trade or business. But the capital-asset provision of § 117 must not be so broadly applied as to defeat rather than further the purpose of Congress. * * * Congress intended that profits and losses arising from the everyday operation of a business be considered as ordinary income or loss rather than capital gain or loss. The preferential treatment provided by § 117 applies to transactions in property which are not the normal source of business income. It was intended "to relieve the taxpayer from * * * excessive tax burdens on gains resulting from a conversion of capital investments, and to remove the deterrent effect of those burdens on such conversions." Burnet v. Harmel, 287 U.S., at 106. Since this section is an exception from the normal tax requirements of the Internal Revenue Code, the definition of a capital asset must be narrowly applied and its exclusions interpreted broadly. This is necessary to effectuate the basic congressional purpose. This Court has always construed narrowly the term "capital assets" in § 117. * * *

We believe that the statute clearly refutes the contention of Corn Products. Moreover, it is significant to note that practical considerations lead to the same conclusion. To hold otherwise would permit those engaged in hedging transactions to transmute ordinary income into capital gain at will. The hedger may either sell the future and purchase in the spot market or take delivery under the future contract itself. But if a sale of the future created a capital transaction while delivery of the commodity under the same future did not, a loophole in the statute would be created and the purpose of Congress frustrated.

The judgment is

Affirmed.

MR. JUSTICE HARLAN took no part in the consideration or decision of this case.

NOTE

The IRS subsequently discovered that it had won the battle, but lost the war by its *Corn Products* victory. The decision repeatedly was invoked to treat losses as ordinary, but seldom used to treat gains as ordinary income. This was largely because revenue agents are unlikely to suspect that anything is amiss when a taxpayer reports capital gain from the sale of property that is typically considered to be a capital asset (a share of stock, for example), but that actually would be ordinary income property under *Corn Products* in the particular circumstances. Revenue agents are more likely to question taxpayers who reported ordinary loss on the sale of such an asset. The Court's decision in *Arkansas Best*, set out below, severely limited the scope of *Corn Products* and thus the cases where the taxpayer might claim an ordinary loss.

Arkansas Best Corporation v. Commissioner

Supreme Court of the United States, 1988, 485 U.S. 212.

JUSTICE MARSHALL delivered the opinion of the Court.

The issue presented in this case is whether capital stock held by petitioner Arkansas Best Corporation (Arkansas Best) is a "capital asset" as defined in § 1221 of the Internal Revenue Code regardless of whether the stock was purchased and held for a business purpose or for an investment purpose.

I

Arkansas Best is a diversified holding company. In 1968 it acquired approximately 65% of the stock of the National Bank of Commerce (Bank) in Dallas, Texas. Between 1969 and 1974, Arkansas Best more than tripled the number of shares it owned in the Bank, although its percentage interest in the Bank remained relatively stable. These acquisitions were prompted principally by the Bank's need for added capital. Until 1972, the Bank appeared to be prosperous and growing, and the added capital was necessary to accommodate this growth. As the Dallas real estate market declined, however, so too did the financial health of the Bank, which had a heavy concentration of loans in the local real estate industry. In 1972, federal examiners classified the Bank as a problem bank. The infusion of capital after 1972 was prompted by the loan portfolio problems of the bank.

Petitioner sold the bulk of its Bank stock on June 30, 1975, leaving it with only a 14.7% stake in the Bank. On its federal income tax return for 1975, petitioner claimed a deduction for an ordinary loss of $9,995,688 resulting from the sale of the stock. The Commissioner of Internal Revenue disallowed the deduction, finding that the loss from the sale of stock was a capital loss, rather than an ordinary loss, and that it therefore was subject to the capital loss limitations in the Internal Revenue Code.

Arkansas Best challenged the Commissioner's determination in the United States Tax Court. The Tax Court, relying on cases interpreting Corn Products Refining Co. v. Commissioner, 350 U.S. 46 (1955), held that stock purchased with a substantial investment purpose is a capital asset which, when sold, gives rise to a capital gain or loss, whereas stock purchased and held for a business purpose, without any substantial investment motive, is an ordinary asset whose sale gives rise to ordinary gains or losses. See 83 T.C. 640, 653–654 (1984). The court characterized Arkansas Best's acquisitions through 1972 as occurring during the Bank's " 'growth' phase," and found that these acquisitions "were motivated primarily by investment purpose and only incidentally by some business purpose." Id., at 654. The stock acquired during this period therefore constituted a capital asset, which gave rise to a capital loss when sold in 1975. The court determined, however, that the acquisitions after 1972 occurred during the Bank's " 'problem' phase," and, except for certain minor exceptions, "were made exclusively for business purposes and subsequently held for the same reason." These acquisitions, the court found, were designed to preserve petitioner's business reputation, because without the added capital the Bank probably would have failed. The loss realized on the sale of this stock was thus held to be an ordinary loss.

The Court of Appeals for the Eighth Circuit reversed the Tax Court's determination that the loss realized on stock purchased after 1972 was subject to ordinary-loss treatment, holding that all of the Bank stock sold in 1975 was subject to capital-loss treatment. 800 F.2d 215 (1986). The court reasoned that the Bank stock clearly fell within the general definition of "capital asset" in Internal Revenue Code section 1221, and that the stock did not fall within any of the specific statutory exceptions to this definition. The court concluded that Arkansas Best's purpose in acquiring and holding the stock was irrelevant to the determination whether the stock was a capital asset. We granted certiorari, 480 U.S. 930, and now affirm.

II

Section 1221 of the Internal Revenue Code defines "capital asset" broadly, as "property held by the taxpayer (whether or not connected with his trade or business)," and then excludes five specific classes of property from capital-asset status. In the statute's present form, the classes of property exempted from the broad definition are (1) "property of a kind which would properly be included in the inventory of the taxpayer", (2) real property or other depreciable property used in the taxpayer's trade or business, (3) "a copyright, a literary, musical, or artistic composition," or similar property, (4) "accounts or notes receivable acquired in the ordinary course of trade or business for services rendered" or from the sale of inventory, and (5) publications of the Federal Government. Arkansas Best acknowledges that the Bank stock falls within the literal definition of capital asset in section 1221, and is outside of the statutory exclusions. It asserts, however, that this determination does not end the inquiry. Petitioner argues that in *Corn Products Refining Co. v. Commissioner, supra,* this Court rejected a literal reading of section 1221, and concluded that assets acquired and sold for ordinary business purposes rather than for investment purposes should be given ordinary-asset treatment. Petitioner's reading of *Corn Products* finds much support in the academic literature and in the courts. Unfortunately for petitioner, this broad reading finds no support in the language of § 1221.

In essence, petitioner argues that "property held by the taxpayer (whether or not connected with his trade or business)" does not include property that is acquired and held for a business purpose. In petitioner's view an asset's status as "property" thus turns on the motivation behind its acquisition. This motive test, however, is not only nowhere mentioned in § 1221, but it is also in direct conflict with the parenthetical phrase "whether or not connected with his trade or business." The broad definition of the term "capital asset" explicitly makes irrelevant any consideration of the property's connection with the taxpayer's business, whereas petitioner's rule would make this factor dispositive.[3]

---

3. Petitioner mistakenly relies on cases in which this Court, in narrowly applying the general definition of "capital asset," has "construed 'capital asset' to exclude property representing income items or accretions to the value of a capital asset themselves properly attributable to income," even though these items are property in the broad sense of the word. United States v. Midland–Ross Corp., 381 U.S. 54, 57 (1965). See, e.g., Commissioner v. Gillette Motor Co., 364 U.S. 130 (1960) ("capital asset" does not include compensation awarded taxpayer that represented fair rental value of its facilities); Commissioner v. P.G. Lake, Inc., 356 U.S. 260 (1958) ("capital asset" does not include proceeds from sale of oil payment rights); Hort v. Commissioner, 313 U.S. 28 (1941) ("capital asset" does not include payment to lessor for cancellation of unexpired portion of a lease). This line of cases, based on the premise that section 1221 "property" does not include claims or rights to ordinary income, has no application in the present context. Petitioner sold capital stock, not a claim to ordinary income.

In a related argument, petitioner contends that the five exceptions listed in § 1221 for certain kinds of property are illustrative, rather than exhaustive, and that courts are therefore free to fashion additional exceptions in order to further the general purposes of the capital-asset provisions. The language of the statute refutes petitioner's construction. Section 1221 provides that "capital asset" means "property held by the taxpayer, * * * but does not include" the five classes of property listed as exceptions. We believe this locution signifies that the listed exceptions are exclusive. The body of section 1221 establishes a general definition of the term "capital asset," and the phrase "does not include" takes out of that broad definition only the classes of property that are specifically mentioned. The legislative history of the capital asset definition supports this interpretation, see H.R.Rep. 704, 73d Cong., 2d Sess., 31 (1934) ("[T]he definition includes all property, except as specifically excluded"); H.R.Rep. 1337, 83d Cong., 2d Sess., A273 (1954) ("[A] capital asset is property held by the taxpayer with certain exceptions"), as does the applicable Treasury regulation, see 26 CFR section 1.1221–1(a) (1987) ("The term 'capital assets' includes all classes of property not specifically excluded by section 1221").

Petitioner's reading of the statute is also in tension with the exceptions listed in section 1221. These exclusions would be largely superfluous if assets acquired primarily or exclusively for business purposes were not capital assets. Inventory, real or depreciable property used in the taxpayer's trade or business, and accounts or notes receivable acquired in the ordinary course of business, would undoubtedly satisfy such a business-motive test. Yet these exceptions were created by Congress in separate enactments spanning 30 years. Without any express direction from Congress, we are unwilling to read section 1221 in a manner that makes surplusage of these statutory exclusions.

In the end, petitioner places all reliance on its reading of Corn Products Refining Co. v. Commissioner, 350 U.S. 46 (1955)—a reading we believe is too expansive. In *Corn Products*, the Court considered whether income arising from a taxpayer's dealings in corn futures was entitled to capital–gains treatment. The taxpayer was a company that converted corn into starches, sugars, and other products. After droughts in the 1930's caused sharp increases in corn prices, the company began a program of buying corn futures to assure itself an adequate supply of corn and protect against price increases. The company "would take delivery on such contracts as it found necessary to its manufacturing operations and sell the remainder in early summer if no shortage was imminent. If shortages appeared, however, it sold futures only as it bought spot corn for grinding." The Court characterized the company's dealing in corn futures as "hedging." As explained by the Court of Appeals in *Corn Products*, "[h]edging is a method of dealing in commodity futures whereby a person or business protects itself against price fluctuations at the time of delivery of the product which it sells or buys." In evaluating the company's claim that the sales of corn futures resulted in capital gains and losses, this Court stated:

"Nor can we find support for petitioner's contention that hedging is not within the exclusions of [§ 1221]. Admittedly, petitioner's corn futures do not come within the literal language of the exclusions set out in that section. They were not stock in trade, actual inventory, property held for sale to customers or depreciable property used in a trade or business. But the capital-asset provision of section 1221 must not be so broadly applied as to defeat rather than further the purpose of Congress. Congress intended that profits and losses arising from the everyday operation of a business be considered as ordinary income or loss rather than capital gain or loss. * * * Since this section is an exception from the normal tax requirements of the Internal Revenue Code, the definition of a capital asset must be narrowly applied and its exclusions interpreted broadly." 350 U.S., at 51–52 (citations omitted).

The Court went on to note that hedging transactions consistently had been considered to give rise to ordinary gains and losses, and then concluded that the corn futures were subject to ordinary-asset treatment. Id., at 52–53.

The Court in *Corn Products* proffered the oft-quoted rule of construction that the definition of "capital asset" must be narrowly applied and its exclusions interpreted broadly, but it did not state explicitly whether the holding was based on a narrow reading of the phrase "property held by the taxpayer," or on a broad reading of the inventory exclusion of § 1221. In light of the stark language of § 1221, however, we believe that *Corn Products* is properly interpreted as involving an application of section 1221's inventory exception. Such a reading is consistent both with the Court's reasoning in that case and with § 1221. The Court stated in *Corn Products* that the company's futures transactions were "an integral part of its business designed to protect its manufacturing operations against a price increase in its principal raw material and to assure a ready supply for future manufacturing requirements." The company bought, sold, and took delivery under the futures contracts as required by the company's manufacturing needs. As Professor Bittker notes, under these circumstances, the futures can "easily be viewed as surrogates for the raw material itself" 2 B. Bittker, Federal Taxation of Income, Estates and Gifts paragraph 51.10.3, p. 51–62 (1981). The Court of Appeals for the Second Circuit in *Corn Products* clearly took this approach. That court stated that when commodity futures are "utilized solely for the purpose of stabilizing inventory cost, * * * they cannot reasonably be separated from the inventory items," and concluded that "property used in hedging transactions properly comes within the exclusions of section 1221." This Court indicated its acceptance of the Second Circuit's reasoning when it began the central paragraph of its opinion: "Nor can we find support for petitioner's contention that hedging is not within the exclusions of [§ 1221]." In the following paragraph, the Court argued that the Treasury had consistently viewed such hedging transactions as a form of insurance to stabilize the cost of inventory, and cited a Treasury ruling which concluded that the value of a manufacturer's raw-material inventory should be adjusted to take into account hedging transactions in futures contracts. 350 U.S. at 52–53 (citing G.C.M. 17322, XV–2 Cum.Bull. 151 (1936)). This discussion, read in light of the Second Circuit's holding and the plain language of § 1221, convinces us that although the corn futures were not "actual inventory," their use as an integral part of the taxpayer's inventory-purchase system led the Court to treat them as substitutes for the corn inventory such that they came within a broad reading of "property of a kind which would properly be included in the inventory of the taxpayer" in § 1221.

Petitioner argues that by focusing attention on whether the asset was acquired and sold as an integral part of the taxpayer's everyday business operations, the Court in *Corn Products* intended to create a general exemption from capital-asset status for assets acquired for business purposes. We believe petitioner misunderstands the relevance of the Court's inquiry. A business connection, although irrelevant to the initial determination of whether an item is a capital asset, is relevant in determining the applicability of certain of the statutory exceptions, including the inventory exception. The close connection between the futures transactions and the taxpayer's business in *Corn Products* was crucial to whether the corn futures could be considered surrogates for the stored inventory of raw corn. For if the futures dealings were not part of the company's inventory-purchase system, and instead amounted simply to speculation in corn futures, they could not be considered substitutes for the company's corn inventory, and would fall outside even a broad reading of the inventory exclusion. We conclude that *Corn Products* is properly interpreted as standing for the narrow proposition that hedging transactions that are an integral part of a business' inventory-purchase system fall within the inventory exclusion of § 1221.[4] Arkansas Best, which is not a dealer in securities, has never suggested that the Bank stock falls within the inventory exclusion. *Corn Products* thus has no application to this case.

It is also important to note that the business-motive test advocated by petitioner is subject to the same kind of abuse that the Court condemned in *Corn Products*. The Court explained in *Corn Products* that unless hedging transactions were subject to ordinary gain and loss treatment, taxpayers engaged in such transactions could "transmute ordinary income into capital gain at will." The hedger could garner capital-asset treatment by selling the futures and purchasing the commodity on the spot market, or ordinary-asset treatment by taking delivery under the futures contract. In a similar vein, if capital stock purchased and held for a business purpose is an ordinary asset, whereas the same stock purchased and held with an investment motive is a capital asset, a taxpayer such as Arkansas Best could have significant influence over whether the asset would receive capital or ordinary treatment. Because stock is most naturally viewed as a capital asset, the Internal Revenue Service would be hard pressed to challenge a taxpayer's claim that stock was acquired as an investment, and

---

4. Although congressional inaction is generally a poor measure of congressional intent, we are given some pause by the fact that over 25 years have passed since Corn Products Refining Co. v. Commissioner was initially interpreted as excluding assets acquired for business purposes from the definition of "capital asset," see Booth Newspapers, Inc. v. United States, 157 Ct.Cl. 886, 303 F.2d 916 (1962), without any sign of disfavor from Congress. We cannot ignore the unambiguous language of § 1221, however, no matter how reticent Congress has been. If a broad exclusion from capital-asset status is to be created for assets acquired for business purposes, it must come from congressional action, not silence.

that a gain arising from the sale of such stock was therefore a capital gain. Indeed, we are unaware of a single decision that has applied the business-motive test so as to require a taxpayer to report a gain from the sale of stock as an ordinary gain. If the same stock is sold at a loss, however, the taxpayer may be able to garner ordinary-loss treatment by emphasizing the business purpose behind the stock's acquisition. The potential for such abuse was evidenced in this case by the fact that as late as 1974, when Arkansas Best still hoped to sell the Bank stock at a profit, Arkansas Best apparently expected to report the gain as a capital gain. See 83 T.C. at 647–648.

III

We conclude that a taxpayer's motivation in purchasing an asset is irrelevant to the question whether the asset is "property held by a taxpayer (whether or not connected with his business)" and is thus within section 1221's general definition of "capital asset." Because the capital stock held by petitioner falls within the broad definition of the term "capital asset" in § 1221 and is outside the classes of property excluded from capital-asset status, the loss arising from the sale of the stock is a capital loss. *Corn Products Refining Co. v. Commissioner,* supra, which we interpret as involving a broad reading of the inventory exclusion of § 1221, has no application in the present context. Accordingly, the judgment of the Court of Appeals is affirmed.

It is so ordered.

JUSTICE KENNEDY took no part in the consideration or decision of this case.

NOTE ON HEDGING TRANSACTIONS

The Supreme Court's decision in *Arkansas Best* has had important implications for the treatment of hedging transactions, such as that entered into by Corn Products Refining Co. When *Corn Products* originally was decided, the determination whether an asset was a capital asset in the hedging context had significance only in terms of characterizing the loss or gain on disposition. With the addition of certain mark-to-market and loss deferral rules, however, the determination of what constitutes a capital asset also became important with respect to the timing of income and deductions because the applicability of these timing rules depends in part on whether a transaction produces ordinary income and loss. See § 1256.

Hedging is a risk management technique widely used by businesses to reduce or eliminate certain risks, for example, fluctuations in commodity prices, the relative value of different currencies, or interest rates. Consider the following simple example. T is a corn farmer who plants a crop of corn each spring at a cost of $10 a bushel. T is uncertain about the price at which he can sell the corn at the end of summer, but would like to lock in a $2 profit (i.e., he is willing to sacrifice any additional profit in order to eliminate the risk of a loss.) In order to hedge this price risk, T sells a forward contract for the amount of corn he expects to harvest. A forward contract is the right to purchase a certain quantity of a commodity at a fixed date in the future. T agrees to deliver a certain amount of corn in

August for $12 a bushel. Thus, no matter what happens to the price of corn, T knows he can sell his crop for $12 a bushel. Suppose corn prices rise to $14 a bushel. T could sell his corn at the market price (making a $4 profit per bushel) and purchase corn on the market at $14 a bushel to satisfy the forward contract obligation. The loss on the forward contract transaction ($2) offsets the $4 profit on the corn, netting a $2 profit. If the market price falls to $10 a bushel, T will use his own corn to satisfy the forward contract, obtaining a price of $2 and profiting $2 a bushel.

In reality, T almost never actually delivers the corn. Instead, T will sell the corn at the market price and sell the forward contract at its market price. For example, if corn prices rise to $14 a bushel, T will sell the corn and buy out the holder of the contract for $2, the difference between the forward price ($12) and the market price ($14). If the price drops to $10, T will sell the corn and have no profit, but will have an offsetting gain on the sale of the forward contract of $2.

Notice that in each case, the gain (or loss) on the sale of the corn is reflected in the revenues on the sale of the inventory, which produces ordinary gain or loss. The offsetting loss (or gain) arises on a business hedge, which, for parity, also should produce an ordinary gain or loss. If, however, the loss is capital, the taxpayer may not be able to deduct it; on the other hand, if the gain is capital, the taxpayer obtains an unwarranted benefit.

Almost everyone agreed that supplies used by a business (cattle feed or jet fuel for example) as well as business hedges (the corn farmer's forward contract) should be treated as ordinary assets. But after *Arkansas Best*, there was a good deal of uncertainty and concern that taxpayers would be whipsawed, for example, by being required to report ordinary income on the sale of the inventory and a capital loss on a forward contract used to hedge the inventory price. The IRS responded by adopting regulations that described in great detail those transactions that qualified as business hedges entitled to ordinary income treatment. Congress amended § 1221 in 1999 to clarify the law. The following excerpt describes the changes.

EXCERPT FROM EXPLANATION OF TAX LEGISLATION ENACTED IN THE 106TH CONGRESS STAFF OF THE JOINT COMMITTEE ON TAXATION, 1999

Present and Prior Law

Capital gain treatment applies to gain on the sale or exchange of a capital asset. Capital assets include property other than (1) stock in trade or other types of assets includible in inventory, (2) property used in a trade or business that is real property or property subject to depreciation, (3) accounts or notes receivable acquired in the ordinary course of a trade or business, (4) certain copyrights (or similar property), and (5) U.S. government publications. Gain or loss on such assets generally is treated as ordinary, rather than capital, gain or loss. Certain other code sections also treat gains or losses as ordinary. For example, the gains or losses of securities dealers or certain electing commodities dealers or electing traders in securities or commodities that are subject to "mark-to-market" accounting are taxed as ordinary (sec. 475).

Under case law in a number of Federal courts prior to 1988, business hedges generally were treated as giving rise to ordinary, rather than capital, gain or loss. In 1988, the U.S. Supreme Court rejected this interpretation in Arkansas Best v. Commissioner, which, relying on the statutory definition of a capital asset described above, held that a loss realized on a sale of stock was capital even though the stock was purchased for a business, rather than an investment, purpose.

Treasury regulations (which were finalized in 1994) under prior law require ordinary character treatment for most business hedges and provide timing rules requiring that gains or losses on hedging transactions be taken into account in a manner that matches the income or loss from the hedged item or items. The regulations apply to hedges that meet a standard of "risk reduction" with respect to ordinary property held (or to be held) or certain liabilities incurred (or to be incurred) by the taxpayer and that meet certain identification and other requirements (Treas. Reg. sec. 1.1221–1).

Reasons for Change

Absent an election by a commodities derivatives dealer to be treated the same as a dealer in securities under section 475, the character of the gains and losses with respect to commodities derivative financial instruments entered into by such a dealer may have been unclear under prior law. The Congress was concerned that this uncertainty (i.e., the potential for capital treatment of the commodities derivatives financial instruments) could inhibit commodities derivatives dealers from entering into transactions with respect to commodities derivatives financial instruments that qualify as "hedging transactions" within the meaning of the Treasury regulations under section 1221. The Congress believes that commodities derivatives financial instruments are integrally related to the ordinary course of the trade or business of commodities derivatives dealers and, therefore, such assets should be treated as ordinary assets.

The Congress further believes that ordinary character treatment is proper for business hedges with respect to ordinary property. The Congress believes that the approach taken in the Treasury regulations under prior law with respect to the character of hedging transactions generally should be codified as an appropriate interpretation of prior law. Those Treasury regulations, however, modeled the definition of a hedging transaction after the prior-law definition contained in section 1256, which generally required that a hedging transaction "reduces" a taxpayer's risk. The Congress believes that a "risk management" standard better describes modern business hedging practices that should be accorded ordinary character treatment.

In adopting a risk management standard, however, the Congress did not intend that speculative transactions or other transactions not entered into in the normal course of a taxpayer's trade or business should qualify for ordinary character treatment, and risk management should not be interpreted so broadly as to cover such transactions. In addition, to minimize whipsaw potential, the Congress believes that it is essential for hedging transactions to be properly identified by the taxpayer when the hedging transaction is entered into.

Finally, because hedging status under prior law and present law is dependent upon the ordinary character of the property being hedged, an issue arises with respect to hedges or certain supplies, sales of which could give rise to capital gain, but which are generally consumed in the ordinary course of a taxpayer's trade or business and that would give rise to ordinary deductions. For purposes of defining a hedging transaction, Treasury regulations treat such supplies as ordinary property. The Congress believes that it was appropriate to confirm this treatment by specifying that such supplies are ordinary assets.

Explanation of Provision

The provision adds three categories to the list of assets the gain or loss on which is treated as ordinary (sec. 1221). The new categories are: (1) commodities derivative financial instruments entered into by commodities derivatives dealers, (2) hedging transactions, and (3) supplies of a type regularly consumed by the taxpayer in the ordinary course of a taxpayer's trade or business.

For this purpose, a commodities derivatives dealer is any person that regularly offers to enter into, assume, offset, assign or terminate positions in commodities derivative financial instruments with customers in the ordinary course of a trade or business. A commodities derivative financial instrument means a contract or financial instrument with respect to commodities, the value or settlement price of which is calculated by reference to any combination of a fixed rate, price, or amount, or a variable rate, price, or amount, which is based on current, objectively determinable financial or economic information. This includes swaps, caps, floors, options, futures contracts, forward contracts, and similar financial instruments with respect to commodities. It does not include shares of stock in a corporation; a beneficial interest in a partnership or trust; a note, bond, debenture, or other evidence of indebtedness; or a contract to which section 1256 applies.

In defining a hedging transaction, the provision generally codifies the approach taken by the Treasury regulations under prior law, but modifies the rules. The "risk reduction" standard of the regulations is broadened to "risk management" with respect to ordinary property held (or to be held) or certain liabilities incurred (or to be incurred). In addition, the Treasury Secretary is granted authority to treat transactions that manage other risks as hedging transactions. As under the prior-law Treasury regulations, the transaction must be identified as a hedge of specific property. It is intended that this be the exclusive means through which the gains or losses with respect to a hedging transaction are treated as ordinary. Authority is provided for Treasury regulations that would address improperly identified or non-identified hedging transactions. The Treasury Secretary is also given authority to apply these rules to related parties.

NOTES

(A) *Timing and Character.* The character of a business hedge also may affect its timing. Section 1256 requires the holder of certain financial contracts and options to mark them to market at year end, requiring gain or loss to be recognized at that time. A business hedge that qualifies for ordinary treatment, however, generally is not subject to these mark-to-market rules. § 1256(e). Business hedges that are not eligible for ordinary income treatment are subject to the mark-to-market rules. The gain or loss is reported annually as 40 percent short-term gain or loss and 60 percent long-term gain or loss. § 1256(a). Furthermore, in some cases, taxpayers would not be permitted to take loss positions into account if the gain position was postponed.

(B) *Ongoing Vitality of Corn Products?* Although the Supreme Court's opinion in *Arkansas Best* appeared to sound a death knell for the *Corn Products* doctrine, *Corn Products* continues to have some vitality. Because the opinion did not explicitly overrule *Corn Products*, the lower courts were left to determine the extent of the Supreme Court's retreat in *Arkansas Best*. For example, the Fifth Circuit treated a loss sustained by an employer on the sale of an employee's home as a capital loss. The employer had entered into an agreement to purchase the home if it fired the employee and it argued that the expense was a form of employee compensation. Relying on *Arkansas Best* for the view that a business purpose for acquisition was irrelevant, the court found that the house was not "used in the trade or business" as required by § 1221(a)(2). Azar Nut Co. v. Commissioner, 931 F.2d 314 (5th Cir.1991). Note that if the employer simply had reimbursed the employee for his loss on the sale of the house, the payment would have been deductible as compensation. In a case that treated as capital a taxpayer's loss on the sale of stock of banks that he purchased intending to form a holding company, the first circuit stated that the *Corn Products* doctrine is limited to hedges that are part of an inventory purchase system. Given the addition of § 1221(a)(7) and (8) to the Code, providing that such hedges are ordinary assets, does *Corn Products* have any ongoing vitality?

In Commissioner v. Bagley & Sewall Co., 221 F.2d 944 (2d Cir.1955), decided just before *Corn Products*, the court allowed deduction as an ordinary loss the decline in value of government bonds purchased solely as collateral to guarantee performance of a manufacturing contract. Is it clear that this case is no longer good law following *Arkansas Best* and its legislative aftermath?

7. CAPITAL GAIN ON SMALL BUSINESS STOCK

In order to encourage investment in "small" companies, Congress has conferred capital gains treatment on a special kind of stock. § 1202. An individual can exclude 50 percent of the gain on the sale or exchange of "qualified small business stock" held for at least five years. The includible portion is taxed at a maximum 28 percent rate; thus, the maximum effective tax rate on the gain is 14 percent. The amount of gain eligible for exclusion is the greater of ten times the taxpayer's basis in the stock or $10 million of gain on stock in the corporation. In order to use the exclusion, the taxpayer must have acquired the stock at its original issuance.

An eligible corporation is one whose net worth at the time of the issuance of the stock is $50 million or less. Furthermore, at least 80 percent of its assets must be used in the conduct of an active trade or business during substantially all of the taxpayer's holding period. Finally, the business conducted by the corporation must be something other than one where one of the principal assets of the business is the reputation of one or more of its employees (such as law, accounting, architecture, athletics, and financial services). The business also cannot involve banking, insurance, leasing, financing, investing, farming, or operating a hotel or restaurant. A taxpayer can elect to rollover the taxable portion of the gain on the sale of qualified small business stock by investing the proceeds in new qualified stock. The new stock must meet the active business requirement for the six-month period following the purchase. The holding period of the old stock is tacked to the new stock so that a total holding period of five years will qualify.

B.   JUDICIAL GLOSS ON THE STATUTE—THE COMMON LAW OF CAPITAL GAINS

The language of § 1221 implies that all property qualifies as a capital asset unless it is specifically excluded under the exceptions enumerated in paragraphs (a)(1) to (8) of that section. The favorable tax rates and the vagaries that would result from applying § 1221 literally have prompted the courts to narrow the scope of the definition of capital asset beyond the statutory requirements.

Courts have adopted two general approaches to decide whether assets that literally come within the scope of § 1221 nevertheless should be denied capital gains treatment. These approaches were described in Michot v. Commissioner, 43 T.C.M. 792, 794 (1982).

> First, some cases derive from [Commissioner v.] Gillette Motor Co., [364 U.S. 130 (1960),] the rule that all that is property in a common sense is not property within the meaning of Section 1221. See, *e.g.*, *Commissioner v. Ferrer*, 304 F.2d 125 (2d Cir.1962) * * *. Second, other cases, relying on *Commissioner v. P.G. Lake, Inc.*, 356 U.S. 260 (1958) and *Hort v. Commissioner*, 313 U.S. 28 (1941), deny capital asset status when a substitute for future ordinary income is perceived.

1.   DISPOSITIONS OF LEASES, LIFE ESTATES, CONTRACTS, AND OTHER INTERESTS

This Section examines a variety of controversies over eligibility for capital gain treatment for dispositions of leases, life estates, contracts, and other interests. Often these cases turn on the relationship of the interest transferred to the property retained by the taxpayer. Sometimes, this is done by asking whether there has been a "sale or exchange" of a capital asset. Although there must be both a "sale or exchange" and a capital asset, the two doctrines are often intermingled. Cases dealing explicitly with the sale or exchange requirement are discussed infra at page 622.

The courts' reluctance to find capital gain when the interest disposed of is a portion of a larger property resembles their reluctance to permit effective assignments of income when something less than the taxpayer's entire property interest is transferred. Recall *Horst* and *Blair* from the preceding Chapter. Distinctions routinely are drawn between so-called "vertical slices," transfers of an interest coterminous with the seller's rights, and "horizontal slices," where the disposition involves a right "carved-out" of a larger interest for a shorter period of time. Capital gain treatment is more likely for the former than the latter. As in the assignment of income context, the cases here are haunted by the "fruit v. tree" metaphor.

Hort v. Commissioner

This case appears supra at page 141.

NOTES

(A) *Rights to Future Income*. The court in *Hort* characterized the lump sum payment for cancellation of the lease as a substitute for "nothing more than the relinquishment of the right to future rental payments." Why should this characterization be dispositive of the capital gains issue? Isn't the value of property generally the present value of its future income stream and thus are not all sales of capital assets essentially relinquishments of the right to future ordinary income?

This "substitute for ordinary income" standard, while frequently adopted by the courts, can provide at most only a clue whether ordinary income or capital gains treatment is appropriate. In a rough way, the capital gains provisions require distinguishing returns to capital (interest, dividends, rents, royalties and the like), which should be taxed as ordinary income, from appreciation in the value of an asset, which should qualify as capital gain when the asset is sold.

(B) *Changes in Value Due to Changes in the Economy—the Landlord*. Suppose the tenant in *Hort* had simply prepaid the rent by transferring the present value of all the rental payments. The landlord clearly would have reported ordinary income. In *Hort* the general decline in rental prices caused by the Depression made the lease more valuable to the lessor at the time of the cancellation in 1934 than it had been when entered into in 1927. Is this the kind of appreciation that should be subject to capital gains rates? Is it any different from appreciation of a bond bearing a high interest rate during a period when interest rates are falling? If Hort had sold the building and land subject to the lease, he would have received capital gains treatment. Why does the sale of the lease alone suggest a different result?

(C) *Changes in Value Due to Changes in the Economy—the Tenant*. Suppose the tenant has a lease with terms more favorable than the current market and the tenant sells the leasehold for a premium. The amount received is a capital gain. Rev.Rul. 72–85, 1972–1 C.B. 234. Why are the landlord and the tenant treated differently? Is it because the lease is a "tree" to the tenant but a "fruit" to the landlord? What if the tenant sold only several years worth of his leasehold for a premium?

Commissioner v. P.G. Lake, Inc.

Supreme Court of the United States, 1958. 356 U.S. 260.

MR. JUSTICE DOUGLAS delivered the opinion of the Court.

* * *

Lake is a corporation engaged in the business of producing oil and gas. It has a seven-eighths working interest[1] in two commercial oil and gas leases. In 1950 it was indebted to its president in the sum of $600,000 and in consideration of his cancellation of the debt assigned him an oil payment right in the amount of $600,000, plus an amount equal to interest at 3 percent a year on the unpaid balance remaining from month to month, payable out of 25 percent of the oil attributable to the taxpayer's working interest in the two leases. At the time of the assignment it could have been estimated with reasonable accuracy that the assigned oil payment right would pay out in three or more years. It did in fact pay out in a little over three years.

In its 1950 tax return Lake reported the oil payment assignment as a sale of property producing a profit of $600,000 and taxable as a long-term capital gain under § 117 of the Internal Revenue Code of 1939. The Commissioner determined a deficiency, ruling that the purchase price (less deductions not material here) was taxable as ordinary income, subject to depletion. * * *

First, as to whether the proceeds were taxable as long-term capital gains * * * or as ordinary income subject to depletion. The Court of Appeals started from the premise, laid down in Texas decisions, see especially Tennant v. Dunn, 130 Tex. 285, 110 S.W.2d 53, that oil payments are interests in land. We too proceed on that basis; and yet we conclude that the consideration received for these oil payment rights * * * was taxable as ordinary income, subject to depletion.

The purpose of [the capital gains provision] was "to relieve the taxpayer from * * * excessive tax burdens on gains resulting from a conversion of capital investments, and to remove the deterrent effect of those burdens on such conversions." See Burnet v. Harmel, 287 U.S. 103, 106. And this exception has always been narrowly construed so as to protect the revenue against artful devices. See Corn Products Refining Co. v. Commissioner, 350 U.S. 46, 52.

We do not see here any conversion of a capital investment. The lump sum consideration seems essentially a substitute for what would otherwise be received at a future time as ordinary income. The payout of these particular assigned oil payment rights could be ascertained with considerable accuracy. Such are the stipulations, findings, or clear inferences. * * * [C]ash was received which was equal to the amount of the income to accrue during the term of the assignment, the assignee being compensated by interest on his advance. The substance of what was assigned was the right to receive future income. The substance of what was received was the

1. An oil and gas lease ordinarily conveys the entire mineral interest less any royalty interest retained by the lessor. The owner of the lease is said to own the "working interest" because he has the right to develop and produce the minerals.

In Anderson v. Helvering, 310 U.S. 404, we described an oil payment as "the right to a specified sum of money, payable out of a specified percentage of the oil, or the proceeds received from the sale of such oil, if, as and when produced." Id., at 410. A royalty interest is "a right to receive a specified percentage of all oil and gas produced" but, unlike the oil payment, is not limited to a specified sum of money. The royalty interest lasts during the entire term of the lease. Id., at 409.

present value of income which the recipient would otherwise obtain in the future. In short, consideration was paid for the right to receive future income, not for an increase in the value of the income-producing property.

These arrangements seem to us transparent devices. Their forms do not control. Their essence is determined not by subtleties of draftsmanship but by their total effect. * * * We have held that if one, entitled to receive at a future date interest on a bond or compensation for services, makes a grant of it by anticipatory assignment, he realizes taxable income as if he had collected the interest or received the salary and then paid it over. That is the teaching of Helvering v. Horst, 311 U.S. 112, * * * and it is applicable here. As we stated in Helvering v. Horst, supra, 117, "The taxpayer has equally enjoyed the fruits of his labor or investment and obtained the satisfaction of his desires whether he collects and uses the income to procure those satisfactions, or whether he disposes of his right to collect it as the means of procuring them." There the taxpayer detached interest coupons from negotiable bonds and presented them as a gift to his son. The interest when paid was held taxable to the father. Here, even more clearly than there, the taxpayer is converting future income into present income.

* * *

Reversed.

NOTES

(A) *Nature of the Asset vs. Method of Payment.* Why is the ability to estimate accurately the future payout of the assigned oil payment important to the Court? Has the Court applied *Corn Products* to find no capital asset in this case? Or is the Court relying on the lack of a sale or exchange, that is, the lack of "any conversion of a capital asset?" In other words, is the nature of the assets sold or the method of payment determinative here?

(B) *Sales of Income.* P.G. *Lake* should be compared with Rhodes' Estate v. Commissioner, 131 F.2d 50 (6th Cir.1942), in which the taxpayer owned 600 shares on which a dividend of $20 per share had been declared. He sold his dividend rights for $11,925 before the dividend was payable. The taxpayer argued that the sale of the dividend rights constituted capital gains. In a per curiam opinion, citing assignment of income cases, the court held that the sale of the dividend rights produced ordinary income. In both *P.G. Lake* and *Rhodes' Estate,* future ordinary income was sold for its present value, and the income interest was sold while the income-generating asset was retained. In neither case did the sales price reflect market appreciation or depreciation. Only if one is concerned about bunching of income—in these cases, a taxpayer's voluntary bunching of income—is there an argument for treating the amount received as capital gain.

(C) *Section 636.* The specific result of the *P.G. Lake* case was changed by § 636, which was enacted in 1969 to provide new rules governing production payments. The sale of a carved-out production payment is treated as a loan. The seller remains taxable on the income from the oil produced and is entitled to deductions for depletion. He can deduct the interest element of the payments. The purchaser of the payment is taxable only on the interest and cannot deduct depletion. An owner who sells a well and retains a production payment is treated as having made a sale subject to a mortgage. The purchaser is taxable on the proceeds of production and is entitled to depletion deductions.

(D) *Slicing the Asset: Horizontal vs. Vertical Slices.* What if the taxpayer in *P.G. Lake* had sold the entire leasehold interest? In United States v. Dresser Industries, Inc., 324 F.2d 56 (5th Cir.1963), the taxpayer had been granted an exclusive right to practice a patent on a new method of surveying for oil wells. The taxpayer later relinquished the "exclusive" feature of the contract in exchange for $500,000. The court distinguished *P.G. Lake:*

> The taxpayer here is cutting off a "vertical slice" of its rights, rather than carving out an interest from the totality of its rights under the grant. The interest transferred was not to terminate when a certain amount was paid, as was so in *Lake,* and taxpayer retained no reversionary interest in the "exclusivity" feature transferred. The tree was sold along with the fruit, at least insofar as that branch was concerned.

* * *

> We conclude, therefore, that the sale was not merely the present sale of the right to earned income, to be paid in the future. Taxpayer had an asset, a right, a property which would produce income. The fact that the income which *could* be earned would be ordinary income is immaterial; such would be true of the sale of all income-producing property.

That point was elaborated upon by a concurring judge:

> A person acquires property for one of two, or both reasons. The first is to receive earnings, i.e., income. The other is to hold the property for appreciation resulting from long or short range economic conditions, inflation or the like. Normally, of course, the predominant reason is to acquire the earning capacity represented by the earnings which the property will generate.

> Hence it is that among those who trade in corporate securities on established national exchanges or over-the-counter markets, there are recognized rules of thumb by which the present value, hence market price, is determined for a given stock. The same is true in the contemporary, frequent practice of large-scale corporate acquisitions by one corporation of the stock or assets of another corporation. Value— market or sales price—is determined by capitalizing earnings. Whether the formula is the conservative one of 6 or 7 times earnings, or something less, or one considerably more speculative, what the buyer offers is his estimate of the present, discounted value of the future earnings of the assets or enterprise.

> But although this sales price is determined by future earnings, and to the seller it takes the place of what he would have received had he continued his ownership, under no stretch of the imagination is it "ordinary income" either in the business world or in the sometimes

more weird, tax world. Were this so, then every such sale for a price in excess of cost would entail this analysis and this tax consequence. There would first have to be ascertained what portion of the excess represented the present value of future earnings and what portion represented merely capital appreciation, from enhancement in value caused by inflation, scarcity or the like. Then as a second step, that portion or the excess of sales price representing future earnings would be taxed as ordinary income, the remainder as capital gains.

Conceding that Congress might compel this, that the ubiquitous and voracious tax gatherer might demand it, or that courts might ultimately sustain it, the fact is that as yet none has gone so fast so far. And that is so because of the practical economic realities which are, after all, of dominant significance in tax affairs. Income is one thing. When income, and income alone, is sold or transferred, it keeps this status. But when the thing which generates the income is transferred, what is paid and received is not vicarious income, whether viewed from an economic or a tax standpoint. It is, as the economist and the businessman views it, the present, discounted value of its future earnings. If the "thing" generating such future earnings is "property" of a kind which the tax law recognizes as one entitled to capital gains or losses when used in the tax law sense, that present, discounted value is a capital gain, not ordinary income, notwithstanding the economic fact that without such capacity to earn "ordinary income" in the hands of its owner, the asset would be valueless.

Does the above description of the ordinary income-capital gain distinction clarify *P.G. Lake*'s citation to assignment of income cases, such as *Horst,* which distinguish transfers of rights to income from transfers of income producing property?

(E) *Shifting Risk.* In Rev.Rul. 82–221, 1982–2 C.B. 113, the IRS permitted a taxpayer who received a lump sum payment for a 65 percent interest in minerals in place to report it as capital gain. The IRS noted that ordinary income, rather than capital gain, treatment generally is required where the taxpayer has retained an "economic interest" in minerals in place. In the instant case, the IRS held that the taxpayer had relinquished an economic interest in the 65 percent of the minerals sold because he received a fixed price and no future royalty, he had transferred the risks of mining the minerals, and he sold a fixed quantity of minerals that represented a substantial portion of the total minerals in place.

(F) *Conversion Transactions.* The difference between the maximum tax rate on ordinary income and that on capital gains creates an incentive to convert ordinary income into capital gains. One of the most common ways to do this is to disguise interest—or payments attributable to the time value of money—as capital gain. Increasingly, Congress has adopted statutory provisions designed to prevent this conversion.

Section 1258, for example, recharacterizes the capital gain on a so-called "conversion transaction" as ordinary income. The general idea is to target transactions in which the taxpayer's economic position is similar to that of a lender and thus the return should be treated as ordinary income, as interest is. Broadly speaking, a conversion transaction is one consisting of two or more positions taken with regard to the same or similar property, where substantially all of the taxpayer's return is attributable to the time value of the net investment. The taxpayer bears no significant risks other than those usually borne by a lender. Conversion transactions include straddles, transactions marketed or sold on the basis that they produce capital gain, and the acquisition of property and a contemporaneous agreement to sell the same property in the future. Treasury may designate other conversion transactions. § 1258(c)(2).

The amount of the gain that is treated as ordinary income cannot exceed the interest the taxpayer would have earned if the rate were 120 percent of the applicable federal rate. For example, suppose T purchases stock for $100 on January 1, 2000 and, at the same time, enters into a forward contract to sell the stock for $105 on January 1, 2001. This is economically similar to a loan for a year where T is to receive 5 percent interest. Assuming the applicable federal rate is greater than 4 percent, $5 of the sales price is ordinary income.

Bell's Estate v. Commissioner

Circuit Court of Appeals, Eighth Circuit, 1943. 137 F.2d 454.

SANBORN, CIRCUIT JUDGE: The question for decision is whether * * * the consideration received by the life beneficiary of a trust for the transfer of the life interest to the remainderman was ordinary income or was capital. * * *

Frederic Somers Bell (now deceased) and Frances Laird Bell, husband and wife, of Winona, Minnesota, on April 28, 1932, each created a trust. The corpus of each trust consisted of 550 shares of the common stock of the Thorncroft Company. * * * The trust agreement executed by Frederic S. Bell provided: "The Trustees shall pay to Frances Laird Bell, wife of the Grantor, during her lifetime, the entire net income of the Trust Estate. Upon her death, the Trustees shall pay, deliver, and convey the Trust Estate to Laird Bell, son of the Grantor."

The trust agreement executed by Frances L. Bell provided: "The Trustees shall pay to Frederic Somers Bell, husband of the Grantor, during his lifetime, the entire net income of the Trust Estate. Upon his death, the Trustees shall pay, deliver, and convey the Trust Estate to Laird Bell, son of the Grantor." The shares of stock constituting the corpus of each trust were transferred to the trustees. On February 1, 1936, Frederic S. Bell assigned to Laird Bell "all his [Frederic S. Bell's] right, title and interest in, to and under the [Frances L. Bell trust] in consideration of the receipt of $104,349.26 [cash and securities]" * * * On the same day, Frances L. Bell assigned to Laird Bell "all her right, title and interest, in, to and under the [Frederic S. Bell trust] in consideration of the receipt of $93,060.87 [cash and securities] (being 16.57144% of the agreed value of the trust property) * * *." The consideration delivered by Laird Bell to each of the life beneficiaries represented the value, at the time of the assignments, of their respective life interests, apparently computed upon the basis of a 4% yield on the agreed value of the trust corpus for the life expectancy of each of the life beneficiaries. Laird Bell, having then acquired absolute title to the corpus of each of the trusts, received the trust assets, and the trusts were terminated. In his income tax return for each subsequent year, Laird Bell included the income from the former trust assets.

Frederic S. Bell and Frances L. Bell, in the belief that the consideration which they had received from Laird Bell for the life interests conveyed to him represented the proceeds of a sale of capital assets, made their respective income tax returns for the year 1936 upon that basis, the return of each of them showing a small capital gain resulting from the sale. The Commissioner of Internal Revenue ruled that the entire consideration received by the life beneficiaries was [ordinary] income * * *. The Board of Tax Appeals affirmed the Commissioner, and the decision of the Board is now before this Court for review.

The Commissioner contends that the consideration received by the life beneficiaries for their respective life interests was in reality an advance payment of future income of the trusts during their life expectancies, and was taxable as ordinary income, even if the son, who acquired the interests, is required to include in his returns all income received by him from the former trust assets. This contention is based mainly upon the opinion of the Supreme Court in Hort v. Commissioner, 313 U.S. 28, in which it was held that the amount received by a lessor from a lessee as consideration for the cancellation of a lease was, in effect, a substitute for the future rents reserved in the lease, and was therefore income and not a return of capital. However, there was no transfer of any interest in the lease or of any property involved in that case. The court said (page 32): " * * * The cancellation of the lease involved nothing more than relinquishment of the right to future rental payments in return for a present substitute payment and possession of the leased premises."

If the parents of Laird Bell, instead of creating these trusts in 1932, had transferred the stock in the Thorncroft Company to him in consideration of his agreement to pay to each of them annually a certain sum for life, and if, in 1936, he had purchased from them releases of his obligations to make further annual payments, the consideration received by them in 1936 would unquestionably have been income, under the ruling in the *Hort* case. But that is not the situation here. * * *

There can be no question that in Blair v. Commissioner, [300 U.S. 5], the Supreme Court ruled that assignments of life interests such as those here involved are transfers of interests in the trust assets, and are not merely assignments of income. The Commissioner, however, in seeking for a distinction between that case and these cases, says in his brief: "It is true that in Blair v. Commissioner, supra, it was held that the assignment of the right to receive trust income during the life of the assignor carried with it such a property interest in the fund that the transferee and not the transferor was taxable upon future income. But there the assignments were by way of gift and there was no question such as here presented with respect to the taxability of the consideration. As pointed out by the Board of Tax Appeals and as herein above indicated, that question is answerable by reference to the *Hort* case, Hort v. Commissioner, 313 U.S. 28, where the Court expressly held that simply because the lease was 'property' the amount received for its cancellation was not a return of capital. Similarly, simply because the life interests here may have been property within the scope of the *Blair* case, it does not follow that the amounts received by the transferors did not constitute ordinary income to them. It is submitted that those amounts were ordinary income in the same sense as prepaid rentals, interest or salaries are ordinary income." * * *

In Harrison v. Schaffner, 312 U.S. 579, a life beneficiary of a trust had assigned to her children specified amounts in dollars from her trust income for the year following the assignment. The trustees paid these amounts to the assignees. The Supreme Court, in its opinion holding that the amounts, for tax purposes, remained the income of the assignor, said with respect to Blair v. Commissioner, supra (at p. 582): " * * * It is true, as respondent argues, that where the beneficiary of a trust had assigned a share of the income to another for life without retaining any form of control over the interest assigned, this Court construed the assignment as a transfer in praesenti to the donee, of a life interest in the corpus of the trust property and held in consequence that the income thereafter paid to the donee was taxable to him and not the donor. Blair v. Commissioner, supra. But we think it quite another matter to say that the beneficiary of a trust who makes a single gift of a sum of money payable out of the income of the trust does not realize income when the gift is effectuated by payment, or that he escapes the tax by attempting to clothe the transaction in the guise of a transfer of trust property rather than the transfer of income where that is its obvious purpose and effect."

The Supreme Court has not, expressly or by implication, overruled or modified its decision in Blair v. Commissioner, supra. The assignments in Helvering v. Horst [311 U.S. 112], Helvering v. Eubank [311 U.S. 122], and Harrison v. Schaffner, supra, are distinguishable from the assignments involved in Blair v. Commissioner, supra, and from the assignments involved in the instant cases. The Supreme Court has made the distinction, and it is not for this Court to unmake it. We have already pointed out that Blair v. Commissioner does not conflict with Hort v. Commissioner, 313 U.S. 28, which involved the extinguishment of a contractual right to future rentals, and not an assignment of an interest in property. * * *

Our conclusion is that in 1936 Frederic S. Bell and Frances L. Bell did not sell to Laird Bell income or naked rights to receive income, but sold to him life interests in trust property, and that the considerations received by them were not ordinary income, taxable as such, but were the proceeds of sales of capital assets.

Since the Board was of the opinion that the consideration received by each of the life beneficiaries was ordinary income, it expressed no opinion as to the proper basis for determining the amount of capital gain, if any. The parties are not in accord upon that question, and we are asked to decide it. We think the question should first be determined by the Tax Court. * * *

The decision of the Board is reversed, and the cases are remanded for further proceedings not inconsistent herewith.

WOODROUGH, CIRCUIT JUDGE (dissenting). * * * I think that the ruling in Hort v. Commissioner, 313 U.S. 28, is applicable and controlling in this case rather than that in Blair v. Commissioner, 300 U.S. 5 and that implications fairly to be drawn from Helvering v. Horst, 311 U.S. 112; Helvering v. Eubanks, 311 U.S. 122; Harrison v. Schaffner, 312 U.S. 579; and Hort v. Commissioner, 313 U.S. 28, lend support to the decision below. I would affirm.

NOTES

(A) *Relationship to Hort and P.G. Lake.* What distinguishes the life estate in *Bell's Estate* (which was treated as a capital asset) from the oil productions payment in *P.G. Lake* or from the lease in *Hort* (which were treated as ordinary assets)? Is it the probable term of the future interest? The method of the transfer? The nature of the property transferred? The fact that the transferor conveyed all that he had?

Suppose the consideration for the life estate had been paid in installments over a number of years. Should that have affected the result? Suppose it had been paid in the form of an annuity, payable to the life tenant each year as long as she lived. Would there still be capital gain or loss? Suppose the life tenants had not sold the life estate but collected the income (their only right)?

(B) *Basis.* Is there a basis for Bell's interest—or are the entire proceeds subject to capital gains tax? Compare Regs. § 1.1014–5 and § 1.1014–7, which provide for a basis in a life interest or remainder interest acquired from a decedent, with *P.G. Lake* and *Hort,* where no basis was allocated to the carved-out interest.

The tax law is extremely complex with respect to basis when a gift or bequest of property is divided into two separate interests, one taking effect after the other. The value of the term or life interest plus the remainder interest equals the total value of the property. Recall that the life or term interest will decline in value and the remainder interest will increase in value as the time that the remainderman takes actual possession approaches. Thus, the value of the interests of the life tenant and the remainderman are always changing. The regulations reflect these changes in basis.

When such a term interest acquired by gift or bequest is sold, § 1001(e) requires the taxpayer to take a zero basis. The life tenant is therefore taxable in full on the sale proceeds, although at capital gains rates. The basis of the life tenant who acquired his interest by gift or bequest can be taken into account when he joins with the remainderman to sell the entire interest in a single transaction. The purchaser of a life interest, however, has a basis equal to the amount paid.

2. WHAT IS THE MEANING OF PROPERTY?

Commissioner v. Ferrer

United States Court of Appeals, Second Circuit, 1962. 304 F.2d 125.

FRIENDLY, CIRCUIT JUDGE: This controversy concerns the tax status of certain payments received by José Ferrer with respect to the motion picture "Moulin Rouge" portraying the career of Henri de Toulouse–Lautrec. The difficulties Mr. Ferrer must have had in fitting himself into the shape of the artist can hardly have been greater than ours in determining whether the transaction here at issue fits the rubric "gain from the sale or exchange of a capital asset held for more than 6 months," as the Tax Court held, 35 T.C. 617 (1961), or constitutes ordinary income, as the Commissioner contends. We have concluded that neither party is entirely right, that some aspects of the transaction fall on one side of the line and some on the other, and that the Tax Court must separate the two.

In 1950 Pierre LaMure published a novel, "Moulin Rouge," based on the life of Toulouse–Lautrec. He then wrote a play, "Monsieur Toulouse," based on the novel. On November 1, 1951, LaMure as "Author" and Ferrer, a famous actor but not a professional producer, as "Manager" entered into a contract, called a Dramatic Production Contract, for the stage production of the play by Ferrer.

* * *

By the contract the Author "leased" to the Manager "the sole and exclusive right" to produce and present "Monsieur Toulouse" on the speaking stage in the United States and Canada, and gave certain rights for its production elsewhere. * * *

Article Seventh said that "In the event that under the terms hereof the Manager shall be entitled to share in the proceeds of the Motion Picture and Additional Rights hereafter referred to, it is agreed that the Manager shall receive" 40% for the first ten years and diminishing percentages thereafter. Among the additional rights so described were "Radio and Television."

For the beginning of an answer whether the Manager would be so entitled, we turn to Article IV, § 2, of the Supplemental Provisions. This tells us that "In the event the Manager has produced and presented the play for the 'Requisite Performances and Terms,' the Negotiator shall pay the Manager" the above percentages "of the proceeds, from the disposal of the motion picture rights." Article VI, § 3, contains a similar provision as to payment by the Author of the proceeds of the "additional rights" including radio and television. * * *

Further provisions put flesh on these bones. Article IV, § 1(a), says that "The title" to the motion picture rights "vests in the Author, as provided in Article VIII hereof." Article VIII says, even more broadly, "The Author shall retain for his sole benefit, complete title, both legal and equitable, in and to all rights whatsoever (including, but not by way of limitation, the Motion Picture Rights * * * Radio and Television Rights * * *)," other than the right to produce the play. The Motion Picture Negotiator, a person appointed by the Council of the Dramatists Guild, Article V, §§ 1 and 6, has power to dispose of the motion picture rights. However, he may not do this without the written consent of both Author and Manager "prior to the time the play has been playing for any of the respective periods of time referred to in Article XIII, Section 9(b) hereof," Article IV, § 1(b). This prohibition serves a double purpose—it protects the Manager from dilution of the value of the right to produce the play through too early exhibition of a picture, and it promotes realization of the enhancement in the value of the motion picture rights normally resulting from successful dramatic production. Doubtless for similar reasons, the Author could not, without the consent of the Manager, permit the release of radio and television rights until first-class production of the play had ceased. Article V, § 1(b), decrees that the Manager shall "have no right, title or interest, legal or equitable, in the motion picture rights, other than the right to receive the Manager's share of the proceeds * * *." Article V, § 1(c), lays down that if the Manager deems "himself aggrieved by any disposition of motion picture rights, he shall have no recourse, in law or in equity," against a purchaser, a lessee, or the Negotiator; "the Manager's sole recourse * * * shall be against the Author and only by arbitration as provided hereunder." * * *

Having been somewhat upstaged by these provisions, the Manager then returns toward the center under other clauses. The Negotiator must confer with him, as well as with the Author, on every step in the disposition of the motion picture rights. * * * If the Manager does not like an offer the Negotiator is planning to accept, he has an opportunity to turn up a better one. * * * An insert to one of the "Additional Clauses" provides that if the Manager desires, the Author, not later than three weeks after the New York opening of the play, will "discuss a proposed deal for the Manager to acquire" the motion picture rights. Finally, another "Additional Clause" prescribes that "All dramatic, motion picture, radio and television rights in the novel MOULIN ROUGE shall merge in and with the play during the existence of this contract," and if the Manager produces and presents the play for a sufficient period, "throughout the copyright period of the play."

Shortly after signature of the Dramatic Production Contract, John Huston called Ferrer to ask whether he would be interested in playing Toulouse–Lautrec in a picture based upon "Moulin Rouge." On getting an affirmative indication, Huston said he would go ahead and acquire the motion picture rights. Ferrer replied, in somewhat of an exaggeration, "When you get ready to acquire them talk to me because I own them."

Both Huston and Ferrer then had discussions with LaMure. Ferrer expressed a willingness "to abandon the theatrical production in favor of the film production, provided that, if the film production were successful I would be recompensed for my abandoning the stage production." * * * LaMure's lawyer prepared a letter of agreement, dated February 7, 1952, whereby Ferrer would cancel and terminate the Contract. Ferrer signed the letter but instructed his attorney not to deliver it until the closing of a contract between himself and the Company that was to produce the picture; the letter was not delivered until May 14, 1952.

Meanwhile, on May 7, 1952, Ferrer entered into a contract with Huston's company, Moulin Productions, Inc. ("Moulin"), hereafter the Motion Picture Contract. This was followed by an agreement and assignment dated May 12, 1952, whereby LaMure sold Huston all motion picture rights to his novel, including the right to exploit the picture by radio and television. * * *

The Motion Picture Contract said that Romulus Films Limited, of London, proposed to produce the picture "Moulin Rouge," that Moulin would be vested with the Western Hemisphere distribution rights, and that Moulin on behalf of Romulus was interested in engaging Ferrer's service to play the role of Toulouse–Lautrec. Under clause 4(a), Ferrer was to receive $50,000 to cover 12 weeks of acting, payments to be made weekly as Ferrer rendered his services. Ferrer's performance was to begin between June 1 and July 1, 1952. By clause 4(b), Ferrer was to receive $10,416.66 per week for each additional week, but this, together with an additional $50,000 of salary provided by clause 4(c), was "deferred and postponed" and was payable only out of net receipts. Finally, clauses 4(d) and (e) provided "percentage compensation" equal to stipulated percentages of the net profits from distribution of the picture in the Western and Eastern Hemispheres respectively—17% of the Western Hemisphere net profits until Ferrer had received $25,000 and thereafter 12¾% (such payments to "be made out of sixty-five (65%) percent of the net profits," whatever that may mean), and 3¾% of the Eastern Hemisphere net profits. If Ferrer's services were interrupted by disability or if production of the picture had to be suspended for causes beyond Moulin's control, but the picture was thereafter completed and Ferrer's "acts, poses, and appearances therein" were recognizable to the public, he was to receive a proportion of the compensation provided in clauses 4(c), (d) and (e) corresponding to the ratio of his period of acting to 12 weeks. The same was true if Ferrer failed to "conduct himself with due regard to public conventions and morals" etc. and Moulin cancelled on that account. The absence of any similar provision with respect to termination for Ferrer's wilful refusal or neglect to perform services indicates that all his rights, except that for compensation already due under clause 4(a), would be forfeited in that event. Over objections by the Commissioner, Ferrer offered testimony by Huston's attorney, who was also president of Moulin, that in the negotiation "it was said that the ultimate percentage payment to be made to Ferrer would be his compensation for giving up his interest in the dramatization guild," and a letter from the same attorney, dated March 3, 1953, confirming that in the negotiations with Ferrer's attorney "for the sale of the dramatic rights held by you to the property entitled 'MONSIEUR TOULOUSE' and the novel 'MOULIN ROUGE,' it was understood that the consideration for such sale price was the payments due, or to become due, to you under Clause 4(d) and Clause 4(e)," and also that LaMure "refused to sell the motion picture rights for the production of the motion picture known as 'MOULIN ROUGE' unless you sold the aforesaid dramatic rights." Ferrer's agent testified, again over objection, that the largest salary Ferrer had previously received for a moving picture appearance was $75,000.

Moulin's books showed $109,027.74 as a salary payment to Ferrer in August, 1953, and $178,751.46 at various later dates in 1953 as the payment of "Participating Interests" under clause 4(d). Ferrer's 1953 return reported the former as ordinary income, and the latter, less expenses of $26,812.72, as a long-term capital gain. The Commissioner determined a deficiency on the basis that the difference, $151,938.74, constituted ordinary income; from the Tax Court's annulment of that determination he has taken this appeal.

Section 117(a) of the 1939 Code, now § 1221 of the 1954 Code, tells us, not very illuminatingly, that " 'capital asset' means property held by the taxpayer (whether or not connected with his trade or business), but does not include" four (now five) types of property therein defined. However, it has long been settled that a taxpayer does not bring himself within the capital gains provision merely by fulfilling the simple syllogism that a contract normally constitutes "property," that he held a contract, and that his contract does not fall within a specified exclusion * * *. This is easy enough; what is difficult, perhaps impossible, is to frame a positive definition of universal validity. * * *

* * * [T]he principal relevant authorities on the two sides of the line in the Supreme Court and in the courts of appeals are as follows: There is no sale or exchange of a capital asset when a lessor receives payment for releasing a lessee from an obligation to pay future rent * * *. The same was true of the cancellation of an exclusive distributorship, * * *, although § 1241 of the 1954 Code * * * now rules otherwise if the distributor has a substantial capital investment therein. The transfer of exclusive agency rights to a third person likewise did not qualify * * *; whether it now does if the capital investment requirement of § 1241 is met is another question. The sale of oil payment rights, * * * the temporary taking of a taxpayer's right to use his own transportation assets, * * * and the surrender of an exclusive contract to purchase coal * * * do not meet the statutory test. Neither does the receipt of a lump sum in liquidation of a percentage of the gross receipts of motion pictures otherwise payable to a producer solely in return for personal services not yet performed * * *. On the other hand, a lessee's surrender of his lease to the lessor, * * * now in effect ratified by § 1241 of the 1954 Code, his relinquishment of a right to restrict the lessor's renting to another tenant in the same business, * * * and his release of his entire interest to a sublessee * * * constitute the sale or exchange of a capital asset. So does the abandonment of an option to acquire a partnership interest * * *.

One common characteristic of the group held to come within the capital gain provision is that the taxpayer had either what might be called an "estate" in * * *, or an "encumbrance" on * * *, or an option to acquire an interest in * * * property which, if itself held, would be a capital asset. In all these cases the taxpayer had something more than an opportunity, afforded by contract, to obtain periodic receipts of income, by dealing with another * * *, or by rendering services, * * * or by virtue of ownership of a larger "estate" * * *. We are painfully aware of the deficiencies of any such attempt to define the wavering line even in this limited area, but it is the best we can do. We add, with greater confidence, that more recent cases * * * have moved away from the distinction * * * between a sale to a third person that keeps the "estate" or "encumbrance" alive, and a release that results in its extinguishment. Indeed, although reasoning from another section of a statute so full of anomalies is rather treacherous business, we take § 1241 of the 1954 Code as indicating Congressional disenchantment with this formalistic distinction. In the instant case we can see no sensible business basis for drawing a line between a release of Ferrer's rights to LaMure for a consideration paid by Moulin, and a sale of them, with LaMure's consent, to Moulin or to a stranger who would then release them. Moulin's attorney, as we have seen, did not care a fig whether there was "an annulment or conveyance" of the Dramatic Production Contract. Tax law is concerned with the substance, here the voluntary passing of "property" rights allegedly constituting "capital assets" not with whether they are passed to a stranger or to a person already having a larger "estate." So we turn to an analysis of what rights Ferrer conveyed.

Two issues can be eliminated before we do this. We need no longer concern ourselves, as at one time we might have been obliged to do, over the alleged indivisibility of a copyright; the Commissioner is now satisfied that sales and exchanges of less than the whole copyright may result in capital gain * * *. Neither do we have in this case any issue of excludability under § 117(a)(1)(A), [now § 1221(a)(1)]; Ferrer was not in the "trade or business" of acquiring either dramatic production rights or motion picture rights.

When Huston displayed an interest in the motion picture rights in November, 1951, Ferrer was possessed of a bundle of rights, three of which are relevant here. First was his "lease" of the play. Second was his power, incident to that lease, to prevent any disposition of the motion picture rights until June 1, 1952, or, on making an additional $1500 advance, to December 1, 1952, and for a period thereafter if he produced the play, and to prevent disposition of the radio and television rights even longer. Third was his 40% share of the proceeds of the motion picture and other rights if he produced the play. All these, in our view, Ferrer "sold or exchanged," although the parties set no separate price upon them. To be sure, Moulin had no interest in producing the play. But Ferrer did, unless a satisfactory substitute was provided. Hence Moulin had to buy him out of that right, as well as to eliminate his power temporarily to prevent a sale of the motion picture, radio and television rights and to liquidate his option to obtain a share of their proceeds.

(1) Surrender of the "lease" of the play sounds like the transactions held to qualify for capital gain treatment in [cases involving a lessee's surrender of his lease to his lessor]. * * * [C]ourts would have enjoined LaMure, or anyone else, from interfering with this, unless the Dramatic Production Contract dictated otherwise. None of its many negations covered this basic grant. Ferrer thus had an "equitable interest" in the copyright of the play.

The Commissioner did not suggest in the Tax Court, and does not here, that this interest or, indeed, any with which we are concerned in this case, fell within § 117(a)(1)(C) of the 1939 Code, [now § 1221(a)(3)], excluding from the term "capital asset" "a copyright; a literary, musical, or artistic composition; or similar property; held by—

"(i) a taxpayer, whose personal efforts created such property * * *."

He was right in not doing this. * * * Yet the legislative history * * * shows that § 117(a)(1)(C), initially added by the Revenue Act of 1950, 64 Stat. 906, 933, was intended to deal with personal efforts and creation in a rather narrow sense. Ferrer's role as producer, paying large sums to the theatre, the actors, other personnel, and the author, is not analogous to that of the writer or even the "creator" of a radio program mentioned by the Committee. Moreover, the dramatic producer does not normally "sell" the production to a single purchaser, as an author or radio program "creator" usually does—he offers it directly to public custom.

We see no basis for holding that amounts paid Ferrer for surrender of his lease of the play are excluded from capital gain treatment because receipts from the play would have been ordinary income. The latter is equally true if a lessee of real property sells or surrenders a lease from which he is receiving business income or subrentals; yet [other courts have] held such to be the sale or exchange of a capital asset, as § 1241 now provides. Likewise we find nothing in the statute that forbids capital gain treatment because the payment to Ferrer might be spread over a number of years rather than coming in a lump sum; although prevention of the unfairness arising from applying ordinary income rates to a "bunching" of income may be one of the motivations of the "capital gain" provisions, the statute says nothing about this. * * * Finally, with respect to the lease of the play, there was no such equivalence between amounts paid for its surrender and income that would have been realized by its retention * * *.

(2) Ferrer's negative power, as an incident to the lease, to prevent any disposition of the motion picture, radio and television rights until after production of the play, was also one which, under the cases previously cited * * * would be protected in equity unless he had contracted to the contrary, and would thus constitute an equitable interest in this portion of the copyright. Although we should not regard Articles IV, § 1(a) and VIII as outlawing equitable relief to protect the rights granted as to the play, a literal reading of Article V, § 1(c), quoted above, would negate Ferrer's power to enjoin disposition of the motion picture rights prior to production of the play and would remit him to arbitration—a consequence serious from the standpoint of definition of a capital asset * * *. In the absence of authority, we should not read the clause so broadly; we would construe it as relating to disputes as to the manner of disposition of the rights after the Negotiator had become entitled to dispose of them, not as closing the door on the only effective method for protecting the Manager's important interest against premature disposition. As a practical matter, this feature of the Dramatic Production Contract "clouded" LaMure's title, despite the Contract's contrary assertion. Huston would not conclude with LaMure and LaMure would not conclude with Huston unless Ferrer released his rights; Huston's attorney testified that a contract like Ferrer's "imposes an encumbrance on the motion picture rights." Ferrer's dissipation of the cloud arising from the negative covenant seems analogous to the tenant's relinquishment of a right to prevent his landlord from leasing to another tenant in the same business, [which has been] held to be the sale or exchange of a capital asset. * * * What we have said in (1) with respect to possible grounds for disqualification as a capital asset is *a fortiori* applicable here.

(3) We take a different view with respect to the capital assets status of Ferrer's right to receive 40% of the proceeds of the motion picture and other rights if he produced "Monsieur Toulouse."

We assume, without deciding, that there is no reason in principle why if the holder of a copyright grants an interest in the portion of a copyright relating to motion picture and other rights contingent on the production of a play, or, to put the matter in another way, gives the producer an option to acquire such an interest by producing the play, the option would not constitute a "capital asset" unless the producer is disqualified by § 117(a)(1)(A), [now § 1221(a)(1)]. Although the copyright might not be such an asset in the owner's hands because of that section or § 117(a)(1)(C)(i), [now § 1221(a)(3)(A)], the latter disqualification would not apply to the producer * * *, and the former would not unless the producer was a professional. However, it is equally possible for the copyright owner to reserve the entire "property" both legal and equitable in himself and agree with the producer that a percentage of certain avails shall be paid as further income from the lease of the play—just as the lessor of real estate might agree to pay a lessee a percentage of what the lessor obtained from other tenants attracted to the building by the lessee's operations. In both instances such payments would be ordinary income. If the parties choose to cast their transaction in the latter mold, the Commissioner may take them at their word.

Here the parties were at some pains to do exactly that. LaMure was to "retain for his sole benefit, complete title, both legal and equitable, in and to all rights whatsoever" other than the right to produce the play. Ferrer was to "have no right, title or interest, legal or equitable, in the motion picture rights, other than the right to receive the Manager's share of the proceeds"; even as to that, he was to have "no recourse, in law or in equity" against a purchaser, a lessee, or the Negotiator, but only a right to arbitration against the Author. We cannot regard all this as mere formalism. The Contract is full of provisions designed to emphasize the Negotiator's freedom to act—provisions apparently stemming from a fear that, without them, the value of the motion picture rights might disintegrate in controversy. [Authority] greatly relied upon by the taxpayer does not show that, despite the contrary language of the Contract, Ferrer had, or ever would have, an affirmative equitable interest in the motion picture or other rights, as distinguished from his temporary negative "encumbrance" on them. * * *

It follows that if Ferrer had produced the play and LaMure had sold the motion picture, radio and television rights for a percentage of the profits, Ferrer's 40% of that percentage would have been ordinary income and not the sale or exchange of a capital asset. The [authorities] point to what would seem the inevitable corollary that if, on the same facts, Ferrer had then sold his rights to a percentage of the profits for a lump sum, that, too, would have been ordinary income. The situation cannot be better from Ferrer's standpoint because he had merely a contingent right to, or an option to obtain, the 40% interest. * * *

The situation is thus one in which two of the rights that Ferrer sold or exchanged were "capital assets" and one was not. Although it would be easy to say that the contingent contract right to a percentage of the avails of the motion picture, radio and television rights was dominant and all else incidental, that would be viewing the situation with the inestimable advantage of hindsight. In 1952 no one could tell whether the play might be a huge success and the picture a dismal failure, whether the exact opposite would be true, whether both would succeed or both would fail. We cannot simply dismiss out of hand the notion that a dramatic production, presenting an actor famous on the speaking stage and appealing to a sophisticated audience, might have had substantial profit possibilities, perhaps quite as good as a film with respect to a figure, not altogether attractive and not nearly so broadly known then as the success of the picture has made him now, which presumably would require wide public acceptance before returning production costs. At the very least, when Ferrer gave up his lease of the play, he was abandoning his bet on two horses in favor of a bet on only one.

In such instances, where part of a transaction calls for one tax treatment and another for a different kind, allocation is demanded. * * * If it be said that to remand for this purpose is asking the Tax Court to separate the inseparable, we answer that no one expects scientific exactness; that however roughly hewn the decision may be, the result is certain to be fairer than either extreme; and that similar tasks must be performed by the Tax Court in other areas. * * *

Still we have not reached the end of the road. The Commissioner contends that, apart from all else, no part of the payments here can qualify for capital gain treatment, since Ferrer could receive "percentage compensation" only if he fulfilled his acting commitments, and all the payments were thus for personal services. * * *

On the basis of this evidence the Tax Court found that the percentage compensation was not "to any extent the consequence of, or consideration for, petitioner's personal services." In one sense, this is hardly so. Under the Motion Picture Contract, Ferrer would receive no percentage compensation if he wrongfully refused to furnish acting services, and none or only a portion if, for reasons beyond his control, he furnished less than all. Since that must have been as plain to the Tax Court as to us, we read the finding to mean rather that Ferrer and Moulin adopted the percentage of profits formula embodied in clauses 4(d) and (e) as an equivalent and in lieu of a fixed sum payable in all events for the release of the Dramatic Production Contract. If they had first agreed on such a sum and had then substituted the arrangement here made, it would be hard to say that although payments under their initial arrangement would not be disqualified for capital gain treatment, payments under the substituted one would be. Ferrer was already bound to play the role of Toulouse–Lautrec, at a salary implicitly found to constitute fair compensation for his services; adoption of a formula whereby his receipt of percentage compensation for releasing his rights was made contingent on his fulfilling that undertaking does not mean that the percentage compensation could not be solely for his release of the Contract. The Tax Court was not bound to accept the testimony that this was the intent—it could lawfully have found that the percentage compensation was in part added salary for Ferrer's acting services and in part payment for the release. However, it found the contrary, and we cannot say that in doing so it went beyond the bounds to which our review of its fact findings is confined. * * * Since, on the taxpayer's own evidence, the percentage compensation was for the totality of the release of his rights under the Dramatic Production Contract, allocation is required as between rights which did and rights which did not constitute a "capital asset."

We therefore reverse and remand to the Tax Court to determine what portion of the percentage compensation under clauses 4(d) and (e) of the Motion Picture Contract constituted compensation for Ferrer's surrendering his lease of the play and his incidental power to prevent disposition of the motion picture and other rights pending its production, as to which the determination of deficiency should be annulled, and what part for the surrender of his opportunity to receive 40% of the proceeds of the motion picture and other rights as to which it should be sustained. The expenses allowed as basis must likewise be allocated. * * *

NOTES

(A) *Reliance on the Common Law.* Judge Friendly's opinion places great weight on an analysis of common law doctrine in determining what portion of Ferrer's rights constituted an "equitable estate." Is this approach based in any way on the policies supporting favorable treatment of capital gains? In this respect, the *Ferrer* opinion is quite different from many of the cases studied in this Section. For example, why did the government not rely on *Corn Products,* supra at page *, to argue that the contract, even if a capital asset, was incidental to Ferrer's business—the production of a play?

(B) *Separation of the Contract into a "Bundle of Rights."* Does the court's separation of the contract in this case into a "bundle of rights" illuminate or obscure the capital gain vs. ordinary income issue? Does the opinion permit the transformation of income received by Ferrer for personal services into capital gain? If the contract were viewed as a whole, would you expect ordinary income or capital gains treatment? In other words, was it principally an employment contract compensating Ferrer for his acting, with an incidental provision for the release of his dramatic production rights, or vice versa? Would these two characterizations suggest different results?

(C) *The "Sale or Exchange" Requirement.* In prior cases, the Second Circuit had relied upon the "sale or exchange" requirement to hold that the cancellation of contract rights produced ordinary income. In *Ferrer,* the court refused to rely upon the "sale or exchange" requirement, choosing instead to look at the nature of the rights transferred rather than the method of the transfer. Is not the method of the transfer more important to the basic policies of capital gains taxation than the court's opinion suggests? Would viewing the contract as one step in an ongoing venture—the production of a movie that would produce ordinary income—have suggested a different result?

(D) *Some of the Aftermath.* The taxpayer in King Broadcasting Co. v. Commissioner, 48 T.C. 542 (1967), sold service contracts for the transmission of Muzak programming to subscribers. The IRS denied capital gains treatment on the basis of Judge Friendly's distinction in *Ferrer* between contractual rights that represent an "estate," "encumbrance" or option to purchase a capital asset, as opposed to contractual rights that merely offer an opportunity to obtain periodic income. The court observed that:

> the service program agreements represent mere contractual opportunities to obtain periodic receipts of income. Essentially, the program service agreements were for the transmission of recorded Muzak programs and, unlike the [franchise agreement between the taxpayer and Muzak], cannot be considered an "enforceable estate" or an "encumbrance" or an interest in property. They were mere opportunities afforded by contract, to obtain receipts of income, as consideration for the transmission of prerecorded programs.

(E) *Common Law Analysis vs. Policy Analysis.* Compare *Ferrer* with Bellamy v. Commissioner, 43 T.C. 487 (1965), in which the actor Ralph Bellamy had a contractual right to prevent the distribution and showing of certain films. He sold his rights under this contract for $89,000 and contended that the amount received represented a long-term capital gain. The court held, however, that his contract rights did not qualify as a capital asset, and that the proceeds were taxable in full as ordinary income, stating:

> The petitioner contends * * * that, although he did not own the films themselves, he had the absolute right under the agreement * * * to prevent the distribution and showing of the films; that this right constituted a proprietary interest in the films, and hence "property"; that since such "property" does not fall within any of the exclusions of section 1221, it must be considered as a capital asset; and that such capital asset was sold * * * for $89,000, resulting in the receipt of long-term capital gain.
>
> * * *
>
> It is well established that not everything which can be called property in the ordinary sense, and which is outside the statutory exclusions, qualifies as a capital asset; and that a capital asset is something in which the taxpayer has an investment, and hence a basis.
>
> * * *
>
> While the right which the petitioner granted * * * to distribute and show the films might, in the ordinary sense, be characterized as a property right, he had no investment therein, aside from the services which he had performed in connection with the making of the films, and hence such rights had no cost basis in his hands. Such right was "not of the type which gives rise to the hardship of the realization in 1 year of an advance in value over cost built up in several years, which is what Congress sought to ameliorate by the capital gains provisions."
>
> We note that in the agreement * * * it was provided that the grant * * * included the petitioner's rights to "the results and proceeds of the Actor's services rendered to the Producer in connection with the Series" and that the $89,000 payment and any additional percentage payments were "in lieu of any and all payments that are or might become due or payable to the Actor pursuant to any agreements between the Actor and Producer or otherwise, by way of series compen-

sation, theatrical exhibition compensation, percentage of gross receipts or net profits compensation or otherwise." Whether the $89,000 which the petitioner received * * * represented, in whole or in part, commutation of the petitioner's right to compensation for past services, or whether it represented, in whole or in part, proceeds from the sale of property which was not a capital asset, the result would be the same, i.e., the $89,000 would be taxable as ordinary income.

We have given careful consideration to the petitioner's contention that the instant case is governed by Commissioner v. Ferrer * * *. It will be seen that the facts in the *Ferrer* case are substantially different from those obtaining here. There the right which was transferred was incidental to a property interest, namely, the "lease" of the play, in which the taxpayer had an investment, and was not a right stemming from a contract of employment. Clearly the amount in question in the instant case did not represent, to any extent, consideration for the transfer of any property interest comparable to that involved in the *Ferrer* case. We do not consider that case as applicable here.

Shortly before *Ferrer* was decided, the Second Circuit held that amounts received by the widow of Glenn Miller from Universal Pictures in exchange for the grant of the "exclusive right" to produce a film based on her late husband's life were ordinary income. The Court expressed some doubt that Mrs. Miller even had such a right, but in any event, what she sold was not "property." Miller v. Commissioner, 299 F.2d 706 (2d Cir. 1962). What would be the result if the estate of Elvis Presley sold its right to publicize and market his name, visage, and "persona"? See Factors Etc., Inc. v. Creative Card Co., 444 F.Supp. 279 (S.D.N.Y.1977), holding those rights (at least with regard to Elvis) to be "a species of property," assignable and descendible. When the contract rights are concerned exclusively with the provision of personal services, the courts are more reluctant to permit capital gain treatment.

(F) *Body Parts.* Suppose a taxpayer sells blood, eggs, an embryo, or other body parts. The cash received is clearly income, but is it capital or ordinary? That depends on whether the donor has transferred property or has rendered services. In Rev. Rul. 53–162, 1953–2 C.B. 127, the Service held that the donation of blood is a contribution of services and thus not eligible for a charitable contribution deduction. Green v. Commissioner, 74 T.C. 1229 (1980), however, held that a sale of blood constituted the sale of property rather than a transfer of services. In dictum, the court noted that the taxpayer, who had a rare type of blood that was much in demand was in the trade or business of selling her blood plasma and therefore the gain was ordinary under § 1221(a)(1). If a body part is property, and the taxpayer contributes only once or rarely, the statute seems to treat it as a capital asset. Is this the type of property that should receive favorable capital gains treatment?

Gladden v. Commissioner

United States Tax Court, 1999. 112 T.C. 209.

SWIFT, JUDGE:

[In 1976 the taxpayers formed a partnership (the "Saddle Mountain Ranch" partnership) and for about $675,000 acquired farmland in Harquak Valley, Maricopa County, Arizona. In 1983 the Interior Department allocated to an Arizona water conservation district ("CAP") and a local irrigation district ("HID"), both governmental subdivisions, rights to receive up to a specified amount of Colorado River water each year. Although not a party to the contracts between these organizations and the Interior Department, the taxpayers' partnership was entitled to receive each year a specified quantity of available Colorado River water. The partnership, along with other landowners, was required to pay HID each year for the Colorado River water they received. The landowners could sell their beneficial interests in Colorado River water rights to third parties but only as a part of a sale of their ownership interests in the land. In 1992 HID relinquished its Colorado River rights for a total payment of $24.6 million from the Interior Department. The taxpayers' partnership received $1,088,132 for relinquishing its share of the Colorado River water rights and entered into an agreement providing that it would return its share of any "relinquishment funds" it received in error or if HID incurred a liability for repayment.]

Capital Asset Treatment of Water Rights

* * * [P]etitioners contend, as a matter of law * * * that the water rights of the partnership constitute capital assets and that relinquishment thereof by the partnership constituted a sale or exchange. Respondent contends, also as a matter of law * * * that relinquishment by the partnership of water rights did not constitute a sale or exchange of a capital asset and therefore that the $1,088,132 the partnership received in 1993 should be treated as ordinary income.

In order for contract rights to qualify as capital assets under section 1221, the contract rights must constitute "property" of the taxpayer and not constitute any of the * * * types of property excluded from capital gain treatment under section 1221. * * *

Neither party herein suggests that any of the above five statutory exceptions applies to the water rights in issue. Petitioners, in their briefs, note that if the water rights in issue were to be treated as "real property" used in the trade or business of the partnership's farming activity, and therefore as excluded from capital asset treatment under section 1221, gain realized on the sale of the water rights would, in any event, be treated as capital gain under section 1231. Neither party, however, pursues this possible treatment of the partnership's water rights as section 1231 "real property". Thus, the only question before us is whether the partnership's water rights constitute "property" and capital assets under section 1221.

The policy considerations and rule of construction concerning what constitutes capital assets have been explained as follows:

> The preferential treatment afforded by the capital gains provisions, 26 U.S.C.A. secs. 1201–1202, 1221–1223, was designed "to relieve the taxpayer from * * * excessive tax burdens on gains resulting from a conversion of capital investment * * *." *Burnet v. Harmel*, 287 U.S. 103, 106, 53 S. Ct. 74, 75, 77 L. Ed. 199. In *Commissioner of Internal*

Revenue v. Gillette Motor Transport, Inc., 364 U.S. 130, 134, 80 S. Ct. 1497, 1500, 4 L. Ed. 2d 1617, the Court held that it was "the purpose of Congress to afford capital-gains treatment only in situations typically involving the realization of appreciation in value accrued over a substantial period of time, and thus to ameliorate the hardship of taxation of the entire gain in one year." *Commissioner of Internal Revenue v. P.G. Lake, Inc., supra; Burnet v. Harmel, supra.* * * *

* * * [N]o single definitive explanation is available of what types of property qualify as capital assets under section 1221.

Over the years, court decisions have recognized limitations on the types of property which qualify as capital assets under section 1221. In *Corn Prods. Ref. Co. v. Commissioner*, 350 U.S. 46, 51 (1955), assets that were an integral part of a taxpayer's business were held not to qualify as capital assets. In that case, the Supreme Court held that although corn futures contracts did not fall expressly within the statutory exclusions, profits received from the purchase and sale of futures contracts entered into in order to assure a reasonably priced supply of corn inventory for the taxpayer's business did not qualify for capital gain treatment. The Court observed that "Congress intended that profits and losses arising from the everyday operation of a business be considered as ordinary income or loss rather than capital gain or loss." Id. at 52.

In 1988, in *Arkansas Best Corp. v. Commissioner*, 485 U.S. 212, 219 (1988), the Supreme Court clarified that the *Corn Products* judicial exception is more properly interpreted as involving an application of the statutory exception for inventory under section [1221(a)(1)]. Respondent does not contend that petitioners' contract rights fall within the inventory exception to capital asset treatment.

Another limitation on the types of property which qualify for treatment as capital assets was explained by the Supreme Court in *Commissioner v. P.G. Lake, Inc.*, 356 U.S. 260 (1958). Thereunder, a mere right to receive ordinary income generally will not qualify as a capital asset. The issue in *Commissioner v. P.G. Lake, Inc., supra*, was whether a transfer of royalty rights associated with the production of oil constituted sale of a capital asset. After the transfer, the taxpayer retained a reversionary interest in the underlying oil and gas leases, and the purchaser acquired nothing more than a right to receive a portion of the royalties for a limited time. The Supreme Court noted that the amount received for the transfer was virtually equivalent to the amount of royalty income that otherwise would have been received. The Supreme Court concluded that the only right the taxpayer sold was the right to receive ordinary income and held that the royalty right did not constitute a capital asset. The Supreme Court noted as follows:

> The substance of what was assigned was the right to receive future income. The substance of what was received was the present value of income which the recipient would otherwise obtain in the future. In short, consideration was paid for the right to receive future income, not for an increase in the value of the income-producing property. [*Id.* at 266.].

Subsequent decisions have attempted to clarify the holding of the Supreme Court in *P.G. Lake, Inc.* With respect to the broad proposition that amounts received for the transfer of a right to receive future income will not qualify for capital gain treatment, the Court of Appeals for the Fifth Circuit in *United States v. Dresser Indus., Inc.*, 324 F.2d 56 (5th Cir.1963), explained:

> As a legal or economic position, this cannot be so. The only commercial value of any property is the present worth of future earnings or usefulness. If the expectation of earnings of stock rises, the market value of the stock may rise; at least a part of this increase in price is attributable to the expectation of increased income. The value of a vending machine, as metal and plastic, is almost nil; its value arises from the fact that it will produce income. [*Id.* at 59.].

In applying the *P.G. Lake, Inc.* limitation on what property qualifies as a capital asset, courts generally consider the entire economics of a transaction, * * * and evaluate all of the rights of the taxpayer, as well as all of the risks and obligations of the taxpayer associated with ownership of the property before the transfer. For example, in an attempt to explain *P.G. Lake, Inc.*, we stated in *Guggenheim v. Commissioner*, 46 T.C. 559 (1966):

> The Court in *Lake* was faced with the problem whether a transfer of part of a capital asset is itself the transfer of a capital asset. That part was defined and delineated by the taxpayer in such a manner as to consist essentially of only the rights to income. The transferee assumed few of the risks identified with the holding of a capital asset; he assumed only a nominal risk of his oil payment right decreasing in value and none of the possibility of the oil payment right increasing in value. On the other hand, the taxpayer, after the transfer, retained essentially all of the investment risks involved in his greater interest to the same extent as before the transfer. [*Id.* at 569.].

The above statement implies that whether investment risks are associated with contract rights transferred is a particularly relevant consideration in determining whether the rights are to be treated as capital assets.

In *Commissioner v. Ferrer*, 304 F.2d 125, 130 (2d Cir.1962), revg. in part and remanding 35 T.C. 617 (1961), the Court of Appeals for the Second Circuit concluded, among other things, that where a taxpayer's "bundle of rights" reflected "something more than an opportunity, afforded by contract, to obtain periodic receipts of income," and where they included "equitable interests" similar to those of an owner of property, they were to be treated as capital assets

The basic proposition of *Commissioner v. P.G. Lake, Inc.* is still viable. Where a taxpayer merely "[substitutes] the right to receive ordinary income from one source for the right to receive ordinary income from another [source]," the rights transferred will not be considered a capital asset.

To summarize, in determining whether a taxpayer's contract rights that are transferred constitute capital assets, courts generally consider all aspects of the taxpayer's bundle of rights and responsibilities that are transferred, specifically including the following six factors:

(1) How the contract rights originated;

(2) How the contract rights were acquired;

(3) Whether the contract rights represented an equitable interest in property which itself constituted a capital asset;

(4) Whether the transfer of contract rights merely substituted the source from which the taxpayer otherwise would have received ordinary income;

(5) Whether significant investment risks were associated with the contract rights and, if so, whether they were included in the transfer; and

(6) Whether the contract rights primarily represented compensation for personal services.

Both parties herein rely on certain Supreme Court cases that involve general, nontax issues regarding water rights. * * *

In *Nevada v. United States*, [463 U.S. 110, 126 (1983)], the Supreme Court explained that "the beneficial interest in the rights confirmed to the Government resided in the owners of the land within the Project to which these water rights became appurtenant upon the application of Project water to the land," and that "the law of Nevada, in common with most other western States, requires for the perfection of a water right for agricultural purposes that the water must be beneficially used by actual application on the land."

In *Ickes v. Fox*, [300 U.S. 82, 94–95 (1937)], the Supreme Court stated:

Although the government diverted, stored and distributed the water, the contention of petitioner that thereby ownership of the water or water-rights became vested in the United States is not well founded. Appropriation was made not for the use of the government, but, under the Reclamation Act, for the use of the land owners; and by the terms of the law and of the contract already referred to, the water-rights became the property of the land owners, wholly distinct from the property right of the government in the irrigation works. * * *

As stated, the water rights and allocations involved in both *Nevada* and *Ickes* were based on the Reclamation Act passed by Congress in 1902. Thereunder, it was expressly provided that "the right to the use of water acquired under the provisions of this Act shall be appurtenant to the land irrigated, and beneficial use shall be the basis, the measure, and the limit of the right." Ch. 1093, sec. 8, 32 Stat. 390.

Consistently with the above statutory language, the underlying contracts involved in *Nevada* between the U.S. Government and the landowners provided generally "for a permanent water right for the irrigation of and to be appurtenant to all of the irrigable area now or hereafter developed under the [Newlands Reclamation Project]". *Nevada v. United States, supra* at 127 n. 9. Similarly, the underlying contracts involved in *Ickes* between the U.S. Government and the landowners provided generally that the "rights shall be, and thereafter continue to be, forever appurtenant to designated lands owned by such shareholders." *Ickes v. Fox, supra* at 89.

Petitioners argue that the above language from *Nevada* and *Ickes* supports a conclusion that the Harquahala Valley landowners' water rights under the Subcontract were appurtenant to the landowners' land.

Respondent relies on the same cases and emphasizes differences in the relevant Federal law and the underlying contracts that were involved in those cases and in the Boulder Canyon Project Act that is involved in the instant case.

We now apply the law, as set forth and discussed above, to the undisputed facts of this case. The participation and rights of the partnership in which petitioners invested in Colorado River water originated in 1983 only as a result of and in direct proportion to the partnership's ownership interest in Harquahala Valley land. The 1983 allocation of water rights to HID under the Subcontract and through HID to the partnership under Arizona law was directly linked to and dependent upon the partnership's ownership of the land and on irrigation of the land in prior years.

Ariz. Rev. Stat. Ann. sec. 48–2990, relating to water rights and irrigation districts, and under which the partnership in 1983 received its Colorado River water rights, provides in part as follows: "Subject to the law of priority, all water of the district available for distribution shall be apportioned to the lands thereof pro rata".

The water rights of the partnership were linked to the partnership's ownership interest in the land, to its farming operations and activities on the land, and to its capital investment in the land. The water rights, and particularly the decision in 1992 to relinquish the water rights, affected the partnership's farming activity and the investment risks associated with that farming activity—especially the financial risks associated with purchasing water on the open market.

From 1983 through 1992, use of the water rights did not produce for the partnership, in any direct or immediate sense, ordinary income. Rather, using water received, land was planted, fertilized, and irrigated. Crops grew. Eventually, crops were harvested, transported, and sold. The water rights at issue simply represent one component of the partnership's investment in and operation of its farming activity.

Certainly, the $1,088,132 the partnership received in 1993 upon relinquishment of the water rights did not represent merely a substitute for ordinary income the partnership otherwise would have received. Rather, it represented payments the partnership received in exchange for making a shift in one significant aspect of its farming activity; i.e., a shift in the source of its irrigation water from the Colorado River at fixed prices to the market place at market prices.

The above undisputed facts surrounding the origination, allocation, and use of the water rights support the conclusion that the partnership's water rights should be treated as capital assets. We so hold.

In spite of differences between the language of the Reclamation Act, involved in *Nevada v. United States*, *supra*, and *Ickes v. Fox*, *supra*, and the language of the Boulder Canyon Project Act, involved in the instant case, we agree generally with petitioners that such differences in the underlying statutory language and in the above nontax opinions of the Supreme Court do not support a conclusion that the water rights involved herein do not constitute capital assets of the partnership. To the contrary, as we read the above authority, we believe they support the conclusion that the water rights allocated to the partnership for use in its farming activity, constitute contractual rights that are to be regarded as integral to the partnership's farming activity (whether technically appurtenant to the land or not) and as capital assets of the partnership.

* * *

Lastly, we note that respondent's rulings often treat as capital assets allocations or rights that taxpayers receive from governmental agencies. See Rev. Rul. 66–58, 1966–1 C.B. 186 (cotton acreage allotments treated as capital assets); Rev. Rul. 70–644, 1970–2 C.B. 167 (milk allocation rights treated as capital assets); see also *Madera Irrigation Dist. v. Hancock*, 985 F.2d 1397, 1401 (9th Cir.1993) (the parties and the Court of Appeals for the Ninth Circuit treated water rights as property rights protected by the Fifth Amendment); *First Victoria Natl. Bank v. United States*, 620 F.2d 1096, 1106–1107 (5th Cir.1980) (rice production histories and rights to receive allotments of rice, if and when issued, were treated as property rights includable in a decedent's gross estate).

On this issue, we grant petitioners' motion for partial summary judgment, and we deny respondent's motion for partial summary judgment.

Sale or Exchange

If petitioners' water rights in Colorado River water are to be treated as capital assets, petitioners and respondent cross-move for partial summary judgment on the issue of whether, for Federal income tax purposes, relinquishment of the water rights by the partnership and receipt of $1,088,132 by the partnership constituted a sale or exchange. Respondent contends that the $1,088,132 was transferred to the partnership either for the partnership's commitment to indemnify HID for unexpected future liabilities that might arise or as a mere windfall distribution to the partnership of HID surplus funds.

The undisputed evidence establishes that the form and substance of the transfers of funds that occurred at both levels (from CAP to HID and from HID to the partnership) were based on and occurred as a result of the partnership's relinquishment or exchange of rights to Colorado River water. Respondent's contention that the transfer of funds from HID to the partnership did not constitute a sale or exchange but was based on some indemnification commitment or windfall distribution of surplus funds ignores the substance of the transaction by which the partnership relinquished its water rights in return for the $1,088,132.

Respondent's arguments are without merit. The transaction before us constitutes a sale or exchange by the partnership of water rights for the $1,088,132 received by the partnership.

We grant petitioners' motion for partial summary judgment on this issue.

NOTE

The Tax Court's opinion was reversed in part by the Fifth Circuit. Gladden v. Commissioner, 262 F.3d 851 (9th Cir.2001). The Tax Court refused to allocate any of the partnership's basis in the land to the water rights because the water rights had not vested when the land was acquired by the partnership. The Fifth Circuit found that the partnership had a "realistic expectation that water rights would eventually attach to the land" and thus a portion of the purchase price for the land could be allocated to the water rights. The court noted that the purchase price undoubtedly included a premium based on the expectation that the land would receive water rights. The allocation of basis is discussed supra at 139.

3.   SALE OF A GOING BUSINESS

Williams v. McGowan

United States Circuit Court of Appeals, Second Circuit, 1945. 152 F.2d 570.

L.   HAND, CIRCUIT JUDGE:

[Williams and Reynolds were partners in a hardware business in which Williams was entitled to two-thirds of the profits and Reynolds to one-third. Williams had a capital investment of $89,053.02 in the partnership, and Reynolds had a capital investment of $29,029.03. Williams acquired Reynolds' interest for $12,187.90 upon the latter's death in 1940.]

* * * On September 17th of the same year, Williams sold the business as a whole to the Corning Building Company for $63,926.28—its agreed value as of February 1, 1940—"plus an amount to be computed by multiplying the gross sales of the business from the first day of February, 1940 to the 28th day of September, 1940," by an agreed fraction. This value was made up of cash of about $8100, receivables of about $7000, fixtures of about $800, and a merchandise inventory of about $49,000, less some $1000 for bills payable. To this was added about $6,000 credited to Williams for profits under the language just quoted, making a total of nearly $70,000. Upon this sale Williams suffered a loss upon his original two-thirds of the business, but he made a small gain upon the one-third which he had bought from Reynolds' executrix and in his income tax return he entered both as items of "ordinary income," and not as transactions in "capital assets." This the Commissioner disallowed and recomputed the tax accordingly; Williams paid the deficiency and sued to recover it in this action. The only question is whether the business was "capital assets" under [§ 1221] of the Internal Revenue Code * * *.

It has been held that a partner's interest in a going firm is for tax purposes to be regarded as a "capital asset." * * * If a partner's interest in a going firm is "capital assets" perhaps a dead partner's interest is the same. * * * We need not say. When Williams bought out Reynolds' interest, he became the sole owner of the business, the firm had ended upon any theory, and the situation for tax purposes was no other than if Reynolds had never been a partner at all, except that to the extent of one-third of the "amount realized" on Williams' sale to the Corning Company, his "basis" was different. * * * We have to decide only whether upon the sale of a going business it is to be comminuted into its fragments, and these are to be separately matched against the definition in [§ 1221], or whether the whole business is to be treated as if it were a single piece of property.

* * * [I]n this instance the section itself furnishes the answer. It starts in the broadest way by declaring that all "property" is "capital assets," and then makes three exceptions. The first is "stock in trade * * * or other property of a kind which would properly be included in the inventory"; next comes "property held * * * primarily for sale to customers"; and finally, property "used in the trade or business of a character which is subject to * * * allowance for depreciation." In the face of this language, although it may be true that a "stock in trade," taken by itself, should be treated as a "universitas facti,"* by no possibility can a whole business be so treated; and the same is true as to any property within the other exceptions. Congress plainly did mean to comminute the elements of a business; plainly it did not regard the whole as "capital assets."

As has already appeared, Williams transferred to the Corning Company "cash," "receivables," "fixtures" and a "merchandise inventory." "Fixtures" are not capital because they are subject to a depreciation allowance; the inventory, as we have just seen, is expressly excluded. So far as appears, no allowance was made for "good-will"; but, even if there had been, we held in Haberle Crystal Springs Brewing Company v. Clarke, Collector, 2 Cir., 30 F.2d 219, that "goodwill" was a depreciable intangible. * * * There can of course be no gain or loss in the transfer of cash; and, although Williams does appear to have made a gain of $1072.71 upon the "receivables," the point has not been argued that they are not subject to a depreciation allowance. That we leave open for decision by the district court, if the parties cannot agree. The gain or loss upon every other item should be computed as an item in ordinary income.

Judgment reversed.

FRANK, CIRCUIT JUDGE (dissenting in part):

I agree that it is irrelevant that the business was once owned by a partnership. For when the sale to the Corning Company occurred, the partnership was dead, had become merely a memory, a ghost. To say that the sale was of the partnership's assets would, then, be to indulge in animism.

But I do not agree that we should ignore what the parties to the sale, Williams and the Corning Company, actually did. They did not arrange for a transfer to the buyer, as if in separate bundles, of the several ingredients of the business. They contracted for the sale of the entire business as a going concern. * * *

To carve up this transaction into distinct sales—of cash, receivables, fixtures, trucks, merchandise, and good will—is to do violence to the realities. I do not think Congress intended any such artificial result. In the Senate Committee Report on the 1942 amendment to [§ 1221], it was said:

* "By universitas facti is meant a number of things of the same kind which are regarded as a whole; e.g., a herd, a stock of wares." Mackeldey, Roman Law § 162.

"It is believed that this Senate amendment will be of material benefit to businesses which, due to depressed conditions, have been compelled to dispose of their plant or equipment at a loss. The bill defines property used in a trade or business as property used in the trade or business of a character which is subject to the allowance for depreciation, and real property held for more than six months which is not properly includible in the inventory of the taxpayer if on hand at the close of the taxable year or property held by the taxpayer primarily for sale to customers in the ordinary course of his trade or business. If a newspaper purchased the plant and equipment of a rival newspaper and later sold such plant and equipment at a loss, such plant and equipment, being subject to depreciation, would constitute property used in the trade or business within the meaning of this section." These remarks show that what Congress contemplated was not the sale of a going business but of its dismembered parts. Where a business is sold as a unit, the whole is greater than its parts. Businessmen so recognize; so, too, I think, did Congress. Interpretation of our complicated tax statutes is seldom aided by saying that taxation is an eminently practical matter (or the like). But this is one instance where, it seems to me, the practical aspects of the matter should guide our guess as to what Congress meant. I believe Congress had those aspects in mind and was not thinking of the nice distinctions between Roman and Anglo–American legal theories about legal entities.

NOTE

The rule of *Williams v. McGowan* was in substance approved by the Supreme Court in Watson v. Commissioner, 345 U.S. 544, 552 (1953).

It is often difficult to allocate the purchase price of an unincorporated business to specific assets in accordance with their relative values. Section 1060 requires both buyers and sellers of unincorporated businesses to allocate the purchase price (and therefore basis) to specific assets in accordance with regulations promulgated under § 338(b)(5). This provision is intended to restrict taxpayers' ability to allocate excessive amounts of the purchase price to depreciable assets. Historically, there was often a conflict between the buyer and seller. The seller wanted to minimize his ordinary income and maximize capital gain, while the buyer preferred to allocate a higher basis to ordinary income items, especially items that might be depreciated over a short period of time. The usual tension involved goodwill, which generally produced capital gain for the seller, but was not depreciable by the purchaser. However, now that goodwill is amortizable under § 197, although still resulting in capital gain, the seller and purchaser's interests may coalesce.

4.   EFFECT OF PRIOR TRANSACTIONS

Cummings v. Commissioner

United States Court of Appeals, Second Circuit, 1974. 506 F.2d 449, cert. denied 421 U.S. 913 (1975).

IRVING R. KAUFMAN, CHIEF JUDGE:

The interplay of two distinct statutory schemes often gives rise to some engrossing legal questions. In this case, we are called upon to consider the relationship of the Internal Revenue Code and the securities laws—in particular, the proper tax treatment of a payment made in satisfaction of an apparent liability under § 16(b) of the Securities Exchange Act. We find that the policies of both statutes support the determination of the Commissioner of Internal Revenue that § 16(b) repayments should be treated as long term capital losses, and reverse the decision of the Tax Court allowing a deduction as an ordinary and necessary business expense.

I

Unlike those in many tax cases, the facts here are relatively straightforward. Nathan Cummings, chairman of the board and chief executive officer of Consolidated Food Corporation, was offered a large bloc of stock in Metro–Goldwyn–Mayer, Inc. [MGM] during 1959. He was told that the company was experiencing management problems, and that if he would become a director, three members of the board who were involved in controversy would resign. Cummings then purchased 51,500 shares of MGM stock for something more than $1,030,000, and was elected to the board after the three directors resigned.

The price of MGM stock rose, and on April 17, 1961, Cummings sold 3400 shares for a total of $227,648.28. His profit was properly reported as a long term capital gain on the 1961 tax return which he and his wife jointly filed. Between September 18 and October 2, 1961, however, Cummings bought back 3000 shares for $146,960.89. This purchase, within six months after the sale, brought him within the likely purview of § 16(b) of the Securities Exchange Act, making the difference between the sale price and the purchase price, $53,870.81, recoverable by MGM. Cummings was apparently unaware of his liability until soon after MGM, in preparation for its 1962 annual meeting, submitted its proxy material to the Securities and Exchange Commission. On January 16, 1962, the Division of Corporate Finance of the SEC informed Joseph A. Macchia, secretary of MGM, that if Cummings had realized profits from his sale and purchase, that fact would have to be noted in the proxy statement. Macchia promptly communicated this to Cummings and although Cummings believed that any violation, if it did occur, was inadvertent, he nevertheless decided to remit the $53,870.81 to MGM. Cummings testified that the purpose of the payment was to prevent any delay in the issuance of MGM's proxy statement and also to protect his business reputation, which might be injured by a disclosure of his potential liability because of an alleged securities laws violation. The Tax Court gave credence to Cummings' version. In any event, MGM issued its proxy statement dated January 18, 1962, without reference to any potential liability outstanding from Cummings.

Cummings and his wife treated his repayment as a deduction against ordinary income on their 1962 income tax return, but the Commissioner disallowed this and assessed a deficiency of $45,790.18, maintaining that long term capital loss treatment was appropriate. The Tax Court, 60 T.C. 91 (1973) held that the payment was properly characterized as an ordinary and necessary business expense, incurred to protect Cummings' business reputation. * * *

II

We are not required in this case to write on a tabula rasa, for the Courts of Appeals of two circuits have already rejected the Tax Court's treatment of § 16(b) repayments as ordinary and necessary business expenses. Anderson v. C.I.R., 480 F.2d 1304 (7th Cir.1973), reversing 56 T.C. 1370 (1971); Mitchell v. C.I.R., 428 F.2d 259 (6th Cir.1970), certiorari denied 401 U.S. 909 (1971), rev'g 52 T.C. 170 (1969). Our starting point, as was theirs, is Arrowsmith v. C.I.R., 344 U.S. 6 (1952), which held that an expenditure made for a business purpose will not be treated as an ordinary and necessary business expense if it is sufficiently related to an earlier capital gains transaction. * * *

The *Arrowsmith* rule was explained and applied in United States v. Skelly Oil Co., 394 U.S. 678 (1969).* There, a corporation repaid money which it had recorded in an earlier taxable year as income reduced by the 27½% oil depletion allowance. The Court held that the corporation could not deduct 100% of the repayment as a business expense since only 72½% of the income had been subject to taxation. *Arrowsmith* was held to forbid the windfall which would result if income taxed at a special lower rate when received were deductible on repayment at a different and more favorable rate.

The nexus between the § 16(b) repayment and the earlier capital gains is apparent. The repayment "had its genesis" in the earlier sale, see *Mitchell,* 428 F.2d at 261, which was a prerequisite for § 16(b) liability. As the *Anderson* court noted, 480 F.2d at 1307, "The amount of liability is calculated by subtracting from the sales proceeds the lowest purchase price within the six-month period" so the repayment may properly be viewed as a return of a portion of the sales proceeds or an adjustment of the sales price. In addition, the capital gain appears to include the profits from the sale and purchase. Cummings experienced a gain in the economic sense when he repurchased the stock at a lower price than that at which it was sold. But the only gain which he recognized for tax purposes was the capital gain on his original sale. Thus, for tax purposes, his payment of $53,870.81 profit from the sale and purchase may appropriately be regarded as an adjustment to the amount of that capital gain.

It is apparent, also, that Cummings would obtain a windfall like that condemned in *Skelly Oil* if we were to treat his § 16(b) repayment as an ordinary and necessary business expense. Both before and after the events at issue he owned the 3000 shares of MGM. In the interim, however, he consummated a sale which resulted in the recognition of a gain and a subsequent repurchase within six months—the combination of which violated § 16(b). The § 16(b) repayment was designed, so far as practicable, to restore the status quo prior to the offending sale and purchase. We would be remiss, therefore, if we allowed Cummings a windfall which would flow from permitting his gain to be taxed at a lower capital gains rate and his

___

* [Ed: *Skelly Oil* is set out infra at page 673].

repayment—designed to erase the improper § 16(b) gains—to be deducted at the more favorable ordinary income rate.

The result we reach is supported not only by a proper interpretation of the tax laws, but by the policy of § 16(b) as well. Our longstanding interpretation of that provision, noted over 30 years ago, is that " * * * the statute was intended to be thoroughgoing, to squeeze all possible profits out of stock transactions" within its purview, in order to remove the incentive for short-term trading by corporate insiders. It would defeat this policy if insiders could reap a tax advantage by enjoying the low capital gains rate on realized gains while obtaining a deduction against ordinary income when they surrendered those gains in satisfaction of a § 16(b) liability. In this case, for example, Cummings would benefit by $45,790.18 if he were permitted to deduct his repayment as a business expense, although (assuming that he elected the 25% alternate capital gains tax) he paid taxes of only $13,467.70 when he reported the comparable gain in 1961. Thus, he seeks to profit by $32,322.48 as a result of his § 16(b) transaction. We agree with the Seventh Circuit that, "Without good reason, we are unwilling to interpret the Internal Revenue Code so as to allow this anomalous result which severely and directly frustrates the purpose of Section 16(b)." * * *

Cummings maintains, however, that the statutory policy is irrelevant to this proceeding because he was never adjudicated to be in violation of § 16(b). * * * In particular, he notes two possible defenses—that the MGM board had the discretion not to demand repayment of Cummings's insider profits, and that the "opportunity for speculative abuse," described as the keystone of § 16(b) liability in Kern County Land Co. v. Occidental Petroleum Corp., 411 U.S. 582 (1973), was lacking because the decision to repurchase was made by Cummings's personal financial assistant.

Even a fledgling securities lawyer would recognize that these "defenses" border on the frivolous. There is no evidence that MGM would not have demanded payment. Moreover, the failure of a board of directors to demand repayment of § 16(b) profits scarcely extinguishes an insider's liability, which may readily be collected in a shareholder derivative action that is inevitable when stock is as widely held as MGM's. Nor is Cummings's reliance on *Kern County* plausible. * * * [It involved] a situation hardly comparable to the garden variety sale and purchase which was executed by Cummings.

In any event, we need not conclusively determine that Cummings violated or intended to violate § 16(b) in order to deny him an ordinary and necessary business expense deduction. Section 16(b) is a placid inlet in the chaotic sea of securities law—a statute designed for easy application. The elements of the cause of action are simple, and information about possible violations is widely disseminated. Thus, no proof need be forthcoming that the insider intended at the time he sold to repurchase the securities within six months, or that inside information was actually used. * * * One can hardly imagine a scheme better designed to insure the almost automatic enforcement of a statute, and we decline to subvert it by refusing to squeeze all profits from inside transactions unless liability has been established by a court adjudication.

III

In viewing Cummings's § 16(b) repayment as a long term capital loss rather than a business expense, we do not ignore a third alternative. As Judge Drennan suggested in his dissenting opinion in the Tax Court, the repayment may be viewed as linked to the repurchase, and treated for tax purposes as an addition to the basis of the purchased stock. The effective net result is that the repayment would be treated as a long term capital loss in the year that the repurchased stock is finally sold. It may be that such treatment would in an appropriate case better effectuate the policy of § 16(b) than that which we adopt today. But, by deferring the tax benefit of a payment currently made, the addition to basis would exact a penalty beyond that specified by Congress from an insider whose violation might be only inadvertent. Since neither party urges adoption of Judge Drennan's formula, however, we decline to resolve the issue. Reversed.

J. JOSEPH SMITH, CIRCUIT JUDGE (concurring in the result):

I concur in the reversal of the judgment, but respectfully differ from the rationale adopted.

I do not agree that this case is controlled by Arrowsmith v. C.I.R., 344 U.S. 6 (1952) and United States v. Skelly Oil Co., 394 U.S. 678 (1969). Both of those cases held that, when income is taxed at a reduced rate when received, it cannot be deducted at a more favorable rate if for some reason it has to be repaid. At the heart of those cases is the repayment of an amount which had previously been included in income. * * *

This case, involving a probable sale and repurchase violation of § 16(b), simply does not present that kind of situation. The mere fact that there could be no liability under § 16(b) were there not a sale which (in this case) resulted in taxable income is irrelevant, because the money paid out by Cummings to MGM cannot be treated as an item previously included in income. The amount of income on the sale (determined by the difference between the original purchase price and the sale price) has no bearing on the calculation of the insider's profit (determined, roughly, by the difference between the sale price and the repurchase price). In fact, it is perfectly clear that there can be an insider's profit even if the sale resulted in a loss, because the sale assumes relevance for tax purposes only when linked with the original purchase and the repurchase will not have tax significance until a subsequent sale occurs. The sale and repurchase, which result in § 16(b) liability, do not constitute a transaction with any tax significance whatever, and the insider's profit is not income for tax purposes, regardless of whether it may be considered, as my brother Kaufman considers it, as "gain in the economic sense."

I also disagree with the characterization of the payment to MGM as an adjustment to the sale price of the stock. I cannot subscribe to the view that "the capital gain appears to include the profits from the sale and purchase," * * * because the transaction resulting in capital gain terminated with the sale, and the purchase was the initiation of a new transaction that should be considered entirely separate and independent for tax purposes. * * *

This reasoning applies, of course, only to sale and repurchase violations of § 16(b). The tax significance of a purchase and sale violation would be entirely different. In that case, the insider's profit obviously should be treated as the repayment of an amount included in income. But the fact that one kind of violation of § 16(b) leads to *Arrowsmith/Skelly Oil* treatment does not require that all kinds of violations of § 16(b) be so treated. * * *

Nor do I think Tank Truck Rentals, Inc. v. C.I.R., 356 U.S. 30 (1958) relevant to the litigation before us. That decision—which is to be applied only in a "sharply limited and carefully defined category" of cases, Commissioner v. Tellier, 383 U.S. 687, 694 (1966)—involved the payment of punitive fines assessed after an adjudication of liability. Since the payment here—made in contemplation of potential liability—was remedial and not punitive, * * * this is not an appropriate case for applying a policy designed to avoid the dilution of punishment. * * *

For these reasons, I would not hold that the ordinary loss deduction should be disallowed and treated instead as a capital loss deduction. These transactions should more properly be treated in accordance with the opinion of Judge Drennen below: For tax purposes, the proper treatment would be to add to the repurchase price as the basis for the new shares the amount paid over, and to recognize neither capital gain or loss nor ordinary business expense until the tax year in which the shares are sold.

NOTES

(A) *Post-Arrowsmith Cases.* In *Arrowsmith,* relied on by the court in *Cummings,* the taxpayer liquidated a corporation and properly reported the gain on the redemption of the stock as a capital gain. Subsequently, the taxpayer was required to satisfy a judgement against the corporation. The Court treated the payment as a capital loss because it was linked to the earlier liquidation proceedings, thereby creating the so-called *Arrowsmith* doctrine which, as the *Cummings* court notes, has been read to require capital loss treatment for transactions "sufficiently related" to an earlier capital gains transaction.

See, for example, Kimbell v. United States, 490 F.2d 203 (5th Cir. 1974), in which the taxpayer sold an interest in two oil and gas leases and reported capital gains. When it was discovered that the wells on the leases were constructed illegally, he settled a claim by making a payment. The court found that the payment was not an ordinary and necessary business expense, but rather was a capital loss because it related back to the earlier transaction. See also Rev.Rul. 67–331, 1967–2 C.B. 290, where the taxpayer received a condemnation award that was taxable as a capital gain under § 1231. He had to repay some of the award in a later year, and the IRS ruled that the deduction was a capital loss.

See also the special provisions covering the reacquisitions of real property in § 1038.

(B) *Post-Cummings Cases.* *Cummings* was the third in a series of appellate court reversals of Tax Court decisions on § 16(b) payments. It was followed by the Tenth Circuit in Brown v. Commissioner, 529 F.2d 609

(1976), the Fifth Circuit in Kimbell v. United States, 490 F.2d 203 (1974), and by the IRS in Rev.Rul. 75–210, 1975–1 C.B. 72. In that ruling, a government regulatory agency announced in 1974 that all employees working in its licensing and regulatory functions must divest themselves of stocks, bonds, and other securities in regulated companies. The IRS required the employees to treat their losses on the subsequent sales as capital losses. The securities were deemed to be capital assets because they had been purchased and held for investment purposes even if they had been sold for business purposes.

See also Smith v. Commissioner, 67 T.C. 570 (1976), where the Tax Court considered payment of a § 12(a) penalty for violation of registration requirements of the Securities Act of 1933. The Court found *Arrowsmith* to be applicable because there was a "direct relationship" between the sale of stock and the taxpayer's settlement payments. The Tax Court cases involving payments under § 16(b) were distinguished. In Bradford v. Commissioner, 70 T.C. 584 (1978), the Tax Court required capitalization of expenditures paid in connection with stock in violation of § 10(b) of the Securities Exchange Act. The Tax Court also denied deduction as an ordinary and necessary business expense under § 162 and required capitalization in connection with a payment due to a possible violation of § 16(b) in Mitchell v. Commissioner, 67 T.C.M. 3015 (1994). Thus, in the Tax Court, the position urged by Judge Smith in his concurring opinion in *Cummings* has apparently taken hold.

(C) *Loss Followed by Gain.* The principles of *Arrowsmith* apply to the reverse situation as well, i.e., a loss followed by a subsequent gain. For example, in Lowe v. Commissioner, 44 T.C. 363 (1965), stock was sold in 1955, with a down payment made at that time and notes given for the balance of the purchase price. No gain was reported by the seller because he felt a "return of capital" method of accounting was appropriate. By 1958, $22,500 had been paid, when the buyer defaulted. The buyer then reconveyed the stock to the seller, and the seller released the buyer from any further liability on the notes. Holding that *Arrowsmith* was applicable, the Tax Court held that the $22,500 was taxable as capital gain in 1958.

What if the taxpayer took ordinary deductions with respect to an asset that is subsequently sold at a gain? In some cases, the statute treats the gain as ordinary. See, e.g., § 1245 and the discussion of recapture rules, supra at page 570. In other cases, the court may mandate ordinary treatment. See, e.g., Merchants National Bank of Mobile v. Commissioner, 199 F.2d 657 (5th Cir.1952) (sale of a note previously deducted as worthless produces ordinary gain). Or the court may require capitalization of the expense. Recall *Schultz v. Commissioner*, supra at page 296. But ordinary gain does not always follow ordinary deductions. In Rev.Rul. 85–186, 1985–2 C.B. 84, the IRS permitted the taxpayer to report the gain realized on the sale of technology as capital even though the costs of producing the technology had previously been deducted under § 174.

Section 4.   What is a Sale or Exchange?

In order to report a capital gain or loss, there not only must be a capital asset, but it must be sold or exchanged. Under the various provisions of § 1222, the several types of capital gain and loss all arise on "the sale or exchange of a capital asset." The need for a sale or exchange is also important under § 1231.

The sale or exchange requirement undoubtedly arises because of concern about the "lock-in" problem. Taxpayers are thought to be more likely to dispose of assets if given an incentive to do so. Courts have sometimes invoked the sale or exchange requirement to prevent favorable capital gains treatment when they considered such treatment to be inappropriate. The requirement also has been viewed as a means of preventing the conversion of interest and dividends into capital gain.

Although this Chapter deals with the questions "What is a capital asset?" and "What is a sale or exchange?" as separate issues, the distinction is not as clear in the judicial opinions. For example, in *Hort,* at page 141 supra, the taxpayer realized ordinary income and not capital gain when he sold the right to future rental income and retained the underlying property. It is not clear, however, whether ordinary income treatment resulted from the nature of the asset transferred or because the taxpayer had divided—rather than sold or exchanged—his property interest. In other words, did the retention of the underlying property mean that no capital asset had been transferred or that no sale or exchange occurred?

The *P.G. Lake* case, supra at page 588, and related decisions in the natural resources context, also illustrate the analytical confusion between the nature of the asset and the sale or exchange requirement. In these cases, the taxpayer typically transferred the right to future business income—a production payment or royalties—but retained the operation of the underlying business. The decisions in this area have not turned, however, on the taxpayer's retention of a working interest in the property. In general, whether a transaction has produced capital gain or ordinary income has turned on whether the "carved-out" interest disposed of is coterminous with the interest owned by the taxpayer. If the carved-out interest is coterminous, capital gain results; if not, ordinary income is produced. Again, it is not clear analytically whether the courts deny capital gains treatment because no capital asset was transferred or because no sale or exchange occurred.

Although the issue often is framed as a narrow question—whether there has been a sale or exchange so that the gain is capital—it often has broader implications that would arise even in the absence of a capital gains preference. For example, the form of a transaction may be a "sale" even though the substance is a "gift" or a "lease," the tax consequences of which may be quite different from those if the transaction is treated as a sale.

Many of the problems relating to the "sale or exchange" requirement have been resolved by specific statutory provisions. For example, § 1231 ignores the need for a sale or exchange on a gain arising from an involuntary conversion. Other examples are discussed infra at page 633.

The materials that follow consider some of the more important applications of the "sale or exchange" requirement. The student should be aware, however, that in most cases, the question of whether a sale or exchange has occurred is an easy one.

NOTE ON "SHORT SALES AGAINST THE BOX" AND "CONSTRUCTIVE REALIZATION"

Concerned about taxpayers' ability to engage in transactions that allow them to diversify their portfolio of assets and also to eliminate future benefits of appreciation or risks of depreciation in assets they currently hold without incurring a current capital gains tax, Congress adopted § 1259. The longstanding technique to accomplish diversification without tax had been the short sale against the box. This note provides a brief description of this technique and of § 1259.

The following definition of a short sale, given by the Supreme Court in Provost v. United States, 269 U.S. 443, 450–51 (1926), is as good as any:

> [A] short sale is a contract for the sale of shares which the seller does not own or the certificates for which are not within his control so as to be available for delivery at the time when, under the rules of the [New York Stock] Exchange, delivery must be made.

Tax-oriented short sales usually were made by taxpayers who hold a long position in the same securities (short sales against the box). Generally the taxpayer borrows securities, usually from a broker, and sells them. The taxpayer subsequently closes out the transaction by delivering identical securities to the lender. (The box apparently refers to the historic practice of holding pieces of paper evincing long positions in securities in a dealer's strongbox.)

Under current law, when a taxpayer sells securities, she generally is allowed to identify the securities sold for purposes of determining gain or loss on the disposition. If the taxpayer does not make an adequate identification, she is deemed to have disposed of the securities first acquired. Mutual fund investors, however, are allowed to determine the adjusted bases of their shares based on the average cost of all such shares.

Under prior law, when a taxpayer sold securities specifically identified as borrowed securities, gain or loss could not be computed because the taxpayer's cost for the securities was not known. The recognition of gain or loss generally was postponed until the taxpayer closed the sale by returning identical property to the lender. See Reg. § 1.1233–1(a) ("a short sale is not deemed to be consummated until delivery of property to close the short sale"). The rationale was that the taxpayer had the option of delivering the securities held or newly purchased securities.

These rules allowed a taxpayer to lock in gain on securities when he entered into a short sale against the box, which eliminated risk of loss on the securities. Any decline in the value of the investor's long position was offset by an increase in the value of the short position, just as any increase in the value of the long position resulted in a loss on the short position. In addition, a short-against-the-box sale often monetized the taxpayer's position because it produced cash almost equal to the value of the long position.

For example, suppose T owns 100 shares of Ford stock that it purchased for $40 per share and that currently are worth $100 per share.

Rather than selling the stock for cash, which would produce taxable gain, T could deposit the Ford stock with a broker. The broker then would borrow another 100 shares of Ford stock from a third party and sell the borrowed shares short on the open market on behalf of T. To close out this short sale, T would have to repay the third party 100 shares of Ford stock. Since T already owns 100 shares of Ford stock, any appreciation or depreciation in the Ford stock would have no economic relevance to T because T is both long and short at the same time with respect to 100 shares of Ford stock. Moreover, T could borrow (generally up to 95 percent) of the short sale proceeds and reinvest this cash in assets of its choosing. (Section 1233 limits these transactions to prevent taxpayers from using short sales against the box to accelerate losses or to convert short-term capital gain into long-term capital gain or long-term capital loss into short-term capital loss.) T locked in $60 of profit and converted his Ford stock into cash or another asset deferring tax on the gain until the short sale was closed.

Another way to hedge appreciated securities is to enter into a short forward contract. Such a contract both obligates and entitles the investor to sell the security for a fixed price on a specified date in the future. Because the sales price is fixed, the investor is no longer exposed to movements in the price of the security. The forward contract might be satisfied by the delivery of the securities or settled with cash.

Alternatively, the investor can buy a put option on the security (the right to sell the security) at a price equal to its current price, thereby hedging against declines in the price of the security. The option might be cash settled. In contrast to an investor that sells short against the box or enters into a short forward contract, an investor that uses a put option retains the potential for gain from further appreciation. If the value of the security rises above the option strike price, the holder will fail to exercise the option and can sell on the open market. This upside potential comes at the cost of the option premium.

Short forwards and put options hedge against risk of loss, but do not necessarily monetize a long position. An investor who wishes to monetize a long position, as well as hedge against risk of loss, of course, can borrow money in a separate transaction.

In general, whether these other transactions were successful in avoiding gain recognition seemed to depend on whether the investor remained the owner of the appreciated security for tax purposes or whether the other party to the transaction became the owner. If the other party did not become the owner, the taxpayer probably would not be deemed to have sold the property.

Retention of the ability to transfer property to a third party suggests that the taxpayer continues to own the property. Assume, for example, that a taxpayer owning appreciated securities enters into a forward contract that obligates and entitles the taxpayer to sell those securities on a date in the future. Assume further that identical securities are available in the market (e.g., shares of publicly traded stock) and that the taxpayer's obligations under the contract are not secured by the particular securities owned by the taxpayer at the time that the contract is entered into. The taxpayer is free to transfer the securities it owns to a third party and later to acquire identical securities in the market to perform under the forward contract. In this case, the taxpayer was not viewed as having transferred ownership by entering into the forward contract.

The tax advantage of these types of transactions was substantially curtailed by § 1259. That section taxes the holder on any gain where there is deemed to be a constructive sale of an appreciated financial position. A financial position includes a futures or forward contract, a short sale, or an option with respect to stock, debt, or a partnership interest. A constructive sale is deemed to occur when the taxpayer (or a related person) enters into a short sale or an offsetting notional principal contract with respect to the same or substantially identical property, or enters into a futures or forward contract to deliver the same or substantially identical property. A constructive sale also occurs where the taxpayer holds an appreciated short position in property and acquires a long position in the same property. Sales of nonpublicly traded property, however, are not subject to this rule.

Thus, § 1259 eliminates the tax advantage of a short against the box—upon entering into the short sale, the gain on the underlying appreciated stock is taxed. A taxpayer who enters into a forward contract to sell property, that is, a contract "to deliver a substantially fixed amount of property for a substantially fixed price," also is taxed on the gain on the underlying property. For example, suppose X holds 100 shares of Techno stock with an adjusted basis of $1,000 and a fair market value of $10,000. He enters into a contract to sell the shares one year hence for $11,000. On entering the contract, he is deemed to have sold the shares for $10,000 and must report a gain of $9,000. The remaining $1,000 is reported when the forward contract is closed.

An offsetting notional principal contract is an agreement to pay or credit the investment yield (including appreciation) on such property for a specified period, and a right to be reimbursed for (or receive credit for) any decline in the value of such property. A popular example is an equity swap. Suppose A owns 100 shares of Digico stock worth $20,000 that have appreciated $5,000. Under prior law, an equity swap permitted her to lock in the appreciation on the Digico stock and invest in another asset without reporting the gain on Digico. Here's how: for a five-year period, A agrees to transfer to B annually an amount equal to the dividends paid on the Digico stock plus the amount by which the value of the stock has increased. B agrees to transfer to A annually an amount equal to a market rate of interest on $20,000 plus the amount by which the value of the Digico stock has decreased. A has essentially sold the Digico stock—she will neither enjoy the appreciation or risk a loss in value—and invested in a $20,000 bond. Because the agreement with B is an offsetting notional principal contract, A now is taxed on the gain on the Digico stock on entering into the contract. When A actually sells the stock, she is credited with the gain already taxed.

There are many financial positions and offsetting contracts that could accomplish essentially the same thing as the forward contract or the equity swap. Section 1259 gives the IRS the authority to draft regulations that would treat as constructive sales other transactions that have the same effect as those described above. There are many open questions that the regulations must resolve. For example, what is substantially identical property? What if a taxpayer holds the short position and his wholly-owned corporation owns the long position? For a discussion of many of these questions, see Deborah H. Schenk, Taxation of Equity Derivatives: A Partial Integration Proposal, 50 Tax L. Rev. 571 (1995); for further discussion of similar techniques, see Edward Kleinbard, Risky and Riskless Positions in Securities, 71 Taxes 783 (1993); Robert Scarborough, Proposal Would Tax Short–Against-the-Box Sales, But May Encourage Alternatives That Use Derivatives, Derivatives Magazine (May, 1996), at 217.

A.   SALE VS. ABANDONMENT OR EXTINGUISHMENT OF RIGHTS

Yarbro v. Commissioner

United States Court of Appeals, Fifth Circuit, 1984.
737 F.2d 479, cert. denied 469 U.S. 1189 (1985).

JOHN R. BROWN, CIRCUIT JUDGE:

This case presents the question of whether an individual taxpayer's loss resulting from the abandonment of unimproved real estate subject to a non-recourse mortgage exceeding the market value is an ordinary loss or a capital loss. * * * [W]e affirm the Tax Court's holding that an abandonment of real property subject to non-recourse debt is a "sale or exchange" for purposes of determining whether a loss is a capital loss.

FACTS

James W. Yarbro (Taxpayer) has been a self-employed financial and tax consultant since 1969. In 1972, he acquired a real estate broker's license. In that year, he formed three joint ventures and negotiated a separate land purchase for each of the ventures. Only the land purchase for the last of the three joint ventures is at issue here.

The venture was formed by Taxpayer, together with five other persons, for the purpose of acquiring about 132 acres of undeveloped land on the northern limits of the city of Fort Worth, Texas. The purchase price was $362,132.08. About 10% was paid in cash, and the balance was covered by four non-recourse promissory notes secured by deeds of trust on the property. * * *

In the summer of 1976, the City of Fort Worth decided to raise the real estate taxes on the joint venture's property by 435% from $770 per year to approximately $3,350 per year. At about the same time, real estate activity in the area completely dried up. As a consequence, by November of 1976, the property's fair market value had dropped below the face amount of the nonrecourse mortgage to which it was subject. When confronted with these facts, the joint venture participants decided to abandon the property and not to pay the real estate taxes for 1976 or the $22,811 annual interest payment for that year. Accordingly, on November 15, 1976, Taxpayer, as trustee, notified the Fort Worth National Bank (the trustee of the mortgages) that he was abandoning the property. Although the bank requested Taxpayer to reconvey the property to it, Taxpayer refused to do so, reasoning that he "had nothing to convey and would have nothing to do * * * with the property from that point on."

In June, 1977, the bank obtained title to the property pursuant to foreclosure proceedings. None of the joint venture participants received any consideration from the foreclosure sale.

THE TAX

On his 1976 federal income tax return, Taxpayer claimed an ordinary loss of $10,376 from the abandonment of the joint venture property. The Commissioner, however, determined that Taxpayer's loss was not an ordinary loss, but, rather, constituted a long-term capital loss. The Commissioner took the position that Taxpayer's abandonment of the property constituted a "sale or exchange" within the meaning of Sections 1211 and 1222 of the Code. The Commissioner further contended that Taxpayer held his own interest in the land as an investment and not for use in taxpayer's "trade or business" or "primarily for sale to customers in the ordinary course of business." Thus, the Commissioner contended that the abandonment was a "sale or exchange" of a "capital asset."

The Tax Court agreed with the Commissioner's analysis. Determining that Taxpayer acquired his interest in the property "primarily for investment purposes" the Tax Court held that the property was not used in Taxpayer's financial consulting and property management business within the meaning of Section 1231 of the Code. The Tax Court also concluded that the "casual" rental of the land for grazing purposes at a nominal fee did not evidence use of the land in a bona fide rental business, and that the evidence did not support a finding that the land was held primarily for sale to customers in the ordinary course of business. Finally, the Tax Court, following the course charted in Freeland v. Commissioner, 74 T.C. 970 (1980), and Middleton v. Commissioner, 77 T.C. 310 (1981), aff'd per curiam, 693 F.2d 124 (11th Cir.1982), held that an abandonment of property constituted a "sale or exchange" for purposes of Code Sections 1211 and 1222.

STATUTORY CONTEXT

Section 165(a) of the Internal Revenue Code of 1954 provides, as a general rule, that taxpayers may deduct "any loss sustained during the taxable year and not compensated for by insurance or otherwise." The application of this general rule, however, is limited by Section 165(f), which provides that "losses from *sales or exchanges of capital assets* shall be allowed only to the extent allowed in §§ 1211 and 1212." (emphasis added). Taxpayer, by arguing that the abandonment was not a "sale or exchange," and that the land in the hands of the joint venture was not a "capital asset," seeks to establish that the loss was an ordinary loss. If accepted, this position would allow Taxpayer to avoid the limitations imposed by §§ 1211 and 1212 on the deduction that may be taken for capital losses.

[The court's rejection of the taxpayer's assertion that he was entitled to rely on earlier decisions defining the "sale or exchange" requirement has been omitted.]

* * *

The term "exchange," in its most common, ordinary meaning implies an act of giving one thing in return for another thing regarded as an equivalent. Webster's New International Dictionary (2d ed. 1954). Thus, three things are required: a giving, a receipt, and a causal connection between the two. In the case of abandonment of property subject to nonrecourse debt, the owner gives up legal title to the property. The mortgagee, who has a legal interest in the property, is the beneficiary of this gift, because the mortgagee's interest is no longer subject to the abandoning owner's rights.

In *Middleton,* as in this case, the taxpayer argued that, because the debt was nonrecourse and he therefore had no personal liability for the debt, he received nothing in exchange for his relinquishment of title. In essence, the argument is that because the taxpayer personally had no obligation to repay the debt, the abandonment could not have relieved him of any obligation. This argument is inconsistent with several Supreme Court decisions.

The Supreme Court has held that regardless of the nonrecourse nature of the debt, the taxpayer does receive a benefit from the disposition of the property: he is relieved of his obligation to pay the debt and taxes and assessments against the property. In Crane v. Commissioner, 331 U.S. 1 (1947), the Supreme Court established that, in computing the *amount* of gain on the disposition, the outstanding debt must be included in the "amount realized" by the taxpayer, whether the debt is recourse or non-recourse. However, in that case Mrs. Crane, besides having the vendee take over the loan payments, received $2500 in cash (boot) on the sale. This left open the question of whether the non-recourse debt would be treated the same as recourse debt in situations where the outstanding debt exceeds the fair market value of the property. In such case, the owner-debtor would not obtain any boot by abandoning the property or transferring it subject to the mortgage.

In Commissioner v. Tufts, 461 U.S. 300 (1983), the Supreme Court answered this unanswered question by holding that where the debt exceeded the market value, the entire nonrecourse debt—not just the fair market value—was the "amount realized" by the taxpayer on the disposition of the property.

* * *

Although *Crane* and *Tufts* concerned the *amount* of the gain or loss and not the *character* of the gain or loss, their rationales support the Commissioner's position in the instant case to the extent that the concept of "amount realized" for computing gain or loss may be equated with the concept of consideration for "sale or exchange" purposes.

Indeed, the Supreme Court in two decisions has followed the same approach of *Crane* and *Tufts* in the "sale or exchange" context.

In Helvering v. Hammel, 311 U.S. 504 (1941), and Helvering v. Nebraska Bridge Supply & Lumber Co., 312 U.S. 666 (1941), the Court held that there had been a "sale or exchange" and a capital loss even though the taxpayer had received no boot or other consideration, other than relief from a debt. In *Hammel,* the Court looked to the legislative purpose and history of the capital gain and loss provisions and held that "sale or exchange" included foreclosure sales. The involuntary nature of the transaction and the lack of any surplus from the sale to be returned to the owner did not make the foreclosure any less a "sale or exchange." Soon after *Hammel*, the Supreme Court rendered a decision, the relevance of which to the recourse-nonrecourse "sale or exchange" issue was aptly explained by the Seventh Circuit:

> In Helvering v. Nebraska Bridge Supply & Lumber Co., 312 U.S. 666 (per curiam), the rationale of *Hammel* was extended. The taxpayer in *Nebraska Bridge Supply* owned property on which the real estate taxes were delinquent. The delinquency created no personal liability. The tax lien was thus like a nonrecourse mortgage. Arkansas bid in the property at a tax sale, acquiring it without paying anything. The state was thus like the holder of a nonrecourse mortgage foreclosing on property worth less than the mortgage. The Eighth Circuit had allowed the taxpayer to take an ordinary loss deduction because "[t]he transfer of title to the State is not only involuntary, but is without any consideration moving to the transferor." 115 F.2d 288, 291 (1940). The Supreme Court summarily reversed.

Laport v. Commissioner, 671 F.2d 1028 (7th Cir.1982).

Based on the Supreme Court's reasoning in *Crane, Tufts* and *Nebraska Bridge Supply,* we approve the Tax Court's acceptance of the Commissioner's interpretation that one who abandons property subject to non-recourse debt receives a relief from the debt obligation when he gives up legal title. Moreover, it is clear that the relief from the debt is what causes the abandonment. It was advantageous, in the view of the Supreme Court, for the Taxpayer to relinquish title only because the debt of which he was relieved was greater than the market value. Thus, under the Supreme Court precedents, the abandonment in this case involved a giving in order to receive something in return as the equivalent,[1] and therefore fit within the ordinary meaning of "sale or exchange."

Moreover, an abandonment of property subject to non-recourse debts has the same *practical effect* as several other transactions which have each been held to be a "sale or exchange." The Supreme Court has held that an involuntary foreclosure sale of real estate was a "sale or exchange" and the loss a capital loss. Helvering v. Hammel, 311 U.S. 504 (1941). In *Nebraska Bridge Supply,* the Court held a tax forfeiture to be a "sale or exchange." In Laport v. Commissioner, 671 F.2d 1028 (7th Cir.1982), the Court held that the taxpayer's conveyance to the mortgagee by quitclaim deed in lieu of foreclosure was a "sale or exchange." In Freeland v. Commissioner, 74 T.C. 970 (1980), the Tax Court held that where the value of land sunk below the amount of a nonrecourse debt and the owner conveyed the land to the mortgagee by quitclaim, there was a "sale or exchange" and an ordinary loss.

---

1. The mortgage agreement effectively treated the property and the debt as being equivalent in value.

The abandonment followed by the mortgagee's foreclosure in this case is the functional equivalent of the foreclosure sale in *Hammel,* the tax forfeiture in *Nebraska Bridge Supply,* and the quitclaims in lieu of foreclosure in *Laport* and *Freeland.* In all these transactions, the taxpayer-owner is relieved of his obligation to repay the debt and is relieved of title of the property. Because the mortgagee is legally entitled to recover title to the property in any of these cases, the fact that out of prudence he concludes he must go through foreclosure proceedings to formalize his interest in the land is not a rational basis for altering the character of the gain or loss realized by the taxpayer on the transaction. The differences in these transactions is [sic] not a difference in substance, but only in form.

The taxpayer who has decided that he cannot or should not make further payment on the nonrecourse loan can manipulate the form of the change in ownership of the property simply by either quitclaiming or abandoning the land before the mortgagee forecloses. * * *

Allowing taxpayers to manipulate the character of their losses from capital to ordinary by hastening to abandon rather than allowing foreclosure would frustrate the congressional purpose to treat capital gains and losses on a parity. As explained by the Supreme Court in *Hammel,* the *quid pro quo* of allowing generous tax treatment on capital gains is the limitation imposed on deductions for capital losses. 311 U.S. at 509–10. Thus, where the taxpayer would be eligible for capital gains treatment upon the sale of property had it appreciated in value, he should not be allowed to avoid the limitations on deductions for capital losses by using an artfully timed abandonment rather than a sale, voluntary reconveyance, or foreclosure. Accordingly, we affirm the Tax Court's holding that the Commissioner's interpretation of "sale or exchange" as including an abandonment of property subject to nonrecourse debt is a reasonable one.

* * *

[The discussion of the inapplicability of Regs. § 1.165–2, which distinguishes losses resulting from property being "permanently discarded from use" from losses "sustained upon the sale or exchange of property," and of the court's holding that the land was a capital asset, rather than property used in the taxpayer's trade or business, has been omitted.]

NOTES

(A) *Repayment of a Loan.* In National–Standard Co. v. Commissioner, 80 T.C. 551 (1983), affirmed 749 F.2d 369 (6th Cir.1984), the taxpayer borrowed Belgian francs to buy a foreign asset and later repaid the loan after selling the asset. Between the loan and the repayment, the value of the franc had appreciated with respect to the U.S. dollar. The court ruled that although the francs constituted a capital asset in the hands of the taxpayer separable from the asset they were used to buy, the repayment of the loan did not constitute a "sale or exchange." As a result, the taxpayer was allowed to take an ordinary loss deduction for the additional dollars needed to discharge the debt. Seven judges dissented, arguing that the francs constituted property and that their transfer to satisfy a debt should be regarded as a sale or exchange. Which position is more consistent with *Yarbro?*

(B) *Sale or Extinguishment of Contract Rights.* Does the receipt of a payment in exchange for the termination of contract rights constitute a sale or exchange giving rise to capital gain or loss? The Tax Court's position is that it does not because the asset disappears upon the payment. In Foote v. Commissioner, 81 T.C. 930 (1983), the taxpayer resigned his tenured appointment to a university faculty in exchange for a cash payment. The court ruled that, even if tenure has significant economic value and thus could have been considered an intangible capital asset, the voluntary extinction of tenure did not constitute a sale or exchange. As the court explained:

> The agreement in question simply terminated [the taxpayer's] rights; his tenure did not pass to the university, but was extinguished. Tenure is a personal right. It cannot be transferred to, or utilized by another. * * * Under these circumstances, there is no sale or exchange.

The IRS similarly held in Rev.Rul. 75–527, 1975–2 C.B. 30, that no sale occurred upon the extinguishment of a contract right. A hot water distribution plant had contracted to furnish heat for the taxpayer's building. The supplier sought to avoid the expense of fulfilling its contractual obligation by reimbursing the taxpayer for the cost of converting from the central heating system to an individual heating system. The IRS ruled that no sale had occurred because "the taxpayer's right to have the building heated by the central heating plant was extinguished and did not pass to the supplier."

Note that in *Ferrer,* the Second Circuit explicitly rejected the disappearing asset approach. The court argued that there was no substantive distinction between transfers that resulted in the immediate extinguishment of contract rights and transfers of rights to third parties who could transfer them again through agreements that would then lead to their extinguishment. In a subsequent case, however, the Second Circuit found that a release of rights did not produce capital gain. In Billy Rose's Diamond Horseshoe, Inc. v. United States, 448 F.2d 549 (2d Cir.1971), the lessor of the Ziegfeld Theater received payments from NBC in exchange for a release from lease provisions that required the network to return the theater in the same condition in which it had been leased. The court found that no sale had occurred because "cancellation or release of a contract right does not transfer the rights to the transferee-payor and thus is not a 'sale.' "

What is the character of a payment that the taxpayer previously had purchased? In Nahey v. Commissioner, 111 T.C. 256 (1998), the taxpayer purchased a business, one of whose assets was a lawsuit seeking damages. The lawsuit ultimately was settled and Nahey received a large payment. The court held that the settlement was ordinary for lack of a sale or exchange. The intervening change in ownership should not make a difference. If the original business had collected on settlement, the proceeds clearly would have been ordinary. In effect, the taxpayer purchased ordinary income. What if Nahey had sold the lawsuit claim before it was settled?

B.   SALE VS. LEASE

One way to convert ordinary income into capital gains is to structure as a sale what is essentially a lease. Prior to 1970, many taxpayers were able to convert ordinary business income to capital gains through a so-called "bootstrap sale" or "Clay Brown" transaction. The transaction typically proceeded as follows: The stock of a corporation would be sold to a charitable organization, which made little or no downpayment and agreed to pay the balance of the purchase price out of the profits of the business. The charitable organization then liquidated the corporation and leased the operating assets back to the seller, who formed a new corporation to operate the business. The new corporation paid a large portion of its profits as "rents" to the charitable organization, which, in turn, paid most of these receipts back to the original owner as installment payments on the initial purchase price.

In Commissioner v. Brown, 380 U.S. 563 (1965), the Supreme Court permitted the seller to report a capital gain so long as the original purchase price was reasonable. The Commissioner had argued that since the risk of the business operation remained with the seller, no "sale" had occurred, that a sale requires a transfer of risk by the seller and that where the purchase price is to be paid from the earnings of the transferred assets, the buyer bears no risk, particularly if there is a premium exceeding the fair market value of the assets. The Court described the Commissioner's position as "overkill" that would have represented a "considerable invasion of current capital gains policy." The dissent, on the other hand, thought this was exactly the kind of income that Congress did not intend to bless with preferential treatment, noting that since the entire purchase price was to be paid out of the assets on a recurrent basis (just as before the sale), the transaction was almost identical to a lease with an option to purchase.

These transactions were advantageous to the charity since it was able to acquire businesses without the investment of its own funds. For many charitable organizations, the rental income was tax-exempt. Subsequently, Congress amended § 514 to impose a tax on income of a tax-exempt organization from debt-financed property. The net income from the property is taxable in proportion to the ratio of the debt to the adjusted basis of the property. There is nothing in § 514, however, to discourage a profitable company from entering into a bootstrap sale with a company that has net operating losses.

C.   STATUTORY "SALES OR EXCHANGES"

NOTE ON STATUTORY SALES OR EXCHANGES

Loss by Casualty or Government Seizure. Does a taxpayer suffer an ordinary loss or a capital loss upon the destruction by fire of an uninsured building used for business purposes? Does he recognize ordinary income or capital gain if he receives an amount of insurance in excess of the adjusted basis of the building? What if the government seizes the taxpayer's property under its power of eminent domain? Do such events constitute sales or exchanges?

These questions are covered by § 1231, discussed supra at page 567, which treats aggregate losses on involuntary conversions of business assets as ordinary losses. Aggregate gains may be capital gains, depending on the mix of assets in the § 1231 hotchpot.

Stocks and Bonds That Become Worthless. Instead of being redeemed or paid off, stocks and bonds may become worthless. Although the owner has suffered a loss, there is no "transaction," and therefore nothing that may be regarded as a realization event (much less a sale or exchange). The owner still has the stocks or bonds; they simply have no value. Sections 165(a) and (c)(2) allow the deduction of the loss in such a case. Section 165(g) provides that such losses are capital losses where the security is a capital asset in the hands of the taxpayer. Ordinary loss treatment, however, is provided under § 1244 for loss on worthlessness or sale of certain stock of a "small business corporation."

Nonbusiness Debt Held by an Individual. The deduction of a nonbusiness bad debt by an individual is treated as a short-term capital loss. The treatment of these losses is discussed supra at page 421.

Retirement of Stock. Suppose a corporation makes a distribution in total liquidation, thus retiring all of its own stock. Is this a "sale or exchange"? Section 331 treats such amounts as having been paid "in exchange for the stock." Similarly, a partial liquidation and certain stock redemptions that are not similar to a dividend are treated as an exchange. § 302(b).

Cancellation of Lease or Distributor's Agreement. Section 1241 treats as capital gain or loss amounts received by a lessee (not a lessor) for the cancellation of a lease, or by a distributor (not his supplier) for the cancellation of his distributor's agreement. This provision applies to distributors only if the distributor has a substantial capital investment in the distributorship. There is no similar requirement for a lessee, and the provision thus applies whether or not the lessee has a substantial investment.

This list of statutory sales or exchanges is not exhaustive. There are other provisions in the Code that permit capital gains treatment on certain types of transactions. Often the signal is that the statute says that an amount received "shall be regarded as received on the sale or exchange" of property.

D. "NET" GIFTS

Diedrich v. Commissioner

Supreme Court of the United States, 1982. 457 U.S. 191.

CHIEF JUSTICE BURGER delivered the opinion of the Court.

We granted certiorari to resolve a Circuit conflict as to whether a donor who makes a gift of property on condition that the donee pay the resulting gift tax receives taxable income to the extent that the gift tax paid by the donee exceeds the donor's adjusted basis in the property transferred.

* * * The United States Court of Appeals for the Eighth Circuit held that the donor realized income. * * * We affirm.

I

In 1972 petitioners Victor and Frances Diedrich made gifts of approximately 85,000 shares of stock to their three children, using both a direct transfer and a trust arrangement. The gifts were subject to a condition that the donees pay the resulting federal and state gift taxes. * * * The donors' basis in the transferred stock was $51,073; the gift tax paid in 1972 by the donees was $62,992. Petitioners did not include as income on their 1972 federal income tax returns any portion of the gift tax paid by the donees. After an audit the Commissioner of Internal Revenue determined that petitioners had realized income to the extent that the gift tax owed by petitioners but paid by the donees exceeded the donors' basis in the property. Accordingly, petitioners' taxable income for 1972 was increased by $5,959.[1] * * * The Tax Court held for the taxpayers, concluding that no income had been realized. * * *

* * *

[The discussion of the companion case of United Missouri Bank v. Commissioner has been omitted.]

The United States Court of Appeals for the Eighth Circuit * * * reversed, concluding that "to the extent the gift taxes paid by donees" exceeded the donors' adjusted bases in the property transferred, "the donors realized taxable income." 643 F.2d, at 504. The Court of Appeals rejected the Tax Court's conclusion that the taxpayers merely had made a "net gift" of the difference between the fair market value of the transferred property and the gift taxes paid by the donees. The court reasoned that a donor receives a benefit when a donee discharges a donor's legal obligation to pay gift taxes. * * *

II

A

Pursuant to its constitutional authority, Congress has defined "gross income" as income "from whatever source derived," including "[i]ncome from discharge of indebtedness." [§ 61(12)]. This Court has recognized that "income" may be realized by a variety of indirect means. In *Old Colony Trust Co. v. Commissioner,* 279 U.S. 716 (1929), the Court held that payment of an employee's income taxes by an employer constituted income to the employee. Speaking for the Court, Chief Justice Taft concluded that "[t]he payment of the tax by the employe[r] was in consideration of the services rendered by the employee and was a gain derived by the employee from his labor." Id., at 729. The Court made clear that the substance, not the form, of the agreed transaction controls. "The discharge by a third person of an obligation to him is equivalent to receipt by the person taxed."

---

1. Subtracting the stock basis of $51,073 from the gift tax paid by the donees of $62,992, the Commissioner found that petitioners had realized a long-term capital gain of $11,919. After a 50% reduction in long-term capital gain, [permitted under prior law], the Diedrichs' taxable income increased by $5,959.

Ibid. The employee, in other words, was placed in a better position as a result of the employer's discharge of the employee's legal obligation to pay the income taxes; the employee thus received a gain subject to income tax.

The holding in *Old Colony* was reaffirmed in *Crane v. Commissioner*, 331 U.S. 1 (1947). In *Crane* the Court concluded that relief from the obligation of a nonrecourse mortgage in which the value of the property exceeded the value of the mortgage constituted income to the taxpayer. The taxpayer in *Crane* acquired depreciable property, an apartment building, subject to an unassumed mortgage. The taxpayer later sold the apartment building, which was still subject to the nonrecourse mortgage, for cash plus the buyer's assumption of the mortgage. This Court held that the amount of the mortgage was properly included in the amount realized on the sale, noting that if the taxpayer transfers subject to the mortgage,

> "the benefit to him is as real and substantial as if the mortgage were discharged, or as if a personal debt in an equal amount had been assumed by another." Id., at 14.

Again, it was the "reality," not the form, of the transaction that governed. Ibid. The Court found it immaterial whether the seller received money prior to the sale in order to discharge the mortgage, or whether the seller merely transferred the property subject to the mortgage. In either case the taxpayer realized an economic benefit.

B

The principles of *Old Colony* and *Crane* control. A common method of structuring gift transactions is for the donor to make the gift subject to the condition that the donee pay the resulting gift tax, as was done in each of the cases now before us. When a gift is made, the gift tax liability falls on the donor under 26 U.S.C. § 2502(d).[2] When a donor makes a gift to a donee, a "debt" to the United States for the amount of the gift tax is incurred by the donor. Those taxes are as much the legal obligation of the donor as the donor's income taxes; for these purposes they are the same kind of debt obligation as the income taxes of the employee in *Old Colony*, supra. Similarly, when a donee agrees to discharge an indebtedness in consideration of the gift, the person relieved of the tax liability realizes an economic benefit. In short, the donor realizes an immediate economic benefit by the donee's assumption of the donor's legal obligation to pay the gift tax.

An examination of the donor's intent does not change the character of this benefit. Although intent is relevant in determining whether a gift has been made, subjective intent has not characteristically been a factor in determining whether an individual has realized income. Even if intent were a factor, the donor's intent with respect to the condition shifting the gift tax obligation from the donor to the donee was plainly to relieve the donor

---

2. "The tax imposed by section 2501 shall be paid by the donor." Section 6321 imposes a lien on the personal property of the donor when a tax is not paid when due. The donee is secondarily responsible for payment of the gift tax should the donor fail to pay the tax. 26 U.S.C. § 6324(b). The donee's liability, however, is limited to the value of the gift. This responsibility of the donee is analogous to a lien or security.

of a debt owed to the United States; the choice was made because the donor would receive a benefit in relief from the obligation to pay the gift tax.[4]

Finally, the benefit realized by the taxpayer is not diminished by the fact that the liability attaches during the course of a donative transfer. It cannot be doubted that the donors were aware that the gift tax obligation would arise immediately upon the transfer of the property; the economic benefit to the donors in the discharge of the gift tax liability is indistinguishable from the benefit arising from discharge of a preexisting obligation. Nor is there any doubt that had the donors sold a portion of the stock immediately before the gift transfer in order to raise funds to pay the expected gift tax, a taxable gain would have been realized. 26 U.S.C. § 1001. The fact that the gift tax obligation was discharged by way of a conditional gift rather than from funds derived from a pregift sale does not alter the underlying benefit to the donors.

C

Consistent with the economic reality, the Commissioner has treated these conditional gifts as a discharge of indebtedness through a part gift and part sale of the gift property transferred. The transfer is treated as if the donor sells the property to the donee for less than the fair market value. The "sale" price is the amount necessary to discharge the gift tax indebtedness; the balance of the value of the transferred property is treated as a gift. The gain thus derived by the donor is the amount of the gift tax liability less the donor's adjusted basis in the entire property. Accordingly, income is realized to the extent that the gift tax exceeds the donor's adjusted basis in the property. This treatment is consistent with § 1001 of the Internal Revenue Code, which provides that the gain from the disposition of property is the excess of the amount realized over the transferor's adjusted basis in the property.

III

We recognize that Congress has structured gift transactions to encourage transfer of property by limiting the tax consequences of a transfer. See, e.g., 26 U.S.C. § 102 (gifts excluded from donee's gross income). Congress may obviously provide a similar exclusion for the conditional gift. Should Congress wish to encourage "net gifts," changes in the income tax consequences of such gifts lie within the legislative responsibility. Until such time, we are bound by Congress' mandate that gross income includes income "from whatever source derived." We therefore hold that a donor who makes a gift of property on condition that the donee pay the resulting gift taxes realizes taxable income to the extent that the gift taxes paid by the donee exceed the donor's adjusted basis in the property.

---

4. The existence of the "condition" that the gift will be made only if the donee assumes the gift tax consequences precludes any characterization that the payment of the taxes was simply a gift from the donee back to the donor. A conditional gift not only relieves the donor of the gift tax liability, but also may enable the donor to transfer a larger sum of money to the donee than would otherwise be possible due to such factors as differing income tax brackets of the donor and donee.

The judgment of the United States Court of Appeals for the Eighth Circuit is Affirmed.

JUSTICE REHNQUIST, dissenting.

It is a well-settled principle today that a taxpayer realizes income when another person relieves the taxpayer of a legal obligation in connection with an otherwise taxable transaction. See *Crane v. Commissioner*, 331 U.S. 1 (1947) (sale of real property); *Old Colony Trust Co. v. Commissioner*, 279 U.S. 716 (1929) (employment compensation). In neither *Old Colony* nor *Crane* was there any question as to the existence of a taxable transaction; the only question concerned the amount of income realized by the taxpayer as a result of the taxable transaction. The Court in this case, however, begs the question of whether a taxable transaction has taken place at all when it concludes that "[t]he principles of *Old Colony* and *Crane* control" this case.
* * *

[The discussion of *Old Colony* and *Crane* has been omitted.]

Unlike *Old Colony* or *Crane*, the question in this case is not the amount of income the taxpayer has realized as a result of a concededly taxable transaction, but whether a taxable transaction has taken place at all. Only *after* one concludes that a partial sale occurs when the donee agrees to pay the gift tax do *Old Colony* and *Crane* become relevant in ascertaining the amount of income realized by the donor as a result of the transaction. Nowhere does the Court explain why a gift becomes a partial sale merely because the donor and donee structure the gift so that the gift tax imposed by Congress on the transaction is paid by the donee rather than the donor.

In my view, the resolution of this case turns upon congressional intent: whether Congress intended to characterize a gift as a partial sale whenever the donee agrees to pay the gift tax. Congress has determined that a gift should not be considered income to the donee. 26 U.S.C. § 102. Instead, gift transactions are to be subject to a tax system wholly separate and distinct from the income tax. See 26 U.S.C. § 2501 et seq. Both the donor and the donee may be held liable for the gift tax. §§ 2502(d), 6324(b). Although the primary liability for the gift tax is on the donor, the donee is liable to the extent of the value of the gift should the donor fail to pay the tax. I see no evidence in the tax statutes that Congress forbade the parties to agree among themselves as to who would pay the gift tax upon pain of such an agreement being considered a taxable event for the purposes of the income tax. Although Congress could certainly determine that the payment of the gift tax by the donee constitutes income to the donor, the relevant statutes do not affirmatively indicate that Congress has made such a determination.

I dissent.

NOTES

(A) *Net Gifts Before March 31, 1981.* The Deficit Reduction Act of 1984 provided that the result of *Diedrich* would apply only to net gifts made after March 31, 1981, the time of the Court of Appeals decision in *Diedrich*.

Payment of gift tax by the donee on gifts prior to that date does not produce income to the donor whose gift tax liability was discharged.

(B) *Relief From Obligations as a Sale.* A taxable sale was found to have occurred in both *Diedrich* and *Yarbro,* supra at page 627, because the transaction had relieved the taxpayer of a financial obligation. In *Yarbro,* the obligation arose independently of the abandonment of the property; in *Diedrich,* however, the obligation arose from the gift itself. Is this a distinction that should make a difference? Note that the Supreme Court emphasized in *Diedrich* that "[t]he fact that the gift tax was discharged by way of a conditional gift rather than from funds derived from a pre-gift sale [of a portion of the stock] does not alter the underlying benefit to the donor."

(C) *Why "Net Gifts"?* Why do taxpayers such as the Diedrichs make "net gifts" that may be characterized as part gift and part sale? It has been suggested that the donor may find the prospect of making the gift far more attractive where she can simply give the property away and shift payment of any gift tax to the donee. There often may be less income tax due if the property is sold after the transfer rather than before, because donees tend to be in lower income tax brackets than donors.

It also should be noted that many gifts are not subject to gift tax. For example, a donor is entitled to exclude from gift tax the first $10,000 transferred to each individual in each year. § 2503(b). A married couple may combine their exclusions in order to make annual gifts of up to $20,000. See § 2513. (Donees may increase their basis in the transferred property by a portion of any gift taxes paid. § 1015(d).)

(D) *When Is the Income Recognized?* Does the donor in a case such as *Diedrich* realize income in the year in which the "net gift" is made or in the year in which the gift tax is paid by the donee? The Ninth Circuit held in Estate of Weeden v. Commissioner, 685 F.2d 1160 (1982), that the donor of stock realized income in the year in which the donees paid the gift tax on the transfer. The court noted that the donor, as a cash basis taxpayer, realized income only when received in cash or cash equivalent, rather than when earned; his nephews' promise to pay the gift tax was not the equivalent of cash because it had no ascertainable market value prior to payment. The court further observed that the donor remained primarily liable for the gift tax until the payment was actually made.

Section 5. Holding Period

The dividing line between short-term and long-term capital gains and losses currently is fixed at one year. At other times it has been only six months.

NOTES

(A) *What a Difference a Day Makes.* A capital asset must be held for *more than* one year to produce a long-term gain. Holding for exactly one year will not suffice—as some taxpayers have learned the hard way.

Because the sellers sold securities one day too early in Caspe v. United States, 694 F.2d 1116 (8th Cir.1982), they were assessed a $95,553 deficiency on a gain of $1,186,424 (the difference between long-term and short-term capital gains treatment) and interest of $18,861 on the deficiency.

(B) *Seemed So Simple, Didn't It?* In Rev.Rul. 70–598, 1970–2 C.B. 168, the Service ruled that in counting the holding period, the day an asset is purchased is excluded and the day the asset is sold is included.

In his comprehensive district court opinion in Caspe v. United States, 82–1 U.S.T.C. ¶ 9247 (S.D.Iowa 1982), Judge Vietor explained the logic behind the "less one" rule:

> To avoid duplication of days and to eliminate the need to calculate fractions of days, the holding period is measured by determining the interval between the date of acquisition and the date of disposition and then subtracting one day. This eliminates the need of calculating the actual hours of ownership on the date of acquisition and the actual hours on the date of disposition, and basically evidences a recognition that the ownership of the asset for two partial days would average one whole day.

(C) *Then "Less One" Became "Plus One."* The IRS has ruled that the "less one" rule becomes a "plus one" rule where the period is counted backward from a designated event. See Rev.Rul. 66–6, 1966–1 C.B. 160. That ruling involved § 631(a), which provides capital gains treatment on the sale of timber if the taxpayer owned the timber or had a contract right to cut it for more than one year before the beginning of the taxable year. At the time of the ruling, the required holding period was six months. At issue was whether a taxpayer who acquired timber on December 31 had owned it for more than six months before the beginning of his taxable year on the following July 1. The IRS ruled that:

> [w]hen a prescribed period of months is before a designated day * * *, it is properly computed * * * by excluding the day so designated and computing the period backward to, and including the day designated as its beginning. * * *
>
> For example, the first day of a period six months before June 16, 1963, would be December 16, 1962, determined by excluding June 16, and computing backward from June 15 to the corresponding date of the appropriate preceding month, i.e. December 15, plus one day, to December 16, 1962.
>
> Moreover, when the date before which something must have occurred is the first day of a month, the date which begins the period is determined by going backward to the last day of the appropriate preceding month, plus one.

The taxpayer was therefore eligible for capital gains treatment since he had acquired the timber by January 1.

(D) *Inherited Property.* Capital assets acquired by inheritance are exempted from the holding period requirement by § 1223(11). The inherited property therefore can be sold immediately upon receipt in a transaction that will result in long-term capital gain or loss.

(E) *"Tacking" of Holding Periods.* Section 1223 allows taxpayers in some circumstances to "tack on" to their own holding period a period of time before their acquisition of the capital asset. For example, a taxpayer who receives property by gift combines her own holding period with the holding period of her donor. § 1223(2). See also the discussion of tacking in nonrecognition transactions at page 649 infra.

SECTION 6.   NONRECOGNITION OF GAIN OR LOSS

There are numerous situations where gain or loss realized on the sale, exchange or other disposition of property is not recognized. Sections 1031–1042 deal with many such transactions. There are a number of corporate and partnership nonrecognition provisions as well.

Where such provisions apply, recognition generally is postponed until the taxpayer's investment is significantly altered. Usually, the basis of the property disposed of becomes the basis of the property acquired, thus preserving the gain or loss. The deferral of tax accomplished by the nonrecognition provisions can be very valuable. Recall the discussion of deferral, supra at page 287. Moreover, if the recognition of gain can be deferred until the taxpayer's death, the tax may be eliminated completely because the basis of the property often will be stepped up to its fair market value at the decedent's death. § 1014. The nonrecognition provisions of § 1031 (like-kind exchanges), § 1033 (involuntary conversion), and § 121 (sale of a principal residence) are discussed in the materials that follow.

A.   EXCHANGES OF "LIKE-KIND" PROPERTIES

Under § 1031, no gain or loss is recognized when certain property held for productive use in a trade or business or for investment is exchanged for property "of a like kind." The gain or loss on many common investments cannot be deferred. Stock, certificates of trust or beneficial interests, other securities or evidences of indebtedness, and partnership interests are not eligible for nonrecognition treatment under § 1031. Inventory or other property held primarily for sale is also excluded from § 1031.

When like-kind properties of equal value are exchanged in a nonrecognition transaction, the basis of the property given up becomes the basis of the property received. § 1031(d). A like-kind exchange also may include the transfer of "boot"—that is, money or other nonqualifying property received in addition (or "to boot")—from one party to the other in order to equalize the exchange. In such cases, the taxpayer will recognize gain, but not loss, on the transaction to the extent of any boot received. §§ 1031(b), (c). His transferred basis in the new property is decreased by any money received and increased by any gain recognized. § 1031(d).

For example, suppose A transfers property with a basis of $150 and a fair market value of $200 in exchange for $20 in cash and B's property with a basis of $120 and a value of $180. A realizes gain of $50 on the transaction—$200 fair market value of property received [$180 building + $20 cash] minus $150 basis—but recognizes gain of only $20 (the cash boot). A's basis in the property received remains $150. (His old basis of

$150 is decreased by $20 cash received and increased by the $20 gain recognized.) B realizes gain of $60—$200 fair market value of property received minus $140 basis (property and cash)—but recognizes no gain because he received no boot. The basis of the property he receives is $140.

The term "like-kind" refers to the nature of the property exchanged rather than to its grade or quality. The transfer of real property for personal property does not qualify for § 1031 treatment because the two are not of similar character. The transfer of improved realty for unimproved realty, however, does qualify as a like-kind exchange. A leasehold for 30 years or more is considered to be of like kind to a fee interest in real property. Reg. § 1.1031(a)–1. Recall *Commissioner v. P.G. Lake,* supra at page 588, where the Supreme Court held that the exchange of an oil production payment for an interest in real estate constituted an anticipatory assignment of income rather than an exchange of like-kind property.

Quite often, when the property to be swapped is real estate, it will be subject to a mortgage. When a mortgage is assumed, or the property is taken subject to the mortgage, the outstanding mortgage is treated as cash received and is recognized as boot to the extent it exceeds any mortgage the seller must assume or to which the property he receives is subject.

For example, assume X transfers to Y property with a basis of $100 and a fair market value of $150, which is subject to a $20 nonrecourse mortgage. He receives from Y property with a basis to Y of $120 and a fair market value of $160, which is subject to a $30 nonrecourse mortgage. X has a realized gain of $50 [amount realized of $180 ($160 property plus mortgage relief of $20) minus a basis of $130 ($100 cost of building transferred plus mortgage assumed of $30)], but recognizes no gain. His basis in the new property is $110 [the transferred basis of $130 minus the mortgage relief of $20, which is treated as cash]. Y has a realized gain of $40 [amount realized of $180 ($150 property and $30 mortgage relief) minus a basis of $140 ($120 basis in property transferred plus $20 mortgage assumed)] but recognizes only $10 of gain (the net mortgage in his favor). His basis in his new property is $120 [the transferred basis of $140 plus the $10 gain recognized minus the mortgage relief of $30 treated as cash].

There may be relatively few situations where two taxpayers simply want to trade property with each other. Thus, it is likely that several parties will have to become involved to achieve a like-kind exchange transaction. For example, assume A wants to dispose of Blackacre in a like-kind exchange. B wants to purchase Blackacre for cash. In order to satisfy both objectives, A directs B to purchase Whiteacre, held by C, which B will then swap with A for Blackacre. The traditional position of the IRS and the courts was that multiparty transactions would not qualify for nonrecognition if they had the formal appearance of a sale of property followed by a reinvestment of the proceeds. The application of § 1031 also might be challenged if it appeared that one of the parties was acting as an agent of the other.

Today, however, the courts and the IRS are more liberal in permitting multiparty exchanges to qualify for § 1031 nonrecognition treatment. See, e.g., Rev.Rul. 77–297, 1977–2 C.B. 304 (three-party exchange of real property qualifies for § 1031 treatment). They often focus on whether the parties intended to enter into a like-kind exchange and whether the several steps in the transaction were part of a single integrated plan. Typical of these decisions is the case that follows.

Carlton v. United States

United States Court of Appeals, Fifth Circuit, 1967. 385 F.2d 238.

GEWIN, CIRCUIT JUDGE:

* * *

During the year 1959 and for several years prior thereto the appellants had been engaged in the ranching business. In connection with that business they owned a tract of land in Saint Lucie County, Florida, (ranch property) having a basis of $8,918.91. On October 18, 1958, they executed a contract with General Development Corporation (General) which gave General an option to acquire the ranch property for $250.00 an acre. General paid the appellants $50,000 deposit which was to be credited to the total purchase price should General exercise its option. The contract also provided that the appellant could require General, by notifying it in writing, to acquire such other land as designated by the appellants for the purpose of exchange in lieu of a cash payment or mortgage. General's obligation to supply funds for any down payment which might be needed to bind any contracts to purchase other land for exchange was not to exceed the $50,000 advanced at the time the option was executed. In the event such an exchange could not be effected, General was to pay for the ranch property by cash and a mortgage securing the balance of the purchase price. From the outset of negotiations with General, the appellants desired to continue ranching operations and intended to exchange the ranch property for other property suitable for ranching. They also desired an exchange as opposed to a sale in order to obtain the tax benefits incident to an exchange under § 1031. At all times General desired simply to purchase the ranch property.

Following the execution of the option contract with General, Thad Carlton (Carlton) found two suitable parcels of land, one in Gladen County, Florida (Lyons), and one in Hendry County, Florida (Fernandez). He conducted all the negotiations for the acquisition of these lands and paid the deposit for each by a cashiers check issued by his bank. The total deposit on both pieces of property did not exceed the fifty thousand dollars paid by General. When the negotiations to acquire the Lyons and Fernandez properties were complete, Carlton notified General in writing that he would require it to purchase these lands for the purpose of exchanging them for his ranch property, and the actual agreements of sale were executed by General.[2] On May 11, 1959 General exercised its option to acquire the ranch property and arrangements were made to close the entire transaction around August 1, 1959. * * *

2. * * * The exercise of this option by the appellants obligated General to effect an exchange and thereafter General could no longer purchase the ranch property but was obligated to make an exchange.

In order to avoid unnecessary duplication in title transfer, a procedure was adopted whereby title to the Lyons and Fernandez properties would be conveyed directly to the appellants instead of to General and then to the appellants. To accomplish this result, General, on August 3rd, assigned to the appellants its contracts to purchase the two pieces of property and paid the appellants, by check, the total amount it would have been required to pay if it had actually first purchased the Lyons and Fernandez property in its own name and then conveyed the land to the appellants. Later that same day Carlton took the assignment of the contracts to purchase and purchased the Lyons property, using his personal check to close the sale. On August 4 he purchased the Fernandez property in a similar manner. At the time Carlton issued these checks, the balance in his checking account was too small to cover them, but he deposited the check received from General when the transaction with it was closed to meet these outstanding checks. This check was the balance of the cash purchase price and was in addition to the $50,000.00 paid when the option was executed.

* * *

Section 1031 provides, in pertinent part, that the gain realized on the exchange of property of like kind held for productive use or investment shall not be recognized except to the extent that "boot" or cash is actually received. There is little doubt that the ranch property and the Lyons and Fernandez properties are of like kind, and that the properties were held by the appellants for productive use. The only question presented here is whether the transfer of the properties constituted a sale or an exchange.

Both parties agree that had the appellants followed the original plan, whereby General would have acquired the legal title to the Lyons and Fernandez properties and then transferred the title to such properties to the appellants for their ranch property, the appellants would have been entitled to postpone the recognition of the gain pursuant to § 1031. However, instead of receiving the title to the Lyons and Fernandez properties from General for their ranch property, the appellants received cash and an assignment of General's contract rights to those properties. Thus, the ultimate question becomes whether the receipt of cash by the appellants upon transferring their ranch property to General transformed the intended exchange into a sale. The Government asserts that it does, and, under the facts and in the circumstances of this case, we agree.

Section 1031 was designed to postpone the recognition of gain or loss where property used in a business is exchanged for other property in the course of the continuing operation of a business. In those circumstances, the taxpayer has not received any gain or suffered any loss in a general and economic sense. Nor has the exchange of property resulted in the termination of one venture and assumption of another. The business venture operated before the exchange continues after the exchange without any real economic change or alteration, and without realization of any cash or readily liquefiable asset. The statute specifically limits the nonrecognition of gain or loss to exchanges of property, and it is well settled that a sale and repurchase do not qualify for nonrecognition treatment under the section. Thus, even though the appellants continued their ranching business after the transaction here in question, that does not control the tax consequences of the transfers. Rather, it is essential that the transfers constituted an exchange and not a sale and repurchase if the tax benefits of § 1031 are to be applicable.

The appellants contend that the entire transaction must be viewed as a whole in determining whether a sale or an exchange has occurred. They argue that the transfer of the ranch property to General for the cash and assignments was part of a single unitary plan designed and intended to effect an exchange of their ranch property for other property suitable for ranching. Thus, they conclude, the transfers of property should be construed to be an exchange.

While it is true that the incidence of taxation is to be determined by viewing the entire transaction as a whole, that rule does not permit us to close our eyes to the realities of the transaction and merely look at the beginning and end of a transaction without observing the steps taken to reach that end. The requirement is that the transaction be viewed in its entirety in order to determine its reality and substance, for it is the substance of the transaction which decides the incidence of taxation. In the instant case, while elaborate plans were laid to exchange property, the substance of the transaction was that the appellants received cash for the deed to their ranch property and not another parcel of land. The very essence of an exchange is the transfer of property between owners, while the mark of a sale is the receipt of cash for the property. Where, as here, there is an immediate repurchase of other property with the proceeds of the sale, that distinction between a sale and exchange is crucial. Further, General was never in a position to exchange properties with the appellants because it never acquired the legal title to either the Lyons or the Fernandez property. Indeed, General was not personally obligated on either the notes or mortgages involved in these transactions. Thus it never had any property of like kind to exchange. Finally, it can not be said that General paid for the Lyons and Fernandez properties and merely had the properties deeded directly to the appellants. The money received from General by the appellants for the ranch property was not earmarked by General to be used in purchasing the Lyons or Fernandez properties. It was unrestricted and could be used by the appellants as they pleased. The fact that they did use it to pay for the Lyons and Fernandez properties does not alter the fact that their use of the money was unfettered and unrestrained. It is an inescapable fact that the money received by appellants from General was money paid to them for a conveyance of their land. As a result, the separate transaction between General and the appellants must be construed to be a sale, and the transactions between the appellants and Lyons and Fernandez as a purchase of other property.

The appellants' intention and desire to execute an exchange does not alter the reality and substance of the situation. It is well established that the intention of a taxpayer to avail himself of the advantages of a particular provision of the tax laws does not determine the tax consequences of his action, but what was actually done is determinative of the tax treatment. Thus, the intention of the appellants to effect an exchange does not convert the transfer of property for cash into an exchange. * * *

Therefore, we are compelled to conclude that the transfer of the ranch property to General constituted a sale, and rendered the nonrecognition of gain provisions of § 1031 inapplicable. Considering how close the appellants came to satisfying the requirements of that section and the stipulation that an exchange was intended, this result is obviously harsh. But there is no equity in tax law, and such must the result be if the limitation in § 1031 to exchanges is to have any meaning.

The judgment of the district court is

Affirmed.

NOTES

(A) *Intent.* As noted in *Carlton,* the intent of the taxpayer is important, but not necessarily dispositive, in determining whether the transaction is a sale or a nontaxable exchange. A transaction that is structured as an exchange may be recharacterized as a sale if the taxpayer receives not the property itself but cash that he uses to purchase the property. *Carlton* should be contrasted with another Fifth Circuit case, Biggs v. Commissioner, 632 F.2d 1171 (1980), in which the court rejected the Commissioner's argument that a failure of the transferor to obtain title to the replacement property precluded the use of § 1031. In *Biggs,* the transferor had a contractual obligation to purchase the replacement property. Although he transferred this obligation to Biggs, the court noted that at least for a short period of time, he bore the risk of being required to make payment on promissory notes of a significant amount. The court also emphasized the fact that all the steps in *Biggs* were part of an integrated plan intended to be a like-kind exchange.

Note that the taxpayer who purchases the property to swap generally has no gain or loss. If, however, there is a delay and the property increases in value, he cannot use § 1031 because he was not holding the property for use in his business or for investment.

(B) *Delayed Exchanges and Options to Receive Cash.* Often, the seller may locate a buyer for his property before finding a replacement property for the buyer to exchange. The taxpayers in Starker v. United States, 602 F.2d 1341 (9th Cir.1979), transferred their interest in timber acreage in exchange for a corporation's promise to transfer suitable property within five years or to pay the outstanding balance in cash. The Ninth Circuit found a like-kind exchange despite the possible five-year delay in effectuating the property exchanges and the possibility of a cash transaction. The court observed that:

> [e]ven if the contract right includes the possibility of the taxpayer receiving something other than ownership of like-kind property * * * it is still of a like kind with ownership for tax purposes when the taxpayer prefers property to cash before and throughout the executory period, and only like-kind property is ultimately received.

In order to prevent the tax planning made possible by the use of long delays with options to receive cash or non-like-kind property, the Code now requires the like-kind exchange to be completed within 180 days after the taxpayer relinquishes property. In addition, the property to be received in exchange must be designated as such within 45 days after the transfer. The contract may designate a limited number of possible properties within the 45–day period if the particular property to be transferred is to be determined by contingencies beyond the control of both parties. § 1031(a)(3).

(C) *"Productive Use in a Trade or Business or for Investment."* Property is eligible for § 1031 treatment only if it as well as the replacement property are "held for productive use in a trade or business or for investment." Investment property may be exchanged for property to be used in a trade or business or vice versa. Reg. § 1.1031(a)–1(a). For what period of time before or after the exchange must the property be held for such purposes? In Wagensen v. Commissioner, 74 T.C. 653 (1980), an elderly taxpayer transferred his cattle ranch to a coal company in exchange for cash and another ranch. The taxpayer gave the new ranch to his children nine months later. The Tax Court held that the transfer (aside from the boot) qualified for § 1031 treatment because at the time of the exchange the taxpayer had no concrete plans to give the ranch to his children. The court noted that the taxpayer had operated the property as a productive cattle business until the transfer to his children and that he had not informed his children of his intentions until shortly before he made the gift.

Compare *Wagensen* with Click v. Commissioner, 78 T.C. 225 (1982), where the taxpayer traded her farm for two residential properties selected by her children. The children and their families occupied the residences from the date of the exchange without paying any rent. The taxpayer gave the homes to her children seven months after the exchange. The Tax Court held that the exchange did not qualify for nonrecognition under § 1031 because the taxpayer had acquired the residences with the intent to give them to her children rather than to hold them as investments for eventual sale.

(D) *Loss Transactions.* Where like-kind property is exchanged, § 1031 is mandatory, not elective. Taxpayers sometimes have sought to avoid its provisions where, for example, they wish to recognize loss on the property transferred or to obtain a fair market value basis for depreciation of the property received. Section 1031 may be avoided by structuring a transaction as a sale and reinvestment of sale proceeds, rather than as an exchange. Unless the seller has other losses to offset the income triggered by a sale and reinvestment, the tax deferral accorded by a like-kind exchange under § 1031 is more advantageous than the step-up to fair market value of basis that would occur in a sale and reinvestment transaction.

On the other hand, a taxpayer may be forced to forgo loss recognition if a transaction intended to be a sale is instead deemed to be a like-kind exchange. See, e.g., Godine v. Commissioner, 36 T.C.M. 1595 (1977), where the taxpayers were prevented from recognizing loss on their transfer of an unprofitable residential building in exchange for a duplex.

(E) *Like-Kind Property.* The regulations provide detailed rules concerning depreciable tangible personal property. They include a description of ten classes of property and cross reference to industrial product codes.

Property that is of a like class or has the same product code is presumed to be like-kind although the reverse is not true. That is, property that is not in the same class *could* be like-kind. Reg. § 1.1031(a)–2. For example, an exchange of a heavy-duty truck used in a business for a passenger car to be used in a business might not be a like-kind exchange, but an exchange of a computer for a printer would be.

The regulations do not provide classes for intangible or nondepreciable property, and thus a determination must be made whether properties are similar in nature. The regulations indicate that the gain on an exchange of a copyright on one novel for a copyright on another novel would not be recognized, but an exchange of the former for a copyright on a song would be.

How similar must personal property be in order to be considered of like kind? Section 1031(e) provides that "livestock of different sexes are not property of like kind." The legislative history indicated that the amendment was intended to recognize that livestock of different sexes typically represent different types of investments because one is usually raised for breeding and the other for slaughter. See S.Rep. No. 91–552, 91st Cong., 1st Sess. 102 (1969).

The Ninth Circuit relied on this legislative history in California Federal Life Insurance Co. v. Commissioner, 680 F.2d 85 (1982), to hold that U.S. Double Eagle gold coins (which had a face value of $3,500 and a numismatic value of $43,427) were not of like-kind to modern Swiss currency. The court, after suggesting that § 1031(e) indicated congressional intention to define "like kind" more narrowly with respect to personal property than with respect to realty, observed that the gold coins "are exchanged in the marketplace only by numismatists, and are valued primarily for their rarity, as collector items" whereas the Swiss francs "are currently circulating currency, and to their investors they represent investments in the Swiss national economy." See also Rev.Rul. 79–44, 1979–1 C.B. 265 (holding that U.S. Double Eagles, which constitute an investment in the coins themselves, are not of like-kind to South African Krugerrands, which constitute an investment in gold bullion); Rev.Rul. 82–96, 1982–1 C.B. 113 (holding that an exchange of Canadian Maple Leaf coins whose gold content far exceeded their face value for gold bullion qualified as like-kind exchange); and Rev.Rul. 82–166, 1982–2 C.B. 190 (holding that gold bullion is not an investment of like-kind to silver bullion).

Why should a swap of improved realty (such as an apartment building) for vacant land be a nonrecognition transaction whereas a swap of livestock of different sexes is not?

(E) *Sale-Leasebacks.* As noted previously, an exchange of a fee interest for a leasehold of 30 years or longer is treated as a nonrecognition exchange. Suppose the taxpayer transfers a fee interest in property for cash and a 30–year leasehold in the same property? Is the gain or loss recognized? In Jordan Marsh Co. v. Commissioner, 269 F.2d 453 (2d Cir.1959), the Second Circuit found that a sale leaseback with a 30–year and 30–day lease was in substance a sale and thus a loss was recognized. In Century Electric Co. v. Commissioner, 192 F.2d 155 (8th Cir.1951), however, the

Eighth Circuit treated a sale for cash and a 95–year lease as a like-kind exchange and disallowed the loss.

Does it make a difference whether the cash received for the assets is less than the fair market value or whether the rent is a market rent? See Leslie Co. v. Commissioner, 539 F.2d 943 (3d Cir.1976), which found a "sale-leaseback" to be a nonrecognition exchange where the "sales" price and rent were both of market value.

(F) *Sales to Related Parties*. The ability to use the deferral provided by § 1031 is severely limited where the exchange is between two related parties. Where a taxpayer exchanges like-kind property with a related party (as defined in § 267) and either party disposes of the property within two years, the gain on the original transfer is recognized on the date of the disposition. § 1031(f). (Although the statute technically permits a loss to be recognized as well, it usually will not be because a loss to a related party is disallowed under § 267(a)(1)). A disposition by death, an involuntary conversion, or a disposition that does not have a tax avoidance purpose does not trigger recognition.

(G) *Holding Period*. A taxpayer who receives property in a tax-free exchange (such as an exchange of like-kind property) tacks his holding period for the property that he relinquished onto his holding period for the newly acquired property. § 1223(1). This rule applies only if the taxpayer's basis in the property given up is the same as his basis in the property received and if the property given up was a capital asset or a § 1231 asset at the time of the exchange. The latter requirement is intended to prevent the conversion of ordinary income into capital gain.

(H) *Policy*. What is the justification for not requiring the taxpayer to recognize the appreciation that has been realized on the transfer of like-kind property? Legislative history indicates that Congress was concerned with imposing a tax when the transaction produced no cash with which to pay the tax. But that cannot be the only motivation. In a swap of non-like-kind properties (such as a truck for land), the taxpayer must pay tax on any gain on the truck despite the lack of cash. Congress also was apparently troubled about the difficulty of valuing property. Valuation is also not a sufficient explanation because in any case in which there is boot, the property must valued. Valuation is also required in all non-like-kind exchanges.

Courts often justify § 1031 by noting that the taxpayer has changed only the form and not the substance of his investment and thus there is a continuity of interest in the investment. Does that justification work when the taxpayer swaps an apartment building for a farm? Has the substance of the investment changed when the taxpayer sells for cash and immediately reinvests in similar property? Does the elevation of form over substance enable taxpayers who own assets that qualify for § 1031 treatment in effect to elect whichever tax result—recognition or nonrecognition—is most advantageous? Should nonrecognition be extended to all sale and repurchase transactions? What would be the effect of such an extension on the taxation of capital appreciation generally?

B.   INVOLUNTARY CONVERSIONS

Section 1033 permits nonrecognition of gain resulting from involuntary conversions, such as where property is taken by eminent domain or destroyed by fire or other casualty. The taxpayer must use the proceeds to acquire "property similar or related in service or use" to the property converted, or, in the case of real estate, to acquire property for business or investment use that is of "like kind" to property condemned by the government. See § 1033(a) and (g).

The taxpayer must acquire the new property by the end of the second year following the involuntary conversion. This time limit is extended to the end of the third year for condemnations of real property used for business or investment.

Section 1033, unlike § 1031, is elective if the taxpayer has received money (rather than property) in exchange for the converted property. This is common, for example, when insurance proceeds are received. The section does not apply to losses resulting from involuntary conversions. (The recognition of such losses on property held for personal use is limited by § 165, discussed in Chapter 3, at page 378.)

The purpose of § 1033 is to provide relief where "the taxpayer's property, through some outside force or agency beyond his control, is no longer useful or available to him for his purposes." C.G. Willis, Inc. v. Commissioner, 41 T.C. 468 (1964). Congress considered it unfair to impose tax on those who probably did not intend to dispose of property and thereby realize gains, who may have suffered hardship and who reinvest any conversion proceeds in replacement property. The taxpayer must recognize gain, however, to the extent that proceeds from involuntary conversions exceed the amount reinvested in replacement property.

NOTES

(A) *"One Economic Unit."* Revenue Ruling 59–361, 1959–2 C.B. 183, states:

> [W]here all the facts and circumstances show a substantial economic relationship between the condemned property and the other property sold by the taxpayer so that together they constituted one economic property unit, * * * involuntary conversion treatment for the proceeds of the voluntary sale will be permitted. The taxpayer must show the unavailability of suitable nearby property of a like-kind to that convert- ed and the proceeds of the voluntary sale must be expended in acquiring property of a like-kind.

The IRS allowed nonrecognition of gain from the sale of timber that had been uprooted by a hurricane and was subject to decay or destruction by insects. The taxpayer had used the proceeds from the sale to purchase other standing timber. See Rev.Rul. 80–175, 1980–2 C.B. 230. A prior ruling had refused to apply § 1033 in a similar situation on the grounds that the sale had been voluntary. The IRS reasoned that Congress had intended to provide nonrecognition for taxpayers who had no economic choice but to sell their property. The ruling sought to establish when conversions would be considered economically involuntary:

> First, an event specified by the statute as one that may result in an involuntary conversion occurred. Second, that event rendered the property unfit or impractical for its intended use. Third, the property was sold and the proceeds invested in similar property.

Contrast Rev.Rul. 78–377, 1978–2 C.B. 208, where the IRS held that the proceeds on the sale of a shopping center partially destroyed by fire could not be added to the insurance proceeds and treated as part of the deferrable amount under § 1033.

(B) *Who Can Make a § 1033 Election?* The IRS has attempted to deny nonrecognition of gain under § 1033(a) where taxpayers have died before § 1033 treatment has been elected or before the substitute property has been acquired or constructed. See, e.g., Rev.Rul. 64–161, 1964–1 C.B. 298 (§ 1033 treatment is unavailable where replacement property is purchased by testamentary trustees after death of taxpayer).

The courts, however, have allowed § 1033 treatment where an executor or trustee has carried out the deceased taxpayer's plan to reinvest the proceeds of an involuntary conversion in suitable replacement property. See, e.g., Morris v. Commissioner, 454 F.2d 208 (4th Cir.1972).

(C) *Relationship of § 1033 to Other Provisions.* Note that § 1033(g) (like § 1031(a)) excludes from eligibility for nonrecognition treatment real property which is "stock in trade or property held primarily for sale," an exception obviously derived from the § 1221(a)(1) exclusion from the capital asset definition. Note also the relationship between § 1033 and § 1231. The treatment of involuntary conversions under § 1231 is discussed supra, at page ___.

(D) *Definition of "Involuntary Conversion."* An involuntary conversion of the taxpayer's property may qualify for nonrecognition under § 1033(a) if it is the result of destruction (complete or partial), theft, seizure, requisition or condemnation, or a sale or exchange under threat of condemnation. Generally, if an event constitutes a casualty for purposes of § 165(c), it constitutes an involuntary conversion, but the events covered by § 1033 appear to be somewhat broader. See, e.g., Rev.Rul. 89–2, 1989–1 C.B. 753, where property rendered unsafe for its intended use by chemical contamination was considered "destroyed."

Some sales of property to the government—or to third parties under what the taxpayer might characterize as a threat of government condemnation—may not qualify for nonrecognition under § 1033. The government must have decided to acquire the property for a public purpose and the taxpayer must have had reasonable grounds to believe that the property would be taken. The "reasonable belief" requirement typically is satisfied if the taxpayer has been notified by a responsible public official that a governmental body has decided to acquire his property and if he reasonably concludes that the body will do so by condemnation if it cannot do so by purchase. For example, the taxpayer was denied nonrecognition treatment in Tecumseh Corrugated Box Co. v. Commissioner, 932 F.2d 526 (6th Cir.1991). The taxpayer owned property that was on a list of lots to be condemned by the National Park Service, but the taxpayer's property had a low priority and the NPS and the taxpayer had been unable to negotiate a transfer price. Section 1033 treatment will be denied where the disposition of property appears to have been a matter of business discretion rather than of practical necessity.

(E) *Definition of "Replacement Property."* There is often uncertainty whether replacement property is sufficiently similar to the property replaced for gain on the conversion to go unrecognized under § 1033. Several courts instead have adopted a "similar use test" that focuses not on the two pieces of property themselves but on the uses to which they were put by the taxpayer. For example, in Clifton Investment Co. v. Commissioner, 312 F.2d 719 (6th Cir.1963), a taxpayer invested proceeds from the condemnation of an office building in a hotel. The taxpayer, which had operated the office building itself with the help of two employees, hired professional management to operate the hotel. The court held that the taxpayer's responsibilities with respect to the two properties differed so greatly that they could not be held to be "similar or related in service or use."

Technological, economic or political factors may sometimes make it difficult—if not impossible—for the taxpayer to reinvest condemnation proceeds in similar property. For example, the taxpayer in Davis v. United States, 589 F.2d 446 (9th Cir.1979), for several decades had owned and leased out agricultural property and an adjoining sea fishery in Hawaii. The proceeds from the condemnation of this property were used to improve property that the taxpayer was developing for lease to an industrial customer. The district court had observed that replacement land could not be purchased and rented out profitably in light of the state's shift over time from an exclusively agricultural economy to a mixed industrial, commercial, resort, and agricultural economy. It also noted that acquisition of a replacement sea fishery was virtually impossible because the state had a declared public policy of absorbing ownership of sea fisheries. The Ninth Circuit held that the conversion qualified for nonrecognition under § 1033(a) because of the similarity of the taxpayer's relationship to the two investments. The court made the appropriate link to the underlying policy of § 1033 when it observed that the test was whether

> the taxpayer has achieved a sufficient continuity of investment to justify non-recognition of the gain, or whether the differences in the relationship of the taxpayer to the two investments are such as to compel the conclusion that he has taken advantage of the condemnation to alter the nature of his investment for his own purposes.

Section 1033(g) provides for nonrecognition of gain where real property held for business or investment use is condemned and the proceeds are reinvested in real property of a "like kind" as defined by § 1031. This amendment was added to § 1033 primarily "in order to conform the standard for condemned property to that of voluntary exchanges" under § 1031.

C. SALE OR EXCHANGE OF TAXPAYER'S RESIDENCE

Section 121 allows the taxpayer to exclude $250,000 (or $500,000 if married filing jointly) of gain from the sale of her principal residence provided it had been used by the taxpayer as such for two of the previous five years. A failure to meet this requirement due to a change in the place of employment, health, or other unforeseen circumstances results in the taxpayer excluding a fraction of $250,000 of gain equal to the fraction of the two-year requirement met.

A taxpayer generally can use this provision no more frequently than every two years. If a taxpayer marries a person who used the provision within the previous two years, she nevertheless may use the rollover on up to $250,000 of gain. Similarly, if spouses file jointly but do not share a residence, each may exclude up to $250,000 of gain by reinvesting the sales proceeds in a new residence. If both reside in the residence, they may exclude $500,000 of gain even if only one of them has lived in the home for two of the previous five years.

For example, if a taxpayer purchases a residence for $50,000 and occupies it as his principal residence for three years before selling it for $90,000, he can exclude all $40,000 of gain. If he then purchases a home for $100,000 and sells it six years later for $500,000, he can exclude $250,000 of the $400,000 of gain. If he files a joint return with his spouse who also occupies the residence, he can exclude all $400,000 of gain. A wealthy taxpayer can avoid paying any tax on the appreciation in a residence simply by selling one home and purchasing another as the gain nears $500,000. For example, if a couple purchases a home for $1 million and sells it after four years for $1.5 million, they pay no tax. If they buy a new home for $1.5 million and sell it after six years for $2 million, they pay no tax again. Assuming a federal tax rate on the gain of 40 percent, the exclusion is worth $200,000 on each occasion (or $100,000 at a 20 percent capital gains rate). That's a big incentive to move. For those for whom the transactions costs outweigh the tax benefits or for whom moving is just a big hassle, they may be able to hold on to the house until death, when the property will pass free of income tax to their beneficiaries.

A taxpayer may have only one principal residence for purposes of Section 121 even if he owns several residences. The property where he spends the majority of his time will ordinarily be considered his principal residence.

For example, the taxpayer in Revenue Ruling 77–298, 1977–2 C.B. 308, was a member of Congress, who owned residences in both Washington, D.C. and her congressional district. The taxpayer and her family occupied the Washington residence and the taxpayer's minor children attended school in the Washington area. The taxpayer occasionally used the other residence for lodging during visits to her district. The IRS held that the taxpayer was entitled to nonrecognition of gain on the sale of the Washington residence.

Is an elected official who resides for most of the year in what President Reagan once jokingly called "public housing" entitled to nonrecognition on the sale of a home? One of President Nixon's many tax problems arose out of an ultimately unsuccessful attempt early in his Presidency to exclude gain from the sale of his New York apartment. At the time, the law required that the taxpayer purchase a new principal residence in order to defer the gain. Nixon purchased a San Clemente estate and claimed it as his principal residence. The staff of the Joint Committee on Taxation, which examined the Nixon tax returns in 1974, concluded that the President spent too little time at his "Western White House" for it to qualify as his principal residence. Joint Committee on Internal Revenue Taxation, Examination of President Nixon's Tax Returns for 1969 though 1972. H.Rep. No. 93–996, 93d Cong. 117–18 (1974).

During the 1984 presidential campaign, then Vice President George H. Bush contested a similar IRS position, which prevented him from rolling over the gain from the sale of the Houston home that he occupied before his election as Vice President. He used the sales proceeds to improve his house in Maine, which he claimed was his principal residence. After he lost his claim, he managed to avoid Maine income tax by declaring his principal residence was Texas. His "official" Texas residence was a hotel suite he rented when in Texas. Vice President Bush's case seems even weaker than that of President Nixon, who intended to make San Clemente his principal residence once he left office (and did so somewhat sooner than anticipated) since Vice President Bush consistently maintained he was "still a Texan" and apparently intended to use the Maine home as a vacation retreat.

Section 121 provides that to the extent the gain is attributable to depreciation, which would be the case where it was used as a place of business, it is not excludible. Because the taxpayer need not have resided in the house immediately prior to its sale, he may rent it for a period provided he occupied it as a principal residence for two of the previous five years. If the taxpayer does rent her "principal residence" prior to sale, can she take deductions for depreciation and rental expenses? The Ninth Circuit ruled that she could both deduct the expenses and exclude the gain. The court held that she did not convert the house from "personal use." The dissent agreed with the IRS that depreciation deductions and use of the exclusion were mutually exclusive as a matter of law. Bolaris v. Commissioner, 776 F.2d 1428 (9th Cir.1985).

The exclusion of gain on the sale of a residence, together with the deductions for real estate taxes and for home mortgage interest, is a significant tax expenditure. In 2000, these items were estimated to involve $87 billion in lost revenue.

D.   SMALL BUSINESS INVESTMENT COMPANIES

Section 1044 permits the nonrecognition of gain on the sale of publicly-traded securities provided the proceeds are invested in common stock or a partnership interest in a "specialized small business investment" company within 60 days of the sale of the securities. An SSBIC must be licensed by the Small Business Administration. To the extent the proceeds are not so invested, gain is recognized. The taxpayer's basis in the SSBIC stock or partnership interest is reduced by the gain not recognized on the sale of the securities.

E.   QUALIFIED SMALL BUSINESS STOCK

Taxpayers can elect to defer recognition of gain on the sale of "qualified small business stock" so long as the stock has been held for more than six months and the taxpayer purchases replacement stock in another qualified small business. § 1045. Qualified small business stock is defined in § 1202 and is discussed supra at p. 586. The gain on the sale of the original stock is recognized only to the extent that the sales proceeds exceed the purchase price of the replacement stock. The basis of the replacement stock is the purchase price minus the deferred gain on the sale of the original stock.

CHAPTER 6

WHEN IS IT INCOME? OR DEDUCTIBLE?—ACCOUNTING PROBLEMS

It is obviously not reasonable to wait until a person's death to add up his accounts for his entire lifetime and collect income tax on the net result. As a practical matter, income taxes must be collected on a periodic basis. The period normally selected is the taxable year. The allocation of income to a particular taxable year necessarily involves the application of accounting conventions that often produce controversial results. This Chapter considers the problems that arise from the necessity of assigning particular items of income or deduction to one taxable year or another.

Tax accounting problems are not merely mechanical exercises necessary to calculate taxable income; they frequently present some of the most difficult theoretical and policy issues in income taxation. Two people who have the same economic income and who engage in the same transactions may have different taxable income and tax liabilities, depending only on how they keep their books. As you study the materials in this Chapter, evaluate the policy considerations advanced in support of this "inequality" among similarly situated taxpayers.

The basic statutory provisions on accounting matters are found in §§ 441–483 of the Code. Sections 441, 446, 451(a), and 461(a) and (h) are particularly important and should be examined carefully. They provide, as a general rule, that the accounting method used on the taxpayer's books ordinarily determines when an item of income is taxed or a deduction allowed. "Books" include records kept solely for tax purposes as well as books used for financial reporting purposes.

There are two basic methods of accounting—the cash method and the accrual method. Under the cash method, items ordinarily are included in income in the year in which they are received, and items are taken as deductions in the year in which they are paid. Most individuals and many small businesses use the cash method. Under the accrual method, items generally are included in income in the year in which they are earned, regardless of when they are received, and items are taken as deductions in the year in which they are incurred, regardless of when they are paid. Most corporations and some individuals, partnerships, and trusts use the accrual method. There seems to be considerable academic and congressional sentiment for limiting the categories of taxpayers who are permitted to use the cash method. Section 448 requires Subchapter C corporations and partnerships with a Subchapter C corporation partner that average $5 million or more in sales and all "tax shelters" to use the accrual method of accounting. A special exception is provided for large so-called "personal service providers," including, for example, law and accounting firms, which may continue to use the cash method of accounting regardless of their annual receipts.

The taxpayer's accounting method will govern, however, only if the method "clearly reflects income." The Commissioner is given broad authority to ensure that taxpayers' accounting methods "clearly reflect income" and to permit or refuse changes in methods. If the taxpayer keeps no books, or if his method of accounting does not clearly reflect income, the Commissioner selects an accounting method. § 446(b).

Determining when income is taxed and when deductions are permitted is often as important in terms of a taxpayer's tax liability, as determining what is income and what is deductible. In a period of low interest rates and little or no inflation, one might have dismissed timing questions as trivial. But in an era of high and fluctuating rates of interest and inflation, the economic value of delaying tax liability can be considerable. (This is demonstrated in some detail in the Note on Tax Deferral, page 287 supra, which might profitably be reviewed at this point.) If, for example, tax-exempt interest rates are 7 percent, a taxpayer in a 40 percent bracket who can delay the inclusion of $100,000 for a year, or advance a deduction of $100,000 by a year, can earn $2,800 in tax-exempt interest on the $40,000 that eventually will go to the government in taxes. Furthermore, if an item produces opposite tax consequences for the two parties involved (e.g., a payment is deductible by the payor and includible by the payee) and each uses different accounting rules, the possibility of generating tax savings through deferral can lead to tax-motivated transactions that lack economic purpose. Conversely, if each party is in the same tax bracket and must apply identical accounting rules, the importance of timing issues diminishes, since any advantage to one party produces an offsetting disadvantage to the other. Where differences in tax rates are important, however—for example, where one party is a tax-exempt organization—the Internal Revenue Service cannot rely on the parties' conflicting interests as a policing mechanism. During the past few decades, taxpayers, the Treasury, and Congress have become more sensitive to time value of money and accounting issues.

Other considerations besides the time value of money can influence timing questions. Tax rates may change from year to year because of tax legislation or changes in the taxpayer's income. Sometimes important tax consequences flow from a shift of one or two years in the inclusion of income or allowance of deductions. Tax rates have changed frequently in recent decades. In 1963, for example, tax rates for individuals ranged from 20 percent to 91 percent of taxable income; the range was 16 percent to 77 percent in 1964, and 14 percent to 70 percent in 1965. The maximum rate of tax applicable to earned income was 70 percent in 1970, 60 percent in 1971 and 50 percent in 1972. In some cases, rates move in the opposite direction. In 1992, the top rate was 31 percent; in 1993 the top rate climbed to 39.6 percent. Legislation enacted in 2001 changed tax rates in 2001 to 2011, reducing the top rate to 35 percent beginning in 2006. Indexing of tax rates for inflation became effective in 1985, and tax brackets change annually depending upon the inflation rate.

Even if tax rates remain constant, the progressive rate structure means that an individual may be taxed at a higher marginal rate if her income is received in one year rather than spread over several years. Thus, she might wish to shift deductions to a high-income year or postpone income to a low-income year. So-called "income-averaging" rules, which mitigated the effect of the progressive rate structure to some extent, were repealed when the Tax Reform Act of 1986 flattened tax rates.

There are other factors that make timing important. For example, the statute of limitations may have run on a particular year; if income can be allocated to that year, the Commissioner is precluded from collecting tax. The taxpayer's status may change in a manner that substantially affects tax liability. For example, he may be unmarried in one year and married in the next. Changes in the Internal Revenue Code, the Regulations, or the case law may require different treatment of items of income or deduction in different years.

In sum, the allocation of income or deduction to particular years is quite important in determining tax liability. The significance of these accounting issues, and the broad discretion delegated to the Commissioner to resolve them, have produced considerable dispute over when income is taxable or deductions are allowable. For example, of the thousands of letter rulings issued to taxpayers annually, more than half typically involve requests by taxpayers to change their methods of accounting.

It is important to remember that timing issues generally are discrete from the questions "What is income?" and "What is deductible?" If an item does not represent taxable income, there is no question as to *when* it is taxed. The appropriate time to take into account an expenditure arises only for those expenses that are deductible. Nevertheless, some "timing" rules are imbedded in substantive provisions that apply to all taxpayers regardless of accounting method. See, e.g., § 168 (determining when depreciation deductions are taken); § 165 (providing for a deduction when losses are "sustained"); § 166 (providing for a deduction when a bad debt becomes "worthless").

Although there is considerable similarity between tax accounting and financial accounting, there are also significant differences. This reflects the different goals between financial accounting and tax accounting. As the Supreme Court noted in Thor Power Tool Co. v. Commissioner, 439 U.S. 522 (1979):

> The primary goal of financial accounting is to provide useful information to management, shareholders, creditors, and others properly interested; the major responsibility of the accountant is to protect these parties from being misled. The primary goal of the income tax system, in contrast, is the equitable collection of revenue; the major responsibility of the Internal Revenue Service is to protect the public fisc. Consistently with its goals and responsibilities, financial accounting has as its foundation the principle of conservatism, with its corollary that "possible errors in measurement [should] be in the direction of

understatement rather than overstatement of net income and net assets." In view of the Treasury's markedly different goals and responsibilities, understatement of income is not destined to be its guiding light. Given this diversity, even contrariety, of objective, any presumptive equivalency between tax and financial accounting would be unacceptable.

As you go through the materials on tax accounting, you will note numerous differences between the two systems.

This Chapter deals with the problems that arise because of the necessity of assigning particular elements of income or deductions to one tax year or another. In general, the question of when income is taxed depends on two factors: (1) the taxable year and (2) the taxpayer's method of accounting. Problems relating to the taxable year are considered first.

SECTION 1.   THE TAXABLE YEAR

A.   IN GENERAL

Burnet v. Sanford & Brooks Co.

Supreme Court of the United States, 1931. 282 U.S. 359.

MR. JUSTICE STONE delivered the opinion of the Court.

* * *

From 1913 to 1916, inclusive, respondent, a Delaware corporation engaged in business for profit, was acting for the Atlantic Dredging Company in carrying out a contract for dredging the Delaware River, entered into by that company with the United States. In making its income tax returns for the years 1913 to 1916, respondent added to gross income for each year the payments made under the contract that year, and deducted its expenses paid that year in performing the contract. The total expenses exceeded the payments received by $176,271.88. The tax returns for 1913, 1915, and 1916 showed net losses. That for 1914 showed net income.

In 1915 work under the contract was abandoned, and in 1916 suit was brought in the Court of Claims to recover for a breach of warranty of the character of the material to be dredged. Judgment for the claimant, 53 Ct.Cl. 490, was affirmed by this Court in 1920. United States v. Atlantic Dredging Co., 253 U.S. 1. * * * From the total recovery, respondent received in that year the sum of $192,577.59, which included the $176,271.88 by which its expenses under the contract had exceeded receipts from it, and accrued interest amounting to $16,305.71. Respondent having failed to include these amounts as gross income in its tax returns for 1920, the Commissioner made the deficiency assessment here involved, based on the addition of both items to gross income for that year.

The Court of Appeals ruled that only the item of interest was properly included, holding, erroneously as the government contends, that the item of

$176,271.88 was a return of losses suffered by respondent in earlier years and hence was wrongly assessed as income. Notwithstanding this conclusion, its judgment of reversal and the consequent elimination of this item from gross income for 1920 were made contingent upon the filing by respondent of amended returns for the years 1913 to 1916, from which were to be omitted the deductions of the related items of expenses paid in those years. Respondent insists that as the Sixteenth Amendment and the Revenue Act of 1918, which was in force in 1920, plainly contemplate a tax only on net income or profits, any application of the statute which operates to impose a tax with respect to the present transaction, from which respondent received no profit, cannot be upheld.

If respondent's contention that only gain or profit may be taxed under the Sixteenth Amendment be accepted without qualification, see Eisner v. Macomber, 252 U.S. 189 * * *, the question remains whether the gain or profit which is the subject of the tax may be ascertained, as here, on the basis of fixed accounting periods, or whether, as is pressed upon us, it can only be net profit ascertained on the basis of particular transactions of the taxpayer when they are brought to a conclusion.

All the revenue acts which have been enacted since the adoption of the Sixteenth Amendment have uniformly assessed the tax on the basis of annual returns showing the net result of all the taxpayer's transactions during a fixed accounting period, either the calendar year, or, at the option of the taxpayer, the particular fiscal year which he may adopt. Under sections 230, 232 and 234(a) of the Revenue Act of 1918, 40 Stat. 1057, respondent was subject to tax upon its annual net income, arrived at by deducting from gross income for each taxable year all the ordinary and necessary expenses paid during that year in carrying on any trade or business, interest and taxes paid, and losses sustained, during the year. * * *

That the recovery made by respondent in 1920 was gross income for that year within the meaning of these sections cannot, we think, be doubted. The money received was derived from a contract entered into in the course of respondent's business operations for profit. While it equalled, and in a loose sense was a return of, expenditures made in performing the contract, still, as the Board of Tax Appeals found, the expenditures were made in defraying the expenses incurred in the prosecution of the work under the contract, for the purposes of earning profits. * * * Only by including these items of gross income in the 1920 return would it have been possible to ascertain respondent's net income for the period covered by the return, which is what the statute taxes. The excess of gross income over deductions did not any the less constitute net income for the taxable period because respondent, in an earlier period, suffered net losses in the conduct of its business which were in some measure attributable to expenditures made to produce the net income of the later period.

* * *

But respondent insists that if the sum which it recovered is the income defined by the statute, still it is not income, taxation of which without apportionment is permitted by the Sixteenth Amendment, since the particular transaction from which it was derived did not result in any net gain or profit. But we do not think the amendment is to be so narrowly construed. A taxpayer may be in receipt of net income in one year and not in another. The net result of the two years, if combined in a single taxable period, might still be a loss; but it has never been supposed that that fact would relieve him from a tax on the first, or that it affords any reason for postponing the assessment of the tax until the end of a lifetime, or for some other indefinite period, to ascertain more precisely whether the final outcome of the period, or of a given transaction, will be a gain or a loss.

The Sixteenth Amendment was adopted to enable the government to raise revenue by taxation. It is the essence of any system of taxation that it should produce revenue ascertainable, and payable to the government, at regular intervals. Only by such a system is it practicable to produce a regular flow of income and apply methods of accounting, assessment, and collection capable of practical operation. It is not suggested that there has ever been any general scheme for taxing income on any other basis. * * * While, conceivably, a different system might be devised by which the tax could be assessed, wholly or in part, on the basis of the finally ascertained results of particular transactions, Congress is not required by the amendment to adopt such a system in preference to the more familiar method, even if it were practicable. It would not necessarily obviate the kind of inequalities of which respondent complains. If losses from particular transactions were to be set off against gains in others, there would still be the practical necessity of computing the tax on the basis of annual or other fixed taxable periods, which might result in the taxpayer being required to pay a tax on income in one period exceeded by net losses in another. * * *

The assessment was properly made under the statutes. Relief from their alleged burdensome operation which may not be secured under these provisions, can be afforded only by legislation, not by the courts.

Reversed.

NOTES

(A) *Fiscal Years.* The basic statutory provision on the taxable year is § 441 of the Code. (Note that §§ 1 and 11 impose the individual and corporate income taxes "for each taxable year.") Ordinarily, the taxable year is a relatively simple concept. For most individuals and a great many businesses, it is simply the calendar year—from January 1 through December 31. Individuals and businesses, however, may use a fiscal year ending on the last day of any other month. A fiscal year ordinarily cannot end on a day other than the last day of a month, but taxpayers may report tax based on a year of 52 or 53 weeks that always ends on the same day of the week if they regularly keep their books on this basis. § 441(f).

Usually business factors control the decision to use a fiscal year rather than a calendar year. If the natural business cycle of a taxpayer is slowest during the summer, as with ski resorts, a June 30 fiscal year end may be appropriate for a variety of reasons—for example, inventories will be relatively small and easy to evaluate at that time, adjustments for items spanning two years will be minimized, and there may be more time to deal with bookkeeping matters.

Many restrictions apply to the election of a fiscal year. For example, a sole proprietor of a business may use a fiscal year for reporting her business income only if she also uses the same fiscal year for reporting her personal income. There are similar restrictions on the use of a fiscal year by a partnership or S corporation. A person may use a calendar year for reporting his personal income and a fiscal year for his business income if he incorporates his business, and the corporation is taxable under subchapter C. Are there advantages to the use of a fiscal year that might lead you to advise a client to incorporate?

(B) *Short Taxable Years.* Returns may have to be filed on the basis of a short taxable year as a result of a taxpayer's death, the creation or dissolution of a corporation, or a change in accounting period. A short taxable year generally is treated as a full taxable year for all purposes. See § 443.

(C) *Changes in Accounting Periods.* Changes from one accounting period to another are governed by §§ 442 and 443 of the Code. Section 442 provides that a taxpayer may change his taxable year only with the permission of the Commissioner. The change will not be permitted unless the taxpayer establishes a substantial nontax business purpose for the change. In addition, the Commissioner may require the taxpayer to make certain adjustments so that the change does not produce a substantial reduction or deferral of tax liability. § 481.

B.   MODIFICATIONS OF THE EFFECTS OF THE ANNUAL ACCOUNTING PERIOD CONCEPT

As indicated by the Court's opinion in *Burnet v. Sanford & Brooks Co.,* supra, the concept of the taxable year is fundamental. Tax computations are made with respect to taxable years; Congress has rejected a general transactional approach. For a modern restatement of this principle, see Hershey Foods Corp. v. Commissioner, 76 T.C. 312 (1981):

> Federal income taxes are computed on an annual basis not on a transactional basis. * * * Each year stands on its own. A transactional approach under which we would wait to see the end result of an entire business venture before determining the proper tax consequences might be thought by some to be more equitable, but that is not the approach used in our system of income taxation.

As suggested by the Supreme Court in *Sanford & Brooks,* however, there are situations in which strict application of the annual accounting period would produce hardship. The most frequent problems involve transactions that occur or have effects in two or more years. This may be the case when an item is deducted in one taxable year and recovered in another, when money received in one year must be repaid in a later year, or when income earned over a number of years is paid in one year, or, as in *Sanford & Brooks,* when a taxpayer experiences losses in one year and profits in another. A number of specific statutory provisions and administrative and judicial interpretations have been developed to ameliorate the effect of strict adherence to the taxable year concept.

1.   THE "TAX BENEFIT" CONCEPT

Generally, where a taxpayer deducts an amount from income in one year and recovers or fails to pay the deducted item in a later taxable year, the amount recovered or not paid must be included in income in the later year. This rule commonly is referred to as the "tax benefit" rule (or the inclusionary component of the tax benefit rule). For example, in Chicago, Rock Island & Pacific Railway v. Commissioner, 47 F.2d 990 (7th Cir.1931), cert. denied, 284 U.S. 618 (1931), employees of a railroad performed services for which they were entitled to wages. The company accrued the wages on its books and deducted them on its income tax return. The wages were not paid for two years. Acting under an accounting practice established by the Interstate Commerce Commission, the railroad subsequently credited the wages to profit. The court held that the company had income in the year of credit. See also Fidelity–Philadelphia Trust Co. v. Commissioner, 23 T.C. 527 (1954) (unclaimed deposits transferred to surplus by a bank constitute income).

There is a second aspect to the tax benefit rule that generally is labelled the "exclusionary" component. Originally developed by the courts, and now partially codified in § 111, this rule provides that where a deduction in a prior year produced no "tax benefit"—as, for example, where the taxpayer had no income and hence no tax liability—subsequent recovery or eventual nonpayment of the previously deducted item does not produce taxable income in the year of recovery or nonpayment. Section 111 initially was limited to the recovery of bad debts and taxes, but now extends to recovery of any deduction taken in a prior year to the extent that the deduction did not reduce "the amount of tax imposed by this Chapter." This permits taxpayers to exclude recoveries of amounts that may have reduced taxable income, but not the amount of tax imposed (for example, due to excess tax credits). Suppose the taxpayer paid a $100 medical bill that should have been issued for $10. When the physician returns $90 to the taxpayer, the patient has no income if he did not deduct medical expenses as an itemized deduction in the year of payment because he would have received no tax benefit from the medical expense.

Section 111 also applies to tax credits. Except for the foreign tax credit and the investment tax credit, which have their own recapture rules, § 111 requires an increase in tax imposed in any year in which there was a subsequent recovery with respect to any item for which a tax credit was allowable in a prior year. If a credit did not reduce income taxes in the earlier year, it does not increase income taxes in the later year. § 111(b). For example, assume an individual in one year claims a 25 percent credit for $1,000 of wages paid to a child caretaker (§ 21), but in a subsequent year, $200 of the wages are refunded. Under § 111(b), tax would be increased in the subsequent year by $50 (25 percent of $200) unless the prior year's credit had not reduced tax.

A somewhat related provision is § 186 of the Code, which deals with damage recoveries for antitrust violations, breach of contract, and patent infringement. This section allows a taxpayer to deduct from damage recoveries those losses that did not produce any earlier tax benefit.

The tax benefit rule provides only "rough justice." It does not eliminate differences in tax that result if tax liability was reduced by one rate in the earlier year, but increased by the later recovery at a different rate. See Alice Phelan Sullivan Corp. v. United States, 180 Ct.Cl. 659, 381 F.2d 399 (1967) (taxing the recovery at the rate applicable in the later year regardless of the size of the tax benefit in the earlier year). Suppose, for example, that the taxpayer, who is in a 28 percent bracket, takes a deduction for a $1,000 painting donated to charity. If the charity returns the painting in a year in which he is in a 40 percent bracket, he will pay an additional $400 of taxes on the $1,000 recovery although he saved only $280 in taxes when he took the deduction in the prior year.

Even if the rate brackets remain the same, and the taxpayer's total tax is zero—the position he would have been in by never having donated the painting—he enjoys the advantage of the time value of the earlier savings of taxes.

Hillsboro National Bank v. Commissioner and United States v. Bliss Dairy, Inc.

Supreme Court of the United States, 1983. 460 U.S. 370.

JUSTICE O'CONNOR delivered the opinion of the Court.

These consolidated cases present the question of the applicability of the tax benefit rule to two corporate tax situations: the repayment to the shareholders of taxes for which they were liable but that were originally paid by the corporation; and the distribution of expensed assets in a corporate liquidation. We conclude that, unless a nonrecognition provision of the Internal Revenue Code prevents it, the tax benefit rule ordinarily applies to require the inclusion of income when events occur that are fundamentally inconsistent with an earlier deduction. Our examination of the provisions granting the deductions and governing the liquidation in these cases lead us to hold that the rule requires the recognition of income in the case of the liquidation but not in the case of the tax refund.

I

[Illinois had imposed a property tax on shares of incorporated banks doing business in the state. Hillsboro National Bank paid this tax on behalf of its shareholders, taking the deduction for taxes permitted by § 164(e). The state refunded some of these payments directly to shareholders after the Supreme Court upheld a state constitutional amendment prohibiting ad valorem taxation of personal property owned by individuals. The IRS sought to include the repayment in Hillsboro's income.

Bliss Dairy deducted under § 162 the full cost of cattle feed purchased for use in its operations. Bliss adopted a plan of liquidation in the next taxable year and distributed a substantial amount of remaining feed to its shareholders in a nontaxable transaction. The IRS asserted that Bliss should have taken into income the value of the feed distributed to its shareholders.]

II

The Government in each case relies solely on the tax benefit rule—a judicially developed principle[1] that allays some of the inflexibilities of the annual accounting system. An annual accounting system is a practical necessity if the federal income tax is to produce revenue ascertainable and payable at regular intervals. Burnet v. Sanford & Brooks Co., 282 U.S. 359, 365 (1931). Nevertheless, strict adherence to an annual accounting system would create transactional inequities. Often an apparently completed transaction will reopen unexpectedly in a subsequent tax year, rendering the initial reporting improper. For instance, if a taxpayer held a note that became apparently uncollectible early in the taxable year, but the debtor made an unexpected financial recovery before the close of the year and paid the debt, the transaction would have no tax consequences for the taxpayer, for the repayment of the principal would be recovery of capital. If, however, the debtor's financial recovery and the resulting repayment took place after the close of the taxable year, the taxpayer would have a deduction for the apparently bad debt in the first year under § 166(a) of the Code. * * * Without the tax benefit rule, the repayment in the second year, representing a return of capital, would not be taxable. The second transaction, then, although economically identical to the first, could, because of the differences in accounting, yield drastically different tax consequences. The Government, by allowing a deduction that it could not have known to be improper at the time, would be foreclosed from recouping any of the tax saved because of the improper deduction.[2] Recognizing and seeking to avoid the possible distortions of income,[3] the courts have long required the taxpayer to recognize the repayment in the second year as income.[4]

---

1. Although the rule originated in the courts, it has the implicit approval of Congress, which enacted § 111 as a limitation on the rule.

2. When the event proving the deduction improper occurs after the close of the taxable year, even if the statute of limitations has not run, the Commissioner's proper remedy is to invoke the tax benefit rule and require inclusion in the later year rather than to re-open the earlier year. * * *

3. As the rule developed, a number of theories supported taxation in the later year. One explained that the taxpayer who had taken the deduction "consented" to "return" it if events proved him not entitled to it, while another explained that the deduction offset income in the earlier year, which became "latent" income that might be recaptured. Still a third view maintained that the later recognition of income was a balancing entry. All these views reflected that the initial accounting for the item must be corrected to present a true picture of income. While annual accounting precludes reopening the earlier year, it does not prevent a less precise correction—far superior to none—in the current year, analogous to the practice of financial accountants. This concern with more accurate measurement of income underlies the tax benefit rule and always has.

4. Even this rule did not create complete transactional equivalence. In the second version of the transaction discussed in the text, the taxpayer might have realized no benefit from the deduction, if, for instance, he had no taxable income for that year. Application of the tax benefit rule as originally developed would require the taxpayer to recognize income on the repayment, so that the net result of the collection of the principal amount of the debt would be recognition of income. Similarly, the tax rates might change between the two years, so that a deduction and an inclusion, though equal in amount, would not produce exactly offsetting tax consequences. Congress enacted § 111 to deal with part of this problem. Although a change

The taxpayers and the Government in these cases propose different formulations of the tax benefit rule. The taxpayers contend that the rule requires the inclusion of amounts *recovered* in later years, and they do not view the events in these cases as "recoveries." The Government, on the other hand, urges that the tax benefit rule requires the inclusion of amounts previously deducted if later events are inconsistent with the deductions; it insists that no "recovery" is necessary to the application of the rule. Further, it asserts that the events in these cases are inconsistent with the deductions taken by the taxpayers. We are not in complete agreement with either view.

An examination of the purpose and accepted applications of the tax benefit rule reveals that a "recovery" will not always be necessary to invoke the tax benefit rule. The purpose of the rule is not simply to tax "recoveries." On the contrary, it is to * * * achieve rough transactional parity in tax, and to protect the Government and the taxpayer from the adverse effects of reporting a transaction on the basis of assumptions that an event in a subsequent year proves to have been erroneous. Such an event, unforeseen at the time of an earlier deduction, may in many cases require the application of the tax benefit rule. We do not, however, agree that this consequence invariably follows. Not every unforeseen event will require the taxpayer to report income in the amount of his earlier deduction. On the contrary, the tax benefit rule will "cancel out" an earlier deduction only when a careful examination shows that the later event is indeed fundamentally inconsistent with the premise on which the deduction was initially based. That is, if that event had occurred within the same taxable year, it would have foreclosed the deduction. In some cases, a subsequent recovery by the taxpayer will be the only event that would be fundamentally inconsistent with the provision granting the deduction. In such a case, only actual recovery by the taxpayer would justify application of the tax benefit rule. For example, if a calendar-year taxpayer made a rental payment on December 15 for a 30–day lease deductible in the current year under § 162(a)(3), * * * the tax benefit rule would not require the recognition of income if the leased premises were destroyed by fire on January 10. The resulting inability of the taxpayer to occupy the building would be an event not fundamentally inconsistent with his prior deduction as an ordinary and necessary business expense under § 162(a). The loss is attributable to the business and therefore is consistent with the deduction of the rental payment as an ordinary and necessary business expense. On the other hand, had the premises not burned and, in January, the taxpayer decided to use them to house his family rather than to continue the operation of his business, he would have converted the leasehold to personal use. This would be an event fundamentally inconsistent with the business use on which the deduction was based. In the case of the fire, only if the lessor—by virtue of some provision in the lease—had

in the rates may still lead to differences in taxes due, see Alice Phelan Sullivan Corp. v. United States, 381 F.2d 399, 180 Ct.Cl. 659 (Ct.Cl.1967), § 111 provides that the taxpayer can exclude from income the amount that did not give rise to some tax benefit. See

Dobson v. Commissioner, 320 U.S. 489, 505–506 (1943). This exclusory rule and the inclusionary rule described in the text are generally known together as the tax benefit rule. It is the inclusionary aspect of the rule with which we are currently concerned.

refunded the rental payment would the taxpayer be required under the tax benefit rule to recognize income on the subsequent destruction of the building. In other words, the subsequent recovery of the previously deducted rental payment would be the only event inconsistent with the provision allowing the deduction. It therefore is evident that the tax benefit rule must be applied on a case-by-case basis. A court must consider the facts and circumstances of each case in the light of the purpose and function of the provisions granting the deductions.

When the later event takes place in the context of a nonrecognition provision of the Code, there will be an inherent tension between the tax benefit rule and the nonrecognition provision. * * * We cannot resolve that tension with a blanket rule that the tax benefit rule will always prevail. Instead, we must focus on the particular provisions of the Code at issue in any case.

* * *

In the cases currently before us, then, we must undertake an examination of the particular provisions of the Code that govern these transactions to determine whether the deductions taken by the taxpayers were actually inconsistent with later events and whether specific nonrecognition provisions prevail over the principle of the tax benefit rule.

III

In *Hillsboro,* the key provision is § 164(e). That section grants the corporation a deduction for taxes imposed on its shareholders but paid by the corporation. It also denies the shareholders any deduction for the tax. In this case, the Commissioner has argued that the refund of the taxes by the state to the shareholders is the equivalent of the payment of a dividend from Hillsboro to its shareholders. If Hillsboro does not recognize income in the amount of the earlier deduction, it will have deducted a dividend. Since the general structure of the corporate tax provisions does not permit deduction of dividends, the Commissioner concludes that the payment to the shareholders must be inconsistent with the original deduction and therefore requires the inclusion of the amount of the taxes as income under the tax benefit rule.

In evaluating this argument, it is instructive to consider what the tax consequences of the payment of a shareholder tax by the corporation would be without § 164(e) and compare them to the consequences under § 164(e). Without § 164(e), the corporation would not be entitled to a deduction, for the tax is not imposed on it. * * * If the corporation has earnings and profits, the shareholder would have to recognize income in the amount of the taxes, because a payment by a corporation for the benefit of its shareholders is a constructive dividend. * * * The shareholder, however, would be entitled to a deduction since the constructive dividend is used to satisfy his tax liability. Section 164(a)(2). Thus, for the shareholder, the transaction would be a wash: he would recognize the amount of the tax as income, but he would have an offsetting deduction for the tax. For the corporation, there would be no tax consequences, for the payment of a dividend gives rise to neither income nor a deduction. Section 311(a).

Under § 164(e), the economics of the transaction of course remain unchanged: the corporation is still satisfying a liability of the shareholder and is therefore paying a constructive dividend. The tax consequences are, however, significantly different, at least for the corporation. The transaction is still a wash for the shareholder, although § 164(e) denies him the deduction to which he would otherwise be entitled, he need not recognize income on the constructive dividend, Treas.Reg. § 1.164–7, 26 CFR § 1.164–7 (1982). But the corporation is entitled to a deduction that would not otherwise be available. In other words, the only effect of § 164(e) is to permit the corporation to deduct a dividend. Thus, we cannot agree with the Commissioner that, simply because the events here give rise to a deductible dividend, they cannot be consistent with the deduction. In at least some circumstances, a deductible dividend is within the contemplation of the Code. The question we must answer is whether § 164(e) permits a deductible dividend in these circumstances—when the money, though initially paid into the state treasury, ultimately reaches the shareholder—or whether the deductible dividend is available, as the Commissioner urges, only when the money remains in the state treasury, as properly assessed and collected tax revenue.

Rephrased, our question now is whether Congress, in granting this special favor to corporations that paid dividends by satisfying the liability of their shareholders, was concerned with the *reason* the money was paid out by the corporation or with the *use* to which it was ultimately put. Since § 164(e) represents a break with the usual rules governing corporate distributions, the structure of the Code does not provide any guidance on the reach of the provision. This Court has described the provision as "prompted by the plight of various banking corporations which paid and voluntarily absorbed the burden of certain local taxes imposed upon their shareholders, but were not permitted to deduct those payments from gross income." The section, in substantially similar form, has been part of the Code since the Revenue Act of 1921, * * * . The only discussion of the provision appears to be that between Dr. T.S. Adams and Senator Smoot at the Senate hearings. Dr. Adams' statement explains why the States imposed the property tax on the shareholders and collected it from the banks, but it does not cast light on the reason for the deduction. Senator Smoot's response, however, is more revealing:

> "I have been a director in a bank * * * for over 20 years. They have paid that tax ever since I have owned a share of stock in the bank. * * * I know nothing about it. I do not take 1 cent of credit for deductions, and the banks are entitled to it. They pay it out."

The payment by the corporations of a liability that Congress knew was not a tax imposed on them gave rise to the entitlement to a deduction; Congress was unconcerned that the corporations took a deduction for amounts that did not satisfy their tax liability. It apparently perceived the shareholders and the corporations as independent of one another, each "[knowing] nothing about" the payments by the other. In those circumstances, it is difficult to conclude that Congress intended that the corporation have no deduction if the State turned the tax revenues over to these independent parties. We conclude that the purpose of § 164(e) was to provide relief for corporations making these payments, and the focus of Congress was on the act of payment rather than on the ultimate use of the funds by the state. As long as the payment itself was not negated by a refund to the corporation, the change in the character of the funds in the hands of the state does not require the corporation to recognize income, and we reverse the judgment below.

IV

The problem in *Bliss* is more complicated. Bliss took a deduction under § 162(a), so we must begin by examining that provision. Section 162(a) permits a deduction for the "ordinary and necessary expenses" of carrying on a trade or business. The deduction is predicated on the consumption of the asset in the trade or business. See Treas.Reg. § 1.162–3 (1982) ("Taxpayers * * * should include in expenses the charges for materials and supplies only in the amount that they are *actually consumed and used in operation* in the taxable year. * * * ") (emphasis added). If the taxpayer later sells the assets rather than consuming it in furtherance of his trade or business, it is quite clear that he would lose his deduction, for the basis of the asset would be zero, * * * so he would recognize the full amount of the proceeds on sale as gain. See § 1001(a), (c). In general, if the taxpayer converts the expensed asset to some other, non-business use, that action is inconsistent with his earlier deduction, and the tax benefit rule would require inclusion in income of the amount of the unwarranted deduction. That non-business use is inconsistent with a deduction for an ordinary and necessary business expense is clear from an examination of the Code. While § 162(a) permits a deduction for ordinary and necessary business expenses, § 262 explicitly denies a deduction for personal expenses. * * * Thus, if a corporation turns expensed assets to the analog of personal consumption, as Bliss did here—distribution to shareholders—it would seem that it should take into income the amount of the earlier deduction.

That conclusion, however, does not resolve this case, for the distribution by Bliss to its shareholders is governed by a provision of the Code that specifically shields the taxpayer from recognition of gain—§ 336.* We must therefore proceed to inquire whether this is the sort of gain that goes unrecognized under § 336. Our examination of the background of § 336 and its place within the framework of tax law convinces us that it does not prevent the application of the tax benefit rule.

[The Court's discussion of § 336 is omitted.]

Thus, the legislative history of § 336, the application of other general rules of tax law, and the construction of the identical language in § 337 all indicate that § 336 does not permit a liquidating corporation to avoid the tax benefit rule. Consequently, we reverse the judgment of the Court of Appeals and hold that, on liquidation, Bliss must include in income the amount of the unwarranted deduction.

---

* Editor's Note—This "gain-shielding" quality of § 336 was removed by the Tax Reform Act of 1986.

V

Bliss paid the assessment on an increase of $60,000 in its taxable income. In the District Court, the parties stipulated that the value of the grain was $56,565, but the record does not show what the original cost of the grain was or what portion of it remained at the time of liquidation. The proper increase in taxable income is the portion of the cost of the grain attributable to the amount of grain on hand at the time of liquidation. In *Bliss,* then, we remand for a determination of that amount. In *Hillsboro,* the taxpayer sought a redetermination in the Tax Court rather than paying the tax, so no further proceedings are necessary, and the judgment of the Court of Appeals is reversed.

It is so ordered.

[The dissenting opinion of JUSTICE BRENNAN in *Hillsboro National Bank* and the opinion of JUSTICE STEVENS joined by JUSTICE MARSHALL, concurring in *Hillsboro National Bank* and dissenting in *Bliss Dairy* have been omitted.]

[JUSTICE BLACKMUN, dissenting in both cases, would have required the corporations in both cases to have amended their tax returns and remove the deductions for the year in which the deductions were claimed. An excerpt from his dissent follows.]

I have no difficulty in favoring some kind of "tax benefit" adjustment in favor of the Government for each of these situations. An adjustment should be made, for in each case the beneficial deduction turned out to be improper and undeserved because its factual premise proved to be incorrect. Each taxpayer thus was not entitled to the claimed deduction, or a portion of it, and this nonentitlement should be reflected among its tax obligations.

This takes me, however, to the difficulty I encounter with * * * the unraveling or rectification of the situation. The Commissioner and the United States in these respective cases insist that the Bank and the Dairy should be regarded as receiving income in the very next tax year when the factual premise for the prior year's deduction proved to be incorrect. I could understand that position, if, in the interim, the bar of a statute of limitations had become effective or if there were some other valid reason why the preceding year's return could not be better corrected and additional tax collected. But it seems to me that the better resolution of these two particular cases and others like them—and a resolution that should produce little complaint from the taxpayer—is to make the necessary adjustment, whenever it can be made, in the tax year for which the deduction was originally claimed. This makes the correction where the correction is due and it makes the amount of the net income for each year a true amount and one that accords with the facts, not one that is unstructured, imprecise, and fictional. This normally would be accomplished either by the taxpayer's filing an amended return for the earlier year, with payment of the resulting additional tax, or by the Commissioner's assertion of a deficiency followed by collection. This actually is the kind of thing that is done all the time, for when a taxpayer's return is audited and a deficiency is asserted due to an overstated deduction, the process equates with the filing of an amended return.

* * *

This, in my view, is the way these two particular tax controversies should be resolved. I see no need for anything more complex in their resolution than what I have outlined. Of course, if a statute of limitations problem existed, or if the facts in some other way prevented reparation to the Government, the cases and their resolution might well be different.

I realize that my position is simplistic, but I doubt if the judge-made tax benefit rule really was intended, at its origin, to be regarded as applicable in simple situations of the kind presented in these successive-tax-year cases. So often a judge-made rule, understandably conceived, ultimately is used to carry us further than it should.

I would vacate the judgment in each of these cases and remand each case for further proceedings consistent with this analysis.

NOTES

(A) *"Fundamentally Inconsistent" Events.* The Supreme Court's decisions in *Hillsboro* and *Bliss Dairy* make it clear—contrary to some prior appellate court decisions—that the tax benefit rule does not require an economic or physical "recovery" of an item or a cancellation of a liability; all that is required is an event "fundamentally inconsistent" with the earlier deduction. Beyond that, however, the majority opinion does little to define a "fundamentally inconsistent event." The refund of taxes to shareholders in *Hillsboro* was deemed not to trigger the tax benefit rule because of the majority's reading of the legislative history of § 164(e). The dissenting Justices disagreed with the conclusion of the majority that the "focus of Congress was on the act of payment rather than on the ultimate use of the funds by the state;" even granting the majority's conclusion, the dissent argued that the refund of the taxes to the shareholders could easily have been classified as "fundamentally inconsistent" with the earlier deduction. The facts of *Hillsboro* seem unique (as does the debate over the legislative purpose of § 164(e)), and the Court here provides little guidance for the application of the tax benefit doctrine in future cases.

The Court's opinion in *Bliss Dairy* creates considerable uncertainty about when courts will intervene to recapture other "fundamentally inconsistent" deductions. For example, the Ninth Circuit refused to treat as a fundamentally inconsistent event the distribution on liquidation of unharvested crops, where the corporation had previously deducted the costs of production. Rojas v. Commissioner, 901 F.2d 810 (9th Cir.1990). The Court distinguished *Bliss Dairy* on the ground that in that case, the feed that had been deducted was distributed, whereas in *Rojas* the seed, fertilizer, and other expensed assets were consumed. It rejected the Service's position that consumption required the production of income, stating that this would "extend the tax benefit rule well beyond the parameters outlined in *Bliss Dairy.*" If the feed in *Bliss Dairy* had been eaten by the cattle which were then distributed, what result? If the cattle in *Bliss Dairy* had been eaten by a horse, which in turn, was eaten by an old lady who had swallowed a fly, what result? (She died, of course.)

(B) *A Transactional Approach.* Would Justice Blackmun's position have the effect of replacing annual accounting with a full transactional system? Compare § 1341, discussed infra at page 677, which allows taxpayers who take a deduction for the surrender of an item previously included in income to calculate their tax savings by reference to either the year of inclusion or the year of deduction. Why should this option be allowed only where a taxpayer first pays taxes and later seeks a refund, and not where the taxpayer first lowers taxes through a deduction and subsequently increases income?

(C) *Items Erroneously Deducted in the Earlier Year.* What if the taxpayer erroneously claimed a deduction in the earlier year? In Mayfair Minerals, Inc. v. Commissioner, 56 T.C. 82 (1971), affirmed 456 F.2d 622 (5th Cir.1972), the Tax Court required a subsequent recovery to be included in income even though the original deduction had been improperly taken. The court held that the taxpayer had "misled" the revenue agents by treating the deduction improperly in the earlier year.

In Unvert v. Commissioner, 72 T.C. 807 (1979), affirmed 656 F.2d 483 (9th Cir.1981), cert. denied 456 U.S. 961 (1982), the taxpayer first deducted as prepaid interest an initial payment for the purchase of condominium units. He later recovered this sum. He argued that the initial outlay really had been a nondeductible deposit and that its recovery constituted a nontaxable restoration of capital. He attempted to invoke the erroneous deduction exception to defeat the application of the tax benefit rule to the recovery. The Tax Court invoked *Mayfair's* estoppel rule and required the taxpayer to include the returned money in income. On appeal, the Ninth Circuit ignored the Tax Court's "quasi-estoppel" theory and affirmed on the ground that the statute of limitations should never bar the inclusion of the recovery of an earlier erroneous deduction. The Fifth Circuit also has rejected the erroneous deduction exception. In Hughes & Luce L.L.P. v. Commissioner, 70 F.3d 16 (5th Cir.1995), a law firm deducted "service costs" that the IRS determined were nondeductible loans. The Fifth Circuit found that reimbursement of the loans triggered income under the tax benefit rule.

(D) *Amount of the Inclusion.* Where the taxpayer transfers property and takes a deduction and the property is later returned to her, the fair market value of the property may have increased or decreased. In *Alice Phelan Sullivan Corp.,* supra, the IRS only attempted to tax the later recovery of property previously donated to charity to the extent of fair market value at the time of the deduction, which was the amount deducted. The Tax Court has held that the inclusion is the lesser of the amount of the deduction or the fair market value of the property when returned. Rosen v. Commissioner, 71 T.C. 226 (1978), affirmed 611 F.2d 942 (1st Cir.1980). If the taxpayer had previously received no tax benefit from the deduction, but the property had increased in value, should there be any taxable income on the return of the property?

(E) *Later Transactions.* Taxpayers sometimes argue—usually without success—that later transactions are related to earlier transactions that produced unusable deductions in order to invoke the exclusionary leg of the tax benefit rule. For example, in Rev.Rul. 66–320, 1966–2 C.B. 37, the taxpayer accepted property worth $3,000 in satisfaction of a $5,000 debt and took a $2,000 bad debt deduction, which produced no tax benefit. Later the taxpayer sold the property for $5,000. The IRS ruled that the sale was a separate transaction, not protected by § 111.

2.   CLAIM OF RIGHT–INCOME RECEIVED SUBJECT TO CONTINGENCIES OR LIABILITIES

Problems similar to those discussed in connection with the tax benefit rule arise in converse situations where taxpayers receive income in one year and are required to repay the amount received in a later year. The courts have had to decide how rigorously to apply the taxable year concept as described in *Sanford & Brooks*.

The issue arises whenever it turns out that the taxpayer did not have an absolute right to the money or property, but only a "claim of right." The general rule is that amounts received under a "claim of right" must be included in income when received and may be deducted if subsequently repaid. The subsequent repayment does not affect the initial inclusion. United States v. Lewis, 340 U.S. 590 (1951). As the Court noted in North American Oil Consolidated v. Burnet, 286 U.S. 417, 424 (1932):

> If a taxpayer receives earnings under a claim of right and without restriction as to its disposition, he has received income which he is required to [report on his tax return], even though it may still be claimed that he is not entitled to retain the money, and even though he may still be adjudged liable to restore its equivalent.

The case that follows discusses § 1341, which in some cases affects the amount of the deduction, and seems to add a "tax detriment" limitation to the subsequent deduction.

United States v. Skelly Oil Co.

Supreme Court of the United States, 1969. 394 U.S. 678.

MR. JUSTICE MARSHALL delivered the opinion of the Court.

During its tax year ending December 31, 1958, respondent refunded $505,536.54 to two of its customers for overcharges during the six preceding years. Respondent, an Oklahoma producer of natural gas, had set its prices during the earlier years in accordance with a minimum price order of the Oklahoma Corporation Commission. After that order was vacated as a result of a decision of this Court, * * * respondent found it necessary to settle a number of claims filed by its customers; the repayments in question represent settlements of two of those claims. Since respondent had claimed an unrestricted right to its sales receipts during the years 1952 through 1957, it had included the $505,536.54 in its gross income in those years. The amount was also included in respondent's "gross income from the property" as defined in § 613 of the Internal Revenue Code of 1954, the section which allows taxpayers to deduct a fixed percentage of certain receipts to compensate for the depletion of natural resources from which they derive income. Allowable percentage depletion for receipts from oil and gas wells is fixed at 27½% of the "gross income from the property." Since respondent claimed and the Commissioner allowed percentage depletion deductions during these years, 27½% of the receipts in question was added to the depletion allowances to which respondent would otherwise have been entitled. Accordingly, the actual increase in respondent's taxable income attributable to the receipts in question was not $505,536.54, but only $366,513.99. Yet, when respondent made its refunds in 1958, it attempted to deduct the full $505,536.54. The Commissioner objected and assessed a deficiency. * * * The Government won in the District Court, but the Court of Appeals for the Tenth Circuit reversed, 392 F.2d 128 (1968). Upon petition by the Government, we granted certiorari, 393 U.S. 820 (1968), to consider whether the Court of Appeals decision had allowed respondent "the practical equivalent of double deduction," * * * in conflict with past decisions of this Court and sound principles of tax law. We reverse.

I

The present problem is an outgrowth of the so-called "claim-of-right" doctrine. Mr. Justice Brandeis, speaking for a unanimous Court in North American Oil Consolidated v. Burnet, 286 U.S. 417, 424 (1932), gave that doctrine its classic formulation. "If a taxpayer receives earnings under a claim of right and without restriction as to its disposition, he has received income which he is required to [report on his tax return], even though it may still be claimed that he is not entitled to retain the money, and even though he may still be adjudged liable to restore its equivalent." Should it later appear that the taxpayer was not entitled to keep the money, Mr. Justice Brandeis explained, he would be entitled to a deduction in the year of repayment; the taxes due for the year of receipt would not be affected. This approach was dictated by Congress' adoption of an annual accounting system as an integral part of the tax code. See Burnet v. Sanford & Brooks Co., 282 U.S. 359, 365–366 (1931). Of course, the tax benefit from the deduction in the year of repayment might differ from the increase in taxes attributable to the receipt; for example, tax rates might have changed, or the taxpayer might be in a different tax "bracket." * * *

Section 1341 of the 1954 Code was enacted to alleviate some of the inequities which Congress felt existed in this area.[1] * * * As an alternative to the deduction in the year of repayment which prior law allowed, § 1341(a)(5) permits certain taxpayers to recompute their taxes for the year of receipt. Whenever § 1341(a)(5) applies, taxes for the current year are to be reduced by the amount taxes were increased in the year or years of receipt because the disputed items were included in gross income. Nevertheless, it is clear that Congress did not intend to tamper with the underlying claim-of-right doctrine; it only provided an alternative for certain cases in which the new approach favored the taxpayer. When the

---

1. * * * Section 1341(b)(2) contains an exclusion covering certain cases involving sales of stock in trade or inventory. However, because of special treatment given refunds made by regulated public utilities, both parties agree that § 1341(b)(2) is inapplicable to this case and that, accordingly, § 1341(a) applies.

new approach was not advantageous to the taxpayer, the old law was to apply under § 1341(a)(4).

In this case, the parties have stipulated that § 1341(a)(5) does not apply. Accordingly, as the courts below recognized, respondent's taxes must be computed under § 1341(a)(4) and thus, in effect, without regard to the special relief Congress provided through the enactment of § 1341. Nevertheless, respondent argues, and the Court of Appeals seems to have held, that the language used in § 1341 requires that respondent be allowed a deduction for the full amount it refunded to its customers. We think the section has no such significance.

In describing the situations in which the section applies, § 1341(a)(2) talks of cases in which "a deduction is allowable for the taxable year because it was established after the close of [the year or years of receipt] that the taxpayer did not have an unrestricted right to such item. * * *" The "item" referred to is first mentioned in § 1341(a)(1); it is the item included in gross income in the year of receipt. The section does not imply in any way that the "deduction" and the "item" must necessarily be equal in amount. In fact, the use of the words "a deduction" and the placement of § 1341 in subchapter Q—the subchapter dealing largely with side-effects of the annual accounting system—make it clear that it is necessary to refer to other portions of the Code to discover how much of a deduction is allowable. The regulations promulgated under the section make the necessity for such a cross-reference clear. Treas.Reg. § 1.1341–1 (1957). * * *

II

Under the annual accounting system dictated by the Code, each year's tax must be definitively calculable at the end of the tax year. * * * In cases arising under the claim-of-right doctrine, this emphasis on the annual accounting period normally requires that the tax consequences of a receipt should not determine the size of the deduction allowable in the year of repayment. There is no requirement that the deduction save the taxpayer the exact amount of taxes he paid because of the inclusion of the item in income for a prior year. * * *

Nevertheless, the annual accounting concept does not require us to close our eyes to what happened in prior years. For instance, it is well settled that the prior year may be examined to determine whether the repayment gives rise to a regular loss or a capital loss. Arrowsmith v. Commissioner, 344 U.S. 6 (1952). The rationale for the *Arrowsmith* rule is easy to see; if money was taxed at a special lower rate when received, the taxpayer would be accorded an unfair tax windfall if repayments were generally deductible from receipts taxable at the higher rate applicable to ordinary income. The Court in *Arrowsmith* was unwilling to infer that Congress intended such a result.

This case is really no different.[2] In essence, oil, and gas producers are taxed on only 72½% of their "gross income from the property" whenever

---

2. The analogy would be even more striking if in *Arrowsmith* the individual taxpayer had not utilized the alternative tax for

capital gains, as they were permitted to do by what is now § 1201 of the 1954 Code. Where the 25% alternative tax is not used, individu-

they claim percentage depletion. The remainder of their oil and gas receipts is in reality tax exempt. We cannot believe that Congress intended to give taxpayers a deduction for refunding money that was not taxed when received. * * * Accordingly, *Arrowsmith* teaches that the full amount of the repayment cannot, in the circumstances of this case, be allowed as a deduction.

This result does no violence to the annual accounting system. Here, as in *Arrowsmith,* the earlier returns are not being reopened. And no attempt is being made to require the tax savings from the deduction to equal the tax consequences of the receipts in prior years.[3] In addition, the approach here adopted will affect only a few cases. The percentage depletion allowance is quite unusual; unlike most other deductions provided by the Code, it allows a fixed portion of gross income to go untaxed. As a result, the depletion allowance increases in years when disputed amounts are received under claim of right; there is no corresponding decrease in the allowance because of later deductions for repayments. Therefore, if a deduction for 100% of the repayments were allowed, every time money is received and later repaid the taxpayer would make a profit equivalent to the taxes on 27½% of the amount refunded. In other situations when the taxes on a receipt do not equal the tax benefits of a repayment, either the taxpayer or the Government may, depending on circumstances, be the beneficiary. Here, the taxpayer always wins and the Government always loses. We cannot believe that Congress would have intended such an inequitable result. * * *

Reversed.

[The dissenting opinion of JUSTICE DOUGLAS and the dissenting opinion of JUSTICE STEWART in which JUSTICE HARLAN and JUSTICE DOUGLAS joined are omitted.]

NOTES

(A) *A "Tax Detriment" Rule?* Does the Supreme Court's opinion in *Skelly Oil* suggest a "tax detriment" rule, i.e., that the tax benefit in the subsequent year of deduction should correspond to the tax detriment of the income inclusion in the earlier year? Does the Court's reasoning suggest that rate differentials generally should be taken into account under the

---

al taxpayers are taxed at ordinary rates on 50% of their capital gains. See § 1202. [Ed. note: Both sections were subsequently repealed.] In such a situation, the rule of the *Arrowsmith* case prevents taxpayers from deducting 100% of an item refunded when they were taxed on only 50% of it when it was received. Although *Arrowsmith* prevents this inequitable result by treating the repayment as a capital loss, rather than by disallowing 50% of the deduction, the policy behind the decision is applicable in this case. Here it would be inequitable to allow a 100% deduction when only 72½% was taxed on receipt.

3. Compare the analogous approach utilized under the "tax benefit" rule. Alice Phelan Sullivan Corp. v. United States, 381 F.2d 399 (Ct.Cl.1967); see Internal Revenue Code of 1954 § 111. In keeping with the analogy, the Commissioner has indicated that the Government will only seek to reduce the deduction in the year of repayment to the extent that the depletion allowance attributable to the receipt directly or indirectly reduced taxable income. * * *.

claim of right doctrine? When the tax benefit rule is applied? Or could disenchantment with the percentage depletion deduction distinguish *Skelly Oil* from other situations?

The *Arrowsmith* case relied upon by the Court in *Skelly Oil* is discussed at page 621 supra.

(B) *Section 1341.* As suggested in *Skelly Oil,* § 1341 overruled the prior case law that permitted the subsequent deduction to reduce taxes only at the rate applicable in the year of repayment. Section 1341 allows taxpayers to reduce tax liability in the year of repayment by amount of the tax on the income in the year of inclusion. This eliminates discrepancies due to different years and thereby effects a more thorough revision of the taxable year concept than does the tax benefit rule.

Section 1341, however, operates only where it "appeared" in the earlier year "that the taxpayer had an unrestricted right" to the income. In Revenue Ruling 68–153, 1968–1 C.B. 371, the IRS ruled that refunds made to customers by a railroad because of subsequent administrative findings that the rates were excessive or because of retroactive rate changes qualified for the favorable treatment of § 1341 because the railroad appeared to have an unrestricted right to the income in the year of inclusion. The ruling also holds that refunds because of erroneous billing or as a result of subsequent events, such as passenger ticket refunds, do not qualify for the benefits of § 1341. Similarly, Revenue Ruling 65–254, 1965–2 C.B. 50, held that § 1341 was not applicable to the repayment of embezzled funds since the taxpayer had no "unrestricted right" to the funds in the year of embezzlement. The taxpayer would have only a loss deduction under § 165 in the year of repayment.

In addition, voluntary repayments do not qualify for § 1341 treatment. In Pike v. Commissioner, 44 T.C. 787 (1965), acq. 1968–2 C.B. 2, a lawyer received a payment in 1957 from a corporation represented by his law firm. In 1958, a controversy arose about this payment. The lawyer contended that his position was sound, but he repaid the amount in order to preserve the good relations of the parties involved. The Tax Court held that the repayment, while deductible when made, did not come within § 1341 since it was never "established * * * [that the taxpayer] 'did not have an unrestricted right' " to the original payment as provided in § 1341. It is not necessary that the taxpayer contest the repayment to qualify under § 1341, however.

(C) *Repayment of "Unreasonable" Salaries.* Recall that under § 162 a deduction is permitted for "reasonable" salaries. It is not uncommon for a business to have a provision requiring repayment of any salary that is determined by the IRS to be "unreasonable." In Revenue Ruling 69–115, 1969–1 C.B. 50, the Service held that § 1341 does not apply to such a payment. In Van Cleave v. United States, 718 F.2d 193 (6th Cir.1983), the court held that the § 1341 adjustment was available for such a repayment by a controlling stockholder-employee. In reversing the district court opinion, the court remarked:

The district court seemed to be persuaded by the argument that, if Mr. Van Cleave were allowed section 1341 treatment under these circumstances, this would open the door to tax avoidance in that taxpayers who controlled corporations could "test the waters" in setting their compensation without risk of an adverse tax result. We believe, however, that such possibility of tax avoidance is not a proper consideration in applying this statute, and that the consideration is a legislative rather than a judicial consideration. Moreover, as Mr. Van Cleave suggests, the possibility of tax avoidance could be reduced by requiring the corporation and recipient of compensation to state in their returns that such compensation was paid subject to an obligation to reimburse in the event a deduction is disallowed to the corporation.

(D) *Source of the Deduction.* As the Court in *Skelly Oil* points out, the taxpayer must first find a source for the deduction of the repayment before turning to § 1341. If the deduction is not permitted, § 1341 has no application. For example, in Wood v. United States, 863 F.2d 417 (5th Cir.1989), the court refused to permit a taxpayer to use § 1341 to take a deduction for the forfeiture of drug sale proceeds because a deduction was denied under § 165 on public policy grounds.

Similarly, even though the taxpayer is unable to use the deduction, no adjustment is made to the earlier income inclusion. In Butchko v. Commissioner, 638 F.2d 1214 (9th Cir.1981), a racetrack teller had shortage amounts deducted from his wages by the racetrack. He was required to include these amounts in income, although he had not received them, because they were used to satisfy his obligations for shortages under his employment contract. Because they were employee business expenses, they were deductible from adjusted gross income and thus no deduction was permitted unless the taxpayer itemized deductions.

3.   NET OPERATING LOSS DEDUCTION

Section 172 greatly reduces the possibility that there will not be any tax benefit from a business deduction. In general, § 172 provides that a taxpayer may apply a loss incurred in one taxable year against income earned in another taxable year. The taxpayer may carry back a net operating loss two years and then carry it forward 20 years. (In 2001 and 2002 only to provide additional cash flow to businesses during a recession, the carryback period is five years). A taxpayer who can obtain no tax benefit in the year of deduction may still receive a tax savings if the loss from that year is applied against the income of another year during the 23-year period. Thus, no more business income will be taxed than the aggregate net income over the period that consists of the two years of carryback, the tax year in which the deduction occurs, and the 20 years of carryover.

The net operating loss deduction is treated much like any other deduction. Section 172(c) defines a net operating loss as the excess of deductions allowed over gross income. This general rule is modified by § 172(d) so that the carryover rules apply only to business losses by disallowing nonbusiness deductions in excess of nonbusiness income. The deduction then is taken into account in computing taxable income and thereby tax liability. A loss that is carried back to an earlier taxable year ordinarily can be deducted only by filing a refund claim to recover the tax already paid for that year. (Section 6164 allows a corporation expecting a net operating loss to postpone the payment of its tax for the immediately preceding year.)

Congress originally adopted the net operating loss concept in 1918 during the transition from wartime to peacetime. Many manufacturers who realized large profits during World War I anticipated losses in converting factories to peacetime production. Congress was persuaded that the two periods should not be treated independently.

Today the primary justification for the net operating loss deduction is "to ameliorate the unduly drastic consequences of taxing income strictly on an annual basis." Libson Shops, Inc. v. Koehler, 353 U.S. 382, 386 (1957). Absent an ability to offset lean years against lush years, the Code would favor those businesses with steady income streams. In addition, one can argue that a person's tax burden should reflect to some extent her overall economic ability to bear that burden over a period extending beyond the taxable year. Finally, the net operating loss deduction has been perceived as stimulating capital investment by encouraging taxpayers to take financial risks in speculative or cyclical ventures.

NOTES

(A) *Expenses Attributable to a Trade or Business*. In order to use a net operating loss deduction, the taxpayer must be in a trade or business. Furthermore, the expenses must be related to the trade or business. For examples of decisions holding that particular expenses were not attributable to the taxpayer's trade or business for purposes of the § 172 net operating loss provisions, see Todd v. Commissioner, 77 T.C. 246 (1981), affirmed per curiam 682 F.2d 207 (9th Cir.1982) (doctor could not claim net operating loss on abandonment of plans to construct apartment building because he was not in trade or business of renting apartments); Payte v. United States, 626 F.2d 400 (5th Cir.1980) (interest on loan obtained to purchase share of business partner); Mannette v. Commissioner, 69 T.C. 990 (1978) (loss from repayment of embezzled funds not related to business as securities trader even though embezzled funds used in that business).

(B) *Joint Returns*. Married taxpayers who file join returns may use the net operating losses from the business of one spouse to offset income from the other spouse's business in carryover years. But if one spouse dies and the other subsequently incurs a net operating loss, that loss cannot be carried back and used against income reported on the joint return when all the earlier income was earned by the decedent. Zeeman v. United States, 395 F.2d 861 (2d Cir.1968).

(C) *Death*. The usual rule is that an NOL carryover expires at the death of the taxpayer who incurred the loss even where there is a surviving spouse. An NOL in the year of death may not be carried over to the estate or to subsequent years, but may be used only on the decedent's final return or in the three preceding years. Rev.Rul. 74–175, 1974–1 C.B. 52.

(D) *Bankruptcy*. Sections 1398(g), (i), and (j) govern the transfer of net operating losses and other tax attributes from debtors to their successors in bankruptcy. Although the rules often are quite complex, the estate in bankruptcy generally succeeds to the net operating losses and any losses remaining after the bankruptcy estate ceases to exist are carried forward by the individual taxpayer.

(E) *Statute of Limitations.* Should a taxpayer who carries back a net operating loss to a year otherwise barred by the statute of limitations be able to deduct an item originally overlooked in preparing that year's return? Several court decisions indicate that taxable income for purposes of § 172(b)(2) means correct taxable income, without regard to the statute of limitations. See, e.g., ABKCO Industries, Inc. v. Commissioner, 56 T.C. 1083 (1971), affirmed on other grounds 482 F.2d 150 (3d Cir.1973); State Farming Co. v. Commissioner, 40 T.C. 774 (1963). The IRS, however, ruled in Revenue Ruling 81–88, 1981–1 C.B. 585, that if a net operating loss is carried back to a year in which there is a barred adjustment that would decrease taxable income, the net operating loss must be the first adjustment to reported taxable income. Any barred adjustments that would increase taxable income are offset against the net operating loss. Adjustments that would decrease taxable income are allowed in the carryback year only to offset adjustments that would increase taxable income.

(F) *Related Special Rules.* A special rule applies to losses resulting from the expropriation of property by a foreign government. Another rule applies to deductible expenditures incurred as a result of statutory or common law tort liability that arises at least three years after the acts or omissions that created liability; a similar rule applies to products liability resulting from injuries incurred after manufacture of the product had ended. See §§ 172(b), (h), (j), and (k). Losses due to patent infringement, breach of contract or fiduciary duty, or an antitrust violation may be used to offset any compensation ultimately received if they cannot be deducted in the year of injury. See § 186.

(G) *Relationship to Tax Benefit Rules.* Where the carryback and carryforward of a loss provide no tax benefit, the tax benefit rule may allow taxpayers, in effect, to use the deduction when they later recover an amount that they had deducted in computing a net loss in an earlier year. See Reg. § 1.111–1(b)(2). There is no time limit on the application of the tax benefit rule as there is for the net operating loss deduction. Recall the statement in *Burnet v. Sanford & Brooks*, supra, to the effect that "[o]nly by [annual taxable periods] is it practicable to produce a regular flow of income and apply methods of accounting, assessment, and collection capable of practical operation." The tax benefit rule and the net operating loss deduction surely minimize the Court's choice in the *Sanford & Brooks* case to accept hardship to the taxpayer in order to achieve administrative convenience.

SECTION 2. METHODS OF ACCOUNTING

The allocation of items of income and deduction to the proper taxable year generally is governed by the taxpayer's method of accounting. Section 446 of the Code provides that taxpayers shall compute taxable income "under the method of accounting on the basis of which the taxpayer regularly computes his income in keeping his books" so long as that method "clearly reflects income." Section 451 of the Code requires taxpayers to include items in gross income in the taxable year of receipt unless their method of accounting requires that the income be included in a different taxable year. Section 461 provides that deductions and credits "shall be taken for the taxable year which is the proper taxable year under the method of accounting used in computing taxable income."

The methods most commonly used are the cash method and the accrual method. There are, in addition, special rules for particular types of transactions, such as installment sales. See § 453 of the Code, and page 743 infra. Moreover, some Code sections provide rules for determining the timing of particular deductions. For example, § 213 provides that medical expenses are deductible when "paid."

The cash method has the virtue of simplicity. Most individuals use the cash method and, because this method affords opportunities to obtain tax deferral, so do many service companies such as accounting and law firms. Although the cash method is relatively simple, many commentators believe that it fails to measure income accurately when the taxpayer's activities are more complex. Examples include when expenses accrue in one year that are not paid until the following year, income is earned in one year and cash will not be received until a future year, or cash is prepaid for services and goods to be received in the future.

The accrual method is widely thought to give a more accurate reflection of economic gain and is used by most businesses in presenting the results of operations to management, investors, and creditors. The regulations mandate the accrual method whenever inventories are required, i.e., whenever the sale of goods is a material income producing factor.

Subchapter C corporations, partnerships with a C corporation as a partner, and tax shelters must use the accrual method. § 448. Subchapter C corporations and partnerships with C corporation partners are exempt from this rule if they average less than $5 million in gross receipts annually over the period of three taxable years before the taxable year in question. See § 448(b)(3) and (c). There is also an exception—the fruit of much lobbying, including some rather aggressive lawyering by a large group of former IRS Commissioners and Treasury Assistant Secretaries for Tax Policy who are now partners in large law firms—for "qualified personal service corporations," which may continue to use the cash method (as may partnerships with such corporations as a partner) regardless of the amount of their annual gross receipts. To qualify, substantially all of an entity's activities must be within one of a number of specified fields, including law, health, engineering, architecture, accounting, actuarial science, performing arts, and consulting. In addition, 95 percent of the corporation's stock must be held by past (retired) or present employees who performed or perform services in connection with the corporation's field of activity. See § 448(d)(2).

Although the accrual method of accounting generally is considered more accurate in measuring economic income, it is not without problems. Historically, the accrual method has taken income and deduction items into account at their stated amount rather than at their discounted present value even if they are to be received or paid in the future. The ability, for example, to deduct now amounts to be paid far in the future creates a time value of money advantage for taxpayers and, in effect, mismeasures income. On the other hand, because income sometimes is subject to tax before cash is received, there may be liquidity problems for the taxpayer. The government may face enforcement obstacles when the taxpayer receives cash before the income accrues. As you review the materials on the accrual method, you will discover that the Service and the courts have responded by creating what is, in fact, a hybrid method of accounting, departing from accrual accounting where it creates problems for tax collection.

Taxpayers are required to use an accounting method that "clearly reflects income," and the IRS has the power to require taxpayers to use a method that does so. § 446(b).

In upholding the Commissioner's authority to require a newspaper company to change from the cash to the accrual method of accounting in Knight–Ridder Newspapers v. United States, 743 F.2d 781 (11th Cir.1984), Judge Goldberg waxed eloquent (or went off the deep end) in characterizing the two methods and the tax law's attitude toward them:

These * * * two most common accounting methods * * * could be said to emblematize the polar nature of the human spirit. The cash method—simple, plodding, elemental—stands firmly in the physical realm. It responds only through the physical senses, recognizing only the tangible flow of currency. Money is income when this raw beast actually feels the coins in its primal paw; expenditures are made only when the beast can see that it has given the coins away.

The accrual method, however, moves in a more ethereal, mystical realm. The visionary prophet, it recognizes the impact of the future on the present, and with grave foreboding or ecstatic anticipation, announces the world to be. When it becomes sure enough of its prophecies, it actually conducts life as if the new age has already come to pass. Transactions producing income or deductions spring to life in the eyes of the seer though nary a dollar has moved.

The Internal Revenue Code, the ultimate arbiter, stands to the side, shifting its eyes uneasily from the one being to the other. The Code is possessed of great wisdom and tolerance. It knows that man must generally choose his own way. Therefore, it leaves to the Taxpayer the original choice of which accounting method to use. Section 446(c) specifically authorizes both the cash and accrual methods.

Yet the Code also understands that either extreme possesses inherent weaknesses and can become blinded to reality. Thus the Code and subsequent Treasury Regulations empower the Secretary of the Treasury and the Commissioner of Internal Revenue to cure the blindness. * * *

Of course, in deciding whether the Commissioner has abused his discretion, we immediately face an age-old philosopher's dilemma: how can we mere mortals know who sees the truth most vividly? How can we know whether the primal cash method or the mystical accrual method sees income more clearly without knowing what income really is? If it is really cash on hand, then the cash method is more accurate. If it is really fixed obligations, then the accrual method is more accurate. By embracing both conceptions, the Code provides no general baseline against which to assess the accuracy of an accounting method. In effect, we risk being led in circular fashion to arbitrarily choose one method as accurately reflecting income. When another method differs from it, that other must not clearly reflect income.

* * *

Fortunately, we need not be so arbitrary in this case. The Code and regulations do provide guidance in the case of businesses that sell merchandise. Such businesses are generally required to use inventories, and where the taxpayer uses inventories, it must use the accrual method. Section 471 of the Code * * *.

This Section considers the methods of accounting, beginning with the cash method. This Chapter generally ignores accounting methods of special and limited application, such as the special method of accounting for long-term contracts, which has wide application in the construction industry.

A. CASH METHOD

Under the cash method of accounting, items of income ordinarily are included in the year in which they are "received," and items of deduction are taken in the year in which they are "paid." Usually, there is not much doubt about the time for inclusion or deduction for a cash basis taxpayer.

In order to prevent cash basis taxpayers from having complete freedom to decide when to report income, the receipt concept has been expanded to include the notion of "constructive receipt." Special problems also arise when a taxpayer receives something other than cash, such as a check or a note. Checks, which are mechanisms for making payment, are treated like cash. On the other hand, since notes (and accounts receivable) are mechanisms to defer payment, rather than mechanisms of payment, their inclusion in income immediately upon receipt would have the effect of obliterating the basic distinction between the cash and accrual methods of accounting. Thus, special rules are needed to preserve the distinction, yet prevent abuse.

There also have been disputes concerning the treatment under the cash method of payments received by a third person (such as an escrow agent) on the taxpayer's behalf. Other problems concern whether an amount received is income or a "deposit." Finally, there are important limitations on taxpayers' flexibility under the cash method to postpone income (for example, by refraining from sending out bills) and to accelerate deductions (by making deductible expenditures before the close of the taxable year). The materials that follow illustrate some of these issues.

1. THE "CONSTRUCTIVE RECEIPT" DOCTRINE

Cash, property, and services are taxable to cash method taxpayers when "actually or constructively received." Reg. § 1.446–1(c)(1). The "constructive receipt" doctrine, set forth in § 1.451–2(a) of the Regulations, requires inclusion of income when a taxpayer has the immediate power to receive the income:

> Income although not actually reduced to a taxpayer's possession is constructively received by him in the taxable year during which it is credited to his account, set apart for him, or otherwise made available so that he may draw upon it at any time, or so that he could have drawn upon it during the taxable year if notice of intention to withdraw had been given. However, income is not constructively received if the taxpayer's control of its receipt is subject to substantial limitations or restrictions.

In Ross v. Commissioner, 169 F.2d 483, 491 (1st Cir.1948), the court described the purpose of the constructive receipt doctrine:

> The doctrine of constructive receipt was, no doubt, conceived by the Treasury in order to prevent taxpayers from choosing the year in which to return income merely by choosing the year in which to reduce it to possession. Thereby the Treasury may subject income to taxation when the only thing preventing its reduction to possession is the volition of the taxpayer.

The government typically raises constructive receipt issues in urging that an item be included in income earlier than desired by the taxpayer. The following case, however, illustrates that taxpayers sometimes urge that the doctrine apply.

Carter v. Commissioner

Tax Court of the United States, 1980. 40 T.C.M. 654.

WILBUR, JUDGE:

* * * The only issue for decision is whether $1,073.01 in wages for services rendered during November and December 1974 but not received by petitioner until 1975, were constructively received by petitioner in 1974 within the meaning of section 451.

* * *

Robert J. Carter * * * reported his income for 1975 as a cash basis taxpayer. Mr. Carter was unemployed from January through September 1974. He began working for the city of New York as a laboratory technician in the Office of the Chief Medical Examiner in October 1974. Several weeks later, he transferred to the City Health Department. Petitioner worked as a laboratory technician at the Health Department also, with the added benefit of a permanent job title. He received continuous service credit for the time he was with the Chief Medical Examiner. Subsequent to Mr. Carter's transfer, there was a delay in processing his payroll checks, arising out of tardiness in forwarding his records from the Chief Medical Examiner and a backlog in payroll processing in the Health Department. Consequently, despite numerous protests and demands for his past due salary, Mr. Carter did not get paid for 6 weeks. He was paid $1,073.01 in gross wages on January 3, 1975. This represented 4 weeks back pay ($715.34) and 2 weeks timely pay ($357.67). From this point, his paycheck was up to date.

Had Mr. Carter received the 4 weeks back wages on time, in 1974, he would have owed no extra taxes. His total income for 1974 would have been $818.30. Petitioner was advised by an Internal Revenue employee who assisted him in preparing his 1975 Federal income tax return to exclude the $1,073.01 from his 1975 wages because it was attributable to 1974. Petitioner did so. Respondent assessed a $195 deficiency in petitioner's 1975 taxes.

Petitioner contends that he constructively received the income in 1974, because the work was performed in 1974. He argues that he had a permanent job title, and the funds necessary to pay him were in the city budget. He argues that this constitutes constructive receipt since all that was necessary was for the city to transfer the funds from its budget to his budget. Respondent's position is that Mr. Carter must be taxed when he actually received the money in 1975. While we sympathize with petitioner's plight, we hold that there was no constructive receipt of income in 1974 and petitioner must be taxed in 1975 when he was finally paid.

Petitioner is a cash basis taxpayer. All items which constitute gross income are to be included for the taxable year in which actually or constructively received. * * *

The petitioner did not have the free and unrestricted control of his wages prior to actual receipt that this Court has required in order to find constructive receipt. * * * Indeed, he tried repeatedly to obtain his back wages during the month of December but was unsuccessful. His control over his wages was clearly subject to substantial limitations or restrictions. Their mere presence in the New York City budget is insufficient to find constructive receipt.

Petitioner appears to recognize that this is the rule of law applicable to his case, but urges that we make an exception in his case that the average man would expect in view of the compelling equities involved. However, as we explained to petitioner at trial, the typical taxpayer expects to pay tax when he receives the income, because only then does he have the money in hand to make the payment. This is the essence of the cash system—an item is income when received and a deduction when paid—and it accords with the practical exigencies as well as obviates requiring the average taxpayer to deal with the complex concepts of more sophisticated accounting systems.

Petitioner would have owed no tax on the income had he received it in 1974, rather than in 1975. But under the cash basis of reporting income, it is taxable in the year received and not in the year producing the smallest tax burden. The rules are clear and must be so for the convenience of all citizens subject to the tax.

While it is truly unfortunate that Mr. Carter became a victim of bureaucratic inefficiency, he clearly did not constructively receive the income in 1974, and as a cash basis taxpayer is taxable on the wages when he actually received them in 1975. We sustain respondent's determination.

NOTES

(A) *Other Taxpayers Urging Constructive Receipt.* In Hornung v. Commissioner, 47 T.C. 428 (1967), the taxpayer was awarded a 1962 Corvette by Sport Magazine for his outstanding performance in a football game held in Green Bay, Wisconsin on Sunday, December 31, 1961. The award was announced at 4:30 p.m. that day in Green Bay, but the person who announced the award had neither the title nor the keys to the car. Hornung actually received the car in New York on January 3, 1962. Hornung's claim that the award was taxable income in 1961 (a year closed by the statute of limitations) was rejected by the Tax Court:

> [S]ince December 31, 1961, was a Sunday, it is doubtful whether the car could have been transferred to petitioner before Monday even with the cooperation of the editor in chief of Sport. The New York dealership at which the car was located was closed. The car had not been set aside for petitioner's use and delivery was not dependent solely upon the volition of petitioner. The doctrine of constructive receipt is therefore inapplicable, and we hold that petitioner received the Corvette for income tax purposes in 1962.

See also Fetzer Refrigerator Co. v. United States, 437 F.2d 577 (6th Cir.1971), where the court upheld the taxpayer's claim that he had "constructively received" certain rents due him from his corporation. The taxpayer, as controlling shareholder and officer of the corporation, had the authority to draw checks upon the bank accounts of the corporations. The amounts in question had been accrued as payable on the books of the corporations at the time they became due. A different result was reached in Hyland v. Commissioner, 175 F.2d 422 (2d Cir.1949), where the record failed to show that the controlling shareholder had the power to pay the amounts owed by the corporation. The IRS announced that it will follow the *Fetzer* case. Rev.Rul. 72–317, 1972–1 C.B. 128.

(B) *Refusing to Take Compensation.* In Commissioner v. Mott, 85 F.2d 315 (6th Cir.1936), the taxpayer was entitled to take three percent of the income from a trust as compensation for his services as trustee. In fact, he took nothing. The court found that he was not taxable on the amount that he might have taken. Suppose he draws a check to his own order for the commissions but does not cash it? See Anderson v. Bowers, 170 F.2d 676 (4th Cir.1948), cert. denied 337 U.S. 918 (1949), where the court held the taxpayer liable for tax.

(C) *Delaying Payment by Contract.* In Schniers v. Commissioner, 69 T.C. 511 (1977), the Tax Court upheld for tax purposes a deferred payment arrangement entered into in December 1973, whereby a cotton farmer delayed until January 1974 receipt of income from crops harvested and warehoused in 1973. The Commissioner had argued for constructive receipt on the ground that the deferred payment contracts were entered into voluntarily by the taxpayer for the sole purpose of delaying the reporting of income. The Tax Court found that the contracts were valid and binding on the taxpayer and remarked:

> The point is that income is not realized by a cash basis farmer from merely harvesting his crops. He receives income only when he

actually or constructively receives income from the sale of those crops. He is not required to sell the crops in the year in which he harvests them. He may decide not to sell them until the following year. Nor is he required, if he decides to sell them in the year of harvest, to contract for immediate payment for his crops. The contract may call for payment after the close of the harvest year and he does not realize income in the year of sale if the contract is a valid, enforceable one.

Taxpayers do not have constructive receipt merely because they could have entered into an arrangement to receive payment earlier. Thus, the fact that the payor is solvent or would have been willing to enter into a contract to pay earlier is irrelevant.

(D) *Delaying Payment by Amending Contracts.* In Oates v. Commissioner, 18 T.C. 570 (1952), affirmed 207 F.2d 711 (7th Cir.1953), the taxpayers were insurance agents who, at retirement, amended their agency contracts with the insurance company to provide for the payment of future renewal commissions in equal monthly installments over a 15-year period, regardless of when and in what amounts the renewal commissions would have become due under the original agency agreement. The amounts payable for any year, however, were limited to amounts that already had been earned. The Commissioner asserted that the agents were taxable on the renewal commissions as they accrued under the original contract. Both the Tax Court and the Seventh Circuit rejected the Commissioner's position. They found that the amended contract constituted a novation, that the old contract had been extinguished, and that the taxpayers had no right to demand compensation for services other than as set out in the new contract. The Tax Court pointed out that the taxpayers "under their amended contracts * * * were not entitled to receive any more than they did in fact receive and that being on the cash basis they can only be taxed on [those amounts actually received]."

In Commissioner v. Olmsted Inc. Life Agency, 304 F.2d 16 (8th Cir.1962), affirming 35 T.C. 429 (1960), a life insurance agency assigned to an insurance company all rights to renewal commissions on previously written life insurance policies. In return, the agency was to receive fixed monthly payments based on the estimated present value of the renewals over a 15–year period. Finding *Oates* to be controlling, both the Tax Court and the Eighth Circuit held the transaction to be a novation rather than a "sale or other disposition" within the meaning of § 1001 of the Code. The cash method agency could be taxed on the payments only as received. The courts, however, did not agree with the IRS that the difference between *Olmsted* and *Oates* justified different results. In *Oates*, the contract was not transferable, the contractual rights were not assignable, and the total payment per year was limited to the renewal commissions actually earned; in *Olmsted*, there were no such limitations. The IRS announced its acquiescence in *Oates*, 1960–1 C.B. 5, but its nonacquiescence in *Olmsted*, 1961–2 C.B. 6.

Is the *Olmsted* case consistent with *Cottage Savings*, supra at page 156? Under Reg. § 1.1001–1(a), why isn't the assignment of the commissions for the annuity an "exchange of property for other property differing materially either in kind or in extent"? Is it because the unfunded promise to pay the renewal commissions is not "property"? Is it because the taxpayer in *Cottage Savings* swapped with a third party whereas the taxpayer in *Olmsted* revised its contract with the original party? Suppose the life insurance agency had sold its rights to the renewal commissions to a third party for an annuity. Would the result be different? *Oates* and *Olmsted* should be revisited in connection with the materials on nonqualified deferred compensation, infra at page 757.

(E) *Agency Arrangements*. The general rule that receipt by an agent is receipt by the principal is normally followed in tax cases. See Maryland Casualty Co. v. United States, 251 U.S. 342 (1920). Escrows can be distinguished from agency arrangements because the escrow intermediary often has obligations to both parties to a transaction while an agent normally acts exclusively for his principal. Cases frequently state that a "deferred escrow arrangement that is not part of a bona fide agreement between the buyer and the seller-taxpayer, but rather is a 'self-imposed limitation' created by the seller-taxpayer, is legally ineffective to shift tax liability from one year to the next." A number of cases, however, illustrate that a legally binding sale via an escrow arrangement often will be effective to shift income to the following year. See, e.g., Busby v. United States, 679 F.2d 48 (5th Cir.1982) (escrow for payments to Texas cotton grower held to be agent of the buyer not the seller; therefore no constructive receipt); Johnston v. Commissioner, 14 T.C. 560 (1950) (sale proceeds held by escrowee under deferred payment agreement not subject to taxpayer's immediate demand, so not constructively received).

In Dennis v. Commissioner, 437 F.2d 123 (9th Cir.1970), reversing 51 T.C. 46 (1968), the husband paid $15,000 to his wife's attorney in December 1964 in settlement of his wife's claims for alimony. The attorney was to deliver the money to the wife when she executed a formal release of all further claims against her husband. She did not execute the release and receive the money until January 1965. The court of appeals held that she had constructively received the money in 1964, and that the husband was entitled to a deduction in that year for alimony paid.

(F) *Embezzlement*. Royalties due an author were paid in 1954 by the publisher, pursuant to a customary arrangement, to the author's literary agent, who embezzled them. The author sued the agent and recovered part of the royalties in 1958. The court held that the amount recovered by the author (who was on the cash basis) in 1958 was income in 1958. The amounts received by the literary agent were not regarded as constructively received by the author. Alsop v. Commissioner, 290 F.2d 726 (2d Cir.1961).

3. RECEIPT OF THE EQUIVALENT OF CASH OR "ECONOMIC BENEFIT"

Generally, when a taxpayer actually receives cash or property, no timing question arises; taxation occurs on receipt. But where the taxpayer receives a right to receive money in the future, a persistent problem is whether this right is "equivalent" to cash. For example, the taxpayer may receive a check or a note or a contract right. It may be nontransferable or negotiable only at a substantial discount. It may be placed in escrow or secured by other property. Although the courts are uniform in holding that a "cash equivalent" is taxable upon receipt, there is disagreement as to what types of property interests are cash equivalents.

Revenue Ruling 80–52

Internal Revenue Service, 1980. 1980–1 C.B. 100.

ISSUE

What is the amount includible in gross income as a result of the bartering transactions described below, and when is the amount includible in gross income?

FACTS

A and B are both members of a barter club. The barter club operates as a vehicle for the exchange of property and services among the members. The club uses "credit units" as a medium of exchange and makes available to members information concerning property and services other members are offering for exchange. The club debits or credits members' accounts for goods or services received from or rendered to other members. Exchanges are made on the basis that one credit unit equals one dollar of value. The rules of the club require that the value placed on goods or services exchanged be equal to the member seller's normal retail price. The transfer of credit units between members is accomplished by various source documents, such as invoices, and the club charges the member purchaser a 10 percent commission payable in cash on barter purchases. Any barter transaction between members is reflected in the form of bookkeeping entries on the books and records of the club. The club does not guarantee that a member will be able to use all of that member's credit units and does not pay a member cash for any credit units not used. However, a member's credit units can be used immediately to purchase goods or services offered by other members of the club, and the member may transfer or sell the member's credit units to another member of the club.

Situation 1. Both A and B use the cash receipts and disbursements method of accounting. Through the club, A bartered to B for 200 credit units services that A would normally perform for $200. During the same taxable year, B bartered to A for 200 credit units services that B would normally perform for $200.

Situation 2. C is an employee of the barter club. During the taxable year, C, who uses the cash receipts and disbursements method of accounting, received from the club in exchange for C's services gross wages of $20,000, $10,000 in cash and 10,000 credit units. C is entitled to use the credit units in the same manner as other members of the club. However, the club does not charge C a commission on C's barter purchases.

LAW AND ANALYSIS

Section 61 of the Internal Revenue Code and regulations thereunder provide that, except as otherwise provided by law, gross income means all income from whatever source derived.

Section 1.61–1 of the Income Tax Regulations provides, in part, that gross income includes income realized in any form, whether in money, property, or services.

Section 1.61–2(d)(1) of the regulations provides that, if services are paid for other than in money, the fair market value of the property or services taken in payment must be included in income as compensation.

* * *

Section 451 of the Code provides that the amount of any item of gross income is includible in the gross income for the taxable year in which received by the taxpayer, unless, under the method of accounting used in computing taxable income, such amount is to be properly accounted for as of a different period.

Section 1.451–1(a) of the regulations provides that income is includible in gross income for the taxable year in which it is actually or constructively received by the taxpayer, unless it is includible in a different year in accordance with the taxpayer's method of accounting.

Rev.Rul. 70–331, 1970–1 C.B. 14, concerns "prize points" that are earned by salespersons and are redeemable for merchandise prizes listed in a catalog. That revenue ruling holds that the fair market value of the prize points awarded to a salesperson who uses the cash receipts and disbursements method of accounting is includible in the salesperson's gross income when the prize points are paid or otherwise made available to the salesperson, whichever is earlier. The prize points in Rev.Rul. 70–331 and the credit units in this revenue ruling both represent payment for services in a form other than money.

In this case A, B, and C received income in the form of a valuable right represented by credit units that can be used immediately to purchase goods or services offered by other members of the barter club. There are no restrictions on their use of the credit units because A, B, and C are free to use the credit units to purchase goods or services when the credit units are credited to their accounts.

HOLDINGS

Situation 1. A and B must include $200 in their gross incomes for the taxable year in which the credit units are credited to their accounts. If A and B were merchants who used the accrual method of accounting and bartered goods to one another, $200 would be includible in their gross receipts.

Situation 2. C must include $20,000 in C 's gross income for the taxable year. * * *

If the commission paid to the barter club by a member purchaser was paid to acquire an item for use in connection with the member purchaser's trade or business, the amount of the commission is deductible as a business expense under section 162 of the Code, provided the item received in the barter transaction meets the requirements of that section. If the commission was paid to acquire a capital item, the amount of the commission must be capitalized pursuant to section 263. If the commission was paid to acquire an item for personal purposes, the amount of the commission is not deductible, pursuant to section 262.

Where members of a barter club exchange goods and services directly with one another and no credit units are received, see Rev.Rul. 79–24, 1979–1 C.B. 60.

NOTES

(A) *Checks.* A check, which is a mechanism for making payment, rather than a promise to pay, generally is treated as cash. A number of disputes, however, have arisen when a taxpayer received a check at year end, but did not cash the check until early in the following year. For example, in Lavery v. Commissioner, 158 F.2d 859 (7th Cir.1946), a taxpayer who received a check on December 30 that was not deposited until January 2 had income in the earlier year because the taxpayer could have cashed the check in the year it was received. See also Bright v. United States, 926 F.2d 383 (5th Cir.1991), where the taxpayer had income in 1985 due to a check deposited with a bank, although the bank withheld funds until it had collected from the drawee bank in 1986. The court noted that the taxpayer could have had access to the funds in 1985 by opening an account at the drawee bank. Compare Baxter v. Commissioner, 816 F.2d 493 (9th Cir.1987), where the court held that a check constituted income in 1980 under circumstances where the funds could not have been credited to the cash basis taxpayer by his bank until January 2, 1980. The facts that the monies were earned in 1979, the check was dated December 30, 1979, and the check could have been picked up by the taxpayer on that date if he had driven to its location 40 miles from his home did not make the amount taxable in 1979. The court pointed out that December 30 was a Saturday and the banks were not open until January 2. These cases appear to be based on constructive receipt—that is, the taxpayer could have "actually" received the cash and thus constructively was deemed to have received it.

Other cases take the position that a check is a cash equivalent and whether the taxpayer has the ability to turn it into cash is irrelevant. For example, in Kahler v. Commissioner, 18 T.C. 31 (1952), the court found that a taxpayer who received a check after banking hours on December 31 was required to include it in income in that year because he had received property with a fair market value. In Revenue Ruling 73–486, 1973–2 C.B. 153, the taxpayer received a check made out for the wrong amount. He returned the check and received one for the correct amount in the following taxable year. The IRS held that a check for the wrong amount is income when received unless the recipient either was not entitled to any excess or would prejudice a further claim by cashing the check for less than the amount due.

On the other hand, constructive receipt questions can arise with regard to checks when the taxpayer does not actually obtain possession of the check in the first year. For example, in Revenue Ruling 76–3, 1976–1 C.B. 114, the Post Office attempted to deliver a check sent by certified mail on December 31, 1974, but the taxpayer was not home to sign for the check. Nevertheless, the Service held that the check was taxable in the first year because the fact that the taxpayer could not sign for the check was not a "limitation or restriction on receipt of the payment." Davis v. Commissioner, 37 T.C.M. 42 (1978), holds to the contrary. In Avery v. Commissioner, 292 U.S. 210, 215 (1934), a corporation declared a dividend payable on December 31, and checks were mailed to the stockholders on that day. The cash method taxpayer received his check on January 2. The Court held that the petitioner was taxable in the year in which the check was received, saying: "In the disclosed circumstances the dividends cannot properly be considered as cash or other property unqualifiedly subject to the petitioner's demand on December 31st. * * * The checks did not constitute payments prior to their actual receipt."

(B) *The "Cash Equivalence" Doctrine.* Unlike the constructive receipt doctrine, the "cash equivalence" or "economic benefit" doctrine requires the *actual* receipt of property or of a right to receive property in the future. This doctrine inquires whether the property or right received confers a present—and often marketable—economic benefit. The doctrine originated in deferred compensation cases, where taxpayers had attempted to receive benefits without recognizing income, but has been applied in a variety of other contexts. Compare, for example, Kuehner v. Commissioner, 214 F.2d 437 (1st Cir.1954), which required the taxpayer to recognize income on the deposit of amounts into an escrow account that he controlled on the ground that his property interest in the escrow account was "equivalent to cash," with Reed v. Commissioner, 723 F.2d 138, 146–47 (1st Cir.1983), reversing 45 T.C.M. 398 (1982), where the court of appeals refused to follow a Tax Court decision applying the "economic benefit" doctrine to an escrow agreement. The court stated in the latter case that to do so "would be at odds with the well established principle that a deferred payment arrangement is effective to defer income recognition to a cash basis taxpayer, provided it is part of an arms-length agreement between the purchaser and seller." The court asserted that extension of the economic benefit doctrine to such cases "would significantly erode the distinction between the cash and accrual methods of accounting."

In Revenue Ruling 73–173, 1973–1 C.B. 40, the IRS held that receipt of breeding rights in thoroughbred stallions by a cash basis taxpayer should be included in income at the time of receipt when the breeding rights are "freely transferable," "readily marketable," and "immediately convertible to cash." When the breeding rights are not transferable, and therefore not marketable, the ruling holds that the taxpayer will not realize any income at the time he enters into the contract.

(C) *Notes.* Much of the difficulty with the "economic benefit" or "cash equivalence" doctrine has involved transfers of notes or other transferable contract rights. In Cowden v. Commissioner, 289 F.2d 20 (5th Cir.1961), the Fifth Circuit found the receipt of a contract right to receive amounts in the next two years to be immediately taxable as the receipt of the equivalent of cash. The court enumerated the qualities that would make a contract or note (or other debt instrument) the equivalent of cash:

> A promissory note, negotiable in form, is not necessarily the equivalent of cash. Such an instrument may have been issued by a maker of doubtful solvency or for other reasons such paper might be

denied a ready acceptance in the market place. We think the converse of this principle ought to be applicable. We are convinced that if a promise to pay of a solvent obligor is unconditional and assignable, not subject to set-offs and is of a kind that is frequently transferred to lenders or investors at a discount not substantially greater than the generally prevailing premium for the use of money, such promise is the equivalent of cash and taxable in like manner as cash would have been taxable had it been received by the taxpayer rather than the obligation. The principle that negotiability is not the test of taxability in an equivalent of cash case such as is before us, is consistent with the rule that men may, if they can, so order their affairs as to minimize taxes, and points up the doctrine that substance and not form should control in the application of income tax laws.

On remand, the Tax Court found that the taxpayers "received income in the form of the equivalent of cash in the amount of the then fair market value" of the contracts upon the execution of the agreement. Cowden v. Commissioner, 20 T.C.M. 1134 (1961).

In Williams v. Commissioner, 28 T.C. 1000 (1957), the taxpayer received a note at a time when its maker was without funds; he tried to sell it without success. The court held that the note was not the equivalent of cash, and not income when received. The Commissioner acquiesced in this decision. 1958–1 C.B. 8.

In Schlemmer v. United States, 94 F.2d 77 (2d Cir.1938), the taxpayer, as director of a contracting business, had voted himself $30,000 in salary for 1927. At the end of the year, the company was unable to pay the salary and gave the taxpayer an unendorsed and unsecured note for the amount due. Both the company and the taxpayer were on the cash basis. The company deducted the amount of the note from its income, and the taxpayer paid tax on it, but the note was never paid. The court allowed the taxpayer's later claim for a refund on the ground that the note should not have been included in his income, finding that the note was not payment of the original debt but only evidence thereof and that it could not be treated as cash income. The *Schlemmer* court emphasized that the parties did not intend the note as payment. Should the intent of the parties determine the time for imposition of tax? Would it make a difference if the note were negotiable?

In Newmark v. Commissioner, 311 F.2d 913 (2d Cir.1962), the taxpayer and another man owned all of the stock of a corporation. Their yearly salaries as the president and the treasurer of the company, respectively, were fixed at $15,600. The taxpayer received $2,600 of this in cash and the balance in the form of monthly demand notes. The corporation had funds at all times. The court held that the taxpayer was in control of the situation and was taxable on the face amount of the notes. The *Schlemmer* case was not cited.

(D) *Accounts Receivable.* A law firm on the cash method of accounting performs services for a large solvent bank and notifies the client of the amount due. Is this account receivable taxable to the law firm under the cash equivalency doctrine prior to collection? Accounts receivable, non-negotiable notes or other debt instruments typically are not included in income when received by a cash method taxpayer. Requiring all debt instruments to be included immediately in income would obliterate the fundamental distinction between the cash and accrual methods of accounting.

(E) *The "Economic Benefit" Doctrine.* Although courts often refer separately to the economic benefit doctrine, the distinction between it and the cash equivalence doctrine is unclear. In Pulsifer v. Commissioner, 64 T.C. 245 (1975), the taxpayers were minor children who won the Irish Hospital Sweepstakes. The funds were deposited in a bank account until the children reached age 21 or until their legal representative applied for release of the funds. The court held that they were taxable currently under the economic benefit doctrine on "the economic and financial benefit derived from the absolute right to income in the form of a fund which has been irrevocably set aside." The distinction between the economic benefit doctrine and constructive receipt is also not always obvious. In Anastasio v. Commissioner, 67 T.C. 814 (1977), affirmed in an unpublished opinion, 573 F.2d 1287 (2d Cir.1977), the court taxed a minor who won the New York State lottery in 1970. The winnings were paid in 1970 to his parents as custodians under the state's Uniform Gifts to Minors Act. The prize money and interest earned thereon were paid over to the winner in 1971. The Tax Court held that the minor "received sufficient economic and financial benefits" from both the lottery prize and the interest to be taxable in 1970. The court claimed to rely on the concept of "economic benefit," which it said "significantly differs from the doctrine of constructive receipt." The court acknowledged, however, in something of an understatement, that "the decided cases have not always been models of clarity in respect of the distinction."

4. PAYMENTS

Section 1.461–1(a)(1) of the regulations provides that under the cash method, allowable deductions are taken into account for the taxable year in which paid. As the following notes and cases illustrate, controversies sometimes arise as to what constitutes "payment."

Revenue Ruling 80–335

Internal Revenue Service, 1980. 1980–2 C.B. 170.

ISSUE

What is the date of payment when a taxpayer uses a "pay by phone" account maintained at a financial institution to pay creditors?

FACTS

A, who uses the cash receipts and disbursements method of accounting, maintains a "pay by phone" account with *M,* a financial institution, whereby *A,* by telephoning *M,* can authorize *M* to make payments to *A* 's creditors as *A* 's agent. * * * *M* pays the bills by charging *A* 's account and either mailing checks to the creditors, transferring funds to the creditors' accounts if the creditors maintain them with *M*, or actually delivering checks to the creditors. * * *

LAW AND ANALYSIS

Section 461 of the Internal Revenue Code provides the general rule that the amount of any allowable deduction shall be taken for the taxable year that is the proper year under the method of accounting used by the taxpayer in computing taxable income.

Section 1.461–1(a)(1) of the Income Tax Regulations provides that under the cash receipts and disbursements method of accounting, amounts representing allowable deductions are taken into account for the taxable year in which paid.

If a taxpayer, who uses the cash receipts and disbursements method of accounting, mails checks to creditors, the taxpayer is entitled to allowable deductions therefor on the day the checks are placed in the mail, provided the checks are subsequently paid by the bank. * * *

If the taxpayer, who uses the cash receipts and disbursements method of accounting, authorizes payment by the taxpayer's agent, payment occurs on the date the agent, on behalf of the taxpayer, delivers a check to the payee. * * * In the present case *M* is acting as the agent of *A*, and therefore, if *M* mails checks to *A* 's creditors, transfers funds to creditors' accounts, or actually delivers checks to creditors, the payments are made on the date of the mailings, transfers, or deliveries, as the case may be. * * *

HOLDING

The date reported by *M* on the monthly statement indicating when payment was made is the date of payment by *A* for purposes of determining when an allowable deduction may be taken.

Revenue Ruling 78–38

Internal Revenue Service, 1978. 1978–1 C.B. 67.

The Internal Revenue Service has given further consideration to Rev. Rul. 71–216, 1971–1 C.B. 96, which holds that a taxpayer who used a bank credit card to contribute to a qualified charity may not deduct any part of the contribution under section 170(a)(1) of the Internal Revenue Code of 1954 until the year the cardholder makes payment of the amount of the contribution to the bank.

Rev.Rul. 71–216 cites [the predecessor to current section 1.170A–1(a)(1) of the regulations] which provides that a deduction is only allowable to an individual under section 170 of the Code for charitable contributions "actually paid" during the taxable year, regardless of when pledged and regardless of the method of accounting employed by the taxpayer in keeping books and records.

In Rev.Rul. 71–216 the assumption was made that a charitable contribution made by a taxpayer by use of a credit card was tantamount to a charitable contribution made by the issuance and delivery of a debenture bond or a promissory note by the obligor to a charitable organization * * *.

Upon further study, it has been concluded that there are major distinctions between contributions made by the use of credit cards and contributions made by debenture bonds and promissory notes. In Rev.Rul. 68–174, the charitable organization that received the debenture bond or promissory note from the obligor received no more than a mere promise to pay. Conversely, the credit card holder in Rev.Rul. 71–216, by using the credit card to make the contribution, became immediately indebted to a third party (the bank) in such a way that the cardholder could not thereafter prevent the charitable organization from receiving payment. The credit card draft received by the charitable organization from the credit card holder in Rev.Rul. 71–216 was immediately creditable by the bank to the organization's account as if it were a check.

Since the cardholder's use of the credit card creates the cardholder's own debt to a third party, the use of a bank credit card to make a charitable contribution is equivalent to the use of borrowed funds to make a contribution.

The general rule is that when a deductible payment is made with borrowed money, the deduction is not postponed until the year in which the borrowed money is repaid. Such expenses must be deducted in the year they are paid and not when the loans are repaid. * * *

Accordingly, the taxpayer discussed in Rev.Rul. 71–216, who made a contribution to a qualified charity by a charge to the taxpayer's bank credit card, is entitled to a charitable contribution deduction under section 170(a) of the Code in the year the charge was made and the deduction may not be postponed until the taxpayer pays the indebtedness resulting from such charge.

NOTES

(A) *Payments Made by Borrowing from Third Parties.* Checks, pay-by-phone devices, and electronic fund transfers are means for making payment and, as Revenue Ruling 80–335 indicates, are treated as such for tax purposes. Typically, accounts and notes payable are means for deferring payment, and a cash method taxpayer will not be allowed deductions until such items are paid. Difficulties may arise, however, because a deduction is normally allowed when an item is paid with funds borrowed from a third party. Revenue Ruling 78–38, while reflecting this general rule, allows a deduction for charitable contributions made by charge account; the ruling distinguishes contributions made by a debenture or promissory note, which it describes as a "mere promise to pay." See also Rev.Rul. 78–39, 1978–1 C.B. 73, where the IRS held that a cash basis taxpayer had made a "payment," deductible under § 213, upon charging medical expenses on a bank credit card.

This distinction for borrowing from third parties led the Service to the conclusion that payments of deductible expenses were deductible when charged to a bank credit card but not deductible until paid if charged to a credit card issued by the vendor. Thus, for example, whether gasoline purchased by a traveling salesman was deductible turned on which credit card she used. Despite the "tax logic" of the IRS position, it was incomprehensible—or even viewed as a bad joke—by normal people and ultimately was abandoned to allow deduction when the charge appears on the taxpayer's credit card statement. A small triumph for common sense.

(B) *"Paying" By Delivering a Note.* The Supreme Court has held that the transfer of the taxpayer's own note does not constitute payment. Helvering v. Price, 309 U.S. 409 (1940) (a secured note satisfying taxpayer's guaranty obligation did not give rise to a deduction because it was not the equivalent of cash).

In Rev.Rul. 70–647, 1970–2 C.B. 38, the taxpayer gave his note in payment of a loan and accrued interest thereon, as evidence of additional new indebtedness. The lender treated the outstanding interest as having been paid by the note and informed the taxpayer that the interest had been "paid by new loan." The ruling held, however, that the taxpayer was not entitled to a deduction, stating: "[t]he 'payment' required as a basis for the deduction by a cash basis taxpayer is the payment of cash or its equivalent, and the giving of the taxpayer's own note is not equivalent of cash entitling the taxpayer to the deduction." Would it matter if the note were negotiable and readily marketable?

In Anthony P. Miller, Inc. v. Commissioner, 164 F.2d 268 (3d Cir. 1947), the court treated a solvent corporation's delivery of negotiable promissory notes, payable on demand, as payment under the predecessor of § 267 of the Code. The court rejected the Commissioner's argument that the amount was not "paid" until the corporation discharged its obligation by payment. In Revenue Ruling 55–608, 1955–2 C.B. 546, the Service indicated that it would accept the result of the *Anthony P. Miller* case.

In Don E. Williams Co. v. Commissioner, 429 U.S. 569 (1977), the Supreme Court held that a corporation's delivery of promissory notes to the trustees of its qualified profit-sharing pension trust did not constitute the "payment" required by § 404(a). The Court stated: "[R]egardless of the method of accounting, all taxpayers must pay out cash or its equivalent by the end of the [statutory] grace period in order to qualify for the § 404(a) deduction."

In Vander Poel, Francis & Co., Inc. v. Commissioner, 8 T.C. 407 (1947), a cash basis corporation deducted salaries in the year in which they were credited to officers' accounts on its books. The corporation had sufficient cash to pay the salaries, and the officers were authorized to write checks for the salaries. The Tax Court refused to apply a doctrine of "constructive payment" to permit deduction by the corporation prior to actual payment even though the salaries were constructively received by the officers. See Reg. § 1.446–1(c)(1), which provides that expenditures are deductible by cash basis taxpayers for the year in which "actually made."

(C) *Payment by Borrowing from the Payee.* In Cleaver v. Commissioner, 158 F.2d 342 (7th Cir.1946), the taxpayer borrowed money by giving a note to a bank. He received from the bank the face amount of the note, less a discount. The court held that he was not entitled to an interest deduction until he paid the note. But compare Burgess v. Commissioner, 8 T.C. 47 (1947), where the taxpayer borrowed money to pay interest on another note and was entitled to a deduction for interest paid.

The Fifth Circuit rekindled doubt about the validity of *Burgess* in Battelstein v. Internal Revenue Service, 631 F.2d 1182 (5th Cir.1980) (en banc), which disallowed interest deductions by a cash basis taxpayer who borrowed the interest from the original lender. The taxpayer had borrowed additional funds on a construction loan, deposited the funds in a checking account, and then written a check for the interest due. The majority cited *Don E. Williams Co.,* supra. The court found no evidence of the commingling of the borrowed funds with other assets that had occurred in *Burgess.* The money did not actually pass into the taxpayer's hands and become mixed with other funds. The court concluded: "[i]f the second loan was for the purpose of financing the interest due on the first loan, then the taxpayer's interest obligation on the first loan has not been paid * * * it has merely been postponed," adding that "the taxpayer's reliance on * * * *Burgess* is * * * misplaced, even assuming that *Burgess* is good law." Ten judges dissented to this *en banc* opinion.

The Tax Court has interpreted *Battelstein* to mean that the taxpayer must have unrestricted control over the borrowed funds before the funds are used to pay the interest to the lender. Noble v. Commissioner, 79 T.C. 751 (1982). In *Noble,* the court rejected the Commissioner's argument that the taxpayer could never have unrestricted control over the funds because of a state law right of set-off.

What if the debtor goes to a second bank and borrows funds to pay the interest? See Crown v. Commissioner, 77 T.C. 582 (1981) (permitting a deduction).

Note that the test for whether a note is income to a cash basis taxpayer is different from the test for whether it constitutes payment. This is illustrated by Revenue Ruling 76–135, 1976–1 C.B. 114, in which a client paid a lawyer with a negotiable promissory note. The ruling held that the cash basis lawyer, who discounted the note at a bank, had income on the discounted value of the note when received. The cash basis client had a deduction only when he made actual payments to the bank.

(D) *Paying and Dying.* A person drew and delivered checks for charitable contributions on December 30 and 31. They were paid by his bank on January 4 and 11, respectively. The drawer of the checks died on January 8. The Tax Court held that both items were deductible as charitable contributions paid in December. Estate of Spiegel v. Commissioner, 12 T.C. 524 (1949), acq. 1949–2 C.B. 3.

Compare Estate of Hubbell v. Commissioner, 10 T.C. 1207 (1948), where the taxpayer mailed a check for state taxes on July 1. The check was received in due course and the bank had sufficient funds. The person died on July 20. The check was not presented to his bank until after that date, and the bank refused payment because of his death. His executor thereupon issued a new check for the taxes. The executor endeavored to deduct the taxes for the period prior to the decedent's death, but the Tax Court held that the state tax had not been "paid" before the decedent's death.

5. EXPENSES PAID IN ADVANCE–PREPAYMENTS

Commissioner v. Boylston Market Ass'n

United States Circuit Court of Appeals, First Circuit, 1942. 131 F.2d 966.

MAHONEY, CIRCUIT JUDGE:

* * *

The taxpayer in the course of its business, which is the management of real estate owned by it, purchased from time to time fire and other insurance policies covering periods of three or more years. It keeps its books and makes its returns on a cash receipts and disbursements basis. The taxpayer has since 1915 deducted each year as insurance expenses the amount of insurance premiums applicable to carrying insurance for that year regardless of the year in which the premium was actually paid. This method was required by the Treasury Department prior to 1938 * * *.

We are asked to determine whether a taxpayer who keeps his books and files his returns on a cash basis is limited to the deduction of the insurance premiums actually paid in any year or whether he should deduct for each tax year the pro rata portion of the prepaid insurance applicable to that year. * * *

The arguments * * * in favor of treating prepaid insurance as an ordinary and necessary business expense are persuasive. We are, nevertheless, unable to find a real basis for distinguishing between prepayment of rentals, Baton Coal Co. v. Commissioner, 3 Cir., 1931, 51 F.2d 469, certiorari denied 284 U.S. 674; * * * bonuses for the acquisition of leases, Home Trust Co. v. Commissioner, 8 Cir., 1933, 65 F.2d 532; * * * bonuses for the cancellation of leases, Steele–Wedeles Co. v. Commissioner, 30 B.T.A. 841, 842; * * * commissions for negotiating leases, see Bonwit Teller & Co. v. Commissioner, 2 Cir., 1931, 53 F.2d 381, 384, 82 A.L.R. 325, and prepaid insurance. Some distinctions may be drawn in the cases cited on the basis of the facts contained therein, but we are of the opinion that there is no justification for treating them differently insofar as deductions are concerned. All of the cases cited are readily distinguishable from such a clear-cut case as a permanent improvement to a building. This latter is clearly a capital expenditure. * * * In such a case there is the creation of a capital asset which has a life extending beyond the taxable year and which depreciates over a period of years. The taxpayer regardless of his method of accounting can only take deductions for depreciation over the life of the asset.

Advance rentals, payments of bonuses for acquisition and cancellation of leases, and commissions for negotiating leases are all matters which the taxpayer amortizes over the life of the lease. Whether we consider these payments to be the cost of the exhaustible asset, as in the case of advance rentals, or the cost of acquiring the asset, as in the case of bonuses, the payments are prorated primarily because the life of the asset extends beyond the taxable year. To permit the taxpayer to take a full deduction in the year of payment would distort his income. Prepaid insurance presents the same problem and should be solved in the same way. Prepaid insurance for a period of three years may be easily allocated. It is protection for the entire period and the taxpayer may, if he desires, at any time surrender the insurance policy. It thus is clearly an asset having a longer life than a single taxable year. The line to be drawn between capital expenditures and ordinary and necessary business expenses is not always an easy one, but we are satisfied that in treating prepaid insurance as a capital expense we are obtaining some degree of consistency in these matters. * * *

The decision of Board of Tax Appeals is affirmed.

NOTES

(A) *Capital Expenditures.* A cash basis taxpayer may not be able to deduct all payments in the year made. As *Boylston* indicates, a cash basis taxpayer clearly cannot deduct capital expenditures, such as a building or a substantial improvement to a building, merely because she pays cash for it. Reg. § 1.461–1(a) in this regard does not distinguish between cash and accrual method taxpayers. If an expenditure results in the creation of an asset having a useful life which extends substantially beyond the close of the taxable year, such an expenditure may not be deductible, or may be deductible only in part, for the taxable year in which made. See also Chapter 3, at page 320 supra.

(B) *Interest.* Prepayments of deductible items by cash method taxpayers have caused problems for the income tax for a long time. Prepayments of interest, for example, were a common method of tax deferral and in the 1970's and 1980's became an important component of tax shelter investments in real estate, farming, motion pictures, and the like. Section 461(g) now requires a cash method taxpayer to allocate and deduct prepaid interest over the loan period, in effect, putting cash method taxpayers on an accrual method for interest deductions. This rule applies to all prepayments of interest, whether on a business or investment debt or on a home mortgage. An exception is provided for "points" on the taxpayer's home mortgage in certain cases.

(C) *Farming Expenses.* Many disputes over prepayments involved farming expenses. Because farming had become a tax shelter vehicle, in 1986 Congress prevented large farming syndicates from using the cash method of accounting. A tortuous flipping among Code sections containing cross references that are almost impossible to follow reveals that § 448 puts farming syndicates on the accrual method. See also § 263A, which requires farming syndicates to capitalize farm supplies as part of the inventory costs of plants or animals raised on the farm.

(D) *The Zaninovich Rule.* The treatment of prepaid expenses other than interest and farming costs remain somewhat unclear. In Zaninovich v. Commissioner, 616 F.2d 429 (9th Cir.1980), the court adopted a "one-year" guidepost to determine whether an expenditure results in the creation of an asset having a useful life extending substantially beyond the end of the taxable year. Under this formulation, prepayments generally may be deducted if they do not provide benefits that extend beyond one year. It is not clear how widely this approach will be followed. *Zaninovich* itself approved the deduction of a lease payment in December for the following year. The Tax Court has refused to follow *Zaninovich*, finding that there is no generally accepted one-year rule as adopted by that case. The court maintains that there is no current deduction for expenses with a useful life of less than 12 months that provide benefits beyond the current taxable year. USFreightways v. Commissioner, 113 T.C. 329 (1999). The Tax Court also takes the position that the one-year exception does not apply to an accrual basis taxpayer in any event. The Seventh Circuit rejected both positions. It concluded that an accrual basis taxpayer can expense short-term items, including those whose benefits extend into the next taxable year. In language remarkably similar to *PNC Bancorp*, supra at page 305, the court permitted deduction of "ordinary" one-year items that recur "with clockwork regularity." 270 F.3d 1137 (7th Cir. 2001).

Many of these cases have arisen from the Commissioner's efforts to disallow deductions for prepaid expenses under the § 446(b) authority to challenge accounting methods that do not clearly reflect income. *Zaninovich* relied heavily on cases concerning the distinction between capital and noncapital expenditures in fashioning its one-year guideline for prepaid rents. In 2002, when the IRS issued its advanced notice of proposed rulemaking, supra at page 312, it proposed to adopt a one-year guideline for many expenses. An expenditure could be deducted so long as it did not create benefits that extended beyond the earlier of 12 months after the first date on which the taxpayer realizes benefits or the end of the taxable year following the taxable year in which the expenditure is incurred.

(E) *Tax Shelters.* Because many tax shelters depended on the deductibility of year-end payments for expenses allocable to the following years, Congress initially put tax shelters on the accrual method with regard to prepayments, but ultimately decided to attack tax shelters directly by requiring them to use the accrual method of accounting. § 448.

(F) *The Economics of Prepayments.* A taxpayer who arranges to prepay for goods or services to be delivered in the future may be regarded as having engaged in two transactions: (1) a purchase of goods or services and (2) a loan to the transferee of the prepaid funds until the goods are delivered or the services performed. The transferee has the use of the funds during the interval between payment and economic performance. The delay of the payor's deduction (as in § 461(i)) until economic performance has an effect similar to the general rule that loans are neither includible in the income of the recipient nor deductible by the payor. In the prepayment case, however, the interest on the "loan" typically is reflected in the price of the goods and services and is not separately stated. Since the payor cannot earn the interest income on the funds, she will be unwilling to prepay the amount that normally would be required at the time of economic performance. By the same token, since the seller has the use of the money in the interval (thereby earning interest income or avoiding interest charges on alternative borrowing), he should be willing to reduce the amount that he otherwise would ask at the later date. The payor thus obtains the benefit of tax-free interest income and the recipient forgoes the deduction of an interest expense in return for the earlier use of the funds. When both parties are subject to the same marginal tax rate, the Treasury gains as much from the interest deduction forgone by the seller as it loses from the interest income excluded by the buyer. The Treasury loses revenue, however, when the prepayment is made by a taxpayer in a higher bracket to a taxpayer in a lower bracket or to a tax-exempt entity. The benefits of shifting the taxation of the interest income to the lower-rate taxpayer may be reduced or eliminated by delaying the payor's deduction until economic performance occurs.

For example, assume A would normally pay B $110 for deductible services, but pays only $100 when the services are to be rendered one year in the future. Separating the transaction into a sale of services and a loan suggests that A has loaned B $100 for one year, at the end of which B will repay A $100 and $10 interest, which A will retransfer to B as payment for the services. In the year the services are performed, A should be allowed a deduction for $110 and charged with $10 interest income. The net result is the same as allowing a deduction of $100 in the year the services are performed. If B were permitted a deduction for the interest, the effect is to shift the investment income to A.

If, however, the prepayment was for two years—and the $100 charge would be $121 if paid at the later date—the results will not be exactly equivalent. Separating the transaction into its two components, a loan and a sale of services, would produce interest income to A of $10 in the first year and $11 in the second year and a deduction of $121 in the second year. Permitting A to deduct $100 in the second year is not the same.

Where payments are deferred until after economic performance, the transaction can be divided into a sale and a loan in the opposite direction—from the seller to the buyer. The tax on interest income then may be shifted from a higher-rate seller to a lower-rate (or tax-exempt) buyer.

Similar opportunities for shifting interest income may involve prepayments of nondeductible amounts. Consider, for example, a tax-exempt university that charges $11,000 a year for tuition but will accept $10,000 if paid one year in advance. A high-bracket taxpayer, in effect, can avoid the tax on the interest income by prepaying the expense.*

A comprehensive approach to the economics of prepayments (and deferred payments) therefore would require recharacterizing such transactions to reflect the existence of a loan. Interest then would be imputed on the loan part of the transaction. The below-market and interest-free loan provisions of § 7872 (described at page 748 infra) seem to provide the IRS with authority to adopt such an approach where the potential for tax avoidance is substantial, but only at the cost of significant additional complexity. For a comprehensive analysis of prepayments and related transactions, see Daniel I. Halperin, "Interest in Disguise: Taxing the Time Value of Money," 95 Yale L.J. 506 (1986).

(G) *The Special Problem of Year–End Payments.* An expense that is paid on December 31 of Year 1 is deductible on the Year 1 tax return of a cash method, calendar year taxpayer. If the expense is paid the next day, it is not deductible until the cash basis taxpayer files its tax return for Year 2. Thus, a one-day delay in payment can mean a one-year delay in deduction. Cash basis taxpayers therefore will attempt to pay their deductible expenses on December 31 and receive income on January 1, all other things being equal.

B. ACCRUAL METHOD

We now turn to the accrual method, which is the method of accounting used by most corporate taxpayers and some individuals, partnerships, and trusts. The accrual method generally requires that items of income be taxed in the year in which they are earned, regardless of when they are received, and that items of expense be deducted in the year in which they are incurred, regardless of when they are paid. In studying the materials that follow, consider the proper role of the accrual method of accounting in

---

* Congress has approved income shifting through prepaid tuition plans in some circumstances. See § 529.

the tax system. There are two basic positions. One view is that accrual accounting is necessary to determine net income properly. That is because generally accepted techniques of accrual accounting are thought to reflect taxpayers' reasonable expectations of revenues and expenses and thereby to match income with any related expenses. This view regards the cash method of accounting simply as a concession to the unsophisticated.

A second view is that the amount by which a taxpayer's current receipts exceed his current expenses properly reflects his current ability to pay taxes, without regard to whether this excess reflects income earned in the current year or in some other year. Given this view, accrual accounting for tax purposes may be regarded as merely a convenience for taxpayers who keep their business records on an accrual basis.

One's acceptance of one or the other of these radically different views towards accrual accounting for tax purposes significantly influences one's perception of the cases and statutory provisions in this Section. Most of the problems of applying the accrual method arise in three contexts: (1) where uncertainty exists as to whether an amount will be received or paid, (2) where an amount is received before it has been earned, and (3) where an obligation to pay an amount is fixed long before the time when payment will be made.

1.   THE "ALL EVENTS" TEST

The "all events" test is the general test for determining whether items of income and deduction have accrued for tax purposes. A statutory definition can be found in § 461(h)(4), which provides that the "all events" test is met with respect to a deductible item if "all events have occurred which determine the fact of liability and the amount of such liability can be determined with reasonable accuracy." The statute codified longstanding regulatory provisions defining the test for deductions, § 1.461–1(a)(2), and parallels complementary regulatory language requiring items to be included in income under the accrual method "when all the events have occurred which fix the right to receive such income and the amount thereof can be determined with reasonable accuracy." Reg. § 1.451–1(a).

The "all events" test originated in United States v. Anderson, 269 U.S. 422 (1926), where the munitions tax on the profits from a munitions manufacturer's 1916 sales became due and was paid in 1917. The taxpayer deducted this amount from its 1917 income (preferring that year of high tax rates). The Supreme Court held that the taxpayer's books were kept on the accrual basis and that the tax was deductible in 1916, not 1917. The Court said:

> In a technical legal sense it may be argued that a tax does not accrue until it has been assessed and becomes due; but it is also true that in advance of the assessment of a tax, all the events may occur which fix the amount of the tax and determine the liability of the taxpayer to pay it. In this respect, for purposes of accounting and of ascertaining true income for a given accounting period, the munitions tax here in question did not stand on any different footing than other accrued expenses appearing on appellee's books. In the economic and

bookkeeping sense with which the statute and Treasury decision were concerned, the taxes had accrued.

In Spring City Foundry Co. v. Commissioner, 292 U.S. 182 (1934), the Supreme Court applied the "all events test" to require inclusion of items in income. In that case, the taxpayer shipped goods during the year 1920, but it did not receive payment. Before the close of the year, a bankruptcy petition was filed against the purchaser. Several years later, the taxpayer received a little more than a quarter of the sales price from the trustee in bankruptcy of the purchaser. The Court held that the entire sales price was accrued income in 1920, stating: "[I]t is the *right* to receive and not the actual receipt that determines the inclusion of the amount in gross income. When the right to receive an amount becomes fixed, the right accrues." The law applicable to that year contained no provision (as there is now in § 166(a)(2)) for the deduction of a partially worthless debt. As the claim still had some value, no adjustment could be made with respect to it during 1920.

The requirement that accrual occur when the amount of income or liability can be determined with "reasonable accuracy" naturally raises issues of what kinds and degrees of uncertainty will preclude accrual. The "all events" test is less precise in application than its language might suggest. Moreover, to divorce the time of accrual from the time of payment raises questions as to the effect of income received prior to the normal time for accrual and of payments made long after the "all events" test has been satisfied. We consider each of these issues in turn.

2.   ACCRUAL OF INCOME

Hallmark Cards, Inc. v. Commissioner

United States Tax Court, 1988. 90 T.C. 26.

KORNER, JUDGE:

* * * Petitioner's primary business is the manufacture and sale of greeting cards, giftwrap, ribbon, stationery, and related products. * * * [P]etitioner embarked on a policy of shipping seasonal merchandise to customers in advance of the period during which the merchandise would normally be displayed and sold. As to Christmas merchandise, customers were generally willing to accept this merchandise in advance. * * * [P]etitioner's customers were less disposed to receiving Valentine shipments in advance. St. Valentine's Day falls shortly after Christmas, the busiest retail season of the year. Merchants were unwilling to accept large shipments of Valentine merchandise while their stores were filled with Christmas merchandise. Additionally, many calendar year customers were concerned over the financial impact of inclusion of large amounts of Valentine merchandise in their yearend inventories. There also was an unwillingness to bear the cost of personal property tax on Valentine merchandise included in yearend inventory. * * *

In 1958, petitioner concluded that it could * * * satisfy customer concerns over its early shipment (other than physical storage) by changing its terms of sale as regards Valentine merchandise. Shipments of Valentine merchandise would be made during the later part of the year preceding Valentine's Day; however, the terms of sale were that title to the goods and risk of loss would not pass to the buyer until January 1 of the following year. Although customers were in physical possession of the merchandise at yearend, they did not own it and therefore were not required to include it in yearend inventory or pay personal property taxes on it. The terms of sale of all other merchandise remained the same (i.e., title and risk of loss passed at time of shipment). Petitioner revised its order forms, sales invoices, and shipping documents to reflect this change in sales terms for Valentine merchandise, and made substantial efforts to apprise its customers of the new policy. Customer reaction to the revised sales terms was generally favorable. * * *

Respondent * * * determined deficiencies in tax [for the years 1975, 1976, 1977 and 1978] attributable to petitioner's allegedly improper deferral of income from Valentine sales until the calendar year following the year of shipment. The notices determined that this practice was inconsistent with petitioner's method of accounting for sales of other merchandise and resulted in a distortion of income. * * *

Petitioner utilizes the calendar year as its accounting period and has employed an accrual method of accounting for both tax and financial accounting purposes. When an accrual method of accounting is utilized, an item of income is included in the taxpayer's gross income for the accounting period during which all the events have occurred which fix the taxpayer's right to receive the item of income, and the amount thereof can be determined with reasonable accuracy. Petitioner contends that, as regards Valentine merchandise shipped prior to yearend, this "all events" test is not satisfied until January 1 of the following year when title to the merchandise and risk of loss pass to the customer. Respondent argues that the all events test is satisfied, at the very latest, at midnight on December 31 of the year in which the merchandise was shipped. We agree with petitioner.

At what point in time a sale takes place is to be determined from the totality of the circumstances. While no single factor is controlling, passage of title is perhaps the most significant factor to be considered, although the transfer of possession is also significant. The objective is to determine at what point in time the seller acquired an unconditional right to receive payment under the contract. Lucas v. North Texas Lumber, 281 U.S. 11, 13 (1930).

Based on the record before us, it is indisputable that petitioner's rights under the sales contracts for Valentine merchandise do not mature until January 1 of the new year. Not until this point in time did petitioner relinquish the benefits and burdens of ownership of the merchandise in exchange for a right to receive payment. Since petitioner had no right to income prior to January 1, the first prong of the all-events test is not met until that date.[1] We cannot agree with respondent's characterization of the

---

1. Since no right to receive income exists in the year of shipment, the second prong of the all-events test—whether the value of that right can be reasonably estimated—is never reached.

passage of title and risk of loss on January 1 as a mere "ministerial act" or "formality." Far from being a ministerial act, the passage of title and risk of loss to the buyer constitutes the very heart of the transaction and is the sine qua non to petitioner's right to receive payment. Until that moment in time when title passes, the potential buyer has mere possession of the merchandise and nothing more. Should it be destroyed while in his possession, the loss is suffered by petitioner. Should he decide that he does not wish to proceed with the transaction, he may return the merchandise to petitioner without penalty. The fact that customers rarely exercised this right is of no consequence; it is existence of the right which controls.

Respondent's heavy reliance on United States v. Hughes Properties, Inc., 476 U.S. 593 (1986), is in our view misplaced. That case concerned the deductibility by the taxpayer, a casino operator, of properly accrued progressive slot machine jackpots which remained unpaid at yearend. The Court allowed the deductions, holding that at the end of its taxable year, the taxpayer's liability for the accrued amounts was definite and fixed pursuant to Nevada law. The Court held that the remote possibility that the casino would cease operations—or the even more remote possibility that people would cease to gamble—went to whether the liability would eventually be paid—not to whether it had been incurred.

Respondent argues that since the Court in *Hughes* ignored these highly remote contingencies in allowing expense accruals, we should accrue Valentine income as of midnight, December 31, of the year of shipment, since at that point of time, there is no doubt that the sale will occur in the next instant.

Respondent misinterprets *Hughes*. In that case, all the events necessary to make the taxpayer's liability for the accrued amounts fixed and definite had occurred by the end of its tax year. The remote contingencies in *Hughes* were found to go to whether the liability would be paid; as to the liability itself, there were no contingencies. Here, in contrast, petitioner does not possess any fixed and definite rights to payment at yearend. The fact that at the stroke of midnight petitioner knows with absolute certainty, that in the next instant, these rights will arise, cannot compensate for the fact that as of the close of the old year, they do not exist. The all-events test is based on the existence or nonexistence of legal rights or obligations at the close of a particular accounting period, not on the probability—or even absolute certainty—that such right or obligation will arise at some point in the future. We thus hold that as to merchandise sold by petitioner pursuant to its deferred Valentine program, the all-events test is not satisfied until January 1, and that income from those sales is not accruable by petitioner until that date.[2]

* * *

2. The business reasons for petitioner's adoption of the Jan. 1 passage of title and risk of loss are sound and have not been disputed. Thus, this is not a case where a taxpayer has deliberately manipulated the terms of sale so as to prevent income from accruing that it would otherwise become entitled to prior to the end of its taxable year. We express no opinion as to the tax consequences of such a situation.

Respondent's theory that petitioner employs a hybrid accounting method is premised on a basic misunderstanding of section 1.446–1(c)(ii), Income Tax Regs. Respondent alleges that the "shipment method" is petitioner's predominant method of accounting which it uses for the sale of all merchandise with the exception of Valentine merchandise, income from the sale of which is accounted for using the "title method." However, the regulation reference to accounting for the sale of an item when shipped, delivered, accepted, or when title to the merchandise passes, does not refer to different accounting methods, but is merely illustrative of the different points in time at which an accrual method taxpayer may accrue an item of income. The touchstone for determining when an item may be accrued is the all-events test. For any given manufacturer, this test may be satisfied when merchandise is shipped, accepted, delivered, or at some other point in time, depending upon the particular circumstances. Petitioner's change in the point of time at which it recognizes income from Valentine sales was in recognition of a change in the contractual terms under which it sold Valentine merchandise. A change in treatment of an item of income resulting from a change in underlying facts does not constitute a change in method of accounting. Sec. 1.446–1(e)(2)(ii)(b), Income Tax Regs. To hold otherwise would effectively give respondent the right to dictate to petitioner the terms under which it may sell its merchandise, clearly "an odious propagation of the tentacles of the government anemone." We therefore conclude that petitioner has consistently used an accrual method of accounting for all sales both before and after its 1958 adoption of revised terms of sale as to Valentine merchandise. Since petitioner has consistently utilized a permissible method of accounting which is deemed to clearly reflect income, respondent abused his discretion in requiring petitioner to adopt a different method of accounting for Valentine sales.

NOTES

(A) *Time of Accrual of Sales of Goods.* When does income accrue from a sale of goods? When the order is given or accepted, when the goods are billed or shipped, or at some other time? In Pacific Grape Products Co. v. Commissioner, 219 F.2d 862 (9th Cir.1955), the taxpayer contracted to sell goods and billed them to its customers, in accordance with established practice, before receiving shipping instructions. No specific goods were set aside to meet specific orders. When shipping instructions were received, the taxpayer shipped goods from its general warehouse. The court held that the income accrued on billing, in accordance with the taxpayer's longstanding practice, although no title passed until the goods were set aside and shipped. It also allowed the deduction of an accrual for shipping expenses and brokerage fees. See § 1.446–1(c)(1)(ii)(C) of the Regulations, which provides:

> The method used by the taxpayer in determining when income is to be accounted for will generally be acceptable if it accords with generally accepted accounting principles, is consistently used by the taxpayer from year to year, and is consistent with the Income Tax Regulations. For example, a taxpayer engaged in a manufacturing business may account for sales of the taxpayer's product when the

goods are shipped, when the product is delivered or accepted, or when title to the goods passes to the customers, whether or not billed, depending upon the method regularly employed in keeping the taxpayer's books.

This requirement of consistency with the seller's standard method of accounting provides greater flexibility than is suggested by the requirement of the "all events" test that income be reported when the seller's "right to payment" becomes "fixed."

Section 458, added to the Code in 1978, permits accrual method taxpayers to exclude from income amounts attributable to sales price adjustments for records, magazines and paperback books returned within a specified period ending shortly after the close of the taxable year.

(B) *Relation to Expenses.* Many taxpayers, faced with the refusal of courts to permit deferral of income, have attempted to offset the immediate inclusion of income by immediately deducting the costs that would be incurred in earning the income. The courts have been more inclined to defer the accrual of deductions than to defer the accrual of income. But see ABKCO Industries, Inc. v. Commissioner, 482 F.2d 150 (3d Cir.1973), affirming 56 T.C. 1083(1971) (amount of royalty payments owed to Chubby Checker—the inventor of "The Twist"—sufficiently contingent to require postponement of accrual).

(C) *Reserve Accounts.* Commissioner v. Hansen, 360 U.S. 446 (1959), involved automobile dealers who kept their books on the accrual basis. They followed a common practice of selling cars in exchange for a trade-in, a downpayment, and a negotiable instrument. Such transactions were secured by conditional sale or chattel mortgage agreements. The dealer then discounted the instrument with a finance company. The finance company paid the dealer most of the purchase price immediately, but retained a portion of the amount in a "dealer's reserve account" in the name of the particular dealer. The amount in this "dealer's reserve account" eventually was paid to the dealer when the purchasers had made all the payments.

The dealers included in their income the cash received from the finance companies, "but they did not accrue on their books or include in their returns the percentage of the price that was retained by the finance companies and credited to their reserve accounts." The Supreme Court held that the amounts credited to the reserve accounts were accrued income to the dealers at the time of the credit and were taxable at that time. *Hansen* was followed in Resale Mobile Homes, Inc. v. Commissioner, 91 T.C. 1085 (1988).

(D) *Substantial Uncertainty About Collectibility.* There is a difference between a contingent receivable, which an accrual basis taxpayer does not include because it is unclear whether she has earned it, and an amount that has been earned, which must be accrued unless the financial condition of the debtor creates a substantial likelihood that the debt will not be paid. Mere doubt about collectibility is not sufficient to prevent accrual. Similarly, legal unenforceability of the debt does not prevent accrual. See, e.g., Flamingo Resort, Inc. v. United States, 664 F.2d 1387 (9th Cir.1982) and

Rev.Rul. 83–106, 1983–2 C.B. 77 (casino required to accrue gambling winnings from patrons using credit when gambling occurred despite unenforceability of markers representing the debt because debts typically are paid).

The accrual of income is not required when a fixed right to receive it arises if there is not a reasonable expectancy that the claim will be paid. In Georgia School–Book Depository, Inc. v. Commissioner, 1 T.C. 463 (1943), the taxpayer was a broker for the purchase of school books for the state of Georgia. For a commission of 8 percent of the sales price, the taxpayer arranged for books to be shipped, stored them until needed, and distributed them to the schools. The commissions were payable only from the "Free Textbook Fund," a trust fund comprised solely of revenues from the state's excise tax on beer. During the years in question, the amount in the fund was inadequate to pay the liabilities. The taxpayer argued that its commissions should not be accrued until payment. The court rejected the taxpayer's argument on the ground that, under the accrual method, the right to receive rather than actual receipt determines the time of accrual. Since the taxpayer had earned its commissions, it had to accrue the income unless it could show "a reasonable expectancy that the claim will never be paid." This exception to accrual was limited to situations where "the right itself is in litigation or * * * the debtor is insolvent." The court concluded that, even though the fund was inadequate, there was no reasonable expectation that the commissions would not be paid:

> Georgia is a state possessing great resources and a fine record of fiscal probity, and undoubtedly it can and will meet its obligations. The fact that petitioner * * * continued to sell and deliver school books to the state indicates that there was no serious doubt as to the ultimate collection of the amounts here involved.

In the *Georgia School–Book Depository* case, there were legal restrictions preventing payment in the year in which the court required accrual. Should legal restrictions on payment be given greater weight by the courts and the IRS? Or should accrual be deferred only where there is a substantial economic uncertainty that the amount will be paid?

In Jones Lumber Co. v. Commissioner, 404 F.2d 764 (6th Cir.1968), the taxpayer sold "shell houses," taking as part payment second mortgage notes from the purchasers with payments beginning from seven to fifteen years after the date of sale. No evidence about the purchasers' financial condition was introduced at trial, but the taxpayer did show "that the second mortgage notes were not assignable and had no ascertainable market value in the opinion of witnesses representing various lending institutions." The court held that the entire sales price was accruable at the time of sale. (The taxpayers were ineligible to use the installment method of reporting such sales, which is described at page 743 infra.) See also Rev.Rul. 79–292, 1979–2 C.B. 287 (observing in a similar situation that a cash method taxpayer would have been allowed to discount the second mortgages to fair market value.)

3. ADVANCE PAYMENTS FOR UNEARNED ITEMS

One of the most intensely disputed issues in tax law is when an accrual basis taxpayer must include in income amounts that actually have been received but have not yet been earned. Under generally accepted account-ing principles, the income is properly accrued when earned by delivery of goods or services. The Commissioner has taken the position, however, that such amounts are income when received. In the early cases, the inclusion of unearned items in income was based on the claim of right doctrine established in *North American Oil Consolidated v. Burnet,* supra at page 673.

After the repeal of § 452, which excluded prepaid receipts from income until earned, taxpayers enjoyed some success in court challenging the Commissioner's policy of requiring immediate reporting of prepaid amounts. See, e.g., Beacon Publishing Co. v. Commissioner, 218 F.2d 697 (10th Cir.1955), reversing 21 T.C. 610 (1954), which permitted an accrual basis taxpayer to defer income from prepaid subscriptions until the year when the liability to furnish the newspaper, magazine or other periodical arose. (Deferral or prepaid subscription income is now permitted under § 455, and deferral of prepaid dues of nonprofit membership organizations is permitted under § 456.)

But three Supreme Court decisions in 1957, 1961, and 1963 required accrual basis taxpayers to include advance payments in income when received, even though accounting principles would indicate deferral. The case that follows discusses these cases and illustrates the application of these Supreme Court decisions.

RCA Corp. v. United States

United States Court of Appeals, Second Circuit, 1981. 664 F.2d 881, cert. denied 457 U.S. 1133 (1982).

KEARSE, CIRCUIT JUDGE:

This appeal requires us to determine whether the Commissioner of Internal Revenue ("Commissioner") properly exercised his discretion when he rejected as "not clearly reflect[ing] income" within the meaning of § 446(b) of the Internal Revenue Code of 1954 * * * the accrual method of accounting used in 1958 and 1959 by plaintiff RCA Corporation ("RCA") to account for revenues received from the prepayment of fees associated with certain service contracts entered into with purchasers of its products. The [district court] held, after a bench trial, that the Commissioner had abused his discretion in rejecting RCA's accrual method of accounting, and award-ed judgment to RCA in the amount of $5,956,039.25, plus [interest], on its claim for a refund of corporate income taxes for the years 1958 and 1959. Believing that the Commissioner properly exercised his discretion, we reverse.

I

* * * Since 1946 RCA has carried on a business, either directly or through [a] wholly-owned subsidiary, of servicing television sets and other consumer products it sold. In the typical service arrangement, the purchas-er of an RCA product would contract, at the time of purchase, to receive service and repair of the product for a stated period in exchange for prepayment of a single lump sum. Under these agreements, service was

available to the purchaser on demand at any time during the contract term, which might range from three to twenty-four months. * * *

[RCA] employed an accrual method of accounting for service contract revenues * * *. For each group of service contracts of a given duration entered into in a given month, the seller credited to current income a sum that represented the actual cost of selling and processing the contracts, plus a profit. The balance of the revenues derived from each group of contracts, i.e., the portion to be earned through future performance under them, was credited to a deferred income account. Each month thereafter, the seller journaled from the deferred income account to current income that proportion of the revenues from each group of contracts that the seller estimated had been earned in the month through actual performance. For the most part, the seller's estimates of its rate of performance for a particular class of contracts were based on its past experience in the business, and took into account such factors as seasonal repair patterns, variations in average daily workloads, and the number of working days in each month. Although these forecasts were not perfect and may have rested to some extent on untested assumptions, they matched service contract revenues and related expenses with reasonable accuracy.

* * *

After an audit of RCA's tax returns for 1958 and 1959, the Internal Revenue Service ("IRS") required RCA to report its service contract revenues upon receipt, rather than deferring recognition of any portion of them. * * * RCA commenced this litigation on June 18, 1969, and, after what seems to have been a lengthy interregnum of fruitless settlement talks, the case was tried in 1979.

At trial, RCA contended, first, that its accrual method of tax accounting for prepaid service contract revenues "clearly reflect[ed] income" within the meaning of I.R.C. § 446(b), and that the Commissioner had therefore abused his discretion in rejecting that method. * * * Finally, RCA asserted that its accrual method was acceptable because certain revenue rulings, Rev.Proc. 71–21, 1971–2 C.B. 549, and Rev.Rul. 71–299, 1971–2 C.B. 218, promulgated by the Commissioner in 1971 and permitting limited use of accounting procedures such as RCA's, are retroactive in effect.[1]

For its part, the government argued that under a trio of Supreme Court cases, Automobile Club of Michigan v. Commissioner, 353 U.S. 180 (1957), ("Michigan"); American Automobile Association v. United States, 367 U.S. 687 (1961) ("AAA"), and Schlude v. Commissioner, 372 U.S. 128

---

1. Section 3.02 of Revenue Procedure 71–21, on which RCA relies, provides, in relevant part:

An accrual method taxpayer who, pursuant to an agreement (written or otherwise), receives a payment in one taxable year for services, where all of the services under such agreement are required by the agreement as it exists at the end of the taxable year of receipt to be performed by him before the end of the next succeeding taxable year, may include such payment in gross income as earned through the performance of the services. * * *

Revenue Ruling 71–299 simply states that Revenue Procedure 71–21 supercedes several earlier revenue rulings to the extent that they are inconsistent with the new Revenue Procedure.

(1963) ("Schlude"), methods of accrual accounting based on projections of customers' demands for services do not "clearly reflect income," and that in view of these decisions the Commissioner did not abuse his discretion in rejecting RCA's method. The government also pressed a broader argument that accrual accounting is *never* permissible without express legislative authorization and the Commissioner's consent. In addition, the government contended that RCA was not entitled to a refund because its adoption of the accrual method was a change of accounting methods for which it was required to, but did not, obtain the Commissioner's consent under I.R.C. § 446(e). Finally, the government argued that * * * Rev.Proc. 71–21 and Rev.Rul. 71–299 are not retroactive.

After reviewing the stipulated facts and hearing the testimony of the one live witness, an accounting expert, the district court ruled for RCA. The court read *Michigan, AAA,* and *Schlude, supra,* to proscribe, as "not clearly reflect[ing] income," only those methods of deferring recognition of income that are not based on demonstrably accurate projections of future expenses required to earn the income. * * * Finding that RCA's accrual method matched service contract revenues and related expenses "with reasonable precision" and therefore "clearly reflect[ed] income," the court held that the Commissioner had abused his discretion under I.R.C. § 446(b) in rejecting RCA's method and imposing on RCA a cash method of accounting.

* * *

The court found it unnecessary, in view of its disposition of the other issues, to discuss the parties' contentions concerning the retroactivity of Rev.Proc. 71–21 and Rev.Rul. 71–299.

* * *

On appeal, the Commissioner renews the various contentions he pressed at trial, two of which have merit. We conclude that the district court erred in holding * * * that the Commissioner abused his discretion in rejecting RCA's accrual method of accounting for prepaid service contract revenues * * * *

II

This case well illustrates the fundamental tension between the purposes of financial accounting and those of tax accounting. As the Supreme Court has recognized, these two systems of accounting have "vastly different objectives" * * * Thor Power Tool Co. v. Commissioner, 439 U.S. 522, 542 (1979) * * *. The case also highlights the fundamentally different perspective that courts must adopt when reviewing the propriety of an exercise of administrative discretion rather than deciding a naked question of substantive law. We conclude that the district court gave too little weight to the objectives of tax accounting and to the Commissioner's wide discretion in implementing those objectives.

Section 446 of the Internal Revenue Code of 1954 provides that "[t]axable income shall be computed under the method of accounting on the basis of which the taxpayer regularly computes his income in keeping his books," unless "the method used does not clearly reflect income"; in the latter event "the computation of taxable income shall be made under such method as, in the opinion of the Secretary [of the Treasury], does clearly reflect income." I.R.C. § 446(a), (b). It is well established that the Commissioner enjoys "broad discretion" to determine whether, " 'in [his] opinion,' " a taxpayer's accounting methods clearly reflect income, *Thor Power Tool, supra,* 439 U.S. at 540 (quoting 26 C.F.R. § 1.446–1(a)(2)), and the Commissioner's exercise of his discretion must be upheld unless it is clearly unlawful.

* * *

The task of a reviewing court, therefore, is not to determine whether in its own opinion RCA's method of accounting for prepaid service contract income "clearly reflect[ed] income," but to determine whether there is an adequate basis in law for the Commissioner's conclusion that it did not. Our review of the relevant decisions persuades us that the law adequately supports the Commissioner's action.

In *Michigan, supra,* the first Supreme Court ruling on tax accounting for income received in respect of services to be performed in the future upon demand, the taxpayer received income in the form of prepaid membership dues and promised, in exchange, to perform various services for its members upon demand at any time during the twelve-month term of the membership agreement. In order to match prepaid dues revenues with related expenses, the taxpayer assumed that members would demand services at a constant rate during the contract term and credited prepaid membership dues to current income on a monthly pro rata basis to match the hypothetical rate of demand for services. The Supreme Court upheld the Commissioner's rejection of this method, reasoning that it was "purely artificial and [bore] no relation to the services which [the taxpayer] may in fact be called upon to render." 353 U.S. at 189.

* * *

Subsequently, in *AAA, supra,* a Supreme Court case that involved a method of deferring recognition of prepaid membership dues income "substantially identical," 367 U.S. at 691, to that employed by the taxpayer in *Michigan,* the taxpayer argued that the Commissioner had abused his discretion in rejecting its deferral method of accounting because it had shown at trial that its method accorded with generally accepted accounting principles and was justified by its past experience in providing services. Despite this showing, the Court upheld the Commissioner's rejection of the method. The Court stated as follows:

> When [the] receipt [of prepaid dues] as earned income is recognized ratably over two calendar years, without regard to correspondingly fixed individual expense or performance justification, but consistently with overall experience, their accounting doubtless presents a rather accurate image of the total financial structure, but fails to respect the criteria of annual tax accounting and may be rejected by the Commissioner.

[F]indings merely reflecting statistical computations of average monthly cost per member on a group or pool basis are without determinate significance to our decision that the federal revenue cannot, without legislative consent and over objection of the Commissioner, be made to depend upon average experience in rendering performance and turning a profit.

Id. at 692–93.

Finally, in *Schlude,* supra, the third Supreme Court case on the subject, the taxpayers, operators of a dance studio, contracted with some of their students to provide a specified number of dancing lessons in exchange for a prepaid fee; the lessons were to be given from time to time, as the student specified, during the contract term. For both tax and book accounting purposes, the taxpayers credited contract prepayments to a deferred income account, and then at the end of each fiscal period credited to current income for that period the fraction of the contract price that represented the fraction of the total number of hours of instruction available under the contract that the student had actually used during the period. In addition, if for more than a year a student failed to request any lessons, the taxpayer treated the contract as cancelled and recognized gain to the extent of the amount of the student's prepayment. Despite the fact that the taxpayer's method of accounting was based largely on its actual performance of services during the taxable year, the court upheld the Commissioner's rejection of the method, viewing the case as "squarely controlled" by *AAA,* 372 U.S. at 134, because the taxpayer was required to perform services under its contracts only at the student's demand, id. at 135.

The policy considerations that underlie *Michigan, AAA,* and *Schlude* are quite clear. When a taxpayer receives income in the form of prepayments in respect of services to be performed in the future upon demand, it is impossible for the taxpayer to know, at the outset of the contract term, the amount of service that his customer will ultimately require, and, consequently, it is impossible for the taxpayer to predict *with certainty* the amount of net income, i.e., the amount of the excess of revenues over expenses of performance, that he will ultimately earn from the contract. For purposes of financial accounting, this uncertainty is tolerable; the financial accountant merely estimates future demands for performance and defers recognition of income accordingly. Tax accounting, however, "can give no quarter to uncertainty." Thor Power Tool, supra, 439 U.S. at 543. The entire process of government depends on the expeditious collection of tax revenues. Tax accounting therefore tends to compute taxable income on the basis of the taxpayer's present ability to pay the tax, as manifested by his current cash flow, without regard to deductions that may later accrue. * * * By the same token, tax accounting is necessarily hostile to accounting practices that defer recognition of income, and thus payment of the tax on it, on the basis of estimates and projections that may ultimately prove unsound.

In view of the relevant Supreme Court decisions and the policies they reflect, we cannot say that the Commissioner abused his discretion in rejecting RCA's method of accounting for service contract income. Like the service agreements at issue in *Michigan, AAA,* and *Schlude,* RCA's service contracts obligated it to perform services only upon the customer's demand. Thus, at the beginning of the contract term, RCA could not know the extent of the performance that the customer might ultimately require, and it could not be certain of the amount of income that it would ultimately earn from the contract. The Commissioner was not required to subject the federal revenues to the vicissitudes of RCA customers' future demands for services. Accordingly, he acted within his discretion in requiring RCA to report its prepaid service contract income upon receipt.

* * *

* * * RCA's efforts to distinguish *AAA* and *Schlude* [are unpersuasive.] RCA contends that the accounting practices at issue in those cases, which were based on the past demand for services, differ significantly from its own, which was based on relatively scientific projections of the future demand for services, and that its accounting method was valid under *AAA* and *Schlude* * * *. We think, however, that the differences between RCA's method and the others are immaterial in the present context. As noted above, the vice of the systems treated in *AAA* and *Schlude* was their tendency to subject government revenues to the uncertainties inherent in prognostications about the rate at which customers would demand services in the future. RCA's system shared this vice. Although RCA's predictions may have been more accurate than those of the taxpayers in *AAA* and *Schlude,* they were predictions nonetheless, and the Commissioner was not required to accept them as determinants of the federal revenue.

RCA's other arguments on this score require but brief discussion. While the Commissioner has permitted certain forms of accrual accounting in Rev.Proc. 71–21, supra, and Rev.Rul. 71–299, supra, that does not necessarily mean, as RCA asserts, that the Commissioner has conceded the correctness of RCA's position in this litigation. As we have emphasized above, the Commissioner possesses considerable discretion in these matters, and he was at liberty to alter his stance toward the accounting practices at issue here in light of his greater experience with them and their effect on revenue collection. In addition, although the district court found that RCA's accounting practices did "clearly reflect income," we are not bound by that finding under the "clearly erroneous" standard of Fed.R.Civ.P. 52. The issue before the district court was not whether RCA's accounting method adequately reflected income, but whether the Commissioner abused his discretion in determining that it did not. The latter question is one of law, and for the reasons stated above we conclude that the Commissioner did not abuse his discretion.[2]

* * *

Finally, we conclude that we need not decide whether Rev.Proc. 71–21 and Rev.Rul. 71–299 are retroactive. Both require the taxpayer to obtain the Commissioner's consent before employing the accounting procedures

---

2. In view of our disposition of this issue, we do not address the government's argument that, absent express legislative authorization and the Commissioner's consent, deferring recognition of income items in accordance with the principles of accrual accounting is never permissible.

permissible under them. * * * RCA has neither sought nor obtained the Commissioner's consent to adopt those procedures. Accordingly, it may not use them even if the Procedure and Ruling are retroactive.

For the reasons stated above, we reverse the judgment of the district court and remand the matter with instructions to dismiss the complaint.

NOTES

(A) *Other Post–Trilogy Litigation.* Following the three Supreme Court decisions described in *RCA Corp.,* the Commissioner enjoyed great success in taxing prepaid but unearned income. See, e.g., Decision, Inc. v. Commissioner, 47 T.C. 58 (1966) (prepaid advertising income); Travis v. Commissioner, 406 F.2d 987 (6th Cir.1969) (prepaid dance lessons). Although the three Supreme Court decisions all involved prepayments for services, in Hagen Advertising Displays, Inc. v. Commissioner, 407 F.2d 1105 (6th Cir.1969), the court held advance payments for manufactured signs to be delivered in the future to be taxable when received. Accord, Modernaire Interiors, Inc. v. Commissioner, 27 T.C.M. 1334 (1968) (sale of custom-made furniture).

The Seventh Circuit permitted deferral, however, in Artnell Co. v. Commissioner, 400 F.2d 981 (7th Cir.1968), reversing 48 T.C. 411 (1967). *Artnell* involved receipts by the Chicago White Sox in one taxable year for tickets, parking, and broadcasting rights for baseball games to be played in the following taxable year. The court sustained the taxpayer's deferral on the ground that the time and extent of the future services were so definite that the taxpayer's method could "so clearly reflect income" that the Commissioner's refusal to permit deferral would be an abuse of his discretion under § 446. The Supreme Court decisions were distinguished on the basis of uncertainty in those cases about the time and extent of the performance of services. The court remanded the case to the Tax Court for a determination whether the White Sox method of accounting clearly reflected income. On remand, the Tax Court found that the White Sox method, while not perfect in matching income with expenses, was more desirable than the Commissioner's proposed method and approved deferral. 29 T.C.M. 403 (1970).

The taxpayer in Boise Cascade Corp. v. United States, 530 F.2d 1367 (Ct.Cl.), cert. denied 429 U.S. 867 (1976), also was permitted to defer receipt of prepaid income. The taxpayer correctly accrued income from the performance of engineering services when performed that were billed subsequently, but attempted to defer income when it was prepaid for services. The court rejected the Commissioner's attempt to require the taxpayer to report the payments that were made before services were rendered. Noting that this had the effect of putting the taxpayer on the cash method as to those receipts, the court expressed the view that the Commissioner's method "would appear to the ordinary mind to distort income instead of clearly reflecting it." The court also criticized the apparent inconsistency of treatment between the two types of payments. As the *RCA* case demonstrates, while the Commissioner's method overstates the taxpayer's income in the year of payment, discretion to do so has been granted by the Supreme Court in *American Automobile Association* and *Schlude.*

(B) *Revenue Procedure 71–21 and Regulation § 1.451–5.* Revenue Procedure 71–21, 1971–2 C.B. 549, cited in *RCA,* permits payments received in one taxable year for services to be performed by the close of the subsequent taxable year to be included in the income of accrual basis taxpayers when earned rather than when received. If the services are not completed by the end of the second year, the amounts paid must be included in income without regard to when the services actually are performed. Thus, the income from many two-year service contracts is taxed as earned. Revenue Procedure 71–21 contains similar rules for income from sales of streetcar tokens, transportation tickets with open dates, photographic mailers, or other photographic processing arrangements. The procedure contains a "booking requirement" that the amount included in income for tax purposes be no less than the amount reported as income for financial reporting purposes. Revenue Procedure 71–21 explicitly does not apply to prepaid rents or interest or amounts received under guaranty or warranty contracts.

In 1971, the Treasury issued Reg. § 1.451–5 to permit advance payments for goods sold to customers in the ordinary course of business to be deferred until the year in which the goods are shipped. This regulation, like Revenue Procedure 71–21, generally limits deferral of payments for the sale of goods in inventory or readily available to the seller to the second taxable year following receipt of the payment.

The rules of Revenue Procedure 71–21 and Reg. § 1.451–5 obviously were designed to reduce litigation over advance payments and to reconcile the tax rules with generally accepted accounting principles. The promulgation of these rules was severely criticized, however, as beyond the Commissioner's authority, given the legislative history and Supreme Court decisions in this area. Do you view Revenue Procedure 71–21 and Reg. § 1.451–5 as appropriate exercises of the Commissioner's discretion? Why are there different rules for goods and services? The existence of the three Supreme Court decisions on income from services obviously influenced the IRS to issue a revenue procedure for prepayments for services and to amend the regulations for prepayments for goods.

Although Rev. Proc. 71–21 was designed to reduce litigation, it has not ended it. Contrast two Tax Court cases in which banks attempted to use Rev. Proc. 71–21 to include credit card fees over a two-year period. In both cases, the fee was deemed to be for services. In Barnett Banks of Florida Inc. v. Commissioner, 106 T.C. 103 (1996), the bank was permitted to prorate the fees because the fee was refundable and thus the bank did not have unrestricted access to the funds. In Signet Banking Corp. v. Commissioner, 106 T.C. 117 (1996), however, the taxpayer was required to accrue the entire amount in the year of receipt because the only service required was the issuance of the card and a credit limit.

Congress has adopted a number of other industry-specific exceptions to the prepaid income rule. Section 456 permits certain membership organizations (such as the American Automobile Association) to defer prepaid dues ratably over the period during which there is a liability to perform services.

Section 455 permits newspaper and periodical publishers to elect to defer prepaid subscriptions.

(C) *Non-Cash Prepayments.* The prepayment need not always be in the form of cash. In T.F.H. Publications, Inc. v. Commissioner, 72 T.C. 623 (1979), an accrual basis taxpayer acquired printing and publishing assets in 1971 for a price that included a credit on the first $40,000 of advertising placed by the seller in the taxpayer's publications. The Tax Court held that the assets received in 1971 constituted payment for future advertising services that must be included in income under *Schlude.*

(D) *Prepayments vs. Security Deposits.* Often the issue arises whether a receipt is an advance payment for services, which is taxable on receipt, or a security deposit, which is not. For example, in Commissioner v. Indianapolis Power and Light Co., 493 U.S. 203 (1990), the Supreme Court treated as nontaxable security deposits amounts received by a utility from its customers to secure their performance. The Court distinguished advance payments from security deposits by looking at the rights and obligations of the parties at the time the payments were made. An individual who makes an advance payment has no right to a refund if the recipient fulfills the contract. A customer who gives a security deposit to a utility, like a lender, retains the right to repayment in cash. The Court noted that the customer has no obligation to buy electricity even if he may apply his deposit against such purchases. The Tax Court has broadly interpreted *Indianapolis Power & Light.* For example, in Oak Industries, Inc. v. Commissioner, 96 T.C. 559 (1991), the court treated as excludable deposits amounts received by a cable television service even though they were noninterest bearing because they were conditionally refundable.

(E) *Policy of Treatment of Prepayments.* As the court noted in *Boise Cascade,* supra, an accrual basis taxpayer is put on the cash method with regard to prepayments. If the accrual method generally is superior to the cash method in accurately measuring income, why does the Commissioner urge the courts to abandon the accrual method in this situation? Does the answer lie in administrative concerns? The IRS is often troubled when the tax liability arises after the taxpayer has received cash or property. Questions of collectibility and enforcement inevitably arise. This is not the first time we have seen administrative concerns trump accurate income measurement. The cash method generally and the realization requirement, which permit taxpayers to defer income until receipt, also are often justified on similar grounds. With a solvent taxpayer like RCA Corp., do the concerns about collectibility justify the Commissioner's position? Why should prepaid services be treated differently from advance payments for goods?

4. EXPENSES

The timing of the deduction for accrual method taxpayer turns on the "all events" test. Section 461(h)(4) states that the all events test is met "if all events have occurred which determine the fact of liability and the amount of such liability can be determined with reasonable accuracy." This test is limited by § 461(h)(1), which provides that the all events test will not be deemed to be satisfied until there is "economic performance."

Before Congress and the courts became concerned with the time value of money advantages that accrual basis taxpayers might obtain by deducting liabilities long before they were paid, controversies involving the accrual of deductions turned on whether the liability was sufficiently contingent to delay accrual under the all events test. The case that follows illustrates the kinds of questions that arise. It was decided only one year after the Supreme Court had decided in *Hughes Properties, Inc.*, 476 U.S. 593 (1986), that an accrual method casino could deduct amounts guaranteed at year end, but not paid, as payoffs on "progressive" slot machines. (As every school child knows, these machines pay a "progressive" jackpot, the amount of which increases as amounts are gambled, when a specified combination of symbols appears on the slot machines' payoff line.)

United States v. General Dynamics Corp.

Supreme Court of the United States, 1987. 481 U.S. 239.

JUSTICE MARSHALL delivered the opinion of the Court.

The issue in this case is whether an accrual-basis taxpayer providing medical benefits to its employees may deduct at the close of the taxable year an estimate of its obligation to pay for medical care obtained by employees or their qualified dependents during the final quarter of the year, claims for which have not been reported to the employer.

I

Taxpayers, respondents herein, are the General Dynamics Corporation and several of its wholly-owned subsidiaries (General Dynamics). General Dynamics uses the accrual method of accounting for federal tax purposes; its fiscal year is the same as the calendar year. From 1962 until October 1, 1972, General Dynamics purchased group medical insurance for its employees and their qualified dependents from two private insurance carriers. Beginning in October, 1972, General Dynamics became a self-insurer with regard to its medical care plans. Instead of continuing to purchase insurance from outside carriers, it undertook to pay medical claims out of its own funds, while continuing to employ private carriers to administer the medical care plans.

To receive reimbursement of expenses for covered medical services, respondent's employees submit claims forms to employee benefits personnel, who verify that the treated persons were eligible under the applicable plan as of the time of treatment. Eligible claims are then forwarded to the plan's administrators. Claims processors review the claims and approve for payment those expenses that are covered under the plan.

Because the processing of claims takes time, and because employees do not always file their claims immediately, there is a delay between the provision of medical services and payment by General Dynamics. To account for this time lag, General Dynamics established reserve accounts to reflect its liability for medical care received, but still not paid for, as of December 31, 1972. It estimated the amount of those reserves with the assistance of its former insurance carriers.

* * * [General Dynamics claims] it was entitled to deduct its reserve as an accrued expense, and seek[s] a refund. The IRS disallowed the deduction, and General Dynamics sought relief in the Claims Court.

The Claims Court sustained the deduction, holding that it satisfied the "all events" test embodied in Treas.Reg. 1.461–1(a)(2), 26 CFR 1.461–1(a)(2) (1986), since "all events" which determined the fact of liability had taken place when the employees received covered services, and the amount of liability could be determined with reasonable accuracy. * * * The Court of Appeals for the Federal Circuit affirmed, largely on the basis of the Claims Court opinion. 773 F.2d 1224, 1226 (1985). * * *

* * * We reverse.

II

As we noted in United States v. Hughes Properties, Inc., 476 U.S. 593, 600 (1986), whether a business expense has been "incurred" so as to entitle an accrual-basis taxpayer to deduct it under § 162(a) of the Internal Revenue Code, 26 U.S.C. § 162(a), is governed by the "all events" test that originated in United States v. Anderson, 269 U.S. 422, 441 (1926). In *Anderson,* the Court held that a taxpayer was obliged to deduct from its 1916 income a tax on profits from munitions sales that took place in 1916. Although the tax would not be assessed and therefore would not formally be due until 1917, all the events which fixed the amount of the tax and determined the taxpayer's liability to pay it had occurred in 1916. The test is now embodied in Treas.Reg. 1.461–1(a)(2), 26 CFR § 1.461–1(a)(2) (1986), which provides that "[u]nder an accrual method of accounting, an expense is deductible for the taxable year in which all the events have occurred which determine the fact of the liability and the amount thereof can be determined with reasonable accuracy."[1]

It is fundamental to the "all events" test that, although expenses may be deductible before they have become due and payable, liability must first be firmly established. This is consistent with our prior holdings that a taxpayer may not deduct a liability that is contingent * * * or contested * * *. Nor may a taxpayer deduct an estimate of an anticipated expense, no matter how statistically certain, if it is based on events that have not occurred by the close of the taxable year. Brown v. Helvering, 291 U.S. 193, 201 (1934) * * *.

---

1. The regulation in force in 1972 was identical to the present version.

The "all events" test has been incorporated into the Internal Revenue Code by the Deficit Reduction Act of 1984, Pub.L. 98–369, 98 Stat. 598, 607, 26 U.S.C. § 461(h)(4) (1982 ed., Supp. III). Section 461(h) imposed limits on the application of the test, providing that "in determining whether an amount has been incurred with respect to any item during any taxable year, the all events test shall not be treated as met any earlier than when economic performance with respect to such item occurs." § 461(h)(1). * * *

Section 461(h) does not apply in this case. It became effective as of July 18, 1984, the date of the enactment of the Deficit Reduction Act. * * * We do not address how this case would be decided under § 461(h), but note that the legislative history of the Act indicates that, "[i]n the case of * * * employee benefit liabilities, which require a payment by the taxpayer to another person, economic performance occurs as the payments to such person are made." H.R.Rep. No. 98–432, pt. 2, p. 1255 (1984); see also H.Conf.Rep. No. 98–861, p. 872 (1984). * * *

We think that this case, like *Brown,* involves a mere estimate of liability based on events that had not occurred before the close of the taxable year, and therefore the proposed deduction does not pass the "all events" test. We disagree with the legal conclusion of the courts below that the last event necessary to fix the taxpayer's liability was the receipt of medical care by covered individuals. A person covered by a plan could only obtain payment for medical services by filling out and submitting a health-expense-benefits claim form. * * * Employees were informed that submission of satisfactory proof of the charges claimed would be necessary to obtain payment under the plans. * * * General Dynamics was thus liable to pay for covered medical services *only* if properly documented claims forms were filed.[2] Some covered individuals, through oversight, procrastination, confusion over the coverage provided, or fear of disclosure to the employer of the extent or nature of the services received, might not file claims for reimbursement to which they are plainly entitled. Such filing is not a mere technicality. It is crucial to the establishment of liability on the part of the taxpayer. Nor does the failure to file a claim represent the type of "extremely remote and speculative possibility" that we held in *Hughes,* 476 U.S., at 601, did not render an otherwise fixed liability contingent. * * * Mere receipt of services for which, in some instances, claims will not be submitted does not, in our judgment, constitute the last link in the chain of events creating liability for purposes of the "all events" test.

The parties stipulated in this case that as of December 31, 1972, the taxpayer had not received all claims for medical treatment services rendered in 1972, and that some claims had been filed for services rendered in 1972 that had not been processed. * * * The record does not reflect which portion of the claims against General Dynamics for medical care had been filed but not yet processed and which portion had not even been filed at the close of the 1972 tax year. The taxpayer has the burden of proving its entitlement to a deduction. * * * Here, respondent made no showing that, as of December 31, 1972, it knew of specific claims which had been filed but which it had not yet processed. Because the taxpayer failed to demonstrate that any of the deducted reserve represented claims for which its liability was firmly established as of the close of 1972, all the events necessary to establish liability were not shown to have occurred, and therefore no deduction was permissible.

This is not to say that the taxpayer was unable to forecast how many claims would be filed for medical care received during this period, and estimate the liability that would arise from those claims. Based on actuarial data, General Dynamics may have been able to make a reasonable estimate of how many claims would be filed for the last quarter of 1972. But that alone does not justify a deduction. * * * A reserve based on the proposition that a particular set of events is likely to occur in the future may be an appropriate conservative accounting measure, but does not warrant a tax

---

2. General Dynamics could not avoid its obligation to pay for services after they were received by, for example, discharging the employee. If an employee were terminated after receiving covered services but before filing a claim, the taxpayer would still be obliged to reimburse that employee, but *only in the event* that the employee filed a claim form. The filing of the claim is thus a true condition precedent to liability on the part of the taxpayer.

deduction. See American Automobile Assn. v. United States, 367 U.S., at 692; Lucas v. American Code Co., 280 U.S., at 452.

That these estimated claims were not intended to fall within the "all events" test is further demonstrated by the fact that the Internal Revenue Code specifically permits insurance companies to deduct additions to reserves for such "incurred but not reported" (IBNR) claims. See 26 U.S.C. § 832(b)(5) (providing that an insurance company may treat as losses incurred "all unpaid losses outstanding at the end of the taxable year"); § 832(c)(4) (permitting deduction of losses incurred as defined in § 832(b)(5)).[3] If the "all events" test permitted the deduction of an estimated reserve representing claims that were actuarially likely but not yet reported, Congress would not have needed to maintain an explicit provision that insurance companies could deduct such reserves.

General Dynamics did not show that its liability as to any medical care claims was firmly established as of the close of the 1972 tax year, and is therefore entitled to no deduction. The judgment of the Court of Appeals is

Reversed.

Justice O'Connor, with whom Justice Blackmun and Justice Stevens join, dissenting.

* * * Under the "all events" test, long applied by this Court and the Internal Revenue Service, an expense may be accrued and deducted when all the events that determine the fact of liability have occurred, and the amount of the liability can be determined with reasonable accuracy. * * * Because the Court today applies a rigid version of the "all events" test that retreats from our most recent application of that test, and unnecessarily drives a greater wedge between tax and financial accounting methods, I respectfully dissent.

This case calls for the Court to revisit the issue addressed only last Term in United States v. Hughes Properties, Inc., 476 U.S. 593 (1986). At issue in *Hughes Properties* was whether a casino operator utilizing the accrual method of accounting could deduct amounts guaranteed for payment on "progressive" slot machines but not yet won by a playing patron. * * * Under Nevada law, a casino operator is prohibited from reducing the amount of the progressive jackpot. We concluded, therefore, that all the events had occurred that determine the fact of the casino operator's liability despite the fact that the jackpot might not be won for as long as four years. We rejected the argument made by the United States that the casino operator's obligation to pay the jackpot arose only upon a winning patron's pull of the handle, even though it was conceivable that the jackpot might never be won. * * *

In my view, the circumstances of this case differ little from those in *Hughes Properties*. The taxpayer here is seeking to deduct the amounts reserved to pay for medical services that are determined to have been provided to employees in the taxable year, whether or not the employees'

---

3. During the time that private insurance carriers provided insurance coverage for General Dynamics employees, the insurers maintained reserves for IBNR claims and deducted those reserves in the tax year in which the services were received.

claims for benefits have been received. The taxpayer's various medical benefits plans provided schedules for the medical and hospital benefits, and created a contractual obligation by the taxpayer to pay for the covered services upon presentation of a claim. The courts below found that the obligation to pay became fixed once the covered medical services were received by the employee. * * * Once the medical services were rendered to an employee while the relevant benefit plan was in effect, General Dynamics could not avoid liability by terminating the plan prior to the filing of a claim. * * * Neither could General Dynamics extinguish its liability by firing an employee before the employee filed a claim for benefits. * * *

It is true, of course, that it was theoretically possible that some employees might not file claim forms. In my view, however, this speculative possibility of nonpayment differs not at all from the speculation in *Hughes Properties* that a jackpot might never be paid by a casino. As we observed in *Hughes Properties*, the potential of nonpayment of a liability always exists, and it alone does not prevent accrual. The beneficiary of a liability always has the option of waiving payment, but a taxpayer is still unquestionably entitled to deduct the liability. An injured employee entitled absolutely to reimbursement for medical services under a worker's compensation statute, for example, may fail to utilize the medical services. The employer, however, has been held to be entitled to deduct the expected medical expenses because the worker's compensation law creates liability. * * * Similarly, any business liability could ultimately be discharged in bankruptcy, or a check might never be cashed by its recipient. There can be no doubt, however, that these remote possibilities alone cannot defeat an accrual basis taxpayer's right to deduct the liability when incurred.

The Claims Court found that the processing of the employees' claims was "routine" and "ministerial in nature" * * * and the majority does not question that finding. * * * Instead, the majority holds that "as a matter of law, the filing of a claim was necessary to create liability." * * * Even if, in a technical sense, the Court is correct that the filing of a claim is a necessary precondition to liability as a matter of law, the failure to file a claim is at most a "merely formal contingenc[y], or [one] highly improbable under the known facts," that this Court has viewed as insufficient to preclude accrual and deductibility. * * * Clearly, the right to reimbursement for medical benefits under any of the medical benefits plans at issue in this case arises once medical services are rendered; the filing and processing of a claim is purely routine and ministerial, and in the nature of a formal contingency, as correctly perceived by the courts below.

The holding of the Court today unnecessarily burdens taxpayers by further expanding the difference between tax and business accounting methods without a compelling reason to do so. Obviously, tax accounting principles must often differ from those of business accounting. The goal of business accounting "is to provide useful and pertinent information to management, shareholders, and creditors," while "the responsibility of the Internal Revenue Service is to protect the public fisc." United States v. Hughes Properties, Inc., 476 U.S., at 603. Therefore, while prudent businesses will accrue expenses that are merely reasonably foreseeable, for tax purposes the liability must be fixed. But Congress has expressly permitted taxpayers to use the accrual method of accounting, and from its inception in United States v. Anderson, supra, the "all-events" test has been a practical adjustment of the competing interests in permitting accrual accounting and protecting the public fisc. Unfortunately, the Court today ignores the pragmatic roots of the all events test and instead applies it in an essentially mechanistic and wholly unrealistic manner. Because the liability in this case was fixed with no less certainty than the range of expenses both routinely accrued by accrual method taxpayers and approved as deductible for tax purposes by this Court and other courts in a variety of circumstances, I respectfully dissent.

NOTES

(A) *Contested Liabilities.* Many of the early accrual accounting cases involved the timing of deduction of contested liabilities. For example, in Dixie Pine Products v. Commissioner, 320 U.S. 516 (1944), the Supreme Court prohibited accrual of a state gasoline tax while the taxpayer was contesting its liability, stating:

> It has never been questioned that a taxpayer who accounts on the accrual basis may, and should, deduct from gross income a liability which really accrues in the taxable year. It has long been held that in order truly to reflect the income of a given year, all the events must occur in that year which fix the amount and the fact of the taxpayer's liability for items of indebtedness deducted though not paid; and this cannot be the case where the liability is contingent and is contested by the taxpayer. Here the taxpayer was strenuously contesting liability in the courts and, at the same time, deducting the amount of the tax, on the theory that the state's exaction constituted a fixed and certain liability. This it could not do. It must, in the circumstances, await the event of the state court litigation and might claim a deduction only for the taxable year in which its liability for the tax was finally adjudicated.

See also Security Flour Mills Co. v. Commissioner, 321 U.S. 281 (1944), where the taxpayer in 1935 accrued on its books processing taxes that it contested and did not pay. In 1936, the tax was held unconstitutional. Thereafter, the taxpayer made refunds to some of its customers for the amount of the tax that it had included in the price of goods sold. The Court held that no deduction was allowable for 1935.

United States v. Consolidated Edison Co., 366 U.S. 380 (1961), involved a contested New York City real estate tax. Local procedure required the taxpayer to pay the entire tax before it could bring suit to recover any excessive amount. The Supreme Court held that the disputed portion of the tax did not accrue as long as the litigation was pending, even though the tax had actually been paid. Section 461(f), which treats a contested item as accruing no later than the date of payment effectively overrules *Consolidated Edison*.

(B) *Contingencies.* As the dissent in *General Dynamics* points out, the analysis of the majority opinion in *Hughes Properties* of what sorts of contingencies are sufficient to defer accruals of deductions under the "all events" tests seems to have been substantially undermined by the majority opinion only one year later in *General Dynamics*. Ultimately, in light of *General Dynamics* and the addition of § 461(h), the *Hughes Properties* case probably will stand only for the rather narrow proposition that the identity of the payee need not necessarily be known in order for a deduction to accrue for tax purposes.

On the other hand, if the Supreme Court can manage to maintain a somewhat steady course, the *General Dynamics* case may prove of more lasting significance. Section 461(h) requires the "all events" test of prior law (which was codified in language similar to the regulations of prior law in § 461(h)(4)) be satisfied in addition to economic performance and provides in § 461(h)(1) that the "all events" test shall not be treated as met *"any earlier than when economic performance* with respect to such items occurs" (emphasis added). *General Dynamics*, therefore, provides an illustration of an instance where economic performance occurs prior to the time when the traditional "all events" test would be satisfied and that test defers the accrual of deductions to that later time.

The outstanding contingencies in *General Dynamics*—viz., that claims have not been filed and, perhaps, approved—seems more substantial than the contingency in *Hughes Properties* that the jackpots may never be paid because the casino might go out of business (or be sold, a prospect ignored by the majority opinion). Although the *General Dynamics* majority did not distinguish *Hughes Properties* on this ground, *Hughes Properties* also seems a somewhat stronger case for accrual since the fact and the amount of liability were both known to the casino, while *General Dynamics* might be regarded as urging the Court to allow an estimate of the fact of liability, as well as the amount, with respect to persons who had not yet filed claims. On the other hand, the prospects for delay in the time between accrual and payment—the time value of money aspect that concerned the Congress in 1984 and to which it enacted § 461(h) to respond—is greater in *Hughes Properties*.

(C) *Reserves*. The prohibition on accruing contested or contingent liabilities often creates a mismatching of income and expenses that violates financial accounting principles, which frequently require reserves for estimated expenses to prevent the overstatement of current income. The 1986 Act repealed the reserve method for computing the deduction for bad debts for all taxpayers, other than commercial banks whose assets do not exceed $500 million and thrift institutions. Thus, taxpayers (other than certain financial institutions) are required to use the specific charge-off method in accounting for losses on bad debts. The specific charge-off method allows a deduction at the time and in the amount that any individual debt is wholly or partially worthless. The staff of the Joint Committee on Taxation, in its General Explanation of the Tax Reform Act of 1986 offers the following reasons for the change:

> The Congress believed that the use of the reserve method for determining losses from bad debts resulted in deductions being allowed for tax purposes for losses that statistically occur in the future. Thus, the Congress believed that the use of the reserve method for determining losses from bad debts allowed a deduction to be taken prior to the

time that the loss actually occurred. This treatment under prior law was not consistent with the treatment of other deductions under the all events test. If a deduction is allowed prior to the taxable year in which the loss actually occurs, the value of the deduction to the taxpayer is overstated and the overall tax liability of the taxpayer understated.

There is no general provision for reserve accounting, even though normal accounting principles permit the use of reserves to match income and expenses. Some courts have permitted reserves in limited cases. For example, in Schuessler v. Commissioner, 230 F.2d 722 (5th Cir.1956), the Fifth Circuit allowed the taxpayer a deduction for a reserve for the estimated expenses of honoring guarantees on the furnaces that he sold. In Harrold v. Commissioner, 192 F.2d 1002 (4th Cir.1951), the taxpayer was allowed to deduct reserves estimating the cost of back-filing, fertilizing and replanting after strip mining. Congress enacted § 462 to provide for general reserve accounting in 1954 but repealed it retroactively in 1955 because of a large anticipated revenue loss.

(D) *Obligations to Related Taxpayers.* Where an accrual basis taxpayer accrues a liability to a cash basis taxpayer, there may be a mismatch of deductions and income. Ordinarily, a lessor or creditor has no interest in postponing receipt of interest or rent. Where, however, the parties are related, the cash basis recipient receives an indirect benefit from the deduction taken by the accrual basis taxpayer. Suppose, for example, that a corporation rents property from a controlling shareholder. Even if the accrual basis corporation does not actually pay the rent, the corporation would have a deduction, which would reduce its taxes and therefore increase its profits, an obvious benefit to the shareholder. To prevent this type of avoidance, § 267(a)(2) defers the accrual method taxpayer's deduction until the year the income is includible by the cash method related party. Related parties are defined in § 267(b).

––––––––

The following case illustrates the kind of problem that gave rise to § 461(h). The taxpayer attempted to accrue current deductions of $24.6 million to be paid far in the future, which had a present value of only $4.4 million. The case was decided after § 461(h) was amended to add economic performance to the all events test, but involves taxable years before that amendment.

Ford Motor Company v. Commissioner

United States Court of Appeals, Sixth Circuit, 1995. 71 F.3d 209.

MILBURN, CIRCUIT JUDGE:

Petitioner Ford Motor Company ("Ford") appeals the decision of the United States Tax Court upholding respondent Commissioner of Internal Revenue's ("Commissioner") reduction of petitioner's deductions for its obligations under agreements it entered into in settlement of tort lawsuits against it. On appeal, the issue is whether respondent Commissioner abused her discretion in determining that petitioner's method of accounting for its structured settlements was not a clear reflection of income under 26 U.S.C. § 446(b) and in ordering petitioner to limit its deduction in 1980 to the cost of the annuity contracts it purchased to fund the settlements. For the reasons that follow, we affirm.

I

A

Petitioner Ford Motor Company is engaged in a number of businesses, including the manufacture of cars and trucks, and it maintains its books and records and files its income taxes using the accrual method of accounting. In the years preceding 1980, some of Ford's cars and trucks were involved in automobile accidents, and in 1980, Ford entered into 20 structured settlement agreements in settlement of personal injury or accidental death claims with persons who were injured in the accidents and with survivors of persons who died as a result of the accidents. In these structured settlement agreements, Ford agreed to make periodic payments of tort damages, yearly or monthly, in exchange for a release of all claims against it. The payments were to be made over various periods of time, the longest of which was 58 years. All but three of the settlements provided for payments over a period of 40 years or more. The agreements were of three types: (I) those that required petitioner to make periodic payments for a period certain ("Type I settlements"); (II) those that required petitioner to make periodic payments for the remainder of a claimant's life ("Type II settlements"); and (III) those that required petitioner to make periodic payments for the longer of a period certain or the remainder of a claimant's life ("Type III settlements"). In total, the structured settlement agreements provided for payments of $24,477,699.

To provide it with funds to cover the periodic payments, Ford purchased single premium annuity contracts at a cost of $4,424,587. The annuity contracts were structured so that the yearly annuity payments would equal the yearly amount owed to the claimants under the structured settlement agreements. None of the settlement agreements released petitioner from liability following the purchase of the annuity contract, and, in the event of a default on an annuity, petitioner would be required to pay the remaining balance owed to the tort claimants. The parties stipulated that the present value of the deferred payments that petitioner agreed to make to the claimants did not exceed the cost of the annuity contracts.

On its 1980 tax return, petitioner claimed deductions for the various types of structured settlements as follows: for the Type I settlements, it claimed the total amount of all periodic payments due; for the Type II settlements, it claimed the amounts it actually paid during 1980; and for the Type III settlements, it claimed the total amount of all payments due for the period certain portion of the settlement. These deductions totaled $10,636,994, which petitioner included as part of a product liability loss that it carried back to its 1970 taxable year pursuant to 26 U.S.C. § 172(b)(1)(I). It also reported the annuity income on its 1980 federal income tax return under 26 U.S.C. § 72. For financial accounting purposes, petitioner reported the 1980 structured settlements by expensing the cost of the annuity in the year of the settlement. * * *

Respondent Commissioner determined that Ford's method of accounting for its structured settlements did not clearly reflect income under 26 U.S.C. § 446(b) and disallowed the deductions petitioner claimed in excess of the cost of the annuities petitioner purchased. Respondent also excluded from petitioner's income the amounts required to be reported as income from annuity contracts, which was $323,340 in 1980. As a result, respondent determined a deficiency in petitioner's 1970 federal income tax liability of $3,300,151.

B

Petitioner Ford * * * claimed that it was entitled to deduct in 1980 the full amount of all payments to be made under the structured settlements, basing its valuation of the life settlements on the life expectancies of the claimants. The total deduction Ford claimed was $24,477,699.

The parties submitted the case to the United States Tax Court with all facts fully stipulated. A divided court upheld the Commissioner's position. * * *

II

A

Section 446 of the Internal Revenue Code provides the general rule governing use of methods of accounting by taxpayers. Section 446(b) provides that, if the method of accounting used by the taxpayer to compute income does not clearly reflect income, "the computation of taxable income shall be made under such method as, in the opinion of the Secretary or his delegate, does clearly reflect income." The Commissioner has broad discretion under § 446(b) to determine whether a particular method of accounting clearly reflects income. Thor Power Tool Co. v. Commissioner, 439 U.S. 522 (1979). "Since the Commissioner has 'much latitude for discretion,' his interpretation of the statute's clear-reflection standard 'should not be interfered with unless clearly unlawful.' " 439 U.S. at 532 (quoting Lucas v. American Code Co., 280 U.S. 445, 449 (1930)). Once the Commissioner has determined that a method of accounting does not clearly reflect income, she may substitute a method that, in her opinion, does clearly reflect income.

* * * All facts in this case were stipulated, and the issue before us is a question of ultimate fact, which we review de novo.

B

There are three stages to our analysis in this case: first, we decide whether the application of § 446(b) was appropriate; second, we decide whether the tax court correctly determined that petitioner's method of accounting did not clearly reflect income; and third, we address the appropriateness of the method of accounting that the Commissioner imposed in its place.

First, petitioner argues that the tax court erred in allowing the Commissioner to require Ford to change its method of accounting because, in the absence of abuse or manipulation, an accrual method taxpayer clearly reflects its income when its reporting satisfies the "all events" test. Therefore, it argues that, because its accrual of deductions satisfied the all events test, the Commissioner had no authority to invoke § 446(b).

Ford Motor Company is an accrual method taxpayer. The accrual method of accounting takes income into account when the right to payment is earned, even if payment is not received until later, and expenses into account when they are incurred, even if payment is not made until a later time. Financial accounting systems differ regarding the time that an expense is "incurred" and therefore should be accrued, but, under the tax law, the standard for determining when an expense is "incurred" is the "all events" test. This test provides that an accrual method taxpayer must deduct an expense in the taxable year when all the events have occurred that establish the fact of liability giving rise to the deduction and the amount of the liability can be determined with reasonable accuracy. Id. The tax court assumed for purposes of discussion that Ford's deductions satisfied the all events test, and for purposes of our review, we will make this assumption as well.

It is a well established principle that the Commissioner may not invoke her authority under § 446(b) to require a taxpayer to change from an accounting method that clearly reflects income, even if she believes that a second method might more clearly reflect income. However, we hold that satisfaction of the all events test by an accrual method taxpayer does not preempt the Commissioner's authority under § 446(b) to determine that a taxpayer's method of accounting does not clearly reflect income.

Section 446(c) of the Internal Revenue Code provides that, subject to the provisions of subsections (a) and (b), a taxpayer may compute taxable income under the accrual method of accounting. The all events test, which is merely a means devised to define the years in which income and deductions accrue, clearly is subordinate to the clear reflection standard contained in subsection (b). The tax court stated:

> The provisions of section 446 make it clear that a taxpayer's ability to use one or more of the methods of accounting listed in 446(c) is contingent upon the satisfaction of subsections 446(a) and (b). The statute does not limit the Commissioner's discretion under section 446(b) by the taxpayer's mere compliance with the methods of accounting generally permitted under section 446(c). * * * In short, the statute clearly provides that the taxpayers may use an accrual method so long as it clearly reflects income.

The language of § 446 is clear on its face, and we agree with the tax court's interpretation of the statute. See Mooney Aircraft, Inc. v. United States, 420 F.2d 400, 406 (5th Cir.1969) ("The 'all events test,' however, is not the only basis upon which the Commissioner can disallow a deduction. Under 446(b) he has discretion to disallow any accounting method which does not clearly reflect income.").

Petitioner argues that Congress acknowledged that the Commissioner's discretion under § 446(b) does not extend to situations such as the present case when it changed the Internal Revenue Code, effective in 1984, to provide in § 461(h)(2)(c) that accrual method taxpayers cannot deduct tort liabilities until the year in which payment is made. Ford points to the legislative history of § 461, which states that "the rules relating to the time for accrual of a deduction by a taxpayer using the accrual method of accounting should be changed to take into account the time value of money." It argues that this statement indicates a recognition by Congress that the Commissioner was not authorized to deny the sort of accrual that Ford is attempting prior to 1984.

The tax court held that the change in prior law to which the legislative history refers is the all events test contained in the Income Tax Regulations and that Congress did not intend "to limit respondent's authority under section 446(b) in any way by enacting section 461(h) in 1984." We agree that the change that this passage references is a modification of the all events test and conclude that nothing in the legislative history of § 461(h) limits the Commissioner's authority under § 446(b). Section 461(h) was a Congressional effort to remedy an accounting distortion by placing all accrual method taxpayers on the cash method of accounting for tort liabilities, regardless of the length of the payout period and without any consideration of whether accrual of an expense in an earlier year would distort income. Its enactment does not preclude the Commissioner from applying the clear reflection standard of § 446(b) on a case-by-case basis to taxpayers in tax years prior to 1984.

C

Having determined that expenses that satisfy the all events test can be disallowed when accrual would not result in a clear reflection of income, we now examine the correctness of the Commissioner's determination that Ford's method of accounting for its tort obligations did not clearly reflect income. * * *

[The court's discussion of the Tax Court's conclusion, by way of an example, that the tax savings from a current deduction would make Ford better off financially by having accidents is omitted. The court accepted Ford's contention that the Tax Court's calculation was incorrect, but concluded that this factor was not determinative to the Tax Court but merely highlighted the distortion of income.]

[E]ven viewing petitioner's numerical example as correct, the gross distortion of income that it demonstrates between the economic and tax results persuades us that the tax court's decision was not improper. Given the length of the payment periods, allowing a deduction for the full amount of liability in 1980 could lead to the result that the tax benefit from the deduction would fund the full amounts due in future years and leave petitioner with a profit. Such a result extends the accrual method of accounting beyond its inherent limitations.

Our task on appeal is to determine whether there is an adequate basis in law for the Commissioner's conclusion that Ford's method of accounting did not clearly reflect income. See RCA Corp., 664 F.2d at 886. We find several cases from other circuits that support our finding that the Commissioner's exercise of her discretion was proper. * * *

[I]n this case, assuming that the all events test for accrual is satisfied, the long time period between the deductions and eventual payment of the obligations causes a distortion of petitioner's income.

Petitioner also argues that the tax court's decision that petitioner's method of accounting did not clearly reflect income was improper because it "authorizes arbitrary and unprincipled use of the Commissioner's section 446(b) power." It asserts that the tax court failed to provide any principles "to delineate the scope of section 446(b)," and that, in doing so, it created an "arbitrary system * * * that requires all accrual taxpayers to account for their liabilities when they become fixed, yet makes the validity of that reporting method subject to the unconstrained whim of the Commissioner."

We are not persuaded by this policy-based argument. The tax court concluded its opinion stating:

> Finally, we want to make clear that the mere fact that a deduction which accrues prior to the time payment is made (the timing factor) does not, by itself, cause the accrual to run afoul of the clear reflection of income requirement. Inherent in the use of an accrual method is the fact that a deduction may be allowed in advance of payment. Our holding in the instant case is not intended to draw a bright line that can be applied mechanically in other circumstances. We decide only the ultimate question of fact in the instant case; namely, whether, for tax purposes, petitioner's method of accounting for its obligations under the structured settlements clearly reflects income. We hold that it does not and that the Government did not abuse its discretion in making that determination.

As the tax court observed, "the issue of whether the taxpayer's method of accounting clearly reflects income is a question of fact to be determined on a case-by-case basis." We find the tax court's language sufficient to limit its holding to extreme cases such as this one in which the economic results are grossly different from the tax results and therefore conclude that the tax court's decision does not allow the Commissioner arbitrary or unprincipled discretion.

D

Given that a change was necessary because Ford's accrual of its settlement obligations in 1980 did not clearly reflect income, Ford argues that the method of accounting that the Commissioner imposed in its place was improper. Ford asserts that the Commissioner lacked the authority to impose the method of accounting that she did because it is "inconsistent with the plain dictates of the Code and regulations and the undisputed facts of this case."

The method of accounting that the Commissioner imposed was to allow Ford a deduction for the amount that it paid for the annuities with no further deductions for the future payments that Ford will make to the claimants. To offset her disallowance of future deductions, the Commissioner will permit Ford to exclude its income from the annuity contracts. Petitioner asserts that this scheme violates established tax law for several reasons and forces Ford to use a tax treatment that it could not have adopted on its own.

First, petitioner argues that the Commissioner is imposing on it a present value method of accounting which should only be imposed in the presence of a directive by Congress to do so. Ford additionally argues that this method impermissibly allows it only to deduct the approximately $4 million it paid for the annuities without ever allowing a deduction for the additional approximately $20 million it will pay to the claimants and that the Commissioner's method is arbitrary because it is not a method that Ford could have adopted on its own.

Respondent counters that its method of accounting is a modified cash basis method that allows Ford "a dollar for dollar deduction, albeit in the form of an offset against its annuity income, for the full face amount of its future payments of approximately $24 million." Respondent points out that, because she allowed Ford to deduct the full cost of the annuity contracts in 1980, it has no basis in the contracts and would be fully taxable on the annuity income of $24,477,699 as it is received. However, the payments Ford is required to make to the tort claimants, which correspond exactly to the amount of its annuity income, give rise to deductions that offset the income and create a wash. Respondent argues that, because she has relieved taxpayer of the obligation to report the annuity income as it is received, she should not allow Ford any deductions for the required payments.

We find no merit in petitioner's assertion that this methodology is improper because it reduces the amount of the deductions to the present value of the payments petitioner is obligated to make. The Commissioner reduced petitioner's deduction to the cost of the annuity contracts. The stipulated facts provided only that the present value of the payments petitioner is obligated to make did not exceed this amount. There is no indication that respondent was imposing a present value method of accounting on petitioner.

Furthermore, we find no authority that prohibits the tax accounting treatment that the Commissioner and the tax court imposed here. The Commissioner's discretion to impose an alternate method of accounting under § 446(b) is not limited to methods that Ford could have adopted on its own. While we recognize that to require Ford to account for its tort obligations on the cash method might have been a more logical alternative, we cannot find that the Commissioner's exercise of her discretion was arbitrary because it resulted in an accounting treatment more favorable to Ford that a straight cash method would be. The only difference between the Commissioner's method of accounting and the cash basis method is that petitioner receives an immediate deduction for the cost of its annuities rather than recovering that cost over the terms of the annuities under 26 U.S.C. § 72, and this difference inures to Ford's benefit. We therefore conclude that the tax court's decision regarding the accounting method the Commissioner imposed was proper.

III

For the reasons stated, the judgment of the tax court is AFFIRMED.

NOTES

(A) *Time Value of Money and Accrual Accounting.* Prior to *Ford Motor Co.*, the government had little success in convincing courts to apply time value of money principles (and three Tax Court judges even dissented in *Ford*). Congress responded in 1984 by enacting § 461(h), which allows deductions for tort liabilities only as payments are made, but that statute was not applicable in the *Ford* case. The government's only previous significant victory on time value of money grounds had been in *Mooney Aircraft, Inc. v. United States*, 420 F.2d 400 (5th Cir.1969), which involved an average twenty-year delay between accrual and payment. In that case, the court acknowledged that the "all events" test was satisfied but held that a long delay between accrual and payment would necessarily violate the requirement that accounting methods "clearly reflect income," stating:

> There is no contingency in this case as to the *fact* of liability itself; the only contingency relates to *when* the liability will arise. * * *
>
> The most salient feature in this case is the fact that many or possibly most of the expenses which taxpayer wishes to presently deduct will not actually be paid for 15, 20 or even 30 years (the taxpayer has not attempted to deny this). In no other case coming to our attention have we found anything even comparable to the time span involved in this case. * * * We therefore find no difficulty in concluding that the Commissioner had a reasonable basis for disallowing the deduction as not clearly reflecting income.

More typical was the Supreme Court's opinion in *Hughes Properties, Inc.*, distinguished in *Ford*, in which the Supreme Court dismissed the Commissioner's time value concerns. The court in *Ford Motor Co.* notes that the Commissioner's tax avoidance concerns in *Hughes* might not have been dismissed so easily if the "progressive" slot machine payouts at issue there had been extended for a longer period. But it is not clear that the Supreme Court would have ruled differently. The Supreme Court apparently believed there was no "potential for tax avoidance" despite the Commissioner's urging that the taxpayer's discretion to set very high odds against progressive payoffs and to place into operation additional progressive slot machines at the end of each taxable year created opportunities to inflate deductions for amounts that would not be paid until some time in the distant future. The Court found no tax avoidance motive or behavior in the case and, in an extraordinary exercise of judicial non-notice, concluded that it was not in the casino's self interest to set the odds so high as to defer payoffs too far in the future because "customers will refuse to play and will gamble elsewhere." It is difficult to imagine where the Court might have been looking when it reached that conclusion. Are the Justices so insulated from ordinary life that they do not know of the extraordinary economic success of state lotteries that routinely raise enormous sums of money from untold numbers of people who avidly want—rather than shrink from—gambles that couple huge payoffs with extremely long odds? Could their law clerks also live lives so sheltered that they too are oblivious to this phenomenon?

In *Mooney Aircraft,* the court noted that the longer the delay between accrual and payment, the less probable the payment. In *Mooney Aircraft,* the taxpayer had made no payments and the court apparently feared it would never do so. In *Ford Motor Co.,* however, the taxpayer had purchased an annuity equal to the present value of its obligations. If it had not done so, how would the Tax Court have determined the present value of Ford's future liability? Concerns over the inability to determine present value for lack of a discount rate prompted Congress to choose the approach of § 461(h) that denies a deduction until there is economic performance (defined to be payment in the case of structured settlements) rather than permitting a current deduction for the present value of the liability. The equivalency of various methods is discussed in the Note infra at page 737.

(B) *Section 461(h).* Although § 461(h) technically changes the "all events test" applicable to accrual basis taxpayers, its effect is essentially to move those taxpayers closer to the cash method for expenditures. The House Report accompanying the 1984 Act, which adopted § 461(h), explained the reasons for change:

> The committee believes that the rules relating to the time for accrual of a deduction by a taxpayer using the accrual method accounting should be changed to take into account the time value of money. * * * Allowing a taxpayer to take deductions currently for an amount to be paid in the future overstates the true cost of the expense to the extent the time value of money is not taken into account; the deduction is overstated by the amount the face value exceeds the present value of the expense.

H.R.Rep. 98–432, 9th Cong., 2d Sess. 1254 (1984).

Under § 461(h), all the events that establish liability for a deductible expenditure for an accrual basis taxpayer are not treated as having occurred any earlier than the time "economic performance" occurs.

Economic Performance. Neither the statute nor the regulations define "economic performance," but the House Report explains that "[e]conomic performance with respect to a particular liability generally occurs when the activities that the taxpayer is obligated to do to satisfy the liability actually are performed." Section 461(h) provides specific rules for certain situations. For example, if the liability of the taxpayer arises out of the provision of services or property by the taxpayer, economic performance occurs as the taxpayer provides the services or property. Thus, if A in Year 1 incurs a fixed liability to pay B $100 in Year 3 for services to be performed in Year 3, A may deduct the $100 only in Year 3. Even if A paid the $100 in Year 1, the deduction could only be taken in Year 3 when economic performance occurs.

In some cases, payment is required to trigger economic performance. The regulations provide that economic performance occurs only on payment with respect to liabilities for rebates and refunds, awards, prizes and jackpots, insurance, warranty and service contracts, taxes, and any liability not specifically covered by another rule. Reg. § 1.461–4(g). Cash basis principles are used to determine payment. Reg. § 1.461–4(g)(1)(ii)(A).

Recurring Items Exception. The principal exception to the economic performance rule is for recurring items. A taxpayer may deduct expenditures for recurring items as soon as the "all events" test is met, so long as economic performance occurs no later than eight and a half months after the close of the taxable year and either the item is immaterial or all events accounting results in a better matching of the liability with the income to which it relates than would result from accruing the liability when economic performance occurs. § 461(h)(3). The Conference Committee Report for the 1984 Act gives the following examples of when the "all events" test does a better job than the "economic performance" test of picking the taxable year for deduction:

> For example, a sales commission agreement may require certain collection activities to be performed in a year subsequent to the year in which sales income is reported. In such a case, economic performance with respect to some portion of the liability to pay the commission may not occur until the following year. Nevertheless, deducting the commission expense in the year in which the sales income is reported results in a better matching of the commission expense with the sales income. Likewise, if income from the sale of goods is recognized in one year, but the goods are not shipped until the following year, the shipping costs are more properly matched to income in the year the goods are sold rather than in the year the goods are shipped.

In applying the recurring items exception, the consistency of the taxpayer's tax and financial statement accounting methods is taken into account. Tort and workers' compensation liabilities are not eligible for the exception. See § 461(h)(3). The regulations also exempt from the recurring items rule fines and liabilities arising out of breach of contract. Reg. § 1.461–5(c).

Liabilities. On its face, § 461(h) does not apply to all premature accruals. It is limited to liabilities arising out of the provision of services or property, or a payment arising from workers' compensation or a tort. The statute, however, gives the Service the authority to issue regulations determining economic performance for other liabilities. Regulations cover liabilities arising out of breach of contract or violation of law, rebates and refunds, awards, prizes, and jackpots, amounts paid for insurance, warranty and service contracts, and taxes.

(C) *Alternative Approaches.* As *Ford Motor Co.* illustrates, there is more than one approach to premature accruals. Congress rejected the approach chosen by the courts in that case—permitting a current deduction for the present value of the future liability. The House Report explained why that alternative was not chosen:

> The committee recognizes that in the case of noncapital items, a taxpayer, theoretically, should be allowed a deduction for either the full amount of a liability when the liability is satisfied or a discounted amount at an earlier time. However, the committee also recognizes that determining the discounted values for all kinds of future expenses would be extraordinarily complex and would be extremely difficult to administer. For instance, a system that allowed current deductions for discounted future expenses would have to include a complex set of

rules for recalculating overstated and understated deductions when the future liabilities are re-estimated or are actually satisfied at a time, or in an amount, different from that originally projected; a complex recapture mechanism would be required. Furthermore, in the case of capital items, an appropriate discounting system may be equally complex. Therefore, in order to prevent deductions for future expenses in excess of their true cost while avoiding the complexity of a system of discounted valuation, the committee believes that expenses should be accrued only when economic performance occurs.

Another alternative is to permit a deduction when payment is made. This option can be justified because it is equivalent to taking a current deduction for the present value of the liability (assuming an after-tax discount rate is used). The legislative history does not address that option, although in many cases waiting until payment would defer the deduction even longer. It is important to note, however, that "economic performance" may occur *after* payment and thus an accrual basis taxpayer may be treated more harshly than a cash basis taxpayer.

(D) *Special Rules for Nuclear Decommissioning and Coal Mine Reclamation Expenses.* The 1984 legislation also provided elective alternative treatments for the expenses of decommissioning nuclear power plants, reclaiming coal mines, and for certain waste disposal sites. See §§ 468A and 468 of the Code. Under § 468A, taxpayers may deduct, subject to an annual limitation, contributions to a qualified nuclear decommissioning reserve fund. The taxpayer must obtain an IRS ruling in order to take such deductions. The taxpayer must actually set aside the amounts in a segregated fund to be used exclusively for the payment of decommissioning costs or taxes and management costs of the fund. The reserve fund is treated as a separate taxable entity and is taxed at the maximum corporate tax rate unless exempt under another provision of the Code. Contributions to the fund are not subject to tax. Other rules prohibit self-dealing or the purchase of assets of a related party. Withdrawals from the fund for any purpose except payment of taxes and management costs are includible in the income of the nuclear plant. The withdrawal then may be deducted from the gross income of the plant if paid for reasonable decommissioning expenditures. Any funds remaining in the reserve when the decommissioning is complete must be included in the taxable income of the plant.

Section 468 provides an elective method for deducting the costs of future reclamation and closing costs of coal mines or certain waste disposal sites required by federal or state law. Taxpayers are allowed a current deduction for reasonable additions to a reserve based upon the amount of surface disturbed by the mining or solid waste activity. An annual interest charge, specified by statute, is imputed on the reserve account and serves to limit future deductions. Amounts charged against the reserve at the time of reclamation or closing are not deductible and any excess of the reserve balance over the estimated or actual costs is immediately taxable. In effect, the taxpayer is treated as realizing taxable income equal to a statutorily imputed rate of interest on amounts held for future expenditures as measured by the reserve. The relationship of §§ 468 and 468A to the economic performance requirement of § 461(h) is discussed in the following note.

NOTE ON THE ECONOMIC EQUIVALENCE OF §§ 461(H), 468A, AND 468: THE CONCEPT OF NON–ADVANTAGEOUS TAX DEFERRAL

In an earlier note, we discussed the equivalence of allowing a deduction earlier than it should be allowed and providing an interest-free loan from the government to the taxpayer of the tax savings resulting from the accelerated deduction. See the Note on Tax Deferral, page 287 supra.[1] Taxpayers could achieve similar tax advantages before 1984 by the use of what the tax-writing committees of Congress labeled "premature accruals"—immediate deduction of nominal costs to be paid in the future. Thus, taxpayers who could deduct expenses to be paid many years hence were able to earn interest (or other investment income) on the tax saved without paying offsetting interest (or increased taxes) to the government. "Structured settlements," such as those at issue in the *Ford Motor Co.* case, are one such example.

The rules of §§ 461(h), 468A and 468 are all attempts to correct the failure of prior law to take into account the "time value of money." These provisions respond to the problem of premature accruals either by deferring the deduction or discounting it to the present value. Section 461(h) deals with the problem by deferring the deduction until "economic performance." Section 468A allows a current deduction, limited to an amount that is expected grow in time to provide the needed decommissioning funds, but requires the deducted amount to be set aside in a special fund whose earnings are taxed at the top corporate rate. Section 468 allows the immediate deduction of an amount estimated to be needed for reclamation expenses but, in effect, taxes imputed interest on the amount deducted. In theory, §§ 468A and 468 are economically equivalent to the delay in deduction required by § 461(h) and therefore should not be viewed as intended to provide special advantages to nuclear decommissioning or coal mine reclamation expenses. Rather, these provisions should be viewed as alternative mechanisms for taking into account the time value of money.

Demonstrating that this is so is best done by reviewing four examples that rely on a number of common assumptions. (Following the examples, the significance of these assumptions is explored.) First, the taxpayer is assumed to be subject to a 40 percent marginal tax rate on all relevant amounts (and for offsetting all relevant deductions) for all taxable years. Second, pretax rates of return are assumed to be 10 percent a year, therefore yielding a 6 percent after-tax rate of return. Third, it is assumed that "economic performance" occurs in Year 4 and that $100 will be spent in Year 4 on the activity giving rise to the deduction.

---

1. That Note also points out that, under certain conditions, the immediate deduction of capital expenditures is equivalent to the exemption from tax of the yield from the capital asset. This suggests the important relationship between the timing of tax deductions and the taxation of investment income, a matter that is discussed in some detail in this Note.

Example 1: The Tax Advantage of Immediate Deduction of the Future Cost. If we assume that the $100 deduction *should* be permitted in the year of payment or economic performance, the advantage of accelerating the deduction can be demonstrated as follows: (1) the $100 deduction in *Year 4* would save (at a 40 percent tax rate) $40 of taxes in Year 4. (2) If the deduction for $100 is permitted in Year 1, the tax savings of $40 will occur in Year 1 and will grow to $47.64 in Year 4 (at a 6 percent after-tax return compounded annually). The taxpayer's advantage from accelerating the deduction is his ability to earn interest on the tax savings without paying interest to the government on this amount.

Example 2: The Equivalence of Delaying Deductions and Allowing Immediate Deduction of Present Value. (1) The taxpayer saves $40 of tax in Year 4—the year of economic performance and payment—if the $100 deduction is delayed until that year. This would be required under § 461(h).

(2) Allowing a deduction currently for the present value of the Year 4 deduction—$100 discounted at the *after-tax* rate of return of 6 percent—would produce a deduction in Year 1 of $84.[2] At a 40 percent tax rate, an $84 deduction saves $33.60 in tax in Year 1. At a 6 percent after-tax rate of return, compounded annually, the Year 1 tax savings of $33.60 would grow to $40 in Year 4. This amount is equal to the tax that would be saved in Year 4 if the deduction were deferred until that time.[3]

Example 3: The Equivalence of § 461(h) and § 468A (Nuclear Decommissioning Expenses). (1) Under § 461(h), as above, the $100 deduction is deferred until Year 4; the tax savings is $40 at that time at a 40 percent tax rate.

(2) Under § 468A, the present value of future nuclear decommissioning expenses ($84) can be deducted currently and set aside in a fund taxable at the top corporate rate (which will be assumed here to be 40 percent). The results for each year are as follows:

Year 1:	Amount into Fund		$84.00
	Earnings of Fund (at 10 percent)	$8.40	
	Less tax (at 40 percent)	$3.36	
	Addition to Fund		$5.04
Fund in Year 2			$89.04

Without belaboring similar computations, the fund will grow to $94.38 in Year 3 and $100.05 in Year 4 (at a 6 percent after-tax rate of return). The tax saved in Year 1 from the $84 deduction is $33.60; that

2. Tables of Present Value are set forth in the Appendix at page 849, infra.

3. Legislative history indicates that Congress was unclear whether the perceived problem with pre–1984 law was that deductions were taken too soon or that the deductions allowed were too large. The House Re-port seems to imply that the timing was correct but the amount wrong. In this light, the economic performance test is a mechanism to avoid the administrative difficulties of allowing current deductions at present value. As discussed subsequently in this Note, that conclusion seems correct for some items covered by § 461(h), but wrong for others.

amount will grow to $40 in Year 4 (at a 6 percent after-tax rate of return).[4]

Example 4: The Equivalence of § 461(h) and § 468 (Coal Mine Reclamation Expenses). (1) Again, as above, a $100 deduction in Year 4 under § 461(h) saves $40 in taxes that year.

(2) Under § 468, an amount equal to the present estimate of future coal mine reclamation expenses can be deducted currently. The "present value" concept is accomplished by annually adding an imputed interest return to the reserve. The reserve is taxable in any year to the extent that the reserve amount exceeds the estimated reclamation costs; any remaining excess in the reserve is taxed at the time of reclamation. Amounts charged against the reserve for reclamation costs are not deductible at that time. The results under § 468 are as follows:

Year 1: Amount deducted and added to the reserve $100

Tax savings to a 40 percent taxpayer $40

Year 2: If the imputed interest rate were equal to the *after-tax* rate of return, $6 of imputed interest would be taxed in Year 2 (since the fund would exceed the estimated reclamation expenses by that amount). This would increase taxes by $2.40 in Year 2. The tax savings of $40 in Year 1 would earn $2.40 (at a 6 percent after-tax rate of return) leaving a net savings of $40. Identical results would occur in Years 3 and 4 ($6 imputed income, increasing taxes by $2.40, exactly offsetting the $2.40 after-tax earnings on the $40 tax savings of Year 1), leaving a net tax savings in Year 4 of $40, an amount identical to that under § 461(h).[5]

(3) The results would not change if, instead of taxing the imputed return of the reserve annually, the imputed return were allowed to

---

4. Perhaps surprisingly, *so long as the assumptions hold,* the value of the tax savings under § 468A will not vary, regardless of the amount put into the fund. Assume, for example, that $200 instead of $84 is set aside in the fund in Year 1. The results will be as follows:

Year 1:	Amount into fund	$200
	Earnings of fund (at 10 percent)	$20
	Less tax (at 40 percent)	$8
	Addition to Fund	$12

| Fund in Year 2 | $212 |

At a 6 percent after-tax rate of return, $212 will grow to $238.20 in Year 4. If $100 is spent on nuclear decommissioning, the excess of $138.20 in the fund will then be taxed. The tax consequences are as follows: The $200 deduction in Year 1 saves $80 in taxes (at a 40 percent rate); that amount accumulates to $95.28 in Year 4 (at a 6 percent after-tax rate of return). But, in Year 4, the $138.20 excess in the fund triggers $55.28 in taxes (at a 40 percent rate), leaving a net tax savings in Year 4 dollars of $40, the identical amount under paragraphs (1) and (2) above. Given these relationships, might the § 468A restrictions on amounts that may be contributed to the fund suggest congressional concern that standard economic assumptions of these examples might not always be realistic in practice?

5. This result should not be surprising in light of footnote 4, supra, which shows that, in the nuclear decommissioning approach, the after-tax savings does not increase in present value terms so long as the investment return is taxed, allowing the fund to compound at an after-tax amount that is then taxed if not spent on the deductible activity.

compound and the compounded return were all taxed in Year 4. The additional tax in Year 4 would then fully offset the after-tax return earned on the $40 tax savings in Year 1. The net effect would be $40 of tax saved in Year 4.

(4) If the return imputed to the § 468 reserve is different from the after-tax rate of return, results identical to delaying the deduction will not occur. Under § 468, the imputed return, after a phase-in period, is a "federal" rate, which is defined in § 1274 of the Code as a rate on U.S. Treasury bonds and, in that section and elsewhere in the Code, is regarded as a pretax rate of return. If the taxpayer's after-tax rate of return is less than the imputed rate (which it will be if the taxpayer earns a pretax rate equal to the federal funds rate), § 468 will produce a lesser tax savings in present value terms than either § 461(h) or § 468A. On the other hand, if the taxpayer earns an after-tax return greater than the rate imputed under § 468, the provision will result in a greater tax savings in present value terms than under either § 461(h) or § 468A. Some of the problems resulting from variations of the actual and imputed returns are avoided in § 468A, which requires the deducted amount actually to be set aside in a fund whose income is taxed at the top corporate tax rate.

Other "Equivalent" Ways of Dealing with the Time Value of Money. Under certain conditions, therefore, §§ 461(h), 468, and 468A can be viewed as economically equivalent means of eliminating the tax advantages of allowing undiscounted deductions to be taken before the expenses are paid.[6] The approach of § 461(h) is the most straightforward since it simply defers the deduction. The other sections allow earlier deductions but either limit these deductions to present value and tax the investment returns from the deducted amounts as in the case of § 468A, or, as in the case of § 468, allow current deductions of the full value; both provisions tax invested returns and include in income in a subsequent year the amount of the deduction compounded at the after-tax rate of return.

Other approaches to "time value of money" issues can be found in the Code. For example, the taxpayer might be allowed to take the deduction at the earlier time but be required to invest the tax savings in a no-interest bond issued by the federal government. This would recapture for the government the value of the "interest-free loan." This approach can be found in § 832(e), which relates to certain mortgage guarantee insurance

---

6. The examples in this note all assume that economic performance and payment occur at the same time, but § 461(h) generally turns on the time of economic performance rather than the time of payment (except in the case of workers' compensation and tort liabilities where § 461(h)(2)(C) provides that economic performance occurs as payments are made). Since the present value of future costs turns on the time of payment, the House Report implies (by equating the deferral of deduction until economic performance

to the current deduction of the present value of the future payment) that economic performance and payment will occur at approximately the same time. Where payment occurs significantly earlier or later than economic performance, it would seem possible to recharacterize a portion of the transaction as a loan and to impute interest income and deductions to avoid distortion of income. See page 748 infra, dealing with the rules governing the timing of interest income and deductions.

companies; this rather obscure provision requires that tax benefits from current deductions be invested in special-issue U.S. bonds that are not transferable and pay no interest.

Payments that are accelerated or deferred often could be separated into two transactions: first, a purchase of goods or services, and second, a loan from one party to the other (depending on whether the payment is accelerated or deferred). If interest income and deductions on the "loan" were imputed and allocated to the parties, the time value of money would be appropriately reflected. This approach is discussed at page 748 supra.

A third approach would explicitly increase the amount of tax deferred by an interest charge. For example, the taxpayer would be allowed a full-value current deduction but also would be charged to compensate the government for the delay in the collection of tax. This would convert the "interest-free" loan into an interest-bearing loan and thereby eliminate the advantage of tax deferral. See, e.g., § 995(f), (requiring payment of such interest on "DISC-related deferred tax liability"). The interest charge is tied to comparable rates on U.S. Treasury bills with one-year maturities. Compare § 668 (charging simple 6 percent interest on tax deferred on income received by a U.S. beneficiary of an "accumulation distribution" from a foreign trust); § 453A (charging interest on deferred tax liability on installment notes at general tax underpayment rates); § 1291 (charging interest on deferred tax on "passive foreign investment companies" at the tax underpayment rate); § 460(b) (charging or paying interest on deferred (or accelerated) tax on completed contract project at the tax overpayment rate).

Finally, the advantage of tax deferral might be redressed by imposing a substitute tax on another taxpayer. This approach produces results that would be equivalent to the government and to the taxpayers if the same tax rates and rates of return apply to both taxpayers. These notions seem to inform those provisions that require "matching" of the time of the payor's deduction with the time of the recipient's inclusion of the payment in income. See, e.g., §§ 267(a)(2), 404(d).

The Concept of Non–Advantageous Deferral. The alternative approaches described above, as well as those of §§ 461(h), 468A, and 468, seem to imply that Congress, to some extent at least, may be indifferent to the timing of income or deductions so long as no tax advantage results. Non-advantageous tax deferral occurs when the taxpayer is no better off in present value terms than he would have been by taking the deduction in the proper year. The most obvious ways of eliminating the advantages of tax deferral are delaying deductions, or charging interest on the deferred tax, or requiring the taxpayer to purchase non-interest bearing government bonds with the tax savings. As the foregoing illustrations demonstrate, there are other ways to eliminate the advantages of tax deferral. Accelerating deductions will not be advantageous if the tax collected in a later year is larger in amount than, and equal in present value to, the tax forgone in the earlier year. More precisely, taxpayers will not benefit if the investment return is taxed currently and the amount of the deduction that would have been available in the later year is equal to the earlier deduction adjusted to reflect the after-tax investment return. Taxpayers will be advantaged, however, if tax deferral permits either compounding of income at something greater than the taxpayer's after-tax rate of return (for example, because the pretax investment income is tax-exempt or is taxed at a lower rate) or if the deferral is not compensated for either by subsequently including in income an amount compounded at the after-tax rate of return or by discounting the earlier deduction at the after-tax rate of return.[7]

Conditions Required for the Equivalences to Hold. It is no coincidence that the examples demonstrating the equivalence among §§ 461(h), 468A, and 468 assumed that (1) the same tax rate applied to all relevant income in each relevant taxable year and (2) that pretax rates of return were invariant and that they were taxable currently, yielding an after-tax rate of return equal to the (unchanging) pretax rate reduced by the (unchanging) tax rate. When these conditions do not hold, the timing of income and deductions may produce greater or lesser tax in present value terms than is shown in the examples. Alternative approaches to time value of money issues therefore must be sensitive to the assumptions necessary to such economic equivalence so that tax-avoidance opportunities will be minimized.

The Need for a Norm. The above analysis compared alternative rules on the assumption that the proper amount and time for the deduction were known. In some cases, the proper result will be apparent and timing variations may be readily compared. For example, some deductions of accrual basis taxpayers seem appropriately delayed until the time of economic performance, regardless of when the fact and amount of liability become fixed; rental payments may be a good example of expenses that should be deducted only upon economic performance. Different results, however, seem appropriate for other kinds of expenses. For example, the expenses of removing oil pipelines or offshore drilling rigs, of nuclear decommissioning, and of coal mine reclamation all seem analogous to capital expenditures, but incurred at the end of an asset's life rather than at the beginning; these expenses are necessary in order to produce income over a number of years. Therefore, the normal rules regarding the recovery of capital expenditures suggest that such expenses should be deductible not in the year of economic performance, but over a period of years, perhaps in accordance with depreciation allowances for other capital expenses. (Recall the airplane maintenance costs discussed in Rev. Rul. 2001–4, supra, at page 323). If this is the case, the assumption in the above examples that a $100 deduction should occur in Year 4 would be wrong and the fact that §§ 461(h), 468A and 468 all reach economically equivalent results would merely show them to be equally inappropriate. On the other hand, since these expenses typically relate to the production of *past* income, many would argue that immediate deduction is proper.

---

7. Even if the taxpayer receives no advantage from deferring tax, the government may independently care about the timing of tax collections. The government may be concerned, for example, because of the size of an annual deficit or surplus or because the government discount rate is different from the taxpayer's after-tax rate of return or other compensating charge imposed by the Code. Since government revenues are calculated on a cash basis, consequences under federal budget legislation often turn on which year taxes will be paid.

Relationship to the Taxation of Interest Income. Both this Note and prior materials indicate that the timing of deductions relates directly to the timing of the taxation of interest income. The rules for such taxation are taken up at page 748, infra.

The concepts discussed in this Note are discussed in greater detail in Daniel I. Halperin, "Interest in Disguise: Taxing the Time Value of Money," 95 Yale L.J. 506 (1986); Noël Cunningham, "A Theoretical Analysis of the Tax Treatment of Future Costs," 40 Tax L.Rev. 577 (1985), and are generalized in Alvin Warren, "The Timing of Taxes," 34 Nat'l Tax J. 499 (1986).

———

C. INSTALLMENT METHOD

NOTE ON INSTALLMENT SALES

Where a taxpayer receives a note or installment obligation on the sale of appreciated property, there may be a liquidity concern in imposing tax on the gain immediately because the seller has not received cash or other property, but merely a right to receive cash in the future. Congress has provided special rules for the disposition of property where at least one payment is to be received in a year after the year of sale. Section 453 typically permits sellers to defer payment of tax by spreading the gain over a number of years, treating a portion of each payment as gain and a portion as a recovery of the taxpayer's basis in the property. The rule has broad application, applying not only to taxpayers with liquidity problems, but also to those who simply want to defer payment of taxes.

This is not the only possible approach to future payments. The Supreme Court in Burnet v. Logan, 283 U.S. 404 (1931), had permitted even more favorable treatment than under the installment method where a sales price was contingent on future events. In that case, the cash method taxpayer sold stock for cash and a right to receive 60 cents for each ton of ore removed from a certain mine. The Court held that there was no income until her basis had been recovered fully, saying:

> The promise was in no proper sense equivalent to cash. It had no ascertainable fair market value. The transaction was not a closed one. Respondent might never recoup her capital investment from payments only conditionally promised. * * * She properly demanded the return of her capital investment before assessment of any taxable profit based on conjecture.

Although the IRS tried to limit the application of this "open transaction" approach to cases where "the uncertainties * * * might prevent the return of capital," they were largely unsuccessful in litigation. When cash method taxpayers received notes with no ascertainable fair market value or where the total sales price was contingent on future events, the transaction was considered an open transaction with gain reportable on a "cost recovery" basis: payments were first applied to basis and gain was recognized only after the recovery of basis. Section 453 eliminates such "cost recovery" treatment for fixed price sales and curtails it for contingent payment sales.

Availability of the Installment Method. Section 453 makes the installment method available to any nondealer who sells real property or non inventory personal property if payment of at least part of the purchase price is deferred to a future year. Section 453(k) denies installment sales treatment to any installment obligations arising from the sale of stock or securities that are traded on an established securities market or arising from sales of other property of a kind regularly traded on an established market and from sales under a revolving credit plan. Furthermore, dealers in personal or real property cannot use the installment method. §§ 453(b)(2) and 453(*l*).

The installment method applies where the seller has a recognized gain; it does not apply to losses. The taxpayer may file an election to opt out of the installment method. § 453(d). If this election is made, gain is recognized in accordance with the seller's regular method of accounting. This results in more, or perhaps all, of the gain being recognized in the year of sale.

Computation of Reported Gain. Where the installment method applies, a portion of every "payment" is treated as gain and a portion is treated as a recovery of basis. The reportable gain equals the "payments" received in the taxable year multiplied by the ratio of "gross profit" on the sale to the "contract price." § 453(c). The "gross profit" is the "selling price" of the property minus its adjusted basis. The "contract price" is the total amount paid for the property. (Adjustments for any indebtedness assumed or taken subject to by the buyer are discussed later in this Note). Temp.Reg. § 15A.453–1(b)(2). The installment obligation itself does not constitute a "payment" unless the buyer's note is payable on demand or is issued by a corporation or government and is readily tradeable. § 453(f)(4).

If there is no interest on the obligation or an insufficient amount of stated interest is payable annually, part of the principal will be redesignated as interest and taxed as accrued. The imputation of interest is discussed in the next principal Note.

Example. S has a basis in Blackacre of $200. In Year 1, he transfers it to B for a $500 note, with adequately stated interest.[1] B is to pay $100 in Year 1, $150 (plus interest) in Year 2, and $250 (plus interest) in Year 3. S's gain and gross profit is $300 ($500 sales price minus $200 adjusted basis). The contract price is $500. Because the gross profit is 60 percent of the contract price, 60 percent of each payment is recognized as gain.

	Year 1	Year 2	Year 3
Payment	$100	$150	$250
Basis	40	60	100
Taxable Gain	60	90	150

Note that the total taxable gain is the same as it would have been if only cash were received, but the timing of the gain differs. In this example, S is able to defer taxes on $240 of the gain.

---

1. Interest at a rate equal to the rate on bonds of the federal government, see the Note at page 748 infra.

Where the sales price is uncertain due to contingencies, regulations provide that basis is recovered ratably in each year of payment. For an unsuccessful effort by taxpayers to manipulate this rule to their advantage see the *ACM Partnership* case, infra at page 814.

Mortgaged Property. An assumption of a "qualifying indebtedness" on the property is not treated as a payment. A "qualifying indebtedness" is a mortgage or other encumbrance on the property that the purchaser assumes or takes subject to as part of the acquisition cost of the property. It does not include indebtedness that is unrelated to the property. Temp.Reg. 15A.453–1(b)(2)(iv).

The full mortgage is included in the selling price for purposes of calculating the gross profit. The contract price does not include the mortgage except to the extent it exceeds the seller's adjusted basis, thus generally reflecting cash payments. The excess of the mortgage over the seller's adjusted basis is treated as a payment in the year of sale. Temp. Reg. § 15A.453–1(b)(3)(i). The effect of these rules is to permit the seller to offset the entire basis against the mortgage, thus allocating more (or all) of the gain to the future cash payments.

Example. In Year 1 S sells Blackacre in which he has a basis of $200 and which is subject to a $100 mortgage. The value of the property is $500. B assumes the mortgage and gives S a note for $400 with $150 to be paid in Year 2 and $250 to be paid in Year 3. S's gain and gross profit is $300 ($500 selling price minus $200 adjusted basis) and the contract price is $400. The gross profit ratio is 75 percent ($300/$400). The amount of gain to be recognized on each payment is:

	Year 1		Year 2	Year 3	Total
Qualified Indebtedness	$100		0	0	$100
Payment	0	(mortgage)	$150.00	$250.00	400
Basis	100		38.50	62.50	200
Gain	0		112.50	187.50	300

Suppose instead that the mortgage were $250 and B paid $250 on the notes ($100 in Year 2 and $150 in Year 3). The gross profit remains $300 and the contract price is also $300 because it includes the notes ($250) and the amount by which the mortgage exceeds the basis or $50 ($250—$200). The gross profit percentage therefore is 100 percent and the gain is reported:

	Year 1		Year 2	Year 3	Total
Qualified Indebtedness	$250		0	0	$250
Payment	250	(mortgage)	100	$150	250
Basis	200		0	0	200
Gain	50		100	150	300

Installment Sales Between Related Parties. Section 453(e) provides special rules for installment sales to certain related parties who subsequently dispose of the property. The rule is designed to prevent deferral of gain recognition by the seller where the related party buyer disposes of the property to a third party within a short period of time after the initial sale.

Without this rule, family members could transfer property out of the family unit for cash without immediate recognition of gain.

Section 453(e) applies to a sale by a related party purchaser within two years of the installment sale by the initial related party seller. The initial seller must recognize gain on resale of the property by the related installment purchaser to the extent the amount realized from the second disposition exceeds the actual payments made under the installment sale. The initial seller recovers subsequent payments tax-free until they equal the amount realized from the resale that triggered his recognition of gain. A second disposition by involuntary conversion or death does not cause the original seller to receive a deemed payment. § 453(e)(6). If the taxpayer can demonstrate that neither disposition was motivated by tax avoidance, the rule does not apply. § 453(e)(7). Related parties are defined in § 267(b).

Example. Dad sells real property with an adjusted basis of $50,000 to Daughter for $100,000. Daughter transfers $10,000 in cash to Dad in the year of sale and gives him a note for $90,000 with adequately stated interest. Dad's gain is $50,000 ($100,000 − $50,000) and his gross profit percentage is 50 percent ($50,000/$100,000). In the year of sale, he reports $5,000 ($10,000 × 50 percent). One year later Daughter sells the property for $105,000 cash. The cash is treated as a payment received by Dad, but is limited to the original contract price ($100,000) minus amounts previously taken into account ($10,000) or $90,000. Dad reports $45,000 ($90,000 × 50 percent) in the second year. In year 5 when the Daughter pays off the $90,000 note, Dad reports nothing.

Character of Gain. Whether the reported gain is capital gain or ordinary income generally is governed by the normal capital gain rules, including the "recapture rules," which produce ordinary income. See Chapter 5. Any recapture income must be recognized in the year of disposition of the property. § 453(i). Therefore, only gain in excess of recapture income may be taken into account under the installment method. The seller must report the recapture income in the year of sale even if no payments are received that year. The basis of the property is increased by the recapture income in computing the gross profit ratio so that the gain will not be taxed twice.

Disposition of Installment Obligations. The disposition of an installment obligation generally triggers any remaining gain on the original sale, in many cases even if the disposition is not a taxable event. § 453B. This section applies on the sale, exchange, transfer, gift, cancellation, or unenforceability of the installment obligation. It does not apply to a transfer at death or to a transfer between spouses subject to § 1041. There is, however, no step-up in the basis of an installment obligation at the decedent's death, § 1014(c), and the estate or the beneficiary reports the gain as payments are received using the decedent's profit ratio.

On the disposition of an installation obligation, gain or loss is recognized equal to the difference between the amount realized on the disposition and the taxpayer's basis in the installment obligation. The amount realized on a transfer other than a sale or exchange is the fair market value of the obligation. The taxpayer's basis in the obligation is the difference between the face value of the obligation and the amount that would be reported as income if the obligation were satisfied in full.

Example. S transfers Blackacre in exchange for an installment obligation of $100,000 to be paid in equal installments over 10 years. S's adjusted basis in Blackacre is $20,000. The gross profit ratio is 80 percent. After three payments have been made, S sells the installment obligation for $65,000. S's adjusted basis in the installment obligation is the face value ($70,000) minus the income that would be reported if paid in full ($70,000 × 80 percent = $56,000) or $14,000. Thus, S's gain on the sale of the note is $51,000 ($65,000 − $14,000).

NOTES

(A) *Payments.* A guarantee of the buyer's obligation does not create a payment nor does a standby letter of credit issued as security for the sale. § 453(f)(3); Temp.Reg. § 15A.453–1(b)(3)(i). See, e.g., Estate of Silverman v. Commissioner, 98 T.C. 54 (1992) (guarantee by Federal Deposit Insurance Corp. of nontransferable certificates of deposit issued by bank in exchange for property is not a payment). If, however, the security is provided by an escrow account funded with cash or a cash equivalent, the secured indebtedness is treated as a payment. Temp.Reg. § 15A.453–1(b)(3)(i).

(B) *Interest on Deferred Tax Liability.* The installment method essentially provides the taxpayer with an interest-free loan from the government for the period the taxes are deferred on the gain. In order to limit this significant advantage to casual sellers of property, § 453A imposes an interest charge on the deferred tax liability on any sale where the sales price exceeds $150,000 and the taxpayer has outstanding installment obligations that arose during the taxable year exceeding $5 million. The interest rate is the rate on tax deficiencies under § 6621(a)(2). This rule does not apply to the sale of farms.

Sellers of time-share units and other residential lots are permitted to use the installment method—unlike other dealers in real property—but they must pay interest on the deferred tax liability.

(C) *Election Not to Use Installment Method.* What does the taxpayer report who receives notes in a transaction not covered by the installment method or for which the taxpayer elects not to use the installment method? In Warren Jones Co. v. Commissioner, 524 F.2d 788 (9th Cir.1975), the taxpayer sold property under a transferable contract that had a fair market value, but the contract could be sold only at a discount of about 50 percent. The court held that if the contract had a fair market value, it had to be included in the amount realized regardless of the discount. The court took the view that the cash equivalency doctrine does not apply to cash basis taxpayers on deferred payment sales. The court's position in *Warren Jones* as to the inapplicability of the cash equivalency doctrine is reflected in two sets of regulations. Temp.Reg. § 15A.453–1(d)(2) provides that where a taxpayer has elected out of the installment sale rules, the "[r]eceipt of an installment obligation shall be treated as a receipt of property, in an amount equal to the fair market value of the installment obligation, whether or not such obligation is the equivalent of cash." The regulations also say that the fair market value of the obligation cannot be less than the fair market value of the property, minus any other consideration received. See Reg. § 1.1001–1(g), which would treat as part of the amount realized on the sale of property any debt obligation (including a contractual obligation). Assuming adequate interest is stated, the amount of the debt obligation would be treated as the fair market value of the property transferred. Even where substantial uncertainty or contingent payments exist, the IRS tends to treat contingent price sales as if they involved a fixed price equal to the fair market value of the property sold. Temp.Reg. § 15A.453–1(d)(2)(iii). Only in "rare and extraordinary" cases will a contingent obligation be treated as not having a fair market value. Don't all assets and all rights have a value?

SECTION 3.   UNSTATED OR IMPUTED INTEREST

NOTE ON UNSTATED OR IMPUTED INTEREST

The time value of money typically is reflected as interest. If money is to be paid at a future time, the amount to be paid will reflect the ability of the payor to earn interest in the interim on the deferred payment. Interest that is not paid as it is earned may be reinvested to earn more interest, which is why interest normally accrues at a compound rate.

By the same token, amounts to be paid currently can be compared to amounts to be paid in the future by "discounting" the future amount to its "present value." Present discounted value is the value now of money to be paid in the future. The value is determined by asking how much money would have to be put aside today—assuming it can earn a specified rate of compound interest—to fund the future payment. Discounting to present value, therefore, is merely the reverse of compounding to future value. Both computations compare amounts to be paid at different times by adjusting these amounts to reflect the ability to earn a compound rate of interest over the relevant period. The accrual of compound interest is typically referred to as "economic," "actuarial," or "constant" interest, terms regarded here as interchangeable. Any pattern of cash payments can be valued with reference to an economic accrual of compound interest to reflect either present value or future value.[1]

The Internal Revenue Code did not recognize the significance of compound interest until 1982 and even now uses compound interest concepts only in certain contexts. Identifying the economic interest element in a transaction is important under the income tax for four reasons. First, it provides a theoretically consistent method for comparing cash flows at different times—of measuring and adjusting income and deductions (and therefore tax liability) to take into account the time value of money. Second, interest income is taxed as ordinary income and thus must be

---

1. Tables of discounted present values and compounded future values can be found in the Appendix at page 849.

distinguished from appreciation in the value of assets over time, which often is eligible for favorable capital gain treatment. Third, interest expense is often (although not always) deductible whereas a repayment of principal, is not. Fourth, interest income and expense must be allocated to the proper taxpayer to prevent shifting of these items among taxpayers subject to different tax rates. The relevant income tax rules can be seen in four contexts: (1) original issue discount, (2) market discount, (3) deferred payment sales, and (4) interest-free or below-market loans.

Original Issue Discount. Original issue discount (OID) exists when the original "issue price" of a debt instrument (a bond, note, or other evidence of indebtedness) is less than the amount to be paid at maturity. Original issue discount typically is present when bonds are issued with no interest payable currently (zero coupon bonds) or a below-market rate of interest payable currently. The difference between the amount received by the borrower (the "issue price") and the amount to be repaid (the "stated redemption price at maturity") is compensation to the lender for the use of money and is functionally equivalent to interest.

Initially, the rules were limited to ensuring that OID would be taxed to the lender as ordinary income, not capital gains. The current rules are designed to treat an original issue discount bond equivalently to one currently paying a market rate of interest. In general, they require the lender to report as interest income annually the amount of OID that economically accrues on the debt instrument. The borrower treats an identical amount as interest that he may deduct, subject to the limitations on interest deductions.

Although the OID rules apply in a number of contexts, we first consider their application when a debt instrument is issued in exchange for cash. Then we will turn to debt instruments issued for property.

If a debt obligation is subject to the OID rules of § 1272, imputed interest is required to be included in income and may be deducted annually on an economic accrual basis, whether or not paid. A debt obligation is subject to the rules if it has OID, which is defined as the excess of the stated redemption price at maturity over the issue price. § 1273(a)(1). Where a debt instrument is issued for cash, the "issue price" is the cash paid by the buyer (the lender). § 1273(b)(2). The "stated redemption price at maturity" is the amount to be paid by the borrower on the maturity date, but excludes any interest payments made at regular intervals of a year or less. § 1273(a)(2). The lender is required to include the "daily portions" of OID in its income for each taxable year it holds the bond. § 1272(a)(1). The OID for each accrual period is determined by multiplying the adjusted issue price at the beginning of the period by the yield to maturity. § 1272(a)(3). The OID that is reported for each accrual period is added to the adjusted issue price of the bond (and to the holder's adjusted basis). § 1272(a)(4)(B). Generally, the accrual period is six months. § 1272(a)(5). The borrower deducts the same amount as interest. § 163(e). It is helpful to think of an OID obligation as being like a bank savings account from which there are no withdrawals; interest accrues on the original principal as well as on the interest from prior periods that was not withdrawn.

Example. B issues a bond for $7,462 with a redemption price of $10,000 on the maturity date three years from the issue date. As the issue price is $7,462 and the redemption price is $10,000, there is $2,548 of OID. L, who purchases the bond, must include the "daily portions" of OID in income for each six-month accrual period. As the yield to maturity on this instrument is 10 percent compounded semiannually, the OID for each six-month period is:

Period	Adjusted Issue Price	Yield	OID
First	$7,462	.05	$373
Second	7,835	.05	392
Third	8,227	.05	411
Fourth	8,638	.05	432
Fifth	9,070	.05	454
Sixth	9,524	.05	476
Redemption	$10,000		

Thus, in the first year, L would report $765 of interest (the OID for the first two accrual periods). If, for example, B used the proceeds of the loan for business purposes, B would deduct $765 of interest in the first year.

Note that the borrower's and lender's methods of accounting are irrelevant. The effect of §§ 1272 and 163(e) is to put both parties on the accrual method with respect to original issue discount.

The OID rules do not apply to tax-exempt obligations, U.S. savings bonds, or short-term obligations (those with a term of a year or less). They also do not apply to loans between natural persons if the total outstanding loans between the borrower and the lender are $10,000 or less, the loan has not made as part of the lender's trade or business, and there is no tax avoidance purpose. § 1272(a)(2).

These rules are quite complex, as even this simple example illustrates. What is the harm if the borrower and lender want to treat all interest as accruing on the maturity date or interest as accruing ratably over the term of the loan? As students should by now know well, taxpayers will take advantage of such mismeasurements of taxable income. For example, suppose an accrual basis taxpayer issues an OID obligation to a cash basis lender. Absent § 1272, the borrower would accrue interest deductions annually, but the lender would include nothing in income until he was paid interest at maturity. Any method of accounting for OID interest other than as it economically accrues will mismeasure income. A ratable allocation of interest would attribute more interest to earlier periods than economically accrues. Thus, both interest income and interest deductions would be accelerated. This leads to transactions between accrual basis borrowers, who would take advantage of the accelerated deductions and tax-exempt lenders, who would be unaffected by the earlier inclusion of income.

Deferred Payment Sales. Suppose a taxpayer sells property worth $7,462 today in exchange for a note with a face value of $10,000 to be paid in three years. The seller, of course, has demanded more for the property than he would receive currently because he is to receive the cash in the future. If, however, the seller and the buyer were permitted simply to characterize the sales price as $10,000, the sales price would be overstated, and income would be measured incorrectly in several ways. Characterizing the full $10,000 as the sales price would benefit the seller, if the property was a capital asset, by transforming ordinary interest income into capital gain. The seller also would be able to report his income only when payments were received rather than accruing interest over time. The buyer also might benefit, if the property was eligible for depreciation deductions, because depreciation would be calculated on an overstated basis, and because depreciation is often accelerated, the buyer might save taxes by substituting depreciation deductions for the interest deductions that might otherwise be available. In effect, the seller has both sold an asset and made a loan to the buyer; by paying $10,000 rather than the property's $7,462 value, the buyer is compensating the seller for the use of the purchase price for three years.

The original issue discount rules apply to impute interest to deferred payment sales to prevent these sorts of machinations. If a debt instrument is issued in exchange for property, the OID rules apply whenever there is unstated interest. The OID rules, in effect, recharacterize a portion of the "sales price" as interest. Interest is imputed, however, only if "adequate stated interest" is not provided in the debt instrument. There is adequate stated interest if the stated principal amount of the debt is less than or equal to the "imputed principal amount" of the debt. § 1274(c)(2). The "imputed principal amount" is the present discounted value of all payments due under the debt instrument. § 1274(b)(1). In calculating this amount, the stream of payments is discounted using the current interest rate on federal debt of a comparable term, compounded semiannually. This rate is known as the applicable federal rate or the AFR. Therefore, there will be adequate stated interest (and none will be imputed) whenever the debt instrument provides stated interest at a rate equal to at least the AFR, compounded semiannually.

In the example above, there is no stated interest because the buyer is to make one $10,000 payment three years hence. If the applicable discount rate (the AFR) is 10 percent, the imputed principal amount would be $7,462 (the present value of all payments). This becomes the issue price of the debt instrument, and thus because the issue price of $7,462 is less than the redemption price of $10,000, the debt instrument is an OID obligation. The issue price of the debt instrument is treated as the sales price of the property; the timing of the taxation of the gain or loss on the sale depends upon whether the installment method applies. Unless the seller elects out of the installment method (see discussion supra at page 743), he will report as gain or loss the difference between his adjusted basis in the property and the sales price of $7,462 at the time the payment is made. During the three years the note is outstanding, he will include in income the interest that economically accrues (as shown in the table above). The buyer will have an adjusted basis in the property of $7,462 and will deduct as interest the OID that economically accrues during each accrual period.

These rules of § 1274 do not apply to the sale of a principal residence, a debt instrument traded or issued for publicly traded property, a sale of a patent where part of the sales price is contingent on use, or the sale of a farm by an individual or small business for $1 million or less. § 1274(c).

With the exception of patents, these transactions are subject to § 483. Section 483, rather than § 1274, also applies to sales of property involving total payments of $250,000 or less. Section 483 changes only the character and not the timing of imputed interest. If the transaction is governed by § 483, the imputed interest is allocated among the principal payments under the contract using an economic accrual computation, but the amounts so allocated are reported as interest by cash basis taxpayers at the time of payment rather than when they accrue. The other major difference between § 1274 and § 483 is that in the case of a sale of land between related individuals, a 6 percent discount rate is used under § 483 to determine whether there is unstated interest, so long as the total sales price for all such sales between the individuals during the year does not exceed $500,000.

Section 1274A provides that the discount rate for purposes of §§ 483 and 1274 cannot exceed 9 percent for seller-financed sales of property where the stated principal does not exceed $2.8 million. In addition, a borrower and lender may jointly elect to have § 1274 not apply and to report interest under the cash method. To qualify for this election, the stated principal of the debt instrument cannot exceed $2 million and the lender can neither be a dealer with respect to the property sold nor use the accrual method of accounting.

Market Discount. Market discount occurs when the value of a debt obligation declines after it is issued, typically because market rates of interest increase. For example, a $1,000 bond paying 10 percent interest will decline in value if the market rate of interest rises from 10 percent to 12 percent. The purchaser of such a bond who, for example might pay only $900 for the bond, will—absent tax considerations—be indifferent whether the discount is market or original; the total amount of "interest" income will be the same. The tax treatment of original and market discount, however, is not identical. Whereas the OID rules affect both the timing and the character of the "interest," the market discount rules affect only the character. Section 1276 treats the market discount as ordinary interest income on a compound interest basis, but does not require cash basis holders of market discount obligations to report the interest until the bond is disposed of. On retirement or sale of the bond, the accrued market discount is reported as ordinary income. Furthermore, unless the holder elects otherwise, the interest is deemed to accrue on a ratable, rather than a constant interest basis. A market discount bond is one in which the stated redemption price exceeds the holder's basis in the bond at the time of its acquisition. § 1278(a)(2). Where a bond originally was issued with OID, the determination of market discount is more complex.

Example. Assume T buys a $1,000 bond, which was originally issued at its face value, for $850. Because the stated redemption price of $1,000 exceeds X's adjusted basis of $850, the bond has market discount of $150. The market discount is allocated ratably over the remaining three-year term. If T holds the bond until redemption, he would report $150 of ordinary income. If T sold the bond at the end of one year for $930, he would report $50 as ordinary interest income (one-third of the market discount) and $30 of capital gain.

Section 1277 defers and limits interest deductions related to market discount bonds. The interest deduction on indebtedness incurred or continued to purchase or carry market discount bonds is disallowed to the extent of market discount income allocable to the current taxable year. Any interest deduction disallowed under this rule can be deducted when the taxpayer sells or retires the market discount bond. This rule may provide a reason for a taxpayer to elect to accrue market discount on an economic basis rather than ratably. Discount accrues less rapidly under the economic interest method than under the ratable method. If the interest expense exceeds the amount of market discount allocable under both the economic accrual approach and the ratable approach, the election to use the economic accrual approach will produce a larger interest deduction in the early portion of the period in which the bond is held.

It is not clear why these interest disallowance rules were considered preferable to allocating and reporting market discount in a manner similar to OID.

Low-Interest or Interest–Free Loans. Ordinarily, a lender will demand a market rate of interest for the use of his money. But there are situations where the lender may agree to forgo market interest. For example, where an employer makes an interest-free loan to an employee, the employee has received an economic benefit equal to the market rate of interest she otherwise would have paid. It is as if the employer paid the employee additional wages, which the employee then remitted to the employer as interest on the loan. Similarly, when a parent makes an interest-free loan to a child, the child has received a gift equal to the forgone interest.

Section 7872 generally precludes the use of interest-free or low-interest loans between employers and employees to avoid employment taxes or limitations on interest deductions, between family members to shift income from high-rate taxpayers to low-rate taxpayers, and between corporations and their shareholders to disguise dividends. Section 7872 applies to below-market loans that are characterized as gift loans, compensation-related loans, corporate-shareholder loans, and tax avoidance loans. § 7872(c).

A below-market *demand loan* (any gift loan or a loan payable on demand) is one in which the interest payable on the loan is less than the applicable federal rate. § 7872(f). Under § 7872(a), for each taxable year the loan is outstanding, the amount of interest that would have been payable if the interest rate had been the AFR is treated as if it had been transferred by the lender to the borrower and then retransferred to the lender as interest.

Example: An employer lends an employee $100,000 payable on demand at a time when the AFR is 10 percent. On the last day of the year, the employer is deemed to transfer $10,250 to the employee (the amount of interest that would have been due if interest had been stated at 10 percent compounded semiannually). This is treated as taxable compensation income to the employee and deductible compensation to the employer. The employee is then deemed to transfer $10,250 of interest to the employer. This will be deductible to the employee only if the interest is deductible under § 163. The employer reports $10,250 of interest income.

In many cases the income tax consequences of employer loans will net out to zero, but employment taxes will apply to the additional compensation. There may be significant income tax consequences, however, if the loan is a gift loan. In the above example, the deemed transfer of $10,250 from a donor to a donee would be a gift, not taxable for income tax purposes, but possibly subject to gift tax, payable by the donor. The donor would have no deduction for the transfer of the gift, but would be taxable on the deemed interest income. The donee may be entitled to a deduction for the deemed interest paid under § 163, but may not be, for example, if the loan is used for personal purposes or if he does not itemize deductions. Where the total outstanding loans between the donor and the donee are less than $100,000, the amount of interest deemed transferred by the borrower is limited to the borrower's net investment income. This appropriately taxes the lender on the income produced by the principal, rather than shifting it to a lower-bracket donee.

A *term loan* is a below-market loan if the amount loaned exceeds the present value of all payments to be made under the loan, using the AFR at the date the loan is entered into as the discount rate. § 7872(e). If there is no interest, or if the interest (either stated or OID) is less than the AFR, § 7872 will apply. On the date of the loan, the lender is treated under § 7872 as having transferred cash equal to the amount loaned over the present value of all payments required to be made. The latter amount becomes the issue price of the debt obligation, which will be less than the redemption price, creating OID. The borrower is treated as paying interest at the statutory rate for each accrual period; this results in income that is taxed to the lender on an economic accrual basis and, generally, in a deduction for the borrower. The compensation (in an employer-employee context) or a dividend (in a corporation-shareholder context) is treated as being fully paid in the year a term loan is made, while the interest accrues economically over the loan period. This results in a tax advantage in terms of the time value of money to the lender, who realizes interest income over the life of the loan, and a disadvantage to the borrower, who realizes the entire amount of compensation or dividend in the initial year of the loan.

Example. An employer loans an employee $100,000 to be repaid at the end of three years. There is no stated interest; the AFR is 10 percent compounded semiannually. Because this is a below-market loan, the employer is treated under § 7872 as if he loaned the employee $74,620 and transferred $25,380 of additional compensation on the date of the loan. The employer deducts and the employee includes $25,380 of additional compensation, which is subject to any applicable employment taxes. In addition, because the issue price of the loan ($74,620) is less than the redemption price ($100,000), it is an OID obligation. The employee is treated as if he paid to the employer interest each six months at the AFR. For the first year, the employee would be deemed to have paid $7,650 in interest (which may be deductible) and the employer is treated as if he received $7,650 of interest income, which is taxable.

Section 7872 does not apply to any gift loan between individuals so long as the outstanding amount of loans between them does not exceed $10,000 and the proceeds are not used to purchase or carry income producing assets. There is also a de minimis exception for compensation and corporate-shareholder loans not exceeding $10,000 so long as one of the principal purposes of the loan arrangement is not tax avoidance.

NOTES

(A) *Relationship of § 7872 to Income Shifting Rules.* Section 7872 is necessary to prevent avoidance of the assignment of income and grantor trust rules. If the lender had assigned the income from an amount equal to the proceeds of the loan to the borrower, the assignment of income doctrine would tax the lender on the income. Similarly, if the lender had created a revocable grantor trust, he would continue to be taxed on the income.

(B) *Low-Interest Loans Not Covered by § 7872.* Section 7872 does not cover all below-market loans. The legislative history indicates that Congress thought that gift loans, compensation-related loans, and corporation-shareholder loans were most susceptible to abuse. Under proposed regulations, § 7872 generally does not apply to loans in connection with the sale or exchange of property. Would a prepayment for services be within § 7872?

A popular plan at a number of universities is to permit prepayment of tuition. Suppose tuition is $10,000, but if tuition is paid one year in advance, the fee is $9,000. The payor shifts the interest income on the $9,000 to the tax-exempt university for one year. How would the payor be treated if she loaned $9,000 to the university and received $10,000 one year later? Is this an example of a tax avoidance loan under § 7872(c)(1)(D)?

Many states and private educational institutions have adopted similar plans. Parents or other interested individuals can make contributions to a state fund that will be used to pay tuition at state universities many years hence. Section 529 provides for tax-free accumulations of income and so long as the withdrawals are used to pay for higher education, the distribution is taxed neither to the contributor nor the student. Beginning in 2004 similar plans established at private institutions will receive identical treatment. A parent who saves for college expenses by investing in a normal bank account, for example, would need to save a larger amount since the investment return would be subject to tax.

(C) *Recharacterizing Transactions as Loans.* Recharacterizing transactions involving deferred payment or prepayment as routinely involving a loan with interest imputed on an economic accrual basis might produce a theoretically consistent method for dealing with time value of money issues. These might include situations where an accrual basis taxpayer accrues a liability to be paid in the future (see, for example, *Ford Motor Co.*, supra at page 726), where a cash basis taxpayer prepays for services or goods (see *Boylston Market,* supra at page 698), or where an accrual basis taxpayer receives payment before services are performed (see *RCA Corp.,* supra at page 710). Compare the tax results that would follow from recharacterizing these transactions as loans with an economic accrual of interest.

(D) *Short-term, Stripped, and Tax–Exempt Bonds.* For special provisions regarding short-term obligations and stripped bonds (where one party owns the bond and another owns the interest coupons that have not yet become payable), see §§ 1281–1283 and 1286, respectively. See also § 1287, denying capital gain treatment to certain debt obligations not issued in registered form.

OID on tax-exempt bonds is covered by § 1288. In general, the OID is deemed to accrue as on any other OID obligation, although the holder of the bond is not subject to tax on the interest. The basis of the bond is increased, however, by the accrued OID so that the holder is not subject to tax on redemption.

(E) *Junk Bond "Interest."* Section 163 limits the interest deduction allowed to corporations issuing a high-yield bond with significant OID. Congress saw these bonds as representing both debt and equity interests in the corporation. Assuming the high "interest" rate is compensation for risk, the lender may resemble an equity investor whose "repayment" depends on the success of the underlying business. Section 163(e)(5) denies a deduction for a portion of extremely high interest and prevents the issuer from deducting the deductible portion until payment even if the lender includes the OID in income. The amount treated as excessive interest is clearly arbitrary and stemmed from Congress's concern with high interest rates and the proliferation of leveraged buy-outs. The details of these rules, however, are too complex to warrant explaining here.

(F) *Rent.* A concept similar to the OID rules applies to rental payments. Suppose a lessor agrees to accept a single payment of $300,000 at the end of a three-year lease. Absent special rules, an accrual basis lessee would deduct $100,000 each year. A cash basis lessor would including nothing until the $300,000 payment was made. Section 467 requires the parties to calculate the rent that economically accrues, by determining what the constant rental stream would have to be for the three years so that the present value would be equal to the present value of $300,000 to be paid in three years. The lessor includes and the lessee deducts that amount each year. Of course, the lessee does not actually pay that amount so § 467 treats the lessor as having loaned that amount to the lessee, triggering imputed interest. The details are far too complex to relate here. We are already in danger of disqualifying this course for its common appellation: "Baby Tax."

SECTION 4.   THE SPECIAL CASE OF DEFERRED COMPENSATION

Employers frequently pay compensation for personal services not as the services are rendered but instead in a later year. Compensation may be deferred in order to spread over a number of years the income of those whose earnings are concentrated in a few years. Thus, an author may receive royalties over a period of time instead of as her books are sold, or a baseball player may receive payments over several years instead of in the year that he plays. Compensation also may be deferred to provide employees income during retirement and, in some cases, so that employees will be taxed on the income after retirement, when they may be in lower tax brackets.

There are two types of deferred compensation arrangements: nonqualified and qualified plans. Qualified plans are subject to a number of stringent statutory rules in both the Internal Revenue Code and under the Employee Retirement Income Security Act of 1974 (ERISA) in exchange for favorable tax treatment. For example, qualified plans are forbidden to discriminate in favor of highly compensated employees. With qualified plans, employers are allowed to deduct deferred compensation currently, and employees are not taxed currently, but instead are taxed only when the compensation is paid during retirement. The investment income on the deferred compensation is not taxed to the "pension trust" that invests the moneys that have been set aside to fund the deferred compensation. Thus, in the case of qualified plans, the investment income is untaxed. This treatment is similar to that of an IRA, discussed infra at p. 773. Nonqualified plans, by contrast, are not subject to ERISA and there are no Code sections directly regulating them, although, § 404(a)(5) requires the employer to defer deduction of the compensation until it is included in the employee's income.

The ruling that follows describes some of the basic rules for the inclusion of nonqualified deferred compensation.

Revenue Ruling 60–31

Internal Revenue Service, 1960. 1960–1 C.B. 174.

Advice has been requested regarding the taxable year of inclusion in gross income of a taxpayer, using the cash receipts and disbursements method of accounting, of compensation for services received under the circumstances described below.

(1) On January 1, 1958, the taxpayer and corporation X executed an employment contract under which the taxpayer is to be employed by the corporation in an executive capacity for a period of five years. Under the contract, the taxpayer is entitled to a stated annual salary and to additional compensation of 10x dollars for each year. The additional compensation will be credited to a bookkeeping reserve account and will be deferred, accumulated, and paid in annual installments equal to one-fifth of the amount in the reserve as of the close of the year immediately preceding the year of first payment. The payments are to begin only upon (a) termination of the taxpayer's employment by the corporation; (b) the taxpayer's becoming a part-time employee of the corporation; or (c) the taxpayer's becoming partially or totally incapacitated. Under the terms of the agreement, corporation X is under a merely contractual obligation to make the payments when due, and the parties did not intend that the amounts in the reserve be held by the corporation in trust for the taxpayer.

The contract further provides that if the taxpayer should fail or refuse to perform his duties, the corporation will be relieved of any obligation to make further credits to the reserve (but not of the obligation to distribute amounts previously contributed) * * *. There is no specific provision in the contract for forfeiture by the taxpayer of his right to distribution from the reserve; and, in the event he should die prior to his receipt in full of the balance in the account, the remaining balance is distributable to his personal representative at the rate of one-fifth per year for five years, beginning three months after his death.

* * *

(4) In June 1957, the taxpayer, a football player, entered into a two-year standard player's contract with a football club in which he agreed to play football and engage in activities related to football during the two-year term only for the club. In addition to a specified salary for the two-year term, it was mutually agreed that as an inducement for signing the contract the taxpayer would be paid a bonus of 150x dollars. The taxpayer could have demanded and received payment of this bonus at the time of signing the contract, but at his suggestion * * * an escrow agreement was executed on June 25, 1957, in which the club agreed to pay 150x dollars on that date to the Y bank, as escrow agent; and the escrow agent agreed to pay this amount, plus interest, to the taxpayer in installments over a period of five years. The escrow agreement also provides that the account established by the escrow agent is to bear the taxpayer's name; that payments from such account may be made only in accordance with the terms of the agreement; that the agreement is binding upon the parties thereto and their successors or assigns; and that in the event of the taxpayer's death during the escrow period the balance due will become part of his estate.

* * *

[T]he individual concerned in each of the situations described above, employs the cash receipts and disbursements method of accounting. Under that method, * * * he is required to include the compensation * * * in gross income only for the taxable year in which it is actually or constructively received. Consequently, the question for resolution is whether in each of the situations described the income in question was constructively received in a taxable year prior to the taxable year of actual receipt.

A mere promise to pay, not represented by notes or secured in any way, is not regarded as a receipt of income within the intendment of the cash receipts and disbursements method. * * *

This should not be construed to mean that under the cash receipts and disbursements method income may be taxed only when realized in cash. For, under that method a taxpayer is required to include in income that which is received in cash or cash equivalent. * * * And, as stated in the * * * regulations, the "receipt" contemplated by the cash method may be actual or constructive.

* * *

[U]nder the doctrine of constructive receipt, a taxpayer may not deliberately turn his back upon income and thereby select the year for which he will report it. * * * Nor may a taxpayer, by a private agreement, postpone receipt of income from one taxable year to another. * * *

However, the statute cannot be administered by speculating whether the payor would have been willing to agree to an earlier payment. See * * * C.E. Gullett, et al., v. Commissioner, 31 B.T.A. 1067, in which the court, citing a number of authorities for its holding, stated:

> It is clear that the doctrine of constructive receipt is to be sparingly used; that amounts due from a corporation but unpaid, are not to be included in the income of an individual reporting his income on a cash receipts basis unless it appears that the money was available to him, that the corporation was able and ready to pay him, that his right to receive was not restricted, and that his failure to receive resulted from exercise of his own choice.

Consequently, it seems clear that in each case involving a deferral of compensation a determination of whether the doctrine of constructive receipt is applicable must be made upon the basis of the specific factual situation involved.

Applying the foregoing criteria to the situations described above, the following conclusions have been reached:

(1) The additional compensation to be received by the taxpayer under the employment contract concerned will be includible in his gross income only in the taxable years in which the taxpayer actually receives installment payments in cash or other property previously credited to his account.

* * *

(4) In arriving at a determination as to the includibility of the 150x dollars concerned in the gross income of the football player, under the circumstances described, in addition to the authorities cited above, consideration also has been given to Revenue Ruling 55–727, C.B. 1955–2, 25, and to the decision in E.T. Sproull v. Commissioner, 16 T.C. 244.

[The IRS distinguished Rev.Rul. 55–727 on the ground that the bonus received by a baseball player in that situation had not been placed in an escrow account.]

In E.T. Sproull v. Commissioner, 16 T.C. 244, affirmed 194 F.2d 541, the petitioner's employer in 1945 transferred in trust for the petitioner the amount of $10,500. The trustee was directed to pay out of principal to the petitioner the sum of $5,250 in 1946 and the balance including income, in 1947. In the event of the petitioner's prior death, the amounts were to be paid to his administrator, executor, or heirs. The petitioner contended that the Commissioner erred in including the sum of $10,500 in his taxable income for 1945. In this connection, the court stated:

> The question then becomes * * * was "any economic or financial benefit conferred on the employee as compensation" in the taxable year. If so, it was taxable to him in that year. This question we must answer in the affirmative. The employer's part of the transaction terminated in 1945. It was then that the amount of the compensation was fixed at $10,500 and irrevocably paid out for petitioner's sole benefit.

Applying the principles stated in the *Sproull* decision to the facts here, it is concluded that the 150x–dollar bonus is includible in the gross income of the football player concerned in 1957, the year in which the club unconditionally paid such amount to the escrow agent.

* * *

As previously stated, in each case involving a deferral of compensation, a determination of whether the doctrine of constructive receipt is applicable must be made upon the basis of the specific factual situation involved.

* * *

With respect to deductions for payments made by an employer under a deferred compensation plan, see section 404(a)(5) of the 1954 Code and section 1.404(a)–12 of the Income Tax Regulations.

In the application of those sections to unfunded plans, no deduction is allowable for any compensation paid or accrued by an employer on account of any employee under such a plan except in the year when paid and then only to the extent allowable under section 404(a). Thus, under an unfunded plan, if compensation is paid by an employer directly to a former employee, such amounts are deductible under section 404(a)(5) when *actually* paid *in cash or other property to the employee,* provided that such amounts meet the requirements of section 162 or section 212.

NOTE

Revenue Ruling 60–31 indicates that the Service does not take either the constructive receipt or the cash equivalency doctrine very seriously when voluntary agreements to defer compensation are at issue. At least for advance ruling purposes, the Commissioner has suggested that the agreement to defer compensation must be made before the performance of services begins. Rev.Rul. 67–449, 1967–2 C.B. 173; Rev.Proc. 71–19, 1971–1 C.B. 698. The courts seem to be more lenient. See, e.g., the discussion of the *Oates* and *Olmsted* cases at page 687, supra.

As indicated in Revenue Ruling 60–31, the Service will not urge application of the cash equivalency doctrine to require immediate inclusion in income of the present value of an unfunded deferred compensation contract even when the employees' rights are nonforfeitable and the employer has unquestionable ability to pay. Instead, the ruling states that the question in each case is whether the constructive receipt doctrine applies. The ruling does indicate, however, that the cash equivalency doctrine might apply if something more than a mere promise guarantees the employees' right to receive payment. Henritze v. Commissioner, 41 B.T.A. 505 (1940), cited in the unedited version of the ruling, involved an assignment of debt to a third party. Payment of the debt to the third party was treated as the receipt of the equivalent of cash by the assignor. Further, in case (4) of the ruling, the football player is subject to immediate taxation when his bonus was placed in escrow. In general, although taxpayers are constantly trying to push the limits, nonforfeitable "funded" deferred compensation—for example, amounts transferred in trust or to an escrow account—must be included in current income under Revenue Ruling 60–31, § 402(b), and the case law.

Recall the requirements of Cowden v. Commissioner, supra, page 692. Under the *Cowden* cash equivalency test, unfunded deferred compensation contracts presumably would not be currently includible in income because such contracts are neither "readily marketable" nor "frequently transferred * * * at a discount not substantially greater than the generally prevailing premium for the use of money." Should "transferability" or "marketability" be the test? Or should the constructive receipt principles be broadened to include in current income an employee's nonforfeitable deferred compensation benefits whenever the employer is solvent?

Consider the following excerpt from the report of the Ways and Means Committee on its version of the Tax Reform Act of 1969:

> It is anomalous that the tax treatment of deferred compensation should depend on whether the amount to be deferred is placed in a trust or whether it is merely accumulated as a reserve on the books of the employer corporation. An employee who receives additional compensation in the form of a promise to pay him that compensation in the future made by a large, financially sound corporation, is probably as likely to receive the compensation as an employee whose deferred compensation is placed in trust.

H.Rep. No. 91–413, 91st Cong., 1st Sess. 90 (1969).

NOTE ON NONQUALIFIED DEFERRED COMPENSATION

As the preceding materials in the Chapter have detailed, if tax rates change or even if tax rates do not change, postponement of tax may be intrinsically valuable. In the case of nonqualified deferred compensation, however, any "missing" tax may be supplied by the employer who, for example, is required by § 404(a)(5) to defer any deduction of the salary payment until the amount is includible in the employee's income. This is an example of surrogate taxation. This provision eliminates any deferral advantage *as long as the tax on the investment income earned on the amount deferred is the same for the employer as it would have been for the employee.*

This is illustrated by the following example in which it is assumed that an employee is entitled to a $10,000 bonus, the interest rate is 10 percent, and both the employer and the employee are subject to tax at a marginal rate of 40 percent. It is also assumed that the amounts of the bonus and the tax savings are invested as is any interest earned thereon.

Case 1: Bonus Paid Currently

	Employee		Employer
Employee Receives	$10,000	Employer	
Tax at 40 percent	4,000	Tax Savings	$4,000
After–Tax Investment	6,000		
Year 1 Interest Earned	600		400
Tax Liability	240		160
After–Tax Interest	360		240
Total Accumulation	6,360		4,240
Year 2 Interest Earned	636		424
Tax Liability	254.40		169.60
After–Tax Interest	381.60		254.40
Total Accumulation	$6,741.60		$4,494.40

Case 2: Bonus Deferred for Two Years

	Employee	Employer
Employer Invests	$10,000	
Year 1 Interest Earned	1,000	
Tax Liability	400	
After–Tax Interest	600	
Total Accumulation	10,600	
Year 2 Interest Earned	1,060	
Tax Liability	424	
After–Tax Interest	636	
Total Accumulation		
Paid to Employee	11,236	Employer
		Tax Savings $4,494.40
Tax at 40 percent	4,494.40	
Net to Employee	$6,741.60	

If, however, the employer is tax-exempt or subject to a lower marginal tax rate than the employee, or if the employer can earn a higher rate of return than the employee, or if the employer obtains a deduction before the employee includes the compensation in income, the fund will grow at a faster rate in the hands of the employer. Consequently, there will be more money available if the employee defers compensation, instead of receiving it currently. This additional amount may inure to the benefit of the employer or the employee or be divided between them depending upon their relative bargaining power. See generally Daniel I. Halperin, "Interest in Disguise: Taxing the Time Value of Money," 95 Yale L.J. 506 (1986).

The case that follows reflects one taxpayer's effort to structure a nonqualified deferred compensation plan to obtain much of the advantage of a qualified plan without the restrictions applicable to the latter.

Albertson's, Inc. v. Commissioner

United States Court of Appeals, Ninth Circuit, 1994.
42 F.3d 537.

REINHARDT, CIRCUIT JUDGE:

I. BACKGROUND

Deferred compensation agreements ("DCAs") are agreements in which certain employees and independent contractors ("DCA participants") agree to wait a specified period of time ("deferral period") before receiving the annual bonuses, salaries, or director's fees that they would otherwise receive on a current basis. During the deferral period, the employer uses the basic amounts of deferred compensation ("basic amounts"), which accumulate on an annual basis, as a source of working capital. At the end of the deferral period, the employer pays the participating individuals the basic amounts and an additional amount for the time value of the deferred payments that have accumulated on the basic amounts ("additional amount"). The time-value-of-money sums are also computed on a yearly basis. The total of these basic amounts and the amounts attributable to compensation for the delay in payment of those amounts constitutes the whole of the deferred compensation ("deferred compensation"). The time-value-of-money component may be measured by interest rate indices, equity fund indices, or cost of living increases, or it may simply be included within a lump-sum payment.

Prior to 1982, Albertson's entered into DCAs with eight of its top executives and one outside director. The parties agreed that their deferred compensation would include the annual basic amounts plus additional amounts calculated annually in accordance with an established formula. The DCA participants would be eligible to receive the deferred compensation (the total sum) upon their retirement or termination of employment with Albertson's. The DCA participants also had the option of further deferring payment for up to fifteen years thereafter. During that extra period, the additional amounts would continue to accrue on an annual basis.

In 1982, Albertson's requested permission from the IRS to deduct the additional amounts (but not the basic amounts) during the year in which they accrued instead of waiting until the end of the deferral period. In 1983, the IRS granted Albertson's request. Accordingly, Albertson's claimed deductions of $667,142 for the additional amounts that had already accrued, even though it had not yet paid the DCA participants any sums under the deferred compensation agreements. In 1987, the IRS changed its policy, however, and sought a deficiency for the additional amounts, contending that all amounts provided for in the deferred compensation agreements were deductible only when received by Albertson's employees. Albertson's filed a petition with the Tax Court, claiming that the additional amounts constituted "interest" and thus could be deducted as they accrued.

In a sharply divided opinion, the Tax Court rejected Albertson's position. The court found that the additional amounts represented compensation, not interest, and were therefore not deductible until the end of the deferral period under I.R.C. § 404(a)(5) & (d).

We reversed the decision of the Tax Court. We held that the additional amounts constituted interest within the definition of I.R.C. § 163(a) and that interest payments were not governed by the timing restrictions of section 404. The government petitioned for rehearing due to the significant fiscal impact of the panel's opinion which it estimates will cause a $7 billion loss in tax revenues.

II. REHEARING

We agreed to rehear this issue after lengthy consideration and reflection. In our original opinion, we stated that the plain language of the statute strongly supported Albertson's interpretation and, accordingly, we adopted it. Nevertheless, we expressed sympathy for the Commissioner's argument that Congress intended the timing restrictions of I.R.C. § 404 to apply to all payments made under a deferred compensation plan and recognized that our plain language interpretation seemed to undercut Congress' purpose.

We have now changed our minds about the result we reached in our original opinion and conclude that our initial decision was incorrect. The question is not an easy one, however. We have struggled with it unsuccessfully at least once, and it may, indeed, ultimately turn out that the United States Supreme Court will tell us that it is this opinion which is in error. This is simply one of those cases—and there are more of them than judges generally like to admit—in which the answer is far from clear and in which there are conflicting rules and principles that we are forced to try to apply simultaneously. Such accommodation sometimes proves to be impossible. In some cases, as here, convincing arguments can be made for both possible results, and the court's decision will depend on which of the two competing legal principles it chooses to give greater weight to in the particular circumstance. Law, even statutory construction, is not a science. It is merely an effort by human beings, albeit judges, to do their best with imperfect tools to arrive at a correct result.

There is a question whether, having once decided a case, we should change our decision when we are not entirely certain that the result we reached is wrong. One response is that, if the issue could be resolved with that degree of certainty, it is unlikely that we would have decided the case incorrectly the first time. Moreover, if certainty were the standard, we would probably never reverse ourselves. There is actually no clear set of rules that tells us when a case warrants our changing our decision on rehearing. We start with the premise that doing so is not generally desirable, and that it runs contrary to the sense of stability and finality that the law seeks to foster. We also know that it is often better to have a definitive answer, whatever it is, than to have continuing reexaminations or self-questioning.

On the other hand, we judges do not just bury our mistakes. We display them publicly in the Federal Reporters and, while we may then as individuals move on to more decision-making, the opinions we have published continue to haunt indefinitely not just the parties, but often numerous other persons whose affairs and fortunes will be governed by them. Because all of us make hundreds of difficult decisions a year involving complex legal questions, we know that we will make a certain number of errors. All that we can do is to try our best to hold them to a minimum. At the same time, if a rehearing is requested and we have a strong sense that we may have erred in the particular case, we should not hesitate to undertake a reexamination of the issue. This is particularly so when significant individual rights or interests are at stake or when a number of parties may be seriously affected by a decision that may be erroneous. Given all of this, our conclusion is that, while we should not ordinarily abandon the decisions we have just reached following full deliberation, we must be willing to take that unusual step—at least in cases of some significance—when ultimately we are fairly persuaded that our decision is in error. This is such a case.

In its petition for rehearing, the government, far more forcefully and clearly than it did originally, has articulated the purpose of the timing restrictions outlined in I.R.C. § 404: to encourage employers to invest in qualified compensation plans by requiring inclusions and deductions of income and expense to be "matched" for nonqualified plans. The matching principle, widely recognized to be the key to I.R.C. § 404, provides significant tax incentives for employers to invest in qualified deferred compensation plans, which are nondiscriminatory and ensure that employees receive the compensation promised to them. As the Commissioner forcefully argues, our original interpretation of I.R.C. § 404 undercut the essential purpose of that provision by violating the matching principle and creating a taxation scheme that favors the type of plan that Congress intended to discourage. For this reason, we granted the Commissioner's petition for rehearing. We now withdraw the portion of our earlier opinion that dealt with deferred compensation, and affirm the Tax Court's decision, although not for the reasons upon which the Tax Court majority relied.

III. ANALYSIS

Albertson's again urges this court (1) to characterize the additional amounts as interest as defined by I.R.C. § 163(a), and (2) to find that such "interest" payments are deductible under I.R.C. § 404. However, we have now concluded that, notwithstanding the statutory language on which Albertson's relies, to hold the additional amounts to be deductible would contravene the clear purpose of the taxation scheme Congress created to govern deferred compensation plans. * * *

A. A Comparison of Qualified and Nonqualified Plans

An examination of the differences between qualified and nonqualified plans is essential to an understanding of the purpose of the congressional scheme governing deferred compensation agreements. Congress has imposed few restrictions upon nonqualified deferred compensation plans. An employer may limit participation in a nonqualified plan to highly paid executives, and it need not guarantee equal benefits for all participants. In addition, the employer is not required to set aside any funds or provide any guarantees (beyond the initial contractual promise) that its employees will receive the compensation. Thus, promised benefits for unfunded, nonqualified plans are subject to the claims of the employer's general creditors.

Under a qualified plan, in contrast, an employer may not discriminate in favor of officers, shareholders, or highly compensated employees. I.R.C. § 401(a)(4) & (a)(5). In addition, a qualified plan must satisfy minimum participation and coverage standards concerning eligibility and actual rates of participation. I.R.C. §§ 401(a)(2) & (a)(26), 410. The amounts which an employer may contribute to qualified plans and the benefits which qualified plans may provide are also restricted. I.R.C. §§ 401(a)(17), 415.

A qualified plan also provides significant guarantees that employees will receive the compensation promised to them. It generally must be funded through a trust. I.R.C. § 401(a). Neither the corpus nor the income of the trust may be diverted for any purpose; they can only be used for the exclusive benefit of the participants. I.R.C. § 401(a)(2). Under certain qualified plans, the employer's contributions must meet strict funding requirements, and minimum standards govern the vesting of participants' benefits. I.R.C. §§ 401(a)(1) & (a)(7), 411, 412.

It is clear that few employers would adopt a qualified deferred compensation plan, with all of its burdensome requirements, if the taxation scheme favored nonqualified plans or treated nonqualified and qualified plans similarly. * * * Thus, the extensive regulations Congress has imposed upon qualified plans would serve little purpose unless employers had an incentive to adopt such plans. As we discuss in the next part, section 404 provides the incentive necessary to encourage employers to adopt qualified plans by providing significantly more favorable tax treatment of qualified plans than of nonqualified ones.

The most significant difference between the two types of plans, for purposes of tax deductibility, is that under a qualified plan the employer must turn over annually to a third party the basic amounts that are deferred and may not use those amounts for the employer's own benefit. Thus, the employer, in effect, is required to make the deferred payments at the time the employee is earning the compensation. It is only the employee's right to receive the funds that is delayed. In contrast, an employer with a nonqualified plan is not required to turn any funds over to anyone until the end of the deferred compensation period. Such an employer may use those funds for its own purposes for a period of many years. In a nonqualified plan, it is not only the employee's right to receive the funds that is deferred; the employer's obligation to part with the funds is deferred as well. If one could simply retain the funds and receive tax benefits similar to those one would receive if those amounts were paid out, there would clearly be little incentive to establish a qualified plan.

B.   The Purpose of Section 404

Congress enacted section 23(p), the forerunner to section 404, in 1942. Prior to 1942, corporations were allowed to deduct DCA-related expenses as they accrued each year, even though employees did not recognize any income until a subsequent taxable year. In 1942, Congress eliminated this favorable treatment for deductions relating to "nonqualified" deferred compensation agreements, such as the DCAs at issue in this case. In so doing, Congress forced employers who chose to retain their funds for their own use to wait until the end of the deferral period, when these amounts were includible in plan participants' taxable income, before they could take deductions for deferred compensation payments. However, employers who maintained a "qualified" plan that met the rigorous requirements of the Internal Revenue Code (and now ERISA), including turning over the sums involved to a trust fund (or purchasing an annuity), were allowed to continue to take the annual deductions even though their employees would not receive the deferred compensation until a later year. See, e.g., I.R.C. §§ 404(a) & (d).

Congress provided a single explanation for the timing restrictions of section 404: to ensure matching of income inclusion and deduction between employee and employer under nonqualified plans. As both the House and Senate Reports note, "if an employer on the accrual basis defers paying any compensation to the employee until a later year or years * * * he will not be allowed a deduction until the year in which the compensation is paid."

C.   The Effects of Albertson's Proposal

Albertson's maintains that section 404 only requires that the basic amounts of compensation be matched; it argues that all additional amounts paid to compensate an employee for the time value of money represent "interest" payments for which an employer may take an immediate deduction. In light of the clear purpose underlying section 404—to encourage employers to create qualified plans for their employees—we decline to ascribe such an intention to Congress.

First, Albertson's proposal appears to undermine the effectiveness of the timing restrictions by reducing the significance of the incentive structure created by section 404. In order to adopt Albertson's proposal and allow employers to take current deductions for additional "interest" payments, we would be required to conclude that Congress created a system in which employers could deduct a substantial portion of the nonqualified deferred compensation package long before its employees had received any of those funds. For example, when the additional amounts are calculated for a compensation package deferred over a fifteen-year period using an interest rate similar to that used by Albertson's [14.8 percent], an employer can classify more than seventy percent of the deferred compensation package as "interest payments." If the additional amounts were calculated at an eight percent interest rate, compounded annually, almost fifty percent of the compensation package could be characterized as "interest" under Albertson's approach. Even under a deferred compensation package with an interest rate one-third as high as Albertson's, one third of the amount paid to the employee at the end of a fifteen-year period would consist of "interest." Moreover, we note that, under Albertson's deferred compensation agreement, participants have the option of deferring payment of the total sum available to them upon retirement for an additional period of up to fifteen years. All payments during that additional period would also constitute "interest," and the deductible portion of the final compensation package would thus increase exponentially.

Albertson's has been unable to explain why Congress, in designing a taxation scheme to encourage the creation of qualified plans, would require an employer that maintains a nonqualified plan to defer taking a deduction on the basic amounts of a promised compensation package but nevertheless allow that employer to take current deductions on amounts that constitute a substantial portion of the compensation package, merely because that portion is classified as "interest." Given that the interest payments will often constitute the bulk of the total compensation package that an employee under a nonqualified plan ultimately receives, it would make little sense to impose a matching requirement upon "basic" payments but not upon "interest" payments. Albertson's interpretation of section 404 would seriously undermine the incentive structure designed by Congress to encourage employers to establish qualified plans.

An additional reason to reject Albertson's statutory interpretation of section 404 is that, in certain cases, Albertson's approach might actually create an incentive for employers to establish nonqualified plans. Whereas an employer who maintains a qualified plan may only take a current deduction for the basic amounts of promised compensation, an amount it actually has paid out, under Albertson's approach an employer that maintains a nonqualified plan could take current deductions for "interest" payments that substantially exceed the basic amounts even though it has paid out none of these funds. Moreover, the employer could take advantage of these tax benefits without being constrained by the burdensome requirements associated with qualified plans. For this reason, characterizing the additional amounts as deductible interest, as Albertson's suggests, would encourage employers to maintain nonqualified plans and thus directly contradict the statutory purpose underlying I.R.C. § 404.[1]

Albertson's rests its argument upon its contention that, because the plain language of § 404 only refers to "compensation" rather than "interest," the employers have a statutory right to deduct the additional amounts as interest under § 163. In this connection, Albertson's points out that section 404 prohibits deduction under sections 162 and 212 but not under section 163, and it is the latter section that governs the deduction of interest. Albertson's argument as to the plain language of the statute is a strong one. We certainly agree that the additional payments resemble "interest" and that, under a literal reading of the statutory language, the deduction of interest is not affected by section 404. However, holding such payments to be deductible "interest" under section 404 would lead to an anomalous result: a taxation scheme designed to make nonqualified plans less attractive would in many cases provide incentives for adopting such plans, and a provision intended to apply the matching principle to nonqualified deferred compensation agreements would exempt substantial portions of DCA payments from its application.

In the end we are forced, therefore, to reject Albertson's approach. We may not adopt a plain language interpretation of a statutory provision that directly undercuts the clear purpose of the statute. * * * In reaching our conclusion, we followed the Supreme Court's approach in United States v. American Trucking Ass'ns., 310 U.S. 534 (1940). There the Court noted that "when [a given] meaning has led to absurd results * * * this Court has looked beyond the words to the purpose of the act. Frequently, however, even when the plain meaning did not produce absurd results but merely an unreasonable one 'plainly at variance with the policy of the legislation as a whole,' this Court has followed that purpose, rather than the literal words." American Trucking Ass'ns., 310 U.S. at 543. * * *

---

1. We also note the government's argument concerning the possible consequences of a finding in favor of Albertson's. According to the Commissioner, under a long-standing administrative practice, employees are currently not taxed upon the benefits they receive from deferred compensation plans until they actually receive them, precisely because employers have not taken deductions for those amounts. Because section 404 only exempts payments under qualified plans from the matching principle, were we to uphold Albertson's approach, the Commissioner suggests that we would be required to conclude that employer deductions for interest accruing under nonqualified plans must be "matched" by the inclusion of those amounts in employees' current taxable income. As is clear from the foregoing discussion, such an unrealized addition to the employees' income for tax purposes would indeed be substantial and, as far as the employees are concerned, harshly inequitable. We express no opinion about the merits of the government's argument.

In rejecting Albertson's appeal, we take heed of the Supreme Court's instructions concerning the proper interpretation of the Internal Revenue Code when the plain language of the provision leads to an unreasonable result and directly contradicts its underlying purpose: the provision "must be analyzed and construed within the framework of the Internal Revenue Code and against the background of the congressional purposes." Id. For the reasons we have expressed, we conclude that, despite the literal wording of the statute, Congress could not have intended to exclude interest payments, a substantial part of the deferred compensation package, from the rule prohibiting deductions until such time as the employee receives the benefits. Indeed, the matching principle would not be much of a principle if so substantial a part of the deferred compensation package were excluded from its operation. * * *

NOTES

(A) *Giving the Advantage of Qualified Plans to Nonqualified Deferred Compensation.* The court's opinion in *Albertson's* rejects its earlier approach of construing the statute literally and allowing the deduction, principally because it believes that to do so would give nonqualified plans the major tax advantage provided to qualified plans, viz., the exemption of investment income from tax. But—in sharp contrast to its eloquence in describing the difficulties of statutory construction and the reasons it granted rehearing in this case—the court's opinion is far from clear about why this would be so.

As the Note on Nonqualified Deferred Compensation at page 761 supra, immediately preceding the *Albertson's* case, demonstrates, when employer and employee tax rates are the same, matching the time of the employer's deduction and the employee's inclusion when the payment is made eliminates any tax advantage from nonqualified deferred compensation, and when their tax rates differ, this matching has the effect of taxing the investment income from such plans at the employer's tax rate. In present value terms, the employer's delayed deduction is equivalent to the amount of compensation deferred and the employee's inclusion at the time of payment is equivalent to the amount of compensation originally earned. (Refer back to the example in the Note at page 761 to confirm this conclusion.) If, however, the employer is allowed a deduction for the "additional amount"—the interest element of the payment—as the interest accrues, this deduction will shelter from tax the interest earnings on the amount of compensation deferred. Rather than being taxed currently at the employer's rate, the interest income will not be taxed until the time of payment when it will be taxed to the employee but not allowed as a deduction to the employer (having already been deducted previously). Thus, the result urged on the Court by Albertson's (and accepted in its first opinion) would defer the tax on the investment income for 15–30 years, as the court states in its opinion.

This result would give nonqualified deferred compensation most of the tax benefits available to qualified plans, with qualified plans having only the additional advantage of an earlier deduction for the original amount of compensation deferred. In a nonqualified plan, the employer's deduction of that amount in all events would be deferred until the time the compensation is paid. As Daniel Halperin asked about the court's first *Albertson's* opinion:

> What reason is there to believe that Congress would have wanted to create a uniquely favorable tax regime for unqualified deferred compensation arrangements that must be limited under ERISA to management and highly paid individuals? The more favorable the treatment of unqualified deferred compensation, the less the incentive for qualified plans. Yet federal policy clearly contemplates the maximum incentive for the creation of qualified plans that provide (retirement) protection for employees at all income levels.

Daniel I. Halperin, "Ninth Circuit's Decision in Albertson's is Outrageous," 62 Tax Notes 1083 (1994).

(B) *Annuities Compared.* Compare the treatment of annuities where payments are deferred until retirement (or age 59½), supra at page 161. Here a lengthy deferral of tax on investment income is available. Is there reason to believe that this arrangement poses substantially less threat to qualified deferred compensation plans than the arrangement sought by Albertson's ?

(C) *The Matching Principle.* Although § 404 specifically requires matching of the time of the employer's deduction with the employee's inclusion in income in the case of nonqualified deferred compensation, there is no general matching principle in the Code and no general requirement that in order for a payor to get a deduction, the payee must be taxed on the income. Indeed, there are many cases where there is no matching. For example, a deductible expenditure by an accrual basis transferor to a cash basis transferee often results in a deduction in a year prior to the inclusion. Moreover, whenever a taxable payor transfers interest or rent to a tax-exempt entity, the payor has a deduction but the recipient reports no income. In some cases, however, Congress has mandated matching. See, e.g., §§ 267, 404(a). Indeed, *Albertson's* is on firm ground in the way it construes the matching requirement of § 404(a) in light of the overall structure of the Code and congressional policies regarding deferred compensation, but the court's reliance on the so-called matching principle cannot be taken as a general guide to statutory interpretation. A complete matching principle would obliterate the differences between cash and accrual accounting.

Consider the application of the matching principle described in footnote 1 of the court's opinion. The government argued that if the court permitted Albertson's to deduct the "interest," then it would be required to hold that the employees had income at the same time. Is that correct? If so, why would such a result be "harshly inequitable"?

NOTE ON QUALIFIED PENSION PLANS

Sections 401–404 and 410–416 provide more favorable tax treatment for pension, profit-sharing, and "stock bonus" plans that are "qualified." Employees are not taxed on their interests in qualified plans until they actually receive benefits even though the plans are funded. On the other hand, contributions to the plan are immediately deductible by the employer. Thus, unlike nonqualified plans subject to § 404(a)(5), qualified plans do not provide for "matching" of income and deductions. Moreover, the pension trust or fund is itself tax-exempt.

To be "qualified," the plan must meet certain prescribed conditions, for example, that it not discriminate in favor of officers, stockholders, or other highly compensated employees. §§ 401(a)(4) and (a)(5) and (20). See also § 414(a). Retirement plans can be divided into two main categories:

(1) "Defined benefit plans," under which the employee is entitled to specified benefits (e.g., $10 per month per year of service or 40 percent of average earnings for the three years prior to retirement) and the employer makes whatever contributions are required to provide such benefits.

(2) "Defined contribution plans," under which the employer makes a specific contribution (e.g., 10 percent of pay), the contributions are credited to an employee's account, and the retirement benefit is whatever amount can be provided by the accumulated fund.

Nondiscrimination Requirements for Qualified Plans. Extensive legislative efforts since 1974 have required qualified plans to provide more protection for rank-and-file employees and limited the total amount that can be set aside for highly-paid employees. These efforts, including the nondiscrimination test, have been aimed at encouraging employers to supplement the Social Security retirement benefits provided to their low- and moderate-income employees. For example, the 1986 Act strengthened the nondiscrimination standards and rules permitting integration of employer-provided pension plans and Social Security.

In theory, the nondiscrimination requirements are present in the Code for the purpose of inhibiting tax abuses and ensuring that employer-provided pensions satisfy retirement income security goals. These requirements operate by permitting pension plan contributions and earnings to qualify for tax-advantaged treatment only if a substantial number of lower-paid employees participate in the plan. The basic requirement is stated as a minimum level of coverage necessary for a plan to qualify for favorable tax treatment. Specifically, the nondiscrimination requirement is satisfied if the percentage of employees covered under the plan who do not earn high wages is at least 70 percent of the percentage of highly compensated employees covered under the plan and, for defined benefit plans, if the lesser of 50 employees or 40 percent of all employees are covered by the plan. See §§ 410(b)(1) and 401(a)(26).

These rules seem inadequate to ensure that the tax advantages of qualified plans provide retirement security for rank-and-file workers. A number of important exceptions to the nondiscrimination requirements remain, and coverage of low-and moderate-income employees remains restricted by the ability of employers to "integrate" their pension plans with Social Security benefits. Such "integration" allows employers to treat retirement benefits provided under Social Security as if they were provided by the employer in testing whether the employer's pension plan satisfies the Code's nondiscrimination tests. See § 401(*l*). Many plans meet the nondiscrimination standards only if the Social Security benefits or payments by an employer are taken into account as if they were pension benefits provided under a pension plan, thereby allowing employer plans to take into account the disproportionately larger benefits of Social Security for low- and moderate-income workers and earners.

Vesting Requirements for Qualified Plans. Employers have some flexibility in giving employees vested rights to benefits, i.e., the right to receive benefits if the employee leaves or loses his job before retirement. An employer must either fully vest pension benefits in workers after five years of service or vest 20 percent of benefits each year beginning at the end of three years of service, so that such employees will be fully vested at the end of seven years of service. Under legislation enacted in 2001, faster vesting of benefits is required for employer contributions matching those of employees. Either 100 percent of such contributions must vest after three years of service or 20 percent must vest each year beginning with the second year of service so that 100 percent is vested after six years of service. See § 411. These requirements represent a substantial improvement on the pre–1986 ERISA standards. If a five-year standard had been applicable in 1985, almost 21 million additional workers would have been entitled to vested benefits—a 7 percent increase in the number of men and a 10 percent increase in women. Greater coverage requirements would have made 6.3 million more women eligible for pension benefits than under prior law. The length of employment conditions are a means of promoting stability in the workforce and avoiding the additional administrative costs of an immediate vesting standard. These rules, however, do not seem likely to attain either the retirement security or tax justice advantages of an immediate vesting rule.

Pre-Retirement Withdrawals. Tax penalties are imposed when employees withdraw their pension funds prior to retirement. The Code imposes tax penalties for most early distributions from qualified plans to recoup the initial tax advantage gained. With some exceptions, the Code applies an additional 10 percent income tax to all early distributions included in gross income. § 72(t). These provisions were adopted principally as a means of ensuring that tax advantages intended for retirement savings will be recaptured whenever such savings do not satisfy the retirement security goal and to create a disincentive for early withdrawals. There are also restrictions on borrowing against pension assets. § 72(p). In both cases, Congress seemed to be concerned principally with the tax abuse potential inherent in a regime that would allow pre-retirement withdrawals.

Funding and Termination of Qualified Plans. To guard against inadequate funding by employers of pension benefits promised to their employees, § 412 imposes funding requirements as a condition of favorable tax treatment. Employers also are required to guarantee benefits to protect employees when plans are terminated before they are completely funded, and a government agency, the Pension Benefit Guaranty Corporation ("PBGC") has been created to provide "plan termination insurance" when neither funding nor the employer guarantee is sufficient. PBGC is funded by mandatory employer premiums.

Limits on Contributions and Benefits. Section 415 limits the maximum amount of contributions to pension plans and pension benefits. These limits were lowered from time to time in the 1980's and 1990's, principally to increase current revenues in connection with deficit reduction efforts. The 2001 legislation, however, raised these limits. Beginning in 2002, the maximum annual contribution is $40,000 for defined contribution plans. The maximum annual benefit is $160,000 for defined benefit plans. And these limits are indexed for inflation. The same limitations apply to self-employed people and partners as to corporate employees.

"Top–Heavy" Plans. Special limitations are imposed on "top-heavy" plans, which primarily benefit high-earning individuals, to require a minimum pension contribution and faster vesting for lower-level employees. § 416.

NOTE ON INDIVIDUAL RETIREMENT ACCOUNTS ("IRAs")

Before 1974, employees generally could not obtain any tax benefits for creating their own retirement plans even if their employer did not take advantage of the Code's qualified pension plan provisions. Between 1974 and 1981, the Code permitted a limited deduction for contributions to individual retirement accounts set up by those who were not active participants in a qualified § 401 plan. Between 1981 and 1986, all wage earners could deduct up to $2,000 a year (or the amount of compensation for services received, if it was less) of contributions made to an individual retirement account. Moreover, during that period, a taxpayer could deduct contributions of up to $2,000 to an account created for a spouse who had no wage income.

The 1981 extension of IRA eligibility to all workers produced a revenue loss more than six times greater than that originally estimated. Although the bulk of this revenue loss was concentrated among high-earning employees, the mass marketing of IRAs by savings institutions apparently induced large numbers of moderate-income taxpayers to shift away from general savings accounts, which are not eligible for tax savings, to tax-preferred retirement savings.

The 1986 Tax Reform Act once again restricted the ability to enjoy the full benefits of IRAs to individuals not covered by employer plans. The Code provided that single persons with more than $25,000 of income and married couples with more than $40,000 of income who are covered by employer plans were no longer eligible to deduct IRA contributions, but they may continue to receive tax-free accumulations of investment income both on their pre–1986 contributions to IRAs and on additional annual IRA contributions of not more than $2,000 a year. §§ 219 and 408.

Under current law, the maximum amounts that can be contributed to an IRA and deducted is $3,000 ($4,000 in 2005 through 2007, and $5,000 beginning in 2008). At age 50, people are allowed to contribute an extra $500 ($1,000 in 2006 or later years). If, however, the individual is an active participant in a qualified plan, the deduction is phased out for taxpayers with income between $50,000–$60,000 ($30,000–$40,000 for single taxpayers). By 2007 this phaseout range increases to $80,000–$100,000 ($50,000–$60,000 for single taxpayers).

Generally, taxpayers who withdraw savings from an IRA before age 59½ are subject to a 10% withdrawal penalty. This penalty does not apply to withdrawals to pay medical expenses, health insurance premiums, or education expenses.

A second type of IRA reverses the usual deduction/inclusion posture. A nondeductible contribution of up to $2,000 annually may be made to a so-called Roth IRA and distributions for certain purposes are excludible. Qualified distributions are those made at least five years after the first contribution and which are either made after the taxpayer reaches age 59½, made to a beneficiary after the death of the contributor or made because the contributor is disabled or to a first-time home buyer. The use of a Roth IRA is phased out for a single taxpayer with income between $95,000–$110,000 ($150,000–$160,000 if married filing jointly). A taxpayer can contribute to both a regular and a Roth IRA but total contributions cannot exceed $2,000 annually. Under the 2001 Act, the $2,000 limit increases to $5,000 as described above. Those with income of less than $100,000 were permitted to convert a regular IRA to a Roth IRA. The early withdrawal penalty does not apply to a distribution to a first-time homeowner.

Congress intended to create an incentive to save for retirement by creating a tax advantage for investment in an IRA. In a traditional IRA, the incentive is in the form of a current deduction for amounts contributed and thus is a deferral of taxation of that amount, as well as the investment income. In a Roth IRA, the incentive is the exemption from taxation of all withdrawals, including the investment income. As demonstrated in the Note on Tax Deferral, supra at page 287, if tax rates are constant, the two forms of IRA are generally economically equivalent. The following example illustrates this equivalence. Assume T, who is in the 40 percent tax bracket, earns $2,000, which he invests in a traditional IRA for which he receives a deduction. Assume the yield on the IRA is 10 percent and at the end of 10 years has grown to $5,188. After paying a tax of $2,075, T is left with $3,113. Alternatively, T could have invested $1,200 in a Roth IRA, after paying $800 in taxes. At 10 percent, the $1,200 will grow to $3,113, which he can withdraw tax-free. Since, however, the ceilings on the amounts that can be contributed to either type of IRA are the same—$2,000—the Roth IRA permits larger accumulations.

If investment yields are not constant, the Roth IRA has the curious effect of taxing two individuals with wildly different amounts of income at the same rate. Suppose, for example, that A and B both invest $2,000 a year for five years in an IRA and retire 50 years later. A invests in a stock that does very poorly and in fact, has only the original $10,000 at retirement. B invests in stocks that grow at 15 percent a year, yielding a retirement fund of $11 million.* A and B of course would pay very different taxes on withdrawal. But if A and B had invested in a Roth IRA, each would have been taxed the same on the $2,000 contributions and would not be taxed at all on withdrawal.

---

* This example is drawn from Gene Steuerle, Back–Loaded IRAs: Head Taxes Re-place Income and Consumption Taxes, 77 Tax Notes 109 (Oct. 9, 1997).

NOTES

(A) *Cash or Deferred Arrangements ("CODAs").* The Code contains an increasingly important set of provisions that allow employees to make their own contributions to retirement savings plans in lieu of receiving cash salary and, by so doing, to achieve tax savings comparable to those available for employer contributions to employer-sponsored pension plans. The most important of these salary reduction plans are so-called 401(k) plans, also known as cash or deferred arrangements (CODAs). Similar optional salary reduction plans are available to employees of certain tax-exempt institutions under other sections of the Internal Revenue Code. See § 403(b); see also §§ 402(g)(4), 457 and 501(c)(18). These plans are subject to a variety of constraints, along the lines of rules applicable to employer pension plan contributions, principally designed to allow employees opportunities for additional tax-preferred retirement savings so long as these opportunities are not limited to high-earning employees.

The 2001 Act significantly liberalized the rules governing such plans and increased the maximum amounts that can be contributed.

(B) *Tax Credit for Contributions to IRAs and CODAs.* In 2001 Congress enacted a temporary nonrefundable tax credit for contributions to an IRA or a CODA, including 401(k) plans, by lower and middle income taxpayers. The maximum annual contribution eligible for the credit is $2,000. For taxpayers with adjusted gross income of zero to $15,000 (zero to $30,000 for married couples filing jointly), the credit is equal to 50 percent of the amount contributed, for a maximum credit of $1,000. Above these income levels, the maximum amount of the credit declines sharply to 20 percent of the amount contributed if AGI is between $15,000–$16,250 ($30,000–$32,500 on joint returns), and 10 percent if AGI is between $16,250 and $25,000 ($32,500–$50,000 for married couples filing jointly). No credit is available for single taxpayers with AGI above $25,000 or married couples with AGI above $50,000. This credit, which is in effect a government matching contribution to individuals' retirement savings accounts, is intended to encourage more moderate income taxpayers to take advantage of the tax benefits of saving through IRAs or CODAs. This credit is scheduled to disappear in 2007.

(C) *Fairness for Women?* The 2001 legislation contains several retirement savings provisions under the heading "Enhancing Fairness for Women." These include some provisions, such as faster vesting of employer contributions to a qualified plan and liberalizing somewhat the treatment of certain transfers of CODA assets incident to a divorce, that will principally benefit women. And—if anyone takes advantage of it—a new provision permitting the establishment of relatively simple pension plans for domestic workers will primarily benefit women. But the most costly provision under this heading allows a special catch-up contribution of up to $5,000 a year to a CODA by any employee over age 50, a provision that almost certainly will be used by more men than women. Congress apparently has not lost it sense of humor.

(D) *Employee Stock Ownership Plans ("ESOPs").* ERISA and subsequent legislation have provided special advantages for the Employee Stock

Ownership Plans (ESOPs) that promote employee ownership of businesses. An ESOP is a qualified deferred compensation employee trust fund that invests in the company's stock and gives employees a right to demand distribution of the stock on retirement or other termination of employment. § 409. As qualified plans, ESOPs are subject to the general rules applicable to such plans. Certain special tax advantages are available to ESOPs, however. See, e.g., § 133 (excluding from income one-half of the interest received by financial institutions on loans to finance ESOP stock acquisitions) and § 1042 (providing nonrecognition treatment for certain ESOP transactions). In addition, the standard qualified deferred compensation plan benefits of an immediate deduction to employers and deferral of employee recognition of income until withdrawals from the trust actually made are still available and somewhat widely used. The Code also provides special estate tax benefits for ESOPs.

(E) *Policy Issues.* Reliance on tax inducements to encourage employers voluntarily to establish and fund retirement income plans for their employees necessarily involves compromises. Congress has endeavored to ensure that the tax subsidy to employer plans is justified by an adequate distribution of benefits and curtailment of risks to low-and moderate-income workers, but, at the same time, has been fearful of enacting harsh rules that will stimulate employers to refuse to establish or curtail voluntary pension or profit-sharing plans. Less restrictive alternative vehicles for tax-preferred savings and low tax rates on investment income generally reduce Congress's ability to impose requirements on qualified deferred compensation plans. As a result, ensuring that such voluntary plans remain an important source of retirement security for the nation's workers is a tightrope act that many analysts think offers little hope for genuine retirement income security for middle-income employees. This voluntary employer-based pension system seems to have reached a ceiling in its participation rate at about one-half the working population. Both the tax savings and distribution of benefits from private pensions disproportionately benefit higher-income workers and employees of large firms. This system is shifting more responsibility and financial rights (and rewards) to individual workers. It is vulnerable to disruption from independent changes in tax policy. Increases in the size of the elderly population and in life expectancies should prompt a thorough reexamination of the nation's system of protecting retirement income. See, e.g., Michael J. Graetz & Jerry L. Mashaw, True Security: Rethinking American Social Insurance, chs. 5, 13 (2000); Daniel I. Halperin, "Special Tax Treatment for Employer–Based Retirement Programs: Is It 'Still' Viable as a Means of Increasing Retirement Income? Should It Continue?," 49 Tax L.Rev. 1 (1993).

NOTE ON STOCK OPTIONS

A very popular form of deferred compensation is a stock option. Generally, executives in consideration for services are given an option to purchase a set number of shares of the employer's stock at a fixed price at given date in the future. These options may be taxed in three different ways:

Incentive Stock Options. Under §§ 421 and 422 of the Code, "incentive stock options" are not taxable at the time they are granted or exercised, and the employee usually obtains capital gain treatment when she ultimately sells the stock. The employer ordinarily may not deduct the option as compensation, and the difference between the fair market value of the stock and its purchase price to the employee constitutes an item of tax preference for purposes of calculating the employee's alternative minimum tax liability. See Chapter 7.

To qualify as an ISO, the option price cannot be less than the fair market value of the stock at the time the option is granted. The taxpayer cannot dispose of the stock within two years after receiving the option or within one year after exercising the option. If she does not meet these holding requirements, the portion of gain that represents the difference between the value of the stock when the option was exercised and her purchase price will constitute ordinary income. The employer will receive a deduction at that time to the extent that the employee recognizes ordinary income. The holding period requirements do not apply if the employee dies.

Suppose, for example, that X Co. granted an option to its CEO to acquire 1000 shares of X Co. stock for $10 each in two years at a time when the stock is worth $10. When the CEO exercises the option, the stock is worth $100. A year later, the CEO sells the stock for $120,000. The CEO has no income at the time he receives the option even though he has received a valuable right. Although the option is not "in the money," the CEO will enjoy the benefit of any increase in the value of the stock above $10 and suffers no loss if the stock price declines below $10. Furthermore, he has no income on the spread between $10 and $100 when he exercises the option. He would report the difference between the sales price of $120,000 and his basis of $10,000 as capital gain on the disposition of the stock.

Congress adopted preferential treatment for ISOs as "an important incentive device for corporations to attract new management and to retain the service of executives who might otherwise leave." Staff of the Joint Comm. on Tax'n, General Explanation of the Economic Recovery Act of 1981, 97th Cong. 157 (1981).

Nonstatutory Stock Options. Suppose at the time the CEO was granted the option in the above example, the stock was worth $50. Because the option price is less than the value of the stock when the option is granted, the option cannot be an ISO. Recall the previous discussion of § 83 at page 119 supra. If the option has a "readily ascertainable market value" (which under the regulations is difficult to achieve), the option is included in the CEO's income. § 83(a). The employer has a deduction of the same amount. There is no additional income at the time of exercise. If the CEO exercises the option, he will not be taxed on the difference between the exercise price ($10) and the market value ($100) (as is true for regular stock options). § 83(e)(4). Again, the additional gain will be reported on the disposition of the shares. If the option expires (because the price falls below $10), the CEO would have a capital loss equal to the amount previously included in income.

Suppose in addition that the CEO will forfeit the stock if he leaves X Co. within five years of receiving the option. Because the stock is subject to restrictions, the CEO has no income on receipt. When the option vests, the CEO includes its value at that time and the employer takes a deduction. If, however, the CEO elects under § 83(b) to report the option when received, he will have ordinary income equal to the value of the option and X Co. will have a deduction of the same amount. There would be no further income when the option is exercised. On disposition of the shares, the CEO reports the difference between the sales price of $120,000 and his basis (the $10,000 paid plus the amount previously included in income).

Compensatory stock options are often very difficult to value and if there is no readily ascertainable value, there is no income on the receipt of the option. At the time of exercise, the CEO has income equal to the spread between the exercise price and the value of the stock or $90,000. Commissioner v. LoBue, 351 U.S. 243 (1956); Reg. § 1.83–7. If the CEO never exercises the option, he has no income and the employer has no deduction.

SECTION 5.   INVENTORIES

NOTE ON INVENTORY VALUATION

When a manufacturer or retailer sells goods, the amount received ordinarily is readily ascertainable. This amount, however, is not gross income, for deduction of the cost of goods sold must be allowed before there is gross income. This may be represented by:

$$(1) \qquad \text{GI} = \text{GR} - \text{CGS}$$

where GI is gross income, GR is gross receipts, and CGS is cost of goods sold.

The problem is to find the cost of goods sold. In some cases (as, say, with a dealer in automobiles), it may be possible to tell the exact cost of each item sold. Generally, however, as with a manufacturer or a department store, it is not possible to know the exact cost of each item sold. Moreover, there may be fluctuations in the value of items on hand, even when they can be identified, which may affect the computation. Inventory accounting rules have been developed to deal with this problem. See §§ 471 and 472.

To calculate gross income, we need to know the cost of goods sold during the accounting period. The stock of goods from which sales have been made is composed of two classes of items: (1) the goods on hand at the beginning of the period and (2) the goods purchased during the period. By subtracting (3) the goods on hand at the end of the period, we can measure those sold during the period. This may be represented by the following:

$$(2) \qquad \text{CGS} = I_o + P - I_c$$

where I_o is the opening inventory, P is the cost of purchases during the period, and I_c is the closing inventory.

Substituting equation (2) in equation (1), we have:

(3) $GI = GR - (I_o + P - I_c)$
or (4) $GI = GR - I_o - P + I_c$

Thus, gross income is reduced as the opening inventory is increased, and is increased through any increase in the closing inventory. But the closing inventory of one year is the opening inventory of the following year. Thus, any change in the closing inventory of one year affects the income of that year in one way and the income of the next year in precisely the opposite way. Inventory adjustments consequently become a means of allocating income to one year or another.

Difficulties arise in identifying and valuing the inventory. By a process of counting or measuring or weighing, it is ordinarily fairly easy to determine the number of units in the inventory at any given time. But tax computations must be made in dollars, and to put the inventory into dollars requires assigning a value in dollars or cents to each unit in the inventory. What value should be used? The figure might be based upon cost, or upon market value at the time the inventory is counted. If the market price has been going up, an inventory valued at market would include in income the unrealized increase in market value of the goods still on hand. On the other hand, where the market value has gone down, an inventory valuation based on market will reduce the income of the year by the unrealized loss in market value of the goods still on hand. There are no rigid rules here, except that the method used must be used consistently year after year. Any practice adopted is simply a convention. Long before the income tax entered the picture, it had become conservative accounting practice in many industries to value inventories at "cost or market, whichever is lower." On this basis, you will note, decreases in market value will lower the inventory figure, and thus reduce income for the year, even though the goods have not been sold, and the inventory loss may in fact never be realized.

Whether the inventory is based on "cost" or on "cost or market, whichever is lower," some means must be used to determine cost. Ordinarily, the actual cost of the items on hand at the close of the period cannot be ascertained. Consider, for example, the hardware dealer who sells nails at retail and keeps his stock in a barrel. As customers come to the store, he scoops out nails, weighs them, and includes the sales price in his gross receipts. When the supply of nails in the barrel runs low, he orders new ones that he dumps into the barrel on top of those already there. Sometimes he may get to the very bottom of the barrel. Other times, he may replenish the supply when the barrel is half or a quarter full. It is obviously impossible to mark the nails to show when any particular nails were bought or the price paid for them.

Some convention must be adopted. For many years, the only method allowed for tax purposes was "first in, first out," known as FIFO. This may be illustrated as follows:

Opening inventory   50   units valued (on some basis) @ $10 per unit

Purchases: Jan.   10   units   @   9   cost (determined from invoices)
              Feb.   12   @ 10

Mar.	8	@ 11
Apr.	12	@ 10
May	14	@ 11
June	10	@ 12
July	12	@ 12
Aug.	13	@ 13
Sept.	14	@ 12
Oct.	8	@ 13
Nov.	11	@ 14
Dec.	12	@ 15

Closing inventory   64   units

On a first in, first out basis, the items on hand at the beginning of the year, and those earliest bought, would be the first to go. Those remaining at the end of the year would be those most recently purchased—first in, first out is the equivalent of last in, last out. Thus, the closing inventory of 64 units would be treated as made up of those most recently purchased, going back as far as necessary until the total of 64 units was made up. On the facts given, this would take in all of those bought in December, November, October, September, August, and six of those bought in July. Thus the closing inventory would be:

July	6	units	@ 12	72
Aug.	13		@ 13	169
Sept.	14		@ 12	168
Oct.	8		@ 13	104
Nov.	11		@ 14	154
Dec.	12		@ 15	180
Total	64			847

Note that prices generally were rising during the year in question. The effect of using the FIFO convention is that the increase in costs during the year is reflected in the closing inventory and the gross income taxable for the year will reflect the lower earlier costs. And this would be true, even if the nails actually on hand were those at the bottom of the barrel that have been there for many years.

Many businesses felt that this method was unsound. Consider, for example, a pipeline company that has to have a large quantity of oil in its pipeline just to keep operating. Although this oil is constantly changing, the company has to keep oil on hand to keep the pipeline filled; it cannot operate without it. The oil is really as much a part of its equipment as the pipe or the pumps. We would not take into account (in computing annual income) fluctuations in the value of the pipes or pumps or storage tanks. Why should fluctuations in the value of the oil in the pipeline be reflected in gross income? Or consider a winery, which has to keep a number of years' supply of wine aging as long as it plans to keep on operating.

In 1939, Congress authorized the "last in, first out" method of inventory valuation, commonly known as LIFO, and this is now set out in detail in § 472. Under this method, the convention to be used in valuing the closing inventory at cost is reversed; it is assumed that the items on hand at the close of the year are those bought longest ago. "Last in, first out" is the equivalent of "first in, last out." Thus, on the basis of the example set out above, if LIFO were used, the closing inventory of 64 units would be made up of those earliest acquired. These would be the 50 units on hand at the beginning of the year, plus the ten acquired in January, and four of those acquired in February. This may be tabulated as follows:

Opening inventory	50	units	@ 10	500
	Jan.	10		@ 9	90
	Feb.	4		@ 10	40
Total		64			630

Thus, the closing inventory on LIFO is 630, while we have ascertained that on FIFO the closing inventory is 847. A substantial difference in the amount of taxable income for the year therefore often depends simply on the method of inventory valuation used; gross income for the year is $217 less under LIFO than FIFO. The use of FIFO means that both increases and decreases in the market value of items in the inventory are reflected in income; however, under LIFO neither increases nor decreases in market value are reflected with respect to the number of units that have been on hand throughout the period. (Note that if, in the example, the closing inventory had been less than 50 units, it would have been necessary to analyze it, and to determine the cost of the number of units in the closing inventory that had been earliest acquired.)

LIFO can be regarded as a sort of averaging device. From the beginning to the end of a complete operation, both FIFO and LIFO will necessarily produce exactly the same aggregate net income. But FIFO will produce more fluctuations. Inventories will go up when prices go up, and inventories will go down when prices go down, with corresponding effects on taxable income. Under LIFO, fluctuations in the value of a more or less permanent inventory—the amount of goods the business has to have on hand if it is to keep operating—will not enter into the income computation as long as the volume of goods on hand does not fall below the opening inventory figure.

LIFO has not been as commonly used as would be expected of a method that would decrease tax liability during a period of increasing prices, such as in the United States since the 1960's. Principally, businesses have been unwilling to adopt LIFO because of the "booking" requirement of § 472(c) that the company must use LIFO for reporting income to shareholders and creditors if it is used for tax purposes. Many companies are concerned that reporting the lower income to shareholders that would result under LIFO would depress the value of their stock in the market, and they have paid many billions of dollars in "voluntary" taxes rather than lower the earnings they report to shareholders. In addition, the LIFO regulations are very complex and require inventory to be valued at cost, not at the lower of cost or market. In the 1990's Treasury estimated that as much as two-thirds of total inventories in the United States was based on FIFO accounting despite its effect in increasing tax liabilities in times of inflation.

Treasury proposed that taxpayers be permitted to use an "indexed FIFO" method, which would adjust FIFO inventories by annual increases in the Consumer Price Index. 2 Treasury Dep't, Report to the President,

Tax Reform for Fairness, Simplicity and Economic Growth 189–93 (1984). Coupled with a repeal of the LIFO conformity requirement, these proposed changes were expected to produce a widespread shift to LIFO or to indexed FIFO. Probably because this would result in a large tax reduction, Congress failed to act.

Thor Power Tool Co. v. Commissioner

Supreme Court of the United States, 1979. 439 U.S. 522.

MR. JUSTICE BLACKMUN delivered the opinion of the Court.

* * *

In 1964, petitioner Thor Power Tool Co. (hereinafter sometimes referred to as the "taxpayer"), in accord with "generally accepted accounting principles," wrote down what it regarded as excess inventory to Thor's own estimate of the net realizable value of the excess goods. Despite this write-down, Thor continued to hold the goods for sale at original prices. * * * The Commissioner of Internal Revenue, maintaining that the write-down did not serve to reflect income clearly for tax purposes, disallowed the offset and the [loss carryback it produced.]

* * *

A

Taxpayer * * * manufactures hand-held power tools, parts and accessories, and rubber products. At its various plants and service branches, Thor maintains inventories of raw materials, work-in-process, finished parts and accessories, and completed tools. At all times relevant, Thor has used, both for financial accounting and for income tax purposes, the "lower of cost or market" method of valuing inventories. * * *

Thor's tools typically contain from 50 to 200 parts, each of which taxpayer stocks to meet demands for replacements. Because of the difficulty, at the time of manufacture, of predicting the future demand for various parts, taxpayer produced liberal quantities of each part to avoid subsequent production runs. * * *

In late 1964, new management took control and promptly concluded that Thor's inventory in general was overvalued. After "a physical inventory taken at all locations" of the tool and rubber divisions * * * management wrote off approximately $2.75 million of obsolete parts, damaged or defective tools, demonstration or sales samples, and similar items. * * * The Commissioner allowed this writeoff because Thor scrapped most of the articles shortly after their removal from the 1964 closing inventory. Management also wrote down $245,000 of parts stocked for three unsuccessful products. * * * The Commissioner allowed this write-down too, since Thor sold these items at reduced prices shortly after the close of 1964. * * *

This left some 44,000 assorted items, the status of which is the inventory issue here. Management concluded that many of these articles, mostly spare parts, were "excess" inventory, that is, that they were held in excess of any reasonably foreseeable future demand. It was decided that this inventory should be written down to its "net realizable value," which, in most cases, was scrap value. * * *

Two methods were used to ascertain the quantity of excess inventory. Where accurate data were available, Thor forecast future demand for each item on the basis of actual 1964 usage, that is, actual sales for tools and service parts, and actual usage for raw materials, work-in-process, and production parts. Management assumed that future demand for each item would be the same as it was in 1964. Thor then applied the following aging schedule: the quantity of each item corresponding to less than one year's estimated demand was kept at cost; the quantity of each item in excess of two years' estimated demand was written off entirely; and the quantity of each item corresponding to from one to two years' estimated demand was written down by 50% or 75%. Thor presented no statistical evidence to rationalize these percentages or this time frame. In the Tax Court, Thor's president justified the formula by citing general business experience, and opined that it was "somewhat in between" possible alternative solutions. This first method yielded a total write-down of $744,030. * * *

At two plants where 1964 data were inadequate to permit forecasts of future demand, Thor used its second method for valuing inventories. At these plants, the company employed flat percentage write-downs of 5%, 10% and 50% for various types of inventory. Thor presented no sales or other data to support these percentages. Its president observed that "this is not a precise way of doing it," but said that the company "felt some adjustment of this nature was in order, and these figures represented our best estimate of what was required to reduce the inventory to net realizable value." This second method yielded a total write-down of $160,832.

Although Thor wrote down all its "excess" inventory at once, it did not immediately scrap the articles or sell them at reduced prices, as it had done with the $3 million of obsolete and damaged inventory, the write-down of which the Commissioner permitted. Rather, Thor retained the "excess" items physically in inventory and continued to sell them at original prices. The company found that, owing to the peculiar nature of the articles involved, price reductions were of no avail in moving this "excess" inventory. As time went on, however, Thor gradually disposed of some of these items as scrap; the record is unclear as to when these dispositions took place.

* * *

* * * The Company contended that, by writing down excess inventory to scrap value, and by thus carrying all inventory at "net realizable value," it had reduced its inventory to "market" in accord with its "lower of cost or market" method of accounting. On audit, the Commissioner disallowed the write-down in its entirety, asserting that it did not serve clearly to reflect Thor's 1964 income for tax purposes.

The Tax Court, in upholding the Commissioner's determination, found as a fact that Thor's write-down of excess inventory did conform to "generally accepted accounting principles"; indeed, the court was "thoroughly convinced * * * that such was the case." The court found that if Thor had failed to write down its inventory on some reasonable basis, its accountants would have been unable to give its financial statements the desired certification. The court held, however, that conformance with "generally accepted accounting principles" is not enough; § 446(b), and § 471 as well, of the 1954 Code, prescribe, as an independent requirement, that inventory accounting methods must "clearly reflect income." The Tax Court rejected Thor's argument that its write-down of "excess" inventory was authorized by Treasury Regulations, and held that the Commissioner had not abused his discretion in determining that the write-down failed to reflect 1964 income clearly.

Inventory accounting is governed by §§ 446 and 471 of the Code. Section 446(a) states the general rule for methods of accounting: "Taxable income shall be computed under the method of accounting on the basis of which the taxpayer regularly computes his income in keeping his books." Section 446(b) provides, however, that if the method used by the taxpayer "does not clearly reflect income, the computation of taxable income shall be made under such method as, in the opinion of the [Commissioner], does clearly reflect income." Regulations promulgated under § 446 and in effect for the taxable year 1964, state that "no method of accounting is acceptable unless, in the opinion of the Commissioner, it clearly reflects income." Treas.Reg. § 1.446–1(a)(2).

Section 471 prescribes the general rule for inventories. It states:

> "Whenever in the opinion of the [Commissioner] the use of inventories is necessary in order clearly to determine the income of any taxpayer, inventories shall be taken by such taxpayer on such basis as the [Commissioner] may prescribe as conforming as nearly as may be to the best accounting practice in the trade or business and as most clearly reflecting the income."

As the Regulations point out, § 471 obviously establishes two distinct tests to which an inventory must conform. First, it must comply "as nearly as may be" with the "best accounting practice," a phrase that is synonymous with "generally accepted accounting principles." Second, it "must clearly reflect the income." Treas.Reg. § 1.471–2(a)(2).

It is obvious that on their face, §§ 446 and 471, with their accompanying Regulations, vest the Commissioner with wide discretion in determining whether a particular method of inventory accounting should be disallowed as not clearly reflective of income. This Court's cases confirm the breadth of this discretion. In construing § 446 and its predecessors, the Court has held that "[t]he Commissioner has broad powers in determining whether accounting methods used by a taxpayer clearly reflect income." Commissioner of Internal Revenue v. Hansen, 360 U.S. 446, 467 (1959). * * *

As has been noted, the Tax Court found as a fact in this case that Thor's write-down of "excess" inventory conformed to "generally accepted accounting principles" and was "within the term, 'best accounting practice,' as that term is used in section 471 of the Code and the regulations promulgated under that section." Since the Commissioner has not challenged this finding, there is no dispute that Thor satisfied the first part of § 471's two-pronged test. The only question, then, is whether the Commissioner abused his discretion in determining that the write-down did not satisfy the test's second prong in that it failed to reflect Thor's 1964 income clearly. Although the Commissioner's discretion is not unbridled and may not be arbitrary, we sustain his exercise of discretion here, for in this case the write-down was plainly inconsistent with the governing Regulations which the taxpayer, on its part, has not challenged.

It has been noted above that Thor at all pertinent times used the "lower of cost or market" method of inventory accounting. The rules governing this method are set out in Treas.Reg. § 1.471–4. That Regulation defines "market" to mean, ordinarily, "the current bid price prevailing at the date of the inventory for the particular merchandise in the volume in which usually purchased by the taxpayer." § 1.471–4(a). The courts have uniformly interpreted "bid price" to mean replacement cost, that is, the price the taxpayer would have to pay on the open market to purchase or reproduce the inventory items. Where no open market exists, the Regulations require the taxpayer to ascertain "bid price" by using "such evidence of a fair market price at the date or dates nearest the inventory as may be available, such as specific purchases or sales by the taxpayer or others in reasonable volume and made in good faith, or compensation paid for cancellation of contracts for purchase commitments." § 1.471–4(b).

The Regulations specify two situations in which a taxpayer is permitted to value inventory below "market" as so defined. The first is where the taxpayer in the normal course of business has actually offered merchandise for sale at prices lower than replacement cost. Inventories of such merchandise may be valued at those prices less direct cost of disposition, "and the correctness of such prices will be determined by reference to the actual sales of the taxpayer for a reasonable period before and after the date of the inventory." The Regulations warn that prices "which vary materially from the actual prices so ascertained will not be accepted as reflecting the market."

The second situation in which a taxpayer may value inventory below replacement cost is where the merchandise itself is defective. If goods are "unsalable at normal prices or unusable in the normal way because of damage, imperfections, shop wear, changes of style, odd or broken lots, or other similar causes," the taxpayer is permitted to value the goods "at bona fide selling prices less direct cost of disposition." § 1.471–2(c). The Regulations define "bona fide selling price" to mean an "actual offering of goods during a period ending not later than 30 days after inventory date." The taxpayer bears the burden of proving that "such exceptional goods as are valued upon such selling basis come within the classifications indicated," and is required to "maintain such records of the disposition of the goods as will enable a verification of the inventory to be made." Ibid.

From this language, the regulatory scheme is clear. The taxpayer must value inventory for tax purposes at cost unless the "market" is lower. "Market" is defined as "replacement cost," and the taxpayer is permitted to depart from replacement cost only in specified situations. When it makes any such departure, the taxpayer must substantiate its lower inventory valuation by providing evidence of actual offerings, actual sales, or actual contract cancellations. In the absence of objective evidence of this kind, a taxpayer's assertions as to the "market value" of its inventory are not cognizable in computing its income tax.

It is clear to us that Thor's procedures for writing down the value of its "excess" inventory were inconsistent with this regulatory scheme. Although Thor conceded that "an active market prevailed" on the inventory date it "made no effort to determine the purchase or reproduction cost" of its "excess" inventory. Thor thus failed to ascertain "market" in accord with the general rule of the Regulations. In seeking to depart from replacement cost, Thor failed to bring itself within either of the authorized exceptions. Thor is not able to take advantage of § 1.471–4(b) since, as the Tax Court found, the company failed to sell its excess inventory or offer it for sale at prices below replacement cost. Indeed, Thor concedes that it continued to sell its "excess" inventory at original prices. Thor also is not able to take advantage of § 1.471–2(c) since, as the Tax Court and the Court of Appeals both held, it failed to bear the burden of proving that its excess inventory came within the specified classifications. Actually, Thor's "excess" inventory was normal and unexceptional, and was indistinguishable from and intermingled with the inventory that was not written down.

More importantly, Thor failed to provide any objective evidence whatever that the "excess" inventory had the "market value" management ascribed to it. The Regulations demand hard evidence of actual sales and further demand that records of actual dispositions be kept. The Tax Court found, however, that Thor made no sales and kept no records. Thor's management simply wrote down its closing inventory on the basis of a well-educated guess that some of it would never be sold. The formulae governing this write-down were derived from management's collective "business experience"; the percentages contained in those formulae seemingly were chosen for no reason other than that they were multiples of five and embodied some kind of analogical symmetry. The Regulations do not permit this kind of evidence. If a taxpayer could write down its inventories on the basis of management's subjective estimates of the goods' ultimate salability, the taxpayer would be able, as the Tax Court observed, id., "to determine how much tax it wanted to pay for a given year."

For these reasons, we agree with the Tax Court and with the Seventh Circuit that the Commissioner acted within his discretion in deciding that Thor's write-down of "excess" inventory failed to reflect income clearly. In the light of the well-known potential for tax avoidance that is inherent in inventory accounting, the Commissioner in his discretion may insist on a high evidentiary standard before allowing write-downs of inventory to "market." Because Thor provided no objective evidence of the reduced market value of its "excess" inventory, its write-down was plainly inconsistent with the Regulations, and the Commissioner properly disallowed it.

C

The taxpayer's major argument against this conclusion is based on the Tax Court's clear finding that the write-down conformed to "generally accepted accounting principles." Thor points to language in Treas.Reg. § 1.446–1(a)(2), to the effect that "[a] method of accounting which reflects the consistent application of generally accepted accounting principles * * * *will ordinarily be regarded* as clearly reflecting income" (emphasis added). Section 1.471–2(b) of the Regulations likewise stated that an inventory taken in conformity with best accounting practice "can, *as a general rule,* be regarded as clearly reflecting * * * income" (emphasis added). These provisions, Thor contends, created a *presumption* that an inventory practice conformable to "generally accepted accounting principles" is valid for income tax purposes. Once a taxpayer has established this conformity, the argument runs, the burden shifts to the Commissioner affirmatively to demonstrate that the taxpayer's method does *not* reflect income clearly. * * *

If the Code and Regulations did embody the presumption petitioner postulates, it would be of little use to the taxpayer in this case. As we have noted, Thor's write-down of "excess" inventory was inconsistent with the Regulations; any general presumption obviously must yield in the face of such particular inconsistency. We believe, however, that no such presumption is present. Its existence is insupportable in light of the statute, the Court's past decisions, and the differing objectives of tax and financial accounting.

First, as has been stated above, the Code and Regulations establish two distinct tests to which an inventory must conform. The Code and Regulations, moreover, leave little doubt as to which test is paramount. While § 471 of the Code requires only that an accounting practice conform "as nearly as may be" to best accounting practice, § 1.446–1(a)(2) of the Regulations states categorically that "*no* method of accounting is acceptable unless, in the opinion of the Commissioner, it clearly reflects income" (emphasis added). Most importantly, the Code and Regulations give the Commissioner broad discretion to set aside the taxpayer's method if, "in [his] opinion," it does not reflect income clearly. This language is completely at odds with the notion of a "presumption" in the taxpayer's favor. The Regulations embody no presumption; they say merely that, in most cases, generally accepted accounting practices will pass muster for tax purposes. And in most cases they will. But if the Commissioner, in the exercise of his discretion, determines that they do not, he may prescribe a different practice without having to rebut any presumption running against the Treasury.

Second, the presumption petitioner postulates finds no support in this Court's prior decisions. It was early noted that the general rule specifying use of the taxpayer's method of accounting "is expressly limited to cases where the Commissioner believes that the accounts clearly reflect the net income." Lucas v. American Code Co., 280 U.S., at 449. More recently, it was held in American Automobile Assn. v. United States [367 U.S. 687 (1961)] that a taxpayer must recognize prepaid income when received, even though this would mismatch expenses and revenues in contravention of "generally accepted commercial accounting principles." 367 U.S., at 690. "[T]o say that in performing the function of business accounting the method employed by the Association 'is in accord with generally accepted commercial accounting principles and practices,'" the Court concluded, "is not to hold that for income tax purposes it so clearly reflects income as to be binding on the Treasury." Id., at 693. "[W]e are mindful that the characterization of a transaction for financial accounting purposes, on the one hand, and for tax purposes, on the other, need not necessarily be the same." Frank Lyon Co. v. United States, 435 U.S. 561, 577 (1978). * * * Indeed, the Court's cases demonstrate that divergence between tax and financial accounting is especially common when a taxpayer seeks a current deduction for estimated future expenses or losses. * * * The rationale of these cases amply encompasses Thor's aim. By its president's concession, the company's write-down of "excess" inventory was founded on the belief that many of the articles inevitably would become useless due to breakage, technological change, fluctuations in market demand, and the like. Thor, in other words, sought a current "deduction" for an estimated future loss. Under the decided cases, a taxpayer so circumstanced finds no shelter beneath an accountancy presumption.

Third, the presumption petitioner postulates is insupportable in light of the vastly different objectives that financial and tax accounting have. The primary goal of the income tax system, in contrast, is the equitable collection of revenue; the major responsibility of the Internal Revenue Service is to protect the public fisc. Consistently with its goals and responsibilities, financial accounting has as its foundation the principle of conservatism, with its corollary that "possible errors in measurement [should] be in the direction of understatement rather than overstatement of net income and net assets." In view of the Treasury's markedly different goals and responsibilities, understatement of income is not destined to be its guiding light. Given this diversity, even contrariety, of objectives, any presumptive equivalency between tax and financial accounting would be unacceptable.

* * *

Finally, a presumptive equivalency between tax and financial accounting would create insurmountable difficulties of tax administration. Accountants long have recognized that "generally accepted accounting principles" are far from being a canonical set of rules that will ensure identical accounting treatment of identical transactions. "Generally accepted accounting principles," rather, tolerate a range of "reasonable" treatments, leaving the choice among alternatives to management. Such, indeed, is precisely the case here. Variances of this sort may be tolerable in financial reporting, but they are questionable in a tax system designed to ensure as far as possible that similarly situated taxpayers pay the same tax. If management's election among "acceptable" options were dispositive for tax purposes, a firm, indeed, could decide unilaterally—within limits dictated only by its accountants—the tax it wished to pay. Such unilateral decisions would not just make the Code inequitable; they would make it unenforceable.

D

Thor complains that a decision adverse to it poses a dilemma. According to the taxpayer, it would be virtually impossible for it to offer objective evidence of its "excess" inventory's lower value, since the goods cannot be sold at reduced prices; even if they could be sold, says Thor, their reduced-price sale would just "pull the rug out" from under the identical "non-excess" inventory Thor is trying to sell simultaneously. The only way Thor could establish the inventory's value by a "closed transaction" would be to scrap the articles at once. Yet immediate scrapping would be undesirable for demand for the parts ultimately might prove greater than anticipated. The taxpayer thus sees itself presented with "an unattractive Hobson's choice: either the unsalable inventory must be carried for years at its cost instead of net realizable value, thereby overstating taxable income by such overvaluation until it is scrapped, or the excess inventory must be scrapped prematurely to the detriment of the manufacturer and its customers."

If this is indeed the dilemma that confronts Thor, it is in reality the same choice that every taxpayer who has a paper loss must face. It can realize its loss now and garner its tax benefit, or it can defer realization, and its deduction, hoping for better luck later. Thor, quite simply, has suffered no present loss. It deliberately manufactured its "excess" spare parts because it judged that the marginal cost of unsalable inventory would be lower than the cost of retooling machinery should demand surpass expectations. This was a rational business judgment and, not unpredictably, Thor now has inventory it believes it cannot sell. Thor, of course, is not so confident of its prediction as to be willing to scrap the "excess" parts now; it wants to keep them on hand, just in case. This, too, is a rational judgment, but there is no reason why the Treasury should subsidize Thor's hedging of its bets. There is also no reason why Thor should be entitled, for tax purposes, to have its cake and to eat it, too.

* * *

The judgment of the Court of Appeals is affirmed.

NOTES

(A) *Hobson's Choice.* To illustrate the Hobson's choice that Thor Power claimed it was faced with, suppose Thor has parts for which it has costs of $200,000, which it considers "excess inventory." It could scrap these parts immediately and, assuming it was in a 36 percent bracket, it would realize an immediate $72,000 tax benefit. It prefers not to scrap the parts, however, because it would be poor business policy not to retain parts for tools that are still held by consumers. Assume Thor estimates that a sufficient quantity of these tools will have worn out in five years, so that it can scrap the parts at that time. Thor estimates that it will collect about $20,000 over the five-year period by continuing to sell the parts at their original price. If it does that, it will have a tax loss of $180,000 ($200,000 − $20,000 in sales), which will produce a tax benefit in year 5 of $64,800. The present value of $64,800 five years from now at a discount rate of 8 percent is approximately $41,540. Assume for ease of computation, that the entire sales of $20,000 take place three years from now. The present value of those proceeds at an 8 percent discount rate is $15,880. Thus, the taxpayer's choice is between scraping the parts for a current benefit of $72,000 or retaining the parts for a combined future sales and tax benefit with a present value of $54,420. Of course, this calculation does not take into account any public relations detriment or loss of future business from Thor telling its customers that it has no replacement parts for tools it sold. Thor thought this was not much of a choice.

Is Thor's "dilemma" different from that faced by any taxpayer holding any loss asset? Shortly after the *Thor* decision, publishers and book dealers generated much adverse publicity for the IRS by complaining that the IRS required them to burn or otherwise destroy books that they otherwise would have warehoused for subsequent sales at deep discounts.

(B) *Manipulation of Inventories.* After *Thor,* the IRS issued Rev.Rul. 80–60, 1980–1 C.B. 97, and Rev.Proc. 80–5, 1980–1 C.B. 582, which (1) directed all taxpayers with improper inventory accounting methods under *Thor* to change their method retroactively for their first taxable year ending on or after December 25, 1979, (2) gave all affected taxpayers blanket consent to make such a change, and (3) stated that failure to make the required change would mean that "the taxpayer will have filed a return not in accordance with the law." This represents a much tougher response than is generally the case for changes in accounting methods (see discussion at page 792 infra).

Efforts to manipulate inventories are quite commonplace. See, e.g., Rev.Rul. 83–39, 1983–1 C.B. 103, holding that sales of "excess" inventory by a manufacturer under conditions where it might be repurchased at the seller's option are not bona fide sales for tax purposes. For a case upholding a criminal tax fraud conviction of taxpayers who engaged in purchase and resale agreements to inflate LIFO inventories, see United States v. Ingredient Technology Corp., 698 F.2d 88 (2d Cir.1983).

(C) *When Are Inventories Required?* Section 471 empowers the Commissioner to require the use of inventories when "necessary in order clearly to determine the income of any taxpayer." Section 1.471–1 of the Regulations provides that "[i]n order to reflect taxable income correctly, inventories * * * are necessary in every case in which the production, purchase or sale of merchandise is an income producing factor." The regulatory scheme is completed by Reg. § 1.446–1(c)(2)(i), which states that "[i]n any case in which it is necessary to use an inventory the accrual method of accounting must be used with regard to purchases and sales unless otherwise authorized." For examples of application of these rules, see, e.g., Knight–Ridder Newspapers, Inc. v. United States, 743 F.2d 781 (11th Cir.1984) (although nearly 80 percent of the company's revenues came from advertisers, the sale of newspapers is a material income producing factor and the company must keep inventories and use the accrual method of accounting); Wilkinson–Beane, Inc. v. Commissioner, 420 F.2d 352 (1st Cir.1970) (holding that caskets sold in connection with an undertaking establishment's provision of a "complete funeral service" are both merchandise and a substantial income producing factor and therefore that inventories and an accrual method of accounting are required); Rev.Rul. 73–384, 1973–2 C.B. 150 (requiring a cash method corporation that fabricated and fit artificial limbs and orthopedic braces for physically handicapped persons, instructed the individuals in their use, and periodically adjusted and evaluated the fit, to use inventories under § 471 and change to an accrual method of accounting). Compare W.C. and A.N. Miller Development Co. v. Commissioner, 81 T.C. 619 (1983) and Homes by Ayres v. Commissioner, 795 F.2d 832 (9th

Cir.1986) (both holding that homes and lots sold by real estate developers do not constitute "merchandise" under Reg. § 1.471–1 and upholding the Commissioner's refusal to permit the taxpayers to use a LIFO inventory method in accounting for the costs of homes they constructed).

(D) *LIFO Conformity Requirement.* The Service has not strictly construed the conformity requirement of § 472(c), which requires a company to use LIFO for reporting income to shareholders and creditors if it is used for tax purposes. For example, in Revenue Ruling 73–66, 1973–1 C.B. 218, the Service ruled that a taxpayer that adopts the LIFO inventory method may include on its balance sheet a footnote or parenthetical statement indicating what the inventory values would have been if the FIFO method had been used without violating the conformity requirement. See also Rev.Rul. 75–50, 1975–1 C.B. 152 (taxpayer may disclose in a footnote or parenthetical statement on its balance sheet the "excess of replacement cost or current cost over LIFO stated value" rather than the excess of "FIFO over LIFO cost"); Rev.Proc. 75–10, 1975–1 C.B. 651 (LIFO election will not be terminated solely because a taxpayer complies with financial disclosure requirements of the FASB and the SEC, which require that footnotes or commentary on annual reports and financial statements disclose the effect on income of the change to the LIFO method, provided that such disclosure is made only for the taxable year of the change to LIFO). In Revenue Ruling 88–84, 1988–2 C.B. 124, the Service permitted use of an inventory method other than LIFO in financial forecasts.

Compare the conformity requirement for LIFO inventories with the treatment of depreciation. No conformity requirement applies to depreciation when taxpayers are permitted to and typically use more accelerated methods for tax purposes than for financial reporting purposes.

(E) *Mark-to-Market Accounting for Securities Dealers.* Securities dealers are required to mark to market at year end securities that are included in their inventory. § 475. They also must recognize gain or loss on non inventory securities as if the security was sold for the fair market value at year end.

(F) *Uniform Capitalization Rules.* As indicated in the Note on inventories, the items comprising opening and closing inventory are selected through use of a convention such as LIFO or FIFO. In determining the costs of goods sold, the costs of the items selected must be determined by including the relevant costs of purchasing or manufacturing the inventory. A failure to capitalize the costs of inventory, including such indirect costs as overhead, would result in a mismatch of the expenses and the related income. Section 263A requires that many indirect costs must be capitalized and included in the costs of inventory. Thus, these costs are taken into account in the determination of costs of goods sold. These rules are often referred to as the "uniform capitalization rules" because Congress intended to provide a single set of capitalization rules to replace a variety of previous rules that had depended on the type of property and its intended use.

Section 263A requires capitalization not only of the direct costs, but also an allocable portion of most indirect costs of assets produced or acquired for resale. This includes most administrative and overhead costs, and indirect expenses for employees, such as pension contributions and fringe benefits. Research and experimentation costs otherwise deductible under § 174 are not required to be capitalized, and according to the legislative history of § 263A, selling, marketing, advertising, and distribution costs are not subject to the capitalization requirement.

In the best congressional tradition, special rules are provided under § 263A for farmers and ranchers as well as for timber and Christmas trees and the real property under those trees. See, e.g., §§ 263A(d)(1); 263A(e)(4)(B), and 263A(c)(5). An additional exception is applied to small wholesalers and retailers, viz, those whose average annual gross receipts (determined on a three-year moving average basis) do not exceed $10 million.

SECTION 6.   CHANGE OF ACCOUNTING METHOD

NOTE ON CHANGE OF ACCOUNTING METHOD

A taxpayer may seek to change its method of accounting; for example, a retailer with a large stockpile of an obsolete product might wish to change its basis for valuation of inventories from cost to the lower of cost or market. Or the taxpayer may be required by the IRS to abandon an accounting method that does not accurately reflect income or that is otherwise unacceptable.

Taxpayers would have many opportunities to avoid tax if they had unconstrained ability to shift from one accounting method to another. Consider, for example, a taxpayer with accounts receivable earned in Year 1 but not collected until Year 2. The receivables might never be included in income if the taxpayer changed from the cash method of accounting in Year 1 to the accrual method in Year 2. The Code contains two provisions, however, that are designed to limit such opportunities.

Section 446(e) gives the IRS broad discretion to approve or deny requests by taxpayers who desire to change their methods of accounting. This discretion applies both when taxpayers seek to change from an incorrect accounting method to a correct method and when they seek to change from one correct method to another. This treatment of changes of accounting method should be contrasted with the treatment of an initial selection of accounting method; a taxpayer selecting an accounting method for the first time may choose any approved method that accurately reflects income without first obtaining the consent of the IRS.

Issues often arise over whether a procedure used to calculate tax liability constitutes a "method of accounting" that cannot be changed without IRS approval. The regulations define a change of accounting method as a "change in the overall plan of accounting for gross income or deductions or a change in the treatment of any material item used in such overall plan." The regulations further explain that a method of accounting is generally not established with respect to an item without "a pattern of consistent treatment." Reg. § 1.446–1(e)(2)(ii)(a).

The IRS considers a change in "the overall plan of accounting" to include, for example, a change from the cash method of accounting to the accrual method (or vice versa), a change in the method of valuing inventories, a change in depreciation method, or a change involving the adoption, use or discontinuance of a special method of computing taxable income, such as the long-term contract method. A change in "the treatment of any material item" includes, for example, a change by an accrual basis taxpayer from accruing property taxes when paid to accruing them when due. The regulations provide that "a material item is any item which involves the proper time for the inclusion of the item in income or the taking of a deduction." Reg. § 1.446–1(e)(2)(ii)(a). Thus, a change in the timing of income or deduction may constitute a change of accounting method even where the dollar amount of income or deduction remains constant in nominal terms. The correction of a mathematical error in the computation of tax liability is not a change of accounting method.

The IRS decides whether to permit the taxpayer to change his accounting method on the basis of all the facts and circumstances, including:

(1) whether the new method is consistent with the Code, regulations, revenue rulings, revenue procedures, and decisions of the Supreme Court;

(2) whether the new method will clearly reflect income;

(3) the reasons for the change; and

(4) the tax effects of the adjustment.

The courts have indicated that the IRS cannot attach unreasonable conditions to a grant of permission to a taxpayer to change his method of accounting. In practice, the IRS routinely grants requests for a change in accounting method if based on adequate business reasons and if the taxpayer agrees to adjust taxable income to compensate for the change. The IRS may withdraw its permission, however, if it discovers that the taxpayer did not disclose all material facts relevant to the change of method.

The ability of the IRS to insist on adjustments as a condition for its consent to a taxpayer's change in accounting method is complemented by the adjustment rules of § 481. These rules apply both to taxpayers who are required by the IRS to abandon an incorrect method and to taxpayers who change methods voluntarily (sometimes without IRS consent, for example, where the Code allows changes at the taxpayer's option). Section 481 requires such taxpayers to take into account "those adjustments which are determined to be necessary solely by reason of the change in order to prevent amounts from being duplicated or omitted." Adjustments may be required to correct distortions attributable to tax years closed by the statute of limitations, but, in the case of pre–1954 tax years, only where the change was initiated by the taxpayer rather than by the IRS.

The period over which the adjustment may be taken into account depends on several factors. If the taxpayer is changing from an impermissible to a permissible method and the adjustment results in increasing taxable income for the adjustment year, the spread period is three years. In some situations, shorter periods are mandated to encourage use of a permissible period initially. If the taxpayer is changing from one permissible method to another, the spread period is six years. If the adjustment results in decreasing taxable income for the year of adjustment, the adjustment is taken into account that year. The IRS frequently issues revenue procedures governing changes in methods of accounting. Sometimes these set forth procedures that are generally applicable; sometimes they describe specific changes common to a particular industry.

Taxpayers and the IRS often dispute whether a change of accounting method is adopted voluntarily or involuntarily. The IRS has frequently sought to treat as voluntary a change of accounting method that resulted from an IRS audit, but several courts have treated such changes as involuntary.

CHAPTER 7

Minimum Taxes

As the preceding chapters have demonstrated, many provisions of the Internal Revenue Code are designed to encourage specified expenditures and activities rather than accurately measure a taxpayer's economic income. As a result, a taxpayer may owe little or no taxes even though he has a substantial amount of economic income. Congress apparently also has long believed, however, that some income tax should be imposed on all taxpayers whose economic income reflects a substantial ability to pay taxes, and has been concerned that the public will regard the income tax as unfair if high income individuals and large profitable corporations pay no income tax. Thus, the Code imposes a minimum tax on those taxpayers who have used income tax exclusions, deductions, or credits to reduce their tax below a specified minimum level.

Individuals are subject to the alternative minimum tax ("AMT") only if the computation of the minimum tax produces a tax greater than that under the regular income tax computation. The tax is imposed at lower rates than the regular tax on a broadened tax base. This base gradually has been expanded to include not only tax credits, exclusions, and deductions, but also some preferences representing deferral of taxes. Corporations also are subject to a minimum tax. It is very similar in structure to the individual minimum tax, although the rate is lower and several of the tax preferences are different. This Chapter primarily focuses on the individual minimum tax.

The minimum tax is a powerful revenue source with widespread impact on the tax planning of high income individuals. It not only raises revenue paid as minimum tax, but also serves to increase the regular income tax paid by taxpayers who limit their use of preferences or deductions to avoid triggering the minimum tax. In recent years the minimum tax has applied to increasing numbers of middle-income taxpayers whom Congress did not intend to be included in its scope. This Chapter offers only a clue about the dramatic effect of the minimum tax in complicating income tax reporting and planning.

Although the AMT does not apply to all tax preferences, it provides an opportunity to explore what is meant by a comprehensive income tax base. As you study the AMT, focus on what provisions might be included in a broadened base and on whether there are simpler, more equitable, and more efficient ways to accomplish the goals of the AMT.

This Chapter provides an introduction to the minimum tax. The history and intellectual origins of the minimum tax are described first. A Note on the role of the minimum tax, a basic outline of the minimum tax provisions and a discussion of the fundamental design issues involved in enacting a minimum tax follow. The Chapter concludes with a brief evaluation of the minimum tax in terms of the fundamental criteria of a good tax—equity, economic efficiency and simplification.

SECTION 1.   AN OVERVIEW OF THE MINIMUM TAX

NOTE ON THE EVOLUTION OF THE MINIMUM TAX

The initial political precursor of the minimum tax was a call in 1964 by Senator Russell Long for the enactment of a plan to provide an alternative broadened tax base. He proposed to give taxpayers the option to compute taxable income in the normal manner and apply the regular rates or to apply a lower rate schedule to an expanded tax base that would include certain exclusions and deductions. He called his system an "optional simplified tax." Although his proposal would have included many items then exempted from income, it also would have excluded many items that would be included by proponents of a comprehensive income tax base.

Senator Long's proposal was the forerunner of a minimum tax recommendation offered by the Treasury Department in tax reform studies published in 1969. Under Treasury's proposal, an individual would have computed tax liability under the regular rules and also would have made a special tax computation by applying tax rates equal to one-half the applicable regular income tax rates to an expanded tax base that would have included tax-exempt interest on local bonds, the appreciation in value on property donated to charity, the excluded portion of capital gains, and percentage depletion after the cost of property has been recovered. Treasury also proposed allocating itemized deductions between taxed income and exempt income and disallowing those allocated to the latter.

Congress reacted to a public statement in January, 1969 by outgoing Treasury Secretary Joseph Barr that 154 taxpayers had adjusted gross incomes of $200,000 or more but taxable incomes of zero. This statement generated more letters to Congress that year than the extremely unpopular war in Vietnam. The most notorious of these taxpayers within Congress was Mrs. Dodge, who had $1 million of income from tax-exempt state and local bonds. Congress did not attack the exclusions or deductions directly even though many other taxpayers were using these provisions to reduce tax revenues by far more significant amounts. Nor did it accept the alternative minimum tax approach proposed by Treasury; instead, Congress ultimately adopted an "add-on minimum" tax under which certain tax preferences were subjected to a separate tax surcharge. This tax was imposed at a rate of 10 percent that applied to the amount by which certain tax preferences exceeded a statutory exemption amount plus the amount of regular income taxes. This tax was payable in addition to the regular income tax. This provision remained effective until 1976 with some minor modifications of the list of tax preferences to which it applied.

In 1976, Congress again rejected a Treasury proposal for an alternative minimum tax, opting instead for substantial increases in the add-on tax. The rate was increased to 15 percent, the exemption amount was decreased, and new tax preferences were added, including "excess itemized deductions.'' The reduction in the minimum tax exemption had the effect of substantially increasing the number of people who were required to pay minimum tax and, in combination with the rate increase and reduction of the offset for regular income taxes, significantly increased the total amount of minimum tax collected. The principal effect of adding ''excess itemized deductions'' as a tax preference was the imposition of an additional tax on individuals who had a high amount of adjusted gross income but low taxable income due to large itemized deductions, principally for interest, taxes, and charitable contributions.

The most significant effect of the minimum tax prior to 1978 had been to increase the tax on capital gains. Concerned with promoting ''capital formation,'' Congress in 1978 lowered the top capital gains rate and eliminated capital gains as an item of tax preference subject to the additional minimum tax. Congress added an alternative minimum tax, which included as tax preferences only capital gains and adjusted itemized deductions and which was payable only if it exceeded the regular tax. It claimed this new provision would ensure that ''capital formation will be facilitated, and also that every individual will pay at least a reasonable minimum amount of tax with respect to large capital gains.'' In 1982, Congress repealed the add-on minimum tax for individuals and expanded the individual alternative minimum tax. The 1982 Act essentially brought the minimum tax for individuals full circle back to its initial conception as an alternative tax. The tax preferences that had been subject to the add-on minimum tax became the tax preferences for the alternative minimum tax. The tax preference for ''excess itemized deductions'' was repealed, but only certain itemized deductions—not including state taxes or personal exemptions—were allowed in computing the AMT. The 1986 Act expanded the tax base and replaced a three-tier rate schedule with a single 21 percent rate. The 1986 legislation also replaced the add-on minimum tax for corporations with an alternative minimum tax imposed at a 20 percent rate.

The legislative history of the 1986 Act reveals a bit of schizophrenia about the purpose of the AMT. On the one hand, Congress wants to prevent individuals with high economic income from escaping tax:

> [T]he minimum tax should serve one overriding objective: to ensure that no taxpayer with substantial economic income can avoid significant tax liability by using exclusions, deductions, and credits. Although these provisions may provide incentives for worthy goals, they become counterproductive when taxpayers are allowed to use them to avoid virtually all tax liability. The ability of high-income taxpayers to pay little or no tax undermines respect for the entire tax system and, thus, for the incentive provisions themselves. In addition, even aside from public perceptions, Congress concluded that it is inherently unfair for high-income taxpayers to pay little or no tax due to their ability to utilize tax preferences.

Staff of the Joint Committee on Taxation, General Explanation of the Tax Reform Act of 1986, at 429 (1987).

On the other hand, Congress also appears to see the AMT as a vehicle for general base broadening, applicable to all individuals whether or not they manage to eliminate regular tax liability:

Congress viewed the minimum taxes under [pre–1986 law] as not adequately addressing the problem [because they were] not designed to define a comprehensive tax base [and] did not sufficiently approach the measurement of economic income. By leaving out many important tax preferences, or defining preferences overly narrowly, the individual * * * minimum taxes permitted some taxpayers with substantial economic incomes to report little or no minimum taxable income and thus to avoid all liability.

Id. at 432–33.

Since 1986, Congress has not made substantial changes to the to the base of the AMT but has changed the rates and the exemption level. In 1991, the AMT tax rate increased from 21 to 24 percent; in 1994, it increased to 26 percent, and a new 28 percent bracket was added for higher income levels. In 2001 Congress increased the AMT exemption amount by $4,000 for married couples filing jointly and $2,000 for single people, effective for the years 2001–2004.

This brief review of the legislative history of minimum taxes demonstrates that this has not been a stable area of the law. Given the importance of minimum taxes as a revenue source, Congress continues to be likely to revisit these taxes. The role of the AMT has become quite controversial largely because the number of taxpayers subject to the tax has increased dramatically. In 1999, Congress passed legislation that would have ultimately repealed the AMT but it was vetoed by President Clinton. The following table sets forth the number of taxpayers subject to minimum tax and the revenue production of the individual minimum taxes since their initial enactment in 1969:

Year	Number of Taxpayers (000)	Amount ($Millions)
1970	18.9	122.0
1975	20.2	144.1
1980	217.3	1262.9
1985	427.7	3791.7
1990	132.1	830.3
1998	853.4	5014.5

Prior to the reductions in the regular income tax rates by the 2001 legislation, the Staff of the Joint Committee on Taxation estimated that the number of individual taxpayers subject to the AMT would rise from 1.9 million in 2002 to 16.4 million in 2011, or 11 percent of all returns. In addition, another 6.3 million would have personal credits reduced or limited. This increase is largely due to two factors. First, the AMT exemption is not indexed for inflation and thus in the last decade, fewer taxpayers have been automatically exempt from the AMT. Expressed in constant 1982 dollars, for example, the revenue from the AMT grew more than 500% from 1990 to 1998. Second, as the AMT expanded to include more non-preference items, such as state income taxes or nonrefundable personal credits, it affected more middle-class taxpayers, a group that Congress apparently did not intend to be AMT filers.

When Congress lowered tax rates as President George W. Bush proposed in 2001, even more taxpayers became potentially subject to the AMT.

The temporary increase in the AMT exemption level included in the 2001 legislation means that about 5.3 million taxpayers will pay the AMT (compared to 1.4 million in 2001). But because this small fix expires in 2005, the Joint Committee estimates that the AMT will apply to 35.5 million taxpayers in 2010 and will raise revenue of $133 billion.

The AMT has been a perennial target of those who hope to simplify the Code. For example, the Staff of the Joint Committee on Taxation in 2001 called for its repeal because it contributes to complexity by requiring taxpayers to calculate income tax liability under both systems. But Congress has shown no signs of interest perhaps because of the huge amount of revenue involved.

NOTE ON THE ROLE OF A MINIMUM TAX

The following excerpt from Michael J. Graetz and Emil M. Sunley, "Minimum Taxes and Comprehensive Tax Reform," in Uneasy Compromise: Problems of a Hybrid Income–Consumption Tax (1988) describes the competing goals for a minimum tax:

> Purists would view the enactment of minimum taxes as a sign that basic, comprehensive tax reform has failed or is unattainable. If the United States ever adopts a truly comprehensive income tax or a truly comprehensive consumption tax, a minimum tax with all its complexities would presumably not be needed. In fact, the November 1984 income tax proposals of the Treasury Department (Treasury I) would have repealed the minimum tax. The Treasury did suggest, however, that if its base-broadening proposals were not fully enacted, a minimum tax might still be necessary.

> We do not view the enactment of a minimum tax as a sign of failure. Instead, it is an admission that the U.S. income tax involves trade-offs among competing objectives. Congress wants to use income tax provisions to encourage particular economic investments or activities and to promote certain societal goals. At the same time, it wants to ensure that the income tax burden is distributed generally in accordance with taxpayers' abilities to pay. A minimum tax is necessary because the ability of a few large, profitable companies or high-income families to pay little or no U.S. income tax is inherently unfair and undermines public confidence in the tax system by inducing widespread perceptions of tax inequity. A well-designed minimum tax should be able to ensure that no taxpayers with substantial economic income can reduce their tax liabilities to zero by combining tax-preferred exclusions, deductions, and credits. But this objective can be achieved only by incurring considerable complexity and by blunting the effectiveness of tax incentives. On balance, we favor minimum taxes for both individuals and corporations under the current income tax; the improvements in both the fairness of the distribution of the tax burden and the perception of tax fairness by the populace outweigh the costs.

> In broad conceptual terms, the minimum tax has been closely linked to the goal of comprehensive income taxation. This linkage suggests that support for a comprehensive minimum tax depends heavily on the theoretical model against which it is measured. Realis-

tically, the U.S. income tax has never been either a pure income-based or a consumption-based tax, but rather has been a hybrid that exempts to varying degrees many forms of consumption, savings, and investment. Given this hybrid character, the scholarly and political debate over the minimum tax often has mirrored underlying preferences for aligning the tax system more closely to the theoretical poles of income-based or consumption-based taxation.

Those who support the latter form of tax system necessarily consider the minimum tax to be a step in the wrong direction. The primary justification for substituting some type of consumption or expenditure tax for the present system is that an income-based tax distorts economic behavior by creating a preference for current over future consumption. The reason is that under an income tax both the amount of saving and the return on saving are subject to taxation. For those who prefer consumption taxes, current income tax preferences designed to create savings and investment incentives are desirable offsets to the distortions between current and future consumption created by income taxation. Therefore, proponents of consumption taxes would oppose any limitation—including a minimum tax—on the use of tax preferences, especially those related to investment activity, because such limitations reduce desired savings and investment incentives and the neutrality between current and future consumption.

Supporters of broad-based income taxation, on the other hand, tend to have less dispute with the goals of a minimum tax and instead focus their criticism on its effectiveness and appropriateness as a means of achieving its goals. The corporate minimum tax debate, even among supporters of broad-based income taxation, has also reflected disagreements over the appropriate role for a corporate tax in an income-based tax system. As we later explain, those who believe that the separate corporate tax should be eliminated and corporate income imputed fully to shareholders would also probably favor similar integration of the corporate and individual minimum taxes. By the same reasoning, proponents of corporate tax reductions on earnings distributed to shareholders as dividends would tend to support similar dividend relief for minimum tax purposes, although they might regard some corporate minimum tax as an essential antidote to the perceived unfairness that would result under such a regime if profitable corporations avoided all corporate-level tax simply by paying dividends.

Political support for a minimum tax appears to have waxed and waned with shifting short-term economic policy concerns and with the political primacy of different models of the tax system overall and the system of business taxation in particular. The conceptual link between minimum taxes and comprehensive taxation of economic income, perhaps as a consequence, has seemed at times tenuous as a political force.

NOTE

Of course, the authors support for a "well-designed minimum tax" does not necessarily imply support for the AMT of current law. In addition to the function described above, a broad-based minimum tax also might serve generally as a transition mechanism towards a more comprehensive income tax. Over time, such a minimum tax, by reducing tax benefits or preferences, might wean taxpayers away from a preference-riddled tax base toward a more comprehensive tax base. As the gaps in both tax bases and in rates between the regular and minimum tax narrows, one or the other eventually might be repealed. Perhaps rather than accepting the recommendation of the Staff of the Joint Committee on Taxation that the AMT be repealed, Congress should keep the AMT and repeal the regular tax. See Michael J. Graetz, "The 1982 Minimum Tax Amendments as a First Step in the Transition to a 'Flat–Rate' Tax," 56 S.Cal.L.Rev. 527 (1983).

NOTE OUTLINING THE BASIC STRUCTURE OF THE INDIVIDUAL MINIMUM TAX

Taxpayers must pay the higher of their regular tax liability or their minimum tax liability. § 55(a). The minimum tax rate is 26 percent on the first $175,000 of the base and 28 percent on the excess. The base is the taxpayer's alternative minimum taxable income ("AMTI") reduced by the allowable exemption amount. The exemption amount for married taxpayers filing jointly is $45,000, $22,500 for married taxpayers filing separately, and $33,750 for single taxpayers. (Under legislation enacted in 2001, these amounts are $49,000, $24,750, and $35,750, respectively, for the years 2001, 2002, and 2004.) The exemption amount is reduced 25 cents for each dollar by which AMTI exceeds $150,000 ($112,500 for single taxpayers and $75,000 for married taxpayers filing separate returns). § 55(d). As a result, the exemption is completely phased out for married taxpayers filing joint returns who have AMTI of at least $330,000. The exemption, phase-out amounts, and the bracket threshold are not indexed for inflation. The lower tax rates applicable to capital gains under § 1(h) also apply to capital gains under the AMT.

To compute AMTI, the taxpayer begins with taxable income and adds back specified tax preferences and makes certain adjustments. § 56(a). In essence, for certain items the taxpayer recomputes the amount taken into account for taxable income. Most of these adjustments involve using slower rates for depreciation allowances than are used for regular tax purposes, in effect, reducing the deferral of income otherwise available under the regular tax computations. In addition, the taxpayer makes adjustments to taxable income, adding back certain itemized deductions that are allowed under the regular tax but not the AMT. Then the taxpayer adds various tax preference items to the tax base. Each of these adjustments are discussed later in this Note. The result is the AMTI.

The alternative minimum tax rate is applied to the excess of the AMTI over the exemption amount (the "taxable excess"). The tax is reduced by the alternative minimum tax foreign tax credit, but it can be used to offset only up to 90 percent of the minimum tax liability. Thus companies with highly taxed foreign source income will still pay at least a minimum tax. To reinforce the inescapability of the minimum tax, net operating loss carryovers are allowed to offset no more than 90 percent of AMTI. This amount—the "tentative minimum tax"—is reduced by the regular tax.

Taxpayers may offset their entire tax liability, including the AMT, by their personal nonrefundable credits. Thus, an individual can use the child credit, the education credits, the dependent care credits, the credit for the elderly and disabled, the adoption credit, and the retirement account credit to offset AMT liability. Conversely, the earned income tax credit and the refundable portion of the child credit must be reduced by both the regular and AMT tax liability.

Some of the adjustments and items of tax preference relate to deferrals of income rather than exclusions. Congress intended to permit taxpayers to offset the minimum tax paid on such deferral items against the regular tax paid when the deferral expired. To the extent of these deferral items, the AMT paid may be carried forward as a credit against any subsequent year's regular tax in excess of the minimum tax. § 53. This "minimum tax credit" can be carried forward indefinitely.

The tax preferences and adjustments for the individual AMTI are as follows:

Depreciation. In determining AMTI, depreciation on assets (other than real estate) placed in service after 1986 must be calculated using a less accelerated method. § 56(a)(1). The AMTI deduction for depreciation for personal property that is depreciated on an accelerated method under MACRS is calculated using a 150 percent declining balance method (switching to straight line in the year it produces a higher deduction). Several types of properties are excluded from these rules. § 56(a)(1)(B). Furthermore, no adjustment is required for the deduction for tangible depreciable property permitted under § 179. For assets using an accelerated method of depreciation for regular tax purposes, the AMTI depreciation deduction usually will be lower in the early years of the recovery period and higher in the later years.

In calculating gain or loss on the disposition of an asset for which an AMTI adjustment was made in calculating depreciation, the basis of the asset is adjusted by the AMTI depreciation rather than the regular tax depreciation. § 56(a)(6). Thus, the gain or loss for AMTI purposes will be different than the gain or loss for regular tax purposes. Similar adjustments to AMTI are made for sales of other assets where the AMT allows smaller deductions than the regular tax.

For property placed in service before 1987, a portion of the depreciation deduction is included as a tax preference and added to AMTI. § 57(a)(6).

Percentage Depletion. The extent to which the taxpayer's deduction for percentage depletion exceeds the adjusted basis in the property is a tax preference item. § 57(a)(1). The depletion deduction for certain amounts of domestic crude oil and domestic natural gas (permitted by § 613A(c)) is not a tax preference item.

Intangible Drilling Costs. Generally, taxpayers are permitted to deduct the costs of drilling for oil, gas, and geothermal property rather than capitalizing and amortizing the cost. For integrated oil companies, the excess of the additional deduction over 65 percent of their net income from that activity is an item of tax preference. § 57(a)(2). Independent producers are not subject to this rule; however, their AMTI cannot be reduced by more than 40 percent of the AMTI that otherwise would be due if the taxpayer were subject to this preference. § 57(a)(2)(E).

Circulation Expenditures. The costs of establishing, maintaining or increasing a newspaper's, magazine's, or other periodical's circulation, which are deductible under § 173, must be capitalized and amortized over a three-year period for AMTI purposes. § 56(b)(2).

Research and Experimental Expenditures. Costs that may be expensed under § 174 must be amortized on a straight line basis over a ten-year period in calculating AMTI. § 56(b)(2). This rule does not apply to research and development expenses incurred with respect to an activity in which the taxpayer materially participates. § 56(b)(2)(D).

Mining Exploration and Development Costs. For regular tax purposes, a taxpayer may expense mining exploration and development costs or amortize them under § 291. In computing AMTI, the costs must be capitalized and amortized on a straight line basis over ten years. § 56(a)(2).

Pollution Control Facilities. Taxpayers using the five-year amortization method for depreciating pollution control facilities under § 169 must recompute the deduction using the alternative depreciation system of § 168(g) for AMTI purposes. § 56(a)(5).

Tax-Exempt Interest. Interest on certain tax-exempt private activity bonds issued after 1986 is an item of tax preference. § 57(a)(5)(C)(i). The amount of the preference is reduced by deductions that were not permitted, but would have been allowed if the tax-exempt interest had been included in taxable income. § 57(a)(5)(A). Other tax-exempt interest is not a tax preference under the minimum tax.

Qualified Small Business Stock. Forty-two percent of the gain excluded from the sale or disposition of qualified small business stock is a tax preference. § 57(a)(7). Recall that 50 percent of the gain on the sale of the stock of certain small businesses that is held for more than five years is excluded from income. § 1202 (see page 586 supra).

Incentive Stock Options. The tax treatment of incentive stock options provided in § 421 cannot be used for AMTI purposes. The AMTI must be increased by the amount by which the option's fair market value at the time the taxpayer's rights to the stock are freely transferable or are not subject to a substantial risk of forfeiture exceeds the price paid by the taxpayer. § 56(b)(3).

Tax Shelter Farm Losses. No loss may be deducted for a tax shelter farming activity where the taxpayer is not a material participant. § 58(a). This would include farm syndicates, § 464(c), or passive farm activities, § 469(c). Tax shelter farm gains and losses cannot be netted. Thus, a loss on one activity is a tax preference even though there is a gain on another activity. Losses that have been disallowed for AMTI purposes in a prior year may be taken as a deduction from farm income from the same activity in the succeeding year. In the year of disposition, taxpayers may claim their losses in calculating AMTI. § 58(c)(2).

Passive Activity Losses. The rules limiting deductions for passive losses, § 469, apply for minimum tax purposes. In calculating the passive loss, however, any AMTI adjustments and tax preferences under §§ 56 and 57 are taken into account. § 58(b).

Long-Term Contracts. A taxpayer who is permitted to use the completed contract method of accounting for long-term contracts must substitute the percentage of completion method in calculating AMTI. § 56(a)(3).

Net Operating Loss Deduction. In calculating the net operating loss deduction, the taxpayer must take into account tax preference items and AMTI adjustments under §§ 56 and 57. This is referred to as the "alternative tax net operating loss" and may be used to offset future income subject to the alternative minimum tax. The deduction for any taxable year is limited to 90 percent of the taxpayer's AMTI (not taking the NOL into account). § 56(a)(4), (d).

Itemized Deductions. Some itemized deductions that may be taken for regular tax purposes may not be used in calculating AMTI.

Medical expenses can be deducted but only to the extent they exceed 10 percent of the taxpayer's adjusted gross income (as opposed to 7.5 percent for regular tax purposes). § 56(b)(1)(B).

No deduction is permitted for state, local, and foreign taxes on income or on real or personal property; refunds are not included in AMTI. § 56(b)(1)(A), (D). To the extent these taxes are deductible in computing AGI (for example, by a self-employed taxpayer in a trade or business), they are deductible for AMTI purposes.

Miscellaneous itemized deductions that are subject to the two percent floor are not deductible at all under the AMT. § 56(b)(1)(A)(i).

Investment interest expense is limited to net investment income. § 56(b)(1)(C). A taxpayer may deduct "qualified housing interest," which is qualified residence interest, as defined by § 163(h)(3), that is paid or accrued on a debt incurred to acquire, construct, or substantially improve a principal residence and one other personally used dwelling. Interest on a refinancing is also deductible if the loan does not exceed the balance remaining on the original mortgage. § 56(e).

The § 68 limitation on itemized deductions of high income taxpayers does not apply for AMTI purposes. § 56(b)(1)(F).

Personal Exemptions and Standard Deduction. The standard deduction and the deduction for personal exemptions are not allowed in calculating AMTI. § 56(b)(1)(E).

NOTES

(A) *The Spread of the AMT.* Many of the taxpayers who are new to the AMT are those with no preferences who are subject to the tax because AMTI is calculated without regard to exemptions or state and local taxes. Taxpayer who live in states with high income taxes (such as New York) are often subject to the AMT solely because they have deducted state taxes.

A typical example is the Klaasens who filed a return with $83,000 of AGI on which they claimed their 10 children as dependents, took a deduction for state and local taxes, and calculated a medical deduction based on the 7.5% limitation. They paid $5,100 of tax on taxable income of $34,000. Not exactly high-flyers. The IRS helpfully pointed out they were subject to the AMT. Once all the exemptions were eliminated, the state and local tax deduction was erased, and the medical deduction was calculated using a 10% floor, the Klaasens were hit with an additional tax bill of $1,000. The Tenth Circuit rejected their argument that the AMT violates the free exercise of religion (the commandment in Genesis to be fruitful and multiply). The court noted that if Congress wanted to avoid this result, it easily could have drafted the statute to do so. Klaassen v. Commissioner, 182 F.3d 932 (10th Cir.1999).

To date, Congress has shown relatively little interest in this inexorable march of the AMT down through the tax brackets. The increase in the AMT exemption level under the 2001 Act is only a temporary palliative. The number of people subject to the AMT will grow dramatically once that provision expires. Further action by Congress is necessary, but only a crisis seems likely to provide sufficient motivation.

For example, due to a complicated limitation on nonrefundable personal credits, like the child credit and the Hope Credit, families in the 15 percent bracket are required to determine their AMT liability in order to calculate the amount of the credit. Perhaps it was the fact that the IRS estimated that it takes six hours to fill out the AMT form that motivated Congress to pass a two-year fix for that problem set to expire after 2001. No word yet on whether all low-bracket taxpayers will permanently join the ranks of AMT filers.

On the other hand, if Congress fails to take action and enough taxpayers become subject to the minimum tax, perhaps the regular tax will be repealed. When that happens, we will give the materials in this Chapter greater prominence.

(B) *Incentive Stock Options.* The tax treatment of incentive stock options is a good example of an unintended consequence of the AMT. Employees do not recognize taxable income on the exercise of an ISO; regular tax is not due until the stock is sold. See discussion at page 777 supra. To take advantage of this rule, most employees must hold the stock for two years after the grant of the option and one year after its exercise. When the option is exercised, however, the spread between the exercise price and the value of the stock at the time of exercise is subject to the AMT. During the dot.com craze early in the new millennium, many employees received and exercised ISOs in companies whose stock had appreciated wildly in value. The employees were required to hold on to the stock and during that period, the value of the stock plummeted such that the ultimate sale of the stock produced little cash. Nevertheless, the employees had huge AMT liabilities triggered by the appreciation that accrued by the exercise date. Congress was besieged by dot.com employees who could not pay off the AMT liability even if they sold all their stock in their employer. Of course, if they had sold the stock immediately after exercise, they would have owed regular tax liability, but would have had the cash to pay the tax. Nevertheless, Congress seems likely to remedy this situation.

(C) *Economic Income.* Is a taxpayer's economic income measured by the combination of the regular and AMT tax bases? Some items, such as the interest on most municipal bonds, is excluded from both bases. At one time, gains deferred under the installment method for regular tax purposes were added back to the AMT base. Are there other examples of deferred income that are not subject to the AMT?

(D) *Evaluating the Minimum Tax.*[1] As discussed in Chapter One, the criteria for a good tax are routinely grouped under three headings—equity, efficiency and simplicity.

Simplicity. The AMT is surely not simple. Nor can a minimum tax be simple when deferral preferences are included in the tax base and the tax takes the form of an alternative tax. Minimum taxes complicate tax planning, particularly for taxpayers who do not readily know whether they are going to be subject to the regular tax or to the AMT and for taxpayers subject to the regular tax in some years and to the minimum tax in others. Only if a minimum tax reduces taxpayers' tendencies to use tax preferences and engage in tax planning does it simplify. But no one advocates minimum taxes on simplification grounds. Minimum taxes are supposed to improve equity.

Equity. Many analysts believe that the exclusions, deductions, credits, and other allowances permitted under the regular tax violate both horizontal and vertical equity. Horizontal equity is violated because tax preferences allow taxpayers with equal economic incomes to pay different amounts of tax. Vertical equity is violated because the relative tax burdens intended to apply to taxpayers with different levels of economic income under the regular income tax rate structure are not, in fact, imposed. If high-economic-income taxpayers can use tax preferences to reduce their effective tax rate disproportionately relative to low-or middle-income taxpayers and pay low or zero income tax, a minimum tax may be necessary to restore tax equity. Moreover, taxpayer perceptions of tax unfairness may be of independent concern because people who believe the income tax is unfair may be less willing to comply with it.

Economic Efficiency. Minimum taxes may rank low on simplification grounds, and higher on equity grounds, but what about economic efficiency? Any minimum tax blunts the incentive effects of tax preferences. If a business engages only a small amount in activities or investments encouraged by tax subsidies, no minimum tax will be imposed; if the business specializes in tax-preferred activities, it will owe minimum tax, perhaps putting it at a competitive disadvantage. On efficiency grounds, no one should care if ten companies each invest a little in a tax-preferred activity or one company invests a lot.

Nevertheless, a minimum tax may improve efficiency in certain situations. Consider tax-exempt bonds. The traditional analysis assumes that

---

1. This evaluation is based on Michael Graetz & Emil Sunley, "Minimum Taxes and Comprehensive Tax" in Uneasy Compromise: Problems of a Hybrid Income–Consumption Tax 396–400 (1988).

the yield differential between taxable and tax-exempt bonds is established by the marginal tax rate of the marginal investor. High-tax-bracket investors in tax-exempt bonds, therefore, are able to enjoy inframarginal windfalls that the Treasury might capture by including tax-exempt interest in the minimum tax base. See page 212 supra.

Assessing the effect of a minimum tax on economic efficiency is complex. If a minimum tax narrows differences in effective tax rates across industries, allocative efficiency should be improved. On the other hand, minimum taxes may introduce new economic inefficiencies among companies in the same industry. Finally, the minimum tax has an uncertain effect in inducing inefficient mergers and acquisitions.

CHAPTER 8

CORPORATE TAX SHELTERS AND ETHICAL RESPONSIBILITIES OF TAX LAWYERS

SECTION 1. CORPORATE TAX SHELTERS

EXCERPT FROM THE PROBLEM OF CORPORATE TAX SHELTERS: DISCUSSION, ANALYSIS AND LEGISLATIVE PROPOSALS

United States Treasury Department, 1999

There is widespread agreement and concern among tax professionals that the corporate tax shelter problem is large and growing.

The American Bar Association, in an appearance before the House Ways and Means Committee, noted its "growing alarm [at] the aggressive use by large corporate taxpayers of tax 'products' that have little or no purpose other than the reduction of Federal income taxes," and its concern at the "blatant, yet secretive marketing" of such products.

The New York State Bar Association, in testimony before the Senate Finance Committee, stated: "We believe that there are serious, and growing, problems with aggressive, sophisticated and, we believe in some cases, artificial transactions designed principally to achieve a particular tax advantage. * * * There is obviously an effect on revenue. While we are unable to estimate the amount of this revenue loss, anecdotal evidence and personal experience leads us to believe that it is likely to be quite significant."

In the 1999 Erwin N. Griswold Lecture before the American College of Tax Counsel, former ABA Tax Section president James Holden stated: "Many of us have been concerned with the recent proliferation of tax shelter products marketed to corporations. * * * [T]he marketing of these products tears at the fabric of the tax law. Many individual tax lawyers with whom I have spoken express a deep sense of personal regret that this level of Code gamesmanship goes on."

The Tax Executives Institute recently testified before the Senate Finance Committee, that: "TEI is not among those who believe no problem exists. But the problem confronting the tax system is not simple, and care must be taken to ensure that the solutions are measured and balanced and, further, that they do not add even more complexity to the already overburdened tax law."

A recent cover story in Forbes magazine was devoted to the "thriving industry of hustling corporate tax shelters." This article quoted a partner in a major accounting firm who described the development and highly selective marketing of "black box" strategies for tax avoidance that can save its purchasers from tens of millions to hundreds of millions of dollars at the expense of other U.S. taxpayers.

While corporate tax payments have been rising, taxes have not grown as fast as have corporate profits. One hallmark of corporate tax shelters is a reduction in taxable income with no concomitant reduction in book income. The ratio of book income to taxable income has risen fairly sharply in the last few years. Some of this decline may be due to tax shelter activity. * * *

There are several reasons to be concerned about the proliferation of corporate tax shelters. These concerns range from the short-term revenue loss to the tax system, to the potentially more troubling long-term effects on our voluntary income tax system.

Short-term revenue loss

Corporate tax shelters reduce the corporate tax base, raising the tax burden on other taxpayers.

Disrespect for the system

Corporate tax shelters breed disrespect for the tax system—both by the people who participate in the tax shelter market and by others who perceive unfairness. A view that well-advised corporations can and do avoid their legal tax liabilities by engaging in these tax-engineered transactions may cause a "race to the bottom." If unabated, this could have long-term consequences to our voluntary tax system far more important than the short-term revenue loss we are experiencing.

The New York State Bar Association recently noted the "corrosive effect" of tax shelters: "The constant promotion of these frequently artificial transactions breeds significant disrespect for the tax system, encouraging responsible corporate taxpayers to expect this type of activity to be the norm, and to follow the lead of other taxpayers who have engaged in tax advantaged transactions."

Complexity

Piecemeal legislative remedies complicate the Code and call into question the viability of common law tax doctrines. In the past few years alone, nearly 30 narrow statutory provisions have been adopted responding to perceived abuses.

Uneconomic use of resources

Significant resources, both in the private sector and the Government, are currently being wasted on this uneconomic activity. Private sector resources used to create, implement and defend complex sheltering transactions could be better used in productive activities. Similarly, the Congress (particularly the tax-writing committees and their staffs), the Treasury Department, and the IRS must expend significant resources to address and combat these transactions.

The ACM Partnership v. Commissioner case alone cost the Federal Government over $2 million to litigate. In addition, there are a number of docketed cases involving almost identical shelter products.

Peter Cobb, former Deputy Chief of Staff of the Joint Committee on Taxation recently stated: "You can't underestimate how many of America's greatest minds are being devoted to what economists would all say is totally useless economic activity."

* * *

Because corporate tax shelters take many different forms and utilize many different structures, they are difficult to define with a single formulation. A number of common characteristics, however, can be identified that are useful in crafting an approach to solving the corporate tax shelter problem.

Lack of economic substance—Professor Michael Graetz recently defined a tax shelter as "a deal done by very smart people that, absent tax considerations, would be very stupid." This definition highlights one of the most important characteristics common to most corporate tax shelters—the lack of any significant economic substance or risk to the participating parties. Through hedges, circular cash flows, defeasements and the like, the participant in a shelter is insulated from any significant economic risk.

Inconsistent financial accounting and tax treatments—There is a current trend among public companies to treat corporate in-house tax departments as profit centers that strive to keep the corporation's effective tax rate (i.e., the ratio of corporate tax liability to book income) low and in line with that of competitors. Accordingly, in most recent corporate tax shelters involving public companies, the financial accounting treatment of the shelter item has been inconsistent with the claimed Federal income tax treatment.

Tax-indifferent parties—Many recent shelters have relied on the use of "tax-indifferent" parties—such as foreign or tax-exempt entities—who participate in the transaction in exchange for a fee to absorb taxable income or otherwise deflect tax liability from the taxable party.

Marketing activity—Promoters often design tax shelters so that they can be replicated multiple times for use by different participants, rather than to address the tax planning issues of a single taxpayer. This allows the shelter "product" to be marketed and sold to many different corporate participants, thereby maximizing the promoter's return from its shelter idea.

Confidentiality—Similar to marketing, maintaining confidentiality of a tax shelter transaction helps to maximize the promoter's return from its shelter idea—it prevents expropriation by others and it protects the efficacy of the idea by preventing or delaying discovery of the idea by the Treasury Department and the IRS. In the past, promoters have required prospective participants to sign a non-disclosure agreement that provides for million dollar payments for any disclosure of the "proprietary" advice. * * *

Contingent or refundable fees and rescission or insurance arrangement—Corporate tax shelters often involve contingent or refundable fees in order to reduce the cost and risk of the shelter to the participants. In a contingent fee arrangement, the promoter's fee depends on the level of tax savings realized by the corporate participant. Some corporate tax shelters also involve insurance or rescission arrangements. Like contingent or refundable fees, insurance or rescission arrangements reduce the cost and risk of the shelter to the participants.

High transaction costs—Corporate tax shelters carry unusually high transaction costs. For example, the transaction costs in the ASA case ($24,783,800) were approximately 26.5 percent of the purported tax savings (approximately $93,500,000).

NOTES

(A) *The Threat.* Tax-motivated transactions have a long history. Recall *Knetsch,* supra at page 363, in which the taxpayer attempted to deduct interest on a non-economic transaction, or *P.G. Lake,* supra at page 588, in which a taxpayer accelerated income to offset losses. Uneasiness over individual tax shelters abated after the Tax Reform Act of 1986, which added the passive loss rules. In recent years, however, there has been renewed concern about the current crop of tax shelters, generally marketed to corporations, that are not subject to § 469. There is some disagreement about whether corporate tax shelters present a serious threat. Treasury (as well as many academics and practitioners) has argued that the tax system faces a crisis, contending that these shelters, many of which would fail if detected, threaten to undermine the corporate tax. Supporters of this view tend to favor giving the IRS broad additional discretionary power to attack shelters. Critics—many of whom are the promoters selling the shelters— argue that there is not a serious problem and that it is a bad idea to give the IRS additional broad powers. Both sides agree that this is a problem that cannot be solved in an easy or straightforward manner.

(B) *You Know It When You See It.* The corporate tax shelter controversy is mired in definitional issues, not the least of which is defining "tax shelter." A definition is essential if statutory penalties or loss or tax credit disallowance rules are to apply only to tax shelters. A tax shelter is somewhat like pornography—you know it when you see it—but that will not work as a statutory definition. Many observers describe a tax shelter as a transaction that would not happen were it not for the tax advantages, as opposed to business deals that do not depend on the tax consequences. Both Treasury and the Staff of the Joint Committee on Taxation have offered definitions that try to draw that line.

JCT Staff Definition:

Corporate tax shelter—A partnership, entity, plan, or arrangement (collectively referred to as an "arrangement") involving a corporate participant will be considered to have a significant purpose of Federal income tax avoidance or evasion under section 6662 if it satisfies *one* of five corporate tax shelter indicators. The mere purchase or sale of an asset will not constitute an arrangement for these purposes.

Corporate tax shelter indicators—

(1) The present value of the reasonably expected pre-tax profit from the arrangement is insignificant relative to the present value of the reasonably expected net tax benefits.

(2) The arrangement involves a tax-indifferent participant, and (a) results in taxable income materially in excess of economic income to the tax-indifferent participant, (b) permits a corporate participant to characterize items of income, gain, loss, deductions, or credits in a more favorable manner than it otherwise could without the involvement of the tax-indifferent participant, or (c) results in a noneconomic increase, creation, multiplication, or shifting of basis for the benefit of the corporate participant, and results in the recognition of income or gain that is not subject to Federal income tax because the tax consequences are borne by the tax-indifferent participant.

(3) The arrangement involves significant reasonably expected net tax benefits and a tax indemnity or similar agreement.

(4) The arrangement involves significant reasonably expected net tax benefits and a reasonably expected "permanent difference" for U.S. financial reporting purposes under generally accepted accounting principles.

(5) The arrangement involves significant reasonably expected net tax benefits and the corporate participant incurs little (if any) additional economic risk.

The Senate Finance Committee proposed legislation that followed this indicator approach, but abandoned it in favor of a 40 percent penalty that would apply to any "abusive tax shelter device," defined as any device lacking either a material non-tax business purpose or economic substance.

Treasury Definition:

Corporate tax shelter—Any entity, plan, or arrangement in which a direct or indirect corporate participant attempts to obtain a "tax benefit" in a "tax avoidance transaction."

Tax benefit—Includes any reduction, exclusion, avoidance, or deferral of tax, or an increase in a refund, but would not include a tax benefit clearly contemplated by the applicable provision.

Tax avoidance transaction—(1) Any transaction in which the present value of the reasonably expected pre-tax profit of the transaction is insignificant relative to the present value of the reasonably expected net tax benefits, and (2) In the case of financing transactions, any transaction in which the present value of the tax benefits of the taxpayer to whom the financing is provided is significantly in excess of the present value of the pre-tax profit or return of the person providing the financing.

How would the transaction entered into by the bank in *Cottage Savings*, supra at page 156, fare under the Treasury definition? Is the "transaction" in that case the swap of the mortgages, where there is no expectation of pre-tax profit and thus tax benefits clearly dominate, or is the "transaction" the original loan?

(C) *Literalism.* One of the problems in crafting a definition of tax shelter (or for that matter "tax avoidance") is that many of these transactions are based on a literal reading of the Code or a regulation to obtain tax benefits that were not intended by Congress. A serious question is whether taxpayers should be able to rely on the literal language of the statutes and regulations. This view is expressed by Senator John Breaux who noted that many taxpayers and their advisors do not have access to sophisticated professional advice and ought to be able to assume that a regulation means what it says.

But those who believe that literal compliance with the statute and regulations is not sufficient cannot agree on how to implement this principle. Some favor leaving it up to the courts to use common law doctrines that would deny tax benefits—relying in particular on the requirements that a transaction have economic substance and a business purpose to be respected for tax purposes.

(D) *Why Now?* The dramatic increase in corporate tax shelters is probably due to a variety of factors, not all tax related. For example, many express the view that corporate tax departments have become potential profit centers due to a change in the culture of corporate management that encourages corporations to look favorably on shelters. Others cite the enlarged role played in tax planning by investment banks and accounting firms and the huge fees to be earned by peddling shelters. The development of more complete capital markets that enable corporations to use derivatives to hedge away almost all economic risk has surely made these transactions more attractive to risk-adverse firms.

But the tax system itself clearly is at fault as well. As the Code has become more and more complex, it has become less coherent, less understandable, and more open to manipulation. Even when Congress responds to abuses, it often does so in broad brush ways that open the door to additional abuses. Recall the IRS position in *Corn Products*, supra at page 574 and in *Cottage Savings*, supra at page 156. These are examples where the government won the battle but lost the war. In its decision to eliminate tax advantages for one taxpayer, the government often creates advantages for others. And there are structural aspects of the Code that invite creative tax planning. The realization rule, for example, often makes the timing of gains and losses elective. A major change made by the Tax Reform Act of 1986 may also have spurred corporations to look for shelters. That Act caused corporations to recognize gain on corporate distributions and dispositions of appreciated assets and many companies began to search for losses (preferably non-economic, artificial losses) to be used to offset these gains.

In the final analysis, however, the decline in audit rates and the inability of the IRS to detect shelters during audits of large companies is keeping the industry afloat. As noted in Chapter 1, the audit rate has declined precipitously, encouraging otherwise risk-adverse taxpayers to play the audit lottery. And even large corporations, who are constantly under audit, play their own sophisticated form of the audit lottery. IRS agents frequently do not have the training or resources to ferret out shelters that are not disclosed on the corporation's return.

The following case illustrates how the economic doctrines have been used to attack an abusive corporate tax shelter.

ACM Partnership v. Commissioner

157 F.3d 231 (3d Cir.1998).

This appeal concerns the tax consequences of a series of transactions executed between November 1989 and December 1991 by appellant ACM, a partnership formed on October 27, 1989, with its principal place of business in Curacao, Netherlands Antilles. Each of ACM's three partners was created as a subsidiary of a larger entity several days before ACM's formation. Southampton was incorporated under Delaware law on October 24, 1989, as a wholly-owned subsidiary of Colgate–Palmolive Company ("Colgate"), an international consumer products company. Kannex Corporation N.V. ("Kannex") was incorporated under Netherlands Antilles law on October 25, 1989, as an entity controlled by Algemene Bank Nederland N.V. ("ABN"), a major Dutch bank. ACM's third partner, Merrill Lynch MLCS, Inc. ("MLCS"), was incorporated under Delaware law on October 27, 1989, as a wholly owned subsidiary of Merrill Lynch Capital Services, an affiliate of the financial services holding company Merrill Lynch & Co., Inc. ("Merrill Lynch"). * * *

The concept behind the ACM partnership originated in a proposal which Merrill Lynch presented to Colgate in May 1989. During the previous year, Colgate had reported $104,743,250 in long-term capital gains which were attributable in significant part to the sale of its wholly owned subsidiary The Kendall Company ("Kendall"). Colgate had considered and rejected several proposals to reduce the tax liability arising from those 1988 capital gains, when Merrill Lynch * * * approached Colgate * * * in May 1989 and proposed an investment partnership that would generate capital losses which Colgate could use to offset some of its 1988 capital gains.[1]

Colgate's Vice President of Taxation * * * expressed reservations because the plan entailed substantial costs, might not be recognized for tax purposes, and did not seem to serve Colgate's non-tax business purposes, and thus might not be well-received by Colgate's legal, financial, and accounting departments who would be required to participate in the plan. Colgate consulted a law firm for advice on the proposed transaction, which the law firm summarized as follows:

A (a foreign entity), B, and C form the ABC Partnership (ABC) on June 30, 1989 with respective cash contributions of $75, $24 and $1. Immediately thereafter, ABC invests $100 in short-term securities which it sells on December 30, 1989, to an unrelated party. The fair market value and face amount of the short-term securities at the time of the sale is still $100. In consideration for the sale, ABC receives $70 cash and an installment note that provides for six semiannual payments. * * * Each payment equals the sum of a notional principal amount multiplied by the London

---

1. The proposal was premised on I.R.C. § 1212(a), which permits a [corporate] taxpayer to carry back a capital loss to offset capital gains recognized within the preceding three years.

Interbank Offering Rate (LIBOR) at the start of the semiannual period.[2] ABC uses the $70 cash and the first payment on the installment note to liquidate A's interest in ABC and uses the subsequent interest payments to purchase long-term securities.

The law firm advised that the sale of the short-term securities would be reported as a contingent installment sale under the installment method which governs "disposition[s] of property where at least 1 payment is to be received after the close of the taxable year in which the disposition occurs," I.R.C. § 453, and the ratable basis recovery rule which provides that, [w]hen a stated maximum selling price cannot be determined as of the close of the taxable year in which the sale or other disposition occurs, but the maximum period over which payments may be received under the contingent sale price agreement is fixed, the taxpayer's basis (inclusive of selling expenses) shall be allocated to the taxable years in which payment may be received under the agreement in equal annual increments. Temp. Treas. Reg. § 15a.453–1(c)(3)(i). Thus, the law firm advised, ABC would recover $25 of its basis in each of the 4 taxable years from 1989 through 1992, and ABC would recognize gain to the extent that the payments received in any year exceeded the $25 or loss to the extent that the payments fell below the $25, but only if the loss were carried over to a year with sufficient reported gains against which to offset that loss.

* * * Colgate was interested in the concept of using the proposed partnership to invest in its own debt because of recent developments which had weighted Colgate's debt portfolio toward fixed-rate long-term debt, leaving Colgate vulnerable to a decline in interest rates. Moreover, persistent rumors that Colgate was a likely target for a hostile takeover or leveraged buyout had decreased the value of Colgate's debt issues due to the risk that Colgate's credit rating would be downgraded if Colgate became more highly leveraged. Because of these factors, Colgate perceived an opportunity to rebalance its debt profile, thus decreasing its exposure to falling interest rates, by acquiring its long-term debt issues at their presently discounted prices.

Colgate and Merrill Lynch discussed the possibility of using the proposed partnership to achieve these objectives. The acquisition of its own debt issues would decrease Colgate's exposure to falling interest rates because by acquiring those debt issues as an asset, Colgate effectively would reap the benefits of receiving the above-market interest payments due on those issues, thus hedging against the burdens associated with owing those payments. Acquiring the debt through the partnership instead of directly would keep the acquisitions off Colgate's books, thus permitting Colgate to carry out its debt acquisition strategy without alerting potential acquirors to the internal accumulation of debt issues which, by increasing the capacity for internal leverage, would increase Colgate's vulnerability to a hostile takeover bid. Thus, the acquisition of Colgate debt through the partnership would allow Colgate to use partnership capital to acquire its debt issues immediately at advantageous prices, then to retire and reissue the debt when market conditions were more favorable. In the interim, the

2. The LIBOR [London Interbank Offering Rate] is the primary fixed income index reference rate used in [European financial] markets.

debt effectively would be retired because Colgate would not owe the obligations thereon to third parties, yet the debt would remain outstanding for accounting purposes, reducing Colgate's vulnerability to potential acquirors.

On July 28, 1989, Merrill Lynch presented a proposed partnership transaction summary which incorporated Colgate's debt acquisition objectives into the tax reduction proposal involving the contingent installment sale which Merrill Lynch had presented to Colgate in May 1989. Merrill Lynch revised its proposals throughout the summer and approached ABN about participating in the partnership with Colgate and Merrill Lynch. Merrill Lynch explained to ABN that the partnership would invest in Colgate long-term debt to serve Colgate's debt management objectives, would engage in a contingent installment sale, and would require ABN's participation for no more than 2–3 years.

* * *

A representative of ABN's legal department testified that the partnership, as he understood it, was to:

> enter into transactions that would create a capital gain and in a later stage a capital loss, and that * * * depending on the percentage of your participation, you would either take part in the gain or the loss. So by having us being the majority partner at the start, we would take the majority of the gain, while in a later stage one of the other partners would take the loss.

* * *

A September 20, 1989 document delineated the details of the proposed partnership transactions and their anticipated tax consequences under I.R.C. § 453 and the ratable basis recovery rule, Temp. Treas. Reg. § 15a.453. The document contemplated using the partnership's $200 million in cash investments to acquire short-term notes, disposing of the short-term notes in exchange for $140 million in cash and LIBOR instruments which would generate contingent payments with a present value of $60 million, and using the $140 million in cash to purchase Colgate debt. Because the partnership was to receive payments on the exchange over the course of six years, the $200 million basis in the short-term notes was to be recovered ratably over six tax years in equal increments of $33.3 million per year pursuant to § 15a.453. Thus, according to this document, the transaction would result in significant capital gains in the first year, consisting of the $106.7 million difference between the $140 million cash received that year and the $33.3 million basis recovered that year, and would result in capital losses in each of the ensuing years because the contingent payments received in each of those years * * * would fall short of the $33.3 million basis to be recovered in each of those years. The aggregate projected capital losses in the ensuing years equaled precisely the amount of capital gains reported in the first year, and the document stated that the recognition of those losses "may be accelerated in any year subsequent to 1989 by sale of the remaining LIBOR notes."

The document also contemplates Colgate's increasing its share in the partnership from 15% to 97% after the partnership recognized the $106.7 million capital gain in the year 1 but before it recognized the capital losses in the ensuing years. According to the document, the LIBOR notes eventually would be sold for a capital loss of $80 million, 97% of which would be allocated to Colgate based on its 97% partnership interest by the time the loss was incurred.

Between October 24 and October 27, 1989, ABN established Kannex, Colgate established Southampton, and Merrill Lynch established MLCS to participate in the ACM partnership. The October 27, 1989 partnership agreement among these newly created entities provided that Kannex was to receive a preferred return of the first $1.24 million in any partnership profits otherwise allocable to Southampton.

[The partnership was subsequently formed and the amounts contributed by the partners were used to purchase Citicorp notes. These notes were subsequently sold for cash and installment notes whose interest rate was based on LIBOR.[3] In exchange for the $175 million Citicorp notes, ACM received total consideration of $174.4 million, consisting of $140 million in cash and the LIBOR notes, which had a present value of $34.4 million. The payments on the notes were used to purchase Colgate debt. In 1991, through a series of transactions involving Colgate, Southampton, and the ACM partnership, Kannex's interest in the partnership was purchased and redeemed, leaving Colgate–Southampton with a combined 99.7 ownership interest in the partnership.]

On its partnership return for the tax year ended November 30, 1989, ACM treated the [sale] of the Citicorp notes as an installment sale under I.R.C. § 453, as ACM was to receive part of the consideration for that exchange "after the close of the taxable year in which the disposition occurs" pursuant to § 453(b)(1). Because the quarterly LIBOR note payments would vary based on fluctuations in the LIBOR, there was no "stated maximum selling price" that could be identified "as of the close of the taxable year in which the * * * disposition occurs." Thus, the transaction came within the terms of Temp. Treas. Reg. § 15a.453–1(c), whose ratable basis recovery rule provides that the taxpayer's basis "shall be allocated to the taxable years in which payment may be received under the agreement in equal annual increments."

Accordingly, ACM divided its $175,504,564 basis in the Citicorp notes * * * equally among the six years over which payments were to be received in exchange for those notes, and thus recovered one sixth of that basis, or $29,250,761, during 1989. Subtracting this basis from the $140 million in cash consideration for the Citicorp notes, ACM reported a 1989 capital gain of $110,749,239.42 which it allocated among its partners according to their partnership shares, resulting in an allocation of $91,516,689 of the gain to Kannex, $18,908,407 to Southampton, and $324,144 to MLCS. Southamp-

---

3. Ed. Note: The LIBOR notes provided for a stream of 20 quarterly contingent payments beginning March 1, 1990, whose amount was derived from multiplying the LIBOR rate times a notional principal amount of $97.76 million. The national principal amount did not represent an amount owed but was simply a multiplier to determine the amount of the LIBOR-based contingent payments.

ton and MLCS were subject to United States income tax on their respective shares of the gain, but Kannex as a foreign corporation was not.[4]

Under the ratable basis recovery rule the tax basis remaining to be recovered over the following five years became $146,253,803, representing the difference between the $175,504,564 value of the Citicorp notes which ACM relinquished to acquire those notes and the $29,250,761 in basis recovered during the first year of the transaction. * * * [This left $146,253,803 remaining basis attributable to the LIBOR notes, whose actual cost totaled $35,504,564. ACM subsequently sold or distributed the LIBOR notes, which produced an $85 million capital loss in 1991. Some of the LIBOR notes were distributed to Southampton, Colgate's partnership entity, and Southampton sold them at roughly a $34 million capital loss in 1989, the same year in which it was allocated a gain, resulting in a net capital loss of about $13.5 million. During the time ACM held the LIBOR notes, they declined in value by nearly $6 million due to declining interest rates.]

[T]he Commissioner of Internal Revenue ("Commissioner") issued ACM a Notice * * * eliminating ACM's $110,749,239.42 installment gain from the sale of the Citicorp notes in November 1989, redetermining ACM's tax basis in the * * * LIBOR notes distributed in December 1989, and disallowing the $84,997,111 capital loss deduction which ACM reported in 1991. In writing this opinion we primarily focus on the capital loss aspects of the case, though it should be understood that the gain and loss are part of a single integrated plan. The Commissioner asserted * * * that the transactions involving the purchase and sale of the Citicorp notes in exchange for cash and LIBOR notes, "were shams in that they were prearranged and predetermined. * * * [S]aid transactions were devoid of economic substance necessary for recognition for federal income tax purposes and were totally lacking in economic reality. The transactions were created solely for tax motivated purposes without any realistic expectation of profit."

The Tax Court * * * issued a memorandum opinion upholding the Commissioner's adjustments on the grounds that "[a] taxpayer is not entitled to recognize a phantom loss from a transaction that lacks economic substance." In reaching the conclusion that ACM was not entitled to deduct its claimed capital losses, the court examined the stated purposes and anticipated economic consequences of the transaction, and found that the claimed losses were "not economically inherent in" the transactions but rather were "created artificially" by machinations whose only purpose and effect was to give rise to the desired tax consequences. * * *

ACM contends that, because its transactions on their face satisfied each requirement of the contingent installment sale provisions and regulations thereunder, it properly deducted the losses arising from its "straightforward application" of these provisions, which required it to recover only one sixth of the basis in the Citicorp notes during the first of the six years

---

4. According to the Tax Court the share allocated to Kannex was not taxed in any jurisdiction but we, of course, are focusing only on the United States tax aspects of the transaction.

over which it was to receive payments. * * * Thus, ACM contends, it properly subtracted the basis in the LIBOR notes to include the remaining five-sixths of the basis in the Citicorp notes used to acquire them. Consequently, ACM argues it properly subtracted the approximately $96 million remaining unrecovered basis in the LIBOR notes from the approximately $11 million consideration it received upon disposition of those notes, and correctly recognized and reported the gains and losses arising from its sale or exchange of property in accordance with I.R.C. § 1001.

While ACM's transactions, at least in form, satisfied each requirement of the contingent installment sale provisions and ratable basis recovery rule, ACM acknowledges that even where the "form of the taxpayer's activities indisputably satisfie[s] the literal requirements" of the relevant statutory language, the courts must examine "whether the substance of those transactions was consistent with their form," because a transaction that is "devoid of economic substance * * * simply is not recognized for federal taxation purposes."

We begin our economic substance analysis with Gregory v. Helvering, the Supreme Court's foundational exposition of economic substance principles under the Internal Revenue Code. In *Gregory*, as in this case, the transactions on their face satisfied "every element required by" the relevant statutory language. The taxpayer, instead of transferring stock from her wholly owned corporation directly to herself which would have generated taxable dividends, created a new corporation, transferred the stock to the new corporation, then liquidated the new corporation, transferred the stock to herself, and asserted that she had not recognized any taxable gain because she had received the stock "in pursuance of a plan of reorganization" within the meaning of I.R.C. § 112(g). Although the transactions satisfied each element of the statute, which defined "reorganization" as a transfer of assets between corporations under common control, the Court found that "[t]he whole undertaking, though conducted according to the [statutory] terms * * * was in fact an elaborate and devious form of conveyance masquerading as a corporate reorganization."

The Court stated that "if a reorganization in reality was effected" any "ulterior [tax avoidance] purpose * * * will be disregarded" and the transaction will be respected for tax purposes. The Court emphasized, however, that where the transactions merely "put on the form of a corporate reorganization as a disguise for concealing its real character" which was a "preconceived plan * * * not to reorganize a business," but rather "to transfer * * * shares to the [taxpayer]," the transaction was not, in reality, "the thing which the statute intended." Viewed according to their substance rather than their form, the Court found, the transactions fell "outside the plain intent of the statute" and therefore could not be treated in accordance with their form without "exalt[ing] artifice above reality." Thus, pursuant to *Gregory*, we must "look beyond the form of [the] transaction" to determine whether it has the "economic substance that [its] form represents," because regardless of its form, a transaction that is "devoid of economic substance" must be disregarded for tax purposes and "cannot be the basis for a deductible loss."[5]

In applying these principles, we must view the transactions "as a whole, and each step, from the commencement * * * to the consummation * * * is relevant." The inquiry into whether the taxpayer's transactions had sufficient economic substance to be respected for tax purposes turns on both the "objective economic substance of the transactions" and the "subjective business motivation" behind them. However, these distinct aspects of the economic sham inquiry do not constitute discrete prongs of a "rigid two-step analysis," but rather represent related factors both of which inform the analysis of whether the transaction had sufficient substance, apart from its tax consequences, to be respected for tax purposes. For the reasons that follow, we find that both the objective analysis of the actual economic consequences of ACM's transactions and the subjective analysis of their intended purposes support the Tax Court's conclusion that ACM's transactions did not have sufficient economic substance to be respected for tax purposes.[6]

1. Objective Aspects of the Economic Sham Analysis

In assessing the economic substance of a taxpayer's transactions, the courts have examined "whether the transaction has any practical economic effects other than the creation of income tax losses," and have refused to recognize the tax consequences of transactions that were devoid of "nontax substance" because they "did not appreciably affect [the taxpayer's] beneficial interest except to reduce his tax." Knetsch v. United States, 364 U.S. 361, 366 (1960). [The court then discusses *Knetsch*, set forth at page 363 supra, and similar cases.]

* * * In light of these cases, we must determine whether the Tax Court erred in concluding that ACM's exchange of the Citicorp notes for contingent-payment LIBOR notes which gave rise to the tax consequences at issue generated only "a phantom loss" that was not "economically inherent in the object of the sale" and did not have "economic substance separate and distinct from economic benefit achieved solely by tax reduction." For the following reasons, we conclude that it did not.

2. Objective Economic Consequences of ACM's Transactions

While the Tax Court's analysis focused on the lack of non-tax purposes behind ACM's transactions rather than on their objective economic conse-

---

5. The courts have distinguished between "shams in fact" where the reported transactions never occurred and "shams in substance" which "actually occurred but that lack the substance their form represents." Because it is undisputed that ACM's transactions actually occurred, we confine our inquiry to the question of whether their economic substance corresponds to their form.

6. While it is clear that a transaction such as ACM's that has neither objective non-tax economic effects nor subjective non-tax purposes constitutes an economic sham whose tax consequences must be disregarded, and equally clear that a transaction that has both objective non-tax economic significance and subjective non-tax purposes constitutes an economically substantive transaction whose tax consequences must be respected, it is also well established that where a transaction objectively affects the taxpayer's net economic position, legal relations, or non-tax business interests, it will not be disregarded merely because it was motivated by tax considerations. * * *

quences, the court made numerous findings that were indicative of the lack of objective economic consequences arising from ACM's shortswing acquisition and disposition of the Citicorp notes. * * * The court noted that ACM sold the Citicorp notes "for consideration equal to [their] purchase price" and thus did not realize any gain or loss in the notes' principal value. Moreover, as the court observed, the lack of change in principal value was not merely coincidental, but was inherent in the terms of the notes and of the transactions in which they were traded. Likewise, the court found that the interest income generated by the notes could not have a material effect on ACM's financial position because the Citicorp notes paid interest at a rate that varied only nominally from the rate that ACM's cash contributions "were already earning * * * in * * * deposit accounts before the notes were acquired," resulting in only a $3,500 difference in yield over the 24–day holding period, a difference which was obliterated by the transaction costs associated with marketing private placement notes to third parties. * * * These transactions, which generated the disputed capital losses by triggering the application of the ratable basis recovery rule, offset one another with no net effect on ACM's financial position. Examining the sequence of ACM's transactions as a whole as we must in assessing their economic substance, we find that these transactions had only nominal, incidental effects on ACM's net economic position.

Viewed according to their objective economic effects rather than their form, ACM's transactions involved only a fleeting and economically inconsequential investment in and offsetting divestment from the Citicorp notes. In the course of this brief interim investment, ACM passed $175 million of its available cash through the Citicorp notes before converting 80% of them, or $140 million, back into cash while using the remaining 20%, or $35 million, to acquire an amount of LIBOR notes that was identical, apart from transaction costs, to the amount of such notes that ACM could have acquired by investing its $35 million in cash directly into such assets. Thus, the transactions with respect to the Citicorp notes left ACM in the same position it had occupied before engaging in the offsetting acquisition and disposition of those notes.[7]

* * *

Gregory requires us to determine the tax consequences of a series of transactions based on what "actually occurred." Just as the *Gregory* Court found that the intervening creation and dissolution of a corporation and transfer of stock thereto and therefrom was a "mere device which put on the form of a corporate reorganization as a disguise for concealing its real character" which amounts to a mere "transfer * * * of corporate shares to the [taxpayer]," so we find that ACM's intervening acquisition and disposi-

---

7. The variable rate on the Citicorp notes presented a theoretical possibility that the consequences of owning those notes would vary from the consequences of leaving ACM's funds on deposit at a rate of interest virtually identical to the initial rate on the Citicorp notes. However, ACM's exposure to any fluctuation in the rate of return on its Citicorp note investment was illusory, as the interest rates were scheduled to be reset only once per month and ACM had arranged to hold the notes for only 24 days, encompassing only one interest rate adjustment on November 15 that would affect the notes for only 12 days before their disposition.

tion of the Citicorp notes was a mere device to create the appearance of a contingent installment sale despite the transaction's actual character as an investment of $35 million in cash into a roughly equivalent amount of LIBOR notes. Thus, the acquisition and disposition of the qualifying private placement Citicorp notes, based upon which ACM characterized its transactions as a contingent installment sale subject to the ratable basis recovery rule, had no effect on ACM's net economic position or non-tax business interests and thus, as the Tax Court properly found, did not constitute an economically substantive transaction that may be respected for tax purposes.[8]

ACM contends that the Tax Court was bound to respect the tax consequences of ACM's exchange of Citicorp notes for LIBOR notes because, under Cottage Sav. Ass'n v. Commissioner, 499 U.S. 554, an exchange of property for "materially different" assets is a substantive disposition whose tax effects must be recognized. We find Cottage Savings inapposite. * * * The distinctions between the exchange at issue in this case and the exchange before the Court in *Cottage Savings* predominate over any superficial similarities between the two transactions. The taxpayer in *Cottage Savings* had an economically substantive investment in assets which it had acquired a number of years earlier in the course of its ordinary business operations and which had declined in actual economic value by over $2 million from approximately $6.9 million to approximately $4.5 million from the time of acquisition to the time of disposition. The taxpayer's relinquishment of assets so altered in actual economic value over the course of a long-term investment stands in stark contrast to ACM's relinquishment of assets that it had acquired 24 days earlier under circumstances which assured that their principal value would remain constant and that their interest payments would not vary materially from those generated by ACM's cash deposits.

While the dispositions in *Cottage Savings* and in this case appear similar in that the taxpayer exchanged the assets for other assets with the same net present value, beneath this similarity lies the more fundamental distinction that the disposition in *Cottage Savings* precipitated the realization of actual economic losses arising from a long-term, economically significant investment, while the disposition in this case was without economic effect as it merely terminated a fleeting and economically inconsequential investment, effectively returning ACM to the same economic position it had occupied before the notes' acquisition 24 days earlier.[9]

8. [Each of the cases discussed above] involved objective acts which satisfied the technical requirements of the Internal Revenue Code provisions that the taxpayer sought to invoke, but which the courts disregarded for tax purposes because they lacked any net effect on the taxpayer's economic position or non-tax business interests. Accordingly, we are unpersuaded by ACM's argument that its transactions must be regarded as economically substantive because it actually and objectively engaged in them.

9. ACM contends that its disposition of the Citicorp notes was substantive because it "relinquished the benefits and burdens of owning the Citicorp notes for the distinct benefits and burdens of owning $140 million of cash and the LIBOR notes." This argument, however, erroneously assumes that ACM had acquired the benefits and burdens associated with the Citicorp notes in an economically substantive sense, when in reality ACM's brief investment in and offsetting divestment from these assets exposed ACM

As the Supreme Court emphasized in *Cottage Savings*, deductions are allowable only where the taxpayer has sustained a " 'bona fide' " loss as determined by its " '[s]ubstance and not mere form.' " According to ACM's own synopsis of the transactions, the contingent installment exchange would not generate actual economic losses. Rather, ACM would sell the Citicorp notes for the same price at which they were acquired, generating only tax losses which offset precisely the tax gains reported earlier in the transaction with no net loss or gain from the disposition.[10] Tax losses such as these, which are purely an artifact of tax accounting methods and which do not correspond to any actual economic losses, do not constitute the type of "bona fide" losses that are deductible under the Internal Revenue Code and regulations.

While ACM contends that "it would be absurd to conclude that the application of the Commissioner's own [ratable basis recovery] regulations results in gains or losses that the Commissioner can then deem to be other than 'bona fide,' " its argument confounds a tax accounting regulation which merely prescribes a method for reporting otherwise existing deductible losses that are realized over several years with a substantive deductibility provision authorizing the deduction of certain losses. In order to be deductible, a loss must reflect actual economic consequences sustained in an economically substantive transaction and cannot result solely from the application of a tax accounting rule to bifurcate a loss component of a transaction from its offsetting gain component to generate an artificial loss which, as the Tax Court found, is "not economically inherent in" the transaction.[11] Based on our review of the record regarding the objective economic consequences of ACM's short-swing, offsetting investment in and divestment from the Citicorp notes, we find ample support for the Tax Court's determination that ACM's transactions generated only "phantom losses" which cannot form the basis of a capital loss deduction under the Internal Revenue Code.[12]

only to de minimis risk of changes in principal value or interest rates.

10. The participation of a foreign partner that was impervious to tax considerations and that claimed most of the reported gains while allocating to Colgate virtually all of the losses allowed Colgate as ACM's major U.S. partner to reap the benefits of the tax losses without sustaining the burdens of the offsetting tax gains.

11. Because the ratable basis recovery rule simply provides a method for reporting otherwise existing economically substantive losses, we find it irrelevant that the rule recognizes that its application could "inappropriately defer or accelerate recovery of the taxpayer's basis," resulting in " 'substantial distortion' " of the tax consequences realized in any particular year of a transaction. Temp. Treas. Reg. §§ 15a.453–1(c)(3), (c)(7). While the rule contemplates some distortion as to the timing of when actual gains or losses are

reported over the span of a contingent installment sale, it does not contemplate the reporting of losses which are not the bona fide result of an economically substantive transaction. Thus, contrary to ACM's argument, the tax losses it reported are not "precisely what the [regulations] intended."

12. Having found ample support for the Tax Court's conclusion that ACM's transactions lacked economic substance and thus cannot give rise to taxable gains or deductible losses regardless of how those gains and losses are allocated, we need not address the Commissioner's alternative argument that the tax consequences of the transaction must be disregarded because ACM's partnership structure artificially "bifurcated the tax consequences of the transaction" by allocating taxable gains to a foreign partner and offsetting tax losses to the taxpayer in a manner which the relevant statute and regulations did not intend.

3.   Subjective Aspects of the Economic Sham Analysis

* * *

We * * * find that the Tax Court's analysis properly rested on economic substance cases applying provisions which, like those relevant in this case, do not by their terms require a business purpose or profit motive. [The court then discusses cases where an inquiry into profit motive or business purpose was undertaken despite the lack of such a requirement in the statute.] [W]e find no merit in ACM's argument that the Tax Court erred as a matter of law by scrutinizing the asserted business purposes and profit motives behind ACM's transactions.

* * *

4.   Intended Purposes and Anticipated Profitability of ACM's Transactions

Before the Tax Court, ACM conceded that there were tax objectives behind its transactions but contended that "tax independent considerations informed and justified each step of the strategy." ACM asserted that its transactions, in addition to presenting "a realistic prospect that ACM would have made a profit" on a pre-tax basis, also served the tax-independent purposes of providing an interim investment until ACM needed its cash to acquire Colgate debt and a hedge against interest rate risk within the partnership. The Tax Court, however, found that the record did not support ACM's assertions that the transactions were designed either to serve these non-tax objectives or to generate a pre-tax profit, and * * * we agree.

* * *

In addition to rejecting ACM's asserted non-tax justifications for its sequence of investments and dispositions, the Tax Court also rejected ACM's contention that its transactions were reasonably expected to yield a pre-tax profit because the court found ACM had planned and executed its transactions without regard to their pretax economic consequences. The evidence in the record overwhelmingly supports this conclusion. The documents outlining the proposed transactions, while quite detailed in their explication of expected tax consequences, are devoid of such detailed projections as to the expected rate of return on the private placement notes and contingent payment notes that were essential components of each proposal.

Moreover, ACM's partners were aware before they entered the partnership that the planned sequence of investments would entail over $3 million in transaction costs. Yet Colgate, which effectively bore virtually all of these costs pursuant to the terms of the partnership agreement, did not attempt to assess whether the transactions would be profitable after accounting for these significant transaction costs. Furthermore, while ACM planned to dispose of the Citicorp notes after a brief holding period for an amount equal to their purchase price, its proposed transactions contemplated holding for two years the LIBOR notes whose principal value would decline in the event of the falling interest rates which ACM's partners predicted.

Thus, while the Citicorp note investment which was essential to structuring the transaction as a contingent installment sale was economically inconsequential, the LIBOR note investment which was equally essential to achieving the desired tax structure was economically disadvantageous under the market conditions which Colgate predicted and which actually transpired. ACM's lack of regard for the relative costs and benefits of the contemplated transaction and its failure to conduct a contemporaneous profitability analysis support the Tax Court's conclusion that ACM's transactions were not designed or reasonably anticipated to yield a pre-tax profit, particularly in view of the significant transactions costs involved in exchanging illiquid private placement instruments. * * *

ACM also argues that the Tax Court's profitability analysis was flawed because the court adjusted the income expected to be generated by the LIBOR notes to its net present value. * * * In transactions that are designed to yield deferred rather than immediate returns, present value adjustments are, as the courts have recognized, an appropriate means of assessing the transaction's actual and anticipated economic effects. * * * We find no basis in the law for precluding a tax court's reliance on a present value adjustment where such an adjustment, under the surrounding circumstances, will serve as an accurate gauge of the reasonably expected economic consequences of the transaction.

* * *

[The portion of the court's opinion allowing a deduction for the approximately $6 million economic loss on the LIBOR notes, due to a decline in interest rates while the partnership held them, is omitted.]

McKEE, CIRCUIT JUDGE, dissenting.

By finding that ACM's sales of the Citicorp notes for cash and LIBOR Notes "satisfied each requirement of the contingent installment sales provisions and the ratable basis recovery rule," yet, simultaneously subjecting these transactions to an economic substance and sham transaction analysis, the majority has ignored the plain language of IRC § 1001, and controlling Supreme Court precedent. We have injected the "economic substance" analysis into an inquiry where it does not belong. Therefore, I respectfully dissent.

ACM, like all taxpayers, has the absolute right to decrease or to avoid the payment of taxes so long as that goal is achieved legally. Gregory v. Helvering. * * * [In *Gregory*] the Court disregarded the transaction, even though the form of the transaction satisfied the literal requirements of the IRC's reorganization provisions, because it found that the entire transaction was nothing but "an elaborate and devious form of conveyance masquerading as a corporate reorganization, and nothing else." In other words, the transaction was one which "upon its face lies outside the plain intent of the statute." Consequently, "the rule which excludes from consideration the motive of tax avoidance" did not apply.

Accordingly, I am not as persuaded as my colleagues that *Gregory* should guide our inquiry into these transactions. Here, the sales of the Citicorp Notes for cash and LIBOR Notes were clearly "legitimate" sales in the nontax sense. Under IRC § 1001, the tax consequences of a gain or loss in the value of property are deferred until the taxpayer realizes the gain or loss. *Cottage Savings Assoc. v. Commissioner.* * * * I believe that, under *Cottage Savings*, the tax loss here should have been allowed. ACM's sales of the Citicorp Notes for cash and LIBOR Notes resulted in the exchange of materially different property with "legally distinct entitlements." Consequently, the sales were substantive dispositions, and the tax effects of those transactions should be recognized. *Cottage Savings*, as well as the plain language of IRC § 1001, demands that result. * * * Here, the "economic substance" inquiry must be governed by the "material difference requirement" of *Cottage Savings*, not by the tax avoidance intent of the taxpayers. As recited earlier, ACM's sales of the Citicorp Notes for cash and LIBOR Notes resulted in the exchange of materially different property. I believe our inquiry should proceed no further, and reverse the holding of the Tax Court eliminating the capital gains and losses attributable to ACM's application of the contingent installment sale provisions and the ratable basis recovery rule to its disposition of the Citicorp Notes.

I can't help but suspect that the majority's conclusion to the contrary is, in its essence, something akin to a "smell test." If the scheme in question smells bad, the intent to avoid taxes defines the result as we do not want the taxpayer to "put one over." However, the issue clearly is not whether ACM put one over on the Commissioner, or used LIBOR notes to "pull the wool over his eyes." The issue is whether what ACM did qualifies for the tax treatment it seeks under § 1001. The fact that ACM may have "put one over" in crafting these transactions ought not to influence our inquiry. Our inquiry is cerebral, not visceral. To the extent that the Commissioner is offended by these transactions he should address Congress and/or the rulemaking process, and not the courts.

NOTES

(A) *Just the Facts, Ma'am.* The D.C. Circuit denied the tax losses in a transaction identical to the one in *ACM Partnership* but on the ground that the partnership was a sham. In ASA Investerings Partnership v. Commissioner, 201 F.3d 505 (D.C.Cir.2000), Allied–Signal also entered into a transaction peddled by Merrill Lynch in which the gains on an installment sale were allocated to a foreign tax-exempt entity. As in *ACM*, by using the basis-recovery rule large losses were created and allocated to Allied Signal, who used them to offset a capital gain on the sale of its interests in another company. The court found that the partnership was created solely to avoid taxes and therefore was not a valid separate entity. Although the court basically found it was not necessary to pursue the economic substance doctrine once it found the partnership was a sham, its analysis in making the determination that the partnership had no purpose other than tax avoidance is very similar to that used by the Third Circuit in *ACM*.

Judge Williams, who wrote the circuit court's opinion in *ASA* remarked that "[t]he hardest aspect of this case is simply getting a handle on the facts." He attempted to make them manageable in the following simplified summary, which may be helpful in understanding the essence of the transaction in *ACM*:

> [S]uppose A finds a way of allocating the nominal tax gain to a tax-free entity, reserving for himself a nominal tax loss? Here is how he might do it: He forms a partnership with a foreign entity not subject to U.S. tax, supplying the partnership with $100,000 and inducing the "partner" to supply $900,000. The "partnership" buys for $1,000,000 property eligible for installment sale treatment under § 453, and, as the ink is drying on the purchase documents, sells the property, * * * for $500,000 in cash and an indefinite five-year debt instrument. The cash payment produces a gain of $300,000, 90% of which goes to the nontaxable foreign entity. Then ownership adjustments are made so that A owns 90% of the partnership. In Year 2 the instrument is sold, yielding a tax loss of $300,000, 90% of which is allocable to A. Presto: A has generated a tax loss of $240,000 ($270,000 loss in Year 2, offset by $30,000 gain in Year 1), with no material change in his financial position—other than receipt of the valuable tax loss. This example is [this] case stripped to its essentials.

201 F.3d at 507. On the other hand, the D.C. District Court upheld a transaction very similar to that in *ACM* on slightly more favorable facts. Boca Investerings Partnership v. United States, 167 F.Supp.2d 298 (D.D.C. 2001).

(B) *You Win Some, You Lose Some.* After a string of judicial victories in corporate tax shelter cases, the IRS suffered a series of reverses that made it less likely that the courts will be effective in shutting down the shelters. The IRS used a variety of judicial doctrines, such as lack of economic substance, no business purpose, or the sham doctrine to deny the promised tax benefits, but courts often find a scintilla of business motive or profit is sufficient to sustain the transaction.

In Compaq Computer Corp. v. Commissioner, 113 T.C. 214 (1999), the court denied the taxpayer's use of foreign tax credits that it had acquired for close to zero cost on the ground that the transaction lacked economic substance. Compaq purchased trust trading units that represented a foreign corporation's stock after dividends had been declared but before the payment date. The foreign corporation paid dividends to Compaq, withholding foreign tax. Compaq immediately sold the trading units at the lower ex-dividend price, and claimed a short-term capital loss, dividend income, and a large foreign tax credit. The court found that the deal had no nontax business purpose and exposed Compaq to no significant economic risk. According to the court, there was simply the "illusion of profit," created when Compaq essentially purchased a foreign tax credit. The Fifth Circuit, however, found that the taxpayer did have a pretax profit and therefore there was economic substance separate from the tax savings. 277 F.3d 778 (5th Cir.2001).

Winn–Dixie's shelter involved the use of leveraged corporate-owned life insurance. The company purchased cash-value life insurance on many of its employees, paying a $100 million premium. It borrowed almost the entire cost against the policies, leaving a net premium of $7 million. It then claimed millions in interest deductions. The scheme was to last for 60 years, which would produce a positive after-tax cash flow. The Tax Court held the transaction to be a sham, finding no business purpose, and this time the Circuit Court agreed. Winn–Dixie Stores, Inc. v. Commissioner, 113 T.C. 254 (1999), aff'd, 254 F.3d 313 (11th Cir.2001). The courts noted that the pre-tax economic effect was a substantial loss. The court also rejected Winn–Dixie's argument that it complied with the literal requirements of § 264 with respect to life insurance policies, holding that the general rules for interest deductions under § 163 controlled. A number of cases involving similar transactions have denied interest deductions on leveraged corporate-owned life insurance. But many corporations are engaged in such transactions and there is a boat load of disputed taxes at issue so further litigation seems inevitable.

The Tax Court also refused to let The Limited rely on the literal statutory language in a case involving a complex transaction in which a foreign subsidiary purchased assets from a domestic subsidiary. The court found that The Limited had structured a transaction to avoid repatriation of the parent corporation's earnings by arguing that its funds were invested with someone "carrying on the banking business," in which case the earnings were excluded from U.S. tax. Despite the fact that the domestic subsidiary was involved in issuing credit cards, the court interpreted "banking business" to require that the entity must perform the range of activities performed by a bank and not just one of them. It did so because it believed that Congress had not intended the statute to be used in this way. The Limited Inc. v. Commissioner, 113 T.C. 169 (1999).

The Service was not so lucky in challenging the shelter entered into by United Parcel Service. The Tax Court disallowed tax savings in connection with United Parcel Service's efforts to restructure its system for compensating certain losses on its shipping of parcels by creating a Bermuda insurance subsidiary and engaging in transactions not at arm's-length. The court concluded that UPS failed to prove that its restructuring of this activity "was motivated by nontax business reasons or that the restructuring had economic substance." To the contrary, the court found that the transactions were done for "the purpose of avoiding taxes," "had no economic substance or business purpose," and were "sham transaction[s] with no economic effect." United Parcel Service of America v. Commissioner, T.C. Memo 1999–268 (1999). The Eleventh Circuit disagreed, however, finding that there was enough economic substance to the activity to avoid labelling it a sham. The Court believed that subsidiary was independent and that the transaction had a business purpose other than tax avoidance. 254 F.3d 1014 (11th Cir.2001).

The IRS has also issued a significant number of revenue rulings and notices denying purported tax benefits associated with a number of shelters. See, e.g., Rev. Rul. 2000–12, 2000–1 C.B. 744 (disallowing losses on the sale of one debt instrument when a taxpayer acquired instruments structured with offsetting contingencies so that if the value of one decreases, the value of the other will increase). The effect of the rulings has been to shut down the specific transaction since a potential user no longer would have any basis on which to claim that the transaction was valid.

The transactions involved in these cases share a number of traits. Usually, a promoter packaged and marketed a deal to the taxpayer, which made the courts suspicious of the corporation's alleged business purpose. The taxpayers also had little or no downside risk since they were fully hedged by derivatives and no significant upside potential, particularly when very large transaction costs and fees were taken into account. To the extent that ownership of a risky asset was essential, it was typically momentary. Usually a tax-indifferent party was used to absorb any profits while the taxpayer attempted to take advantage of a temporary artificial loss. In addition to the foreign entities, tax-exempt Native American tribes have often been willing to play the role of the tax-indifferent part—for a fee, of course.

(B) *Proposed Codification of Judicial Doctrines.* As *ACM* illustrates, tax shelters often are based on discontinuities in statutory or regulatory rules that under current law can be combated through administrative rulemaking and judicial doctrines. In its report excerpted above, Treasury considered a statutory rule that would disallow tax benefits by overriding technical rules. Treasury argued that "(1) policymakers do not have the knowledge, expertise and time to continually address these transactions, (2) adding more mechanical rules to the Code adds to complexity, unintended results, and potential fodder for new shelters, (3) the approach may reward taxpayers and promoters who rush to complete transactions before the anticipated prospective effective date of any reactive legislation, and (4) the approach results in further misuse and neglect of common law tax doctrines." Critics argue, however, that it is impractical to codify the judicial doctrines, contend that statutory rules will catch legitimate transactions in their sweep, and argue that they will not be effective in eliminating shelters.

This is a variant of the ancient rules versus standards debate: Is it better to have specific statutory rules that create clear boundaries (and thus permit transactions one step over the line to obtain desirable tax consequences) or vaguer standards that provide more flexibility to the IRS but make it much harder for taxpayers and their advisors to know when they are in compliance?

Even if one favors a substantive disallowance rule, there remains the thorny problem of how to define those transactions in which tax benefits will be disallowed. One suggestion has been to codify the business purpose and economic substance doctrines. Why is this regarded as an improvement in the law? While tax professionals have some concept of what the terms "business purpose" and "economic substance" mean, it is very difficult to define them in statutory language. Just what are the indicia of economic substance? One possibility is legal ownership, but clearly that is not sufficient since one can have title and nothing more. Generally, it requires some economic risk—and to avoid momentary risk (for example, the taxpayer in *Compaq* had a downside risk for a mere hour), some minimum period of time would need to be specified. Once specified, that minimum will serve as a roadmap to tax savings.

With respect to business purpose, the main idea is that there must be some business reason for entering into the transaction other than a desire to save taxes. But most corporations find it very easy to "find or create" a business purpose. Recall that in *ACM*, Colgate claimed it entered into the partnership as a way to manage the term structure of its debt. Winn–Dixie claimed the insurance policies helped to fund an employee business plan. In each case, the court easily dismissed the alleged business purpose.

In its Fiscal Year 2001 Budget, Treasury proposed a substantive statutory disallowance rule, essentially repeating its definition of a tax shelter set out at page 812 supra:

> The proposal would codify and clarify the economic substance doctrine. The proposal would disallow tax benefits from any transaction in which the reasonably expected pre-tax profit (determined on a present value basis, after taking into account foreign taxes as expenses and transaction costs) of the taxpayer from the transaction is insignificant relative to the reasonably expected net tax benefits (i.e., tax benefits in excess of the tax liability arising from the transaction, determined on a present value basis) of the taxpayer from such transaction. With respect to financing transactions, tax benefits would be disallowed if the present value of the tax benefits of the taxpayer to whom the financing is provided are significantly in excess of the present value of the pre-tax profit or return of the person providing the financing.

This approach also has difficulties. Can expected profit be measured objectively? How much nontax economic profit is sufficient? And why is it that the tax consequences cannot be taken into account in determining whether the investment makes economic sense? Clearly no one thinks that taking into account the tax savings from accelerated depreciation turns the purchase of a machine into a transaction with no economic substance. And purchasing a municipal bond without considering its tax exemption is not smart. Treasury has thus suggested another possible approach: Permit the taxpayer to enjoy tax benefits where Congress intended them to be used and deny them in circumstances where Congress did not intend them to be available. But how does one determine such Congressional intent? By looking at legislative history, such as committee reports? By considering transactions at which a particular section was aimed? By inferring intent from the overall structure of the Code? Or may the IRS or a court simply adopt what it considers the best policy result?

(C) *Sunlight.* The Treasury Department has issued proposed and temporary regulations requiring increased disclosure of corporate tax shelters. The regulations are premised on the notion that if the shelters were exposed to scrutiny, corporations might be less likely to invest in questionable transactions. In any event, their likely discovery and challenge by the IRS would become part of the corporation's cost-benefit analysis. At the very least, they would give the IRS a clue as to where the tax savings are buried.

The disclosure requirement is triggered by transactions producing tax savings exceeding specific dollar thresholds. Under temporary regulations under § 6011 issued in 1999 corporations must report any transaction that is (1) the same or substantially similar to a list of reportable tax shelter transactions (which will be updated by Treasury as it uncovers new techniques), and (2) expected to reduce the corporation's federal income tax liability by more than $1 million in a single tax year, or more than $2 million for any combination of tax years. The regulations also require corporations to report any transaction that (1) is expected to reduce the corporation's federal income tax liability by more than $5 million in a single tax year, or more than $10 million for any combination of tax years, and (2) features at least *two* of the following six characteristics relating to the terms of the deal. Those characteristics are confidentiality, contingent fees, recission rights or indemnities, marketing, a book/tax difference exceeding $5 million, a tax-indifferent party, and cross-border tax arbitrage.

Businesses and their representatives have complained that the reporting requirements are too burdensome and frequently would apply to routine business transactions. In an attempt to accommodate legitimate business transactions, the temporary regulations exempt from disclosure transactions carried out in the ordinary course of business consistently with customary commercial practice. To qualify for this exception, the corporation would have to show either that it would have entered the transaction irrespective of tax benefits or that there is a longstanding and generally accepted understanding in the public domain of the expected tax treatment. Also considered to be part of the ordinary course of business are transactions involving the acquisition, disposition, or restructuring of a business, a recapitalization of a business, or the acquisition of capital for use in a business. Nevertheless, some accounting firms have claimed that the proposed rules would cover a "large percentage of everything we do."

One technique often used by tax shelter promoters is to require as a condition of viewing a particular gimmick that the potential investor sign a confidentiality agreement forbidding it to disclose or discuss the shelter with anyone even if the corporation does not "purchase" the shelter. Section 6111(d) requires registration of any arrangement if a significant purpose is the avoidance of tax by a participating corporation, if an offering is made to any potential participant under conditions of confidentiality and if its promoters may receive a combined amount greater than $100,000. The proposed and temporary regulations under § 6111 define "a significant purpose of federal tax avoidance" as one of the following if: (1) The transaction is listed in published guidance as required to be registered, or otherwise identified in guidance as a tax avoidance transaction, (2) The transaction would not pass the economic substance test (see Notice 98–5, 1998–3 IRB 49), i.e., whether the reasonably expected pre-tax profit (determined on a present value basis) is insignificant relative to the reasonably expected net tax benefits, (3) Tax benefits are an important intended result of the deal, and the promoter expects to market the deal to more than one potential customer. There is no significant purpose of tax avoidance for transactions that the promoter believes are part of the ordinary course of the customer's business, consistent with customary commercial practice, and for which there is a longstanding and generally accepted understanding of the expected tax treatment or for which the promoter believes there is no reasonable basis under the federal tax law for denial of the expected tax benefits.

Apparently, the government's expectation was that these transactions would no longer be offered under conditions of confidentiality and thus the IRS estimated that only four shelters would be registered under the temporary regulations.

Section 6112 requires promoters to maintain lists of those who purchased a shelter that is required to be registered. Temporary and proposed regulations under § 6112 require customer lists to be maintained for transactions having a significant purpose of federal tax avoidance under the § 6111 regulations regardless of the size of the fees or whether the deals were offered under conditions of confidentiality.

The ink had hardly dried on these proposed regulations before Treasury reached the conclusion that they probably would not result in sufficient disclosure. In 2001 only 272 transactions were disclosed by 99 corporate taxpayers. So in March 2002, Treasury offered new proposals that were incorporated into the Tax–Shelter Transparency Act introduced by Senators Baucus and Grassley. The new approach sticks with disclosure but combines it with stiff penalties for a failure to disclose. For example, a failure to disclose a so-called listed transaction—one classified by the Treasury as a really bad transaction—would result in a strict liability, nonwaivable penalty of $200,000, which must be reported to the SEC. If the transaction ultimately results in an understatement, the substantial understatement penalty increases. The Act would also impose penalties on tax shelter promoters who do not maintain lists of investors and would give Treasury the power to censure or impose monetary sanctions against tax advisors and firms that participate in shelter activities. It remains to be seen whether transparency will have the desired effect.

(D) *Proposed Penalties*. Another suggested approach is to change the cost-benefit analysis of tax shelters by increasing the costs if the shelter fails. To this end, both Treasury and the Joint Committee have proposed increasing penalties on understatements attributable to tax shelters. They suggest that Congress impose a 40 percent "strict liability" penalty on substantial understatements of tax arising from any undisclosed "corporate tax shelter," where a corporate tax shelter is defined as "any entity, plan or arrangement in which a direct or indirect corporate participant attempts to obtain a tax benefit in a 'tax avoidance transaction'." The Treasury proposal would reduce the 40 percent rate to 20 percent if certain disclosures are made. The Senate Finance Committee introduced legislation that provides no escape from penalties for "highly abusive shelters." For merely "abusive" shelters, the penalty is reduced or in some cases eliminated if the corporate taxpayer (1) satisfies disclosure requirements, (2) has substantial authority for its position, and (3) reasonably believes its treatment more like than not is correct.

Treasury also proposed adding significant penalties for failure to disclose tax shelters under the temporary regulations discussed in Note (C) above. Treasury also would require a corporate participant to disclose to its shareholders the payment (including the amount and transaction details) of an understatement penalty of at least $1 million that was attributable to a corporate tax shelter.

(E) The Use of Opinion Letters. Opinion letters drafted by attorneys are often the linchpin of shelter offerings because they provide the taxpayer an assurance that a certain tax consequence will prevail, and perhaps more importantly, provide penalty protection if the transaction fails. Rules with respect to opinion letter are discussed in the following section.

In January, 2001, the IRS published proposed regulations that would tighten standards under Circular 230 for issuing tax shelter opinion letters. Circular 230 provides standards for attorneys, accountants and others who represent taxpayers before the IRS. These proposed rules would strengthen the standards for factual due diligence, including the pre-tax profitability of the transaction, and require legal analysis of all "material" tax issues, including the application of anti-abuse rules. The amendments would also prohibit tax practitioners from taking a fee contingent on whether the expected tax treatment of the transaction is upheld. Although Circular 230 applies only to those who practice before the IRS and thus has no effect on practitioners willing to forgo this privilege, the preamble to the proposal rules indicates that regulations are expected to be issued that provide that opinions that do not comply with the Circular 230 standards cannot be relied upon to protect taxpayers against the imposition of penalties. The proposed amendments to Circular 230 were clearly intended to have a chilling effect on practitioners promoting corporate tax shelters. Many observers are skeptical that they will prove effective. The principal sanction under Circular 230 is public reprimand and censure. Some promoters of corporate tax shelters may regard censure by the IRS simply as good advertising.

SECTION 2.   ETHICAL RESPONSIBILITIES OF TAX PRACTITIONERS

The organized bar promulgates ethical standards for its members, and tax lawyers, like other lawyers, are subject to the ethical codes of the state in which they are admitted. Tax lawyers are also subject to the practice standards established by the Treasury Department under Circular 230 for all those who engage in practice before the Internal Revenue Service. These standards describe minimum acceptable conduct. Finally, lawyers who are also "tax return preparers" are subject to rules and penalties imposed by the Internal Revenue Code itself.

One of the most important and controversial ethical issues facing tax practitioners involves the standard to be applied in giving tax advice. For many years, the most important authority delineating the tax lawyer's ethical obligations was ABA Opinion 314. It provided:

> In practice before the Internal Revenue Service, which is itself an adversary party rather than a judicial tribunal, the lawyer is under a duty not to mislead the Service, either by misstatement, silence, or through his client, but is under no duty to disclose the weaknesses of his client's case. He must be candid and fair, and his defense of his client must be exercised within the bounds of the law and without resort to any manner of fraud or chicane.

The opinion permitted lawyers who advise clients on the preparation of tax returns to urge positions favorable to the client as long as there was a "reasonable basis" for doing so. The opinion explained:

> where the lawyer believes there is a reasonable basis for a position that a particular transaction does not result in taxable income, or that certain expenditures are properly deductible as expenses, the lawyer has no duty to advise that riders be attached to the client's tax return explaining the circumstances surrounding the transaction or the expenditure.

The "reasonable basis" standard was widely criticized, and in response, the ABA issued Opinion 85–352. Opinion 314 still retains some validity in other areas.

Formal Opinion 85–352

American Bar Association, July 7 (1985).

The Committee has been requested by the Section of Taxation of the American Bar Association to reconsider the "reasonable basis" standard in the Committee's Formal Opinion 314 governing the position a lawyer may advise a client to take on a tax return.

Opinion 314 (April 27, 1965) was issued in response to a number of specific inquiries regarding the ethical relationship between the Internal Revenue Service and lawyers practicing before it. The opinion formulated general principles governing this relationship, including the following:

> [A] lawyer who is asked to advise his client in the course of the preparation of the client's tax returns may freely urge the statement of positions most favorable to the client just as long as there is a *reasonable basis* for this position. (Emphasis supplied).

The Committee is informed that the standard of "reasonable basis" has been construed by many lawyers to support the use of any colorable claim on a tax return to justify exploitation of the lottery of the tax return audit selection process. This view is not universally held, and the Committee does not believe that the reasonable basis standard, properly interpreted and applied, permits this construction.

However, the Committee is persuaded that as a result of serious controversy over this standard and its persistent criticism by distinguished members of the tax bar, IRS officials and members of Congress, sufficient doubt has been created regarding the validity of the standard so as to erode its effectiveness as an ethical guideline. For this reason, the Committee has concluded that it should be restated. Another reason for restating the standard is that since publication of Opinion 314, the ABA has adopted in succession the Model Code of Professional Responsibility (1969, revised 1980) and the Model Rules of Professional Conduct (1983). Both the Model Code and the Model Rules directly address the duty of a lawyer in presenting or arguing positions for a client in language that does not refer to "reasonable basis." It is therefore appropriate to conform the standard of Opinion 314 to the language of the new rules.

This opinion reconsiders and revises only that part of Opinion 314 that relates to the lawyer's duty in advising a client of positions that can be taken on a tax return. It does not deal with a lawyer's opinion on tax shelter investment offerings, which is specifically addressed by this Committee's Formal Opinion 346 (Revised), and which involves very different considerations, including third party reliance.

The ethical standards governing the conduct of a lawyer in advising a client on positions that can be taken in a tax return are no different from those governing a lawyer's conduct in advising or taking positions for a client in other civil matters. Although the Model Rules distinguish between the roles of advisor and advocate,[2] both roles are involved here, and the ethical standards applicable to them provide relevant guidance. In many cases a lawyer must realistically anticipate that the filing of the tax return may be the first step in a process that may result in an adversary relationship between the client and the IRS. This normally occurs in situations when a lawyer advises an aggressive position on a tax return, not when the position taken is a safe or conservative one that is unlikely to be challenged by the IRS.

Rule 3.1 of the Model Rules, which is in essence a restatement of DR 7–102(A)(2) of the Model Code,[3] states in pertinent part:

> A lawyer shall not bring or defend a proceeding, or assert or controvert an issue therein, unless there is a basis for doing so that is not frivolous, which includes a good faith argument for an extension, modification or reversal of existing law.

Rule 1.2(d), which applies to representation generally, states:

> A lawyer shall not counsel a client to engage, or assist a client, in conduct that the lawyer knows is criminal or fraudulent, but a lawyer may discuss the legal consequences of any proposed course of conduct with a client and may counsel or assist a client to make a good faith effort to determine the validity, scope, meaning or application of the law.

On the basis of these rules and analogous provisions of the Model Code, a lawyer, in representing a client in the course of the preparation of the client's tax return, may advise the statement of positions most favorable to the client if the lawyer has a good faith belief that those positions are warranted in existing law or can be supported by a good faith argument for an extension, modification or reversal of existing law. A lawyer can have a good faith belief in this context even if the lawyer believes the client's position probably will not prevail.[4] However, good faith requires that there be some realistic possibility of success if the matter is litigated.

---

2. *See, e.g.,* Model Rules 2.1 and 3.1.

3. DR 7–102(A)(2) states:

In his representation of a client, a lawyer shall not:

* * *

(2) Knowingly advance a claim or defense that is unwarranted under existing law, ex-cept that he may advance such claim or defense if it can be supported by good faith argument for an extension, modification or reversal of existing law.

4. Comment to Rule 3.11; *see also* Model Code EC 7–4.

This formulation of the lawyer's duty in the situation addressed by this opinion is consistent with the basic duty of the lawyer to a client, recognized in ethical standards since the ABA Canons of Professional Ethics, and in the opinions of this Committee: zealously and loyally to represent the interests of the client within the bounds of the law.

Thus, where a lawyer has a good faith belief in the validity of a position in accordance with the standard stated above that a particular transaction does not result in taxable income or that certain expenditures are properly deductible as expenses, the lawyer has no duty to require as a condition of his or her continued representation that riders be attached to the client's tax return explaining the circumstances surrounding the transaction or the expenditures.

In the role of advisor, the lawyer should counsel the client as to whether the position is likely to be sustained by a court if challenged by the IRS, as well as of the potential penalty consequences to the client if the position is taken on the tax return without disclosure. Section 6661 of the Internal Revenue Code imposes a penalty for substantial understatement of tax liability which can be avoided if the facts are adequately disclosed or if there is or was substantial authority for the position taken by the taxpayer.[5] Competent representation of the client would require the lawyer to advise the client fully as to whether there is or was substantial authority for the position taken in the tax return. If the lawyer is unable to conclude that the position is supported by substantial authority, the lawyer should advise the client of the penalty the client may suffer and of the opportunity to avoid such penalty by adequately disclosing the facts in the return or in a statement attached to the return. If after receiving such advice the client decides to risk the penalty by making no disclosure and to take the position initially advised by the lawyer in accordance with the standard stated above, the lawyer has met his or her ethical responsibility with respect to the advice.

In all cases, however, with regard both to the preparation of returns and negotiating administrative settlements, the lawyer is under a duty not to mislead the Internal Revenue Service deliberately, either by misstatements or by silence or by permitting the client to mislead. Rules 4.1 and 8.4(c); DRs 1–102(A)(4), 7–102(A)(3) and (5).

In summary, a lawyer may advise reporting a position on a return even where the lawyer believes the position probably will not prevail, there is no "substantial authority" in support of the position, and there will be no disclosure of the position in the return. However, the position to be asserted must be one which the lawyer in good faith believes is warranted in existing law or can be supported by a good faith argument for an extension, modification or reversal of existing law. This requires that there be some realistic possibility of success if the matter is litigated. In addition, in his role as advisor, the lawyer should refer to potential penalties and other legal consequences should the client take the position advised.

---

5. This penalty is now imposed by section 6662. The penalty can be avoided by disclosure only if the taxpayer has a reasonable basis for the position taken.—Ed.

NOTES

(A) *Some Realistic Possibility of Success.* A task force of the ABA Section of Taxation has expressed the view that "a position having only a 5% or 10% likelihood of success, if litigated, should not meet the new standard. A position having a likelihood of success closely approaching one-third should meet the standard." Paul Sax, James P. Holden, Theodore Tannenwald Jr., David Watts & Bernard Wolfman, "Report of the Special Task Force Report on Formal Opinion 85–352," *reprinted in* 39 Tax Lawyer 633, 638–39 (1986). How easy is it to quantify the likelihood of success? Surely a lawyer can differentiate between a one-third chance and a 10 percent chance.

The reasonable basis standard of ABA Opinion 314 was often referred to as a "laugh aloud" standard, suggesting an attorney could urge any position that he could state without laughing aloud. Although the "realistic possibility of success" standard expressed in Opinion 85–352 is surely more stringent than the reasonable basis standard, is it anything more than a "giggle test"?

Whether or not Opinion 85–352 is an improvement, it may have little practical impact because no one is enforcing it. Provisions of the law and administrative requirements are more apt to have a real impact.

(B) *Tax Preparer Rules.* An income tax return preparer is subject to a penalty of $250 if any part of an understatement of liability on a return or claim for refund is due to a position for which there was not a "realistic possibility of being sustained on its merits." The penalty applies only (1) if the preparer knew or reasonably should have known that the position was adopted on the return, (2) if the position was not adequately disclosed (or, even if disclosed, it was frivolous), and (3) if the preparer is unable to establish that there was reasonable cause for the understatement and that he acted in good faith. A position is considered to have a realistic possibility of being sustained on its merits if a reasonable and well-informed analysis by a person knowledgeable in the tax law would lead such a person to conclude that the position has approximately a one-in-three, or greater, likelihood of being sustained on its merits. Reg. § 1.6694–2(b). Reliance on another competent professional is sufficient for a preparer to establish reasonable cause and good faith.

(C) *Circular 230.* Under 31 U.S.C. § 230, the Secretary of the Treasury has the authority to establish practice standards for those who practice before the IRS. The Secretary has exercised this authority by issuing regulations known as "Circular 230." Violation of Circular 230 standards can result in disbarment from practice before the IRS.

Circular 230 permits a practitioner to sign a return that includes a position that does not have a realistic possibility of being sustained on the merits if it is not frivolous and it is disclosed. He may advise the taxpayer to take such a position if the position is not frivolous and he advises the client that the client can avoid penalties by disclosing the position. The standards adopted in Circular 230 conform closely to the standards of § 6694 and Opinion 85–352.

(D) *Opinion Letters and Tax Shelters.* Circular 230 also governs tax shelter opinion letters. Concerned that practitioners were providing opinions on tax shelters essentially as "penalty insurance," the Treasury Department in January 2001 issued proposed regulations that would substantially tighten the restrictions on such letters.

The new standards would require basic factual due diligence and prohibit reliance on unreasonable factual representations or assumptions. Factual representations and assumptions cannot be incorrect, incomplete, inconsistent, or implausible. Because a valid business purpose is often critical to sustaining a shelter, factual representations regarding business purpose are not reasonable without describing the transaction's profitability. The opinion must consider all potentially relevant judicial doctrines, including the step transaction, business purpose, economic substance, substance over form, and sham transaction doctrines, as well as potentially relevant anti-abuse rules.

In most cases, a tax shelter opinion could not be used for penalty insurance because the writer is unable to opine that the transaction more likely than not will succeed for tax purposes. In addition, such an opinion must state prominently that it does not provide a basis for avoiding a penalty. Only in cases where the transaction is likely to succeed—highly unlikely with respect to most tax shelters—could it be relied on for penalty protection.

The proposed rules would prohibit contingent fee arrangements where the practitioner's fee is based on the tax benefit being sustained. They also would require that practitioners in firms who have responsibility for a firm's tax practice take reasonable steps to put in place adequate procedures to ensure compliance with the Circular 230 standards.

As we stated earlier, it is difficult to know if these new standards will help to staunch the flow of tax shelters. Most shelters already come with a more-likely-than-not opinion although it is not generally based on the type of factual and legal analysis called for by the proposed regulations. In cases where the shelter depends on a literal reading of the statute, regulations or a ruling, invalidation may depend on a vague doctrine such as economic substance and practitioners may well differ as to the likely results.

(E) *Other Ethical Issues.* Tax lawyers face ethical issues in many contexts other than advice regarding a position on a tax return. Lawyers are likely to face significant ethical issues when representing a taxpayer before the Service or in court when planning transactions, when writing opinions for use by third parties or in many other situations. A comprehensive study of these issues is found in Bernard Wolfman, James P. Holden & Deborah H. Schenk, Ethical Problems in Federal Tax Practice (1995).

The following article elaborates on the professional responsibilities of a tax lawyer and provides examples to illustrate the rules.

Examining the Line—Balancing the Duty to the Client With the Duty to the Tax System

Harvey Coustan & John S. Nolan, Taxes 824 (Dec. 1997).

I. *The Nature and Source of Tax Practice and Standards*

Practice standards are ethical principles that guide the tax practitioner in balancing *duty to client* with *duty to "system."* The tax practitioner owes various duties to client, but primary among them are loyalty, which requires an absence of conflicting interests; confidentiality, which requires that the clients' confidences and secrets be protected from disclosure; and competence, which requires that the client's objectives be pursued with diligence, adequate tax knowledge and skills, thoroughness, preparation, and due care.

While practitioners are expected to pursue the interests of their clients with zeal and skill, there are limits beyond which the practitioner may not go in pursuit of client interest. A practitioner may not assist a client in unlawful conduct, must be truthful in dealing with others, and must be candid with a tribunal. A practitioner should act with integrity and not subordinate his or her judgment to others. The practitioner may find it necessary to withdraw from a representation that challenges these absolutes. In the tax field, duty to system also requires that practitioners observe specific standards relating to the quality of advice given and the accuracy of tax return positions. These accuracy standards, applicable to both taxpayers and their advisors, effectively serve as additional tax practice standards.

* * *

II.   Duty to Client—Absence of Conflicting Interests

It is fundamental to the professional relationship that the client commands the undivided loyalty of the professional. Loyalty, in this context, includes an absence of conflicting interests.

Under the ABA Model Rules, representation is prohibited if the representation will be *directly adverse* to another client unless both clients consent *and* the lawyer reasonably believes that the representation will not adversely affect the relationship with the existing client.[4] A representation may not be undertaken if it would be materially limited by the lawyer's responsibilities to another client or to a third person, or to the lawyer's own interest, unless the lawyer reasonably believes that the representation would not be adversely affected, and the client consents.[5] A representation that may be materially adverse to a former client is also prohibited if the subject matter of the proposed representation is substantially related to that of the former client.[6] Finally, if a lawyer is prohibited from representing a client, no other lawyer in the same firm may accept that representation.[7]

Special conflict of interest rules apply to lawyers who move between government employment and private practice. Generally, a lawyer may not represent a private client with respect to a matter in which the lawyer participated personally and substantially as a public officer or employee.[8]

* * *

---

4. Model Rules of Professional Conduct (hereinafter "ABA Model") Rule 1.7(a) (1983).

5. Id. Rule 1.7(b).

6. Id. Rule 1.9.

7. Id. Rule. 1.10.

8. Id. Rule 1.11. See also 18 U.S.C. § 207, which sets forth statutory limitations on representation by former government employees.

Circular 230 also contains anti-conflict rules. Persons who practice before the Internal Revenue Service may not represent conflicting interests except by express consent of all directly interested persons after full disclosure. * * *

The Tax Court has not only adopted the ABA Model Rules; the Court has also adopted a special rule relating to conflicts of interest. The Tax Court Rule 24(f) requires that a lawyer who was involved—

(i) in planning or promoting a transaction or operating an entity connected to an issue in a case;

(ii) or who represents more than one person with differing interests in a case; or

(iii) who may be witness in a case, take certain steps.

Except in (iii) above, the lawyer may proceed with the representation if he or she obtains the informed consent of the client. Otherwise, the lawyer must withdraw unless other steps can be taken to obviate a conflict of interest or other violation of the ABA Model Rules. If the lawyer may be a witness in the case, informed consent of the client will not suffice; the lawyer must withdraw unless as above, there are other steps that can be taken to prevent a conflict of interest or other violation of the ABA Rules.[14]

* * *

Consider [the following] potential conflict situation.

K represented Mr. And Mrs. Coleman in a tax dispute with the IRS. When it became apparent that the matter would require litigation, Mr. And Mrs. Coleman replaced K with the law firm of R & H. R & H filed a petition on behalf of Mr. And Mrs. Coleman, raising the innocent spouse defense on behalf of Mrs. Coleman. Sometime later, Mr. And Mrs. Coleman were divorced, but they made no change in their joint representation in the tax matter. Prior to trial, Mr. Coleman entered into settlement negotiations with the IRS. K had continued to represent Mrs. Coleman in various matters after the divorce, and Mr. Coleman communicated to K the proposed settlement terms so that K could explain them to Mrs. Coleman.

Acting on behalf of Mrs. Coleman, K then revoked the R & H authority to represent her and undertook that representation himself, actions to which Mr. Coleman took strong objection. The proposed settlement was later presented to the Court without disclosure of the dispute over representation, and a decision was entered based on the settlement agreement. Six months later, Mrs. Coleman, acting through K, moved to vacate the earlier decision on grounds of conflict of interest by R & H in their representation of her. That motion was granted. Mr. Coleman now moves to disqualify K from further representation of Mrs. Coleman in the tax dispute. How should the Court rule?

14. ABA Model Rule 3.7 generally precludes a lawyer from representing a client in a proceeding where the lawyer is likely to be a witness with respect to a contested issue. It is unclear whether Tax Court Rule 24(f) adds something not already in the Model Rules.

III.   Duty to Client—Confidentiality

Virtually all professional organizations impose an obligation of confidentiality on members of their profession with respect to client affairs. A lawyer may not reveal information relating to a representation of a client or former client without the client's consent except where necessary to prevent the client from "committing a criminal act that the lawyer believes is likely to result in imminent death or substantial bodily harm."[15] This rule is modified in some states, however, to permit the lawyer to disclose fraud under some circumstances.

This ethical obligation of confidentiality is to be distinguished from the attorney-client privilege, which is a rule of evidence rather than an ethical rule. The attorney-client privilege is more durable than the obligation of confidentiality. For example, if appropriately claimed, the privilege may survive a court order to testify. In contrast, the ethical obligation ends whenever the practitioner encounters a legal obligation to make disclosure. The attorney-client privilege is available for only a limited class of communications, *i.e.*, those that were delivered in confidence in the course of rendering legal advice and were not disclosed beyond lawyer and client. On the other hand, the ethical obligation is very broad and attaches to all information that the client might wish to be held confidential, even though already communicated beyond practitioner and client.

* * *

The tax practitioner who knows that a client has not complied with the revenue laws, or has made an error in or omission from any return, document, affidavit, or other paper required to be executed, is required to advise the client promptly of the fact of such non-compliance, error, or omission. Disclosure to the IRS is not required or authorized even with client's permission.[26]

The principal difficulty arising under these various confidentiality rules occurs when the practitioner feels a need to disclose information when the client has acted in a fraudulent or otherwise illegal manner. ABA Formal Opinion 314 addresses this problem. The lawyer may not mislead the IRS deliberately and affirmatively, either by misstatements or by knowingly permitting the client to mislead. A lawyer who represents a client before the IRS may stress the strong points of the client's case and is not required to disclose weakness in that case. When a client has made misstatements to the IRS, the lawyer must counsel the client to correct them, and may, if the client refuses, have a duty to withdraw. The lawyer may not, however, disclose the misstatement without the client's permission.

Consider the following examples:

15. ABA Model Rule 1.6. There is a limited exception where the disclosure is necessary to establish a claim or defense on behalf of the lawyer in a controversy between the lawyer and the client.

26. Circular 230, 31 CFR Part 10, § 10.21.

You represent the sole proprietor of a business that is being audited by the Service. You are making good progress with the agent on the matters that have been raised by the Service. In the course of gathering information requested by the agency, you become aware of the fact that the client neglected to report a capital gain unrelated to the issues raised by the Service. The gain was realized in the year under audit. While there is no doubt that a gain was realized, you conclude that the nonreporting was a result of error rather than an intent to evade tax liability. You call this error to the attention of the client, who asks you if he is obligated to correct it. He also asks if he will violate any law by not doing so. Then he asks if you can continue to represent him in the audit if he does not disclose the error. How do you respond to these questions? Would it matter if the issues raised by the Service included another unrelated capital gain issue so that the taxpayer's Schedule D was at issue?

You can and should advise the client that he or she is not obligated to report the gain; the return was not filed with intent to evade tax. You urge him nonetheless to report it. If the client does not grant you permission to report the error, however, you should advise him that it would not be wise for you to continue to represent him, because you cannot mislead the agent. If the agent should ask you if, to the best of your understanding, the return is otherwise correct, you could not answer Yes. You would be forced to tell the agent he or she must ask the client, and if the agent should do so, you should advise the client that he may not lie to the agent. Even telling the agent he must ask the client is likely to raise the agent's suspicion.

* * *

What do you do? Should you have intervened when the taxpayer misstated the facts? For a discussion of a comparable fact situation, see ABA Formal Opinion, 93–375, August 6, 1993. * * *

You must counsel the client to advise the [IRS] that her understanding of the facts if not correct, but you yourself cannot do so unless the client consents. ABA Formal Opinion 314 makes it clear that proceedings before the IRS are not proceedings before a "tribunal", and Model Rule 1.6 prohibits you from correcting the client's misstatement because there is no risk of death or substantial bodily harm involved.

You must again advise the [IRS] to ask the client. If the [IRS] persists, you must decline to answer, obviously creating suspicion. * * *

In any event, you must continue to urge the client to correct the misstatement to avoid the risk of possible criminal liability of the client for having made a deliberate misstatement of fact to a federal official. * * *

IV. Duty to Clients—Competence

ABA Model Rule 1.1 requires that a lawyer provide competent representation to a client. The text of the rule states that competent representation requires "the legal knowledge, skill, thoroughness and preparation reasonably necessary for the representation."

If a professional fails to provide competent representation, there is not only an ethical violation; there is a serious risk that such conduct may result in professional liability.

Violation of an ethical standard may be relevant, though generally is not conclusive, in determining whether a practitioner has engaged in malpractice. Most ethical codes, including the ABA Model Rules, disclaim a connection between violation of an ethical rule and malpractice.

In the view of most courts, violation of an ethical standard intended to protect a person in the claimant's position will constitute evidence of professional malpractice. The elements of a cause of action for professional malpractice are as follows: a duty of care is owed to a client or to another person and the professional violates that duty; there is injury to the claimant; and the injury results from the breach.

The professional's duty of care may be summarized as follows: he or she is obligated to exercise the competence and diligence ordinarily exercised by others in the profession under similar circumstances. A professional is not merely required to exercise "average" competence: a professional who holds out greater competence, such as a tax specialist, is held to the higher standard applicable to that specialty. The standard is one of reasonable competence under all circumstances.

Injury to the claimant will generally consist of the economic benefits that were reasonably anticipated from the representation. Injury to the claimant generally does not occur (and hence the statute of limitations does not begin to run) until the later of: the time the representation ends; the professional's conduct produces significant injury to the claimant; or the client has become aware (or reasonably should have become aware) of the malpractice that has produced injury.

In tax cases, special considerations often apply. Injury to the claimant generally does not occur until the IRS has assessed the disputed tax liability. The claimant's pursuit of the tax controversy process is consistent with the claimant's duty to mitigate damages. If the claimant would have owed the taxes in any event (as where the malpractice consists of failure to file a return), the injury should be limited to penalties, interest, and professional fees incurred to resolve the underpayment. If, however, the malpractice involved failure to structure a transaction in a way that would have avoided a tax liability, the injury may include the tax unnecessarily incurred. * * *

[An example] will illustrate the professional's duty of care.

* * *

You are negotiating the settlement of a Tax Court case with counsel for the IRS. The terms are agreed and both parties are ready to proceed. It is apparent to you that counsel for the IRS does not appreciate how favorable the settlement will be for your client because IRS counsel is not taking account the impact of the settlement in several areas. If IRS counsel were aware of this, the language of the settlement documents could easily preclude these unanticipated benefits. Do you have any obligation to disclose this to IRS counsel?

You have no duty to advise IRS counsel that he or she is not fully aware of the effects of the settlement. To the contrary, you have a duty not to do so because of your duty of loyalty and confidentiality to your client.* * * The fact that respondent's counsel may have overlooked a Code provision which substantially reduced the amount to be paid by the taxpayer is not a basis for setting aside the agreement as previously submitted to and approved by the Court even though taxpayer's counsel was aware of the fact that respondent's counsel was overlooking the effect of that Code provision.

V.   Duty to System

A.   Criminal or Fraudulent Conduct

The ABA Model Rules contain explicit provisions as to criminal or fraudulent activity by a lawyer. A lawyer may not counsel a client to engage in, or assist a client in, conduct that the lawyer knows is criminal or fraudulent. A lawyer may, however, discuss the legal consequences of any proposed course of conduct with a client and may counsel a client with respect to the validity, scope, meaning, or application of the law.[42] Hence, a lawyer may not participate in a sham transaction, such as a plan to effectuate criminal or fraudulent escape of tax liability.[43]

The fact that a client uses advice obtained from a professional in the course of action that is criminal or fraudulent does not, of course, of itself make the professional a party to the course of action. There is a critical distinction between presenting an analysis of legal aspects of questionable conduct and recommending the means by which a crime or fraud may be committed.[44] A lawyer may not disclose a client's wrongdoing, but the lawyer is required to avoid furthering the purpose by suggesting, for example, how it might be concealed.[45]

The circumstances under which a lawyer must or may withdraw from a representation by reason of the client's illegal or fraudulent activity are more explicit. A lawyer may not represent a client, or *shall* withdraw from an ongoing representation, if the representation will result in violation of the rules of professional conduct or other law.[47] The lawyer is not obliged to withdraw, however, if the client suggests it for the purpose, for example, of seeking to avoid the lawyer's professional obligations upon withdrawal.

A lawyer *may* withdraw if the client persists in a course of action involving the lawyer's services that the lawyer reasonably believes is criminal or fraudulent, or the client has used the lawyer's services to perpetrate a crime or fraud.[48] Withdrawal in these circumstances is permissible even if that action will "materially prejudice the client."[49] The lawyer's duty or right to withdraw is not as clear, however, where the act of withdrawal would have the effect of disclosing a client confidence in

---

42. ABA Model Rule 1.2(d). This rule applies whether or not the defrauded person is a party to the transaction.

43. ABA Model Rule 1.2(d) Comment.

44. Id.

45. ABA Model Rule 1.2(d). This rule applies whether or not the defrauded person is a party to the transaction.

47. ABA Model Rule 1.16(a).

48. ABA Model Rule 1.16(b).

49. ABA Model Rule 1.16(b) Comment.

violation of ABA Model Rule 1.6. Where, however, the lawyer's representation is likely to be known to and relied on by third persons to whom fraudulent conduct by the client is directed, an affirmative disavowal by the lawyer of his or her work product to the third parties (a so-called "noisy" withdrawal) may be required without regard to ABA Model Rule 1.6.[50]

An example will indicate the difficulties a professional may face under these rules.

In recent months, you provided a client with an opinion concerning the tax consequences of a proposed investment transaction. You understood that the client would use the opinion in the course of marketing this investment product. The opinion concludes that it is more likely than not that the intended tax benefits of the investment will be available. Although you used due care in preparing the opinion, you now learn that some of the material facts supplied to you by the client are incorrect and that the intended tax consequences cannot, on the correct facts, reasonably be anticipated. You discuss the matter with the client and are convinced that the client knowingly misled you. The client adamantly denies you leave to disclose the inaccuracies. What steps are you permitted to take?

A lawyer has an ethical obligation under Model Rule 4.1(a) not to mislead a third party. A lawyer may not assist a client in conduct that the lawyer knows is criminal or fraudulent. A lawyer may not make a false statement of fact or law to a third person, and must disclose a material fact to a third person when disclosure is necessary to avoid assisting in a criminal or fraudulent act by a client *unless disclosure is prohibited by Rule 1.6.*[51] As has been previously indicated, some state adoptions of the Model Rules explicitly permit, and sometimes mandate, the lawyer to disclose a client fraud. Under the Commentary to Model Rule 1.6, a lawyer may not disclose past frauds unknown to the lawyer at the time the lawyer's services were used. Under Opinion 92–366, a lawyer may not disavow previous work product if the client's fraud is complete, rather than ongoing.

Under the circumstances presented in the foregoing situation, you should advise the client not to use your opinion in its present form and that if the client does so, you may be forced publicly to disclaim it in a manner designed to reach third parties who may have received it and are considering making the investment or who have already done so. If the client has already distributed your opinion, or disregards your instructions and thereafter distributes it, you must evaluate the likelihood investors will rely on it, and if it is at all likely they will do so, you must consider whether you have an obligation to disaffirm it publicly in light of the Comment to Model Rule 1.6 and ABA Formal Opinions 92–366 and 93–375, depending upon the circumstances.

* * *

B.   Candor Toward a Tribunal

A lawyer may not knowingly fail to disclose a material fact to a "tribunal" when disclosure is necessary to avoid assisting a criminal or

---

50. ABA Formal Opinion 92–366.   **51.** ABA Model Rule 1.2(d).

fraudulent act by the client.[53] A tribunal is a trial-type proceeding in which witnesses are questioned, evidence is presented, and a decision is ordered by a fact-finder. It includes administrative agency quasi-judicial proceedings. Proceedings before the IRS are not, however, viewed as a "tribunal" entitled to the benefit of this disclosure mandate.[54]

This duty of disclosure may, however, conflict with the duty to keep the client's confidences. When such conflict arises, the lawyer is directed to seek to persuade the client that disclosure is necessary. If unsuccessful, the general rule, except in criminal cases, is that the lawyer must disclose the existence of the client's deception. Such disclosure may result in "grave consequences" to the client, but the undesirable alternative is that the truth finding process, implemented by the adversary system, will be subverted.[55]

C. Truthfulness in Dealing with Others

As previously indicated, a lawyer may not, in the course of representing a client, fail to disclose a material fact to a third person when disclosure is necessary to avoid assisting a criminal or fraudulent act by a client, unless disclosure is prohibited by Rule 1.6.[56] Accordingly, disclosure to avoid assisting in a criminal or fraudulent act by a client is required only where the lawyer reasonably believes that disclosure is necessary to prevent the client from committing a criminal act that the lawyer believes is likely to result in imminent death or substantial bodily harm.

* * *

[The authors discussion of penalties on taxpayers from inaccurate returns or underpayments of tax has been omitted. For a discussion of some of the more important penalties see pages 74–75, supra. The discussion of the tax practitioners' obligations regarding tax returns is also omitted, having been covered earlier in this Section. Problems illustrating application of these standards follow.]

C. *Problems—Tax Preparer Obligations*

The following circumstances illustrate a number of the tax preparer's accuracy obligations.

Your client, a closely held corporation, is considering a plan to refinance certain outstanding indebtedness. The plan would achieve modest business savings but would also substantially reduce the company's income tax liabilities for several years. The plan would require that the company take a position on its return which is contrary to a regulation. The company's tax director advises you that he has studied the regulation carefully and believes that it is not valid because it incorrectly interprets the controlling statute. The company asks you to review the matter and advise it with respect to adopting a plan and adopting a tax return position with respect to the plan.

---

53. ABA Model Rule 3.3(a).

54. ABA Formal Opinion 314 (1965).

55. ABA Model Rule 3.3(a) Comment.

56. ABA Model Rule 4.1.

You research the matter and learn that several law review articles criticize the regulation and question its validity. In addition, one federal District Court case held the regulation invalid, but the case was reversed on other grounds by the U.S. Court of Appeals for that circuit. Your client is not located in that district or circuit. Upon finishing your research, you conclude that the taxpayer's proposed position would probably lose if it were challenged by the Service. You believe, however, that the taxpayer's odds of prevailing are somewhere between 25% and 35%.

Before reporting back to the taxpayer, you think about this very carefully. If you advise the taxpayer to adopt the proposed return position, what risks do you face? Of course, you always face the possibility that your advice in a given position might be questioned and your own client could bring a suit against you for malpractice. A carefully-worded letter of advice to the client spelling out all of the risks and a statement as to the possibility of success should, however, overcome this possibility.

It appears that the position would constitute a "substantial portion of the return;" accordingly, you would be a preparer and the various preparer penalties could apply to you.[103] If you are signing the corporate tax return as preparer, then you could be liable for a preparer penalty,[104] but if someone else in your firm is signing the return, he or she will be subject to the penalties. If a person from another firm is signing the return, and is assessed a preparer penalty, you could nevertheless also be assessed a penalty as a "non-signing" preparer.

In the instant situation, you would most likely not be subject to the penalty imposed on preparers for a position which lacks a "realistic possibility of success"[105] because your analysis showed that the position has approximately a one in three chance of success. The penalty for an understatement due to reckless or intentional disregard of rules or regulations[106] may only be avoided, however, if the position is not frivolous and is adequately disclosed. In addition, the position must represent a good faith challenge to the validity of the regulation.

* * *

If the client adopts your recommendation, the client should avoid the "disregard component" of the accuracy penalty[107] with the disclosure described above so long as adequate books and records are kept and the item is properly substantiated. The negligence component of that penalty should be avoided because the tax return position appears to have a "reasonable basis." The substantial understatement penalty will also be avoided with disclosure.[108]

After digesting the above information, you discuss it with your client's tax director. He advises you that the return position in question, will be adopted, that there will be no disclosure of the position in the return, and

---

103. Code Sec. 7701(a)(36).

104. Code Sec. 6694.

105. Code Sec. 6694(a).

106. Code Sec. 6694(b).

107. Code Sec. 6662(b)(1).

108. Code Sec. 6662(d)(2)(B).

that he wants a written opinion from you expressing your professional views.

If the client does not disclose the position, this might be a situation where the "reasonable cause and good faith" exception is not available because the taxpayer may not have bene acting in good faith by failing to disclose the position.[109] Even your opinion that such a position could be taken might not qualify the client for a "reasonable cause, good faith" exception if you have advised the client to disclose, and the client has not followed that advice. The taxpayer has not relied on your advice and thus may not have acted in good faith.[110]

You should caution the client that a written opinion from you would, of necessity, include a recommendation to disclose, and if the client chose to disregard that recommendation, the client could be subject to the various taxpayer penalties described above.

The taxpayer files the return, taking the position in question. One year later, the management of the tax department changes, and a new tax director, who is risk adverse, concludes that the company should not be exposed to any penalty risks. The tax director consults you and asks if the company can file an amended return, pay any tax attributable to the reversal of the position in question, and thereby avoid penalty risks. You inform the new tax director that he may indeed file a "qualified amended return" if the corporation has not been contacted by the Internal Revenue Service concerning an examination of the return and can pay the tax in question.[111] In addition, the disclosure described above can also be made on a "qualified amended return" and if all of the criteria are met, the penalties again can be avoided.

Conclusion

There is often a fine line between balancing a tax practitioner's duty to client with the duty to the tax system. As can be seen from the above discussion and illustrations, the tax practitioner often finds himself in difficult positions when his duty to his client seems to conflict with his duty to the system. The various model professional guidelines and interpretations and legislative and regulatory sources provide a background for making the proper decision as to which duty prevails. Careful and thoughtful analysis is generally required to avoid sanctions imposed by various regulatory agencies, professional associations, and the courts in cases involving penalties as well as suits for professional malpractice. The added burden created by this need to balance adds significant time to the already difficult task of interpreting and giving advice on the many complicated substantive provisions of the Internal Revenue Code.

---

109.   Code Sec. 6664(c).

110.   Reg. § 1.6664–4(b)(1).

111.   Reg. § 1.6661–6(c)(1).

APPENDIX A

THE CONCEPT OF PRESENT VALUE

The concept of present value can be summed up in the notion that a dollar today is worth more than a dollar tomorrow. That is because today's dollar can be invested immediately to earn interest for the recipient. Likewise, a dollar that one must pay tomorrow—as income tax, for example—is worth less to the payor than a dollar that must be paid today.

For example, assume that a person could receive a payment either today or 12 months from today. Also assume that he could earn a 6 percent rate of interest on any funds that he invested. If he would accept $100 if the payment were made today, he should demand $106 if the payment were deferred to the later year. Or, assume that the same person owes $500 of tax. Assuming an after-tax interest rate of 6 percent, his tax liability would cost only $471.50 in present value if he could defer payment until the next taxable year.

It follows that a dollar tomorrow is worth more than a dollar the day after tomorrow. The taxpayer in the previous example would thus demand $112 if the payment was not to be received for two years; he would reduce his tax liability to $445 if he did not have to settle up with the IRS for two years.

Present value is thus the amount that one would have to invest today at a specified interest rate in order to have a specified amount at a specified future date. This amount is calculated by discounting the future payment by the rate of return available to the investor over the relevant period. This formula may be expressed as:

$$PV = \frac{C}{(1 + r)^n}$$

where PV equals the present value, r equals the rate of return, C equals the future payment and n equals the number of years of deferral.

The difference in value between a dollar today and a dollar in the future thus depends both upon interest rates and upon the length of deferral. It will also depend in the context of the income tax on the marginal rate of the taxpayer in the two periods.

The following tables list the present value of a dollar received after different lengths of time and at different rates of interest (Table 1) and the future value of a dollar that compounds for different periods of time and at different rates of interest (Table 2).

APPENDIX TABLE 1

Discount factors: Present value of $1 to be received after t years $= 1/(1 + r)^t$

Number of years	Interest rate per year									
	1%	2%	3%	4%	5%	6%	7%	8%	9%	10%
1	.990	.980	.971	.962	.952	.943	.935	.926	.917	.909
2	.980	.961	.943	.925	.907	.890	.873	.857	.842	.826
3	.971	.942	.915	.889	.864	.840	.816	.794	.772	.751
4	.961	.924	.888	.855	.823	.792	.763	.735	.708	.683
5	.951	.906	.863	.822	.784	.747	.713	.681	.650	.621
6	.942	.888	.837	.790	.746	.705	.666	.630	.596	.564
7	.933	.871	.813	.760	.711	.665	.623	.583	.547	.513
8	.923	.853	.789	.731	.677	.627	.582	.540	.502	.467
9	.914	.837	.766	.703	.645	.592	.544	.500	.460	.424
10	.905	.820	.744	.676	.614	.558	.508	.463	.422	.386
11	.896	.804	.722	.650	.585	.527	.475	.429	.388	.350
12	.887	.788	.701	.625	.557	.497	.444	.397	.356	.319
13	.879	.773	.681	.601	.530	.469	.415	.368	.326	.290
14	.870	.758	.661	.577	.505	.442	.388	.340	.299	.263
15	.861	.743	.642	.555	.481	.417	.362	.315	.275	.239
16	.853	.728	.623	.534	.458	.394	.339	.292	.252	.218
17	.844	.714	.605	.513	.436	.371	.317	.270	.231	.198
18	.836	.700	.587	.494	.416	.350	.296	.250	.212	.180
19	.828	.686	.570	.475	.396	.331	.277	.232	.194	.164
20	.820	.673	.554	.456	.377	.312	.258	.215	.178	.149
25	.780	.610	.478	.375	.295	.233	.184	.146	.116	.092
30	.742	.552	.412	.308	.231	.174	.131	.099	.075	.057

Number of years	Interest rate per year									
	11%	12%	13%	14%	15%	16%	17%	18%	19%	20%
1	.901	.893	.885	.877	.870	.862	.855	.847	.840	.833
2	.812	.797	.783	.769	.756	.743	.731	.718	.706	.694
3	.731	.712	.693	.675	.658	.641	.624	.609	.593	.579
4	.659	.636	.613	.592	.572	.552	.534	.516	.499	.482
5	.593	.567	.543	.519	.497	.476	.456	.437	.419	.402
6	.535	.507	.480	.456	.432	.410	.390	.370	.352	.335
7	.482	.452	.425	.400	.376	.354	.333	.314	.296	.279
8	.434	.404	.376	.351	.327	.305	.285	.266	.249	.233
9	.391	.361	.333	.308	.284	.263	.243	.225	.209	.194
10	.352	.322	.295	.270	.247	.227	.208	.191	.176	.162
11	.317	.287	.261	.237	.215	.195	.178	.162	.148	.135
12	.286	.257	.231	.208	.187	.168	.152	.137	.124	.112
13	.258	.229	.204	.182	.163	.145	.130	.116	.104	.093
14	.232	.205	.181	.160	.141	.125	.111	.099	.088	.078
15	.209	.183	.160	.140	.123	.108	.095	.084	.074	.065
16	.188	.163	.141	.123	.107	.093	.081	.071	.062	.054
17	.170	.146	.125	.108	.093	.080	.069	.060	.052	.045
18	.153	.130	.111	.095	.081	.069	.059	.051	.044	.038
19	.138	.116	.098	.083	.070	.060	.051	.043	.037	.031
20	.124	.104	.087	.073	.061	.051	.043	.037	.031	.026
25	.074	.059	.047	.038	.030	.024	.020	.016	.013	.010
30	.044	.033	.026	.020	.015	.012	.009	.007	.005	.004

Number of years	Interest rate per year									
	21%	22%	23%	24%	25%	26%	27%	28%	29%	30%
1	.826	.820	.813	.806	.800	.794	.787	.781	.775	.769
2	.683	.672	.661	.650	.640	.630	.620	.610	.601	.592
3	.564	.551	.537	.524	.512	.500	.488	.477	.466	.455
4	.467	.451	.437	.423	.410	.397	.384	.373	.361	.350
5	.386	.370	.355	.341	.328	.315	.303	.291	.280	.269
6	.319	.303	.289	.275	.262	.250	.238	.227	.217	.207
7	.263	.249	.235	.222	.210	.198	.188	.178	.168	.159
8	.218	.204	.191	.179	.168	.157	.148	.139	.130	.123
9	.180	.167	.155	.144	.134	.125	.116	.108	.101	.094
10	.149	.137	.126	.116	.107	.099	.092	.085	.078	.073
11	.123	.112	.103	.094	.086	.079	.072	.066	.061	.056
12	.102	.092	.083	.076	.069	.062	.057	.052	.047	.043
13	.084	.075	.068	.061	.055	.050	.045	.040	.037	.033
14	.069	.062	.055	.049	.044	.039	.035	.032	.028	.025
15	.057	.051	.045	.040	.035	.031	.028	.025	.022	.020

Number	Interest rate per year									
of years	21%	22%	23%	24%	25%	26%	27%	28%	29%	30%
16	.047	.042	.036	.032	.028	.025	.022	.019	.017	.015
17	.039	.034	.030	.026	.023	.020	.017	.015	.013	.012
18	.032	.028	.024	.021	.018	.016	.014	.012	.010	.009
19	.027	.023	.020	.017	.014	.012	.011	.009	.008	.007
20	.022	.019	.016	.014	.012	.010	.008	.007	.006	.005
25	.009	.007	.006	.005	.004	.003	.003	.002	.002	.001
30	.003	.003	.002	.002	.001	.001	.001	.001	.000	.000

E.g.: If the interest rate is 10 percent per year, the present value of $1 received at the end of year 5 is $0.621.

APPENDIX TABLE 2

Future value of $1 by the end of t years $= (1 + r)^t$

Number	Interest rate per year									
of years	1%	2%	3%	4%	5%	6%	7%	8%	9%	10%
1	1.010	1.020	1.030	1.040	1.050	1.060	1.070	1.080	1.090	1.100
2	1.020	1.040	1.061	1.082	1.102	1.124	1.145	1.166	1.188	1.210
3	1.030	1.061	1.093	1.125	1.158	1.191	1.225	1.260	1.295	1.331
4	1.041	1.082	1.126	1.170	1.216	1.262	1.311	1.360	1.412	1.464
5	1.051	1.104	1.159	1.217	1.276	1.338	1.403	1.469	1.539	1.611
6	1.062	1.126	1.194	1.265	1.340	1.419	1.501	1.587	1.677	1.772
7	1.072	1.149	1.230	1.316	1.407	1.504	1.606	1.714	1.828	1.949
8	1.083	1.172	1.267	1.369	1.477	1.594	1.718	1.851	1.993	2.144
9	1.094	1.195	1.305	1.423	1.551	1.689	1.838	1.999	2.172	2.358
10	1.105	1.219	1.344	1.480	1.629	1.791	1.967	2.159	2.367	2.594
11	1.116	1.243	1.384	1.539	1.710	1.898	2.105	2.332	2.580	2.853
12	1.127	1.268	1.426	1.601	1.796	2.012	2.252	2.518	2.813	3.138
13	1.138	1.294	1.469	1.665	1.886	2.133	2.410	2.720	3.066	3.452
14	1.149	1.319	1.513	1.732	1.980	2.261	2.579	2.937	3.342	3.797
15	1.161	1.346	1.558	1.801	2.079	2.397	2.759	3.172	3.642	4.177
16	1.173	1.373	1.605	1.873	2.183	2.540	2.952	3.426	3.970	4.595
17	1.184	1.400	1.653	1.948	2.292	2.693	3.159	3.700	4.328	5.054
18	1.196	1.428	1.702	2.026	2.407	2.854	3.380	3.996	4.717	5.560
19	1.208	1.457	1.754	2.107	2.527	3.026	3.617	4.316	5.142	6.116
20	1.220	1.486	1.806	2.191	2.653	3.207	3.870	4.661	5.604	6.727
25	1.282	1.641	2.094	2.666	3.386	4.292	5.427	6.848	8.623	10.83
30	1.348	1.811	2.427	3.243	4.322	5.743	7.612	10.06	13.27	17.45

Number	Interest rate per year									
of years	11%	12%	13%	14%	15%	16%	17%	18%	19%	20%
1	1.110	1.120	1.130	1.140	1.150	1.160	1.170	1.180	1.190	1.200
2	1.232	1.254	1.277	1.300	1.323	1.346	1.369	1.392	1.416	1.440
3	1.368	1.405	1.443	1.482	1.521	1.561	1.602	1.643	1.685	1.728
4	1.518	1.574	1.630	1.689	1.749	1.811	1.874	1.939	2.005	2.074
5	1.685	1.762	1.842	1.925	2.011	2.100	2.192	2.288	2.386	2.488
6	1.870	1.974	2.082	2.195	2.313	2.436	2.565	2.700	2.840	2.986
7	2.076	2.211	2.353	2.502	2.660	2.826	3.001	3.185	3.379	3.583
8	2.305	2.476	2.658	2.853	3.059	3.278	3.511	3.759	4.021	4.300
9	2.558	2.773	3.004	3.252	3.518	3.803	4.108	4.435	4.785	5.160
10	2.839	3.106	3.395	3.707	4.046	4.411	4.807	5.234	5.695	6.192
11	3.152	3.479	3.836	4.226	4.652	5.117	5.624	6.176	6.777	7.430
12	3.498	3.896	4.335	4.818	5.350	5.936	6.580	7.288	8.064	8.916
13	3.883	4.363	4.898	5.492	6.153	6.886	7.699	8.599	9.596	10.70
14	4.310	4.887	5.535	6.261	7.076	7.988	9.007	10.15	11.42	12.84
15	4.785	5.474	6.254	7.138	8.137	9.266	10.54	11.97	13.59	15.41
16	5.311	6.130	7.067	8.137	9.358	10.75	12.33	14.13	16.17	18.49
17	5.895	6.866	7.986	9.276	10.76	12.47	14.43	16.67	19.24	22.19
18	6.544	7.690	9.024	10.58	12.38	14.46	16.88	19.67	22.90	26.62
19	7.263	8.613	10.20	12.06	14.23	16.78	19.75	23.21	27.25	31.95
20	8.062	9.646	11.52	13.74	16.37	19.46	23.11	27.39	32.43	38.34
25	13.59	17.00	21.23	26.46	32.92	40.87	50.66	62.67	77.39	95.40
30	22.89	29.96	39.12	50.95	66.21	85.85	111.1	143.4	184.7	237.4

Number	Interest rate per year									
of years	21%	22%	23%	24%	25%	26%	27%	28%	29%	30%
1	1.210	1.220	1.230	1.240	1.250	1.260	1.270	1.280	1.290	1.300
2	1.464	1.488	1.513	1.538	1.563	1.588	1.613	1.638	1.664	1.690
3	1.772	1.816	1.861	1.907	1.953	2.000	2.048	2.097	2.147	2.197
4	2.144	2.215	2.289	2.364	2.441	2.520	2.601	2.684	2.769	2.856

Number of years	Interest rate per year									
	21%	22%	23%	24%	25%	26%	27%	28%	29%	30%
5	2.594	2.703	2.815	2.932	3.052	3.176	3.304	3.436	3.572	3.713
6	3.138	3.297	3.463	3.635	3.815	4.002	4.196	4.398	4.608	4.827
7	3.797	4.023	4.259	4.508	4.768	5.042	5.329	5.629	5.945	6.275
8	4.595	4.908	5.239	5.590	5.960	6.353	6.768	7.206	7.669	8.157
9	5.560	5.987	6.444	6.931	7.451	8.005	8.595	9.223	9.893	10.60
10	6.728	7.305	7.926	8.594	9.313	10.09	10.92	11.81	12.76	13.79
11	8.140	8.912	9.749	10.66	11.64	12.71	13.86	15.11	16.46	17.92
12	9.850	10.87	11.99	13.21	14.55	16.01	17.61	19.34	21.24	23.30
13	11.92	13.26	14.75	16.39	18.19	20.18	22.36	24.76	27.39	30.29
14	14.42	16.18	18.14	20.32	22.74	25.42	28.40	31.69	35.34	39.37
15	17.45	19.74	22.31	25.20	28.42	32.03	36.06	40.56	45.59	51.19
16	21.11	24.09	27.45	31.24	35.53	40.36	45.80	51.92	58.81	66.54
17	25.55	29.38	33.76	38.74	44.41	50.85	58.17	66.46	75.86	86.50
18	30.91	35.85	41.52	48.04	55.51	64.07	73.87	85.07	97.86	112.5
19	37.40	43.74	51.07	59.57	69.39	80.73	93.81	108.9	126.2	146.2
20	45.26	53.36	62.82	73.86	86.74	101.7	119.1	139.4	162.9	190.0
25	117.4	144.2	176.9	216.5	264.7	323.0	393.6	478.9	581.8	705.6
30	304.5	389.8	497.9	634.8	807.8	1026	1301	1646	2078	2620

E.g.: If the interest rate is 10 percent per year, the investment of $1 today will be worth $1.611 at the end of year 5.

INDEX

References are to pages.

†